T0234448

Lecture Notes in Computer Science 13688

Founding Editors

Gerhard Goos
   Karlsruhe Institute of Technology, Karlsruhe, Germany

Juris Hartmanis
   Cornell University, Ithaca, NY, USA

Editorial Board Members

Elisa Bertino
   Purdue University, West Lafayette, IN, USA

Wen Gao
   Peking University, Beijing, China

Bernhard Steffen 📖
   TU Dortmund University, Dortmund, Germany

Moti Yung 📖
   Columbia University, New York, NY, USA

More information about this series at https://link.springer.com/bookseries/558

Shai Avidan · Gabriel Brostow ·
Moustapha Cissé · Giovanni Maria Farinella ·
Tal Hassner (Eds.)

Computer Vision – ECCV 2022

17th European Conference
Tel Aviv, Israel, October 23–27, 2022
Proceedings, Part XXVIII

Springer

Editors
Shai Avidan
Tel Aviv University
Tel Aviv, Israel

Gabriel Brostow ⓘ
University College London
London, UK

Moustapha Cissé
Google AI
Accra, Ghana

Giovanni Maria Farinella ⓘ
University of Catania
Catania, Italy

Tal Hassner ⓘ
Facebook (United States)
Menlo Park, CA, USA

ISSN 0302-9743   ISSN 1611-3349 (electronic)
Lecture Notes in Computer Science
ISBN 978-3-031-19814-4   ISBN 978-3-031-19815-1 (eBook)
https://doi.org/10.1007/978-3-031-19815-1

© The Editor(s) (if applicable) and The Author(s), under exclusive license
to Springer Nature Switzerland AG 2022
This work is subject to copyright. All rights are reserved by the Publisher, whether the whole or part of the material is concerned, specifically the rights of translation, reprinting, reuse of illustrations, recitation, broadcasting, reproduction on microfilms or in any other physical way, and transmission or information storage and retrieval, electronic adaptation, computer software, or by similar or dissimilar methodology now known or hereafter developed.
The use of general descriptive names, registered names, trademarks, service marks, etc. in this publication does not imply, even in the absence of a specific statement, that such names are exempt from the relevant protective laws and regulations and therefore free for general use.
The publisher, the authors, and the editors are safe to assume that the advice and information in this book are believed to be true and accurate at the date of publication. Neither the publisher nor the authors or the editors give a warranty, expressed or implied, with respect to the material contained herein or for any errors or omissions that may have been made. The publisher remains neutral with regard to jurisdictional claims in published maps and institutional affiliations.

This Springer imprint is published by the registered company Springer Nature Switzerland AG
The registered company address is: Gewerbestrasse 11, 6330 Cham, Switzerland

Foreword

Organizing the European Conference on Computer Vision (ECCV 2022) in Tel-Aviv during a global pandemic was no easy feat. The uncertainty level was extremely high, and decisions had to be postponed to the last minute. Still, we managed to plan things just in time for ECCV 2022 to be held in person. Participation in physical events is crucial to stimulating collaborations and nurturing the culture of the Computer Vision community.

There were many people who worked hard to ensure attendees enjoyed the best science at the 16th edition of ECCV. We are grateful to the Program Chairs Gabriel Brostow and Tal Hassner, who went above and beyond to ensure the ECCV reviewing process ran smoothly. The scientific program includes dozens of workshops and tutorials in addition to the main conference and we would like to thank Leonid Karlinsky and Tomer Michaeli for their hard work. Finally, special thanks to the web chairs Lorenzo Baraldi and Kosta Derpanis, who put in extra hours to transfer information fast and efficiently to the ECCV community.

We would like to express gratitude to our generous sponsors and the Industry Chairs, Dimosthenis Karatzas and Chen Sagiv, who oversaw industry relations and proposed new ways for academia-industry collaboration and technology transfer. It's great to see so much industrial interest in what we're doing!

Authors' draft versions of the papers appeared online with open access on both the Computer Vision Foundation (CVF) and the European Computer Vision Association (ECVA) websites as with previous ECCVs. Springer, the publisher of the proceedings, has arranged for archival publication. The final version of the papers is hosted by SpringerLink, with active references and supplementary materials. It benefits all potential readers that we offer both a free and citeable version for all researchers, as well as an authoritative, citeable version for SpringerLink readers. Our thanks go to Ronan Nugent from Springer, who helped us negotiate this agreement. Last but not least, we wish to thank Eric Mortensen, our publication chair, whose expertise made the process smooth.

October 2022

Rita Cucchiara
Jiří Matas
Amnon Shashua
Lihi Zelnik-Manor

Preface

Welcome to the proceedings of the European Conference on Computer Vision (ECCV 2022). This was a hybrid edition of ECCV as we made our way out of the COVID-19 pandemic. The conference received 5804 valid paper submissions, compared to 5150 submissions to ECCV 2020 (a 12.7% increase) and 2439 in ECCV 2018. 1645 submissions were accepted for publication (28%) and, of those, 157 (2.7% overall) as orals.

846 of the submissions were desk-rejected for various reasons. Many of them because they revealed author identity, thus violating the double-blind policy. This violation came in many forms: some had author names with the title, others added acknowledgments to specific grants, yet others had links to their github account where their name was visible. Tampering with the LaTeX template was another reason for automatic desk rejection.

ECCV 2022 used the traditional CMT system to manage the entire double-blind reviewing process. Authors did not know the names of the reviewers and vice versa. Each paper received at least 3 reviews (except 6 papers that received only 2 reviews), totalling more than 15,000 reviews.

Handling the review process at this scale was a significant challenge. To ensure that each submission received as fair and high-quality reviews as possible, we recruited more than 4719 reviewers (in the end, 4719 reviewers did at least one review). Similarly we recruited more than 276 area chairs (eventually, only 276 area chairs handled a batch of papers). The area chairs were selected based on their technical expertise and reputation, largely among people who served as area chairs in previous top computer vision and machine learning conferences (ECCV, ICCV, CVPR, NeurIPS, etc.).

Reviewers were similarly invited from previous conferences, and also from the pool of authors. We also encouraged experienced area chairs to suggest additional chairs and reviewers in the initial phase of recruiting. The median reviewer load was five papers per reviewer, while the average load was about four papers, because of the emergency reviewers. The area chair load was 35 papers, on average.

Conflicts of interest between authors, area chairs, and reviewers were handled largely automatically by the CMT platform, with some manual help from the Program Chairs. Reviewers were allowed to describe themselves as senior reviewer (load of 8 papers to review) or junior reviewers (load of 4 papers). Papers were matched to area chairs based on a subject-area affinity score computed in CMT and an affinity score computed by the Toronto Paper Matching System (TPMS). TPMS is based on the paper's full text. An area chair handling each submission would bid for preferred expert reviewers, and we balanced load and prevented conflicts.

The assignment of submissions to area chairs was relatively smooth, as was the assignment of submissions to reviewers. A small percentage of reviewers were not happy with their assignments in terms of subjects and self-reported expertise. This is an area for improvement, although it's interesting that many of these cases were reviewers hand-picked by AC's. We made a later round of reviewer recruiting, targeted at the list of authors of papers submitted to the conference, and had an excellent response which helped provide enough emergency reviewers. In the end, all but six papers received at least 3 reviews.

The challenges of the reviewing process are in line with past experiences at ECCV 2020. As the community grows, and the number of submissions increases, it becomes ever more challenging to recruit enough reviewers and ensure a high enough quality of reviews. Enlisting authors by default as reviewers might be one step to address this challenge.

Authors were given a week to rebut the initial reviews, and address reviewers' concerns. Each rebuttal was limited to a single pdf page with a fixed template.

The Area Chairs then led discussions with the reviewers on the merits of each submission. The goal was to reach consensus, but, ultimately, it was up to the Area Chair to make a decision. The decision was then discussed with a buddy Area Chair to make sure decisions were fair and informative. The entire process was conducted virtually with no in-person meetings taking place.

The Program Chairs were informed in cases where the Area Chairs overturned a decisive consensus reached by the reviewers, and pushed for the meta-reviews to contain details that explained the reasoning for such decisions. Obviously these were the most contentious cases, where reviewer inexperience was the most common reported factor.

Once the list of accepted papers was finalized and released, we went through the laborious process of plagiarism (including self-plagiarism) detection. A total of 4 accepted papers were rejected because of that.

Finally, we would like to thank our Technical Program Chair, Pavel Lifshits, who did tremendous work behind the scenes, and we thank the tireless CMT team.

October 2022

Gabriel Brostow
Giovanni Maria Farinella
Moustapha Cissé
Shai Avidan
Tal Hassner

Organization

General Chairs

Rita Cucchiara   University of Modena and Reggio Emilia, Italy
Jiří Matas   Czech Technical University in Prague, Czech Republic
Amnon Shashua   Hebrew University of Jerusalem, Israel
Lihi Zelnik-Manor   Technion – Israel Institute of Technology, Israel

Program Chairs

Shai Avidan   Tel-Aviv University, Israel
Gabriel Brostow   University College London, UK
Moustapha Cissé   Google AI, Ghana
Giovanni Maria Farinella   University of Catania, Italy
Tal Hassner   Facebook AI, USA

Program Technical Chair

Pavel Lifshits   Technion – Israel Institute of Technology, Israel

Workshops Chairs

Leonid Karlinsky   IBM Research, Israel
Tomer Michaeli   Technion – Israel Institute of Technology, Israel
Ko Nishino   Kyoto University, Japan

Tutorial Chairs

Thomas Pock   Graz University of Technology, Austria
Natalia Neverova   Facebook AI Research, UK

Demo Chair

Bohyung Han   Seoul National University, Korea

Social and Student Activities Chairs

Tatiana Tommasi   Italian Institute of Technology, Italy
Sagie Benaim   University of Copenhagen, Denmark

Diversity and Inclusion Chairs

Xi Yin   Facebook AI Research, USA
Bryan Russell   Adobe, USA

Communications Chairs

Lorenzo Baraldi   University of Modena and Reggio Emilia, Italy
Kosta Derpanis   York University & Samsung AI Centre Toronto,
                               Canada

Industrial Liaison Chairs

Dimosthenis Karatzas   Universitat Autònoma de Barcelona, Spain
Chen Sagiv   SagivTech, Israel

Finance Chair

Gerard Medioni   University of Southern California & Amazon,
                               USA

Publication Chair

Eric Mortensen   MiCROTEC, USA

Area Chairs

Lourdes Agapito   University College London, UK
Zeynep Akata   University of Tübingen, Germany
Naveed Akhtar   University of Western Australia, Australia
Karteek Alahari   Inria Grenoble Rhône-Alpes, France
Alexandre Alahi   École polytechnique fédérale de Lausanne,
                               Switzerland
Pablo Arbelaez   Universidad de Los Andes, Columbia
Antonis A. Argyros   University of Crete & Foundation for Research
                               and Technology-Hellas, Crete
Yuki M. Asano   University of Amsterdam, The Netherlands
Kalle Åström   Lund University, Sweden
Hadar Averbuch-Elor   Cornell University, USA

Hossein Azizpour	KTH Royal Institute of Technology, Sweden
Vineeth N. Balasubramanian	Indian Institute of Technology, Hyderabad, India
Lamberto Ballan	University of Padova, Italy
Adrien Bartoli	Université Clermont Auvergne, France
Horst Bischof	Graz University of Technology, Austria
Matthew B. Blaschko	KU Leuven, Belgium
Federica Bogo	Meta Reality Labs Research, Switzerland
Katherine Bouman	California Institute of Technology, USA
Edmond Boyer	Inria Grenoble Rhône-Alpes, France
Michael S. Brown	York University, Canada
Vittorio Caggiano	Meta AI Research, USA
Neill Campbell	University of Bath, UK
Octavia Camps	Northeastern University, USA
Duygu Ceylan	Adobe Research, USA
Ayan Chakrabarti	Google Research, USA
Tat-Jen Cham	Nanyang Technological University, Singapore
Antoni Chan	City University of Hong Kong, Hong Kong, China
Manmohan Chandraker	NEC Labs America, USA
Xinlei Chen	Facebook AI Research, USA
Xilin Chen	Institute of Computing Technology, Chinese Academy of Sciences, China
Dongdong Chen	Microsoft Cloud AI, USA
Chen Chen	University of Central Florida, USA
Ondrej Chum	Vision Recognition Group, Czech Technical University in Prague, Czech Republic
John Collomosse	Adobe Research & University of Surrey, UK
Camille Couprie	Facebook, France
David Crandall	Indiana University, USA
Daniel Cremers	Technical University of Munich, Germany
Marco Cristani	University of Verona, Italy
Canton Cristian	Facebook AI Research, USA
Dengxin Dai	ETH Zurich, Switzerland
Dima Damen	University of Bristol, UK
Kostas Daniilidis	University of Pennsylvania, USA
Trevor Darrell	University of California, Berkeley, USA
Andrew Davison	Imperial College London, UK
Tali Dekel	Weizmann Institute of Science, Israel
Alessio Del Bue	Istituto Italiano di Tecnologia, Italy
Weihong Deng	Beijing University of Posts and Telecommunications, China
Konstantinos Derpanis	Ryerson University, Canada
Carl Doersch	DeepMind, UK

Matthijs Douze	Facebook AI Research, USA
Mohamed Elhoseiny	King Abdullah University of Science and Technology, Saudi Arabia
Sergio Escalera	University of Barcelona, Spain
Yi Fang	New York University, USA
Ryan Farrell	Brigham Young University, USA
Alireza Fathi	Google, USA
Christoph Feichtenhofer	Facebook AI Research, USA
Basura Fernando	Agency for Science, Technology and Research (A*STAR), Singapore
Vittorio Ferrari	Google Research, Switzerland
Andrew W. Fitzgibbon	Graphcore, UK
David J. Fleet	University of Toronto, Canada
David Forsyth	University of Illinois at Urbana-Champaign, USA
David Fouhey	University of Michigan, USA
Katerina Fragkiadaki	Carnegie Mellon University, USA
Friedrich Fraundorfer	Graz University of Technology, Austria
Oren Freifeld	Ben-Gurion University, Israel
Thomas Funkhouser	Google Research & Princeton University, USA
Yasutaka Furukawa	Simon Fraser University, Canada
Fabio Galasso	Sapienza University of Rome, Italy
Jürgen Gall	University of Bonn, Germany
Chuang Gan	Massachusetts Institute of Technology, USA
Zhe Gan	Microsoft, USA
Animesh Garg	University of Toronto, Vector Institute, Nvidia, Canada
Efstratios Gavves	University of Amsterdam, The Netherlands
Peter Gehler	Amazon, Germany
Theo Gevers	University of Amsterdam, The Netherlands
Bernard Ghanem	King Abdullah University of Science and Technology, Saudi Arabia
Ross B. Girshick	Facebook AI Research, USA
Georgia Gkioxari	Facebook AI Research, USA
Albert Gordo	Facebook, USA
Stephen Gould	Australian National University, Australia
Venu Madhav Govindu	Indian Institute of Science, India
Kristen Grauman	Facebook AI Research & UT Austin, USA
Abhinav Gupta	Carnegie Mellon University & Facebook AI Research, USA
Mohit Gupta	University of Wisconsin-Madison, USA
Hu Han	Institute of Computing Technology, Chinese Academy of Sciences, China

Bohyung Han	Seoul National University, Korea
Tian Han	Stevens Institute of Technology, USA
Emily Hand	University of Nevada, Reno, USA
Bharath Hariharan	Cornell University, USA
Ran He	Institute of Automation, Chinese Academy of Sciences, China
Otmar Hilliges	ETH Zurich, Switzerland
Adrian Hilton	University of Surrey, UK
Minh Hoai	Stony Brook University, USA
Yedid Hoshen	Hebrew University of Jerusalem, Israel
Timothy Hospedales	University of Edinburgh, UK
Gang Hua	Wormpex AI Research, USA
Di Huang	Beihang University, China
Jing Huang	Facebook, USA
Jia-Bin Huang	Facebook, USA
Nathan Jacobs	Washington University in St. Louis, USA
C.V. Jawahar	International Institute of Information Technology, Hyderabad, India
Herve Jegou	Facebook AI Research, France
Neel Joshi	Microsoft Research, USA
Armand Joulin	Facebook AI Research, France
Frederic Jurie	University of Caen Normandie, France
Fredrik Kahl	Chalmers University of Technology, Sweden
Yannis Kalantidis	NAVER LABS Europe, France
Evangelos Kalogerakis	University of Massachusetts, Amherst, USA
Sing Bing Kang	Zillow Group, USA
Yosi Keller	Bar Ilan University, Israel
Margret Keuper	University of Mannheim, Germany
Tae-Kyun Kim	Imperial College London, UK
Benjamin Kimia	Brown University, USA
Alexander Kirillov	Facebook AI Research, USA
Kris Kitani	Carnegie Mellon University, USA
Iasonas Kokkinos	Snap Inc. & University College London, UK
Vladlen Koltun	Apple, USA
Nikos Komodakis	University of Crete, Crete
Piotr Koniusz	Australian National University, Australia
Philipp Kraehenbuehl	University of Texas at Austin, USA
Dilip Krishnan	Google, USA
Ajay Kumar	Hong Kong Polytechnic University, Hong Kong, China
Junseok Kwon	Chung-Ang University, Korea
Jean-Francois Lalonde	Université Laval, Canada

Ivan Laptev	Inria Paris, France
Laura Leal-Taixé	Technical University of Munich, Germany
Erik Learned-Miller	University of Massachusetts, Amherst, USA
Gim Hee Lee	National University of Singapore, Singapore
Seungyong Lee	Pohang University of Science and Technology, Korea
Zhen Lei	Institute of Automation, Chinese Academy of Sciences, China
Bastian Leibe	RWTH Aachen University, Germany
Hongdong Li	Australian National University, Australia
Fuxin Li	Oregon State University, USA
Bo Li	University of Illinois at Urbana-Champaign, USA
Yin Li	University of Wisconsin-Madison, USA
Ser-Nam Lim	Meta AI Research, USA
Joseph Lim	University of Southern California, USA
Stephen Lin	Microsoft Research Asia, China
Dahua Lin	The Chinese University of Hong Kong, Hong Kong, China
Si Liu	Beihang University, China
Xiaoming Liu	Michigan State University, USA
Ce Liu	Microsoft, USA
Zicheng Liu	Microsoft, USA
Yanxi Liu	Pennsylvania State University, USA
Feng Liu	Portland State University, USA
Yebin Liu	Tsinghua University, China
Chen Change Loy	Nanyang Technological University, Singapore
Huchuan Lu	Dalian University of Technology, China
Cewu Lu	Shanghai Jiao Tong University, China
Oisin Mac Aodha	University of Edinburgh, UK
Dhruv Mahajan	Facebook, USA
Subhransu Maji	University of Massachusetts, Amherst, USA
Atsuto Maki	KTH Royal Institute of Technology, Sweden
Arun Mallya	NVIDIA, USA
R. Manmatha	Amazon, USA
Iacopo Masi	Sapienza University of Rome, Italy
Dimitris N. Metaxas	Rutgers University, USA
Ajmal Mian	University of Western Australia, Australia
Christian Micheloni	University of Udine, Italy
Krystian Mikolajczyk	Imperial College London, UK
Anurag Mittal	Indian Institute of Technology, Madras, India
Philippos Mordohai	Stevens Institute of Technology, USA
Greg Mori	Simon Fraser University & Borealis AI, Canada

Vittorio Murino	Istituto Italiano di Tecnologia, Italy
P. J. Narayanan	International Institute of Information Technology, Hyderabad, India
Ram Nevatia	University of Southern California, USA
Natalia Neverova	Facebook AI Research, UK
Richard Newcombe	Facebook, USA
Cuong V. Nguyen	Florida International University, USA
Bingbing Ni	Shanghai Jiao Tong University, China
Juan Carlos Niebles	Salesforce & Stanford University, USA
Ko Nishino	Kyoto University, Japan
Jean-Marc Odobez	Idiap Research Institute, École polytechnique fédérale de Lausanne, Switzerland
Francesca Odone	University of Genova, Italy
Takayuki Okatani	Tohoku University & RIKEN Center for Advanced Intelligence Project, Japan
Manohar Paluri	Facebook, USA
Guan Pang	Facebook, USA
Maja Pantic	Imperial College London, UK
Sylvain Paris	Adobe Research, USA
Jaesik Park	Pohang University of Science and Technology, Korea
Hyun Soo Park	The University of Minnesota, USA
Omkar M. Parkhi	Facebook, USA
Deepak Pathak	Carnegie Mellon University, USA
Georgios Pavlakos	University of California, Berkeley, USA
Marcello Pelillo	University of Venice, Italy
Marc Pollefeys	ETH Zurich & Microsoft, Switzerland
Jean Ponce	Inria, France
Gerard Pons-Moll	University of Tübingen, Germany
Fatih Porikli	Qualcomm, USA
Victor Adrian Prisacariu	University of Oxford, UK
Petia Radeva	University of Barcelona, Spain
Ravi Ramamoorthi	University of California, San Diego, USA
Deva Ramanan	Carnegie Mellon University, USA
Vignesh Ramanathan	Facebook, USA
Nalini Ratha	State University of New York at Buffalo, USA
Tammy Riklin Raviv	Ben-Gurion University, Israel
Tobias Ritschel	University College London, UK
Emanuele Rodola	Sapienza University of Rome, Italy
Amit K. Roy-Chowdhury	University of California, Riverside, USA
Michael Rubinstein	Google, USA
Olga Russakovsky	Princeton University, USA

Mathieu Salzmann	École polytechnique fédérale de Lausanne, Switzerland
Dimitris Samaras	Stony Brook University, USA
Aswin Sankaranarayanan	Carnegie Mellon University, USA
Imari Sato	National Institute of Informatics, Japan
Yoichi Sato	University of Tokyo, Japan
Shin'ichi Satoh	National Institute of Informatics, Japan
Walter Scheirer	University of Notre Dame, USA
Bernt Schiele	Max Planck Institute for Informatics, Germany
Konrad Schindler	ETH Zurich, Switzerland
Cordelia Schmid	Inria & Google, France
Alexander Schwing	University of Illinois at Urbana-Champaign, USA
Nicu Sebe	University of Trento, Italy
Greg Shakhnarovich	Toyota Technological Institute at Chicago, USA
Eli Shechtman	Adobe Research, USA
Humphrey Shi	University of Oregon & University of Illinois at Urbana-Champaign & Picsart AI Research, USA
Jianbo Shi	University of Pennsylvania, USA
Roy Shilkrot	Massachusetts Institute of Technology, USA
Mike Zheng Shou	National University of Singapore, Singapore
Kaleem Siddiqi	McGill University, Canada
Richa Singh	Indian Institute of Technology Jodhpur, India
Greg Slabaugh	Queen Mary University of London, UK
Cees Snoek	University of Amsterdam, The Netherlands
Yale Song	Facebook AI Research, USA
Yi-Zhe Song	University of Surrey, UK
Bjorn Stenger	Rakuten Institute of Technology
Abby Stylianou	Saint Louis University, USA
Akihiro Sugimoto	National Institute of Informatics, Japan
Chen Sun	Brown University, USA
Deqing Sun	Google, USA
Kalyan Sunkavalli	Adobe Research, USA
Ying Tai	Tencent YouTu Lab, China
Ayellet Tal	Technion – Israel Institute of Technology, Israel
Ping Tan	Simon Fraser University, Canada
Siyu Tang	ETH Zurich, Switzerland
Chi-Keung Tang	Hong Kong University of Science and Technology, Hong Kong, China
Radu Timofte	University of Würzburg, Germany & ETH Zurich, Switzerland
Federico Tombari	Google, Switzerland & Technical University of Munich, Germany

James Tompkin	Brown University, USA
Lorenzo Torresani	Dartmouth College, USA
Alexander Toshev	Apple, USA
Du Tran	Facebook AI Research, USA
Anh T. Tran	VinAI, Vietnam
Zhuowen Tu	University of California, San Diego, USA
Georgios Tzimiropoulos	Queen Mary University of London, UK
Jasper Uijlings	Google Research, Switzerland
Jan C. van Gemert	Delft University of Technology, The Netherlands
Gul Varol	Ecole des Ponts ParisTech, France
Nuno Vasconcelos	University of California, San Diego, USA
Mayank Vatsa	Indian Institute of Technology Jodhpur, India
Ashok Veeraraghavan	Rice University, USA
Jakob Verbeek	Facebook AI Research, France
Carl Vondrick	Columbia University, USA
Ruiping Wang	Institute of Computing Technology, Chinese Academy of Sciences, China
Xinchao Wang	National University of Singapore, Singapore
Liwei Wang	The Chinese University of Hong Kong, Hong Kong, China
Chaohui Wang	Université Paris-Est, France
Xiaolong Wang	University of California, San Diego, USA
Christian Wolf	NAVER LABS Europe, France
Tao Xiang	University of Surrey, UK
Saining Xie	Facebook AI Research, USA
Cihang Xie	University of California, Santa Cruz, USA
Zeki Yalniz	Facebook, USA
Ming-Hsuan Yang	University of California, Merced, USA
Angela Yao	National University of Singapore, Singapore
Shaodi You	University of Amsterdam, The Netherlands
Stella X. Yu	University of California, Berkeley, USA
Junsong Yuan	State University of New York at Buffalo, USA
Stefanos Zafeiriou	Imperial College London, UK
Amir Zamir	École polytechnique fédérale de Lausanne, Switzerland
Lei Zhang	Alibaba & Hong Kong Polytechnic University, Hong Kong, China
Lei Zhang	International Digital Economy Academy (IDEA), China
Pengchuan Zhang	Meta AI, USA
Bolei Zhou	University of California, Los Angeles, USA
Yuke Zhu	University of Texas at Austin, USA

Todd Zickler   Harvard University, USA
Wangmeng Zuo   Harbin Institute of Technology, China

Technical Program Committee

Davide Abati
Soroush Abbasi
    Koohpayegani
Amos L. Abbott
Rameen Abdal
Rabab Abdelfattah
Sahar Abdelnabi
Hassan Abu Alhaija
Abulikemu Abuduweili
Ron Abutbul
Hanno Ackermann
Aikaterini Adam
Kamil Adamczewski
Ehsan Adeli
Vida Adeli
Donald Adjeroh
Arman Afrasiyabi
Akshay Agarwal
Sameer Agarwal
Abhinav Agarwalla
Vaibhav Aggarwal
Sara Aghajanzadeh
Susmit Agrawal
Antonio Agudo
Touqeer Ahmad
Sk Miraj Ahmed
Chaitanya Ahuja
Nilesh A. Ahuja
Abhishek Aich
Shubhra Aich
Noam Aigerman
Arash Akbarinia
Peri Akiva
Derya Akkaynak
Emre Aksan
Arjun R. Akula
Yuval Alaluf
Stephan Alaniz
Paul Albert
Cenek Albl

Filippo Aleotti
Konstantinos P.
    Alexandridis
Motasem Alfarra
Mohsen Ali
Thiemo Alldieck
Hadi Alzayer
Liang An
Shan An
Yi An
Zhulin An
Dongsheng An
Jie An
Xiang An
Saket Anand
Cosmin Ancuti
Juan Andrade-Cetto
Alexander Andreopoulos
Bjoern Andres
Jerone T. A. Andrews
Shivangi Aneja
Anelia Angelova
Dragomir Anguelov
Rushil Anirudh
Oron Anschel
Rao Muhammad Anwer
Djamila Aouada
Evlampios Apostolidis
Srikar Appalaraju
Nikita Araslanov
Andre Araujo
Eric Arazo
Dawit Mureja Argaw
Anurag Arnab
Aditya Arora
Chetan Arora
Sunpreet S. Arora
Alexey Artemov
Muhammad Asad
Kumar Ashutosh

Sinem Aslan
Vishal Asnani
Mahmoud Assran
Amir Atapour-Abarghouei
Nikos Athanasiou
Ali Athar
ShahRukh Athar
Sara Atito
Souhaib Attaiki
Matan Atzmon
Mathieu Aubry
Nicolas Audebert
Tristan T.
    Aumentado-Armstrong
Melinos Averkiou
Yannis Avrithis
Stephane Ayache
Mehmet Aygün
Seyed Mehdi
    Ayyoubzadeh
Hossein Azizpour
George Azzopardi
Mallikarjun B. R.
Yunhao Ba
Abhishek Badki
Seung-Hwan Bae
Seung-Hwan Baek
Seungryul Baek
Piyush Nitin Bagad
Shai Bagon
Gaetan Bahl
Shikhar Bahl
Sherwin Bahmani
Haoran Bai
Lei Bai
Jiawang Bai
Haoyue Bai
Jinbin Bai
Xiang Bai
Xuyang Bai

Yang Bai
Yuanchao Bai
Ziqian Bai
Sungyong Baik
Kevin Bailly
Max Bain
Federico Baldassarre
Wele Gedara Chaminda
  Bandara
Biplab Banerjee
Pratyay Banerjee
Sandipan Banerjee
Jihwan Bang
Antyanta Bangunharcana
Aayush Bansal
Ankan Bansal
Siddhant Bansal
Wentao Bao
Zhipeng Bao
Amir Bar
Manel Baradad Jurjo
Lorenzo Baraldi
Danny Barash
Daniel Barath
Connelly Barnes
Ioan Andrei Bârsan
Steven Basart
Dina Bashkirova
Chaim Baskin
Peyman Bateni
Anil Batra
Sebastiano Battiato
Ardhendu Behera
Harkirat Behl
Jens Behley
Vasileios Belagiannis
Boulbaba Ben Amor
Emanuel Ben Baruch
Abdessamad Ben Hamza
Gil Ben-Artzi
Assia Benbihi
Fabian Benitez-Quiroz
Guy Ben-Yosef
Philipp Benz
Alexander W. Bergman

Urs Bergmann
Jesus Bermudez-Cameo
Stefano Berretti
Gedas Bertasius
Zachary Bessinger
Petra Bevandić
Matthew Beveridge
Lucas Beyer
Yash Bhalgat
Suvaansh Bhambri
Samarth Bharadwaj
Gaurav Bharaj
Aparna Bharati
Bharat Lal Bhatnagar
Uttaran Bhattacharya
Apratim Bhattacharyya
Brojeshwar Bhowmick
Ankan Kumar Bhunia
Ayan Kumar Bhunia
Qi Bi
Sai Bi
Michael Bi Mi
Gui-Bin Bian
Jia-Wang Bian
Shaojun Bian
Pia Bideau
Mario Bijelic
Hakan Bilen
Guillaume-Alexandre
  Bilodeau
Alexander Binder
Tolga Birdal
Vighnesh N. Birodkar
Sandika Biswas
Andreas Blattmann
Janusz Bobulski
Giuseppe Boccignone
Vishnu Boddeti
Navaneeth Bodla
Moritz Böhle
Aleksei Bokhovkin
Sam Bond-Taylor
Vivek Boominathan
Shubhankar Borse
Mark Boss

Andrea Bottino
Adnane Boukhayma
Fadi Boutros
Nicolas C. Boutry
Richard S. Bowen
Ivaylo Boyadzhiev
Aidan Boyd
Yuri Boykov
Aljaz Bozic
Behzad Bozorgtabar
Eric Brachmann
Samarth Brahmbhatt
Gustav Bredell
Francois Bremond
Joel Brogan
Andrew Brown
Thomas Brox
Marcus A. Brubaker
Robert-Jan Bruintjes
Yuqi Bu
Anders G. Buch
Himanshu Buckchash
Mateusz Buda
Ignas Budvytis
José M. Buenaposada
Marcel C. Bühler
Tu Bui
Adrian Bulat
Hannah Bull
Evgeny Burnaev
Andrei Bursuc
Benjamin Busam
Sergey N. Buzykanov
Wonmin Byeon
Fabian Caba
Martin Cadik
Guanyu Cai
Minjie Cai
Qing Cai
Zhongang Cai
Qi Cai
Yancheng Cai
Shen Cai
Han Cai
Jiarui Cai

Bowen Cai
Mu Cai
Qin Cai
Ruojin Cai
Weidong Cai
Weiwei Cai
Yi Cai
Yujun Cai
Zhiping Cai
Akin Caliskan
Lilian Calvet
Baris Can Cam
Necati Cihan Camgoz
Tommaso Campari
Dylan Campbell
Ziang Cao
Ang Cao
Xu Cao
Zhiwen Cao
Shengcao Cao
Song Cao
Weipeng Cao
Xiangyong Cao
Xiaochun Cao
Yue Cao
Yunhao Cao
Zhangjie Cao
Jiale Cao
Yang Cao
Jiajiong Cao
Jie Cao
Jinkun Cao
Lele Cao
Yulong Cao
Zhiguo Cao
Chen Cao
Razvan Caramalau
Marlène Careil
Gustavo Carneiro
Joao Carreira
Dan Casas
Paola Cascante-Bonilla
Angela Castillo
Francisco M. Castro
Pedro Castro

Luca Cavalli
George J. Cazenavette
Oya Celiktutan
Hakan Cevikalp
Sri Harsha C. H.
Sungmin Cha
Geonho Cha
Menglei Chai
Lucy Chai
Yuning Chai
Zenghao Chai
Anirban Chakraborty
Deep Chakraborty
Rudrasis Chakraborty
Souradeep Chakraborty
Kelvin C. K. Chan
Chee Seng Chan
Paramanand Chandramouli
Arjun Chandrasekaran
Kenneth Chaney
Dongliang Chang
Huiwen Chang
Peng Chang
Xiaojun Chang
Jia-Ren Chang
Hyung Jin Chang
Hyun Sung Chang
Ju Yong Chang
Li-Jen Chang
Qi Chang
Wei-Yi Chang
Yi Chang
Nadine Chang
Hanqing Chao
Pradyumna Chari
Dibyadip Chatterjee
Chiranjoy Chattopadhyay
Siddhartha Chaudhuri
Zhengping Che
Gal Chechik
Lianggangxu Chen
Qi Alfred Chen
Brian Chen
Bor-Chun Chen
Bo-Hao Chen

Bohong Chen
Bin Chen
Ziliang Chen
Cheng Chen
Chen Chen
Chaofeng Chen
Xi Chen
Haoyu Chen
Xuanhong Chen
Wei Chen
Qiang Chen
Shi Chen
Xianyu Chen
Chang Chen
Changhuai Chen
Hao Chen
Jie Chen
Jianbo Chen
Jingjing Chen
Jun Chen
Kejiang Chen
Mingcai Chen
Nenglun Chen
Qifeng Chen
Ruoyu Chen
Shu-Yu Chen
Weidong Chen
Weijie Chen
Weikai Chen
Xiang Chen
Xiuyi Chen
Xingyu Chen
Yaofo Chen
Yueting Chen
Yu Chen
Yunjin Chen
Yuntao Chen
Yun Chen
Zhenfang Chen
Zhuangzhuang Chen
Chu-Song Chen
Xiangyu Chen
Zhuo Chen
Chaoqi Chen
Shizhe Chen

Xiaotong Chen
Xiaozhi Chen
Dian Chen
Defang Chen
Dingfan Chen
Ding-Jie Chen
Ee Heng Chen
Tao Chen
Yixin Chen
Wei-Ting Chen
Lin Chen
Guang Chen
Guangyi Chen
Guanying Chen
Guangyao Chen
Hwann-Tzong Chen
Junwen Chen
Jiacheng Chen
Jianxu Chen
Hui Chen
Kai Chen
Kan Chen
Kevin Chen
Kuan-Wen Chen
Weihua Chen
Zhang Chen
Liang-Chieh Chen
Lele Chen
Liang Chen
Fanglin Chen
Zehui Chen
Minghui Chen
Minghao Chen
Xiaokang Chen
Qian Chen
Jun-Cheng Chen
Qi Chen
Qingcai Chen
Richard J. Chen
Runnan Chen
Rui Chen
Shuo Chen
Sentao Chen
Shaoyu Chen
Shixing Chen

Shuai Chen
Shuya Chen
Sizhe Chen
Simin Chen
Shaoxiang Chen
Zitian Chen
Tianlong Chen
Tianshui Chen
Min-Hung Chen
Xiangning Chen
Xin Chen
Xinghao Chen
Xuejin Chen
Xu Chen
Xuxi Chen
Yunlu Chen
Yanbei Chen
Yuxiao Chen
Yun-Chun Chen
Yi-Ting Chen
Yi-Wen Chen
Yinbo Chen
Yiran Chen
Yuanhong Chen
Yubei Chen
Yuefeng Chen
Yuhua Chen
Yukang Chen
Zerui Chen
Zhaoyu Chen
Zhen Chen
Zhenyu Chen
Zhi Chen
Zhiwei Chen
Zhixiang Chen
Long Chen
Bowen Cheng
Jun Cheng
Yi Cheng
Jingchun Cheng
Lechao Cheng
Xi Cheng
Yuan Cheng
Ho Kei Cheng
Kevin Ho Man Cheng

Jiacheng Cheng
Kelvin B. Cheng
Li Cheng
Mengjun Cheng
Zhen Cheng
Qingrong Cheng
Tianheng Cheng
Harry Cheng
Yihua Cheng
Yu Cheng
Ziheng Cheng
Soon Yau Cheong
Anoop Cherian
Manuela Chessa
Zhixiang Chi
Naoki Chiba
Julian Chibane
Kashyap Chitta
Tai-Yin Chiu
Hsu-kuang Chiu
Wei-Chen Chiu
Sungmin Cho
Donghyeon Cho
Hyeon Cho
Yooshin Cho
Gyusang Cho
Jang Hyun Cho
Seungju Cho
Nam Ik Cho
Sunghyun Cho
Hanbyel Cho
Jaesung Choe
Jooyoung Choi
Chiho Choi
Changwoon Choi
Jongwon Choi
Myungsub Choi
Dooseop Choi
Jonghyun Choi
Jinwoo Choi
Jun Won Choi
Min-Kook Choi
Hongsuk Choi
Janghoon Choi
Yoon-Ho Choi

Yukyung Choi
Jaegul Choo
Ayush Chopra
Siddharth Choudhary
Subhabrata Choudhury
Vasileios Choutas
Ka-Ho Chow
Pinaki Nath Chowdhury
Sammy Christen
Anders Christensen
Grigorios Chrysos
Hang Chu
Wen-Hsuan Chu
Peng Chu
Qi Chu
Ruihang Chu
Wei-Ta Chu
Yung-Yu Chuang
Sanghyuk Chun
Se Young Chun
Antonio Cinà
Ramazan Gokberk Cinbis
Javier Civera
Albert Clapés
Ronald Clark
Brian S. Clipp
Felipe Codevilla
Daniel Coelho de Castro
Niv Cohen
Forrester Cole
Maxwell D. Collins
Robert T. Collins
Marc Comino Trinidad
Runmin Cong
Wenyan Cong
Maxime Cordy
Marcella Cornia
Enric Corona
Huseyin Coskun
Luca Cosmo
Dragos Costea
Davide Cozzolino
Arun C. S. Kumar
Aiyu Cui
Qiongjie Cui

Quan Cui
Shuhao Cui
Yiming Cui
Ying Cui
Zijun Cui
Jiali Cui
Jiequan Cui
Yawen Cui
Zhen Cui
Zhaopeng Cui
Jack Culpepper
Xiaodong Cun
Ross Cutler
Adam Czajka
Ali Dabouei
Konstantinos M. Dafnis
Manuel Dahnert
Tao Dai
Yuchao Dai
Bo Dai
Mengyu Dai
Hang Dai
Haixing Dai
Peng Dai
Pingyang Dai
Qi Dai
Qiyu Dai
Yutong Dai
Naser Damer
Zhiyuan Dang
Mohamed Daoudi
Ayan Das
Abir Das
Debasmit Das
Deepayan Das
Partha Das
Sagnik Das
Soumi Das
Srijan Das
Swagatam Das
Avijit Dasgupta
Jim Davis
Adrian K. Davison
Homa Davoudi
Laura Daza

Matthias De Lange
Shalini De Mello
Marco De Nadai
Christophe De
    Vleeschouwer
Alp Dener
Boyang Deng
Congyue Deng
Bailin Deng
Yong Deng
Ye Deng
Zhuo Deng
Zhijie Deng
Xiaoming Deng
Jiankang Deng
Jinhong Deng
Jingjing Deng
Liang-Jian Deng
Siqi Deng
Xiang Deng
Xueqing Deng
Zhongying Deng
Karan Desai
Jean-Emmanuel Deschaud
Aniket Anand Deshmukh
Neel Dey
Helisa Dhamo
Prithviraj Dhar
Amaya Dharmasiri
Yan Di
Xing Di
Ousmane A. Dia
Haiwen Diao
Xiaolei Diao
Gonçalo José Dias Pais
Abdallah Dib
Anastasios Dimou
Changxing Ding
Henghui Ding
Guodong Ding
Yaqing Ding
Shuangrui Ding
Yuhang Ding
Yikang Ding
Shouhong Ding

Haisong Ding
Hui Ding
Jiahao Ding
Jian Ding
Jian-Jiun Ding
Shuxiao Ding
Tianyu Ding
Wenhao Ding
Yuqi Ding
Yi Ding
Yuzhen Ding
Zhengming Ding
Tan Minh Dinh
Vu Dinh
Christos Diou
Mandar Dixit
Bao Gia Doan
Khoa D. Doan
Dzung Anh Doan
Debi Prosad Dogra
Nehal Doiphode
Chengdong Dong
Bowen Dong
Zhenxing Dong
Hang Dong
Xiaoyi Dong
Haoye Dong
Jiangxin Dong
Shichao Dong
Xuan Dong
Zhen Dong
Shuting Dong
Jing Dong
Li Dong
Ming Dong
Nanqing Dong
Qiulei Dong
Runpei Dong
Siyan Dong
Tian Dong
Wei Dong
Xiaomeng Dong
Xin Dong
Xingbo Dong
Yuan Dong

Samuel Dooley
Gianfranco Doretto
Michael Dorkenwald
Keval Doshi
Zhaopeng Dou
Xiaotian Dou
Hazel Doughty
Ahmad Droby
Iddo Drori
Jie Du
Yong Du
Dawei Du
Dong Du
Ruoyi Du
Yuntao Du
Xuefeng Du
Yilun Du
Yuming Du
Radhika Dua
Haodong Duan
Jiafei Duan
Kaiwen Duan
Peiqi Duan
Ye Duan
Haoran Duan
Jiali Duan
Amanda Duarte
Abhimanyu Dubey
Shiv Ram Dubey
Florian Dubost
Lukasz Dudziak
Shivam Duggal
Justin M. Dulay
Matteo Dunnhofer
Chi Nhan Duong
Thibaut Durand
Mihai Dusmanu
Ujjal Kr Dutta
Debidatta Dwibedi
Isht Dwivedi
Sai Kumar Dwivedi
Takeharu Eda
Mark Edmonds
Alexei A. Efros
Thibaud Ehret

Max Ehrlich
Mahsa Ehsanpour
Iván Eichhardt
Farshad Einabadi
Marvin Eisenberger
Hazim Kemal Ekenel
Mohamed El Banani
Ismail Elezi
Moshe Eliasof
Alaa El-Nouby
Ian Endres
Francis Engelmann
Deniz Engin
Chanho Eom
Dave Epstein
Maria C. Escobar
Victor A. Escorcia
Carlos Esteves
Sungmin Eum
Bernard J. E. Evans
Ivan Evtimov
Fevziye Irem Eyiokur
Yaman
Matteo Fabbri
Sébastien Fabbro
Gabriele Facciolo
Masud Fahim
Bin Fan
Hehe Fan
Deng-Ping Fan
Aoxiang Fan
Chen-Chen Fan
Qi Fan
Zhaoxin Fan
Haoqi Fan
Heng Fan
Hongyi Fan
Linxi Fan
Baojie Fan
Jiayuan Fan
Lei Fan
Quanfu Fan
Yonghui Fan
Yingruo Fan
Zhiwen Fan

Zicong Fan
Sean Fanello
Jiansheng Fang
Chaowei Fang
Yuming Fang
Jianwu Fang
Jin Fang
Qi Fang
Shancheng Fang
Tian Fang
Xianyong Fang
Gongfan Fang
Zhen Fang
Hui Fang
Jiemin Fang
Le Fang
Pengfei Fang
Xiaolin Fang
Yuxin Fang
Zhaoyuan Fang
Ammarah Farooq
Azade Farshad
Zhengcong Fei
Michael Felsberg
Wei Feng
Chen Feng
Fan Feng
Andrew Feng
Xin Feng
Zheyun Feng
Ruicheng Feng
Mingtao Feng
Qianyu Feng
Shangbin Feng
Chun-Mei Feng
Zunlei Feng
Zhiyong Feng
Martin Fergie
Mustansar Fiaz
Marco Fiorucci
Michael Firman
Hamed Firooz
Volker Fischer
Corneliu O. Florea
Georgios Floros

Wolfgang Foerstner
Gianni Franchi
Jean-Sebastien Franco
Simone Frintrop
Anna Fruehstueck
Changhong Fu
Chaoyou Fu
Cheng-Yang Fu
Chi-Wing Fu
Deqing Fu
Huan Fu
Jun Fu
Kexue Fu
Ying Fu
Jianlong Fu
Jingjing Fu
Qichen Fu
Tsu-Jui Fu
Xueyang Fu
Yang Fu
Yanwei Fu
Yonggan Fu
Wolfgang Fuhl
Yasuhisa Fujii
Kent Fujiwara
Marco Fumero
Takuya Funatomi
Isabel Funke
Dario Fuoli
Antonino Furnari
Matheus A. Gadelha
Akshay Gadi Patil
Adrian Galdran
Guillermo Gallego
Silvano Galliani
Orazio Gallo
Leonardo Galteri
Matteo Gamba
Yiming Gan
Sujoy Ganguly
Harald Ganster
Boyan Gao
Changxin Gao
Daiheng Gao
Difei Gao

Chen Gao
Fei Gao
Lin Gao
Wei Gao
Yiming Gao
Junyu Gao
Guangyu Ryan Gao
Haichang Gao
Hongchang Gao
Jialin Gao
Jin Gao
Jun Gao
Katelyn Gao
Mingchen Gao
Mingfei Gao
Pan Gao
Shangqian Gao
Shanghua Gao
Xitong Gao
Yunhe Gao
Zhanning Gao
Elena Garces
Nuno Cruz Garcia
Noa Garcia
Guillermo
    Garcia-Hernando
Isha Garg
Rahul Garg
Sourav Garg
Quentin Garrido
Stefano Gasperini
Kent Gauen
Chandan Gautam
Shivam Gautam
Paul Gay
Chunjiang Ge
Shiming Ge
Wenhang Ge
Yanhao Ge
Zheng Ge
Songwei Ge
Weifeng Ge
Yixiao Ge
Yuying Ge
Shijie Geng

Zhengyang Geng
Kyle A. Genova
Georgios Georgakis
Markos Georgopoulos
Marcel Geppert
Shabnam Ghadar
Mina Ghadimi Atigh
Deepti Ghadiyaram
Maani Ghaffari Jadidi
Sedigh Ghamari
Zahra Gharaee
Michaël Gharbi
Golnaz Ghiasi
Reza Ghoddoosian
Soumya Suvra Ghosal
Adhiraj Ghosh
Arthita Ghosh
Pallabi Ghosh
Soumyadeep Ghosh
Andrew Gilbert
Igor Gilitschenski
Jhony H. Giraldo
Andreu Girbau Xalabarder
Rohit Girdhar
Sharath Girish
Xavier Giro-i-Nieto
Raja Giryes
Thomas Gittings
Nikolaos Gkanatsios
Ioannis Gkioulekas
Abhiram
  Gnanasambandam
Aurele T. Gnanha
Clement L. J. C. Godard
Arushi Goel
Vidit Goel
Shubham Goel
Zan Gojcic
Aaron K. Gokaslan
Tejas Gokhale
S. Alireza Golestaneh
Thiago L. Gomes
Nuno Goncalves
Boqing Gong
Chen Gong

Yuanhao Gong
Guoqiang Gong
Jingyu Gong
Rui Gong
Yu Gong
Mingming Gong
Neil Zhenqiang Gong
Xun Gong
Yunye Gong
Yihong Gong
Cristina I. González
Nithin Gopalakrishnan
  Nair
Gaurav Goswami
Jianping Gou
Shreyank N. Gowda
Ankit Goyal
Helmut Grabner
Patrick L. Grady
Ben Graham
Eric Granger
Douglas R. Gray
Matej Grcić
David Griffiths
Jinjin Gu
Yun Gu
Shuyang Gu
Jianyang Gu
Fuqiang Gu
Jiatao Gu
Jindong Gu
Jiaqi Gu
Jinwei Gu
Jiaxin Gu
Geonmo Gu
Xiao Gu
Xinqian Gu
Xiuye Gu
Yuming Gu
Zhangxuan Gu
Dayan Guan
Junfeng Guan
Qingji Guan
Tianrui Guan
Shanyan Guan

Denis A. Gudovskiy
Ricardo Guerrero
Pierre-Louis Guhur
Jie Gui
Liangyan Gui
Liangke Gui
Benoit Guillard
Erhan Gundogdu
Manuel Günther
Jingcai Guo
Yuanfang Guo
Junfeng Guo
Chenqi Guo
Dan Guo
Hongji Guo
Jia Guo
Jie Guo
Minghao Guo
Shi Guo
Yanhui Guo
Yangyang Guo
Yuan-Chen Guo
Yilu Guo
Yiluan Guo
Yong Guo
Guangyu Guo
Haiyun Guo
Jinyang Guo
Jianyuan Guo
Pengsheng Guo
Pengfei Guo
Shuxuan Guo
Song Guo
Tianyu Guo
Qing Guo
Qiushan Guo
Wen Guo
Xiefan Guo
Xiaohu Guo
Xiaoqing Guo
Yufei Guo
Yuhui Guo
Yuliang Guo
Yunhui Guo
Yanwen Guo

Akshita Gupta
Ankush Gupta
Kamal Gupta
Kartik Gupta
Ritwik Gupta
Rohit Gupta
Siddharth Gururani
Fredrik K. Gustafsson
Abner Guzman Rivera
Vladimir Guzov
Matthew A. Gwilliam
Jung-Woo Ha
Marc Habermann
Isma Hadji
Christian Haene
Martin Hahner
Levente Hajder
Alexandros Haliassos
Emanuela Haller
Bumsub Ham
Abdullah J. Hamdi
Shreyas Hampali
Dongyoon Han
Chunrui Han
Dong-Jun Han
Dong-Sig Han
Guangxing Han
Zhizhong Han
Ruize Han
Jiaming Han
Jin Han
Ligong Han
Xian-Hua Han
Xiaoguang Han
Yizeng Han
Zhi Han
Zhenjun Han
Zhongyi Han
Jungong Han
Junlin Han
Kai Han
Kun Han
Sungwon Han
Songfang Han
Wei Han

Xiao Han
Xintong Han
Xinzhe Han
Yahong Han
Yan Han
Zongbo Han
Nicolai Hani
Rana Hanocka
Niklas Hanselmann
Nicklas A. Hansen
Hong Hanyu
Fusheng Hao
Yanbin Hao
Shijie Hao
Udith Haputhanthri
Mehrtash Harandi
Josh Harguess
Adam Harley
David M. Hart
Atsushi Hashimoto
Ali Hassani
Mohammed Hassanin
Yana Hasson
Joakim Bruslund Haurum
Bo He
Kun He
Chen He
Xin He
Fazhi He
Gaoqi He
Hao He
Haoyu He
Jiangpeng He
Hongliang He
Qian He
Xiangteng He
Xuming He
Yannan He
Yuhang He
Yang He
Xiangyu He
Nanjun He
Pan He
Sen He
Shengfeng He

Songtao He
Tao He
Tong He
Wei He
Xuehai He
Xiaoxiao He
Ying He
Yisheng He
Ziwen He
Peter Hedman
Felix Heide
Yacov Hel-Or
Paul Henderson
Philipp Henzler
Byeongho Heo
Jae-Pil Heo
Miran Heo
Sachini A. Herath
Stephane Herbin
Pedro Hermosilla Casajus
Monica Hernandez
Charles Herrmann
Roei Herzig
Mauricio Hess-Flores
Carlos Hinojosa
Tobias Hinz
Tsubasa Hirakawa
Chih-Hui Ho
Lam Si Tung Ho
Jennifer Hobbs
Derek Hoiem
Yannick Hold-Geoffroy
Aleksander Holynski
Cheeun Hong
Fa-Ting Hong
Hanbin Hong
Guan Zhe Hong
Danfeng Hong
Lanqing Hong
Xiaopeng Hong
Xin Hong
Jie Hong
Seungbum Hong
Cheng-Yao Hong
Seunghoon Hong

Yi Hong
Yuan Hong
Yuchen Hong
Anthony Hoogs
Maxwell C. Horton
Kazuhiro Hotta
Qibin Hou
Tingbo Hou
Junhui Hou
Ji Hou
Qiqi Hou
Rui Hou
Ruibing Hou
Zhi Hou
Henry Howard-Jenkins
Lukas Hoyer
Wei-Lin Hsiao
Chiou-Ting Hsu
Anthony Hu
Brian Hu
Yusong Hu
Hexiang Hu
Haoji Hu
Di Hu
Hengtong Hu
Haigen Hu
Lianyu Hu
Hanzhe Hu
Jie Hu
Junlin Hu
Shizhe Hu
Jian Hu
Zhiming Hu
Juhua Hu
Peng Hu
Ping Hu
Ronghang Hu
MengShun Hu
Tao Hu
Vincent Tao Hu
Xiaoling Hu
Xinting Hu
Xiaolin Hu
Xuefeng Hu
Xiaowei Hu

Yang Hu
Yueyu Hu
Zeyu Hu
Zhongyun Hu
Binh-Son Hua
Guoliang Hua
Yi Hua
Linzhi Huang
Qiusheng Huang
Bo Huang
Chen Huang
Hsin-Ping Huang
Ye Huang
Shuangping Huang
Zeng Huang
Buzhen Huang
Cong Huang
Heng Huang
Hao Huang
Qidong Huang
Huaibo Huang
Chaoqin Huang
Feihu Huang
Jiahui Huang
Jingjia Huang
Kun Huang
Lei Huang
Sheng Huang
Shuaiyi Huang
Siyu Huang
Xiaoshui Huang
Xiaoyang Huang
Yan Huang
Yihao Huang
Ying Huang
Ziling Huang
Xiaoke Huang
Yifei Huang
Haiyang Huang
Zhewei Huang
Jin Huang
Haibin Huang
Jiaxing Huang
Junjie Huang
Keli Huang

Lang Huang
Lin Huang
Luojie Huang
Mingzhen Huang
Shijia Huang
Shengyu Huang
Siyuan Huang
He Huang
Xiuyu Huang
Lianghua Huang
Yue Huang
Yaping Huang
Yuge Huang
Zehao Huang
Zeyi Huang
Zhiqi Huang
Zhongzhan Huang
Zilong Huang
Ziyuan Huang
Tianrui Hui
Zhuo Hui
Le Hui
Jing Huo
Junhwa Hur
Shehzeen S. Hussain
Chuong Minh Huynh
Seunghyun Hwang
Jaehui Hwang
Jyh-Jing Hwang
Sukjun Hwang
Soonmin Hwang
Wonjun Hwang
Rakib Hyder
Sangeek Hyun
Sarah Ibrahimi
Tomoki Ichikawa
Yerlan Idelbayev
A. S. M. Iftekhar
Masaaki Iiyama
Satoshi Ikehata
Sunghoon Im
Atul N. Ingle
Eldar Insafutdinov
Yani A. Ioannou
Radu Tudor Ionescu

Umar Iqbal
Go Irie
Muhammad Zubair Irshad
Ahmet Iscen
Berivan Isik
Ashraful Islam
Md Amirul Islam
Syed Islam
Mariko Isogawa
Vamsi Krishna K. Ithapu
Boris Ivanovic
Darshan Iyer
Sarah Jabbour
Ayush Jain
Nishant Jain
Samyak Jain
Vidit Jain
Vineet Jain
Priyank Jaini
Tomas Jakab
Mohammad A. A. K.
    Jalwana
Muhammad Abdullah
    Jamal
Hadi Jamali-Rad
Stuart James
Varun Jampani
Young Kyun Jang
YeongJun Jang
Yunseok Jang
Ronnachai Jaroensri
Bhavan Jasani
Krishna Murthy
    Jatavallabhula
Mojan Javaheripi
Syed A. Javed
Guillaume Jeanneret
Pranav Jeevan
Herve Jegou
Rohit Jena
Tomas Jenicek
Porter Jenkins
Simon Jenni
Hae-Gon Jeon
Sangryul Jeon

Boseung Jeong
Yoonwoo Jeong
Seong-Gyun Jeong
Jisoo Jeong
Allan D. Jepson
Ankit Jha
Sumit K. Jha
I-Hong Jhuo
Ge-Peng Ji
Chaonan Ji
Deyi Ji
Jingwei Ji
Wei Ji
Zhong Ji
Jiayi Ji
Pengliang Ji
Hui Ji
Mingi Ji
Xiaopeng Ji
Yuzhu Ji
Baoxiong Jia
Songhao Jia
Dan Jia
Shan Jia
Xiaojun Jia
Xiuyi Jia
Xu Jia
Menglin Jia
Wenqi Jia
Boyuan Jiang
Wenhao Jiang
Huaizu Jiang
Hanwen Jiang
Haiyong Jiang
Hao Jiang
Huajie Jiang
Huiqin Jiang
Haojun Jiang
Haobo Jiang
Junjun Jiang
Xingyu Jiang
Yangbangyan Jiang
Yu Jiang
Jianmin Jiang
Jiaxi Jiang

Jing Jiang
Kui Jiang
Li Jiang
Liming Jiang
Chiyu Jiang
Meirui Jiang
Chen Jiang
Peng Jiang
Tai-Xiang Jiang
Wen Jiang
Xinyang Jiang
Yifan Jiang
Yuming Jiang
Yingying Jiang
Zeren Jiang
ZhengKai Jiang
Zhenyu Jiang
Shuming Jiao
Jianbo Jiao
Licheng Jiao
Dongkwon Jin
Yeying Jin
Cheng Jin
Linyi Jin
Qing Jin
Taisong Jin
Xiao Jin
Xin Jin
Sheng Jin
Kyong Hwan Jin
Ruibing Jin
SouYoung Jin
Yueming Jin
Chenchen Jing
Longlong Jing
Taotao Jing
Yongcheng Jing
Younghyun Jo
Joakim Johnander
Jeff Johnson
Michael J. Jones
R. Kenny Jones
Rico Jonschkowski
Ameya Joshi
Sunghun Joung

Felix Juefei-Xu
Claudio R. Jung
Steffen Jung
Hari Chandana K.
Rahul Vigneswaran K.
Prajwal K. R.
Abhishek Kadian
Jhony Kaesemodel Pontes
Kumara Kahatapitiya
Anmol Kalia
Sinan Kalkan
Tarun Kalluri
Jaewon Kam
Sandesh Kamath
Meina Kan
Menelaos Kanakis
Takuhiro Kaneko
Di Kang
Guoliang Kang
Hao Kang
Jaeyeon Kang
Kyoungkook Kang
Li-Wei Kang
MinGuk Kang
Suk-Ju Kang
Zhao Kang
Yash Mukund Kant
Yueying Kao
Aupendu Kar
Konstantinos Karantzalos
Sezer Karaoglu
Navid Kardan
Sanjay Kariyappa
Leonid Karlinsky
Animesh Karnewar
Shyamgopal Karthik
Hirak J. Kashyap
Marc A. Kastner
Hirokatsu Kataoka
Angelos Katharopoulos
Hiroharu Kato
Kai Katsumata
Manuel Kaufmann
Chaitanya Kaul
Prakhar Kaushik

Yuki Kawana
Lei Ke
Lipeng Ke
Tsung-Wei Ke
Wei Ke
Petr Kellnhofer
Aniruddha Kembhavi
John Kender
Corentin Kervadec
Leonid Keselman
Daniel Keysers
Nima Khademi Kalantari
Taras Khakhulin
Samir Khaki
Muhammad Haris Khan
Qadeer Khan
Salman Khan
Subash Khanal
Vaishnavi M. Khindkar
Rawal Khirodkar
Saeed Khorram
Pirazh Khorramshahi
Kourosh Khoshelham
Ansh Khurana
Benjamin Kiefer
Jae Myung Kim
Junho Kim
Boah Kim
Hyeonseong Kim
Dong-Jin Kim
Dongwan Kim
Donghyun Kim
Doyeon Kim
Yonghyun Kim
Hyung-Il Kim
Hyunwoo Kim
Hyeongwoo Kim
Hyo Jin Kim
Hyunwoo J. Kim
Taehoon Kim
Jaeha Kim
Jiwon Kim
Jung Uk Kim
Kangyeol Kim
Eunji Kim

Daeha Kim
Dongwon Kim
Kunhee Kim
Kyungmin Kim
Junsik Kim
Min H. Kim
Namil Kim
Kookhoi Kim
Sanghyun Kim
Seongyeop Kim
Seungryong Kim
Saehoon Kim
Euyoung Kim
Guisik Kim
Sungyeon Kim
Sunnie S. Y. Kim
Taehun Kim
Tae Oh Kim
Won Hwa Kim
Seungwook Kim
YoungBin Kim
Youngeun Kim
Akisato Kimura
Furkan Osman Kınlı
Zsolt Kira
Hedvig Kjellström
Florian Kleber
Jan P. Klopp
Florian Kluger
Laurent Kneip
Byungsoo Ko
Muhammed Kocabas
A. Sophia Koepke
Kevin Koeser
Nick Kolkin
Nikos Kolotouros
Wai-Kin Adams Kong
Deying Kong
Caihua Kong
Youyong Kong
Shuyu Kong
Shu Kong
Tao Kong
Yajing Kong
Yu Kong

Zishang Kong
Theodora Kontogianni
Anton S. Konushin
Julian F. P. Kooij
Bruno Korbar
Giorgos Kordopatis-Zilos
Jari Korhonen
Adam Kortylewski
Denis Korzhenkov
Divya Kothandaraman
Suraj Kothawade
Iuliia Kotseruba
Satwik Kottur
Shashank Kotyan
Alexandros Kouris
Petros Koutras
Anna Kreshuk
Ranjay Krishna
Dilip Krishnan
Andrey Kuehlkamp
Hilde Kuehne
Jason Kuen
David Kügler
Arjan Kuijper
Anna Kukleva
Sumith Kulal
Viveka Kulharia
Akshay R. Kulkarni
Nilesh Kulkarni
Dominik Kulon
Abhinav Kumar
Akash Kumar
Suryansh Kumar
B. V. K. Vijaya Kumar
Pulkit Kumar
Ratnesh Kumar
Sateesh Kumar
Satish Kumar
Vijay Kumar B. G.
Nupur Kumari
Sudhakar Kumawat
Jogendra Nath Kundu
Hsien-Kai Kuo
Meng-Yu Jennifer Kuo
Vinod Kumar Kurmi

Yusuke Kurose
Keerthy Kusumam
Alina Kuznetsova
Henry Kvinge
Ho Man Kwan
Hyeokjun Kweon
Heeseung Kwon
Gihyun Kwon
Myung-Joon Kwon
Taesung Kwon
YoungJoong Kwon
Christos Kyrkou
Jorma Laaksonen
Yann Labbe
Zorah Laehner
Florent Lafarge
Hamid Laga
Manuel Lagunas
Shenqi Lai
Jian-Huang Lai
Zihang Lai
Mohamed I. Lakhal
Mohit Lamba
Meng Lan
Loic Landrieu
Zhiqiang Lang
Natalie Lang
Dong Lao
Yizhen Lao
Yingjie Lao
Issam Hadj Laradji
Gustav Larsson
Viktor Larsson
Zakaria Laskar
Stéphane Lathuilière
Chun Pong Lau
Rynson W. H. Lau
Hei Law
Justin Lazarow
Verica Lazova
Eric-Tuan Le
Hieu Le
Trung-Nghia Le
Mathias Lechner
Byeong-Uk Lee

Chen-Yu Lee
Che-Rung Lee
Chul Lee
Hong Joo Lee
Dongsoo Lee
Jiyoung Lee
Eugene Eu Tzuan Lee
Daeun Lee
Saehyung Lee
Jewook Lee
Hyungtae Lee
Hyunmin Lee
Jungbeom Lee
Joon-Young Lee
Jong-Seok Lee
Joonseok Lee
Junha Lee
Kibok Lee
Byung-Kwan Lee
Jangwon Lee
Jinho Lee
Jongmin Lee
Seunghyun Lee
Sohyun Lee
Minsik Lee
Dogyoon Lee
Seungmin Lee
Min Jun Lee
Sangho Lee
Sangmin Lee
Seungeun Lee
Seon-Ho Lee
Sungmin Lee
Sungho Lee
Sangyoun Lee
Vincent C. S. S. Lee
Jaeseong Lee
Yong Jae Lee
Chenyang Lei
Chenyi Lei
Jiahui Lei
Xinyu Lei
Yinjie Lei
Jiaxu Leng
Luziwei Leng

Jan E. Lenssen
Vincent Lepetit
Thomas Leung
María Leyva-Vallina
Xin Li
Yikang Li
Baoxin Li
Bin Li
Bing Li
Bowen Li
Changlin Li
Chao Li
Chongyi Li
Guanyue Li
Shuai Li
Jin Li
Dingquan Li
Dongxu Li
Yiting Li
Gang Li
Dian Li
Guohao Li
Haoang Li
Haoliang Li
Haoran Li
Hengduo Li
Huafeng Li
Xiaoming Li
Hanao Li
Hongwei Li
Ziqiang Li
Jisheng Li
Jiacheng Li
Jia Li
Jiachen Li
Jiahao Li
Jianwei Li
Jiazhi Li
Jie Li
Jing Li
Jingjing Li
Jingtao Li
Jun Li
Junxuan Li
Kai Li

Kailin Li
Kenneth Li
Kun Li
Kunpeng Li
Aoxue Li
Chenglong Li
Chenglin Li
Changsheng Li
Zhichao Li
Qiang Li
Yanyu Li
Zuoyue Li
Xiang Li
Xuelong Li
Fangda Li
Ailin Li
Liang Li
Chun-Guang Li
Daiqing Li
Dong Li
Guanbin Li
Guorong Li
Haifeng Li
Jianan Li
Jianing Li
Jiaxin Li
Ke Li
Lei Li
Lincheng Li
Liulei Li
Lujun Li
Linjie Li
Lin Li
Pengyu Li
Ping Li
Qiufu Li
Qingyong Li
Rui Li
Siyuan Li
Wei Li
Wenbin Li
Xiangyang Li
Xinyu Li
Xiujun Li
Xiu Li

Xu Li
Ya-Li Li
Yao Li
Yongjie Li
Yijun Li
Yiming Li
Yuezun Li
Yu Li
Yunheng Li
Yuqi Li
Zhe Li
Zeming Li
Zhen Li
Zhengqin Li
Zhimin Li
Jiefeng Li
Jinpeng Li
Chengze Li
Jianwu Li
Lerenhan Li
Shan Li
Suichan Li
Xiangtai Li
Yanjie Li
Yandong Li
Zhuoling Li
Zhenqiang Li
Manyi Li
Maosen Li
Ji Li
Minjun Li
Mingrui Li
Mengtian Li
Junyi Li
Nianyi Li
Bo Li
Xiao Li
Peihua Li
Peike Li
Peizhao Li
Peiliang Li
Qi Li
Ren Li
Runze Li
Shile Li

Sheng Li
Shigang Li
Shiyu Li
Shuang Li
Shasha Li
Shichao Li
Tianye Li
Yuexiang Li
Wei-Hong Li
Wanhua Li
Weihao Li
Weiming Li
Weixin Li
Wenbo Li
Wenshuo Li
Weijian Li
Yunan Li
Xirong Li
Xianhang Li
Xiaoyu Li
Xueqian Li
Xuanlin Li
Xianzhi Li
Yunqiang Li
Yanjing Li
Yansheng Li
Yawei Li
Yi Li
Yong Li
Yong-Lu Li
Yuhang Li
Yu-Jhe Li
Yuxi Li
Yunsheng Li
Yanwei Li
Zechao Li
Zejian Li
Zeju Li
Zekun Li
Zhaowen Li
Zheng Li
Zhenyu Li
Zhiheng Li
Zhi Li
Zhong Li

Zhuowei Li
Zhuowan Li
Zhuohang Li
Zizhang Li
Chen Li
Yuan-Fang Li
Dongze Lian
Xiaochen Lian
Zhouhui Lian
Long Lian
Qing Lian
Jin Lianbao
Jinxiu S. Liang
Dingkang Liang
Jiahao Liang
Jianming Liang
Jingyun Liang
Kevin J. Liang
Kaizhao Liang
Chen Liang
Jie Liang
Senwei Liang
Ding Liang
Jiajun Liang
Jian Liang
Kongming Liang
Siyuan Liang
Yuanzhi Liang
Zhengfa Liang
Mingfu Liang
Xiaodan Liang
Xuefeng Liang
Yuxuan Liang
Kang Liao
Liang Liao
Hong-Yuan Mark Liao
Wentong Liao
Haofu Liao
Yue Liao
Minghui Liao
Shengcai Liao
Ting-Hsuan Liao
Xin Liao
Yinghong Liao
Teck Yian Lim

Che-Tsung Lin
Chung-Ching Lin
Chen-Hsuan Lin
Cheng Lin
Chuming Lin
Chunyu Lin
Dahua Lin
Wei Lin
Zheng Lin
Huaijia Lin
Jason Lin
Jierui Lin
Jiaying Lin
Jie Lin
Kai-En Lin
Kevin Lin
Guangfeng Lin
Jiehong Lin
Feng Lin
Hang Lin
Kwan-Yee Lin
Ke Lin
Luojun Lin
Qinghong Lin
Xiangbo Lin
Yi Lin
Zudi Lin
Shijie Lin
Yiqun Lin
Tzu-Heng Lin
Ming Lin
Shaohui Lin
SongNan Lin
Ji Lin
Tsung-Yu Lin
Xudong Lin
Yancong Lin
Yen-Chen Lin
Yiming Lin
Yuewei Lin
Zhiqiu Lin
Zinan Lin
Zhe Lin
David B. Lindell
Zhixin Ling

Zhan Ling	Jun Liu	Zhenguang Liu
Alexander Liniger	Juncheng Liu	Lin Liu
Venice Erin B. Liong	Jiawei Liu	Lihao Liu
Joey Litalien	Hongyu Liu	Pengju Liu
Or Litany	Chuanbin Liu	Xinhai Liu
Roee Litman	Haotian Liu	Yunfei Liu
Ron Litman	Lingqiao Liu	Meng Liu
Jim Little	Chang Liu	Minghua Liu
Dor Litvak	Han Liu	Mingyuan Liu
Shaoteng Liu	Liu Liu	Miao Liu
Shuaicheng Liu	Min Liu	Peirong Liu
Andrew Liu	Yingqi Liu	Ping Liu
Xian Liu	Aishan Liu	Qingjie Liu
Shaohui Liu	Bingyu Liu	Ruoshi Liu
Bei Liu	Benlin Liu	Risheng Liu
Bo Liu	Boxiao Liu	Songtao Liu
Yong Liu	Chenchen Liu	Xing Liu
Ming Liu	Chuanjian Liu	Shikun Liu
Yanbin Liu	Daqing Liu	Shuming Liu
Chenxi Liu	Huan Liu	Sheng Liu
Daqi Liu	Haozhe Liu	Songhua Liu
Di Liu	Jiaheng Liu	Tongliang Liu
Difan Liu	Wei Liu	Weibo Liu
Dong Liu	Jingzhou Liu	Weide Liu
Dongfang Liu	Jiyuan Liu	Weizhe Liu
Daizong Liu	Lingbo Liu	Wenxi Liu
Xiao Liu	Nian Liu	Weiyang Liu
Fangyi Liu	Peiye Liu	Xin Liu
Fengbei Liu	Qiankun Liu	Xiaobin Liu
Fenglin Liu	Shenglan Liu	Xudong Liu
Bin Liu	Shilong Liu	Xiaoyi Liu
Yuang Liu	Wen Liu	Xihui Liu
Ao Liu	Wenyu Liu	Xinchen Liu
Hong Liu	Weifeng Liu	Xingtong Liu
Hongfu Liu	Wu Liu	Xinpeng Liu
Huidong Liu	Xiaolong Liu	Xinyu Liu
Ziyi Liu	Yang Liu	Xianpeng Liu
Feng Liu	Yanwei Liu	Xu Liu
Hao Liu	Yingcheng Liu	Xingyu Liu
Jie Liu	Yongfei Liu	Yongtuo Liu
Jialun Liu	Yihao Liu	Yahui Liu
Jiang Liu	Yu Liu	Yangxin Liu
Jing Liu	Yunze Liu	Yaoyao Liu
Jingya Liu	Ze Liu	Yaojie Liu
Jiaming Liu	Zhenhua Liu	Yuliang Liu

Yongcheng Liu
Yuan Liu
Yufan Liu
Yu-Lun Liu
Yun Liu
Yunfan Liu
Yuanzhong Liu
Zhuoran Liu
Zhen Liu
Zheng Liu
Zhijian Liu
Zhisong Liu
Ziquan Liu
Ziyu Liu
Zhihua Liu
Zechun Liu
Zhaoyang Liu
Zhengzhe Liu
Stephan Liwicki
Shao-Yuan Lo
Sylvain Lobry
Suhas Lohit
Vishnu Suresh Lokhande
Vincenzo Lomonaco
Chengjiang Long
Guodong Long
Fuchen Long
Shangbang Long
Yang Long
Zijun Long
Vasco Lopes
Antonio M. Lopez
Roberto Javier
    Lopez-Sastre
Tobias Lorenz
Javier Lorenzo-Navarro
Yujing Lou
Qian Lou
Xiankai Lu
Changsheng Lu
Huimin Lu
Yongxi Lu
Hao Lu
Hong Lu
Jiasen Lu

Juwei Lu
Fan Lu
Guangming Lu
Jiwen Lu
Shun Lu
Tao Lu
Xiaonan Lu
Yang Lu
Yao Lu
Yongchun Lu
Zhiwu Lu
Cheng Lu
Liying Lu
Guo Lu
Xuequan Lu
Yanye Lu
Yantao Lu
Yuhang Lu
Fujun Luan
Jonathon Luiten
Jovita Lukasik
Alan Lukezic
Jonathan Samuel Lumentut
Mayank Lunayach
Ao Luo
Canjie Luo
Chong Luo
Xu Luo
Grace Luo
Jun Luo
Katie Z. Luo
Tao Luo
Cheng Luo
Fangzhou Luo
Gen Luo
Lei Luo
Sihui Luo
Weixin Luo
Yan Luo
Xiaoyan Luo
Yong Luo
Yadan Luo
Hao Luo
Ruotian Luo
Mi Luo

Tiange Luo
Wenjie Luo
Wenhan Luo
Xiao Luo
Zhiming Luo
Zhipeng Luo
Zhengyi Luo
Diogo C. Luvizon
Zhaoyang Lv
Gengyu Lyu
Lingjuan Lyu
Jun Lyu
Yuanyuan Lyu
Youwei Lyu
Yueming Lyu
Bingpeng Ma
Chao Ma
Chongyang Ma
Congbo Ma
Chih-Yao Ma
Fan Ma
Lin Ma
Haoyu Ma
Hengbo Ma
Jianqi Ma
Jiawei Ma
Jiayi Ma
Kede Ma
Kai Ma
Lingni Ma
Lei Ma
Xu Ma
Ning Ma
Benteng Ma
Cheng Ma
Andy J. Ma
Long Ma
Zhanyu Ma
Zhiheng Ma
Qianli Ma
Shiqiang Ma
Sizhuo Ma
Shiqing Ma
Xiaolong Ma
Xinzhu Ma

Gautam B. Machiraju
Spandan Madan
Mathew Magimai-Doss
Luca Magri
Behrooz Mahasseni
Upal Mahbub
Siddharth Mahendran
Paridhi Maheshwari
Rishabh Maheshwary
Mohammed Mahmoud
Shishira R. R. Maiya
Sylwia Majchrowska
Arjun Majumdar
Puspita Majumdar
Orchid Majumder
Sagnik Majumder
Ilya Makarov
Farkhod F.
    Makhmudkhujaev
Yasushi Makihara
Ankur Mali
Mateusz Malinowski
Utkarsh Mall
Srikanth Malla
Clement Mallet
Dimitrios Mallis
Yunze Man
Dipu Manandhar
Massimiliano Mancini
Murari Mandal
Raunak Manekar
Karttikeya Mangalam
Puneet Mangla
Fabian Manhardt
Sivabalan Manivasagam
Fahim Mannan
Chengzhi Mao
Hanzi Mao
Jiayuan Mao
Junhua Mao
Zhiyuan Mao
Jiageng Mao
Yunyao Mao
Zhendong Mao
Alberto Marchisio

Diego Marcos
Riccardo Marin
Aram Markosyan
Renaud Marlet
Ricardo Marques
Miquel Martí i Rabadán
Diego Martin Arroyo
Niki Martinel
Brais Martinez
Julieta Martinez
Marc Masana
Tomohiro Mashita
Timothée Masquelier
Minesh Mathew
Tetsu Matsukawa
Marwan Mattar
Bruce A. Maxwell
Christoph Mayer
Mantas Mazeika
Pratik Mazumder
Scott McCloskey
Steven McDonagh
Ishit Mehta
Jie Mei
Kangfu Mei
Jieru Mei
Xiaoguang Mei
Givi Meishvili
Luke Melas-Kyriazi
Iaroslav Melekhov
Andres Mendez-Vazquez
Heydi Mendez-Vazquez
Matias Mendieta
Ricardo A. Mendoza-León
Chenlin Meng
Depu Meng
Rang Meng
Zibo Meng
Qingjie Meng
Qier Meng
Yanda Meng
Zihang Meng
Thomas Mensink
Fabian Mentzer
Christopher Metzler

Gregory P. Meyer
Vasileios Mezaris
Liang Mi
Lu Mi
Bo Miao
Changtao Miao
Zichen Miao
Qiguang Miao
Xin Miao
Zhongqi Miao
Frank Michel
Simone Milani
Ben Mildenhall
Roy V. Miles
Juhong Min
Kyle Min
Hyun-Seok Min
Weiqing Min
Yuecong Min
Zhixiang Min
Qi Ming
David Minnen
Aymen Mir
Deepak Mishra
Anand Mishra
Shlok K. Mishra
Niluthpol Mithun
Gaurav Mittal
Trisha Mittal
Daisuke Miyazaki
Kaichun Mo
Hong Mo
Zhipeng Mo
Davide Modolo
Abduallah A. Mohamed
Mohamed Afham
Mohamed Aflal
Ron Mokady
Pavlo Molchanov
Davide Moltisanti
Liliane Momeni
Gianluca Monaci
Pascal Monasse
Ajoy Mondal
Tom Monnier

Aron Monszpart
Gyeongsik Moon
Suhong Moon
Taesup Moon
Sean Moran
Daniel Moreira
Pietro Morerio
Alexandre Morgand
Lia Morra
Ali Mosleh
Inbar Mosseri
Sayed Mohammad
    Mostafavi Isfahani
Saman Motamed
Ramy A. Mounir
Fangzhou Mu
Jiteng Mu
Norman Mu
Yasuhiro Mukaigawa
Ryan Mukherjee
Tanmoy Mukherjee
Yusuke Mukuta
Ravi Teja Mullapudi
Lea Müller
Matthias Müller
Martin Mundt
Nils Murrugarra-Llerena
Damien Muselet
Armin Mustafa
Muhammad Ferjad Naeem
Sauradip Nag
Hajime Nagahara
Pravin Nagar
Rajendra Nagar
Naveen Shankar Nagaraja
Varun Nagaraja
Tushar Nagarajan
Seungjun Nah
Gaku Nakano
Yuta Nakashima
Giljoo Nam
Seonghyeon Nam
Liangliang Nan
Yuesong Nan
Yeshwanth Napolean

Dinesh Reddy
    Narapureddy
Medhini Narasimhan
Supreeth
    Narasimhaswamy
Sriram Narayanan
Erickson R. Nascimento
Varun Nasery
K. L. Navaneet
Pablo Navarrete Michelini
Shant Navasardyan
Shah Nawaz
Nihal Nayak
Farhood Negin
Lukáš Neumann
Alejandro Newell
Evonne Ng
Kam Woh Ng
Tony Ng
Anh Nguyen
Tuan Anh Nguyen
Cuong Cao Nguyen
Ngoc Cuong Nguyen
Thanh Nguyen
Khoi Nguyen
Phi Le Nguyen
Phong Ha Nguyen
Tam Nguyen
Truong Nguyen
Anh Tuan Nguyen
Rang Nguyen
Thao Thi Phuong Nguyen
Van Nguyen Nguyen
Zhen-Liang Ni
Yao Ni
Shijie Nie
Xuecheng Nie
Yongwei Nie
Weizhi Nie
Ying Nie
Yinyu Nie
Kshitij N. Nikhal
Simon Niklaus
Xuefei Ning
Jifeng Ning

Yotam Nitzan
Di Niu
Shuaicheng Niu
Li Niu
Wei Niu
Yulei Niu
Zhenxing Niu
Albert No
Shohei Nobuhara
Nicoletta Noceti
Junhyug Noh
Sotiris Nousias
Slawomir Nowaczyk
Ewa M. Nowara
Valsamis Ntouskos
Gilberto Ochoa-Ruiz
Ferda Ofli
Jihyong Oh
Sangyun Oh
Youngtaek Oh
Hiroki Ohashi
Takahiro Okabe
Kemal Oksuz
Fumio Okura
Daniel Olmeda Reino
Matthew Olson
Carl Olsson
Roy Or-El
Alessandro Ortis
Guillermo Ortiz-Jimenez
Magnus Oskarsson
Ahmed A. A. Osman
Martin R. Oswald
Mayu Otani
Naima Otberdout
Cheng Ouyang
Jiahong Ouyang
Wanli Ouyang
Andrew Owens
Poojan B. Oza
Mete Ozay
A. Cengiz Oztireli
Gautam Pai
Tomas Pajdla
Umapada Pal

Simone Palazzo
Luca Palmieri
Bowen Pan
Hao Pan
Lili Pan
Tai-Yu Pan
Liang Pan
Chengwei Pan
Yingwei Pan
Xuran Pan
Jinshan Pan
Xinyu Pan
Liyuan Pan
Xingang Pan
Xingjia Pan
Zhihong Pan
Zizheng Pan
Priyadarshini Panda
Rameswar Panda
Rohit Pandey
Kaiyue Pang
Bo Pang
Guansong Pang
Jiangmiao Pang
Meng Pang
Tianyu Pang
Ziqi Pang
Omiros Pantazis
Andreas Panteli
Maja Pantic
Marina Paolanti
Joao P. Papa
Samuele Papa
Mike Papadakis
Dim P. Papadopoulos
George Papandreou
Constantin Pape
Toufiq Parag
Chethan Parameshwara
Shaifali Parashar
Alejandro Pardo
Rishubh Parihar
Sarah Parisot
JaeYoo Park
Gyeong-Moon Park

Hyojin Park
Hyoungseob Park
Jongchan Park
Jae Sung Park
Kiru Park
Chunghyun Park
Kwanyong Park
Sunghyun Park
Sungrae Park
Seongsik Park
Sanghyun Park
Sungjune Park
Taesung Park
Gaurav Parmar
Paritosh Parmar
Alvaro Parra
Despoina Paschalidou
Or Patashnik
Shivansh Patel
Pushpak Pati
Prashant W. Patil
Vaishakh Patil
Suvam Patra
Jay Patravali
Badri Narayana Patro
Angshuman Paul
Sudipta Paul
Rémi Pautrat
Nick E. Pears
Adithya Pediredla
Wenjie Pei
Shmuel Peleg
Latha Pemula
Bo Peng
Houwen Peng
Yue Peng
Liangzu Peng
Baoyun Peng
Jun Peng
Pai Peng
Sida Peng
Xi Peng
Yuxin Peng
Songyou Peng
Wei Peng

Weiqi Peng
Wen-Hsiao Peng
Pramuditha Perera
Juan C. Perez
Eduardo Pérez Pellitero
Juan-Manuel Perez-Rua
Federico Pernici
Marco Pesavento
Stavros Petridis
Ilya A. Petrov
Vladan Petrovic
Mathis Petrovich
Suzanne Petryk
Hieu Pham
Quang Pham
Khoi Pham
Tung Pham
Huy Phan
Stephen Phillips
Cheng Perng Phoo
David Picard
Marco Piccirilli
Georg Pichler
A. J. Piergiovanni
Vipin Pillai
Silvia L. Pintea
Giovanni Pintore
Robinson Piramuthu
Fiora Pirri
Theodoros Pissas
Fabio Pizzati
Benjamin Planche
Bryan Plummer
Matteo Poggi
Ashwini Pokle
Georgy E. Ponimatkin
Adrian Popescu
Stefan Popov
Nikola Popović
Ronald Poppe
Angelo Porrello
Michael Potter
Charalambos Poullis
Hadi Pouransari
Omid Poursaeed

Shraman Pramanick
Mantini Pranav
Dilip K. Prasad
Meghshyam Prasad
B. H. Pawan Prasad
Shitala Prasad
Prateek Prasanna
Ekta Prashnani
Derek S. Prijatelj
Luke Y. Prince
Véronique Prinet
Victor Adrian Prisacariu
James Pritts
Thomas Probst
Sergey Prokudin
Rita Pucci
Chi-Man Pun
Matthew Purri
Haozhi Qi
Lu Qi
Lei Qi
Xianbiao Qi
Yonggang Qi
Yuankai Qi
Siyuan Qi
Guocheng Qian
Hangwei Qian
Qi Qian
Deheng Qian
Shengsheng Qian
Wen Qian
Rui Qian
Yiming Qian
Shengju Qian
Shengyi Qian
Xuelin Qian
Zhenxing Qian
Nan Qiao
Xiaotian Qiao
Jing Qin
Can Qin
Siyang Qin
Hongwei Qin
Jie Qin
Minghai Qin

Yipeng Qin
Yongqiang Qin
Wenda Qin
Xuebin Qin
Yuzhe Qin
Yao Qin
Zhenyue Qin
Zhiwu Qing
Heqian Qiu
Jiayan Qiu
Jielin Qiu
Yue Qiu
Jiaxiong Qiu
Zhongxi Qiu
Shi Qiu
Zhaofan Qiu
Zhongnan Qu
Yanyun Qu
Kha Gia Quach
Yuhui Quan
Ruijie Quan
Mike Rabbat
Rahul Shekhar Rade
Filip Radenovic
Gorjan Radevski
Bogdan Raducanu
Francesco Ragusa
Shafin Rahman
Md Mahfuzur Rahman
    Siddiquee
Hossein Rahmani
Kiran Raja
Sivaramakrishnan
    Rajaraman
Jathushan Rajasegaran
Adnan Siraj Rakin
Michaël Ramamonjisoa
Chirag A. Raman
Shanmuganathan Raman
Vignesh Ramanathan
Vasili Ramanishka
Vikram V. Ramaswamy
Merey Ramazanova
Jason Rambach
Sai Saketh Rambhatla

Clément Rambour
Ashwin Ramesh Babu
Adín Ramírez Rivera
Arianna Rampini
Haoxi Ran
Aakanksha Rana
Aayush Jung Bahadur
    Rana
Kanchana N. Ranasinghe
Aneesh Rangnekar
Samrudhdhi B. Rangrej
Harsh Rangwani
Viresh Ranjan
Anyi Rao
Yongming Rao
Carolina Raposo
Michalis Raptis
Amir Rasouli
Vivek Rathod
Adepu Ravi Sankar
Avinash Ravichandran
Bharadwaj Ravichandran
Dripta S. Raychaudhuri
Adria Recasens
Simon Reiß
Davis Rempe
Daxuan Ren
Jiawei Ren
Jimmy Ren
Sucheng Ren
Dayong Ren
Zhile Ren
Dongwei Ren
Qibing Ren
Pengfei Ren
Zhenwen Ren
Xuqian Ren
Yixuan Ren
Zhongzheng Ren
Ambareesh Revanur
Hamed Rezazadegan
    Tavakoli
Rafael S. Rezende
Wonjong Rhee
Alexander Richard

Christian Richardt
Stephan R. Richter
Benjamin Riggan
Dominik Rivoir
Mamshad Nayeem Rizve
Joshua D. Robinson
Joseph Robinson
Chris Rockwell
Ranga Rodrigo
Andres C. Rodriguez
Carlos Rodriguez-Pardo
Marcus Rohrbach
Gemma Roig
Yu Rong
David A. Ross
Mohammad Rostami
Edward Rosten
Karsten Roth
Anirban Roy
Debaditya Roy
Shuvendu Roy
Ahana Roy Choudhury
Aruni Roy Chowdhury
Denys Rozumnyi
Shulan Ruan
Wenjie Ruan
Patrick Ruhkamp
Danila Rukhovich
Anian Ruoss
Chris Russell
Dan Ruta
Dawid Damian Rymarczyk
DongHun Ryu
Hyeonggon Ryu
Kwonyoung Ryu
Balasubramanian S.
Alexandre Sablayrolles
Mohammad Sabokrou
Arka Sadhu
Aniruddha Saha
Oindrila Saha
Pritish Sahu
Aneeshan Sain
Nirat Saini
Saurabh Saini

Takeshi Saitoh
Christos Sakaridis
Fumihiko Sakaue
Dimitrios Sakkos
Ken Sakurada
Parikshit V. Sakurikar
Rohit Saluja
Nermin Samet
Leo Sampaio Ferraz
    Ribeiro
Jorge Sanchez
Enrique Sanchez
Shengtian Sang
Anush Sankaran
Soubhik Sanyal
Nikolaos Sarafianos
Vishwanath Saragadam
István Sárándi
Saquib Sarfraz
Mert Bulent Sariyildiz
Anindya Sarkar
Pritam Sarkar
Paul-Edouard Sarlin
Hiroshi Sasaki
Takami Sato
Torsten Sattler
Ravi Kumar Satzoda
Axel Sauer
Stefano Savian
Artem Savkin
Manolis Savva
Gerald Schaefer
Simone Schaub-Meyer
Yoni Schirris
Samuel Schulter
Katja Schwarz
Jesse Scott
Sinisa Segvic
Constantin Marc Seibold
Lorenzo Seidenari
Matan Sela
Fadime Sener
Paul Hongsuck Seo
Kwanggyoon Seo
Hongje Seong

Dario Serez
Francesco Setti
Bryan Seybold
Mohamad Shahbazi
Shima Shahfar
Xinxin Shan
Caifeng Shan
Dandan Shan
Shawn Shan
Wei Shang
Jinghuan Shang
Jiaxiang Shang
Lei Shang
Sukrit Shankar
Ken Shao
Rui Shao
Jie Shao
Mingwen Shao
Aashish Sharma
Gaurav Sharma
Vivek Sharma
Abhishek Sharma
Yoli Shavit
Shashank Shekhar
Sumit Shekhar
Zhijie Shen
Fengyi Shen
Furao Shen
Jialie Shen
Jingjing Shen
Ziyi Shen
Linlin Shen
Guangyu Shen
Biluo Shen
Falong Shen
Jiajun Shen
Qiu Shen
Qiuhong Shen
Shuai Shen
Wang Shen
Yiqing Shen
Yunhang Shen
Siqi Shen
Bin Shen
Tianwei Shen

Xi Shen
Yilin Shen
Yuming Shen
Yucong Shen
Zhiqiang Shen
Lu Sheng
Yichen Sheng
Shivanand Venkanna
   Sheshappanavar
Shelly Sheynin
Baifeng Shi
Ruoxi Shi
Botian Shi
Hailin Shi
Jia Shi
Jing Shi
Shaoshuai Shi
Baoguang Shi
Boxin Shi
Hengcan Shi
Tianyang Shi
Xiaodan Shi
Yongjie Shi
Zhensheng Shi
Yinghuan Shi
Weiqi Shi
Wu Shi
Xuepeng Shi
Xiaoshuang Shi
Yujiao Shi
Zenglin Shi
Zhenmei Shi
Takashi Shibata
Meng-Li Shih
Yichang Shih
Hyunjung Shim
Dongseok Shim
Soshi Shimada
Inkyu Shin
Jinwoo Shin
Seungjoo Shin
Seungjae Shin
Koichi Shinoda
Suprosanna Shit

Palaiahnakote
   Shivakumara
Eli Shlizerman
Gaurav Shrivastava
Xiao Shu
Xiangbo Shu
Xiujun Shu
Yang Shu
Tianmin Shu
Jun Shu
Zhixin Shu
Bing Shuai
Maria Shugrina
Ivan Shugurov
Satya Narayan Shukla
Pranjay Shyam
Jianlou Si
Yawar Siddiqui
Alberto Signoroni
Pedro Silva
Jae-Young Sim
Oriane Siméoni
Martin Simon
Andrea Simonelli
Abhishek Singh
Ashish Singh
Dinesh Singh
Gurkirt Singh
Krishna Kumar Singh
Mannat Singh
Pravendra Singh
Rajat Vikram Singh
Utkarsh Singhal
Dipika Singhania
Vasu Singla
Harsh Sinha
Sudipta Sinha
Josef Sivic
Elena Sizikova
Geri Skenderi
Ivan Skorokhodov
Dmitriy Smirnov
Cameron Y. Smith
James S. Smith
Patrick Snape

Mattia Soldan
Hyeongseok Son
Sanghyun Son
Chuanbiao Song
Chen Song
Chunfeng Song
Dan Song
Dongjin Song
Hwanjun Song
Guoxian Song
Jiaming Song
Jie Song
Liangchen Song
Ran Song
Luchuan Song
Xibin Song
Li Song
Fenglong Song
Guoli Song
Guanglu Song
Zhenbo Song
Lin Song
Xinhang Song
Yang Song
Yibing Song
Rajiv Soundararajan
Hossein Souri
Cristovao Sousa
Riccardo Spezialetti
Leonidas Spinoulas
Michael W. Spratling
Deepak Sridhar
Srinath Sridhar
Gaurang Sriramanan
Vinkle Kumar Srivastav
Themos Stafylakis
Serban Stan
Anastasis Stathopoulos
Markus Steinberger
Jan Steinbrener
Sinisa Stekovic
Alexandros Stergiou
Gleb Sterkin
Rainer Stiefelhagen
Pierre Stock

Ombretta Strafforello
Julian Straub
Yannick Strümpler
Joerg Stueckler
Hang Su
Weijie Su
Jong-Chyi Su
Bing Su
Haisheng Su
Jinming Su
Yiyang Su
Yukun Su
Yuxin Su
Zhuo Su
Zhaoqi Su
Xiu Su
Yu-Chuan Su
Zhixun Su
Arulkumar Subramaniam
Akshayvarun Subramanya
A. Subramanyam
Swathikiran Sudhakaran
Yusuke Sugano
Masanori Suganuma
Yumin Suh
Yang Sui
Baochen Sun
Cheng Sun
Long Sun
Guolei Sun
Haoliang Sun
Haomiao Sun
He Sun
Hanqing Sun
Hao Sun
Lichao Sun
Jiachen Sun
Jiaming Sun
Jian Sun
Jin Sun
Jennifer J. Sun
Tiancheng Sun
Libo Sun
Peize Sun
Qianru Sun

Shanlin Sun
Yu Sun
Zhun Sun
Che Sun
Lin Sun
Tao Sun
Yiyou Sun
Chunyi Sun
Chong Sun
Weiwei Sun
Weixuan Sun
Xiuyu Sun
Yanan Sun
Zeren Sun
Zhaodong Sun
Zhiqing Sun
Minhyuk Sung
Jinli Suo
Simon Suo
Abhijit Suprem
Anshuman Suri
Saksham Suri
Joshua M. Susskind
Roman Suvorov
Gurumurthy Swaminathan
Robin Swanson
Paul Swoboda
Tabish A. Syed
Richard Szeliski
Fariborz Taherkhani
Yu-Wing Tai
Keita Takahashi
Walter Talbott
Gary Tam
Masato Tamura
Feitong Tan
Fuwen Tan
Shuhan Tan
Andong Tan
Bin Tan
Cheng Tan
Jianchao Tan
Lei Tan
Mingxing Tan
Xin Tan

Zichang Tan
Zhentao Tan
Kenichiro Tanaka
Masayuki Tanaka
Yushun Tang
Hao Tang
Jingqun Tang
Jinhui Tang
Kaihua Tang
Luming Tang
Lv Tang
Sheyang Tang
Shitao Tang
Siliang Tang
Shixiang Tang
Yansong Tang
Keke Tang
Chang Tang
Chenwei Tang
Jie Tang
Junshu Tang
Ming Tang
Peng Tang
Xu Tang
Yao Tang
Chen Tang
Fan Tang
Haoran Tang
Shengeng Tang
Yehui Tang
Zhipeng Tang
Ugo Tanielian
Chaofan Tao
Jiale Tao
Junli Tao
Renshuai Tao
An Tao
Guanhong Tao
Zhiqiang Tao
Makarand Tapaswi
Jean-Philippe G. Tarel
Juan J. Tarrio
Enzo Tartaglione
Keisuke Tateno
Zachary Teed

Ajinkya B. Tejankar
Bugra Tekin
Purva Tendulkar
Damien Teney
Minggui Teng
Chris Tensmeyer
Andrew Beng Jin Teoh
Philipp Terhörst
Kartik Thakral
Nupur Thakur
Kevin Thandiackal
Spyridon Thermos
Diego Thomas
William Thong
Yuesong Tian
Guanzhong Tian
Lin Tian
Shiqi Tian
Kai Tian
Meng Tian
Tai-Peng Tian
Zhuotao Tian
Shangxuan Tian
Tian Tian
Yapeng Tian
Yu Tian
Yuxin Tian
Leslie Ching Ow Tiong
Praveen Tirupattur
Garvita Tiwari
George Toderici
Antoine Toisoul
Aysim Toker
Tatiana Tommasi
Zhan Tong
Alessio Tonioni
Alessandro Torcinovich
Fabio Tosi
Matteo Toso
Hugo Touvron
Quan Hung Tran
Son Tran
Hung Tran
Ngoc-Trung Tran
Vinh Tran

Phong Tran
Giovanni Trappolini
Edith Tretschk
Subarna Tripathi
Shubhendu Trivedi
Eduard Trulls
Prune Truong
Thanh-Dat Truong
Tomasz Trzcinski
Sam Tsai
Yi-Hsuan Tsai
Ethan Tseng
Yu-Chee Tseng
Shahar Tsiper
Stavros Tsogkas
Shikui Tu
Zhigang Tu
Zhengzhong Tu
Richard Tucker
Sergey Tulyakov
Cigdem Turan
Daniyar Turmukhambetov
Victor G. Turrisi da Costa
Bartlomiej Twardowski
Christopher D. Twigg
Radim Tylecek
Mostofa Rafid Uddin
Md. Zasim Uddin
Kohei Uehara
Nicolas Ugrinovic
Youngjung Uh
Norimichi Ukita
Anwaar Ulhaq
Devesh Upadhyay
Paul Upchurch
Yoshitaka Ushiku
Yuzuko Utsumi
Mikaela Angelina Uy
Mohit Vaishnav
Pratik Vaishnavi
Jeya Maria Jose Valanarasu
Matias A. Valdenegro Toro
Diego Valsesia
Wouter Van Gansbeke
Nanne van Noord

Simon Vandenhende
Farshid Varno
Cristina Vasconcelos
Francisco Vasconcelos
Alex Vasilescu
Subeesh Vasu
Arun Balajee Vasudevan
Kanav Vats
Vaibhav S. Vavilala
Sagar Vaze
Javier Vazquez-Corral
Andrea Vedaldi
Olga Veksler
Andreas Velten
Sai H. Vemprala
Raviteja Vemulapalli
Shashanka
    Venkataramanan
Dor Verbin
Luisa Verdoliva
Manisha Verma
Yashaswi Verma
Constantin Vertan
Eli Verwimp
Deepak Vijaykeerthy
Pablo Villanueva
Ruben Villegas
Markus Vincze
Vibhav Vineet
Minh P. Vo
Huy V. Vo
Duc Minh Vo
Tomas Vojir
Igor Vozniak
Nicholas Vretos
Vibashan VS
Tuan-Anh Vu
Thang Vu
Mårten Wadenbäck
Neal Wadhwa
Aaron T. Walsman
Steven Walton
Jin Wan
Alvin Wan
Jia Wan

Jun Wan
Xiaoyue Wan
Fang Wan
Guowei Wan
Renjie Wan
Zhiqiang Wan
Ziyu Wan
Bastian Wandt
Dongdong Wang
Limin Wang
Haiyang Wang
Xiaobing Wang
Angtian Wang
Angelina Wang
Bing Wang
Bo Wang
Boyu Wang
Binghui Wang
Chen Wang
Chien-Yi Wang
Congli Wang
Qi Wang
Chengrui Wang
Rui Wang
Yiqun Wang
Cong Wang
Wenjing Wang
Dongkai Wang
Di Wang
Xiaogang Wang
Kai Wang
Zhizhong Wang
Fangjinhua Wang
Feng Wang
Hang Wang
Gaoang Wang
Guoqing Wang
Guangcong Wang
Guangzhi Wang
Hanqing Wang
Hao Wang
Haohan Wang
Haoran Wang
Hong Wang
Haotao Wang

Hu Wang
Huan Wang
Hua Wang
Hui-Po Wang
Hengli Wang
Hanyu Wang
Hongxing Wang
Jingwen Wang
Jialiang Wang
Jian Wang
Jianyi Wang
Jiashun Wang
Jiahao Wang
Tsun-Hsuan Wang
Xiaoqian Wang
Jinqiao Wang
Jun Wang
Jianzong Wang
Kaihong Wang
Ke Wang
Lei Wang
Lingjing Wang
Linnan Wang
Lin Wang
Liansheng Wang
Mengjiao Wang
Manning Wang
Nannan Wang
Peihao Wang
Jiayun Wang
Pu Wang
Qiang Wang
Qiufeng Wang
Qilong Wang
Qiangchang Wang
Qin Wang
Qing Wang
Ruocheng Wang
Ruibin Wang
Ruisheng Wang
Ruizhe Wang
Runqi Wang
Runzhong Wang
Wenxuan Wang
Sen Wang

Shangfei Wang
Shaofei Wang
Shijie Wang
Shiqi Wang
Zhibo Wang
Song Wang
Xinjiang Wang
Tai Wang
Tao Wang
Teng Wang
Xiang Wang
Tianren Wang
Tiantian Wang
Tianyi Wang
Fengjiao Wang
Wei Wang
Miaohui Wang
Suchen Wang
Siyue Wang
Yaoming Wang
Xiao Wang
Ze Wang
Biao Wang
Chaofei Wang
Dong Wang
Gu Wang
Guangrun Wang
Guangming Wang
Guo-Hua Wang
Haoqing Wang
Hesheng Wang
Huafeng Wang
Jinghua Wang
Jingdong Wang
Jingjing Wang
Jingya Wang
Jingkang Wang
Jiakai Wang
Junke Wang
Kuo Wang
Lichen Wang
Lizhi Wang
Longguang Wang
Mang Wang
Mei Wang

Min Wang

Peng-Shuai Wang

Run Wang

Shaoru Wang

Shuhui Wang

Tan Wang

Tiancai Wang

Tianqi Wang

Wenhai Wang

Wenzhe Wang

Xiaobo Wang

Xiudong Wang

Xu Wang

Yajie Wang

Yan Wang

Yuan-Gen Wang

Yingqian Wang

Yizhi Wang

Yulin Wang

Yu Wang

Yujie Wang

Yunhe Wang

Yuxi Wang

Yaowei Wang

Yiwei Wang

Zezheng Wang

Hongzhi Wang

Zhiqiang Wang

Ziteng Wang

Ziwei Wang

Zheng Wang

Zhenyu Wang

Binglu Wang

Zhongdao Wang

Ce Wang

Weining Wang

Weiyao Wang

Wenbin Wang

Wenguan Wang

Guangting Wang

Haolin Wang

Haiyan Wang

Huiyu Wang

Naiyan Wang

Jingbo Wang

Jinpeng Wang

Jiaqi Wang

Liyuan Wang

Lizhen Wang

Ning Wang

Wenqian Wang

Sheng-Yu Wang

Weimin Wang

Xiaohan Wang

Yifan Wang

Yi Wang

Yongtao Wang

Yizhou Wang

Zhuo Wang

Zhe Wang

Xudong Wang

Xiaofang Wang

Xinggang Wang

Xiaosen Wang

Xiaosong Wang

Xiaoyang Wang

Lijun Wang

Xinlong Wang

Xuan Wang

Xue Wang

Yangang Wang

Yaohui Wang

Yu-Chiang Frank Wang

Yida Wang

Yilin Wang

Yi Ru Wang

Yali Wang

Yinglong Wang

Yufu Wang

Yujiang Wang

Yuwang Wang

Yuting Wang

Yang Wang

Yu-Xiong Wang

Yixu Wang

Ziqi Wang

Zhicheng Wang

Zeyu Wang

Zhaowen Wang

Zhenyi Wang

Zhenzhi Wang

Zhijie Wang

Zhiyong Wang

Zhongling Wang

Zhuowei Wang

Zian Wang

Zifu Wang

Zihao Wang

Zirui Wang

Ziyan Wang

Wenxiao Wang

Zhen Wang

Zhepeng Wang

Zi Wang

Zihao W. Wang

Steven L. Waslander

Olivia Watkins

Daniel Watson

Silvan Weder

Dongyoon Wee

Dongming Wei

Tianyi Wei

Jia Wei

Dong Wei

Fangyun Wei

Longhui Wei

Mingqiang Wei

Xinyue Wei

Chen Wei

Donglai Wei

Pengxu Wei

Xing Wei

Xiu-Shen Wei

Wenqi Wei

Guoqiang Wei

Wei Wei

XingKui Wei

Xian Wei

Xingxing Wei

Yake Wei

Yuxiang Wei

Yi Wei

Luca Weihs

Michael Weinmann

Martin Weinmann

Congcong Wen
Chuan Wen
Jie Wen
Sijia Wen
Song Wen
Chao Wen
Xiang Wen
Zeyi Wen
Xin Wen
Yilin Wen
Yijia Weng
Shuchen Weng
Junwu Weng
Wenming Weng
Renliang Weng
Zhenyu Weng
Xinshuo Weng
Nicholas J. Westlake
Gordon Wetzstein
Lena M. Widin Klasén
Rick Wildes
Bryan M. Williams
Williem Williem
Ole Winther
Scott Wisdom
Alex Wong
Chau-Wai Wong
Kwan-Yee K. Wong
Yongkang Wong
Scott Workman
Marcel Worring
Michael Wray
Safwan Wshah
Xiang Wu
Aming Wu
Chongruo Wu
Cho-Ying Wu
Chunpeng Wu
Chenyan Wu
Ziyi Wu
Fuxiang Wu
Gang Wu
Haiping Wu
Huisi Wu
Jane Wu

Jialian Wu
Jing Wu
Jinjian Wu
Jianlong Wu
Xian Wu
Lifang Wu
Lifan Wu
Minye Wu
Qianyi Wu
Rongliang Wu
Rui Wu
Shiqian Wu
Shuzhe Wu
Shangzhe Wu
Tsung-Han Wu
Tz-Ying Wu
Ting-Wei Wu
Jiannan Wu
Zhiliang Wu
Yu Wu
Chenyun Wu
Dayan Wu
Dongxian Wu
Fei Wu
Hefeng Wu
Jianxin Wu
Weibin Wu
Wenxuan Wu
Wenhao Wu
Xiao Wu
Yicheng Wu
Yuanwei Wu
Yu-Huan Wu
Zhenxin Wu
Zhenyu Wu
Wei Wu
Peng Wu
Xiaohe Wu
Xindi Wu
Xinxing Wu
Xinyi Wu
Xingjiao Wu
Xiongwei Wu
Yangzheng Wu
Yanzhao Wu

Yawen Wu
Yong Wu
Yi Wu
Ying Nian Wu
Zhenyao Wu
Zhonghua Wu
Zongze Wu
Zuxuan Wu
Stefanie Wuhrer
Teng Xi
Jianing Xi
Fei Xia
Haifeng Xia
Menghan Xia
Yuanqing Xia
Zhihua Xia
Xiaobo Xia
Weihao Xia
Shihong Xia
Yan Xia
Yong Xia
Zhaoyang Xia
Zhihao Xia
Chuhua Xian
Yongqin Xian
Wangmeng Xiang
Fanbo Xiang
Tiange Xiang
Tao Xiang
Liuyu Xiang
Xiaoyu Xiang
Zhiyu Xiang
Aoran Xiao
Chunxia Xiao
Fanyi Xiao
Jimin Xiao
Jun Xiao
Taihong Xiao
Anqi Xiao
Junfei Xiao
Jing Xiao
Liang Xiao
Yang Xiao
Yuting Xiao
Yijun Xiao

Yao Xiao

Zeyu Xiao

Zhisheng Xiao

Zihao Xiao

Binhui Xie

Christopher Xie

Haozhe Xie

Jin Xie

Guo-Sen Xie

Hongtao Xie

Ming-Kun Xie

Tingting Xie

Chaohao Xie

Weicheng Xie

Xudong Xie

Jiyang Xie

Xiaohua Xie

Yuan Xie

Zhenyu Xie

Ning Xie

Xianghui Xie

Xiufeng Xie

You Xie

Yutong Xie

Fuyong Xing

Yifan Xing

Zhen Xing

Yuanjun Xiong

Jinhui Xiong

Weihua Xiong

Hongkai Xiong

Zhitong Xiong

Yuanhao Xiong

Yunyang Xiong

Yuwen Xiong

Zhiwei Xiong

Yuliang Xiu

An Xu

Chang Xu

Chenliang Xu

Chengming Xu

Chenshu Xu

Xiang Xu

Huijuan Xu

Zhe Xu

Jie Xu

Jingyi Xu

Jiarui Xu

Yinghao Xu

Kele Xu

Ke Xu

Li Xu

Linchuan Xu

Linning Xu

Mengde Xu

Mengmeng Frost Xu

Min Xu

Mingye Xu

Jun Xu

Ning Xu

Peng Xu

Runsheng Xu

Sheng Xu

Wenqiang Xu

Xiaogang Xu

Renzhe Xu

Kaidi Xu

Yi Xu

Chi Xu

Qiuling Xu

Baobei Xu

Feng Xu

Haohang Xu

Haofei Xu

Lan Xu

Mingze Xu

Songcen Xu

Weipeng Xu

Wenjia Xu

Wenju Xu

Xiangyu Xu

Xin Xu

Yinshuang Xu

Yixing Xu

Yuting Xu

Yanyu Xu

Zhenbo Xu

Zhiliang Xu

Zhiyuan Xu

Xiaohao Xu

Yanwu Xu

Yan Xu

Yiran Xu

Yifan Xu

Yufei Xu

Yong Xu

Zichuan Xu

Zenglin Xu

Zexiang Xu

Zhan Xu

Zheng Xu

Zhiwei Xu

Ziyue Xu

Shiyu Xuan

Hanyu Xuan

Fei Xue

Jianru Xue

Mingfu Xue

Qinghan Xue

Tianfan Xue

Chao Xue

Chuhui Xue

Nan Xue

Zhou Xue

Xiangyang Xue

Yuan Xue

Abhay Yadav

Ravindra Yadav

Kota Yamaguchi

Toshihiko Yamasaki

Kohei Yamashita

Chaochao Yan

Feng Yan

Kun Yan

Qingsen Yan

Qixin Yan

Rui Yan

Siming Yan

Xinchen Yan

Yaping Yan

Bin Yan

Qingan Yan

Shen Yan

Shipeng Yan

Xu Yan

Yan Yan
Yichao Yan
Zhaoyi Yan
Zike Yan
Zhiqiang Yan
Hongliang Yan
Zizheng Yan
Jiewen Yang
Anqi Joyce Yang
Shan Yang
Anqi Yang
Antoine Yang
Bo Yang
Baoyao Yang
Chenhongyi Yang
Dingkang Yang
De-Nian Yang
Dong Yang
David Yang
Fan Yang
Fengyu Yang
Fengting Yang
Fei Yang
Gengshan Yang
Heng Yang
Han Yang
Huan Yang
Yibo Yang
Jiancheng Yang
Jihan Yang
Jiawei Yang
Jiayu Yang
Jie Yang
Jinfa Yang
Jingkang Yang
Jinyu Yang
Cheng-Fu Yang
Ji Yang
Jianyu Yang
Kailun Yang
Tian Yang
Luyu Yang
Liang Yang
Li Yang
Michael Ying Yang

Yang Yang
Muli Yang
Le Yang
Qiushi Yang
Ren Yang
Ruihan Yang
Shuang Yang
Siyuan Yang
Su Yang
Shiqi Yang
Taojiannan Yang
Tianyu Yang
Lei Yang
Wanzhao Yang
Shuai Yang
William Yang
Wei Yang
Xiaofeng Yang
Xiaoshan Yang
Xin Yang
Xuan Yang
Xu Yang
Xingyi Yang
Xitong Yang
Jing Yang
Yanchao Yang
Wenming Yang
Yujiu Yang
Herb Yang
Jianfei Yang
Jinhui Yang
Chuanguang Yang
Guanglei Yang
Haitao Yang
Kewei Yang
Linlin Yang
Lijin Yang
Longrong Yang
Meng Yang
MingKun Yang
Sibei Yang
Shicai Yang
Tong Yang
Wen Yang
Xi Yang

Xiaolong Yang
Xue Yang
Yubin Yang
Ze Yang
Ziyi Yang
Yi Yang
Linjie Yang
Yuzhe Yang
Yiding Yang
Zhenpei Yang
Zhaohui Yang
Zhengyuan Yang
Zhibo Yang
Zongxin Yang
Hantao Yao
Mingde Yao
Rui Yao
Taiping Yao
Ting Yao
Cong Yao
Qingsong Yao
Quanming Yao
Xu Yao
Yuan Yao
Yao Yao
Yazhou Yao
Jiawen Yao
Shunyu Yao
Pew-Thian Yap
Sudhir Yarram
Rajeev Yasarla
Peng Ye
Botao Ye
Mao Ye
Fei Ye
Hanrong Ye
Jingwen Ye
Jinwei Ye
Jiarong Ye
Mang Ye
Meng Ye
Qi Ye
Qian Ye
Qixiang Ye
Junjie Ye

Sheng Ye
Nanyang Ye
Yufei Ye
Xiaoqing Ye
Ruolin Ye
Yousef Yeganeh
Chun-Hsiao Yeh
Raymond A. Yeh
Yu-Ying Yeh
Kai Yi
Chang Yi
Renjiao Yi
Xinping Yi
Peng Yi
Alper Yilmaz
Junho Yim
Hui Yin
Bangjie Yin
Jia-Li Yin
Miao Yin
Wenzhe Yin
Xuwang Yin
Ming Yin
Yu Yin
Aoxiong Yin
Kangxue Yin
Tianwei Yin
Wei Yin
Xianghua Ying
Rio Yokota
Tatsuya Yokota
Naoto Yokoya
Ryo Yonetani
Ki Yoon Yoo
Jinsu Yoo
Sunjae Yoon
Jae Shin Yoon
Jihun Yoon
Sung-Hoon Yoon
Ryota Yoshihashi
Yusuke Yoshiyasu
Chenyu You
Haoran You
Haoxuan You
Yang You

Quanzeng You
Tackgeun You
Kaichao You
Shan You
Xinge You
Yurong You
Baosheng Yu
Bei Yu
Haichao Yu
Hao Yu
Chaohui Yu
Fisher Yu
Jin-Gang Yu
Jiyang Yu
Jason J. Yu
Jiashuo Yu
Hong-Xing Yu
Lei Yu
Mulin Yu
Ning Yu
Peilin Yu
Qi Yu
Qian Yu
Rui Yu
Shuzhi Yu
Gang Yu
Tan Yu
Weijiang Yu
Xin Yu
Bingyao Yu
Ye Yu
Hanchao Yu
Yingchen Yu
Tao Yu
Xiaotian Yu
Qing Yu
Houjian Yu
Changqian Yu
Jing Yu
Jun Yu
Shujian Yu
Xiang Yu
Zhaofei Yu
Zhenbo Yu
Yinfeng Yu

Zhuoran Yu
Zitong Yu
Bo Yuan
Jiangbo Yuan
Liangzhe Yuan
Weihao Yuan
Jianbo Yuan
Xiaoyun Yuan
Ye Yuan
Li Yuan
Geng Yuan
Jialin Yuan
Maoxun Yuan
Peng Yuan
Xin Yuan
Yuan Yuan
Yuhui Yuan
Yixuan Yuan
Zheng Yuan
Mehmet Kerim Yücel
Kaiyu Yue
Haixiao Yue
Heeseung Yun
Sangdoo Yun
Tian Yun
Mahmut Yurt
Ekim Yurtsever
Ahmet Yüzügüler
Edouard Yvinec
Eloi Zablocki
Christopher Zach
Muhammad Zaigham
 Zaheer
Pierluigi Zama Ramirez
Yuhang Zang
Pietro Zanuttigh
Alexey Zaytsev
Bernhard Zeisl
Haitian Zeng
Pengpeng Zeng
Jiabei Zeng
Runhao Zeng
Wei Zeng
Yawen Zeng
Yi Zeng

Yiming Zeng
Tieyong Zeng
Huanqiang Zeng
Dan Zeng
Yu Zeng
Wei Zhai
Yuanhao Zhai
Fangneng Zhan
Kun Zhan
Xiong Zhang
Jingdong Zhang
Jiangning Zhang
Zhilu Zhang
Gengwei Zhang
Dongsu Zhang
Hui Zhang
Binjie Zhang
Bo Zhang
Tianhao Zhang
Cecilia Zhang
Jing Zhang
Chaoning Zhang
Chenxu Zhang
Chi Zhang
Chris Zhang
Yabin Zhang
Zhao Zhang
Rufeng Zhang
Chaoyi Zhang
Zheng Zhang
Da Zhang
Yi Zhang
Edward Zhang
Xin Zhang
Feifei Zhang
Feilong Zhang
Yuqi Zhang
GuiXuan Zhang
Hanlin Zhang
Hanwang Zhang
Hanzhen Zhang
Haotian Zhang
He Zhang
Haokui Zhang
Hongyuan Zhang

Hengrui Zhang
Hongming Zhang
Mingfang Zhang
Jianpeng Zhang
Jiaming Zhang
Jichao Zhang
Jie Zhang
Jingfeng Zhang
Jingyi Zhang
Jinnian Zhang
David Junhao Zhang
Junjie Zhang
Junzhe Zhang
Jiawan Zhang
Jingyang Zhang
Kai Zhang
Lei Zhang
Lihua Zhang
Lu Zhang
Miao Zhang
Minjia Zhang
Mingjin Zhang
Qi Zhang
Qian Zhang
Qilong Zhang
Qiming Zhang
Qiang Zhang
Richard Zhang
Ruimao Zhang
Ruisi Zhang
Ruixin Zhang
Runze Zhang
Qilin Zhang
Shan Zhang
Shanshan Zhang
Xi Sheryl Zhang
Song-Hai Zhang
Chongyang Zhang
Kaihao Zhang
Songyang Zhang
Shu Zhang
Siwei Zhang
Shujian Zhang
Tianyun Zhang
Tong Zhang

Tao Zhang
Wenwei Zhang
Wenqiang Zhang
Wen Zhang
Xiaolin Zhang
Xingchen Zhang
Xingxuan Zhang
Xiuming Zhang
Xiaoshuai Zhang
Xuanmeng Zhang
Xuanyang Zhang
Xucong Zhang
Xingxing Zhang
Xikun Zhang
Xiaohan Zhang
Yahui Zhang
Yunhua Zhang
Yan Zhang
Yanghao Zhang
Yifei Zhang
Yifan Zhang
Yi-Fan Zhang
Yihao Zhang
Yingliang Zhang
Youshan Zhang
Yulun Zhang
Yushu Zhang
Yixiao Zhang
Yide Zhang
Zhongwen Zhang
Bowen Zhang
Chen-Lin Zhang
Zehua Zhang
Zekun Zhang
Zeyu Zhang
Xiaowei Zhang
Yifeng Zhang
Cheng Zhang
Hongguang Zhang
Yuexi Zhang
Fa Zhang
Guofeng Zhang
Hao Zhang
Haofeng Zhang
Hongwen Zhang

Hua Zhang	Zhizhong Zhang	Bowen Zhao
Jiaxin Zhang	Qilong Zhangli	Pu Zhao
Zhenyu Zhang	Bingyin Zhao	Bingchen Zhao
Jian Zhang	Bin Zhao	Borui Zhao
Jianfeng Zhang	Chenglong Zhao	Fuqiang Zhao
Jiao Zhang	Lei Zhao	Hanbin Zhao
Jiakai Zhang	Feng Zhao	Jian Zhao
Lefei Zhang	Gangming Zhao	Mingyang Zhao
Le Zhang	Haiyan Zhao	Na Zhao
Mi Zhang	Hao Zhao	Rongchang Zhao
Min Zhang	Handong Zhao	Ruiqi Zhao
Ning Zhang	Hengshuang Zhao	Shuai Zhao
Pan Zhang	Yinan Zhao	Wenda Zhao
Pu Zhang	Jiaojiao Zhao	Wenliang Zhao
Qing Zhang	Jiaqi Zhao	Xiangyun Zhao
Renrui Zhang	Jing Zhao	Yifan Zhao
Shifeng Zhang	Kaili Zhao	Yaping Zhao
Shuo Zhang	Haojie Zhao	Zhou Zhao
Shaoxiong Zhang	Yucheng Zhao	He Zhao
Weizhong Zhang	Longjiao Zhao	Jie Zhao
Xi Zhang	Long Zhao	Xibin Zhao
Xiaomei Zhang	Qingsong Zhao	Xiaoqi Zhao
Xinyu Zhang	Qingyu Zhao	Zhengyu Zhao
Yin Zhang	Rui Zhao	Jin Zhe
Zicheng Zhang	Rui-Wei Zhao	Chuanxia Zheng
Zihao Zhang	Sicheng Zhao	Huan Zheng
Ziqi Zhang	Shuang Zhao	Hao Zheng
Zhaoxiang Zhang	Siyan Zhao	Jia Zheng
Zhen Zhang	Zelin Zhao	Jian-Qing Zheng
Zhipeng Zhang	Shiyu Zhao	Shuai Zheng
Zhixing Zhang	Wang Zhao	Meng Zheng
Zhizheng Zhang	Tiesong Zhao	Mingkai Zheng
Jiawei Zhang	Qian Zhao	Qian Zheng
Zhong Zhang	Wangbo Zhao	Qi Zheng
Pingping Zhang	Xi-Le Zhao	Wu Zheng
Yixin Zhang	Xu Zhao	Yinqiang Zheng
Kui Zhang	Yajie Zhao	Yufeng Zheng
Lingzhi Zhang	Yang Zhao	Yutong Zheng
Huaiwen Zhang	Ying Zhao	Yalin Zheng
Quanshi Zhang	Yin Zhao	Yu Zheng
Zhoutong Zhang	Yizhou Zhao	Feng Zheng
Yuhang Zhang	Yunhan Zhao	Zhaoheng Zheng
Yuting Zhang	Yuyang Zhao	Haitian Zheng
Zhang Zhang	Yue Zhao	Kang Zheng
Ziming Zhang	Yuzhi Zhao	Bolun Zheng

Haiyong Zheng
Mingwu Zheng
Sipeng Zheng
Tu Zheng
Wenzhao Zheng
Xiawu Zheng
Yinglin Zheng
Zhuo Zheng
Zilong Zheng
Kecheng Zheng
Zerong Zheng
Shuaifeng Zhi
Tiancheng Zhi
Jia-Xing Zhong
Yiwu Zhong
Fangwei Zhong
Zhihang Zhong
Yaoyao Zhong
Yiran Zhong
Zhun Zhong
Zichun Zhong
Bo Zhou
Boyao Zhou
Brady Zhou
Mo Zhou
Chunluan Zhou
Dingfu Zhou
Fan Zhou
Jingkai Zhou
Honglu Zhou
Jiaming Zhou
Jiahuan Zhou
Jun Zhou
Kaiyang Zhou
Keyang Zhou
Kuangqi Zhou
Lei Zhou
Lihua Zhou
Man Zhou
Mingyi Zhou
Mingyuan Zhou
Ning Zhou
Peng Zhou
Penghao Zhou
Qianyi Zhou

Shuigeng Zhou
Shangchen Zhou
Huayi Zhou
Zhize Zhou
Sanping Zhou
Qin Zhou
Tao Zhou
Wenbo Zhou
Xiangdong Zhou
Xiao-Yun Zhou
Xiao Zhou
Yang Zhou
Yipin Zhou
Zhenyu Zhou
Hao Zhou
Chu Zhou
Daquan Zhou
Da-Wei Zhou
Hang Zhou
Kang Zhou
Qianyu Zhou
Sheng Zhou
Wenhui Zhou
Xingyi Zhou
Yan-Jie Zhou
Yiyi Zhou
Yu Zhou
Yuan Zhou
Yuqian Zhou
Yuxuan Zhou
Zixiang Zhou
Wengang Zhou
Shuchang Zhou
Tianfei Zhou
Yichao Zhou
Alex Zhu
Chenchen Zhu
Deyao Zhu
Xiatian Zhu
Guibo Zhu
Haidong Zhu
Hao Zhu
Hongzi Zhu
Rui Zhu
Jing Zhu

Jianke Zhu
Junchen Zhu
Lei Zhu
Lingyu Zhu
Luyang Zhu
Menglong Zhu
Peihao Zhu
Hui Zhu
Xiaofeng Zhu
Tyler (Lixuan) Zhu
Wentao Zhu
Xiangyu Zhu
Xinqi Zhu
Xinxin Zhu
Xinliang Zhu
Yangguang Zhu
Yichen Zhu
Yixin Zhu
Yanjun Zhu
Yousong Zhu
Yuhao Zhu
Ye Zhu
Feng Zhu
Zhen Zhu
Fangrui Zhu
Jinjing Zhu
Linchao Zhu
Pengfei Zhu
Sijie Zhu
Xiaobin Zhu
Xiaoguang Zhu
Zezhou Zhu
Zhenyao Zhu
Kai Zhu
Pengkai Zhu
Bingbing Zhuang
Chengyuan Zhuang
Liansheng Zhuang
Peiye Zhuang
Yixin Zhuang
Yihong Zhuang
Junbao Zhuo
Andrea Ziani
Bartosz Zieliński
Primo Zingaretti

Nikolaos Zioulis
Andrew Zisserman
Yael Ziv
Liu Ziyin
Xingxing Zou
Danping Zou
Qi Zou

Shihao Zou
Xueyan Zou
Yang Zou
Yuliang Zou
Zihang Zou
Chuhang Zou
Dongqing Zou

Xu Zou
Zhiming Zou
Maria A. Zuluaga
Xinxin Zuo
Zhiwen Zuo
Reyer Zwiggelaar

Contents – Part XXVIII

Salient Object Detection for Point Clouds

Songlin Fan[1,2], Wei Gao[1,2(✉)], and Ge Li[1]

[1] Peking University Shenzhen Graduate School, Shenzhen, China
[2] Peng Cheng Laboratory, Shenzhen, China
{slfan,gaowei262,geli}@pku.edu.cn
https://git.openi.org.cn/OpenPointCloud/PCSOD

Abstract. This paper researches the unexplored task—point cloud salient object detection (SOD). Differing from SOD for images, we find the attention shift of point clouds may provoke saliency conflict, *i.e.*, an object paradoxically belongs to salient and non-salient categories. To eschew this issue, we present a novel view-dependent perspective of salient objects, reasonably reflecting the most eye-catching objects in point cloud scenarios. Following this formulation, we introduce **PCSOD**, the first dataset proposed for point cloud SOD consisting of 2,872 in-/out-door 3D views. The samples in our dataset are labeled with hierarchical annotations, *e.g.*, super-/sub-class, bounding box, and segmentation map, which endows the brilliant generalizability and broad applicability of our dataset verifying various conjectures. To evidence the feasibility of our solution, we further contribute a baseline model and benchmark five representative models for a comprehensive comparison. The proposed model can effectively analyze irregular and unordered points for detecting salient objects. Thanks to incorporating the task-tailored designs, our method shows visible superiority over other baselines, producing more satisfactory results. Extensive experiments and discussions reveal the promising potential of this research field, paving the way for further study.

Keywords: Salient object detection · Point cloud · Dataset · Baseline

1 Introduction

Salient objects describe the most attractive objects with respect to their surroundings. Due to its myriad applications, salient object detection (SOD) can provide the pre-processing results for many vision tasks, such as 3D shape classification [46], compression [32], and quality assessment [30], to name a few. Distinct from the relevant task [6,43,61] for predicting eye fixation positions, namely saliency detection, SOD demands locating salient objects and completely segmenting them further, thus being more challenging. Most existing SOD works [9,12,15,26,37,58] devote their efforts to analyzing salient objects on regular images. With the fast revolution of 3D collection equipment, point clouds as the raw output of many devices (such as LiDAR and depth sensors) have a growing presence in research and applications. Compared with the adoption of alternative 3D formats, data processing directly on point clouds avoids

ⓒ The Author(s), under exclusive license to Springer Nature Switzerland AG 2022
S. Avidan et al. (Eds.): ECCV 2022, LNCS 13688, pp. 1–19, 2022.
https://doi.org/10.1007/978-3-031-19815-1_1

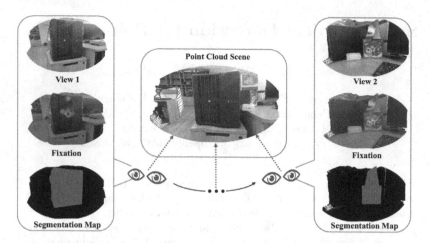

Fig. 1. Illustration of saliency conflict. The variation of attention allocated to the black computer causes a contradiction that the black computer simultaneously belongs to the salient and non-salient objects for this scene. We, therefore, propose to analyze the salient objects of point clouds according to the views.

information loss and computational redundancy in format conversion that may induce performance drops. Despite the flourishing advance of many point-based tasks, *e.g.*, classification [3], object detection [42], and segmentation [16], point cloud SOD is still in its infancy, and many issues have not been discussed yet.

As immersive visual media, point clouds offer a watching experience with six degrees of freedom (6DOF). Unlike the watching of static images, the attention allocation of humans varies when the view changes. The research community dubs the phenomenon that attention being allocated from one region to another as the attention shift [9,44]. However, we find that the attention shift of point clouds may trigger a new thorny problem that we name saliency conflict, *i.e.*, an object paradoxically belongs to salient and non-salient categories for different views of one point cloud scene sample. Figure 1 shows an example of an office scene recorded by point clouds. The attention allocated to the black computer varies as the view changes, which causes the black computer to go from being the salient object to the non-salient object. **Then is the black computer the salient object of this office scene?** The answer matters not only the definition of salient objects in point cloud scenarios but also the relevant dataset construction.

In this paper, we argue that the manifestations of salient objects in point clouds depend on the views, and point cloud SOD is to compute the salient objects of any given view in 3D space. The union of salient objects (segmentation maps) of "given views" indicates the complete description of salient objects for scenes in point clouds. For Fig. 1, different segmentation maps correspond to different views, and the union of segmentation maps represents the salient objects of this office scene. Firstly, this formulation makes it easier to grasp the nature of the SOD problem due to the fact that humans actually observe only one view at a time while the viewpoint is free. Broadly speaking, the image is a special case of only a single view. Secondly, this formulation avoids the complex modeling to handle the whole 3D scene with saliency conflict phenomenon, which can benefit the design of simpler models capable of analyzing different views. Thirdly, this formulation eases the dataset construction with the human-annotated most attractive objects via subjective experiments, since the subjective experiment results of different views sometimes cannot be reflected into a large-scale point cloud sample (such as the office scene sample in Fig. 1) simultaneously without our view-dependent saliency analysis.

Following our formulation of point cloud SOD, we introduce *PCSOD*—the first versatile dataset for point cloud SOD with densely annotated labels. Our dataset contains 2,872 frequent 3D views that belong to over one hundred in-/out-door scenes. The manual data collection phase lasts over one year, and the samples reflect a wide range of scenarios in our lives. Detailed statistics show that our dataset has 138 object categories and 53.4% difficult samples, which ensures its brilliant generalizability. To extend the applicability of this new dataset, we provide hierarchical annotations for each sample, including super-/sub-class, bounding box, and segmentation map. The proposed dataset as a comprehensive platform can conveniently support research on multi-task learning [48] and other valuable vision tasks, not limited to point cloud SOD.

Since point clouds record 3D information in the format of irregular and unordered points, existing SOD models [9,12,15,26,58] for images cannot be transferred for point cloud processing. Additionally, though several representative point-based models [3,16,25,38,59] have been developed for other segmentation tasks, they are incapable of performing well in SOD. These models for other segmentation tasks fail to consider the particularities of SOD, *i.e.*, the benefits of multi-scale features [35] and the refinement of global semantics [4,27]. To prove the feasibility of our solution, we further develop a baseline model and benchmark five representative segmentation models for comparison and analysis of point cloud SOD. Owing to incorporating the task-tailored designs, the proposed baseline model can take full advantage of the multi-scale features and global semantics to locate salient objects and accurately separate them. Extensive experiments verify the effectiveness of our solution for point cloud SOD.

In summary, we conclude the contributions as follows:

1) We propose a novel view-dependent perspective of point cloud SOD. Our formulation avoids the saliency conflict, emphasizes the nature of SOD, and reasonably reflects the most eye-catching objects in point cloud scenarios.
2) We construct the first versatile dataset for point cloud SOD, termed *PCSOD*. Our dataset has brilliant generalizability and broad applicability, expected to be a catalyst for point cloud SOD and many other vision tasks.
3) We develop a baseline model for point cloud SOD. Our baseline model has a full consideration of the particularities of SOD, outperforming other baseline models by a clear margin.
4) We establish the first benchmark of point cloud SOD, conduct a thorough analysis, and bring a new perspective toward point cloud SOD.

2 Related Work

Salient Object Detection. Following the pioneer attempt [17], many early works [24,36,47,53] design hand-crafted features to exploit low-level cues. These methods cannot obtain satisfactory accuracy because of the lack of semantic cues. Thanks to the powerful capability of neural networks in abstracting semantics, the bottleneck of traditional methods is broken. Hou *et al.* [15] introduce short connections into a skip-layer structure. The advanced representations at multiple layers thus can be fully utilized. Siris *et al.* [45] propose a semantic scene context-aware framework to capture sufficient high-level semantics for locating salient objects. To rich the semantic information diluted during the top-down transmission, some recent works [4,27,35] explicitly extract global semantics and append them into low-level features, achieving visible performance improvement. Despite the gratifying achievements of existing RGB image-based methods [28,40,55,60], they still have difficulty understanding complex scenes for lacking spatial geometry information. Consequently, researchers begin extending the task of SOD on 3D images, such as RGB-D images [10,15,20,22,26,56,58] and light field images [23,29,50,57], which show significant potential. A detailed description of these image-based methods is beyond the scope of this article. Please refer to the relevant surveys [11,51,62] for more introduction. We can conclude that all these efforts are confined to the image domain. This work will disentangle the limitation and probe SOD on point clouds.

Regarding the attention modeling on point clouds, we also learn that a few methods [6,13,18,43,46,61] are developed to automatically compute the human attention distribution. The algorithms of these methods merely produce a heatmap of the attention distribution, while the SOD task we study demands completely segmenting the salient objects, thus being more challenging.

Deep Learning on Point Clouds. Processing point clouds has long been a significant challenge. Previous works [19,21] tend to first rearrange raw points via octree or kdtree. The emergence of PointNet/PointNet++ [3,38] shows us a new approach for raw point processing. They employ shared multilayer perceptrons (MLPs) to extract point-wise features and achieve state-of-the-art performance across many vision tasks. Following PointNet, three directions are mainly adopted to improve the performance further, *i.e.*, powerful convolution [25,54], effective neighborhood connection [52,59], and advanced reduction [16,39]. Li *et al.* [25] propose to learn an X-transformation from raw points by imitating the typical convolution, while Wu *et al.* [54] regard the typical convolution as the combination of weight and density functions. ShellNet [59] arranges neighbors into concentric spherical shells that have a convolution order from the inner to the outer shells. Wang *et al.* [52] propose a simple operation known as EdgeConv, which extracts local geometric features while retaining permutation invariance. To explore more advanced reduction operations, Hu *et al.* [16] and Qian *et al.* [39] resort to attentive pooling and anisotropic reduction, respectively. However, these methods are not initially developed for SOD, ignoring the particularities of SOD.

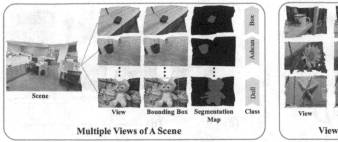 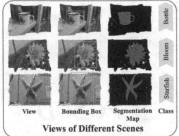

Fig. 2. Examples from our *PCSOD* dataset with hierarchical annotations.

3 Proposed Dataset

Datasets [9,23,41] have become the driving force behind many vision tasks, especially with the emergence of deep learning. With this in mind, we introduce *PCSOD* for: (1) probing a new challenging task, (2) facilitating research on new issues, and (3) verifying new conjectures. Next, we will elaborate more details about our dataset. Besides, some visual examples are shown in Fig. 2 and Fig. 3.

3.1 Dataset Construction

Data Collection. Point clouds in existing datasets [1,2,5,14,34] are often collected for specific scenes (such as outdoor road or indoor office scenes). In contrast, a high-quality SOD dataset [49] demands rich scenes, which motivates us to collect diverse data by ourselves. The data collection phase takes over one year, and we collect 2,872 3D views from over one hundred preset scenes across dozens of cities. Each 3D view has 240,000 points. This process can also simulate the 3D view acquisition when "travelling" in an off-shelf large-scale point cloud sample (such as an office or even a city). As shown in Fig. 2, the 3D views of a scene constitute a series of watching descriptions of this scene whose salient objects can be obtained from subjective experiments without saliency conflict.

Data Annotation. Referring to the determination of salient objects in images [49,50], we employ thirty professional annotators to label the salient objects from given views. Before the labeling, every annotator is pre-trained over fifteen samples. To ensure the annotation accuracy, we divide these thirty annotators into ten groups. Three annotators in one group jointly determine the salient objects, then cross-validated by other groups. An object is regarded as a positive label only if more than eighty percent of annotators verify it. The recently released datasets [9,34] indicate that offering hierarchical annotations benefits the applicability of a new dataset. As shown in Fig. 2, we hierarchically label the determined salient objects and provide three levels of annotations,

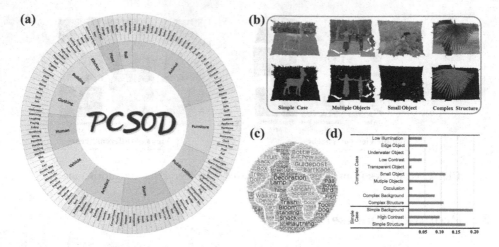

Fig. 3. Statistics of our *PCSOD* dataset. (a) Categories of salient objects. (b) Illustration of challenging samples. (c) Word cloud of salient objects. (d) Histogram distribution of challenging samples.

i.e., class, bounding box, and segmentation map. Each level of annotations is obtained through corresponding professionals. Furthermore, at least two passes of verification are performed for each annotation to ensure its quality.

Data Split. Having a standard dataset split [9,50] is conducive to fairly studying and comparing the pros and cons of algorithms. Following the ratio of 7:3 adopted by many datasets [50], our *PCSOD* is randomly split into 2,000 samples for training and 872 samples for testing.

3.2 Dataset Statistics

Diverse Object Categories. A diverse SOD dataset should have broad coverage of scenes in the real world to ensure brilliant generalizability. Our *PCSOD* covers a wide range of scenarios in our lives. As shown in Fig. 3(a) and Fig. 3(c), the salient object categories have a heterogeneous variety. Specifically, objects in our dataset can be categorized into 12 super-classes, *e.g.*, human, animal, plant, *etc.* These 12 super-classes are further comprised of 138 sub-classes, fully covering the daily situations. The diverse salient object categories enable a comprehensive understanding of the attention allocation of humans in real-world scenes.

Rich Annotations. A versatile dataset should not only support the study of existing issues but also adapt to new research directions. As shown in Fig. 2, our *PCSOD* offers hierarchical annotations, *e.g.*, super-/sub-class, bounding box, and segmentation map. These annotations help researchers understand each sample of our dataset from different aspects (such as object property, object proposal, and scene parsing), sparking novel ideas. Besides, our annotations are very precise. The segmentation maps accurately reflect the structures of objects in 3D scenes, even though some are very complex (see the complex structure case in Fig. 3(b)).

Difficult Samples. A valuable dataset should contain a certain amount of difficult samples and dive into the problems. The difficult samples benefit the performance of models confronting various complex scenes. With this consideration, we add many challenging samples to our dataset, including multiple objects, small objects, complex structures, low illumination, *etc.* Some visual examples are shown in Fig. 3(b). Figure 3(d) further details the proportion of samples with each attribute. Statistics indicate that our dataset has 53.4% difficult samples, which evidences that the proposed *PCSOD* is very challenging.

4   Proposed Method

Extending the concept of salient objects in images to point clouds, we formulate that the salient objects of views from a scene indicate the complete description of salient objects in this scene. Point cloud SOD aims to identify the salient objects of any given view. While various methods have been developed for image-based SOD, they cannot handle irregular and unordered point clouds. Moreover, existing point-based segmentation models for other tasks cannot guarantee the performance of identifying salient objects. These circumstances motivate us to design a baseline model and excavate potential directions for point cloud SOD.

4.1   Overall Architecture

As shown in Fig. 4, the proposed baseline model inherits a typical encoder-decoder architecture. The encoder extracts multi-level features from raw points, while the decoder enhances and fuses the extracted features to predict salient objects. To illustrate the effectiveness of our designs, we introduce the classical PointNet++ [38] as the encoder. It has been studied [27] that high-level features will be gradually diluted when transmitted to low-level ones. To address this issue, some recent image-based methods [4,27,35] explicitly extract global semantics and append them into low-level features, observing gratifying performance improvement. Inspired by the philosophical designs of these methods, we design two key modules, *i.e.*, Point Perception Block (PPB) and Saliency Perception Block (SPB), to take full advantage of the benefits of multi-scale features and the refinement of global semantics for locating salient objects.

Formally, let $\mathcal{V} = \{v_1, v_2, ..., v_N\}$ represent a view of N points with associated point-wise features (*e.g.*, RGB colors), where $v \in \mathbb{R}^{d_{in}}$. To obtain the probabilities $\mathcal{P} = \{p_1, p_2, ..., p_N\}$ of corresponding points being salient, the encoder first extracts multi-level features $\{F_l\}_{l=1}^4$ from raw points $\mathcal{V}$. The lth level features $F_l = \{f_1^l, f_2^l, ..., f_{N_l}^l\}$ have $N_l = \frac{N}{4^l}$ aggregated points with doubling the feature dimension compared with F_{l-1} (except the feature dimension of the first level is

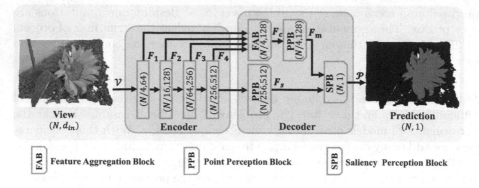

Fig. 4. Overall architecture of the proposed baseline model, which has a typical encoder-decoder architecture.

fixed to 64). Then we aggregate multi-level features $\{F_l\}_{l=1}^4$ into the compact representations F_c via the Feature Aggregation Block (FAB). As shown in Fig. 5, the operations in FAB are very straightforward, *i.e.*, upsampled high-level features are sequentially fused with low-level features. We adopt the common trilinear interpolation as the upsampling operation to match the spatial size of different level features, while the fusion operation we employ is concatenation along the feature dimension followed by MLPs. Following previous works [16,38], the feature concatenation can simultaneously retain the originality of the fused two level features and is proved to be very effective for point cloud feature fusion. Note that the feature fusion in all modules is uniformly through concatenation unless otherwise stated. To prevent the dilution of high-level features, the PPB is proposed to abstract global semantics and strengthen the multi-scale representations. We obtain global semantics F_s and multi-scale features F_m from the highest-level features F_4 and the compact representations F_c, respectively, using two PPBs with different configurations. The global semantics can supplement the diluted high-level features in multi-scale features and alleviate the distraction of non-salient background. To achieve this, we further develop the SPB to integrate multi-scale features F_m and global semantics F_s, and produce the final prediction $\mathcal{P}$. Next, we will elaborate on the details of our PPB and SPB.

4.2   Proposed Modules

Point Perception Block. The global semantics and multi-scale features are important for SOD [4,27,35]. The former helps to locate the positions of salient objects, while the latter is conducive to recognizing salient objects of different sizes. Besides, the acquisition of them demands enlarging the receptive fields of features and capturing the context information. Inspired by the widely used Receptive Field Block [31], we introduce the PPB to achieve this goal.

As shown in Fig. 5, the PPB consists of five branches to capture the context information of point-wise features. The first four branches with similar structures

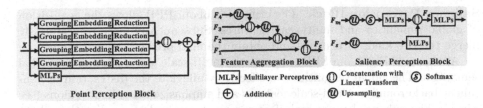

Fig. 5. Details of the components in the proposed baseline model, *i.e.*, Point Perception Block, Feature Aggregation Block, and Saliency Perception Block.

encode center points by their local regions of different sizes. Each branch has three sub-units, *i.e.*, grouping, embedding, and reduction. To be more specific, let $X^p = \{x_1^p, x_2^p, ..., x_M^p\}$ denote the spatial coordinates of input points X with intermediate learned features $X^f = \{x_1^f, x_2^f, ..., x_M^f\}$. M indicates the number of points. For each point $x_i^p \in X^p$, the grouping sub-unit gathers its k nearest neighbors $\mathcal{N}(x_i^p) = \{x_{i,1}^p, x_{i,2}^p, ..., x_{i,k}^p\}$ by K-nearest neighbours (KNN). The spatial size of the local region $\mathcal{N}(x_i^p)$ centered on x_i^p varies as k takes different values. To learn local geometric representations, the embedding sub-unit embeds the relative spatial position between x_i^p and its neighbor $x_{i,j}^p$ as

$$e_i^j = MLPs([x_i^p, x_{i,j}^p, x_i^p - x_{i,j}^p, \mathcal{D}(x_i^p, x_{i,j}^p)]), \qquad (1)$$

where $\mathcal{D}(\cdot)$ and $[]$ denote the Euclidean distance between two points and the concatenation operation, respectively. Because e_i^j merely contains the geometric features and lacks associated point-wise features, we concatenate e_i^j with corresponding point-wise features x_i^f to obtain the advanced representations a_i^j. All advanced representations $\mathcal{A}_i = \{a_i^1, a_i^2, .., a_i^k\}$ of k neighbors express each of their semantic contributions to the center point x_i^p. The reduction sub-unit aggregates the neighborhood semantic contributions by a Mean-max reduction operation

$$\hat{x}_i^f = MLPs([max(\mathcal{A}_i), mean(\mathcal{A}_i)]), \qquad (2)$$

where $max(\cdot)$ and $mean(\cdot)$ denote the max function and mean function, respectively. Compared with the input features X^f, the branch outputs $\hat{X}^f = \{\hat{x}_1^f, \hat{x}_2^f, ..., \hat{x}_M^f\}$ have enlarged receptive fields and capture the context information in local regions. Finally, we fuse the output features $\{\hat{X}_b^f\}_{b=1}^4$ of the first four branches and further introduce a skip connection of the fifth branch to retain the original features

$$\hat{Y}^f = MLPs([\hat{X}_1^f, \hat{X}_2^f, \hat{X}_3^f, \hat{X}_4^f]) + MLPs(X^f). \qquad (3)$$

Similar to the Receptive Field Block, by setting $K = \{k_1, k_2, k_3, k_4\}$ for the first four branches reasonably, the global semantics and multi-scale features can be obtained, respectively. Besides, the input points X and corresponding outputs Y of our PPB share the same feature size. Therefore, our PPB can be easily embedded in various networks to improve their performance.

Saliency Perception Block. The utilization of our PPB allows the acquisition of global semantics and multi-scale features. Subsequently, how to seamlessly merge the two kinds of features and obtain the final prediction is still open.

As shown in Fig. 5, our SPB enhances the multi-scale features using the global semantics. The global semantics can effectively alleviate the distraction of non-salient background in multi-scale features and emphasize the salient regions (see Fig. 8). The enhanced multi-scale features are then used to predict the salient objects. Specifically, the SPB first upsamples the global semantics F_s and multi-scale features F_m to the spatial size of the input $\mathcal{V}$. The upsampling operation is followed by MLPs to reduce the aliasing effect. Then we use the upsampled global semantics to enhance the multi-scale features

$$F_e = MLPs([MLPs(\mathcal{U}(F_s)), \mathcal{S}(MLPs(\mathcal{U}(F_m)))]), \qquad (4)$$

where $\mathcal{U}$ and $\mathcal{S}$ denote the upsampling and softmax operations, respectively. F_e is the enhanced multi-scale features. In this approach, the enhanced multi-scale features include both the accurate positions and fine-grained structures of salient objects. Finally, we use a prediction layer (MLPs) to predict salient objects $\mathcal{P}$ from the enhanced multi-scale features F_e.

5 Experiments

5.1 Experimental Setup

Implementation Details. We use the popular Pytorch framework to implement our method on an NVIDIA TITAN XP GPU. The points in the inputs are represented by nine-dimensional vectors ($d_{in} = 9$) consisting of spatial coordinates, RGB colors, and normalized spatial coordinates. Due to the limitations of memory capacity, we randomly sample $N = 4,096$ points with replacement from inputs in the training stage, while the sampling operations in the testing are without replacement for testing all 240,000 points in a 3D view. We use random rotation to augment data. The parameters K of the PPB for abstracting global semantics are $\{1, 4, 9, 16\}$ while those of another PPB are $\{1, 9, 25, 49\}$. Our loss function is defined on the standard cross-entropy loss. We train the proposed baseline model by Adam optimizer with an initial learning rate of 5e−4 and a weight decay of 1e−4. The total training epochs are 3,000, with a batch size of 32. A three-time voting strategy [38] is adopted to produce the predictions in the testing phase.

Evaluation Metrics. To compare the results of different methods, we adopt four popular evaluation metrics for performance benchmarking, *i.e.*, mean absolute error (MAE), F-measure [33], E-measure [8], and intersection over union (IoU). MAE estimates the point-wise approximation degree between predicted segmentation maps and corresponding ground truths. It can be formulated as MAE $= \frac{1}{N} \sum_{i=1}^{N} |p_i - g_i|$, where $p_i \in \mathcal{P}$ and $g_i \in \mathcal{G}$ are the prediction and ground truth, respectively. F-measure is the harmonic mean value of the precision ($prec$) and recall ($reca$), *i.e.*, F-measure $= \frac{(1-\beta^2)prec \cdot reca}{\beta^2 prec + reca}$, where β^2 is set

Table 1. Benchmarking results of six representative baseline models on our *PCSOD* dataset. "↑"/"↓" suggests that larger/smaller is better. Note that the best results are shown in **boldface**

Methods	Years	MAE ↓	F-measure ↑	E-measure ↑	IoU ↑
PointNet [3]	CVPR'17	0.116	0.632	0.768	0.519
PointNet++ [38]	NeurIPS'17	0.077	0.738	0.816	0.608
PointCNN [25]	NeurIPS'18	0.142	0.409	0.575	0.265
ShellNet [59]	ICCV'19	0.074	0.753	0.848	0.648
RandLA [16]	TPAMI'21	0.127	0.633	0.740	0.517
Ours	–	**0.069**	**0.769**	**0.851**	**0.656**

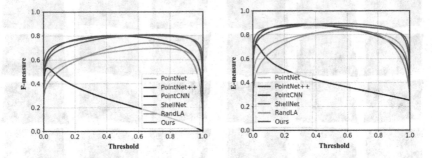

Fig. 6. F-measure and E-measure under different thresholds.

to 0.3 for emphasizing the importance of precision. E-measure captures both the local matching and region-level matching information of segmentation maps for assessment. IoU is a metric describing the extent of overlap between two segmentation maps. It is defined as IoU $= \frac{inter}{union}$, where *inter* and *union* indicate the intersection and union of two segmentation maps, respectively. Note that the relevant concepts of S-measure [7] in 3D space may change, thus being ignored.

5.2   Comparison and Analysis

To the best of our knowledge, there is no deep learning-based method designed for point cloud SOD. Consequently, we introduce five representative baseline models [3,16,25,38,59] from others segmentation tasks for comparison and analysis. PointNet [3] and its improved version, namely PointNet++ [38], are the two most representative models in point cloud processing. PointCNN [25], Shell-Net [59], and RandLA [16] indicate three promising directions of point cloud processing, *i.e.*, powerful convolution, effective neighborhood connection, and advanced reduction. For a fair comparison, we retrain these models on our *PCSOD* dataset according to the recommended parameter settings and produce the final results by the same voting strategy as our method.

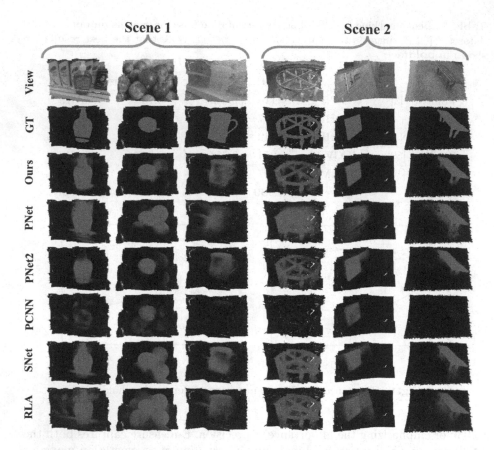

Fig. 7. Qualitative comparison of six baseline models on views of two common scenes, *i.e.*, a supermarket (Scene 1) and a park (Scene 2). Note that "GT", "PNet", "PNet2", "PCNN", "SNet", and "RLA" mean the ground truth, PointNet [3], PointNet++ [38], PointCNN [25], ShellNet [59], and RandLA [16], respectively.

Quantitative Comparison. In Table 1, we list the results of six baseline models on four evaluation metrics. We can learn that the proposed method achieves state-of-the-art performance and outperforms all competitors by a clear margin. Specifically, our model surpasses the second-best model ShellNet by 6.8%, 2.1%, 0.4%, and 1.2% on MAE, F-measure, E-measure, and IoU. RandLA is a recently proposed model with significant superiority over PointNet++ for semantic segmentation. However, experiments in Table 1 show that RandLA has no advantage on SOD and even performs worse than PointNet++, indicating designing tailored models for point cloud SOD is non-trivial. Though our baseline model has the best performance, there is still considerable room for performance improvement, which demands further efforts from the research community. To study the generalizability of these baseline models under different thresholds, we plot the F-measure scores and E-measure scores by taking different thresholds. As shown

Table 2. Ablation analysis of the proposed point cloud SOD model. No. 1–No. 4 study the effectiveness of our SPB and PPB, respectively. "PPB 1" and "PPB 2" denote the PPBs for producing global semantics and multi-scale features, respectively. No. 5–No. 8 investigate the alternative reduction operations.

No.	Methods	MAE ↓	F-measure ↑	E-measure ↑	IoU ↑
1	PointNet++ [38]	0.077	0.738	0.816	0.608
2	+SPB	0.076	0.748	0.828	0.624
3	+SPB, +PPB 1	0.073	0.754	0.840	0.639
4	+SPB, +PPB 1, +PPB 2	**0.069**	**0.769**	**0.851**	**0.656**
5	Mean reduction	0.071	0.764	0.843	0.649
6	Max reduction	0.070	0.765	0.843	0.651
7	Attentive reduction [16]	0.074	0.758	0.847	**0.658**
8	Mean-max reduction	**0.069**	**0.769**	**0.851**	0.656

in Fig. 6, the results of our method are much flatter at most thresholds, which demonstrates that our method has excellent generalizability.

Qualitative Comparison. To further reveal the feasibility of our solution predicting salient objects of any given 3D views, we illustrate the results of several frequent views from two common scenes in Fig. 7. Scene 1 is a supermarket (indoor scene), while Scene 2 is a park (outdoor scene), both of which are unseen by these models. It can be seen that most baseline models can locate the salient objects of given views, except for PointCNN. Though some views are very challenging, *e.g.*, cluttered background (column 2), transparent object (column 3), complex structure (column 4), and random view with non-central object (column 5 and 6), our method can consistently produce accurate and complete segmentation maps with high contrast, which evidences the superiority of our method.

5.3   Ablation Study

To analyze the fundamentals of our baseline model, we conduct extensive ablation experiments in Table 2. The ablation experiments are based on the encoder PointNet++ [38], studying the effectiveness of the designs in our decoder, *i.e.*, key modules and feature reduction operations. In each experiment, only one influential factor is changed as the others keep the same for a fair comparison.

To investigate the contributions from our SPB and PPB separately, we first load the SPB into the encoder. By comparing No. 1 and No. 2 in Table 2, we can learn that the introduction of our SPB can help promote the performance of our model in locating salient objects. However, because the high-level features from the encoder have limited receptive fields, directly utilizing them as the semantics can only achieve suboptimal performance. As demonstrated in Table 2 (No. 3), a properly configured PPB helping acquire semantics with global receptive fields can unlock the potential of the SPB. Besides, the PPB with a different configuration can also strengthen the multi-scale representations of features, which

View   GT   Feature 1   Feature 2   Feature 3   Prediction

Fig. 8. 3D heatmap visualization of feature maps. Feature 1, Feature 2, and Feature 3 represent the multi-scale features, global semantics, and enhanced multi-scale features, respectively.

benefits the perception of objects of different sizes. Therefore, another PPB in the ablation No. 4 can bring orthogonal contributions to SOD. Figure 8 further shows how the feature maps change. Due to the dilution of high-level features, multi-scale features incorrectly focus on the non-salient background, whereas the global semantics have an accurate perception of salient objects. The SPB can correct the deviation of multi-scale features by combining global semantics and obtain the enhanced multi-scale features. The ablations No. 4–No. 8 in Table 2 study various reduction manners. It can be seen that our Mean-max reduction can outperform the individual Mean reduction or Max reduction. Furthermore, compared to the attentive reduction [16], our method has a better performance without increasing the number of network parameters.

6   Conclusion

In this paper, we present the first comprehensive study on point cloud SOD, involving its formulation, dataset construction, and baseline design. To avoid the saliency conflict, we propose a novel view-dependent perspective of salient objects. Our formulation can reasonably reflect the salient objects in point cloud scenarios. Then we elaborately construct a high-quality dataset, namely *PCSOD*, and contribute a baseline model for point cloud SOD. Our dataset has excellent generalizability and broad applicability, expected to boost the advance of SOD and many other vision tasks. We conduct extensive experiments on our dataset to verify the feasibility of our solution. Experimental results show that our baseline model has significant superiority and produces visually favorable predictions. Our work reveals the potential of point cloud SOD and pave the way for further study.

Acknowledgements. This work was supported by National Key R&D Program of China (2020AAA0103501), The Major Key Project of PCL, Natural Science Foundation of China (61801303, 62031013), Guangdong Basic and Applied Basic Research Foundation (2019A1515012031), Shenzhen Fundamental Research Program (GXWD20201231165807007-20200806163656003), and Shenzhen Science and Technology Plan Basic Research Project (JCYJ20190808161805519).

References

1. Armeni, I., Sener, O., Zamir, A.R., Jiang, H., Brilakis, I., Fischer, M., Savarese, S.: 3D semantic parsing of large-scale indoor spaces. In: IEEE/CVF Conference on Computer Vision and Pattern Recognition, pp. 1534–1543 (2016)
2. Behley, J., et al.: SemanticKITTI: a dataset for semantic scene understanding of lidar sequences. In: IEEE/CVF International Conference on Computer Vision, pp. 9297–9307 (2019)
3. Charles, R.Q., Su, H., Kaichun, M., Guibas, L.J.: PointNet: deep learning on point sets for 3D classification and segmentation. In: IEEE/CVF Conference on Computer Vision and Pattern Recognition, pp. 77–85 (2017). https://doi.org/10.1109/CVPR.2017.16
4. Chen, Z., Xu, Q., Cong, R., Huang, Q.: Global context-aware progressive aggregation network for salient object detection. In: AAAI Conference on Artificial Intelligence, vol. 34, pp. 10599–10606 (2020)
5. Dai, A., Chang, A.X., Savva, M., Halber, M., Funkhouser, T., Nießner, M.: Scannet: richly-annotated 3D reconstructions of indoor scenes. In: IEEE/CVF Conference on Computer Vision and Pattern Recognition, pp. 5828–5839 (2017)
6. Ding, X., Lin, W., Chen, Z., Zhang, X.: Point cloud saliency detection by local and global feature fusion. IEEE Trans. Image Process. 28(11), 5379–5393 (2019). https://doi.org/10.1109/TIP.2019.2918735
7. Fan, D.P., Cheng, M.M., Liu, Y., Li, T., Borji, A.: Structure-measure: a new way to evaluate foreground maps. In: IEEE/CVF Conference on Computer Vision and Pattern Recognition, pp. 4548–4557 (2017)
8. Fan, D.P., Gong, C., Cao, Y., Ren, B., Cheng, M.M., Borji, A.: Enhanced-alignment measure for binary foreground map evaluation. arXiv preprint arXiv:1805.10421 (2018)
9. Fan, D.P., Wang, W., Cheng, M.M., Shen, J.: Shifting more attention to video salient object detection. In: IEEE/CVF Conference on Computer Vision and Pattern Recognition, pp. 8546–8556 (2019). https://doi.org/10.1109/CVPR.2019.00875
10. Fan, D.-P., Zhai, Y., Borji, A., Yang, J., Shao, L.: BBS-Net: RGB-D salient object detection with a bifurcated backbone strategy network. In: Vedaldi, A., Bischof, H., Brox, T., Frahm, J.-M. (eds.) ECCV 2020. LNCS, vol. 12357, pp. 275–292. Springer, Cham (2020). https://doi.org/10.1007/978-3-030-58610-2_17
11. Fu, K., Jiang, Y., Ji, G.P., Zhou, T., Zhao, Q., Fan, D.P.: Light field salient object detection: a review and benchmark. arXiv preprint arXiv:2010.04968 (2020)
12. Gao, W., Liao, G., Ma, S., Li, G., Liang, Y., Lin, W.: Unified information fusion network for multi-modal RGB-D and RGB-T salient object detection. IEEE Trans. Circuits Syst. Video Technol., 1 (2021). https://doi.org/10.1109/TCSVT.2021.3082939
13. Guo, Y., Wang, F., Xin, J.: Point-wise saliency detection on 3D point clouds via covariance descriptors. Vis. Comput. 34(10), 1325–1338 (2018)
14. Hackel, T., Savinov, N., Ladicky, L., Wegner, J.D., Schindler, K., Pollefeys, M.: Semantic3D. net: a new large-scale point cloud classification benchmark. arXiv preprint arXiv:1704.03847 (2017)
15. Hou, Q., Cheng, M.M., Hu, X., Borji, A., Tu, Z., Torr, P.H.S.: Deeply supervised salient object detection with short connections. IEEE Trans. Pattern Anal. Mach. Intell. 41(4), 815–828 (2019). https://doi.org/10.1109/TPAMI.2018.2815688

16. Hu, Q., et al.: Learning semantic segmentation of large-scale point clouds with random sampling. IEEE Trans. Pattern Anal. Mach. Intell., 1 (2021). https://doi.org/10.1109/TPAMI.2021.3083288
17. Itti, L., Koch, C., Niebur, E.: A model of saliency-based visual attention for rapid scene analysis. IEEE Trans. Pattern Anal. Mach. Intell. **20**(11), 1254–1259 (1998). https://doi.org/10.1109/34.730558
18. Kim, G., Huber, D., Hebert, M.: Segmentation of salient regions in outdoor scenes using imagery and 3-D data. In: IEEE Workshop on Applications of Computer Vision, pp. 1–8. IEEE (2008)
19. Klokov, R., Lempitsky, V.: Escape from cells: deep Kd-networks for the recognition of 3D point cloud models. In: IEEE/CVF International Conference on Computer Vision, pp. 863–872 (2017). https://doi.org/10.1109/ICCV.2017.99
20. Lang, C., Nguyen, T.V., Katti, H., Yadati, K., Kankanhalli, M., Yan, S.: Depth matters: influence of depth cues on visual saliency. In: Fitzgibbon, A., Lazebnik, S., Perona, P., Sato, Y., Schmid, C. (eds.) ECCV 2012. LNCS, vol. 7573, pp. 101–115. Springer, Heidelberg (2012). https://doi.org/10.1007/978-3-642-33709-3_8
21. Lei, H., Akhtar, N., Mian, A.: Octree guided CNN with spherical kernels for 3D point clouds. In: IEEE/CVF Conference on Computer Vision and Pattern Recognition, pp. 9623–9632 (2019). https://doi.org/10.1109/CVPR.2019.00986
22. Li, C., Cong, R., Piao, Y., Xu, Q., Loy, C.C.: RGB-D salient object detection with cross-modality modulation and selection. In: Vedaldi, A., Bischof, H., Brox, T., Frahm, J.-M. (eds.) ECCV 2020. LNCS, vol. 12353, pp. 225–241. Springer, Cham (2020). https://doi.org/10.1007/978-3-030-58598-3_14
23. Li, N., Ye, J., Ji, Y., Ling, H., Yu, J.: Saliency detection on light field. IEEE Trans. Pattern Anal. Mach. Intell. **39**(8), 1605–1616 (2017). https://doi.org/10.1109/TPAMI.2016.2610425
24. Li, X., Lu, H., Zhang, L., Ruan, X., Yang, M.H.: Saliency detection via dense and sparse reconstruction. In: IEEE/CVF International Conference on Computer Vision, pp. 2976–2983 (2013). https://doi.org/10.1109/ICCV.2013.370
25. Li, Y., Bu, R., Sun, M., Wu, W., Di, X., Chen, B.: PointCNN: convolution on X-transformed points. In: Advances in Neural Information Processing Systems 31 (2018)
26. Liao, G., Gao, W., Jiang, Q., Wang, R., Li, G.: MMNet: multi-stage and multi-scale fusion network for RGB-D salient object detection. In: ACM International Conference on Multimedia, pp. 2436–2444 (2020)
27. Liu, J.J., Hou, Q., Cheng, M.M., Feng, J., Jiang, J.: A simple pooling-based design for real-time salient object detection. In: IEEE/CVF Conference on Computer Vision and Pattern Recognition, pp. 3917–3926 (2019)
28. Liu, N., Han, J.: DHSNet: deep hierarchical saliency network for salient object detection. In: IEEE/CVF Conference on Computer Vision and Pattern Recognition, pp. 678–686 (2016). https://doi.org/10.1109/CVPR.2016.80
29. Liu, N., Zhao, W., Zhang, D., Han, J., Shao, L.: Light field saliency detection with dual local graph learning and reciprocative guidance. In: IEEE/CVF International Conference on Computer Vision, pp. 4712–4721 (2021)
30. Liu, Q., Su, H., Duanmu, Z., Liu, W., Wang, Z.: Perceptual quality assessment of colored 3D point clouds. IEEE Trans. Vis. Comput. Graph., 1 (2022). https://doi.org/10.1109/TVCG.2022.3167151
31. Liu, S., Huang, D., Wang, Y.: Receptive field block net for accurate and fast object detection. In: Ferrari, V., Hebert, M., Sminchisescu, C., Weiss, Y. (eds.) ECCV 2018. LNCS, vol. 11215, pp. 404–419. Springer, Cham (2018). https://doi.org/10.1007/978-3-030-01252-6_24

32. Ma, Y., et al.: Variable rate ROI image compression optimized for visual quality. In: IEEE/CVF Conference on Computer Vision and Pattern Recognition Workshops, pp. 1936–1940 (2021). https://doi.org/10.1109/CVPRW53098.2021.00221
33. Margolin, R., Zelnik-Manor, L., Tal, A.: How to evaluate foreground maps. In: IEEE/CVF Conference on Computer Vision and Pattern Recognition, pp. 248–255 (2014). https://doi.org/10.1109/CVPR.2014.39
34. Mo, K., et al.: PartNet: a large-scale benchmark for fine-grained and hierarchical part-level 3D object understanding. In: IEEE/CVF Conference on Computer Vision and Pattern Recognition, pp. 909–918 (2019)
35. Pang, Y., Zhao, X., Zhang, L., Lu, H.: Multi-scale interactive network for salient object detection. In: IEEE/CVF Conference on Computer Vision and Pattern Recognition, pp. 9410–9419 (2020). https://doi.org/10.1109/CVPR42600.2020.00943
36. Perazzi, F., Krähenbühl, P., Pritch, Y., Hornung, A.: Saliency filters: contrast based filtering for salient region detection. In: IEEE/CVF Conference on Computer Vision and Pattern Recognition, pp. 733–740 (2012). https://doi.org/10.1109/CVPR.2012.6247743
37. Piao, Y., Rong, Z., Zhang, M., Lu, H.: Exploit and replace: an asymmetrical two-stream architecture for versatile light field saliency detection. In: AAAI Conference on Artificial Intelligence, vol. 34, pp. 11865–11873 (2020)
38. Qi, C.R., Yi, L., Su, H., Guibas, L.J.: PointNet++: deep hierarchical feature learning on point sets in a metric space. In: Advances in Neural Information Processing Systems 30 (2017)
39. Qian, G., Hammoud, H., Li, G., Thabet, A., Ghanem, B.: ASSANet: an anisotropic separable set abstraction for efficient point cloud representation learning. In: Advances in Neural Information Processing Systems 34 (2021)
40. Qin, X., Zhang, Z., Huang, C., Gao, C., Dehghan, M., Jagersand, M.: BASNet: boundary-aware salient object detection. In: IEEE/CVF Conference on Computer Vision and Pattern Recognition, pp. 7471–7481 (2019). https://doi.org/10.1109/CVPR.2019.00766
41. Russakovsky, O., et al.: ImageNet large scale visual recognition challenge. Int. J. Comput. Vis. **115**(3), 211–252 (2015)
42. Shi, S., Wang, X., Li, H.: PointRCNN: 3D object proposal generation and detection from point cloud. In: IEEE/CVF Conference on Computer Vision and Pattern Recognition, pp. 770–779 (2019). https://doi.org/10.1109/CVPR.2019.00086
43. Shtrom, E., Leifman, G., Tal, A.: Saliency detection in large point sets. In: IEEE/CVF International Conference on Computer Vision, pp. 3591–3598 (2013). https://doi.org/10.1109/ICCV.2013.446
44. Siris, A., Jiao, J., Tam, G.K., Xie, X., Lau, R.W.: Inferring attention shift ranks of objects for image saliency. In: IEEE/CVF Conference on Computer Vision and Pattern Recognition, pp. 12130–12140 (2020). https://doi.org/10.1109/CVPR42600.2020.01215
45. Siris, A., Jiao, J., Tam, G.K., Xie, X., Lau, R.W.: Scene context-aware salient object detection. In: IEEE/CVF International Conference on Computer Vision, pp. 4156–4166 (2021)
46. Tasse, F.P., Kosinka, J., Dodgson, N.: Cluster-based point set saliency. In: IEEE/CVF International Conference on Computer Vision, pp. 163–171 (2015). https://doi.org/10.1109/ICCV.2015.27

47. Tu, W.C., He, S., Yang, Q., Chien, S.Y.: Real-time salient object detection with a minimum spanning tree. In: IEEE/CVF Conference on Computer Vision and Pattern Recognition, pp. 2334–2342 (2016). https://doi.org/10.1109/CVPR.2016.256

48. Vandenhende, S., Georgoulis, S., Van Gansbeke, W., Proesmans, M., Dai, D., Van Gool, L.: Multi-task learning for dense prediction tasks: A survey. IEEE Trans. Pattern Anal. Mach. Intell., 1 (2021). https://doi.org/10.1109/TPAMI.2021.3054719

49. Wang, L., et al.: Learning to detect salient objects with image-level supervision. In: IEEE/CVF Conference on Computer Vision and Pattern Recognition, pp. 3796–3805 (2017). https://doi.org/10.1109/CVPR.2017.404

50. Wang, T., Piao, Y., Lu, H., Li, X., Zhang, L.: Deep learning for light field saliency detection. In: IEEE/CVF International Conference on Computer Vision, pp. 8837–8847 (2019). https://doi.org/10.1109/ICCV.2019.00893

51. Wang, W., Lai, Q., Fu, H., Shen, J., Ling, H., Yang, R.: Salient object detection in the deep learning era: an in-depth survey. IEEE Trans. Pattern Anal. Mach. Intell. 1 (2021). https://doi.org/10.1109/TPAMI.2021.3051099

52. Wang, Y., Sun, Y., Liu, Z., Sarma, S.E., Bronstein, M.M., Solomon, J.M.: Dynamic graph CNN for learning on point clouds. ACM Trans. Graph. **38**(5), 1–12 (2019)

53. Wei, Y., Wen, F., Zhu, W., Sun, J.: Geodesic saliency using background priors. In: Fitzgibbon, A., Lazebnik, S., Perona, P., Sato, Y., Schmid, C. (eds.) ECCV 2012. LNCS, vol. 7574, pp. 29–42. Springer, Heidelberg (2012). https://doi.org/10.1007/978-3-642-33712-3_3

54. Wu, W., Qi, Z., Fuxin, L.: PointConv: deep convolutional networks on 3D point clouds. In: 2019 IEEE/CVF Conference on Computer Vision and Pattern Recognition (CVPR), pp. 9613–9622 (2019). https://doi.org/10.1109/CVPR.2019.00985

55. Yang, S., Lin, W., Lin, G., Jiang, Q., Liu, Z.: Progressive self-guided loss for salient object detection. IEEE Trans. Image Process. **30**, 8426–8438 (2021). https://doi.org/10.1109/TIP.2021.3113794

56. Zhang, J., et al.: UC-Net: uncertainty inspired RGB-D saliency detection via conditional variational autoencoders. In: IEEE/CVF Conference on Computer Vision and Pattern Recognition, pp. 8579–8588 (2020). https://doi.org/10.1109/CVPR42600.2020.00861

57. Zhang, J., Liu, Y., Zhang, S., Poppe, R., Wang, M.: Light field saliency detection with deep convolutional networks. IEEE Trans. Image Process. **29**, 4421–4434 (2020). https://doi.org/10.1109/TIP.2020.2970529

58. Zhang, M., Fei, S.X., Liu, J., Xu, S., Piao, Y., Lu, H.: Asymmetric two-stream architecture for accurate RGB-D saliency detection. In: Vedaldi, A., Bischof, H., Brox, T., Frahm, J.-M. (eds.) ECCV 2020. LNCS, vol. 12373, pp. 374–390. Springer, Cham (2020). https://doi.org/10.1007/978-3-030-58604-1_23

59. Zhang, Z., Hua, B.S., Yeung, S.K.: ShellNet: efficient point cloud convolutional neural networks using concentric shells statistics. In: IEEE/CVF International Conference on Computer Vision, pp. 1607–1616 (2019). https://doi.org/10.1109/ICCV.2019.00169

60. Zhao, J., Liu, J.J., Fan, D.P., Cao, Y., Yang, J., Cheng, M.M.: EGNet: edge guidance network for salient object detection. In: IEEE/CVF International Conference on Computer Vision, pp. 8778–8787 (2019). https://doi.org/10.1109/ICCV.2019.00887

61. Zheng, T., Chen, C., Yuan, J., Li, B., Ren, K.: PointCloud saliency maps. In: IEEE/CVF International Conference on Computer Vision, pp. 1598–1606 (2019). https://doi.org/10.1109/ICCV.2019.00168
62. Zhou, T., Fan, D.P., Cheng, M.M., Shen, J., Shao, L.: RGB-D salient object detection: a survey. Comput. Vis. Media **7**(1), 37–69 (2021)

Learning Semantic Segmentation from Multiple Datasets with Label Shifts

Dongwan Kim[1(✉)], Yi-Hsuan Tsai[3], Yumin Suh[4], Masoud Faraki[4],
Sparsh Garg[4], Manmohan Chandraker[4,5], and Bohyung Han[1,2]

[1] ECE, Seoul National University, Seoul, South Korea
dongwan123@gmail.com
[2] IPAI, Seoul National University, Seoul, South Korea
[3] Phiar Technologies, Redwood City, USA
[4] NEC Labs America, San Jose, USA
[5] UC San Diego, San Diego, USA

Abstract. While it is desirable to train segmentation models on an aggregation of multiple datasets, a major challenge is that the label space of each dataset may be in conflict with one another. To tackle this challenge, we propose UniSeg, an effective and model-agnostic approach to automatically train segmentation models across multiple datasets with heterogeneous label spaces, without requiring any manual relabeling efforts. Specifically, we introduce two new ideas that account for conflicting and co-occurring labels to achieve better generalization performance in unseen domains. First, we identify a gradient conflict in training incurred by mismatched label spaces and propose a class-independent binary cross-entropy loss to alleviate such label conflicts. Second, we propose a loss function that considers class-relationships across datasets for a better multi-dataset training scheme. Extensive quantitative and qualitative analyses on road-scene datasets show that UniSeg improves over multi-dataset baselines, especially on unseen datasets, e.g., achieving more than 8%p gain in IoU on KITTI. Furthermore, UniSeg achieves 39.4% IoU on the WildDash2 public benchmark, making it one of the strongest submissions in the zero-shot setting. Our project page is available at https://www.nec-labs.com/~mas/UniSeg.

Keywords: Semantic segmentation · Multi-dataset training · Label shift

1 Introduction

Many segmentation datasets, such as Cityscapes [8], BDD [54], IDD [47] and Mapillary [35], have been leveraged by semantic segmentation models to produce high-quality results [5,28,29,43,55,57,58,60]. However, most approaches only exploit labels within a single dataset for training. Given the expense of labeling

Supplementary Information The online version contains supplementary material available at https://doi.org/10.1007/978-3-031-19815-1_2.

© The Author(s), under exclusive license to Springer Nature Switzerland AG 2022
S. Avidan et al. (Eds.): ECCV 2022, LNCS 13688, pp. 20–36, 2022.
https://doi.org/10.1007/978-3-031-19815-1_2

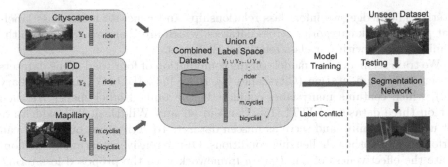

Fig. 1. We tackle the problem of multi-dataset semantic segmentation, where each dataset has a different label space. Directly combining all the datasets and training a model would result in label conflicts within the unified label space. For example, the rider in the right image can be considered as both the "rider" or the "motorcyclist" categories in the unified label space. Therefore, it is important to handle such label conflicts during the training process.

segmentation data, it is important to consider whether labels from multiple datasets can be combined to train more robust models.

One benefit of a model trained on multiple datasets would be the increase in data volume and diversity, which allows a joint model to better reason about challenging objects or scenes. Moreover, if a segmentation model could be trained on a label space that is unified across datasets, we may obtain richer training constraints and inference outputs compared to a model trained from a single dataset. However, combining multiple datasets is non-trivial since their label spaces are heterogeneous and may possibly be in conflict with one another. For example, Cityscapes has 19 categories while Mapillary has 65 more fine-grained categories. A recent work, MSeg [21], deals with this issue by manually defining a taxonomy for the unified label space, which requires re-annotating many images for consistency across datasets. Such a time-consuming solution limits the scalability to more datasets to be collected in the future.

This paper presents a model-agnostic framework called UniSeg, which allows us to employ multiple datasets with heterogeneous label spaces for training semantic segmentation models. First, we observe that the widely-used cross-entropy (CE) loss often leads to conflicting gradients when two datasets contain categories that are in direct conflict with each other (see Fig. 1), e.g., Cityscapes only has the "rider" class, but Mapillary contains both the "motorcyclist" and "bicyclist" categories. To this end, we consider the binary cross-entropy (BCE) loss for semantic segmentation, which allows us to compute separate gradients for each class and resolve the gradient conflict issue during optimization by selectively ignoring certain classes during loss computation. Surprisingly, this simple modification in the loss term, which we call the *Null BCE*, leads to several significant benefits for multi-dataset training, especially on unseen datasets. Second, to utilize class relations across label spaces, we propose *class-relational BCE*, which allows each pixel to be supervised with multiple labels. For example, if we are able to link "bicyclist" from Mapillary to the Cityscapes "rider" class, the training process can be improved by leveraging such a relationship. Without external knowledge, we infer class relationships and generate multi-class labels that properly link categories across datasets, which are then integrated into the training process with our class-relational BCE loss.

We train segmentation models on the combination of four road-scene datasets for semantic segmentation (Cityscapes [8], BDD [54], IDD [47], and Mapillary [35]), which contains many label conflicts in the unified label space. We then test on three datasets, KITTI [15], CamVid [4] and WildDash [56], which are not used for training and serve as unseen datasets to verify that our model can perform well in other challenging conditions. Our extensive experiments demonstrate the effectiveness of our *UniSeg* framework with the proposed loss terms: Null BCE loss and class-relational BCE loss. We compare against baselines using the traditional multi-dataset training. For instance, on the KITTI dataset, our HRNet-W48 [44] model achieves more than 8%p gain in IoU on average across all the settings, and outperforms other methods on the WildDash2 public benchmark. We also conduct qualitative analyses on the output of our UniSeg model and observe that it makes accurate multi-label predictions, especially for classes with label conflict. In summary, the main contributions of this paper are:

- We design a principled model-agnostic framework for multi-dataset semantic segmentation with label shifts, which is free from additional manual annotation costs and prior knowledge.
- We propose a simple yet effective loss terms to handle the label shift problem, while also introducing a new training scheme via class-relational BCE.
- We validate the benefit of using our method in various multi-dataset training settings, showing significant performance improvements over baselines, especially on unseen datasets during training.

2   Related Work

Multi-dataset Semantic Segmentation. Several recent works have considered to use multiple datasets to jointly train a semantic segmentation model [3,18,21,27,32,50]. However, the adopted setting/goal and the perspective of their approaches vary significantly. For instance, [3] uses both the Mapillary [35] and Cityscapes [8] datasets to train a segmentation model on the Cityscapes label space, while detecting outlier regions in an unseen dataset, WildDash [56]. Moreover, [50] considers multi-dataset training using dataset-specific classifiers on the original label space of each dataset. In contrast to our setting, these methods do not consider using a unified label space with a single classifier.

To exploit different label spaces across datasets, two approaches [27,32] adopt the idea of label hierarchy to jointly train on multiple datasets. However, such a strategy requires a manually pre-defined structure of label space, where categories need to be merged, added, or split in the hierarchy tree. Thus it may not be easily scalable to newly introduced datasets. More recently, MSeg [21] proposes to unify multiple datasets via defining a label taxonomy, which maps all the datasets into the same label space. However, this pre-processing scheme requires human re-annotation on a large number of images to ensure label consistency, which is time-consuming and not scalable to more datasets. In contrast, we aim to tackle the multi-dataset setting with label shifts purely from a model-training perspective without requiring any human intervention.

Multi-label Learning. A few works [7,12,20,22,59] proposed methods for effectively training on multi-label settings, where each data sample is accompanied with one or more labels. As an example, Durand *et al.* [12] propose a partial-BCE loss, which computes the loss only on the known classes while ignoring unknown classes. While there exists a technical similarity to the partial-BCE loss, our idea is derived from a different problem setting than partial labels, i.e., the gradient-conflict in multi-dataset training. To alleviate gradient conflict, our Null-BCE reformulates the problem into a partial label problem, and thus, enables better training without sacrificing label granularity of certain datasets.

Domain Adaptation and Generalization. Unsupervised domain adaptation (DA) techniques have been developed to learn domain-invariant features that reduce the gap across the source and target domains in several tasks, such as image classification [14,23,31,39,46], object detection [6,17,19,40], and semantic segmentation [16,26,36,45,48]. Extending from a traditional dual-domains setting, other DA settings have been proposed to consider multi-source [37] and multi-target [9,30] domains. A more challenging setting, universal DA [38,53], deals with various cases across datasets that may have different label spaces. In our multi-dataset setting with supervisions, although there are also domain gaps across datasets similar to the domain adaptation setting, we focus on solving the label shift and conflict issues, which is orthogonal to the adaptation scenario.

Domain generalization assumes multiple training datasets available, and the goal is to learn a model that can generalize well to unseen datasets. Several methods have been developed via learning a share embedding space [11,13,33, 34], domain-specific information [24,41], or meta-learning based approaches [1, 25]. However, these approaches mainly focus on the image classification task, and more importantly, assume a shared label space across the training datasets and any unseen ones, which is different from the setting of this paper, where each dataset may have its own distinct label space.

3 Proposed Method

3.1 Multi-dataset Semantic Segmentation

The typical way to optimize a single-dataset semantic segmentation model is to use a pixel-wise cross-entropy loss. When it comes to multiple datasets, since each dataset has its own label space, there could be two straightforward options to train the model. One method is to construct individually separate classifiers for each dataset. However, this could result in problems during testing, where it may not be clear which classifier should be selected. The second option is to unify all the label spaces and train a single classifier, which is more suitable for our problem context and will be the strategy on which this paper focuses.

Cross-Entropy Formulation. Given an image $X_i \in \mathbb{R}^{H \times W \times 3}$ in dataset D_i and its K_i-categorical one-hot label $Y_i \in \{0,1\}^{H \times W \times K_i}$ in the label space $\mathbb{Y}_i$, we unify the label space as $\mathbb{Y}_u = \mathbb{Y}_1 \cup \mathbb{Y}_2 ... \cup \mathbb{Y}_N$, where N is the number of datasets. Therefore, the original label Y_i is extended to K_u categories, where $K_u \leq \sum_i K_i$ is the number of unified categories. Without any prior knowledge, a natural way to extend Y_i to a K_u-categorical label is to assign all categories in $\mathbb{Y} = \mathbb{Y}_u \setminus \mathbb{Y}_i$ with label 0. As a result, the cross-entropy loss that optimizes the segmentation network $\mathbf{G}$ on multiple datasets can be written as:

$$\mathcal{L}_{seg}^{ce} = -\sum_{i=1}^{N} \sum_{k=1}^{K_u} \sum_{h,w} Y_i^{(h,w,k)} \log(P_i^{(h,w,k)}), \tag{1}$$

where $P_i \in [0,1]^{H \times W \times K_u}$ is the softmax of the segmentation output $O_i = \mathbf{G}(X_i) \in \mathbb{R}^{H \times W \times K_u}$, from the unified classifier. In (1), we omit summation over all samples in each dataset to prevent notations from being over-complicated.

Gradient Conflict in (1). Although unifying the label spaces across datasets enables the standard cross-entropy optimization in (1), it can cause training difficulty when there is a label conflict across datasets. Here, we assume that we do not have prior knowledge regarding the label space and its semantics in the individual datasets. Therefore, such label conflict is likely to occur, as each dataset may define label spaces differently. For instance, Cityscapes only has the "rider" class, while Mapillary does not and has the "motorcyclist" and "bicyclist" categories instead. In this case, the unified label space of $\mathbb{Y}_u$ contains all three categories, "rider", "motorcyclist", and "bicyclist", but during training, images from Mapillary would always treat "rider" with a label of 0.

Based on the example above, such label conflict may cause optimization difficulty with the cross-entropy (CE) loss. To further analyze the negative effect caused by label conflict, we consider the update step of a single parameter θ that contributes to the output O of an arbitrary class k in the last layer of the network. Given an image X_1 from one dataset labeled as k at a position (h, w), the gradient of the loss at a position (h, w) to a parameter θ is calculated as:

$$\frac{\partial \mathcal{L}_{seg}^{ce}}{\partial \theta} = \frac{\partial O_1^{(h,w,k)}}{\partial \theta}(P_1^{(h,w,k)} - Y_1^{(h,w,k)}). \tag{2}$$

Now, consider an identical image X_2 that originates from another dataset with a different label space. Combining the two cases, the gradient for θ becomes:

$$\frac{\partial \mathcal{L}_{seg}^{ce}}{\partial \theta} = \frac{\partial O_1^{(h,w,k)}}{\partial \theta}(P_1^{(h,w,k)} - Y_1^{(h,w,k)}) + \frac{\partial O_2^{(h,w,k)}}{\partial \theta}(P_2^{(h,w,k)} - Y_2^{(h,w,k)}). \tag{3}$$

Note that, since X_1 and X_2 are identical images, $\frac{\partial O_1^{(h,w,k)}}{\partial \theta} = \frac{\partial O_2^{(h,w,k)}}{\partial \theta}$. However, since the two images originate from different datasets, we have $Y_1^{(h,w,k)} \neq Y_2^{(h,w,k)}$ (*i.e.*, if $Y_1^{(h,w,k)} = 1$, $Y_2^{(h,w,k)} = 0$). Thus, the parameter θ receives one gradient that is smaller than 0, and another that is larger than 0, despite coming from identical samples. This is not optimal for training the model, yet can easily occur when training a model on multiple datasets with conflicting label spaces.

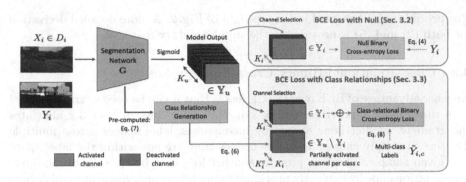

Fig. 2. Overview of the proposed framework using the Null BCE loss (Sect. 3.2) and Class-relational BCE loss (Sect. 3.3): 1) For Null BCE, we replace the original CE loss function to reduce the gradient conflict issue as mentioned in Sect. 3.1. In the loss calculation, we only take the categories in the label space $\mathbb{Y}_i$ of D_i into consideration via (4); 2) For class-relational BCE, through the pre-computed class relationships for each dataset via (8), we incorporate the generated multi-class labels $\tilde{Y}_{i,c}$ via (6) to form (9). Note that only some pixels within the image may have multi-class labels, as illustrated (highlighted in orange). (Color figure online)

3.2 Revisited Binary Cross-Entropy Loss

To resolve the aforementioned issue, we find that the binary cross-entropy (BCE) loss, while similar to the CE loss, exhibits some interesting properties that are desirable for our task setting. First, it does not require a softmax operation, whose value is dependent on the output logits of other classes. Instead, BCE loss is accompanied by a point-wise sigmoid activation. Furthermore, with the BCE loss, we are able to selectively assign labels to each class. Therefore, we design a "Null" class strategy, where we only assign the *valid* labels for each dataset. That is, for images from the D_i dataset, we only assign labels for categories within $\mathbb{Y}_i$, while for other categories $\mathbb{Y} = \mathbb{Y}_u \setminus \mathbb{Y}_i$, we neither assign label 0 nor 1. We name this loss as the "Null BCE loss", which is written as:

$$
\mathcal{L}_{seg}^{bce} = -\sum_{i=1}^{N}\sum_{k=1}^{K_i}\sum_{h,w} Y_i^{(h,w,k)} \log(Q_i^{(h,w,k)}) + (1 - Y_i^{(h,w,k)}) \log(1 - Q_i^{(h,w,k)}) ,
$$

$$(4)$$

where $Q_i \in [0,1]^{H \times W \times K_u}$ is the output from the sigmoid activation. It is important to note that, although there is only a slight difference from (1) in the summation of the loss term, *i.e.*, summed over K_i instead of K_u, this change resolves the gradient conflict issue mentioned in (3) since no loss is calculated for class k for the input image X_2 (see the example in (3)):

$$
\frac{\partial \mathcal{L}_{seg}^{bce}}{\partial \theta} = \frac{\partial O_1^{(h,w,k)}}{\partial \theta}(Q_1^{(h,w,k)} - Y_1^{(h,w,k)}).
$$

$$(5)$$

The procedure is illustrated in the top-right of Fig. 2. A more detailed derivation for both (2) and (5) is provided in the supplementary material.

3.3 Class-Relational Binary Cross-Entropy Loss

Another advantage of BCE over the CE loss is that it can be used to train a model with multi-label supervision. While our Null BCE loss in Sect. 3.2 alleviates the gradient conflict issue caused by inconsistent label spaces across multiple datasets, it simply chooses to ignore classes that are not within the label space of a given sample. Thus, we propose another loss that better utilizes the inter-class relationships by explicitly providing multi-label supervision at pixels where co-occurring labels may exist (bottom-right of Fig. 2).

Multi-class Label Generation. For a class c from dataset D_i, we generate the new multi-class label $\tilde{Y}_{i,c} \in \{0,1\}^{K_u}$. This aims at training the classifier to predict not only the original class but also any co-existing class(es) from the unified label space $\mathbb{Y}_u$. For example, multi-class labels can be generated for subset/superset relationships, $e.g.$, "bicyclist" with "rider" or "crosswalk" with "road", but not classes with similar appearance or high co-occurrence.

Assuming we know these class relationships, we assign additional label $c' \in \mathbb{Y}_u$ only if its similarity to the class $c \in \mathbb{Y}_i$ is sufficiently large,

$$\tilde{Y}_{i,c}^{(c')} = \begin{cases} 1 & \text{if } c' = c \text{ or } \mathbf{s}_{i,c}^{(c')} > \max(\tau, \mathbf{s}_{i,c}^{(c)}) \\ \varnothing & \text{else if } c' \in \mathbb{Y}_u \setminus \mathbb{Y}_i \\ 0 & \text{otherwise} \end{cases}, \tag{6}$$

where $\mathbf{s}_{i,c}^{(c')}$ is the similarity between class c and c' measured in dataset D_i (details for calculation are introduced in the next section) and τ is a threshold. When classes c and c' have a conflict, $e.g.$, when c is "bicyclist" and c' is "rider", we expect the similarity $\mathbf{s}_{i,c}^{(c')}$ to be large. In contrast, we expect it to be small for classes without conflict.

For the choice of τ, we check if the class of the largest score in $\mathbf{s}_{i,c}$ comes from another dataset, D_j, which indicates a high chance of label conflict, and thus, requires multi-class labels. For such cases, we average the largest scores and obtain a value of 0.48 ± 0.01, which is used as the threshold τ. Note that, the max condition in (6) implies that multi-labels are only activated, $i.e.$, $\tilde{Y}_{i,c}^{(c')} = 1$, when similarity for class $c' \in \mathbb{Y}_u \setminus \mathbb{Y}_i$ is higher than that of the original class c, $i.e.$, $\mathbf{s}_{i,c}^{(c')} \geq \mathbf{s}_{i,c}^{(c)}$. This makes label generation more robust to variations in τ. Figure 3 illustrates an example of this process.

Class Relationship Generation. To extract inter-class relationships, we leverage the cosine classifier [49], such that the cosine similarity between the feature and any classifier weight vector can be calculated, even for classes across datasets. Let $\hat{\phi}_c$ denote the ℓ_2-normalized 1×1 convolution weight vector for

Class Relationship and Multi-label Generation

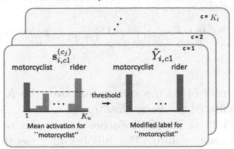

Fig. 3. One example of generating the final multi-class label $\tilde{Y}_{i,c}$ through the mean activation $\mathbf{s}_{i,c}^{(c)}$ for "motorcyclist", where the final multi-class includes the "rider" class.

the cth class, and $\hat{\mathbf{x}}^{(h,w)}$ denote the ℓ_2-normalized input feature vector at location (h, w). Then, the cosine similarity, $S^{(h,w,c)}$, for class c at location (h, w) is calculated as:

$$S^{(h,w,c)} = t \cdot \hat{\phi}_{\mathbf{c}}^{\top} \hat{\mathbf{x}}^{(h,w)} = t \cdot \|\phi_{\mathbf{c}}\| \|\mathbf{x}^{(h,w)}\| \cos \theta_c, \tag{7}$$

where θ_c represents the angle between ϕ_c and $\mathbf{x}^{(h,w)}$, and t is a scaling factor.

We then calculate the mean activation vector of the final output layer as the similarity score, $\mathbf{s}_{i,c} \in [0,1]^{K_u}$, which indicates the relationships between each class c in dataset D_i and all other classes in the unified label space $\mathbb{Y}_u$.

$$\mathbf{s}_{i,c}^{(c')} = \frac{1}{M_{i,c}} \sum_{X_i \in D_i} \sum_{h,w} S_i^{(h,w,c')} \cdot \mathbb{1}_{i,c}^{(h,w)}, \quad \forall i \in \{1, ..., N\}; \forall c' \in \mathbb{Y}_u, \tag{8}$$

where $M_{i,c}$ denotes the number of pixels with ground-truth of c in D_i, X_i represents the samples in D_i, and $\mathbb{1}_{i,c}^{(h,w)} \in \{0,1\}$ is an indicator whose value is 1 if the ground-truth is c at location (h, w) of X_i. Note that, $\mathbf{s}_{i,c}$ can be computed either for each dataset or over all the datasets. In practice, we adopt the dataset-specific similarities to reflect the properties of each individual dataset.

Discussions. In (8), we define the similarity between classes to be asymmetric, i.e., $s_{i,c}^{c'} \neq s_{j,c'}^{c}$, where $i \neq j$ and $c' \in \mathbb{Y}_j$, in order to address the asymmetric relations such as subset/superset. For example, since "rider" is a superset of "motorcyclist", any "motorcyclist" is also a "rider", yet the opposite is not always true. Here, our method is able to implicitly capture such intricate relationships, where the model can generate stronger "rider" activations given inputs of "motorcyclist". On the contrary, the model does not generate strong "motorcyclist" activations on "rider", since a "rider" is not always a "motorcyclist".

Class-Relational BCE Loss. With the the multi-class label $\tilde{Y}_{i,c}$ via (6) that is aware of the class-relationships across datasets, we define our class-relational

BCE Loss as:

$$\mathcal{L}_{seg}^{cl-bce} = -\sum_{i=1}^{N}\sum_{k=1}^{K_i^c}\sum_{h,w}\tilde{Y}_{i,c}^{(h,w,k)}\log(Q_i^{(h,w,k)}) + (1 - \tilde{Y}_{i,c}^{(h,w,k)})\log(1 - Q_i^{(h,w,k)}),$$

(9)

where the difference from (4) is the summation over the K_i^c-categorical multi-label $\tilde{Y}_{i,c}$ that is calculated for each class c. As a result, some of the "Null" categories from Sect. 3.2 can now be incorporated in the loss calculation based on the inferred class relationships. The full list of generated multi-labels are provided in the supplementary material.

3.4 Model Training and Implementation Details

Data Preparation. As noted in Sect. 3.1, given N number of datasets, $D = \{D_1, D_2, ..., D_N\}$, we unify the label space as the union of the N individual label spaces, $\mathbb{Y}_u = \mathbb{Y}_1 \cup \mathbb{Y}_2 ... \cup \mathbb{Y}_N$. We concatenate the N datasets to obtain a single unified dataset. Before doing so, we preprocess each dataset such that the segmentation labels can be re-mapped to the correct index of $\mathbb{Y}_u$. Note that, to make the training batches consistent, we resize all the images with the shorter side as 1080 pixels, and use 713×713 random cropping with standard data augmentations such as random scaling and random horizontal flipping.

Implementation Details. We use the HRNet V2 [44] backbones initialized with weights pre-trained on ImageNet [10]. The batch size is 32/16 with an initial learning rate of 0.02/0.01 for HRNet-W18 and HRNet-W48, respectively. All models are trained using SGD with 0.9 momentum and a polynomial learning rate decay scheme for 150 epochs. To obtain the multi-class labels in our class-relational BCE loss, we pre-train an HRNet-W18 model using the cosine classifier and fix the generated class relationships $s_{i,c}$ for each dataset in all the experiments.

4   Experimental Results

In this section, we first introduce our experimental setting on multi-dataset semantic segmentation. Then, to verify the robustness of our UniSeg model, we present the results trained using different combinations of four driving-scene datasets (Cityscapes [8], BDD [54], IDD [47], and Mapillary [35]), and tested on three unseen datasets (KITTI [15], CamVid [4] and WildDash [56]). Note that we experiment on road-scenes datasets to better highlight the negative effects of label conflict, and to demonstrate that UniSeg can effectively alleviate the label conflict issue. In addition, we diversify our experiments by training models on "Leave-One-Out" settings, where one of the four training datasets acts as a held-out testing set (unseen), and the model is trained on the remaining three datasets. Our quantitative results are accompanied by qualitative results, which provide more insight of our model.

Table 1. mIoU comparisons with baselines using the HRNet-W18 architecture. KITTI, WildDash, and CamVid are fixed as unseen test datasets. "N/A" indicates the setting where there are no multi-labels generated for our final model and thus we only show our Null BCE setting. "C-R BCE" indicates class-relational BCE.

Train datasets	Method	KITTI	WildDash	CamVid	Mean
Single-dataset	Single-best (CE)	41.9	41.2	60.8	48.0
C + I + B	Multi-dataset (CE)	46.2	44.3	70.3	51.6
	UniSeg: Null | C-R BCE	**54.9** | N/A	**44.6** | N/A	**71.8** | N/A	**54.9** | N/A
I + B + M	Multi-dataset (CE)	48.0	47.5	71.2	55.4
	UniSeg: Null | C-R BCE	52.7 | **54.6**	47.7 | **48.3**	**73.2** | 72.7	57.9 | **58.5**
C + I + M	Multi-dataset (CE)	50.2	41.3	72.8	54.8
	UniSeg: Null | C-R BCE	55.9 | **56.5**	44.1 | **44.8**	73.3 | **73.8**	57.8 | **58.4**
C + B + M	Multi-dataset (CE)	55.0	46.2	73.4	58.2
	UniSeg: Null | C-R BCE	59.0 | **59.2**	47.5 | **48.7**	73.8 | **74.0**	60.1 | **60.6**
C + I + B + M (All)	Multi-dataset (CE)	48.8	46.0	72.7	55.8
	UniSeg: Null | C-R BCE	57.6 | **58.9**	47.5 | **48.2**	73.3 | **73.9**	59.5 | **60.3**

4.1 Datasets and Experimental Setting

Here, we describe individual datasets and their dataset-specific characteristics that could affect multi-dataset training on semantic segmentation. In the experiments, we use the official splits for training and evaluation.

The **Cityscapes** and **BDD** datasets are collected from different environments (central Europe and USA, respectively), but both contain the same 19 classes in their label spaces. The **IDD** dataset is collected in India, and provides a hierarchical label space with four levels. We follow a conventional level-3 setting which contains 26 classes. Finally, the **Mapillary** dataset is one of the largest driving scenes dataset, with data collected from around the world, and has a total of 65 fine-grained categories. Overall, the unified label space when training on all four datasets has a total of 70 categories.

KITTI, **WildDash**, and **CamVid** are all small-scale datasets that we use as unseen test datasets. The label spaces of KITTI and WildDash are identical to Cityscapes, while for CamVid, we follow the reduced label space used in [21].

Evaluation. For quantitative evaluation, we follow the standard evaluation protocol for the single class prediction, for simplicity. Specifically, we evaluate on the classes that exist both on the label set where the model is trained from and the label set defined in the test dataset. We select appropriate channels from the model output followed by the argmax operation. Note that our method can also predict the co-occurring categories for each pixel, as demonstrated qualitatively in Sect. 4.4. During testing, following [21], all images are resized so that the height of the image is 1080p (while maintaining the aspect ratio). Intersection-over-union (IoU) score is used to evaluate the segmentation output.

Table 2. mIoU comparisons with baselines using the HRNet-W48 architecture.

Train datasets	Method	KITTI	WildDash	CamVid	Mean
Single-dataset	Single-best (CE)	48.1	48.8	73.6	56.8
C + I + B	Multi-dataset (CE)	54.5	51.5	76.7	60.9
	UniSeg: Null | C-R BCE	**62.9** | N/A	**54.2** | N/A	**76.8** | N/A	**64.6** | N/A
I + B + M	Multi-dataset (CE)	54.4	53.5	77.7	61.9
	UniSeg: Null | C-R BCE	58.4 | **59.3**	**55.9** | 55.7	77.8 | **78.3**	64.0 | **64.4**
C + I + M	Multi-dataset (CE)	56.8	52.9	78.0	62.6
	UniSeg: Null | C-R BCE	63.9 | **65.8**	53.5 | **53.6**	78.4 | **78.7**	65.3 | **66.0**
C + B + M	Multi-dataset (CE)	57.2	54.2	78.2	63.2
	UniSeg: Null | C-R BCE	64.7 | **68.0**	55.3 | **57.8**	78.1 | **78.3**	66.0 | **68.0**
C + I + B + M (All)	Multi-dataset (CE)	57.0	56.0	78.1	63.7
	UniSeg: Null | C-R BCE	64.4 | **65.2**	56.5 | **58.4**	78.2 | **78.6**	66.4 | **67.4**

Table 3. mIoU comparisons with baselines using SegFormer-B1 and B4 architectures.

Method	Arch	KITTI	WildDash	CamVid	Mean
Multi-dataset (CE)	SegFormer B1	55.1	51.4	75.0	60.5
UniSeg: Null | C-R BCE		**59.7** | **60.3**	53.4 | **54.3**	75.5 | **75.7**	62.9 | **63.4**
Multi-dataset (CE)	SegFormer B4	58.4	57.0	78.4	64.6
UniSeg: Null | C-R BCE		**69.1** | 69.0	60.1 | **61.9**	79.2 | **79.6**	69.5 | **70.2**

4.2 Overall Performance

We present our quantitative results for the unseen datasets in Tables 1, 2, and 3, and the leave-one-out setting in Table 4. For more insightful comparisons, we focus on the evaluation of unseen datasets as it is a more interesting setting for validating the generalizability of models, and leave the results for seen datasets in the supplementary material.

Full Setting. In Tables 1 and 2, we show the performance on unseen datasets (KITTI, WildDash, CamVid) for various combinations of the training datasets (*i.e.*, combinations of three or four datasets). In addition to the three methods, we present the "single-best" baseline, where the results are obtained by the best model after training on each of the datasets using the CE loss. That is, we evaluate all single-dataset models and report the strongest result for each unseen dataset. In Table 3, we present the performance of SegFormer [51] models (B1 and B4) trained on all four datasets to demonstrate that UniSeg is model-agnostic.

Leave-One-Out. We employ Leave-One-Out settings with the training datasets to diversify our evaluation. In these settings, one of the four training datasets (*i.e.*, Cityscapes, IDD, BDD, Mapillary) is left out of training and treated as an unseen test dataset. For example, in Table 4, each column presents results of the unseen

Table 4. mIoU comparisons for the Leave-One-Out settings with HRNet-W18 and HRNet-W48. Each column indicates the unseen testing dataset, while the model is trained on the remaining three datasets.

Method	Arch	Cityscapes	IDD	BDD	Mapillary	Mean
Multi-dataset (CE)	HRNet W18	55.0	44.8	52.2	45.7	49.4
UniSeg: Null | C-R BCE		56.1 | **56.8**	46.2 | **47.6**	**52.3** | 52.1	**48.1** | **48.1**	50.7 | **51.2**
Multi-dataset (CE)	HRNet W48	62.1	49.2	56.8	51.8	55.0
UniSeg: Null | C-R BCE		64.6 | **65.8**	**53.3** | 52.9	**58.1** | 57.9	**53.4** | **53.4**	57.4 | **57.5**

test dataset, while the other three serve as train datasets. Note that, when training on "Cityscapes, IDD, BDD", the unified label space is small and no new labels are generated by (6) (*i.e.*, column "Mapillary" of Table 4).

Results. First, we observe that jointly training on multiple datasets generally outperforms the single-best setting, even when the CE loss is used. This shows the advantage of using multi-dataset training, where data diversity and volume are increased. We observe that the two variants of our UniSeg models—Null BCE and class-relational BCE—consistently perform favorably against the multi-dataset baseline with the typical CE loss. For example, using either the HRNet-W18/W-48 model, averaged over all the settings, there is a 7.2%/8.2% gain on KITTI and a 3.3%/3.6% gain on "Mean" in Table 1 and 2, which is considered as a significant improvement in semantic segmentation. Furthermore, the results in Tables 3 (different model architecture) and 4 (diverse dataset combinations) follow a similar trend to Tables 1 and 2, where the UniSeg models consistently outperform the CE baseline. This validates our original intuition that the gradient conflict in the CE loss affects model's robustness, regardless of the model architecture (CNNs in Tables 1 and 2 and Transformers in Table 3) and dataset combination. Finally, comparing between our two model variants, class-relational BCE further improves the overall performance. This shows that providing our generated multi-class labels helps multi-dataset training with conflicting label spaces.

4.3   Results on WildDash2 Benchmark

We further highlight the effectiveness of UniSeg by evaluating on the WildDash2 (WD2) benchmark. The WD2 benchmark is a newer version of the original Wild-Dash dataset, with a few additional classes and negative samples. To evaluate on the WD2 benchmark, we employ the HRNet-W48 "Multi-dataset" and UniSeg models trained on all four datasets (C + I + B + M setting of Table 2). Only the test images are provided to users, while evaluation is done on the WD2 server.

Our UniSeg model currently sits at the fourth place on the public leaderboard[1], only surpassed by three submissions from a single method that uses a

---

[1] https://wilddash.cc/benchmark/summary_tbl?hc=semantic_rob_2020.

Table 5. Class mIoU and negative class mIoU on the WildDash2 benchmark.

Method	Architecture	Class mIoU	Negative mIoU	Meta Avg.
MSeg [21]	HRNet-W48	38.7	24.7	35.2
Yin *et al.* [52]	HRNet-W48	–	–	35.7
Yin *et al.* [52]	Segformer-B5	–	–	37.9
Multi-Dataset (CE)	HRNet-W48	39.0	27.9	36.0
UniSeg (C-R BCE)	HRNet-W48	**41.7**	**34.8**	**39.4**

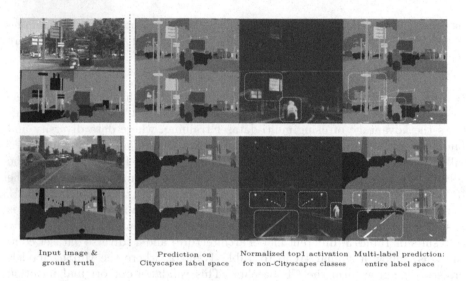

Input image &   Prediction on   Normalized top1 activation   Multi-label prediction:
ground truth   Cityscapes label space   for non-Cityscapes classes   entire label space

Fig. 4. Multi-label predictions on two samples of Cityscapes. For each set of outputs, the first row corresponds to an HRNet-W48 model trained with the CE loss, while the second row corresponds to our C-R BCE model. While both models make strong predictions on the Cityscapes label space (column 2), only the C-R BCE model has high (normalized) activations for non-Cityscapes classes in regions with label conflict (column 3). For example, the C-R BCE model correctly predicts "traffic sign - back" (light brown) and "traffic light" (beige), even though it is not included in the ground-truth for Cityscapes. Furthermore, the C-R BCE model can make more fine-grained predictions, such as "rider" → "motorcyclist" (light purple), "rider" → "bicyclist" (brown), and "road" → "lane marking" (white). (Color figure online)

more powerful architecture and includes WD2 in the training set. In contrast, we do not use any WD2 data during training. A summary of the results in shown in Table 5. Note that, while MSeg [21] merges some important fine-grained classes such as "road markings", our UniSeg model is able to make predictions for such classes. This highlights the benefits of retaining the original fine-grained labels. Here, we also compare with Yin *et al.* [52] which facilitates multi-dataset training by replacing class labels with text descriptions, while also using open datasets [2, 42] for training.

4.4   Qualitative Analysis

To better understand the full capacity of our UniSeg model, we visualize the output predictions of the UniSeg (C-R BCE) and CE models on two samples of the Cityscapes validation set in Fig. 4. We first normalize the logits for each model's output, which is done by computing the softmax across all 70 classes for the CE model, and an element-wise sigmoid operation for the UniSeg model. The classes of Cityscapes with the top-1 scores are plotted to obtain the predictions in column 2. Next, we identify the top-1 classes among the non-Cityscapes classes and plot the scores in column 3. Finally, we obtain multi-label predictions by thresholding the scores of the non-Cityscapes classes: if the score is above a set threshold, the original class is replaced with the non-Cityscapes class. Here, we use 0.5 as the threshold for the UniSeg model, and 0.1 for the CE model.

Through this visualization, we observe that our model exhibits interesting properties beyond quantitative results. First, we find that our model can **make accurate predictions even for regions where Cityscapes does not provide a ground truth**: in the first sample, although the backside of the traffic signs are not labeled (black in ground truth) in Cityscapes, our model outputs high scores for these pixels (column 3) and overrides the original prediction to the "traffic sign - back" class from the Mapillary dataset (column 4). Furthermore, in the second sample, we observe similar behavior for "street lights" (beige).

Our model also **effectively handles cases with direct label conflict**. In the first sample we see men on a motorcycle, which is given the "rider" label in Cityscapes (column 2). However, since our model is also trained on the "motorcyclist" class, and is able to alleviate the gradient conflict between "rider" and "motorcyclist", our model generates large activations for "motorcyclist" (light purple in column 4) as well. Similar results can be seen for the second sample, where the "lane marking" class (white) replaces parts of the "road" class, and the "bicyclist" class (brown) overrides the "rider" class. Note that, unlike the UniSeg model, the model trained on CE cannot produce large activations for these conflicting labels.

5   Conclusion

In this paper, we proposed UniSeg, which is an effective method to train multi-dataset segmentation models with different label spaces. To alleviate the gradient conflict issue caused by conflicting labels across datasets, we designed a "Null" class strategy using the class-independent BCE loss. To further reap the benefits of multi-dataset training, we incorporated learned class-relationships into the class-relational BCE loss. Our experiments demonstrate that UniSeg improves performance over ordinary multi-dataset training, especially for the unseen datasets.

Acknowledgements. This work was done during the first author's internship at NEC Labs America, and was supported by the NRF Korea grant [No. 2022R1A2C3012210] and the IITP grants [No. 2021-0-01343] funded by the Korean government (MSIT).

References

1. Balaji, Y., Sankaranarayanan, S., Chellappa, R.: MetaReg: towards domain generalization using meta-regularization. In: NeurIPS (2018)
2. Benenson, R., Popov, S., Ferrari, V.: Large-scale interactive object segmentation with human annotators. In: CVPR (2019)
3. Bevandic, P., Kreso, I., Orsic, M., Segvic, S.: Simultaneous semantic segmentation and outlier detection in presence of domain shift. In: German Conference on Pattern Recognition (2019)
4. Brostow, G.J., Fauqueur, J., Cipolla, R.: Semantic object classes in video: a high-definition ground truth database. Pattern Recognit. Lett. **30**(2), 88–97 (2009)
5. Chen, L.C., Papandreou, G., Kokkinos, I., Murphy, K., Yuille, A.L.: DeepLab: semantic image segmentation with deep convolutional nets, atrous convolution, and fully connected CRFs. CoRR abs/1606.00915 (2016)
6. Chen, Y., Li, W., Sakaridis, C., Dai, D., Gool, L.V.: Domain adaptive faster R-CNN for object detection in the wild. In: CVPR (2018)
7. Cole, E., Mac Aodha, O., Lorieul, T., Perona, P., Morris, D., Jojic, N.: Multi-label learning from single positive labels. In: CVPR (2021)
8. Cordts, M., et al.: The cityscapes dataset for semantic urban scene understanding. In: CVPR (2016)
9. Dai, S., Sohn, K., Tsai, Y.H., Carin, L., Chandraker, M.: Adaptation across extreme variations using unlabeled domain bridges. arXiv preprint arXiv:1906.02238 (2019)
10. Deng, J., Dong, W., Socher, R., Li, L.J., Li, K., Fei-Fei, L.: ImageNet: a large-scale hierarchical image database. In: CVPR (2009)
11. Dou, Q., Castro, D.C., Kamnitsas, K., Glocker, B.: Domain generalization via model-agnostic learning of semantic features. In: NeurIPS (2019)
12. Durand, T., Mehrasa, N., Mori, G.: Learning a deep convnet for multi-label classification with partial labels. In: CVPR (2019)
13. Faraki, M., Yu, X., Tsai, Y.H., Suh, Y., Chandraker, M.: Cross-domain similarity learning for face recognition in unseen domains. In: CVPR (2021)
14. Ganin, Y., et al.: Domain-adversarial training of neural networks. In: JMLR (2016)
15. Geiger, A., Lenz, P., Urtasun, R.: Are we ready for autonomous driving? The KITTI vision benchmark suite. In: CVPR (2012)
16. Hoffman, J., et al.: CyCADA: cycle-consistent adversarial domain adaptation. In: ICML (2018)
17. Hsu, C.-C., Tsai, Y.-H., Lin, Y.-Y., Yang, M.-H.: Every pixel matters: center-aware feature alignment for domain adaptive object detector. In: Vedaldi, A., Bischof, H., Brox, T., Frahm, J.-M. (eds.) ECCV 2020. LNCS, vol. 12354, pp. 733–748. Springer, Cham (2020). https://doi.org/10.1007/978-3-030-58545-7_42
18. Kalluri, T., Varma, G., Chandraker, M., Jawahar, C.V.: Universal semi-supervised semantic segmentation. In: ICCV (2019)
19. Kim, T., Jeong, M., Kim, S., Choi, S., Kim, C.: Diversify and match: a domain adaptive representation learning paradigm for object detection. In: CVPR (2019)
20. Kundu, K., Tighe, J.: Exploiting weakly supervised visual patterns to learn from partial annotations. In: Advances in Neural Information Processing Systems (2020)
21. Lambert, J., Liu, Z., Sener, O., Hays, J., Koltun, V.: MSeg: a composite dataset for multi-domain semantic segmentation. In: CVPR (2020)
22. Lanchantin, J., Wang, T., Ordonez, V., Qi, Y.: General multi-label image classification with transformers. In: CVPR (2021)

23. Lee, S., Kim, D., Kim, N., Jeong, S.G.: Drop to adapt: Learning discriminative features for unsupervised domain adaptation. In: ICCV (2019)
24. Li, D., Yang, Y., Song, Y.Z., Hospedales, T.M.: Deeper, broader and artier domain generalization. In: ICCV (2017)
25. Li, D., Yang, Y., Song, Y.Z., Hospedales, T.M.: Learning to generalize: meta-learning for domain generalization. In: AAAI (2018)
26. Li, Y., Yuan, L., Vasconcelos, N.: Bidirectional learning for domain adaptation of semantic segmentation. In: CVPR (2019)
27. Liang, X., Zhou, H., Xing, E.: Dynamic-structured semantic propagation network. In: CVPR (2018)
28. Lin, G., Shen, C., van dan Hengel, A., Reid, I.: Efficient piecewise training of deep structured models for semantic segmentation. In: CVPR (2016)
29. Liu, Z., Li, X., Luo, P., Loy, C.C., Tang, X.: Semantic image segmentation via deep parsing network. In: ICCV (2015)
30. Liu, Z., et al.: Open compound domain adaptation. In: CVPR (2020)
31. Long, M., Cao, Y., Wang, J., Jordan, M.: Learning transferable features with deep adaptation networks. In: ICML (2015)
32. Meletis, P., Dubbelman, G.: Training of convolutional networks on multiple heterogeneous datasets for street scene semantic segmentation. In: IEEE Intelligent Vehicles Symposium (IV) (2018)
33. Motiian, S., Piccirilli, M., Adjeroh, D.A., Doretto, G.: Unified deep supervised domain adaptation and generalization. In: ICCV (2017)
34. Muandet, K., Balduzzi, D., Schölkopf, B.: Domain generalization via invariant feature representation. In: ICML (2013)
35. Neuhold, G., Ollmann, T., Bulo, S.R., Kontschieder, P.: The Mapillary vistas dataset for semantic understanding of street scenes. In: ICCV (2017)
36. Paul, S., Tsai, Y.-H., Schulter, S., Roy-Chowdhury, A.K., Chandraker, M.: Domain adaptive semantic segmentation using weak labels. In: Vedaldi, A., Bischof, H., Brox, T., Frahm, J.-M. (eds.) ECCV 2020. LNCS, vol. 12354, pp. 571–587. Springer, Cham (2020). https://doi.org/10.1007/978-3-030-58545-7_33
37. Peng, X., Bai, Q., Xia, X., Huang, Z., Saenko, K., Wang, B.: Moment matching for multi-source domain adaptation. In: ICCV (2019)
38. Saito, K., Kim, D., Sclaroff, S., Saenko, K.: Universal domain adaptation through self-supervision. In: NeurIPS (2020)
39. Saito, K., Watanabe, K., Ushiku, Y., Harada, T.: Maximum classifier discrepancy for unsupervised domain adaptation. In: CVPR (2018)
40. Saito1, K., Ushiku, Y., Harada, T., Saenko, K.: Strong-weak distribution alignment for adaptive object detection. In: CVPR (2019)
41. Seo, S., Suh, Y., Kim, D., Kim, G., Han, J., Han, B.: Learning to optimize domain specific normalization for domain generalization. In: Vedaldi, A., Bischof, H., Brox, T., Frahm, J.-M. (eds.) ECCV 2020. LNCS, vol. 12367, pp. 68–83. Springer, Cham (2020). https://doi.org/10.1007/978-3-030-58542-6_5
42. Shao, S., et al.: Objects365: a large-scale, high-quality dataset for object detection. In: ICCV (2019)
43. Shelhamer, Evan an Long, J., Darrell, T.: Fully convolutional networks for semantic segmentation. TPAMI (2016)
44. Sun, K., et al.: High-resolution representations for labeling pixels and regions. arXiv:1904.04514 (2019)
45. Tsai, Y.H., Sohn, K., Schulter, S., Chandraker, M.: Domain adaptation for structured output via discriminative patch representations. In: ICCV (2019)

46. Tzeng, E., Hoffman, J., Saenko, K., Darrell, T.: Adversarial discriminative domain adaptation. In: CVPR (2017)
47. Varma, G., Subramanian, A., Namboodiri, A.M., Chandraker, M., Jawahar, C.V.: IDD: a dataset for exploring problems of autonomous navigation in unconstrained environments. In: WACV (2019)
48. Vu, T.H., Jain, H., Bucher, M., Cord, M., Pérez, P.: Advent: adversarial entropy minimization for domain adaptation in semantic segmentation. In: CVPR (2019)
49. Wang, H., et al.: CosFace: large margin cosine loss for deep face recognition. In: CVPR (2018)
50. Wang, L., Li, D., Zhu, Y., Tian, L., Shan, Y.: Cross-dataset collaborative learning for semantic segmentation. In: CVPR (2021)
51. Xie, E., Wang, W., Yu, Z., Anandkumar, A., Alvarez, J.M., Luo, P.: SegFormer: simple and efficient design for semantic segmentation with transformers. In: NeurIPS (2021)
52. Yin, W., Liu, Y., Shen, C., van den Hengel, A., Sun, B.: The devil is in the labels: semantic segmentation from sentences. arXiv:2202.02002 (2022)
53. You, K., Long, M., Cao, Z., Wang, J., Jordan, M.I.: Universal domain adaptation. In: CVPR (2019)
54. Yu, F., et al.: Bdd100k: a diverse driving dataset for heterogeneous multitask learning. In: CVPR (2020)
55. Yu, F., Koltun, V.: Multi-scale context aggregation by dilated convolutions. In: ICLR (2016)
56. Zendel, O., Honauer, K., Murschitz, M., Steininger, D., Domínguez, G.F.: Wild-Dash - creating hazard-aware benchmarks. In: Ferrari, V., Hebert, M., Sminchisescu, C., Weiss, Y. (eds.) ECCV 2018. LNCS, vol. 11210, pp. 407–421. Springer, Cham (2018). https://doi.org/10.1007/978-3-030-01231-1_25
57. Zhang, H., et al.: Context encoding for semantic segmentation. In: CVPR (2018)
58. Zhao, H., Shi, J., Qi, X., Wang, X., Jia, J.: Pyramid scene parsing network. In: CVPR (2017)
59. Zhao, X., et al.: Object detection with a unified label space from multiple datasets. In: Vedaldi, A., Bischof, H., Brox, T., Frahm, J.-M. (eds.) ECCV 2020. LNCS, vol. 12359, pp. 178–193. Springer, Cham (2020). https://doi.org/10.1007/978-3-030-58568-6_11
60. Zheng, S., et al.: Conditional random fields as recurrent neural networks. In: ICCV (2015)

Weakly Supervised 3D Scene Segmentation with Region-Level Boundary Awareness and Instance Discrimination

Kangcheng Liu[1]($\boxtimes$), Yuzhi Zhao[2], Qiang Nie[3], Zhi Gao[4], and Ben M. Chen[1]

[1] The Chinese University of Hong Kong, Shatin, China
{kcliu,bmchen}@mae.cuhk.edu.hk
[2] City University of Hong Kong, Kowloon, China
[3] Tencent Youtu Lab, Shanghai, China
[4] Wuhan University, Wuhan, China
yzzhao2-c@my.cityu.edu.hk

Abstract. Current state-of-the-art 3D scene understanding methods are merely designed in a full-supervised way. However, in the limited reconstruction cases, only limited 3D scenes can be reconstructed and annotated. We are in need of a framework that can concurrently be applied to 3D point cloud semantic segmentation and instance segmentation, particularly in circumstances where labels are rather scarce. The paper introduces an effective approach to tackle the 3D scene understanding problem when labeled scenes are limited. To leverage the boundary information, we propose a novel energy-based loss with boundary awareness benefiting from the region-level boundary labels predicted by the boundary prediction network. To encourage latent instance discrimination and guarantee efficiency, we propose the first unsupervised region-level semantic contrastive learning scheme for point clouds, which uses confident predictions of the network to discriminate the intermediate feature embeddings in multiple stages. In the limited reconstruction case, our proposed approach, termed WS3D, has pioneer performance on the large-scale ScanNet on semantic segmentation and instance segmentation. Also, our proposed WS3D achieves state-of-the-art performance on the other indoor and outdoor datasets S3DIS and SemanticKITTI.

Keywords: 3D scene understanding · Weakly-supervised/Semi-supervised learning · Region-level contrast · Energy function · Segmentation

1 Introduction

The 3D scene segmentation problem, which typically consists of two important downstream tasks: point cloud semantic segmentation and instance

Y. Zhao and Q. Nie—Co-second authors.

Supplementary Information The online version contains supplementary material available at https://doi.org/10.1007/978-3-031-19815-1_3.

© The Author(s), under exclusive license to Springer Nature Switzerland AG 2022
S. Avidan et al. (Eds.): ECCV 2022, LNCS 13688, pp. 37–55, 2022.
https://doi.org/10.1007/978-3-031-19815-1_3

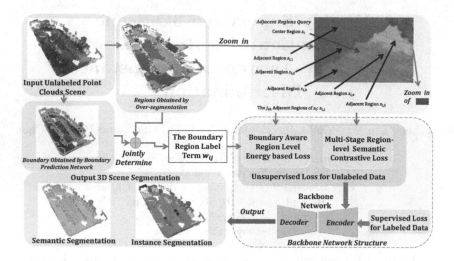

Fig. 1. The illustration of the **overall framework** of our proposed **WS3D**.

segmentation, becomes increasingly important recently with the wide deployment of 3D sensors, such as LiDAR and RGB-D cameras [3]. Point clouds are the raw sensor data obtained by 3D sensors and the most common 3D data representation for 3D scene understanding in robotics and autonomous driving. However, the majority of point cloud understanding methods rely on heavy annotations [4,7,15]. Annotations of 3D point cloud requires a large amount of time and huge labours. For instance, it requires approximately half an hour per scene for ScanNet [10] or S3DIS [2] with even thousands of scenes. Though existing point cloud understanding methods [4,7,15] have achieved good results on these datasets, it is difficult to directly extend them to new scenes when high-quality labels are scarce. And limited number of scenes can be reconstructed in reality [18]. Therefore, developing methods that can be trained with limited 3D labels in complex scenes, termed as weakly supervised learning (WSL)-based or semi-supervised learning (SSL)-based 3D point cloud understanding, becomes in high demand. Recently, motivated by the success of WSL in images [54], many works start to tackle WSL with fewer labels in 3D, but great challenges remain. The challenges involve the meaningful information loss when 3D scenes are transformed to image [50], reliance on fully supervised image segmentation [50], sophisticated pre-processing and pre-training [55], customized labeling strategy and reliance on scene class labels for sub-clouds [52], lack of relationship mining both in low-level geometry and high-level semantics [18]. Hence, developing an effective 3D WSL framework to effectively exploit the information in limited 3D labeled data for the scene segmentation task becomes extremely important.

Weakly supervised image semantic and instance segmentation is a vehement research focus in recent years. Some simple but effective methods have been proposed for WSL-based semantic understanding such as contrastive learning [19,55] and conditional random field (CRF) [6,43]. However, there still exist four main challenging unsolved issues. **Firstly**, the widely adopted energy-function-based conditional random field segmentation [6] relies on handcrafted feature similarities, and does not consider the boundary information. It attaches equal importance to pixels on the semantic boundary and within the same semantic object, which can cause vague and inaccurate predictions in pixel-level segmentation at the object boundaries. And how to leverage boundary information has been explored in 2D but rarely explored in 3D WSL. **Secondly**, the computation costs are both very high when applying pixel-level contrastive learning or pixel-level energy-based segmentation in a high-resolution image for every pixel pair. Furthermore, the large-scale point cloud scenes even contain billions of points, making the point-level contrastive learning intractable. **Thirdly**, the existing unsupervised contrastive-learning-based pre-training for point clouds [18,55] only regards the geometrically registered point cloud pairs as positive samples, while does not take their important correlated semantics into consideration. **Finally**, although existing state-of-the-art detection and segmentation methods [31,63] succeed in using multi-level feature representations in 2D, it remains challenging to design efficient 3D multi-stage contrastive learning strategies to establish more distinctive feature representations at each stage of the feature pyramid.

As depicted in Fig. 1, we propose a unified **WS3D** framework which simultaneously solves the 3D semantic segmentation and instance segmentation. We firstly use the oversegmentation [46] to obtain regions, and use a boundary prediction network as an intermediate tool to obtain boundary region labels. Then, high-confidence boundary region labels serve as guidance for our proposed unsupervised region-level energy-based loss. Meanwhile, we propose an unsupervised multi-stage region-level confidence-guided contrastive loss to enhance instance discrimination. Combined with supervised loss, complete 3D scene segmentation is achieved. Specifically, our **WS3D** includes two novel designs to address the challenging issues mentioned above and to enhance the performance. Firstly, to encourage latent instance discrimination and to guarantee efficiency, an efficient region-level contrastive learning strategy is proposed to guide network training at multiple stages, which realizes unsupervised instance discrimination. Also, to leverage boundary information as labels for semantic divisions, an energy-based loss with guidance from the semantic boundary regions is proposed to make the maximum utilization of the unlabeled data in network training.

The main contributions of our work are highlighted as follows:

1. We propose an unsupervised region-level energy-based loss to achieve region-level boundary awareness, which utilizes boundaries as additional information to assist the 3D scene segmentation.
2. We propose the first unsupervised region-level semantic contrastive learning strategy for multi-stage feature discrimination. The energy-based loss and the contrastive loss are jointly optimized for the segmentation network in a complementary manner to make full use of the unlabeled data.
3. We propose the first weakly supervised framework that can be simultaneously applied for 3D semantic segmentation and instance segmentation. We conduct a lot of experiments on ScanNet and other indoor/outdoor bench-

marks such as S3DIS and SemanticKITTI with different annotation ratios. It is demonstrated State-of-the-art performance has been attained.

2 Related Work

Machine Learning for 3D Scene Understanding. Point cloud processing has become increasingly important in robotic control and scene understanding applications [33–38]. Deep-learning-based approaches are commonly selected for the downstream high-level tasks of 3D scene understanding. The deep-learning-based point cloud processing approaches can be roughly divided into voxelization-based approaches [8,42,45,47,59], transformation-based approaches [13,14,27,30,53,56], and point-based approaches [1,12,23,28,29,35,36,39,41,58, 60,62]. The typical point-based method is the superpoint-graph [28] proposing graph-based deep metric learning for point clouds oversegmentation, which has inspired our work. Different from them, we use the oversegmentation result as the intermediate tool to obtain the boundary region labels. Typical voxel-based method is the Sparseconv [16]. We use it as the backbone network in the task of semantic segmentation because of its high performance in inferring 3D semantics.

Pre-training for the Point Clouds Understanding. Many recent works proposed to pre-train networks on source datasets with auxiliary tasks such as the low-level point cloud geometric registration [55], the local structure prediction [48], the completion of the occluded point clouds [51], and the high-level supervised point cloud semantic segmentation [11], with effective learning strategies such as contrastive learning [55] and generative models [11]. Then, they finetuned the weights of the trained networks for the target 3D understanding tasks to boost performance on the target dataset. However, two major challenges still exist. Firstly, all the mentioned approaches depended on high-quality full annotations, which are hard to obtain for large-scale 3D scenes. Secondly, the large-scale pre-training requires a huge number of computational resources even for image understanding tasks [65]. Thus, the pre-training for large-scale point clouds understanding is hard to put into practice. The unsupervised pre-training [18] showed great capacity in unleashing the potential of a large amount of training data to serve for complicated tasks, e.g., instance segmentation. But merely utilizing unsupervised pre-training cannot explicitly make the utilization of unlabeled scenes, which results in unsatisfactory performance. Unlike previous methods benefiting a lot from pre-training, our proposed approach is trained in an end-to-end manner without pre-training.

WSL for 3D Semantic/Instance Segmentation. A large number of recent works focused on the task of 3D semantic and instance segmentation [21,25,30, 44] with full labels. However, applying current State-of-the-art methods (SOTAs) in a direct way for training often results in a great decrease in performance [20] for WSL, if the percentage of labeled data drops to a certain value, e.g., less than 30%. Recently, many works started to focus more on point cloud semantic segmentation with partially labeled data. Wang et al. [50] chose to transform 3D point clouds representations to 2D images, but pixel-level semantic segmentation

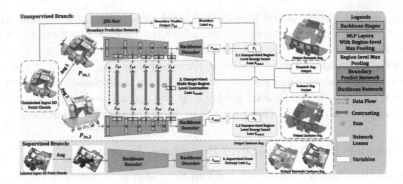

Fig. 2. WS3D architecture overview. **WS3D** consists of three modules: 1. **Unsupervised** region-level energy-based optimization guided by boundary labels; 2. **Unsupervised** multi-stage region-level contrastive learning with high confidence; 3. **Supervised** region-level semantic contrastive learning with labeled data. The backbone network adopts the encoder-decoder structures. The weights of the backbone network are shared in the supervised and unsupervised branch. Our framework can be integrated seamlessly to any off-the-shelf point-based or voxel-based backbones.

labels are still in need during network training. Sub-cloud-level labels [52] needed additional large amount of labor to divide the whole scene into point cloud sub-scenes and to annotate the divided 3D scans into diverse categories. The iterative self-training approaches [40] took advantage of designing a sequential learning strategy, which was made up of two steps to provide pseudo supervisions from limited annotations. However, the OTOC merely works for the task of semantic segmentation. And it can not be easily generalized to more complicated tasks such as instance segmentation. Xu et al. [57] designed a learning framework that merely relies on a small portion of points to be annotated during training. It was designed to approximate the gradient during the learning process, where the auxiliary 3D spatial constraints and color-level evenness were also considered in the network optimizations. However, the approach was restricted to the object part segmentation, and it is difficult to annotate points in a well-proportioned and homogeneous as required. Like Xu et al. [57], we interchangeably use the terms weakly-supervised and semi-supervised for the limited reconstruction cases in this work. In summary, weakly/semi-supervised 3D semantic and instance segmentation are far from mature. More effective methods should be proposed to extract meaningful information from the unlabeled data when limited 3D scenes can be labeled.

3   Proposed Methodology

We propose a general **WS3D** framework to tackle weakly supervised 3D understanding with limited labels, as shown in Fig. 2. We choose different backbone networks for semantic and instance segmentation tasks. For semantic segmentation, we choose the effective backbone Sparseconv [16]. For instance segmentation, our backbone and point clustering procedure follow widely-used Point-Group [25]. **WS3D** consists of three modules for the network optimization:

1. Unsupervised energy-based loss guided by boundary awareness and highly confident predictions for unlabeled data, which is discussed in Subsect. 3.1; **2.** Unsupervised multi-stage region-level contrastive learning with highly confident predictions for unlabeled data, which is discussed in Subsect. 3.2. **3.** Supervised semantic contrastive learning for labeled data, which is discussed in Subsect. 3.3. The three modules are integrated jointly into the optimization function for network training to accomplish the semantic or instance segmentation task.

3.1 Unsupervised Region-Level Boundary Awareness

Energy-function-based conditional random field segmentation was proposed in [6] and has been widely applied. However, it works in a fully supervised manner and does not consider the semantic boundary information, which is a great indication of semantic partitions in point clouds scenes. In this Subsection, we develop a boundary-aware energy-based loss for unsupervised learning. As shown in Fig. 1, to obtain robust boundaries for unlabeled 3D points, we first perform point cloud oversegmentation [46], and also extract boundary points using an off-the shelf semantic boundary prediction network, which are both subsequently used as the conditions to define boundary regions for 3D points. Then, we propose a region-level energy-based loss based on obtained boundary region labels.

Point Clouds Oversegmentation. To obtain boundary regions, and facilitate subsequent region-level affinity computation and region-level contrastive learning, we first perform a region-level coarse clustering based on point cloud oversegmentation. The previous method depended on the region growing [46] to do oversegmentation, which relied heavily on the accurate normal estimation and were easily influenced by noises. In our work, we choose to use normal, curvature to provide the initial oversegmentation. And the oversegmentation results are shown in Fig. 1 and 4. Denote original point clouds as P_{in}. After oversegmentation, they are partitioned into Q subregions $S = \{s_1, s_2, ..., s_q\}$, where $s_i \cap s_k = \emptyset$ for any $s_i \neq s_k$ as shown in Fig. 1 and 4.

Boundary Points Extraction. As shown in Fig. 1, in addition to the oversegmentation results, we extract the semantic boundary points to further identify boundary regions. The semantic boundary often indicates the distinguishment between various semantic classes. We extract semantic boundary points by JSENet [22], as shown in Fig. 2. As for training, we first define semantic boundary points from the limited labeled scenes as ground truth. With definition of the ground truth boundary points, we design the loss following JSENet except substituting the binary cross entropy loss L_{bce} with the focal loss L_{foc} [32] to tackle the large class imbalance between the boundary points and non-boundary points. L_{foc} is as follows:

$$L_{foc} = -\frac{1}{N_i} \sum_{i=1}^{N_i} (1 - b_i)^{\alpha} b_i^{gt} log(b_i) + (b_i)^{\alpha} (1 - b_i^{gt}) log(1 - b_i), \tag{1}$$

where b_i denotes the binary predicted boundary map and b_i^{gt} denotes the ground truth boundary map. N_i is the total number of input points for training. We select $\alpha = 2$ based on the original design [32]. After its convergence, we apply the trained network to the remaining unlabeled scenes to obtain their boundary points. Examples of predicted boundary points of ScanNet [10] are shown in Fig. 4, which clearly reveal distinctions between diverse semantic classes.

Boundary Labels. After extracting semantic boundary points, we utilize them as labels of discrimination between diverse semantic categories. As shown in Fig. 1, denote the j_{th} adjacent regions of the center region s_i as $s_{i,j}$. The adjacent region query is realized by fast Octree-based K-nearest neighbour search [5]. Then, we determine the two adjacent regions as boundary regions if both s_i and $s_{i,j}$ contain boundary points. The label for boundary region $w_{i,j}$ is designed as:

$$w_{i,j} = \begin{cases} 1 & if\ s_i,\ s_{i,j}\ both\ contain\ boundary\ points; \\ 0 & otherwise. \end{cases} \tag{2}$$

The label $w_{i,j}$ denotes semantic boundaries of adjacent regions, which is then used to guide the optimization of the energy function for segmentation.

Energy Loss Guided by Boundary Labels. As shown in Fig. 2, we first perform data augmentation (detailed in the Appendix) for the input point clouds $\mathbf{P}_{in}$ to obtain two transformed point clouds $\mathbf{P}_{in,1}$ and $\mathbf{P}_{in,2} \in \mathbb{R}^{N \times C_{in}}$, where N is the numbers of points. C_{in} and C_{out} are the numbers of input and output feature channels, respectively. Utilizing the backbone network Sparseconv [16], we can obtain point cloud predictions $\mathbf{P}_{out,1}$ and $\mathbf{P}_{out,2}$. Then, applying region-level max pooling on the same subregions, we obtain the predicted classes $\mathbf{P}_1$, and $\mathbf{P}_2 \in \mathbb{R}^{M \times C_{out}}$ of the specific subregions. $\mathbf{P} = \{p(s_1), p(s_2), ...p(s_i), ..., p(s_R)\}$, where R is the total number of regions obtained by oversegmentation. Denote the prediction of the j_{th} neighbouring region of center region s_i as $p(s_{i,j})$. Taking the unary network prediction and pairwise affinity between the neighbouring region into account, inspired by conditional random field (CRF) in DeepLab [6], we formulate the optimization energy function E_{sum} as follows:

$$E_{sum} = \sum_i E_i(s_i) + \sum_{i<j}^{adjacent} E_{i,j}(s_i, s_{i,j}). \tag{3}$$

The first unary network prediction item $E_i(s_i)$ is the entropy regularization term. It encourages region-level prediction with high confidence, which also facilitates the contrastive learning introduced subsequently. It is formulated as:

$$E_i(s_i) = -log\,p(s_i). \tag{4}$$

We propose the pairwise affinity term of E_{sum} as:

$$E_{i,j}(s_i, s_{i,j}) = H_{i,j}w_{i,j}[\epsilon - \|p(s_i) - p(s_{i,j})\|]^2_+ \\ + H_{i,j}(1 - w_{i,j})\|p(s_i) - p(s_{i,j})\|^2. \tag{5}$$

The $H_{i,j}$ is the confidence indicator. $H_{i,j} = 1$, if the probabilities which produce $p(s_i)$ and $p(s_{i,j})$ are both larger than a threshold γ. Otherwise, it equals 0.

ϵ can be any value in the range of $(0, 1)$. $p(s_i)$ and $p(s_{i,j})$ are the semantic predictions for the i_{th} center region and the j_{th} neighbouring region, respectively. And $[x]_+$ is the maximum function $max(0, x)$. For adjacent boundary regions, we encourage their confident semantic or instance predictions to be different (i.e., larger $\|p(s_i) - p(s_{i,j})\|$); while for non-boundary adjacent regions, we force their semantic predictions to be the same (i.e., $\|p(s_i) - p(s_{i,j})\| = 0$). Different from the traditional energy function in DeepLab [6], which used handcrafted features to compare similarities, we propose to use the learned boundary region labels to guide the network's confident max-pooled region-level predictions. Therefore, the proposed boundary-aware energy function better encourages semantic separations at boundaries. Furthermore, we only consider pairwise affinity between adjacent regions instead of all pixel pairs, which greatly reduces computation costs, and avoids noises induced by distant unrelated pairs in the meanwhile.

3.2   Unsupervised Region-Level Instance Discrimination

After applying entropy regularization term $E_i(s_i)$, we can obtain region-level predictions with high confidence. Note that confident region-level predictions further improve the latent feature discrimination capacity of the network, which makes contrastive learning in the latent space feasible. Therefore, we further propose **a multi-stage region-level contrastive learning** for unlabeled data. Compared with previous work only using contrastive learning with low-level geometric registrations [55], our work unleashes potentials of contrastive learning with instance discrimination to enhance distinct feature learning in latent space.

The key of semantic/instance segmentation is to maintain discriminative feature representations at different stages of the backbone network [63]. Inspired by the feature pyramid network [31,63], we propose a simple but effective multi-stage contrastive learning approach for point clouds in an unsupervised setting. As shown in Fig. 2, given the input augmented point clouds $P_{in,1}$ and $P_{in,2}$, we feed them into the backbone encoder. We add five additional MLP heads with region-level max-pooling to obtain region-level segmentation predictions at the m_{th} backbone stage, denoted as $\mathbf{f}_{g,m}$ and $\mathbf{f}_{h,m}$, respectively (five stages in our case, denote M as the total network stages. i.e., $M = 5$). After we apply the MLP heads to the extracted features at different stages, we can obtain the hierarchical feature embeddings. Unlike existing pixel-level [9] (or point-level for point clouds) contrastive learning, our proposed contrastive learning performs on the region level. The region-level semantic contrastive loss is formulated as:

$$L_{contrast}^m = -\frac{1}{\mathbf{S}_p} \sum_{(a,b) \in S_p} log \frac{H_{i,j} exp(\mathbf{f}_{g,m}^a \cdot \mathbf{f}_{h,m}^+ / \tau)}{\sum_{(\cdot,c) \in S_p} H_{i,j} exp(\mathbf{f}_{g,m}^a \cdot \mathbf{f}_{h,m}^- / \tau))}, \quad (6)$$

where $(a, b) \in \mathbf{S}_p$ are latent confident predicted positive region pairs, and $(a, c) \in \mathbf{S}_p$ are latent negative region pairs. As mentioned before, $H_{i,j}$ is designed for eliminating contrastive learning candidates with low confidence degrees. Reliable region-level contrastive learning is only applied to confident predictions by the network. Note that although a recent work **GPC** [24] proposed methods to perform contrastive learning on the point clouds in a SSL manner, our work is different from their method in two aspects. Firstly, our contrastive learning is conducted at region level while **GPC** conducted contrastive learning at point level. Secondly, **GPC** focused on the selection of the positive and negative point-set samples to perform contrastive learning in a pseudo-label supervised manner on two different 3D scene samples, while we focus on unsupervised contrastive learning which disentangles different feature representations in latent spaces on the same augmented 3D scene sample, guided by confident network predictions.

The final proposed multi-stage contrastive learning loss is formulated as the sum of losses at every network stage:

$$L_{multi} = \sum_{m=1}^{M} L_{contrast}^{m}. \tag{7}$$

After applying the multi-stage contrastive loss L_{multi}, the output at each stage of the network will provide more distinctive representations to attain a better performance. From our ablation experiments, the performance can be boosted by applying multi-stage contrastive loss. Combining proposed loss items $E_{sum,1}$, $E_{sum,2}$ (see Eq. 3) for the two augmented scenes $P_{in,1}$, $P_{in,2}$, and L_{multi} (see Eq. 7), we formulate the overall loss $L_{unlabeled}$ for the **WS3D** training with unlabeled data: $L_{unlabeled} = E_{sum,1} + E_{sum,2} + L_{multi}$.

3.3 Supervised Learning for Labeled Data

We also guide the network optimization by using supervision from the labeled data. As shown in Fig. 2, we use the cross-entropy loss L_{ce} to guide the supervised learning on the labeled data in the supervised branch. The loss term for the **WS3D** training with the labeled data is $L_{labeled} = L_{ce}$.

3.4 The Overall Optimization Loss Function

Leveraging our proposed region-level energy-based loss and region-level constrastive learning, the network can make use of the unlabeled data for better feature learning to boost performance. As shown in Fig. 2, for semantic segmentation and instance segmentation, we train the network in an end-to-end manner for both supervised and unsupervised branches to make full use of labeled and unlabeled data. The overall optimization function L_{total} is formulated as follows:

$$L_{total} = L_{labeled} + L_{unlabeled}. \tag{8}$$

4 Experiments

4.1 Experimental Settings

Datasets. To demonstrate the effectiveness of our proposed **WS3D** for WSL under the limited reconstruction labeling scheme, we have tested it on various of benchmarks, including S3DIS [2], ScanNet [17], and SemanticKITTI [4] for

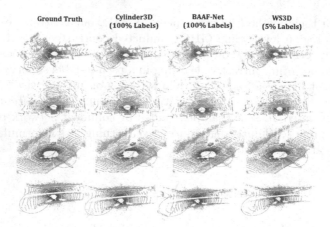

Fig. 3. Qualitative **semantic segmentation** results of proposed **WS3D** on SemanticKITTI Val. Set with 5% labeling percentage, compared with fully supervised arts Cylinder3D [64], and BAAF-Net [44] with semantics indicated by different colors. The red circles highlight the performance difference between diverse methods.

semantic segmentation, and ScanNet [17] for instance segmentation, respectively. The detailed information of each dataset is put in the Appendix.

Training Set Partition. Following the typical setting in data-efficient learning in the limited reconstruction case [18,24], we partition the training set of all tested datasets into labeled data and unlabeled data with various of labeling points proportion, e.g., {1%, 5%, 10%, 15%, 20%, 25%, 30%, 40%, 100%}. For the limited reconstruction case, noted that to partition the labeled points into a specific labeling ratio, we probably need to split a maximum of one scene into two sub-scenes. One of the sub-scenes belongs to the labeled data and the other sub-scenes belong to the unlabeled data.

Implementation Details. For the task of semantic segmentation, we train the network for 500 epochs on a single NVIDIA 1080Ti GPU with a batch size of 16 during training. The initial learning rate is 1×10^{-3} and is multiplied with 0.2 every 50 epochs. We implement it by *PyTorch* and optimize it with Adam optimizer [26]. We set the hyperparameter γ as 0.8 to ensure merely highly confident prediction can be used for the network optimization. ϵ is set to 0.5. For the instance segmentation, we train the network for 580 epochs on a single NVIDIA 1080Ti GPU with a batch size of 8 during training. The other settings are the same as the semantic segmentation task.

4.2   WSL-Based 3D Semantic Segmentation

Overall Experimental Results. For semantic segmentation, we tested **WS3D** on various indoor and outdoor benchmarks, including ScanNet [10], S3DIS [2], and SemanticKITTI [4]. We have done experiments with limited labeled data, e.g., only {1%, 5%, 10%, 15%, 20%, 25%, 30%, 40%, 100%} data in the training set are used as labeled data. As mentioned, we have used the voxel-based method

Table 1. Comparison of **semantic segmentation** results with different labeling percentages on ScanNet val. set, and S3DIS val. set (Area 5), and SemanticKITTI val. set. 'Sup-only-GPC' denotes **GPC** model trained with only labeled data. 'WS3D' denotes model trained with our proposed methods. We have shown the performance increase in the last row for each dataset, compared to merely trained models with labeled data (the left value) and to the SOTAs **GPC** [24] (the right value).

Datasets	Network model	Semantic segmentation mIOU (%) on the validation set according to supervision level (%)								
		1%	5%	10%	15%	20%	25%	30%	40%	100%
ScanNet	Sup-only-GPC	40.9	48.1	57.2	61.3	64.0	65.3	67.1	68.8	72.9
	GPC [24]	46.6	54.8	60.5	63.3	66.7	67.5	68.9	71.3	74.0
	WS3D	49.9	56.2	62.2	65.8	68.5	69.4	70.3	73.4	76.9
	↑	+9.0/+3.3	+8.1/+1.4	+5.0/+1.7	+4.5/+2.5	+4.5/+1.8	+4.1/+1.9	+3.2/+1.4	+4.6/+2.1	+4.0/+2.9
S3DIS	Sup-only-GPC	36.3	45.0	52.9	55.3	59.9	60.3	61.2	62.6	66.4
	GPC [24]	38.2	53.0	57.7	60.2	63.5	63.9	64.9	65.0	68.8
	WS3D	45.3	54.6	59.3	62.3	65.7	66.5	67.2	69.5	72.9
	↑	+9.0/+7.1	+9.6/+1.6	+6.4/+1.6	+7.0/+2.1	+5.8/+2.2	+6.2/+2.6	+6.0/+2.3	+6.9/+4.5	+6.5/+4.1
SemanticKITTI	Sup-only-GPC	28.6	34.8	43.9	47.9	53.8	55.1	55.4	57.4	65.0
	GPC [24]	34.7	41.8	49.9	53.1	58.8	59.1	59.4	59.9	65.8
	WS3D	38.9	43.7	52.3	55.5	61.4	61.7	62.1	63.2	66.9
	↑	+10.3/+4.2	+8.9/+1.9	+8.4/+2.4	+7.6/+2.4	+7.6/+2.6	+6.6/+2.6	+6.7/+2.7	+5.8/+3.3	+1.9/+1.1

Sparseconv [16] as the backbone. The qualitative results are shown in Fig. 3. And the quantitative semantic segmentation performance in terms of mIOU is summarized in Table 1. Our WSL model significantly surpasses the supervised-only model in **GPC** that is merely trained with labeled data, showing that our WSL can make use of the unlabeled data to enhance the feature discrimination capacity of the model. Also, it can be observed that compared with Sup-only-GPC models, the increment of performance is more obvious when the unlabeled data percentage is larger. For example, the performance increase on SemanticKITTI is 10.3% for the 1% labeling percentage, 5.8% for the 40% labeling percentage, and 1.9% for the 100% labeling percentage. This can be possibly explained by the fact that for more unlabeled data, our proposed **WS3D** can extract more meaningful semantic information from the unlabeled data based on our boundary-guided energy-based loss and confidence-guided region-level contrastive learning design. In addition, compared with current SOTAs **GPC**, our proposed **WS3D** also achieves consistently better results in semantic segmentation performance, especially when faced with very limited label circumstances (e.g., 1% labeling points). In that case, **WS3D** outperforms **GPC** by 3.3%, 7.1%, and 4.2% for ScanNet, S3DIS, and SemanticKITTI, respectively. Figure 3 shows that we can provide comparable performance compared with fully supervised SOTAs BAAF-Net [44] and Cylinder3D [64] on SemanticKITTI with 5% labels.

Comparisons with SOTAs in the Fully Supervised Mode. To demonstrate the feature learning capacity of our proposed **WS3D**, we have also experimented with the 100% labeling percentage for a fair comparison with fully supervised SOTAs. The results are shown in Table 2 and the last column of Table 1. We have fed the whole training set into the supervised branch and unsupervised branch in Fig. 2 simultaneously. Therefore, our proposed energy-based loss and region-level contrastive learning strategy operate as additional optimization guidance for the network training. Table 2 demonstrates that we can realize at least comparable or even better results, compared with fully supervised SOTAs.

Table 2. Comparison of SOTAs methods in the semantic segmentation performance on ScanNet validation set, S3DIS validation set (Area 5), and on SemanticKITTI validation set and test set. All results are based on the 100% label ratio. Top-two results are highlighted.

Approaches	Venue	ScanNet Val	S3DIS Val. (Area 5)	SemanticKITTI Val	SemanticKITTI Test
Minkow-Network [8]	CVPR19	72.2	65.4	61.1	63.1
PointASNL [58]	CVPR20	66.4	62.6	–	58.8
KPConv [49]	ICCV19	69.2	67.1	–	46.8
SPV-NAS [47]	ECCV20	–	–	64.7	66.4
Fusion-Net [61]	ECCV20	–	67.2	63.7	61.3
MV-Fusion [27]	ECCV20	76.4	65.4	–	–
Cylinder3D [64]	CVPR21	–	–	**65.9**	**67.8**
BAAF-Net [44]	CVPR21	–	**72.1**	61.2	59.9
Sup-only-GPC	–	72.9	66.4	65.0	65.4
GPC	ICCV21	**74.0**	68.8	65.8	67.7
WS3D	-		**76.9**	**72.9**	**66.9**	**69.0**

Table 3. Comparison of experimental results on 20% and fully labeled case for the task of inductive and transductive learning, respectively. In transductive learning, the test set is also utilized for network training. We test on the task of semantic segmentation on ScanNet, S3DIS, and SemanticKITTI with the evaluation metric of mIOU(%).

Datasets	20% label			100% label		
	Base	Induct	Transduct.	Base	Induct	Transduct
ScanNet Val.	64.0	68.5	71.4	72.9	76.9	77.6
S3DIS Area5 Val.	59.9	65.7	66.6	66.4	72.9	73.5
Semantic KITTI Val.	53.8	61.4	64.5	65.0	66.9	68.2
Semantic KITTI Test.	55.7	62.5	63.6	65.4	68.1	71.3

Transductive Learning. Similar to the experimental setting of [24], we have also conducted experiments evaluating the performance of **WS3D** in transductive learning. Different from inductive learning we tested above that requires the trained model to be generalized to an unseen test set, transductive learning can exploit the testing set when training. Compared with inductive learning, we add the test set as part of the unlabeled data in transductive learning. As is demonstrated in Table 3, the sem. seg. mIOU becomes higher if the network is learned in a transductive way, both for the fully labeled case with 100% labels and the weakly labeled case with 20% labels. It demonstrates that our proposed WSL approaches, including the energy-based boundary-aware loss and the region-level contrastive learning, can leverage the unlabeled data for feature learning effectively in an implicit way to enhance the final segmentation performance.

4.3 WSL-Based 3D Instance Segmentation

As our method can be integrated seamlessly into various network backbones and applied to different highly-level understanding tasks, we have also integrated our method with Point-Group [25] for the instance segmentation on ScanNet with results shown in Table 4. Noticed that the performance increase is 21.7% when merely 1% data is labeled compared with the sup-only case. It further demonstrates that our proposed approaches for the unsupervised branch have effectively exploited the unlabeled data to improve the feature learning capacity of the model. As shown in Fig. 4, our proposed approach can provide explicit boundary guidance for separating diverse semantic classes, and the instance segmentation performance is comparable to those fully supervised counterparts.

Table 4. Comparison of the performance of **instance segmentation**, under various levels of supervision on ScanNet validation set. 'Sup-only-GPC' denotes the model trained with only labeled data. '**WS3D**' denotes the model trained with our proposed methods. We have shown the performance increase of **WS3D** in the last row.

Tested Dataset	Network Model	Ins. Seg. Results with the metric of AP@50%								
		1%	5%	10%	15%	20%	30%	35%	40%	100%
ScanNet	Sup-only-GPC	10.8	33.6	42.8	45.3	48.2	49.0	49.5	50.2	56.8
	WS3D	32.5	45.6	49.2	51.1	51.3	51.9	52.5	53.0	58.7
	↑	**+21.7**	**+12.0**	**+6.4**	**+5.8**	**+3.1**	**+2.9**	**+3.0**	**+2.8**	**+1.9**

Table 5. WS3D ablation studies on ScanNet (Left Value) and S3DIS (Right Value) Val. Set, for semantic segmentation (Metric: mIOU%) and on ScanNet Val. set for instance segmentation (Metric: AP@50%), both tested with the 5% labeled case.

Cases	Base	$w_{i,j}$	$H_{i,j}$ in EF	$H_{i,j}$ in UCSL	UCSL	MS-UCSL	SCE	mIOU%	AP@50%
No. 1	✓	✓	✓	✓		✓	✓	**56.2/54.6**	**45.6**
No. 2	✓		✓	✓		✓	✓	51.0/49.3	39.9
No. 3	✓			✓		✓	✓	49.9/47.2	37.0
No. 4	✓	✓		✓		✓	✓	51.6/52.1	40.1
No. 5	✓	✓	✓			✓	✓	51.1/51.4	40.7
No. 6	✓	✓	✓	✓	✓		✓	52.5/50.9	42.2
No. 7	✓	✓	✓				✓	49.3/48.0	38.1
No. 8	✓	✓	✓	✓		✓		54.3/52.8	42.9
No. 9	✓						✓	48.1/45.0	34.8

4.4 Ablation Study

Ablations: In this Subsection, to analyze the significance and demonstrate the effectiveness of various components in **WS3D**, we have done comprehensive ablations on ScanNet and S3DIS datasets for different network modules on both semantic segmentation and instance segmentation tasks. The final results are summarized in Table 5. We have ablated network modules in all combinations of settings as follows. Take the ScanNet instance segmentation at AP@50% as examples: **Case 1**: The full **WS3D**. **Case 2**: Removing the boundary prediction network, and not using the guidance of $w_{i,j}$. The framework still consists of the supervised branch, unsupervised guidance of the energy function based on the predicted confident pseudo label, and contrastive learning. This setting leads to a significant drop of 5.7% on AP. **Case 3**: Removing the pairwise term in the energy-based optimization function E_{sum}, the AP drops largely by 8.6%. **Case 4**: Removing $H_{i,j}$ in the energy function, the performance drops by 5.5%. **Case 5**: Removing $H_{i,j}$ in the unsupervised contrastive learning, the performance drops by 4.9%. **Case 6**: Conducting contrastive learning only with the region-level feature $\mathbf{f}_{g,5}$ and $\mathbf{f}_{h,5}$ at the fifth network stage, rather than at multiple stages. The performance drops by 3.4%. **Case 7**: Removing the unsupervised region-level contrastive learning branch, the performance drops largely by 7.5%. **Case 8**: Removing the supervised learning branch with the cross-entropy loss, the performance drops by 2.7%. **Case 9**: Only using the supervised branch, the ins. seg. performance drops significantly by 10.8%.

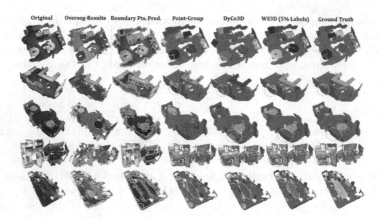

Fig. 4. Qualitative **instance segmentation** results of proposed **WS3D** on ScanNet with the 5% labeling ratio, compared with fully supervised arts, with instances indicated by different colors. And the intermediate oversegmentation results for obtaining regions and boundary predictions, with boundary points (pts.) indicated by blue.

Analyses: From the above ablations, some important findings are summarized: **Firstly**, not using our designed modules results in a significant performance drop (Cases No. 3, No. 7, and No. 9), which demonstrates the effectiveness of the proposed unsupervised branch and learning strategies to leverage the unlabeled data. **Secondly**, our proposed learning strategies with boundary label $w_{i,j}$ (Case No. 2), energy function design (No. 3), high-confidence prediction based energy function design (No. 4), high-confidence based region-level contrastive learning strategy (No. 5), multi-stage contrastive learning network design (No. 6), all have a boost on the overall semantic/instance segmentation performance. The results demonstrate that the proposed energy loss is significant for semantic/instance seg. performance, because semantic boundary labels are crucial for identifying diverse objects. **Thirdly**, removing the supervision (Case No. 8), our method still maintains the performance with a slight drop of performance by 2.7%. It further validates the robustness and feature learning capacity of our approach.

5   Conclusion

In summary, we propose a general **WS3D** framework for WSL-based 3D scene segmentation with SOTAs performance. We propose an unsupervised boundary-aware energy-based loss and a novel region-level multi-stage semantic contrastive learning strategy, which are complementary to each other to make the network learn more meaningful and discriminative features from the unlabeled data. The effectiveness of our approach is verified across three diverse large-scale 3D scene understanding benchmarks under various experiment circumstances.

Acknowledgments. This work is mainly supported by the Hong Kong PhD Fellowship Scheme awarded to Dr. Kangcheng Liu. This work is partially supported by the Hubei Province Natural Science Foundation (Grant No. 2021CFA088), and Wuhan University-Huawei Geoinformatics Innovation Laboratory.

References

1. Ao, S., Hu, Q., Yang, B., Markham, A., Guo, Y.: SpinNet: learning a general surface descriptor for 3D point cloud registration. In: Proceedings of the IEEE/CVF Conference on Computer Vision and Pattern Recognition (CVPR), pp. 11753–11762 (2021)
2. Armeni, I., et al.: 3D semantic parsing of large-scale indoor spaces. In: Proceedings of the IEEE Conference on Computer Vision and Pattern Recognition (CVPR), pp. 1534–1543 (2016)
3. Behley, J., et al.: Towards 3D LiDAR-based semantic scene understanding of 3D point cloud sequences: the semanticKITTI dataset. Int. J. Robot. Res. (IJRR), 02783649211006735 (2021)
4. Behley, J., et al.: SemanticKITTI: a dataset for semantic scene understanding of lidar sequences. In: Proceedings of the IEEE International Conference on Computer Vision (ICCV), pp. 9297–9307 (2019)
5. Behley, J., Steinhage, V., Cremers, A.B.: Efficient radius neighbor search in three-dimensional point clouds. In: 2015 IEEE International Conference on Robotics and Automation (ICRA), pp. 3625–3630. IEEE (2015)
6. Chen, L.C., Papandreou, G., Kokkinos, I., Murphy, K., Yuille, A.L.: DeepLab: semantic image segmentation with deep convolutional nets, atrous convolution, and fully connected CRFs. IEEE Trans. Pattern Anal. Mach. Intell. **40**(4), 834–848 (2017)
7. Cheng, R., Razani, R., Taghavi, E., Li, E., Liu, B.: 2–S3Net: attentive feature fusion with adaptive feature selection for sparse semantic segmentation network. In: Proceedings of the IEEE/CVF Conference on Computer Vision and Pattern Recognition (CVPR), pp. 12547–12556 (2021)
8. Choy, C., Gwak, J., Savarese, S.: 4D spatio-temporal convnets: Minkowski convolutional neural networks. In: Proceedings of the IEEE Conference on Computer Vision and Pattern Recognition (CVPR), pp. 3075–3084 (2019)
9. Cui, J., Zhong, Z., Liu, S., Yu, B., Jia, J.: Parametric contrastive learning. In: Proceedings of the IEEE/CVF International Conference on Computer Vision (ICCV), pp. 715–724 (2021)
10. Dai, A., Chang, A.X., Savva, M., Halber, M., Funkhouser, T., Nießner, M.: ScanNet: richly-annotated 3D reconstructions of indoor scenes. In: Proceedings of the IEEE Conference on Computer Vision and Pattern Recognition (CVPR), pp. 5828–5839 (2017)
11. Eckart, B., Yuan, W., Liu, C., Kautz, J.: Self-supervised learning on 3D point clouds by learning discrete generative models. In: Proceedings of the IEEE/CVF Conference on Computer Vision and Pattern Recognition (CVPR), pp. 8248–8257 (2021)
12. Fan, H., Yu, X., Ding, Y., Yang, Y., Kankanhalli, M.: PSTNET: point spatio-temporal convolution on point cloud sequences. In: International Conference on Learning Representations (ICLR) (2020)

13. Feng, Y., Zhang, Z., Zhao, X., Ji, R., Gao, Y.: GVCNN: group-view convolutional neural networks for 3D shape recognition. In: Proceedings of the IEEE Conference on Computer Vision and Pattern Recognition (CVPR), pp. 264–272 (2018)
14. Gojcic, Z., Zhou, C., Wegner, J.D., Guibas, L.J., Birdal, T.: Learning multiview 3D point cloud registration. In: Proceedings of the IEEE/CVF Conference on Computer Vision and Pattern Recognition (CVPR), pp. 1759–1769 (2020)
15. Gong, J., et al.: Omni-supervised point cloud segmentation via gradual receptive field component reasoning. In: Proceedings of the IEEE/CVF Conference on Computer Vision and Pattern Recognition (CVPR), pp. 11673–11682 (2021)
16. Graham, B., Engelcke, M., van der Maaten, L.: 3D semantic segmentation with submanifold sparse convolutional networks. In: Proceedings of the IEEE Conference on Computer Vision and Pattern Recognition (CVPR), pp. 9224–9232 (2018)
17. Hou, J., Dai, A., Niessner, M.: 3D-SIS: 3D semantic instance segmentation of RGB-D scans. In: Proceedings of the IEEE/CVF Conference on Computer Vision and Pattern Recognition (CVPR), June 2019
18. Hou, J., Graham, B., Nießner, M., Xie, S.: Exploring data-efficient 3D scene understanding with contrastive scene contexts. In: Proceedings of the IEEE/CVF Conference on Computer Vision and Pattern Recognition (CVPR), pp. 15587–15597 (2021)
19. Hu, H., Cui, J., Wang, L.: Region-aware contrastive learning for semantic segmentation. In: Proceedings of the IEEE/CVF International Conference on Computer Vision (ICCV), pp. 16291–16301 (2021)
20. Hu, Q., et al.: SQN: weakly-supervised semantic segmentation of large-scale 3D point clouds with 1000x fewer labels. arXiv preprint arXiv:2104.04891 (2021)
21. Hu, Q., et al.: RandLA-Net: efficient semantic segmentation of large-scale point clouds. In: Proceedings of the IEEE/CVF Conference on Computer Vision and Pattern Recognition (CVPR), pp. 11108–11117 (2020)
22. Hu, Z., Zhen, M., Bai, X., Fu, H., Tai, C.: JSENet: joint semantic segmentation and edge detection network for 3D point clouds. In: Vedaldi, A., Bischof, H., Brox, T., Frahm, J.-M. (eds.) ECCV 2020. LNCS, vol. 12365, pp. 222–239. Springer, Cham (2020). https://doi.org/10.1007/978-3-030-58565-5_14
23. Huang, S., Gojcic, Z., Usvyatsov, M., Wieser, A., Schindler, K.: Predator: registration of 3D point clouds with low overlap. In: Proceedings of the IEEE/CVF Conference on Computer Vision and Pattern Recognition (CVPR), pp. 4267–4276 (2021)
24. Jiang, L., et al.: Guided point contrastive learning for semi-supervised point cloud semantic segmentation. In: Proceedings of the IEEE/CVF International Conference on Computer Vision (ICCV), pp. 6423–6432 (2021)
25. Jiang, L., Zhao, H., Shi, S., Liu, S., Fu, C.W., Jia, J.: PointGroup: dual-set point grouping for 3D instance segmentation. In: Proceedings of the IEEE/CVF Conference on Computer Vision and Pattern Recognition, pp. 4867–4876 (2020)
26. Kingma, D.P., Ba, J.: Adam: a method for stochastic optimization. arXiv preprint arXiv:1412.6980 (2014)
27. Kundu, A., Yin, X., Fathi, A., Ross, D., Brewington, B., Funkhouser, T., Pantofaru, C.: Virtual multi-view fusion for 3D semantic segmentation. In: Vedaldi, A., Bischof, H., Brox, T., Frahm, J.-M. (eds.) ECCV 2020. LNCS, vol. 12369, pp. 518–535. Springer, Cham (2020). https://doi.org/10.1007/978-3-030-58586-0_31
28. Landrieu, L., Boussaha, M.: Point cloud oversegmentation with graph-structured deep metric learning. In: Proceedings of the IEEE/CVF Conference on Computer Vision and Pattern Recognition, pp. 7440–7449 (2019)

29. Lei, H., Akhtar, N., Mian, A.: Spherical kernel for efficient graph convolution on 3D point clouds. IEEE Trans. Pattern Anal. Mach. Intell. **43**, 3664–3680(2020)
30. Li, L., Zhu, S., Fu, H., Tan, P., Tai, C.L.: End-to-end learning local multi-view descriptors for 3D point clouds. In: Proceedings of the IEEE/CVF Conference on Computer Vision and Pattern Recognition (CVPR), pp. 1919–1928 (2020)
31. Lin, T.Y., Dollár, P., Girshick, R., He, K., Hariharan, B., Belongie, S.: Feature pyramid networks for object detection. In: Proceedings of the IEEE Conference on Computer Vision and Pattern Recognition (CVPR), pp. 2117–2125 (2017)
32. Lin, T.Y., Goyal, P., Girshick, R., He, K., Dollár, P.: Focal loss for dense object detection. In: Proceedings of the IEEE International Conference on Computer Vision, pp. 2980–2988 (2017)
33. Liu, K.: Robust industrial UAV/UGV-based unsupervised domain adaptive crack recognitions with depth and edge awareness: from system and database constructions to real-site inspections. In: 30th ACM International Conference on Multimedia (ACM MM) (2022)
34. Liu, K., Gao, Z., Lin, F., Chen, B.M.: FG-Net: fast large-scale LiDAR point cloudsUnderstanding network leveraging correlated feature mining and geometric-aware modelling. arXiv preprint arXiv:2012.09439 (2020)
35. Liu, K., Gao, Z., Lin, F., Chen, B.M.: FG-Conv: large-scale lidar point clouds understanding leveraging feature correlation mining and geometric-aware modeling. In: 2021 IEEE International Conference on Robotics and Automation (ICRA), pp. 12896–12902. IEEE (2021)
36. Liu, K., Gao, Z., Lin, F., Chen, B.M.: FG-Net: a fast and accurate framework for large-scale lidar point cloud understanding. IEEE Trans. Cybern. (2022)
37. Liu, K., Han, X., Chen, B.M.: Deep learning based automatic crack detection and segmentation for unmanned aerial vehicle inspections. In: 2019 IEEE International Conference on Robotics and Biomimetics (ROBIO), pp. 381–387. IEEE (2019)
38. Liu, K., Qu, Y., Kim, H.M., Song, H.: Avoiding frequency second dip in power unreserved control during wind power rotational speed recovery. IEEE Trans. Power Syst. **33**(3), 3097–3106 (2017)
39. Liu, Y., Fan, B., Meng, G., Lu, J., Xiang, S., Pan, C.: DensePoint: learning densely contextual representation for efficient point cloud processing. In: Proceedings of the IEEE International Conference on Computer Vision (ICCV), pp. 5239–5248 (2019)
40. Liu, Z., Qi, X., Fu, C.W.: One thing one click: a self-training approach for weakly supervised 3D semantic segmentation. In: Proceedings of the IEEE/CVF Conference on Computer Vision and Pattern Recognition (CVPR), pp. 1726–1736 (2021)
41. Liu, Z., Tang, H., Lin, Y., Han, S.: Point-voxel CNN for efficient 3D deep learning. In: Advances in Neural Information Processing Systems (NIPS), pp. 965–975 (2019)
42. Noh, J., Lee, S., Ham, B.: HVPR: hybrid voxel-point representation for single-stage 3D object detection. In: Proceedings of the IEEE/CVF Conference on Computer Vision and Pattern Recognition, pp. 14605–14614 (2021)
43. Obukhov, A., Georgoulis, S., Dai, D., Van Gool, L.: Gated CRF loss for weakly supervised semantic image segmentation. arXiv preprint arXiv:1906.04651 6 (2019)
44. Qiu, S., Anwar, S., Barnes, N.: Semantic segmentation for real point cloud scenes via bilateral augmentation and adaptive fusion. In: Proceedings of the IEEE/CVF Conference on Computer Vision and Pattern Recognition (CVPR), pp. 1757–1767 (2021)
45. Que, Z., Lu, G., Xu, D.: VoxelContext-Net: an octree based framework for point cloud compression. In: Proceedings of the IEEE/CVF Conference on Computer Vision and Pattern Recognition (CVPR), pp. 6042–6051 (2021)

46. Rusu, R.B., Cousins, S.: 3D is here: Point cloud library (PCL). In: 2011 IEEE International Conference on Robotics and Automation (ICRA), pp. 1–4. IEEE (2011)
47. Tang, H., et al.: Searching efficient 3D architectures with sparse point-voxel convolution. arXiv preprint arXiv:2007.16100 (2020)
48. Thabet, A., Alwassel, H., Ghanem, B.: Self-supervised learning of local features in 3D point clouds. In: Proceedings of the IEEE/CVF Conference on Computer Vision and Pattern Recognition Workshops (CVPRW), pp. 938–939 (2020)
49. Thomas, H., Qi, C.R., Deschaud, J.E., Marcotegui, B., Goulette, F., Guibas, L.J.: kPConv: flexible and deformable convolution for point clouds. In: Proceedings of the IEEE International Conference on Computer Vision (ICCV), pp. 6411–6420 (2019)
50. Wang, H., Rong, X., Yang, L., Feng, J., Xiao, J., Tian, Y.: Weakly supervised semantic segmentation in 3D graph-structured point clouds of wild scenes. arXiv preprint arXiv:2004.12498 (2020)
51. Wang, H., Liu, Q., Yue, X., Lasenby, J., Kusner, M.J.: Unsupervised point cloud pre-training via occlusion completion. In: Proceedings of the IEEE/CVF International Conference on Computer Vision, pp. 9782–9792 (2021)
52. Wei, J., Lin, G., Yap, K.H., Hung, T.Y., Xie, L.: Multi-path region mining for weakly supervised 3D semantic segmentation on point clouds. In: Proceedings of the IEEE/CVF Conference on Computer Vision and Pattern Recognition (CVPR), pp. 4384–4393 (2020)
53. Wu, B., Zhou, X., Zhao, S., Yue, X., Keutzer, K.: SqueezeSegV 2: improved model structure and unsupervised domain adaptation for road-object segmentation from a lidar point cloud. In: 2019 International Conference on Robotics and Automation (ICRA), pp. 4376–4382. IEEE (2019)
54. Wu, T., et al.: Embedded discriminative attention mechanism for weakly supervised semantic segmentation. In: Proceedings of the IEEE/CVF Conference on Computer Vision and Pattern Recognition (CVPR), pp. 16765–16774 (2021)
55. Xie, S., Gu, J., Guo, D., Qi, C.R., Guibas, L., Litany, O.: PointContrast: unsupervised pre-training for 3D point cloud understanding. In: Vedaldi, A., Bischof, H., Brox, T., Frahm, J.-M. (eds.) ECCV 2020. LNCS, vol. 12348, pp. 574–591. Springer, Cham (2020). https://doi.org/10.1007/978-3-030-58580-8_34
56. Xu, C., et al.: SqueezeSegV3: spatially-adaptive convolution for efficient point-cloud segmentation. arXiv preprint arXiv:2004.01803 (2020)
57. Xu, X., Lee, G.H.: Weakly supervised semantic point cloud segmentation: towards 10x fewer labels. In: Proceedings of the IEEE/CVF Conference on Computer Vision and Pattern Recognition (CVPR), pp. 13706–13715 (2020)
58. Yan, X., Zheng, C., Li, Z., Wang, S., Cui, S.: PointASNL: robust point clouds processing using nonlocal neural networks with adaptive sampling. In: Proceedings of the IEEE/CVF Conference on Computer Vision and Pattern Recognition (CVPR), pp. 5589–5598 (2020)
59. Ye, M., Xu, S., Cao, T.: HVNet: hybrid voxel network for LiDAR based 3D object detection. In: Proceedings of the IEEE/CVF Conference on Computer Vision and Pattern Recognition (CVPR), pp. 1631–1640 (2020)
60. Yin, T., Zhou, X., Krahenbuhl, P.: Center-based 3D object detection and tracking. In: Proceedings of the IEEE/CVF Conference on Computer Vision and Pattern Recognition (CVPR), pp. 11784–11793 (2021)
61. Zhang, F., Fang, J., Wah, B., Torr, P.: Deep FusionNet for point cloud semantic segmentation. In: Vedaldi, A., Bischof, H., Brox, T., Frahm, J.-M. (eds.) ECCV

2020. LNCS, vol. 12369, pp. 644–663. Springer, Cham (2020). https://doi.org/10. 1007/978-3-030-58586-0_38

62. Zhang, Z., Hua, B.S., Yeung, S.K.: ShellNet: efficient point cloud convolutional neural networks using concentric shells statistics. In: Proceedings of the IEEE International Conference on Computer Vision (ICCV), pp. 1607–1616 (2019)

63. Zhao, H., Shi, J., Qi, X., Wang, X., Jia, J.: Pyramid scene parsing network. In: Proceedings of the IEEE Conference on Computer Vision and Pattern Recognition (CVPR), pp. 2881–2890 (2017)

64. Zhu, X., et al.: Cylindrical and asymmetrical 3D convolution networks for LiDAR-based perception. IEEE Trans. Pattern Anal. Mach. Intell. (2021)

65. Zoph, B., et al.: Rethinking pre-training and self-training. Adv. Neural Inf. Process. Syst. **33**, 3833–3845 (2020)

Towards Open-Vocabulary Scene Graph Generation with Prompt-Based Finetuning

Tao He[1], Lianli Gao[2], Jingkuan Song[2], and Yuan-Fang Li[1(✉)]

[1] Faculty of Information Technology, Monash University, Melbourne, Australia
{tao.he,yuanfang.li}@monash.edu
[2] Center for Future Media, University of Electronic Science and Technology of China, Chengdu, China
lianli.gao@uestc.edu.cn, jingkuan.song@gmail.com

Abstract. Scene graph generation (SGG) is a fundamental task aimed at detecting visual relations between objects in an image. The prevailing SGG methods require all object classes to be given in the training set. Such a closed setting limits the practical application of SGG. In this paper, we introduce *open-vocabulary* scene graph generation, a novel, realistic and challenging setting, in which a model is trained on a set of base object classes but is required to infer relations for unseen target object classes. To this end, we propose a two-step method which firstly pre-trains on large amounts of coarse-grained region-caption data and then leverages two prompt-based techniques to finetune the pre-trained model without updating its parameters. Moreover, our method is able to support inference over completely unseen object classes, which existing methods are incapable of handling. On extensive experiments on three benchmark datasets, Visual Genome, GQA and Open-Image, our method significantly outperforms recent, strong SGG methods on the setting of Ov-SGG, as well as on the conventional closed SGG.

Keywords: Open-vocabulary scene graph generation ·
Visual-language model pretraining · Prompt-based finetuning

1 Introduction

Scene Graph Generation (SGG) [38–40,49,53] aims at generating visual relation triples in a given image and is one of the fundamental tasks in computer vision. It has wide applications in a suite of high-level image understanding tasks, including visual captioning [46–48], visual question answering [1,41], and 3D scene understanding [2,54].

It was not until recently that the long-tail distribution in SGG datasets was identified [53]. Following this discovery, a number of works [6,12,21,25,40,43] endeavoured to reduce the impact of the biases in data by exploiting debiasing techniques [18,21,39]. Although remarkable improvements in the performance of

© The Author(s), under exclusive license to Springer Nature Switzerland AG 2022
S. Avidan et al. (Eds.): ECCV 2022, LNCS 13688, pp. 56–73, 2022.
https://doi.org/10.1007/978-3-031-19815-1_4

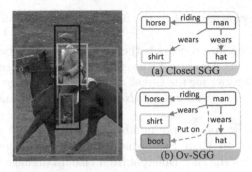

Fig. 1. An illustration of the conventional closed SGG *vs.* Ov-SGG. For the unseen target object **boot**, closed SGG methods such as EBM [38] and Motifs [53], cannot predict any relation regarding **boot** whilst our Ov-SGG method is able to.

unbiased SGG have been made, these state-of-the-art methods are limited to predicting relationships between pre-defined object classes only. In real-world scenarios, however, it is highly likely that an SGG model encounters objects of *unseen* categories that do not appear in the training set. In this more realistic and practical setting, the performance of these conventional SGG models [18,39,53] degrades, and dramatically so when inferring over completely unseen object classes, as can be seen in Table 1 in Sect. 5). This motivates us to ask the question, *can we predict visual relationships for unseen objects?* Formally, we call this problem setting **Open-vocabulary Scene Graph Generation** (Ov-SGG).

In Ov-SGG, the model is trained on objects belonging to a set of seen (i.e. base) object categories $\mathcal{O}^b$ and then predicts relationships on unseen (i.e. target) object categories $\mathcal{O}^t$, both of which are subsets of the open-vocabulary object class set $\mathcal{O} = \mathcal{O}^b \cup \mathcal{O}^t$. This is distinct from, and more challenging than, most existing zero-shot scene graph generation (Zs-SGG) settings [27] or weakly supervised scene graph generation (Ws-SGG) settings [50]. More specifically, Zs-SGG [27] is dedicated to predicting the relationship of objects whose combinations do not emerge in the training set, where the objects are all from seen categories. In contrast, in Ov-SGG, at inference time, not only object combinations may be novel, object categories themselves may not have been seen by the model during training. Zhong *et al.* [58] extends weakly supervised scene graph generation [50] to learning scene graphs from image-caption pairs and demonstrates their model's capability of open-set SGG. In their open-set configuration, the model is trained with a large object set (4,273 classes) and a predicate set (677 categories), and the object categories for testing are included in the training object set. In other words, both settings assume $\mathcal{O}^t \subseteq \mathcal{O}^b$ should be seen beforehand. In contrast, in our open-vocabulary setting, the model is presented with some unseen object classes at inference time, i.e., $\mathcal{O}^t \setminus \mathcal{O}^b \neq \varnothing$, and in the extreme case, completely unseen object classes, i.e., $\mathcal{O}^t \cap \mathcal{O}^b = \varnothing$. Learning scene graphs for unseen object categories has so far remained unexplored. Fig. 1 illustrates a comparison between Ov-SGG and its closed-world counterpart. Moreover, we propose a more realistic and more challenging setting, in which the test set contains novel relation predicates not seen during training. We name this task as *general open-vocabulary* SGG, or gOv-SGG. For instance, in Fig. 1, the novel relation "put on" makes this task gOv-SGG.

The main challenge for Ov-SGG is the knowledge gap between the base and target object categories, i.e., how to leverage the learned visual patterns from the limited base categories for the target categories. To bridge this gap, we propose a two-step method of *visual-relation pre-training* and *prompt-based finetuning*.

Firstly, we capitalize on a large number of visual-textual pairs to pre-train a cross-modal model to align the visual concepts with their corresponding unbounded textual descriptions. Different from visual-language models [33,37,56] that are pre-trained on whole images and their captions, we leverage the dense captions of Visual Genome that focus on detailed regional semantics, as we believe that the dense captions can provide more localised relational information. Secondly, we design two prompt-based learning strategies, hard prompt and soft visual-relation prompt. The pre-trained model makes predictions by *filling in the blank* in the designed prompt.

Finetuning has been widely employed to further reduce the knowledge gap between the pre-trained model and downstream tasks [23,37,57] . However, the standard finetuning practice does not lead to promising results on Ov-SGG, as the newly introduced task-specific prediction heads cannot well handle unseen scenarios, as observed recently [26]. Prompt-based learning [7,8,22] has enjoyed remarkable success in a variety of downstream tasks in natural language processing, including relation extraction [7], commonsense knowledge mining [8] and text generation [22]. This is achieved by learning a small amount of parameters for prompt generation without the need to update parameters of the large underlying pre-trained model. As a result, compared to standard finetuning, prompt-based learning suffers less from task interference and thus enjoys better zero-shot learning ability .

Our contributions can be summarized as follows.

- We propose the new, practical and challenging tasks of *open-vocabulary scene graph generation* (**Ov-SGG**), together with a more challenging setting, *general* open-vocabulary SGG (**gOv-SGG**). We believe that Ov-SGG and gOv-SGG represent a firm step towards the real application of SGG.
- We propose a two-step method that firstly *pre-trains a visual-relation model* on large amounts of available region-caption pairs aiming for visual-relation alignment with open-vocabulary textual descriptions, and secondly finetunes the pre-trained model by two *prompt-based finetuning strategies*: hard prompt and soft visual-relation prompt. To our best knowledge, this is the first investigation of prompt-based finetuning for SGG.
- Extensive experiments on three standard SGG datasets, VG [19], GQA [14] and Open-Image [20], demonstrate our model's significant superiority over state-of-the-art SGG methods on the task of Ov-SGG. Moreover, our method is the only one capable of handling the more challenging zero-shot object SGG. Finally, our model also consistently surpasses all compared baselines on the standard closed SGG task.

2 Related Work

Scene Graph Generation (SGG) [5] aims to detect and localise visual relation between objects. Primary works [15,36] mainly view scene graphs as auxiliary information to improve the quality of image retrieval. Later on, a couple of following arts [41,46,47] demonstrate that scene graphs can be applied to various visual tasks and significantly improve their performance, particularly because scene graphs can provide those models with structured visual representations and facilitate image understanding. With the standard SGG benchmark dataset Visual Genome [19] coming forth for the public, a number of researchers [6,38,40,45,53, 55] started put their efforts to SGG. Xu et al. [45] leveraged an iterative message passing technique derived from graph convolution network [16] to refine object features and improve the quality of generated scene graphs. Yang et al. [46] developed an auto-encoder network by incorporating image-caption into SGG. Zeller et al. [53] first pointed out the bias of relation distribution in the VG dataset and revealed that even using the statistic frequency can obtain the comparable SOTA performance at that time. Thus, a suit of subsequent works [6,25,38–40] started to work on tackling the tricky bias problem in SGG. However, many researchers ignore a common issue that is the SGG models' generalizability. Although some works [3,31,48] proposed the task of weakly supervised scene graph generation, they typically focus on generating scene graphs without localisaed clues, e.g., from image-caption pairs [48] or VCR [52].

Pretrained Visual-Language (VL) Models have been widely applied for tremendous visual-language tasks [33,37,44,57]. Without of loss generality, we could divide those works into two stages: (1) a cross-modal model is first pretrained by natural supervision, e.g., image-caption pairs, to align visual features with their corresponding textual semantics in the common space by a contrastive learning [33,57] or masked token loss [37,56], and (2) developing a suite of visual-language fusion mechanisms, e.g., concatenation of both features [9], and then finetuning the pretrained VL model for downstream VL tasks, such as image caption [37] and visual dialog [44]. Recently, CLIP [33] used massive image-text data to train two encoders for images and texts solely by a simple contrastive loss and showed promising results on a wide-range of image classification tasks, especially in the zero-shot scenario.

Prompt-Based Learning [26] has gained extensive attention in natural language processing due to successful applications of large-scale pretrained language models such as Bert [10] and GPT-3 [4]. Early studies [29,34] typically focused on finetuning the pretrained language models to adapt the model to different downstream tasks by training new parameters via task-specific objective functions. With the advent of prompt-based learning [42], following works [7,8,22] turn to prompt engineering by designing appropriate prompts for the pretrained language model without adding task-specific training or modifying the language parameters. Chen et al. [7] develops an adaptive prompt finetuning strategy for entity relation extraction. Li et al. [22] proposes a lightweight prefix-tuning strategy which enables the mode to fix the parameters of the pretrained language model during training while learns continuous task-specific vectors for text generation.

3   Problem Definition

Scene graph generation (SGG) aims to detect and localize the relationship between objects in an image. *Open-vocabulary* scene graph generation (**Ov-SGG**) is a more challenging problem that works in a more generic scenario, i.e., trained on a set of base object but predicting the relationship for target objects. Formally, let us consider a set of base object categories $\mathcal{O}^b$ where c_k denotes a semantic label of an object. To model the realistic open-world scenario, we assume that there also exists another set of target object classes $\mathcal{O}^t$, where $\mathcal{O}^t \setminus \mathcal{O}^b \neq \emptyset$, i.e., the target set $\mathcal{O}^t$ contains *novel classes* not found in the base set $\mathcal{O}^b$. Moreover, all entities in relation triples in the training set are labeled only by the base object classes in $\mathcal{O}^b$, i.e., $\mathcal{D}^t = \{(x_i, \boldsymbol{y}_i)\}_{i=1}^M$, where M is the number of training images; x_i denotes the i-th image and $\boldsymbol{y}_i$ is the corresponding scene graph that comprises the set of n_i annotated relation triples, i.e., $\boldsymbol{y}_i = \{(s_j, r_j, o_j)\}_{j=1}^{n_i}$ where $s_j, o_j \in \mathcal{O}^b$ are the subject and object respectively; $r_j \in \mathcal{R}$ is the relation predicate; and $\mathcal{Y}$ is the set of all relation predicate words.

The goal of Ov-SGG is to train a model $\mathcal{M}$ on $\mathcal{D}^b$ so that during the inference stage, $\mathcal{M}$ can predict not only relations of $\mathcal{O}^b \times \mathcal{O}^b$ pairs, but also of $\mathcal{O} \times \mathcal{O}$, where $\mathcal{O} = \mathcal{O}^b \cup \mathcal{O}^t$ and $\times$ is the Cartesian product operation. At the same time, a derivative task, zero-shot object SGG (**ZsO-SGG**) requires a model $\mathcal{M}$ trained on $\mathcal{O}^b$ to predict over $\mathcal{O}^t \times \mathcal{O}^t$, where additionally, $\mathcal{O}^t$ contains novel classes only, i.e., $\mathcal{O}^t \cap \mathcal{O}^b = \emptyset$. We also define a more challenging setting, general Ov-SGG (**gOv-SGG**), in which the predication set $\mathcal{R}$ contains novel predicates in the testing stage that are not seen in training. I.e., $\mathcal{R} = \mathcal{R}^b \cup \mathcal{R}^t$ and $\mathcal{R}^t \setminus \mathcal{R}^b \neq \emptyset$.

4   Method

Figure 2 shows the overview of our Ov-SGG framework, which is based on a pretrained visual-relation model (VRM) by tremendous visual-textual corpus, and finetuned on the base objects in a prompt-based learning manner. More specifically, we first train two transformer encoders for image and text, as in [33], to align the visual concepts with their open-vocabulary relational description. With the pretrained VRM, we devise two prompt-based finetuning strategies to reduce the knowledge gap between VRM and SGG by a fill-in-the-blank paradigm.

4.1   Pretrained Context-Aware Visual-Relation Model

An intuitive idea to pretrain a visual-relation model is to use the relation triples subject-predicate-object (SPO) comprised of $\mathcal{O}^b$ to train such a visual-relation space. However, this practice could result in heavily overfitting issue due to the small number of $|\mathcal{O}^b|$. Thus, we consider to use unbounded vocabulary relation

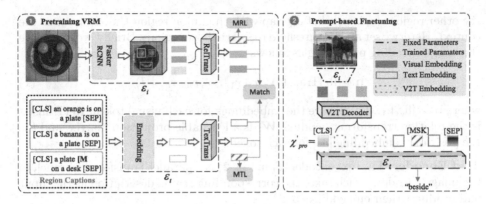

Fig. 2. The overview of our framework for Ov-SGG. **Left**: the architecture of pretraining VRM, which consists of two encoders for regions and dense captions in VG trained by three losses: masked region loss (MRL), match loss and masked token loss (MTL). **Right**: our proposed soft visual-relation prompt for finetuning, which leverages the off-the-shell VRM and optimizes a visual to textual (V2T) decoder network to produce soft prompts.

corpus to train the model. Additionally, the majority of VL models [13,33] totally attempt to align visual concepts with their global textual semantic from image-caption pairs in a fixed scheme, but the identical object in an image could have different relation in an SG, which depends on the other object in a pair. Hence, the pre-trained model should be able to map a visual component into various relation concepts according to its regional context. This ability is not available for the previous pretrained models [13,23,33]. Toward this goal, we propose to train a regional context-aware visual-relation model on the dense-caption of VG by two Transformer-based encoders for images and texts (left of Fig. 2).

Training Data. We collect the dense-caption in the training set of Visual Genome (VG) as our pretrained data with ∼2.6 million region-caption pairs with bounding box information. More specifically, each image on average consists of ∼50 various dense region descriptions. Note that the dense caption is different from the image caption, e.g., MSCOCO [24] with a general global structured description, while the dense caption generally depicts an object's relation with another object within a region. In VG, the vast majority of region captions describe relationships. For more dataset statistic details, please refer to [19].

Image Encoder. The image encoder ($\mathcal{E}_i$ in Fig. 2) consists of two modules: a region proposal feature extractor (e.g., Faster-RCNN [35]) and a relation Transformer embedding module. The Transformer network takes the region proposals r as input visual tokens. Since our model attempts to encode the relation-specific regional context, we do not feed all regions into the encoder like in previous works [33,37,56]. Instead, we propose a union region based sampling strategy that samples feasible regions as the regional context. Concretely, we first randomly sample two anchor regions as the top left r_t and bottom right r_b region and then select the other regions $[r_1...r_m]$ that overlap with the union region $\text{Union}(r_t, r_b)$ as the context. Here, we set an IoU threshold to select those regions. Briefly, we formulate the image encoding processing as follows:

$$\mathbf{h} = \text{RelTrans}(\boldsymbol{W}_1[r_t, r_1, \ldots, r_m, r_b] + \boldsymbol{l}) \tag{1}$$

where $\mathbf{h} = [\mathbf{h}_t, \mathbf{h}_1...\mathbf{h}_m, \mathbf{h}_b]$ are the embeddings for each visual token; $\text{RelTrans}(\cdot)$ is the relation transformer module; $\boldsymbol{W}_1$ is a learnable projection matrix; and $\boldsymbol{l}$ is the positional embedding [33] for each token.

Text Encoder. The text encoder ($\mathcal{E}_t$ in Fig. 2) is a parallel Transformer branch to the image encoder, which takes the corresponding region description as the input and produces their embeddings by:

$$e_i = \text{TexTrans}(\boldsymbol{W}_2 [\texttt{CLS}, w_1, w_2, \ldots, w_k, \texttt{EOF}] + \boldsymbol{l}') \tag{2}$$

where $\boldsymbol{c}_i = [w_1, w_2, \ldots, w_k]$ denotes k words in the dense-caption of region r_i; $\boldsymbol{l}'$ is the position embeddings for each token; and [CLS] and [EOF] are learnable special tokens, denoting the first and last word, respectively. Note that we choose the embedding of [EOF] as the embedding of $\boldsymbol{c}_i$.

Pre-trained Loss Function. The training loss is designed from two main perspectives: image-text matching loss [51] and masked token loss [23]. For the former, we adopt the cosine contrastive loss $\mathcal{L}_c$ [33] to force the visual region embedding to match the embedding of its corresponding dense-caption. For the latter, regarding to RelTrans, we mask any region in $\mathbf{h}$, i.e., replacing it by the special token [mask], with 15% probabilities and let $\mathbf{h}_{[\text{mask}]}$ be close to the embedding of its ground-truth caption by the contrastive loss, denoted as masked region loss $\mathcal{L}_{\text{MRL}}$. As for the text encoder, we follow the standard masked language models [44,51] to train TexTrans by a cross-entropy loss, which we denote by $\mathcal{L}_{\text{MTL}}$. The total pre-trained loss is defined as:

$$\mathcal{L}_{pre} = \mathcal{L}_{\text{MRL}} + \mathcal{L}_{\text{MTL}} + \mathcal{L}_c \tag{3}$$

4.2 Prompt-Based Finetuning for Ov-SGG

In this section, we introduce our proposed prompted-based finetuning method for Ov-SGG, which exploits the rich visual relationship knowledge in the visual-relational model (VRM) to equip the SGG model with the open-vocabulary capability.

Standard Finetuning Strategy. It is intuitive to utilise some standard finetuning techniques [10,37] to deploy a task-specific prediction head for relation prediction and update the pretrained VRM. Following this setup, we could naïvely design a finetuning strategy on the VRM.

Let r_{so} denote the union region of subject r_s and object r_o, and $r_1, \ldots, r_m$ are the object proposals overlapping with r_{so}. We feed them into the pretrained image encoder as in Eq. (1) to produce visual embeddings $\mathbf{h}$. Then, we simply leverage two classifiers to predict the predicate and object label by a cross-entropy loss:

$$\mathcal{L}_f = \text{CE}(\boldsymbol{W}_r \cdot \text{h}_r) + \sum_{h \in \{\text{h}_s, \text{h}_o\}} \text{CE}(\mathbf{W}_c \cdot \text{h}) \tag{4}$$

where h_r is the embedding of the union region of r_s and r_o; $\text{h}_r = \text{LN}(\text{h}_s, \text{h}_{so}, \text{h}_o)$ where $\text{LN}(.)$ is a linear project function; and $\boldsymbol{W}_r$ is the randomly initialized relation classifier. Different from relation classification, we utilize a zero-shot classification setting to predict object labels, that is, using the fixed embeddings of object categories $\mathbf{W}_c$ by our pre-trained text encoder as the object classifier. In this way the model can predict unseen object categories; and CE is the cross-entropy function. At finetuning, all other parameters are updated, as in [37].

However, in practice, we find that the above finetuning strategy does not gain satisfying performance for SGG, particularly in the open-vocabulary scenario. The main reason is updating all parameters could modified the preserved knowledge in the VRM and damage the model's capability of generalization.

Prompt-Based Finetuning for Ov-SGG. Inspired by the success of prompt-based learning [22,30,42] on large-scale pre-trained language models such as GPT-3 [4], we propose two prompt-based finetuning strategies, hard prompt and soft visual-relation prompt (SVRP), for Ov-SGG based on our pre-trained VRM. A key advantage of our prompt-based tuning strategies is that they allow our pre-trained VRM to be optimized on task-specific data without updating its parameters. Doing so avoids altering the learned (open-vocabulary) knowledge during training, and thus supports predictions over unseen object labels at inference time.

The core of prompt-based learning is the design of *templates* to convert the input sequence, x_{in}, into a textual prompt $\mathcal{X}_{pro}$ with unfilled cloze-style slots. The VRM then makes a prediction by filling the slot with the candidate of the maximum probability in the label space. Without loss of generality, a prompt contains two key parts: a template $\mathcal{T}$ that can been manually designed [42] or learned from the training data [32]; and a label mapping function $\mathcal{M} : \mathcal{Y} \rightarrow \mathcal{V}$ that maps a downstream task's labels $\mathcal{Y}$ to the vocabulary $\mathcal{V}$ of a pre-trained model. Note that in this work, $\mathcal{Y} = \mathcal{R}$ is the set of relation labels $\mathcal{R}$ as defined in Sect. 3, while $\mathcal{V} = \{w_i\}_{i=1}^{|\mathcal{V}|}$ is the set of words in the dense captions.

Hard Prompt Based Finetuning. Since relations in SGG are represented as SPO triples, we could readily formulate a relation prompt as follows:

$$\mathcal{X}_{pro} = \mathcal{T}(x_{in}) = [\text{CLS}] x_s [\text{MASK}] x_o [\text{SEP}] \tag{5}$$

where x_s and x_o denote the label of the subject and object, and [MASK] is the slot for candidate predicate labels. Note that the labels of x_s and x_o are produced in an zero-shot manner describing in the second term of Eq. (4). Then, we could predict the relation label by:

$$\hat{y} = \underset{y \in \mathcal{Y}}{\text{argmax}} \, P\left(f_{\text{fill}}\left(\mathcal{X}_{pro}, \mathcal{M}(y)\right) \mid \text{h}_r; \boldsymbol{\theta}\right) \tag{6}$$

where $f_{\text{fill}}(.)$ is a function that fills the slot [MASK] in $\mathcal{X}_{pro}$ with a label word $\mathcal{M}(r) \in \mathcal{V}$, $\text{h}_r = \text{LN}(\text{h}_s, \text{h}_{so}, \text{h}_o)$ is defined as in Eq. (4), and $\boldsymbol{\theta}$ are the parameters of the linear projection function LN (updated) and of VRM (frozen). For the prediction score P, we also use Cosine similarity to calculate it:

$$P\left(p \mid \text{h}_r, \mathcal{X}_{pro}\right) = \frac{\exp\left(\cos\left(\text{h}_r, \text{e}_{\text{in}}(p)\right)\right)}{\sum_q \exp\left(\cos\left(\text{h}_r, \text{e}_{\text{in}}(q)\right)\right)} \tag{7}$$

where $p = f_{\text{fill}}(\mathcal{X}_{pro}, \mathcal{M}(p))$ represents a filled prompt, $\text{e}_{\text{in}}(p) = \text{TexTrans}(p)$ denotes the textual embedding of p, and q ranges over all filled prompts.

Soft Visual-Relation Prompt (SVRP) Based Finetuning. The above hard prompt employs a fixed template as shown in Eq. (5), where only object label information is used. In contrast, SVRP learns a *prefix* visual-to-textual vector as the context to complement the hard prompt, that is,

$$\mathcal{X}'_{pro} = [\text{CLS}][x'_s, \dots, x'_o], x_s [\text{MASK}] x_o [\text{SEP}] \tag{8}$$

where $[x'_s, \dots, x'_o]$ denotes the prefix contextual vector.

To this end, we deploy a visual-to-textual decoder network $\mathbb{T}$ to decode the visual cues into the textual context, i.e., $[x'_s, \dots, x'_o] = \mathbb{T}(\mathbf{h})$, where $\mathbf{h} = [\text{h}_s, \text{h}_1, \dots, \text{h}_m, \text{h}_o]$ is produced by Eq. (1). Thus, we rewrite Eq. (8) as: $\mathcal{X}'_{pro} = \mathbb{T}(\mathcal{X}_{pro} \mid \mathbf{h})$. Similar to Eq. (6), the prediction can be formulated as:

$$\hat{y} = \underset{y \in \mathcal{Y}}{\text{argmax}}\, P\left(f_{\text{fill}}\left(\mathcal{X}'_{pro}, \mathcal{M}(y)\right); \boldsymbol{\theta}'\right) \tag{9}$$

where $\boldsymbol{\theta}'$ are the trainable parameters of $\mathbb{T}$ and the fixed VRM. In this way, we view $\mathcal{X}'_{pro}$ as an input of a masked language model and feed it into the pre-trained TexTrans network to find the token that maximizes the probability of [MASK]. Thus, we could rewrite the prediction by:

$$\begin{aligned} P\left(r \mid \mathcal{X}'_{pro}\right) &= P\left([\text{MASK}] = \mathcal{M}(r) \mid \mathcal{X}'_{pro}\right) \\ &= \frac{\exp\left(\cos\left(\mathbf{w}_r, \text{e}_{[\text{MASK}]}\right)\right)}{\sum_{r' \in \mathcal{R}} \exp\left(\cos\left(\mathbf{w}_{r'}, \text{e}_{[\text{MASK}]}\right)\right)} \end{aligned} \tag{10}$$

where $\mathbf{w}_r$ is the embedding of r by $\mathcal{E}_t$, and $\text{e}_{[\text{MASK}]}$ is the output of the token [MASK] in $\mathcal{X}'_{pro}$ by $\mathcal{E}_t$. During finetuning, we inject the supervised examples $\{(\boldsymbol{h}, \boldsymbol{y})\}$ to the model and utilise cross-entropy loss to optimize Eq. (10).

5   Experiments

We evaluate our method on the task of SGG in both the new open-vocabulary and conventional closed-set settings on three benchmark datasets: Visual Genome (VG) [19], GQA [14] and Open-Image [20]. Implementation details can be found in the supplementary materials.

5.1   Datasets

Visual Genome (VG) is the mainstream benchmark dataset for SGG. Following previous works [39,45,53], we use the pre-processed VG with 150 object classes and 50 predicates [45]. VG consists of 108k images, of which 57,723 images are used for training and 26,443 for testing. Additionally, 5,000 images make up the validation set.

GQA is a more challenging dataset derived from VG images. It contains 1,704 object categories and 311 predicate words. Following [17], we have 66,078 training images, 4,903 validation images, and 10,055 test images.

Open-Image(v_6) consists of 301 object categories and 31 predicate categories. Following the split of [11], the training set has 126,368 images while the validation and test sets contain 1,813 and 5,322 images respectively.

5.2   Evaluation Settings

We evaluate model performance in Ov-SGG as well as two other related settings: closed-set SGG and zero-shot object SGG. Before training, we fist randomly split all the object classes into two groups, *base classes* and *target classes*, on each exper- imental dataset, with 70% objects for the base group whilst the remaining 30% for the target.

Closed-set SGG (Cs-SGG) is the conventional standard SGG evaluation proto- col in which a model predicts the relation between base objects only, i.e., $\mathcal{O}^b \times \mathcal{O}^b$. We report the results on the two subtasks: Predicate Classification (PREDCLS) and Scene Graph Classification (SGCLS).

Open-vocabulary SGG (Ov-SGG) aims to evaluate the model's ability to rec- ognize the relationship between open-vocabulary objects, i.e., $\mathcal{O} \times \mathcal{O}$. We discard the third subtask SGDET in this setting, as the object detection network [56] can not handle open-vocabulary object detection.

Zero-shot Object SGG (ZsO-SGG) is different from the previous Zero-shot SGG [38,39], which simply aims to evaluate a model's capability of predicting unseen object pairs, i.e., the combinations of subject and object classes has not appeared in the training set. In contrast, we set the zero-shot configuration on the object level, that is, to predict the predicate between two object classes completely unseen during training, i.e., $\mathcal{O}^t \times \mathcal{O}^t$. Thus, this setting can be regarded as a special case of Ov-SGG.

Metrics. For VG and GQA, we mainly report Recall@K (R@K). As the bias of R@K has been widely acknowledged [38,39], we further report the results on mR@K. For Open-Image, following the settings of [11], we report three metrics: Recall@50, weighed mean Average Precision (wmAP) and mean Average Preci- sion (mAP) of triples.

Baselines. We compare with recent and strong SGG methods: VTransE [55], IMP [45], Motifs [53], VCtree [40], TDE [39], GCA [18], and EBM [38]. Since TDE and EBM are model-free, for a fair comparison, we choose VCTree as their baseline model to apply their techniques.

Table 1. The comparison Recall@K results of Visual Genome and GQA datasets with other state-of-the-arts SGG models on the tasks of closed SGG, ov-SGG and ZsO-SGG, where we use 70% object for training and the remaining 30% as the unseen objects for testing. All compared methods use the same backbone of ResNet-50 as in [11]. '–' indicates models incapable of obtaining the result. Note that following [17], we report the results of GQA under the setting of graph unconstraint.

	Models	Cs-SGG(70%)				Ov-SGG(70%+30%)				ZsO-SGG(30%)			
		PREDCLS		SGCLS		PREDCLS		SGCLS		PREDCLS		SGCLS	
		R@50	R@100	R@50	R@100	R@50	R@100	R@50	R@100	R@50	R@100	R@50	R@100
VG	IMP [45]	46.93	48.12	28.20	28.91	40.02	43.40	23.86	25.71	37.01	39.46	–	–
	Motifs [53]	49.41	50.71	29.65	30.43	41.14	44.70	24.02	27.12	39.53	41.14	–	–
	VCtree [40]	50.13	52.50	30.09	31.02	42.56	45.84	25.24	28.47	41.27	42.52	–	–
	TDE [39]	45.21	46.03	27.14	27.64	38.29	40.38	22.56	24.22	34.15	36.37	–	–
	GCA [18]	51.15	53.38	29.89	32.10	43.48	46.26	25.71	27.40	42.56	43.18	–	–
	EBM [38]	52.81	54.91	31.64	32.95	44.09	46.95	26.03	28.03	43.27	44.03	–	–
Ablations	**SVRP**	**54.39**	**56.42**	**32.75**	**33.87**	**47.62**	**49.94**	**28.40**	**30.13**	**45.75**	**48.39**	**9.30**	**11.32**
	FT-p	48.13	50.05	28.82	29.12	42.13	45.10	24.47	26.64	41.02	44.10	–	–
	FT	51.42	53.51	29.13	30.46	44.73	46.49	26.24	28.02	42.86	46.25	5.16	7.42
	HardPro	46.83	54.12	30.93	32.41	46.34	48.02	26.87	29.41	43.42	47.05	6.61	8.13
	SVRP-d	47.05	54.27	31.05	32.20	46.96	48.29	27.68	29.89	44.31	47.53	7.84	10.25
GQA	IMP [45]	50.73	54.44	17.28	20.16	30.60	34.30	9.61	11.86	24.34	28.85	–	–
	Motifs [53]	51.74	56.10	18.93	21.02	32.24	36.04	12.37	13.40	28.24	31.34	–	–
	VCtree [40]	51.02	55.78	19.31	21.76	32.06	36.86	12.86	13.73	30.83	33.17	–	–
	TDE [39]	48.30	52.69	16.45	18.50	29.15	33.37	10.36	11.42	24.16	26.83	—	–
	GCA [18]	53.83	57.85	20.73	22.84	33.47	37.11	13.13	14.57	32.73	34.24	–	–
	EBM [38]	53.27	58.16	20.01	22.52	33.03	36.82	13.01	14.34	32.10	34.65	–	–
Ablations	**SVRP**	**55.85**	**61.21**	**22.54**	**24.38**	**35.26**	**39.03**	**15.16**	**16.42**	**34.70**	**36.79**	**1.72**	**2.35**
	FT-p	50.22	54.93	17.38	19.11	31.37	35.02	11.22	12.46	27.58	30.13	–	–
	FT	52.14	56.17	19.49	21.63	33.08	36.77	13.35	14.38	29.51	32.42	.19	.80
	HardPro	54.81	58.92	20.10	22.03	34.19	37.05	14.18	14.90	32.64	34.01	1.04	1.43
	SVRP-d	55.13	59.86	20.52	22.75	34.62	37.98	14.75	15.42	33.53	35.24	1.12	1.72

5.3   Results and Analysis

Table 1 presents the comparison results on VG and GQA with other state-of-the-arts models on the three tasks: Cs-SGG, Ov-SGG and ZsO-SGG. It is worth noting that for the task of ZsO-SGG, the conventional SGG models are incapable of predicting object labels of unseen classes and thus we do not report their results. For GQA, we follow the setting of [17] and compute recalls without the graph constraint.

Cs-SGG. In this conventional setting, we could observe that our SVRP on both VG and GQA consistently surpasses all the compared baselines, even the recent, SOTA models GCA [18] and EBM [38]. For instance, SVPR on VG gains averagely about 1.55 and 1.02 points of improvements on the task of PREDCLS and SGCLS when compared to EBM. Compared to the other models, e.g., IMP and Motifs, SVPR exceed them by even larger margins, e.g., about 6.32 points better than IMP on average.

Table 2. Results on Open-Image(v6) in the closed-set and open-vocabulary settings. All methods used the X152FPN network [11] pretrained on Open Images.

Models	Cs-SGG(70%)			Ov-SGG(70%+30%)		
	R@50	mAP	wmAP	R@50	mAP	wmAP
IMP [45]	71.54	34.67	30.01	51.38	24.15	21.62
Motifs [53]	72.05	32.70	29.16	50.47	23.03	20.51
VCtree [40]	72.41	33.08	30.15	52.12	24.29	22.14
TDE [39]	70.52	30.10	31.68	49.50	21.38	18.33
EBM [38]	71.26	34.46	30.25	52.03	24.59	23.31
SVRP	**72.84**	**35.32**	**33.11**	**54.45**	**27.97**	**25.36**

Ov-SGG. The middle block shows the results of the new, challenging Ov-SGG setting, in which all models suffer considerable performance drops when compared to Cs-SGG. However, our SVRP technique still obtains the best results, on average 3.91 and 2.71 points higher than GCA in terms of PREDCLS and SGCLS, respectively. The conventional models such as Motifs and VCTree, which were designed for Cs-SGG, struggle on this task. We posit the main reason to be their reliance on manually-designed external knowledge, e.g., word embeddings from GLOVE [28]. Although beneficial for Cs-SGG, this knowledge damages the model's generalizability for open-vocabulary objects, as they do not see the embeddings of the target object during training, and are prone to overfitting on the base object classes. In contrast, through pre-training on massive dense-caption corpus, our pre-trained VRM directly learns to align the visual and relation knowledge, which can avoid the overfitting problem on the base classes. Additional, our prompt-based mechanisms allow us to finetune VRM without modifying its parameters, which makes it possible to extend the generalizability of VRM to Ov-SGG.

ZsO-SGG. The rightmost block shows the results of ZsO-SGG. Again, our SVRP is superior to all baseline models in PREDCLS on the two datasets. In particular, SVRP on average exceeds the strong EBM and GCA by about 3.42 and 4.20, respectively. Moreover, our method is the only one that is capable of handling SGCls in this setting. Table 2 shows the results on Open-Image. Interestingly, we could find that the performance of ZsO-SGG is significantly higher than the conventional Zs-SGG [39], possibly because the majority of predicates in the ZsO-SGG are frequent relationships and this is in favor of better results with the biased metric R@K.

Fully-closed scene graph generation. We further evaluate our technique for fully closed scene graph generation, as shown in Table 3. Specifically, we use all object classes in VG to train following the conventional setting [40]. We discard all the statistical bias prior information for all compared methods. From the results, we could observe that our SVRP surpasses all compared baselines, except for mR@100 on the task of PREDCLS, our SVRP has 0.7 points lower than EBM.

Table 3. The results of fully closed scene graph generation on VG and K is set to 50/100. All compared methods use the object detection network from [11] with ResNet-50 as the backbone.

Models	PredCls		SGCls		SGDet	
	R@K	mR@K	R@K	mR@K	R@K	mR@K
IMP [45]	54.1/57.9	9.3/10.2	30.3/32.2	5.8/6.2	19.7/24.6	1.3/7.6
Motifs [53]	60.1/61.5	13.8/15.1	32.1/34.5	7.3/8.0	26.2/28.3	5.2/6.3
VCtree [40]	59.6/60.4	16.7/18.4	33.0/35.7	9.1/10.3	25.9/30.0	8.2/10.1
TDE [39]	50.2/55.8	20.3/24.2	27.2/30.4	10.4/12.5	22.6/25.9	8.6/10.5
GCA [18]	58.9/60.9	22.2/23.3	29.1/33.3	11.4/13.1	–/–	–/–
EBM [38]	59.8/61.7	24.1/**26.0**	32.0/34.6	13.1/14.9	26.8/33.7	9.2/11.6
SVRP	**60.2/62.3**	**24.3/25.3**	**33.9/35.2**	**12.5/15.3**	**31.8/35.8**	**10.5/12.8**
FT-p	56.0/60.5	20.1/23.6	31.7/32.1	10.1/11.4	26.7/32.5	7.3/9.4
FT	58.8/62.2	22.7/24.5	32.4/34.8	11.3/13.5	27.0/33.2	9.0/10.5
HardPro	60.5/63.1	23.2/25.0	32.1/34.5	13.2/14.9	30.2/34.1	9.8/12.0
SVRP-d	60.2/62.7	23.8/25.3	33.5/35.0	14.0/15.2	31.3/34.8	10.2/12.7

Ablations. We evaluate the effectiveness of our model components in several variants: (1) FT-p uses the pretrained model from [56] instead of our VRM, i.e., without pre-training; (2) FT uses the standard finetuning strategy described in Sect. 4.2; (3) HardPro uses hard prompt finetuning described in Sect. 4.2; and (4) SVRP-d removes the decoder network $\mathbb{T}$ for SVRP. The ablation results on the VG and GQA datasets are shown in Table 1 and 3, respectively. With the pre-trained VRM removed (FT-p *vs.* FT), we could find that our VRM can bring 2–3 points improvements, which suggests that simply using the visual-language model [56] for SGG does not bring much benefit, possibly because the visual-language model trained on the global image-caption pairs focuses on the images' global semantics, but ignores the regional semantics. However, those regional cues play an important role in SGG. Furthermore, our two prompt-based finetuning techniques present clear superiority to the standard finetuning strategy, especially in the open-vocabulary scenarios, since the prompt-based strategies directly leverage knowledge preserved in the pre-trained model, which equips the downstream SGG model with the zero-shot capability, whilst the standard finetuning strategy updates the pre-trained model and therefore creates interference between tasks. With respect to the decoder network (SVRP-d), the results confirm solely feeding plain region embeddings to the language model does not generate good prefix contexts for prompts.

gOv-SGG. Additionally, we also provide a baseline for the challenging task of gOv-SGG, in which the model needs to make predictions on novel relation predicates during inference. In this setting, the model sees 70% objects and 70% predicates in the training stage. Specifically, the finetuning predicate set $\mathcal{R}$ in Eq. (10) only account for 70% of all predicates. The model then tries to predict the remaining 30% predicates words on the whole of objects. Since none of the baseline methods can handle this task, we only report the results of our models and its ablated variants, as shown in Table 4. We could obviously see that our SVPR still achieves the best results over all metrics.

Table 4. The results of gOv-SGG on VG where K is set to 50/100.

Models	PredCls				SGCls			
	R@50	R@100	mR@50	mR@100	R@50	R@100	mR@50	mR@100
SVRP	**33.5**	**35.9**	**8.3**	**10.8**	**19.1**	**21.5**	3.2	**4.5**
FT-p	29.4	31.3	5.8	6.7	16.9	18.0	2.3	2.7
HardPro	30.0	32.6	6.9	8.1	17.2	18.6	3.0	4.1
SVRP-d	31.3	33.2	7.6	9.0	18.3	19.7	3.2	4.4

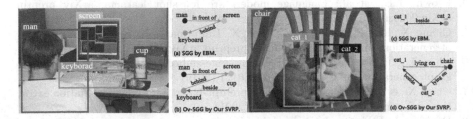

Fig. 3. Qualitative results of our SVRP and EBM [38] on the VG test set for Ov-SGG. EBM is unable to detect relations on the unseen 'cup' and 'chair' classes while our method can.

Qualitative Analysis. On the task of Ov-SGG, we visualize the scene graphs produced by our technique as well as by the representative closed SGG model EMB [38], as shown in Fig. 3. For the left image, EBM cannot detect any relation regrading the unseen target object "cup", while our SVRP can predict the "beside" relationship between the keyboard and cup. Similarly for the right image, EBM is unable to make predictions about the unseen object class "chair" while our method can.

6 Conclusion

We propose the new practical and challenging open-vocabulary scene graph generation (Ov-SGG) setting and design a two-step method that firstly pre-trains a visual-relation model on large-scale region-caption data. We develop two prompt-based strategies to finetune the visual-relation model for the downstream Ov-SGG task without modifying the pret-rained model parameters. Our extensive experiments on three benchmark datasets show that our method significantly outperforms recent, strong SGG methods on the setting of Ov-SGG, gOv-SGG and the closed SGG. In the future, we hope to integrate open-vocabulary object detection into Ov-SGG.

Acknowledgments. This work was partially funded by DARPA CCU program (HR001121S0024).

References

1. Antol, S., et al.: VQA: visual question answering. In: CVPR, pp. 2425–2433 (2015)
2. Armeni, I., et al.: 3D scene graph: a structure for unified semantics, 3D space, and camera. In: Proceedings of the IEEE/CVF International Conference on Computer Vision, pp. 5664–5673 (2019)
3. Baldassarre, F., Smith, K., Sullivan, J., Azizpour, H.: Explanation-based weakly-supervised learning of visual relations with graph networks. In: Vedaldi, A., Bischof, H., Brox, T., Frahm, J.-M. (eds.) ECCV 2020. LNCS, vol. 12373, pp. 612–630. Springer, Cham (2020). https://doi.org/10.1007/978-3-030-58604-1_37
4. Brown, T.B., et al.: Language models are few-shot learners. arXiv preprint arXiv:2005.14165 (2020)
5. Chang, X., Ren, P., Xu, P., Li, Z., Chen, X., Hauptmann, A.: Scene graphs: a survey of generations and applications. arXiv preprint arXiv:2104.01111 (2021)
6. Chen, T., Yu, W., Chen, R., Lin, L.: Knowledge-embedded routing network for scene graph generation. In: CVPR, pp. 6163–6171 (2019)
7. Chen, X., et al.: AdaPrompt: adaptive prompt-based finetuning for relation extraction. arXiv preprint arXiv:2104.07650 (2021)
8. Davison, J., Feldman, J., Rush, A.M.: Commonsense knowledge mining from pre-trained models. In: Proceedings of the 2019 Conference on Empirical Methods in Natural Language Processing and the 9th International Joint Conference on Natural Language Processing (EMNLP-IJCNLP), pp. 1173–1178 (2019)
9. Deng, J., Yang, Z., Chen, T., Zhou, W., Li, H.: TransVG: end-to-end visual grounding with transformers. In: ICCV (2021)
10. Devlin, J., Chang, M.W., Lee, K., Toutanova, K.: BERT: pre-training of deep bidirectional transformers for language understanding (2019)
11. Han, X., Yang, J., Hu, H., Zhang, L., Gao, J., Zhang, P.: Image scene graph generation (SGG) benchmark. arXiv preprint arXiv:2107.12604 (2021)
12. He, T., Gao, L., Song, J., Cai, J., Li, Y.F.: Learning from the scene and borrowing from the rich: tackling the long tail in scene graph generation. In: IJCAI (2020)
13. Huang, Z., Zeng, Z., Liu, B., Fu, D., Fu, J.: Pixel-BERT: aligning image pixels with text by deep multi-modal transformers. arXiv preprint arXiv:2004.00849 (2020)
14. Hudson, D.A., Manning, C.D.: GQA: a new dataset for real-world visual reasoning and compositional question answering. In: Proceedings of the IEEE/CVF Conference on Computer Vision and Pattern Recognition, pp. 6700–6709 (2019)
15. Johnson, J., et al.: Image retrieval using scene graphs. In: Proceedings of the IEEE Conference on Computer Vision and Pattern Recognition, pp. 3668–3678 (2015)
16. Kipf, T.N., Welling, M.: Semi-supervised classification with graph convolutional networks. In: ICLR (2017)
17. Knyazev, B., de Vries, H., Cangea, C., Taylor, G.W., Courville, A., Belilovsky, E.: Graph density-aware losses for novel compositions in scene graph generation. In: BMVC (2020)
18. Knyazev, B., de Vries, H., Cangea, C., Taylor, G.W., Courville, A., Belilovsky, E.: Generative compositional augmentations for scene graph prediction. In: Proceedings of the IEEE/CVF International Conference on Computer Vision (ICCV), pp. 15827–15837, October 2021
19. Krishna, R., et al.: Visual genome: Connecting language and vision using crowd-sourced dense image annotations. IJCV **123**(1), 32–73 (2017)
20. Kuznetsova, A., et al.: The open images dataset V4. Int. J. Comput. Vis. **128**(7), 1956–1981 (2020)

21. Li, R., Zhang, S., Wan, B., He, X.: Bipartite graph network with adaptive message passing for unbiased scene graph generation. In: Proceedings of the IEEE/CVF Conference on Computer Vision and Pattern Recognition, pp. 11109–11119 (2021)
22. Li, X.L., Liang, P.: Prefix-tuning: optimizing continuous prompts for generation. In: ACL (2021)
23. Li, X., et al.: OSCAR: object-semantics aligned pre-training for vision-language tasks. In: Vedaldi, A., Bischof, H., Brox, T., Frahm, J.-M. (eds.) ECCV 2020. LNCS, vol. 12375, pp. 121–137. Springer, Cham (2020). https://doi.org/10.1007/978-3-030-58577-8_8
24. Lin, T.-Y., et al.: Microsoft COCO: common objects in context. In: Fleet, D., Pajdla, T., Schiele, B., Tuytelaars, T. (eds.) ECCV 2014. LNCS, vol. 8693, pp. 740–755. Springer, Cham (2014). https://doi.org/10.1007/978-3-319-10602-1_48
25. Lin, X., Ding, C., Zeng, J., Tao, D.: GPS-Net: graph property sensing network for scene graph generation. In: IEEE/CVF Conference on Computer Vision and Pattern Recognition (CVPR), June 2020
26. Liu, P., Yuan, W., Fu, J., Jiang, Z., Hayashi, H., Neubig, G.: Pre-train, prompt, and predict: a systematic survey of prompting methods in natural language processing. arXiv preprint arXiv:2107.13586 (2021)
27. Lu, C., Krishna, R., Bernstein, M., Fei-Fei, L.: Visual relationship detection with language priors. In: Leibe, B., Matas, J., Sebe, N., Welling, M. (eds.) ECCV 2016. LNCS, vol. 9905, pp. 852–869. Springer, Cham (2016). https://doi.org/10.1007/978-3-319-46448-0_51
28. Pennington, J., Socher, R., Manning, C.D.: Glove: global vectors for word representation. In: Proceedings of the 2014 Conference on Empirical Methods in Natural Language Processing (EMNLP), pp. 1532–1543 (2014)
29. Peters, M.E., et al.: Deep contextualized word representations. In: NAC-ACL (2018)
30. Petroni, F., et al.: Language models as knowledge bases? In: EMNLP-IJCNLP (2019)
31. Peyre, J., Sivic, J., Laptev, I., Schmid, C.: Weakly-supervised learning of visual relations. In: Proceedings of the IEEE International Conference on Computer Vision, pp. 5179–5188 (2017)
32. Qin, G., Eisner, J.: Learning how to ask: querying LMS with mixtures of soft prompts. In: ACL (2021)
33. Radford, A., et al.: Learning transferable visual models from natural language supervision. In: ICML (2021)
34. Radford, A., Narasimhan, K., Salimans, T., Sutskever, I.: Improving language understanding by generative pre-training (2018)
35. Ren, S., He, K., Girshick, R., Sun, J.: Faster R-CNN: towards real-time object detection with region proposal networks. In: NIPS, pp. 91–99 (2015)
36. Schuster, S., Krishna, R., Chang, A., Fei-Fei, L., Manning, C.D.: Generating semantically precise scene graphs from textual descriptions for improved image retrieval. In: Proceedings of the fOurth Workshop on Vision and Language, pp. 70–80 (2015)
37. Su, W., et al.: VL-BERT: pre-training of generic visual-linguistic representations. In: ICLR (2020)
38. Suhail, M., et al.: Energy-based learning for scene graph generation. In: Proceedings of the IEEE/CVF Conference on Computer Vision and Pattern Recognition, pp. 13936–13945 (2021)
39. Tang, K., Niu, Y., Huang, J., Shi, J., Zhang, H.: Unbiased scene graph generation from biased training. In: CVPR (2020)

40. Tang, K., Zhang, H., Wu, B., Luo, W., Liu, W.: Learning to compose dynamic tree structures for visual contexts. In: Proceedings of the IEEE/CVF Conference on Computer Vision and Pattern Recognition, pp. 6619–6628 (2019)
41. Teney, D., Liu, L., van Den Hengel, A.: Graph-structured representations for visual question answering. In: CVPR, pp. 1–9 (2017)
42. Trinh, T.H., Le, Q.V.: A simple method for commonsense reasoning. arXiv preprint arXiv:1806.02847 (2018)
43. Wang, T.J.J., Pehlivan, S., Laaksonen, J.: Tackling the unannotated: Scene graph generation with bias-reduced models. In: BMVC (2020)
44. Wang, Y., Joty, S., Lyu, M.R., King, I., Xiong, C., Hoi, S.C.: VD-BERT: a unified vision and dialog transformer with BERT. In: EMNLP (2020)
45. Xu, D., Zhu, Y., Choy, C.B., Fei-Fei, L.: Scene graph generation by iterative message passing. In: Proceedings of the IEEE Conference on Computer Vision and Pattern Recognition, pp. 5410–5419 (2017)
46. Yang, X., Tang, K., Zhang, H., Cai, J.: Auto-encoding scene graphs for image captioning. In: CVPR, pp. 10685–10694 (2019)
47. Yao, T., Pan, Y., Li, Y., Mei, T.: Exploring visual relationship for image captioning. In: Ferrari, V., Hebert, M., Sminchisescu, C., Weiss, Y. (eds.) Computer Vision – ECCV 2018. LNCS, vol. 11218, pp. 711–727. Springer, Cham (2018). https://doi.org/10.1007/978-3-030-01264-9_42
48. Ye, K., Kovashka, A.: Linguistic structures as weak supervision for visual scene graph generation. In: Proceedings of the IEEE/CVF Conference on Computer Vision and Pattern Recognition, pp. 8289–8299 (2021)
49. Zareian, A., Karaman, S., Chang, S.-F.: Bridging knowledge graphs to generate scene graphs. In: Vedaldi, A., Bischof, H., Brox, T., Frahm, J.-M. (eds.) ECCV 2020. LNCS, vol. 12368, pp. 606–623. Springer, Cham (2020). https://doi.org/10.1007/978-3-030-58592-1_36
50. Zareian, A., Karaman, S., Chang, S.F.: Weakly supervised visual semantic parsing. In: Proceedings of the IEEE/CVF Conference on Computer Vision and Pattern Recognition, pp. 3736–3745 (2020)
51. Zareian, A., Rosa, K.D., Hu, D.H., Chang, S.F.: Open-vocabulary object detection using captions. In: Proceedings of the IEEE/CVF Conference on Computer Vision and Pattern Recognition, pp. 14393–14402 (2021)
52. Zellers, R., Bisk, Y., Farhadi, A., Choi, Y.: From recognition to cognition: visual commonsense reasoning. In: The IEEE Conference on Computer Vision and Pattern Recognition (CVPR), June 2019
53. Zellers, R., Yatskar, M., Thomson, S., Choi, Y.: Neural motifs: scene graph parsing with global context. In: CVPR, pp. 5831–5840 (2018)
54. Zhang, C., Yu, J., Song, Y., Cai, W.: Exploiting edge-oriented reasoning for 3D point-based scene graph analysis. In: Proceedings of the IEEE/CVF Conference on Computer Vision and Pattern Recognition, pp. 9705–9715 (2021)
55. Zhang, H., Kyaw, Z., Chang, S.F., Chua, T.S.: Visual translation embedding network for visual relation detection. In: Proceedings of the IEEE Conference on Computer Vision and PATTERN RECOGNITION, pp. 5532–5540 (2017)
56. Zhang, P., et al.: VINVL: revisiting visual representations in vision-language models. In: CVPR, pp. 5579–5588 (2021)

57. Zhang, Y., Jiang, H., Miura, Y., Manning, C.D., Langlotz, C.P.: Contrastive learning of medical visual representations from paired images and text. arXiv preprint arXiv:2010.00747 (2020)
58. Zhong, Y., Shi, J., Yang, J., Xu, C., Li, Y.: Learning to generate scene graph from natural language supervision. In: Proceedings of the IEEE/CVF International Conference on Computer Vision, pp. 1823–1834 (2021)

Variance-Aware Weight Initialization for Point Convolutional Neural Networks

Pedro Hermosilla[1(✉)], Michael Schelling[1], Tobias Ritschel[2], and Timo Ropinski[1]

[1] Ulm University, Ulm, Germany
pedro-1.hermosilla-casajus@uni-ulm.de
[2] University College London, London, UK

Abstract. Appropriate weight initialization has been of key importance to successfully train neural networks. Recently, batch normalization has diminished the role of weight initialization by simply normalizing each layer based on batch statistics. Unfortunately, batch normalization has several drawbacks when applied to small batch sizes, as they are required to cope with memory limitations when learning on point clouds. While well-founded weight initialization strategies can render batch normalization unnecessary and thus avoid these drawbacks, no such approaches have been proposed for point convolutional networks. To fill this gap, we propose a framework to unify the multitude of continuous convolutions. This enables our main contribution, variance-aware weight initialization. We show that this initialization can avoid batch normalization while achieving similar and, in some cases, better performance.

1 Introduction

Weight initialization schemes play a crucial role when training deep neural networks. By initializing weights appropriately, it can be avoided that layer activations diminish or explode during a forward pass through the network. Accordingly, researchers have dedicated great efforts in order to optimize the weight initialization process, such that these downsides are circumvented [7]. As modern weight initialization schemes have been developed for structured CNNs, they are based on a few assumptions, that do not hold (as well show in Sect. 4.2), when learning on unstructured point cloud data. Nevertheless, it is common practice, to overlook this discrepancy, and to apply these initialization schemes. These initialization schemes result in exploding or vanishing variance in layer activations, when learning on point cloud data. To overcome this shortcoming, usually batch normalization is applied, as it helps to rescale activations based on the current batch. While this approach is highly effective when learning on some moderate-resolution image data, where many training samples fit into memory and thus can be considered in one batch, it has severe downsides when learning on point clouds. Due to memory limitations, these data sets usually only allow for rather small batch sizes. This makes the sample mean and variance of each individual batch usually not

Supplementary Information The online version contains supplementary material available at https://doi.org/10.1007/978-3-031-19815-1_5.

ⓒ The Author(s), under exclusive license to Springer Nature Switzerland AG 2022
S. Avidan et al. (Eds.): ECCV 2022, LNCS 13688, pp. 74–89, 2022.
https://doi.org/10.1007/978-3-031-19815-1_5

representative of the entire training set. Therefore, in order to use batch normalization on point clouds, researchers are usually forced to reduce the point cloud resolution or to process each scene in chunks. However, as recently shown by Nekrasov et al. [15] and Choy et al. [3], the sampling resolution and the context size play crucial roles in the final prediction of the model. Whilst methods exist to increase the batch size virtually during training, such as accumulating the gradients over several batches or using multiple GPUs, batch normalization has the same limitations in these setups since the mean and standard deviation are computed separately in each iteration/GPU.

Within this paper, we tackle the drawbacks which result from applying weight initialization schemes, originally developed for structured data, when learning on point clouds. Based on our observations of layer activations in point convolutional networks, we are able to derive a variance-aware initialization scheme, which avoids the aforementioned downsides. To this end, we make the following contributions:

- A unified mathematical framework for 3D point convolutional neural networks.
- We show that spatial autocorrelation increases with the depth of point convolutional networks, and show how to account for it with variance-aware weight initialization.
- We demonstrate how the proposed weight initialization scheme can be generalized across training data sets, and thus does not require additional preprocessing.

Since the proposed weight initialization scheme is variance-aware, we are able to omit batch normalization during the training process. Thus we do not only avoid the aforementioned issues which come with batch normalization, but we also are able to use larger point clouds during training and therefore arrive at en-par or sometimes even better results. To our knowledge, the proposed initialization scheme is the first one, which has been specifically developed for point convolutional neural networks.

2 Related Work

Training of deeper convolutional neural networks (CNNs) [18] is a challenging optimization and hence benefits from suitable initialization. Simonyan and Zisserman [18] simply used Gaussian noise with a small standard deviation. Improving upon this, He et al. [7] proposed an initialization that takes into account the effect variance of the activations. These directly affect the numeric quality of the gradients and can be important for convergence. Their design is specific to convolutions with certain non-linearities. Mishkin and Matas [14] and Krähenbühl et al. [11] have devised alternative inits for CNNs which initialize layer-by-layer such that the variance of the activation affect each layer remains constant, e.g. close to one. Alternative to good initialization, batch normalization [10] can serve a similar purpose: instead of changing the tunable parameters (weights), additional normalization using the statistics of each batch is employed. These deteriorate if the sample statistics are not representative of the true statistics, which is pressing if models are complex and batches are small. Our work aims to enable the same benefits of good initialization found for CNNs on images on unstructured convolutions [1,6,8,12,19,21] as used for 3D point clouds.

3   Formalizing Point Cloud Convolution

We propose a formalization to cover a large range of existing 3D point cloud convolutions. Our contribution is to derive an initialization based on that.

Convolution of output feature F^l at layer l is defined as:

$$F^l(\mathbf{x}) = \sum_{c=0}^{C} \int F_c^{l-1}(\mathbf{x} + \tau)\kappa_c(\tau)\mathrm{d}\tau \tag{1}$$

where C is the number of input features, κ is the convolution kernel and τ an offset. This formulation alone is well-known. What is not formalized so far, however, is the many different learnable point cloud convolutions.

To represent κ, we use a $w_{c,i}$-weighted sum of the projection of the offset τ into a set of K basis functions b_i:

$$\kappa_c(\tau) = \sum_{i=0}^{K} b_i(\tau)w_{c,i}, \tag{2}$$

resulting in the following definition of convolution:

$$F^l(\mathbf{x}) = \sum_{c=0}^{C} \int F_c^{l-1}(\mathbf{x} + \tau) \sum_{i=0}^{K} b_i(\tau)w_{c,i}\mathrm{d}\tau. \tag{3}$$

This definition of convolution covers many existing state-of-the-art methods, as well as the common discrete convolution used for images. We will first show how discrete convolution can be represented by Eq. 3, before applying it to continuous convolutions.

3.1   Discrete Convolution

Here, the bases b_i are Dirac delta functions on the positions of the kernel points $\mathbf{p}_i$:

$$b_i(\tau) = \delta(\tau - \mathbf{p}_i) \tag{4}$$

In images, these points are placed on a regular grid in each axis. Therefore, if pixels are laid out on a regular grid, the kernel can be reduced to a matrix indexed by pixel displacements, a summation over the neighboring pixels:

$$F^l(x) = \sum_{c=0}^{C} \sum_{i=-\tau}^{\tau} F_c^{l-1}(\mathbf{x} + i)w_{c,i}. \tag{5}$$

3.2   Continuous Convolution

Several methods have been proposed to perform a convolution in the continuous domain, as it is beneficial when learning on point clouds. As stated above, many of these methods can be expressed through the mathematical framework introduced in Sect. 3. To illustrate this, we have selected the most commonly used and highly cited continuous convolutions to be expressed in our framework as summarized in Table 1. This "zoo" can be structured along two axis: the basis (Sec. 3.3) and the integral estimation (Sect. 3.4).

Table 1. Taxonomy of continuous convolutions.

Method	Basis	Estim.	Init
Atzmon et al. [1]	Gauss	$\hat{A}_{\mathrm{MC}}$	He et al. [7]
Lei et al. [12]	Box	$\hat{A}_{\mathrm{Avg}}$	He et al. [7]
Thomas et al. [19]	Lin. Corr.	$\hat{A}_{\mathrm{Sum}}$	He et al. [7]
Hermosilla et al. [8]	MLP	$\hat{A}_{\mathrm{MC}}$	He et al. [7]
Wu et al. [21]	MLP	$\hat{A}_{\mathrm{NN}}$	He et al. [7]
Groh et al. [6]	Dot	$\hat{A}_{\mathrm{Sum}}$	He et al. [7]
Hua et al. [9]	Box	$\hat{A}_{\mathrm{Avg}}$	He et al. [7]
Mao et al. [13]	Lin. Corr.	$\hat{A}_{\mathrm{Avg}}$	He et al. [7]
Boulch [2]	MLP Corr.	$\hat{A}_{\mathrm{Avg}}$	He et al. [7]

3.3 Zoo Axis 1: Basis

We will here show how most published work on deep point cloud learning (those that are convolutional, which would not include the acclaimed PoinNet architecture [16]) can be expressed in the framework of different basis functions (Fig. 1), allowing to derive a joint way of initialization.

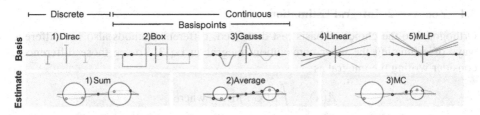

Fig. 1. Our framework organizes continuous convolution along the basis function (top) and convolution integral estimation (bottom) axis.

In **PCCNN**, Atzmon et al. [1] define the basis b_i as Gaussians of the distance to a set of kernel points $\mathbf{p}_i$:

$$b_i(\tau) = \exp\left(-\frac{\|\mathbf{p}_i - \tau\|^2}{s}\right), \tag{6}$$

where s is a bandwidth parameter.

For **PointWiseCNN**, Hua et al. [9] also used a set of kernel points as PCCNN. However, the authors used a box function as point correlation:

$$b_i(\tau) = \begin{cases} 1 & \operatorname*{argmin}_{j}(\|\mathbf{p}_j - \tau\|) = i \\ 0 & \operatorname*{argmin}_{j}(\|\mathbf{p}_j - \tau\|) \neq i \end{cases} \tag{7}$$

This approach was also adopted by Lei et al. [12] in **SPHConv**, but in spherical coordinates.

In **KPConv**, Thomas et al. [19] also used a set of kernel points as PCCNN. However, the authors used linear correlation instead of a Gaussian:

$$b_i(\tau) = \max\left(1 - \frac{\|\mathbf{P}_i - \tau\|}{s}, 0\right). \tag{8}$$

Here, kernel points are arranged as the vertices of platonic solids.

Linear correlation was also used by He et al. [7] in their convolution operation **InterpCNN** with kernel points arranged in a grid.

In **ConvPoint**, Boulch [2] also used kernel points. However, the correlation function was learned by an MLP instead.

In the **MCConv** work of Hermosilla et al. [8], the basis b_i is defined as the output of an MLP $\alpha(\tau)$ with a structure too complex to be written as an equation here. According to our taxonomie's axes, **PointConv** by Wu et al. [21] is the same as MCConv and only differs in the implementation of the MLP and along the integration design axis.

The **FlexConv** approach by Groh et al. [6] uses a single basis $\mathbf{v}_i$ for each input feature and it is defined as the affine projection $\cdot_1$ of the point to the learned vector:

$$b_i(\tau) = \mathbf{v}_i^T \cdot_1 \tau \tag{9}$$

These basis functions can be interpreted as a learned unit vector scaled by the convolution weight.

3.4 Zoo Axis 2: Integral Estimation

Orthogonal to the choice of basis just discussed, different methods also use different ways of estimating the inner convolution integral in Eq. 3. To see those differences, consider writing the integral as

$$A(\mathbf{x}) = \int a(\mathbf{x}, \tau) d\tau \quad \text{where}$$

$$a(\mathbf{x}, \tau) = F_c^{l-1}(x + \tau) \sum_{i=0}^{K} b_i(\tau) \mathbf{w}_{c,i}. \tag{10}$$

In point cloud processing, several ways have been proposed to estimate this integral, based on summing, averaging, MC estimation and MC with learned density:

$$\hat{A}_{\text{Sum}}(\mathbf{x}) = \sum_{y \in \mathcal{N}(\mathbf{x})} a(y) \qquad\qquad [6, 19], \tag{11}$$

$$\hat{A}_{\text{Avg}}(\mathbf{x}) = \sum_{y \in \mathcal{N}(\mathbf{x})} a(y)/|\mathcal{N}(\mathbf{x})| \qquad\qquad [9, 12], \tag{12}$$

$$\hat{A}_{\text{MC}}(\mathbf{x}) = \sum_{y \in \mathcal{N}(\mathbf{x})} a(y)/(p(y)|\mathcal{N}(\mathbf{x})|) \qquad\qquad [1, 8], \tag{13}$$

$$\hat{A}_{\text{NN}}(\mathbf{x}) = \sum_{y \in \mathcal{N}(\mathbf{x})} a(y)/\pi(p(y)) \qquad\qquad [21]. \tag{14}$$

The most similar approach to the discrete convolution case is to use a sum (Eq. 11) over the neighboring samples [6,19]. Although easy to implement, it is sensitive to neighborhoods with a variable number of samples, as well as to non-uniformly sampled point clouds (second row in Fig. 1). To consider this shortcoming, other approaches normalize over the average (Eq. 12) of the neighboring contributions [2,9,12,13]. This is robust to neighborhoods with a different number of samples. However, they are not robust under non-uniformly sampled point clouds. To be able to learn robustly on non-uniformly sampled point clouds, other methods have used a weighted sum Eq. 13, where weights depend on the density of the points, following the principles of Monte Carlo integration [1,8]. Wu et al. [21] additionally propose an MPL π to map the estimated density to a corrected density as per Eq. 14. These methods are robust under different numbers of neighboring samples, as well as non-uniformly sampled point clouds.

4 Weight Initialization

We will now derive weights w that are *optimal in terms of feature variance* for the general form of convolution we describe in Eq. 18, for any form of convolution integral estimation and any basis.

Weights are optimal, if the variance of the features does not increase/decrease for increasing layer depth [7]. This is best understood from plots where the horizontal axis is network layer and the vertical axis is variance (Fig. 2). A method, such as uniform initialization will have increasing/decreasing variance for increasing depth. Previous work [7] has enabled keeping the variance constant as shown by the pink curve. All the continuous methods use similar initializations where variance decreases (solid red curves). Our contribution is the blue curve: variance remains constant for the continuous case.

Based on the convolution framework introduced in Sect. 3, we will in this section, first describe the weight initialization commonly used for discrete convolutions, before detailing the currently used weight initialization for point convolutional neural networks. Based on the shortcomings of these initialization schemes, we will further introduce our new initialization scheme, which we have developed for point convolutional neural networks.

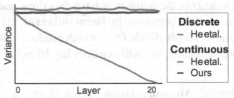

Fig. 2. Good weight initialization prevents decreasing variance (vertical axis) with increasing layer depth (horizontal axis).

4.1 Discrete Convolutions

The weight parameters of a discrete convolution are usually initialized independently with respect to the input data. The underlying idea is to initialize the weights in such a way, that the variance of the output features is the same as the variance of the input. The weights are therefore initialized using a normal distribution with a carefully selected variance. This variance is computed, by relying on several assumptions. First, that the weights are independent of each other, and second, that the features of each pixel are independent of each other. Following these assumptions, He et al. [7] derived the appropriate variance of the weights for convolutional neural networks with ReLUs:

$$\mathbb{V}[w] = \frac{2}{NC}, \tag{15}$$

where N is the number of pixels in the kernel, and C is the number of input features.

4.2 Continuous Convolutions

In this section, we discuss the implications that arise, when applying classical weight initialization approaches in the context of point convolutional neural networks, and further propose our weight initialization approach, specifically tailored to point convolutional neural networks.

Common Practices. A naïve approach would be to use the same initialization scheme for continuous convolution as the one used for discrete convolutions. However, the number of neighboring points highly depends on the data to process, e.g. convolution on samples on a plane will have fewer neighbors than convolutions on molecular data. Therefore, a common approach is to rely on the standard weight initialization schemes provided by the software packages, which in the best case results in the following variance:

$$\mathbb{V}[w] = \frac{2}{BC} \tag{16}$$

where B is the number of basis functions and C is the number of features. Other methods such as presented by Hermosilla et al. [8] and Thomas et al. [19], in their implementation, simply divide by C which produces an even more biased variance and, therefore, worse results. We will consider Eq. 16 as the standard initialization.

Spatial Autocorrelation. Even though approximating the number of neighbors by the number of basis functions is a crude approximation, this initialization scheme is designed using some assumptions that do not hold, when considering the continuous case. The derivations for the discrete case assumed, that features from neighboring pixels are independent of each other. In the continuous case, however, they are correlated.

Figure 3 shows the empirical correlogram of the features of different layers of a point convolutional neural network. To obtain this data, we used the simplest 1D point cloud and the simplest continuous convolution conceivable (Fig. 3,a): As a point cloud we sample positions from the uniform random distribution on $(0, 1)$, and the initial features from a normal distribution with variance 0.1. As a basis we use three boxes separated by $r = .05$ and Eq. 11 to estimate the integral. Figure 3,b depicts the correlation as a function of the distance between points for different layer depth. We can see that no clear pattern for the spatial autocorrelation in the initial features (Input) emerges. However, after the initial convolution, the correlation increases for close points, and this

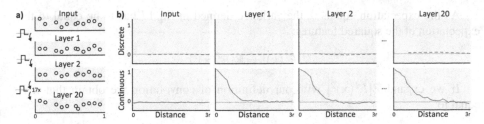

Fig. 3. a: Minimal setting for continuous convolution: Starting from the top 1D point cloud we convolve with a 1D 3-tap box kernel 20 times. **b**: Spatial autocorrelation of features in each layer as a function of the distance between points this setting. The top row shows that there is no spatial autocorrelation for the discrete case. However, for continuous convolutions, we can see high spatial autocorrelation for close points and an increase with the depth of the network.

correlation slightly increases and widens with the depth of the network. This is empirical evidence, how the assumption of independence of features between neighbors does not hold in the continuous case, and thus an initialization scheme rooted on this might be suboptimal.

Variance-Aware Weight Initialization To obtain a more suitable weight initialization scheme for point convolutional neural networks, we start our derivation with the definition of the variance of layer l:

$$\mathbb{V}[F^l(\mathbf{x})] = \mathbb{E}[F^l(\mathbf{x})^2] - \mathbb{E}[F^l(\mathbf{x})]^2 \qquad (17)$$

We will perform the derivations for a single input channel and use the assumption that each feature channel is independent of each other to scale the resulting variance by the number of channels, C.

Starting with Eq. 17, we compute the expectation of the output features of layer l. Therefore, we assume that each weight w_i is independent of each other, as well as from the basis functions and features, and that they are further initialized from a normal distribution centered at 0. Accordingly, we can reformulate the expectation of the output features of layer l as follows:

$$\mathbb{E}[F^l(\mathbf{x})] = \mathbb{E}\left[\int F^{l-1}(x+\tau)\sum_{i=0}^{K} b_i(\tau)w_{c,i}\mathrm{d}\tau\right]$$

$$= \int \sum_{i=0}^{K} \mathbb{E}\left[F^{l-1}(\mathbf{x}+\tau)b_i(\tau)\right]\mathbb{E}\left[w_{c,i}\right]\mathrm{d}\tau$$

$$= \int \sum_{i=0}^{K} \mathbb{E}\left[F^{l-1}(x+\tau)b_i(\tau)\right]0\mathrm{d}\tau$$

$$= 0$$

As the expectation equals 0, the variance defined in Eq. 17 has to be equal to the expectation of the squared features:

$$\mathbb{V}[F^l(\mathbf{x})] = \mathbb{E}[F^l(\mathbf{x})^2]$$

If we expand $\mathbb{E}[F^l(\mathbf{x})^2]$ with our definition of convolution we obtain that it is equal to

$$\mathbb{E}\left[\int G_1 \sum_{i=0}^{K} H_{i,1} w_{k,i} d\tau_1 \int G_2 \sum_{j=0}^{K} H_{j2} w_{l,j} d\tau_2\right],$$

where $G_{1/2} = F^{l-1}(x + \tau_{1/2})$ and $H_{i1/2} = b_i(\tau_{1/2})$. Since w is independent of the features and basis functions, we can re-arrange the terms to obtain

$$\int\int \sum_{i=0}^{K} \sum_{j=0}^{K} \mathbb{E}\left[G_1 G_2 H_{i1} H_{j2}\right] \mathbb{E}\left[w_{ki} w_{lj}\right] d\tau_1 d\tau_2.$$

This equation can be simplified using the assumption that each weight is also independent of each other, and that the weights are drawn from a distribution centered at 0:

$$\sum_{i=0}^{K} \sum_{j=0}^{K} \mathbb{E}\left[w_i w_j\right] = \sum_{i=0}^{K} \sum_{j=0}^{K} \mathbb{C}[w_i, w_j] + \mathbb{E}[w_i]\mathbb{E}[w_j] = \sum_{i=0}^{K} \mathbb{V}[w] + 0$$

Thus, we can reformulate $\mathbb{E}[F^l(\mathbf{x})^2]$ as:

$$\int\int \sum_{i=0}^{K} \mathbb{E}\left[G_1 G_2 H_{i,1} H_{i,2}\right] \mathbb{V}[w] d\tau_1 d\tau_2$$

Finally, we can arrange the terms to isolate the variance of the weights w on one side of the equality, and thus obtain a closed form to determine the optimal variance for our weights. When additionally including the constant C, to account for the number of input features, we obtain:

$$\mathbb{V}[w] = \frac{\mathbb{V}[F^l(\mathbf{x})]}{C z_l} \qquad \text{where} \tag{18}$$

$$z_l = \mathbb{E}\left[\sum_{i=0}^{K} \int G_{k2} H_{i2} \int G_{k1} H_{i1} d\tau_1 d\tau_2\right]. \tag{19}$$

This accounts for the spatial autocorrelation of the input features ($G_{k1} G_{k2}$) as well as the basis functions ($H_{i1} H_{i2}$).

4.3 Variance Computation

In order to apply this initialization, we have to compute Eq. 18. First, we specify the desired variance in the output of each layer, $\mathbb{V}[F^l(\mathbf{x})]$, which can be chosen to be a constant such as 1. This leaves us with computing Eq. 19, a statement for layer l given the features in the previous layer $l - 1$. Hence, the computation proceeds by-layers, starting at the first layer, adjusting variance and proceeding to the next layer as seen in the outer loop in Algorithm 1.

Algorithm 1. Weight initialization.

1: **for** $l \in$ Layers **do**
2:     $z_l \leftarrow 0$
3:     **for** 1 to N **do**   ▷ Eq. 19
4:         $\mathcal{P} \leftarrow \texttt{samplePointCloud()}$
5:         $\bar{z}_l \leftarrow \texttt{estimate}(\mathcal{P}, l)$
6:         $z_l \leftarrow z_l + \bar{z}_l$
7:     **end for**
8:     $z_l \leftarrow z_l / N$
9: **end for**

The outer expectation in Eq. 19 is estimated by sampling N random point clouds $\mathcal{P}$. The inner double-integral for each point cloud is a double convolution with the same structure as the convolution Eq. 10. Hence, it can be estimated using one of the techniques defined by Eq. 11, Eq. 12 or Eq. 13. Depending on which technique is used, this might or might not be an unbiased estimator of the true convolution integral, but at any rate, for the initialization to work, the same estimation has to be used that will later be used for actual learning. The function $\texttt{estimate}(\mathcal{P}, l)$ executes the estimation with the weights already initialized up to level $l - 1$ on the point cloud $\mathcal{P}$.

As we will show later, this algorithm can be used to estimate z_l from the training data for a specific architecture or can be pre-computed from a set of representative point clouds. In the latter case, the z_l is estimated for a set of consecutive layers where each will capture the spatial autocorrelation introduced by previous layers. These z_l values can be later queried for another network architecture based on the depth of each layer, scaling them by the number of input features, and use the result to initialize the layer.

5 Experiments

5.1 Operators

In order to evaluate the proposed initialization scheme, we have selected widely used point convolution approaches, that can be expressed in our framework introduced in Sect. 3. During the selection process, we have ensured, that we cover a variety of different basis functions as well as integral approximations and have selected PCCNN [1], KPConv [19], SPHConv [12], MCConv [8], and PointConv [21].

5.2 Variance Evaluation

To empirically validate our derivations, we compare the variance of each layer in a 25-layer network initialized with the standard initialization (Eq. 16) and initialized with ours (Eq. 18). Figure 4 shows the results obtained from this experiment. As we can see, while the variance of each layer exponentially approaches zero for the standard initialization, ours maintains a constant variance over all layers for all tested convolution operators.

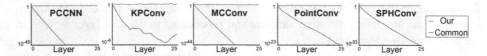

Fig. 4. Comparison of the variance of each layer when applying standard weight initialization (*red*), and when applying our weight initialization (*blue*). The plots show the results for different point convolution operators. Note the vertical axis to be in log-scale.

5.3 Classification

We validate our algorithm on the task of shape classification on the SCANOBJECTNN data set [20]. Since all shapes contain similar numbers of points, this is an ideal setup to observe the effects of our initialization scheme under varying batch sizes.

Data Set: The data set is composed of 2, 902 real objects from 15 different categories, obtained from real 3D scans of the SCANNET data set [4]. For this experiment, we use the data set in which only points from the object are used as input to the network, i.e., the background points have been removed. We use the official training/test split which uses 80 % objects for training and 20 % for testing. We sample 1, 024 random points from each object from the 2, 048 points provided in the data set. As initial point features, we use a single float with the value of 1.0, while we use random anisotropic scaling on the point coordinates (random scaling in each axis independently between 0.9 and 1.1) and random rotation along the vertical axis for data augmentation. Performance is measured as overall accuracy accumulating the predicted probabilities for each model with different data augmentations.

Network Architecture: We used an encoder network with three resolution levels, and two convolution layers per level (see Fig. 5). In order to compute the point cloud levels, we used Poisson disk sampling with radii [0.1, 0.2, 0.4], and three times this radius as the convolution's receptive field. This results in a total of six convolution layers. We also used an increasing number of features per level, [128, 256, 512], and a global average pooling layer on the resulting features to create the global shape descriptor. This descriptor was then processed by a single layer MLP with 512 hidden units, which generates the resulting

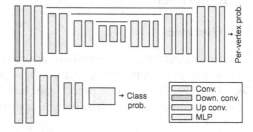

Fig. 5. Network architectures used for the SCANNET data set on the task of semantic segmentation (top) and the SCANOBJECTNN data set for the task of classification (bottom).

probabilities. In order to have the same number of parameters for all different convolution operations, we used 16 basis functions for all of them, which enables analyzing the effect of our initialization scheme, while avoiding overfitting issues.

Training: We trained the models using SGD with momentum for 650 epochs, batch size between 2 and 16, and an initial learning rate of 0.005. To enable convergence for all methods, we scaled the learning rate by 0.1 after 500 epochs. In order to prevent overfitting, we used a dropout value of 0.2 before each convolution and 0.5 on the final MLP, and we used weight decay loss scaled by 0.0001.

Table 2. Comparison of ours and standard initialization, Group Normalization, and batch normalization on the SCANOBJECTNN data set for different batch sizes.

Batch size →	2				4			8			16		
	Ours	He	Xav.	GN	BN	Ours	GN	BN	Ours	GN	BN	Ours	GN	BN
PCCNN [1]	85.7	13.5	13.5	**86.1**	23.3	85.5	86.7	**87.3**	85.2	86.7	**87.3**	83.5	86.6	**87.9**
KPConv [19]	**84.8**	78.9	13.5	83.8	17.7	**84.5**	83.8	83.4	**85.1**	84.6	84.8	84.1	84.1	**85.3**
MCConv [8]	**86.3**	13.5	13.5	85.5	21.3	**85.9**	85.7	83.5	85.7	85.6	**85.9**	84.4	85.0	**85.6**
PointConv [21]	**85.7**	85.1	85.3	85.0	20.1	**85.2**	84.8	83.4	85.4	84.6	**85.9**	85.4	84.9	85.4
SPHConv [12]	**82.2**	13.5	13.5	79.8	26.2	**81.9**	80.8	81.6	81.0	80.3	**82.8**	81.0	80.8	**83.4**

Results: The resulting accuracy for different methods and different batch sizes is shown in Table 2. This table shows that our initialization allows to eliminate batch normalization from the network without a significant decrease in performance for most convolution operators. Moreover, we can see that for low batch sizes, our initialization obtains better performance than batch normalization, whose performance reduces with the batch size. Lastly, we can see that our initialization scheme outperforms batch normalization for some convolution operators (MCConv), where a small batch size acts as regularization during training. When compared to standard initialization schemes, such as He [7] or Xavier [5], our method always obtains better performance while these methods are not able to converge for most of the convolution operators. Moreover, we compare our initialization scheme with Group Normalization [22], a common normalization technique used for small batch sizes. Table 2 shows that, although Group Normalization enables network training with small batch sizes, with most convolution operators and batch sizes, our initialization scheme obtains better results.

5.4 Semantic Segmentation

We also evaluated our method on the task of semantic segmentation of the SCANNET data set [4]. In this task, each scene is too big to be processed as a whole and it has to be processed in blocks, allowing us to validate our initialization for different scene sizes.

Data Set: The SCANNET data set [4] is composed of real 3D scans from 1, 513 different rooms, where the network has to predict the class of the object to which each point belongs to. We use the official splits, corresponding to 1, 045 rooms for training, 156 rooms for validation, and 312 rooms for testing. Since the ground truth annotation for the test set is not publicly available, we evaluated the methods on the validation set. We sample each scan with a sphere of radius r_1 around a random point in the scene and using another sphere of bigger radius, r_2, to select the context, i.e., the points of the bigger sphere are input to the network but we only perform predictions for the points inside the small sphere. We use two sets of radii in our experiments. First, we use $r_1 = 2$ m and $r_2 = 4$ m, resulting in point clouds of around 120 k points for the bigger sphere and around 45 k for the smaller one. In this setup, we fill the available memory in our system and use only a point cloud from a single room in each training step. Then, we also use $r_1 = 1$ m and $r_2 = 2$ m, resulting in smaller point clouds of around 12 k and 45 k points. These radii provide a smaller context for the prediction but allow us to process four rooms in each batch. We use random rotation along the up vector and anisotropic scaling to augment the data during training. Performance is measured as Intersection Over Union (IoU), by accumulating the predicted probabilities of each point sampled from different spheres and with different random rotations and scalings.

Network Architecture: We used a U-Net architecture [17] with four different levels and with two convolution layers in each level (see Fig. 5). The different levels are computed using Poisson Disk sampling with different radii, $[0.03, 0.06, 0.12, 0.24]$, and the receptive field of the convolution layers uses three times the Poisson radius of the level. The number of features increases per level in the encoder and decreases per level in the decoder, resulting in $[64, 128, 256, 512, 256, 128, 64]$. The up-sampling operations in the decoder are also continuous convolutions, which results in 19 convolution layers in total. As before, we used 16 basis functions for all tests and all methods.

Training: We trained the models using SGD with momentum for 500 epochs, and, for each epoch, we sample 3000 point clouds. We used an initial learning rate of 0.005, which was scaled by 0.25 after 300 and again by 0.25 after 400, allowing all methods to converge. In order to prevent overfitting, we used a dropout value of 0.2 before each convolution and weight decay loss scaled by 0.0001.

Results: When we train the models with a single scene per batch, Table 3 shows that batch normalization is not able to successfully learn the task. Our initialization scheme, on the other hand, enables us to eliminate batch normalization obtaining competitive IoUs. Moreover, we can see that for some methods, such as KPConv, MCConv, and SPHConv, using standard initialization without batch norm can result in an improvement on performance wrt. batch

Table 3. Comparison of our initialization on different convolution operations, for Semantic Segmentation on SCANNET, on different batch sizes.

Batch size →		1			4	
	BN	NoBN			BN	NoBN
			Ours			Ours
	Std	Std	Dir.	Tran.	Std	Dir.
PCCNN [1]	32.4	13.3	**65.1**	63.6	**65.7**	62.6
KPConv [19]	33.9	52.5	**66.1**	64.9	66.0	**67.7**
MCConv [8]	40.3	58.8	67.4	**67.9**	**66.1**	65.1
PointConv [21]	41.4	1.6	**62.3**	61.7	**64.2**	62.5
SPHConv [12]	28.1	46.4	**60.7**	60.6	59.5	**60.1**

norm. However, these results do not match the IoU obtained with our initialization scheme. This is true for both variants of ours, the "direct" and the "transfer" one, as shown in the table. The direct one will perform the initialization based on access to the data to choose weights optimally. For the "transfer" one, we computed Eq. 19 on synthetic shapes from the MODELNET40 data set [23] on a network with 25 consecutive layers without any pooling operation or skip connections. Then, we used this initialization on the network for the semantic segmentation task. The only additional step is to select the appropriate w_l value based on the layer depth and scale this value by the number of input channels C of the layer. We see that this transfer of weight initialization can work, as performance remains similar while retaining all the benefits and avoiding the need to do anything when deploying our initialization for a specific architecture. Table 3 also shows the results obtained when the networks are trained with four small point clouds per batch. We can see that in this setup, batch normalization achieves high IoU. However, for some methods, MCConv and SPHConv, using larger point clouds with our initialization significantly increases the obtained IoU.

6   Limitations

Our method is not exempt from limitations. The main limitation of our method is that, contrary to most initialization schemes used for CNN in images, it is data-dependent and requires processing the data first. This pre-processing overhead is negligible to the overall training time: for the SCANNET task results in 47.5 additional seconds from a total of 3 days of training, and for the SCANOBJECTNN task results in 6.1 additional seconds from a total of 4 hours of training. However, we also propose a method to transfer weight initialization's between tasks that does not require pre-processing the data, i.e. our "transfer" setup. However, a large difference between the shapes used to transfer the weight initialization and different statistics between the input features of the data sets could lead to low performance for some operators.

7   Conclusions

In this paper, we have introduced a novel, variance-aware weight initialization scheme, developed for point convolutional neural networks. By exploiting spatial autocorrelation within the layers of a point convolutional neural network, we were able to derive the weight variance used for initialization. In contrast to standard weight initialization schemes, which have been developed for structured data, our proposed weight initialization scheme allows omitting batch normalization, which leads to several issues in the learning process. We have shown, that when using our weight initialization scheme, we are able to neglect batch normalization, and still obtain the same or sometimes even better learning performance. Moreover, we have shown that our weight initialization allows training with small batch sizes and, therefore, larger point clouds, the main limitation of using batch normalization on point clouds. We believe, that the proposed weight initialization scheme, is the first one developed for point convolutional neural networks, and we hope that it will establish itself as the standard method in this subfield.

In the future, we see several endeavors for future work. Same as He et al. [7], we assume features to be independent, which would not be true for positions and normals (one is approximately the derivative of the other) or position or orientation and color (due to shading). Further, we would like to investigate the impact of our weight initialization scheme in other domains, such as graphs and problems such as protein learning.

Acknowledgements. This work was partially funded by the Deutsche Forschungsgemeinschaft (DFG) under grant 391088465 (ProLint) and by the Federal Ministry of Health (BMG) under grant ZMVI1-2520DAT200 (AktiSmart-KI).

References

1. Atzmon, M., Maron, H., Lipman, Y.: Point convolutional neural networks by extension operators. In: ACM Transactions on Graphics (Proc. SIGGRAPH) (2018)
2. Boulch, A.: ConvPoint: continuous convolutions for point cloud processing. Comput. Graph. **88**, 24–34 (2020)
3. Choy, C., Gwak, J., Savarese, S.: 4D spatio-temporal convnets: minkowski convolutional neural networks. In: Proceedings of the IEEE Conference on Computer Vision and Pattern Recognition, pp. 3075–3084 (2019)
4. Dai, A., Chang, A.X., Savva, M., Halber, M., Funkhouser, T., Nießner, M.: ScanNet: richly-annotated 3D reconstructions of indoor scenes. In: Proceedings of the IEEE Conference on Computer Vision and Pattern Recognition, pp. 5828–5839 (2017)
5. Glorot, X., Bengio, Y.: Understanding the difficulty of training deep feedforward neural networks. In: Proceedings of the Thirteenth International Conference on Artificial Intelligence and Statistics (2010)
6. Groh, F., Wieschollek, P., Lensch, H.P.A.: Flex-convolution (million-scale point-cloud learning beyond grid-worlds). In: ACCV (2018)
7. He, K., Zhang, X., Ren, S., Sun, J.: Delving deep into rectifiers: surpassing human-level performance on ImageNet classification. In: ICCV, pp. 1026–1034 (2015)
8. Hermosilla, P., Ritschel, T., Vazquez, P.P., Vinacua, A., Ropinski, T.: Monte Carlo convolution for learning on non-uniformly sampled point clouds. In: ACM Transactions on Graphics (Pro. of SIGGRAPH Asia) (2018)
9. Hua, B.S., Tran, M.K., Yeung, S.K.: Pointwise convolutional neural networks. In: Computer Vision and Pattern Recognition (CVPR) (2018)
10. Ioffe, S., Szegedy, C.: Batch normalization: accelerating deep network training by reducing internal covariate shift. In: International Conference on Machine Learning, pp. 448–456. PMLR (2015)
11. Krähenbühl, P., Doersch, C., Donahue, J., Darrell, T.: Data-dependent initializations of convolutional neural networks. arXiv:1511.06856 (2015)
12. Lei, H., Akhtar, N., Mian, A.: Octree guided CNN with spherical kernels for 3D point clouds. In: CVPR (2019)
13. Mao, J., Wang, X., Li, H.: Interpolated convolutional networks for 3D point cloud understanding. In: International Conference on Computer Vision (ICCV) (2019)
14. Mishkin, D., Matas, J.: All you need is a good init. arXiv:1511.06422 (2015)
15. Nekrasov, A., Schult, J., Litany, O., Leibe, B., Engelmann, F.: Mix3D: out-of-context data augmentation for 3D scenes. In: International Conference on 3D Vision (3DV) (2021)
16. Qi, C.R., Su, H., Mo, K., Guibas, L.J.: PointNet: deep learning on point sets for 3D classification and segmentation. In: CVPR, pp. 652–660 (2017)

17. Ronneberger, O., Fischer, P., Brox, T.: U-Net: convolutional networks for biomedical image segmentation. In: Navab, N., Hornegger, J., Wells, W.M., Frangi, A.F. (eds.) MICCAI 2015. LNCS, vol. 9351, pp. 234–241. Springer, Cham (2015). https://doi.org/10.1007/978-3-319-24574-4_28
18. Simonyan, K., Zisserman, A.: Very deep convolutional networks for large-scale image recognition. arXiv:1409.1556 (2014)
19. Thomas, H., Qi, C.R., Deschaud, J.E., Marcotegui, B., Goulette, F., Guibas, L.J.: KPConv: flexible and deformable convolution for point clouds. In: ICCV (2019)
20. Uy, M.A., Pham, Q.H., Hua, B.S., Nguyen, D.T., Yeung, S.K.: Revisiting point cloud classification: A new benchmark dataset and classification model on real-world data. In: International Conference on Computer Vision (ICCV) (2019)
21. Wu, W., Qi, Z., Fuxin, L.: PointConv: deep convolutional networks on 3D point clouds. In: CVPR (2019)
22. Wu, Y., He, K.: Group normalization. In: Ferrari, V., Hebert, M., Sminchisescu, C., Weiss, Y. (eds.) ECCV 2018. LNCS, vol. 11217, pp. 3–19. Springer, Cham (2018). https://doi.org/10.1007/978-3-030-01261-8_1
23. Wu, Z., et al.: 3D shapeNets: a deep representation for volumetric shape modeling. In: Proceedings of 28th IEEE Conference on Computer Vision and Pattern Recognition (CVPR) (2015)

Break and Make: Interactive Structural Understanding Using LEGO Bricks

Aaron Walsman[1](✉), Muru Zhang[1], Klemen Kotar[2], Karthik Desingh[1], Ali Farhadi[1], and Dieter Fox[1,3]

[1] University of Washington, Seattle, USA
awalsman@cs.washington.edu
[2] Allen Institute for Artificial Intelligence, Seattle, USA
[3] NVIDIA, Santa Clara, USA

Abstract. Visual understanding of geometric structures with complex spatial relationships is a fundamental component of human intelligence. As children, we learn how to reason about structure not only from observation, but also by interacting with the world around us – by taking things apart and putting them back together again. The ability to reason about structure and compositionality allows us to not only build things, but also understand and reverse-engineer complex systems. In order to advance research in interactive reasoning for part-based geometric understanding, we propose a challenging new assembly problem using LEGO bricks that we call **Break and Make**. In this problem an agent is given a LEGO model and attempts to understand its structure by interactively inspecting and disassembling it. After this inspection period, the agent must then prove its understanding by rebuilding the model from scratch using low-level action primitives. In order to facilitate research on this problem we have built **LTRON**, a fully interactive 3D simulator that allows learning agents to assemble, disassemble and manipulate LEGO models. We pair this simulator with a new dataset of fan-made LEGO creations that have been uploaded to the internet in order to provide complex scenes containing over a thousand unique brick shapes. We take a first step towards solving this problem using sequence-to-sequence models that provide guidance for how to make progress on this challenging problem. Our simulator and data are available at github.com/aaronwalsman/ltron. Additional training code and PyTorch examples are available at github.com/aaronwalsman/ltron-torch-eccv22.

1 Introduction

The physical world is made out of objects and parts. Buildings are made out of roofs, rooms and walls, chairs are made out of seats, backs and legs, and cars have doors, wheels and windshields. The ability to reason about these parts and the structural relationships between them are a key component of our ability to build tools and shelters, solve complex organizational problems and manipulate the

---

Supplementary Information The online version contains supplementary material available at https://doi.org/10.1007/978-3-031-19815-1_6.

© The Author(s), under exclusive license to Springer Nature Switzerland AG 2022
S. Avidan et al. (Eds.): ECCV 2022, LNCS 13688, pp. 90–107, 2022.
https://doi.org/10.1007/978-3-031-19815-1_6

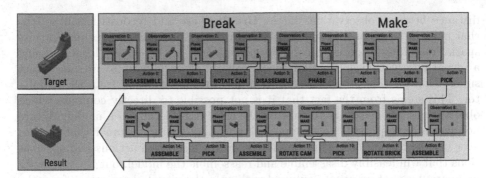

Fig. 1. A training example of the **Break and Make** task on a four-brick model in our dataset. During **Break** phase, the agent must learn to disassemble removable parts based on RGB images to understand the underlying structure. During the second **Make** phase, the agent must learn to pick bricks and reassemble the scene based on all past observations.

world around us. Building part-based reasoning capability into intelligent agents has been a long-standing goal of the computer vision, robotics and broader AI communities.

In this paper we propose **Break and Make**, a challenging new problem designed to investigate interactive structural reasoning using LEGO bricks. This problem is designed to simulate the process of reverse engineering: taking apart a complex object to learn more about its structure, and then using this newfound knowledge to put it back together again. This task is naturally divided into two phases. In the first **Break** phase, a learning agent is presented with a previously unseen LEGO model and has the opportunity to disassemble and inspect it in order to observe its internal structural and hidden components. After this, in the second **Make** phase, the agent is presented with an empty scene and must use the information gathered during the **Break** phase to rebuild the model from scratch. Both phases must be completed using visual action primitives designed to simulate the LEGO construction process. These actions require an agent to reason not only about individual bricks, but also the connection points between them.

In order to facilitate research on this challenging problem, we provide a dataset of 1727 ethically-sourced fan-made LEGO models with generous public licensing. These models range in size from 5 to 7302 individual bricks and use a library of 1790 distinct brick shapes. We also include a set of augmentations and a random model generator in order to provide more examples for large-scale training. Finally, we provide a 3D simulator and interactive learning environment with an OpenAI gym interface designed to train agents on this problem. Our simulator is compatible with a file format commonly used in the LEGO fan community, and is therefore capable of displaying and manipulating a wide range of models found online.

The **Break and Make** problem presents a difficult challenge for a number of reasons. First, the interchangeable nature of LEGO bricks and the large number of distinct brick shapes results in a very large state and action space. Second, this problem requires precise memory in order to bridge the long-term temporal distance between observations in the **Break** phase and reconstruction actions that must be taken in the **Make** phase. Third, this problem also requires precise spatial reasoning in order to carefully place bricks in the correct location using a visual observation and action space. Finally, it is difficult to provide direct supervision for this problem, even with accurate information from the simulator. This stems from the fact that it is not possible to directly compute which observations are necessary to capture the structural details of a model. We are however able to provide noisy supervision using a custom planner that reasons over visual observations. This planner generates a series of actions and observations that will feasibly disassemble and reassemble the model, but it comes with no guarantee that an agent equipped with only the visual observations from the sequence would have enough information to make the necessary decisions.

Despite these challenges, we show that progress can be made on LEGO assemblies containing up to 8 bricks using sequence-to-sequence models based on Transformers and LSTMs. We detail a suite of experiments that show the current capability of these models and demonstrate how performance deteriorates as the problem becomes more complex in terms of both model size and variety of brick shapes.

Our primary contributions are:

1. We introduce a challenging new interactive problem **Break and Make** requiring complex scene understanding and construction. Section 3 describes this problem in detail.
2. We present **LTRON**, a new simulator and dataset that allow interactive learning agents to build and manipulate LEGO models. Sections 3.2 and 3.4 provide details.
3. We also present a transformer-based network architecture **StudNet**, designed to make progress on this challenging problem. We compare this with with other sequence-to-sequence models and demonstrate the difficulty of attacking this problem using current techniques. Section 4 provides details on these approaches and Sect. 5.1 discusses their results.

2   Related Work

2.1   Understanding Compositional Structures

Interactive scene understanding and reasoning about compositional structure has origins in the early days of AI. An early example is Winograd's SHRDLU system [55] that used language instructions to interactively stack virtual blocks and answer questions posed by a human operator.

More recently researchers have introduced a number of interactive environments such as RoboThor [5], iGibson [43], Habitat [48] and MultiON [53] designed to simulate indoor environments for embodied learning agents. Many tasks have been proposed for these environments, such as goal-directed navigation [60], interactive question answering [4,11] and instruction following [44]. While many of these tasks and environments offer some degree of object manipulation, most of these interactions involve only a small number of object classes, and do not require the agent to reason about complex compositional structures. In contrast the **Break and Make** task requires an agent to reason in detail about these structures and how to build them from a library of 1790 unique parts.

In the non-interactive domain, researchers have released a number of simulated tasks and datasets [2,29,34] designed to provide access to a diverse set of objects with increasing detail, part structure and complexity. Others such as CLEVR [20], CLEVERER [59], and CATER [10] are designed around answering questions about object relationships in images and videos. In these settings, it is easy to procedurally generate a large dataset using randomization, but it has been difficult to generate datasets with large object and relationship vocabularies. Researchers have also taken great effort to annotate natural images and videos with detailed attributes [7], parts [52] and relationships [25].

Scene understanding via active or interactive perception is a classic way for robots and embodied agents to explore and model their environment. Researchers have investigated varying levels of detail and semantics in this space [32,39,41,46,47,51]. Previously it has been difficult to explore objects with fine-grained part structure in these settings due to the difficulty in collecting and annotating this data. **LTRON** provides complex models in an interactive environment, allowing agents to collect large amounts of data for researching complex cluttered environments with compositional structures. Another recent line of work explores learning physical properties of the world either from observations of rigid body interactions [56–58] or unsupervised physical interaction with a robot [8]. While we do not provide explicit rigid body dynamics in **LTRON**, we allow agents to explore extremely detailed physical structures with complex part-interactions at a scope that has not been practical in the past.

2.2   Building 3D Structures

In robotics, there has been a long-standing interest in enabling robots to build or assemble structured objects. Several authors have explored assembling IKEA furniture [27,30,45]. Others [16,42] have used Deep Reinforcement Learning and Learning from Demonstration methods to teach robots high precision assembly tasks using a real robot. While LTRON does not offer the realistic dynamics necessary to support traditional robotic manipulation, it does offer a high degree of scene complexity and compositionality which allows researchers to explore fine-grained spatial reasoning.

Recently construction and object-centric reasoning have become important topics in the reinforcement learning and AI community. Multiple datasets [21,54] have been developed to train agents to build and reason about geometric forms using CAD software. While they support a small number of primitive-based modelling tools, our building environment supports constructing models from over one thousand discrete brick types. Other recent works [1,9] have used reinforcement learning for block-stacking problems, and to create structures designed to achieve goals such as connecting or covering other blocks.

Researchers have also investigated the task of generating programs to describe and/or assemble shapes out of low level primitives [22,35] and reason about the relationships between them [15].

LEGO bricks are popular construction toys that are often an early entry point for children to learn about building. They are also an excellent abstraction for real-world construction problems, which has led other researchers to explore using LEGO for various construction problems. Several approaches have been proposed to automatically construct LEGO assemblies from a reference 3D body [23]. For example, multiple authors [26,36] have suggested methods for automated reconstruction based on genetic and evolutionary algorithms. Duplo bricks have also been used for tracking human demonstrations and assembly [12].

In contrast to these approaches, recent works have suggested data-driven deep learning approaches for LEGO problems based on generative models of graphs [49], and image to voxel reconstruction [28]. Similar to **Break and Make**, Chung et al. [3] propose a method for assembling LEGO structures from a reference image using interactive learning. Unlike **LTRON** these approaches use a use only a limited number of bricks, and do not support the large variety of bricks in the LEGO universe.

3   Task and Data

The **Break and Make** task requires an agent to learn how to inspect a LEGO assembly using rendered images, and then use the information gathered in this way to rebuild the assembly from scratch. Both the inspection phase and the construction phase are inherently interactive problems that require multi-step reasoning due to the ambiguities resulting from occlusions and the iterative nature of the building process. Many LEGO bricks have groups of similar neighbors which may appear identical under partial occlusion. Furthermore, complex structures often contain interior bricks that are not visible at all unless outer bricks are removed. These two factors mean that for many assemblies, there is no single viewpoint that completely captures an entire structure. Therefore in order to solve this problem an agent must often consider multiple viewpoints and take apart the assembly in order to fully understand it.

3.1   LEGO Bricks

A LEGO **brick** describes the shape and connection-point structure of a single LEGO part. While most LEGO bricks are a single rigid shape, some such as ropes and connector hoses are flexible. **LTRON** currently does not support these flexible components, so they are removed from all models before training. Some other bricks have moving parts, but in this case we break each of these into a separate brick shape for each moving component. We use polygon meshes extracted from the LDraw [19] package to represent all bricks. The **color** of a brick is represented as a single integer that refers to a specific RGB color value in a lookup table, which is consistent with LDraw conventions.

Each brick also contains a number of **connection points**. These describe how bricks may be connected to each other. The prototypical connection point is the short cylindrical stud that covers the top of many bricks in a rectangular grid, and the corresponding holes that cover the bottom. However, there are a large number of additional connection point types that exist in the LEGO universe, including technic pins, axles, clips, poles and ball/socket joints. In developing **LTRON** we have tried to faithfully represent as many of these as possible in order to provide a rich action space for interactive learning. Each of these connection points has a number of attributes related to its physical dimensions and compatibility with other bricks. One important attribute of all connection points is **polarity**, which describes whether the connection point is an extrusion (positive polarity) or cavity (negative polarity). We use part metadata from the LDCAD [33] software package in order to detect these connection points on bricks and provide manipulation actions for them.

We refer to a collection of multiple bricks and their 3D locations as an **assembly**. Mathematically, this can be modelled as a set tuples $a = \{b_1, b_2, \ldots b_n\}$ where each tuple $b_i = (s_i, c_i, R_i, t_i)$ represents an **instance** of a single brick. Each of these instances b_i contains a brick shape index $s_i \in N_{shapes}$, a color index $c_i \in N_{colors}$, a 3D rotation $R_i \in SO(3)$ and a 3D translation $t_i \in \mathbb{R}^3$. The relative placement of the instances, combined with their shapes and the connection points associated with those shapes allow us to construct a set of **connections** describing a pair of connection points that are in very close proximity to each other and are mutually compatible.

3.2   Environment

In order to manipulate an assembly, our environment provides two virtual work spaces. The first, which we refer to as the **table** work space contains the agent's work in progress towards inspecting or assembling a model. The second work space, which we refer to as the **hand** contains only a single brick that the agent is about to place, or has just removed from the table workspace. Each workspace provides a 2D image rendered from a camera viewpoint that can be controlled by the agent. The table is rendered at 256×256 pixels and the hand is rendered at 96×96 pixels. Many of the actions below require the agent to select one or more connection points on bricks in the hand or table workspace. To do this the agent must specify a 2D location in screen space, and the polarity of the connection point it wishes to select. This is similar to the Alfred dataset [44] and AI2 THOR 2.0 [24] which allow interaction with objects using pixel-based selection. To reduce the size of this action space, the resolution of this selection space is downsampled by 4 to 64×64 for the table and 24×24 for the hand. **LTRON** uses these workspaces to provide the following manipulation actions as shown in Fig. 2.

Disassemble: The agent must select a valid connection point in the table workspace. If the brick can be removed without causing collision, the associated brick instance is removed from the table work space and replaces any brick instance currently in the hand workspace.

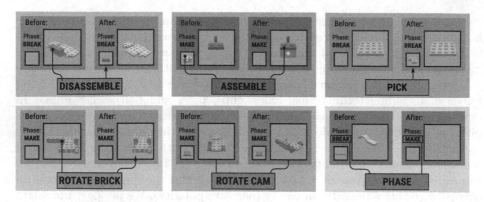

Fig. 2. We define in total six different actions. **Disassemble** removes a brick from the table workspace by selecting a connection point to detach. **Assemble** moves a brick from the hand workspace to the scene by attaching a pair of specified connection points. **Pick** selects a new brick shape and color and adds it to the hand workspace. **Rotate Brick** rotates the assembled brick at the selected connection point. **Rotate Camera** rotates the camera to reduce the ambiguity caused by occlusions. **Switch Phase** switches between break phase and make phase.

Assemble: The agent must specify valid and compatible connection points on one brick in the hand workspace and another in the table workspace. If the brick may be placed without collision, the brick in the hand is removed and placed into the table workspace attached to the specified connection point. If the table workspace is empty and there is no destination connection point to select, the agent may select a valid connection point in the hand workspace alone. This will remove the brick from the hand workspace and add it to the table workspace by placing the specified connection point at the origin.

Pick: The agent specifies a shape id and color id. A new brick with the specified shape and color replaces any brick instance currently in the hand work space.

Rotate 90/180/270: The agent must select a valid connection point on a brick in the table workspace. If rotating the brick will not cause collision, the brick is rotated by the specified angle about the primary axis of the connection point.

Rotate Camera Left/Right/Up/Down/Frame: In some cases it may be necessary to view an assembly from different viewpoints in order to effectively manipulate it, so we provide five actions for each workspace that the agent can use to manipulate the camera. The first four rotate the camera up, down, left or right about a fixed center point. Rotating left and right rotates by 45°C about the scene's up-axis, while rotating up and down alternate between a downward viewing angle 30°C above the center point and an upward viewing angle 30°C below the center point. The fifth **Frame** camera action moves the camera's fixed center point to the centroid of the current brick assembly.

Switch Phase: Finally there are two additional actions that switch from the Break phase to the Make phase, and that end the episode when the agent is finished building. Switching from the Break phase to the Make phase clears both workspaces.

3.3 Evaluation

The **Break and Make** task requires a learning agent to visually inspect a LEGO assembly in order to gather enough information to then build it again from scratch. In order to assess the capability of a learned model, it is necessary to compare the generated assembly that it builds with the target assembly it is trying to copy. We provide four different metrics that attempt to estimate various aspects of the agent's success.

F1$_b$ Score: The first metric is an F1 score over bricks in the two assemblies which we refer to as $F1_b$. This metric ignores pose and simply measures whether the agent was able to add the correct bricks to its estimated assembly regardless of how they are connected together. For this metric, we first remove pose information from the generated assembly $\hat{a}$ and the target assembly a^* to produce a multi-set of brick shape and colors $m^* = \{(s_0^*, c_0^*) \ldots (s_n^*, c_n^*)\}$ for the target assembly and another $\hat{m} = \{(\hat{s}_0, \hat{c}_0) \ldots (\hat{s}_n, \hat{c}_n)\}$ for the assembly the agent generated. We can the compute true positives, false positives and false negatives as:

$$TP_b = m^* \cap \hat{m}, \quad FP_b = \hat{m} - m^*, \quad FN_b = m^* - \hat{m}$$

We then use these three quantities to compute an F1 score. Getting a score of 1.0 on this problem is necessary to rebuilding the assembly correctly, but it is not sufficient. This metric is still useful though because it allows us to categorize errors. If the agent was not able to rebuild the structure, but was able to identify the necessary bricks for that structure, then it may give us guidance for which aspect of the system needs the most improvement.

F1$_a$ Score: Unlike $F1_b$, $F1_a$ includes pose and is designed to measure the accuracy if the entire assembly. In this metric, we first define a rotation threshold θ_ϵ and a distance threshold d_ϵ and say that two bricks i and j are *aligned* iff they have the same shape $s_i = s_j$ and color $c_i = c_j$ and their centers are close $||t_i - t_j|| < d_\epsilon$ and the geodesic distance between their orientations is close $G(R_i, R_j) < \theta_\epsilon$.

Given that we care more about the *relative* position of bricks to each other, than their *absolute* position in the scene, we first compute a single rotation R_0 and translation t_0 that bring as many bricks in a^* into alignment with $\hat{a}$ as possible. We then consider each brick in $\hat{a}$ to be a true positive if it is aligned with another brick in a^* and consider it to be a false negative otherwise. Any brick in a^* that is not aligned to a brick in $\hat{a}$ is a false negative. We then use these quantities to compute $F1_a$.

Assembly Edit Distance (AED): While this $F1_a$ metric gives us a useful measure of similarity between two assemblies, it is possible that it may over-penalize some small mistakes. Consider the case where a long chain of bricks has been reconstructed correctly except for a single mistake in the middle. Because of the single rigid transform R_0 and t_0, we can only align either the top half or the bottom half of the reconstruction $\hat{a}$ with the target assembly a^*, and will incur a massive penalty for this single mistake. To mitigate this, we introduce Assembly Edit Distance (AED): we compute R_0 and t_0 as before, but once this is done, we mark all bricks that are aligned under this transformation and remove them from their respective assemblies. We then repeat this process with the remaining bricks and count how many rigid alignments must be computed until either the scene is empty, or the remaining bricks cannot be aligned because their shapes or colors do not match. We then add an additional edit penalty of 1, representing a single edit to remove the brick, for each brick in $\hat{a}$ left at the end of this process, and a penalty of 2, representing an edit to add the brick to the assembly and an edit to move it into place, for each brick in a^* left at the end of the sequence.

F1$_e$ Score: An added bonus of the **AED** metric is that it can be used to compute a matching between each brick in the generated assembly $\hat{a}$ and the target assembly a^*. This matching allows us to compute one final metric: an F1 score over edges ($F1_e$), or connections between two bricks. We consider every pair of bricks that are connected to each other in the generated assembly $\hat{a}$ to be a true positive edge if both of those bricks have been matched to a brick in the target assembly a^* and the matching bricks in the target assembly are also connected to each other. Otherwise the connected pair is a false positive. Any connected pair in the target assembly a^* that is not matched in this way is a false negative. Like $F1_b$ this metric can be considered necessary but insufficient, but again it is useful because it lets us characterize the errors made during the build process. If the agent was not able to determine the correct spatial alignment of the bricks, but is able to connect the right bricks together, then it may tell us the agent is struggling with the precise placement necessary to align bricks correctly. This is similar to a metric used in Visual Genome [25], but uses our iterative matching edit distance to compute assignment and has no action/attribute labels on individual edges.

3.4 Dataset

We provide two sources of scene files to train and evaluate agents on these tasks. The first is a set of fan-made reproductions of official LEGO sets that have been uploaded to the Open Model Repository (OMR) [18], while the second is a set of randomly constructed models that we have generated with the **LTRON** simulator.

The OMR contains 1727 files that are incredibly diverse, ranging in size from 5 to 7302 bricks. The sets come from over fifty distinct product categories such as "City," "Castle," and "Star Wars" that have been released over a span of several decades and use 1790 distinct brick shapes. These files have many properties in common with other naturally occurring data sources such as a long tail of increasingly rare bricks, and edge-cases that are difficult to model. This is a blessing to researchers who are interested in building models that can handle complex data distributions, and a curse to those looking for quick progress. In general these models are much larger than we are presently able to train on. Both the mean and the median number of bricks in a scene is more than one hundred, while our experiments below show that current methods struggle with scenes containing only eight bricks. In order to generate a large amount of training data with smaller scenes, we have sliced these models into compact connected components using the connection points to find groups of connected bricks. In all cases we have used a master train/test split on the original files to inform the train/test on all slices of those files. Table 1 shows the train test splits for these slices. See the supplementary material for more details on the statistics, slicing procedure and cleaning process of this data.

In contrast to the OMR data above, our randomly generated models are constructed by iteratively selecting brick shapes and colors at random and attempting to connect them to other bricks using randomly selected compatible connection points. This provides a much larger source of data that is in many ways easier to use for training, but unfortunately has many qualitative differences from the more natural OMR data. For example OMR scenes with a similar number of bricks tend to be much more compact than our randomly generated files as a byproduct of the human designers' preferences for tightly fitting configurations. Similarly, the OMR scenes exhibit more symmetry, and more high-level structure such as clearly identifiable walls and branching structures. Despite these issues, this randomly constructed data is still very useful as a way to explore how the problem becomes easier as we reduce the number of brick shapes.

Table 1. Train/test split sizes for the Open Model Repository and our Randomly Generated Data.

Open model repository	Train scenes	Test scenes	Total scenes
Original Scenes	1360	367	1727
2 Brick Slices	136072	2000	138072
4 Brick Slices	61514	2000	63514
8 Brick Slices	28094	2000	30094
Random construction	Train scenes	Test scenes	Total scenes
2 Bricks	50000	2000	52000
4 Bricks	50000	2000	52000
8 Bricks	50000	2000	52000

4   Methods

4.1   Model

Our StudNet models are based on the popular Transformer [50] architecture. In this model, the input images are first broken into 16×16 pixel tiles similar to the VIT architecture [6]. The model then extracts features from each tile using a learned linear layer and two positional embeddings, one that encodes the tile's XY coordinates in the image and another that encodes the tile's frame id in the temporal sequence. We unroll the XY coordinates of the image into a single one-dimensional coordinate space and concatenate the coordinates of the table image and the hand image so that a single index can be used to determine which image the tile belongs to and its 2D location. These tile features are then fed into a transformer that uses GPT-style [37] causal masking to prevent tokens that occur early in the sequence from paying attention to later tokens.

Transformer models notoriously require very large memory due to the N^2 attention mechanism that allows for long-range connectivity between tokens in the sequence. In order to make this architecture tractable on the long sequences of tokens produced by **LTRON**, we employ a simple but effective data compression technique: at each step we only include image tiles which have changed since the previous frame. In the first frame, we also remove all tiles that contain only the solid background color. Given that manipulating a single brick usually only changes a small portion of the image, this results in substantial savings. In addition to the image tiles, we provide a token that specifies the current phase (**Break** or **Make**).

The **Break and Make** task requires an agent to take both discrete high-level actions as well as select low-level pixel locations to assemble and disassemble bricks. We model this using five separate heads: a mode head that selects one of the primary action types (see Fig. 2) to take at each step, a shape selector head and color selector head that are used when picking up a new brick, and a table location and hand location heatmap that is used to select pixel locations for brick interaction. The shape and color heads are linear layers that project from the transformer hidden dimension to the number of shapes and colors used in a particular experiment. Unfortunately we cannot decode a dense heatmap for the pixel locations directly from the tokens coming out of the transformer encoder because our compression strategy throws many of these tokens away. We experiment with two different decoder styles to address this issue.

The first, which we refer to as StudNet-A uses a separate transformer decoder layer. This layer receives a dense positional encoding as the query tokens, and the output of the encoder as the key and value tokens resulting in a dense output. Although some details differ, this is similar to the Perceiver IO [17] and MAE [13] models that do primary computation at a lower resolution and use cross-attention to expand to dense output when necessary. We decode at 16×16 resolution and upsample to 64×64.

The second decoder, which we refer to as StudNet-B, feeds the input images through a small convolutional network to produce a 64×64 feature map for the table and a 24×24 feature map for the hand. In our experiments we use the first layer of a Resnet-18 [14] for this. Two additional heads, one for the table workspace and another for the hand workspace, compute a single feature from a per-frame readout token, and use dot-product attention with the convolutional feature map to produce a heatmap of click locations.

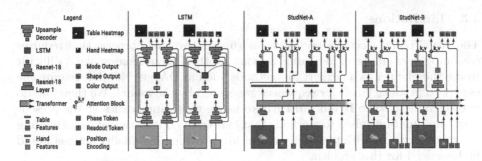

Fig. 3. Network architectures used in our experiments.

We compare these models against a convolution and LSTM baseline. This model takes guidance from the ALFRED Dataset [44] which similarly requires an agent to reason about high level actions as well as pixel-based selection. In this network, the images from both the table and hand workspaces are fed through a Resnet-18 backbone [14], and are then concatenated and passed to an LSTM. The output of this LSTM is then decoded using five heads. The first three produce the mode, shape and color actions. The second and third heads tile the LSTM feature to match the shape of the table and hand resnet features, then upsample these with UNET-style [38]/FPN [31]-style lateral connections from the image encoder to produce a dense feature that is used to select cursor locations. In experiments we use two versions of this model, one trained from scratch, and another where the Resnet-18 backbone has been pretrained on a pixel-labeling task designed to densely predict brick shapes and colors.

4.2   Training

We train the models above using behavior cloning on offline sequences. In order to generate these sequences, we have developed a visual planner that interfaces directly with **LTRON**. This planner uses hidden state information combined with rendered occlusion maps to reason about which bricks are currently visible in the scene and plan assembly and disassembly sequences accordingly. While this information allows the planner to determine which bricks can be manipulated, it does not strictly guarantee that the visual information acquired during the planning process is enough to unambiguously resolve the full 3D structure of the scene, or correctly identify the shapes of every brick. This is due to the fact that many brick shapes look identical to others when viewed from certain angles or under partial occlusion, and so it may be important to change the camera viewpoint or disassembly order to resolve these ambiguities. Due to the large number of brick shapes, we have not attempted to exhaustively catalogue when and how these ambiguities arise for every combination of brick shapes. Therefore the planner currently has no way of knowing when these conditions occur.

4.3　Limitations

The visual planner can be quite slow and uses a two-stage process that requires reasoning over groups of individual actions. Both of these issues make it difficult to use the planner as an expert for methods such as DAgger [40] that require the expert to produce labels for sequences generated by the model. We therefore do not attempt to solve **Break and Make** using these approaches at the present time, and limit ourselves to methods that can train on a static dataset. Building improved planners with the ability to quickly provide high-quality actions would be beneficial for this problem.

5　Experiments

5.1　Break and Make

We evaluate the models above on the Random Construction and Sliced OMR datasets at three fixed scene sizes: two bricks, four bricks and eight bricks. While these scenes are quite small compared to the complete models in the Open Model Repository, they often require dozens of interaction steps to complete and present a challenging problem.

On the random construction data with six brick types and six colors, all models make substantial progress on small scenes. Table 2 shows the models' performance on each of these tasks under the four metrics described in Sect. 3.3. Note that performance drops substantially as the scenes get larger.

Table 2. Test results of our four models on randomly constructed assemblies across three scene sizes. See Sect. 3.3 for details on metrics.

Random construction												
Metric	2 bricks				4 bricks				8 bricks			
	$F1_b$	$F1_e$	$F1_a$	AED	$F1_b$	$F1_e$	$F1_a$	AED	$F1_b$	$F1_e$	$F1_a$	AED
LSTM	0.61	0.38	0.43	2.16	0.41	0.09	0.13	7.25	0.02	0.00	0.02	16.05
Pretr. LSTM	0.70	0.51	0.45	1.89	0.25	0.01	0.08	8.46	0.03	0.00	0.02	16.09
StudNet-A	0.90	0.86	0.58	1.11	0.56	0.29	0.24	5.80	0.02	0.01	0.01	15.87
StudNet-B	0.87	0.77	0.57	1.30	0.64	0.34	0.25	5.48	0.38	0.14	0.12	13.90

The Sliced OMR dataset contains 1790 brick shapes and 98 colors making it structurally and visually significantly more challenging than the random construction dataset. Table 3 illustrates that all of the models we tested score significantly lower on this dataset. In particular our StudNet-A transformer architecture fails to correctly learn to switch from disassembling to rebuilding the LEGO models and thus scores very poorly across all of our metrics. Our StudNet-B architecture shows the best overall performance, demonstrating that progress can be made even on the most challenging 8 brick dataset. This illustrates not only that **Break and Make** is a fundamentally hard problem, but also that its difficulty can be regulated by the dataset selection while maintaining the same action space and problem structure. This allows future work to make meaningful progress on simple datasets like Random Construction and then progress to ever more difficult datasets.

Table 3. Test results of our four models on OMR assemblies across three scene sizes. See Sect. 3.3 for details on metrics.

Open model repository												
Metric	2 bricks				4 bricks				8 bricks			
	$F1_b$	$F1_e$	$F1_a$	AED	$F1_b$	$F1_e$	$F1_a$	AED	$F1_b$	$F1_e$	$F1_a$	AED
LSTM	0.43	0.33	0.31	2.76	0.10	0.03	0.07	7.67	0.01	0.00	0.01	16.01
Pretr. LSTM	0.45	0.34	0.33	2.86	0.04	0.01	0.03	8.16	0.00	0.00	0.00	15.97
StudNet-A	0.00	0.00	0.00	3.99	0.00	0.00	0.00	8.08	0.00	0.00	0.00	16.01
StudNet-B	0.36	0.18	0.29	3.74	0.14	0.02	0.12	8.30	0.05	0.00	0.04	16.05

5.2 Ablations and Failure Analysis

Given the relatively low performance of the models presented here on the break and make task, we also conducted several experiments designed to discover which part of this problem is most difficult for future research. Appendix D.1 contains the details of these experiments. We also attempt to pretrain a model on the randomly generated assemblies and fine-tune on the OMR data. Appendix D.2 contains details. Finally we also provide a human baseline to verify the tractability of this problem in Appendix D.3.

6 Conclusion

LTRON and the **Break and Make** challenge offer an ideal environment to study a number of important technical problems in Machine Learning and Artificial Intelligence. First, the **LTRON** simulator offers an environment to explore interactive building and construction problems at a level of detail and granularity that has not previously been possible. Second, while we have only been able to make progress on very small LEGO models in this paper, **LTRON** has the ability to represent very large assemblies with hundreds and even thousands of bricks. Our hope is that the existence of these very difficult large-scale tasks that are currently beyond the scope of modern temporal-spatial visual modelling techniques will inspire researchers to explore new ways to scale algorithms and hardware to accomplish the goals. Finally **Break and Make** provides an ideal setting to explore interactive learning algorithms designed for long-term credit assignment, as agents must connect low-level actions taken during disassembly and inspection with reward signals collected in the distant future during reassembly.

References

1. Bapst, V., et al.: Structured agents for physical construction. In: International Conference on Machine Learning, pp. 464–474. PMLR (2019)
2. Chang, A.X., et al.: ShapeNet: an information-rich 3D model repository. arXiv preprint arXiv:1512.03012 (2015)
3. Chung, H., et al.: Brick-by-brick: combinatorial construction with deep reinforcement learning. In: Advances in Neural Information Processing Systems, vol. 34, pp. 5745–5757 (2021)
4. Das, A., Datta, S., Gkioxari, G., Lee, S., Parikh, D., Batra, D.: Embodied question answering. In: Proceedings of the IEEE Conference on Computer Vision and Pattern Recognition, pp. 1–10 (2018)
5. Deitke, M., et al.: Robothor: an open simulation-to-real embodied AI platform. In: Proceedings of the IEEE/CVF Conference on Computer Vision and Pattern Recognition, pp. 3164–3174 (2020)
6. Dosovitskiy, A., et al.: An image is worth 16x16 words: transformers for image recognition at scale. arXiv preprint arXiv:2010.11929 (2020)
7. Farhadi, A., Endres, I., Hoiem, D., Forsyth, D.: Describing objects by their attributes. In: 2009 IEEE Conference on Computer Vision and Pattern Recognition, pp. 1778–1785. IEEE (2009)
8. Finn, C., Goodfellow, I., Levine, S.: Unsupervised learning for physical interaction through video prediction. arXiv preprint arXiv:1605.07157 (2016)
9. Ghasemipour, S.K.S., Kataoka, S., David, B., Freeman, D., Gu, S.S., Mordatch, I.: Blocks assemble! learning to assemble with large-scale structured reinforcement learning. In: International Conference on Machine Learning, pp. 7435–7469. PMLR (2022)
10. Girdhar, R., Ramanan, D.: Cater: A diagnostic dataset for compositional actions and temporal reasoning. arXiv:abs/1910.04744 (2020)
11. Gordon, D., Kembhavi, A., Rastegari, M., Redmon, J., Fox, D., Farhadi, A.: IQA: visual question answering in interactive environments. In: Proceedings of the IEEE Conference on Computer Vision and Pattern Recognition, pp. 4089–4098 (2018)
12. Gupta, A., Fox, D., Curless, B., Cohen, M.: DuploTrack: a reatime system for authoring and guiding Duplo model assembly. In: Proceedings of the 25th Annual ACM Symposium Adjunct on User Interface Software and Technology. ACM, New York (2012)
13. He, K., Chen, X., Xie, S., Li, Y., Dollár, P., Girshick, R.: Masked autoencoders are scalable vision learners. arXiv preprint arXiv:2111.06377 (2021)
14. He, K., Zhang, X., Ren, S., Sun, J.: Deep residual learning for image recognition. In: Proceedings of the IEEE Conference on Computer Vision and Pattern Recognition, pp. 770–778 (2016)
15. Huang, J., Smith, C., Bastani, O., Singh, R., Albarghouthi, A., Naik, M.: Generating programmatic referring expressions via program synthesis. In: International Conference on Machine Learning, pp. 4495–4506. PMLR (2020)
16. Inoue, T., De Magistris, G., Munawar, A., Yokoya, T., Tachibana, R.: Deep reinforcement learning for high precision assembly tasks. In: 2017 IEEE/RSJ International Conference on Intelligent Robots and Systems (IROS), pp. 819–825. IEEE (2017)
17. Jaegle, A., et al.: Perceiver IO: a general architecture for structured inputs & outputs. arXiv preprint arXiv:2107.14795 (2021)
18. Jessiman, J., et al.: Open Model Repository. https://omr.ldraw.org

19. Jessiman, J., et al.: LDraw. https://www.ldraw.org (2022)
20. Johnson, J., Hariharan, B., van der Maaten, L., Fei-Fei, L., Zitnick, C.L., Girshick, R.: CLEVR: a diagnostic dataset for compositional language and elementary visual reasoning. In: CVPR (2017)
21. Jones, B., Hildreth, D., Chen, D., Baran, I., Kim, V.G., Schulz, A.: Automate: a dataset and learning approach for automatic mating of cad assemblies. ACM Trans. Graph. (TOG) **40**(6), 1–18 (2021)
22. Jones, R.K., et al.: Shapeassembly: learning to generate programs for 3D shape structure synthesis. ACM Trans. Graph. (TOG) **39**(6), 1–20 (2020)
23. Kim, J.: Survey on automated LEGO assembly construction (2015)
24. Kolve, E., et al.: AI2-THOR: an interactive 3D environment for visual AI. arXiv preprint arXiv:1712.05474 (2017)
25. Krishna, R., et al.: Visual genome: connecting language and vision using crowd-sourced dense image annotations (2016). https://arxiv.org/abs/1602.07332
26. Lee, S., Kim, J., Kim, J.W., Moon, B.R.: Finding an optimal LEGO brick layout of voxelized 3D object using a genetic algorithm. In: Proceedings of the 2015 Annual Conference on Genetic and Evolutionary Computation, pp. 1215–1222 (2015)
27. Lee, Y., Hu, E.S., Lim, J.J.: Ikea furniture assembly environment for long-horizon complex manipulation tasks. In: 2021 IEEE International Conference on Robotics and Automation (ICRA), pp. 6343–6349. IEEE (2021)
28. Lennon, K., et al.: Image2Lego: customized LEGO set generation from images. arXiv preprint arXiv:2108.08477 (2021)
29. Li, Y., Mo, K., Shao, L., Sung, M., Guibas, L.: Learning 3D part assembly from a single image. In: Vedaldi, A., Bischof, H., Brox, T., Frahm, J.-M. (eds.) ECCV 2020. LNCS, vol. 12351, pp. 664–682. Springer, Cham (2020). https://doi.org/10.1007/978-3-030-58539-6_40
30. Lim, J.J., Pirsiavash, H., Torralba, A.: Parsing IKEA objects: fine pose estimation. In: Proceedings of the IEEE International Conference on Computer Vision, pp. 2992–2999 (2013)
31. Lin, T.Y., Dollár, P., Girshick, R., He, K., Hariharan, B., Belongie, S.: Feature pyramid networks for object detection. In: Proceedings of the IEEE Conference on Computer Vision and Pattern Recognition, pp. 2117–2125 (2017)
32. McCormac, J., Clark, R., Bloesch, M., Davison, A., Leutenegger, S.: Fusion++: Volumetric object-level slam. In: 2018 International Conference on 3D vision (3DV), pp. 32–41. IEEE (2018)
33. Melkert, R.: LDCad (2017). https://www.melkert.net/LDCad
34. Mo, K., et al.: PartNet: a large-scale benchmark for fine-grained and hierarchical part-level 3D object understanding. In: Proceedings of the IEEE/CVF Conference on Computer Vision and Pattern Recognition, pp. 909–918 (2019)
35. Nandi, C., et al.: Synthesizing structured cad models with equality saturation and inverse transformations. In: Proceedings of the 41st ACM SIGPLAN Conference on Programming Language Design and Implementation, pp. 31–44 (2020)
36. Peysakhov, M., Regli, W.: Using assembly representations to enable evolutionary design of LEGO structures. Artif. Intell. Eng. Des. Anal. Manuf. **17**, 155–168 (2003)
37. Radford, A., Narasimhan, K., Salimans, T., Sutskever, I.: Improving language understanding by generative pre-training (2018)
38. Ronneberger, O., Fischer, P., Brox, T.: U-Net: convolutional networks for biomedical image segmentation. In: Navab, N., Hornegger, J., Wells, W.M., Frangi, A.F. (eds.) MICCAI 2015. LNCS, vol. 9351, pp. 234–241. Springer, Cham (2015). https://doi.org/10.1007/978-3-319-24574-4_28

39. Rosinol, A., Gupta, A., Abate, M., Shi, J., Carlone, L.: 3D dynamic scene graphs: actionable spatial perception with places, objects, and humans (2020)
40. Ross, S., Gordon, G., Bagnell, D.: A reduction of imitation learning and structured prediction to no-regret online learning. In: Proceedings of the Fourteenth International Conference on Artificial Intelligence and Statistics, pp. 627–635. JMLR Workshop and Conference Proceedings (2011)
41. Salas-Moreno, R.F., et al.: Slam++: simultaneous localisation and mapping at the level of objects. In: Proceedings of the IEEE Conference on Computer Vision and Pattern Recognition, pp. 1352–1359 (2013)
42. Savarimuthu, T.R., et al.: Teaching a robot the semantics of assembly tasks. IEEE Trans. Syste. Man Cybern. Syst. **48**(5), 670–692 (2017)
43. Shen, B., et al.: iGibson, a simulation environment for interactive tasks in large realisticscenes. arXiv preprint arXiv:2012.02924 (2020)
44. Shridhar, M., et al.: Alfred: a benchmark for interpreting grounded instructions for everyday tasks. In: Proceedings of the IEEE/CVF Conference on Computer Vision and Pattern Recognition, pp. 10740–10749 (2020)
45. Suárez-Ruiz, F., Zhou, X., Pham, Q.C.: Can robots assemble an IKEA chair? Sci. Robot. **3**(17), eaat6385 (2018)
46. Sucar, E., Wada, K., Davison, A.: NodeSLAM: neural object descriptors for multi-view shape reconstruction. In: 2020 International Conference on 3D Vision (3DV), pp. 949–958. IEEE (2020)
47. Sui, Z., Chang, H., Xu, N., Jenkins, O.C.: Geofusion: geometric consistency informed scene estimation in dense clutter. IEEE Robot. Autom. Lette. **5**(4), 5913–5920 (2020)
48. Szot, A., et al.: Habitat 2.0: training home assistants to rearrange their habitat. In: Advances in Neural Information Processing Systems, vol. 34, 251–266 (2021)
49. Thompson, R., Ghalebi, E., DeVries, T., Taylor, G.W.: Building LEGO using deep generative models of graphs. arXiv preprint arXiv:2012.11543 (2020)
50. Vaswani, A., et al.: Attention is all you need. arXiv preprint arXiv:1706.03762 (2017)
51. Vineet, V., et al.: Incremental dense semantic stereo fusion for large-scale semantic scene reconstruction. In: 2015 IEEE International Conference on Robotics and Automation (ICRA), pp. 75–82. IEEE (2015)
52. Wah, C., Branson, S., Perona, P., Belongie, S.: Multiclass recognition and part localization with humans in the loop. In: 2011 International Conference on Computer Vision, pp. 2524–2531. IEEE (2011)
53. Wani, S., Patel, S., Jain, U., Chang, A.X., Savva, M.: Multi-on: benchmarking semantic map memory using multi-object navigation. In: Neural Information Processing Systems (NeurIPS) (2020)
54. Willis, K.D., et al.: Fusion 360 gallery: a dataset and environment for programmatic cad reconstruction. arXiv preprint arXiv:2010.02392 (2020)
55. Winograd, T.: SHRDLU: a system for dialog (1972)
56. Wu, J., Lim, J.J., Zhang, H., Tenenbaum, J.B., Freeman, W.T.: Physics 101: learning physical object properties from unlabeled videos. In: BMVC, vol. 2, p. 7 (2016)
57. Wu, J., Lu, E., Kohli, P., Freeman, B., Tenenbaum, J.: Learning to see physics via visual de-animation. In: NIPS, pp. 153–164 (2017)
58. Wu, J., Yildirim, I., Lim, J.J., Freeman, B., Tenenbaum, J.: Galileo: Perceiving physical object properties by integrating a physics engine with deep learning. In: Advances in Neural Information Processing Systems, vol. 28, pp. 127–135 (2015)

59. Yi, K., et al.: CLEVRER: collision events for video representation and reasoning (2020)
60. Zhao, X., Agrawal, H., Batra, D., Schwing, A.: The surprising effectiveness of visual odometry techniques for embodied PointGoal navigation. In: Proceedings of the ICCV (2021)

Bi-PointFlowNet: Bidirectional Learning for Point Cloud Based Scene Flow Estimation

Wencan Cheng[1](✉)[ID] and Jong Hwan Ko[2][ID]

[1] Department of Artificial Intelligence, Sungkyunkwan University, Suwon 16419, South Korea
{cwc1260,jhko}@skku.edu
[2] College of Information and Communication Engineering, Sungkyunkwan University, Suwon 16419, South Korea

Abstract. Scene flow estimation, which extracts point-wise motion between scenes, is becoming a crucial task in many computer vision tasks. However, all of the existing estimation methods utilize only the unidirectional features, restricting the accuracy and generality. This paper presents a novel scene flow estimation architecture using bidirectional flow embedding layers. The proposed bidirectional layer learns features along both forward and backward directions, enhancing the estimation performance. In addition, hierarchical feature extraction and warping improve the performance and reduce computational overhead. Experimental results show that the proposed architecture achieved a new state-of-the-art record by outperforming other approaches with large margin in both FlyingThings3D and KITTI benchmarks. Codes are available at https://github.com/cwc1260/BiFlow.

Keywords: Scene flow estimation · Point cloud · Bidirectional learning

1 Introduction

A scene flow estimation task is to capture the point-wise motion from two consecutive frames. As it provides the fundamental low-level information of dynamic scenes, it has become an essential step in various high-level computer vision tasks including object detection and motion segmentation. Therefore, accurate scene flow estimation is crucial for perceiving dynamic environment in real-world applications such as autonomous driving and robot navigation [16,42].

Early scene flow estimation approaches employed RGB images as an input. However, due to the increasing applications of LiDAR sensors that can capture dynamic scenes in the form of three-dimensional (3D) point clouds, scene flow estimation using point cloud has been actively studied. FlowNet3D [21] proposed the first point cloud based estimation model using the hierarchical architecture of PointNet++ [32]. Based on this scheme, several studies [9,37]

ⓒ The Author(s), under exclusive license to Springer Nature Switzerland AG 2022
S. Avidan et al. (Eds.): ECCV 2022, LNCS 13688, pp. 108–124, 2022.
https://doi.org/10.1007/978-3-031-19815-1_7

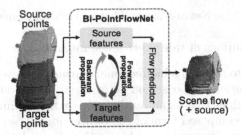

Fig. 1. Illustration of the bidirectional learning for scene flow estimation. The features extracted from each input frame are propagated bidirectionally for generating augmented feature representations that benefit scene flow estimation. The estimated scene flows are warped with the source frame for a clear comparison with the target frame.

proposed the multi-scale correlation propagation structure for more accurate estimation. Recently, PointPWC [46] significantly improved the estimation performance using regression of multi-scale flows in a coarse-to-fine manner. Another study [30] proposed integration of an optimal transport-solving module in a neural network for estimating scene flow.

All of these existing methods utilized only the unidirectional feature propagation (i.e., propagating source point features to target points) for calculating flow correlations. Meanwhile, various models for natural language processing (NLP) tasks [6,8,18,33] showed that the bidirectionally-learned features can significantly improve the performance due to their strong contextual information.

Since scene flow estimation is also a temporal sequence processing task, bidirectional learning can boost the estimation performance. Bidirectional configuration has already proved its effectiveness on optical flow estimation, which is similar representation as scene flow estimation [11,12,14,20,43]. However, to the best of our knowledge, there is no prior work that utilized bidirectional learning for the estimation of scene flow in the 3D space.

Based on this motivation, we propose Bi-PointFlowNet, a novel bidirectional architecture for point cloud based scene flow estimation. As shown in Fig. 1, the bidirectional correlations can be learned by forward-propagation from the source features and backward-propagation from the target features. Therefore, each frame contains knowledge from the other, allowing the features to produce stronger correlations. In addition, the proposed Bi-PointFlowNet adopts the coarse-to-fine method for multi-scale bidirectional correlation extraction.

We evaluated the proposed model on two challenging benchmarks, the FlyingThings3D [23] and KITTI [26] datasets, under both occluded and non-occluded conditions. On the FlyingThings3D dataset, Bi-PointFlowNet outperforms all existing methods with more than 44% and 32% of estimation error reduction on the non-occluded cases and the occluded cases, respectively. To evaluate generalization performance, we trained the models on the synthetic (FlyingThings3D) dataset and evaluated on the real-world LiDAR scan (KITTI Scene Flow 2015) dataset without fine-tuning. Compared to the existing approaches, the results show that Bi-PointFlowNet achieves improved generality with 44% and 21% lower error on the non-occluded and occluded cases, respectively. Our Bi-PointFlowNet also showed better time efficiency while maintaining high accuracy.

The key contributions of this paper are summarized as follows:

- We are the first to apply the bidirectional learning architecture used for a 3D scene flow estimation task based on point cloud. The model can extract bidirectional correlations that significantly improve flow estimation performance.
- We propose a decomposed form of the bidirectional layer that optimizes the computation count for accelerated bidirectional correlations extraction.
- The proposed model achieves the state-of-the-art performance and generality on the synthetic FlyingThings3D and real-world KITTI benchmarks in both occluded and non-occluded conditions.

2   Related Work

2.1   Scene Flow Estimation

The 3D scene flow, first introduced by [39], represents a dense 3D motion vector field for each point on every surface in the scene. Early dense scene flow estimation approaches [3,10,23,25,29,38,40,44] used stereo RGB images as an input. With the rapid development of 3D sensors and the emergence of point cloud based networks [31,32,45], a line of studies proposed estimating the scene flow using the raw 3D point clouds. FlowNet3D [21] was the first study that estimated the scene flow from two raw point cloud frames through a deep neural network. However, the performance of FlowNet3D was restricted by its single flow correlation. To address this drawback, Gu et al. proposed HPLFlownet [9] that captures multi-scale correlations using a bilateral convolutional layer [13,34]. PointPWC-Net [46] further improved the performance and efficiency by hierarchically regressing scene flow in a coarse-to-fine manner. There are several other approaches that leveraged the all-to-all correlation, including FLOT [30] that learns the all-to-all correlation by solving an optimal transport problem, and FlowStep3D [16] that iteratively aligns point clouds based on the iterative closest point (ICP) algorithm [2,5]. However, learning an all-to-all correlation matrix is computationally inefficient when the input point clouds contain a large number of points.

Our Bi-PointFlowNet is inspired by these point cloud based methods. It also adopts the coarse-to-fine architecture to capture the multi-level correlation and to reduce computational overhead. However, the proposed method is different from the existing models as it utilizes bidirectional learning, which collects the contextual information from both source and target features for more accurate estimation.

2.2   Bidirectional Models

The bidirectional models aim to extract features based on both the current and future states. They are able to capture strong contextual information with future

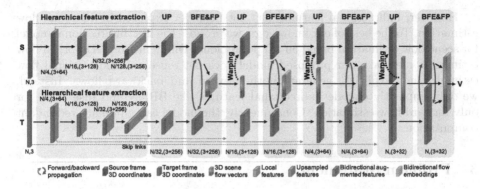

Fig. 2. Architecture of Bi-PointFlowNet for scene flow estimation. (**UP** stands for an upsampling layer. **BFE&FP** stand for a bidirectional flow embedding layer and a flow prediction layer. They are visualized in the same block for a clear representation.) First, we feed two consecutive input point frames into the shared hierarchical feature extraction module for multilevel feature extraction. Then the upsampling layers propagate features from high levels to low levels and the warping operations are directly applied upon the upsampled points. After each upsampling layer, a bidirectional flow embedding layer is adopted for bidirectional feature (forward feature and backward features) propagation and flow embedding generation. The flow embeddings are immediately fed into the flow prediction layer for scene flow regression according to the current level. The figure is best viewed in color. (Color figure online)

knowledge, which is helpful for many time-sequence processing tasks such as natural language processing (NLP). The bidirectional model was first proposed in a bidirectional RNN (BRNN) [33] that learns sequence representations forward and backward through two separate networks. Subsequently, a more powerful structure called bidirectional long short-term memory (BiLSTM) [8] was proposed and successfully applied in frame-wise phoneme classification. Based on these fundamental studies, various approaches [1,24,28,49] have been actively explored. In recent years, the bidirectional encoder representation transformer (BERT) [6] and its variants [17,22] have achieved overwhelming performance in various applications including language understanding [18,47,48].

Recently, a series of studies showed that 2D optical flow estimation can also benefit from bidirectional learning, because optical flow estimation is a type of time series-based task as well. MirrorFlow [11] reused a symmetric optical flow algorithm bidirectionally to extract forward and backward optical flows, which are then constrained by the bidirectional motion and occlusion consistency. Similarly, Wang et al. [43] also proposed an approach that generates bidirectional optical flows but by reusing a neural network. In addition, Janai et al. [14] proposed a method that extracts bidirectional optical flows in a coarse-to-fine manner based on a pyramid structure. Based on the bidirectional models, Hur et al. [12] implemented an architecture that iteratively refines the optical flow estimation by using the previous output.

However, bidirectional learning has not been yet explored in 3D scene flow estimation. To the best of our knowledge, we propose the first bidirectional model for scene flow estimation based on 3D point cloud. Different from 2D optical flow estimation methods, our proposed model does not reuse an unidirectional flow estimator nor explicitly generate both forward and backward flows. Instead, we only implicitly encode bidirectional features like BRNN and fuse them for only forward flow estimation. Consequently, the model can eliminate redundant computations.

3   Problem Statement

Scene flow estimation using a point cloud is to estimate a 3D point-wise motion field in a dynamic scene. The inputs are two consecutive point cloud frames, the source frame $S = \{p_i = (x_i, f_i)\}_{i=1}^N$ and target frame $T = \{q_j = (y_j, g_j)\}_{j=1}^M$, where each point consists of a 3D coordinate $x_i, y_j \in \mathbb{R}^3$ and its corresponding feature $f_i, g_j \in \mathbb{R}^c$. The outputs are 3D motion field vectors $V = \{v_i \in \mathbb{R}^3\}_{i=1}^N$ that represent the point-wise non-rigid transformation from the source frame toward the target frame. Our goal is to estimate the best non-rigid transformation V that represents the best alignment from the source frame towards the target frame. Note that N and M denote the number of points in the source and target frame, respectively. However, N and M are not required to be equal because of sparsity and occlusion in a point cloud. Therefore, learning the hard correspondence between the two frames is not feasible. Instead, we directly learn the flow vector for each point in the source frame, as in the most of the recent methods [9,16,19,21,30,46].

4   Bi-PointFlowNet

The proposed Bi-PointFlowNet estimates scene flow using a hierarchical architecture with bidirectional flow embedding extraction. The network accepts two consecutive point cloud frames S and T as an input. The output of the network is the estimated scene flow vectors V. As shown in Fig. 2, Bi-PointFlowNet consists of four components. First, a hierarchical feature extractor extracts multi-level local features in both input frames. Second, novel bidirectional flow embedding layers are applied at different upsampled levels for multi-level bidirectional correlation extraction. Third, upsampling and warping layers propagate features from higher levels to lower levels. Finally, the flow predictor aggregates bidirectional correlations and propagated features to obtain the flow estimation for each level.

4.1   Hierarchical Feature Extraction

To extract informative features from point clouds more efficiently and effectively, we adopt the hierarchical feature extraction scheme commonly used in point cloud processing [32,45]. Feature extractions proceed in L levels for generating

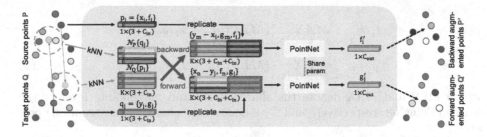

Fig. 3. Bidirectional feature propagation in the novel Bidirectional Flow Embedding layer. Each point first groups the nearest neighbors from the other point cloud forming a local region. (Forward grouping: a source point groups points from the target points. Backward grouping: a target point groups points from the source points.) Each point in the local region is then concatenated with its own local features propagated from previous feature upsampling. Finally, a PointNet layer with shared parameters accepts the local regions as input and updates the bidirectional augmented features for each point.

hierarchical features from dense to sparse. At each level l, dense input points and their corresponding features are first subsampled through the *furthest point sampling*, which forms a sparse point set. Then, the *k-nearest neighbor* is used to locally group dense points around every subsampled sparse point. Finally, a *Pointconv* [45] layer aggregates the features and coordinates from the grouped local points, and generates the local feature for each subsampled point.

4.2   Bidirectional Flow Embedding

Unlike conventional correlation extraction that uses only unidirectional features between two consecutive frames, we propose a novel bidirectional flow embedding (BFE) layer that provides rich contextual information. The BFE layer first generates bidirectional augmented feature representations through a bidirectional feature propagation (BFP) module, as shown in Fig. 3. Then, a conventional *flow embedding* (FE) layer is followed to extract correlation embeddings for flow regression.

Let the inputs to the BFP module be P and Q, where $P \subset S$ and $Q \subset T$ are the subsampled points. For each point $p_i \in P$ in the target frame, the BFP module first collects the nearest points from the source frame that forms the group $\mathcal{N}_Q\{p_i\}$. Likewise, the BFP module collects points from the target frame for each point $q_j \in Q$ in the source frame that forms group $\mathcal{N}_P\{q_j\}$. Subsequently, the points p_i, q_j and their groups $\mathcal{N}_Q\{p_i\}$, $\mathcal{N}_P\{q_j\}$ are simultaneously processed by a shared PointNet [31,32] layer to generate the bidirectionally-augmented point representations. Thus, the bidirectional-augmented point features, which are backward augmented feature f'_i for p_i and forward augmented feature g'_j for q_j, are respectively represented as:

$$f_i' = \underset{(y_m, g_m) \in \mathcal{N}_Q \{p_i\}}{MAX} (MLP([y_m - x_i, g_m, f_i])), \qquad (1)$$

$$g_j' = \underset{(x_n, f_n) \in \mathcal{N}_P \{q_j\}}{MAX} (MLP([x_n - y_j, f_n, g_j])), \qquad (2)$$

where MLP and MAX denote the shared MLP and maxpooling layer of the learned PointNet, respectively, and '$[\cdot, \cdot]$' denotes the channel concatenation operator.

Since the output estimation are only forward directed, a normal unidirectional *flow embedding* (FE) correlation layer captures correlations from the source bidirectionally-augmented points to the target bidirectionally-augmented points after the BFP. We name the correlation as the bidirectional flow embedding, because they are extracted from the bidirectional features. Note that, the generated augmented points are also fed to the subsequent upsampling layer for hierarchical feature propagation, which will be elaborated in Sect. 4.4.

4.3 Decomposed Form of Bidirectional Flow Embedding

The aforementioned BFE layer directly follows the standard procedure (i.e. grouping $\rightarrow$ concatenation $\rightarrow$ MLP $\rightarrow$ max-pooling) to fuse the local information, as presented in [32]. However, this procedure requires a large number of operations as it should be executed for each point of the input point cloud. Let the inputs to the BFE module be $P = \{(x_i, f_i) \in \mathbb{R}^{3+C}\}_{i=1}^{N'}$ and $Q = \{(y_j, g_j) \in \mathbb{R}^{3+C}\}_{j=1}^{M'}$, and the number of grouping points to be K. For convenient analysis, we assume a one-layer MLP whose weights are $W \in \mathbb{R}^{(3+C+C) \times C'}$. Then, $(3 + C + C) \times C'$ MLP computations are required for $(N' + M') \times K$ times. Therefore, the total operation count of BFE is $(N' + M') \times K \times (3 + C + C) \times C'$. However, as the total number of input points is $(N' + M')$, every K neighbor points are grouped into $(N' + M')$ groups and then calculated by the MLP. Thus, at least $(N' + M') \times (K - 1)$ MLP operations are repeatedly calculated.

To optimize this redundancy, we propose a decomposed form of BFE. First, we decompose the MLP weights W into three sub-weights: the weights for local position encoding $W_p \in \mathbb{R}^{3 \times C'}$, the weights for the bidirectional propagated feature $W_b \in \mathbb{R}^{C \times C'}$ and the weights for the replicated feature $W_r \in \mathbb{R}^{C \times C'}$. W_b and W_r are performed at both P and Q before grouping, thus forming transformed features $W_b f_i$, $W_b g_j$, $W_r f_i$ and $W_r g_j$. These transformed features and their corresponding coordinates are then supplied for grouping. Afterwards, only W_p is used for transformation of the grouped local coordinates. Finally, we simply add the transformed local coordinates with the transformed features together and apply the activation function. Therefore, Eq. 1 and 2 can be transformed as:

$$f_i' = \underset{(y_m, W_b g_m) \in \mathcal{N}_Q \{p_i = (x_i, W_r f_i)\}}{MAX} \sigma(W_p(y_m - x_i) + W_b g_m + W_r f_i), \qquad (3)$$

$$g'_j = \underset{(x_n, W_b f_n) \in \mathcal{N}_P \{q_j = (y_j, W_r g_j)\}}{MAX} \sigma(W_p(x_n - y_j) + W_b f_n + W_r g_j), \qquad (4)$$

where σ represents the activation function. Thus, computing W_b, W_r at P, Q only requires $(N' + M') \times (C + C) \times C'$ operations, while local coordinate transformation requires $(N' + M') \times (K \times 3) \times C'$ operations. As a result, the total computations count of decomposed BFE is reduced to $(N' + M') \times (K \times 3 + C + C) \times C'$.

4.4   Upsampling and Warping

The upsampling (UP) layer can propagate features (including flows, local features, and bidirectional augmented points) from sparse levels to dense levels. To reduce the computational cost, we adopt the 3D interpolation using the inverse-distance weighted function based on the k nearest neighbors. Let $\{(x^l_j, f^l_j)\}^{N^l}_{j=1}$ denotes the coordinates and features from a high level, and $\{x^{l-1}_i\}^{N^{l-1}}_{i=1}$ denotes the coordinates from a low level through a super link, where N^{l-1} and N^l are the number of points and $N^{l-1} > N^l$. The interpolated feature of a dense point $\{x^l_i\}$ is defined as:

$$f^{l-1}_i = \frac{\sum^k_{j=1} w(x^l_j, x^{l-1}_i) f^l_j}{\sum^k_{j=1} w(x^l_j, x^{l-1}_i)}, \qquad (5)$$

where $w(x^l_j, x^{l-1}_i) = 1/||x^l_j - x^{l-1}_i||_2$, and $k = 3$ by default.

The upsampled scene flows are immediately accumulated to the source frame in order to obtain a frame closer to the corresponding target frame through a warping layer. This process can be simply denoted as $x^l_w = x^l + v^l$ for each source point x^l from the l-th level, where v^l denotes an upsampled flow vector. Through warping, the warped points gradually become close to the target frame. Thus, the subsequent BFE layer can easily group more valuable points with high semantic similarity that can promote more accurate flow estimation. In addition, accurate flow estimation of the current level also enhances warping at the next level.

4.5   Scene Flow Prediction

We implement a scene flow predictor in order to regress the scene flow vector. For each level, the inputs are the upsampled flows and features from the upsampling layer, and bidirectional flow embeddings from the BFE layer. First, the predictor uses a *Pointconv* to produce smooth features by locally fusing these features and flows around each warped source point. Subsequently, a MLP transforms the smooth high-dimensional features into 3-dimensional scene flow vectors for all points. Since the predictor only focuses on a small region around each warped source point, the outputs from the last MLP layer are point-wise flow residuals, as in [27,41]. Afterwards, the residuals are further accumulated with the upsampled flows forming the output flow estimation for the current level.

4.6 Loss Function

The training process adopts the multi-level supervision manner used in previous studies for optical flow estimation [7,35] and scene flow estimation [42,46]. At each level, the estimated flows are supervised by the L2 loss. Let $\{v_i^l\}_{i=1}^{N^l}$ denote the scene flow vectors estimated from the l-th level and $\{\hat{v}_i^l\}_{i=1}^{N^l}$ denote the ground truth scene flow vectors of the l-th level. The training loss is defined as:

$$\mathcal{L} = \sum_{l=0}^{L-1} \alpha^l \sum_{i=1}^{N^l} \|\hat{v}_i^l - v_i^l\|_2, \tag{6}$$

where α^l is the weight of the loss function at level l. The weights are set to be $\alpha^0 = 0.16$, $\alpha^1 = 0.08$, $\alpha^2 = 0.04$, $\alpha^3 = 0.02$ by default.

5 Experiments

5.1 Experimental Settings

We conducted experiments on an NVIDIA TITAN RTX GPU with PyTorch. As shown in Fig. 2, we implemented a hierarchical model with $L = 4$ levels. We used $N = M = 8,192$ points as inputs. The numbers of subsampled points of each level are defined as $N^1 = 2,048$, $N^2 = 512$, $N^3 = 256$, and $N^4 = 64$. As in the previous methods, we first trained and evaluated networks on the synthetic FlyingThings3D [23] dataset (Sect. 5.3). Then, to validate the generalization ability, the trained model was directly evaluated on the real-world KITTI Scene Flow 2015 [26] dataset without any fine-tuning (Sect. 5.4).

5.2 Evaluation Metrics

For a fair comparison, we adopted the same evaluation metrics as used in recent works [9,16,19,30,46].

- **EPE3D**$_{full}$ **(m):** the main evaluation metric measuring end-point-error $\|\hat{v}_i^l - v_i^l\|_2$ averaged over **all** point.
- **EPE3D (m):** the main evaluation metric measuring end-point-error $\|\hat{v}_i^l - v_i^l\|_2$ averaged each **non-occluded** point.
- **ACC3DS:** the percentage of points whose EPE3D <0.05 m or relative error <5%.
- **ACC3DR:** the percentage of points whose EPE3D < 0.1 m or relative error <10%.
- **Outliers3D:** the percentage of points whose EPE3D >0.3 m or relative error >10%.
- **EPE2D (px):** 2D end-point-error measured by projecting points back to the 2D image plane, which is a common metric for optical flow evaluation.
- **ACC2D:** the percentage of points whose EPE2D <3 px or relative error <5%.

Table 1. Comparison of the proposed method with previous state-of-the-art methods on the non-occluded $FT3D_s$ and $KITTI_s$ datasets. All methods are trained only on the $FT3D_s$ dataset.

Dataset	Method	EPE3D (m) ↓	ACC3D S ↑	ACC3D R ↑	Outliers 3D ↓	EPE2D (px) ↓	ACC 2D ↑
$FT3D_s$	FlowNet3D [21]	0.113	0.412	0.771	0.602	5.974	0.569
	HPLFlowNet [9]	0.080	0.614	0.855	0.429	4.672	0.676
	PointPWC [46]	0.059	0.738	0.928	0.342	3.239	0.799
	FLOT [30]	0.052	0.732	0.927	0.357	–	–
	HCRF-Flow [19]	0.048	0.835	0.950	0.261	2.565	0.870
	FlowStep3D [16]	0.045	0.816	0.961	0.216	–	–
	Ours	**0.028**	**0.918**	**0.978**	**0.143**	**1.582**	**0.929**
$KITTI_s$	FlowNet3D [21]	0.177	0.374	0.668	0.527	7.214	0.509
	HPLFlowNet [9]	0.117	0.478	0.778	0.410	4.805	0.593
	PointPWC [46]	0.069	0.728	0.888	0.265	1.902	0.866
	FLOT [30]	0.056	0.755	0.908	0.242	–	–
	HCRF-Flow [19]	0.053	0.863	0.944	0.179	2.070	0.865
	FlowStep3D [16]	0.054	0.805	0.925	0.149	–	–
	Ours	**0.030**	**0.920**	**0.960**	**0.141**	**1.056**	**0.949**

Table 2. Comparison of the proposed method with previous state-of-the-art methods on the occluded $FT3D_o$ and $KITTI_o$ datasets. All methods are trained only on the $FT3D_o$ dataset.

Dataset	Method	EPE3D$_{full}$ (m) ↓	EPE3D (m) ↓	ACC3D S ↑	ACC3D R ↑	Outliers 3D ↓
$FT3D_o$	FlowNet3D [21]	0.211	0.157	0.228	0.582	0.804
	HPLFlowNet [9]	0.201	0.168	0.262	0.574	0.812
	FLOT [30]	0.250	0.153	0.396	0.660	0.662
	PointPWC [46]	0.195	0.155	0.416	0.699	0.638
	OGSFNet [27]	0.163	0.121	0.551	0.776	0.518
	RAFT-3D (16 iters) [36]	–	**0.064**	**0.837**	0.892	–
	Ours	**0.102**	0.073	0.791	**0.896**	**0.274**
$KITTI_o$	FlowNet3D [21]	0.183	–	0.098	0.394	0.799
	HPLFlowNet [9]	0.343	–	0.103	0.386	0.814
	FLOT [30]	0.130	–	0.278	0.667	0.529
	PointPWC [46]	0.118	–	0.403	0.757	0.496
	OGSFNet [27]	0.075	–	0.706	0.869	0.327
	Ours	**0.065**	–	**0.769**	**0.906**	**0.264**

5.3 Training and Evaluation on FlyingThings3D

FlyingThing3D [23] is a synthetic dataset composed of 19,640 pairs of frames for training and 3,824 pairs of frames for testing. Each frame consists of stereo and RGB-D images rendered from scenes with multiple moving objects sampled from

ShapeNet [4] dataset. We trained and evaluated our proposed model based on two versions of datasets prepared by different pre-processing methodologies. The first version is FT3D$_s$, which removes the occluded points after transforming the image data into points, as suggested in [9,16,30,46]. The second version, FT3D$_o$ introduced by [21,27,30], remains the occluded points. The input points of $N = 8,192$ are randomly sampled from each frame with non-correspondence.

For training, we used the Adam optimizer [15] with beta1 = 0.9, beta2 = 0.999, and starting learning rate $\alpha = 0.0001$. The learning rate is reduced by half every 80 epochs. We trained the model for 560 epochs.

Results. We report the performance of the proposed model compared to other state-of-the-art approaches [9,16,21,27,30,46]. On the non-occluded FlyingThings3D dataset, the proposed Bi-PointFlowNet achieved a new state-of-the-art record on all evaluation metrics based on point cloud, as shown in Table 1. It outperformed all recent state-of-the-art methods with more than 44% reduction of estimation error. When compared to the similar coarse-to-fine PointPWC [46], our model achieved an error reduction of 52%. On the other hand, Table 2 also shows remarkable performance of our work when handling occluded data. Our Bi-PointFlowNet improved the state-of-the-art performance by 32%. In addition, we also compared our method with RGB-D image-based RAFT-3D [36]. Table 2 shows that our method achieved comparable performance than Raft-3D with 16 iterations. Although our method did not achieve better EPE3D and ACC3DS, it outperformed Raft-3D for the ACC3DR metric. Despite a minor increase in errors, we report that our model requires significant less computation (13.3GFLOPs) and parameter size (7.9M) than RAFT-3D (329GFLOPs, 45M), making it more applicable to time-sensitive low-power applications. According to [36], we expect that RAFT-3D having similar computation to ours with less iteration will yield much worse accuracy than ours.

5.4   Generalization on KITTI

In order to evaluate the generalization ability of Bi-PointFlowNet to real-world data, we followed the same evaluation strategy as in the recent studies [9,16,21, 27,30,46]. We directly tested the trained model on the real-world KITTI [26] dataset without fine-tuning. The KITTI dataset contains 200 training and 200 testing sets. However, due to unprovided disparities in the testing set and in parts of the training set, we used 142 scenes (non-occluded) and 150 scenes (occluded) from the training set with available raw point clouds. For fair comparison of our method with the previous approaches [9,16,21,27,30,46], we followed the common step that removes ground points by height <0.3 m. According to the preparation of the FlyingThings3D dataset, both the non-occluded KITTI$_s$ and occluded KITTI$_o$ datasets are created.

Results. The generalization results on KITTI$_s$ and KITTI$_o$ are listed in Table 1 and 2, respectively. Our method significantly outperforms other methods on all metrics by a large margin. Table 1 represents that the model outperforms the previous state-of-the-art method by 44% on the main EPE3D metric. Compared with previous coarse-to-fine network, PointPWC-Net [46], our method achieves 56%

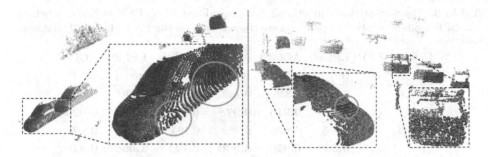

Fig. 4. Qualitative results of Bi-PointFlowNet on the non-occluded KITTI$_s$ dataset. Points are colored to indicate points as from source frame, target frame, unidirectional PointPWCNet estimated points (source frame + scene flow) or as bidirectional Bi-PointFlowNet estimated points (source frame + scene flow). (Color figure online)

error reduction. Meanwhile, Table 2 shows that our model outperforms the previous state-of-the-art method by 21% of error reduction. In addition, we present the qualitative results on the non-occluded cases of the KITTI$_s$ dataset in Fig. 4. The results show that our Bi-PointFlowNet reduced the estimation error for all points compared to the unidirectional coarse-to-fine PointPWC-Net. Furthermore, Bi-PointFlowNet is able to keep more accurate surface and contour details than PointPWC-Net (marked in the yellow circles in Fig. 4).

5.5 Ablation Study

Ablation of the Bidirectional Flow Embedding Layer. As described in Sect. 4.2, the key component of the proposed bidirectional flow embedding layer is the bidirectional feature propagation module, which is followed by the conventional unidirectional flow embedding layer. To evaluate the contribution of BFP, we implemented an ablation model that removes the BFP module resulting in a unidirectional network. We compare the performance of this ablation model with our proposed full model in Table 3. The results show that the proposed BFP module significantly improved the performance on all metrics with a large margin. Especially, the EPE3D error of the generality test on the KITTI$_s$ dataset was reduced by 43%, which shows important implications in the real-world applications. In addition, the ablation model without BFP and original PointPWC-Net are both coarse-to-fine architectures. However, due to the introduction of the residual in the flow predictor, the ablation model still outperformed PointPWC-Net, according to Table 1 and 3.

Ablation of the Decomposed form for BFE. We performed two comparative experiments to evaluate the effectiveness and efficiency of the proposed decomposed form of BFE. The one is Bi-PointFlowNet with original BFE (Sect. 4.2) and the other one is the model with the decomposed BFE (Sect. 4.3). Table 4 shows that the model using the decomposed form significantly reduces

Table 3. Ablation of the bidirectional flow embedding layer. BFP indicates whether the BFP module is used. All methods are trained only on the FlyingThings3D dataset.

Dataset	BFP	EPE3D (m) ↓	ACC3D S ↑	ACC3D R ↑	Outliers 3D ↓	EPE2D (px) ↓	ACC 2D ↑
FT3D$_s$	×	0.042	0.836	0.962	0.263	2.270	0.882
	√	**0.028**	**0.918**	**0.978**	**0.143**	**1.582**	**0.929**
KITTI$_s$	×	0.053	0.858	0.930	0.194	1.894	0.880
	√	**0.030**	**0.920**	**0.960**	**0.141**	**1.056**	**0.949**

Table 4. Ablation of the decomposed form of the bidirectional flow embedding layer. Decomp. indicates whether using decomposed form of BFE. GFLOPs indicates the total operation count. All methods are trained only on the FT3D$_s$ dataset.

Dataset	Decomp.	EPE3D (m) ↓	ACC3D S ↑	ACC3D R ↑	Outliers 3D ↓	EPE2D (px) ↓	ACC 2D ↑	GFLOPs	Runtime (ms)
FT3D$_s$	×	0.029	0.917	0.977	**0.142**	1.633	0.928	23.8	61.2
	√	**0.028**	**0.918**	**0.978**	0.143	**1.582**	**0.929**	13.3	40.5
KITTI$_s$	×	0.030	**0.925**	**0.965**	**0.133**	1.079	**0.951**	23.8	61.2
	√	**0.030**	0.920	0.960	0.141	**1.056**	0.949	13.3	40.5

Table 5. Comparison of the bidirectional feature propagation on PointPWC and FlowNet3D. Although the selected baselines showed strong performance, our proposed BFP still reduced the errors by large margins.

Model	FT3D EPE3D (m)	KITTI EPE3D (m)	Param size (M)
PointPWC	0.059	0.069	7.72M
PointPWC + BFP	**0.051**	**0.059**	7.98M
FlowNet3D	0.157	0.173	1.23M
Deeper FlowNet3D	0.160	0.197	1.33M
FlowNet3D + BFP	**0.138**	**0.118**	1.33M

the total operation count by 44% and accelerates the inference by 33% while maintaining the accuracy, compared with the original model.

Ablation of Our Contribution to FlowNet3D and PointPWC. We validate the contribution of the proposed bidirectional learning method by applying the BFP module into other state-of-the-art methods, FlowNet3D [21] and Point-PWC [46]. We built two models by directly inserting BFPs before their flow correlation modules. Since adding BFP requires additional parameters, we also implemented a deeper FlowNet3D network with an equivalent amount of parameters as the model with BFP. Please note that, the experiments related to FlowNet3D were evaluated on the occluded datasets while the PointPWC-based experiments

Table 6. Runtime comparison. The results are evaluated on a single TITAN RTX GPU.

Method	PointPWC [46]	FLOT [30]	FlowStep3D [16]	Ours
Runtime (ms)	51.3	289.6	820.8	40.5

were tested on the non-occluded datasets. Table 5 indicates that the proposed BFP achieves the excellent efficiency and effectiveness. With 0.2M (only 3% of total) additional parameters to the PointPWC, the performance is improved with a 13% error reduction. Moreover, the combination of FlowNet3D and BFP significantly reduce the generalization error by 31%. Furthermore, the ablation of the deeper FlowNet3D reveals the improved performance is owing to the bidirectional strategy rather than an effect of increased number of parameters.

5.6 Runtime

We compare the running time of our proposed methods to that of other state-of-the-art approaches in Table 6. We measured the runtimes of all methods on a single NVIDIA TITAN RTX GPU. The model ran in 40.5 ms, which is faster than the coarse-to-fine PointPWC [46] due to the use of the BFE decomposition. Moreover, compared with other recent advanced approaches [16, 30], our methods outperformed by a large margin in terms of running time while achieving superior accuracy and generality.

6 Conclusion

We presented Bi-PointFlowNet for accurate and fast scene flow estimation. Our proposed network leverages a novel bidirectional flow embedding module that worked with hierarchical feature extraction and propagation to accurately estimate flow. For further accelerating inference, the proposed method applied the decomposed form of the bidirectional flow embedding layer that removes the redundant computations. Experimental results on two challenging datasets showed our network significantly outperformed previous state-of-the-art methods under both non-occluded and occluded conditions. The proposed models also demonstrated excellent time efficiency, allowing the models to be further applied to resource-limited devices, such as wearable devices, drones, IoT edge devices, etc.

Acknowledgement. This work was partly supported by the National Research Foundation (NRF) grants (2022R1F1A1074142, 2022R1A4A3032913) and Institute of Information and Communication Technology Planning & Evaluation (IITP) grants (IITP-2019-0-00421, IITP-2020-0-00821, IITP-2021-0-02052, IITP-2021-0-02068), funded by the MSIT (Ministry of Science and ICT) of Korea. Wencan Cheng was partly supported by the China Scholarship Council (CSC).

References

1. Baldi, P., Brunak, S., Frasconi, P., Soda, G., Pollastri, G.: Exploiting the past and the future in protein secondary structure prediction. Bioinformatics **15**(11), 937–946 (1999)
2. Besl, P.J., McKay, N.D.: Method for registration of 3-D shapes. In: Sensor Fusion IV: Control Paradigms and Data Structures, vol. 1611, pp. 586–606. International Society for Optics and Photonics (1992)
3. Čech, J., Sanchez-Riera, J., Horaud, R.: Scene flow estimation by growing correspondence seeds. In: CVPR 2011, pp. 3129–3136. IEEE (2011)
4. Chang, A.X., et al.: ShapeNet: an information-rich 3D model repository. arXiv preprint arXiv:1512.03012 (2015)
5. Chen, Y., Medioni, G.: Object modelling by registration of multiple range images. Image Vis. Comput. **10**(3), 145–155 (1992)
6. Devlin, J., Chang, M.W., Lee, K., Toutanova, K.: BERT: pre-training of deep bidirectional transformers for language understanding. arXiv preprint arXiv:1810.04805 (2018)
7. Dosovitskiy, A., et al.: FlowNet: learning optical flow with convolutional networks. In: Proceedings of the IEEE International Conference on Computer Vision, pp. 2758–2766 (2015)
8. Graves, A., Schmidhuber, J.: Framewise phoneme classification with bidirectional LSTM and other neural network architectures. Neural Netw. **18**(5–6), 602–610 (2005)
9. Gu, X., Wang, Y., Wu, C., Lee, Y.J., Wang, P.: HPLFlowNet: hierarchical permutohedral lattice FlowNet for scene flow estimation on large-scale point clouds. In: Proceedings of the IEEE/CVF Conference on Computer Vision and Pattern Recognition, pp. 3254–3263 (2019)
10. Huguet, F., Devernay, F.: A variational method for scene flow estimation from stereo sequences. In: 2007 IEEE 11th International Conference on Computer Vision, pp. 1–7. IEEE (2007)
11. Hur, J., Roth, S.: MirrorFlow: exploiting symmetries in joint optical flow and occlusion estimation. In: Proceedings of the IEEE International Conference on Computer Vision, pp. 312–321 (2017)
12. Hur, J., Roth, S.: Iterative residual refinement for joint optical flow and occlusion estimation. In: Proceedings of the IEEE/CVF Conference on Computer Vision and Pattern Recognition, pp. 5754–5763 (2019)
13. Jampani, V., Kiefel, M., Gehler, P.V.: Learning sparse high dimensional filters: image filtering, dense CRFs and bilateral neural networks. In: Proceedings of the IEEE Conference on Computer Vision and Pattern Recognition, pp. 4452–4461 (2016)
14. Janai, J., Güney, F., Ranjan, A., Black, M., Geiger, A.: Unsupervised learning of multi-frame optical flow with occlusions. In: Ferrari, V., Hebert, M., Sminchisescu, C., Weiss, Y. (eds.) ECCV 2018. LNCS, vol. 11220, pp. 713–731. Springer, Cham (2018). https://doi.org/10.1007/978-3-030-01270-0_42
15. Kingma, D.P., Ba, J.: Adam: a method for stochastic optimization. arXiv preprint arXiv:1412.6980 (2014)
16. Kittenplon, Y., Eldar, Y.C., Raviv, D.: FlowStep3D: model unrolling for self-supervised scene flow estimation. In: Proceedings of the IEEE/CVF Conference on Computer Vision and Pattern Recognition, pp. 4114–4123 (2021)

17. Lan, Z., Chen, M., Goodman, S., Gimpel, K., Sharma, P., Soricut, R.: ALBERT: A lite BERT for self-supervised learning of language representations. arXiv preprint arXiv:1909.11942 (2019)
18. Lee, J., et al.: BioBERT: a pre-trained biomedical language representation model for biomedical text mining. Bioinformatics 36(4), 1234–1240 (2020)
19. Li, R., Lin, G., He, T., Liu, F., Shen, C.: HCRF-flow: scene flow from point clouds with continuous high-order CRFs and position-aware flow embedding. In: Proceedings of the IEEE/CVF Conference on Computer Vision and Pattern Recognition, pp. 364–373 (2021)
20. Liu, P., Lyu, M., King, I., Xu, J.: SelFlow: self-supervised learning of optical flow. In: Proceedings of the IEEE/CVF Conference on Computer Vision and Pattern Recognition, pp. 4571–4580 (2019)
21. Liu, X., Qi, C.R., Guibas, L.J.: FlowNet3D: learning scene flow in 3D point clouds. In: Proceedings of the IEEE/CVF Conference on Computer Vision and Pattern Recognition, pp. 529–537 (2019)
22. Liu, Y., et al.: RoBERTa: a robustly optimized BERT pretraining approach. arXiv preprint arXiv:1907.11692 (2019)
23. Mayer, N., et al.: A large dataset to train convolutional networks for disparity, optical flow, and scene flow estimation. In: Proceedings of the IEEE Conference on Computer Vision and Pattern Recognition, pp. 4040–4048 (2016)
24. Melamud, O., Goldberger, J., Dagan, I.: context2vec: learning generic context embedding with bidirectional LSTM. In: Proceedings of the 20th SIGNLL Conference on Computational Natural Language Learning, pp. 51–61 (2016)
25. Menze, M., Geiger, A.: Object scene flow for autonomous vehicles. In: Proceedings of the IEEE Conference on Computer Vision and Pattern Recognition, pp. 3061–3070 (2015)
26. Menze, M., Heipke, C., Geiger, A.: Object scene flow. ISPRS J. Photogramm. Remote Sens. 140, 60–76 (2018)
27. Ouyang, B., Raviv, D.: Occlusion guided scene flow estimation on 3D point clouds. In: Proceedings of the IEEE/CVF Conference on Computer Vision and Pattern Recognition, pp. 2805–2814 (2021)
28. Peters, M.E., et al.: Deep contextualized word representations. arXiv preprint arXiv:1802.05365 (2018)
29. Pons, J.P., Keriven, R., Faugeras, O.: Multi-view stereo reconstruction and scene flow estimation with a global image-based matching score. Int. J. Comput. Vis. 72(2), 179–193 (2007)
30. Puy, G., Boulch, A., Marlet, R.: FLOT: scene flow on point clouds guided by optimal transport. In: Vedaldi, A., Bischof, H., Brox, T., Frahm, J.-M. (eds.) ECCV 2020. LNCS, vol. 12373, pp. 527–544. Springer, Cham (2020). https://doi.org/10.1007/978-3-030-58604-1_32
31. Qi, C.R., Su, H., Mo, K., Guibas, L.J.: PointNet: deep learning on point sets for 3D classification and segmentation. In: Proceedings of the IEEE Conference on Computer Vision and Pattern Recognition, pp. 652–660 (2017)
32. Qi, C.R., Yi, L., Su, H., Guibas, L.J.: PointNet++: deep hierarchical feature learning on point sets in a metric space. arXiv preprint arXiv:1706.02413 (2017)
33. Schuster, M., Paliwal, K.K.: Bidirectional recurrent neural networks. IEEE Trans. Signal Process. 45(11), 2673–2681 (1997)
34. Su, H., et al.: SPLATNet: sparse lattice networks for point cloud processing. In: Proceedings of the IEEE Conference on Computer Vision and Pattern Recognition, pp. 2530–2539 (2018)

35. Tam, G.K., et al.: Registration of 3D point clouds and meshes: a survey from rigid to nonrigid. IEEE Trans. Visual. Comput. Graph. **19**(7), 1199–1217 (2012)
36. Teed, Z., Deng, J.: RAFT-3D: scene flow using rigid-motion embeddings. In: Proceedings of the IEEE/CVF Conference on Computer Vision and Pattern Recognition, pp. 8375–8384 (2021)
37. Tishchenko, I., Lombardi, S., Oswald, M.R., Pollefeys, M.: Self-supervised learning of non-rigid residual flow and ego-motion. In: 2020 International Conference on 3D Vision (3DV), pp. 150–159. IEEE (2020)
38. Valgaerts, L., Bruhn, A., Zimmer, H., Weickert, J., Stoll, C., Theobalt, C.: Joint estimation of motion, structure and geometry from stereo sequences. In: Daniilidis, K., Maragos, P., Paragios, N. (eds.) ECCV 2010. LNCS, vol. 6314, pp. 568–581. Springer, Heidelberg (2010). https://doi.org/10.1007/978-3-642-15561-1_41
39. Vedula, S., Baker, S., Rander, P., Collins, R., Kanade, T.: Three-dimensional scene flow. In: Proceedings of the Seventh IEEE International Conference on Computer Vision, vol. 2, pp. 722–729. IEEE (1999)
40. Vogel, C., Schindler, K., Roth, S.: Piecewise rigid scene flow. In: Proceedings of the IEEE International Conference on Computer Vision, pp. 1377–1384 (2013)
41. Wang, G., Hu, Y., Wu, X., Wang, H.: Residual 3D scene flow learning with context-aware feature extraction. arXiv preprint arXiv:2109.04685 (2021)
42. Wang, G., Wu, X., Liu, Z., Wang, H.: Hierarchical attention learning of scene flow in 3D point clouds. IEEE Trans. Image Process. **30**, 5168–5181 (2021)
43. Wang, Y., Yang, Y., Yang, Z., Zhao, L., Wang, P., Xu, W.: Occlusion aware unsupervised learning of optical flow. In: Proceedings of the IEEE Conference on Computer Vision and Pattern Recognition, pp. 4884–4893 (2018)
44. Wedel, A., Rabe, C., Vaudrey, T., Brox, T., Franke, U., Cremers, D.: Efficient dense scene flow from sparse or dense stereo data. In: Forsyth, D., Torr, P., Zisserman, A. (eds.) ECCV 2008. LNCS, vol. 5302, pp. 739–751. Springer, Heidelberg (2008). https://doi.org/10.1007/978-3-540-88682-2_56
45. Wu, W., Qi, Z., Fuxin, L.: PointConv: deep convolutional networks on 3D point clouds. In: Proceedings of the IEEE/CVF Conference on Computer Vision and Pattern Recognition, pp. 9621–9630 (2019)
46. Wu, W., Wang, Z.Y., Li, Z., Liu, W., Fuxin, L.: PointPWC-Net: cost volume on point clouds for (self-)supervised scene flow estimation. In: Vedaldi, A., Bischof, H., Brox, T., Frahm, J.-M. (eds.) ECCV 2020. LNCS, vol. 12350, pp. 88–107. Springer, Cham (2020). https://doi.org/10.1007/978-3-030-58558-7_6
47. Wu, X., Lv, S., Zang, L., Han, J., Hu, S.: Conditional BERT contextual augmentation. In: Rodrigues, J.M.F., Cardoso, P.J.S., Monteiro, J., Lam, R., Krzhizhanovskaya, V.V., Lees, M.H., Dongarra, J.J., Sloot, P.M.A. (eds.) ICCS 2019. LNCS, vol. 11539, pp. 84–95. Springer, Cham (2019). https://doi.org/10.1007/978-3-030-22747-0_7
48. Yang, W., Zhang, H., Lin, J.: Simple applications of BERT for ad hoc document retrieval. arXiv preprint arXiv:1903.10972 (2019)
49. Zhou, P., et al.: Attention-based bidirectional long short-term memory networks for relation classification. In: Proceedings of the 54th Annual Meeting of the Association for Computational Linguistics (Volume 2: Short Papers), pp. 207–212 (2016)

3DG-STFM: 3D Geometric Guided Student-Teacher Feature Matching

Runyu Mao[1], Chen Bai[2], Yatong An[2], Fengqing Zhu[1], and Cheng Lu[2(✉)]

[1] Purdue University, West Lafayette, USA
`mao111@purdue.edu`
[2] XPeng Motors, Guangzhou, China
{`chenbai,yatongan,luc`}`@xiaopeng.com`

Abstract. We tackle the essential task of finding dense visual correspondences between a pair of images. This is a challenging problem due to various factors such as poor texture, repetitive patterns, illumination variation, and motion blur in practical scenarios. In contrast to methods that use dense correspondence ground-truths as direct supervision for local feature matching training, we train 3DG-STFM: a multi-modal matching model (Teacher) to enforce the depth consistency under 3D dense correspondence supervision and transfer the knowledge to 2D unimodal matching model (Student). Both teacher and student models consist of two transformer-based matching modules that obtain dense correspondences in a coarse-to-fine manner. The teacher model guides the student model to learn RGB-induced depth information for the matching purpose on both coarse and fine branches. We also evaluate 3DG-STFM on a model compression task. To the best of our knowledge, 3DG-STFM is the first student-teacher learning method for the local feature matching task. The experiments show that our method outperforms state-of-the-art methods on indoor and outdoor camera pose estimations, and homography estimation problems. Code is available at: https://github.com/Ryan-prime/3DG-STFM.

1 Introduction

Establishing correspondences between overlapped images is critical for many computer vision tasks including structure from motion (SfM), simultaneous localization and mapping (SLAM), visual localization, etc. Most existing methods that tackle this problem follow the classical tri-stage pipeline, i.e., feature detection [27,36], feature description [3,11,12,22,27,48], and feature matching [27,33,39]. To improve efficiency, HLoc [38] was proposed to incorporate these matching techniques for visual localization. Several recent works [23,33,34,42] attempted to avoid the detection step and established a dense matching by considering all points from a regular grid. These dense matching approaches aim to

---

Supplementary Information The online version contains supplementary material available at https://doi.org/10.1007/978-3-031-19815-1_8.

© The Author(s), under exclusive license to Springer Nature Switzerland AG 2022
S. Avidan et al. (Eds.): ECCV 2022, LNCS 13688, pp. 125–142, 2022.
https://doi.org/10.1007/978-3-031-19815-1_8

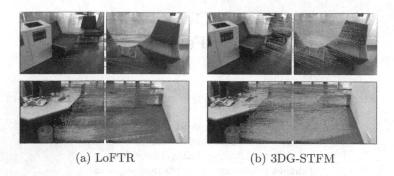

(a) LoFTR   (b) 3DG-STFM

Fig. 1. Comparison between dense local feature matching method LoFTR [42] and the proposed method 3DG-STFM. This example demonstrates that our approach, embedded the depth distribution via student-teacher learning, could find the correct correspondences under challenging scenario with repetitive patterns and low-texture regions. The red color indicates epipolar error beyond 5×10^{-4} (in the normalized image coordinates). (Color figure online)

supply interest points in low-texture regions and provide sufficient candidates for the matching purpose.

To generate dense ground-truth correspondences as supervision, depth maps, camera intrinsic and extrinsic matrices are used for the calculation of point reprojections from one image to the other [23,39,42]. Although photometric objective, widely used in optical flow estimation [20,30,31], could provide dense correspondences, its constant brightness assumption is not allowed to be generalized for the geometric matching problem. One typical adversarial scenario is image pairs taken under radically different illumination. On the other hand, given a set of images with dense correspondences, triangulation could easily reconstruct the 3D scene and depth maps. Therefore, depth information is implicitly provided by dense correspondence supervision.

However, to the best of our knowledge, none of the existing methods explored the depth modality distribution during the training phase. Depth maps, unlike RGB images, provide 3D information, which depicts the geometry distribution in an explicit manner. We argue that the introduction of depth modality distribution can provide two-fold benefits. First, depth information, even if in lower quality or sparse, can remove lots of ambiguity in 2D image space and enforce geometric consistency for feature matching, which is very difficult using only RGB inputs. That is particularly true when there are multiple similar objects within the image pair. In that case, most of existing methods tend to find implausible matching candidates since they purely discriminate 2D descriptors without depth or size knowledge. An example is shown in the first row of Fig. 1, where the baseline method is confused by the similar 2D appearance and incorrectly matches the closer chair to the further one. Second, as the example shown in the second row of Fig. 1, low texture area of single object haunts 2D descriptor in terms of enforcing dense and consistent matching. That deficiency can also be nicely regularized by leveraging the discrimination of depth modality.

Despite the advantage of depth information, high quality RGB-D inputs can only be collected in well-controlled lab environment, and very few, especially low cost devices can capture similar well aligned RGB-D pairs in real world scenarios. Most imaging systems are only equipped with RGB sensors as input and cannot afford high computational cost stemmed from multi-modal inference. That makes naive multi-modal fusion of RGB and depth inputs during both inference and training a restrictive solution. Consequently, a good way of transferring expensive RGB-D knowledge into RGB modality inference is needed in practical scenarios, considering constraints from both hardware and computational load.

Motivated by these observations, we propose 3DG-STFM, a student-teacher learning framework, to transfer depth knowledge learned by a multi-modal teacher model to a unimodal student model to improve the local feature matching. To the best of our knowledge, 3DG-STFM is the first student-teacher learning architecture to transfer cross-modal knowledge on the image matching problem. The method aims to find the depth and RGB correlational distribution in RGB-D images and transfer the knowledge to the RGB student branch by maintaining such distribution. Therefore, depth modality is not explicitly required in the actual inference process (student branch).

We propose attention mechanisms to guide the student model to study the teacher model's matching distribution and learning priority. Therefore, with RGB images as input, the student unimodal model could explore RGB-induced depth information and learn multi-modal matching strategies. The main contributions of this paper are summarized as follows:

- We propose the first student-teacher learning architecture on the local feature matching problem that learns the induced depth distribution distilled from dense RGB-D correspondence supervision.
- We propose attentive knowledge transfer strategies to help the student model understand the matching distribution and learning priority during the training instead of learning point-to-point matching.
- We show that the proposed model produces high-quality dense correspondences on a range of matching tasks and achieves state-of-the-art results on both camera pose and homography estimation tasks.

2   Related Work

2.1   Learning-Based Dense Local Feature Matching

In the past decades, many groups made great efforts to improve the local feature matching pipeline, i.e., feature detection, feature description and feature matching, and achieved promising performance by leveraging learning-based techniques. DeTone et al. proposed Superpoint [12], a self-supervised learnable interest point detector and descriptor. ViewSynth [29] designed a depth map keypoint detection method without using RGB domain information. Instead of learning better task-agnostic local features, SuperGlue [39] built a densely connected graph between two sets of keypoints by leveraging a Graph Neural Network (GNN). Geometric correlation of the keypoints and their visual features are integrated and exchanged within the GNN using the self and cross attention mechanism. However, those detector-based local feature matching algorithms only produced sparse keypoints, especially in low-texture regions.

To address the above problem, detector-free methods [21,23,34,42] proposed pixel-wise dense matching methods. [9] and [40] used contrastive loss to learn dense feature descriptors and were followed by the nearest neighbor search for the matching purpose. NCNet [33] proposed an end-to-end approach by directly learning the dense correspondences. It enumerated all possible matches between two images and constructed a 4D correlation tensor map. The 4D neighborhood consensus networks learned to identify reliable matching pairs and filtered out unreliable matches accordingly. Based on this concept, Sparse NCNet [34] improved NCNet's efficiency and performance by processing the 4D correlation map with submanifold sparse convolutions [16]. And DRC-Net [23] proposed a coarse-to-fine approach to generate higher accuracy dense correspondences. Recently, LoFTR [42] was proposed to learn global consensus between image correspondences by leveraging Transformers. Inspired by [39], the attention mechanism was used to learn the mutual relationship among features. For memory efficiency, the coarse matching features were first predicted and then fed to a small transformer to produce the final fine-level matches. Benefiting from the global receptive field of Transformers, LoFTR improved the matching performance by a large margin. All above mentioned dense local feature matching approaches needed dense ground-truth correspondences as supervision. None of the dense matching methods has explored any modality beyond 2D image space in which the feature ambiguities often exist due to the missing information in depth.

2.2   Student-Teacher Learning

Student-teacher learning has been actively studied in knowledge transfer context including model compression [1,18], acceleration [8,51], and cross-modal knowledge transfer [15,17]. Given a well-trained teacher model with large weight, the goal of the student-teacher learning is to distill and compress the knowledge from the teacher, and guides the lightweight student model for better performance. On the other hand, data with multiple modalities commonly provides more valuable supervisions than single modality data and could benefit model performance. However, due to the lack of data or labels for some modalities during training or testing, it is important to transfer knowledge between different modalities.

Due to different network architectures, many different knowledge transfer approaches have been proposed. The most popular response-based knowledge for image classification was Knowledge Distillation (KD) loss proposed by [18]. In this method, KD loss employed the distribution of neural response of the last output layer, logits layer, of the teacher model and guided the student to learn the distribution. Besides the output, the intermediate layer's feature representation was also used to train the student model [35]. Zagoruyko et al. [52] proposed a method to transfer the attention instead of the feature representations to achieve a better distillation performance. And NST [19] provided a method to learn a similar activation of the neurons. Moreover, there are many other related approaches [6,26,43,45,47,49]. However, none of them provided a knowledge

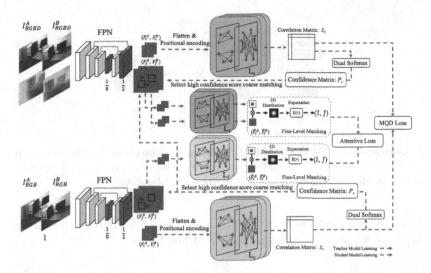

Fig. 2. Overview of 3DG-STFM. For each of student or teacher branch, Feature Pyramid Networks (FPN) [25] are used to extract coarse-level local features (F_c^A, F_c^B) and fine-level features (F_f^A, F_f^B) with $\frac{1}{8}$ and $\frac{1}{2}$ of the original image resolution. The coarse level transformer consisting of L_c attention layers finds coarse pairs and their matching scores. Matches with high confidence scores will be selected and mapped to a fine-level feature map. Surrounding features on F_f^A, F_f^B are collected by the $w \times w$ size window and fed to a fine-level transformer with L_f attention layers. The fine-level matching module is applied to predict correspondences $(\hat{i}, \hat{j})$ on subpixel-level. The teacher model is first trained under direct supervision. During student training, it will be frozen and provide additional supervision via attentive loss and Mutual Query Divergence (MQD) loss.

transfer solution for correspondence matching problems, which need to consider all mutual relationships among local features of different images.

3   Method

Our proposed system, 3DG-STFM, is to train a unimodal local feature matching model (Student) by leveraging the knowledge from a well-trained multi-modal model (Teacher). As shown in Fig. 2, the RGBD image pairs (I_{RGBD}^A, I_{RGBD}^B) and RGB image pairs (I_{RGB}^A, I_{RGB}^B) are fed to teacher and student branches separately. The labels of dense correspondences provide direct supervision during the teacher or student training. Once we reach a well-trained multi-modal teacher model, two strategies are proposed for cross-modal knowledge transfer: (1) Using the Mutual Query Divergence (MQD) loss guides the student model to learn the coarse-level matching distributions embedded in the teacher model's correlation matrix S_c. (2) Using the attentive loss guides the student at the fine-level module to pay more attention to the teacher's confident predictions and learn the matching distribution with priority.

Our method is based on the matching strategies mentioned in LoFTR [42] due to their high performances. In this section, we will first introduce the

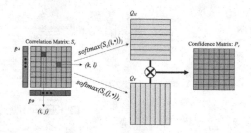

Fig. 3. Coarse-level differentiable matching mechanism. Transformer outputs are correlated to generate correlation matrix S_c. Dual-softmax [33,44] operation is applied on two dimensions to obtain the matching probability.

transformer-based model in Sect. 3.1. Section 3.2 and 3.3 will describe our knowledge transfer strategies over both coarse and fine levels.

3.1 Transformer-Based Local Feature Matching

As shown in Fig. 2, two transformer-based matching modules, inspired by [42], are adopted in both teacher and student branches of our 3DG-STFM system.

Coarse-Level Matching. Given the coarse-level feature map in dimension $h \times w \times c$, we flatten them into $hw \times c$ and do the positional encoding [5]. The encoded local feature vector will be fed to a coarse-level matching transformer. Unlike classical vision transformer [5,13,46] focusing on self-attention, the matching transformer adds a cross-attention layer to consider the relations between pixels from different images. We interleave the self-attention and cross-attention layers in matching transformer modules by L_c times. As shown in Fig. 3, the output of the coarse matching transformer $\{\hat{F}^A, \hat{F}^B\}$ corresponding to two different images $\{I^A, I^B\}$ will be used to calculate correlation matrix S_c by $S_c(i,j) = Corr(\hat{F}_i^A, \hat{F}_j^B)$, in which $\hat{F}_i^A$ and $\hat{F}_j^B$ indicate local feature at position i of I^A and local feature at position j of I^B. The dual-softmax [33,44], two softmax operations with temperature $\tau = 0.1$ in horizontal and vertical directions, is applied on the correlation matrix to calculate forward and backword matching probability: $P_{A \to B}(i,j) = softmax(\frac{1}{\tau} S_c(i, \cdot))_j$ and $P_{A \leftarrow B}(i,j) = softmax(\frac{1}{\tau} S_c(\cdot, j))_i$. The confidence matrix P_c with the final matching probabilities has same dimension as S_c and is calculated by: $P_c(i,j) = P_{A \to B}(i,j) \cdot P_{A \leftarrow B}(i,j)$. We call the output of horizontal and vertical softmax as query matrix $\{Q_H, Q_V\}$ since they depict query results of each feature from one image to another and vice versa. Given the ground-truth matrix derived from correspondence labels, we calculate the cross-entropy loss:

$$\mathcal{L}_c = -\frac{1}{|\mathcal{M}_{gt}|} \sum_{(i,j) \in \mathcal{M}_c^{gt}} FL(P_c(i,j)) \log P_c(i,j) \tag{1}$$

$$FL(p) = \alpha(1 - \hat{p})^\gamma, \hat{p} = \begin{cases} p & \text{if y=1} \\ 1 - p & \text{otherwise} \end{cases} \tag{2}$$

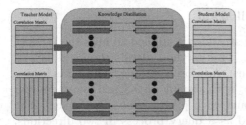 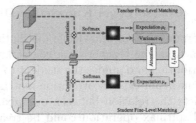

(a) Coarse-level knowledge transfer.　　(b) Fine-level attentive knowledge transfer

Fig. 4. Knowledge transfer on coarse-level and fine-level. (a) The correlation matrix is decomposed into multiple independent distributions depicting mutual query processes for the student learning.(b) One center point of a fine-level feature is selected and correlates with all points of the other feature map for heatmap distribution generation. Both expectation and variance of teacher branch's heatmap are used for fine-level knowledge transfer.

in which P_c is the confidence matrix and $\mathcal{M}_{gt}$ is the correspondence set generated by ground-truth labels. We follow [42] to set a focal loss term, FL with predicted probability p, to address the imbalance between matching and non-matching pairs.

Fine-Level Matching. Based on the confidence matrix P_c, matching pairs with probability scores higher than a threshold θ_c are selected and refined by a fine-level matching module. The selected coarse-level features are upsampled and concatenated to fine-level features cropped by $w \times w$ size windows before passing to the fine-level matching transformer.

The fine-level matching transformer is a lightweight transformer containing L_f attention layers. It aggregates the contextual information to generate features $\{\tilde{F}_f^A, \tilde{F}_f^B\}$ and passes them to a differentiable matching module. Instead of generating a confidence matrix, the fine-level matching module selects the center feature of $\tilde{F}_f^A$ and correlates with all features in $\tilde{F}_f^B$. The similarity distribution is generated and the expectation μ is treated as the prediction. The final loss based on direct supervision is calculated by:

$$\mathcal{L}_f = \frac{1}{|\mathcal{M}_f|} \sum_{(\hat{i},\hat{j}) \in \mathcal{M}_f} \frac{1}{\sigma^2(\hat{i})} ||\mu(\hat{i}) - \hat{j}_{gt}||_2^2 \tag{3}$$

where $\hat{j}_{gt}$ is the ground-truth position we wrap from image solution to fine-level heatmap scale. $\mu(\hat{i})$ is the prediction associated to coarse position $\hat{i}$ and $\sigma^2(\hat{i})$ is the total variance of heatmap distribution. $\mathcal{M}_f$ is the set of fine matches predicted by module. The total variance of the similarity distribution is treated as uncertainty to assign a weight to each fine-level match. The larger total variance indicates it is an uncertain prediction and associate with low weights.

3.2   Coarse-Level Knowledge Distillation

A response-based knowledge distillation strategy is applied to help the student learn from the teacher on a coarse level. This method distills the logits layer's distribution and guides the student to learn. As aforementioned, the logits layer's output in our case is correlation matrix S_c with size $hw \times hw$. Each row or column depicts the relation between one pixel and each pixel of the other image. The dual softmax operation could be treated as a query process in two directions. Local features at position $i \in F_c^A$ retrieve the closest feature from all positions $j \in F_c^B$ and vice versa. Many existing response-based knowledge [17,18] distillation methods treat the logits layer's output as a single distribution. However, as shown in Fig. 3, exploring the relationship between $S_c(i,j)$ and $S_c(k,l)$ in different row and column is meaningless for matching purpose. These uninterpretable relations could produce extra loss that confuses the knowledge transfer process.

Instead of learning a single distribution from the correlation matrix S_c in teacher, we split the distribution into two matching query matrices, as shown in Fig. 4a, to avoid the unpredictable correlations between them. Based on Knowledge Distillation (KD) loss [18], we propose Mutual Query Divergence loss $\mathcal{L}_{MQD}$ that employs all $2 \times hw$ mutual query distributions:

$$\mathcal{L}_{MQD} = \frac{1}{n}\Big(-\sum_{i=1}^{n} FL(p_S^{(i)})\hat{p}_S^{(i)} \log(\hat{p}_T^{(i)})\Big) \tag{4}$$

$$p_S^{(l)} = \frac{\exp(o_S^{(k)})}{\sum_{k=1}^{L} \exp(o_S^k)}, \hat{p}_S^{(l)} = \frac{\exp(\frac{o_S^{(k)}}{T})}{\sum_{k=1}^{L} \exp(\frac{o_S^k}{T})}, \hat{p}_T^{(l)} = \frac{\exp(\frac{o_T^{(k)}}{T})}{\sum_{k=1}^{L} \exp(\frac{o_T^k}{T})} \tag{5}$$

in which $\hat{p}_S^l$ and $\hat{p}_T^l$ are student and teacher's query distributions distilled from their logits layer's outputs o_S and o_T at temperature T. Additional focal loss weight FL (Eq. 2) is added to balance the matching/unmatching ground-truth pairs. p_S^l is the standard confidence score predicted by student model expressed in Eq. 5. The $\mathcal{L}_{MQD}$ on coarse level is the mean of KD loss of all n distribution, where n is equal to $2 \times hw$ in our case. Based on this loss, the coarse level matching module pays attention to the distributions benefit matching and ignores noisy information across distributions.

3.3   Fine-Level Attentive Knowledge Transfer

After transferring the coarse level matching knowledge from the teacher model with the mutual query distribution distillation, an attentive loss ($\mathcal{L}_{att}$) is proposed for the student's fine-level matching module. Instead of learning point-to-point matching under the supervision of ground-truth, $\mathcal{L}_{att}$ explores the matching distribution and learning priority of the teacher model.

As shown in Fig. 4b, the fine-level local feature matching is based on the differentiable matching approach that could produce a heatmap that represents the matching probability of each pixel in the neighborhood of j with i. By computing expectation μ over the probability distribution, we get the final position $\hat{j}$ with sub-pixel accuracy on I^B. The uncertainty of the prediction is also measured by the total variance of the correlation distribution. During the student-teacher learning process, both branches could generate heatmaps. We treat heatmaps of teacher model and student model as gaussian distributions $\mathcal{N}_t(\mu_t, \sigma_t^2)$ and $\mathcal{N}_s(\mu_s, \sigma_s^2)$. The Kullback-Leibler (KL) divergence loss ($\mathcal{L}_{KL}$) is applied to help the student learn the distribution from the teacher. The KL divergence of two gaussian distributions could be written as:

$$\mathcal{L}_{KL}(\mathcal{N}_s, \mathcal{N}_t) = \log(\frac{\sigma_t}{\sigma_s}) + \frac{\sigma_s^2 + (\mu_s - \mu_t)^2}{2\sigma_t^2} - \frac{1}{2} \tag{6}$$

Although total variance $\{\sigma_t, \sigma_s\}$, and $\sigma(\hat{i})$ (Eq. 3) are included in the loss, the optimizer would decrease loss by increase the total variance. To avoid the incorrect loss, the gradient is not backpropagated through σ_s, σ_t, and $\sigma(\hat{i})$. Therefore, we generate $\mathcal{L}_{att}$ by removing those constant variable of $\mathcal{L}_{KL}$:

$$\mathcal{L}_{att} = \frac{1}{|\mathcal{M}_f|} \sum_{(\hat{i}, \hat{j}) \in \mathcal{M}_f} \frac{(\mu_s^{(\hat{i})} - \mu_t^{(\hat{i})})^2}{2\sigma_t^{(\hat{i})2}} \tag{7}$$

where the $\mu_s^{(\hat{i})}$ and the $\mu_t^{(\hat{i})}$ are the expectations of student's and teacher's output distributions which corresponding to match $(\hat{i}, \hat{j})$ in fine-level correspondence set $\mathcal{M}_f$. Therefore, the total loss is a mean of the weighted sum of all the fine-level pairs' l_2 loss in matching set $\mathcal{M}_f$. We call this attentive loss since it could be treated as a l_2 distance loss that pays more attention to the prediction associated with large attention weight $\frac{1}{2\sigma_t^2}$. The total variance is commonly treated as a metric for certainty measure. The teacher prediction with a small total variance indicates the teacher is quite certain about the location of the correspondence. In this case, the loss is assigned with a large weight to guide the student model to learn those certain predictions from the teacher in priority.

3.4   Supervision

Both teacher and student training processes are under the direct supervision provided by correspondence ground-truths. The teacher model provides extra supervision during the student model training. For direct supervision, we follow the same procedure mentioned in [33,39,42] that uses the camera intrinsic, extrinsic matrices, and depth maps to compute the dense correspondences. To supervise coarse-level matching training, mutual nearest neighbors of the two sets of $\frac{1}{8}$-resolution grids are selected as ground-truth $\mathcal{M}_c^{gt}$. The pixel-level matching positions could be used for l_2 loss and supervise the fine-level matching learning. The final loss for the teacher and student model is:

$$\mathcal{L}_{teacher} = \lambda_0 \mathcal{L}_c + \lambda_1 \mathcal{L}_f \tag{8}$$

$$\mathcal{L}_{student} = \lambda_0 \mathcal{L}_c + \lambda_1 \mathcal{L}_f + \lambda_2 \mathcal{L}_{MQD} + \lambda_3 \mathcal{L}_{att} \tag{9}$$

in which $\mathcal{L}_c$ and $\mathcal{L}_f$ are coarse-level and fine-level loss under direct supervision described in Eq. 1 and Eq. 3. The student model is also guided by the teacher model via Mutual Query Divergence loss $\mathcal{L}_{MQD}$ and attentive loss $\mathcal{L}_{att}$ for the coarse and the fine level knowledge transfer.

3.5   Implementation Details

We train the indoor model of 3DG-STFM on the ScanNet [10] dataset and the outdoor model on the MegaDepth [24] dataset. The coarse-level transformer contains 4 attention layers, and the fine-level transformer has 1 attention layer. Each attention layer consists of a self-attention and a cross-attention layer with 8 heads. The focal loss parameters $\{\alpha, \gamma\}$ are set as $\{0.25, 2.0\}$. The confidence score threshold θ_c is set to 0.2 to remove unreliable correspondences. The window size w is 5. For indoor dataset ScanNet, the models are trained using AdamW with an initial learning rate of 6×10^{-3} on 32 2080Ti GPUs. All images are resized to 640×480. The weights of losses $\{\lambda_0, \lambda_1, \lambda_2, \lambda_3\}$ are set as $\{0.25, 0.25, 4.0, 0.25\}$. The outdoor models for Megadepth are trained using AdamW with an initial learning rate of 8×10^{-3} on 16 P100 GPUs. The weights of losses $\{\lambda_0, \lambda_1, \lambda_2, \lambda_3\}$ are set as $\{0.25, 0.25, 1.0, 0.25\}$. It is worth mentioning that our method is based on LoFTR [42], which provides two version implementations for the outdoor dataset in their official code. One is for 840×840 resolution image and consumes 24 GB RAM during the training. The other is training on 640×640 image pairs and feasible for 16 GB RAM GPUs. In this work, we treat the latter one as the baseline for the outdoor pose estimation and homography estimation tasks, and our 3DG-STFM is also trained on images resized to 640×640 with padding. We normalize depth maps in both ScanNet and Megadepth in the training process. The depth maps of ScanNet are in the range of 0 to 10 m. We normalize it to $[0, 1]$ and concatenate it to RGB images for multi-modal training. On the other hand, Megadepth's depth maps are relative estimations that come from COLMAP [41] reconstructions and have a pretty large range. We normalized them to $[0, 1]$ for each pair of images for teacher model training.

4   Experiments

4.1   Indoor Pose Estimation

Dataset. We use ScanNet [10], a large-scale indoor scene dataset composed of 1613 monocular sequences with depth maps and camera poses. This dataset is quite challenging due to extensive texture-less regions and repetitive patterns. Following the [39,42], we sample 230M image pairs with overlap scores between 0.4 and 0.8 for training and the student model is evaluated on the 1500 testing pairs. The images are resized to 640×480 to fit the depth map's dimension.

Evaluation Protocol. Following [42], we report the AUC of the pose error at thresholds $(5°, 10°, 20°)$. The pose error is defined as the maximum of angular error in rotation and translation. The predicted matches are used to solve the essential matrix with RANSAC.

Table 1. Evaluation on ScanNet [10] for indoor pose estimation. The AUC of the pose error in percentage is reported.

Category	Method	Pose estimation AUC		
		@5°	@10°	@20°
Multi-modal	3DG-STFM teacher	27.93	47.11	63.74
Detector-based	ORB [37]+GMS [4]	5.21	13.65	25.36
	D2-Net [14]+NN	5.25	14.53	27.96
	ContextDesc [28]+Ratio Test [27]	6.64	15.01	25.75
	SP [12]+NN	9.43	21.53	36.40
	SP [12]+PointCN [50]	11.40	25.47	41.41
	SP [12]+OANet [53]	11.76	26.90	43.85
	SP [12]+SGMNet [7]	15.40	32.06	48.32
	SP [12]+SuperGlue [39]	16.16	33.81	51.84
Detector free	LoFTR [42]	22.06	40.80	57.62
	3DG-STFM student	**23.58**	**43.60**	**61.17**

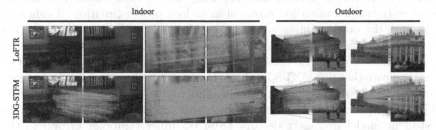

Fig. 5. Qualitative results. Our student model is compared to LoFTR [42] in indoor and outdoor scenes. Our method performs better in challenge scenarios with repetitive pattern and low texture region. The red color indicates epipolar error beyond 5×10^{-4} for indoor scenes and 1×10^{-4} for outdoor scenes (in the normalized image coordinates). More qualitative results in the supplementary. (Color figure online)

Results. Since the released DRC-Net is trained on MegaDepth and LoFTR is proved to have better performance, we only consider LoFTR as the state-of-the-art for comparison. The results in Table 1 show that our student model learns from the teacher model and outperforms all unimodal competitors. For detector free methods, our student model outperforms LoFTR by $\sim 3\%$ at AUC@10°.

For the visual comparison in Fig. 5, our student model shows denser and more reliable correspondences than LoFTR does, especially in regions with repetitive patterns. In addition, our model provides more robust correspondences in the low-texture region, which also benefits the pose estimation. On average, our student model detects **1192.84** inlier (epipolar error less than 5×10^{-4} in the normalized image coordinates) correspondences on each pair of indoor images, which is much higher than **887.04** inlier correspondences of LoFTR. Both numeric and qualitative results demonstrate the effectiveness of our student model that learns the RGB-induced depth distribution from the teacher model.

Table 2. Evaluation on MegaDepth [24] for outdoor pose estimation. The AUC of the pose error in percentage is reported.

Category	Method	Pose estimation AUC		
		@5°	@10°	@20°
Multi-modal	3DG-STFM teacher	53.43	69.81	81.79
Detector-based	SP [12]+SuperGlue [39]	42.18	61.16	75.96
Detector free	DRC-Net [23]	27.01	42.96	58.31
	LoFTR [42]	51.38	67.11	79.29
	3DG-STFM student	**52.58**	**68.46**	**80.04**

4.2 Outdoor Pose Estimation

Dataset. We use MegaDepth [24], a dataset consisting of 1M internet images of 196 different outdoor scenes, for outdoor pose estimation evaluation. We follow DISK [44] to select 1500 pairs for validation.

Results. We resize the images with the long side to 1200 during the inference and follow the same evaluation protocol as indoor pose estimation. As shown in Fig. 5, since the outdoor images contain less low texture regions and repetitive patterns, the unimodal model baseline (LoFTR) could also predict many correct correspondences for robust camera pose estimations. However, the results in Table 2 indicate that our 3DG-STFM teacher model achieves better performance by leveraging the relative depth. The student model learned from the teacher could also outperform LoFTR, the state-of-art unimodal competitor. We find our student model averagely detects **1864.63** inlier (epipolar error less than 1×10^{-4} in the normalized image coordinates) correspondences on each outdoor image pair, which is also higher than LoFTR's **1694.60** inlier detections.

4.3 Homography Estimation

We also evaluate our student model for homography estimation on HPatches dataset [2]. Following previous work [39,42], we select 108 image sequences under large illumination changes or significant viewpoint variations for evaluation. Every test image sequence contains one reference image and five pairing images.

Evaluation Protocol. We resize the original images with shorter dimensions equal to 480 and find the top 1K correspondences for each pair for detector free methods. Our 3DG-STFM student model is trained on Megadepth [24] mentioned in Sect. 4.2. All baseline results are reported using their original default implementation hyperparameters. Homography estimation is performed by the OpenCV RANSAC implementation. Following [12], we compute the reprojected mean error of the four corners of the image and report the area under the cumulative curve (AUC) up to three values: 3, 5, and 10 pixels in Table 3.

Results. Our 3DG-STFM student model is generalized well on the homography estimation task and achieves best performance compare with detector free

Table 3. Homography estimation on HPatches [2]. The AUC of the corner error in percentage is reported.

Category	Method	Homography est. AUC			#matches
		@3px	@5px	@10px	
Detector-based	D2Net [14]+NN	23.2	35.9	53.6	0.2k
	R2D2 [32]+NN	50.6	63.9	76.8	0.5k
	DISK [44]+NN	52.3	64.9	78.9	1.1k
	SP [12]+SuperGlue [39]	53.9	68.3	**81.7**	0.6k
Detector free	Sparse-NCNet [34]	48.9	54.2	67.1	1.0k
	DRC-Net [23]	50.6	56.2	68.3	1.0k
	LoFTR [42]	63.4	71.9	79.9	1.0k
	3DG-STFM	**64.7**	**73.1**	81.0	1.0k

Fig. 6. Visualization of matching distribution change for better understand student-teacher learning. The color of correspondence scatter is determined by the confidence score predictions of each model. The teacher model not only guide the student model to find more correspondences, but also teaches the confidence score distribution to the student model. (Color figure online)

methods as shown in Table 3. The method based on Superpoint [12] and Superglue [39] get better performance at AUC@10px than our approach. However, the 3DG-STFM student model shows more accurate performances under the other two strict metrics. We provide more details in the supplementary material.

4.4 Student-Teacher Learning Understanding

Visualizing Knowledge Transfer. To understand how our teacher model transfers knowledge to the student, we visualize the matching details to compare our student model and teacher model on ScanNet. We remove the teacher branch and training student branch solely based on direct supervision and treat it as the vanilla unimodal model for comparisons. Since we adopt the LoFTR's matching strategy, this vanilla unimodal model is the same as LoFTR. In Fig. 6, we plot all the predicted matches of models with a confidence score higher than 0.2. We show in the first row of Fig. 6 that both the teacher and student model find much more correspondences around low-texture regions than state-of-the-art. The teacher model explores the depth modality and then guides the student model to learn the RGB-induced depth information to increase the discriminant

Table 4. Ablation study.

Method	Pose estimation AUC		
	@5°	@10°	@20°
Multi-model teacher	18.41	36.53	54.07
Unimodal	14.78	31.47	48.44
Unimodal+MQD	16.46	33.62	51.70
Unimodal+MQD+Att	**17.05**	**34.77**	**52.26**

Table 5. Model compression study.

Method	L_c	L_f	Pose estimation AUC		
			@5°	@10°	@20°
Teacher Model	4	1	18.41	36.53	54.07
Full-Size Student Model	4	1	17.05	34.77	52.26
Full-Size Model	4	1	**14.78**	31.47	48.44
Slim Model	2	1	14.18	29.68	46.45
Slim Student Model	2	1	14.49	**31.76**	**49.51**

features in areas with low texture but depth variations. We also show that the student follows the teacher's confidence score pattern, while both have different patterns compared to LoFTR, shown in the second row of Fig. 6. The confidence scores are indicated by color, high in red, low in blue. This knowledge transfer is achieved by proposed MQD loss and attentive loss for coarse-level and fine-level matching for our student-teacher architecture.

Ablation Study. To better understand the contribution in each module, we randomly select 150 scenes from ScanNet as a mini version dataset and test different variants of our model. The test set is the same as the original ScanNet. As shown in Table 4, the teacher model achieves the best performance and is used to teach the two models, i.e., Unimodal+MQD and Unimodal+MQD+Att. The unimodal model is trained under direct supervision provided by dense correspondences labels based on Eq. 8. Compared with the unimodal model, both MQD and attentive loss help the knowledge transfer from teacher to student.

Model Compression Performance. Our architecture can also be generalized to model compression tasks. We implement the model compression experiments on the mini version of ScanNet. The results shown in Table 5 indicate our slim model has the competitive performance with the uncompressed model. In Table 5, the slim matching model is proposed with half attention layers on the coarse-level transformer L_c. The Slim Student Model is trained with our student-teacher architecture, while both the Full-Size Model and the Slim Model are trained under the direct supervision provided by ground-truth. By learning knowledge from the Teacher Model, the Slim Student Model improves 2% compared to the Slim Model and also shows better performance than the Full-Size Model at AUC@10° and @20°. More details are provided in the supplementary.

5   Conclusion

In this paper, we propose 3DG-STFM: a novel student-teacher learning framework for the dense local feature matching problem. Our proposed framework mines depth knowledge from one multi-modal teacher model to guide the student model to learn the hidden depth information embedded in the RGB domain. Two attentive mechanisms, i.e., MQD loss and attentive loss, are proposed to help the knowledge transfer. Our student model is evaluated on several image matching and camera pose estimation tasks on indoor and outdoor datasets and achieves state-of-the-art performances. Our 3DG-STFM also shows generalization ability on model compression tasks.

References

1. Ba, L.J., Caruana, R.: Do deep nets really need to be deep? arXiv preprint arXiv:1312.6184 (2013)
2. Balntas, V., Lenc, K., Vedaldi, A., Mikolajczyk, K.: HPatches: a benchmark and evaluation of handcrafted and learned local descriptors. In: Proceedings of the IEEE Conference on Computer Vision and Pattern Recognition, pp. 5173–5182 (2017)
3. Bay, H., Tuytelaars, T., Van Gool, L.: SURF: speeded up robust features. In: Leonardis, A., Bischof, H., Pinz, A. (eds.) ECCV 2006. LNCS, vol. 3951, pp. 404–417. Springer, Heidelberg (2006). https://doi.org/10.1007/11744023_32
4. Bian, J., Lin, W.Y., Matsushita, Y., Yeung, S.K., Nguyen, T.D., Cheng, M.M.: GMS: grid-based motion statistics for fast, ultra-robust feature correspondence. In: Proceedings of the IEEE Conference on Computer Vision and Pattern Recognition, pp. 4181–4190 (2017)
5. Carion, N., Massa, F., Synnaeve, G., Usunier, N., Kirillov, A., Zagoruyko, S.: End-to-end object detection with transformers. In: Vedaldi, A., Bischof, H., Brox, T., Frahm, J.-M. (eds.) ECCV 2020. LNCS, vol. 12346, pp. 213–229. Springer, Cham (2020). https://doi.org/10.1007/978-3-030-58452-8_13
6. Chen, H., et al.: Data-free learning of student networks. In: Proceedings of the IEEE/CVF International Conference on Computer Vision, pp. 3514–3522 (2019)
7. Chen, H., et al.: Learning to match features with seeded graph matching network. In: Proceedings of the IEEE/CVF International Conference on Computer Vision, pp. 6301–6310 (2021)
8. Chen, T., Goodfellow, I., Shlens, J.: Net2Net: accelerating learning via knowledge transfer. arXiv preprint arXiv:1511.05641 (2015)
9. Choy, C.B., Gwak, J., Savarese, S., Chandraker, M.: Universal correspondence network. In: Advances in Neural Information Processing Systems (2016)
10. Dai, A., Chang, A.X., Savva, M., Halber, M., Funkhouser, T., Nießner, M.: Scan-Net: richly-annotated 3D reconstructions of indoor scenes. In: Proceedings of the IEEE Conference on Computer Vision and Pattern Recognition, pp. 5828–5839 (2017)
11. DeTone, D., Malisiewicz, T., Rabinovich, A.: Toward geometric deep SLAM. arXiv preprint arXiv:1707.07410 (2017)
12. DeTone, D., Malisiewicz, T., Rabinovich, A.: SuperPoint: self-supervised interest point detection and description. In: Proceedings of the IEEE Conference on Computer Vision and Pattern Recognition Workshops, pp. 224–236 (2018)
13. Dosovitskiy, A., et al.: An image is worth 16×16 words: transformers for image recognition at scale. arXiv preprint arXiv:2010.11929 (2020)
14. Dusmanu, M., et al.: D2-Net: a trainable CNN for joint description and detection of local features. In: Proceedings of the IEEE/CVF Conference on Computer Vision and Pattern Recognition, pp. 8092–8101 (2019)
15. Garcia, N.C., Morerio, P., Murino, V.: Modality distillation with multiple stream networks for action recognition. In: Ferrari, V., Hebert, M., Sminchisescu, C., Weiss, Y. (eds.) ECCV 2018. LNCS, vol. 11212, pp. 106–121. Springer, Cham (2018). https://doi.org/10.1007/978-3-030-01237-3_7
16. Graham, B., Engelcke, M., Van Der Maaten, L.: 3D semantic segmentation with submanifold sparse convolutional networks. In: Proceedings of the IEEE Conference on Computer Vision and Pattern Recognition, pp. 9224–9232 (2018)

17. Gupta, S., Hoffman, J., Malik, J.: Cross modal distillation for supervision transfer, pp. 2827–2836 (2016)
18. Hinton, G., Vinyals, O., Dean, J.: Distilling the knowledge in a neural network. arXiv preprint arXiv:1503.02531 (2015)
19. Huang, Z., Wang, N.: Like what you like: knowledge distill via neuron selectivity transfer. arXiv preprint arXiv:1707.01219 (2017)
20. Yu, J.J., Harley, A.W., Derpanis, K.G.: Back to basics: unsupervised learning of optical flow via brightness constancy and motion smoothness. In: Hua, G., Jégou, H. (eds.) ECCV 2016. LNCS, vol. 9915, pp. 3–10. Springer, Cham (2016). https://doi.org/10.1007/978-3-319-49409-8_1
21. Jiang, W., Trulls, E., Hosang, J., Tagliasacchi, A., Yi, K.M.: COTR: correspondence transformer for matching across images. In: Proceedings of the IEEE/CVF International Conference on Computer Vision (ICCV), pp. 6207–6217, October 2021
22. Leutenegger, S., Chli, M., Siegwart, R.Y.: BRISK: binary robust invariant scalable keypoints. In: 2011 International Conference on Computer Vision, pp. 2548–2555 (2011)
23. Li, X., Han, K., Li, S., Prisacariu, V.: Dual-resolution correspondence networks. In: Advances in Neural Information Processing Systems 33 (2020)
24. Li, Z., Snavely, N.: MegaDepth: learning single-view depth prediction from internet photos. In: Proceedings of the IEEE Conference on Computer Vision and Pattern Recognition, pp. 2041–2050 (2018)
25. Lin, T.Y., Dollár, P., Girshick, R., He, K., Hariharan, B., Belongie, S.: Feature pyramid networks for object detection. In: Proceedings of the IEEE Conference on Computer Vision and Pattern Recognition, pp. 2117–2125 (2017)
26. Liu, Y., et al.: Knowledge distillation via instance relationship graph. In: Proceedings of the IEEE/CVF Conference on Computer Vision and Pattern Recognition, pp. 7096–7104 (2019)
27. Lowe, D.G.: Distinctive image features from scale-invariant keypoints. Int. J. Comput. Vis. **60**(2), 91–110 (2004)
28. Luo, Z., et al.: ContextDesc: local descriptor augmentation with cross-modality context. In: Proceedings of the IEEE/CVF Conference on Computer Vision and Pattern Recognition, pp. 2527–2536 (2019)
29. Mahmud, J., Singh, R.V., Akiva, P., Kundu, S., Peng, K., Frahm, J.: ViewSynth: learning local features from depth using view synthesis. In: 31st British Machine Vision Conference (2020)
30. Meister, S., Hur, J., Roth, S.: Unflow: unsupervised learning of optical flow with a bidirectional census loss. In: Thirty-Second AAAI Conference on Artificial Intelligence (2018)
31. Ren, Z., Yan, J., Ni, B., Liu, B., Yang, X., Zha, H.: Unsupervised deep learning for optical flow estimation. In: Thirty-First AAAI Conference on Artificial Intelligence (2017)
32. Revaud, J., De Souza, C., Humenberger, M., Weinzaepfel, P.: R2D2: reliable and repeatable detector and descriptor. In: Advances in Neural Information Processing Systems 32, pp. 12405–12415 (2019)
33. Rocco, I., Cimpoi, M., Arandjelović, R., Torii, A., Pajdla, T., Sivic, J.: Neighbourhood consensus networks. In: Proceedings of the 32nd Conference on Neural Information Processing Systems (2018)

34. Rocco, I., Arandjelović, R., Sivic, J.: Efficient neighbourhood consensus networks via submanifold sparse convolutions. In: Vedaldi, A., Bischof, H., Brox, T., Frahm, J.-M. (eds.) ECCV 2020. LNCS, vol. 12354, pp. 605–621. Springer, Cham (2020). https://doi.org/10.1007/978-3-030-58545-7_35
35. Romero, A., Ballas, N., Kahou, S.E., Chassang, A., Gatta, C., Bengio, Y.: FitNets: hints for thin deep nets. arXiv preprint arXiv:1412.6550 (2014)
36. Rosten, E., Drummond, T.: Machine learning for high-speed corner detection. In: Leonardis, A., Bischof, H., Pinz, A. (eds.) ECCV 2006. LNCS, vol. 3951, pp. 430–443. Springer, Heidelberg (2006). https://doi.org/10.1007/11744023_34
37. Rublee, E., Rabaud, V., Konolige, K., Bradski, G.: ORB: an efficient alternative to SIFT or SURF. In: 2011 International Conference on Computer Vision, pp. 2564–2571 (2011)
38. Sarlin, P.E., Cadena, C., Siegwart, R., Dymczyk, M.: From coarse to fine: robust hierarchical localization at large scale. In: Proceedings of the IEEE/CVF Conference on Computer Vision and Pattern Recognition, pp. 12716–12725 (2019)
39. Sarlin, P.E., DeTone, D., Malisiewicz, T., Rabinovich, A.: SuperGlue: learning feature matching with graph neural networks. In: Proceedings of the IEEE/CVF Conference on Computer Vision and Pattern Recognition, pp. 4938–4947 (2020)
40. Schmidt, T., Newcombe, R., Fox, D.: Self-supervised visual descriptor learning for dense correspondence. IEEE Robot. Autom. Lett. 2(2), 420–427 (2016)
41. Schönberger, J.L., Frahm, J.M.: Structure-from-motion revisited. In: Conference on Computer Vision and Pattern Recognition (CVPR) (2016)
42. Sun, J., Shen, Z., Wang, Y., Bao, H., Zhou, X.: LoFTR: detector-free local feature matching with transformers. In: Proceedings of the IEEE/CVF Conference on Computer Vision and Pattern Recognition, pp. 8922–8931 (2021)
43. Tarvainen, A., Valpola, H.: Weight-averaged consistency targets improve semi-supervised deep learning results. CORR abs/1703.01780. arXiv preprint arXiv:1703.01780 (2017)
44. Tyszkiewicz, M.J., Fua, P., Trulls, E.: DISK: learning local features with policy gradient. arXiv preprint arXiv:2006.13566 (2020)
45. Wang, H., Lian, D., Ge, Y.: Binarized collaborative filtering with distilling graph convolutional networks. arXiv preprint arXiv:1906.01829 (2019)
46. Wang, H., Zhu, Y., Green, B., Adam, H., Yuille, A., Chen, L.-C.: Axial-DeepLab: stand-alone axial-attention for panoptic segmentation. In: Vedaldi, A., Bischof, H., Brox, T., Frahm, J.-M. (eds.) ECCV 2020. LNCS, vol. 12349, pp. 108–126. Springer, Cham (2020). https://doi.org/10.1007/978-3-030-58548-8_7
47. Wang, Z., Deng, Z., Wang, S.: Accelerating convolutional neural networks with dominant convolutional kernel and knowledge pre-regression. In: Leibe, B., Matas, J., Sebe, N., Welling, M. (eds.) ECCV 2016. LNCS, vol. 9912, pp. 533–548. Springer, Cham (2016). https://doi.org/10.1007/978-3-319-46484-8_32
48. Yang, T.Y., Hsu, J.H., Lin, Y.Y., Chuang, Y.Y.: DeepCD: learning deep complementary descriptors for patch representations. In: Proceedings of the IEEE International Conference on Computer Vision, pp. 3314–3322 (2017)
49. Yang, Y., Qiu, J., Song, M., Tao, D., Wang, X.: Distilling knowledge from graph convolutional networks. In: Proceedings of the IEEE/CVF Conference on Computer Vision and Pattern Recognition, pp. 7074–7083 (2020)
50. Yi, K.M., Trulls, E., Ono, Y., Lepetit, V., Salzmann, M., Fua, P.: Learning to find good correspondences. In: Proceedings of the IEEE Conference on Computer Vision and Pattern Recognition, pp. 2666–2674 (2018)
51. Yim, J., Joo, D., Bae, J., Kim, J.: A gift from knowledge distillation: fast optimization, network minimization and transfer learning, pp. 4133–4141 (2017)

52. Zagoruyko, S., Komodakis, N.: Paying more attention to attention: improving the performance of convolutional neural networks via attention transfer. arXiv preprint arXiv:1612.03928 (2016)
53. Zhang, J., et al.: Learning two-view correspondences and geometry using order-aware network. In: Proceedings of the IEEE/CVF International Conference on Computer Vision, pp. 5845–5854 (2019)

Video Restoration Framework and Its Meta-adaptations to Data-Poor Conditions

Prashant W. Patil(✉)[ID], Sunil Gupta[ID], Santu Rana[ID],
and Svetha Venkatesh[ID]

A2I2, Deakin University, Geelong Waurn Ponds Campus, Geelong, VIC, Australia
prashant.patil@deakin.edu.au

Abstract. Restoration of weather degraded videos is a challenging problem due to diverse weather conditions e.g., rain, haze, snow, *etc.*. Existing works handle video restoration for each weather using a different custom-designed architecture. This approach has many limitations. First, a custom-designed architecture for each weather condition requires domain-specific knowledge. Second, disparate network architectures across weather conditions prevent easy knowledge transfer to novel weather conditions where we do not have a lot of data to train a model from scratch. For example, while there is a lot of common knowledge to exploit between the models of different weather conditions at day or night time, it is difficult to do such adaptation. To this end, we propose a generic architecture that is effective for any weather condition due to the ability to extract robust feature maps without any domain-specific knowledge. This is achieved by novel components: spatio-temporal feature modulation, multi-level feature aggregation, and recurrent guidance decoder. Next, we propose a meta-learning based adaptation of our deep architecture to the restoration of videos in data-poor conditions (night-time videos). We show comprehensive results on video de-hazing and de-raining datasets in addition to the meta-learning based adaptation results on night-time video restoration tasks. Our results clearly outperform the state-of-the-art weather degraded video restoration methods. The source code is available at: https://github.com/pwp1208/Meta_Video_Restoration.

Keywords: Spatio-temporal feature modulation · Meta-adaptation · Day and night-time video restoration

1 Introduction

Fog, snow, rain, and haze are different types of adverse weather conditions that often degrade the quality of images or videos recorded for computer vision applications such as video surveillance, traffic monitoring, and autonomous driving.

Supplementary Information The online version contains supplementary material available at https://doi.org/10.1007/978-3-031-19815-1_9.

© The Author(s), under exclusive license to Springer Nature Switzerland AG 2022
S. Avidan et al. (Eds.): ECCV 2022, LNCS 13688, pp. 143–160, 2022.
https://doi.org/10.1007/978-3-031-19815-1_9

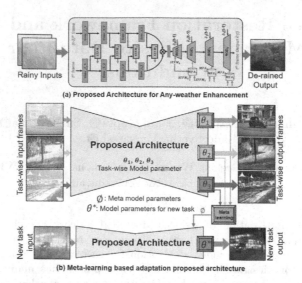

(a) Proposed Architecture for Any-weather Enhancement

(b) Meta-learning based adaptation proposed architecture

Fig. 1. (a) A generic architecture is provided for restoring any weather degraded video. This architecture outperforms the existing custom-designed architectures and lends itself to easy meta- learning based adaptations permitting sample-efficient learning for novel data-poor weather conditions. (b) A meta-learning (ϕ) adaptation from previous models (θ_1, θ_2, θ_3) to a new model (θ^*) for novel weather condition.

These applications routinely involve subtasks such as optical flow estimation [40], object detection [15], depth estimation [33], which use algorithms or models expecting clean data (image or video) as their input. The research on weather-degraded restoration is quite active [4,17,22,34,35]. Earlier works mainly focused on single image restoration. Most of them are focused on a weather while some of them [4,22] have also extended for multi-weather conditions, *i.e.* use the *same* architecture to train a model for a given weather condition. The extension to video restoration includes [9,19,43–45,49]. Many of these models have achieved remarkable success *e.g.,* video de-hazing [18,49], video de-raining [44,45] and video de-raining with veiling effect [41,43].

However, these methods for video restoration have a crucial limitation. They use different architectures for handling different weather conditions. Since a system usually needs to deal with multiple weather conditions, when working with models with disparate architectures, the design process becomes cumbersome. The models of different weather conditions have a great deal of similarity (*e.g.,* in the feature extraction step), which can be exploited to adapt these models to novel conditions that are data-poor using recent machine learning techniques such as few-shot learning [1], meta-learning [11], *etc.* However, this cannot be easily done unless we use the same architecture across different conditions. For example, if using the same architecture, we can use meta-learning to efficiently adapt a *day-time* video restoration model to *night-time* condition. Therefore, we need a generic architecture for video restoration that allows learning across multiple weather conditions and permits transfer to novel conditions.

For designing a single architecture that works across multi-weather video restoration, we need to extract robust feature maps. For this, we propose three modules: *spatio-temporal feature modulator* (STFM) to interlink features at multiple spatial and temporal scales, *multi-level feature aggregation* module for combining different STFM outputs, and *recurrent guidance decoder* to generate temporally consistent content. This proposed architecture does not require prior domain-specific knowledge and is agnostic to weather conditions. Further, our generic architecture is amenable to model adaptation through meta-learning [11]. We provide an efficient adaptation scheme wherein our architecture can be used in combination with the popular meta-learning algorithm-MAML [11].

In experiments, we first demonstrate that our generic architecture outperforms state-of-the-art (SOTA) for video de-hazing and de-raining tasks using REVIDE [49] and RainSynAll100 [42] datasets respectively. Next, we demonstrate how our model can be efficiently adapted to novel weather conditions. Particularly, we examine adaptation for night-time video restoration that has limited availability of weather degraded night-time videos. In this meta-learning setting, we first train the meta-model and task-wise models for day-time haze, rain, and rain with veiling effects removal tasks. We then show that our meta-model can be adapted to night-time haze, rain, and rain with veiling effects removal in a more sample-efficient manner than training from scratch or fine-tuning the day-time trained models with night-time data. Finally, we also make available a synthetic night-time weather degraded database for de-hazing, de-raining, and de-raining with veiling effects useful to the community given the lack of such datasets. Overview of proposed architecture for weather-degraded restoration and its meta-learning based adaptation for new weather condition is depicted in Fig. 1. Our major contributions are:

- A novel architecture is proposed for any-weather degraded video restoration based on spatio-temporal feature modulation with multi-level feature aggregation and recurrent guidance decoder.
- We propose a meta-learning based adaptation of this architecture for handling novel data-poor weather-degraded conditions.
- We first show comprehensive results on video de-hazing and de-raining datasets. We then show the meta-learning based adaptation results for night-time weather-degraded video restoration. We obtain superior performance for rain, haze, and rain with veiling effect removal for day and night conditions.

To the authors' best knowledge, this is the first video restoration contribution that uses the same architecture across weather conditions, and it is also the first meta-learning adaptation of video restoration models to new conditions. Our approach does not require domain-specific knowledge (*transmission map* [41], *future frames* [44]) during training, unlike the current SOTA approaches.

2   Literature Survey

Video De-raining Methods: The first study on video rain removal is done in [13], which utilizes the space-time correlation model to capture the dynamics of raindrops. In [24], a hybrid rain model and motion segmentation context information is integrated with a dynamic routing residue recurrent network for video rain removal. The discriminative prior knowledge-based video rain streak removal approach is proposed by Jiang *et al.* [17]. This approach captures inherent features related to rain streaks based on sparse coding in [20]. Chen *et al.* [5] proposed a novel content alignment and compensation approach for video rain removal. The sparse coding with a multi-scale approach is proposed in [20] to deliver the former characteristic of rain streaks. Any video-based application needs to capture temporal consistency effectively for superior performance. In [44], the temporal correlation and consistency among consecutive video frames are learnt for video rain streak removal. To impose the inter-frame consistency constraint, five successive video frames are used. They estimate the optical flow and warped with input frames. Further, the prediction network is proposed for video rain streak removal. Due to degraded input frames, optical flow may cause many problems. In [41], the robust self-aligned video de-raining approach with transmission depth consistency is proposed. Recently, Yue *et al.* [45] proposed semi-supervised video de-raining approach with dynamic rain generation process.

Video De-hazing Methods: Many algorithms are proposed for image dehazing with [8,36] and without [9,34] prior information. Dhara [8] *et al.* proposed weighted least squares filtering with adaptive air-light refinement and non-linear color balancing approach for image de-hazing. Zhang *et al.* [48] proposed illumination balancing approach for night-time image de-hazing. Further, maximum reflectance prior [47] and multiple light colors [23] based approaches are proposed for night-time dehazing. These approaches may perform poorly for video de-hazing task and may achieve better results by considering the temporal consistency. In 2018, the first attempt for video de-hazing with multi-frame multi-level fusion strategy was made by Li *et al.* [18]. Further, the transmission map-based video de-hazing module is proposed in [33]. Video de-hazing approaches received less attention as video de-hazing databases were not available. But, a real-world video de-hazing database has become recently available [49].

These existing works are able to handle single weather (haze or rain) efficiently through disparate architectures. Since a system usually needs to deal with multiple weather conditions, when working with models with disparate architectures, the design process becomes cumbersome. Also, using disparate architectures prevents easy adaptation to novel weather-degraded conditions.

Multi-weather Video Restoration Methods: Few researchers proposed multi-weather single image restoration approaches [22,46]. First attempt with a gated context aggregation network was proposed by Chen *et al.* [4] to restore the haze and rain-free image directly. In [22], rain, fog, snow, and adherent raindrops weather conditions are handled using multiple task-specific encoders with neural architectures. Despite excellent performance in multi-weather degraded image restoration, these methods may fail for video restoration due to a lack of temporal consistency. In this context, Yang *et al.* [42] proposed the first video de-raining approach by considering the veiling effect. The veiling effect is rain-streak accumulation in the line of sight. Similar to [44], the recurrent multi-frame de-raining with veiling effect approach is proposed in [43] with physics model and adversarial learning. To maintain the temporal consistency, they considered five consecutive frames including **future frames** to enhance the current frame with multi-stage process. Recently, Li *et al.* [19] proposed multi-frame based rain and snow removal approach.

Meta-learning Methods: Meta-learning aims to extract meta-knowledge from historical tasks to accelerate learning on new tasks by transferring previously learned knowledge. Meta-learning has been applied to many applications like video interpolation [6], object segmentation [2], action recognition [7] and object tracking [38]. In [6], authors considered the interpolation of a single video as one task. They analysed the effect of existing SOTA networks with scratch training, fine-tuning and meta-learning. Xinjian *et al.* [12] used meta-learning to transfer embeddings across rainy and clean images. In contrast, meta-learning in our architecture is used to adapt the day time (haze, rain and rain with veil) video restoration model to night-time conditions. However, none of these works have focused on multi-weather degradation restoration.

3   Proposed Video Restoration Framework

In this section, we describe the proposed architecture and its meta-learning adaptation to adapt the model for data-poor weather conditions.

3.1   Network Architecture

The overview of the proposed architecture for multi-weather video restoration is illustrated in Fig. 2 and 3 which comprises of three major components: (1) Spatio-temporal feature modulation (STFM), (2) Multi-level feature aggregation (MFA), and (3) Recurrent guided decoder (RGD).

Spatio-Temporal Feature Modulation: The efficient feature fusion of different time instances plays an important role in video processing applications. To effectively interlink the multi-frame features, we propose the STFM module. The STFM module effectively extracts the multi-frame features through scale and temporal modulations. As $(t-1)^{th}$ frame output is provided at decoder recurrently, the tth and $(t-2)^{th}$ frames are given to two different encoder paths as inputs. The feature maps of both the frames at each encoder level are given to STFM modules. In the STFM module, each of these feature maps (t^{th} and $(t-2)^{th}$ frames) are passed through multi-scale convolution block (convolution with filter size $1, 3, 5$). Further, these multi-scale feature maps are processed through scale modulation to interlink the information at different scales. The scale modulation helps the network to boost the feature maps by incorporating the feature maps from multi-scales. Scale modulation (SM) is defined as:

$$SM_{a,b} = \alpha \left[f_{Sc\_a} \copyright f_{Sc\_b} \right] + \beta; \quad a \neq b \tag{1}$$

where, f_{Sc_a}, f_{Sc_b} are outcomes of multi-scale convolution block ($a, b \in (1, 3, 5)$), $\alpha = \gamma[\mathbb{C}^3\{ \underset{c \in (1,C)}{\text{avg}} (f_{Sc\_a}, f_{Sc\_b})\}]$, $\beta = \gamma[\mathbb{C}^3\{f_{Sc\_a} \copyright f_{Sc\_b}\}]$, γ is global average

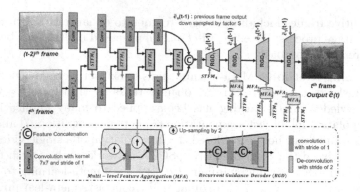

Fig. 2. Proposed architecture for weather-degraded video restoration (*STFM: spatio-temporal feature modulation*).

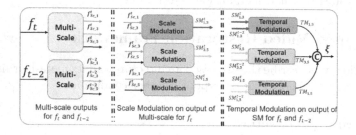

Fig. 3. Proposed spatio-temporal feature modulation (STFM).

pooling, © is concatenation, C is total number of channels and $\mathbb{C}^3$ is convolution with kernel 3×3 (see Fig. 3). As video-based frameworks need to deal with multi-frame information correlation, the scale modulated feature maps are temporally modulated. Temporal features of tth and $(t-2)^{th}$ frames are modulated as:

$$TM_{a,b} = \alpha \left[SM_{a,b}^t © SM_{a,b}^{t-2} \right] + \beta; \quad a \neq b \tag{2}$$

where, $\alpha = \gamma[\mathbb{C}^3\{ \underset{c \in (1,C)}{\text{avg}} (SM_{a,b}^t, SM_{a,b}^{t-2})\}]$, and $\beta = \gamma[\mathbb{C}^3\{SM_{a,b}^t © SM_{a,b}^{t-2}\}]$. This process helps to learn the inter-frame information. Here, the α and β in both SM and TM are mainly proposed for scaling and shifting (modulation) of the multi-scale feature maps and the feature maps of different time instance respectively. Finally, three temporally modulated features ($TM_{1,3}, TM_{3,5}, TM_{1,5}$) are merged and considered as the output (ξ) of STFM module.

Multi-level Feature Aggregation: The proposed STFM module interlinks the multi-frame feature maps through scale and temporal modulation. Multi-level feature interlinking is a crucial task to enlarge the overall receptive field of the network. To do this, the multi-level feature aggregation (MFA) module is proposed. This MFA module is hierarchical, which takes the multi-level STFM

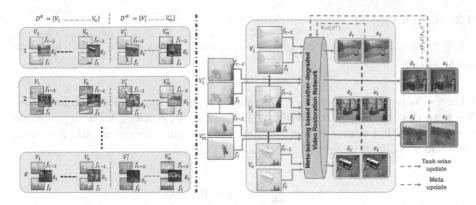

Fig. 4. Overview of the proposed meta-learning based weather-degraded video restoration framework. ***Left:*** Each task $\in (1, K)$ consists of n number of training videos and m number of validation videos. These train videos, V_1 to V_n, are used for task-wise update (*i.e.*, the inner loop) and validation videos, V_1' to V_m', are used for meta-update (*i.e.*, the outer loop). ***Right:*** The training videos V_1 to V_n from each task 1 to k in $D^k$are used to adapt θ_k using task-wise optimizers for inner loop and validation videos V_1' to V_m' from each task 1 to k in D'^k are used to adapt meta optimizer for outer loop.

features to capture and fuse the effective information at different levels. Also, compared to normal feature aggregation/concatenation operation, the proposed MFA obtains a wide-ranging vision field to further guide the feature maps as:

$$MFA_l = \begin{cases} \left[\xi_{(4-l)}\copyright\xi^2_{(5-l)}\right]\copyright\xi^2_{(5-l)}; \ l = 1 \\ \left[xi_{(4-l)}\copyright xi^2_{(5-l)}\right]\copyright MFA^2_{(l-1)}; \ l > 1 \end{cases} \tag{3}$$

where, ξ are STFM feature maps, ξ^2 are corresponding up-sampled STFM feature maps and MFA^2 are respective up-sampled MFA feature maps. In the proposed network, we have used three MFA blocks with sequential input.

Recurrent Guided Decoder: The proposed RGD module takes advantage of the spatio-temporally modulated features, multi-level feature aggregation features, and previous frame output feedback for the effective restoration of the current frame. The RGD module at each scale correlates the previous frame output maps ($\tilde{e}(t-1)$) and respective MFA feature maps to learn the temporally consistant content of the current frame. Initially, the MFA feature maps are merged with previous scale RGD feature maps. These features are correlated through the convolution operation. In [28], the authors argued that the feedback from either decoder level features or simply the output of the previous frame works very effectively for video-based applications. Therefore, these correlated feature maps are merged with the subsequent scale of the previous frame output maps ($\tilde{e}_s(t-1)$) to restore temporally consistent current frame.

3.2   Learning the Model Parameters

The proposed network parameters are optimized using $\mathbb{L}_1$ i.e. Least absolute deviations as:

$$\mathbb{L}_1 = |(e_t - \tilde{e}_t)| \tag{4}$$

where, e_t is target frame and $\tilde{e}_t$ is an restored frame using proposed architecture. We note that the $\tilde{e}_t$ is a function of f_t, f_{t-2} and $\tilde{e}_{t-1}$. Along with $\mathbb{L}_1$, to guide the model with textural and structural information, the perceptual loss with pre-trained VGG19 model [37] is calculated as:

$$\mathbb{L}_P = \sum_{l=1}^{L} \|\psi_l(\tilde{e}_t) - \psi_l(e_t)\|_1 \tag{5}$$

where, $\psi_l(.)$ represents l^{th} pooling layer of VGG-19 model. Further, we have considered structural similarity index (SSIM) loss to preserve high frequency information [31]. The SSIM loss function is defined as:

$$\mathbb{L}_S = 1 - SSIM(\tilde{e}_t, e_t) \tag{6}$$

The combination of SSIM loss with edge loss has been shown to work well [10]. So, the edge loss is also considered to focus on the edge restoration while training the proposed network. Edge loss is formulated with Sobel operator ($\mathbb{S}$) as:

$$\mathbb{L}_{ed} = \|\mathbb{S}(\tilde{e}_t) - \mathbb{S}(e_t)\|_1 \tag{7}$$

Thus, the overall loss ($\mathbb{L}_{Total}$) for training the proposed network is given as:

$$\mathbb{L}_{Total} = \lambda_1 \mathbb{L}_1 + \lambda_{ed} \mathbb{L}_{ed} + \lambda_P \mathbb{L}_P + \lambda_S \mathbb{L}_S \tag{8}$$

where, λ_{loss} are the weights assigned for the respective loss functions.

3.3   Meta-learning Based Adaptation

The proposed framework deals with six different weather-degraded scenarios: day-time (haze, rain, rain with veiling effect), and night-time (haze, rain and rain with veiling effect). The overview of the proposed meta-learning framework is depicted in Fig. 4 and summarised in Algorithm 1. In general, we have K different tasks in training set, $D = \{D^1, D^2, ...D^K\}$ and dataset for each task contains n data points as $D^k = \{V_1, V_2, ...V_n\}$ where $V_n = \{(f_{t-2}, f_t), e_t \mid t > 2\}$ as pair of inputs (f_{t-2}, f_t) and target frame (e_t) at time $t \in (3, ...F)$ and F being the total number of frames in each video. Similarly, the validation set used to update the meta model $D' = \{D'^1, D'^2, ...D'^K\}$ contains $D'^k = \{V'_1, V'_2, ...V'_m\}$. **Left** part of Fig. 4 shows the training and validation splits.

While training, a copy of the proposed architecture is kept as the meta-model and denoted as ϕ. The proposed architecture is first trained task-wise

---

Algorithm 1 : Pseudocode for meta-adaptation

Input: Training D^k and validation D'^k datasets, learning rate α
Initialize ϕ
while not done **do**
    for k in $\{1, 2, ...K\}$ **do**
        Initialize θ_k
        Optimize the θ_k as
        $\theta_k \leftarrow \phi - \alpha \bigtriangledown_\phi \mathbb{L}_{Total}\left(\theta_k, D^k\right)$
    end for
    Update $\phi \leftarrow \phi - \alpha \sum_{k=1}^{K} \bigtriangledown_\phi \mathbb{L}_{Total}\left(\theta_k, D'^k\right)$
end while

---

using training data D to learn task-specific parameters θ_k. The task-specific parameters are optimized using D^k as:

$$\theta_k \leftarrow \phi - \alpha \bigtriangledown_\phi \mathbb{L}_{Total}\left(\theta_k, D^k\right) \tag{9}$$

where, ϕ is meta-model parameter, α is learning rate, θ_k are task-wise parameters to be optimized using gradients $\bigtriangledown_\phi$ with respective losses ($\mathbb{L}_{Total}$) on training split (D^k) and by $\mathbb{L}_{Total}(\theta_k, D^k)$, we mean the $\mathbb{L}_{Total}$ computed on model with parameters θ_k using dataset D^k. The gradients of task-wise adapted model are then used to update the meta model parameters as:

$$\phi \leftarrow \phi - \alpha \sum_{k=1}^{K} \bigtriangledown_\phi \mathbb{L}_{Total}\left(\theta_k, D'^k\right) \tag{10}$$

4   Multi-weather Database Generation

The collection of real-world weather degraded day-night video with respective clean video is a challenging task. Therefore, many weather-specific synthetic video databases are introduced in the literature only with day-time scenarios. No single video dataset is generated for night-time weather degraded restoration. Therefore, in this work, we synthetically generate the day and night-time haze, rain and rain with veiling effect video datasets for meta-learning based training and new task adaptation purpose. For the synthetic day-time multi-weather video database generation, we have used a popular outdoor DAVIS-2016 [29] video database. Also, the night-time videos are downloaded from https:// www.pexels.com/videos/. The depth maps from [32] and procedure for synthetic database generation is adapted from [21]. Few samples from the synthesized day and night-time haze, rain and rain with veiling effect datasets are shown in Fig. 5. In total, 30 (20: task-wise training *i.e. task-specific model update* and 10: validation *i.e. meta model update*) videos for each day-time and 30 (10: meta-training and 20: meta-model testing) videos for each night-time weather degraded tasks are generated for meta-learning based weather-degraded video restoration (*see supp. material for more details*).

Fig. 5. Synthetically generated video frames (*first three columns: day-time and last three columns: night-time*).

Table 1. Quantitative results with GDN [26], DuRN [27], KDNN [14], FFA [30], EDVR [39], MSBD [9], IDN [49] on REVIDE [49] database for video de-hazing (*all quantitative values are collected from* [49] and PM: Proposed Method).

Methods →	GDN	DuRN	KDNN	FFA	EDVR	MSBD	IDN	PM
PSNR	19.69	18.51	16.32	16.65	21.22	22.01	23.21	**26.36**
SSIM	0.8545	0.8272	0.7731	0.8133	0.8707	0.8759	0.8836	**0.9044**

5   Experiments

5.1   Implementation Details

Losses in Eq. (8) are considered when training a proposed architecture for de-hazing and de-raining and adapting it to night-time weather conditions. The values of λ_{loss} are set (verified experimentally) as $\lambda_{ed} = 0.7$, $\lambda_P = 0.5$, $\lambda_S = 0.5$ and $\lambda_1 = 1$. The proposed network implemented with Tensorflow 2.0 library on NVIDIA DGX Tesla V100 32 GB GPU.

We compare the proposed method with existing SOTA approaches on REV-IDE and RainSynAll100 datasets for video de-hazing and de-raining tasks. We used the same train-test splits as provided in the respective datasets. Weights are initialized randomly and optimized with Adam optimizer. For the meta-learning based adaptation results, we use our synthetically generated day and night-time haze, rain, and rain with veiling effect video datasets: training the model on day videos and then efficiently adapting to night conditions. We compare the results of the meta-learnt model vs. learning from scratch on night conditions. PSNR (luminance channel) and SSIM are used as evaluation metrics.

5.2   Analysis of Proposed Architecture

De-hazing: The proposed network is tested on REVIDE [49] video de-hazing database. The SOTA de-hazing methods GDN [26], DuRN [27], KDNN [14], MSBDN [9], FFA [30], EDVR [39], CG-IDN [49] are used for analysis. The quantitative results' analysis of proposed method with SOTA methods is given in Table 1 for video de-hazing. The qualitative results on REVIDE database and real world video are shown in Fig. 6. From Table 1, and Fig. 6, we can see that

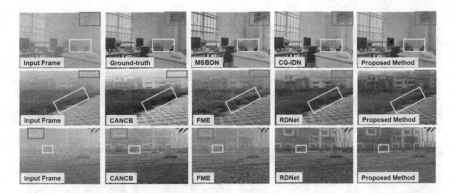

Fig. 6. Qualitative result analysis (*first row: REVIDE, last two rows: Real world*) for video de-hazing (MSBDN [9], CG-IDN [49] and CANCB [8], FME [51], RDNet [50]).

Table 2. Quantitative analysis with DIP [16], EVD [18], SCNN [5], MRF [3], J4RNet [25], DLF [42] and RMFD [43] on RainSynAll100 [42] database († *and* ‡ *represent method is used as pre and post-processing respectively*).

Methods →	DIP†+EVD‡	SCNN†+EVD‡	DIP†+MRF‡	SCNN†+MRF‡	J4RNet	DLF	RMFD	PM
PSNR	18.28	17.87	18.79	18.39	22.93	25.72	25.14	**28.39**
SSIM	0.6804	0.6423	0.6914	0.6469	0.7746	0.8989	0.9172	**0.9317**

the proposed network achieves superior performance for video de-hazing. We note that CG-IDN [49] has ∼**23M** compared our proposed network with ∼**10M** parameters. *Computational complexity analysis is given in supp. material.*

De-raining with Veiling Effect: The proposed network is tested on Rain-SynAll100 [42] dataset. J4RNet [25], DLF [42], RMFD [43] SOTA methods are used as baselines. To do more analysis, the combination of de-hazing and de-raining approaches are used similar to [43]. The quantitative result analysis for RainSynAll100 datasets is given in the Table 2. Also, the proposed architecture compared qualitatively on RainSynAll100 database and real world rainy videos is illustrated in Fig. 7 (*see* Sect. 3 *from supp. material*). 3dB performance improvement is achieved compared to recent RMFD [43] on RainSynAll100 dataset. Also from visual results, it is evident that the DLF and RFMD suffers from rainy streaks effect, veil effect and true color restoration whereas the proposed architecture produces the results without any rain streaks with veil effect removal and true color restoration. Also, the RMFD [43] has ∼**29M** whereas our proposed network has only ∼**10M** parameters.

5.3   Ablation Study on Proposed Architecture

The REVIDE database is used to examine the individual contributions (STFM, MFA, $\tilde{e}_{t-1}$) in the proposed network in terms of average PSNR and SSIM.

The STFM (comprising of SM and TM) interlinks the multi-frame features spatially and temporally. **How does this scale and temporal feature modu-**

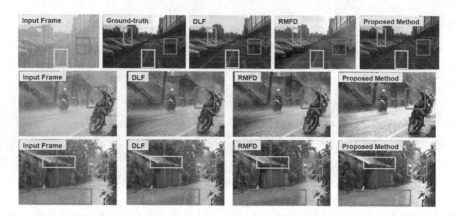

Fig. 7. Qualitative result analysis (*first row: RainSynAll100* and *last two rows: Real world videos*) for video de-raining with veiling effect (DLF [42] and RMFD [43]).

Table 3. Ablation study analysis of proposed modules (M: Modulation, MFA: multi-level feature aggregation, and $\tilde{e}_{t-1}$: feedback of previous frame output).

Network ↓	Scale M	Temporal M	MFA	$\tilde{e}_{t-1}$	PSNR	SSIM
I					22.74	0.8489
II	✓				23.69	0.8566
III		✓			23.95	0.8609
IV	✓	✓			24.64	0.8749
V	✓	✓	✓		25.42	0.8814
VI	✓	✓	✓	✓	**26.36**	**0.9044**

lation help the network to integrate the effective multi-frame features? To scrutinize this, the results of the proposed network are analyzed with and without scale and temporal modulation by keeping all other modules the same and results are given in Table 3. STFM module helps the network for inter-frame feature fusion which yields towards effective restoration. This is easily conveyed from results reported in Table 3 (Networks II–IV).

Next, we study the multi-level feature aggregation - the MFA module. **Is interlinking multi-level feature maps through MFA effective?** To analyse this, we examine the accuracy of the proposed network with and without the MFA module. From Network IV and V of Table 3, it is clear that the presence of the proposed MFA module improves performance.

As the motion between two consecutive frames is very minute, the t and $(t-2)$ frames are given as input to get temporal consistency. The enhanced frame $\tilde{e}_{t-1}$ is used to further ensure temporal consistency. **Whether sharing of the previous enhanced frame helps the network to get temporally consistent results?** We analyse the efficiency of the network with and without this recurrent guidance. From results reported in Table 3 (Networks VI), it is

Table 4. Analysis of scratch (Scrt), Fine, Combined (Comb) and meta training for night-time video restoration tasks.

Metrics →	PSNR				SSIM			
Night tasks ↓	Scrt	Fine	Comb	Meta	Scrt	Fine	Comb	Meta
De-hazing	21.99	22.01	22.97	**23.67**	0.6505	0.6615	0.6995	**0.7178**
De-raining	23.57	22.78	23.45	**24.71**	0.6695	**0.7102**	0.6845	0.7029
De-raining w/ veil	22.21	22.88	22.69	**23.49**	0.6723	0.6845	0.6937	**0.7171**

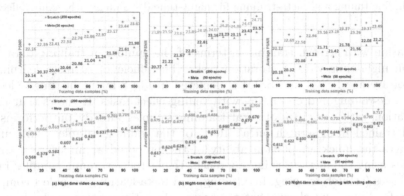

Fig. 8. Scratch and meta-training analysis with respect to different training samples in terms of average PSNR and SSIM for night-time weather degraded restoration tasks.

clear that conditioning the decoder with $(t - 1)^{th}$ frame output leads to better temporal consistency. Also, we use 2 past frames and argue that our method will be less affected by any sudden temporal change (e.g. the first few frames are bright while the later ones are dark) compared to a method [43] that uses more number of previous frames as our restoration is less reliant on past frames. *The ablation study on losses is provided in the supp. material.*

5.4   Analysis of Meta-adaptation

The meta-learning based adaptation of the proposed architecture is trained end-to-end. Initially, the task-wise and meta-model are initialised randomly and follow the iterative steps for inner and outer loop parameter optimization with day-time tasks (*haze, rain, and rain with veiling effects*) following Algorithm 1. After 250 epochs, the trained meta-model is used to adapt to new tasks: night-time (*haze, rain and rain with veiling effects*) weather degraded video restoration.

In this section, the proposed network is analysed with scratch training, fine-tuning, combined training and meta-learning based adaptation for night-time practical scenarios like haze, rain, and rain with veiling effect. As meta-learning helps the proposed architecture for quick adaptation of new task with few numbers of training samples, we compared the effectiveness of meta-learning based

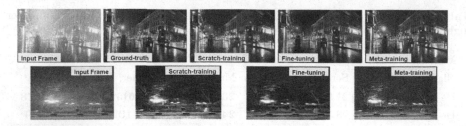

Fig. 9. Qualitative analysis (1st row: synthetic and 2nd row: real world data) with scratch, fine-tuning and meta-training for night-time de-raining with veiling effect.

adaptation with scratch training in terms of the number of training data samples on night-time video restoration tasks. The efficiency of meta learning in term of average PSNR and SSIM is depicted in Fig. 8 for night-time video dehazing, de-raining and de-raining with veiling effect tasks. It shows that meta-adaptation with just 10% of total training samples already outperforms the model trained from scratch on all 100% of the training samples. This analysis shows the quick adaptation ability of the proposed architecture with few samples using the meta-learning approach. Using 100% training samples in the three cases (scratch training, fine-tuning, and meta-learning), Table 4 compares the performance and shows that the meta adaptation performs the best (see Fig. 9).

6   Conclusion

This work is a general restoration framework which benefits the day, and night-time weather degraded video restoration through the proposed architecture and its meta-learning based adaptation. The proposed architecture makes use of multi-frame based spatio-temporal feature modulation with multi-level feature aggregation and recurrent guidance decoder. Further, the proposed work incorporates the meta-learning based adaptation of the proposed architecture for weather degraded night-time video restoration. To the best of the authors' knowledge, this is the first video restoration attempt to address the problem caused by diverse weather (haze, rain, and rain with veiling effect) in day and night-time through meta-learning based adaptation. As night-time weather degraded video restoration receives less attention due to the limited availability of datasets, we provided the synthetic comprehensive night-time haze, rain, and rain with veiling effects datasets. The comprehensive results on video de-hazing and de-raining datasets in addition to the meta-learning based adaptation on night-time weather degraded video restoration proves the effectiveness of the proposed architecture.

Acknowledgement. This research was partially funded by the Australian Government through the Australian Research Council (ARC). Prof. Svetha Venkatesh is the recipient of an ARC Australian Laureate Fellowship (FL170100006).

References

1. Baik, S., Choi, J., Kim, H., Cho, D., Min, J., Lee, K.M.: Meta-learning with task-adaptive loss function for few-shot learning. In: Proceedings of the IEEE/CVF International Conference on Computer Vision (ICCV), pp. 9465–9474, October 2021
2. Behl, H.S., Naja, M., Arnab, A., Torr, P.H.: Meta-learning deep visual words for fast video object segmentation. In: 2020 IEEE/RSJ International Conference on Intelligent Robots and Systems (IROS), pp. 8484–8491. IEEE (2020)
3. Cai, B., Xu, X., Tao, D.: Real-time video dehazing based on spatio-temporal MRF. In: Chen, E., Gong, Y., Tie, Y. (eds.) PCM 2016. LNCS, vol. 9917, pp. 315–325. Springer, Cham (2016). https://doi.org/10.1007/978-3-319-48896-7_31
4. Chen, D., et al.: Gated context aggregation network for image dehazing and deraining. In: 2019 IEEE Winter Conference on Applications of Computer Vision (WACV), pp. 1375–1383. IEEE (2019)
5. Chen, J., Tan, C.H., Hou, J., Chau, L.P., Li, H.: Robust video content alignment and compensation for rain removal in a CNN framework. In: Proceedings of the IEEE Conference on Computer Vision and Pattern Recognition, pp. 6286–6295 (2018)
6. Choi, M., Choi, J., Baik, S., Kim, T.H., Lee, K.M.: Scene-adaptive video frame interpolation via meta-learning. In: Proceedings of the IEEE/CVF Conference on Computer Vision and Pattern Recognition, pp. 9444–9453 (2020)
7. Coskun, H., et al.: Domain-specific priors and meta learning for few-shot first-person action recognition. IEEE Trans. Pattern Anal. Mach. Intell., 1 (2021). https://doi.org/10.1109/TPAMI.2021.3058606
8. Dhara, S.K., Roy, M., Sen, D., Biswas, P.K.: Color cast dependent image dehazing via adaptive airlight refinement and non-linear color balancing. IEEE Trans. Circuits Syst. Video Technol. 31(5), 2076–2081 (2020)
9. Dong, H., et al.: Multi-scale boosted dehazing network with dense feature fusion. In: Proceedings of the IEEE/CVF Conference on Computer Vision and Pattern Recognition, pp. 2157–2167 (2020)
10. Dudhane, A., Biradar, K.M., Patil, P.W., Hambarde, P., Murala, S.: Varicolored image de-hazing. In: Proceedings of the IEEE/CVF Conference on Computer Vision and Pattern Recognition, pp. 4564–4573 (2020)
11. Finn, C., Abbeel, P., Levine, S.: Model-agnostic meta-learning for fast adaptation of deep networks. In: International Conference on Machine Learning, pp. 1126–1135. PMLR (2017)
12. Gao, X., Wang, Y., Cheng, J., Xu, M., Wang, M.: Meta-learning based relation and representation learning networks for single-image deraining. Pattern Recogn. 120, 108124 (2021)
13. Garg, K., Nayar, S.K.: Detection and removal of rain from videos. In: Proceedings of the 2004 IEEE Computer Society Conference on CVPR, CVPR 2004, vol. 1, pp. I. IEEE (2004)
14. Hong, M., Xie, Y., Li, C., Qu, Y.: Distilling image dehazing with heterogeneous task imitation. In: Proceedings of the IEEE/CVF Conference on CVPR, pp. 3462–3471 (2020)
15. Huang, Z., Zou, Y., Kumar, B., Huang, D.: Comprehensive attention self-distillation for weakly-supervised object detection. In: Advances in Neural Information Processing Systems 33 (2020)

16. Jiang, T.X., Huang, T.Z., Zhao, X.L., Deng, L.J., Wang, Y.: A novel tensor-based video rain streaks removal approach via utilizing discriminatively intrinsic priors. In: Proceedings of the IEEE Conference on CVPR, pp. 4057–4066 (2017)
17. Jiang, T.X., Huang, T.Z., Zhao, X.L., Deng, L.J., Wang, Y.: FastDeRain: a novel video rain streak removal method using directional gradient priors. IEEE Trans. Image Process. **28**(4), 2089–2102 (2018)
18. Li, B., Peng, X., Wang, Z., Xu, J., Feng, D.: End-to-end united video dehazing and detection. In: Proceedings of the AAAI Conference on Artificial Intelligence, vol. 32 (2018)
19. Li, M., Cao, X., Zhao, Q., Zhang, L., Meng, D.: Online rain/snow removal from surveillance videos. IEEE Trans. Image Process. **30**, 2029–2044 (2021)
20. Li, M., et al.: Video rain streak removal by multiscale convolutional sparse coding. In: Proceedings of the IEEE Conference on CVPR, pp. 6644–6653 (2018)
21. Li, R., Cheong, L.F., Tan, R.T.: Heavy rain image restoration: integrating physics model and conditional adversarial learning. In: Proceedings of the IEEE/CVF Conference on Computer Vision and Pattern Recognition, pp. 1633–1642 (2019)
22. Li, R., Tan, R.T., Cheong, L.F.: All in one bad weather removal using architectural search. In: Proceedings of the IEEE/CVF Conference on Computer Vision and Pattern Recognition, pp. 3175–3185 (2020)
23. Li, Y., Tan, R.T., Brown, M.S.: Nighttime haze removal with glow and multiple light colors. In: Proceedings of the IEEE International Conference on Computer Vision, pp. 226–234 (2015)
24. Liu, J., Yang, W., Yang, S., Guo, Z.: D3R-Net: dynamic routing residue recurrent network for video rain removal. IEEE Trans. Image Process. **28**(2), 699–712 (2018)
25. Liu, J., Yang, W., Yang, S., Guo, Z.: Erase or fill? Deep joint recurrent rain removal and reconstruction in videos. In: Proceedings of the IEEE Conference on CVPR, pp. 3233–3242 (2018)
26. Liu, X., Ma, Y., Shi, Z., Chen, J.: GridDehazeNet: attention-based multi-scale network for image dehazing. In: Proceedings of the IEEE/CVF International Conference on Computer Vision, pp. 7314–7323 (2019)
27. Liu, X., Suganuma, M., Sun, Z., Okatani, T.: Dual residual networks leveraging the potential of paired operations for image restoration. In: Proceedings of the IEEE/CVF Conference on Computer Vision and Pattern Recognition, pp. 7007–7016 (2019)
28. Patil, P.W., Biradar, K.M., Dudhane, A., Murala, S.: An end-to-end edge aggregation network for moving object segmentation. In: Proceedings of the IEEE/CVF Conference on Computer Vision and Pattern Recognition, pp. 8149–8158 (2020)
29. Perazzi, F., Pont-Tuset, J., McWilliams, B., Van Gool, L., Gross, M., Sorkine-Hornung, A.: A benchmark dataset and evaluation methodology for video object segmentation. In: Proceedings of the IEEE Conference on CVPR, pp. 724–732 (2016)
30. Qin, X., Wang, Z., Bai, Y., Xie, X., Jia, H.: FFA-Net: feature fusion attention network for single image dehazing. In: Proceedings of the AAAI Conference on Artificial Intelligence, vol. 34, pp. 11908–11915 (2020)
31. Que, Y., Li, S., Lee, H.J.: Attentive composite residual network for robust rain removal from single images. IEEE Trans. Multimedia **23**, 3059–3072 (2020)
32. Ranftl, R., Lasinger, K., Hafner, D., Schindler, K., Koltun, V.: Towards robust monocular depth estimation: mixing datasets for zero-shot cross-dataset transfer. IEEE Trans. Pattern Anal. Mach. Intell. **44**, 1623–1637 (2020)
33. Ren, W., et al.: Deep video dehazing with semantic segmentation. IEEE Trans. Image Process. **28**(4), 1895–1908 (2018)

34. Shao, Y., Li, L., Ren, W., Gao, C., Sang, N.: Domain adaptation for image dehazing. In: Proceedings of the IEEE/CVF Conference on Computer Vision and Pattern Recognition, pp. 2808–2817 (2020)
35. Sharma, A., Tan, R.T.: Nighttime visibility enhancement by increasing the dynamic range and suppression of light effects. In: Proceedings of the IEEE/CVF Conference on Computer Vision and Pattern Recognition, pp. 11977–11986 (2021)
36. Shin, J., Kim, M., Paik, J., Lee, S.: Radiance-reflectance combined optimization and structure-guided norm for single image dehazing. IEEE Trans. Multimedia **22**(1), 30–44 (2019)
37. Simonyan, K., Zisserman, A.: Very deep convolutional networks for large-scale image recognition. arXiv preprint arXiv:1409.1556 (2014)
38. Wang, G., Luo, C., Sun, X., Xiong, Z., Zeng, W.: Tracking by instance detection: a meta-learning approach. In: Proceedings of the IEEE/CVF conference on Computer Vision and Pattern Recognition, pp. 6288–6297 (2020)
39. Wang, X., Chan, K.C., Yu, K., Dong, C., Change Loy, C.: EDVR: video restoration with enhanced deformable convolutional networks. In: Proceedings of the IEEE/CVF Conference on CVPR Workshops (2019)
40. Yan, W., Sharma, A., Tan, R.T.: Optical flow in dense foggy scenes using semi-supervised learning. In: Proceedings of the IEEE/CVF Conference on Computer Vision and Pattern Recognition, pp. 13259–13268 (2020)
41. Yan, W., Tan, R.T., Yang, W., Dai, D.: Self-aligned video deraining with transmission-depth consistency. In: Proceedings of the IEEE/CVF Conference on Computer Vision and Pattern Recognition, pp. 11966–11976 (2021)
42. Yang, W., Liu, J., Feng, J.: Frame-consistent recurrent video deraining with dual-level flow. In: Proceedings of the IEEE/CVF Conference on Computer Vision and Pattern Recognition, pp. 1661–1670 (2019)
43. Yang, W., Tan, R.T., Feng, J., Wang, S., Cheng, B., Liu, J.: Recurrent multi-frame deraining: combining physics guidance and adversarial learning. IEEE Trans. Pattern Anal. Mach. Intell. **44**, 8569–8586 (2021)
44. Yang, W., Tan, R.T., Wang, S., Liu, J.: Self-learning video rain streak removal: when cyclic consistency meets temporal correspondence. In: Proceedings of the IEEE/CVF Conference on Computer Vision and Pattern Recognition, pp. 1720–1729 (2020)
45. Yue, Z., Xie, J., Zhao, Q., Meng, D.: Semi-supervised video deraining with dynamical rain generator. In: Proceedings of the IEEE/CVF Conference on Computer Vision and Pattern Recognition, pp. 642–652 (2021)
46. Zamir, S.W., et al.: Multi-stage progressive image restoration. In: Proceedings of the IEEE/CVF Conference on Computer Vision and Pattern Recognition, pp. 14821–14831 (2021)
47. Zhang, J., Cao, Y., Fang, S., Kang, Y., Wen Chen, C.: Fast haze removal for nighttime image using maximum reflectance prior. In: Proceedings of the IEEE conference on Computer Vision and Pattern Recognition, pp. 7418–7426 (2017)
48. Zhang, J., Cao, Y., Wang, Z.: Nighttime haze removal based on a new imaging model. In: 2014 IEEE International Conference on Image Processing (ICIP), pp. 4557–4561. IEEE (2014)
49. Zhang, X., et al.: Learning to restore hazy video: a new real-world dataset and a new method. In: Proceedings of the IEEE/CVF Conference on Computer Vision and Pattern Recognition, pp. 9239–9248 (2021)

50. Zhao, S., Zhang, L., Shen, Y., Zhou, Y.: RefineDNet: a weakly supervised refinement framework for single image dehazing. IEEE Trans. Image Process. **30**, 3391–3404 (2021)
51. Zhu, Z., Wei, H., Hu, G., Li, Y., Qi, G., Mazur, N.: A novel fast single image dehazing algorithm based on artificial multiexposure image fusion. IEEE Trans. Instrum. Meas. **70**, 1–23 (2020)

MonteBoxFinder: Detecting and Filtering Primitives to Fit a Noisy Point Cloud

Michaël Ramamonjisoa[1]([✉]), Sinisa Stekovic[2], and Vincent Lepetit[1,2]

[1] LIGM, Ecole des Ponts, Univ Gustave Eiffel, CNRS, Marne-la-vallée, France
{michael.ramamonjisoa,vincent.lepetit}@enpc.fr
[2] Institute for Computer Graphics and Vision, Graz University of Technology, Graz, Austria
sinisa.stekovic@icg.tugraz.at
https://michaelramamonjisoa.github.io/projects/MonteBoxFinder

Abstract. We present MonteBoxFinder, a method that, given a noisy input point cloud, fits cuboids to the input scene. Our primary contribution is a discrete optimization algorithm that, from a dense set of initially detected cuboids, is able to efficiently filter good boxes from the noisy ones. Inspired by recent applications of MCTS to scene understanding problems, we develop a stochastic algorithm that is, by design, more efficient for our task. Indeed, the quality of a fit for a cuboid arrangement is invariant to the order in which the cuboids are added into the scene. We develop several search baselines for our problem and demonstrate, on the ScanNet dataset, that our approach is more efficient and precise. Finally, we strongly believe that our core algorithm is very general and that it could be extended to many other problems in 3D scene understanding.

Keywords: Primitive fitting · Discrete optimization · MCTS

1 Introduction

Representing a 3D scene with a set of simple geometric primitives is a long-standing computer vision problem [23]. Solving it would provide a light representation of 3D scenes that is arguably easier to exploit by many downstream applications than a 3D point cloud for example. But maybe more importantly, this would also demonstrate the ability to reach a "high-level understanding" of the scene's geometry, by creating a drastically simplified representation (Fig. 1).

In this work, we start from a point cloud of a indoor scene, which can be obtained by 3D reconstruction from images or scanning with an RGB-D camera. Recent works have considered representing 3D point clouds with primitives [9,10,20,21]; however they consider "ideal 3D input data", in the sense that the point cloud is complete and noise-free. By contrast, point clouds from 3D reconstruction or scans are typically very noisy with missing data, and robust methods are required to handle this real data.

Supplementary Information The online version contains supplementary material available at https://doi.org/10.1007/978-3-031-19815-1_10.

ⓒ The Author(s), under exclusive license to Springer Nature Switzerland AG 2022
S. Avidan et al. (Eds.): ECCV 2022, LNCS 13688, pp. 161–177, 2022.
https://doi.org/10.1007/978-3-031-19815-1_10

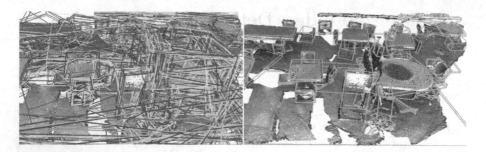

Fig. 1. Given a noisy 3D scan with missing data, our method extracts many possible cuboids, and then efficiently selects the subset that fits the scan best.

To be robust to noise and missing data, we propose a discrete optimization-based method. Our approach does not require any training data, which would be very cumbersome to create manually. Given a point cloud, we extract a large number of primitives. While in our experiments we consider only cuboids as our primitives, our approach can be generalized to other choices of primitives. We rely on a simple *ad hoc* algorithm [24] to obtain an initial set of primitives. We expect this algorithm to generate correct primitives but also many false positives. Our problem then becomes the identification of the correct primitives while rejecting the incorrect ones, by searching the subset of primitives that explains the scene point cloud the best.

While the theoretical combinatorics of this search are huge, as they grow exponentially with the number of extracted primitives, the search is structured by some constraints. For example two primitives should not intersect. To tackle this problem, we take inspiration from a recent work on 3D scene understanding [13]. [13] proposes to rely on the Monte Carlo Tree Search (MCTS) algorithm to handle a similar combinatorial problem to select objects' 3D models: The MCTS algorithm is probably best known as the algorithm used by AlphaGo [28]. It is typically used to explore the tree of possible moves in the game Go because it scales particularly well to high combinatorics. [13] adapts it to 3D models selection by considering a move as the selection of a 3D model for one object, and showed it performs significantly better than the simple hill-climbing algorithm that is sometimes used for similar problems [33]. Another advantage of this approach is that it does not impose assumptions on the form of the objective function, unlike other approaches based on graphs, for example [25].

While exploring the solution tree with MCTS as done in [13] is efficient, we show we can still speed up the search for a solution significantly more. The tree structure imposes an ordering of the possible 3D models to pick from. Such sequential structures are necessary when MCTS is applied to games as game moves depend on the previous ones, but we argue that there is a more efficient alternative in the case of object detection and selection for scene understanding.

As illustrated in Fig. 2, MCTS works by performing multiple iterations over the tree structure, focusing on the most promising moves. The estimate of how much a move is promising is updated at each iteration. For our problem of prim-

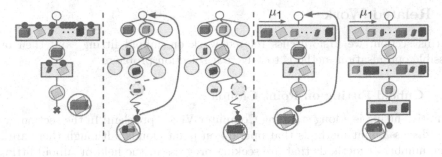

Hill-Climbing   2 iterations of MCTS   2 iterations of our algorithm

Fig. 2. Comparative overview The hill-climbing algorithm—simply taking the primitive that improves the most the objective function— can terminate × quickly as it gets stuck into a local minimum because of the constraints between primitives. MCTS as used in [13] explores iteratively the solution tree by traversing blue paths, updating which primitives are the most promising ones, but keeping the tree structure fixed. At each iteration, our approach also updates (→) which primitives are the most promising ones, and starts with them. This makes our approach identify a good solution much faster than MCTS in general. Red circles ● represent objective function evaluations. Hill-climbing has to evaluate the complete objective function each time it considers a primitive, while MCTS and our algorithm evaluate the objective function only at the end of an iteration when a complete solution is complete. (Color figure online)

itive selection, we propose to also proceed by iteration. Instead of considering a tree search, at the end of each iteration, we sort the primitives according to how likely they are to belong to the correct solution. The next iteration will thus evaluate a solution that integrates the most promising primitives. Our experiments show that this converges much faster to a correct solution.

To evaluate our approach, we experiment on the ScanNet dataset [8], a large and challenging set of indoor 3D RGB-D scans. It contains 3D point clouds of real scenes, with noisy captures and large missing parts, as some parts were not scanned and dark or specular materials are not well captured by the RGB-D cameras. We did not find any previous work working on similar problems, but we adapted other algorithms, namely a simple hill-climbing approach [33] and the MCTS algorithm of [13] to serve as our baselines for comparison. To do so, we introduce several metrics to evaluate the fit quality.

Our algorithm is conceptually simple, and can be written in a few lines of pseudo-code. We believe it is much more general than the cuboid fitting problem. It could first be extended to other type of primitives, and applied to many other selection problems with high combinatorics, and could be applied to other 3D scene understanding problems, for auto-labelling for example. We hope it will inspire other researchers for their own problems.

2   Related Work

In this section, we first discuss related work on cuboid fitting, and then on possible optimisation methods to solve our selection problem.

2.1   Cuboid Fitting on Point Clouds

Primitive fitting is a long standing Computer Vision problem. In the section, we only discuss about methods that operate on point clouds, although there are a large number of methods that are seeking progress in the field of cuboid fitting from 2D RGB images [12,17,23].

Object Scale. Sung *et al.* [30] leveraged cuboids decompositions to improve 3D object completion of scans of synthetic objects. Tulsiani *et al.* [31] introduced object abstraction using cuboids on more challenging objects from the Shapenet [4] dataset. Paschalidou *et al.* [21] extended [31] by using the more expressive superquadrics to fit 3D objects. However these methods only operate at the scale of a single objects, on synthetic data, and always assume or are limited to a moderate number of primitives. Some older work related to us have focused on parsing an input point cloud as a decomposition into primitives. Li *et al.* [19] decompose a *real* scan of an object into primitives by extracting a set of primitives with RANSAC, which they refine by reasoning on relationship between these primitives. However their method works only on very clean scans, and using object that were *built* as a set of primitives. Furthermore, since they reason about interaction between primitives using a graph, the complexity of there method quickly becomes untractable.

Room-Scale Cuboid Detection. Another class of works has focused on room-scale 3D point cloud parsing with cuboids. A large number of works focused on detecting object bounding boxes in 3D scans have recently emerged since the deep learning era [22,26,27]. Guo *et al.* [11] wrote a great survey regarding these methods. Contrary to these methods, our method is able to parse 3D scans with cuboids at the granularity level of parts of objects. Liang *et al.* [16] used RGB-D images to fit cuboids to the point cloud obtained by the depth map. In contrast to us, they operate using single-view images, but also leverage color cues via superpixels. Shao *et al.* [25] also parse depth maps with cuboids. Given an initial set of cuboids, they build a graph to exploit physical constraints between them to refine the cuboids arrangement. However, they still require human-in-the-loop for challenging scenes, and their graph based method limits the number of cuboids that can be retrieved without exceeding complexity. Our method, in contrast, can deal with number of cuboids that are an order of magnitude larger.

2.2   Solution Search for Scene Understanding

We focus here on scene understanding methods which, like us, do not rely on supervised training data for complete scenes, even if some of them require training data to recognize the objects. These methods typically start from a set of possible hypotheses for the objects present in the scene (similar to the primitives in our case), and choose the correct ones with some optimization algorithms.

Monte Carlo Markov Chain (MCMC) [2] is a popular algorithm to select the correct objects in a scene by imposing constraints on their arrangement. MCMCs can be applied to a parse graph [6,7,14,32] that defines constraints between objects. However, this parse graph needs to be defined manually or learned from manual annotations. Also, MCMCs typically converge very slowly.

Greedy approaches were also used in previous works [15], and they rely on a hill-climbing method to find the objects' poses [15]. [33] selects objects using hill-climbing as well by starting from the objects with the best fits to an RGB-D image. While simple and greedy, this approach can work well on simple scenes. However, it can easily get stuck on complex situations, as our experiments show. [18] uses beam search but this is also an approximation as it also cuts some hypotheses to speed up the search.

Monte Carlo Tree Search (MCTS) was recently used in [13], where they proposed to use MCTS as an optimization algorithm to choose objects that explain an RGB-D sequence. [13] adapts MCTS by considering the selection of one object as a possible move in a game. The moves are selected to optimize an objective function based on the semantic segmentation of the images and the depth maps. The advantage of this approach is that MCTS can scale to complex scenes, while optimizing a complex objective function.

Our approach is motivated by [13]. However, we generate the primitives in a very different way, but more importantly, we propose a novel optimization algorithm, which, contrary to MCTS, does not rely on a tree structure, making it is simpler and significantly more efficient than MCTS, as demonstrated by our experiments (Table 1).

Table 1. Properties of different solution search methods. Our method leverages all popular mechanisms for efficient solution search while leveraging the structure of the problem, which does not require employing tree structures for solution search.

Method	Uphill	MCTS	Ours
Exploratory	✗	✓	✓
Stochastic	✗	✓	✓
Leverage order invariance	✓	✗	✓

3   Method

In this section, we first describe how we extract a large pool of cuboids from a given 3D scan. Then, we formalize the selection of the optimal cuboid arrangement. Finally, we detail the solution we propose.

3.1   Generating Cuboid Proposals from Noisy Scans

Figure 3 summarizes our cuboid proposal generation pipeline. The goal of this pipeline is to provide a large pool of cuboids. Some extracted cuboids can be

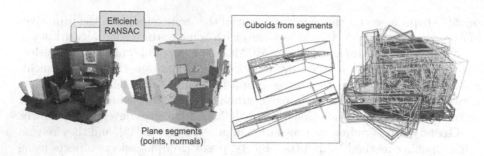

Fig. 3. Overview of our cuboid generation pipeline. After extracting plane segments using an off-the-shelf algorithm [24], we construct cuboids around these segments and pairs of adjacent segments. The result is a dense set of cuboids, which may contain many false positives.

false positives at this stage. The correct subset of cuboids will be selected by the next stage. In this way, we can be robust to noise and missing data in the 3D scan. Our pipeline can be divided in 3 steps: (1) we first extract plane segments; (2) we construct cuboids from pairs of plane segments; (3) we also construct *thin* cuboids by fitting a 3D bounding box to the each plane segment individually. These thin cuboids allow us to represent planar surfaces as well in the final representation. On average, we obtain 880 cuboids and 174 *thin* cuboids per scene.

Extracting Planes Segments. We use Efficient-RANSAC by Schnabel *et al.* [24] to extract 3D planes from the input point cloud. Efficient-RANSAC identifies and returns planar connected components made of 3D points. It is controlled by three hyperparameters: a threshold on the plane-to-point distance to count the inliers, a threshold on the cosine-similarity between normals to points, and a connectivity radius. We use the same hyperparameters for all the scenes in ScanNet, although we could run RANSAC multiple times with various geometric parameters in order to adapt to various types of noise, and still be able to efficiently filter out false positives.

Constructing Boxes from Pairs of Planes. Given a set of planes segments $\{\pi_i = (X_i, \mathbf{N}_i)\}$, where a plane segment π is represented as a point cloud X and its fitted plane normal $\mathbf{N}$, we construct bounding boxes from all pairs of planes (π_A, π_B) that satisfy two criteria, *alignment* and *proximity*. Alignment means that the two normals should be orthogonal or co-linear. Proximity enforces planes segments to have at least one connected component in 3D. We then employ two Gram-Schmidt orthonormalizations to obtain the frame coordinate of two bounding boxes, which are computed to enclose $X_A \cup X_B$. More details can be found in the supplementary material.

Fitting 3D Bounding Boxes to 3D Plane Segments. Since we want our method to also retrieve thin objects that may not have compatible neighbors, we therefore fit a 3D oriented bounding box to each plane segment's point cloud X, using the efficient *"Oriented Bounding Box"* method from [5].[1]

---

[1] We used CGAL's [1] implementation of [5, 24].

Algorithm 1: Loss function ●

---

procedure evalObjFunc(*S, Y*)

    Input   : Set of cuboids S, target point cloud Y and its normals $\mathbf{N}(Y)$;

    $(X, \mathbf{N}(X)) \leftarrow$ sample_mesh_surface(S);

    $\ell_c :=$ ChamferDistance($X \rightarrow Y$) + ChamferDistance($Y \rightarrow X$);

    $\ell_n :=$ CosineDissimilarity($\mathbf{N}(X) \rightarrow \mathbf{N}(Y)$) + CosineDissimilarity($\mathbf{N}(Y) \rightarrow$
    $\mathbf{N}(X)$);

    return $\ell_c \cdot (1 + 0.25 \cdot \exp(\ell_n))$;

3.2 The Cuboids Arrangement Search Problem

We now want to select a subset $\mathcal{S}'$ of $\mathcal{S}$, the set of cuboids generated in Sect. 3.1, which fits well the input point cloud X of the scene. The cuboids in $\mathcal{S}'$ should not mutually intersect to ensure a minimal representation of this scene.

To solve this problem, we consider (1) an objective function ℓ, defined in Algorithm 1, which will guide the search towards the best solution, and (2) a search algorithm such as the baselines described in Sect. 3.3, that should be designed to converge to the best solution as efficiently as possible. To better present the algorithms, we introduce a Cuboid Class, which we present first.

Cuboid Class. We define a Cuboid class to instantiate cuboids for our solution search algorithms. It is described by its faces normals and its 8 corners, yielding a surface mesh from which we can sample 3D points. Other attributes can be added to a Cuboid , depending on the needs of a particular algorithm, e.g. the number of times a Cuboid s has been used in a solution can be denoted as $s.n_1$.

To enforce constraints between cuboids, we need to test if the intersection between two cuboids is small enough. We define this criterion using a variation of the measure of a Intersection-over-Union criterion, and provide its pseudo-code in Supp Mat. isCompatible(s_1, s_2, η) measures the ratio between the volume $vol(s_1 \cap s_2)$ of the intersection between both cuboids s_1 and s_2, and the minimum of the volumes of each cuboid $vol(s_1)$ and $vol(s_2)$. In practice, we approximate these volumes by uniformly randomly sampling points from both cuboids and count the points that are inside both s_1 and s_2. The volume ratio is then compared to a threshold η, to decide if the two Cuboid intersect. While this test can be performed *"on the fly"* when searching solutions, we pre-compute the pair-wise Cuboid compatibility matrix in advance for efficiency.

Objective Function. We aim to minimize the distance between our cuboids and the target point cloud, while keeping its normals aligned with the point-cloud's normals. We use Chamfer Distance (CD) and Cosine Dissimilarity, *i.e.* the complement of Cosine Similarity, as our distance and normals deviation losses, yielding full objective function is described in Algorithm 1. In the loss, we truncate CD to $\tau = 0.1$, and normalize it by τ.

3.3 Solution Search Baseline Algorithms

Hill-Climbing Algorithm. The first baseline for our discrete optimization problem is the Hill-Climbing algorithm [29], a naive greedy descent algorithm. This algorithm constructs a solution iteratively, where at each iteration, it comprehensively searches for the proposal that best improves the loss function of a solution $\mathcal{S}_F$, while leaving the solution valid *i.e.* with no incompatibilities. If no proposal is available nor can improve the objective function, the algorithm stops ✕. The pseudo code for Hill-Climbing is given in the supplementary material.

MCTS Algorithm. We first describe here the MCTS algorithm, as it inspired our algorithm. [3] provides a full description of the MCTS algorithm. We present it in the context of our cuboid selection problem, following what was done in [13] for 3D model selection. [13] provides a pseudo code for MCTS.

MCTS is able to efficiently explore the large trees that result from the high combinatorics of some games such as Go. As represented in Fig. 2, the nodes of the tree correspond to possible states, and the branches to possible moves. MCTS does not build explicitly the entire tree—this would not be tractable anyway—, but only a portion of it, starting from the root at the top.

⤳*Simulation Step.* Nodes are thus created progressively at each iteration. To decide which nodes should be created, the existing nodes contain in addition to a state an estimate V of the *value* of this state. To initialize V, MCTS uses a *simulation step* denoted ⤳ in Fig. 2, which explores randomly the rest of the tree until reaching a leaf without having to build the tree explicitly. For games, reaching a leaf corresponds to either winning or loosing the game. If the game is won, V should be large; if the game is lost, V should be small.

Adaptation to Our Problem. Figure 2 shows that in our case, a state in a node is the set of primitives that have been selected so far. A "move" corresponds to adding a primitive to the selected primitives. The children of a node contain primitives that are mutually incompatible, and compatible with the primitives in the ancestor nodes: Such structure ensures that every path in the tree represents a valid solution. In this paper, we consider two possibilities: A varying number of children as in [13] and MCTS-Binary, a binary tree version of MCTS: In MCTS-Binary, a node has two children, corresponding to selecting or skipping a primitive. More details are provided in the supplementary material.

✕ "Reaching a leaf" happens when no more primitives can be added, because we ran out of primitives or because all the remaining primitives intersect with the primitives already selected. The value V of the new nodes are initialized after the simulation step by evaluating the objective function ●for the set of primitives for the leaf. We take this objective function as a fitness measure between the primitives and the point cloud. Note that this function does not need to have special properties, nor do we need heuristics to guide the tree search.

Selection and Expansion Steps. At each iteration, MCTS traverses the tree starting from the root node, often using the standard Upper Confidence Bound (UCB) criterion [3] to choose which branch to follow. A high UCB score for a node means that it is more likely to be part of the correct solution. This criterion depends on the values V stored in the nodes and balances exploitation and exploration: When at a node N, we continue with its child node N' that maximizes the UCB score, which depends on the number of times N and N' have been visited so far. This criterion allows MCTS to balance exploration and exploitation.

At some point of this traversal procedure, we will encounter a node with a child node N that has not been created yet, we add the child node to the tree. We use the simulation step described above to initialize $V(N)$ and initialize $n(N)$ to 1.

$\rightarrow$ *Update Step.* MCTS also uses the value $V(N)$ to improve the value estimate of each node N' visited during the tree traversal. Different ways to do so are possible, and we found that for our problem, it is better to take the maximum between the current estimate $V(N')$ and $V(N)$: $V(N') \leftarrow \max(V(N'), V(N))$. $n(N')$, the number of times the node was visited is also incremented.

Final Solution. After a chosen number of iterations, MCTS stops. For our problem, we obtain a set of primitives by doing a tree traversal starting from the root node and following the nodes with the highest values V.

3.4 Our Algorithm: MonteBoxFinder

We first review the issues when using MCTS for our problem, then give an overview of our algorithm and its components. Finally, we provide some details for each component.

Moving from MCTS. Our primitives selection algorithm is inspired by MCTS, and it is motivated by two observations that show that MCTS is not optimal for our selection problem:

- the order we select the primitives does not matter. However, MCTS keeps growing its tree without modifying the nodes already created. This implies that if a primitive appears at the top of the tree but does not actually belong to the correct solution, it will slow down the convergence of MCTS towards this solution.
- if a node corresponding to adding some primitive P has a high value V, the node corresponding to not keeping P should have a low value, and vice versa. There is no mechanism in MCTS as used in [13] to ensure this. This is unfortunate as one iteration could be used to update more nodes than only the visited nodes.

Algorithm 2: Our MonteBoxFinder Algorithm

Result: Set of selected Cuboid $\mathcal{S}_F$
Input: Set of available Cuboid $\mathcal{S}$;
Number of evaluations N_{eval} ;
Threshold η ;
Current solution $\mathcal{S}_c := \emptyset$;
Final solution $\mathcal{S}_F := \emptyset$;
Current best loss $\ell^* := +\infty$;
procedure InitializeNodes($\mathcal{S}$)
  Input: Pool of Cuboid $\mathcal{S}$;
  $\mathcal{S} \leftarrow$ Shuffle($s \in \mathcal{S}$);
  $\mathcal{S}_c \leftarrow$ Simulate($\mathcal{S}$, η);
  $\ell \leftarrow$ evalObjFunc($\mathcal{S}_c$);
  // Update ALL Cuboid states
  $\mathcal{S} \leftarrow$ Update($\mathcal{S}$, $\mathcal{S}_c$, ℓ);
  return $\mathcal{S}$

// MonteBoxFinder Core Algorithm
$\mathcal{S} \leftarrow$ InitializeNodes($\mathcal{S}$);
for (iter=0; iter$\neq N_{eval}$; iter++) {
  $\mathcal{S} \leftarrow$ Sorted$_{\downarrow}$($s \in \mathcal{S}$, $s \mapsto s.\mu_1$);
  $\mathcal{S}_c \leftarrow$ Simulate($\mathcal{S}$, η);
  $\ell \leftarrow$ evalObjFunc($\mathcal{S}_c$);
  // Update ALL Cuboid states
  $\mathcal{S} \leftarrow$ Update($\mathcal{S}$, $\mathcal{S}_c$, ℓ);
  if $\ell < \ell^*$ **then**
    $\ell^* \leftarrow \ell$;
    $\mathcal{S}_F \leftarrow \mathcal{S}_c$;
return Best solution $\mathcal{S}_F$;

Overview. We give an overview of our algorithm in Algorithm 2. To exploit the two observations described above, we do not use a tree structure. Instead, we use the list of primitives which we sort at each iteration, by exploiting our current estimate for each primitive to be part of the current solution. Our method progressively estimates and exploits a prior probability $\mathcal{P}$ for a primitive to belong to the solution based on our adaptation of the Upper Bounding Criterion (UCB) that balances the exploitation vs. exploration trade-off.

Algorithm 3: Simulate($\rightsquigarrow$) and Update($\rightarrow$) functions of our algorithm

---

Input: Exploration probability $\mathcal{P}_\epsilon$;
Threshold δ;
procedure Simulate($\mathcal{S}_A$, η)
  Input: Pool of available Cuboid $\mathcal{S}_A$,
    threshold η
  Output $\mathcal{S}_F := \emptyset$;
  for ($s \in \mathcal{S}_A$) {
    if s.isCompatible($\mathcal{S}_F$, η) **then**
      $\epsilon := $ uniform_sample([0, 1]);
      if ($\epsilon < \mathcal{P}_\epsilon$) **then**
        if ($s.\mu_1 > s.\mu_0$) **then**
          $\mathcal{S}_F$.add(s)
      else
        if ($s.\mu_1 < s.\mu_0$) **then**
          $\mathcal{S}_F$.add(s)
  return $\mathcal{S}_F$

procedure Update($\mathcal{S}$, $\mathcal{S}_F$, ℓ)
  Input: Full pool of Cuboid $\mathcal{S}$;
  Selected set of Cuboid $\mathcal{S}_F \subset \mathcal{S}$;
  Solution score ℓ;
  for ($s \in \mathcal{S}$) {
    if $s \in \mathcal{S}_F$ **then**
      // Update best ℓ when kept
      $s.\ell_1 \leftarrow \min(\ell, s.\ell_1)$
      $s.n_1 \leftarrow s.n_1 + 1$
      $s.\mu_1 \leftarrow -s.\ell_1 + \sqrt{\ln(1/\delta)/s.n_1}$
    else
      // Update best ℓ when rejected
      $s.\ell_0 \leftarrow \min(\ell, s.\ell_0)$
      $s.n_0 \leftarrow s.n_0 + 1$
      $s.\mu_0 \leftarrow -s.\ell_0 + \sqrt{\ln(1/\delta)/s.n_0}$
  return $\mathcal{S}$

Initialization. We initialize the run with a few random traversals in order to initialize the states of each `Cuboid` proposal.

Simulate ($\leadsto$). At every iteration we first sort primitives $\mathcal{S}_A$ according to their confidence value $s.\mu_1$ in descending order, hence more confident primitives will be more likely selected. Afterwards, we perform the simulation that pops primitives s from sorted $\mathcal{S}_A$. With probability $\mathcal{P}_\epsilon = 0.3$, we perform exploitation and add s to the list of selected proposals $\mathcal{S}_F$ if $(s.\mu_1 > s.\mu_0)$. Otherwise, we perform exploration and add s to $\mathcal{S}_F$ if $(s.\mu_1 < s.\mu_0)$.

UCB Criterion. We modified the UCB score to fit our algorithm, which does not rely on a tree structure. We use this modified term to estimate two confidence measures $s.\mu_0$ and $s.\mu_1$ reflecting how much a cuboid s is likely to belong to the correct solution or not:

$$s.\mu_0 = -s.\ell_0 + \sqrt{\ln(1/\delta)/s.n_0}, \quad s.\mu_1 = -s.\ell_1 + \sqrt{\ln(1/\delta)/s.n_1}, \qquad (1)$$

where $s.\rho_0$ and $s.\rho_1$ are the minimum loss values reached when rejecting and accepting primitive s, $s.n_0$ and $s.n_1$ denote the number of times that the primitive were rejected and selected respectively, and $\delta = 0.03$ is a hyperparameter modifying the exploration rate, smaller δ implies larger exploration.

Update ($\rightarrow$). In comparison with the *update step* of MCTS described in Sect. 3.3, our MonteBoxFinder algorithm updates *all* primitives states after an iteration. If a primitive s was selected, we update its $s.\ell_1$, $s.\mu_1$, and $s.n_1$ values based on the obtained loss ℓ and our adapted UCB criterion, otherwise we update its $s.\ell_0$, $s.n_0$, and $s.\mu_0$ values instead. In the next iteration during simulation, we use these value to determine whether to select or reject the primitive.

4   Experiments

4.1   Dataset

ScanNet [8] is a dataset that contains noisy 3D scans of 1613 indoor scenes. We evaluate our method on the full dataset, where for each scene, we used the decimated and cleaned point clouds provided in [8] both for the box proposals generation step and for the solution search step.

4.2   Metrics

Fitness Measures. The most direct way to measure the quality of a solution is to measure the loss function ℓ described in Algorithm 1. Indeed, we want to evaluate the ability of our algorithm to search the solution space. Additionally, we measure a bi-directional precision metric Pr_τ. Pr_τ is computed as the proportion of points successfully matched between the *"synthetic"* point cloud X, generated by sampling 3D points from retrieved 3D cuboid meshes, and the 3D

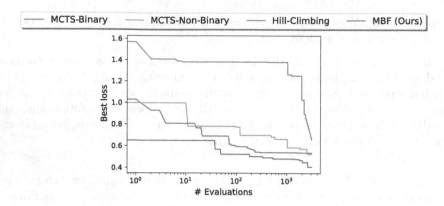

Fig. 4. Value of the objective function for the best found solution as a function of the number of evaluations for Hill-Climbing, MCTS, MCTS-Binary, and our MonteBoxFinder (MBF) method. Hill-Climbing requires many evaluations before finding a reasonable solution, which explains the flat curve at the beginning. It also gets stuck into a local minimum and stops improving. In this experiment, we give the number of evaluations Hill-Climbing used before getting stuck to the three other methods. Our method converges significantly faster than the other methods towards a better solution. Similar graphs for other scenes are provided in the supplementary.

scan Y. A point is successfully matched if its Chamfer Distance $(CD)^2$ value is below a threshold $\tau = 0.2$:

$$\mathrm{Pr}_\tau = \frac{|\{x \in X \text{ s.t. } CD[x \to Y] \leq \tau\}|}{2|X|} + \frac{|\{y \in Y \text{ s.t. } CD[y \to X] \leq \tau\}|}{2|Y|}. \quad (2)$$

Efficiency Measure. The motivation for developing our approach compared to [13] is to converge faster towards a good solution. In order to measure efficiency of a given method, we consider the curve of the objective function of the best found solution as a function of the iteration, as the ones showed in Fig. 4. We use the Area Under the Curve (AUC) given a maximum budget of iterations N_{eval}: the lower the AUC, the faster the convergence. We also report AUC (norm), which normalizes the AUC values of the different between 0 and 1, with 0 being the value of the best performing method and 1 being the value of the worst performing method.

Complexity Measure. We observe that bad solutions tend to contain a small number of selected primitives. This is because it is challenging to find a large subset of cuboids with no intersection between any pair of cuboids. Hence we also report the number of cuboids in the retrieved solutions.

---

[2] In this case, we do not apply the normalization discussed in Algorithm 1.

Table 2. Comparison between our method and our baselines. Our method outperforms all baselines on all metrics computed on ScanNet. We retrieve a more accurate fit, while being able to find more non-intersecting cuboids.

	Loss↓	Precision ↑	AUC ↓	AUC (norm) ↓	Avg. # Cuboids ↑
Hill-Climbing	0.383	0.928	0.871	0.998	12
MCTS	0.247	0.966	0.427	0.225	28
MCTS-Binary	0.292	0.961	0.370	0.102	35
Ours (MonteBoxFinder)	**0.201**	**0.982**	**0.322**	**0.018**	**37**

4.3   Evaluation Protocol

For all scenes from the ScanNet dataset [8], we run the Hill-Climbing method, and obtain its solution $\mathcal{S}_{HC}$. We then consider the number N_{eval} of evaluations of the objective that were required by Hill-Climbing to construct this solution. We then run MCTS and our algorithm using the same number of evaluations N_{eval}. This ensures the three methods are compared fairly, as they are given the same evaluation budget, which is by far the most costly step of all three algorithms.

4.4   Quantitative Results

Table 2 provides the results of our experimental comparisons. As expected, the Hill-Climbing algorithm performs worst: By greedily selecting proposals that minimize the loss, it gets stuck to local minimum solutions consisting of large proposals. It can also provide a complete solution only once it converged, while MCTS, MCTS-Binary and our method can provide a good solution much faster. The table also shows that our algorithm converges significantly faster than MCTS and MCTS-Binary, which was the desired goal. Interestingly, MCTS-Binary performs better than the original MCTS method of [13]. In the supplementary material, we discuss in details the links between our method and MCTS-Binary.

4.5   Qualitative Results

Figure 5 shows qualitative results. Hill-climbing focuses on large cuboids to describe the scene. MCTS often selects many true positives but misses some of the proposals because it cannot explore deeper levels of the tree for the given iteration budget. In contrast, our algorithm is able to successfully retrieve cuboid primitives for objects of different sizes, such as walls, floors, and furniture.

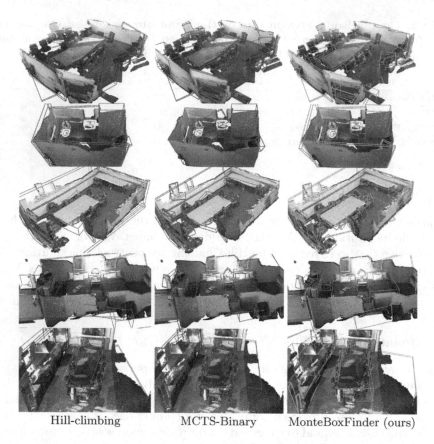

Hill-climbing   MCTS-Binary   MonteBoxFinder (ours)

Fig. 5. Qualitative results. Hill-climbing often selects large cuboids that span across multiple different objects (first, third, fourth rows, and fifth rows). MCTS does better, but does not sufficiently explore the solution space (second row). In contrast, our algorithm outperforms both methods and is able to successfully reconstruct many chairs in first, third, and fifth rows, and bedroom furniture in fourth row. *More qualitative results are provided in the supplementary material.*

5   Conclusion

We proposed a method for efficiently and robustly finding a set of cuboids that fits well a 3D point cloud, even under noise and missing data. Our algorithm is not restricted to cuboids, and could consider other primitives. Only a procedure to identify the primitives is required, even if it generates many false positives as our algorithm can reject them. Moreover, the output of our algorithm could be used to generate labeled data for training a deep architecture for fast inference. This could be done to predict cuboids from point clouds, but also from RGB-D images, since the 3D scans of ScanNet were created from RGB-D images By simply reprojecting the cuboids retrieved by our method, we can obtain RGB-D images annotated with the visible cuboids.

Acknowledgments. We would like to thank Pierre-Alain Langlois for his suggestions and help with CGAL. We thank Gul Varol, Van Nguyen Nguyen and Georgy Ponimatkin for our helpful discussions. This project has received funding from the CHISTERA IPALM project.

References

1. CGAL User and Reference Manual
2. Andrieu, C., Freitas, N.D., Doucet, A., Jordan, M.I.: An introduction to MCMC for machine learning. Mach. Learn. **50**, 5–43 (2003). https://doi.org/10.1023/A: 1020281327116
3. Browne, C., et al.: A survey of Monte Carlo tree search methods. IEEE Trans. Comput. Intell. AI Games **4**(1), 1–43 (2012)
4. Chang, A.X., et al.: ShapeNet: an information-rich 3D model repository. Technical report arXiv:1512.03012 [cs.GR], Stanford University – Princeton University – Toyota Technological Institute at Chicago (2015)
5. Chang, C.T., Gorissen, B., Melchior, S.: Fast oriented bounding box optimization on the rotation group $SO(3, R)$. ACM Trans. Graph. **30**(5) (2011). https://doi. org/10.1145/2019627.2019641
6. Chen, Y., Huang, S., Yuan, T., Qi, S., Zhu, Y., Zhu, S.C.: Holistic++ scene understanding: single-view 3D holistic scene parsing and human pose estimation with human-object interaction and physical commonsense. In: International Conference on Computer Vision (ICCV) (2019)
7. Choi, W., Chao, Y.W., Pantofaru, C., Savarese, S.: Understanding indoor scenes using 3D geometric phrases. In: International Conference on Computer Vision and Pattern Recognition (CVPR) (2013)
8. Dai, A., Chang, A.X., Savva, M., Halber, M., Funkhouser, T., Nießner, M.: ScanNet: richly-annotated 3D reconstructions of indoor scenes. In: International Conference on Computer Vision and Pattern Recognition (CVPR) (2017)
9. Deprelle, T., Groueix, T., Fisher, M., Kim, V., Russell, B., Aubry, M.: Learning elementary structures for 3D shape generation and matching. In: Advances in Neural Information Processing Systems (NeurIPS), pp. 7433–7443 (2019)
10. Groueix, T., Fisher, M., Kim, V.G., Russell, B., Aubry, M.: AtlasNet: a Papier-Mâché approach to learning 3D surface generation. In: International Conference on Computer Vision and Pattern Recognition (CVPR) (2018)
11. Guo, Y., Wang, H., Hu, Q., Liu, H., Liu, L., Bennamoun, M.: Deep learning for 3D point clouds: a survey. IEEE Trans. Pattern Anal. Mach. Intell. **43**(12), 4338–4364 (2020)
12. Gupta, A., Efros, A.A., Hebert, M.: Blocks world revisited: image understanding using qualitative geometry and mechanics. In: Daniilidis, K., Maragos, P., Paragios, N. (eds.) ECCV 2010. LNCS, vol. 6314, pp. 482–496. Springer, Heidelberg (2010). https://doi.org/10.1007/978-3-642-15561-1_35
13. Hampali, S., Stekovic, S., Sarkar, S.D., Kumar, C.S., Fraundorfer, F., Lepetit, V.: Monte Carlo scene search for 3D scene understanding. In: International Conference on Computer Vision and Pattern Recognition (CVPR) (2021)
14. Huang, S., Qi, S., Zhu, Y., Xiao, Y., Xu, Y., Zhu, S.-C.: Holistic 3D scene parsing and reconstruction from a single RGB image. In: Ferrari, V., Hebert, M., Sminchisescu, C., Weiss, Y. (eds.) ECCV 2018. LNCS, vol. 11211, pp. 194–211. Springer, Cham (2018). https://doi.org/10.1007/978-3-030-01234-2_12

15. Izadinia, H., Shan, Q., Seitz, S.M.: Im2CAD. In: International Conference on Computer Vision and Pattern Recognition (CVPR) (2017)
16. Jiang, H., Xiao, J.: A linear approach to matching cuboids in RGBD images. In: International Conference on Computer Vision and Pattern Recognition (CVPR) (2013)
17. Kluger, F., Ackermann, H., Brachmann, E., Yang, M.Y., Rosenhahn, B.: Cuboids revisited: learning robust 3D shape fitting to single RGB images. In: International Conference on Computer Vision and Pattern Recognition (CVPR), pp. 13070–13079, June 2021
18. Lee, D.C., Gupta, A., Hebert, M., Kanade, T.: Estimating spatial layout of rooms using volumetric reasoning about objects and surfaces. In: Advances in Neural Information Processing Systems (NeurIPS) (2010)
19. Li, Y., Wu, X., Chrysanthou, Y., Sharf, A., Cohen-Or, D., Mitra, N.J.: GlobFit: consistently fitting primitives by discovering global relations. ACM Trans. Graph. **30**(4), 52:1-52:12 (2011)
20. Paschalidou, D., van Gool, L., Geiger, A.: Learning unsupervised hierarchical part decomposition of 3D objects from a single RGB image. In: International Conference on Computer Vision and Pattern Recognition (CVPR) (2020)
21. Paschalidou, D., Ulusoy, A.O., Geiger, A.: Superquadrics revisited: learning 3D shape parsing beyond cuboids. In: International Conference on Computer Vision and Pattern Recognition (CVPR) (2019)
22. Qi, C.R., Litany, O., He, K., Guibas, L.J.: Deep Hough voting for 3D object detection in point clouds. In: Proceedings of the IEEE International Conference on Computer Vision (2019)
23. Roberts, L.G.: Machine perception of three-dimensional solids. Ph.D. thesis, Massachusetts Institute of Technology (1963)
24. Schnabel, R., Wahl, R., Klein, R.: Efficient RANSAC for point-cloud shape detection. Comput. Graph. Forum **26**, 214–226 (2007). https://doi.org/10.1111/j.1467-8659.2007.01016.x
25. Shao, T., Monszpart, A., Zheng, Y., Koo, B., Xu, W., Zhou, K., Mitra, N.: Imagining the Unseen: Stability-based Cuboid Arrangements for Scene Understanding. In: ACM SIGGRAPH Asia 2014 (2014). * Joint first authors
26. Shi, S., Guo, C., Jiang, L., Wang, Z., Shi, J., Wang, X., Li, H.: PV-RCNN: point-voxel feature set abstraction for 3D object detection. In: Proceedings of the IEEE/CVF Conference on Computer Vision and Pattern Recognition (CVPR), June 2020
27. Shi, W., Rajkumar, R.: Point-GNN: graph neural network for 3D object detection in a point cloud. In: Proceedings of the IEEE/CVF Conference on Computer Vision and Pattern Recognition, pp. 1711–1719 (2020)
28. Silver, D., et al.: Mastering the game of Go with deep neural networks and tree search. Nature **529**(7587), 484–489 (2016)
29. Skiena, S.: The Algorithm Design Manual. Springer, Cham (2010). https://doi.org/10.1007/978-3-030-54256-6
30. Sung, M., Kim, V.G., Angst, R., Guibas, L.: Data-driven structural priors for shape completion. ACM Trans. Graph. **34**, 1–11 (2015). Proc. of SIGGRAPH Asia
31. Tulsiani, S., Su, H., Guibas, L.J., Efros, A.A., Malik, J.: Learning shape abstractions by assembling volumetric primitives. In: International Conference on Computer Vision and Pattern Recognition (CVPR) (2017)
32. Zhao, Y., Zhu, S.C.: Scene parsing by integrating function, geometry and appearance models. In: International Conference on Computer Vision and Pattern Recognition (CVPR) (2013)

33. Zou, C., Guo, R., Li, Z., Hoiem, D.: Complete 3D scene parsing from an RGBD image. Int. J. Comput. Vis. **127**(2), 143–162 (2018). https://doi.org/10.1007/s11263-018-1133-z

Scene Text Recognition with Permuted Autoregressive Sequence Models

Darwin Bautista(✉) and Rowel Atienza

Electrical and Electronics Engineering Institute,
University of the Philippines, Diliman, Quezon City, Philippines
{darwin.bautista,rowel}@eee.upd.edu.ph

Abstract. Context-aware STR methods typically use internal autoregressive (AR) language models (LM). Inherent limitations of AR models motivated two-stage methods which employ an external LM. The conditional independence of the external LM on the input image may cause it to erroneously rectify correct predictions, leading to significant inefficiencies. Our method, PARSeq, learns an ensemble of internal AR LMs with shared weights using Permutation Language Modeling. It unifies context-free non-AR and context-aware AR inference, and iterative refinement using bidirectional context. Using synthetic training data, PARSeq achieves state-of-the-art (SOTA) results in STR benchmarks (91.9% accuracy) and more challenging datasets. It establishes new SOTA results (96.0% accuracy) when trained on real data. PARSeq is optimal on accuracy vs parameter count, FLOPS, and latency because of its simple, unified structure and parallel token processing. Due to its extensive use of attention, it is robust on arbitrarily-oriented text, which is common in real-world images. Code, pretrained weights, and data are available at: https://github.com/baudm/parseq.

Keywords: Scene text recognition · Permutation language modeling · Autoregressive modeling · Cross-modal attention · Transformer

1 Introduction

Machines read text in natural scenes by first detecting text regions, then recognizing text in those regions. The task of recognizing text from the cropped regions is called Scene Text Recognition (STR). STR enables the reading of road signs, billboards, paper bills, product labels, logos, printed shirts, *etc.* It has practical applications in self-driving cars, augmented reality, retail, education, and devices for the visually impaired, among others. In contrast to Optical Character Recognition (OCR) in documents where the text attributes are more uniform, STR has to deal with varying font styles, orientations, text shapes,

Supplementary Information The online version contains supplementary material available at https://doi.org/10.1007/978-3-031-19815-1_11.

© The Author(s), under exclusive license to Springer Nature Switzerland AG 2022
S. Avidan et al. (Eds.): ECCV 2022, LNCS 13688, pp. 178–196, 2022.
https://doi.org/10.1007/978-3-031-19815-1_11

illumination, amount of occlusion, and inconsistent sensor conditions. Images captured in natural environments could also be noisy, blurry, or distorted. In essence, STR is an important but very challenging problem.

STR is mainly a vision task, but in cases where parts of the text are impossible to read, $e.g.$ due to an occluder, the image features alone will not be enough to make accurate inferences. In such cases, language semantics is typically used to aid the recognition process. Context-aware STR methods incorporate semantic priors from a word representation model [48] or dictionary [45], or learned from data [3,9,21,32,33,50,52,53,69] using sequence modeling [6,60].

Sequence modeling has the advantage of learning end-to-end trainable language models (LM). STR methods with *internal* LMs jointly process image features and language context. They are trained by enforcing an autoregressive (AR) constraint on the language context where *future* tokens are conditioned on *past* tokens but not the other way around, resulting in the model $P(\mathbf{y}|\mathbf{x}) = \prod_{t=1}^{T} P(y_t|\mathbf{y}_{<t}, \mathbf{x})$ where $\mathbf{y}$ is the T-length text label of the image $\mathbf{x}$. AR models have two inherent limitations arising from this constraint. First, the model is able to learn the token dependencies in one direction only—usually the left-to-right (LTR) direction. This unidirectionality causes AR models to be biased towards a single reading direction, resulting in spurious addition of suffixes or direction-dependent predictions (illustrated in Appendix A). Second, during inference, the AR model can only be used to output tokens serially in the same direction used for training. This is called next-token or monotonic AR decoding.

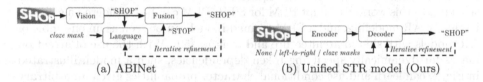

(a) ABINet   (b) Unified STR model (Ours)

Fig. 1. (a) State-of-the-art method ABINet [21] uses a combination of context-free vision and context-aware language models. The language model functions as a *spell checker* but is prone to erroneous rectification of correct initial predictions due to its conditional independence on the image features. (b) Our proposed method performs both initial decoding and iterative refinement by jointly processing image and context features, resulting in a single holistic output. This eschews the need for separate language and fusion models, resulting in a more efficient and robust STR method

To address these limitations, prior works have combined left-to-right and right-to-left (RTL) AR models [9,53], or opted for a two-stage approach using an ensemble of a context-free STR model with a standalone or external LM [21,69]. A combined LTR and RTL AR model still suffers from unidirectional context, but works around it by performing two separate decoding streams—one for each direction—then choosing the prediction with the higher likelihood. Naturally, this results in increased decoding time and complexity. Meanwhile, two-stage ensemble approaches like in Fig. 1a obtain their initial predictions using parallel non-AR decoding. The initial context-less prediction is decoded directly from the image using the context-free model $P(\mathbf{y}|\mathbf{x}) = \prod_{t=1}^{T} P(y_t|\mathbf{x})$. This enables the external LM, $P(\mathbf{y}) = \prod_{t=1}^{T} P(y_t|\mathbf{y}_{\neq t})$ in ABINet [21] for example, to use bidirectional context since all characters are available at once. The LM functions as a *spell checker* and rectifies the initial prediction, producing a context-based output. The conditional independence of the LM from the input image may cause it to erroneously rectify correct predictions if they appear misspelled, or if a similar word with a higher likelihood exists. This is evident in the low word accuracy of the LM in SRN (27.6%) and in ABINet (41.9%) when used as a spell checker [21]. Hence, a separate fusion layer is used to combine the features from the initial prediction and the LM prediction to get the final output. A closer look at the LM of ABINet (Appendix B) reveals that it is inefficient for STR. It is underutilized relative to its parameter count, and it exhibits dismal word accuracy despite using a significant chunk of the overall compute requirements of the full ABINet model.

In sequence model literature, there has been recent interest in generalized models of sequence generation. Various neural sequence models, such as AR and refinement-based non-AR, were shown to be special cases in the generalized framework proposed by Mansimov *et al.* [40]. This result posits that the same generalization can be done in STR models, unifying context-free and context-aware STR. While the advantages of this unification are not apparent, we shall show later that such a generalized model enables the use of an internal LM while maintaining the refinement capabilities of an external LM.

Permutation Language Modeling (PLM) was originally proposed for large-scale language pretraining [68], but recent works [47,58] have adapted it for learning Transformer-based generalized sequence models capable of different decoding schemes. In this work, we adapt PLM for STR. PLM can be considered a generalization of AR modeling, and a PLM-trained model can be seen as an ensemble of AR models with shared architecture and weights [59]. With the use of attention masks for dynamically specifying token dependencies, such a model, illustrated in Fig. 2, can learn and use conditional character probabilities given an arbitrary subset of the input context, enabling monotonic AR decoding, parallel non-AR decoding, and even iterative refinement.

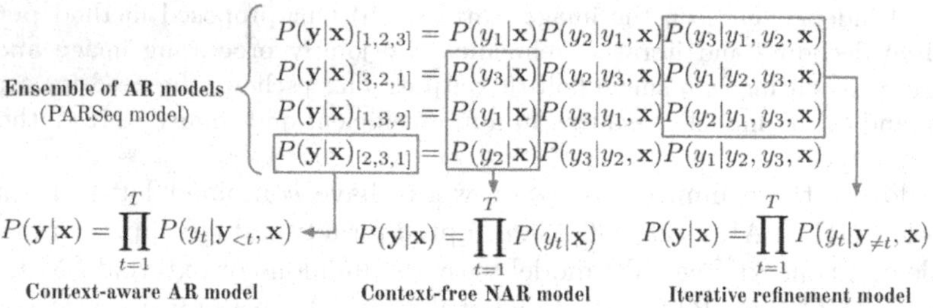

$$
\begin{aligned}
&\text{Ensemble of AR models}\\
&\quad\text{(PARSeq model)}
\end{aligned}
\left\{
\begin{array}{l}
P(\mathbf{y}|\mathbf{x})_{[1,2,3]} = P(y_1|\mathbf{x})P(y_2|y_1,\mathbf{x})\boxed{P(y_3|y_1,y_2,\mathbf{x})}\\[4pt]
P(\mathbf{y}|\mathbf{x})_{[3,2,1]} = \boxed{P(y_3|\mathbf{x})}P(y_2|y_3,\mathbf{x})P(y_1|y_2,y_3,\mathbf{x})\\[4pt]
P(\mathbf{y}|\mathbf{x})_{[1,3,2]} = P(y_1|\mathbf{x})P(y_3|y_1,\mathbf{x})\boxed{P(y_2|y_1,y_3,\mathbf{x})}\\[4pt]
\boxed{P(\mathbf{y}|\mathbf{x})_{[2,3,1]}} = \boxed{P(y_2|\mathbf{x})}P(y_3|y_2,\mathbf{x})P(y_1|y_2,y_3,\mathbf{x})
\end{array}
\right.
$$

$$
\underbrace{P(\mathbf{y}|\mathbf{x}) = \prod_{t=1}^{T} P(y_t|\mathbf{y}_{<t},\mathbf{x})}_{\text{Context-aware AR model}}
\qquad
\underbrace{P(\mathbf{y}|\mathbf{x}) = \prod_{t=1}^{T} P(y_t|\mathbf{x})}_{\text{Context-free NAR model}}
\qquad
\underbrace{P(\mathbf{y}|\mathbf{x}) = \prod_{t=1}^{T} P(y_t|\mathbf{y}_{\neq t},\mathbf{x})}_{\text{Iterative refinement model}}
$$

Fig. 2. Illustration of NAR and iterative refinement (cloze) models in relation to an ensemble of AR models for an image $\mathbf{x}$ with a three-element text label $\mathbf{y}$. Four different factorizations of $P(\mathbf{y}|\mathbf{x})$ (out of six possible) are shown, with each one determined by the factorization order shown in the subscript

In summary, state-of-the-art (SOTA) STR methods [21,69] opted for a two-stage ensemble approach in order to use bidirectional language context. The low word accuracy of their external LMs, despite increased training and runtime requirements, highlights the need for a more efficient approach. To this end, we propose a permuted autoregressive sequence (PARSeq) model for STR. Trained with PLM, PARSeq is a unified STR model with a simple structure, but is capable of both context-free and context-aware inference, as well as iterative refinement using bidirectional (*cloze*) context. PARSeq achieves SOTA results on the STR benchmarks for both synthetic and real training data (Table 6) across all character sets (Table 4), while being optimal in its use of parameters, FLOPS, and runtime (Fig. 5). For a more comprehensive comparison, we also benchmark on larger and more difficult real datasets which contain occluded and arbitrarily-oriented text (Fig. 4b). PARSeq likewise achieves SOTA results in these datasets (Table 5).

2   Related Work

The recent surveys of Long *et al.* [38] and Chen *et al.* [12] provide comprehensive discussions on different approaches in STR. In this section, we focus on the use of language semantics in STR.

Context-free STR methods directly predict the characters from image features. The output characters are conditionally-independent of each other. The most prominent approaches are CTC-based [22] methods [10,37,51,63], with a few using different approaches such as self-attention [20] for pooling features into character positions [2], or casting STR as a multi-instance classification problem [11,25]. Ensemble methods [21,69] use an attention mechanism [6,60] to produce the initial context-less predictions. Since context-free methods rely solely on the image features for prediction, they are less robust against corruptions like occluded or incomplete characters. This limitation motivated the use of language semantics for making the recognition model more robust.

Context-aware STR methods typically use semantics learned from data to aid in recognition. Most approaches [3,13,32,52,53] use RNNs with attention [6] or Transformers [9,33,50] to learn internal LMs using the standard AR training. These methods are limited to monotonic AR decoding. Ensemble methods [21,69] use bidirectional context via an external LM for prediction refinement. The conditional independence of the external LM on image features makes it prone to erroneous rectification, limiting usefulness while incurring significant overhead. VisionLAN [66] learns semantics by selectively masking image features of individual characters during training, akin to denoising autoencoders and Masked Language Modeling (MLM) [19]. In contrast to prior work, PARSeq learns an internal LM using PLM instead of the standard AR modeling. It supports flexible decoding by using a parameterization which decouples the target decoding position from the input context, similar to the *query stream* of two-stream attention [68]. Unlike ABINet [21] which uses the *cloze* context for both training and inference, PARSeq uses it for iterative refinement only. Moreover, as said earlier, the refinement model of ABINet is conditionally independent of the input image, while PARSeq considers both input image and language context in the refinement process.

Generation from Sequence Models can be categorized into two contrasting schemes: autoregressive (one token at a time) and non-autoregressive (all tokens predicted at once). Mansimov *et al.* [40] proposed a generalized framework for sequence generation which unifies the said schemes. BANG [47] adapted two-stream attention [68] for use with MLM, in contrast to our use of PLM. PMLM [34] is trained using a generalization of MLM where the masking ratio is stochastic. A variant which uses a uniform prior was shown to be equivalent to a PLM-trained model. Closest to our work is Tian *et al.* [58] which adapts the two-stream attention parameterization [68] to decoders by interspersing the content and query streams from different layers. In contrast, our decoder does not use self-attention and does not intersperse the two streams. This allows our single layer decoder to use the query stream only, and avoid the overhead of the unused content stream.

3   Permuted Autoregressive Sequence Models

In this section, we first present the Transformer-based model architecture of PARSeq. Next, we discuss how to train it using Permutation Language Modeling. Lastly, we show how to use the trained model for inference by discussing the different decoding schemes and the iterative refinement procedure.

3.1   Model Architecture

Multi-head Attention (MHA) [60] is extensively used by PARSeq. We denote it as $MHA(\mathbf{q}, \mathbf{k}, \mathbf{v}, \mathbf{m})$, where $\mathbf{q}$, $\mathbf{k}$, and $\mathbf{v}$ refer to the required parameters *query*, *key*, and *value*, while $\mathbf{m}$ refers to the optional attention mask. We provide the background material on MHA in Appendix C.

PARSeq follows an encoder-decoder architecture, shown in Fig. 3, commonly used in sequence modeling tasks. The encoder has 12 layers while the decoder is only a single layer. This *deep-shallow* configuration [28] is a deliberate design choice which minimizes the overall computational requirements of the model while having a negligible impact in performance. Details in Appendix D.

ViT Encoder. Vision Transformer (ViT) [20] is the direct extension of the Transformer to images. A ViT layer contains one MHA module used for *self-attention*, *i.e.* $\mathbf{q} = \mathbf{k} = \mathbf{v}$. The encoder is a 12-layer ViT without the classification head and the [CLS] token. An image $\mathbf{x} \in \mathbb{R}^{W \times H \times Ch}$, with width W, height H, and number of channels Ch, is *tokenized* by evenly dividing it into $p_w \times p_h$ patches, flattening each patch, then linearly projecting them into d_{model}-dimensional tokens using a patch embedding matrix $\mathbf{W}^p \in \mathbb{R}^{p_w p_h Ch \times d_{model}}$,

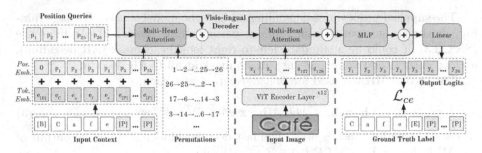

Fig. 3. PARSeq architecture and training overview. *LayerNorm* and *Dropout* layers are omitted due to space constraints. [B], [E], and [P] stand for *beginning-of-sequence (BOS), end-of-sequence (EOS)*, and *padding* tokens, respectively. $T = 25$ results in 26 distinct *position* tokens. The position tokens both serve as query vectors and position embeddings for the input context. For [B], no position embedding is added. Attention masks are generated from the given permutations and are used only for the *context-position* attention. $\mathcal{L}_{ce}$ pertains to the cross-entropy loss

resulting in $(WH)/(p_w p_h)$ tokens. Learned position embeddings of equal dimension are added to the tokens prior to being processed by the first ViT layer. In contrast to the standard ViT, all output tokens $\mathbf{z}$ are used as input to the decoder:

$$\mathbf{z} = Enc(\mathbf{x}) \in \mathbb{R}^{\frac{WH}{p_w p_h} \times d_{model}} \tag{1}$$

Visio-Lingual Decoder. The decoder follows the same architecture as the pre-*LayerNorm* [5,65] Transformer decoder but uses twice the number of attention heads, *i.e.* $nhead = d_{model}/32$. It has three required inputs consisting of *position*, *context*, and *image* tokens, and an optional attention mask.

In the following equations, we omit *LayerNorm* and *Dropout* for brevity. The first *MHA* module is used for *context–position* attention:

$$\mathbf{h}_c = \mathbf{p} + MHA(\mathbf{p}, \mathbf{c}, \mathbf{c}, \mathbf{m}) \in \mathbb{R}^{(T+1) \times d_{model}} \tag{2}$$

where T is the context length, $\mathbf{p} \in \mathbb{R}^{(T+1) \times d_{model}}$ are the position tokens, $\mathbf{c} \in \mathbb{R}^{(T+1) \times d_{model}}$ are the context embeddings with positional information, and $\mathbf{m} \in \mathbb{R}^{(T+1) \times (T+1)}$ is the optional *attention mask*. Note that the use of special *delimiter* tokens ([B] or [E]) increases the total sequence length to $T + 1$.

The *position* tokens encode the target position to be predicted, each one having a direct correspondence to a specific position in the output. This parameterization is similar to the *query stream* of two-stream attention [68]. It decouples the context from the target position, allowing the model to learn from PLM. Without the position tokens, *i.e.* if the context tokens are used as *queries* themselves like in standard Transformers, the model will not learn anything meaningful from PLM and will simply function like a *standard* AR model.

The supplied mask varies depending on how the model is used. During training, masks are generated from random permutations (Sect. 3.2). At inference (Sect. 3.3), it could be a standard left-to-right lookahead mask (AR decoding), a *cloze* mask (iterative refinement), or no mask at all (NAR decoding).

The second MHA is used for *image–position* attention:

$$\mathbf{h}_i = \mathbf{h}_c + MHA(\mathbf{h}_c, \mathbf{z}, \mathbf{z}) \in \mathbb{R}^{(T+1) \times d_{model}} \tag{3}$$

where no attention mask is used. The last decoder hidden state is the output of the MLP, $\mathbf{h}_{dec} = \mathbf{h}_i + MLP(\mathbf{h}_i) \in \mathbb{R}^{(T+1) \times d_{model}}$.

Finally, the output logits are $\mathbf{y} = Linear(\mathbf{h}_{dec}) \in \mathbb{R}^{(T+1) \times (C+1)}$ where C is the size of the character set (charset) used for training. The additional character pertains to the [E] token (which marks the end of the sequence). In summary, given an attention mask $\mathbf{m}$, the decoder is a function which takes the form:

$$\mathbf{y} = Dec(\mathbf{z}, \mathbf{p}, \mathbf{c}, \mathbf{m}) \in \mathbb{R}^{(T+1) \times (C+1)} \tag{4}$$

3.2 Permutation Language Modeling

Given an image $\mathbf{x}$, we want to maximize the likelihood of its text label $\mathbf{y} = [y_1, y_2, \ldots, y_T]$ under the set of model parameters θ. In standard AR modeling, the likelihood is factorized using the chain rule according to the canonical ordering, $[1, 2, \ldots, T]$, resulting in the model $\log p(\mathbf{y}|\mathbf{x}) = \sum_{t=1}^{T} \log p_\theta(y_t|\mathbf{y}_{<t}, \mathbf{x})$. However, Transformers process all tokens in parallel, allowing the output tokens to *access* or be conditionally-dependent on all the input tokens. In order to have a valid AR model, *past* tokens cannot have access to *future* tokens. The AR property is enforced in Transformers with the use of attention masks. For example, a standard AR model for a three-element sequence $\mathbf{y}$ will have the attention mask shown in Table 1a.

The key idea behind PLM is to train on all $T!$ factorizations of the likelihood:

$$\log p(\mathbf{y}|\mathbf{x}) = \mathbb{E}_{\mathbf{z} \sim \mathcal{Z}_T} \left[\sum_{t=1}^{T} \log p_\theta(y_{z_t}|\mathbf{y}_{\mathbf{z}_{<t}}, \mathbf{x}) \right] \tag{5}$$

where $\mathcal{Z}_T$ denotes the set of all possible permutations of the index sequence $[1, 2, \ldots, T]$, and z_t and $\mathbf{z}_{<t}$ denote the t-th element and the first $t-1$ elements, respectively, of a permutation $\mathbf{z} \in \mathcal{Z}_T$. Each permutation $\mathbf{z}$ specifies an ordering which corresponds to a distinct factorization of the likelihood.

To implement PLM in Transformers, we do **not** need to actually permute the text label $\mathbf{y}$. Rather, we craft the attention mask to *enforce* the ordering specified by $\mathbf{z}$. As a concrete example, shown in Table 1 are attention masks for four different permutations of a three-element sequence. Notice that while the order of the input and output sequences remains constant, all four correspond to distinct AR models specified by the given permutation or factorization order. With this in mind, it can be seen that the standard AR training is just a special case of PLM where only one permutation, $[1, 2, \ldots, T]$, is used.

In practice, we cannot train on all $T!$ factorizations due to the exponential increase in computational requirements. As a compromise, we only use K of the possible $T!$ permutations. Instead of sampling uniformly, we choose the K permutations in a specific way. We use $K/2$ permutation pairs. The first half consists of the *left-to-right* permutation, $[1, 2, \ldots, T]$, and $K/2 - 1$ randomly sampled permutations. The other half consists of *flipped* versions of the first. We found that this sampling procedure results in a more stable training.

With K permutations and the ground truth label $\hat{\mathbf{y}}$, the full training loss is the mean of the individual cross-entropy losses for each permutation-derived attention mask $\mathbf{m}_k$:

$$\mathcal{L} = \frac{1}{K} \sum_{k=1}^{K} \mathcal{L}_{ce}(\mathbf{y}_k, \hat{\mathbf{y}}) \tag{6}$$

where $\mathbf{y}_k = Dec(\mathbf{z}, \mathbf{p}, \mathbf{c}, \mathbf{m}_k)$. *Padding* tokens are ignored in the loss computation. More PLM details are in Appendix E.

Table 1. Illustration of AR attention masks for each permutation. The table header (with the [B] token) pertains to the input context, while the header column (with the [E] token) corresponds to the output tokens. *1* means that the output token has conditional dependency on the corresponding input token. *0* means that no information flows from input to output

(a) $[1, 2, 3]$					(b) $[3, 2, 1]$					(c) $[1, 3, 2]$					(d) $[2, 3, 1]$				
	[B]	y_1	y_2	y_3		[B]	y_1	y_2	y_3		[B]	y_1	y_2	y_3		[B]	y_1	y_2	y_3
y_1	1	0	0	0	y_1	1	0	1	1	y_1	1	0	0	0	y_1	1	0	1	1
y_2	1	1	0	0	y_2	1	0	0	1	y_2	1	1	0	1	y_2	1	0	0	0
y_3	1	1	1	0	y_3	1	0	0	0	y_3	1	1	0	0	y_3	1	0	1	0
[E]	1	1	1	1	[E]	1	1	1	1	[E]	1	1	1	1	[E]	1	1	1	1

3.3 Decoding Schemes

PLM training coupled with the correct parameterization allows PARSeq to be used with various decoding schemes. In this work, we only use two contrasting schemes even though more are theoretically supported. Specifically, we elaborate the use of monotonic AR and NAR decoding, as well as iterative refinement.

Autoregressive (AR) decoding generates one new token per iteration. The *left-to-right* attention mask (Table 2a) is always used. For the first iteration, the context is set to [B], and only the first position query token $\mathbf{p}_1$ is used. For any succeeding iteration i, position queries $[\mathbf{p}_1, \ldots, \mathbf{p}_i]$ are used, while the context is set to the previous output, $argmax(\mathbf{y})$ prepended with [B].

Non-autoregressive (NAR) decoding generates all output tokens at the same time. All position queries $[\mathbf{p}_1, \ldots, \mathbf{p}_{T+1}]$ are used but no attention mask is used (Table 2b). The context is always [B].

Iterative refinement can be performed regardless of the initial decoding method (AR or NAR). The previous output (truncated at [E]) serves as the context for the current iteration similar to AR decoding, but all position queries $[\mathbf{p}_1, \ldots, \mathbf{p}_{T+1}]$ are always used. The *cloze* attention mask (Table 2c) is used. It is created by starting with an all-one mask, then masking out the matching token positions.

Table 2. Illustration of information flow for the different decoding schemes. Conventions follow Table 1. In NAR decoding, no mask is used; this is equivalent to using an all-one mask. "..." pertains to elements y_3 to y_{T-1}

(a) *left-to-right* AR mask

	[B]	y_1	y_2	...	y_T
y_1	1	0	0	0	0
y_2	1	1	0	0	0
...	1	1	1	...	0
y_T	1	1	1	1	0
[E]	1	1	1	1	1

(b) NAR mask

	[B]
y_1	1
y_2	1
...	1
y_T	1
[E]	1

(c) *cloze* mask

	[B]	y_1	y_2	...	y_T
y_1	1	0	1	1	1
y_2	1	1	0	1	1
...	1	1	1	...	1
y_T	1	1	1	1	0
[E]	1	1	1	1	1

4   Results and Analysis

In this section, we first discuss the experimental setup including the datasets, pre-processing methods, training and evaluation protocols, and metrics used. Next, we present our results and compare PARSeq to SOTA methods in terms of the said metrics and commonly used computational cost indicators.

4.1   Datasets

STR models are traditionally trained on large-scale synthetic datasets because of the relative scarcity of labelled real data [3]. However, in recent years, the amount of labelled real data has become sufficient for training STR models. In fact, training on real data was shown to be more sample-efficient than on synthetic data [4]. Hence, in addition to the commonly used synthetic training datasets MJSynth (MJ) [25] and SynthText (ST) [23], we also use real data for training. Specifically, we use COCO-Text (COCO) [61], RCTW17 [54], Uber-Text (Uber) [73], ArT [14], LSVT [57], MLT19 [44], and ReCTS [72]. A comprehensive discussion about these datasets is available in Baek *et al.* [4]. In addition, we also use two recent large-scale real datasets based on Open Images [30]: TextOCR [55] and annotations from the OpenVINO toolkit [31]. More details in Appendix F.

Following prior works [3], we use IIIT 5k-word (IIIT5k) [42], CUTE80 (CUTE) [49], Street View Text (SVT) [64], SVT-Perspective (SVTP) [46], ICDAR 2013 (IC13) [27], and ICDAR 2015 (IC15) [26] as the datasets for evaluation. Baek *et al.* [3] provides an in-depth discussion of these datasets. We use the case-sensitive annotations of Long and Yao [39] for IIIT5k, CUTE, SVT, and SVTP. Note that IC13 and IC15 have two *versions* of their respective *test* splits commonly used in the literature—857 and 1,015 for IC13; 1,811 and 2,077 for IC15. To avoid confusion, we refer to the *benchmark* as the union of IIIT5k, CUTE, SVT, SVTP, IC13 *(1,015)*, and IC15 *(2,077)*.

These six benchmark datasets only have a total of 7,672 test samples. This amount pales in comparison to benchmark datasets used in other vision tasks such as ImageNet [18] (*classification*, 50k samples) and COCO [35] (*detection*, 40k samples). Furthermore, the said datasets largely contain horizontal text only, as shown in Fig. 4a, except for SVT, SVTP, and IC15 *2,077* which contain a number of rotated text. In the real world, the conditions are less ideal, and captured text will most likely be blurry, vertically-oriented, rotated, or even occluded. In order to have a more comprehensive comparison, we also use the test sets of more recent datasets, shown in Fig. 4b, such as COCO-Text (9.8k samples; low-resolution, occluded text), ArT [14] (35.1k samples; curved and rotated text), and Uber-Text [73] (80.6k samples; vertical and rotated text).

(a) Samples from the *benchmark* datasets   (b) Samples from Uber, COCO, ArT

Fig. 4. Sample test images from the datasets used

4.2 Training Protocol and Model Selection

All models are trained in a mixed-precision, dual-GPU setup using PyTorch DDP for 169,680 iterations with a batch size of 384. Learning rates vary per model (Appendix G.2). The Adam [29] optimizer is used together with the 1cycle [56] learning rate scheduler. At iteration 127,260 (75% of total), Stochastic Weight Averaging (SWA) [24] is used and the 1cycle scheduler is replaced by the SWA scheduler. Validation is performed every 1,000 training steps. Since SWA averages weights at the end of each epoch, the last checkpoint at the end of training is selected. For PARSeq, $K = 6$ permutations are used (Sect. 4.4). A patch size of 8×4 is used for PARSeq and ViTSTR. More details are in Appendix G.

Label preprocessing is done following prior work [53]. For training, we set a maximum label length of $T = 25$, and use a charset of size $C = 94$ which contains mixed-case alphanumeric characters and punctuation marks.

Image preprocessing is done like so: images are first augmented, resized, then finally normalized to the interval $[-1, 1]$. The set of augmentation operations consists primarily of RandAugment [16] operations, excluding `Sharpness`. `Invert` is added due to its effectiveness in house number data [15]. `GaussianBlur` and `PoissonNoise` are also used due to their effectiveness in STR data augmentation [1]. A RandAugment policy with 3 layers and a magnitude of 5 is used. RGB images are used, which are resized unconditionally to 128×32 pixels.

4.3   Evaluation Protocol and Metrics

All experiments are performed on an NVIDIA Tesla A100 GPU system. Reported mean $\pm$ SD values are obtained from four replicates per model. A t-test ($\alpha = 0.05$) is used to determine if model differences are statistically-significant. There can be multiple *best* results in a column if the differences are not statistically-significant. PARSeq results are obtained from the **same** model using two different decoding schemes: PARSeq$_A$ denotes AR decoding with one refinement iteration, while PARSeq$_N$ denotes NAR decoding with two refinement iterations (ablation study in Appendix H).

Word accuracy is the primary metric for STR benchmarks. A prediction is considered correct if and only if characters at all positions match.

Charset may vary at inference time. Subsets of the training charset can be used for evaluation. Specifically, the following charsets are used: 36-character (lowercase alphanumeric), 62-character (mixed-case alphanumeric), and 94-character (mixed-case alphanumeric with punctuation). In Python, these correspond to array slices `[:36]`, `[:62]`, and `[:94]` of `string.printable`, respectively.

4.4   Ablation on Training Permutations vs Test Accuracy

As discussed in Sect. 3.2, training on all possible permutations is not feasible in practice due to the exponential increase in computational requirements. We instead sample a number of permutations from the pool of all possible permutations. Table 3 shows the effect of the number of training permutations on the test accuracy for all decoding schemes. With $K = 1$, only the left-to-right ordering is used and the training simplifies to the standard AR modeling. In this setup, NAR decoding does not work at all, while AR decoding works well as expected. Meanwhile, the refinement or *cloze* accuracy is at a dismal 71.14% (this is very low considering that the ground truth itself is used as the initial prediction). All decoding schemes start to perform satisfactorily only at $K >= 6$. This result shows that PLM is indeed required to achieve a unified STR model. Intuitively, NAR decoding will not work when training on just the forward and/or reverse orderings ($K <= 2$) because the variety of training contexts is insufficient. NAR decoding relies on the priors for each character which could only be sufficiently trained if all characters in the charset naturally exist as the first character of a sequence. Ultimately, $K = 6$ provides the best balance between decoding accuracy and training time. The very high cloze accuracy ($\sim$94%) of our internal LM highlights the advantage of jointly using image features and language context for prediction refinement. After all, the primary input signal in STR is the image, not the language context.

Table 3. 94-char word accuracy (real training data) on the benchmark vs number of permutations (K) used for training PARSeq. No refinement iterations were used for both AR and NAR decoding. *cloze acc.* pertains to the word accuracy of one refinement iteration. It was measured by using the ground truth label as the initial prediction

K	AR acc.	NAR acc.	Cloze acc.	Training hours
1	93.04	0.01	71.14	5.86
2	93.48	22.69	94.55	7.30
6	93.34	92.22	94.81	8.48
12	92.91	91.71	94.59	10.10
24	92.67	91.72	94.36	13.53

4.5   Comparison to State-of-the-Art (SOTA)

We compare PARSeq to popular and recent SOTA methods. In addition to the published results, we reproduce a select number of methods for a fair comparison [3]. In Table 6, most reproduced methods attain higher accuracy compared to the original results. The exception is ABINet (around 1.4% decline in combined accuracy) which originally used a much longer training schedule (with pretraining of 80 and 8 epochs for LM and VM, respectively) and additional data (WikiText-103). For both synthetic and real data, PARSeq$_A$ achieves the highest word accuracies, while PARSeq$_N$ consistently places second or third. When real data is used, all reproduced models attain much higher accuracy compared to the original reported results, while PARSeq$_A$ establishes new SOTA results.

In Table 4, we show the mean accuracy for each charset. When synthetic data is used for training, there is a steep decline in accuracy from the 36- to the 62- and 94-charsets. This suggests that diversity of cased characters is lacking in the synthetic datasets. Meanwhile, PARSeq$_A$ consistently achieves the highest accuracy on all charset sizes for both synthetic and real training data. Finally in Table 5, PARSeq is the most robust against occlusion and text orientation

Table 4. Mean word accuracy on the benchmark vs evaluation charset size

Method	Train data	36-char	62-char	94-char
CRNN	S	83.2 ± 0.2	56.5 ± 0.3	54.8 ± 0.2
ViTSTR-S	S	88.6 ± 0.0	69.5 ± 1.0	67.7 ± 1.0
TRBA	S	90.6 ± 0.1	71.9 ± 0.9	69.9 ± 0.8
ABINet	S	89.8 ± 0.2	68.5 ± 1.1	66.4 ± 1.0
PARSeq$_N$	S	90.7 ± 0.2	72.5 ± 1.1	70.5 ± 1.1
PARSeq$_A$	S	**91.9 ± 0.2**	**75.5 ± 0.6**	**73.0 ± 0.7**
CRNN	R	88.5 ± 0.1	87.2 ± 0.1	85.8 ± 0.1
ViTSTR-S	R	94.3 ± 0.1	92.8 ± 0.1	91.8 ± 0.1
TRBA	R	95.2 ± 0.2	93.7 ± 0.1	92.5 ± 0.1
ABINet	R	95.2 ± 0.1	93.7 ± 0.1	92.4 ± 0.1
PARSeq$_N$	R	95.2 ± 0.1	93.7 ± 0.1	92.7 ± 0.1
PARSeq$_A$	R	**96.0 ± 0.0**	**94.6 ± 0.0**	**93.3 ± 0.1**

Table 5. 36-char word accuracy on large-scale and more challenging datasets

Method	Train data	Test datasets and # of samples			
		ArT	COCO	Uber	Total
		35,149	9,825	80,551	125,525
CRNN	S	57.3 ± 0.1	49.3 ± 0.6	33.1 ± 0.3	41.1 ± 0.3
ViTSTR-S	S	66.1 ± 0.1	56.4 ± 0.5	37.6 ± 0.3	47.0 ± 0.2
TRBA	S	68.2 ± 0.1	61.4 ± 0.4	38.0 ± 0.3	48.3 ± 0.2
ABINet	S	65.4 ± 0.4	57.1 ± 0.8	34.9 ± 0.3	45.2 ± 0.3
PARSeq$_N$	S	69.1 ± 0.2	60.2 ± 0.8	39.9 ± 0.5	49.7 ± 0.3
PARSeq$_A$	S	**70.7 ± 0.1**	**64.0 ± 0.9**	**42.0 ± 0.5**	**51.8 ± 0.4**
CRNN	R	66.8 ± 0.2	62.2 ± 0.3	51.0 ± 0.2	56.3 ± 0.2
ViTSTR-S	R	81.1 ± 0.1	74.1 ± 0.4	78.2 ± 0.1	78.7 ± 0.1
TRBA	R	82.5 ± 0.2	77.5 ± 0.2	81.2 ± 0.3	81.3 ± 0.2
ABINet	R	81.2 ± 0.1	76.4 ± 0.1	71.5 ± 0.7	74.6 ± 0.4
PARSeq$_N$	R	83.0 ± 0.2	77.0 ± 0.2	82.4 ± 0.3	82.1 ± 0.2
PARSeq$_A$	R	**84.5 ± 0.1**	**79.8 ± 0.1**	**84.5 ± 0.1**	**84.1 ± 0.0**

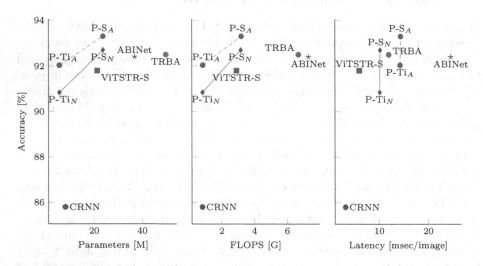

Fig. 5. 94-char mean word accuracy (real training data) vs computational cost. *P-S* and *P-Ti* are shorthands for PARSeq-S and PARSeq-Ti, respectively. For TRBA and PARSeq$_A$, FLOPS and latency correspond to mean values measured on the benchmark

variability. Appendix J contains more experiments on arbitrarily-oriented text. Altogether, bigger charsets and more challenging large-scale test datasets provide a more stringent evaluation and reveal wider performance gaps between methods.

Figure 5 shows the cost-quality trade-offs in terms of accuracy and commonly used cost indicators like parameter count, FLOPS, and latency. PARSeq-S is the base model used for all results, while -Ti is its scaled down variant (details in Appendix D). Note that for PARSeq, the parameter count is fixed regardless of the decoding scheme. PARSeq-S achieves the highest mean word accuracy and exhibits very competitive cost–quality characteristics across the three indicators.

Table 6. Word accuracy on the six benchmark datasets (36-char). For *Train data*: Synthetic datasets (**S**) - MJ [25] and ST [23]; Benchmark datasets (**B**) - SVT, IIIT5k, IC13, and IC15; Real datasets (**R**) - COCO, RCTW17, Uber, ArT, LSVT, MLT19, ReCTS, TextOCR, and OpenVINO; "*" denotes usage of character-level labels. In our experiments, bold indicates the highest word accuracy per column. [1]Used with SCATTER [36]. [2]SynthText without special characters (5.5M samples). [3]LM pretrained on WikiText-103 [41]. Combined accuracy values are available in Appendix K

Method		Train data	Test datasets and # of samples							
			IIIT5k	SVT	IC13		IC15		SVTP	CUTE
			3,000	647	857	1,015	1,811	2,077	645	288
Published results	PlugNet [43]	S	94.4	92.3	–	95.0	–	82.2	84.3	85.0
	SRN [69]	S	94.8	91.5	95.5	–	82.7	–	85.1	87.8
	RobustScanner [70]	S,B	95.4	89.3	–	94.1	–	79.2	82.9	92.4
	TextScanner [62]	S*	95.7	92.7	–	94.9	–	83.5	84.8	91.6
	AutoSTR [71]	S	94.7	90.9	–	94.2	81.8	–	81.7	–
	RCEED [17]	S,B	94.9	91.8	–	–	–	82.2	83.6	91.7
	PREN2D [67]	S	95.6	94.0	96.4	–	83.0	–	87.6	91.7
	VisionLAN [66]	S	95.8	91.7	95.7	–	83.7	–	86.0	88.5
	Bhunia et al. [8]	S	95.2	92.2	–	95.5	–	84.0	85.7	89.7
	CVAE-Feed.[1] [7]	S	95.2	–	–	95.7	–	84.6	88.9	89.7
	STN-CSTR [11]	S	94.2	92.3	96.3	94.1	86.1	82.0	86.2	–
	CRNN [4]	S	84.3	78.9	–	88.8	–	61.5	64.8	61.3
	ViTSTR-B [2]	S[2]	88.4	87.7	93.2	92.4	78.5	72.6	81.8	81.3
	TRBA [4]	S	92.1	88.9	–	93.1	–	74.7	79.5	78.2
	ABINet [21]	S[3]	96.2	93.5	97.4	–	86.0	–	89.3	89.2
Experiments	CRNN	S	91.2±0.2	85.7±0.7	92.1±0.7	90.9±0.5	74.4±1.0	70.8±0.9	73.5±0.6	78.7±0.7
	ViTSTR-S	S	94.0±0.2	91.7±0.4	95.1±0.7	94.2±0.7	82.7±0.1	78.7±0.1	83.9±0.6	88.2±0.6
	TRBA	S	96.3±0.2	**92.8±0.9**	96.3±0.3	95.0±0.4	84.3±0.1	80.6±0.2	86.9±1.3	91.3±1.6
	ABINet	S	95.3±0.2	**93.4±0.2**	**97.1±0.4**	95.0±0.3	83.1±0.3	79.1±0.2	87.1±0.6	89.7±2.3
	PARSeq_N (Ours)	S	95.7±0.2	92.6±0.3	96.3±0.4	**95.5±0.6**	85.1±0.1	81.4±0.1	87.9±0.9	91.4±1.5
	PARSeq_A (Ours)	S	**97.0±0.2**	**93.6±0.4**	**97.0±0.3**	**96.2±0.4**	**86.5±0.2**	**82.9±0.2**	**88.9±0.9**	**92.2±1.2**
	CRNN	R	94.6±0.2	90.7±0.4	94.1±0.4	94.5±0.3	82.0±0.2	78.5±0.2	80.6±0.3	89.1±0.4
	ViTSTR-S	R	98.1±0.2	95.8±0.4	97.6±0.3	97.7±0.3	88.4±0.4	87.1±0.3	91.4±0.2	96.1±0.4
	TRBA	R	98.6±0.1	97.0±0.2	97.6±0.3	97.6±0.2	89.8±0.4	88.7±0.4	93.7±0.3	**97.7±0.2**
	ABINet	R	98.6±0.2	**97.8±0.3**	**98.0±0.4**	97.8±0.2	**90.2±0.2**	88.5±0.2	93.9±0.8	**97.7±0.7**
	PARSeq_N (Ours)	R	98.3±0.1	97.5±0.4	**98.0±0.4**	98.1±0.1	89.6±0.2	88.4±0.4	94.6±1.0	**97.7±0.9**
	PARSeq_A (Ours)	R	**99.1±0.1**	**97.9±0.2**	98.3±0.2	**98.4±0.2**	**90.7±0.3**	**89.6±0.3**	**95.7±0.9**	**98.3±0.6**

Compared to ABINet and TRBA, PARSeq-S uses significantly less parameters and FLOPS. In terms of latency (details in Appendix I), PARSeq-S with AR decoding is slightly slower than TRBA, but is still significantly faster than ABINet. Meanwhile, PARSeq-Ti achieves a much higher word accuracy vs CRNN in spite of similar parameter count and FLOPS. PARSeq-S is Pareto-optimal, while -Ti is a compelling alternative for low-resource applications.

5   Conclusion

We adapted PLM for STR in order to learn PARSeq, a unified STR model capable of context-free and -aware decoding, and iterative refinement. PARSeq achieves SOTA results in different charset sizes and real-world datasets by jointly conditioning on both image and text representations. By unifying different decoding schemes into a single model and taking advantage of the parallel computations in Transformers, PARSeq is optimal on accuracy vs parameter count, FLOPS, and latency. Due to its extensive use of *attention*, it also demonstrates robustness on vertical and rotated text common in many real-world images.

Acknowledgments. This work was funded in part by CHED-PCARI IIID-2016-005 (Project AIRSCAN). We are also grateful to the PCARI PRIME team, led by Roel Ocampo, who ensured the uptime of our GPU servers.

References

1. Atienza, R.: Data augmentation for scene text recognition. In: 2021 IEEE/CVF International Conference on Computer Vision Workshops (ICCVW), pp. 1561–1570 (2021). https://doi.org/10.1109/ICCVW54120.2021.00181
2. Atienza, R.: Vision transformer for fast and efficient scene text recognition. In: International Conference on Document Analysis and Recognition (ICDAR) (2021)
3. Baek, J., et al.: What is wrong with scene text recognition model comparisons? Dataset and model analysis. In: Proceedings of the IEEE/CVF International Conference on Computer Vision (ICCV), October 2019
4. Baek, J., Matsui, Y., Aizawa, K.: What if we only use real datasets for scene text recognition? Toward scene text recognition with fewer labels. In: Proceedings of the IEEE/CVF Conference on Computer Vision and Pattern Recognition (CVPR), pp. 3113–3122, June 2021
5. Baevski, A., Auli, M.: Adaptive input representations for neural language modeling. In: International Conference on Learning Representations (2019). https://openreview.net/forum?id=ByxZX20qFQ
6. Bahdanau, D., Cho, K., Bengio, Y.: Neural machine translation by jointly learning to align and translate. In: Bengio, Y., LeCun, Y. (eds.) 3rd International Conference on Learning Representations, ICLR 2015, San Diego, CA, USA, 7–9 May 2015. Conference Track Proceedings (2015)
7. Bhunia, A.K., Chowdhury, P.N., Sain, A., Song, Y.Z.: Towards the unseen: Iterative text recognition by distilling from errors. In: Proceedings of the IEEE/CVF International Conference on Computer Vision (ICCV), pp. 14950–14959, October 2021
8. Bhunia, A.K., Sain, A., Kumar, A., Ghose, S., Chowdhury, P.N., Song, Y.Z.: Joint visual semantic reasoning: multi-stage decoder for text recognition. In: Proceedings of the IEEE/CVF International Conference on Computer Vision (ICCV), pp. 14940–14949, October 2021
9. Bleeker, M., de Rijke, M.: Bidirectional scene text recognition with a single decoder. In: ECAI 2020, pp. 2664–2671. IOS Press (2020)
10. Borisyuk, F., Gordo, A., Sivakumar, V.: Rosetta: large scale system for text detection and recognition in images. In: Proceedings of the 24th ACM SIGKDD International Conference on Knowledge Discovery and Data Mining, pp. 71–79 (2018)
11. Cai, H., Sun, J., Xiong, Y.: Revisiting classification perspective on scene text recognition (2021). https://arxiv.org/abs/2102.10884
12. Chen, X., Jin, L., Zhu, Y., Luo, C., Wang, T.: Text recognition in the wild: a survey. ACM Comput. Surv. (CSUR) **54**(2), 1–35 (2021)
13. Cheng, Z., Bai, F., Xu, Y., Zheng, G., Pu, S., Zhou, S.: Focusing attention: towards accurate text recognition in natural images. In: Proceedings of the IEEE International Conference on Computer Vision, pp. 5076–5084 (2017)
14. Chng, C.K., et al.: ICDAR 2019 robust reading challenge on arbitrary-shaped text-RRC-ArT. In: 2019 International Conference on Document Analysis and Recognition (ICDAR), pp. 1571–1576. IEEE (2019)

15. Cubuk, E.D., Zoph, B., Mané, D., Vasudevan, V., Le, Q.V.: AutoAugment: learning augmentation strategies from data. In: 2019 IEEE/CVF Conference on Computer Vision and Pattern Recognition (CVPR), pp. 113–123 (2019). https://doi.org/10.1109/CVPR.2019.00020

16. Cubuk, E.D., Zoph, B., Shlens, J., Le, Q.V.: RandAugment: practical automated data augmentation with a reduced search space. In: Proceedings of the IEEE/CVF Conference on Computer Vision and Pattern Recognition Workshops, pp. 702–703 (2020)

17. Cui, M., Wang, W., Zhang, J., Wang, L.: Representation and correlation enhanced encoder-decoder framework for scene text recognition. In: Lladós, J., Lopresti, D., Uchida, S. (eds.) ICDAR 2021. LNCS, vol. 12824, pp. 156–170. Springer, Cham (2021). https://doi.org/10.1007/978-3-030-86337-1_11

18. Deng, J., Dong, W., Socher, R., Li, L.J., Li, K., Fei-Fei, L.: ImageNet: a large-scale hierarchical image database. In: CVPR 2009 (2009)

19. Devlin, J., Chang, M.W., Lee, K., Toutanova, K.: BERT: pre-training of deep bidirectional transformers for language understanding. In: Proceedings of the 2019 Conference of the North American Chapter of the Association for Computational Linguistics: Human Language Technologies, Volume 1 (Long and Short Papers), Minneapolis, Minnesota, pp. 4171–4186. Association for Computational Linguistics, June 2019. https://doi.org/10.18653/v1/N19-1423. https://aclanthology.org/N19-1423

20. Dosovitskiy, A., et al.: An image is worth 16 × 16 words: transformers for image recognition at scale. In: International Conference on Learning Representations (2020)

21. Fang, S., Xie, H., Wang, Y., Mao, Z., Zhang, Y.: Read like humans: autonomous, bidirectional and iterative language modeling for scene text recognition. In: Proceedings of the IEEE/CVF Conference on Computer Vision and Pattern Recognition (CVPR), pp. 7098–7107, June 2021

22. Graves, A., Fernández, S., Gomez, F., Schmidhuber, J.: Connectionist temporal classification: labelling unsegmented sequence data with recurrent neural networks. In: Proceedings of the 23rd International Conference on Machine Learning, pp. 369–376 (2006)

23. Gupta, A., Vedaldi, A., Zisserman, A.: Synthetic data for text localisation in natural images. In: IEEE Conference on Computer Vision and Pattern Recognition (2016)

24. Izmailov, P., Podoprikhin, D., Garipov, T., Vetrov, D., Wilson, A.: Averaging weights leads to wider optima and better generalization. In: Silva, R., Globerson, A., Globerson, A. (eds.) 34th Conference on Uncertainty in Artificial Intelligence 2018, UAI 2018, pp. 876–885. Association For Uncertainty in Artificial Intelligence (AUAI) (2018)

25. Jaderberg, M., Simonyan, K., Vedaldi, A., Zisserman, A.: Synthetic data and artificial neural networks for natural scene text recognition. In: Workshop on Deep Learning. NIPS (2014)

26. Karatzas, D., et al.: ICDAR 2015 competition on robust reading. In: 2015 13th International Conference on Document Analysis and Recognition (ICDAR), pp. 1156–1160. IEEE (2015)

27. Karatzas, D., et al.: ICDAR 2013 robust reading competition. In: 2013 12th International Conference on Document Analysis and Recognition, pp. 1484–1493. IEEE (2013)

28. Kasai, J., Pappas, N., Peng, H., Cross, J., Smith, N.: Deep encoder, shallow decoder: Reevaluating non-autoregressive machine translation. In: International Conference on Learning Representations (2021). https://openreview.net/forum?id=KpfasTaLUpq

29. Kingma, D.P., Ba, J.: Adam: a method for stochastic optimization. In: International Conference on Learning Representations (ICLR) (2015)

30. Krasin, I., et al.: OpenImages: a public dataset for large-scale multi-label and multi-class image classification (2017). Dataset https://github.com/openimages. https://storage.googleapis.com/openimages/web/index.html

31. Krylov, I., Nosov, S., Sovrasov, V.: Open images V5 text annotation and yet another mask text spotter. In: Balasubramanian, V.N., Tsang, I. (eds.) Proceedings of the 13th Asian Conference on Machine Learning. Proceedings of Machine Learning Research, vol. 157, pp. 379–389. PMLR, 17–19 November 2021. https://proceedings.mlr.press/v157/krylov21a.html

32. Lee, C.Y., Osindero, S.: Recursive recurrent nets with attention modeling for OCR in the wild. In: Proceedings of the IEEE Conference on Computer Vision and Pattern Recognition (CVPR), June 2016

33. Lee, J., Park, S., Baek, J., Oh, S.J., Kim, S., Lee, H.: On recognizing texts of arbitrary shapes with 2D self-attention. In: Proceedings of the IEEE/CVF Conference on Computer Vision and Pattern Recognition Workshops, pp. 546–547 (2020)

34. Liao, Y., Jiang, X., Liu, Q.: Probabilistically masked language model capable of autoregressive generation in arbitrary word order. In: Proceedings of the 58th Annual Meeting of the Association for Computational Linguistics, pp. 263–274 (2020)

35. Lin, T.-Y., et al.: Microsoft COCO: common objects in context. In: Fleet, D., Pajdla, T., Schiele, B., Tuytelaars, T. (eds.) ECCV 2014. LNCS, vol. 8693, pp. 740–755. Springer, Cham (2014). https://doi.org/10.1007/978-3-319-10602-1_48

36. Litman, R., Anschel, O., Tsiper, S., Litman, R., Mazor, S., Manmatha, R.: SCATTER: selective context attentional scene text recognizer. In: IEEE/CVF Conference on Computer Vision and Pattern Recognition (CVPR), June 2020

37. Liu, W., Chen, C., Wong, K.Y.K., Su, Z., Han, J.: STAR-Net: a spatial attention residue network for scene text recognition. In: BMVC. vol. 2, p. 7 (2016)

38. Long, S., He, X., Yao, C.: Scene text detection and recognition: the deep learning era. Int. J. Comput. Vis. 129(1), 161–184 (2021)

39. Long, S., Yao, C.: UnrealText: synthesizing realistic scene text images from the unreal world. In: Proceedings of the IEEE Conference on Computer Vision and Pattern Recognition (CVPR) (2020)

40. Mansimov, E., Wang, A., Welleck, S., Cho, K.: A generalized framework of sequence generation with application to undirected sequence models. arXiv preprint arXiv:1905.12790 (2019)

41. Merity, S., Xiong, C., Bradbury, J., Socher, R.: Pointer sentinel mixture models. In: 5th International Conference on Learning Representations, ICLR 2017, Toulon, France, 24–26 April 2017. Conference Track Proceedings. OpenReview.net (2017). https://openreview.net/forum?id=Byj72udxe

42. Mishra, A., Alahari, K., Jawahar, C.: Scene text recognition using higher order language priors. In: BMVC-British Machine Vision Conference. BMVA (2012)

43. Mou, Y., et al.: PlugNet: degradation aware scene text recognition supervised by a pluggable super-resolution unit. In: Vedaldi, A., Bischof, H., Brox, T., Frahm, J.-M. (eds.) ECCV 2020. LNCS, vol. 12360, pp. 158–174. Springer, Cham (2020). https://doi.org/10.1007/978-3-030-58555-6_10

44. Nayef, N., et al.: ICDAR 2019 robust reading challenge on multi-lingual scene text detection and recognition-RRC-MLT-2019. In: 2019 International Conference on Document Analysis and Recognition (ICDAR), pp. 1582–1587. IEEE (2019)
45. Nguyen, N., et al.: Dictionary-guided scene text recognition. In: Proceedings of the IEEE/CVF Conference on Computer Vision and Pattern Recognition (CVPR), pp. 7383–7392 (6 2021)
46. Phan, T.Q., Shivakumara, P., Tian, S., Tan, C.L.: Recognizing text with perspective distortion in natural scenes. In: Proceedings of the IEEE International Conference on Computer Vision, pp. 569–576 (2013)
47. Qi, W., et al.: BANG: bridging autoregressive and non-autoregressive generation with large scale pretraining. In: International Conference on Machine Learning, pp. 8630–8639. PMLR (2021)
48. Qiao, Z., Zhou, Y., Yang, D., Zhou, Y., Wang, W.: SEED: semantics enhanced encoder-decoder framework for scene text recognition. In: IEEE/CVF Conference on Computer Vision and Pattern Recognition (CVPR), June 2020
49. Risnumawan, A., Shivakumara, P., Chan, C.S., Tan, C.L.: A robust arbitrary text detection system for natural scene images. Expert Syst. Appl. 41(18), 8027–8048 (2014)
50. Sheng, F., Chen, Z., Xu, B.: NRTR: a no-recurrence sequence-to-sequence model for scene text recognition. In: 2019 International Conference on Document Analysis and Recognition (ICDAR), pp. 781–786. IEEE (2019)
51. Shi, B., Bai, X., Yao, C.: An end-to-end trainable neural network for image-based sequence recognition and its application to scene text recognition. IEEE Trans. Pattern Anal. Mach. Intell. 39(11), 2298–2304 (2016)
52. Shi, B., Wang, X., Lyu, P., Yao, C., Bai, X.: Robust scene text recognition with automatic rectification. In: Proceedings of the IEEE Conference on Computer Vision and Pattern Recognition, pp. 4168–4176 (2016)
53. Shi, B., Yang, M., Wang, X., Lyu, P., Yao, C., Bai, X.: ASTER: an attentional scene text recognizer with flexible rectification. IEEE Trans. Pattern Anal. Mach. Intell. 41(9), 2035–2048 (2018)
54. Shi, B., et al.: ICDAR 2017 competition on reading Chinese text in the wild (RCTW-17). In: 2017 14th IAPR International Conference on Document Analysis and Recognition (ICDAR), vol. 1, pp. 1429–1434. IEEE (2017)
55. Singh, A., Pang, G., Toh, M., Huang, J., Galuba, W., Hassner, T.: TextOCR: towards large-scale end-to-end reasoning for arbitrary-shaped scene text. In: Proceedings of the IEEE/CVF Conference on Computer Vision and Pattern Recognition, pp. 8802–8812 (2021)
56. Smith, L.N., Topin, N.: Super-convergence: very fast training of neural networks using large learning rates. In: Artificial Intelligence and Machine Learning for Multi-Domain Operations Applications, vol. 11006, p. 1100612. International Society for Optics and Photonics (2019)
57. Sun, Y., et al.: ICDAR 2019 competition on large-scale street view text with partial labeling-RRC-LSVT. In: 2019 International Conference on Document Analysis and Recognition (ICDAR), pp. 1557–1562. IEEE (2019)
58. Tian, C., Wang, Y., Cheng, H., Lian, Y., Zhang, Z.: Train once, and decode as you like. In: Proceedings of the 28th International Conference on Computational Linguistics, pp. 280–293 (2020)
59. Uria, B., Murray, I., Larochelle, H.: A deep and tractable density estimator. In: International Conference on Machine Learning, pp. 467–475. PMLR (2014)
60. Vaswani, A., et al.: Attention is all you need. In: Guyon, I., et al. (eds.) Advances in Neural Information Processing Systems, vol. 30. Curran Associates, Inc. (2017)

61. Veit, A., Matera, T., Neumann, L., Matas, J., Belongie, S.: COCO-text: dataset and benchmark for text detection and recognition in natural images. arXiv preprint arXiv:1601.07140 (2016). http://vision.cornell.edu/se3/wp-content/uploads/2016/01/1601.07140v1.pdf
62. Wan, Z., He, M., Chen, H., Bai, X., Yao, C.: TextScanner: reading characters in order for robust scene text recognition. In: Proceedings of the AAAI Conference on Artificial Intelligence, vol. 34, pp. 12120–12127 (2020)
63. Wang, J., Hu, X.: Gated recurrent convolution neural network for OCR. In: Proceedings of the 31st International Conference on Neural Information Processing Systems, pp. 334–343 (2017)
64. Wang, K., Babenko, B., Belongie, S.: End-to-end scene text recognition. In: 2011 International Conference on Computer Vision, pp. 1457–1464. IEEE (2011)
65. Wang, Q., et al.: Learning deep transformer models for machine translation. In: Proceedings of the 57th Annual Meeting of the Association for Computational Linguistics, pp. 1810–1822 (2019)
66. Wang, Y., Xie, H., Fang, S., Wang, J., Zhu, S., Zhang, Y.: From two to one: A new scene text recognizer with visual language modeling network. In: Proceedings of the IEEE/CVF International Conference on Computer Vision (ICCV), pp. 14194–14203, October 2021
67. Yan, R., Peng, L., Xiao, S., Yao, G.: Primitive representation learning for scene text recognition. In: Proceedings of the IEEE/CVF Conference on Computer Vision and Pattern Recognition (CVPR), pp. 284–293, June 2021
68. Yang, Z., Dai, Z., Yang, Y., Carbonell, J., Salakhutdinov, R.R., Le, Q.V.: XLNet: generalized autoregressive pretraining for language understanding. In: Advances in Neural Information Processing Systems 32 (2019)
69. Yu, D., Li, X., Zhang, C., Liu, T., Han, J., Liu, J., Ding, E.: Towards accurate scene text recognition with semantic reasoning networks. In: Proceedings of the IEEE/CVF Conference on Computer Vision and Pattern Recognition, pp. 12113–12122 (2020)
70. Yue, X., Kuang, Z., Lin, C., Sun, H., Zhang, W.: RobustScanner: dynamically enhancing positional clues for robust text recognition. In: Vedaldi, A., Bischof, H., Brox, T., Frahm, J.-M. (eds.) ECCV 2020. LNCS, vol. 12364, pp. 135–151. Springer, Cham (2020). https://doi.org/10.1007/978-3-030-58529-7_9
71. Zhang, H., Yao, Q., Yang, M., Xu, Y., Bai, X.: AutoSTR: efficient backbone search for scene text recognition. In: Vedaldi, A., Bischof, H., Brox, T., Frahm, J.-M. (eds.) ECCV 2020. LNCS, vol. 12369, pp. 751–767. Springer, Cham (2020). https://doi.org/10.1007/978-3-030-58586-0_44
72. Zhang, R., et al.: ICDAR 2019 robust reading challenge on reading Chinese text on signboard. In: 2019 International Conference on Document Analysis and Recognition (ICDAR), pp. 1577–1581. IEEE (2019)
73. Zhang, Y., Gueguen, L., Zharkov, I., Zhang, P., Seifert, K., Kadlec, B.: Uber-Text: a large-scale dataset for optical character recognition from street-level imagery. In: SUNw: Scene Understanding Workshop - CVPR 2017, Hawaii, USA (2017). http://sunw.csail.mit.edu/abstract/uberText.pdf

When Counting Meets HMER: Counting-Aware Network for Handwritten Mathematical Expression Recognition

Bohan Li[1,2], Ye Yuan[1], Dingkang Liang[2], Xiao Liu[1], Zhilong Ji[1], Jinfeng Bai[1], Wenyu Liu[2], and Xiang Bai[2(✉)]

[1] Tomorrow Advancing Life, Beijing, China
jizhilong@tal.com
[2] Huazhong University of Science and Technology, Wuhan, China
{bohan1024,dkliang,liuwy,xbai}@hust.edu.cn

Abstract. Recently, most handwritten mathematical expression recognition (HMER) methods adopt the encoder-decoder networks, which directly predict the markup sequences from formula images with the attention mechanism. However, such methods may fail to accurately read formulas with complicated structure or generate long markup sequences, as the attention results are often inaccurate due to the large variance of writing styles or spatial layouts. To alleviate this problem, we propose an unconventional network for HMER named Counting-Aware Network (CAN), which jointly optimizes two tasks: HMER and symbol counting. Specifically, we design a weakly-supervised counting module that can predict the number of each symbol class without the symbol-level position annotations, and then plug it into a typical attention-based encoder-decoder model for HMER. Experiments on the benchmark datasets for HMER validate that both joint optimization and counting results are beneficial for correcting the prediction errors of encoder-decoder models, and CAN consistently outperforms the state-of-the-art methods. In particular, compared with an encoder-decoder model for HMER, the extra time cost caused by the proposed counting module is marginal. The source code is available at https://github.com/LBH1024/CAN.

Keywords: Handwritten mathematical expression recognition · Attention mechanism · Counting

1 Introduction

Handwritten mathematical expression recognition (HMER) is an important task of document analysis, which has broad applications including assignment grading, digital library service, and office automation. Despite the great successes of

---

B. Li and Y. Yuan—Contribute equally.

ⓒ The Author(s), under exclusive license to Springer Nature Switzerland AG 2022
S. Avidan et al. (Eds.): ECCV 2022, LNCS 13688, pp. 197–214, 2022.
https://doi.org/10.1007/978-3-031-19815-1_12

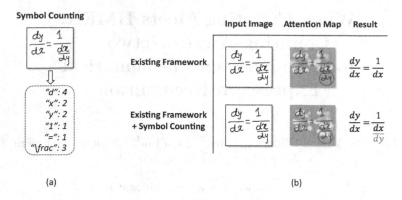

Fig. 1. (a) Illustration of the symbol counting task. (b) Comparison between the existing framework (e.g., DWAP [40]) and the proposed framework (CAN). By visualizing the attention map, we can observe that the existing framework misses the denominator "dy" while our CAN correctly locate it after using symbol counting.

the current OCR systems, HMER still remains a very challenging problem due to the complex structures of formulas or irregular writings.

Encoder-decoder architectures are extensively used in the recent HMER approaches [1,31,40], which formulate HMER as an image-to-sequence translation problem. Given a handwritten formula, such methods predict its corresponding markup sequence (e.g., LaTeX) with the attention mechanism. However, encoder-decoder models often cannot guarantee the accuracy of attention, especially when the structure of a handwritten formula is complicated or the markup sequence is long.

In this paper, we propose an unconventional method for improving the robustness of the encoder-decoder models for HMER. We argue that counting and HMER are two complementary tasks, and using counting can improve the performance of HMER. In this community, object counting [12,15] has been intensively studied, but has seldom been applied in the OCR area. Our intuition includes two aspects: 1) symbol counting (as illustrated in Fig. 1(a)) is able to provide the symbol-level position information, which can make the attention results more accurate. 2) The counting results, representing the number of each symbol class, can serve as additional global information to promote recognition accuracy.

Specifically, we design a weakly-supervised counting module named MSCM, which can be easily plugged into existing encoder-decoder networks and optimized jointly in an end-to-end manner. With this counting module, an encoder-decoder model can be better aware of each symbol's position, as shown in Fig. 1(b). It is worth noticing that the proposed counting module just needs original HMER annotations (LaTeX sequences) without extra labeling work. We combine our counting module with a typical encoder-decoder model (e.g., DWAP [40]), proposing a unified network for HMER named Counting-Aware Network (CAN). We test it on the benchmark datasets and observe that both

HMER and symbol counting gain obvious and consistent performance improvement. In particular, compared with the original model, the extra time cost brought by MSCM is marginal.

In summary, the main contributions of this paper are two-fold. 1) To the best of our knowledge, we are the first to bring symbol counting into HMER and reveal the relevance and the complementarity of HMER and symbol counting. 2) We propose a new method that jointly optimizes symbol counting and HMER, which consistently improves the performance of the encoder-decoder models for HMER.

To be specific about the performance, with adopting DWAP [40] as the baseline network, our method achieves state-of-the-art (SOTA) recognition accuracy on the widely-used CROHME dataset (57.00% on CROHME 2014, 56.06% on CROHME 2016, 54.88% on CROHME 2019). Moreover, with adopting the latest SOTA method ABM [1] as the baseline network, CAN achieves new SOTA results (57.26% on CROHME 2014, 56.15% on CROHME 2016, 55.96% on CROHME 2019). This indicates that our method can be generalized to various existing encoder-decoder models for HMER and boost their performance.

2 Related Work

2.1 HMER

Traditional HMER methods usually take a three-step approach: a symbol segmentation step, a symbol recognition step, and a grammar-guided structure analysis step. Classic classification techniques such as HMM [8,11,29], Elastic Matching [2,26] and Support Vector Machines [10] are mainly used in the recognition step. In the structure analysis step, formal grammars are elaborately designed to model the 2D and syntactic structures of formulas. Lavirotte *et al.* [13] propose to use graph grammar to recognize mathematical expression. Chan *et al.* [3] incorporate correction mechanism into a parser based on definite clause grammar (DCG). However, limited feature learning ability and complex grammar rules make the traditional methods far to meet real-world application.

Recently, deep learning has rapidly boosted the performance of HMER. The mainstream framework is the encoder-decoder network [1,5,24,30,31,40,42,43, 46]. Deng *et al.* [5] first apply an attention-based encoder-decoder model in HMER, inspired by its success in image caption task [34]. Zhang *et al.* [43] also present a similar model named WAP. In their model, they apply a FCN as the encoder and utilize the coverage attention, which is the sum of all past attention weights, to alleviate the lack of coverage problem [25]. Wu *et al.* [30,31] focus on the pair-wise adversarial learning strategy to improve the recognition accuracy. Later, Zhang *et al.* [42] devise a tree-based decoder to parse formulas. At each step, a parent and child node pair is generated and the relation between parent node and child node reflects the structure type. Bi-directional learning has been proven effective to improve model recognition performance [23]. Zhao *et al.* [46] design a bi-directionally trained transformer framework and Bian

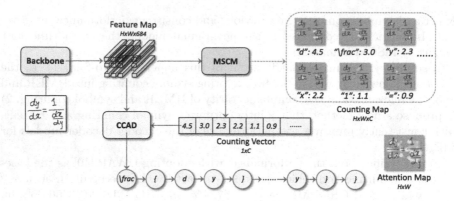

Fig. 2. Structure of the proposed CAN, which consists of a backbone network, a multi-scale counting Module (MSCM) and a counting-combined attentional decoder (CCAD).

et al. [1] propose an bi-directional mutual learning network. They further prove bi-directional learning can also significantly improve the HMER performance.

2.2 Object Counting

Object counting can be roughly divided into two categories, detection-based and regression-based. The detection-based methods [17,21] obtain the number by detecting each instance. The regression-based methods [15,33] learn to count by regressing a density map, and the predicted count equals the integration of the density map. To improve the counting accuracy, multi-scale strategy [44], attention mechanism [39] and perspective information [35] are widely adopted in the regression-based methods. Nevertheless, both detection-based and density map regression-based methods need the object position annotations (fully-supervised), such as box-level [17,21] and point-level [15,33,44] annotations. To relieve the expensive and laborious labeling work, several approaches [27,36] that only use count-level annotations (weakly-supervised) are proposed. And they find that the visualized feature map can accurately reflect the object regions. Different from most of the previous counting modules that are category specifically (e.g., crowd counting), our counting module is designed for multi-class object counting since formulas usually contains various symbols. In the OCR area, Xie *et al.* [32] propose a counting-based loss function mainly designed for scene texts (words or text-lines), while our model can exploit the counting information of more complicated texts (e.g., mathematical expressions) at both the feature level and the loss level.

3 Methodology

3.1 Overview

As shown in Fig. 2, our Counting-Aware Network (CAN) is a unified end-to-end trainable framework that comprises a backbone, a multi-scale counting module (MSCM) and a counting-combined attentional decoder (CCAD). Following DWAP [40], we apply DenseNet [9] as the backbone. Given a gray-scale image $\mathcal{X} \in \mathbb{R}^{H' \times W' \times 1}$, the backbone is first used to extract 2D feature map $\mathcal{F} \in \mathbb{R}^{H \times W \times 684}$, where $\frac{H'}{H} = \frac{W'}{W} = 16$. The feature map $\mathcal{F}$ will be used by both the MSCM and the CCAD. The counting module MSCM is used to predict the number of each symbol class and generate the 1D counting vector $\mathcal{V}$ that represents the counting results. The feature map $\mathcal{F}$ and the counting vector $\mathcal{V}$ will be fed into the CCAD to get predicted output.

3.2 Multi-Scale Counting Module

In this part, we present the detail of the proposed multi-scale counting module (MSCM), which is designed to predict the number of each symbol class. Specifically, as depicted in Fig. 3, MSCM consists of multi-scale feature extraction, channel attention and sum-pooling operator. Formula images usually contain various sizes of symbols due to different writing habits. Single kernel size can not effectively handle the scale variations. To this end, we first utilize two parallel convolution branches to extract multi-scale features by using different kernel sizes (set to 3×3 and 5×5). Following the convolution layer, the channel attention [7] is adopted to enhance the feature information further. Here, we choose one of the branches for simple illustration. Let us denote $\mathcal{H} \in \mathbb{R}^{H \times W \times C'}$ as the extracted feature map from the convolution (3×3 or 5×5) layer. The enhanced feature S can be written as:

$$Q = \sigma(W_1(G(\mathcal{H})) + b_1), \tag{1}$$

$$\mathcal{S} = \mathcal{Q} \otimes g(W_2\mathcal{Q} + b_2), \tag{2}$$

where G is the global average pooling. σ and $g(\cdot)$ refer to ReLU and sigmoid function, respectively. $\otimes$ denotes channel-wise product and W_1, W_2, b_1, b_2 are trainable weights.

After getting the enhanced feature $\mathcal{S}$, we use a 1×1 convolution to reduce the channel number from C' to C, where C is the number of symbol classes. Ideally, the symbol counting result should mainly calculate from the foreground (symbols), i.e., the response of the background should be close to zero. Thus, following the 1×1 convolution, we utilize a sigmoid function to yield the value in a range of (0,1) to generate counting map $\mathcal{M} \in \mathbb{R}^{H \times W \times C}$. For each $\mathcal{M}_i \in \mathbb{R}^{H \times W}$, it is supposed to effectively reflect the position of the i-th symbol class, as shown

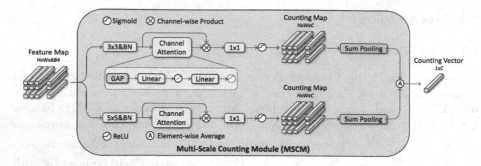

Fig. 3. Structure of the proposed multi-scale counting module (MSCM).

in Fig. 2. In this sense, each $\mathcal{M}_i$ is actually a pseudo density map, and we can utilize sum-pooling operator to obtain counting vector $\mathcal{V} \in \mathbb{R}^{1 \times C}$:

$$\mathcal{V}_i = \sum_{p=1}^{H} \sum_{q=1}^{W} M_{i,pq} \tag{3}$$

Here, $\mathcal{V}_i \in \mathbb{R}^{1 \times 1}$ is the predicted count of the i-th class symbol. It is noteworthy that the feature maps of different branches contain different scale information and are highly complementary. Thus, we combine the complementary counting vectors and use the average operator to generate the final result $\mathcal{V}^f \in \mathbb{R}^{1 \times C}$, which is then fed into the decoder CCAD.

3.3 Counting-Combined Attentional Decoder

The structure of our counting-combined attentional decoder (CCAD) is shown in Fig. 4. Given the 2D feature map $\mathcal{F} \in \mathbb{R}^{H \times W \times 684}$, we first use a 1×1 convolution to change the number of channel and get transformed feature $\mathcal{T} \in \mathbb{R}^{H \times W \times 512}$. Then, to enhance model's awareness of spatial position, we use a fixed absolute encoding $\mathcal{P} \in \mathbb{R}^{H \times W \times 512}$ to represent different spatial positions in $\mathcal{T}$. Specifically, we adopt the spatial positional encoding [20], which independently uses sine and cosine functions with different frequencies for both spatial coordinates.

During the decoding process, when decoding at step t, we pass the embedding of symbol y_{t-1} into a GRU cell [4] to get a hidden state $h_t \in \mathbb{R}^{1 \times 256}$. With the transformed feature $\mathcal{T}$ and the spatial encoding $\mathcal{P}$, we can then get the attention weights $\alpha_t \in \mathbb{R}^{H \times W}$ as follows:

$$e_t = w^T \tanh(\mathcal{T} + \mathcal{P} + W_a \mathcal{A} + W_h h_t) + b, \tag{4}$$

$$\alpha_{t,ij} = \exp(e_{t,ij}) / \sum_{p=1}^{H} \sum_{q=1}^{W} e_{t,pq}, \tag{5}$$

where w, b, W_a, W_h are trainable weights and coverage attention $\mathcal{A}$ is the sum of all past attention weights.

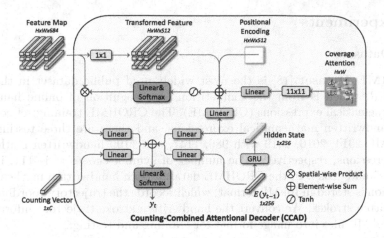

Fig. 4. Structure of the proposed counting-combined attentional decoder (CCAD).

Applying spatial-wise product to the attention weights α_t and the feature map $\mathcal{F}$, we can get context vector $\mathcal{C} \in \mathbb{R}^{1 \times 256}$. In most of the previous HMER methods, they predict y_t only using the context vector $\mathcal{C}$, the hidden state h_t and the embedding $E(y_{t-1})$. Actually, $\mathcal{C}$ just corresponds to a local region of the feature map $\mathcal{F}$. And we argue that h_t and $E(y_{t-1})$ also lack global information. Considering that the counting vector $\mathcal{V}$ is calculated from a global counting perspective, which can serve as additional global information to make the prediction more accurate, we combine them together to predict y_t as follows:

$$p(y_t) = \text{softmax}(w_o^T (W_c \mathcal{C} + W_v \mathcal{V} + W_t h_t + W_e E) + b_o, \qquad (6)$$

$$y_t \sim p(y_t), \qquad (7)$$

where w_o, b_o, W_c, W_v, W_t, W_e are trainable weights.

3.4 Loss Function

The overall loss function consists of two parts and is defined as follows:

$$\mathcal{L} = \mathcal{L}_{cls} + \mathcal{L}_{counting}, \qquad (8)$$

where $\mathcal{L}_{cls}$ is a common-used cross entropy classification loss of the predicted probability $p(y_t)$ with respect to its ground-truth. Denoting the counting ground truth of each symbol class as $\hat{\mathcal{V}}$, $\mathcal{L}_{counting}$ is a smooth $L1$ [22] regression loss defined as follows:

$$\mathcal{L}_{counting} = smooth_{L1}(\mathcal{V}, \hat{\mathcal{V}}) \qquad (9)$$

4 Experiments

4.1 Datasets

CROHME Dataset [18] is the most widely-used public dataset in the field of HMER, which is from the competition on recognition of online handwritten mathematical expressions (CROHME). The CROHME training set contains 8836 handwritten mathematical expressions, and there are three testing sets: CROHME 2014, 2016, 2019 with 986, 1147, and 1199 handwritten mathematical expressions, respectively. The number of symbol classes C is 111, including "*sos*" and "*eos*". In the CROHME dataset, each handwritten mathematical expression is stored in InkML format, which records the trajectory coordinates of handwritten strokes. We convert the handwritten stroke trajectory information in the InkML files into image format for training and testing.

Fig. 5. Some example images from the HME100K dataset.

HME100K Dataset [37] is a real scene handwritten mathematical expression dataset, consisting of 74,502 images for training and 24,607 images for testing. The number of symbol classes C is 249 including "*sos*" and "*eos*". These images are from tens of thousands of writers, mainly captured by cameras. Consequently, HME100K is more authentic and realistic with variations in color, blur, and complicated background. Some example images are shown in Fig. 5.

4.2 Implementation Details

The proposed CAN is implemented in PyTorch. We use a single Nvidia Tesla V100 with 32GB RAM to train our model with batch size 8 and the Adadelta optimizer [38]. The learning rate starts from 0 and monotonously increases to 1 at the end of the first epoch and decays to 0 following the cosine schedules [45]. For the CROHME dataset, the total training epoch is set to 240, and we separately present the results with and without data augmentation. Compared with previous methods, we use different data augmentation (rotation, affine, perspective, erosion and dilation) to explore the ability of our method. For the HME100K dataset, the total training epoch is set to 30 without data augmentation.

It is noteworthy that when counting the symbols in the handwritten mathematical expression, six classes of symbols are ignored by assigning their counting ground truth as zero because they are invisible: "sos", "eos", "^", "_", "{", "}". Counting these symbols will confuse the model and bring lower accuracy.

Input Image	DWAP (Baseline)	CAN-DWAP (Ours)
 *log*	\log g	\log
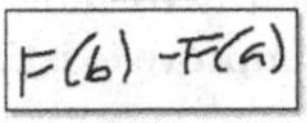 F(b) -F(a)	F (b) - F (G)	F (b) - F (a)
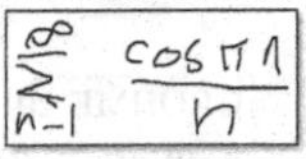 ∑ cos π / n	\sum_ { n = 1 } ^ { \infty } \frac { \cos \pi } { n }	\sum_ { n = 1 } ^ { \infty } \frac { \cos \pi } { n }
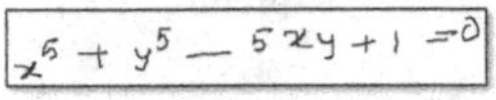 x⁵ + y⁵ − 5xy + 1 = 0	x ^ { 5 } + y ^ { 5 } - x y + 1 = 0	x ^ { 5 } + y ^ { 5 } - 5 x y + 1 = 0
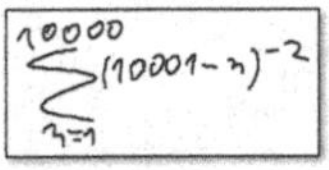 ∑ (10001−n)⁻²	\sum_ { n = 1 } ^ { 1000 000001 - n) ^ { -2 }	\sum_ { n = 1 } ^ { 1000 0 } (10001 - n) ^ { -2 }

Fig. 6. Some recognition cases of DWAP and CAN-DWAP.

4.3 Evaluation Metrics

Expression Recognition. Expression recognition rate (ExpRate), defined as the percentage of correctly recognized expressions, is used to evaluate the performance of different methods on mathematical expression recognition. Moreover, ≤ 1 and ≤ 2 are also used, indicating that the expression recognition rate is tolerable at most one or two symbol-level errors.

Symbol Counting. The mean absolute error (MAE) and the mean squared error (MSE) are the primary metrics in the object counting task. In our multi-class symbol counting task, we use MAE and MSE to evaluate the counting performance for each formula image, and then average the counting results of all formula images to get MAE_{Ave} and MSE_{Ave}:

$$MAE = \frac{1}{C} \sum_{i=1}^{C} |\mathcal{V}_i - \hat{\mathcal{V}}_i|, \quad MSE = \sqrt{\frac{1}{C} \sum_{i=1}^{C} |\mathcal{V}_i - \hat{\mathcal{V}}_i|^2}, \tag{10}$$

$$MAE_{Ave} = \frac{1}{N} \sum_{i=1}^{N} MAE_i, \quad MSE_{Ave} = \frac{1}{N} \sum_{i=1}^{N} MSE_i, \tag{11}$$

where C denotes the number of symbol classes, N is the number of images in the testing set, $\mathcal{V}_i$ and $\hat{\mathcal{V}}_i$ are the predicted count and its corresponding ground truth of a symbol class respectively.

4.4 Comparison with State-of-the-Art

To demonstrate the superiority of our method, we compare it with previous state-of-the-art (SOTA) methods. Table 1 shows the expression recognition rate (ExpRate) on the CROHME dataset. Most of the previous methods do not use data augmentation, so we mainly focus on the results produced without data augmentation.

Table 1. Results on the CROHME dataset. * indicates using stoke trajectory coordinates annotations. † indicates our reproduced result. CAN-DWAP and CAN-ABM represent using DWAP and ABM as the baseline respectively. Note that we use different data augmentation than previous methods. Our intention is to show that even with data augmentation, our counting module can still stably improve existing HMER methods' performance.

Method	CROHME 2014			CROHME 2016			CROHME 2019		
	ExpRate ↑	≤1 ↑	≤2 ↑	ExpRate ↑	≤1 ↑	≤2 ↑	ExpRate ↑	≤1 ↑	≤2 ↑
Without data augmentation									
UPV [18]	37.22	44.22	47.26	–	–	–	–	–	–
TOKYO [19]	–	–	–	43.94	50.91	53.70	–	–	–
PAL [30]	39.66	56.80	65.11	–	–	–	–	–	–
WAP [43]	46.55	61.16	65.21	44.55	57.10	61.55	–	–	–
PAL-v2 [31]	48.88	64.50	69.78	49.61	64.08	70.27	–	–	–
TAP [41]*	48.47	63.28	67.34	44.81	59.72	62.77	–	–	–
DLA [14]	49.85	–	–	47.34	–	–	–	–	–
DWAP [40]	50.10	–	–	47.50	–	–	–	–	–
DWAP-TD [42]	49.10	64.20	67.80	48.50	62.30	65.30	51.40	66.10	69.10
DWAP-MSA [40]	52.80	68.10	72.00	50.10	63.80	67.40	47.70	59.50	63.30
WS-WAP [24]	53.65	–	–	51.96	64.34	70.10	–	–	–
MAN [28]*	54.05	68.76	72.21	50.56	64.78	67.13	–	–	–
BTTR [46]	53.96	66.02	70.28	52.31	63.90	68.61	52.96	65.97	69.14
ABM [1]	56.85	73.73	81.24	52.92	69.66	78.73	53.96	71.06	78.65
DWAP (baseline)†	51.48	67.01	73.30	50.65	63.30	70.88	50.04	65.39	69.39
CAN-DWAP (ours)	**57.00**	74.21	80.61	**56.06**	71.49	79.51	**54.88**	71.98	79.40
ABM (baseline)†	56.04	73.10	79.90	53.36	70.01	78.12	53.71	71.23	78.23
CAN-ABM (ours)	**57.26**	74.52	82.03	**56.15**	72.71	80.30	**55.96**	72.73	80.57
With data augmentation									
Li *et al.* [16]	56.59	69.07	75.25	54.58	69.31	73.76	–	–	–
Ding *et al.* [6]	58.72	–	–	57.72	70.01	76.37	61.38	75.15	80.23
DWAP (baseline)†	57.97	73.81	79.19	55.97	71.40	79.86	56.05	72.23	79.15
CAN-DWAP (ours)	**65.58**	77.36	83.35	**62.51**	74.63	82.48	**63.22**	78.07	82.49
ABM (baseline)†	63.76	76.35	83.05	60.86	73.93	81.17	62.22	77.23	81.90
CAN-ABM (ours)	**65.89**	77.97	84.16	**63.12**	75.94	82.74	**64.47**	78.73	82.99

As shown in Table 1, with adopting DWAP [40] as the baseline, CAN-DWAP achieves SOTA results on CROHME 2014, CROHME 2016, CROHME 2019 and outperforms the latest SOTA method ABM [1] on CROHME 2016 by a significant margin of 3.14%. Figure 6 shows some qualitative recognition results of DWAP and CAN-DWAP. We can observe that our method is less likely to miss symbols or predict redundant symbols.

To further verify the effectiveness of our method, we reproduce the latest SOTA method ABM [1] and adopt it as our baseline to construct CAN-ABM. As shown in Table 1, CAN-ABM outperforms its baseline and achieves new SOTA results. This indicates that our method can be generalized to various existing encoder-decoder models for HMER and boost their performance.

4.5 Results on the HME100K Dataset

Although the CROHME dataset has been widely used and has great influence in the field of HMER, its small size limits the performance of different methods. Hence, we further evaluate our method on the HME100K dataset, which is nearly ten times larger than the CROHME dataset and has more variations in color, blur, and background. The quantitative results are listed in Table 2, CAN-DWAP and CAN-ABM largely outperform their baseline DWAP [40] and ABM [1] respectively.

4.6 Inference Speed

To explore the efficiency of our proposed method, we evaluate its speed on the HME100K dataset with a single Nvidia Tesla V100. As shown in Table 3, compared with the baseline model, the extra parameters and FLOPs are mainly brought by the counting module's two convolution layers with kernels of sizes 3×3 and 5×5. As to the inference speed, the extra time cost brought by the counting module is marginal.

4.7 Ablation Study

Component Analysis. In our method, symbol counting serves as an auxiliary task and influences the feature learning together with the primary task HMER through joint optimization. Meanwhile, adding counting vector during the decoding process also has an impact on the performance. So, to verify the effectiveness of the three components: positional encoding, joint optimization, and counting vector, we conduct experiments and the results are listed in Table 4. We can observe that both joint optimization and counting vector can boost the performance to a certain degree, and adding positional encoding can also slightly improve the recognition accuracy.

Table 2. Results on the HME100K dataset. [†] indicates our reproduced result. CAN-DWAP and CAN-ABM represent using DWAP and ABM as the baseline respectively.

Method	HME100K		
	ExpRate ↑	≤1 ↑	≤2 ↑
DWAP-TD [42][†]	62.60	79.05	85.67
DWAP [40] (baseline)[†]	61.85	70.63	77.14
CAN-DWAP (ours)	67.31	82.93	89.17
ABM [1] (baseline)[†]	65.93	81.16	87.86
CAN-ABM (ours)	**68.09**	**83.22**	**89.91**

Table 3. Comparison on parameters, FLOPs, and FPS.

Method	HME100K			
	#Params	Input size	FLOPs	FPS
DWAP [40] (baseline)	4.7M	(1,1,120,800)	9.7G	23.3
CAN-DWAP (ours)	17.0M	(1,1,120,800)	14.7G	21.7

Impact of Convolution Kernel in Counting Module. In our counting module MSCM, we adopt a multi-scale strategy by using convolution layer with different sizes of kernels (3×3 and 5×5). To explore the impact of different convolution kernels, we conduct experiments on CROHME 2014 with using different sizes of convolution kernels. As shown in Table 5, using 3×3 and 5×5 convolution kernels together achieves the best results (57.00% ExpRate, 0.033 MAE_{Ave} and 0.037 MSE_{Ave}). Using either 3×3 or 5×5 convolution kernel will get lower counting accuracy and lower ExpRate. We think this phenomenon indicates that multi-scale information obtained with different kinds of convolution kernels can help the counting module better tackle the size variations.

Table 4. Ablation study of different components.

Method	CROHME 2014			CROHME 2016			CROHME 2019		
	ExpRate ↑	≤1 ↑	≤2 ↑	ExpRate ↑	≤1 ↑	≤2 ↑	ExpRate ↑	≤1 ↑	≤2 ↑
DWAP [40] (baseline)	51.48	67.01	73.30	50.65	63.30	70.88	50.04	65.39	69.39
+ Positional encoding	51.88	68.12	74.21	51.00	64.06	71.37	50.96	66.14	70.48
+ Joint optimization	55.23	72.18	78.17	54.11	68.00	76.37	53.13	69.89	76.00
+ Counting vector	**57.00**	**74.21**	**80.61**	**56.06**	**71.49**	**79.51**	**54.88**	**71.98**	**79.40**

Table 5. Ablation study of different convolution kernels in counting module.

Method	CROHME 2014				
	ExpRate ↑	≤1 ↑	≤2 ↑	MAE_{Ave} ↓	MSE_{Ave} ↓
CAN-DWAP (3×3)	54.92	71.26	78.07	0.048	0.046
CAN-DWAP (5×5)	55.53	71.88	78.58	0.044	0.043
CAN-DWAP (3×3 & 5×5)	**57.00**	**74.21**	**80.61**	**0.033**	**0.037**

Impact of Counting Vector on HMER. To explore the impact of counting vector, we use the ground truth of counting vector and add different random disturbances to it (e.g., randomly add or subtract 1) so that we can get several counting vectors with different MAE_{Ave} and MSE_{Ave}. By providing these

Table 6. Ablation study of different counting vectors. * indicates adding random disturbance to counting vector. The latter counting GT with * is added with more disturbances than the former one.

Method	CROHME 2014				
	ExpRate ↑	≤1 ↑	≤2 ↑	MAE_{Ave} ↓	MSE_{Ave} ↓
CAN-DWAP	57.00	74.21	80.61	0.033	0.037
CAN-DWAP (counting GT)*	58.28	74.92	81.02	0.027	0.025
CAN-DWAP (counting GT)*	60.10	76.04	81.73	0.019	0.016
CAN-DWAP (counting GT)	62.44	76.14	82.23	0.000	0.000

counting vectors to the decoder during training and testing, we conduct several experiments and the results are shown in Table 6. When using the ground truth of counting vector, the ExpRate on CROHME 2014 reaches 62.44%. As more disturbances are added, the counting vector becomes more inaccurate, and the ExpRate drops consequently.

Table 7. Ablation study of HMER's impact on symbol counting.

Method	CROHME 2014	
	MAE_{Ave} ↓	MSE_{Ave} ↓
Counting w/o HMER	0.048	0.044
Counting w HMER	**0.033**	**0.037**

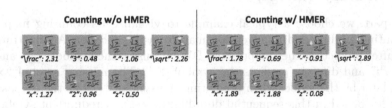

Fig. 7. Counting map generated with and without HMER task.

Impact of HMER on Symbol Counting. Through joint optimization, symbol counting can promote the performance of HMER. To find out whether HMER can also promote the performance of symbol counting, we train CAN only with the symbol counting task and compare it with CAN trained with two tasks. As shown in Table 7, HMER can boost the performance of symbol counting with improving MAE_{Ave} by 31.25% and MSE_{Ave} by 15.91%.

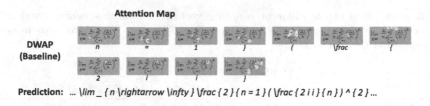

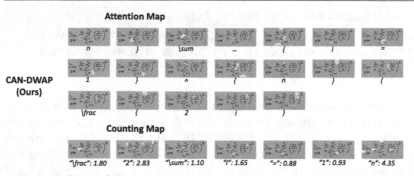

Fig. 8. Counting map and attention map of DWAP and CAN-DWAP.

Some visual results are shown in Fig. 7. We can observe that when training only with the symbol counting task, some symbols are wrongly located (e.g., "−") or partially counted (e.g., "2"). Counting with the HMER task can alleviate this problem by providing context-aware information, which is gained through the context-aware decoding process in the decoder CCAD.

4.8 Case Study with Maps

In this part, we choose a typical example to visualize its counting map from the counting module and its attention map from the decoder. As illustrated in Fig. 8, after predicting the symbol "n", DWAP misses the symbol "$\sum$" and the symbol "i" and directly predicts the symbol "$=$". The missing symbol "$\sum$" is noticed later by the model when predicting the symbol "(" but the mistake has already happened in this sequential decoding process. A redundant symbol "i" is also wrongly predicted, and the attention map shows that this mistake is due to the model's repeated attention on the symbol "i".

In contrast, our method CAN-DWAP predicts the formula correctly. From the counting map, we can see that almost all symbols are accurately located (note that we do not use symbol-level position annotations). And the predicted count of each symbol class, which is calculated by summing each counting map, is very close to its ground truth. These phenomenons demonstrate that by counting each symbol class, the model becomes more aware of each symbol, especially their positions. As a result, the model has more accurate attention results (seen from the attention map) during the decoding process and is less likely to miss or predict redundant symbols.

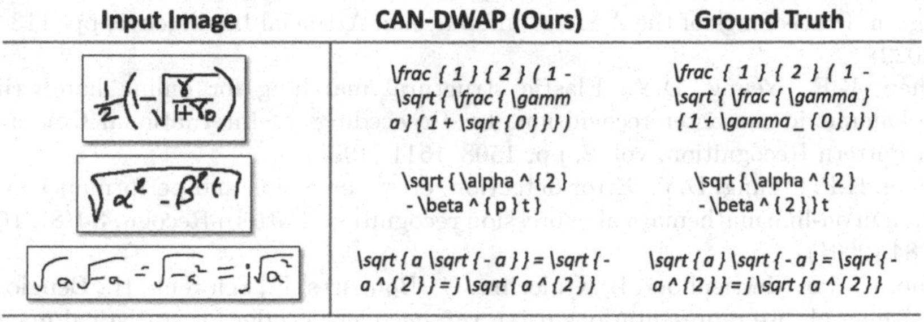

Input Image	CAN-DWAP (Ours)	Ground Truth
$\frac{1}{2}\left(1-\sqrt{\frac{Y}{H+Y_0}}\right)$	\frac { 1 } { 2 } (1 - \sqrt { \frac { \gamm a } { 1 + \sqrt { 0 } } })	\frac { 1 } { 2 } (1 - \sqrt { \frac { \gamma } { 1 + \gamma _ { 0 } } })
$\sqrt{\alpha^2 - \beta^2 t}$	\sqrt { \alpha ^ { 2 } - \beta ^ { p } t }	\sqrt { \alpha ^ { 2 } - \beta ^ { 2 } } t
$\sqrt{a}\sqrt{-a} = \sqrt{-a^2} = j\sqrt{a^2}$	\sqrt { a \sqrt { - a } } = \sqrt { - a ^ { 2 } } = j \sqrt { a ^ { 2 } }	\sqrt { a } \sqrt { - a } = \sqrt { - a ^ { 2 } } = j \sqrt { a ^ { 2 } }

Fig. 9. Some failure cases of our CAN-DWAP.

4.9 Limitation

Despite the significant performance improvement brought by symbol counting, the variations in writing styles still cause some recognition problems and cannot be solved very well with symbol counting, as shown in Fig. 9. Moreover, since we do not explicitly model structure grammar, our method may make some mistakes when extreme fine structure perception ability is needed.

5 Conclusion

In this paper, we design a counting module MSCM, which can perform symbol counting just relying on the original HMER annotations (LaTeX sequences). By plugging this counting module into an attention-based encoder-decoder network, we propose an unconventional end-to-end trainable network for HMER named CAN, which jointly optimizes HMER and symbol counting. Experiments on the benchmark datasets for HMER validate three main conclusions. 1) Symbol counting can consistently improve the performance of the encoder-decoder models for HMER. 2) Both joint optimization and counting results contribute to this improvement. 3) HMER can also increase the accuracy of symbol counting through joint optimization.

Acknowledgements. This work was done when Bohan Li was an intern at Tomorrow Advancing Life, and was supported in part by the National Natural Science Foundation of China 61733007 and the National Key R&D Program of China under Grant No. 2020AAA0104500.

References

1. Bian, X., Qin, B., Xin, X., Li, J., Su, X., Wang, Y.: Handwritten mathematical expression recognition via attention aggregation based bi-directional mutual learning. In: Proceedings of the AAAI Conference on Artificial Intelligence, pp. 113–121 (2022)
2. Chan, K.F., Yeung, D.Y.: Elastic structural matching for online handwritten alphanumeric character recognition. In: Proceedings of International Conference on Pattern Recognition, vol. 2, pp. 1508–1511 (1998)
3. Chan, K.F., Yeung, D.Y.: Error detection, error correction and performance evaluation in on-line mathematical expression recognition. Pattern Recogn. **34**(8), 1671–1684 (2001)
4. Cho, K., van Merrienboer, B., Gulcehre, C., Bougares, F., Schwenk, H., Bengio, Y.: Learning phrase representations using rnn encoder-decoder for statistical machine translation. In: Conference on Empirical Methods in Natural Language Processing (2014)
5. Deng, Y., Kanervisto, A., Ling, J., Rush, A.M.: Image-to-markup generation with coarse-to-fine attention. In: Proceedings of International Conference on Machine Learning, pp. 980–989 (2017)
6. Ding, H., Chen, K., Huo, Q.: An encoder-decoder approach to handwritten mathematical expression recognition with multi-head attention and stacked decoder. In: Lladós, J., Lopresti, D., Uchida, S. (eds.) ICDAR 2021. LNCS, vol. 12822, pp. 602–616. Springer, Cham (2021). https://doi.org/10.1007/978-3-030-86331-9_39
7. Hu, J., Shen, L., Sun, G.: Squeeze-and-excitation networks. In: Proceedings of IEEE International Conference on Computer Vision and Pattern Recognition, pp. 7132–7141 (2018)
8. Hu, L., Zanibbi, R.: HMM-based recognition of online handwritten mathematical symbols using segmental k-means initialization and a modified pen-up/down feature. In: Proceedings of International Conference on Document Analysis and Recognition, pp. 457–462 (2011)
9. Huang, G., Liu, Z., Van Der Maaten, L., Weinberger, K.Q.: Densely connected convolutional networks. In: Proceedings of IEEE International Conference on Computer Vision and Pattern Recognition, pp. 4700–4708 (2017)
10. Keshari, B., Watt, S.: Hybrid mathematical symbol recognition using support vector machines. In: Proceedings of International Conference on Document Analysis and Recognition, vol. 2, pp. 859–863 (2007)
11. Kosmala, A., Rigoll, G., Lavirotte, S., Pottier, L.: On-line handwritten formula recognition using hidden Markov models and context dependent graph grammars. In: Proceedings of International Conference on Document Analysis and Recognition, pp. 107–110 (1999)
12. Laradji, I.H., Rostamzadeh, N., Pinheiro, P.O., Vazquez, D., Schmidt, M.: Where are the blobs: counting by localization with point supervision. In: Ferrari, V., Hebert, M., Sminchisescu, C., Weiss, Y. (eds.) ECCV 2018. LNCS, vol. 11206, pp. 560–576. Springer, Cham (2018). https://doi.org/10.1007/978-3-030-01216-8_34
13. Lavirotte, S., Pottier, L.: Mathematical formula recognition using graph grammar. In: Document Recognition V, vol. 3305, pp. 44–52 (1998)
14. Le, A.D.: Recognizing handwritten mathematical expressions via paired dual loss attention network and printed mathematical expressions. In: Proceedings of IEEE International Conference on Computer Vision and Pattern Recognition Workshops, pp. 566–567 (2020)

15. Li, Y., Zhang, X., Chen, D.: CSRNet: dilated convolutional neural networks for understanding the highly congested scenes. In: Proceedings of IEEE International Conference on Computer Vision and Pattern Recognition (2018)
16. Li, Z., Jin, L., Lai, S., Zhu, Y.: Improving attention-based handwritten mathematical expression recognition with scale augmentation and drop attention. In: Proceedings of International Conference on Frontiers in Handwriting Recognition, pp. 175–180 (2020)
17. Liu, W., et al.: SSD: single shot MultiBox detector. In: Leibe, B., Matas, J., Sebe, N., Welling, M. (eds.) ECCV 2016. LNCS, vol. 9905, pp. 21–37. Springer, Cham (2016). https://doi.org/10.1007/978-3-319-46448-0_2
18. Mouchere, H., Viard-Gaudin, C., Zanibbi, R., Garain, U.: ICFHR 2014 competition on recognition of on-line handwritten mathematical expressions (CROHME 2014). In: Proceedings of International Conference on Frontiers in Handwriting Recognition, pp. 791–796 (2014)
19. Mouchère, H., Viard-Gaudin, C., Zanibbi, R., Garain, U.: ICFHR 2016 CROHME: competition on recognition of online handwritten mathematical expressions. In: Proceedings of International Conference on Frontiers in Handwriting Recognition, pp. 607–612 (2016)
20. Parmar, N., et al.: Image transformer. In: Proceedings of International Conference on Machine Learning, pp. 4055–4064 (2018)
21. Ren, S., He, K., Girshick, R., Sun, J.: Faster R-CNN: towards real-time object detection with region proposal networks. In: Proceedings of Advances in Neural Information Processing Systems 28 (2015)
22. Ren, S., He, K., Girshick, R., Sun, J.: Faster R-CNN: towards real-time object detection with region proposal networks. IEEE Trans. Pattern Anal. Mach. Intell. **39**(06), 1137–1149 (2017)
23. Shi, B., Yang, M., Wang, X., Lyu, P., Yao, C., Bai, X.: ASTER: an attentional scene text recognizer with flexible rectification. IEEE Trans. Pattern Anal. Mach. Intell. **41**(9), 2035–2048 (2018)
24. Truong, T.N., Nguyen, C.T., Phan, K.M., Nakagawa, M.: Improvement of end-to-end offline handwritten mathematical expression recognition by weakly supervised learning. In: Proceedings of International Conference on Frontiers in Handwriting Recognition, pp. 181–186 (2020)
25. Tu, Z., Lu, Z., Liu, Y., Liu, X., Li, H.: Modeling coverage for neural machine translation. In: Proceedings of the Association for Computational Linguistics, pp. 76–85 (2016)
26. Vuong, B.Q., He, Y., Hui, S.C.: Towards a web-based progressive handwriting recognition environment for mathematical problem solving. Expert Syst. Appl. **37**(1), 886–893 (2010)
27. Wang, C., Zhang, H., Yang, L., Liu, S., Cao, X.: Deep people counting in extremely dense crowds. In: Proceedings of ACM Multimedia, pp. 1299–1302 (2015)
28. Wang, J., Du, J., Zhang, J., Wang, Z.R.: Multi-modal attention network for handwritten mathematical expression recognition. In: Proceedings of International Conference on Document Analysis and Recognition, pp. 1181–1186 (2019)
29. Winkler, H.J.: HMM-based handwritten symbol recognition using on-line and off-line features. In: IEEE International Conference on Acoustics, Speech, and Signal Processing Conference Proceedings, vol. 6, pp. 3438–3441 (1996)
30. Wu, J.-W., Yin, F., Zhang, Y.-M., Zhang, X.-Y., Liu, C.-L.: Image-to-markup generation via paired adversarial learning. In: Berlingerio, M., Bonchi, F., Gärtner, T., Hurley, N., Ifrim, G. (eds.) ECML PKDD 2018. LNCS (LNAI), vol. 11051, pp. 18–34. Springer, Cham (2019). https://doi.org/10.1007/978-3-030-10925-7_2

31. Wu, J.W., Yin, F., Zhang, Y.M., Zhang, X.Y., Liu, C.L.: Handwritten mathematical expression recognition via paired adversarial learning. Int. J. Comput. Vis. **128**(10), 2386–2401 (2020)
32. Xie, Z., Huang, Y., Zhu, Y., Jin, L., Liu, Y., Xie, L.: Aggregation cross-entropy for sequence recognition. In: Proceedings of IEEE International Conference on Computer Vision and Pattern Recognition, pp. 6538–6547 (2019)
33. Xu, C., Liang, D., Xu, Y., Bai, S., Zhan, W., Bai, X., Tomizuka, M.: AutoScale: learning to scale for crowd counting. Int. J. Comput. Vis. **130**, 405–434 (2021). https://doi.org/10.1007/s11263-021-01542-z
34. Xu, K., et al.: Show, attend and tell: neural image caption generation with visual attention. In: Proceedings of International Conference on Machine Learning, pp. 2048–2057 (2015)
35. Yan, Z., et al.: Perspective-guided convolution networks for crowd counting. In: Proceedings of IEEE International Conference Computer Vision (2019)
36. Yang, Y., Li, G., Wu, Z., Su, L., Huang, Q., Sebe, N.: Weakly-supervised crowd counting learns from sorting rather than locations. In: Vedaldi, A., Bischof, H., Brox, T., Frahm, J.-M. (eds.) ECCV 2020. LNCS, vol. 12353, pp. 1–17. Springer, Cham (2020). https://doi.org/10.1007/978-3-030-58598-3_1
37. Yuan, Y., et al.: Syntax-aware network for handwritten mathematical expression recognition. In: Proceedings of IEEE International Conference on Computer Vision and Pattern Recognition, pp. 4553–4562 (2022)
38. Zeiler, M.D.: ADADELTA: an adaptive learning rate method. arXiv preprint arXiv:1212.5701 (2012)
39. Zhang, A., et al.: Attentional neural fields for crowd counting. In: Proceedings of IEEE International Conference on Computer Vision (2019)
40. Zhang, J., Du, J., Dai, L.: Multi-scale attention with dense encoder for handwritten mathematical expression recognition. In: Proceedings of International Conference on Pattern Recognition, pp. 2245–2250 (2018)
41. Zhang, J., Du, J., Dai, L.: Track, attend, and parse (TAP): an end-to-end framework for online handwritten mathematical expression recognition. IEEE Trans. Multimedia **21**(1), 221–233 (2018)
42. Zhang, J., Du, J., Yang, Y., Song, Y.Z., Wei, S., Dai, L.: A tree-structured decoder for image-to-markup generation. In: Proceedings of International Conference on Machine Learning, pp. 11076–11085 (2020)
43. Zhang, J., et al.: Watch, attend and parse: an end-to-end neural network based approach to handwritten mathematical expression recognition. Pattern Recogn. **71**, 196–206 (2017)
44. Zhang, Y., Zhou, D., Chen, S., Gao, S., Ma, Y.: Single-image crowd counting via multi-column convolutional neural network. In: Proceedings of IEEE International Conference on Computer Vision and Pattern Recognition (2016)
45. Zhang, Z., He, T., Zhang, H., Zhang, Z., Xie, J., Li, M.: Bag of freebies for training object detection neural networks. arXiv preprint arXiv:1902.04103 (2019)
46. Zhao, W., Gao, L., Yan, Z., Peng, S., Du, L., Zhang, Z.: Handwritten mathematical expression recognition with bidirectionally trained transformer. In: Proceedings of International Conference on Document Analysis and Recognition, pp. 570–584 (2021)

Detecting Tampered Scene Text in the Wild

Yuxin Wang[1], Hongtao Xie[1](✉), Mengting Xing[1], Jing Wang[2],
Shenggao Zhu[2], and Yongdong Zhang[1]

[1] University of Science and Technology of China, Hefei, China
{wangyx58,htxie,metingx,zhyd73}@mail.ustc.edu.cn
[2] Huawei Cloud, Shenzhen, Guangdong, China
{wangjing105,zhushenggao}@huawei.com

Abstract. Text manipulation technologies cause serious worries in
recent years, however, corresponding tampering detection methods have
not been well explored. In this paper, we introduce a new task, named
Tampered Scene Text Detection (TSTD), to localize text instances and
recognize the texture authenticity in an end-to-end manner. Different
from the general scene text detection (STD) task, TSTD further introduces the fine-grained classification, *i.e.* the tampered and real-world
texts share a semantic space (text position and geometric structure) but
have different local textures. To this end, we propose a simple yet effective modification strategy to migrate existing STD methods to TSTD
task, keeping the semantic invariance while explicitly guiding the class-
specific texture feature learning. Furthermore, we discuss the potential
of frequency information for distinguishing feature learning, and propose
a parallel-branch feature extractor to enhance the feature representation
capability. To evaluate the effectiveness of our method, a new TSTD
dataset (Tampered-IC13) is proposed and released at https://github.
com/wangyuxin87/Tampered-IC13.

Keywords: Tampered scene text detection · Parallel-branch feature
extractor · Deep learning

1 Introduction

As an important media for information transmission, scene text contains
amounts of important and sensitive information [3,22,31,33]. With the development of text manipulation technologies [21,34,38], computers can automatically
tamper with the important and sensitive content into fake information, being
used in fraud, marketing or other illegal purposes. In contrast, methods for the
tampered text detection field are currently blank. To fill such a research blank,

Supplementary Information The online version contains supplementary material
available at https://doi.org/10.1007/978-3-031-19815-1_13.

© The Author(s), under exclusive license to Springer Nature Switzerland AG 2022
S. Avidan et al. (Eds.): ECCV 2022, LNCS 13688, pp. 215–232, 2022.
https://doi.org/10.1007/978-3-031-19815-1_13

Fig. 1. The visualization of TSTD task. TSTD methods need to firstly locate all the text regions and then determine whether the text has been tampered with. Left: original image; right: tampered image. Green box: real-world texts; red box: tampered texts. (Color figure online)

we propose a new task named Tampered Scene Text Detection (TSTD) in this paper. On the basis of face forgery detection task [12,17] that tampering detection approaches should not focus on only the tampered class, TSTD task needs to locate all the texts in scene images and determine whether the text has been tampered with (shown in Fig. 1).

TSTD task has two main challenges: 1) **Fine-grained perception.** The tampered and real-world texts share a semantic space (text position and geometric structure) but have local texture differences. As shown in Fig. 1, both tampered and real-world texts exist in the same position (*e.g.* board, bus, etc.) and have the identical geometric structure (*e.g.* horizontal/oriented posture and text shape), while tampered texts contain different local textures (*e.g.* smoothness) than real-world ones. Thus, TSTD methods need to maximize the discrimination of class-specific texture features while maintaining the semantic invariance. 2) **The limited size of high-quality annotated tampered text images.** At present, the results of existing text manipulation methods [34,38] are still a long way from practical application. In general, manual refinement in the post processing is necessary for the visualization improvement, which inevitably results in lots of human cost. Thus, how to construct a TSTD method with low data-dependency is necessary.

Firstly, to inherit the advantages (*e.g.* multi-scale text modeling [32,37], etc) of general scene text detection (STD) methods [43,44], we argue that TSTD methods should evolve from the STD approaches but not an entire new architecture. In this paper, we propose a Separating Segmentation while Sharing Regression (S3R) modification strategy to construct TSTD approaches based on existing STD ones. The S3R strategy follows the phenomenon that tampered and real-word texts only have local texture differences, but contain the same global semantics (text position and geometric structure). In the previous STD works, the pixel-level segmentation and distance regression show impressive performance to model local texture [33] and global semantics [37] respectively in STD task. Thus, the S3R strategy aims to maximize the discrimination of class-specific texture features while maintaining the semantic invariance by sharing/separating the segmentation/regression branches between tampered and real-world texts. On the one hand, S3R strategy separates the segmentation branches between tampered and real-world texts, and introduces a representation suppression loss L_{rs} for class-specific texture feature learning. On the other hand, S3R strategy shares the regression branch between tampered and real-world texts to learn the invariant semantics (text position and geometric structure). The proposed S3R strategy can be effectively embedded into any current scene text detectors, migrating the general STD methods to TSTD task without introducing obvious speed decrease (detailed in Sect. 4.3).

Secondly, image manipulations are proved to leave high-frequency traces [17,41]. However, such variant high-frequency information is difficult to be captured in the RGB domain. Thus, the network needs amounts of tampered images for the better convergency on tampered textures, resulting in a high data-dependency. To this end, we introduce a parallel-branch feature extractor to capture the high-frequency information in frequency domain. Through aggregating the RGB and high-frequency features, our parallel-branch feature extractor can easily capture the high-frequency traces to assist the prediction and cause in low data-dependency (detailed in Sect. 4.4).

In addition, a new word-level tampered TSTD dataset named Tampered-IC13 is proposed (shown in Fig. 5). Tampered-IC13 is generated by tampering with the text in the most well-known scene text detection benchmark ICDAR2013 [10]. To the best of our knowledge, this is the first world-level TSTD dataset, which will greatly promote the development of TSTD task.

The contribution of this paper can be summarized as following three points:

- We introduce a new tampered scene text detection (TSTD) task to fill the research blank. Furthermore, the proposed united modification strategy (S3R) can be embedded into any current scene text detection methods, helping them to migrate to TSTD task without introducing obvious speed decrease.
- A parallel-branch feature extractor is constructed to capture both characteristics in RGB and frequency domains, which is first introduced in TSTD task. The exhaustive experiments prove its effectiveness in feature representation enhancement and data-dependency reduction.
- We construct a new word-level TSTD dataset (Tampered-IC13) to evaluate the effectiveness of our method, which is released publicly.

2   Related Work

2.1   Scene Text Detection

Scene text detection (STD) networks [27,35,37] contain two processes: text localization (TL) and geometric prediction (GP). TL process determines the position of text instances (*e.g.* center point/line) and GP process aims to accurately reconstruct the text regions (*e.g.* contour line). Previous methods [32,33] mainly divide the scene text detection methods based on the GP process, and classify detection methods to GP-REG and GP-SEG ones. Here, SEG means that pixel-level segmentation is utilized and REG refers to regressing the distance. As the TL process is also important in the detection process and has various implementations [26,40,43], we provide a more detailed classification of STD methods by taking the TL process into account: TL-SEG + GP-REG, TL-SEG + GP-SEG,

TL-REG + GP-SEG and TL-REG + GP-REG. In this section, we will detail the differences among these four-category methods respectively.

TL-SEG + GP-REG methods [23,27,37,43] use pixel-level segmentation to represent the text center location, *e.g.* shrinked polygons, while regressing the distance to the border for geometric prediction. EAST [43] predicts the shrinked polygon for text center localization to avoid the overlapping of adjacent texts. Then, distance regression to the four borders is utilized to reconstruct the text regions. Similarly, to further handle the arbitrary-shaped texts, MSR [37] regresses the distance from the closest border point to the center point. Thus, arbitrary-shaped polygon can be obtained by clustering all the border points. CentripetalText [23] proposes to use text kernels and centripetal shifts to present text instances. First, it generates shrinked polygons to coarsely locate text instances. The predicted centripetal shifts are then utilized to determine the boundaries of text instances. FCENet [44] models text instances in the Fourier domain via the Fourier transformation, and regresses compact Fourier signatures to represent the contour of arbitrary-shaped texts in GP process.

TL-SEG + GP-SEG approaches [26,28,29] regard scene text detection task as a pure pixel-level classification task. PSENet [28] predicts kernels with different scales for text reconstruction. To handle the adjacent text instances, the kernel map with minimum scale is used to separate adjacent texts, and other kernel maps constrain the geometric representation during the reconstruction process. To further simplify the reconstruction rules, PAN [29] only uses two different scales of kernel maps (shrinked polygon and full text region) for text localization and geometric prediction respectively, and proposes a low computational-cost segmentation head for real-time text detection. Similarly, Tian *et al.* [26] proposes a learnable post-processing (embedding feature) for accurate arbitrary-shaped text representation. To be specific, pixels of the full text are assigned to different text centers based on the pixel embedding distance.

TL-REG + GP-SEG methods [33,35,36] are mainly inspired by general two-stage [7,20] object detection methods, which firstly regress the coarse location of text region (*e.g.* text proposals). Then, pixel-level segmentation is implemented in the region of interests (RoIs) for geometric prediction. To handle the large-scale variance problem, ContourNet [33] firstly constructs an Adaptive-RPN to perceive the shape characteristics, which is supervised under the scale-invariance metric. Then, an orthogonal correction module is used to suppress the false-positive contour points. To further supplement the limited correction capability in 2D-space [33], LEMNet [36] distinguishes the false-positive samples in a high-level semantic dimension. Besides, SPCNet [35] introduces a semantic segmentation branch to enhance the feature representation capability and re-score the box confidence.

TL-REG + GP-REG methods [30,45] have the similar architecture to TL-REG + GP-SEG approaches. Instead of simply regarding geometric prediction as the pure segmentation task, these methods try to regress the text-specific geometric properties to handle the complex geometric variance. SLPR [45] uses slide lines to regress the outline points in horizontal and vertical directions respectively. To iteratively refine the contour points, ATRR [30] uses RNNs [39] to regress the border points based on the region of interests (RoIs).

Special Cases. We discuss some specific cases that can not be easily distinguished: 1) Compared with TL process, GP process is usually more complex in scene text detectors. For example, LOMO [40] predicts both text segmentation and border distance for text reconstruction. Thus, the GP process in LOMO [40] can be regarded as a combination of GP-SEG and GP-REG. 2) For the detection methods constructed on the one-stage detection framework [14,15] without introducing an explicit TL process, we simply classify these methods based on the GP process.

2.2   Scene Text Editing and Tampering Detection

Scene text editing task aims to end-to-end tamper with text content in scene images. As deep learning becomes the most promising machine learning tool [2,4,13,42], scene text editing has achieved remarkable improvement in recent years. ETW [34] splits the text editing process into three sub-networks: text conversion network, background inpainting network and fusion network. The text transfer network learns to transform the style of input text image. Then, the background inpainting network erases the text content in the source image and reconstructs the background texture. Finally, the fusion network aggregates the style-transferred text images and text erased images to generate the final tampered sample. Based on ETW [34], SwapText [38] introduces TPS to handle the severe geometric distortion cases. To edit the specific character in text images, STEFANN [21] proposes a character-level text editing network. Though text manipulation technologies have been well developed in recent years, methods for tampered text detection field are almost blank. [1,11,18,24] regard tampered text detection task as a pure classification task, and the detection process is not included in their approaches. Benefiting from the gradient spread and shared features between detection and classification branches, the end-to-end detection framework is proved to be significant in both detection accuracy enhancement and model complexity reduction [16,19]. Thus, the end-to-end tampered text detection approaches need to be explored.

Although the face forgery detection methods achieve promising results in capturing tampered textures, it is impossible to directly use the face-specific texture learning (e.g. lips [6], eyes and nose [9]) to handle text-specific tampered samples. Thus, it is necessary to explore a text-specific tampering detection method for accurate tampered text detection.

3   Our Method

In this section, we firstly introduce the proposed S3R modification strategy in Sect. 3.1. Then, the parallel-branch feature extractor is detailed in Sect. 3.2. Finally, we introduce the proposed Tampered-IC13 dataset in Sect. 3.3.

3.1   The S3R Strategy

As tampered and real-word texts only have local texture differences but the same global semantics (appearance and geometric structure), the S3R strategy mainly focuses on one point: *"shall we separate the TL and GP processes of tampered text from the real-world one?"*.

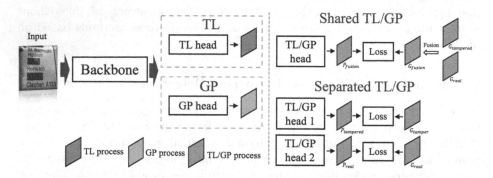

Fig. 2. The pipeline of our S3R strategy. TL is short for text localization process and GP is short for geometric prediction process. TL and GP process are parallel branches in [28,43], but are serial branches in [30,33]. P is short for prediction. $G_{tampered}$ and G_{real} are the ground truth of tampered and real-world texts respectively. *Fusion* is the element-wise addition operation.

As shown in the right top of Fig. 2, the shared TL/GP process means that we aggregate the tampered and real-world ground truth in a single map and use one TL/GP head for prediction. In contrast, separated TL/GP (right bottom of Fig. 2) means that we use two independent heads to handle tampered and real-world texts respectively. In general, 1) for shared TL/GP process, we firstly aggregate the ground truth map of tampered texts $G_{tampered} \in R^{H \times W \times C}$ and real-world texts $G_{real} \in R^{H \times W \times C}$ to a single map $G_{fusion} \in R^{H \times W \times C}$ through element-wise addition. H, W and C mean height, width and the channel number respectively. Thus, the fused ground-truth map G_{fusion} guides the network to eliminate the class difference between tampered and real-world texts. Then, we use a single head to predict the shared feature map P_{fusion}, and calculate the loss between the P_{fusion} and G_{fusion}. 2) For separated TL/GP process, we simply use two independent heads for tampered ($P_{tampered}$) and real-world (P_{real}) feature map prediction. The final loss function is the sum of the losses in these two branches, calculated between $[P_{tampered}, G_{tampered}]$ and $[P_{real}, G_{real}]$ respectively.

In S3R strategy, we use the separated TL/GP process for segmentation, and use shared TL/GP process for regression. Specially, in order to guide the class-specific texture learning in the segmentation branch, we introduce a representation suppression loss L_{rs} in separated segmentation branches, which is formulated in Eq. (1). $L_{tampered,real}$ is the loss to suppress the representation

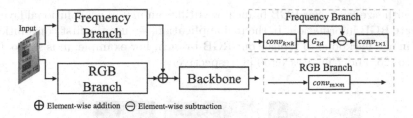

Fig. 3. The structure of our parallel feature extractor. *conv* is the convolutional layer. G_{2d} is the 2d Gaussian kernel.

of tampered prediction in the real-world segmentation branch, which punishes the tampered pixels activated in the real-world segmentation map. Similarly, $L_{real,tampered}$ suppresses the representation of real-world prediction in tampered segmentation branch. As the pixel-level segmentation and distance regression shows an impressive performance in modeling local texture [33] and global semantics [37], S3R helps the model to explicitly classify class-aware textures while keeping semantic invarance (*e.g.* text appearance, textual shape) between tampered and real-world texts (detailed in Sect. 4.3).

$$L_{rs} = L_{tampered,real} + L_{real,tampered} \tag{1}$$

3.2 The Parallel-branch Feature Extractor

Though image manipulations leave high-frequency traces [17,41] in the tampered image, it is difficult for the network to capture the variant high-frequency information in the RGB domain. According to this observation, we propose a parallel-branch feature extractor with the goal of considering the characteristics in both RGB and frequency domain. As shown in Fig. 3, our parallel-branch feature extractor contains two parts: frequency branch and RGB branch. Firstly, the input image is processed by these two branches respectively. Then, the information captured from two branches is fused by element-wise addition. Finally, the aggregated features are sent to the backbone.

For the frequency branch, inspired from [17,41], we adopt Laplacian of Gaussian (LoG) to capture high-frequency information. For input image I, a convolutional layer with size $k \times k$ is firstly utilized for feature enhancement. The value of k represents how much information can be perceived in the frequency branch, which is an ablation study in our experiments. Then, a 2d Gaussian kernel is used to smooth the features. Finally, a skip-connection and a 1×1 convolutional layer are used for generating high-frequency information and dimension alignment respectively. The detailed formulation of frequency branch is shown in Eq. (2):

$$F_{fre} = w_{1\times1}(x - w_g x) \tag{2}$$

To be specific, w_g is the 2d Gaussian kernel, $w_{1\times1}$ means the convolutional layer with size 1×1. $x = w_{k\times k}I$. I is the input image and $w_{k\times k}$ is the convolutional layer with size $k \times k$. For RGB branch, we utilize an $m \times m$ convolutional layer to generate RGB information. In the real application, we use the first convolutional layer in the backbone to replace our RGB branch. For example, m is set to 3 for VGG16 [25] and 7 for ResNet50 [8] respectively.

Fig. 4. The visualization of feature maps in parallel-branch feature extractor. (a): input image; (b): the feature map in frequency branch; (c) the feature map in RGB branch.

Fig. 5. Some examples in Tampered-IC13. Left: original images; right: our tampered images. The tampered texts contain a high similarity to the real-world ones.

To better understand how frequency information helps the network for prediction, we visualize the extracted features from frequency branch and RGB branch. We normalize each map to [0, 1] for better visualization. As shown in Fig. 4, different from RGB branch mainly focuses on the text content in the RGB domain, the frequency branch effectively captures the high-frequency characteristics in the outline areas. By fusing the features captured from both frequency and RGB branches, the parallel-branch feature extractor is able to learn distinguishing features between tampered and real-world texts.

3.3   Tampered-IC13 Dataset

The difficulty of the TSTD task lies in how the network can better distinguish the tampered class from the real class, which puts higher requirements on the data generation process to ensure the texture consistency and background integrity in the tampered region. Considering that ICDAR2013 (IC13) dataset is one of the most well-known datasets in scene text detection community during the past five years, we use IC13 dataset as the benchmark data to generate our tampered dataset. Some examples of Tampered-IC13 are shown in Fig. 5. The details of Tampered-IC13 dataset are available in the supplementaries.

Dataset Challenge. Benefiting from the sophisticated tampering process and effective later interventions, the proposed Tampered-IC13 achieves high-quality tampered text textures, consistent text-free areas and smooth transmission in the contour regions. Thus, it is quite a challenge to achieve the accurate detection on Tampered-IC13 and the detection results on Tampered-IC13 can well reflect the performance of TSTD detectors.

4 Experiment

In this section, we firstly introduce the evaluation metrics and implementation details in Sect. 4.1 and Sect. 4.2 respectively. Next, we evaluate the effectiveness of S3R strategy in Sect. 4.3. Finally, the performance of parallel-branch feature extractor and some discussions are shown in Sect. 4.4 and Sect. 4.5.

4.1 Evaluation Metric

Following the general scene text detection methods, we adopt precision (P), recall (R) and F-measure (F) to evaluate the detection results of tampered and real-world texts. To evaluate the average performance between tampered and real-world detection results, we propose a new mean F-measure (mF), which is inspired by mAP [20] Eq. (4). $F_{tampered}$ and F_{real} are F-measure calculated by Eq. (3) for tampered and real-world texts respectively. In order to treat tampered and real-world results equally, we set $\lambda_1, \lambda_2 = 1$.

$$F = 2 \times P \times R/(P + R) \tag{3}$$

$$mF = (\lambda_1 F_{tampered} + \lambda_2 F_{real})/2 \tag{4}$$

4.2 Implementation Details

We conduct the experiments on four well-known models to evaluate the effectiveness of our method. To be specific, EAST [43] (TL-SEG + GP-REG), PSENet [28] (TL-SEG + GP-SEG), ContourNet [33] (TL-REG + GP-SEG) and ATRR [30] (TL-REG + GP-REG) are used in our experiments. Specially, we simplify the prediction head in ATRR [30] and use a convolutional layer to replace RNNs [39] to improve its generalization. All the models are constructed based on the publicly released code[1,2,3,4]. As there is not a published code in ATRR [30], we

---

[1] https://github.com/SakuraRiven/EAST.
[2] https://github.com/whai362/PSENet.
[3] https://github.com/wangyuxin87/ContourNet.
[4] https://github.com/facebookresearch/maskrcnn-benchmark.

reconstruct the model based on the structure of Mask-RCNN [7]. The training settings follow the details in the corresponding paper. The training and testing sets in Tampered-IC13 are used to train and evaluate our model respectively. During the inference, we resize the image to 748×748, 736×736, 1200×2000 and 1200×2000 for EAST, PSENet, ContourNet and ATRR respectively, where each size reflects the best performance in the corresponding model.

Table 1. The detection performance of different modification strategies. Sep and Sha are shorts for separated and shared. TL and GP are the TL process and GP process. SEG+REG, SEG+SEG, REG+SEG and REG+REG mean TL-SEG+GP-REG, TL-SEG+GP-SEG, TL-REG+GP-SEG and TL-REG+GP-REG respectively. R-T, P-T and F-T are the recall, precision and F-measure of tampered detection results. R-R, P-R and F-R are the recall, precision and F-measure of real-world detection results. mF is the mean F-measure. To better understand the table, we set "separated" (Sep) and "segmentation" (SEG) to red, and set "shared" (Sha) and "regression" (REG) to blue.

	TL		GP		Accuracy						
	Sha	Sep	Sha	Sep	R-T	P-T	F-T	R-R	P-R	F-R	mF
EAST [43] (SEG+REG)	✓		✓		68.68	70.11	69.39	23.18	46.61	31.39	50.39
		✓	✓		**69.97**	**70.23**	**69.94**	**27.32**	**50.46**	**35.45**	**52.70**
	✓			✓	53.97	31.74	39.97	15.40	40.97	22.38	31.18
PSENet [28] (SEG+SEG)	✓			✓	77.39	77.24	77.31	38.25	51.45	43.88	60.60
		✓		✓	**79.43**	**79.92**	**79.67**	**41.89**	**61.56**	**49.85**	**64.76**
	✓	✓			65.58	53.76	59.08	21.69	12.46	15.83	37.46
ContourNet [33] (REG+SEG)	✓		✓		91.24	85.33	88.19	54.77	76.32	63.77	75.98
		✓	✓		79.23	75.39	77.26	46.85	66.75	55.06	66.16
	✓			✓	**91.45**	**86.68**	**88.99**	**54.80**	**77.88**	**64.33**	**76.66**
ATRR [30] (REG+REG)	✓		✓		**90.63**	**84.60**	**87.52**	**54.63**	**76.74**	**63.83**	**75.68**
	✓			✓	90.43	83.77	86.97	52.15	74.82	61.46	74.22
		✓	✓		86.97	72.87	79.29	51.29	66.93	58.08	68.69

4.3   The Evaluation of S3R Strategy

The detailed modifications to four models in Table 1 are available in the supplementary materials. As shown in Table 1, we summarize two conclusions: 1) Separating the SEG branch benefits the class-specific texture learning between tampered and real-world texts. For example, EAST, PSENet and ContourNet obtains 2.31%(52.7% vs 50.39%), 27.30% (64.76% vs 37.46%) and 0.68% (76.66% vs 75.98%) improvement in mF respectively. 2) Sharing the REG branches helps the learning of invariant semantics. For example, when we shared the GP process in EAST, there exists 21.52% improvement in the mF (52.70% vs 31.18%). Based on the above two conclusions, our S3R strategy shows significance in both tampered and real-world text detection. As shown in Table 1, the model implemented with S3R strategy (separating segmentation while sharing regression) outperforms other modification strategies by a large margin. To be specific, the S3R strategy helps EAST [43], PSENet [28], ContourNet [33] and ATRR [30] to obtain 52.70%, 64.76%, 76.66% and 75.68% in mF respectively.

How Does S3R Strategy Achieve Class-specific Texture Learning in Separated Segmentation? We conduct an additional experiment to illustrate how does S3R achieve the class-specific texture learning. Specially, ContourNet [33] (TL-REG + GP-SEG) is used in this experiment. The results in Table 2 illustrate several conclusions: 1) Simply constructing the separated segmentation branches without representation suppression (L_{rs} in Eq. (1)) between two branches is even harmful to performance (74.18% of Separated GP vs 75.98% of Shared GP in mF). Thus, such an implicit separated structure has no capability to learn class-specific texture features, and the extra introduced parameters further increase the network learning difficulty. 2) By implementing a shared segmentation head and only separating the segmentation map in the last convolutional layer with the representation suppression, it obtains a slight improvement in mF (76.16% of Shared GP + Sup vs 75.98% of Shared GP). The implementation of Shared GP + Sup is similar to Softmax loss, predicting multi-class segmentation maps and suppressing the representation between each other. 3) When we separate the segmentation head and further use the representation suppression between two heads (Separated GP + Sup), the model obtains the best results (76.66% in mF). Compared with separating only the last convolutional layer (Shared GP + Sup), the separated segmentation heads have more powerful capability for class-specific texture learning. Furthermore, such explicit separated structure also benefits the model convergency (compared with Separated GP). 4) As EAST [43] and PSENet [28] segment the text regions in the entire image rather than RoI-based prediction (*e.g.* shared-TL sends class-independent proposals to both tampered and real-world heads), the ground-truth segmentation maps in separated branches are mutually exclusive. Thus, the natural representation suppression in separated segmentation branches of EAST [43] and PSENet [28] helps the model to learn class-specific texture features (Table 1). Based on above analyses, the separated structure and representation suppression between

Table 2. The evaluation of S3R strategy in class-specific texture learning. Sup is short for representation suppression. GP is short for geometric prediction process.

Method	Implementation	Accuracy						
		R-T	P-T	F-T	R-R	P-R	F-R	mF
ContourNet [33]	Shared GP	91.24	85.33	88.19	54.77	76.32	63.77	75.98
	Separated GP	86.35	85.66	86.00	52.12	77.62	62.36	74.18
	Shared GP + Sup	91.33	85.27	88.20	**54.80**	77.29	64.12	76.16
	Separated GP + Sup	**91.45**	**86.68**	**88.99**	**54.80**	**77.88**	**64.33**	**76.66**

two branches together promote the class-specific texture learning, and improve the detection performance to a new level. Specially, the implementation details of L_{rs} in ContourNet [33] are shown in the supplementaries.

Why is It Important to Maintain Semantic Invariance? We infer that the shared feature learning of global semantics helps the TSTD network converge. As the distance regression is proved to perform well in modeling the text position [33] and geometric structure [37], independently modeling these class-invariant semantics will not introduce new information and the additionally introduced parameters are harmful to the network convergency.

Table 3. The comparison of testing speed. As the original ATRR [30] shares TL and GP process, S3R strategy does not introduce extra computations.

Method	Original (FPS)	Modified (FPS)
EAST [43]	6.7	5.8
PSENet [28]	8.9	7.4
ATRR [30]	3.2	3.2
ContourNet [33]	3.7	3.6

Table 4. The comparison of parallel-branch feature extractor implemented with different k. Specially, EAST is pre-trained on the SynthText [5] for a better convergency.

kernel size ($k \times k$)	Accuracy						
	R-T	P-T	F-T	R-R	P-R	F-R	mF
5×5	74.75	72.39	73.55	41.39	**64.77**	50.50	60.03
7×7	**75.15**	**73.21**	**74.17**	**44.04**	62.74	**51.75**	**62.96**
9×9	74.74	72.37	73.55	43.38	61.93	51.10	62.33

The Influence in Testing Speed. We conduct several experiments to compare the testing speed between original and our modified models. As shown in Table 3, our S3R strategy only introduces a slight speed decrease to the original model.

4.4   The Effectiveness of Parallel-branch Feature Extractor

The Evaluation of k. We conduct several experiments to study the relationship between the k and the detection performance. The value of k determines how much information can be perceived in the frequency branch. As shown in Table 4, the kernel with size 7×7 obtains the best results. Thus, we set kernel size to 7×7 in the later experiments.

The Effectiveness in Performance Boosting. We embed parallel-branch feature extractor into existing detection methods to evaluate its effectiveness. As shown in Table 5, our parallel-branch feature extractor is able to improve both tampered and real-world text detection results. The relative improvement for EAST [43] and ATRR [28] are 2.57% and 0.67% in mF respectively. We summarize the impressive improvement to that the high-frequency information effectively assists the network to learn distinguishing features between tampered and real-world texts. More experiments conducted on other models are available in the supplementary materials.

Table 5. The detection results of models with/without introducing parallel-branch feature extractor. Specially, EAST is pre-trained on the SynthText [5] for a better convergency. The evaluation on more models are available in the supplementary materials.

	Frequency	Accuracy						
		R-T	P-T	F-T	R-R	P-R	F-R	mF
EAST [43]	–	74.54	70.25	72.33	40.23	60.90	48.45	60.39
	✓	**75.15**	**73.21**	**74.17**	**44.04**	**62.74**	**51.75**	**62.96**
ATRR [30]	–	90.63	84.60	87.52	54.63	76.74	63.83	75.68
	✓	**90.84**	**86.10**	**88.40**	**55.13**	**77.08**	**64.29**	**76.35**

Table 6. The evaluation of parallel-branch feature extractor in data dependency reduction. EAST [43] is used in this experiment. To ensure a better convergency, SynthText [5] is used to pre-train the model. *Half* means that we only use a half of images in the training set.

Frequency	Data	Accuracy							
		R-T	P-T	F-T	R-R	P-R	F-R	mF	↓mF
–	Full	74.54	70.25	72.33	40.23	60.90	48.45	60.39	–
	Half	72.91	68.71	70.75	37.09	57.14	44.98	57.87	2.52
✓	Full	75.15	73.21	74.17	44.04	62.74	51.75	62.96	–
	Half	73.11	71.80	72.45	41.48	59.39	49.12	60.79	**2.17**

The Effectiveness in Data-dependency Reduction. We further reduce the training images to evaluate our effectiveness in data-dependency reduction. As show in Table 6, we summarize two conclusions: 1) Model implemented with our parallel-branch feature extractor obtains less performance decrease with fewer training images (2.17% vs 2.52% decrease in mF). 2) Compared with the model without implementing parallel-branch feature extractor, our method can obtain comparable even better detection performance with only a half of training images (60.79% vs 60.39% in mF). Based on above analyses, our parallel-branch feature extractor effectively reduces the data dependency of the network.

4.5   Discussion

The Generalization on Detecting Low-quality Images. As images on the web have different quality, we think it is necessary to evaluate the generalization of TSTD methods on detecting low-quality images. Specifically, we use the ffmpeg compression algorithm to reduce the image quality. Details are available in the supplementaries.

The Qualitative Analysis. We visualize some detection results in Fig. 6. From the first and second rows, we find that the modified four models can effectively handle most cases in TSTD task. We further provide some failure cases to discuss the limitation of these methods. As shown in the third row of Fig. 6, methods implemented with TL-SEG process (EAST [43] and PSENet [28]) fail to handle the texts with extreme ratios (word "management" and string "002101"). We infer that the simplicity of these two methods makes them difficult to consider the long-range geometric structure [27].

Fig. 6. The visualization of detection results from four models. From left to right: ground truth, EAST [43], PSENet [28], ATRR [30], ContourNet [33]. Red boxes: tampered texts; green boxes: real-world texts. (Color figure online)

Limitation. In this paper, we focus on only the word-level tampered text detection and propose the relatively word-level detection method. The character-level and line-level tampered cases are not included in this paper. As the first work for TSTD task, we think that our word-level detection approach also gives lots of insights to TSTD community. Furthermore, we believe the methods proposed in this paper can also be used in character-level and line-level tampered text detection methods, *e.g.* the S3R strategy and parallel-branch feature extractor.

5   Conclusion

This paper introduces a new task, named Tampered Scene Text Detection (TSTD), to localize text instances and recognize the texture authenticity. We propose a unified modification (S3R) strategy to migrate the general STD method to TSTD task while keeping high detection performance and inference speed. The S3R strategy successfully maintains the semantic invariance and explicitly guides the class-specific texture feature learning between tampered and real-world texts. Furthermore, a parallel-branch feature extractor is constructed for the feature representation capability enhancement and data-dependency reduction. The exhaustive experiments on the proposed Tampered-IC13 demonstrate the effectiveness of our methods, and will give lots of insights to the TSTD community.

Acknowledgement. This work is supported by the National Nature Science Foundation of China (62121002, 62022076, U1936210), the Fundamental Research Funds for the Central Universities under Grant WK3480000011, the Youth Innovation Promotion Association Chinese Academy of Sciences (Y2021122). We acknowledge the support of GPU cluster built by MCC Lab of Information Science and Technology Institution, USTC.

References

1. Bibi, M., Hamid, A., Moetesum, M., Siddiqi, I.: Document forgery detection using printer source identification-a text-independent approach. In: 2019 International Conference on Document Analysis and Recognition Workshops (ICDARW), vol. 8, pp. 7–12. IEEE (2019)
2. Du, Y., et al.: SVTR: scene text recognition with a single visual model. In: IJCAI (2022)
3. Fang, S., Xie, H., Wang, Y., Mao, Z., Zhang, Y.: Read like humans: autonomous, bidirectional and iterative language modeling for scene text recognition. In: Proceedings of the IEEE/CVF Conference on Computer Vision and Pattern Recognition, pp. 7098–7107 (2021)
4. Ge, J., Xie, H., Min, S., Zhang, Y.: Semantic-guided reinforced region embedding for generalized zero-shot learning. In: Proceedings of the AAAI Conference on Artificial Intelligence, vol. 35, pp. 1406–1414 (2021)
5. Gupta, A., Vedaldi, A., Zisserman, A.: Synthetic data for text localisation in natural images. In: Proceedings of the IEEE Conference on Computer Vision and Pattern Recognition, pp. 2315–2324 (2016)
6. Haliassos, A., Vougioukas, K., Petridis, S., Pantic, M.: Lips don't lie: a generalisable and robust approach to face forgery detection. In: Proceedings of the IEEE/CVF Conference on Computer Vision and Pattern Recognition, pp. 5039–5049 (2021)
7. He, K., Gkioxari, G., Dollár, P., Girshick, R.: Mask r-CNN. In: Proceedings of the IEEE International Conference on Computer Vision, pp. 2961–2969 (2017)
8. He, K., Zhang, X., Ren, S., Sun, J.: Deep residual learning for image recognition. In: Proceedings of the IEEE Conference on Computer Vision and Pattern Recognition, pp. 770–778 (2016)

9. Hu, Z., Xie, H., Wang, Y., Li, J., Wang, Z., Zhang, Y.: Dynamic inconsistency-aware deepfake video detection. In: IJCAI (2021)

10. Karatzas, D., et al.: ICDAR 2013 robust reading competition. In: 2013 12th International Conference on Document Analysis and Recognition, pp. 1484–1493. IEEE (2013)

11. Kundu, S., Shivakumara, P., Grouver, A., Pal, U., Lu, T., Blumenstein, M.: A new forged handwriting detection method based on fourier spectral density and variation. In: Palaiahnakote, S., Sanniti di Baja, G., Wang, L., Yan, W.Q. (eds.) ACPR 2019. LNCS, vol. 12046, pp. 136–150. Springer, Cham (2020). https://doi.org/10.1007/978-3-030-41404-7_10

12. Li, J., Xie, H., Li, J., Wang, Z., Zhang, Y.: Frequency-aware discriminative feature learning supervised by single-center loss for face forgery detection. In: Proceedings of the IEEE/CVF Conference on Computer Vision and Pattern Recognition, pp. 6458–6467 (2021)

13. Li, P., Li, Y., Xie, H., Zhang, L.: Neighborhood-adaptive structure augmented metric learning. In: AAAI (2022)

14. Liao, M., Shi, B., Bai, X.: Textboxes++: a single-shot oriented scene text detector. IEEE Trans. Image Process. 27(8), 3676–3690 (2018)

15. Liao, M., Shi, B., Bai, X., Wang, X., Liu, W.: Textboxes: a fast text detector with a single deep neural network. In: Thirty-first AAAI Conference on Artificial Intelligence (2017)

16. Liu, Y., Chen, H., Shen, C., He, T., Jin, L., Wang, L.: Abcnet: real-time scene text spotting with adaptive bezier-curve network. In: Proceedings of the IEEE/CVF Conference on Computer Vision and Pattern Recognition, pp. 9809–9818 (2020)

17. Masi, I., Killekar, A., Mascarenhas, R.M., Gurudatt, S.P., AbdAlmageed, W.: Two-branch recurrent network for isolating deepfakes in videos. In: Vedaldi, A., Bischof, H., Brox, T., Frahm, J.-M. (eds.) ECCV 2020. LNCS, vol. 12352, pp. 667–684. Springer, Cham (2020). https://doi.org/10.1007/978-3-030-58571-6_39

18. Nandanwar, L., et al.: Forged text detection in video, scene, and document images. IET Image Process. 14(17), 4744–4755 (2020)

19. Qiao, L., et al.: Mango: a mask attention guided one-stage scene text spotter. In: Proceedings of the AAAI Conference on Artificial Intelligence, vol. 35, pp. 2467–2476 (2021)

20. Ren, S., He, K., Girshick, R., Sun, J.: Faster r-cnn: towards real-time object detection with region proposal networks. Adv. Neural Inf. Process. Syst. 28 (2015)

21. Roy, P., Bhattacharya, S., Ghosh, S., Pal, U.: STEFANN: scene text editor using font adaptive neural network. In: Proceedings of the IEEE/CVF Conference on Computer Vision and Pattern Recognition, pp. 13228–13237 (2020)

22. Sheng, F., Chen, Z., Xu, B.: NRTR: a no-recurrence sequence-to-sequence model for scene text recognition. In: 2019 International Conference on Document Analysis and Recognition (ICDAR), pp. 781–786. IEEE (2019)

23. Sheng, T., Chen, J., Lian, Z.: Centripetaltext: an efficient text instance representation for scene text detection. Adv. Neural Inf. Process. Syst. 34, 335–346 (2021)

24. da Silva Barbosa, R., Lins, R.D., De Lira, E.D.F., Camara, A.C.A.: Later added strokes or text-fraud detection in documents written with ballpoint pens. In: 2014 14th International Conference on Frontiers in Handwriting Recognition, pp. 517–522. IEEE (2014)

25. Simonyan, K., Zisserman, A.: Very deep convolutional networks for large-scale image recognition. arXiv preprint arXiv:1409.1556 (2014)

26. Tian, Z., Shu, M., Lyu, P., Li, R., Zhou, C., Shen, X., Jia, J.: Learning shape-aware embedding for scene text detection. In: Proceedings of the IEEE/CVF Conference on Computer Vision and Pattern Recognition, pp. 4234–4243 (2019)

27. Wang, P., et al.: A single-shot arbitrarily-shaped text detector based on context attended multi-task learning. In: Proceedings of the 27th ACM International Conference on Multimedia, pp. 1277–1285 (2019)

28. Wang, W., Xie, E., Li, X., Hou, W., Lu, T., Yu, G., Shao, S.: Shape robust text detection with progressive scale expansion network. In: CVPR, pp. 9336–9345 (2019)

29. Wang, W., et al.: Efficient and accurate arbitrary-shaped text detection with pixel aggregation network. In: Proceedings of the IEEE/CVF International Conference on Computer Vision, pp. 8440–8449 (2019)

30. Wang, X., Jiang, Y., Luo, Z., Liu, C.L., Choi, H., Kim, S.: Arbitrary shape scene text detection with adaptive text region representation. In: CVPR, pp. 6449–6458 (2019)

31. Wang, Y., Xie, H., Fang, S., Wang, J., Zhu, S., Zhang, Y.: From two to one: a new scene text recognizer with visual language modeling network. In: ICCV, pp. 14194–14203 (2021)

32. Wang, Y., Xie, H., Fu, Z., Zhang, Y.: DSRN: a deep scale relationship network for scene text detection. In: IJCAI, pp. 947–953 (2019)

33. Wang, Y., Xie, H., Zha, Z.J., Xing, M., Fu, Z., Zhang, Y.: Contournet: taking a further step toward accurate arbitrary-shaped scene text detection. In: CVPR, pp. 11753–11762 (2020)

34. Wu, L., Zhang, C., Liu, J., Han, J., Liu, J., Ding, E., Bai, X.: Editing text in the wild. In: ACM MM, pp. 1500–1508 (2019)

35. Xie, E., Zang, Y., Shao, S., Yu, G., Yao, C., Li, G.: Scene text detection with supervised pyramid context network. In: Proceedings of the AAAI Conference on Artificial Intelligence, vol. 33, pp. 9038–9045 (2019)

36. Xing, M., et al.: Boundary-aware arbitrary-shaped scene text detector with learnable embedding network. IEEE Trans. Multimedia **24**, 3129–3143 (2021)

37. Xue, C., Lu, S., Zhang, W.: Msr: multi-scale shape regression for scene text detection. arXiv preprint arXiv:1901.02596 (2019)

38. Yang, Q., Huang, J., Lin, W.: Swaptext: image based texts transfer in scenes. In: Proceedings of the IEEE/CVF Conference on Computer Vision and Pattern Recognition, pp. 14700–14709 (2020)

39. Zaremba, W., Sutskever, I., Vinyals, O.: Recurrent neural network regularization. arXiv preprint arXiv:1409.2329 (2014)

40. Zhang, C., Liang, B., Huang, E.A.: Look more than once: an accurate detector for text of arbitrary shapes. In: CVPR, pp. 10552–10561 (2019)

41. Zhang, X., Karaman, S., Chang, S.F.: Detecting and simulating artifacts in GAN fake images. In: 2019 IEEE International Workshop on Information Forensics and Security (WIFS), pp. 1–6. IEEE (2019)

42. Zheng, T., Chen, Z., Fang, S., Xie, H., Jiang, Y.G.: Cdistnet: Perceiving multi-domain character distance for robust text recognition. arXiv preprint arXiv:2111.11011 (2021)

43. Zhou, X., et al.: East: an efficient and accurate scene text detector. In: Proceedings of the IEEE conference on Computer Vision and Pattern Recognition, pp. 5551–5560 (2017)

44. Zhu, Y., Chen, J., Liang, L., Kuang, Z., Jin, L., Zhang, W.: Fourier contour embedding for arbitrary-shaped text detection. In: Proceedings of the IEEE/CVF Conference on Computer Vision and Pattern Recognition, pp. 3123–3131 (2021)
45. Zhu, Y., Du, J.: Sliding line point regression for shape robust scene text detection. In: ICPR, pp. 3735–3740. IEEE (2018)

Optimal Boxes: Boosting End-to-End Scene Text Recognition by Adjusting Annotated Bounding Boxes via Reinforcement Learning

Jingqun Tang[1] , Wenming Qian[2], Luchuan Song[3] , Xiena Dong[4], Lan Li[5],
and Xiang Bai[6(✉)]

[1] Ant Group, Hangzhou, China
jingquntang@163.com
[2] NetEase Fuxi AI Lab, Hangzhou, China
wenmingqian@corp.netease.com
[3] University of Rochester, Rochester, USA
lsong11@ur.rochester.edu
[4] Hangzhou Dianzi University, Hangzhou, China
dxn@hdu.edu.cn
[5] Wuhan University, Wuhan, China
2016302580090@whu.edu.cn
[6] Huazhong University of Science and Technology, Hangzhou, China
xbai@hust.edu.cn

Abstract. Text detection and recognition are essential components of a modern OCR system. Most OCR approaches attempt to obtain accurate bounding boxes of text at the detection stage, which is used as the input of the text recognition stage. We observe that when using tight text bounding boxes as input, a text recognizer frequently fails to achieve optimal performance due to the inconsistency between bounding boxes and deep representations of text recognition. In this paper, we propose Box Adjuster, a reinforcement learning-based method for adjusting the shape of each text bounding box to make it more compatible with text recognition models. Additionally, when dealing with cross-domain problems such as synthetic-to-real, the proposed method significantly reduces mismatches in domain distribution between the source and target domains. Experiments demonstrate that the performance of end-to-end text recognition systems can be improved when using the adjusted bounding boxes as the ground truths for training. Specifically, on several benchmark datasets for scene text understanding, the proposed method outperforms state-of-the-art text spotters by an average of 2.0% F-Score on end-to-end text recognition tasks and 4.6% F-Score on domain adaptation tasks.

Keywords: End-to-End text recognition · Reinforcement learning · Optimal bounding boxes

J. Tang and W. Qian—Equal contribution.

Supplementary Information The online version contains supplementary material available at https://doi.org/10.1007/978-3-031-19815-1_14.

© The Author(s), under exclusive license to Springer Nature Switzerland AG 2022
S. Avidan et al. (Eds.): ECCV 2022, LNCS 13688, pp. 233–248, 2022.
https://doi.org/10.1007/978-3-031-19815-1_14

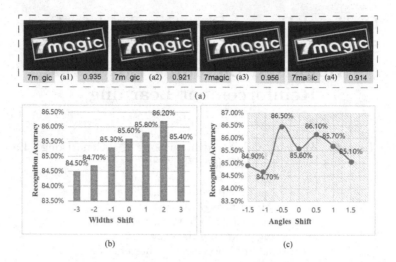

Fig. 1. (a) The red boxes represent the ground-truth bounding boxes, while the others are randomly shifted. Fig.(a1) represents the recognition confidence and recognition results with the ground-truth bounding box, while Fig.(a2) to Fig.(a4) with randomly shifted bounding boxes. The recognition results are presented on the left of (a1) to (a4), and the recognition confidence on the right; (b) text recognition accuracy with adjusting widths of the ground-truth bounding boxes; (c) text recognition accuracy with adjusting angles of the ground-truth bounding boxes. (Color figure online)

1   Introduction

In modern society, text plays a more important role than ever before as an essential tool for communication and collaboration. Meanwhile, scene text reading has become an active research area due to its wide applications in the real world, such as image instant translation [6,28], image search [25,30], and industrial automation [1,10].

Text detection and recognition can be roughly divided into two categories: two-step systems and end-to-end systems. For two-step systems [2,16,19,26,27, 29,33], since detected texts are cropped from the image, detection and recognition are two separate steps. Some of these methods first generate text proposals using a text detection model and then recognize them with a text recognition model [7,11,18]. For end-to-end systems, many end-to-end trainable networks [3,4,9,15,21] have recently been proposed [4,9,21] develop unified text detection and recognition systems with very similar overall architectures, which consist of a recognition branch and a detection branch. However, current models simply use tight annotated text bounding boxes as the ground truth, ignoring the inconsistency between bounding boxes and deep representations of text recognition. So, are tight bounding boxes the most suitable for recognition tasks? Through a series of experiments, we observe that a text recognizer frequently fails to achieve its best performance when using tight bounding boxes as inputs. As shown in Fig. 1(a), with suitable adjustments to the bounding boxes, we can get higher recognition confidence and correct recognition results (see Fig. 1(a3)). As shown in Fig. 1(b) and Fig. 1(c), the text recognizer can perform better when adjusting the widths or rotation angles of the ground-truth bounding boxes. The above experiments show a certain inconsistency between bounding boxes and deep representations of text recognition. Additionally, unlike in COCO [20], where clipping two pixels off an object does not prevent recognition, a 1–2 pixel error in text boxes may render the correct recognition prediction unrecoverable. The text recognition result is more sensitive to changes in the bounding box. To address the aforementioned problems, this paper presents a reinforcement learning-based method for adjusting the shape of each ground-truth bounding box so that it is more compatible with the text recognition task.

We propose a reinforcement learning-based method named Box Adjuster, which mitigates the inconsistency between bounding boxes and deep representations of text recognition. Our method can be summarized as follows: Firstly, we choose a range of representative text recognizers and regard the average recognition confidence as a reward. Secondly, the **Box** Adjusting **D**eep **Q** **N**etwork (BoxDQN) with Feature Fusion Module (FFM) is trained, which can automatically adjust bounding boxes according to the text recognition reward. Finally, we train the end-to-end scene text recognition model with the refined ground-truth bounding boxes for better recognition. Furthermore, as a preprocessing method, it is only applied in the process of creating training datasets. Thus, there is no additional computational cost in the forward phase.

Additionally, the proposed Box Adjuster is beneficial for resolving cross-domain problems such as synthetic-to-real, in which the source domain represents labeled synthetic data and the target domain represents unlabeled real data. To prove the effectiveness and generalization of our approach, we conduct experiments on standard benchmarks, including ICDAR 2013 [13], ICDAR 2015 [12], ICDAR 19-ReCTS [32] and ICDAR 19-MLT [24] datasets. The proposed method achieves better performance on the datasets when compared with the existing state-of-the-art methods. Besides, we demonstrate the efficacy of our approach on domain adaptation tasks.

Our contributions can be summarized as follows:

- We introduce the Box Adjuster, which adjusts the shape of each annotated text bounding box to make it more compatible with text recognition models. Besides, a text recognition-based reward is proposed to train our BoxDQN model in order to capture optimal annotated bounding boxes.
- Our proposed Feature Fusion Module (FFM), which integrates foreground, background, and box coordinates, considerably enhances BoxDQN in terms of application scope and accuracy.
- Our approach is generalized and can be easily applied to boost existing OCR systems without any additional computational cost during the inference phase. Concurrently, the proposed method outperforms state-of-the-art text spotters by an average of 2.0% F-Score on public datasets.

– When utilized in the cross-domain area, the proposed method significantly mitigates inconsistency between source and target domains, resulting in an average improvement of 4.6% for state-of-the-art text spotters.

2   Related Works

The related work mainly consists of two-step OCR systems, end-to-end OCR systems and reinforcement learning. Please refer to the supplementary material for a detailed description.

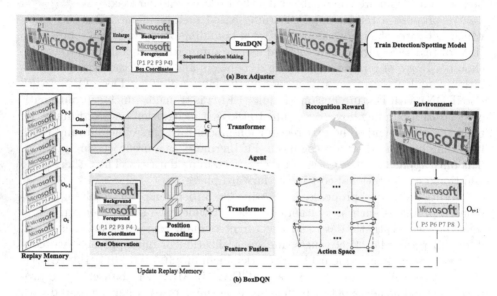

Fig. 2. Overview of our proposed method Box Adjuster and the details of BoxDQN model architecture. In order to mitigate the inconsistency between bounding boxes and deep representations of text recognition, we utilize Box Adjuster to adjust ground-truth bounding boxes and train the text spotter with them. BoxDQN is a method based on reinforcement learning with the reward of recognition confidence.

3   Methodology

This paper aims to mitigate the inconsistency problem between bounding boxes and deep representations of text recognition. A reasonable solution is to train the detection module with suitable bounding boxes that can boost the performance of the recognition module. Thus, the issue is how to obtain these appropriate bounding boxes. As illustrated in Fig. 2(a), we propose a method with the BoxDQN model structure termed Box Adjuster for adjusting bounding boxes to obtain suitable shapes. BoxDQN accepts an initial bounding box and adjusts it continuously throughout the loop. Then we train the text spotter with adjusted annotated bounding boxes.

The bounding box adjustment is formulated as a sequential decision-making process. In the decision-making process, the agent constantly interacts with the environment and takes a sequence of actions to adjust the bounding box. As shown in Fig. 2(b), the agent chooses which action from action space to perform based on the input of four consecutive observations. Following the environment's execution of the selected action, the agent receives the next state and current reward, which can be used to guide the agent's action policy until it achieves a reasonable bounding box by maximising the cumulative rewards. In this section, we first introduce the state, action space, and reward of our model, then describe the components of BoxDQN and its training process. Finally, we detail how our method can be applied to cross-domain problems.

3.1 State and Action Space

Based on the current state and reward, the agent chooses which action to take from action space. So it is crucial to capture abundant information from the state. However, one observation can only provide limited information for the agent, and it is necessary to make full use of historical observations for making decisions. Thus, we choose four serial observations as the state and the current state can be defined as $s_t = \{o_{t-3}, o_{t-2}, o_{t-1}, o_t\}$, where o_t denotes the current observation at step t. A single observation is composed of background, foreground, and box-coordinates, denoted by $o_t = \{background, foreground_t, box\text{-}coordinates_t\}$. The background area is four times the size of the initial bounding box. The $foreground_t$ is cropped from the background by a minimum enclosing rectangle of the bounding box at step t. The $box\text{-}coordinates_t$ represents the coordinates of text in background at step t. We have 16 actions in action space which are combinations of 4 vertexes and 4 directions. As we can see from Fig. 2(b), the first action in action spaces implies that the top-left vertex of the quadrangle moves down by one pixel.

3.2 Text Recognition-based Reward

The goal of BoxDQN is to capture appropriate bounding boxes for better recognition. Therefore, a reliable reward is needed to guide the agent to automatically adjust the bounding boxes. We select a few representative text recognition algorithms, including CRNN [26], RARE [27] and others. The average recognition confidence among them is regarded as a reward, so the reward at step t can be formulated as $r_t = conf_{t+1} - conf_t$, where $conf_t = Conf(foreground_t)$, $conf_t$ denotes the recognition confidence at step t.

$$conf_t = \sum_{k=0}^{N_P} conf_k / max(N_G, N_P), \tag{1}$$

where N_P denotes the number of characters in a prediction word and N_G denotes the number of characters in a ground-truth word. The aim of reinforcement learning is to maximize the cumulative rewards:

$$G_t = \sum_{k=0}^{T} \gamma^k r_{t+k}, \tag{2}$$

where γ denotes the discount factor and $\gamma \in [0,1]$. Ignoring the discount factor, the cumulative reward is equal to $conf_T - conf_0$, where $conf_T$ refers to the recognition confidence of foreground in the terminal state, T means the maximum number of steps and $conf_0$ refers to the recognition confidence of foreground in the initial state. Because $conf_0$ is invariant and only determined by the initial bounding box, maximizing cumulative rewards means maximizing $conf_T$ without γ.

3.3   BoxDQN Model

With the defined action space, state, and reward, the details of BoxDQN are illustrated in Fig. 2(b). The agent is composed of a feature fusion module (FFM) and a transformer encoder [31]. It accepts a single state with four observations as input and outputs 16 dimensional vectors, each of which specifies the appropriate action to take. With two deep convolutional neural networks [14] and a transformer encoder, the FFM is proposed to integrate background, foreground, and box-coordinates. During a bounding box adjustment, BoxDQN receives four observations and outputs the corresponding action according to the current state. Every observation needs to be fused by the FFM successively. The feature maps of the background and foreground are extracted from two convolution neural networks, respectively. We concatenate two image feature maps and the position encoding as the input of the transformer in the FFM. After all four observations are passed through the FFM, the transformer in the agent selects an action from the action space based on the concatenation of four fused feature maps. The bounding box moves in response to the selected action, changing both the box-coordinates and the minimum enclosing rectangle of the box-coordinates, and then the next state starts.

3.4   Domain Adaptation

In many cases, due to the absence of labeled real data, we train and test models using synthetic data. However, the domain gap between synthetic and real data degrades performance on real data. To address domain shift problems, we propose a domain-adaptive approach based on our BoxDQN. As shown in Fig. 3, our method consists of four steps: (1) refer to the labeled synthetic data domain as the source domain and the unlabeled real data domain as the target domain, (2) train a text spotter with the labeled synthetic data, (3) use the trained text spotter to generate pseudo-labels on real data and adjust the pseudo-labels by employing the BoxDQN mentioned above, (4) finetune the text spotter with the adjusted bounding boxes on real data.

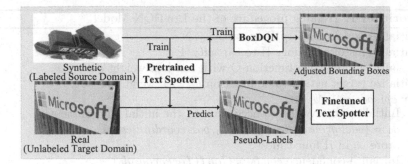

Fig. 3. Illustration of the pipeline with BoxDQN in the area of OCR domain adaptation. We propose a solution that utilizes BoxDQN to tackle domain shift problems.

3.5 Training BoxDQN Model

We use a value-based reinforcement learning method to adjust the bounding boxes, and the training process is presented in Algorithm 1. During the inner loop of the algorithm, BoxDQN can only adjust one bounding box in a single iteration. Thus, we crop all backgrounds from the source images by the bounding boxes in advance. M is the number of backgrounds. Firstly, the agent selects and executes an action according to an ϵ-greedy policy. The ϵ gradually decreases with iterations from 1.0 to 0.2. Secondly, we present two methods to determine whether the BoxDQN has reached the terminal state. Thirdly, we store a transition $\{s_t, a_t, r_t, s_{t+1}, Term_{t+1}\}$ and sample random mini-batch of transitions in replay memory D. The a_t represents the action at step t and $Term_{t+1}$ represents the terminal state at step t+1, respectively. $Term_{t+1}$ has two types: 0 and 1, where 0 and 1 represent termination and continuance, respectively. Finally, we refer to the training method in the paper [23] that uses a separate network termed $\hat{Q}$ for generating the targets y_j in the Q-learning update. Q represents the BoxDQN agent and has the same network structures as $\hat{Q}$. The $\hat{Q}$-network parameters θ^- are only updated with the Q-network parameters θ every C steps and are held fixed between individual updates. The parameters of Q are updated by optimizing the loss function with stochastic gradient descent. The training loss function is defined as follows:

$$loss = (y_j - Q(s_j, a_j; \theta))^2, \tag{3}$$

where y_j can be formulated as follows:

$$y_j = r_j + (1 - Term_{j+1}) * \gamma * max_{a'}\hat{Q}(a', s_{j+1}; \theta^-). \tag{4}$$

Algorithm 1: Training procedure of the BoxDQN Model

Initialize replay memory D to capacity N
Initialize history memory H to capacity 4
Initialize action-value function Q with random weight θ
Initialize target action-value function $\hat{Q}$ with weight $\theta^- = \theta$
for *episode* $= 1, M$ **do**
    Initialize observation o_0 according to the initial environment
    $o_0 = \{background, foreground_0, box\text{-}coordinates_0\}$
    Store o_0 in H four times
    Initialize confidence $conf_0 = Conf(foreground_0)$
    for $t = 1, T$ **do**
        With probability ϵ select a random action a_t
        Otherwise select $a_t = argmax_a Q(s_t, a; \theta)$
        Execute action a_t, observe reward r_t, new
        observation o_{t+1} and new confidence $conf_{t+1}$
        if $conf_{t+1} >= 1.2 * conf_0$ or $t+1==T$: **then**
         | $Term_{t+1} = 1$
        else
         | $Term_{t+1} = 0$
        end
        Get state s_t from H
        Update H by using o_{t+1}
        Get state s_{t+1} from H
        Store transition $(s_t, a_t, r_t, s_{t+1}, Term_{t+1})$ in D
        Sample random mini-batch of transitions
        $(s_j, a_j, r_j, s_{j+1}, Term_{j+1})$ from D
        Set $s_j = H(j)$ and $s_{j+1} = H(j+1)$
        Set $y_j = r_j + (1 - Term_{j+1}) * \gamma * max_{a'}\hat{Q}(a', s_{j+1}; \theta^-)$
        Perform a gradient descent step on $(y_j - Q(a_j, s_j; \theta))^2$ with
        respect to the network paremeters θ
        Every C steps reset $\hat{Q} = Q$
        if $Term_{t+1} == 1$ **then**
         | break out
        end
    end
end

---

4 Experiments

4.1 Datasets

To verify the effectiveness of our method for the end-to-end text spotting methods and the classic two-step methods, we perform experiments on four different datasets. Furthermore, we conduct domain-shift experiments on these datasets to show the robustness of our method in general scenarios. A detailed description of the relevant datasets is given in the supplementary material.

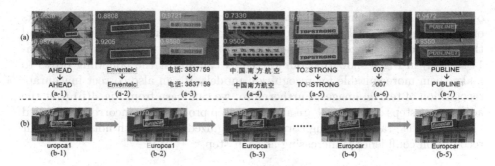

Fig. 4. Qualitative results of BoxDQN. Each pair in (a) is a comparison between the original label (top) and our adjusted bounding boxes (bottom). (a-1) to (a-3) are the results of manual ground truth, and (a-4) to (a-7) are the results on domain-shift, whose bounding boxes are pseudo labels. (b) is a visual display of the adjustment process of BoxDQN. The upper left corner of each image uses red numbers to indicate the recognition confidence.

4.2   Implementation Details

Baseline. The baseline methods are divided into two distinct categories: (1) two-step methods and (2) end-to-end methods. For two-step methods, due to detected texts are cropped from the image, the detection and recognition are two separate steps. We choose EAST [33] and DBNET [19] to detect the position of the characters, and then CRNN [26] and RARE [27] recognize the content within the bounding boxes. For end-to-end methods, we adopt FOTS [21], ABCNET [22], and MTS-V3 [17].

Training. A Linux workstation with 32 NVIDIA GeForce 2080Ti (11 GB) is used in our experiments. We train the recognition models in advance on SynthText-80k (for IC13 and IC15) and SynthText-MLT (for MLT19 and ReCTS) as well as on the corresponding real datasets. The trained recognition models are then used in BoxDQN training to continuously adjust and optimize the bounding boxes. The training phase of BoxDQN costs 2 days.

Inference. We evaluate the trained BoxDQN on the training set of the corresponding data and adjust the bounding boxes as the new ground truth to train the detection or spotting models, respectively. The average time taken for BoxDQN to adjust a bounding box is 25 ms. In the process of baseline methods evaluation, we follow the official public code repository for training and testing. The datasets in the Sect. 4.1 are involved in evaluation.

4.3   Qualitative Results

Our method mainly focuses on adjusting annotated bounding boxes for better text recognition. To verify its effectiveness, we conduct experiments on the four datasets, *i.e.*IC13, IC15, MLT19 and ReCTS. We show the adjustment results of our method on the bounding boxes of different datasets. The qualitative results of bounding boxes in English and Chinese are represented in Fig. 4. We find that our bounding boxes can achieve higher credibility in recognition. The (a-1) to (a-3) in Fig. 4 show that our BoxDQN can adjust the bounding boxes to make them more suitable for recognition models. It can also correct inaccurate recognition of text in images. Furthermore, we can learn from Fig. 4(b) that the adjustment steps of BoxDQN are a step-by-step process. The incorrectly labelled "Europcar" is gradually being correctly recognized. It is worth noting that our recognition confidence is increasing at each step.

4.4   Quantitative Results

To verify the robustness of our method with those baseline methods, we use the annotated bounding boxes refined by BoxDQN to train the baseline methods. During the quantitative evaluation, the same dataset with the original annotations is also used for training the baseline methods as a comparison. Finally, we test the F-Score metrics of our adjusted bounding boxes under recognition. The gain in Table 1 indicates the gain after including our BoxDQN.

Two-Step Methods. Two-step methods are those in which the detection model and the recognition model work separately. We choose the combination of [EAST, DBNET] for detection and [CRNN, RARE] for recognition in our experiments. The BoxDQN enhances the bounding boxes, and the detection models are then trained on the adjusted training part of the datasets. The trained models are then evaluated on the test datasets, respectively. From Table 1, when any combination of two-step pipelines is trained on our BoxDQN refined data, the metrics obtained are greatly improved. We find that our method has a greater improvement for MLT19 in Table 1. The gain of [EAST+CRNN] on the IC15 is 1.7%, but for the same pipeline on MLT19, the gain is 3.0%. For more complex OCR scenarios, our method has a more significant improvement. Regardless of any pipeline, the gain of the F-Score can obtain an improvement of at least 1.6%, which is robust to two-step methods.

End-to-End Methods. There are some differences between the end-to-end methods and the two-step methods, mainly in the independence of the detection branch and the recognition branch. We adopt the bounding boxes adjusted by BoxDQN to train the whole end-to-end models rather than the detection models and test the appearance of each metric. Table 2 shows the results of different end-to-end methods. Our BoxDQN is also helpful for the end-to-end text spotting methods, especially for ABCNET, whose gain is 3.3% and 2.6% on the MLT19 and ReCTS, respectively. The gain of the end-to-end methods is slightly lower compared with the two-step methods. This may be due to the fact that the end-to-end training of text spotters can slightly mitigate inconsistencies in detection and recognition.

Table 1. The quantitative results of our method on the two-step methods. Gain stands for the improvement of the F-Score with and without BoxDQN. We bold the results of each gain to highlight the improvement of the effect by BoxDQN.

Methods	BoxDQN	IC13		IC15		MLT19		ReCTS	
		F-score	Gain	F-score	Gain	F-score	Gain	F-score	Gain
[EAST+CRNN]	−	84.7	**2.1**	82.2	**1.7**	53.9	**3.0**	69.7	**2.8**
	✓	86.8		83.9		56.9		72.5	
[EAST+RARE]	−	85.5	**1.8**	83.7	**1.9**	55.5	**2.9**	71.1	**2.6**
	✓	87.3		85.4		58.1		73.7	
[DBNET+CRNN]	−	85.2	**1.9**	83.4	**1.7**	55.9	**2.7**	70.0	**2.9**
	✓	87.1		85.1		58.6		72.9	
[DBNET+RARE]	−	85.4	**1.8**	84.7	**1.6**	57.2	**2.4**	73.4	**2.1**
	✓	87.2		86.3		59.6		75.5	

Table 2. The quantitative results of our method on the end-to-end methods. The metrics are the same as the Table 1.

Methods	BoxDQN	IC13 [13]		IC15 [12]		MLT19 [24]		ReCTS [32]	
		F-Score	Gain	F-Score	Gain	F-Score	Gain	F-Score	Gain
FOTS [21]	−	83.7	**1.9**	81.5	**1.8**	53.0	**3.1**	70.2	**2.7**
	✓	85.6		83.3		56.1		72.9	
ABCNET [22]	−	86.8	**1.6**	82.4	**1.7**	56.2	**3.3**	72.5	**2.6**
	✓	88.4		84.1		59.5		75.1	
MTS-V3 [17]	−	87.6	**1.5**	83.1	**1.4**	61.2	**2.8**	73.4	**2.3**
	✓	89.1		84.5		64.0		75.7	

4.5 Domain Adaption

Taking into account the domain gap between the synthetic pretraining datasets and the in-the-wild data, we conduct cross-domain experiments to verify the generalization of our method. In detail, we pretrain BoxDQN on the synthetic datasets (SynthText-80k [8] and Synthetic-MLT [24]). After that, we adopt the pre-trained detection models on the relevant real datasets to obtain pseudo bounding boxes. The BoxDQN adjusts the pseudo bounding boxes, and finally the recognition models work on the adjusted bounding boxes to obtain the recognition results. We simulate in-the-wild data through unlabeled IC15 and MLT19, and verify the domain adaptability of our BoxDQN. The results of domain adaption experiments are shown in Table 3 and Fig. 4(a-1,2,3). From Fig. 4(a-4,5,6,7), although our method has a slight visual deviation in the adjustment of pseudo-labels, it can improve the confidence and correct the wrong recognition results. Table 3 proves that our method can improve at least 4.4% in cross-domain datasets.

Table 3. The experiments results on the cross-domain unlabeled datasets, the annotation information do not used in the datasets. We bold the gain of each pipelines.

Methods	BoxDQN	IC15 [12]		MLT19 [24]	
		F-Score	Gain	F-Score	Gain
[EAST [33]+CRNN [26]]	–	67.1	**5.4**	41.3	**7.0**
	✓	72.5		48.3	
[EAST [33]+RARE [27]]	–	68.3	**5.3**	42.9	**6.7**
	✓	73.6		49.6	
[DBNET [19]+CRNN [26]]	–	68.3	**5.2**	42.7	**5.4**
	✓	73.5		48.1	
[DBNET [19]+RARE [27]]	–	69.4	**5.3**	44.3	**6.2**
	✓	74.7		50.5	
[FOTS [21]]	–	66.6	**4.8**	39.8	**5.8**
	✓	71.4		45.6	
[ABCNET [22]]	–	69.4	**4.4**	44.4	**5.1**
	✓	73.8		49.5	
[MTS-V3 [17]]	–	71.3	**4.7**	46.7	**4.6**
	✓	76.0		51.3	

Table 4. Ablation study on grid search. The effect comparison under our BoxDQN and the grid search policy. The experimental dataset is based on IC15 [12].

Methods	Grid search			BoxDQN		
	Precision	Recall	F-Score	Precision	Recall	F-Score
[EAST [33]+CRNN [26]]	90.3	76.4	82.8	91.0	77.8	**83.9**
[DBNET [19]+RARE [27]]	91.9	80.3	85.7	92.5	80.8	**86.3**
[ABCNET [22]]	93.6	74.5	83.0	94.6	75.7	**84.1**
[MTS-V3 [17]]	93.5	75.2	83.4	94.8	76.2	**84.5**

4.6   Ablation Study

Grid Search. To verify that our BoxDQN is reasonable for adjusting annotated bounding boxes, we compare our method with a grid search policy and include the metric of F-Score in this experiments. In detail, we perform a grid search in each bounding box's four vertices in the directions of up, down, left, and right with a step length of one pixel. The recognition models are trained in advance and give the results with the highest confidence after 10 rounds of grid search as the new ground truth. Refer to Table 4 for the quantitative results. When compared with grid search, BoxDQN can improve recognition accuracy. This qualifies it as an appropriate bounding-box adjustment method in OCR systems and indicates that it does not over-fit the datasets.

Table 5. Ablation study on the DQN with only foreground image as input. The effect between our BoxDQN and the original DQN is shown below. The dataset is IC15 [12].

Methods	DQN			BoxDQN		
	Precision	Recall	F-Score	Precision	Recall	F-Score
[EAST [33]+CRNN [26]]	90.5	77.2	83.3	91.0	77.8	**83.9**
[DBNET [19]+RARE [27]]	92.3	79.9	85.7	92.5	80.8	**86.3**
[ABCNET [22]]	94.0	74.5	83.1	94.6	75.7	**84.1**
[MTS-V3 [17]]	94.1	75.5	83.8	94.8	76.2	**84.5**

Table 6. Ablation study on the number of iterations of BoxDQN. Each row shows the F-Score of the BoxDQN with a different iteration number. We bold the best value of each column.

Iter	[EAST+CRNN]	[DBNET+RARE]	[FOTS]	[ABCNET]	[MST-V3]
5	82.9	85.2	82.3	82.9	83.5
10	83.3	85.8	82.7	83.4	84.0
20	83.9	**86.3**	**83.3**	84.1	84.5
40	**84.0**	86.2	83.1	**84.3**	**84.6**

Only Foreground Image as Input. Our BoxDQN model adopts a FFM that fuses the foreground, background, and coordinates from the text images. The experimental settings in this section are the same as those in the Sect.4.2. The comparison results are shown in Table 5, demonstrating that the BoxDQN with more prior information outperforms the classic DQN (86.3 vs. 85.7, [DBNET [19]+RARE [27]] row). And for all of the representative methods, our method has a steady improvement on them. This verifies the robustness of our BoxDQN. More importantly, with the background image as input, our model can handle cases such as those shown in Fig. 4(a-7) where the bounding box is slightly shorter than the text transcription.

BoxDQN Under Different Iterations. Since our BoxDQN is sensitive to the times of iterations, different iterations have a great impact on the effect. We test the BoxDQN under different iterations and compare the number of iterations corresponding to the best BoxDQN. As shown in Table 6, the best performance of BoxDQN can be achieved when the number of iterations is set at 20, with minimal resource consumption. This is the same as the number of iterations (20) set in our experiments.

4.7 Exploration on Arbitrarily-shaped Text Based on Bezier Curves

To further explore the potential of our approach, we perform experiments on arbitrarily shaped text (TotalText [5] dataset). Our BoxDQN method requires a text representation with a fixed number of boundary points for optimization, so we have to convert polygon contour points that do not have a fixed number of

Table 7. The quantitative results of our method on TotalText. The baseline model is ABCNet with Bezier curves.

Methods	BoxDQN	TotalText [5]	
		F-Score	Gain
ABCNet [33]	−	61.5	**2.3**
	✓	63.8	

points to a representation that does. We can currently only convert arbitrarily-shaped text to a fixed number of control points (8) with the help of Bezier curves. We train our BoxDQN on the SynText150k [22] dataset which contains 150k synthetic arbitrary-shaped text annotated by Bezier curves. Then, we use BoxDQN to adjust the control points of the Bezier curve to obtain the optimal ground truth. The rest of the experimental settings is consistent with the multi-oriented text datasets, except for the differences mentioned above. From Table 7, we can find there is a considerable improvement(61.5 *vs.* 63.8) in recognition performance when training with the ground-truth Bezier curves optimized by BoxDQN. This experiment illustrates the possibility of extending our approach to arbitrarily-shaped text if there is a more general representation of text boxes.

5 Conclusion and Future Work

In this work, we first analyze the inconsistency between bounding boxes and text recognition, and then present a novel and general preprocessing method called Box Adjuster, which learns the optimal distribution of the text recognition module and delivers it to detection via bounding box adjustment. Our proposed approach is employed exclusively during the training phase, with no additional calculations during the prediction phase. More significantly, the cross-domain problems will be alleviated by utilizing the Box Adjuster. Comprehensive experiments have demonstrated that the proposed approach rationally addresses the aforementioned inconsistency and significantly improves the performance of both two-step and end-to-end text spotting approaches on standard datasets. In the future, we hope to extend our method for arbitrary-shaped text spotting.

Acknowledgements. This work was supported by the National Natural Science Foundation of China 61733007.

References

1. Aftabchowdhury, M.M., Deb, K.: Extracting and segmenting container name from container images. Int. J. Comput. Appl. **74**(19), 18–22 (2013)
2. Baek, Y., Lee, B., Han, D., Yun, S., Lee, H.: Character region awareness for text detection. In: Proceedings of CVPR, pp. 9365–9374 (2019)

3. Bartz, C., Yang, H., Meinel, C.: SEE: towards semi-supervised end-to-end scene text recognition. In: McIlraith, S.A., Weinberger, K.Q. (eds.) Proceedings of the Thirty-Second AAAI Conference on Artificial Intelligence, (AAAI-18), the 30th innovative Applications of Artificial Intelligence (IAAI-18), and the 8th AAAI Symposium on Educational Advances in Artificial Intelligence (EAAI-18), New Orleans, Louisiana, USA, February 2–7, 2018, pp. 6674–6681. AAAI Press (2018). https://www.aaai.org/ocs/index.php/AAAI/AAAI18/paper/view/16270

4. Busta, M., Neumann, L., Matas, J.: Deep textspotter: an end-to-end trainable scene text localization and recognition framework. In: 2017 IEEE International Conference on Computer Vision (ICCV), pp. 2204–2212 (2017)

5. Ch'ng, C.K., Chan, C.S.: Total-text: a comprehensive dataset for scene text detection and recognition. In: Proceedings of ICDAR. vol. 1, pp. 935–942 (2017)

6. Dvorin, Y., Havosha, U.E.: Method and device for instant translation (2009). uS Patent App. 11/998,931

7. Gupta, A., Vedaldi, A., Zisserman, A.: Synthetic data for text localisation in natural images. In: IEEE Conference on Computer Vision & Pattern Recognition, pp. 2315–2324 (2016)

8. Gupta, A., Vedaldi, A., Zisserman, A.: Synthetic data for text localisation in natural images. In: Proceedings of CVPR, pp. 2315–2324 (2016)

9. He, T., Tian, Z., Huang, W., Shen, C., Qiao, Y., Sun, C.: An end-to-end textspotter with explicit alignment and attention. In: Proceedings of the IEEE Conference on Computer Vision and Pattern Recognition, pp. 5020–5029 (2018)

10. He, Z., Liu, J., Ma, H., Li, P.: A new automatic extraction method of container identity codes. IEEE Trans. Intell. Trans. Syst. 6(1), 72–78 (2005)

11. Jaderberg, M., Simonyan, K., Vedaldi, A., Zisserman, A.: Reading text in the wild with convolutional neural networks. Int. J. Comput. Vis. 116(1), 1–20 (2016)

12. Karatzas, D., et al.: ICDAR 2015 competition on robust reading. In: ICDAR, pp. 1156–1160 (2015)

13. Karatzas, D., et al.: ICDAR 2013 robust reading competition. In: Proceedings of ICDAR, pp. 1484–1493 (2013)

14. Krizhevsky, A., Sutskever, I., Hinton, G.E.: Imagenet classification with deep convolutional neural networks. In: Pereira, F., Burges, C.J.C., Bottou, L., Weinberger, K.Q. (eds.) Advances in Neural Information Processing Systems, vol. 25, pp. 84–90. Curran Associates, Inc. (2012). https://proceedings.neurips.cc/paper/2012/file/c399862d3b9d6b76c8436e924a68c45b-Paper.pdf

15. Li, H., Wang, P., Shen, C.: Towards end-to-end text spotting with convolutional recurrent neural networks. In: Proceedings of the IEEE International Conference on Computer Vision (ICCV), pp. 5238–5246 (2017)

16. Li, H., Wang, P., Shen, C., Zhang, G.: Show, attend and read: a simple and strong baseline for irregular text recognition. In: Proceedings of the AAAI Conference on Artificial Intelligence, vol. 33, pp. 8610–8617 (2019)

17. Liao, M., Pang, G., Huang, J., Hassner, T., Bai, X.: Mask textSpotter v3: segmentation proposal network for robust scene text spotting. In: Vedaldi, A., Bischof, H., Brox, T., Frahm, J.-M. (eds.) ECCV 2020. LNCS, vol. 12356, pp. 706–722. Springer, Cham (2020). https://doi.org/10.1007/978-3-030-58621-8_41

18. Liao, M., Shi, B., Bai, X., Wang, X., Liu, W.: Textboxes: a fast text detector with a single deep neural network. In: Thirty-first AAAI Conference on Artificial Intelligence (2017)

19. Liao, M., Wan, Z., Yao, C., Chen, K., Bai, X.: Real-time scene text detection with differentiable binarization. In: Proceedings of AAAI, pp. 11474–11481 (2020)

20. Lin, T.-Y., Maire, M., Belongie, S., Hays, J., Perona, P., Ramanan, D., Dollár, P., Zitnick, C.L.: Microsoft COCO: common objects in context. In: Fleet, D., Pajdla, T., Schiele, B., Tuytelaars, T. (eds.) ECCV 2014. LNCS, vol. 8693, pp. 740–755. Springer, Cham (2014). https://doi.org/10.1007/978-3-319-10602-1_48

21. Liu, X., Ding, L., Shi, Y., Chen, D., Yan, J.: Fots: fast oriented text spotting with a unified network. In: 2018 IEEE/CVF Conference on Computer Vision and Pattern Recognition (CVPR), pp. 5676–5685 (2018)

22. Liu, Y., Chen, H., Shen, C., He, T., Wang, L.: Abcnet: real-time scene text spotting with adaptive bezier-curve network. In: 2020 IEEE/CVF Conference on Computer Vision and Pattern Recognition (CVPR), pp. 9809–9818 (2020)

23. Mnih, V., Kavukcuoglu, K., Silver, D., Rusu, A.A., Veness, J., Bellemare, M.G., Graves, A., Riedmiller, M., Fidjeland, A.K., Ostrovski, G., Petersen, S., Beattie, C., Sadik, A., Antonoglou, I., King, H., Kumaran, D., Wierstra, D., Legg, S., Hassabis, D.: Human-level control through deep reinforcement learning. Nature 518(7540), 529–533 (2015). https://doi.org/10.1038/nature14236

24. Nayef, N., et al.: ICDAR 2019 robust reading challenge on multi-lingual scene text detection and recognition-rrc-mlt-2019. In: 2019 International Conference on Document Analysis and Recognition (ICDAR), pp. 1582–1587. IEEE (2019)

25. Schroth, G., Hilsenbeck, S., Huitl, R., Schweiger, F., Steinbach, E.G.: Exploiting text-related features for content-based image retrieval. In: 2011 IEEE International Symposium on Multimedia, ISM 2011, Dana Point, CA, USA, December 5–7, 2011, pp. 77–84 (2011)

26. Shi, B., Bai, X., Yao, C.: An end-to-end trainable neural network for image-based sequence recognition and its application to scene text recognition. IEEE Trans. Pattern Anal. Mach. Intell. 39(11), 2298–2304 (2016)

27. Shi, B., Wang, X., Lyu, P., Yao, C., Bai, X.: Robust scene text recognition with automatic rectification. In: Proceedings of the IEEE Conference on Computer Vision and Pattern Recognition (CVPR), pp. 4168–4176 (2016)

28. Song, L., Yin, G., Liu, B., Zhang, Y., Yu, N.: Fsft-Net: face transfer video generation with few-shot views. In: 2021 IEEE International Conference on Image Processing (ICIP), pp. 3582–3586. IEEE (2021)

29. Tang, J., et al.: Few could be better than all: feature sampling and grouping for scene text detection. In: Proceedings of the IEEE/CVF Conference on Computer Vision and Pattern Recognition, pp. 4563–4572 (2022)

30. Tsai, S.S., Chen, H., Chen, D.M., Schroth, G., Girod, B.: Mobile visual search on printed documents using text and low bit-rate features. In: IEEE International Conference on Image Processing, pp. 2601–2604 (2011)

31. Vaswani, A., et al.: Attention is all you need. In: Guyon, I., Luxburg, U.V., Bengio, S., Wallach, H., Fergus, R., Vishwanathan, S., Garnett, R. (eds.) Advances in Neural Information Processing Systems, vol. 30. Curran Associates, Inc. (2017). https://proceedings.neurips.cc/paper/2017/file/3f5ee243547dee91fbd053c1c4a845aa-Paper.pdf

32. Zhang, R., et al.: ICDAR 2019 robust reading challenge on reading Chinese text on signboard. In: 2019 International Conference on Document Analysis and Recognition (ICDAR), pp. 1577–1581. IEEE (2019)

33. Zhou, X., Yao, C., Wen, H., Wang, Y., Zhou, S., He, W., Liang, J.: East: an efficient and accurate scene text detector. In: Proceedings CVPR, pp. 5551–5560 (2017)

GLASS: Global to Local Attention for Scene-Text Spotting

Roi Ronen[1], Shahar Tsiper[2(✉)], Oron Anschel[2], Inbal Lavi[2],
Amir Markovitz[2], and R. Manmatha[3]

[1] Viterbi Faculty of Electrical and Computer Engineering, Technion, Haifa, Israel
[2] AWS AI Labs, Tel Aviv, Israel
tsiper@amazon.com
[3] AWS AI Labs, San Francisco, CA, USA

Abstract. In recent years, the dominant paradigm for text spotting is to combine the tasks of text detection and recognition into a single *end-to-end* framework. Under this paradigm, both tasks are accomplished by operating over a shared global feature map extracted from the input image. Among the main challenges that end-to-end approaches face is the performance degradation when recognizing text across scale variations (smaller or larger text), and arbitrary word rotation angles. In this work, we address these challenges by proposing a novel global-to-local attention mechanism for text spotting, termed GLASS, that fuses together global and local features. The global features are extracted from the shared backbone, preserving contextual information from the entire image, while the local features are computed individually on resized, high resolution rotated word crops. The information extracted from the local crops alleviates much of the inherent difficulties with scale and word rotation. We show a performance analysis across scales and angles, highlighting improvement over scale and angle extremities. In addition, we introduce an orientation-aware loss term supervising the detection task, and show its contribution to both detection and recognition performance across all angles. Finally, we show that GLASS is general by incorporating it into other leading text spotting architectures, improving their text spotting performance. Our method achieves state-of-the-art results on multiple benchmarks, including the newly released TextOCR.

Keywords: Text spotting · Text detection · Text recognition · Language understanding

---

R. Ronen and S. Tsiper—Equal contibution.
Code available at https://www.github.com/amazon-research/glass-text-spotting.

Supplementary Information The online version contains supplementary material available at https://doi.org/10.1007/978-3-031-19815-1_15.

© The Author(s), under exclusive license to Springer Nature Switzerland AG 2022
S. Avidan et al. (Eds.): ECCV 2022, LNCS 13688, pp. 249–266, 2022.
https://doi.org/10.1007/978-3-031-19815-1_15

1   Introduction

Text spotting, the task of detecting text instances in the wild and recognizing them, has seen a notable increase in performance in recent years. It is now commonly used in many real-life scenarios and applications. Demanding areas such as autonomous driving, document analysis, and geo-localization, where accurate text transcription is a must, all rely on text spotting. The challenge lies in the fact that some words may span the entire image, while other words, even in the same image, may be hard to read, e.g., appear on a traffic sign barely seen from across the street.

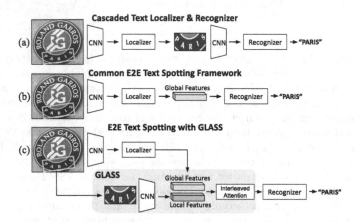

Fig. 1. An overview of text spotting approaches. (a) Cascaded. A standalone text detector followed by a standalone recognizer. Each is trained separately. **(b)** End-to-end (E2E) text spotting. Detection and recognition are jointly optimized. **(c)** Our approach with GLASS fusion, operating on two separate feature maps taken at different resolutions and contexts, bridging (a) and (b). Feature maps are fused using interleaved attention, improving robustness to scale and rotation, and overall performance.

Two prevalent paradigms exist for text spotting (see Fig. 1): the first is a modular approach, cascading independent text detection and recognition models. The recognition model uses uniformly aligned and resized word-crop images as input with upright orientation, abstracting away scale and rotation. The components in this approach are mostly explored independently in the literature, isolating either the word detection performance (ignoring transcripts) [2,4,21,38,45], or the recognition performance over datasets composed of word-crop images [1,24,30,39]. The second approach is a combined End-to-End (E2E) architecture, adding a recognition branch that operates directly on the detection model's latent features [3,8,16,20,28,32,35]. Feature sampling replaces cropping, allowing detection and recognition to be jointly trained E2E.

With E2E becoming the common paradigm, scale and rotation-free crops were often replaced by sampled CNN features, that are highly sensitive to both scale and rotation [13,44]. While the joint optimization in E2E systems improved performance for average-sized and upright-facing words, scale extremities and strong rotations were overlooked.

In this work, we propose to bridge the two paradigms to get the best out of both worlds. We combine *global* features from the detector's embedding space with *local* cropped word embeddings. The fusion is done using a novel Global-to-Local interleaved attention module, leveraging information from both feature maps. This global-to-local approach enriches the information used by the recognition branch, boosting the overall text spotting accuracy for different scales and rotations. Additional gains for rotated text are obtained by introducing an orientation prediction side-task, aimed at better capturing rotated words, or words in rotated images. The side task is supervised by a new loss term with a πn periodic sine-squared function. The model is optimized end-to-end, benefiting both detection and recognition. We name our approach GLASS - Global to Local Attention for Scene-text Spotting.

Our method achieves state-of-the-art results on ICDAR 2015 [14], Total-Text [6], and Rotated ICDAR 2013 [20] benchmarks. We also present blind evaluation results measured on the recently released TextOCR [40] dataset, largely surpassing the baseline. GLASS is then examined across a range of text scales and orientations in an ablation study. Finally, we incorporate GLASS into recent E2E text spotting approaches, and show gains of 2.3% for Mask TextSpotter v3 [20] and 3.7% for ABCNet v2 [28], when measuring E2E F-score on Total-Text [6]. To summarize, the main contributions of this work are:

1. A new global-to-local attention module improving text spotting performance at scale extremities
2. A periodic orientation loss, further improving detection and recognition results across all angles
3. State-of-the-art results on ICDAR 2015 [14], Total-Text [6], TextOCR [40] and Rotated ICDAR 2013 [20] benchmarks
4. Incorporation of GLASS into other text spotting frameworks, demonstrating consistent gains

2   Background and Related Work

Text Spotting. We compare the two paradigms for text spotting, cascaded and E2E. The cascaded option enjoys modularity, allowing to combine different architectures for detection and recognition. By uniformly scaling and rotating the word crops to their upright orientation, the recognizer is operating on a fixed and less challenging input space. Another benefit is that each part can train using different data. The recognizer can leverage large amounts of synthetically generated word-crops, tailored for specific lexicons and challenging scenarios [12, 19], which cannot be leveraged by the detector. For detection, synthetic images are largely limited to pre-training [10,29]. The main caveat in the cascaded approach is that no contextual information is shared between the predicted words during recognition.

In contrast, in E2E methods the recognizer leverages contextual information from each word's surroundings, which helps disambiguate and overcome challenging scenarios. This is due to the large receptive field of CNN backbones [31]. Furthermore, jointly training detection and recognition, benefits both tasks [37,43], leading to substantial gains. Finally, such methods often enjoy improved latency, since the feature extraction step is done once, and shared by the detector and the recognizer. A main drawback of E2E approaches is the limited resolution at which the recognizer operates. The recognition branch is commonly fed with sampled features at a fixed spatial size [3,20,28,35], which might be insufficient for accurate prediction [24,30,39]. Specifically, the feature sampling operator, which provides the input features to the recognizer, is lossy and may fail to preserve meaningful information. The sampling procedure is sensitive to different text scales and orientations, as discussed in ABCNet v2 [28] and shown below.

Feature Sampling. As recognition operates on features sampled from a latent space, the sampling procedure plays a large role in its success. Different sampling approaches have seen several advancements over the years.

Region of Interest (RoI) Pooling [9] was first introduced for sampling features, and has been widely used since [18,43]. It was replaced with RoIAlign [11] that used a bilinear interpolation for weighted feature sampling, that was also extended for the first time for sampling non axis-aligned (i.e., *rotated*) RoIs [26]. For sampling arbitrarily shaped text, further extensions [16,20,32] added a background mask to the sampling operation for isolating the extracted word only, often relying on segmentation-based detectors or masks.

For text, Mask TextSpotter v3 [20] presented an anchor-free, non-parametric, segmentation proposal network where original detections are in the form of a segmentation map. Features were sampled using hard RoI masking. Recently, Liu *et al.* introduced ABCNet [27] and ABCNet v2 [28] which use a Bézier curve parametrization for localizing curved text. They exploited the parametrization using a BezierAlign operator for feature sampling.

In the above methods, the text recognition module operates only on the limited resolution features pooled from the whole-image, the global feature map. Our method is the first to combine additional information computed directly from a normalized word crop. Since it is not tailored to a specific backbone or pooling layer, GLASS can be added on top of multiple existing E2E frameworks, as we show in Sect. 4.4.

A few notable works predict text without relying on feature sampling. These include CharNet [25], which directly outputs bounding boxes of words and characters with corresponding character labels, and MANGO [35], which divides the input image into grids and coarsely localizes the text sequence using a position-aware attention module.

Global-to-Local Fusion. There have been approaches in the literature for improving object detection performance across a large range of scales. Recent approaches [22,41,42] focused on fusing between different layers of the shared feature extraction backbone. They harness the fact that different layers at differ-

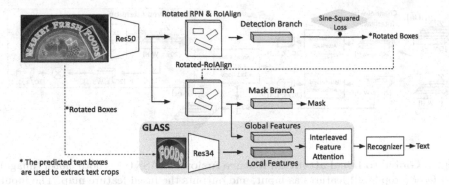

Fig. 2. Global to Local Scene-text Spotting. The global detection branch is a Mask R-CNN variant supervised by our novel sine-squared loss for rotated box prediction. During inference, predicted boxes are used to sample global backbone features and to crop the original image as input for the local feature extractor. Global and local features are fused in GLASS and passed to the recognizer for transcript extraction.

ent depths within the shared backbone have a different receptive field, and are capable of detecting details at a multitude of scales. We leverage the global-to-local key concept from object detection [22,41] and adopt it for the recognition task in E2E text spotting.

Orientation Prediction. Several recent works modeled the text detection problem using a rotated box geometry for the detections. Among the first was EAST [45], that suggested a hybrid approach for regressing both a rotated box and a quadrilateral around text objects. The use of rotated RPN proposals and Rotated-ROIAlign was first suggested in [33], using the regular L_1 loss to regress the output boxes. The authors in [46], identified an ambiguity in the angle prediction, namely that the same box can be described by four valid angles, a different angle perpendicular for each face. They tackled it with a cascaded process where a single correct box orientation is regressed in a gradual manner. In [17] the same ambiguity was handled by optimizing over the minimal angle difference among all of the detected box sides, and in [34] the ambiguity is dealt with by representing the orientation of each box with 8 parameters, and regressing over all of them, while ensuring continuity of the loss function. Our approach tackles the angle regression ambiguity by introducing an orientation-aware, periodic trigonometric loss, as further discussed in Sect. 3.2.

3 Method

3.1 GLASS Fusion Module

Our pipeline is composed of three principal components, seen in Fig. 2: the detection branch, the GLASS fusion module, and the recognition head. The detection branch is used for locating words, predicting their bounding boxes and segmentation masks. It is trained with the added orientation-aware loss, and its backbone

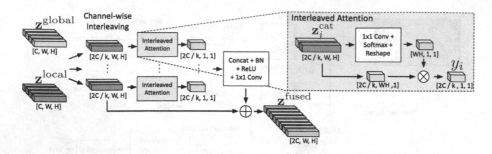

Fig. 3. Global to Local attention feature fusion. GLASS takes both *global* (image) and *local* (crop-level) features as input, and outputs the fused feature map. The input feature maps are channel-wise interleaved, concatenated and split into k blocks. Each block is processed by an attention module, producing k tensor outputs. These are then concatenated, transformed by 1×1 convolution and summed element-wise with the input feature maps. (Color figure online)

is used for extracting the global features. The fusion module combines the global and local features, producing an enriched embedding that is then fed into the recognition head. In this work, we use a Rotated Mask R-CNN [11,33] as the baseline approach for our detection branch, and for the recognition branch we use ASTER [39].

We begin by presenting our global-to-local fusion module in Sect. 3.1, and follow with a description of our orientation-aware loss in Sect. 3.2. Finally, we discuss aspects regarding the overall architecture and training objective in Sect. 3.3.

We propose a fusion module for incorporating the scale and rotation invariance of the local word-crop approach into an end-to-end text spotter, while still using global context. Uniformly scaled and aligned crops abstract away nuisances such as the original word's size and off-axis rotation, and allow us to maximize our ability to extract text.

The predicted boxes of the detection branch are used in two sampling operations. For *global* features, we sample the FPN [22] features from the detection branch. For *local* features, we sample the image directly (i.e. crop), performing an affine transformation that yields a uniformly scaled, axis-aligned word crop. This crop is passed through a local feature extractor.

Formally, we denote the input image $\mathbf{x}$ and its FPN features $\mathbf{z}$. Following detection, the global feature map $\mathbf{z}$ is sampled using the predicted boxes, yielding $\mathbf{z}^{\text{global}}$. Using the same boxes, the image $\mathbf{x}$ is cropped and aligned into $\mathbf{x}^{\text{local}}$, which in turn is embedded using a shallow dedicated backbone into $\mathbf{z}^{\text{local}}$. Every text detection is now represented by two separate feature maps, $\mathbf{z}^{\text{global}}$ and $\mathbf{z}^{\text{local}}$, illustrated in Fig. 3 by light-blue and pink bars, respectively.

Inspired by [30], we propose an interleaved attention procedure that operates over small feature blocks, aiming to combine and use the most relevant information for the text recognition task, from both input features. Attending over small blocks is significantly lighter than standard attention mechanisms in high dimensionality, and is shown to improve robustness for downstream tasks [30].

The interleaved attention combines global and local features in a learned way, maximizing informational content. This dynamic weighting allows the attention mechanism to place greater emphasis on specific relevant context, depending on the input.

The global and local features are first combined to k block tensors by an interleaved concatenation, where $k \ll C$. The ith block is given by

$$\mathbf{z}_i^{\text{cat}} = \left[z_{i \cdot m+1}^{\text{global}}, \ z_{i \cdot m+1}^{\text{local}}, \ \ldots, \ z_{i \cdot m+m}^{\text{global}}, \ z_{i \cdot m+m}^{\text{local}} \right], \tag{1}$$

where $m = \lceil C/k \rceil$. Block indices are given by $i \in \{0, 1, \ldots, k-1\}$, and $z_j^{\text{global}}, z_j^{\text{local}}$ depict the jth channel of $\mathbf{z}^{\text{global}}, \mathbf{z}^{\text{local}}$, for $j \in [1, C]$.

A spatial attention operator is then applied to each of the k blocks in $\mathbf{z}^{\text{cat}}$, as shown in Fig. 3 within the dashed box, such that

$$y_i = \text{vec}(\mathbf{z}_i^{\text{cat}})^T \text{vec}\left(\text{softmax}(v_i^T \mathbf{z}_i^{\text{cat}}) \right), \tag{2}$$

yielding an attentional vector $y_i \in \mathbb{R}^{2C/k}$. Here $v_i \in \mathbb{R}^{2C/k}$ is a learnable vector and $\text{vec}(\cdot)$ reshapes a tensor of size (C, W, H) into a matrix of size (C, WH). Interleaving the two feature maps ensures that in Eq. (2) we mix information that corresponds with both global and local features.

Next we stack the k attention vectors $y_{1 \ldots k}$ channel-wise, apply batch normalization (BN), ReLU and a 1×1 convolution for capturing channel-wise dependencies, resulting in the tensor $\mathbf{y}$. The fused output is an element-wise addition of $\mathbf{y}$ and the interleaved-concatenated feature maps, $\mathbf{z}^{\text{cat}}$, illustrated by the green bars in Fig. 3. Formally,

$$\mathbf{z}^{\text{fused}} = \mathbf{z}^{\text{cat}} + \mathbf{w}^T \text{ReLU}(\text{BN}(\mathbf{y})), \tag{3}$$

where $\mathbf{w} \in \mathbb{R}^{C \times H \times W}$ are learnable weights. The output $\mathbf{z}^{\text{fused}}$ is then used as input to the recognition head.

We note that there are two alternatives to the proposed interleaved attention. The first is a naïve concatenation of the global and local features, which is tested in Sect. 3.2, and is shown to reduce accuracy. The second is performing a full attention computation between the full dimension of local and global features, however, this computation is unfeasible due to computational limitations.

3.2 Orientation Prediction

Unlike objects in other common object-detection benchmarks such as COCO [23] and Pascal VOC [7], text instances are long, narrow and directed. A word extracted upside-down or rotated by 90° is usually non-recoverable in terms of recognition. This makes orientation prediction especially important and meaningful. To this end, we propose a new orientation-aware loss function operating on rotated box detections $\mathbf{r} \in \mathbb{R}^{N \times 5}$, where the first 4 coordinates describe the rotated box center, width and height, and the last coordinate, $\theta \in \mathbb{R}$, depicts its upward facing angle. The loss function for the mth matched detection is given by

$$\mathcal{L}_{\text{rbox}} = \sum_{i=1}^{4} \alpha_i \left| \hat{r}_i - r_i \right| + \alpha_\theta \sin^2 \left(\hat{\theta} - \theta \right), \tag{4}$$

where the hat denotes prediction. The constants α_i for $i \in [1, 4]$ and α_θ are chosen empirically. The sine-squared function has a periodicity of $n\pi$ for $n \in \mathbb{Z}$, leveraging the fact that a rotated rectangle is symmetric to $n\pi$ rotations. This symmetry removes an inherent ambiguity during training, allowing the same prediction for boxes that are either upright or flipped upside-down. This mechanism was empirically shown to improve detection results across all angular range, as further explored in Sect. 4.5 and shown in Fig. 4. For each word, the orientation angle is then used to perform a rotated pooling operation on the shared backbone features, yielding the global feature input. This process is common in additional E2E frameworks [20,28], but without the orientation-aware loss, orientation mistakes in the form of discrete jumps of $k\pi/2, k \in \mathbb{Z}$ degrees are more common. In our implementation, the predicted angle is also used to generate an oriented word-crop, from which the local features are computed, as illustrated in Fig. 2.

3.3 Global to Local End-to-end Text Spotting

Here, we describe our proposed E2E framework with GLASS, shown in Fig. 2. For the shared backbone, we use the commonly used ResNet50 and FPN [22]. Its associated features $\mathbf{z}^{\text{global}}$ are sampled using Rotated-RoIAlign operating directly on the FPN levels as in [37]. For obtaining the local feature maps $\mathbf{z}^{\text{local}}$, we first sample a crop of the text RoI from the input image using Rotated-RoIAlign layer. Then, the crop features are extracted by ResNet34 backbone [5].

Finally, we fuse the global and local feature maps using the interleaved attention operation, described in Sect. 3.1, yielding $\mathbf{z}^{\text{fused}}$, which is the recognition module's input. The recognition head, detailed in the Supplementary Material, provides the transcript for each word. We note that the mask head is used as a parallel branch to the recognizer, and only receives $\mathbf{z}^{\text{global}}$ as input.

The overall loss function $\mathcal{L}$ used for the E2E supervised training is given by

$$\mathcal{L} = \mathcal{L}_{\text{rbox}} + \lambda_1 \mathcal{L}_{\text{mask}} + \lambda_2 \mathcal{L}_{\text{rec}}. \tag{5}$$

Here, the mask loss $\mathcal{L}_{\text{mask}}$ is identical to Mask R-CNN [11] and $\mathcal{L}_{\text{rec}}$ is the recognition loss.

We note that GLASS has no effect on the computational cost of the detector, including its mask branch, and the recognizer head. The computational aspects of GLASS, as well as the loss terms used in training, are further discussed in the Supplementary Material.

4   Experiments

We evaluate the performance of our method on several benchmarks, testing our method's robustness to rotations and text size. First, we compare our full framework with GLASS to current art. Next, we examine GLASS when integrated into two common E2E text spotting architectures, Mask TextSpotter v3 [20] and ABCNet v2 [28]. Finally, we provide a comprehensive ablation study isolating the contribution of GLASS for different data distributions with various settings. Additional ablation studies are presented in the Supplementary Material.

4.1   Datasets

SynthText [10] is a synthetically generated dataset containing approximately 800K images and 6M synthetic text instances. **ICDAR 2013** [15] has 233 testing images containing mostly horizontal text. We synthetically rotate these images by various angles and use it to measure our performance on rotated text. **ICDAR 2015** [14] consists of 1,000 training images and 500 testing images. Most of the images are of low resolution and contain small text instances. **Total-Text** [6] contains 1,255 training and 300 testing images. It offers text instances in a variety of shapes, including horizontal, rotated, and curved text. **TextOCR** [40] is a recently published arbitrary-shaped detection and recognition dataset containing of 21,778 train, 3153 validation and 3232 test images with more than 700k, 100k and 80k annotated words, respectively.

4.2   Implementation Details

We follow the common SynthText pre-training scheme [3, 20]. For Total-Text, we fine-tune using a mixture of Total-Text and SynthText datasets, as in [3]. For ICDAR13 and ICDAR15 results, we train also on both datasets, following [20]. For TextOCR results, we follow the baseline [40] and use all of the datasets mentioned in Sect. 4.1. In the ablation studies (Sect. 4.5), we fine-tune the model for 100k iterations with a batch size of 8 images. In Sect. 4.3, the model is fine-tuned for 250k iterations with a batch size of 24 images. The recognizer used is an off-the-shelf component, based on ASTER [39]. Additional implementation details are found in the Supplementary Material.

4.3   Comparison with State-of-the-Art

Quantitative results for end-to-end text recognition on the ICDAR15, Total-Text and TextOCR datasets are listed in Table 1. For ICDAR15, our method outperforms previously reported word spotting protocol results for all three lexicons, and for the end-to-end evaluation protocol with Generic lexicon. For the Total-Text dataset, our method achieves state-of-the-art F-measure results for both settings in the word spotting evaluation, and for full-lexicon end-to-end. For no-lexicon end-to-end, GLASS outperforms all methods but CRAFTS [3].

We are among the first to report results for the challenging TextOCR test dataset in Table 1. This newly released dataset is an order of magnitude larger than previous ones and has ample variation in scale and rotation. Thresholds for the detection and recognition heads were set using the TextOCR validation set. Our method achieves state-of-the-art F-measure results, surpassing Mask TextSpotter v3 [20] by 16.3% on end-to-end evaluation protocol. Both methods were optimized with a similar data profile, including TextOCR train data [40].

Table 1. Results for ICDAR 2015, Total-Text and TextOCR datasets. 'S', 'W' and 'G' refer to strong, weak and generic lexicons. "None" refers to recognition without any lexicon. "Full" lexicon contains all the words in the test set. (*) refers to using specific lexicons from [20]. (†) indicates IoU of 0.1 was used instead of 0.5 during evaluation. (‡) represents results obtained using method's official source code.

Method	ICDAR 2015						Total-Text				TextOCR
	Word spotting			End-to-End			Word spotting		End-to-End		End-to-End
	S	W	G	S	W	G	None	Full	None	Full	
TextDragon [8]	86.2	81.6	68.0	82.5	78.3	65.2	–	–	48.8	71.8	–
ABCNet v2 [28]	–	–	–	82.7	78.5	73.0	70.4	78.1	–	–	–
MTSv3* [20]	83.1	79.1	75.1	83.3	78.1	74.2	–	–	71.2	78.4	50.8
Text Perc. [36]	84.1	79.4	67.9	80.5	76.6	65.1	69.7	78.3	–	–	–
CRAFTS [3]	–	–	–	83.1	**82.1**	<u>74.9</u>	–	–	**78.7**	–	–
MANGO*† [35]	85.2	81.1	74.6	**85.4**	<u>80.1</u>	73.9	<u>72.9</u>	<u>83.6</u>	68.9‡	<u>78.9‡</u>	–
YAMTS* [16]	**86.8**	<u>82.4</u>	<u>76.7</u>	<u>85.3</u>	79.8	74.0	–	–	71.1	78.4	–
Ours*	**86.8**	**82.5**	**78.8**	84.7	<u>80.1</u>	**76.3**	**79.9**	**86.2**	<u>76.6</u>	**83.0**	**67.1**

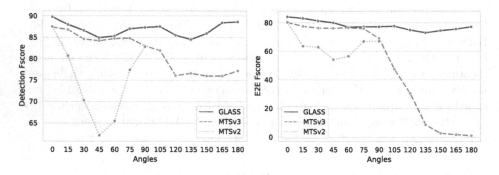

Fig. 4. GLASS contribution for different angles. We measure the performance on the Rotated ICDAR 2013 dataset. Combining GLASS with our novel sine-squared loss improves text detection and recognition across all angles. Notice the 4% detection and 7% recognition gains at angles close to 90°.

To validate our framework performance on oriented text, we show results on the Rotated ICDAR 2013 benchmark [20] in Fig. 4. Our approach with GLASS and the sine-squared loss outperforms previous art on both text detection and recognition across all angles, and especially benefits the detection algorithm on steep angles larger than 60°.

4.4 Incorporating Glass into Other Methods

GLASS can be incorporated into any text spotting architecture that uses a feature pooling module, regardless of its specific pooling mechanism. To demonstrate this, we employ GLASS in two common E2E text spotting works, Mask TextSpotter v3 [20] and ABCNet v2 [28]. We note that Mask TextSpotter v3 and ABCNet v2 use different backbones and RPN modules, different detection and recognition heads, in addition to other minor differences. Importantly, unlike our method which uses Rotated-RoIAlign pooling, Mask TextSpotter v3 uses an axis-aligned RoIAlign with hard feature masking, and ABCNet v2 applies BezierAlign. Despite the differences between all three architectures, the use of GLASS within both Mask TextSpotter v3 and ABCNet v2 is straightforward and requires minimal changes.

Table 2. GLASS results with Mask TextSpotter v3 (MTSv3) [20] and ABC-Net v2 [28]. First and third rows are results reproduced using the official MTSv3 and ABCNet v2 implementations. The second and fourth rows show the effect of incorporating GLASS into MTSv3 and ABCNet v2.

Method	Total-Text		ICDAR 2015	
	E2E Hmean	FPS	E2E Hmean	FPS
MTSv3 [20]	67.5	2.2	68.5	2.6
+ GLASS	69.8 (**+2.3**)	2.0	72.3 (**+3.8**)	2.3
ABCNet v2 [28]	67.6	6.5	–	–
+ GLASS	71.3 (**+3.7**)	6.0	–	–

For each method, we use its publicly available source code[1], [2], and train both architectures with and without the GLASS component, following the training procedure published by the respective authors. Results are shown in Table 2. Adding only minor computational overhead, GLASS provides a considerable benefit to the E2E performance of each method. Further discussion on the computational aspects of GLASS is found in the Supplementary Material.

4.5 Ablation Study

To evaluate the effectiveness of individual parts in our proposed framework, we conduct ablation studies on the Total-Text and ICDAR15 datasets. In Tables 3 to 6 we report the *end-to-end* F-measure (Hmean) as defined in ICDAR15 [14].

---

[1] https://github.com/MhLiao/MaskTextSpotterV3.
[2] https://github.com/aim-uofa/AdelaiDet.

Every model version is pre-trained and fine-tuned as an end-to-end system independently for every experiment.

The **baseline** architecture consists of a Mask R-CNN detection branch with a Rotated-RoIAlign component and our novel rotated box regression loss, as described in Sect. 3.2. The recognizer is set as described in Supplementary Material and receives as input only the *global* features from the shared backbone, as described in Sect. 3.1 and shown in Fig. 1b. The recognition head remains unchanged for all experiments, with the sole difference being the input features selected for it.

Contribution of GLASS to End-to-End Performance. The effect of GLASS on overall performance is presented in Table 3. Different feature map and fusion combinations are compared, all using the baseline architecture for detection. Replacing the global features with local features as recognition input, shown in the second row of the table, causes a 3.2% and 4.6% regression for Total-Text and ICDAR15 datasets, respectively. We identify the main reason for this regression in a noticeable drop in the detection performance (see in Supplementary Material), and the lack of mutual supervision of the detection-recognition.

A simple channel-wise concatenation of global and local features (row 3) improves the results over the baseline by 2.4% and 3.5% on Total-Text and ICDAR15 datasets. Furthermore, using GLASS provides further boosts for both Total-Text and ICDAR15 datasets, reaching 3.1% and 4.6% over the baseline. Overall, adding the GLASS module leads to considerable gains in the E2E performance, while only increasing latency by roughly 10%.

Table 3. Ablation study - Fusion. "Global" and "Local" columns stands for the use of image-level (Global) and cropped (Local) features. "Fusion" column compares two different fusion operations where both features are used: a simple channel-wise concatenation and our fusion method. All rows use the Rotated Mask R-CNN detector and recognition head described in Sect. 3.2 and Sect. 3.3. "FPS" column states the average latency in frames-per-second measured for Total-Text. We measure End-to-End Hmean on Total-Text (TT) and ICDAR15 (IC15).

	Global	Local	Fusion	TT	IC15	FPS
Baseline	✓		–	72.6	69.1	3.0
Baseline + Local		✓	–	69.4 (↓3.2)	64.5 (↓4.6)	2.8
Baseline + Global-Local	✓	✓	Concat.	75.0 (↑2.4)	72.6 (↑3.5)	2.7
Baseline + GLASS	✓	✓	Ours	75.7 (↑3.1)	73.7 (↑4.6)	2.7

Table 4. Ablation study - Orientation loss. We use Total-Text and ICDAR15 to compare the two losses for the rotated box angle: (a) the commonly used L_1 loss and (b) our novel sine-squared loss from Eq. (4). Both experiments use GLASS. The metrics R, P, and H denote detection recall, precision, and Hmean respecively, while E2E denoted End-to-End Hmean.

	Total-Text				ICDAR 2015			
	R	P	H	E2E	R	P	H	E2E
GLASS + L_1 loss	**86.3**	88.2	87.2	75.0	83.4	85.0	84.2	73.5
GLASS + $\sin^2$ loss	85.5	**90.8**	**88.1**	**75.7**	**84.5**	**86.9**	**85.7**	**73.7**

Orientation Robustness Analysis. We compare our framework with two different orientation losses: our proposed sine-squared loss in Eq. (4) and the commonly used L_1 loss. Both models use GLASS. The results on Total-Text and ICDAR15 datasets are presented in Table 4. Relying on the L_1 loss, instead of our $\sin^2$ loss, leads to a result regression of 0.7% on the Total-Text dataset, which emphasizes arbitrarily rotated text.

Scale Robustness Analysis. We establish our method's contribution in challenging cases in both quantitative and qualitative manners. The relative contribution of GLASS at different scales is quantified by performing a custom ablation study using the Total-Text dataset. Total-Text contains a variety of challenging texts at different scales and rotations. First, we divide text instances into four groups: small, medium, large and extra-large, denoted by S, M, L and XL accordingly, and illustrated in Fig. 5. The groups are defined as four equally-sized bins w.r.t. the square root area of their ground-truth text polygon, over the entire dataset.

Table 5. GLASS contribution across different scales. We measure the performance over 4 scale groups in Total-Text: small, medium, large and extra-large, denoted by S, M, L, XL accordingly (see Fig 5). The specific sizes were chosen for creating equally sized bins of ground-truth instances. GLASS outperforms the other configurations, especially on the lower and higher end of the scales. The baseline achieves comparable performance to GLASS on medium and large scales.

	S	M	L	XL
Baseline	71.8	77.8	77.7	79.0
Baseline + Local branch	72.7 (↑1.9)	77.3 (↓0.5)	74.9 (↓2.8)	75.5 (↓3.5)
Baseline + GLASS	**73.9 (↑2.1)**	**78.1 (↑0.3)**	**77.8 (↑0.1)**	**80.8 (↑1.8)**

Table 6. Ablation study - Recognition with ground-truth boxes. To isolate the recognizer's performance, *ground-truth* boxes are used, simulating perfect detections. We compare global, local and fused recognizer inputs on Total-Text and ICDAR15.

	GT Detection	Features Global	Local	Total-Text Hmean	ICDAR15 Hmean
Baseline	✓	✓		75.3	72.8
Baseline + Local branch	✓		✓	74.2 (↓1.1)	78.5 (↑5.7)
Baseline + GLASS	✓	✓	✓	80.5 (↑5.2)	80.0 (↑7.2)

The F-score is measured for each population of prediction and ground-truth polygons independently, shown in Table 5. As expected, most of the gain is achieved over the small and extra-large text groups, compared to the baseline that predicts text solely using the global branch.

A qualitative comparison is shown in Fig. 6, where we picked examples from the Total-Text dataset that contain a mix of small and large scale text. The baseline result, shown in row (a), is under-performing on challenging text instances that are either small, very large or have a steep rotation angle. In row (b), where only the local features are used, there is a notable regression in both detection and recognition accuracy. In row (c) our method is robust to both scale and orientation, and capable of accurately detecting and recognizing text in extreme and challenging scenarios.

Fig. 5. Illustration of text scale groups.

Isolating Recognition Branch Performance. Lastly, we assess the impact of the GLASS module on the recognition task by injecting the ground-truth rotated boxes as the detection output. By overriding the entire detection branch with *oracle* predictions we are able to isolate the recognizer and compare multiple configurations. The results are presented in Table 6, showing that using the fused features from GLASS contributes to a large increase of 5.2% and 7.2% in the recognition performance on Total-Text and ICDAR15 respectively.

Fig. 6. Qualitative results for Total-Text. Predictions from: **(a)** A standard E2E text spotting framework. **(b)** An E2E framework using only the local features for recognition, and **(c)** Our proposed method with the GLASS component. Blue and red represent correct and incorrect predictions, respectively. GLASS improves recognition, specifically for small and large words, matching the results in Table 5.

5   Discussion

We propose two extensions for existing text spotting methods. First is combining global and local features for end-to-end text recognition, and a fusion operator enabling that, termed GLASS. The other is an orientation prediction side task, using the orientation-aware sine-squared objective during optimization.

The proposed algorithm combines highly-contextual global features, which also encode each word's surroundings and allows reading it in-context, like humans do, with uniformly scaled and oriented local features, abstracting away scale and rotation. This improves performance for common cases, and even more so for cases of strong scale and rotation.

Extensive experiments over four benchmarks, including the challenging Rotated ICDAR 2013 and the new TextOCR show state-of-the-art results. Ablation studies highlight our contribution over scale and rotation ranges, as well as our method's applicability to other recent text spotting methods.

References

1. Baek, J., et al.: What is wrong with scene text recognition model comparisons? dataset and model analysis. In: Proceedings of the IEEE International Conference on Computer Vision, pp. 4715–4723 (2019)
2. Baek, Y., Lee, B., Han, D., Yun, S., Lee, H.: Character region awareness for text detection. In: Proceedings of the IEEE Conference on Computer Vision and Pattern Recognition, pp. 9365–9374 (2019)

3. Baek, Y., et al.: Character region attention for text spotting. In: Vedaldi, A., Bischof, H., Brox, T., Frahm, J.-M. (eds.) ECCV 2020. LNCS, vol. 12374, pp. 504–521. Springer, Cham (2020). https://doi.org/10.1007/978-3-030-58526-6_30

4. Bušta, M., Patel, Y., Matas, J.: E2E-MLT - an unconstrained end-to-end method for multi-language scene text. In: Carneiro, G., You, S. (eds.) ACCV 2018. LNCS, vol. 11367, pp. 127–143. Springer, Cham (2019). https://doi.org/10.1007/978-3-030-21074-8_11

5. Cheng, Z., Bai, F., Xu, Y., Zheng, G., Pu, S., Zhou, S.: Focusing attention: towards accurate text recognition in natural images. Proceedings of the IEEE International Conference on Computer Vision, pp. 5076–5084 (2017)

6. Ch'ng, C.K., Chan, C.S.: Total-text: a comprehensive dataset for scene text detection and recognition. In: International Conference on Document Analysis and Recognition, vol. 1, pp. 935–942. IEEE (2017)

7. Everingham, M., Van Gool, L., Williams, C.K.I., Winn, J., Zisserman, A.: The pascal visual object classes (voc) challenge. Int. J. Comput. Vis. **88**(2), 303–338 (2010)

8. Feng, W., He, W., Yin, F., Zhang, X.Y., Liu, C.L.: TextDragon: an end-to-end framework for arbitrary shaped text spotting. In: Proceedings of the IEEE International Conference on Computer Vision, pp. 9076–9085 (2019)

9. Girshick, R.: Fast R-CNN. In: Proceedings of the IEEE International Conference on Computer Vision, pp. 1440–1448 (2015)

10. Gupta, A., Vedaldi, A., Zisserman, A.: Synthetic data for text localisation in natural images. In: Proceedings of the IEEE Conference on Computer Vision and Pattern Recognition, pp. 2315–2324 (2016)

11. He, K., Gkioxari, G., Dollár, P., Girshick, R.: Mask R-CNN. In: Proceedings of the IEEE International Conference on Computer Vision, pp. 2961–2969 (2017)

12. Jaderberg, M., Simonyan, K., Vedaldi, A., Zisserman, A.: Synthetic data and artificial neural networks for natural scene text recognition. In: Workshop on Deep Learning, Advances in Neural Information Processing Systems (2014)

13. Jaderberg, M., Simonyan, K., Zisserman, A., Kavukcuoglu, K.: Spatial transformer networks. Adv. Neural Inf. Process. Syst. **28** (2015)

14. Karatzas, D., et al.: ICDAR 2015 competition on robust reading. In: International Conference on Document Analysis and Recognition, pp. 1156–1160. IEEE (2015)

15. Karatzas, D., et al.: ICDAR 2013 robust reading competition. In: International Conference on Document Analysis and Recognition, pp. 1484–1493. IEEE (2013)

16. Krylov, I., Nosov, S., Sovrasov, V.: Open images v5 text annotation and yet another mask text spotter. arXiv preprint arXiv:2106.12326 (2021)

17. Lee, J., Lee, J., Yang, C., Lee, Y., Lee, J.: Rotated box is back: an accurate box proposal network for scene text detection. In: Lladós, J., Lopresti, D., Uchida, S. (eds.) ICDAR 2021. LNCS, vol. 12824, pp. 49–63. Springer, Cham (2021). https://doi.org/10.1007/978-3-030-86337-1_4

18. Li, H., Wang, P., Shen, C.: Towards end-to-end text spotting with convolutional recurrent neural networks. In: Proceedings of the IEEE International Conference on Computer Vision, pp. 5238–5246 (2017)

19. Li, H., Wang, P., Shen, C., Zhang, G.: Show, attend and read: a simple and strong baseline for irregular text recognition. In: Proceedings of the AAAI Conference on Artificial Intelligence, vol. 33, no. 01, 8610–8617 (2019)

20. Liao, M., Pang, G., Huang, J., Hassner, T., Bai, X.: Mask TextSpotter v3: segmentation proposal network for robust scene text spotting. In: Vedaldi, A., Bischof, H., Brox, T., Frahm, J.-M. (eds.) ECCV 2020. LNCS, vol. 12356, pp. 706–722. Springer, Cham (2020). https://doi.org/10.1007/978-3-030-58621-8_41

21. Liao, M., Wan, Z., Yao, C., Chen, K., Bai, X.: Real-time scene text detection with differentiable binarization. In: Proceedings of the AAAI Conference on Artificial Intelligence, vol. 34, no. 07, pp. 11474–11481 (2020)
22. Lin, T.Y., Dollár, P., Girshick, R., He, K., Hariharan, B., Belongie, S.: Feature pyramid networks for object detection. In: Proceedings of the IEEE Conference on Computer Vision and Pattern Recognition, pp. 2117–2125 (2017)
23. Lin, T.-Y., Maire, M., Belongie, S., Hays, J., Perona, P., Ramanan, D., Dollár, P., Zitnick, C.L.: Microsoft COCO: common objects in context. In: Fleet, D., Pajdla, T., Schiele, B., Tuytelaars, T. (eds.) ECCV 2014. LNCS, vol. 8693, pp. 740–755. Springer, Cham (2014). https://doi.org/10.1007/978-3-319-10602-1_48
24. Litman, R., Anschel, O., Tsiper, S., Litman, R., Mazor, S., Manmatha, R.: SCATTER: selective context attentional scene text recognizer. In: Proceedings of the IEEE Conference on Computer Vision and Pattern Recognition, pp. 11962–11972 (2020)
25. Liu, W., Chen, C., Wong, K.Y.K.: Char-Net: a character-aware neural network for distorted scene text recognition. In: Proceedings of the AAAI Conference on Artificial Intelligence, vol. 32, no. 1 (2018)
26. Liu, X., Liang, D., Yan, S., Chen, D., Qiao, Y., Yan, J.: FOTS: fast oriented text spotting with a unified network. In: Proceedings of the IEEE Conference on Computer Vision and Pattern Recognition, pp. 5676–5685 (2018)
27. Liu, Y., Chen, H., Shen, C., He, T., Jin, L., Wang, L.: Abcnet: real-time scene text spotting with adaptive bezier-curve network. In: Proceedings of the IEEE Conference on Computer Vision and Pattern Recognition, pp. 9809–9818 (2020)
28. Liu, Y., Shen, C., Jin, L., He, T., Chen, P., Liu, C., Chen, H.: ABCNet v2: Adaptive bezier-curve network for real-time end-to-end text spotting. arXiv preprint arXiv:2105.03620 (2021)
29. Long, S., Yao, C.: Unrealtext: Synthesizing realistic scene text images from the unreal world. arXiv preprint arXiv:2003.10608 (2020)
30. Lu, N., Yu, W., Qi, X., Chen, Y., Gong, P., Xiao, R., Bai, X.: Master: multi-aspect non-local network for scene text recognition. Pattern Recogn. **117**, 107980 (2021)
31. Luo, W., Li, Y., Urtasun, R., Zemel, R.: Understanding the effective receptive field in deep convolutional neural networks. Adv. Neural Inf. Process. Syst. **29** (2016)
32. Lyu, P., Liao, M., Yao, C., Wu, W., Bai, X.: Mask textSpotter: an end-to-end trainable neural network for spotting text with arbitrary shapes. In: Proceedings of the European Conference on Computer Vision, pp. 67–83 (2018)
33. Ma, J., et al.: Arbitrary-oriented scene text detection via rotation proposals. IEEE Trans. Multimedia **20**(11), 3111–3122 (2018)
34. Qian, W., Yang, X., Peng, S., Yan, J., Guo, Y.: Learning modulated loss for rotated object detection. In: Proceedings of the AAAI Conference on Artificial Intelligence. vol. 35, no. 3, pp. 2458–2466 (2021)
35. Qiao, L., et al.: MANGO: a mask attention guided one-stage scene text spotter. In: Proceedings of the AAAI Conference on Artificial Intelligence, vol. 35, no. 3, pp. 2467–2476 (2021)
36. Qiao, L., et al.: Text perceptron: towards end-to-end arbitrary-shaped text spotting. In: Proceedings of the AAAI Conference on Artificial Intelligence, vol. 34, no. 07, pp. 11899–11907 (2020)
37. Qin, S., Bissacco, A., Raptis, M., Fujii, Y., Xiao, Y.: Towards unconstrained end-to-end text spotting. In: Proceedings of the IEEE International Conference on Computer Vision, pp. 4704–4714 (2019)
38. Qin, X., et al.: Mask is all you need: Rethinking mask R-CNN for dense and arbitrary-shaped scene text detection. arXiv preprint arXiv:2109.03426 (2021)

39. Shi, B., Yang, M., Wang, X., Lyu, P., Yao, C., Bai, X.: ASTER: an attentional scene text recognizer with flexible rectification. IEEE Trans. Pattern Anal. Mach. Intell. **41**(9), 2035–2048 (2018)
40. Singh, A., Pang, G., Toh, M., Huang, J., Galuba, W., Hassner, T.: Textocr: towards large-scale end-to-end reasoning for arbitrary-shaped scene text. In: Proceedings of the IEEE Conference on Computer Vision and Pattern Recognition, pp. 8802–8812 (2021)
41. Tan, M., Pang, R., Le, Q.V.: EfficientDet: scalable and efficient object detection. In: Proceedings of the IEEE Conference on Computer Vision and Pattern Recognition (2020)
42. Wang, J., et al.: Deep high-resolution representation learning for visual recognition. IEEE Trans. Pattern Anal. Mach. Intell. **43** (10), 3349–3364 (2021)
43. Wang, P., Li, H., Shen, C.: Towards end-to-end text spotting in natural scenes. IEEE Trans. Pattern Anal. Mach. Intell. (2021)
44. Worrall, D.E., Garbin, S.J., Turmukhambetov, D., Brostow, G.J.: Harmonic networks: deep translation and rotation equivariance. In: Proceedings of the IEEE Conference on Computer Vision and Pattern Recognition, pp. 7168–7177 (2017)
45. Zhou, X., et al.: East: an efficient and accurate scene text detector. In: Proceedings of the IEEE Conference on Computer Vision and Pattern Recognition, pp. 5551–5560 (2017)
46. Zhu, Y., Ma, C., Du, J.: Rotated cascade R-CNN: a shape robust detector with coordinate regression. Pattern Recogn. **96**, 106964 (2019)

COO: Comic Onomatopoeia Dataset for Recognizing Arbitrary or Truncated Texts

Jeonghun Baek[✉][ID], Yusuke Matsui[ID], and Kiyoharu Aizawa[ID]

The University of Tokyo, Tokyo, Japan
{baek,matsui,aizawa}@hal.t.u-tokyo.ac.jp

Abstract. Recognizing irregular texts has been a challenging topic in text recognition. To encourage research on this topic, we provide a novel comic onomatopoeia dataset (COO), which consists of onomatopoeia texts in Japanese comics. COO has many arbitrary texts, such as extremely curved, partially shrunk texts, or arbitrarily placed texts. Furthermore, some texts are separated into several parts. Each part is a truncated text and is not meaningful by itself. These parts should be linked to represent the intended meaning. Thus, we propose a novel task that predicts the link between truncated texts. We conduct three tasks to detect the onomatopoeia region and capture its intended meaning: text detection, text recognition, and link prediction. Through extensive experiments, we analyze the characteristics of the COO. Our data and code are available at https://github.com/ku21fan/COO-Comic-Onomatopoeia.

Keywords: Comic onomatopoeia · Arbitrary text · Truncated text · Text detection · Text recognition · Link prediction

1 Introduction

Along with the development of deep neural networks, text recognition methods have significantly improved. Currently, most state-of-the-art methods can easily recognize simple horizontal texts. Recently, the research trend has progressed to recognize more irregular texts: recognizing horizontal text to recognizing arbitrary-shaped text such as curved or perspective text in scene images [10,20,22,23,25,42–45,49,51]. We expect that *studies on more irregular texts will further improve the text recognition methods.*

To encourage these studies, we provide a novel comic onomatopoeia dataset (COO), which contains more irregular texts. After investigating various text datasets from English [9,15–17,30,36,40,50] to other languages [1,8,11,26,27,34, 37,48], we find that onomatopoeia texts in the Japanese comic dataset (Manga10-9 [26]) have arbitrary shapes or are arbitrarily placed in the image. Onomatopoeias are written texts that represent the sound or state of objects (humans, animals,

---

Supplementary Information The online version contains supplementary material available at https://doi.org/10.1007/978-3-031-19815-1_16.

© The Author(s), under exclusive license to Springer Nature Switzerland AG 2022
S. Avidan et al. (Eds.): ECCV 2022, LNCS 13688, pp. 267–283, 2022.
https://doi.org/10.1007/978-3-031-19815-1_16

and so on). To exaggerate the sound or state of the object, onomatopoeias are typically written in irregular shapes or placed at unexpected positions. Fig. 1 (a) illustrates examples of COO: (left) shows extremely curved text, (right) shows partially shrunk text, and part of the text is on the object.

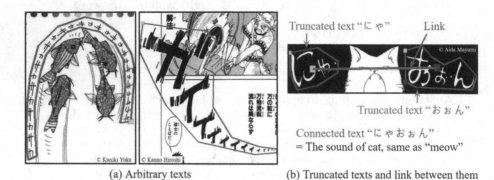

(a) Arbitrary texts   (b) Truncated texts and link between them

Fig. 1. Visualization of comic onomatopoeia dataset *COO*. Red and blue squares denote the start and end points of each annotation, respectively. The purple line denotes the link between truncated texts

Onomatopoeia in Japanese comics is sometimes separated into several parts, as shown in Fig. 1 (b). When separated, each part is a truncated text. Each truncated text does not fully represent the meaning. After truncated texts are connected, the connected text represents the intended meaning. For example, the truncated texts "にゃ" and "おぉん" in Fig. 1 (b) do not represent the meaning independently. When they are connected into "にゃおぉん", the connected text represents the meaning: the sound of cat, same as "meow". To correctly capture the meaning of truncated texts, *we propose a novel task that predicts the link between truncated texts*. By using the link information, we connect truncated texts to capture the intended meaning. To solve this task, we formulate the task as the sequence-to-sequence problem [38], and propose a model named M4C-COO, a variant of multimodal multi-copy mesh (M4C) [13].

Considering truncated texts, we conduct three tasks to detect the onomatopoeia region and capture its intended meaning: 1) Text detection: The model takes an image, and outputs the regions of onomatopoeias. 2) Text recognition: The model takes the region of onomatopoeia, and outputs the text in the region. 3) Link prediction: The model takes the regions and texts of onomatopoeias, and outputs the links between truncated texts. With extensive experiments using state-of-the-art methods, we analyze the characteristics of COO and the limitation of current models. We hope that these analyses inspire and encourage future work on recognizing arbitrary or truncated texts.

Among three tasks, we mainly focus on text recognition and link prediction. Because they are somewhat different from existing tasks, they can hinder using our dataset. To prevent it, we provide decent baselines for them. Traditional

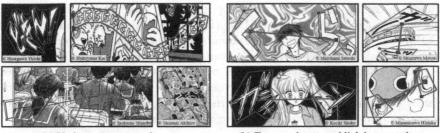

| (a) Various onomatopoeias | (b) Truncated texts and link between them |

Fig. 2. Visualizations of COO. Each example shows diversity of onomatopoeias

text recognition task generally recognizes horizontal or curved texts. However, the COO has many vertically long texts: In 72.5% of onomatopoeia regions, the height is greater than the width. To address vertically long texts, we introduce several effective techniques. In the case of the link prediction task, it is a novel task, and thus we introduce it thoroughly.

In summary, our main contributions are as follows:

- We construct a novel challenging dataset *COO* to encourage the research on recognizing arbitrary or truncated texts.
- COO has many vertically long texts, and we investigate several techniques that are effective to recognize vertically long texts.
- COO has some truncated texts, and they should be linked. We propose a novel task, which predicts the link between truncated texts, and a M4C-COO model for this task.

2 COO: Comic Onomatopoeia Dataset

Most onomatopoeias in COO are arbitrary-shaped or arbitrarily placed. In addition, they are written in informal fonts or various sizes. This section introduces the visualization, annotation guideline, statistics, and analysis of our dataset. More details are presented in the supplementary materials.

2.1 Why Use Onomatopoeias of Japanese Comics?

We use onomatopoeias of Japanese comics rather than English comics. Because of following three reasons:

1. Japanese comics have various types of onomatopoeias. Fig. 1 and Fig. 2 show many arbitrary or truncated texts. As arbitrary texts, Fig. 2 (a) (top row) shows three-dimensional or curved texts. Fig. 2 (a) (bottom row) shows transparent texts on the objects that look similar to background objects. Fig. 2 (b) shows truncated texts.

2. Japanese comics have more onomatopoeias than English comics. We compared Japanese comic dataset Manga109 [26], and English comic dataset COMICS [15]. Manga109 has *5.8 onomatopoeias per page on average*, whereas COMICS has much fewer (492 onomatopoeias in the first 5,000 images).

3. Japanese language has more diverse onomatopoeias than most languages. According to Petersen [28], "The reason sounds in manga are so rich and varied is also in part due to the nature of the Japanese language that has a much wider range of onomatopoeic expressions than most languages."

2.2 Label Annotation

For each comic onomatopoeia, we create annotation data according to three tasks: 1) Text detection: Annotate polygon regions. 2) Text recognition: Annotate texts. 3) Link prediction: Annotate links between truncated texts.

We annotate comic onomatopoeias in Manga109 [26]. Manga109 consists of 109 Japanese comics. Each image in Manga109 consists of two pages (left and right pages) because some objects or onomatopoeias lie across two pages, as shown in Fig. 3.

Fig. 3. Each image in Manga109 consists of two pages, and it is used as input data for text detection task

Polygon Regions of Onomatopoeia. We use polygon annotations instead of bounding box annotations to minimize regions irrelevant with texts. We place the points that represent the contour of the onomatopoeia. The points are placed clockwise starting from the top left of the onomatopoeia and ending with the bottom left. Red and blue squares in Fig. 2 denote start and end points of each annotation, respectively. Because most state-of-the-art methods are developed with single-line annotations, we split a multi-lined onomatopoeia into single lines as much as possible.

Texts of Onomatopoeia. While the Japanese language consists of Hiragana (e.g. "あ", "い"), Katakana (e.g. "ア", "イ"), and Chinese characters (e.g. "任", "意"), Japanese comic onomatopoeias are typically written in Hiragana or Katakana. Thus, Chinese characters are not the target of annotation. We annotate Hiragana, Katakana, and some special symbols for each onomatopoeia. Generally, most comic onomatopoeias are written in informal fonts or by drawing.

Link Between Truncated Texts. Link annotation is conducted on polygon and text annotations. The link between truncated texts is determined by the meaning of onomatopoeia. Onomatopoeias have a link if the following conditions are satisfied: 1) Two or more onomatopoeias are separated in the image. 2) By themselves, they do not fully represent the intended meaning. 3) When they are connected, they represent the intended meaning. The purple line in Fig. 2 denotes the link between truncated texts.

The annotation was performed with an annotation team consisting of 15 annotators and 3 annotation checkers. After all onomatopoeias in 109 comics were annotated, annotation checkers performed the initial check. After that, we (authors) checked the annotations over three times and provided feedback for re-annotation to ensure annotation quality. As a result, annotations have been revised over three times.

2.3 Dataset Analysis

Table 1 presents the statistics of COO dataset. COO has 61,465 polygons in total. If we regard the polygon that has more than 4 points as curved, the ratios of the curved, quadrilateral, and rectangular annotations are 61.3%, 15.4%, and 23.4%, respectively. The average number of points on all polygons is 6.3. COO has 2,261 links in total, and one link appears every five pages on average. Most links are between two truncated texts. The numbers of links made by three, four, and five truncated texts are 132, 11, and 1, respectively.

Table 1. Statistics on the COO dataset

Count type	Total	Train	Valid	Test
Images	10,602	8,763	890	949
Comic volumes	109	89	10	10
Polygon	61,465	50,064	4,636	6,765
Link	2,261	1,923	161	177
Vocabularies	13,272	11,635	1,915	2,251
Character types	182	182	163	166

The number of character types is 182, and Fig. 4 shows all of them. To recognize English texts, one may use 94 characters, including alphanumerics and symbols, as done in ASTER [33]. To recognize general Japanese texts, one should use thousands of Chinese characters. Then, the number of character types exceeds thousands, and the increment of the character types makes text recognition difficult. However, comic onomatopoeias do not include thousands of Chinese characters, and character types do not increment considerably, only 94 to 182. This indicates that the difficulty from the increment of the character types is little, and we can focus on recognizing arbitrary or truncated texts.

ぁあぃいぅうゔぇえぉおかがきぎくぐけげこごさざしじすずせ
ぜそぞただちぢっつづてでとどなにぬねのはばぱひびぴふぶぷ
へべぺほぼぽまみむめもゃやゅゆょよらりるれろゎわをん
ァアィイゥウヴェエォオカガキギクグケゲコゴサザシジスズセ
ゼソゾタダチヂッツヅテデトドナニヌネノハバパヒビピフブプ
ヘベペホボポマミムメモャヤュユョヨラリルレロヮワンヶ
!.?~★☆♡♥♩♪♫♬、。゛゜・ー

Fig. 4. Total 182 character types of COO. Because COO does not contain Chinese characters, the number of character types is much smaller than that in the Japanese language (over 2,000 characters)

COO can be also used for comic analysis or comic translation. For example, 79% of links start from the left and end with the right. This is an interesting characteristic because Japanese comics generally read right to left while the order of most truncated texts is reverse. For other example, in our manual check over each truncated texts, we find that an object is typically placed between

Fig. 5. Examples of truncated texts in English

truncated texts. This is assumed to be a drawing technique to represent the sound or state of the object dramatically.

2.4 Comparison with Existing Arbitrary Scene Text Datasets

Comic onomatopoeias exhibit various shapes and sizes, and are placed arbitrarily in the image. They are close to scene text rather than document text. There are several existing arbitrary-shaped scene text datasets: CUTE [30], CTW1500 [21], Total-Text [9], ArT [8], and TextOCR [36]. They have polygon annotations for curved texts. While these datasets focus on arbitrary-shaped texts, our dataset COO focuses on both arbitrary-shaped texts and arbitrarily placed texts. Furthermore, while most texts in other datasets are horizontal or curved, and are not separated into several parts, our dataset has many vertical texts or texts separated into several parts (truncated texts). Thus, we mainly focus on vertical text recognition and link prediction between truncated texts.

Our dataset contains only Japanese comic onomatopoeias whereas other datasets mainly contain English or Chinese texts. One may concern that methods developed on our dataset may not be generalized to other cases. However, we believe that the algorithm developed on Japanese comic onomatopoeias can be generalized to other cases because the algorithm developed on the small English benchmark data was generalized to other languages. Scene text detection and recognition methods have been developed based on English datasets. According to the benchmark paper of scene text recognition [3], the total number of English benchmark evaluation data is 8,539. The number of character types and vocabulary of the data are 79 and 3,940, respectively. The data definitely do not cover all the texts in real life. However, the developed algorithm for competing on this small English benchmark data did not differ from the winning algorithms in ICDAR2019 competitions to recognize multi-lingual texts [27] and Chinese texts [8, 37, 48].

2.5 Truncated Texts in English

Truncated texts (onomatopoeias) in Japanese comics and link prediction for connecting them might be considered too special. However, it is not, and similar problems also occur in other cases. Fig. 5[1] (left) shows that the words on necklace

---

[1] The images in Fig. 5 can be found here: left, middle, right (accessed 03-08-2022).

are separated into two pieces: "BEST" → "BE" and "ST", and "FRIENDS" →
"FRIE" and "NDS". (middle) shows that the word "Summer" is separated into
"S" and "ummer". (right) shows that the word "SUMMER" is separated into
"SUM" and "MER". Like the (right) image, we sometimes see a word separated
in multiline in the poster or commercials. In general, current state-of-the-art
methods are specialized in single-line recognition, not multiline. Here, we can use
link prediction to connect them ("SUM" and "MER") and capture the intended
meaning ("SUMMER"). Extending the link prediction to these cases can be a
new problem of our community.

3 Methods for Three Tasks

We summarize our methods for three tasks. Text detection and recognition are
well-known tasks; thus, we skip details of model description. Meanwhile, since
link prediction between truncated texts is a novel task proposed in this study,
we thoroughly introduce the M4C-COO model for the task. More details are in
the supplementary materials.

3.1 Text Detection

Text detection methods are mainly categorized into regression-based [10,22,25,
42,45,49,51] and segmentation-based methods [20,23,43,44]. To investigate the
appropriate approach for comic onomatopoeia, we use two methods in each category. Specifically, we use ABCNet v2 [22] and MTS v3 [20] as representatives of
regression-based and segmentation-based methods, respectively. Both methods
were originally proposed for the text spotting task in which text detection and
recognition tasks are combined. However, these methods also provided results of
using only the text detection part and showed state-of-the-art performance. We
take the only text detection part and use them as text detectors. Furthermore,
MTS v3 exhibits superior performance for rotated text detection. We expect
that MTS v3 can also detect vertical texts in our dataset.

3.2 Text Recognition

In this study, the well-known model called TPS-ResNet-BiLSTM-Attention (TR-
BA) [3] is used. TRBA is created by combining existing methods such as RARE
[32] and FAN [7]. TRBA takes four steps to recognize texts: 1) Rectify input
image with TPS transformation [6]. 2) Convert rectified images into visual features by ResNet [12]. 3) Convert visual features into contextual features by
BiLSTM. 4) From contextual features, predict character string with attention
module [4].

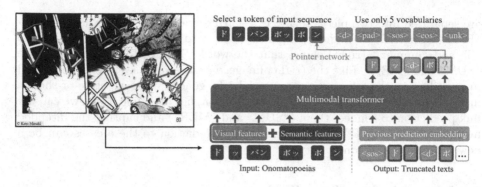

Fig. 6. M4C-COO takes the sequence of all onomatopoeias in an image and outputs the sequence of truncated texts

3.3 Link Prediction

In this study, we formulate the link prediction task into the sequence-to-sequence problem [38]. The model takes the sequence of all onomatopoeias in an image, and outputs the sequence of truncated texts. The sequence of truncated texts consists of pairs of truncated texts and the delimiter symbol <d> which divides pairs of truncated texts. Under this setting, predicting links between truncated texts is the same as predicting the sequence of truncated texts from the input sequence.

An example of input and output sequences is as follows. Given the input sequence as below and truncated texts are (1) "ド" and "ッ" separated from "ドッ", and (2) "ボ" and "ン" separated from "ボン" (when two pairs of truncated texts exist), the output sequence is as follows.

Input sequence: [ド, ッ, バン, ボッ, ボ, ン]
Output sequence: [ド, ッ, <d>, ボ, ン]

By dividing the output sequence with <d>, we obtain two lists [ド, ッ] and [ボ, ン]. By connecting each of the lists, we obtain connected texts "ドッ" and "ボン". Fig. 6 illustrates this example.

To solve this sequence-to-sequence problem, we propose a model named M4C-COO. Fig. 6 illustrates M4C-COO. M4C-COO is a variant of a model called multimodal multi-copy mesh (M4C) [13]. M4C has been used for visual question answering with text (TextVQA [35,36]). M4C takes question word embedding, object, and OCR (text) tokens and fuses them using a multimodal transformer [39]. In addition, M4C uses an iterative answer prediction mechanism to generate a multi-word answer. Based on fused features and iterative answer prediction, M4C predicts the answer of the question. Unlike M4C for TextVQA [13], M4C-COO does not use question word embedding and object part. M4C-COO takes only onomatopoeia tokens and predicts a sequence of truncated texts.

To find truncated texts, we should exploit both visual and semantic (text) features because 1) truncated texts look similar and are close, and 2) They represent the intended meaning if they are connected. M4C-COO exploits both visual and semantic features of onomatopoeias. In M4C-COO, onomatopoeia tokens are embedded into four features, which are categorized as visual and semantic features. For visual features, we use (1) appearance feature (FRCN) from onomatopoeia regions extracted by using Faster RCNN [29] part in MTS v3 [20], and (2) 4-dimensional relative bounding box coordinates (bbox) for each onomatopoeia region. For semantic features, we use (3) fastText [5] and (4) pyramidal histogram of characters (PHOC) [2]. fastText is a word embedding method with sub-word information. fastText is well known for handling out-of-vocabulary words. PHOC counts characters in the word and makes the pyramidal histograms for each word.

Furthermore, the copy mechanism of the pointer network [41] in M4C-COO is exactly what we needed for link prediction. Generally, the copy mechanism selects a token (word) in the input sequence, and the selected token is used as an output token. In other words, it copies the token in the input sequence to the output sequence. In our task, we need to select truncated texts in the input onomatopoeia sequence. This operation is the same as the copy mechanism.

M4C generally uses both thousands of vocabularies and copy mechanism to predict the output sequence. Thousands of vocabularies are used to generate a token that is not in the input sequence. In our task, all the tokens in the output sentence are in input sentence, except for the delimiter symbol <d> and end of sentence token <eos>. Thus, *M4C-COO uses only five vocabularies*: the delimiter symbol <d> and four special tokens for training M4C-COO, padding token <pad>, start and end of sentence tokens (<sos> and <eos>), and unknown token <unk>.

4 Experiment and Analysis

In this section, we present the results of the experiments on three tasks. Through experiments, we analyze the characteristics of COO and the limitations of the current methods. More details of the experimental settings are provided in the supplementary materials.

4.1 Implementation Detail

Model and Training Strategy. For text detection, we use the official codes of ABCNet v2[2] [22] and MTS v3[3] [20]. For text recognition and link prediction, we use the official codes of TRBA[4] [3] and M4C[5] [13], respectively. For the training strategy, we follow the default setting to the extent possible.

Dataset. We split 109 comics of Manga109 into 89, 10, and 10 books and use them as training, validation, and test sets, respectively. For the evaluation, we

---

[2] https://github.com/aim-uofa/AdelaiDet/tree/master/configs/BAText.
[3] https://github.com/MhLiao/MaskTextSpotterV3.
[4] https://github.com/clovaai/deep-text-recognition-benchmark.
[5] https://github.com/facebookresearch/mmf/tree/main/projects/m4c.

Table 2. Ablation study on text detectors ABCNet v2 and MTS v3

#	Method	P	R	H
1	ABCNet v2 [22]-Bounding box	61.9	60.7	61.2
2	ABCNet v2 [22]-Polygon	67.7	64.5	66.0
3	MTS v3 [20]-Bounding box	67.5	58.2	62.5
4	MTS v3 [20]-Polygon	**69.8**	**65.9**	**67.8**

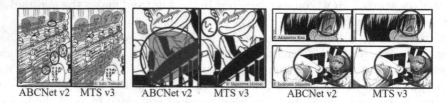

ABCNet v2   MTS v3   ABCNet v2   MTS v3   ABCNet v2   MTS v3

Fig. 7. Text detection on the test set. The green regions are the predicted regions and the red circles are failures

select the model with the best score on the validation set. In each task, we use ground truth information rather than predicted results of other tasks.

Evaluation Metric. For text detection, we use intersection over union to determine whether the model correctly detects the region of onomatopoeia. For text detection and link prediction, we show precision (P), recall (R), and their harmonic mean (H, Hmean). As a default, we mainly use Hmean for comparison. For text recognition, we show word-level accuracy for comparison. We run three trials for all experiments and report average values.

4.2   Text Detection

We compare the effectiveness of bounding box annotation and polygon annotation, and compare the regression-based detector with the segmentation-based detector.

Training with Bounding Box vs. with Polygon. Lines 1 and 3 in Table 2 show the results of training with bounding box (the axis-aligned rectangle that bounds the onomatopoeia region) annotation instead of using polygon annotation. Comparing lines (1 vs. 2) and (3 vs. 4), training with polygon annotation shows better performance than training with bounding box annotation: +4.8% for ABCNet v2 and +5.3% for MTS v3. However, the performance improvement by using polygon annotation is not that considerable. This result may indicate that current detection algorithms may not fully exploit polygon annotation. To improve performance, we may need the algorithm that exploits irregular polygon annotations, such as partially shrunk polygon, more effectively.

Regression vs. Segmentation. ABCNet v2 and MTS v3 are the representatives of regression-based and segmentation-based methods, respectively. Comparing lines 2 and 4 in Table 2, MTS v3 shows better performance +1.8% than ABCNet v2. This result is unexpected and interesting because ABCNet v2 shows better performance than MTS v3 in other benchmark datasets such as MSRA-TD500 [47] (85.2 vs. 83.5). This result indicates that segmentation-based methods can be advantageous for detecting the region of onomatopoeia.

Visualization and Failure Case. Fig. 7 shows the predictions on the test set and failure cases of the current methods. In Fig. 7 (left), MTS v3 correctly detects vertically long onomatopoeias (nine of "ピョン"), whereas ABCNet v2 misses two onomatopoeias ("ピョン") and the part of onomatopoeias ("ン"). According to MTS v3 paper [20], MTS v3 is good at detecting rotated texts. These cases show that MTS v3 can also be used for vertically long texts. In Fig. 7 (middle), MTS v3 sometimes misses small onomatopoeias (the size of onomatopoeia "ひく" is $[width \times height] = [25 \times 28]$ whereas the image size is $[1654 \times 1170]$) and ABCNet v2 misclassifies the text-like part (similar to "ン") as onomatopoeia. Both methods misclassify the text-like part (similar to "サへ") as onomatopoeia (right-top) and miss the occluded texts (right-bottom).

Table 3. Ablation study on text recognizer TRBA

#	Method	Accuracy
1	TRBA [3]	46.3
2	+ Rotation trick	49.8
3	+ SAR decoding	43.2
4	+ Rotation trick + SAR decoding	55.4
5	#4 + Hard RoI (batch 100%)	63.5
6	#4 + Hard RoI (batch 50%)	67.9
7	#6 + 2D attention (height 64)	78.5
8	#6 + 2D attention (height 100)	**81.0**

4.3 Text Recognition

We investigate techniques to address vertically long texts, such as rotation and decoding tricks, Hard RoI masking, and 2D attention.

Rotation and Decoding Tricks. A text recognizer generally takes a text image in which characters are arranged horizontally as input and recognizes each character from left to right. However, if the model takes a text image in which characters are arranged vertically as input, the model cannot recognize each character from left to right. For this case, a simple rotation trick can be useful: Rotates vertical images 90°C to make them horizontal. Here, an image whose height is greater than the width and whose text label contains more than two characters is regarded as a vertical image. Comparing lines 1 to 2 in Table 3, using the rotation trick results in a performance gain of +3.5%.

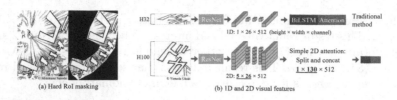

Fig. 8. (*a*) Hard RoI masking removes the region irrelevant to text. (*b*) Traditional methods use 1D attention on 1D features whereas 2D attention exploits 2D features

Fig. 9. Text recognition on the test set. GT denotes the ground truth, and Pred denotes the prediction by TRBA with the best score (#8 in Table 3). Green- and red-colored characters denote correct and incorrect recognition, respectively

Some cases, such as short vertical texts, are correctly recognized without the rotation trick but incorrectly recognized with the rotation trick. For these cases, SAR decoding [19] can be useful. SAR decoding is a decoding trick of the text recognition model SAR [19]: At the test time, if the height of the input image is greater than the width, the model takes three images as input data: the original image and images rotated by –90 and 90°C. The confidence score on recognizing each image is calculated. Next, the model outputs the result with the highest confidence score. Lines 3 and 4 in Table 3 show that solely adding SAR decoding results in a performance drop of –3.1%, whereas using both the rotation trick and SAR decoding improves the original TRBA by +9.1%.

Hard RoI Masking. When the text is diagonally long, the image contains more background noise, as shown in Fig. 8 (a) (left). Background noise may be irrelevant to text and decrease performance. To suppress this region, we use the hard region of interest (Hard RoI) masking [20] that removes this region, as shown in Fig. 8 (a) (right). Comparing lines 4 and 5 in Table 3, using Hard RoI masking shows an improvement by +8.1%. Furthermore, considering that evaluation is conducted without Hard RoI masking, teaching the model how to handle original images can be useful. To do so, we fill half of each mini-batch with original images. As shown in line 6, performance further improves by +4.4%.

2D Attention on 2D Visual Features. The model can benefit from considering the attention on vertical direction. Traditional methods [3,7,31–33] take an image with a height of 32 and make 1D visual features through convolutional networks (ResNet), as shown in Fig. 8 (b) (top): $[height \times width \times channel] = [1 \times 26 \times 512]$ is called 1D because the vertical dimension is squeezed to 1. Because English texts are mainly horizontal, most methods follow this trend. Recently, some methods [14,18,19,24,46] take an image whose height is greater than 32 and make 2D visual features, as shown in Fig. 8 (b) (bottom): $[5 \times 26 \times 512]$ is called 2D because the vertical dimension remains at 5. These methods showed performance improvements by using 2D attention on 2D visual features.

We show the effectiveness of 2D attention with a minimal modification. We use a simple method to exploit 2D visual features, as shown in Fig. 8 (b) (bottom). We use 1D BiLSTM, and we need to make vertical dimension 1 before BiLSTM. To do so, we split vertical features and concatenate them horizontally (e.g., 5×26 to 1×130), as done in EPAN [14]. Lines 7 and 8 in Table 3 show performance improvements. Simple 2D attention improves performance by +10.6% and +13.1% where the heights of images are 64 and 100, respectively.

Visualization and Failure Case. Some vertical or diagonal texts can be correctly recognized, whereas transparent, partially shrunk, or occluded texts are incorrectly recognized. Fig. 9 shows the predictions by TRBA with the best score (#8 in Table 3): TRBA correctly recognizes vertically long texts "パタ ンッ" and "ピンポーン" (row 1, column 1 and 2) whereas incorrectly recognizes transparent texts "ザ" and "ワ" (row 2, column 1 and 2), partially shrunk text (column 3), and texts occluded by objects or a frame (column 4).

Table 4. Ablation study on link prediction model M4C-COO

#	Method	Visual feature	Semantic feature	P	R	H
1	Rule-base	Distance	–	1.1	**74.5**	2.1
2	M4C-COO	FRCN + bbox	fastText + PHOC	**77.2**	68.7	**72.7**
3	+ Vocab. 11,640	FRCN + bbox	fastText + PHOC	55.0	38.7	45.4
4	Only fastText	–	fastText	42.4	30.2	35.2
5	+ PHOC	–	fastText + PHOC	61.7	50.5	55.4
6	+ PHOC + FRCN	FRCN	fastText + PHOC	62.1	53.4	57.2

4.4 Link Prediction

We present the results of the link prediction task, such as a comparison with a rule-based method and ablation studies.

M4C-COO vs. Distance-Based Method. We test the distance-based method as a baseline: 1) Calculate the average distance from one truncated text to another truncated text. 2) For each onomatopoeia, if the other onomatopoeia is closer than the average distance, they are regarded as linked. Line 1 in Table 4 shows that the distance-based method has the highest recall of 74.5% but a considerably low precision of 1.1%. Comparing lines 1 and 2, M4C-COO shows a much better performance of +70.6% (Hmean) than the distance-based method.

Effect of Vocabulary. Comparing lines 2 and 3 in Table 4, *M4C-COO (with only five vocabularies) shows a much better performance of +27.3% than M4C-COO with 11,640 vocabularies (vocabularies of the training set).* This result indicates that using only the copy mechanism is more suitable for this task than using both many vocabularies and the copy mechanism. Many vocabularies may disturb the copy mechanism, and therefore performance decreases.

Ablation Study. Line 4 in Table 4 shows that using only fastText feature for M4C-COO results in a performance drop of −37.5%. Line 5 shows that if we use PHOC together, the performance drastically improves by +20.2%. Line 6 indicates that if FRCN (appearance feature) is added, the performance further improves by +1.8%. However, the performance gain by adding FRCN is considerably less than that by adding PHOC. This result is reasonable considering the drawing style. Because the comic artist is identical in each image, the drawing (writing) style of onomatopoeias in each image is similar. Therefore, exploiting the appearance feature to predict the link is less effective. Comparing lines (2 vs. 6), using bbox (relative coordinate) makes huge improvement by +15.5%. Sometimes there are multiple onomatopoeias whose texts are identical in an image, and only one of them is a truncated text linked to other truncated text. In such cases, the model can benefit from bbox. The model can select the only one truncated text by using coordinate.

Fig. 10. Link prediction on the test set. The purple line denotes the ground truth link between truncated texts, and the orange line denotes the predicted link

Visualization and Failure Case. Some links can be correctly predicted, whereas predicting links between texts similar to background images is difficult. Fig. 10 shows the predictions by M4C-COO: M4C-COO correctly predicts the link between "バ" and "ン" (column 1) and the link between "ザ" and "ワッ" (column 2, row 1), while misses the link between "ド" and "ゴォォ" (column 1) and the link between transparent texts "ザ" and "ワ" (column 2, row 2).

5 Conclusion

We have constructed a novel dataset named COO. COO contains many arbitrary-shaped texts or arbitrarily placed texts. Some texts are separated into several parts, and each part is a truncated text. To capture the intended meaning of truncated texts, we have proposed the link prediction task and the M4C-COO model. We have conducted three tasks (text detection, text recognition, and link prediction) and provided decent baselines. We have experimentally analyzed the characteristics of COO and the limitation of current methods. Detecting the onomatopoeia region and capturing the intended meaning of truncated texts are not straightforward. Thus, COO is a challenging text dataset. We hope that this work will encourage future work on recognizing various types of texts.

Acknowledgements. This work is partially supported by JSPS KAKENHI Grant Number 22J13427, JST-Mirai JPMJMI21H1 and AI center of the University of Tokyo.

References

1. Aizawa, K., et al.: Building a manga dataset manga109 with annotations for multimedia applications. IEEE MultiMedia **2**(27), 8–18 (2020)
2. Almazán, J., Gordo, A., Fornés, A., Valveny, E.: Word spotting and recognition with embedded attributes. TPAMI **36**(12), 2552–2566 (2014)
3. Baek, J., et al.: What is wrong with scene text recognition model comparisons? dataset and model analysis. In: ICCV, pp. 4715–4723 (2019)
4. Bahdanau, D., Cho, K., Bengio, Y.: Neural machine translation by jointly learning to align and translate. In: ICLR (2015)
5. Bojanowski, P., Grave, E., Joulin, A., Mikolov, T.: Enriching word vectors with subword information. TACL **5**, 135–146 (2017)
6. Bookstein, F.L.: Principal warps: thin-plate splines and the decomposition of deformations. TPAMI **11**(6), 567–585 (1989)
7. Cheng, Z., Bai, F., Xu, Y., Zheng, G., Pu, S., Zhou, S.: Focusing attention: towards accurate text recognition in natural images. In: ICCV, pp. 5076–5084 (2017)
8. Chng, C.K., et al.: ICDAR 2019 robust reading challenge on arbitrary-shaped text-rrc-art. In: ICDAR, pp. 1571–1576 (2019)
9. Ch'ng, C.-K., Chan, C.S., Liu, C.-L.: Total-Text: toward orientation robustness in scene text detection. Int. J. Doc. Anal. Recogn. (IJDAR) **23**(1), 31–52 (2019). https://doi.org/10.1007/s10032-019-00334-z
10. Dai, P., Zhang, S., Zhang, H., Cao, X.: Progressive contour regression for arbitrary-shape scene text detection. In: CVPR, pp. 7393–7402 (2021)
11. Guérin, C., et al.: ebdtheque: a representative database of comics. In: ICDAR, pp. 1145–1149 (2013)
12. He, K., Zhang, X., Ren, S., Sun, J.: Deep residual learning for image recognition. In: CVPR, pp. 770–778 (2016)
13. Hu, R., Singh, A., Darrell, T., Rohrbach, M.: Iterative answer prediction with pointer-augmented multimodal transformers for textvqa. In: CVPR, pp. 9992–10002 (2020)

14. Huang, Y., Sun, Z., Jin, L., Luo, C.: EPAN: effective parts attention network for scene text recognition. Neurocomputing **376**, 202–213 (2020)
15. Iyyer, M., Manjunatha, V., Guha, A., Vyas, Y., Boyd-Graber, J., Daume, H., Davis, L.S.: The amazing mysteries of the gutter: drawing inferences between panels in comic book narratives. In: CVPR, pp. 7186–7195 (2017)
16. Karatzas, D., et al.: ICDAR 2015 competition on robust reading. In: ICDAR, pp. 1156–1160 (2015)
17. Karatzas, D., et al.: ICDAR 2013 robust reading competition. In: ICDAR, pp. 1484–1493 (2013)
18. Lee, J., Park, S., Baek, J., Oh, S.J., Kim, S., Lee, H.: On recognizing texts of arbitrary shapes with 2D self-attention. In: Workshop on Text and Documents in the Deep Learning Era, CVPR, pp. 546–547 (2020)
19. Li, H., Wang, P., Shen, C., Zhang, G.: Show, attend and read: a simple and strong baseline for irregular text recognition. In: AAAI, vol. 33, no. 01, pp. 8610–8617 (2019)
20. Liao, M., Pang, G., Huang, J., Hassner, T., Bai, X.: Mask TextSpotter v3: segmentation proposal network for robust scene text spotting. In: Vedaldi, A., Bischof, H., Brox, T., Frahm, J.-M. (eds.) ECCV 2020. LNCS, vol. 12356, pp. 706–722. Springer, Cham (2020). https://doi.org/10.1007/978-3-030-58621-8_41
21. Liu, Y., Jin, L., Zhang, S., Luo, C., Zhang, S.: Curved scene text detection via transverse and longitudinal sequence connection. Pattern Recog. **90**, 337–345 (2019)
22. Liu, Y., et al.: Abcnet v2: adaptive bezier-curve network for real-time end-to-end text spotting. TPAMI (2021)
23. Long, S., Ruan, J., Zhang, W., He, X., Wu, W., Yao, C.: Textsnake: a flexible representation for detecting text of arbitrary shapes. In: ECCV, pp. 20–36 (2018)
24. Lu, N., et al.: Master: multi-aspect non-local network for scene text recognition. Pattern Recogn. **117**, 107980 (2021)
25. Ma, J., et al.: Arbitrary-oriented scene text detection via rotation proposals. TMM **20**(11), 3111–3122 (2018)
26. Matsui, Y., Ito, K., Aramaki, Y., Fujimoto, A., Ogawa, T., Yamasaki, T., Aizawa, K.: Sketch-based manga retrieval using manga109 dataset. Multimedia Tools Appl. **76**(20), 21811–21838 (2016). https://doi.org/10.1007/s11042-016-4020-z
27. Nayef, N., et al.: ICDAR 2019 robust reading challenge on multi-lingual scene text detection and recognition-rrc-mlt-2019. In: ICDAR, vol. 1, pp. 1454–1459 (2019)
28. Petersen, R.S.: The acoustics of manga. In: Heer, J., Worcester, K., (eds.) A Comics Studies Reader, pp. 163–171. University Press of Mississippi (2009)
29. Ren, S., He, K., Girshick, R., Sun, J.: Faster r-cnn: Towards real-time object detection with region proposal networks. In: NeurIPS (2015)
30. Risnumawan, A., Shivakumara, P., Chan, C.S., Tan, C.L.: A robust arbitrary text detection system for natural scene images. ESWA **41**(18), 8027–8048 (2014)
31. Shi, B., Bai, X., Yao, C.: An end-to-end trainable neural network for image-based sequence recognition and its application to scene text recognition. TPAMI **39**(11), 2298–2304 (2016)
32. Shi, B., Wang, X., Lyu, P., Yao, C., Bai, X.: Robust scene text recognition with automatic rectification. In: CVPR, pp. 4168–4176 (2016)
33. Shi, B., Yang, M., Wang, X., Lyu, P., Yao, C., Bai, X.: Aster: an attentional scene text recognizer with flexible rectification. TPAMI **41**(9), 2035–2048 (2018)
34. Shi, B., et al.: ICDAR 2017 competition on reading Chinese text in the wild (RCWT-17). In: ICDAR, vol. 1, pp. 1429–1434 (2017)

35. Singh, A., et al.: Towards vqa models that can read. In: CVPR, pp. 8317–8326 (2019)
36. Singh, A., Pang, G., Toh, M., Huang, J., Galuba, W., Hassner, T.: TextOCR: towards large-scale end-to-end reasoning for arbitrary-shaped scene text. In: CVPR, pp. 8802–8812 (2021)
37. Sun, Y., et al.: ICDAR2019 competition on large-scale street view text with partial labeling-RRC-LSTV. In: ICDAR, pp. 1557–1562 (2019)
38. Sutskever, I., Vinyals, O., Le, Q.V.: Sequence to sequence learning with neural networks. In: NeurIPS **27** (2014)
39. Vaswani, A., et al.: Attention is all you need. In: NeurIPS **30** (2017)
40. Veit, A., Matera, T., Neumann, L., Matas, J., Belongie, S.: Coco-text: Dataset and benchmark for text detection and recognition in natural images. arXiv:1601.07140 (2016)
41. Vinyals, O., Fortunato, M., Jaitly, N.: Pointer networks. In: NeurIPS **28** (2015)
42. Wang, H.: All you need is boundary: toward arbitrary-shaped text spotting. In: AAAI, vol. 34, no. 07, 12160–12167 (2020)
43. Wang, W., et al.: Shape robust text detection with progressive scale expansion network. In: CVPR, pp. 9336–9345 (2019)
44. Wang, W., et al.: Efficient and accurate arbitrary-shaped text detection with pixel aggregation network. In: ICCV, pp. 8440–8449 (2019)
45. Wang, Y., Xie, H., Zha, Z.J., Xing, M., Fu, Z., Zhang, Y.: Contournet: taking a further step toward accurate arbitrary-shaped scene text detection. In: CVPR, pp. 11753–11762 (2020)
46. Yang, X., He, D., Zhou, Z., Kifer, D., Giles, C.L.: Learning to read irregular text with attention mechanisms. In: IJCAI, vol. 1, no. 2, p. 3 (2017)
47. Yao, C., Bai, X., Liu, W., Ma, Y., Tu, Z.: Detecting texts of arbitrary orientations in natural images. In: CVPR, pp. 1083–1090 (2012)
48. Zhang, R., et al.: ICDAR 2019 robust reading challenge on reading Chinese text on signboard. In: ICDAR, pp. 1577–1581 (2019)
49. Zhang, S.X., et al.: Deep relational reasoning graph network for arbitrary shape text detection. In: CVPR, pp. 9699–9708 (2020)
50. Zhang, Y., Gueguen, L., Zharkov, I., Zhang, P., Seifert, K., Kadlec, B.: Uber-text: a large-scale dataset for optical character recognition from street-level imagery. In: Scene Understanding Workshop, CVPR, p. 5 (2017)
51. Zhu, Y., Chen, J., Liang, L., Kuang, Z., Jin, L., Zhang, W.: Fourier contour embedding for arbitrary-shaped text detection. In: CVPR, pp. 3123–3131 (2021)

Language Matters: A Weakly Supervised Vision-Language Pre-training Approach for Scene Text Detection and Spotting

Chuhui Xue[1,2], Wenqing Zhang[2], Yu Hao[2], Shijian Lu[1], Philip H. S. Torr[3], and Song Bai[2(✉)]

[1] Nanyang Technological University, Nanyang, Singapore
[2] ByteDance Inc., Singapore, Singapore
`songbai.site@gmail.com`
[3] University of Oxford, Oxford, UK

Abstract. Recently, Vision-Language Pre-training (VLP) techniques have greatly benefited various vision-language tasks by jointly learning visual and textual representations, which intuitively helps in Optical Character Recognition (OCR) tasks due to the rich visual and textual information in scene text images. However, these methods cannot well cope with OCR tasks because of the difficulty in both instance-level text encoding and image-text pair acquisition (i.e. images and captured texts in them). This paper presents a weakly supervised pre-training method, oCLIP, which can acquire effective scene text representations by jointly learning and aligning visual and textual information. Our network consists of an image encoder and a character-aware text encoder that extract visual and textual features, respectively, as well as a visual-textual decoder that models the interaction among textual and visual features for learning effective scene text representations. With the learning of textual features, the pre-trained model can attend texts in images well with character awareness. Besides, these designs enable the learning from weakly annotated texts (i.e. partial texts in images without text bounding boxes) which mitigates the data annotation constraint greatly. Experiments over the weakly annotated images in ICDAR2019-LSVT show that our pre-trained model improves F-score by +2.5% and +4.8% while transferring its weights to other text detection and spotting networks, respectively. In addition, the proposed method outperforms existing pre-training techniques consistently across multiple public datasets (e.g., +3.2% and +1.3% for Total-Text and CTW1500).

Keywords: Vision-language pre-training · Scene text detection · Scene text spotting

1 Introduction

Optical Character Recognition (OCR) (including scene text detection, recognition, and spotting) has attracted increasing interests in recent years in both

---

Supplementary Information The online version contains supplementary material available at https://doi.org/10.1007/978-3-031-19815-1_17.

© The Author(s), under exclusive license to Springer Nature Switzerland AG 2022
S. Avidan et al. (Eds.): ECCV 2022, LNCS 13688, pp. 284–302, 2022.
https://doi.org/10.1007/978-3-031-19815-1_17

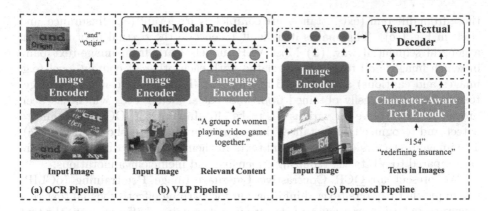

Fig. 1. Illustration of general Optical Character Recognition (OCR), Vision-Language Pre-training (VLP) pipeline, and the proposed pipeline (oCLIP): General OCR pipelines focus only on visual features from images. In addition, general VLP models extract image and language features from input images and corresponding sentence-level text, and model the interaction among all visual and textual features through a multi-modal encoder. Differently, oCLIP extracts instance-level textual features from texts instances in images. It models the interactions between each text instance and its extracted image features which can be trained with weak supervision only (i.e. partial texts in images without text bounding boxes). Our pre-trained model weights can be directly transferred to various scene text detectors and spotters with significant performance improvement.

computer vision and deep learning research communities due to its wide range of applications in multilingual translation, autonomous driving, etc. Most of the existing OCR techniques follow general computer vision pipelines that first extract visual features from the input image and then perform feature regression or classification for text detection or recognition, as shown in Fig. 1 (a). However, we human usually read texts by utilizing not only the visual features of each text but also our linguistic knowledge in our memory. For example, we usually locate and read texts faster and more easily with the knowledge of the corresponding text language. Therefore, both visual and textual information are useful to robust reading of texts from natural scene images.

Recently, joint learning visual and textual representations has been studied in many Vision-Language Pre-training (VLP) techniques [5,40,68], and it greatly promotes various Vision-Language (VL) tasks such as Visual Question Answering (VQA), Image-Text Retrieval, etc. As a language-related task, OCR can intuitively benefit from these VLP techniques. However, most existing VLP methods usually suffer from two typical constraints while being applied to OCR tasks. **(1)** Each image in VL tasks is usually associated with one sentence or paragraph where words or phrases (i.e. tokens) are arranged in reading orders. Instead, an image in OCR tasks often contains many text instances each of which consists of one or multiple tokens. The tokens within one text instance are often closely related to each other (e.g. 'redefining' and 'insurance' in Fig. 1(c)) while those from different text instances are completely irrelevant (e.g. 'insurance' and '154' in Fig. 1(c)). This makes it difficult to encode the textual information in a general sequential way. (2) Most VLP models learn from image-text pairs in which images and texts are correlated with each other at content-level (e.g. images and captions) as illustrated in Fig. 1(b). These content-relevant image-text pairs can be easily obtained from web, social media, etc., which has been proven to be effective for various VL tasks [40]. In contrast, OCR tasks aim to detect and recognize text instances that appear in images as shown in Fig. 1(c). The image-text pairs (i.e. images and texts in them) are more difficult to obtain as compared to VL tasks, requiring expensive and inefficient annotations.

We present an **O**CR **C**ontrastive **L**anguage-**I**mage **P**re-training (oCLIP) technique that exploits textual information for learning effective visual text representations for better scene text detection and spotting. Different from the text encoder in the existing VLP methods [40], we design a character-aware text encoder as illustrated in Fig. 1(c). It extracts language features by encoding textual information from the sequence of characters in each text instance without considering the relations among irrelevant text instances. In addition, we introduce a visual-textual decoder that models the relations between the input image and each labelled text instance only instead of all captured texts in the input image. With the two designs, oCLIP can learn effective visual text representations from weakly-annotated data (i.e. partial text instances in images without text bounding boxes) which greatly mitigates the data acquisition challenge and enables exploitation of large amounts of weakly-annotated images.

The contributions of this paper are three-fold. First, it introduces an end-to-end trainable pre-training network that allows to exploit language supervision to learn effective visual text representations. Second, we design a character-aware text encoder and a visual-textual decoder that can extract effective instance-level textual information and learn from partial text transcriptions without requiring text bounding boxes. Third, extensive experiments over multiple public datasets show that the proposed weakly supervised pre-trained network achieves superior performance on various scene text detection and spotting datasets.

2   Related Work

2.1   Scene Text Detection and Spotting

Most of recent scene text detectors are trained on fully-annotated data which can be broadly classified into two categories. The first category takes a bottom-up approach which first detects low-level text elements like characters [2], text segments [41,47] and text keypoints [65] and then groups them into words or text lines. The second category treats words as one specific type of objects, and many scene text detectors like EAST [76], TextBoxes++ [25], RRD [28] and PSENet [54] are designed to detect text bounding boxes directly with generic object detection or segmentation techniques. Besides, many researchers study the text-specific features for robust text detection through text border or counter [8,59,66,77], deformation convolution [52,61], local refinement [15,73] and so on. Besides, many methods are designed to address the data bias. Some works [11,26,71] aim to synthesize scene text images that can be used for training scene text detection, recognition and spotting models. In addition, WeText [49] and OPM [44] design different weakly supervised mechanisms to use different types of data for training. GA-DAN [72] and TST [60] study the domain adaptation that adapt the synthetic scene text images to real. More recently, STKM [51] is proposed to pre-train a general model backbone for different scene text detectors.

Besides, many end-to-end trainable scene text spotters have been designed in which text detector and recognizer are complementary to each other. Li et al. [21] first integrates the scene text detector and RNN-based recognizer in to a unified network. Liu et al. [29] and He et al. [16] leverage more advanced scene text detectors or recognizers for better text spotting performances. More recently, Mask TextSpotters [23,24,36] adopt Mask R-CNN [13] as text detector and character segmentation or attention module for recognition. ABCNet [30,31] proposes to detect texts with Bezier curves. TextDragon [10] detects center lines of texts along which characters are recognized in sequence. Baek et al. [3] proposes to detect characters by training with weakly supervised mechanism. Xing et al. [62] propose to detects and recognizes characters simultaneously. MANGO [39] is designed for text spotting with mask attention guidance. TextTranSpotter [19] is proposed to leverage the weakly-annotated images for training. Additionally, text recognition with less annotation have been studied in [1,48].

2.2   Vision-Language Pre-training

As inspired by the advanced Transformer-based pre-training techniques [9] in Natural Language Processing (NLP) community, many vision-language pre-training methods have been studied in recent years, which greatly promotes the many multi-modal tasks in computer vision community. ViLBERT [35] and LXMERT [46] present a two-stream framework with a vision-language co-attention module for cross-modal feature fusion. On the other hand, VisualBERT [22], Unicoder-VL [20], VL-BERT [43], and UNITER [4] follow a single-stream framework (i.e. vanilla BERT structure), focusing on generic VL tasks including VCR and VQA. Besides, many VLP methods have been proposed for VL tasks such as RVL-BERT [6] for visual relationship detection, PERVALENT [12] and VLN-BERT [37] for visual navigation, VisualID [38] and VD-BERT [58] for visual dialog, etc.

3   Methodology

We present oCLIP that learns better scene text visual representations by feature alignment with textual information. As shown in Fig. 2, the proposed network first extracts image embeddings from input images by using an image encoder (including a network backbone ResNet-50 [14] followed by a multi-head attention layer). A character-aware text encoder is designed to extract the textual information from the transcriptions of text instances in input images by encoding the sequence of characters in each text instance. The extracted textual and

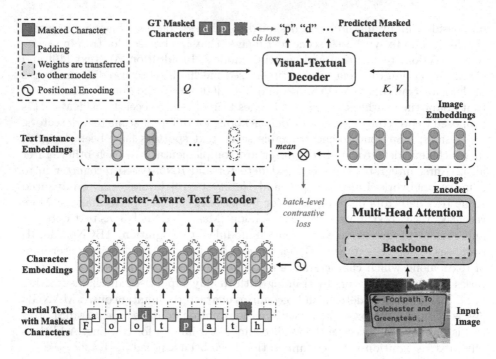

Fig. 2. The framework of oCLIP: Given an input image, an image encoder (including a backbone followed by a multi-head attention layer) first extracts the visual features. Meanwhile, the characters in each text instance are transformed to character embeddings, and a character-aware text encoder further extracts text instance embeddings from the character embeddings. A visual-textual decoder models the interactions between the text instance embeddings and the corresponding image embeddings. During training, a random character in each text instance will be masked (as highlighted by red boxes) and the overall network is optimized by predicting the masked characters.

visual features are passed into a visual-textual decoder which models the interactions among the visual features of input image and the textual features of each individual text instance. During training, we randomly mask a character in each text instance and the network is optimized by predicting the masked characters leveraging the extracted visual and textual features.

3.1   Character-Aware Text Encoder

In general VL tasks, texts (e.g. titles, captions, etc.) are usually sentences that consist of sequences of text tokens. As such, the text encoders for VL tasks are often designed to encode texts in a sequential way. However, the natural scene images in OCR tasks usually contain one or multiple text instances. The text tokens within each text instance are sequentially related to each other while those from different text instances are often completely irrelevant. This makes

Input Image | by General Text Encoder | by Character-Aware Text Encoder

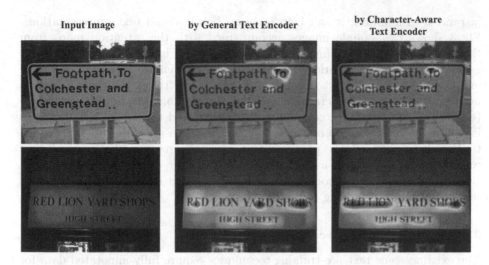

Fig. 3. Illustration of the proposed character-aware text encoder: Given sample images in the first column, columns 2–3 show the attention maps (from the attention layer in the image encoder) that are obtained from models with the general sentence-level text encoder and the proposed character-aware text encoder, respectively. The proposed character-aware text encoder attends better to text regions as compared with the general text encoder, leading to better learning of the scene text visual representations of the network backbone.

it difficult to encode these text instances by using a general text encoder. To address this issue, we design a character-aware text encoder.

The proposed character-aware text encoder extracts instance-level text embeddings with the input text instances as sequences of characters. Given n annotated text instances $T = \{t_0, t_1, ... t_{n-1}\}$ in an image, each text instance t_i consists of a sequence of characters $t_i = [c_0^i, c_1^i, ..., c_{k-1}^i]$. We embed the characters into fixed-sized vectors and add a set of learnt positional encoding [50] $PE = [PE_0, PE_1, ..., PE_k]$ to capture the sequential information of characters in each text instance only, which can be formulated by:

$$ce_j^i = W_c \cdot c_j^i + PE_j, \quad i \in [0, n-1], \quad j \in [0, k-1], \tag{1}$$

where W_c is the character embedding matrix. The encoded character embeddings of $i-th$ text instance $ce^i = [ce_0^i, ce_1^i, ..., ce_{k-1}^i]$ are hence passed into a Transformer [50] encoder which models the interaction among all characters in the text instance and extracts the text instance embeddings te_i from its character embeddings ce_i. As a result, the character-aware text encoder extracts the text instance embeddings $te = \{te_0, te_1, ..., te_{n-1}\}$ from the annotated text instances $t = \{t_0, t_1, ... t_{n-1}\}$. Note a randomly selected character in each text instance is masked during training by setting it to the mask category.

The proposed character-aware text encoder effectively encodes the instance-level textual information and neglects the relations between each pair of text instances. In addition, it can help to learn better visual text representations. Fig. 3 shows two sample images accompanied with the attention maps from the attention layer in the image encoder (details in Fig. 2). As Fig. 3 shows, by extracting textual information from the general text encoder, the overall model only focuses on partial text instances (e.g. 'Foo' and 'th' of 'Footpath'). This is because the tokens in general text encoder usually contain multiple characters (e.g. the token 'Footpath' contains 8 characters) and the model thus tends to focus on the most important parts only in the token according to the linguistic knowledge. Instead, the proposed text encoder can attend better to all text regions in images with the awareness of each character, demonstrating the superiority of the proposed encoder on learning visual text representations for scene text detection and spotting tasks.

3.2   Visual-Textual Decoder

The existing scene text pre-training techniques require fully-annotated data for training where the bounding boxes or transcriptions of all text instances are provided. However, such annotations are often extremely expensive and difficult to obtain. To address the data annotation bias, we present a visual-textual decoder that models the interaction between the input image and each individual annotated text while ignoring the unlabelled texts. The model thus can be trained by using the annotations of partial text instances in the images.

Given an input image I as shown in Fig. 2, we first extract the image embeddings ie and the textual information te by using an image encoder (including a network backbone followed by a multi-head attention layer) and a character-aware text encoder, respectively. The visual-textual decoder hence learns the relationships among ie and each item in te (i.e. embeddings of each text instance) to enhance the learning of visual representations. Specifically, the visual-textual decoder consists of 6 stacked decoder layers each of which contains a multi-head attention layer and a feed-forward network. The text instance embeddings te are passed into the visual-textual decoder as queries and the image embeddings ie are passed into the decoder as keys and values. This allows every text instance alone to attend over all positions in the image embeddings. Note that we don't adopt the self-attention layer in the visual-textual decoder in order to neglect the relationships between each pair of text instances and eliminates the effects of unlabelled text instances. The model thus can effectively learn from partial annotated text instances. Finally, the visual-textual decoder predicts the masked characters in each text instance for optimization.

The masked characters can be predicted by learning the language knowledge from textual information only. We illustrate the attention maps of the decoder in Fig. 4 to demonstrate the effectiveness of the proposed visual-textual decoder. For each sample image in Fig. 4, we pass three text instances (with masked characters [M]) into our network, and we obtain three attention maps and three predicted masked characters each of which corresponds to an input text instance. As Fig. 4 shows, the visual-textual decoder not only predicts the masked characters (e.g. 'I' for 'ST [M]RLING') but also attends the regions of corresponding

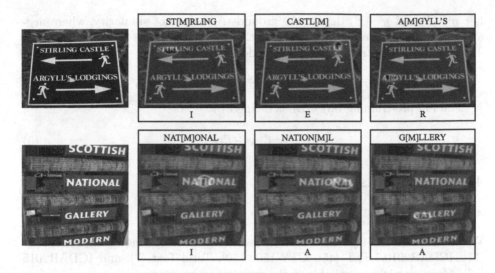

Fig. 4. Illustration of the proposed visual-textual decoder: Given two sample images in the first column, the input text instances (masked characters are highlighted by [M]), corresponding attention maps in the decoder and the predicted masked characters are shown from top to bottom in each box in columns 2–4, respectively. The proposed visual-textual decoder aligns the visual and textual features well, which effectively attends and predicts the masked characters in images.

masked characters well in the images. It can be seen that the proposed decoder aligns the visual and textual features to predict the masked characters (instead of using textual information alone), demonstrating the effectiveness of the proposed visual-textual decoder.

3.3 Network Optimization

During training, the proposed model takes text instances T (with masked characters $\boldsymbol{y}^{msk}$) and images I as inputs, and predicts the masked characters $\boldsymbol{p}^{msk}(I,T)$ for optimization. We consider the masked character prediction as a classification problem and adopt cross-entropy H for optimization:

$$\mathcal{L}_{cls} = \mathbb{E}_{(I,T)\sim D}\mathrm{H}(\boldsymbol{y}^{msk},\boldsymbol{p}^{msk}(I,T)). \tag{2}$$

Besides, as inspired by CLIP [40], we adopt a batch-level contrastive loss for faster convergence. Given N images and N texts in a training batch, we form N^2 (text, image) pairs from all texts and images, where N pairs of texts and images are correlated with each other and $N^2 - N$ pairs are unrelated. For each image and text, we calculate the softmax-normalized image-to-text and text-to-image similarity as:

$$p_b^{i2t}(I) = \frac{\exp(I,T_b)}{\sum_{b=1}^{B}\exp(I,T_b)}, \quad p_b^{t2i}(T) = \frac{\exp(T,I_b)}{\sum_{b=1}^{B}\exp(T,I_b)}. \tag{3}$$

Let $\boldsymbol{y}^{i2t}(I)$ and $\boldsymbol{y}^{t2i}(T)$ denote the ground-truth one-hot similarity, where negative pairs have a probability of 0 and the positive pair has a probability of 1. The batch-level contrastive loss is thus defined by:

$$\mathcal{L}_{bc} = \mathbb{E}_{(I,T)\sim D}[\mathrm{H}(\boldsymbol{y}^{i2t}(I), \boldsymbol{p}^{i2t}(I)) + \mathrm{H}(\boldsymbol{y}^{t2i}(T), \boldsymbol{p}^{t2i}(T))]. \tag{4}$$

The full pre-training objective is defined by:

$$\mathcal{L} = \mathcal{L}_{cls} + \mathcal{L}_{bc}. \tag{5}$$

4 Experiments

4.1 Datasets

We use a number of public datasets in our experiments including SynthText [11], ICDAR2019-LSVT [45], CTW1500 [70], Total-Text [7], and ICDAR2015 [17]. More details are available in the supplementary material.

4.2 Implementation Details

Pre-training: We use ResNet-50 [14] as the backbone in the image encoder of the proposed network. The input images are resized to 512×512 during training. We adopt the Adam optimizer [18] with decoupled weight decay regularization [34] applied to all weights that are not gains or biases. The initial learning rate is $1e^{-4}$ which decays using a cosine schedule [33]. The model is trained end-to-end for 100 epochs on 8 Tesla V100 GPUs with batch size of 640. The length of each text instance is set as 25 following [64,69].

Fine-tuning: We fine-tune several scene text detectors and spotters for evaluation of oCLIP including: 1) PSENet [54], 2) DB [27], 3) FCENet [77], 4) TextBPN [75], and 5) Mask TextSpotter-v3 [24]. More details are available in the supplementary material.

4.3 Experimental Results

We evaluate the proposed oCLIP from three aspects. First, we evaluate the performances of the proposed method by training with weakly annotated data (i.e. with partial annotated text instances available in each image). Second, we compare the proposed method with the existing pre-training techniques in scene text community. Third, we compare the proposed method with the state-of-the-art scene text detectors and spotters.

Table 1. Scene text detection performances of different models on **ICDAR2019-LSVT** dataset. '+oCLIP': Our pre-trained model with 400,000 weakly annotated images in ICDAR2019-LSVT dataset is adopted for fine-tuning.

Model	Precision	Recall	F-score
MSR [67]	86.4	63.4	73.1
Keypoint [65]	78.5	70.1	74.1
DB [27]	76.5	70.5	73.4
DB+oCLIP	**81.5**	**70.9**	**75.8**
PSENet [54]	90.4	63.5	74.6
PSENet+oCLIP	**90.7**	**67.0**	**77.1**

Table 2. Scene text spotting performances of different models on **ICDAR2019-LSVT** dataset. '+oCLIP': Our pre-trained model with 400,000 weakly annotated images in ICDAR2019-LSVT dataset is adopted for fine-tuning. 'P', 'R', 'F', '1-NED', and 'E2E' refer to Precision, Recall, F-score, Normalized metric in terms of Normalized Edit Distance, and end-to-end, respectively.

Method	Detection			E2E spotting			
	P	R	F	1-NED	P	R	F
Mask TextSpotter-V3	80.5	61.0	69.4	35.7	32.1	24.4	27.7
Mask TextSpotter-V3+oCLIP	**80.6**	**61.9**	**70.1**	**39.0**	**37.4**	**28.7**	**32.5**

Weakly Supervised Pre-training: We evaluate the performances of oCLIP on learning visual text representations from weakly annotated data. We first conduct the experiments by pre-training our model on 400,000 weakly annotated images (i.e. only the transcription of the text-of-interest in each image is provided), and fine-tuning different scene text detectors and spotters on 30,000 fully annotated images from ICDAR2019-LSVT dataset. As Table 1 and 2 show, oCLIP improves the performances of different scene text detectors and spotters, demonstrating that the proposed method effectively learns the visual representations from weakly annotated data. Note that most previous approaches are designed to train on fully annotated images and they can't utilize the weakly annotated images from ICDAR2019-LSVT dataset well.

In addition, we conduct an experiment on SynthText dataset to show the effects of the amount of annotated texts on model performances. We first prepare four sets of text annotations from SynthText dataset by randomly selecting different proportions of text instances (i.e. 25%, 50%, 75%, and 100%) in each image (e.g. 1 out of 4 text instances in each image are used for training '25%' model). Next, we pre-train four models on all images in SynthText dataset by using the four sets of text annotations, and then transfer the backbone weights to fine-tune PSENet on Total-Text dataset. For comparison, we report the performances of two additionally models including: 1) 'No Pre-train' model in which

Table 3. The effectiveness of the proposed weakly supervised pre-training technique: We pre-train four models by using different proportions of text instances in SynthText dataset (e.g. 1 out of 4 text instances in each image are used for training for '25%' model), and transfer the models weights to fine-tune PSENet on Total-Text dataset. 'Baseline': Train PSENet on SynthText and then fine-tune on Total-Text.

% Annotated texts	Precision	Recall	F-score
No Pre-train	81.8	75.1	78.3
Baseline	87.8	79.0	82.6
25%	90.2	80.1	84.8
50%	91.1	80.0	85.2
75%	90.6	80.8	85.4
100%	**90.7**	**80.8**	**85.5**

Table 4. Comparison with existing scene text pre-training techniques: by pre-training on the same set of data (i.e. SynthText dataset), the proposed pre-training method outperforms the existing pre-training techniques consistently across different datasets. '+SynthText': Train PSENet with SynthText and then fine-tune with Total-Text.

Model	Total-Text			CTW1500		
	P	**R**	**F**	**P**	**R**	**F**
PSENet [54]	81.8	75.1	78.3	80.6	75.6	78.0
PSENet+SynthText	87.8	79.0	82.6	81.8	77.8	79.7
PSENet+STKM[51]	86.3	78.4	82.2	85.1	78.2	81.5
PSENet+oCLIP[SynthText]	90.7	80.8	85.5	86.3	79.6	82.8
PSENet+oCLIP[Web Images]	**92.2**	**82.4**	**87.0**	**87.5**	**79.9**	**83.5**

no pre-training is adopted, and 2) 'Baseline' model that first trains PSENet on SynthText and then fine-tunes on Total-Text, respectively. As Table 3 shows, all four pre-train models help to improve the performances of PSENet, which outperforms the 'No Pre-train' and 'Baseline' models significantly. Besides, the four models achieve comparable performances on scene text detection task by pre-training on different amount of annotated texts, demonstrating the effectiveness of the proposed weakly supervised learning.

Comparing with Existing Scene Text Pre-training Strageties: We compare the oCLIP with two scene text pre-training strategies including: (1) training PSENet on SynthText dataset and then fine-tuning on real dataset, and (2) pre-training on SynthText by using STKM [51] and transferring the pre-trained weights to fine-tune PSENet on real dataset. For a fair comparison, we pre-train our model on SynthText with full annotations and transfer the backbone weights for fine-tuning PSENet on real datasets. As Table 4 shows, by pre-training on the same set of data, oCLIP outperforms the existing pre-training techniques by +3.3% and +1.3% in F-score on Total-Text and CTW1500 datasets, respectively.

Table 5. Comparison with state-of-the-art scene text detection techniques on **CTW1500** dataset. '+oCLIP' refers to that our pre-trained model on SynthText dataset is adopted for fine-tuning. 'RN50', 'PD', 'Syn', and 'MLT' refer to ResNet-50, pre-training data, SynthText dataset, and ICDAR2027-MLT dataset, respectively

Model	PD	Precision	Recall	F-score
TextSnake [32]	Syn	67.9	**85.3**	75.6
ATRR [57]	–	80.1	80.2	80.1
TextField [63]	Syn	83.0	79.8	81.4
Keypoint [65]	Syn	**88.3**	77.7	82.7
PAN [56]	Syn	88.0	79.4	83.5
CRAFT [2]	Syn	86.4	81.4	83.7
ContourNet [59]	–	83.7	84.1	83.9
SD [61]	MLT	85.8	82.3	84.0
DRRG [74]	MLT	85.9	83.0	84.5
TextBPN [75]	Syn	87.8	81.5	84.5
DB-RN50 [27]	–	81.1	80.6	80.8
DB-RN50+oCLIP	Syn	82.5	81.5	**82.0 (+1.2)**
FCENet-RN50 [77]	–	85.7	80.7	83.1
FCENet-RN50+oCLIP	Syn	87.2	83.9	**85.6 (+2.5)**

Automatic Data Acquisition and Training from Web Images: The proposed oCLIP can be simply applied to an automatic data acquisition and training pipeline due to the success of learning from weakly-annotated images. We extracted texts from 40 million web images and filtered out less-confident ones by using the existing scene text detector and recognizer form model pre-training. As Table 4 shows, by learning from the automatically extracted data from web images, oCLIP significantly improves the performances of PSENet on Total-Text and CTW1500 datasets. More details are available in supplementary material.

Comparing with State-of-the-Art Scene Text Detectors And Spotters: We further conduct experiments to compare oCLIP with state-of-the-art scene text detection and spotting techniques. For a fair comparison, we pre-train a model by our method on SynthText with full annotations and transfer the backbone weights to fine-tune DB, FCENet, TextBPN, and Mask TextSpotter-V3 on real datasets. As Table 5-8 show, the proposed pre-trained model effectively promote the existing scene text detectors to state-of-the-art performances on different dataset. In addition, by transferring the pre-trained weights from our model, the performances of different scene text detectors and spotters are consistently improved by large margins.

4.4 Ablation Studies

We study the contributions of different modules in our method including a character-aware encoder (CAE), a visual-textual decoder (VTD), and a batch-level contrastive loss (BCL). We train four models with different modules included on fully annotated SynthText dataset and fine-tune PSENet on Total-Text dataset. As Table 9 shows, with the inclusion of different modules in our network, the performances of PSENet can be improved consistently, demonstrating the effectiveness of different modules in of network.

Table 6. Comparison with state-of-the-art scene text detection techniques on **Total-Text** dataset. '+oCLIP' refers to that our pre-trained model on SynthText dataset is adopted for fine-tuning. 'RN50', 'PD', 'Syn', and 'MLT' refer to ResNet-50, pre-training data, SynthText dataset, and ICDAR2027-MLT dataset, respectively

Model	PD	Precision	Recall	F-score
TextSnake [32]	Syn	82.7	74.5	78.4
ATRR [57]	–	80.9	76.2	78.5
MSR [67]	Syn	83.8	74.8	79.0
TextField [63]	Syn	81.2	79.9	80.6
PAN [56]	Syn	88.0	79.4	83.5
CRAFT [2]	MLT	87.6	79.9	83.6
Keypoint [65]	Syn	86.1	82.6	84.4
ContourNet [59]	–	86.5	84.9	85.4
DRRG [74]	MLT	86.5	84.9	85.7
SD [61]	MLT	**89.2**	84.7	86.9
DB-RN50 [27]	–	81.7	75.0	78.2
DB-RN50+oCLIP	Syn	86.1	82.1	**84.1 (+5.9)**
TextBPN [75]	–	88.0	82.9	85.4
TextBPN+oCLIP	Syn	89.0	**85.3**	**87.1 (+1.7)**

Table 7. Comparison with state-of-the-art scene text detection techniques on **ICDAR2015** dataset. '+oCLIP' refers to that our pre-trained model on SynthText dataset is adopted for fine-tuning. 'RN50', 'PD', 'Syn', and 'MLT' refer to ResNet-50, pre-training data, SynthText dataset, and ICDAR2027-MLT dataset, respectively.

Model	PD	Precision	Recall	F-score
SegLink [42]	Syn	76.1	76.8	75.0
TextField [63]	Syn	84.3	80.1	82.4
TextSnake [32]	Syn	84.9	80.4	82.6
PAN [56]	Syn	84.0	81.9	82.9
ATRR [57]	–	90.4	83.3	86.8
CRAFT [2]	MLT	89.8	84.3	86.9
ContourNet [59]	–	87.6	86.1	86.9
SD [61]	MLT	88.7	**88.4**	88.6
DB-RN50 [27]	–	89.3	74.0	80.9
DB-RN50+oCLIP	Syn	89.1	82.0	**85.4 (+4.5)**
FCENet-RN50 [77]	–	88.0	81.9	84.9
FCENet-RN50+oCLIP	Syn	**91.2**	82.7	**86.7 (+1.8)**

Table 8. Comparison with state-of-the-art scene text spotting techniques on **ICDAR 2015** and **Total-Text** dataset. '+oCLIP' refers to that the model are fine-tuned from the our pre-trained model on SynthText dataset. 'S', 'W', and 'G' refer to end-to-end recognition with strong, weak, generic lexicon for ICDAR2015. 'Full' refers to full lexicon for Total-Text.

Model	ICDAR2015			Total-Text
	S	W	G	Full
CharNet [62]	80.1	74.5	62.2	–
FOTS [29]	83.6	74.5	62.2	–
TextDragon [10]	82.5	78.3	65.2	74.8
Boundary TextSpotter [53]	79.7	75.2	64.1	–
PAN++ [55]	82.7	78.2	69.2	78.6
ABCNet-V2 [31]	82.7	78.5	73.0	78.1
Mask TextSpotter-V3 [24]	83.3	78.1	74.2	78.4
Mask TextSpotter-V3+oCLIP	**84.1**	**78.6**	**74.3**	**79.6**

Table 9. Ablation study of the proposed method for scene text detection over Total-Text dataset. We fine-tune PSENet by using the pre-trained models with different modules. 'CAE', 'VTD', and 'BCL' refer to character-aware encoder, visual-textual decoder, and batch-level contrastive loss, respectively.

	CAE	VTD	BCL	Precision	Recall	F-score
No Pretrain				81.8	75.1	78.3
1			✓	88.1	77.7	82.6
2	✓		✓	89.6	78.9	83.9
3	✓	✓		89.3	77.4	82.9
4	✓	✓	✓	**90.7**	**80.8**	**85.5**

5   Conclusion

This paper presents a weakly supervised pre-training technique for scene text detection and spotting tasks. It focuses on the joint learning of visual and textual information from images and text transcriptions to enhance the learning of visual representations. It designs a character-aware text encoder and a visual-textual decoder that improves the feasibility of oCLIP on learning from partial text transcriptions only without text bounding boxes. Experimental results show that the proposed method can effectively learn from weakly-annotated scene text datasets which greatly mitigates the data acquisition challenge and significantly promotes different scene text detectors and spotters.

References

1. Baek, J., Matsui, Y., Aizawa, K.: What if we only use real datasets for scene text recognition? toward scene text recognition with fewer labels. In: Proceedings of the IEEE/CVF Conference on Computer Vision and Pattern Recognition, pp. 3113–3122 (2021)
2. Baek, Y., Lee, B., Han, D., Yun, S., Lee, H.: Character region awareness for text detection. In: Proceedings of the IEEE/CVF Conference on Computer Vision and Pattern Recognition, pp. 9365–9374 (2019)
3. Baek, Y., et al.: Character region attention for text spotting. In: Vedaldi, A., Bischof, H., Brox, T., Frahm, J.-M. (eds.) ECCV 2020. LNCS, vol. 12374, pp. 504–521. Springer, Cham (2020). https://doi.org/10.1007/978-3-030-58526-6_30
4. Chen, Y.C., Li, L., Yu, L., El Kholy, A., Ahmed, F., Gan, Z., Cheng, Y., Liu, J.: Uniter: learning universal image-text representations (2019)
5. Chen, Y.C., et al.: UNITER: uNiversal image-TExt representation learning. In: Vedaldi, A., Bischof, H., Brox, T., Frahm, J.-M. (eds.) ECCV 2020. LNCS, vol. 12375, pp. 104–120. Springer, Cham (2020). https://doi.org/10.1007/978-3-030-58577-8_7
6. Chiou, M.J., Zimmermann, R., Feng, J.: Visual relationship detection with visual-linguistic knowledge from multimodal representations. IEEE Access **9**, 50441–50451 (2021)
7. Ch'ng, C.K., Chan, C.S.: Total-text: a comprehensive dataset for scene text detection and recognition. In: 2017 14th IAPR International Conference on Document Analysis and Recognition (ICDAR), vol. 1, pp. 935–942. IEEE (2017)
8. Dai, P., Zhang, S., Zhang, H., Cao, X.: Progressive contour regression for arbitrary-shape scene text detection. In: Proceedings of the IEEE/CVF Conference on Computer Vision and Pattern Recognition, pp. 7393–7402 (2021)
9. Devlin, J., Chang, M.W., Lee, K., Toutanova, K.: Bert: Pre-training of deep bidirectional transformers for language understanding. arXiv preprint arXiv:1810.04805 (2018)
10. Feng, W., He, W., Yin, F., Zhang, X.Y., Liu, C.L.: Textdragon: an end-to-end framework for arbitrary shaped text spotting. In: Proceedings of the IEEE/CVF International Conference on Computer Vision, pp. 9076–9085 (2019)
11. Gupta, A., Vedaldi, A., Zisserman, A.: Synthetic data for text localisation in natural images. In: Proceedings of the IEEE Conference on Computer Vision and Pattern Recognition, pp. 2315–2324 (2016)

12. Hao, W., Li, C., Li, X., Carin, L., Gao, J.: Towards learning a generic agent for vision-and-language navigation via pre-training. In: Proceedings of the IEEE/CVF Conference on Computer Vision and Pattern Recognition, pp. 13137–13146 (2020)

13. He, K., Gkioxari, G., Dollár, P., Girshick, R.: Mask r-cnn. In: Proceedings of the IEEE International Conference on Computer Vision, pp. 2961–2969 (2017)

14. He, K., Zhang, X., Ren, S., Sun, J.: Deep residual learning for image recognition. In: Proceedings of the IEEE Conference on Computer Vision and Pattern Recognition, pp. 770–778 (2016)

15. He, M., et al.: Most: a multi-oriented scene text detector with localization refinement. In: Proceedings of the IEEE/CVF Conference on Computer Vision and Pattern Recognition, pp. 8813–8822 (2021)

16. He, T., Tian, Z., Huang, W., Shen, C., Qiao, Y., Sun, C.: An end-to-end textspotter with explicit alignment and attention. In: Proceedings of the IEEE Conference on Computer Vision and Pattern Recognition, pp. 5020–5029 (2018)

17. Karatzas, D., et al.: ICDAR 2015 competition on robust reading. In: 2015 13th International Conference on Document Analysis and Recognition (ICDAR), pp. 1156–1160. IEEE (2015)

18. Kingma, D.P., Ba, J.: Adam: a method for stochastic optimization. arXiv preprint arXiv:1412.6980 (2014)

19. Kittenplon, Y., Lavi, I., Fogel, S., Bar, Y., Manmatha, R., Perona, P.: Towards weakly-supervised text spotting using a multi-task transformer. In: Proceedings of the IEEE/CVF Conference on Computer Vision and Pattern Recognition, pp. 4604–4613 (2022)

20. Li, G., Duan, N., Fang, Y., Gong, M., Jiang, D.: Unicoder-vl: a universal encoder for vision and language by cross-modal pre-training. In: Proceedings of the AAAI Conference on Artificial Intelligence, vol. 34, no. 07, pp. 11336–11344 (2020)

21. Li, H., Wang, P., Shen, C.: Towards end-to-end text spotting with convolutional recurrent neural networks. In: Proceedings of the IEEE International Conference on Computer Vision, pp. 5238–5246 (2017)

22. Li, L.H., Yatskar, M., Yin, D., Hsieh, C.J., Chang, K.W.: Visualbert: a simple and performant baseline for vision and language. arXiv preprint arXiv:1908.03557 (2019)

23. Liao, M., Lyu, P., He, M., Yao, C., Wu, W., Bai, X.: Mask textspotter: an end-to-end trainable neural network for spotting text with arbitrary shapes. IEEE Trans. Pattern Anal. Mach. Intell. 43(2), 532–548 (2021). https://doi.org/10.1109/TPAMI.2019.2937086

24. Liao, M., Pang, G., Huang, J., Hassner, T., Bai, X.: Mask TextSpotter v3: segmentation proposal network for robust scene text spotting. In: Vedaldi, A., Bischof, H., Brox, T., Frahm, J.-M. (eds.) ECCV 2020. LNCS, vol. 12356, pp. 706–722. Springer, Cham (2020). https://doi.org/10.1007/978-3-030-58621-8_41

25. Liao, M., Shi, B., Bai, X.: Textboxes++: a single-shot oriented scene text detector. IEEE Trans. Image Process. 27(8), 3676–3690 (2018)

26. Liao, M., Song, B., Long, S., He, M., Yao, C., Bai, X.: Synthtext3d: synthesizing scene text images from 3D virtual worlds. Sci. China Inf. Sci. 63(2), 1–14 (2020)

27. Liao, M., Wan, Z., Yao, C., Chen, K., Bai, X.: Real-time scene text detection with differentiable binarization. In: Proceedings of AAAI, vol. 34, no. 07, pp. 11474–11481 (2020)

28. Liao, M., Zhu, Z., Shi, B., Xia, G.s., Bai, X.: Rotation-sensitive regression for oriented scene text detection. In: Proceedings of the IEEE Conference on Computer Vision and Pattern Recognition, pp. 5909–5918 (2018)

29. Liu, X., Liang, D., Yan, S., Chen, D., Qiao, Y., Yan, J.: Fots: fast oriented text spotting with a unified network. In: Proceedings of the IEEE Conference on Computer Vision and Pattern Recognition, pp. 5676–5685 (2018)
30. Liu, Y., Chen, H., Shen, C., He, T., Jin, L., Wang, L.: Abcnet: real-time scene text spotting with adaptive bezier-curve network. In: Proceedings of the IEEE/CVF Conference on Computer Vision and Pattern Recognition, pp. 9809–9818 (2020)
31. Liu, Y., et al.: Abcnet v2: adaptive bezier-curve network for real-time end-to-end text spotting. IEEE Trans. Pattern Anal. Mach. Intell. 1 (2021). https://doi.org/10.1109/TPAMI.2021.3107437
32. Long, S., Ruan, J., Zhang, W., He, X., Wu, W., Yao, C.: Textsnake: a flexible representation for detecting text of arbitrary shapes. In: Proceedings of the European Conference on Computer Vision (ECCV), pp. 20–36 (2018)
33. Loshchilov, I., Hutter, F.: Sgdr: Stochastic gradient descent with warm restarts. arXiv preprint arXiv:1608.03983 (2016)
34. Loshchilov, I., Hutter, F.: Decoupled weight decay regularization. arXiv preprint arXiv:1711.05101 (2017)
35. Lu, J., Batra, D., Parikh, D., Lee, S.: Vilbert: pretraining task-agnostic visiolinguistic representations for vision-and-language tasks. Adv. Neural Inf. Process. Syst. **32** (2019)
36. Lyu, P., Liao, M., Yao, C., Wu, W., Bai, X.: Mask textspotter: an end-to-end trainable neural network for spotting text with arbitrary shapes. In: Proceedings of the European Conference on Computer Vision (ECCV), pp. 67–83 (2018)
37. Majumdar, A., Shrivastava, A., Lee, S., Anderson, P., Parikh, D., Batra, D.: Improving vision-and-language navigation with image-text Pairs from the web. In: Vedaldi, A., Bischof, H., Brox, T., Frahm, J.-M. (eds.) ECCV 2020. LNCS, vol. 12351, pp. 259–274. Springer, Cham (2020). https://doi.org/10.1007/978-3-030-58539-6_16
38. Murahari, V., Batra, D., Parikh, D., Das, A.: Large-scale pretraining for visual dialog: a simple state-of-the-art baseline. In: Vedaldi, A., Bischof, H., Brox, T., Frahm, J.-M. (eds.) ECCV 2020. LNCS, vol. 12363, pp. 336–352. Springer, Cham (2020). https://doi.org/10.1007/978-3-030-58523-5_20
39. Qiao, L., et al.: Mango: a mask attention guided one-stage scene text spotter. In: Proceedings of the AAAI Conference on Artificial Intelligence, pp. 2467–2476 (2021)
40. Radford, A., et al.: Learning transferable visual models from natural language supervision. In: International Conference on Machine Learning, pp. 8748–8763. PMLR (2021)
41. Shi, B., Bai, X., Belongie, S.: Detecting oriented text in natural images by linking segments. In: The IEEE Conference on Computer Vision and Pattern Recognition (CVPR), pp. 2550–2558 (2017)
42. Shi, B., Bai, X., Belongie, S.: Detecting oriented text in natural images by linking segments. In: Proceedings of the IEEE Conference on Computer Vision and Pattern Recognition, pp. 2550–2558 (2017)
43. Su, W., et al.: Vl-bert: pre-training of generic visual-linguistic representations. arXiv preprint arXiv:1908.08530 (2019)
44. Sun, Y., Liu, J., Liu, W., Han, J., Ding, E., Liu, J.: Chinese street view text: Large-scale Chinese text reading with partially supervised learning. In: Proceedings of the IEEE/CVF International Conference on Computer Vision, pp. 9086–9095 (2019)
45. Sun, Y., et al.: ICDAR 2019 competition on large-scale street view text with partial labeling-RRC-LSVT. In: 2019 International Conference on Document Analysis and Recognition (ICDAR), pp. 1557–1562. IEEE (2019)

46. Tan, H., Bansal, M.: Lxmert: learning cross-modality encoder representations from transformers. arXiv preprint arXiv:1908.07490 (2019)

47. Tang, J., Yang, Z., Wang, Y., Zheng, Q., Xu, Y., Bai, X.: Seglink++: detecting dense and arbitrary-shaped scene text by instance-aware component grouping. Pattern Recogn. **96**, 106954 (2019)

48. Tensmeyer, C., Wigington, C.: Training full-page handwritten text recognition models without annotated line breaks. In: 2019 International Conference on Document Analysis and Recognition (ICDAR), pp. 1–8. IEEE (2019)

49. Tian, S., Lu, S., Li, C.: Wetext: scene text detection under weak supervision. In: Proceedings of the IEEE International Conference on Computer Vision, pp. 1492–1500 (2017)

50. Vaswani, A., et al.: Attention is all you need. Adv. Neural Inf. Process. Syst. **30** (2017)

51. Wan, Q., Ji, H., Shen, L.: Self-attention based text knowledge mining for text detection. In: Proceedings of the IEEE/CVF Conference on Computer Vision and Pattern Recognition, pp. 5983–5992 (2021)

52. Wang, F., Zhao, L., Li, X., Wang, X., Tao, D.: Geometry-aware scene text detection with instance transformation network. In: Proceedings of the IEEE Conference on Computer Vision and Pattern Recognition, pp. 1381–1389 (2018)

53. Wang, H., et al.: All you need is boundary: toward arbitrary-shaped text spotting. In: Proceedings of the AAAI Conference on Artificial Intelligence, vol. 34, pp. 12160–12167 (2020)

54. Wang, W., Xie, E., Li, X., Hou, W., Lu, T., Yu, G., Shao, S.: Shape robust text detection with progressive scale expansion network. In: Proceedings of the IEEE/CVF Conference on Computer Vision and Pattern Recognition, pp. 9336–9345 (2019)

55. Wang, W., et alC.: Pan++: towards efficient and accurate end-to-end spotting of arbitrarily-shaped text. IEEE Trans. Pattern Anal. Mach. Intell. **44**(9), 5349–5367 (2021)

56. Wang, W., et al.: Efficient and accurate arbitrary-shaped text detection with pixel aggregation network. In: Proceedings of the IEEE/CVF International Conference on Computer Vision, pp. 8440–8449 (2019)

57. Wang, X., Jiang, Y., Luo, Z., Liu, C.L., Choi, H., Kim, S.: Arbitrary shape scene text detection with adaptive text region representation. In: Proceedings of the IEEE/CVF Conference on Computer Vision and Pattern Recognition, pp. 6449–6458 (2019)

58. Wang, Y., Joty, S., Lyu, M.R., King, I., Xiong, C., Hoi, S.C.: Vd-bert: a unified vision and dialog transformer with bert. arXiv preprint arXiv:2004.13278 (2020)

59. Wang, Y., Xie, H., Zha, Z.J., Xing, M., Fu, Z., Zhang, Y.: Contournet: taking a further step toward accurate arbitrary-shaped scene text detection. In: Proceedings of the IEEE/CVF Conference on Computer Vision and Pattern Recognition, pp. 11753–11762 (2020)

60. Wu, W., et al.: Synthetic-to-real unsupervised domain adaptation for scene text detection in the wild. In: Proceedings of the Asian Conference on Computer Vision (2020)

61. Xiao, S., Peng, L., Yan, R., An, K., Yao, G., Min, J.: Sequential deformation for accurate scene text detection. In: Vedaldi, A., Bischof, H., Brox, T., Frahm, J.-M. (eds.) ECCV 2020. LNCS, vol. 12374, pp. 108–124. Springer, Cham (2020). https://doi.org/10.1007/978-3-030-58526-6_7

62. Xing, L., Tian, Z., Huang, W., Scott, M.R.: Convolutional character networks. In: Proceedings of the IEEE/CVF International Conference on Computer Vision, pp. 9126–9136 (2019)
63. Xu, Y., Wang, Y., Zhou, W., Wang, Y., Yang, Z., Bai, X.: Textfield: learning a deep direction field for irregular scene text detection. IEEE Trans. Image Process. **28**(11), 5566–5579 (2019)
64. Xue, C., Lu, S., Bai, S., Zhang, W., Wang, C.: I2c2w: image-to-character-to-word transformers for accurate scene text recognition. arXiv preprint arXiv:2105.08383 (2021)
65. Xue, C., Lu, S., Hoi, S.: Detection and rectification of arbitrary shaped scene texts by using text keypoints and links. Pattern Recogn. **124**, 108494 (2022)
66. Xue, C., Lu, S., Zhan, F.: Accurate scene text detection through border semantics awareness and bootstrapping. In: Proceedings of the European Conference on Computer Vision (ECCV), pp. 355–372 (2018)
67. Xue, C., Lu, S., Zhang, W.: Msr: Multi-scale shape regression for scene text detection. arXiv preprint arXiv:1901.02596 (2019)
68. Xue, H., et al.: Probing inter-modality: visual parsing with self-attention for vision-and-language pre-training. Adv. Neural Inf. Process. Syst. **34**, 4514–4528 (2021)
69. Yu, D., et al.: Towards accurate scene text recognition with semantic reasoning networks. In: Proceedings of the IEEE/CVF Conference on Computer Vision and Pattern Recognition, pp. 12113–12122 (2020)
70. Yuliang, L., Lianwen, J., Shuaitao, Z., Sheng, Z.: Detecting curve text in the wild: New dataset and new solution. arXiv preprint arXiv:1712.02170 (2017)
71. Zhan, F., Lu, S., Xue, C.: Verisimilar image synthesis for accurate detection and recognition of texts in scenes. In: Proceedings of the European Conference on Computer Vision (ECCV), pp. 249–266 (2018)
72. Zhan, F., Xue, C., Lu, S.: Ga-dan: Geometry-aware domain adaptation network for scene text detection and recognition. In: Proceedings of the IEEE/CVF International Conference on Computer Vision, pp. 9105–9115 (2019)
73. Zhang, C., Liang, B., Huang, Z., En, M., Han, J., Ding, E., Ding, X.: Look more than once: an accurate detector for text of arbitrary shapes. In: Proceedings of the IEEE/CVF Conference on Computer Vision and Pattern Recognition, pp. 10552–10561 (2019)
74. Zhang, S.X., et al.: Deep relational reasoning graph network for arbitrary shape text detection. In: Proceedings of the IEEE/CVF Conference on Computer Vision and Pattern Recognition, pp. 9699–9708 (2020)
75. Zhang, S.X., Zhu, X., Yang, C., Wang, H., Yin, X.C.: Adaptive boundary proposal network for arbitrary shape text detection. In: Proceedings of the IEEE/CVF International Conference on Computer Vision, pp. 1305–1314 (2021)
76. Zhou, X., et al.: East: an efficient and accurate scene text detector. In: The IEEE Conference on Computer Vision and Pattern Recognition (CVPR), pp. 5551–5560 (2017)
77. Zhu, Y., Chen, J., Liang, L., Kuang, Z., Jin, L., Zhang, W.: Fourier contour embedding for arbitrary-shaped text detection. In: Proceedings of the IEEE/CVF Conference on Computer Vision and Pattern Recognition, pp. 3123–3131 (2021)

Toward Understanding WordArt: Corner-Guided Transformer for Scene Text Recognition

Xudong Xie[1], Ling Fu[1], Zhifei Zhang[2], Zhaowen Wang[2], and Xiang Bai[1(✉)]

[1] Huazhong University of Science and Technology, Wuhan, China
{xdxie,ling_fu,xbai}@hust.edu.cn
[2] Adobe Research, San Jose, USA
{zzhang,zhawang}@adobe.com

Abstract. Artistic text recognition is an extremely challenging task with a wide range of applications. However, current scene text recognition methods mainly focus on irregular text while have not explored artistic text specifically. The challenges of artistic text recognition include the various appearance with special-designed fonts and effects, the complex connections and overlaps between characters, and the severe interference from background patterns. To alleviate these problems, we propose to recognize the artistic text at three levels. Firstly, corner points are applied to guide the extraction of local features inside characters, considering the robustness of corner structures to appearance and shape. In this way, the discreteness of the corner points cuts off the connection between characters, and the sparsity of them improves the robustness for background interference. Secondly, we design a character contrastive loss to model the character-level feature, improving the feature representation for character classification. Thirdly, we utilize Transformer to learn the global feature on image-level and model the global relationship of the corner points, with the assistance of a corner-query cross-attention mechanism. Besides, we provide an artistic text dataset to benchmark the performance. Experimental results verify the significant superiority of our proposed method on artistic text recognition and also achieve state-of-the-art performance on several blurred and perspective datasets. The dataset and codes are available at: https://github.com/xdxie/WordArt.

Keywords: Artistic text recognition · Corner point · Attention

1 Introduction

The artistic text is a kind of beautified text that is carefully designed by designers or artists. They use various complex fonts of different styles, combining word

Supplementary Information The online version contains supplementary material available at https://doi.org/10.1007/978-3-031-19815-1_18.

© The Author(s), under exclusive license to Springer Nature Switzerland AG 2022
S. Avidan et al. (Eds.): ECCV 2022, LNCS 13688, pp. 303–321, 2022.
https://doi.org/10.1007/978-3-031-19815-1_18

effects such as shadow, rotation, stereo transformation, deformation, and distortion. Meanwhile, the background patterns and text meaning are considered during the design. Artistic text is widely used in advertisements, slogans, exhibitions, decorations, magazines, and books. Figure 1 shows some typical artistic text images with several unique properties.

(a) Diverse fonts   (b) Background interference   (c) Extreme deformation

(d) Word efsmffect   (e) Artistic design   (f) Overlapping

Fig. 1. The artistic text examples of different types from the WordArt dataset

In view of this, artistic text recognition is an overlooked and extremely challenging task with importance and practicability in a wide range of applications. Unlike scene text recognition (STR) [8,39,41], artistic text recognition often has several difficulties and challenges: (1) As illustrated in Fig. 1(a, c, d), the character appearance varies widely due to the different fonts, artistic design effects, and deformation. (2) In Fig. 1(a, f), there are many complicated connections and overlaps between characters, which makes it difficult to focus on the center or the stroke of a character independently during the recognition process. (3) The design of the artistic text may use background elements to express characters or words and organically combine texts with patterns, causing serious background interference, as shown in Fig. 1(b, e).

It is difficult for existing scene text recognition methods to be competent for this task. The approaches for regular scene text [5,12,15,39] only focus on horizontal text with standard printing fonts and cannot cope with instances with various shapes, artistic effects, and fonts. Other methods utilizing rectification [30,40,41] for irregular scene text recognition can rectify the text line but not the various character shapes. The existing methods based on the attention mechanism [26,27,54] cannot obtain accurate positions of artistic characters, as shown in Fig. 6. In a sense, irregular texts belong to a subset of artistic texts. In addition, handwriting contains a variety of fonts and ligatures, but the background of these instances is very simple without word effects and artistic designs. Therefore, the methods for handwriting recognition [2,9] fail to handle the artistic text with complex background. Recently, some researchers have introduced linguistic knowledge and corpora to help improve the performance of scene text recognition [8,36]. However, as shown in Fig. 5, the language model is also inefficient for the complex artistic text. Therefore, we need to learn more robust and representative visual features.

Considering these challenges, in order to obtain robust visual features to recognize the artistic text accurately, we propose to model image features at three levels. **(1) Local feature within character.** In the artistic text, the appearance and shape of characters vary widely from instance to instance. It is necessary to build an explicit invariant feature within characters to robustly represent the core key points or structures, suppressing the interference of appearance and deformation. Since the corner points [14,42] of the character strokes and the relative positions between these points are invariant, we use the corner point map as a robust representation of the input image. Moreover, the discreteness of the corner point map cuts off the connection and the overlap between characters, and the sparsity suppresses most of the background interference. In addition, we propose a corner-query cross-attention mechanism, treating the corner point as the query and the image as the key to make the corner seek the image features of interest. In this way, the corner guides the model to pay more accurate attention to the core strokes or character centers of the artistic text. **(2) Character-level feature.** Accurate character recognition is critical for text recognition. The huge visual differences between the same characters of artistic texts lead to the scattered distribution of their features in the feature space. To implicitly learn common representations for each class of characters, it is necessary to make the same class instances cluster together in the feature space and different classes away from each other. Therefore, we introduce a loss function based on the contrastive learning [4,23], significantly improving the clustering degree of their features (Fig. 7). For each character in a minibatch, its positive samples are characters of the same class, and other characters are negative samples. **(3) Global feature on image-level.** Global features of images can assist the overall text recognition because the characters can be reasoned through the visual and semantic information from context. Transformer [45] based on the self-attention mechanism has demonstrated its strong advantages and performance [8,26], benefiting from its global modeling ability. Therefore, to extract the global features of artistic text images with arbitrary shapes and model the global relationship of the corner points, we use Transformer [45] as our backbone and propose the CornerTransformer.

To benchmark the performance of different methods on the artistic text recognition task, we propose a dataset named WordArt. Experimental results show that our method outperforms the existing STR models on this challenging task. CornerTransformer performs well on many artistic texts containing complex fonts, ligatures, and overlaps. Furthermore, we achieve competitive or better results than other methods on common STR benchmarks. In particular, our model outperforms the SOTAs on Street View Text [48], SVT-Perspective [35] and ICDAR 2015 [21] benefits from the corner point map, as gradient-based corner point detection is robust to image resolution, noise and blur.

To summarize, the contributions of this paper are four-fold:

(1) We focus on a new challenging task: artistic text recognition, and propose the WordArt dataset to benchmark the performance.

(2) We notice the importance of the corner point on artistic text recognition and present a corner-query cross-attention mechanism, which allows the model to pay more accurate attention to the core strokes or character centers.

(3) We design a character contrastive loss to cluster the same class of character features, enabling the model to learn unified representations for characters.

(4) Our method significantly outperforms other models on artistic text recognition and also achieves new state-of-the-art results on scene text recognition.

2   Related Work

Scene Text Recognition. Scene text can be roughly divided into regular and irregular text. The sequence-to-sequence models based on CTC [12,15,39] and attention [5] for regular text recognition have made a great progress. However, these methods fail to cope with curved or rotated text, so irregular text recognition has recently attracted many research interests. The rectification-based methods [30,40,41,53] utilize the spatial transformer network [20] to transform the text image into a canonical shape, but the predefined transformation space limits the generalization of them. The segmentation-based methods [28,47] formulate the recognition task as a character segmentation problem, but character-level annotations are required. In addition, the recent methods with the 2D attention mechanism [26,27,54] also show strong performance on irregular text recognition, and we choose SATRN [26] as the baseline to build our model. Overall, it is difficult to directly apply these methods to artistic text recognition because of the limitations stated in Sect. 1.

Special Text Recognition. Beyond scene text recognition, other recognition tasks for special text are also significantly important. For example, handwriting recognition [2,17,60] has always been the focus of research given the changeable character shapes and varying writing styles. Another meaningful task that has emerged recently is handwritten mathematical expression recognition [25,51], which has wide applications in education. Manga text recognition [10] is also an interesting problem due to the unconstrained text in the manga. Moreover, Wang *et al.* [50] specifically explore font-independent features of scene texts via a glyph generative adversarial network [11]. Compared with the artistic text, the backgrounds of handwriting and manga images are very simple, and there is no character overlapping, artistic rendering, or word effects. To our knowledge, ours is the first work for artistic text recognition.

Text Recognition with Auxiliary Information. Some segmentation-based methods [28,47] introduce character-level annotations to improve the recognition results. Other recent approaches [8,36] transfer linguistic knowledge to the vision model with a pre-trained language model. Through linguistic information, the model can predict characters according to the context. However, to utilize such information needs to pay the extra cost of data and computing. Besides the deep learning-based methods, other traditional methods explore robust text image presentations, such as SIFT descriptors [35], Strokelets [55], and HOG [43].

Access to such information is automatic and almost cost-free. In this paper, we use the corner point [14,42] to assist the Transformer-based [26,45] method for artistic text recognition.

Text Recognition Dataset. There exist several standard datasets for the task of scene text recognition. IIIT5k-Words (IIIT5k) [33], ICDAR 2013 (IC13) [22], and Street View Text (SVT) [48] only contain horizontal text with standard fonts. ICDAR 2015 (IC15) [21] contains many small, blurred, and irregular text. SVT-Perspective (SVTP) [35] is built based on the original SVT to evaluate perspective distorted text recognition. CUTE80 (CUTE) [37] and Total-Text [6] mainly focus on curved text. COCO-Text [46] is the first large-scale dataset for text in natural images. Besides, there are some multilingual datasets such as CTW [57], LSVT [44] and MLT [34]. However, most images in these datasets do not contain artistic text. Therefore, we construct a new dataset to benchmark the performance of artistic text recognition.

3 Methodology

3.1 Overview

The overall structure of CornerTransformer is shown in Fig. 2. Given an image $X \in \mathbb{R}^{H \times W \times 3}$, we first utilize a corner point detector to generate a corner point map $M \in \mathbb{R}^{H \times W \times 1}$. Then, X and M are fed into two convolutional layers respectively for producing features of $X' \in \mathbb{R}^{\frac{H}{4} \times \frac{W}{4} \times C}$ and $M' \in \mathbb{R}^{\frac{H}{4} \times \frac{W}{4} \times C}$, where C is the feature dimension. On the one hand, X' will learn the global features X'_g of the image through the multi-head self-attention mechanism. On the other hand, M' will combine with X'_g through the multi-head cross-attention mechanism. Then, the encoder output feature and the character sequence embedding will be fed into the Transformer decoder [45] to generate the feature sequence. Finally, we apply two linear branches to calculate the cross-entropy loss and the character contrastive loss separately.

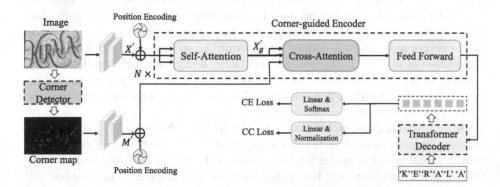

Fig. 2. The overall architecture of CornerTransformer consists of two inputs from different modalities, a corner-guided encoder and a Transformer decoder [45]. CE loss is the cross-entropy loss, and CC loss is our proposed character contrastive loss

Fig. 3. Visualization of corner point detection. **Top:** The detected corner points of artistic text images. **Bottom:** Corner points of a character "M" with various appearances, whose structural relations are similar

3.2 Corner-Guided Encoder

In the task of artistic text recognition, the deformation and distortion of characters are extremely diverse due to various fonts and artistic effects. Thus, it is necessary to transform the artistic text image into a more robust representation. As shown in Fig. 3, we observe that, for the great variance in the appearance of a specific character, the most critical corners of this character can almost always be detected. The structural relations formed by the connection of these key corners are similar. Moreover, these points are the positions that contain rich visual information of the image. Therefore, we utilize the corner map extracted from the image as an auxiliary input to provide an invariant visual representation. In addition, the connection and the position overlap between characters are extremely complicated, while the discrete corner map can naturally cut off the connection and suppress the overlapping effect of strokes. Furthermore, designers often use some background elements when designing the artistic text to perfectly integrate the artistic text with the background, which causes serious interference from the background during the recognition process. However, the corner map only retains the keypoints of the image, suppressing most background elements and making it easier for the model to focus on important text features.

Given an image, we use a classical corner point detector, Shi-Tomasi corner detector [42], to generate its corner map. This detector improves the stability of Harris detector [14], and can produce high-quality corner points. For each pixel (x, y) in the image, we first calculate the image structure tensor S, then the corner response function is defined as $R = \min(\lambda_1, \lambda_2)$, where λ_1 and λ_2 are the eigenvalues of S. If $R > threshold$, pixel (x, y) is a corner point and the value in position (x, y) of the corner map is 1, otherwise it is 0. Therefore, the corner map is a sparse matrix whose element of value 1 only represents the position information of corners.

After obtaining the corner map, considering that there are local correlations between corners instead of being independent of each other, we first use two convolutional layers to model local relations on the corner map and add 2D position encoding [26] to record the corner position information. A natural method to combine image and corner features is to concatenate them together and feed them into the Transformer encoder. However, this can not make full use of the auxiliary information of corners as shown in Table 3. Since the corner map is sparse, the model will still mainly focus on image features. Therefore, we design a corner-guided encoder to fuse corner features at each block. Specifically, we add a multi-head cross-attention layer after the self-attention layer. We utilize the image feature X_g' as the key and value, and the corner feature M' as the query. The corner-query cross-attention mechanism can be formulated as:

$$CA(Q, K, V) = CA(M', X_g', X_g') = softmax(\frac{M'X_g'^T}{\sigma})X_g', \qquad (1)$$

where CA means Cross-Attention and σ is a scaling factor. Since corners represent keypoints inside characters, we use the corner map as a query to make the corner seek the image features of interest. Furthermore, the model can pay more accurate attention to the character positions of the artistic text in the image. For instance, for character "A" in a text image, its top corner point tends to focus on other positions of this character rather than other characters. Our ablation study and visualization analysis also prove the effectiveness of the corner-query cross-attention mechanism.

The corner-guided encoder is composed of a stack of N blocks, where each consists of a self-attention layer, a cross-attention layer, and a feed-forward layer. The query of each cross-attention layer is M'.

3.3 Character Contrastive Loss

Corner-based representation mainly focuses on the local modeling within the character, while Transformer tends to the global modeling of the whole image. To bridge these two representation levels, we introduce a middle-level (character-level) representation learning method. For the artistic text, different instances of the same character show a variety of appearances, including font, shadow, rotation, and other effects. Therefore, in the training process, it is necessary to learn an implicit and unified character-level representation for each character class, so that instances of the same character class are clustered together in the feature space, and features of different classes are far away from each other.

Inspired by the popular thought of contrastive learning [4,23,59], we propose a Character Contrastive loss (CC loss) to achieve our motivation. In short, for a character in a minibatch, the characters of the same class are positive samples, and other characters are negative samples. Specifically, given a minibatch of N images, each image contains variable-length text. We unify the length of text labels to $m = 25$, and there are $N \times m$ characters in a minibatch. For the ith character, x_i is the feature vector and y_i is the class label, where $i \in I \equiv \{1, 2, ..., N \times m\}$. When the ith character is an anchor, its positive set is $P(i) \equiv \{p \in I : y_p = y_i, p \neq i\}$, and the negative set is $N(i) \equiv \{n \in I : y_n \neq y_i, n \neq i\}$. The character contrastive loss can be formulated as:

$$\mathcal{L}_{CC} = \sum_{i \in I} \frac{-1}{N_p} \sum_{p \in P(i)} log \frac{exp(x_i \cdot x_p/\tau)}{\sum_{s \in P(i)} exp(x_i \cdot x_s/\tau) + \sum_{t \in N(i)} exp(x_i \cdot x_t/\tau)}, \qquad (2)$$

where N_p is the number of positive samples, and τ a scaling factor.

Finally, the full optimization objective is defined as:

$$\mathcal{L} = \mathcal{L}_{CE} + \lambda \mathcal{L}_{CC}, \tag{3}$$

where $\mathcal{L}_{CE}$ is the cross entropy loss. We set $\lambda = 0.1$ by default.

4 Experiments

4.1 WordArt Dataset

To benchmark the performance of different models on the artistic text recognition task, we collect a dataset of artistic text named WordArt. Thanks to the TextSeg [52] dataset, which contains images of posters, greeting cards, covers, billboards, handwriting, etc. There exist many artistic texts in these images. In view of this, we first crop the word images with the word bounding box annotations and then carefully pick over the artistic text following the definition of the artistic text as stated in Sect. 1. Finally, our WordArt dataset consists of 6316 artistic text images. Following the splitting rule of TextSeg, the training set contains 4805 images, and the testing set contains 1511 images. The statistical analysis is presented in Fig. 4. The distributions of text length and character frequency roughly align with the English corpus. The qualitative presentation of the WordArt dataset is shown in Fig. 1.

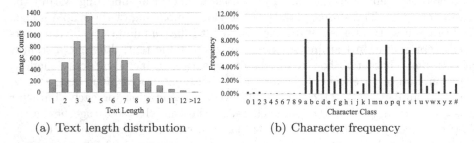

(a) Text length distribution   (b) Character frequency

Fig. 4. Statistical analysis for the WordArt dataset. (a) The number of images with different text lengths. (b) Frequency distribution of all characters in the whole dataset

4.2 Implementation Details

In our CornerTransformer, the feature dimension of all the attention layers is set to 512, with 8 heads for each layer. We set $N = 12$ for the corner-guided encoder. To calculate the character contrastive loss, we add two linear layers with 2048 hidden dimension and an $L2$ normalization to transform the decoder output features into a normalized feature space. By default, we jointly use CE loss and CC loss to train our model. τ in CC loss is set to 0.1. As common practice [1,56], we use two synthetic datasets MJSynth (MJ) [18,19] and SynthText [13] as training datasets and directly evaluate the performance on the WordArt dataset and STR datasets after training. The input images are resized to 32×128 for both training and testing with batch size 256. The model is trained with Adam optimizer [24] with the initial learning rate $3e^{-4}$. The total epoch is 6, and the learning rate will decay to $3e^{-5}$ after 4 epochs. We adopt several data augmentation strategies such as rotation, Gaussian noise, etc.

4.3 Ablation Study

For artistic text recognition, our main contributions to the method are introducing the corner map with designing the corner-query cross-attention and proposing the character contrastive loss. We will verify the effectiveness of each design in detail. Since we need to use the global modeling capabilities of Transformer [45], we choose SATRN [26] as our baseline and reproduce its model by replacing the dimensions the query and key from 128 to 512. To comprehensively evaluate different designs, besides the word accuracy, we present character recall and character precision to assist the evaluation. All the results for the ablation study are evaluated on our WordArt dataset.

The Effectiveness of the Corner Map. Since we add an attention module to fuse the corner map, extra parameters are introduced, increasing the capacity of the model. In order to verify that the performance improvement comes from the role of the corner map rather than the extra parameters, we replace the input of the corner branch in Fig. 2 with the same image as the main branch. The results shown in the third row of Table 1 are lower than baseline. We attribute this to the large amount of noise and redundant information contained in the image, which adds false guidance to the model when directly applying it as a query. Besides, we also remove the extra input branch but retain the added attention module. In this case, the cross-attention turns into self-attention. As shown in the fourth row of Table 1, this only gives a slight boost to the baseline results. Therefore, the role of the corner map is crucial for artistic text recognition, indicating keypoints and filtering out noise.

Table 1. Ablation study about the effectiveness of the corner map

Input	Word acc	Char recall	Char precision
Baseline (Self-attn)	67.0	84.6	84.2
Corner+Image	**69.1**	**85.7**	**84.8**
Image+Image	66.0	83.8	83.3
Self-attn ×2	67.6	85.2	83.3

Different Corner Detectors. In view of the importance of the corner map for model performance, it is necessary to choose a suitable corner detector to obtain high-quality corner maps. The detector used in our model is the Shi-Tomasi corner detector [42]. We also experiment with the Harris detector [14] but found it often produces more extra noise corners, which has slight damage to performance. In addition, we use a deep learning-based corner detector SuperPoint [7].

We load its pre-trained model to produce corner maps, and the results are presented in Table 2. Although SuperPoint can generate high-quality corner maps, it uses an additional neural network model that increases the feed-forward time.

It is worth noting that no matter which detector we use, they can all capture the most critical corner locations and the structure of the text. Therefore, the results in Table 2 using corner maps are better than the other results in Table 1.

Table 2. Results of different corner detectors

Corner detector	Word acc	Char recall	Char precision
Shi-Tomasi [42]	**69.1**	**85.7**	**84.8**
Harris [14]	68.4	85.1	84.6
SuperPoint [7]	69.0	85.3	84.7

Table 3. Results of different fusion strategies

Fusion strategy	Word acc	Char recall	Char precision
Baseline	67.0	84.6	84.2
Corner-query	**69.1**	**85.7**	**84.8**
Corner-key/value	66.9	84.1	84.2
Concat	67.0	84.7	84.4
Add	66.6	84.9	84.3
Multiply	67.4	84.7	84.4

Fusion Strategy. It is crucial to efficiently fuse the features of the corner map and the image, which determines whether the model can make full use of the important information carried by the corners. Given these two features obtained from convolutional layers, we can fuse them into one by Concat, Add and Multiply operations and straightly feed the fused feature to Transformer. As shown in Table 3, there is no significant improvement in these results. Add operation introduces additive noise to image features. Multiply operation makes the image filter out valuable features based on the corners, bringing a slight improvement. Moreover, for the cross-attention module, we swap the roles of corner and image, so that corner features are used as the key and value. But the results are not improved, although this operation introduces extra parameters compared to the baseline. The reason is that a lot of information is lost when the corner map is used as the value. Therefore, our corner-query cross-attention mechanism is an efficient fusion strategy.

Table 4. Ablation study on character contrastive loss

Hyperparameters	Word acc	Char recall	Char precision
$\lambda = 0$ (without CC loss)	67.0	84.6	84.2
$\lambda = 0.1$, $\tau = 0.05$, $d = 512$	66.5	84.0	83.6
$\lambda = 0.1$, $\tau = 0.1$, $d = 512$	68.1	85.5	85.3
$\lambda = 0.1$, $\tau = 0.15$, $d = 512$	67.7	84.9	84.6
$\lambda = 0.1$, $\tau = 0.1$, $d = 2048$	**68.6**	**85.8**	**85.9**
$\lambda = 0.01$, $\tau = 0.1$, $d = 2048$	67.2	84.4	84.3
$\lambda = 1$, $\tau = 0.1$, $d = 2048$	66.6	83.9	83.7

Character Contrastive Loss. According to the previous work of contrastive learning [4,23], the scaling factor τ of the loss function in formula (2) plays an important role in final performance. Relatively low values of τ make hard negatives have more weight but the feature space will be less smooth when τ is extremely low. We conduct an ablation study on τ as shown in Tab. 4, and found $\tau = 0.1$ is optimal. Besides, the dimension of the final output feature vector x_i also affects performance. Generally, higher dimension brings better results because the feature vector represents more information. If the weight of the CC loss is small ($\lambda = 0.01$), it will not bring a significant performance improvement. In contrast, if $\lambda = 1$, it will interfere the joint optimization, resulting in performance degradation. As a result, we adopt $\lambda = 0.1$, $\tau = 0.1$, $d = 2048$ in our model. The results of character recall and character precision show that CC loss actually improves the performance of character recognition.

4.4 Performance for Artistic Text Recognition

In order to demonstrate the superiority of our CornerTransformer on the artistic text recognition task, we compare it with several state-of-the-art scene text recognition methods in Table 5. All the results of these methods are obtained by directly loading their released checkpoints to be evaluated on WordArt. Our CornerTransformer shows a significant superiority, thanks to the corner-query cross-attention and the character contrastive loss. Figure 5 presents some hard examples that are successfully recognized by CornerTransformer. Our model can cope with artistic texts containing complex fonts, ligatures, overlaps, and many extremely curved and deformed texts.

ari arc art   culumn outimm autumn   umrike unrik umrik   santasy suntasy fantasy

yetter spater letter   othe othead ahead   slaws just stars   straject stratect strategy

Fig. 5. Qualitative recognition results on WordArt dataset. Each example is along with the results from ABINet-LV [8], our baseline and the proposed CornerTransformer, separately. Hard examples successfully recognized by CornerTransformer

4.5 Evaluation on STR Benchmarks

To further verify the generalization of CornerTransformer, we also conduct evaluations on six STR benchmarks: IIIT5k [33], IC13 [22], SVT [48], IC15 [21], SVTP [35] and CUTE [37]. The results compared with other state-of-the-art methods are shown in Table 6. We can achieve state-of-the-art results on SVT and IC15 because most images are severely corrupted by noise and blur, while gradient-based corner detection is robust to image resolution, noise and blur. Besides, we also obtain a competitive result on CUTE and the best result on SVTP. The texts in these datasets are perspective and curved, while the relative position between corner points is invariant.

Table 5. Performance comparison with other methods on WordArt dataset. * indicates the baseline of SATRN [26] reimplemented by ourselves, replacing the dimensions of the query and key from 128 to 512. Inference time is estimated using an NVIDIA TITAN Xp by averaging 3 trials, based on Pytorch implementation. † indicates the inference time is estimated based on the TensorFlow implementation. "WiKi" indicates using a language model trained with WiKiText-103 [32].

Methods	Training data	WordArt	Params (M)	Time (ms)
CRNN [39]	ST+MJ	47.5	8.3	9.9
ASTER [41]	ST+MJ	57.9	21	247.9
TRBA [1]	ST+MJ	55.8	49.6	28.8
DAN [49]	ST+MJ	52.4	18.2	41.7
NRTR [38]	ST+MJ	58.5	66.7	350.8
RobustScanner [58]	ST+MJ+SA+R	61.3	48.0	71.0
SAR [27]	ST+MJ+SA+R	63.8	57.5	109.2
SEED [36]	ST+MJ	60.1	25.0	158.8
SCATTER [29]	ST+MJ+SA	64.0	119.7	142.7
SATRN† [26]	ST+MJ	65.7	55.5	494.1
ABINet-LV [8]	ST+MJ+WiKi	67.4	36.7	42.4
Baseline*	ST+MJ	67.0	65.6	274.7
Baseline + Corner	ST+MJ	69.1	80.5	294.9
Baseline + CC loss	ST+MJ	68.6	70.9	274.7
CornerTransformer	ST+MJ	**70.8**	85.7	294.9

4.6   Further Visualization and Analysis

Corner Directs More Accurate Attention. To intuitively verify the effectiveness of our corner-query cross-attention, exploring the essential mechanism why the corner map can improve the model performance, we visualize the feature map of the final output from our corner-guided encoder, as shown in Fig. 6. Evidently, for various text images with deformation, ligature, art design, and curve, our encoder can accurately focus on the position of each character, and there are apparent margins between characters. More importantly, our encoder can sometimes even focus on fine-grained features like character strokes, despite not providing any character-level or stroke-level annotations. All these good properties benefit from the corner-query cross-attention. The corner map contains the keypoints of the character strokes, and the corner-query attention enables the corner to seek the image features of interest (that is to seek other positions of the current character but not another character). Therefore, a corner point can gradually focus on the stroke feature up to the whole character feature. Besides, the corner map is very sparse and naturally separates each character.

Table 6. Accuracy comparison with other STR methods on six standard benchmarks

Methods	Training data	Regular				Irregular			
		IIIT5k	SVT	IC13	Avg	SVTP	IC15	CUTE	Avg
CRNN [39]	ST+MJ	78.2	80.9	89.4	81.0	–	–	–	–
ASTER [41]	ST+MJ	93.4	89.5	91.8	92.5	78.5	76.1	79.5	76.9
TRBA [1]	ST+MJ	87.9	87.5	92.3	88.8	79.2	77.6	74.0	77.6
DAN [49]	ST+MJ	94.3	89.2	93.9	93.5	80.0	74.5	84.4	76.6
NRTR [38]	ST+MJ	90.1	91.5	95.8	91.5	86.6	79.4	80.9	81.1
RobustScanner [58]	ST+MJ	95.3	88.1	94.8	94.2	79.5	77.1	90.3	78.9
SAR [27]	ST+MJ	91.5	84.5	91.0	90.4	76.4	69.2	83.3	72.1
SEED [36]	ST+MJ	93.8	89.6	92.8	93.0	81.4	80.0	83.6	80.6
SCATTER [29]	ST+MJ	93.2	90.9	94.1	93.1	86.2	82.0	84.8	83.2
SATRN [26]	ST+MJ	92.8	91.3	94.1	92.9	86.5	79.0	87.8	81.5
Text is Text [3]	ST+MJ	92.3	89.9	93.3	92.2	84.4	76.9	86.3	79.4
ABINet-LV [8]	ST+MJ+WiKi	**96.2**	93.5	**97.4**	**96.1**	89.3	86.0	89.2	87.0
S-GTR [16]	ST+MJ	95.8	94.1	96.8	95.8	87.9	84.6	**92.3**	86.0
Baseline*	ST+MJ	94.7	92.3	95.5	94.5	87.1	83.3	89.6	84.7
Baseline + Corner	ST+MJ	95.1	94.1	95.7	95.1	90.1	84.9	90.3	86.5
Baseline + CC loss	ST+MJ	95.4	92.0	96.1	95.1	88.2	83.9	89.8	85.4
CornerTransformer	ST+MJ	95.9	**94.6**	96.4	95.8	91.5	**86.3**	92.0	**88.0**

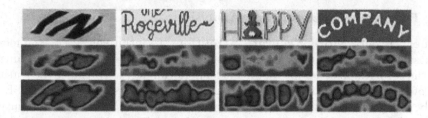

Fig. 6. Visualization for the feature map of the encoder output. First row: input images; Second row: feature maps of the baseline; Third row: feature maps of the baseline equipped with the corner-query cross-attention

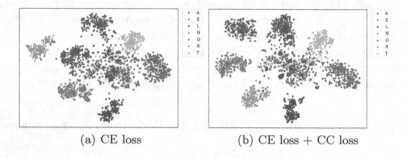

(a) CE loss   (b) CE loss + CC loss

Fig. 7. Visualization for the character feature distribution of the decoder output

Character Contrastive Loss Improves Class Representation. In order to verify the effectiveness of our character contrastive loss and justify the motivation for designing this loss, we perform dimension reduction on the final output features of the CornerTransformer decoder and use t-SNE [31] to visualize the distribution of character features. Figure 7 demonstrates the feature distributions of randomly selected 7 characters. Obviously, compared with the baseline using only the cross-entropy loss, when adding the character contrastive loss, the features of each character class are clustered together, and the features of different classes are far away from each other. This phenomenon is in line with our design that characters of the same category are positive samples and those of different categories are negative samples.

4.7 Limitations

For some extremely difficult artistic texts, CornerTransformer may fail to achieve correct results. A few failure examples are shown in Fig. 8. When decorative patterns from the background have exactly the same appearance and similar shape as the texts, it is difficult to distinguish whether these patterns belong to texts or not. These are indeed challenging examples for any text recognizer.

jmath math   gif mother   billions buch!   shuttle spektoy

Fig. 8. Failure examples for artistic text recognition. Each image is along with our result and the ground truth

5   Conclusion

In this paper, we focus on a new challenging task of artistic text recognition. To tackle the difficulties of this task, we introduce the corner point map as a robust representation for the artistic text image and present the corner-query cross-attention mechanism to make the model achieve more accurate attention. We also design a character contrastive loss to learn the invariant features of characters, leading to tight clustering of features. In order to benchmark the performance of different models, we provide the WordArt dataset. Experimental results demonstrate the remarkable superiority of our CornerTransformer on artistic text recognition. Interestingly, we achieve state-of-the-art results on several scene text datasets with small and blurred images. We hope the proposed WordArt dataset can encourage more advanced text recognition models, and the corner-based design can offer insights to other challenging recognition tasks.

Acknowledgements. This work was supported by the National Natural Science Foundation of China 61733007.

References

1. Baek, J., et al.: What is wrong with scene text recognition model comparisons? dataset and model analysis. In: Proceedings of the IEEE/CVF International Conference on Computer Vision, pp. 4715–4723 (2019)
2. Bhunia, A.K., Ghose, S., Kumar, A., Chowdhury, P.N., Sain, A., Song, Y.Z.: Metahtr: Towards writer-adaptive handwritten text recognition. In: Proceedings of the IEEE/CVF Conference on Computer Vision and Pattern Recognitionm pp. 15830–15839 (2021)
3. Bhunia, A.K., Sain, A., Chowdhury, P.N., Song, Y.Z.: Text is text, no matter what: Unifying text recognition using knowledge distillation. In: Proceedings of the IEEE/CVF International Conference on Computer Vision, pp. 983–992 (2021)
4. Chen, T., Kornblith, S., Norouzi, M., Hinton, G.: A simple framework for contrastive learning of visual representations. In: International Conference on Machine Learning, pp. 1597–1607. PMLR (2020)
5. Cheng, Z., Bai, F., Xu, Y., Zheng, G., Pu, S., Zhou, S.: Focusing attention: Towards accurate text recognition in natural images. In: Proceedings of the IEEE International Conference on Computer Vision, pp. 5076–5084 (2017)
6. Ch'ng, C.K., Chan, C.S., Liu, C.L.: Total-text: toward orientation robustness in scene text detection. Int. J. Document Anal. Recogn. (IJDAR) **23**(1), 31–52 (2020)

7. DeTone, D., Malisiewicz, T., Rabinovich, A.: Superpoint: Self-supervised interest point detection and description. In: Proceedings of the IEEE Conference on Computer Vision and Pattern Recognition Workshops, pp. 224–236 (2018)

8. Fang, S., Xie, H., Wang, Y., Mao, Z., Zhang, Y.: Read like humans: autonomous, bidirectional and iterative language modeling for scene text recognition. In: Proceedings of the IEEE/CVF Conference on Computer Vision and Pattern Recognition, pp. 7098–7107 (2021)

9. Frinken, V., Uchida, S.: Deep blstm neural networks for unconstrained continuous handwritten text recognition. In: 2015 13th International Conference on Document Analysis and Recognition (ICDAR), pp. 911–915. IEEE (2015)

10. Del Gobbo, J., Matuk Herrera, R.: Unconstrained text detection in manga: a new dataset and baseline. In: Bartoli, A., Fusiello, A. (eds.) ECCV 2020. LNCS, vol. 12537, pp. 629–646. Springer, Cham (2020). https://doi.org/10.1007/978-3-030-67070-2_38

11. Goodfellow, I., et al.: Generative adversarial nets. In: Advances in Neural Information Processing Systems 27 (2014)

12. Graves, A., Fernández, S., Gomez, F., Schmidhuber, J.: Connectionist temporal classification: labelling unsegmented sequence data with recurrent neural networks. In: Proceedings of the 23rd International Conference on Machine Learning, pp. 369–376 (2006)

13. Gupta, A., Vedaldi, A., Zisserman, A.: Synthetic data for text localisation in natural images. In: Proceedings of the IEEE Conference on Computer Vision and Pattern Recognition, pp. 2315–2324 (2016)

14. Harris, C., Stephens, M., et al.: A combined corner and edge detector. In: Alvey Vision Conference, vol. 15, pp. 10–5244. Citeseer (1988)

15. He, P., Huang, W., Qiao, Y., Loy, C.C., Tang, X.: Reading scene text in deep convolutional sequences. In: Thirtieth AAAI Conference on Artificial Intelligence (2016)

16. He, Y., et al.: Visual semantics allow for textual reasoning better in scene text recognition. arXiv preprint arXiv:2112.12916 (2021)

17. Hu, J., Brown, M.K., Turin, W.: Hmm based online handwriting recognition. IEEE Trans. Pattern Anal. Mach. Intell. **18**(10), 1039–1045 (1996)

18. Jaderberg, M., Simonyan, K., Vedaldi, A., Zisserman, A.: Synthetic data and artificial neural networks for natural scene text recognition. Eprint Arxiv (2014)

19. Jaderberg, M., Simonyan, K., Vedaldi, A., Zisserman, A.: Reading text in the wild with convolutional neural networks. Int. J. Comput. Vision **116**(1), 1–20 (2016)

20. Jaderberg, M., Simonyan, K., Zisserman, A., et al.: Spatial transformer networks. In: Advances in Neural Information Processing Systems 28 (2015)

21. Karatzas, D., et al.: Icdar 2015 competition on robust reading. In: 2015 13th international conference on document analysis and recognition (ICDAR), pp. 1156–1160. IEEE (2015)

22. Karatzas, D., et al.: Icdar 2013 robust reading competition. In: 2013 12th International Conference on Document Analysis and Recognition, pp. 1484–1493. IEEE (2013)

23. Khosla, P., Teterwak, P., Wang, C., Sarna, A., Tian, Y., Isola, P., Maschinot, A., Liu, C., Krishnan, D.: Supervised contrastive learning. Adv. Neural. Inf. Process. Syst. **33**, 18661–18673 (2020)

24. Kingma, D.P., Ba, J.: Adam: a method for stochastic optimization. arXiv preprint arXiv:1412.6980 (2014)

25. Le, A.D.: Recognizing handwritten mathematical expressions via paired dual loss attention network and printed mathematical expressions. In: Proceedings of the IEEE/CVF Conference on Computer Vision and Pattern Recognition Workshops, pp. 566–567 (2020)
26. Lee, J., Park, S., Baek, J., Oh, S.J., Kim, S., Lee, H.: On recognizing texts of arbitrary shapes with 2d self-attention. In: Proceedings of the IEEE/CVF Conference on Computer Vision and Pattern Recognition Workshops, pp. 546–547 (2020)
27. Li, H., Wang, P., Shen, C., Zhang, G.: Show, attend and read: a simple and strong baseline for irregular text recognition. In: Proceedings of the AAAI Conference on Artificial Intelligence, vol. 33, pp. 8610–8617 (2019)
28. Liao, M., et al.: Scene text recognition from two-dimensional perspective. In: Proceedings of the AAAI Conference on Artificial Intelligence, vol. 33, pp. 8714–8721 (2019)
29. Litman, R., Anschel, O., Tsiper, S., Litman, R., Mazor, S., Manmatha, R.: Scatter: selective context attentional scene text recognizer. In: proceedings of the IEEE/CVF conference on computer vision and pattern recognition. pp. 11962–11972 (2020)
30. Luo, C., Jin, L., Sun, Z.: Moran: A multi-object rectified attention network for scene text recognition. Pattern Recogn. **90**, 109–118 (2019)
31. Van der Maaten, L., Hinton, G.: Visualizing data using t-sne. J. Mach. Learn. Res. **9**(11) (2008)
32. Merity, S., Xiong, C., Bradbury, J., Socher, R.: Pointer sentinel mixture models. arXiv preprint arXiv:1609.07843 (2016)
33. Mishra, A., Alahari, K., Jawahar, C.: Scene text recognition using higher order language priors. In: BMVC-British Machine Vision Conference. BMVA (2012)
34. Nayef, N., et al.: Icdar 2019 robust reading challenge on multi-lingual scene text detection and recognition-rrc-mlt-2019. In: 2019 International Conference on Document Analysis and Recognition (ICDAR), pp. 1582–1587. IEEE (2019)
35. Phan, T.Q., Shivakumara, P., Tian, S., Tan, C.L.: Recognizing text with perspective distortion in natural scenes. In: Proceedings of the IEEE International Conference on Computer Vision, pp. 569–576 (2013)
36. Qiao, Z., Zhou, Y., Yang, D., Zhou, Y., Wang, W.: Seed: Semantics enhanced encoder-decoder framework for scene text recognition. In: Proceedings of the IEEE/CVF Conference on Computer Vision and Pattern Recognition, pp. 13528–13537 (2020)
37. Risnumawan, A., Shivakumara, P., Chan, C.S., Tan, C.L.: A robust arbitrary text detection system for natural scene images. Expert Syst. Appl. **41**(18), 8027–8048 (2014)
38. Sheng, F., Chen, Z., Xu, B.: Nrtr: A no-recurrence sequence-to-sequence model for scene text recognition. In: 2019 International Conference on Document Analysis and Recognition (ICDAR), pp. 781–786. IEEE (2019)
39. Shi, B., Bai, X., Yao, C.: An end-to-end trainable neural network for image-based sequence recognition and its application to scene text recognition. IEEE Trans. Pattern Anal. Mach. Intell. **39**(11), 2298–2304 (2016)
40. Shi, B., Wang, X., Lyu, P., Yao, C., Bai, X.: Robust scene text recognition with automatic rectification. In: Proceedings of the IEEE Conference on Computer Vision and Pattern Recognition, pp. 4168–4176 (2016)

41. Shi, B., Yang, M., Wang, X., Lyu, P., Yao, C., Bai, X.: Aster: an attentional scene text recognizer with flexible rectification. IEEE Trans. Pattern Anal. Mach. Intell. **41**(9), 2035–2048 (2018)
42. Shi, J., et al.: Good features to track. In: 1994 Proceedings of IEEE Conference on Computer Vision and Pattern Recognition, pp. 593–600. IEEE (1994)
43. Su, B., Lu, S.: Accurate scene text recognition based on recurrent neural network. In: Cremers, D., Reid, I., Saito, H., Yang, M.-H. (eds.) ACCV 2014. LNCS, vol. 9003, pp. 35–48. Springer, Cham (2015). https://doi.org/10.1007/978-3-319-16865-4_3
44. Sun, Y., et al.: Icdar 2019 competition on large-scale street view text with partial labeling-rrc-lsvt. In: 2019 International Conference on Document Analysis and Recognition (ICDAR), pp. 1557–1562. IEEE (2019)
45. Vaswani, A., et al.: Attention is all you need. In: Advances in Neural Information Processing Systems 30 (2017)
46. Veit, A., Matera, T., Neumann, L., Matas, J., Belongie, S.: Coco-text: dataset and benchmark for text detection and recognition in natural images. arXiv preprint arXiv:1601.07140 (2016)
47. Wan, Z., He, M., Chen, H., Bai, X., Yao, C.: Textscanner: reading characters in order for robust scene text recognition. In: Proceedings of the AAAI Conference on Artificial Intelligence, vol. 34, pp. 12120–12127 (2020)
48. Wang, K., Babenko, B., Belongie, S.: End-to-end scene text recognition. In: 2011 International Conference on Computer Vision, pp. 1457–1464. IEEE (2011)
49. Wang, T., et al.: Decoupled attention network for text recognition. In: Proceedings of the AAAI Conference on Artificial Intelligence, vol. 34, pp. 12216–12224 (2020)
50. Wang, Y., Lian, Z.: Exploring font-independent features for scene text recognition. In: Proceedings of the 28th ACM International Conference on Multimedia, pp. 1900–1920 (2020)
51. Wu, J.W., Yin, F., Zhang, Y.M., Zhang, X.Y., Liu, C.L.: Handwritten mathematical expression recognition via paired adversarial learning. Int. J. Comput. Vision **128**(10), 2386–2401 (2020)
52. Xu, X., Zhang, Z., Wang, Z., Price, B., Wang, Z., Shi, H.: Rethinking text segmentation: a novel dataset and a text-specific refinement approach. In: Proceedings of the IEEE/CVF Conference on Computer Vision and Pattern Recognition, pp. 12045–12055 (2021)
53. Yang, M., et al.: Symmetry-constrained rectification network for scene text recognition. In: Proceedings of the IEEE/CVF International Conference on Computer Vision, pp. 9147–9156 (2019)
54. Yang, X., He, D., Zhou, Z., Kifer, D., Giles, C.L.: Learning to read irregular text with attention mechanisms. In: IJCAI, vol. 1, p. 3 (2017)
55. Yao, C., Bai, X., Shi, B., Liu, W.: Strokelets: A learned multi-scale representation for scene text recognition. In: Proceedings of the IEEE Conference on Computer Vision and Pattern Recognition, pp. 4042–4049 (2014)
56. Yu, D., Li, X., Zhang, C., Liu, T., Han, J., Liu, J., Ding, E.: Towards accurate scene text recognition with semantic reasoning networks. In: Proceedings of the IEEE/CVF Conference on Computer Vision and Pattern Recognition, pp. 12113–12122 (2020)
57. Yuan, T.L., Zhu, Z., Xu, K., Li, C.J., Mu, T.J., Hu, S.M.: A large Chinese text dataset in the wild. J. Comput. Sci. Technol. **34**(3), 509–521 (2019)

58. Yue, X., Kuang, Z., Lin, C., Sun, H., Zhang, W.: RobustScanner: dynamically enhancing positional clues for robust text recognition. In: Vedaldi, A., Bischof, H., Brox, T., Frahm, J.-M. (eds.) ECCV 2020. LNCS, vol. 12364, pp. 135–151. Springer, Cham (2020). https://doi.org/10.1007/978-3-030-58529-7_9
59. Zhang, X., Zhu, B., Yao, X., Sun, Q., Li, R., Yu, B.: Context-based contrastive learning for scene text recognition. AAAI (2022)
60. Zhang, X.Y., Yin, F., Zhang, Y.M., Liu, C.L., Bengio, Y.: Drawing and recognizing Chinese characters with recurrent neural network. IEEE Trans. Pattern Anal. Mach. Intell. **40**(4), 849–862 (2017)

Levenshtein OCR

Cheng Da, Peng Wang, and Cong Yao[✉]

Alibaba DAMO Academy, Beijing, China
dc.dacheng08@gmail.com, wdp0072012@gmail.com, yaocong2010@gmail.com

Abstract. A novel scene text recognizer based on Vision-Language Transformer (VLT) is presented. Inspired by Levenshtein Transformer in the area of NLP, the proposed method (named Levenshtein OCR, and LevOCR for short) explores an alternative way for automatically transcribing textual content from cropped natural images. Specifically, we cast the problem of scene text recognition as an iterative sequence refinement process. The initial prediction sequence produced by a pure vision model is encoded and fed into a cross-modal transformer to interact and fuse with the visual features, to progressively approximate the ground truth. The refinement process is accomplished via two basic character-level operations: *deletion* and *insertion*, which are learned with imitation learning and allow for parallel decoding, dynamic length change and good interpretability. The quantitative experiments clearly demonstrate that LevOCR achieves state-of-the-art performances on standard benchmarks and the qualitative analyses verify the effectiveness and advantage of the proposed LevOCR algorithm.

Keywords: Scene text recognition · Transformer · Interpretability

1 Introduction

Scene text recognition is a long-standing and challenging problem [4,28,52] that has attracted much attention from the computer vision community. It aims at decoding textual information from natural scene images, which could be very beneficial to down-stream applications, such as traffic sign recognition and content-based image retrieval. However, reading text from natural images is faced with numerous difficulties: variation in text style and shape, non-uniform illumination, partial occlusion, perspective distortion, to name just a few. Recently, various text recognition methods [28] have been proposed to tackle this tough problem and substantial progresses have been observed [8,14,26,32,44,47,48,51].

It has become a trend in the computer vision community to draw inspirations from methods initially proposed for NLP tasks to solve vision problems, for instance, ViT [7], DETR [3] and Swin-Transformer [27]. Also, in the field of scene text recognition, multiple recent works [8,47] start to incorporate linguistic knowledge into the text recognition process, fusing information from both the vision and language modalities for higher text recognition accuracy.

C. Da and P. Wang—Equal contribution.

© The Author(s), under exclusive license to Springer Nature Switzerland AG 2022
S. Avidan et al. (Eds.): ECCV 2022, LNCS 13688, pp. 322–338, 2022.
https://doi.org/10.1007/978-3-031-19815-1_19

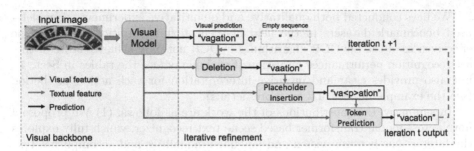

Fig. 1. Schematic overview of LevOCR. LevOCR accomplishes text recognition in an iterative way through two basic operations: *deletion* and *insertion*. Note that in LevOCR the operation of *insertion* is further decomposed into two sub-operations: Placeholder Insertion and Token Prediction.

Inspired by the wisdom from these pioneering works, we propose an alternative algorithm for scene text recognition. The backbone of the proposed model is a Vision-Language Transformer (VLT) [5,20,38], which is employed to perform cross-modal information fusion for more informative representations and better recognition performance. To further facilitate more flexible and interpretable text recognition, we introduce the strategy from Levenshtein Transformer (LevT) [10], which was originally designed for sequence generation and refinement tasks in NLP, into our framework. The core idea is to learn one refinement policy (deletion or insertion) for current iteration from its adversary in the previous iteration, in order to manipulate the basic units in the sequence (corresponding to characters in text recognition) to approach the target sequence. In such a way, the proposed text recognizer Levenshtein OCR (LevOCR for short) can realize text recognition in a progressive fashion, where the final prediction is obtained by iteratively refining an initial or intermediate recognition result until convergence (*i.e.*, post-editing for error correction). An intuitive illustration is depicted in Fig. 1. Note that due to the diversity of data augmentation in the training phase, the proposed model also supports generating the final recognition from an *empty* sequence, which falls back to a text generation task.

Similar to ABINet [8], we also fuse the information of both the vision modality and the language modality in an iterative procedure to predict the final recognition result. However, there are two key differences: (1) The main architecture of LevOCR is a Vision-Language Transformer (VLT), which allows for more sufficient utilization of the interactions between vision and language; (2) More importantly, while ABINet produces whole sequences at each iteration, LevOCR performs *fine-granularity predictions* through character-level operations (deletion or insertion of individual characters), endowing the system with higher flexibility and better *interpretability*, *i.e.*, when a specific decision (deletion or insertion) is made, one can trace back to the input space (image or text) to examine the supporting cues for that decision. This constitutes an unique characteristic of our LevOCR algorithm.

We have conducted both qualitative and quantitative experiments on widely-used benchmark datasets in the field of scene text recognition to verify the effectiveness of the LevOCR algorithm. LevOCR not only achieves state-of-the-art recognition performances on various benchmarks (see the tables in Sect. 4), but also provides clear and intuitive interpretation for each action prediction (see the example in Sect. 4.8 for more details).

In summary, the contributions of the work are as follows: (1) We propose a novel, cross-modal transformer based scene text recognizer, which fully explores the interactions between vision and language modalities and accomplishes text recognition via an iterative process. (2) The proposed LevOCR allows for parallel decoding and dynamic length change, and exhibits good transparency and interpretability in the inference phase, which could be very crucial for diagnosing and improving text recognition models in the future. (3) LevOCR achieves state-of-the-art results on standard benchmarks, and extensive experiments verify the effectiveness and advantage of LevOCR.

2   Related Work

2.1   Scene Text Recognition Methods

Traditional methods directly cast scene text recognition as a sequence classification task, which is purely based on visual features without any explicitly linguistic knowledge. CTC-based methods [13,15,36,41] provide differentiable Connectionist Temporal Classification (CTC) loss for access to end-to-end trainable sequence recognition, among which RNN model is often employed for context modeling of feature maps extracted by CNNs [36]. Segmentation-based methods [25,40] utilize FCN to directly predict the character labels in pixel-level and further group characters into words, in which character-level annotation is required. Opposite to parallel prediction of CTC and segmentation methods, attention-based methods [6,21,37] with encoder-decoder mechanism sequentially generates characters in order via RNN-attention model, where language information between characters can be implicitly captured. Due to the promising results, attention-based methods have previously dominated this field.

2.2   Enhanced Attention-Based Methods

Considering irregular text, previous methods [37,50] integrate spatial transformer module into attention-based framework, which rectifies the input with perspective and curvature distortion into a more canonical form. [6] observes the attention drift problem [42], in which the alignments between feature areas and text targets are not accurate for complicated images, and proposes a focus network to suppress the attention adrift. RobustScanner [48] utilizes positional clues to decode random character sequences effectively, by introducing a position enhancement branch into attention-based framework. Furthermore, SE-ASTER [33] employs a pre-trained language model to predict additional semantic information, which can guide the decoding process.

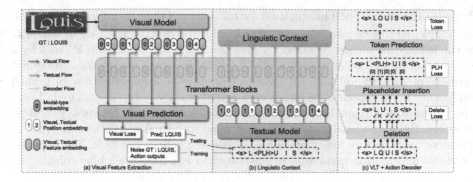

Fig. 2. Overview of the architecture of LevOCR. (Color figure online)

2.3 Transformer-Based Methods

Recently, transformer units [39] are employed in scene text recognition model to replace the complex LSTM blocks of RNN. Some prior methods [22,29,35] provide conventional transformer-based encoder-decoder framework for text recognition, which is based on customized CNNs feature extraction block. Furthermore, TrOCR [23] proposes an encoder-decoder structure with pre-trained transformer-based CV and NLP models, to deal with original image patches directly. ViTSTR [1] then employs vision transformers (ViT) for scene text recognition with image patches, where only transformer encoder is required and so that the characters can be predicted in parallel. To handle the linguistic context well, VisionLAN [45] presents a visual reasoning module to capture the visual and linguistic information simultaneously by masking the input image in the feature level. Additionally, SRN [47] introduces a global semantic reasoning module with transformer units to enhance semantic context. ABInet [8] goes a further step and proposes an explicit language model via transformer.

3 Methodology

LevOCR consists of three essential modules: Visual Feature Extraction (VFE), Linguistic Context (LC) and Vision-Language Transformer (VLT). Given an input image, the CNN model first extracts visual information and makes an initial visual prediction. And the initial visual prediction is further fed into transformer-based textual module to generate linguistic context. Finally, the intermediate visual features and linguistic features are directly concatenated and fed into VLT for sufficient information interaction, without any explicit cross-modal alignments. Additionally, different action decoders are built upon VLT for subsequent task. The schematic pipeline is illustrated in Fig. 2.

3.1 Visual Feature Extraction

Given a image $\mathbf{x} \in \mathbb{R}^{H \times W \times 3}$ and the corresponding text label $\mathbf{y} = (y_1, y_2, \ldots, y_N)$ with N maximum text length, a modified ResNet [12,37] backbone is utilized for visual information extraction, and then transformer units [39] are employed to generate enhanced 2D visual features $\mathbf{F}_v \in \mathbb{R}^{\frac{H}{4} \times \frac{W}{4} \times D}$, where D is the feature dimension. We directly decrease the height of feature $\mathbf{F}_v$ to 3 by 2 convolution layers, generating $\mathbf{V} \in \mathbb{R}^{3 \times \frac{W}{4} \times D}$ as the visual feature for subsequent refinement task. In addition, we construct another position attention [8] branch on feature $\mathbf{F}_v$ to generate the initial visual prediction $\hat{\mathbf{y}} = (\hat{y}_1, \hat{y}_2, \ldots, \hat{y}_N)$. Then, the visual loss L_v can be realized by a cross-entropy loss between $\mathbf{y}$ and $\hat{\mathbf{y}}$. Notably, the pure visual feature $\mathbf{V}$ is not used for visual prediction, in order to preserve more feature information for subsequent refinement task. The pipeline of visual information extraction is illustrated in Fig. 2 (a) with blue color.

3.2 Linguistic Context

NLP community has achieved substantial performance improvement. to model linguistic knowledge. The textual module is constructed with Transformer blocks [39] to model linguistic knowledge. Concretely, the input of textual module is a text sequence that need to be corrected, represented by $\tilde{\mathbf{y}} = (\tilde{y}_1, \tilde{y}_2, \ldots, \tilde{y}_N)$. First, word embedding at character level is used to encode $\tilde{\mathbf{y}}$ into feature $\mathbf{F}_t \in \mathbb{R}^{N \times D}$. Then, multiple transformer blocks transcribe $\mathbf{F}_t$ into refined text feature $\mathbf{T} \in \mathbb{R}^{N \times D}$, where N is the maximum text length and D is the feature dimension. The pipeline of linguistic context is illustrated in Fig. 2(b) with red color.

3.3 Vision-Language Transformer

Text instances in natural scenes do not always conform with linguistic rules. For example, digits and random characters appear commonly. Therefore, Lev-OCR employs VLT [20] to integrate visual and linguistic features. In this way, no enforced alignments as in ABInet [8] of two modalities are required and adaptive weights of two modalities are directly driven by the objective function. Then, action decoder heads are built upon VLT for *deletion* and *insertion* action learning, which can make a complementary judgement on both two modalities and be explicitly examined for good interpretability. Specifically, the visual feature $\mathbf{V} = [\mathbf{v}_1; \mathbf{v}_2; \ldots; \mathbf{v}_{N_v}] \in \mathbb{R}^{N_v \times D}$ and textual feature $\mathbf{T} = [\mathbf{t}_1; \mathbf{t}_2; \ldots; \mathbf{t}_N] \in \mathbb{R}^{N \times D}$ are produced by the corresponding modules, respectively. We directly concatenate these features of two modalities as the input of VLT blocks. In order to discriminate the features with different modalities and positions, position embeddings and modal-type ones are introduced. The detailed process of VLT is formulated as follows:

$$
\begin{aligned}
\overline{\mathbf{V}} &= [\mathbf{v}_1 + \mathbf{p}_1^v; \mathbf{v}_2 + \mathbf{p}_2^v; \ldots; \mathbf{v}_{N_v} + \mathbf{p}_{N_v}^v] + \mathbf{E}_v \\
\overline{\mathbf{T}} &= [\mathbf{t}_1 + \mathbf{p}_1^t; \mathbf{t}_2 + \mathbf{p}_2^t; \ldots; \mathbf{t}_N + \mathbf{p}_N^t] + \mathbf{E}_t \\
\mathbf{H}^{(0)} &= [\mathbf{h}_1^{(0)}; \mathbf{h}_2^{(0)}; \ldots; \mathbf{h}_{N+N_v}^{(0)}] = [\overline{\mathbf{T}}; \overline{\mathbf{V}}] \\
\mathbf{H}^{(l+1)} &= \text{BERT}_l(\mathbf{H}^{(l)}).
\end{aligned}
\tag{1}
$$

Here, N_v is $3 \times \frac{W}{4}$. The visual and textual position embeddings are represented as $[\mathbf{p}_1^v; \mathbf{p}_2^v; \ldots; \mathbf{p}_{N_v}^v] \in \mathbb{R}^{N_v \times D}$ and $[\mathbf{p}_1^t; \mathbf{p}_2^t; \ldots; \mathbf{p}_N^t] \in \mathbb{R}^{N \times D}$. Then, visual and textual modal-type embeddings are denoted as $\mathbf{E}_v \in \mathbb{R}^{1 \times D}$ and $\mathbf{E}_t \in \mathbb{R}^{1 \times D}$. And the l-th transformer block is denoted as BERT$_l$. Thus, the final aggregated feature $\mathbf{H} \in \mathbb{R}^{(N+N_v) \times D}$ are generated by L-th transformer block, in which even the unaligned features of two modalities can be adaptively interacted and fused.

3.4   Imitation Learning

In order to mimic how humans edit text, we cast this text sequence refinement task into a Markov Decision Process (MDP) denoted as a tuple $(\mathcal{Y}, \mathcal{A}, \mathcal{E}, \mathcal{R}, \mathbf{y}^0)$ as in [10]. We define a text as a sequence that consists of digits and characters, and thus $\mathcal{Y}$ is a set of word vocabulary with the dictionary of symbols $\mathcal{V}$. Typically, $\mathbf{y}^0 \in \mathcal{Y}$ represents the initial sequence. For text refinement task, two basic actions *deletion* and *insertion* are defined as the set of actions $\mathcal{A}$. The reward function $\mathcal{R} = -\mathcal{D}(\mathbf{y}, \mathbf{y}^*)$ directly measures the Levenshtein distance between the prediction and the sequence of ground-truth text. Given k-th step text sequence $\mathbf{y}^k$, the agent interacts with the environment $\mathcal{E}$, executes editing actions and returns the modified sequence $\mathbf{y}^{k+1}$, which is denoted as $\mathbf{y}^{k+1} = \mathcal{E}(\mathbf{y}^k, \mathbf{a}^{k+1})$. Our main purpose is to learn a favourable policy π that model the probability distribution over actions $\mathcal{A}$ for maximum reward.

Deletion Action. The input text sequence for imitation learning is also denoted as $\mathbf{y} = (y_1, y_2, \ldots, y_N)$ for simplicity. Deletion policy $\pi^{del}(d|i, \mathbf{y})$ aims to make a binary decision for every character $y_i \in \mathbf{y}$, in which $d = 1$ indicates that this token should be deleted or $d = 0$ for keeping it. Typically, y_1 and y_N are special symbols <s> and </s> for sequence boundary, respectively. Thus, they can not be deleted, which is denoted as $\pi^{del}(0|1, \mathbf{y}) = \pi^{del}(0|N, \mathbf{y}) = 1$. Moreover, based on the aggregated feature $\mathbf{H}$, the deletion classifier can be formulated as follows:

$$\pi_\theta^{del}(d|i, \mathbf{y}) = \text{softmax}(\mathbf{h}_i \mathbf{W}_{del}^T), i = 2, \ldots, N-1, \tag{2}$$

where $\mathbf{W}_{del} \in \mathbb{R}^{2 \times D}$ is the weight of deletion classifier. Note that only the first N sequences of $\mathbf{H}$ are used for prediction, and N is the maximum text length.

Insertion Action. Insertion action is more complicated than deletion one, since the position of insertion need to be predefined. Technically, *insertion* is decomposed into two sub-operations: placeholder insertion and token prediction. Concretely, for each consecutive pairs (y_i, y_{i+1}) in $\mathbf{y}$, placeholder insertion policy $\pi^{plh}(p|i, \mathbf{y})$ predicts the number p of placeholder should be inserted at position i. Thus, the classifier of placeholder insertion is defined as follows:

$$\pi_\theta^{plh}(p|i, \mathbf{y}) = \text{softmax}([\mathbf{h}_i, \mathbf{h}_{i+1}] \mathbf{W}_{plh}^T),$$
$$i = 1, \ldots, N-1, \tag{3}$$

where $\mathbf{W}_{plh} \in \mathbb{R}^{M \times 2D}$ is the weight of the placeholder classifier, and M is the max number of placeholders can be inserted. $[\mathbf{h}_i, \mathbf{h}_{i+1}]$ is the concatenation of $\mathbf{h}_i$ and $\mathbf{h}_{i+1}$.

Referring to the predicted number of placeholder insertion, we can insert a corresponding number of placeholders at the relevant positions. Then, token prediction policy $\pi^{tok}(t|i, \mathbf{y})$ is required to replace placeholder y_i with symbol t in the dictionary $\mathcal{V}$, which is formulated as follows:

$$\pi_\theta^{tok}(t|i, \mathbf{y}) = \text{softmax}(\mathbf{h}_i \mathbf{W}_{tok}^T), \forall_{y_i} = <\text{p}>. \tag{4}$$

Here, $\mathbf{W}_{tok} \in \mathbb{R}^{|\mathcal{V}| \times D}$ is the weight of token predictor, $<\text{p}>$ is the placehoder and $|\mathcal{V}|$ is the size of dictionary.

Training Phase. Notably, *deletion* and *insertion* are alternatively executed. For instance, given a text sequence, deletion policy is first called to delete wrong symbols. Then, placeholder insertion policy inserts some possible placeholders. Finally, token prediction policy replaces all placeholders with right symbols. Typically, these actions are performed in parallel for each position. Moreover, the imitation learning strategy is utilized for LevOCR training, aiming to approximating the expert policy π^* that can be directly and simply derived from the ground-truth text sequence as follows:

$$\mathbf{a}^* = \arg\min_{\mathbf{a}} \mathcal{D}(\mathbf{y}^*, \mathcal{E}(\mathbf{y}, \mathbf{a})). \tag{5}$$

Here, Levenshtein distance $\mathcal{D}$ is used for distance measure. The optimal actions $\mathbf{a}^*$ can represent $\mathbf{d}^*$, $\mathbf{p}^*$, and $\mathbf{t}^*$, which can be produced by dynamic programming efficiently. The loss function of *deletion* is formulated as follows:

$$L_{del} = \mathbb{E}_{\mathbf{y}_{del} \sim d_{\tilde{\pi}_{del}}} \sum_{d_i^* \in \mathbf{d}^*} -\log \pi_\theta^{del}(d_i^*|i, \mathbf{y}_{del}), \tag{6}$$

where $\mathbf{d}^* = (d_1^*, d_2^*, \ldots, d_N^*) \sim \pi^*$ denotes the optimal deletion action for each position of $\mathbf{y}_{del}$, generated by Eq. (5). And $d_{\tilde{\pi}_{del}}$ is a text distribution induced by policy $\tilde{\pi}_{del}$ for the sequence generation with additive noise:

$$d_{\tilde{\pi}_{del}} = \begin{cases} \{\mathcal{E}(\mathcal{E}(\mathbf{y}^0, \tilde{\mathbf{p}}), \tilde{\mathbf{t}})), \tilde{\mathbf{p}} \sim \pi^R, \tilde{\mathbf{t}} \sim \pi^R\}, \alpha < \mu \\ \{\mathcal{E}(\mathcal{E}(\mathbf{y}', \mathbf{p}^*), \tilde{\mathbf{t}})), \mathbf{p}^* \sim \pi_{\theta_*}^{plh}, \tilde{\mathbf{t}} \sim \pi_\theta^{tok}\}, \alpha \geq \mu, \end{cases} \tag{7}$$

where π^R represents a random policy, $\alpha \sim \text{Uniform}[0, 1]$, $\mu \in [0, 1]$ is a mixture factor, $\mathbf{y}^0$ is the initial sequence, and $\mathbf{y}'$ is any sequence ready to insert. For $\mu < \alpha$, we randomly add some symbols on $\mathbf{y}^0$ to generate $\mathbf{y}_{del}$. For $\mu \geq \alpha$, we use expert placeholder policy and the learned token prediction to generate $\mathbf{y}_{del}$ based on $\mathbf{y}'$. This procedure can be regarded as adversarial learning in GAN [9]. Similarly, the loss function of *insertion* is as follows:

$$L_{ins} = \mathbb{E}_{\mathbf{y}_{ins} \sim d_{\tilde{\pi}_{ins}}} \left[\sum_{p_i^* \in \mathbf{p}^*} -\log \pi_\theta^{plh}(p_i^*|i, \mathbf{y}_{ins}) \right.$$
$$\left. + \sum_{t_i^* \in \mathbf{t}^*} -\log \pi_\theta^{tok}(t_i^*|i, \mathbf{y}_{ins}') \right], \tag{8}$$

where $\mathbf{p}^* = (p_1^*, p_2^*, \ldots, p_{N-1}^*) \sim \pi^*$ represents the optimal number of place-holders for each consecutive position pair in $\mathbf{y}_{ins}$, generated by Eq. (5). And $\mathbf{t}^* = (t_1^*, t_2^*, \ldots, t_{N-1}^*) \sim \pi^*$ denotes the optimal symbol for each placeholder in $\mathbf{y}'_{ins}$, where $\mathbf{y}'_{ins} = \mathcal{E}(\mathbf{y}_{ins}, \mathbf{p})$, $\mathbf{p} \sim \pi_\theta^{plh}$. Moreover, $d_{\tilde{\pi}_{ins}}$ is a text distribution induced by policy $\tilde{\pi}_{ins}$ for the sequence generation with deleted noise:

$$d_{\tilde{\pi}_{ins}} = \begin{cases} \{\mathcal{E}(\mathbf{y}^*, \tilde{\mathbf{d}})), \tilde{\mathbf{d}} \sim \pi^R\}, \beta < \mu \\ \{\mathcal{E}(\mathbf{y}^0, \mathbf{d}^*)), \mathbf{d}^* \sim \pi_{\theta_*}^{del}\}, \beta \geqslant \mu, \end{cases} \quad (9)$$

where factor $\beta \sim \text{Uniform}[0, 1]$. We also adopt mixture manner to construct $\mathbf{y}_{ins}$ for insertion learning. For $\beta < \mu$, we randomly delete some symbols on ground-truth $\mathbf{y}^*$ to produce $\mathbf{y}_{ins}$. For $\beta \geqslant \mu$, expert deletion policy is employed to generate $\mathbf{y}_{ins}$ based on initial sequence $\mathbf{y}^0$. The training procedure is illustrated in Fig. 2(c) with green color, and the final loss function is formulated as:

$$L = \lambda_1 L_v + \lambda_2 L_{del} + \lambda_3 L_{ins}, \quad (10)$$

where λ_1, λ_2 and λ_3 are weights for visual prediction, *deletion* and *insertion*.

Notably, the visual model is pre-trained with only images for better initialization by L_v. And the textual model and VLT blocks can also be pre-trained with only texts. Specifically, the input of VLT is $\mathbf{H}^{(0)} = \overline{\mathbf{T}}$ without image feature, which is used for *deletion* and *insertion* learning via L_{del} and L_{ins}. Based on these pre-trained models, LevOCR is further trained by Eq. (10).

Note that the input sequences (*i.e.* $\tilde{\mathbf{y}}$) for *deletion* and *insertion* are indeed different. Typically, $\tilde{\mathbf{y}}$ is not always a "true" word. For instance, $\tilde{\mathbf{y}}$ could be the output of placeholder insertion for token prediction that includes placeholders or even be an empty sequence. Therefore, different input sequences $\tilde{\mathbf{y}}$ should be fed into textual model individually and encoded as the unique text features $\mathbf{T}$ and aggregated features $\mathbf{H}$ for the specific action (deletion, placeholder insertion and token prediction) learning in training phase.

3.5   Inference Phase

We alternatively employ *deletion* and *insertion* to refine text at inference process, until two policies converge (either nothing to delete or insert, or reaching maximum iterations). Concretely, given a image $\mathbf{x}$, we first obtain the visual feature $\mathbf{V}$ and the initial sequence $\mathbf{y}^0$ (*e.g.* visual prediction). And then $\mathbf{y}^0$ is fed into textual module, generating refined text texture $\mathbf{T}$. Furthermore, the visual feature and textual one are interacted and fused in VLT to produce aggregated feature $\mathbf{H}$. Finally, action decoders greedily choose the action with the maximum probability at each position by Eqs. (2) (3) (4) in parallel. Then, *deletion* and *insertion* are executed in turn with new corresponding features $\mathbf{T}$ and $\mathbf{H}$. Note that LevOCR can not only accomplish text refinement on initial visual predictions, but also perform text generation with empty sequence $\mathbf{y}^0$.

4   Experiment

4.1   Datasets

For fair comparison, we follow previous settings [2,8] to train LevOCR on two synthetic datasets MJSynth (MJ) [16,17] and SynthText(ST) [11] without fine-tuning on other datasets. Extensive experiments are conducted on six standard Latin scene text benchmarks, including 3 regular text datasets (IC13 [19], SVT [43], IIIT [30]) and 3 irregular ones (IC15 [18], SVTP [31], CUTE [34]).

ICDAR 2013 (IC13) [19] includes 1095 cropped word images for testing. We evaluate on 857 images with alphanumeric characters and more than 2 characters. **Street View Text (SVT)** [43] contains 647 testing images collected from Google Street View. **IIIT 5K-Words (IIIT5k)** [30] is crawled from Google image search, and consists of 3000 testing images. **ICDAR 2015 (IC15)** [18] includes word patches cropped from incidental scene images captured by Google Glasses. **Street View Text-Perspective (SVTP)** [31] consists of 639 images collected from Google Street View, and many images are heavily distorted. **CUTE80 (CUTE)** [34] contains 80 natural scenes images for curved text recognition. 288 images are cropped from these images for testing.

4.2   Implementation Details

The textual model and VLT block consist of 6 stacked transformer units with 8 heads for each layer, respectively. The number of hidden units in FC-layer of transformer block is 2048, and the dimension D of visual and textual feature is set to 512. Besides, The size of symbol dictionary $|\mathcal{V}|$ is 40, including 0-9, a-z, <s>, </s>, *pad* and <p>. The max length of output sequence N is set to 28, and the max number of placeholders M is set to 28. The mixture factor μ is set to 0.5. λ_1, λ_2 and λ_3 are set to 1. The input images are resized to 32×128. Common data augmentation is employed, such as rotation, affine, perspective distortion, image quality deterioration and color jitter. Our approach is trained on NVIDIA Tesla V100 GPUs with batch size 128. Adadelta [49] optimizer is adopted with the initial learning rate 0.1, and the max training epoch is 10.

4.3   Text Refinement and Text Generation

The initial sequence $\mathbf{y}^0$ is pivotal in LevOCR, which not only determines the final performance, but also endows LevOCR with the ability of highly flexible text editing. To empirically verify the ability of text refinement and generation, we construct 4 kinds of initial sequence: (1) $\mathbf{y}^0_{VP}$: the visual prediction is directly adopted and LevOCR essentially aims to text refinement. (2) $\mathbf{y}^0_{Emp}$: empty sequence is simply used and thus the inference stage falls back to a text generation task. (3) $\mathbf{y}^0_{Rand}$: ground-truth is corrupted by random noise, where we replace one character for 30% text, add one character for 30% text, delete one character for 40% text, and remain the digit text unchangeable. (4) $\mathbf{y}^0_{GT}$: ground-truth. These results with different initial sequences are reported in Table 1.

Table 1. The accuracies of LevOCR with different initial sequences $\mathbf{y}^0$ and max iterations on 6 public benchmarks.

Initial Sequence	Iteration	IC13	SVT	IIIT	IC15	SVTP	CUTE	AVG
LevOCR$_{VP}$	–	95.10	90.57	95.23	83.98	83.41	87.84	90.65
LevOCR + $\mathbf{y}^0_{VP}$	#1	96.50	92.43	96.50	86.09	87.75	91.32	92.55
	#2	96.73	92.89	96.63	86.42	88.06	91.67	92.79
	#3	96.85	92.89	96.63	86.42	88.06	91.67	92.81
LevOCR + $\mathbf{y}^0_{Emp}$	#1	95.45	90.42	95.00	83.99	83.72	88.89	90.64
	#2	96.73	92.43	96.33	86.03	87.60	92.01	92.51
	#3	96.97	92.74	96.37	86.09	88.06	92.01	92.63
LevOCR + $\mathbf{y}^0_{Rand}$	#1	84.83	85.32	87.90	82.05	82.33	84.38	85.20
	#2	84.83	85.63	87.93	82.05	82.33	84.38	85.25
	#3	84.83	85.63	87.93	82.05	82.33	84.38	85.25
LevOCR + $\mathbf{y}^0_{GT}$	#1	99.07	98.15	98.67	92.16	97.83	97.22	96.91
	#2	99.07	98.15	98.67	92.16	97.83	97.22	96.91
	#3	99.07	98.15	98.67	92.16	97.83	97.22	96.91

Table 2. The accuracies of LevOCR with different backbones.

Methods	Backbone	IC13	SVT	IIIT	IC15	SVTP	CUTE	AVG
LevOCR$_{VP}$ w/o LevT	CNN	95.21	90.41	95.30	83.26	83.41	88.88	90.53
LevOCR w/o LevT		95.21	90.42	95.43	83.43	84.03	89.23	90.70
LevOCR$_{VP}$	ViT	94.86	89.18	93.6	82.38	84.18	82.98	89.30
LevOCR		96.15	91.80	95.63	85.81	88.06	86.81	91.87
LevOCR$_{VP}$	CNN	95.10	90.57	95.23	83.98	83.41	87.84	90.65
LevOCR		96.85	92.89	96.63	86.42	88.06	91.67	92.81

The performance of $\mathbf{y}^0_{Rand}$ and $\mathbf{y}^0_{GT}$ can be regarded as the lower bound and upper bound of LevOCR, respectively. Based on the noisy initial sequences, $\mathbf{y}^0_{Rand}$ gets 85.25% average accuracy. This implies that almost 85% noisy texts can be corrected. Moreover, $\mathbf{y}^0_{GT}$ achieves the best accuracy 96.91% than others, proving that better linguistic context can be captured in better initial text sequence, leading to better performance of LevOCR. Additionally, the first line LevOCR$_{VP}$ records the accuracy of pure visual prediction of LevOCR. Both $\mathbf{y}^0_{VP}$ and $\mathbf{y}^0_{Emp}$ can obtain obvious improvements over LevOCR$_{VP}$, showing the effectiveness of text refinement and generation of LevOCR. Generally, the accuracies of 4 constructions (*i.e.* $\mathbf{y}^0_{GT} > \mathbf{y}^0_{VP} > \mathbf{y}^0_{Emp} > \mathbf{y}^0_{Rand}$) suggest that choosing a better $\mathbf{y}^0$ is crucial, and LevOCR indeed adopts linguistic information, not just relies on visual features. These results sufficiently demonstrate the powerful abilities of LevOCR in text refinement and text generation.

4.4   Iterative Refinement

We investigate the influence of various maximum refinement iterations (*i.e.*, $1, 2, 3$) and the results are also shown in Table 1. Notably, even if the maximum

Table 3. The detailed iterative process of LevOCR with different initial sequences on 6 public benchmarks. "Iteration" represents the current number of refinement iteration. "Input" represents the initial sequence or the output of last iteration. "Delete", "PLHIns" and "TokenPred" represent the action output of deletion, placeholder insertion and token prediction, respectively. And <3p> indicates that three consecutive placeholders <p> are inserted into the sequence. Best viewed in colors.

Image	GT	Initial Sequence	Iteration: Input-Delete-PLHIns-TokenPred
1: IC13	service	$\mathbf{y}_{VP}^0$ = servce	#1: servce-sere-ser<3p>e-service
		$\mathbf{y}_{Emp}^0$ = <s> < /s >	#1: <s> < /s >-<s> < /s >-<7p>-serbice
			#2: serbice-serbice-serb<p>ice-serblice
			#3: serblice-serice-ser<p>ice-service
		$\mathbf{y}_{Rand}^0$ = servcce	#1: servcce-servce-serv<p>ce-service
2: SVT	public	$\mathbf{y}_{VP}^0$ = publif	#1: publif-publi-publi<p>-public
		$\mathbf{y}_{Emp}^0$ = <s> < /s >	#1: <s> < /s >-<s> < /s >-<6p>-publif
			#2: publif-publi-publi<p>-public
		$\mathbf{y}_{Rand}^0$ = publcc	#1: publcc-publc-publc<2p>-publcip
			#2: publcip-publi-publi<p>-public
3: IIIT	solaris	$\mathbf{y}_{VP}^0$ = solris	#1: solris-soris-so<2p>ris-solaris
		$\mathbf{y}_{Emp}^0$ = <s> < /s >	#1: <s> < /s >-<s> < /s >-<6p>-solris
			#2: solris-soris-so<2p>ris-solaris
		$\mathbf{y}_{Rand}^0$ = solacis	#1: solacis-solais-sola<p>is-solaris
4: IC15	breakfast	$\mathbf{y}_{VP}^0$ = breakeast	#1: breakeast-breakast-break<p>ast-breakfast
		$\mathbf{y}_{Emp}^0$ = <s> < /s >	#1: <s> < /s >-<s> < /s >-<9p>-breakeast
			#2: breakeast-breakast-break<p>ast-breakfast
		$\mathbf{y}_{Rand}^0$ = breaufast	#1: breaufast-breafast-brea<p>fast-breakfast
5: SVTP	house	$\mathbf{y}_{VP}^0$ = houce	#1: houce-hou-hou<2p>-house
		$\mathbf{y}_{Emp}^0$ = <s> < /s >	#1: <s> < /s >-<s> < /s >-<5p>-houce
			#2: houce-hou-hou<2p>-house
		$\mathbf{y}_{Rand}^0$ = housk	#1: housk-houk-houk<2p>-houke2
			#2: houke2-hou2-hou<p>2-hous2
			#3: hous2-hou-hou<2p>-house
6: CUTE	vacation	$\mathbf{y}_{VP}^0$ = vagation	#1: vagation-vaation-va<p>ation-vacation
		$\mathbf{y}_{Emp}^0$ = <s> < /s >	#1: <s> < /s >-<s> < /s >-<8p>-vacation
		$\mathbf{y}_{Rand}^0$ = vacction	#1: vacction-vaction-vac<p>tion-vacation

iteration is set to 3, the refinement process might be stopped after 2 iterations when the sequence remains the same as the first iteration. Thus the results may be the same under different maximum iterations. Apparently, the results at #1 are already promising, and more iterations lead to further improvements. Therefore, there is no sophisticated setting for the maximum iteration and the adaptive convergence enables access to high efficiency. Thus, the maximum iteration is set to 3 for convenience. It is crucial to note that the accuracy of $\mathbf{y}_{Emp}^0$ at #1 is close to LevOCR$_{VP}$, which is only based on visual feature. While the accuracy of $\mathbf{y}_{Emp}^0$ is greatly increased 2.1% at #2 iteration over #1, demonstrating that LevOCR indeed utilizes language knowledge for further text refinement.

4.5 Effectiveness of Levenshtein Transformer

To further explore the significance of Levenshtein Transformer pipeline for text refinement, we construct some variants of LevOCR and these results are shown in Table 2. We remove the *deletion* and *insertion* losses in Eq.(10) and replace them with only one classification loss, the performance of LevOCR without LevT is not significantly improved and approximate to pure image prediction. While the proposed LevOCR with LevT obtains obvious 2.4% improvement than pure visual prediction. Besides CNN feature, vision transformer (ViT) [7] with 4×4 patches is utilized for image feature extraction. And the proposed *deletion* and *insertion* actions are learned for text refinement. ViT-based LevOCR can also achieve stable improvement 2.9% than visual prediction. These results demonstrate that LevT is a perfect fit for text refinement and the proposed LevOCR works well with CNN and ViT backbones, resulting in promising generalization.

4.6 Qualitative Analyses

It is essential to qualitatively dissect the iterative process of LevOCR. We select 6 exemplar images for qualitative exhibition, of which the visual predictions are incorrect. Generally, these challenging images are with various types of noises, such as motion blur, Gaussian blur, irregular font, occlusion, curved shape, perspective distortion and low resolution. The iterative refinement processes are elaborately reported in Table 3. And different 3 initial sequences as in Sect. 4.3 are adopted to show the amending capability powered by *deletion* and *insertion*.

Deletion action targets at removing wrong letters. As in Img.6, the 'C' is recognized as 'G' by visual model due to the curved shape. By leveraging both visual and linguistic information, 'G' in $\mathbf{y}_{VP}^0$ tends to be deleted. Similarly, deletion is triggered in $\mathbf{y}_{Rand}^0$ to remove a redundant 'C'. Considering placeholder insertion in empty sequence $\mathbf{y}_{Emp}^0$, we clearly observe that the inserted number of placeholder equals to the length of GT, indicating that LevOCR can fully comprehend image. When the length of input text is shorter than GT, placeholder insertion try to add the rest of placeholders at the right position. Consequently, placeholder insertion and deletion endows LevOCR with the ability of directly altering sequence length, which is different from previous methods (such as SRN [47] and ABINet [8]).

As for token prediction, it heavily relies on the output of placeholder insertion. When both predicted placeholders and the rest characters are correct, token prediction can directly make right decision (such as Img.4 and Img.6). However, when the output of deletion or placeholder insertion is incorrect, the refinement might collapse. As shown in Img.5 with $\mathbf{y}_{Rand}^0$, 'k' is not removed and 2 more placeholders are inserted. Fortunately, Img.5 can be successfully corrected after 2 more iterations. This phenomenon demonstrates that *deletion* and *insertion* are well learned by imitation learning, and adversarial learning guarantees that these two actions are complementary and inter-inhibitive. Additionally, token prediction supports inserting not only one character, but also word piece (multiple characters), such as "vic" in Img.1, "la" in Img.3 and "se" in Img.5. These results clearly confirm the superiority of our method.

Table 4. The accuracy comparisons with SOTA methods on 6 public benchmarks. The underlined and bold values represent the second and the best results, respectively.

Methods	Datasets	Regular text			Irregular text			Average
		IC13	SVT	IIIT	IC15	SVTP	CUTE	
TBRA [2]	MJ+ST	93.6	87.5	87.9	77.6	79.2	74.0	84.6
ViTSTR [1]	MJ+ST	93.2	87.7	88.4	78.5	81.8	81.3	85.6
ESIR [50]	MJ+ST	91.3	90.2	93.3	76.9	79.6	83.3	87.1
SAM [24]	MJ+ST	95.3	90.6	93.9	77.3	82.2	87.8	88.3
SE-ASTER [33]	MJ+ST	92.8	89.6	93.8	80.0	81.4	83.6	88.3
TextScanner [40]	MJ+ST	92.9	90.1	93.9	79.4	84.3	83.3	88.5
DAN [44]	MJ+ST	93.9	89.2	94.3	74.5	80.0	84.4	87.2
ScRN [46]	MJ+ST	93.9	88.9	94.4	78.7	80.8	87.5	88.4
RobustScanner [48]	MJ+ST	94.8	88.1	95.3	77.1	79.5	90.3	88.4
PIMNet [32]	MJ+ST	95.2	91.2	95.2	83.5	84.3	84.4	90.5
SATRN [22]	MJ+ST	94.1	91.3	92.8	79.0	86.5	87.8	88.6
MASTER [29]	MJ+ST	95.3	90.6	95.0	79.4	84.5	87.5	89.5
SRN [47]	MJ+ST	95.5	91.5	94.8	82.7	85.1	87.8	90.4
ABINet [8]	MJ+ST	**97.4**	**93.5**	96.2	86.0	**89.3**	89.2	92.6
LevOCR	MJ+ST	96.85	92.89	**96.63**	**86.42**	88.06	**91.67**	**92.81**

4.7 Comparisons with State-of-the-Arts

We compare our LevOCR against thirteen state-of-the-art scene text recognition methods on 6 public benchmarks, and the recognition results are illustrated in Table 4. For fair comparison, we only choose the methods that trained on synthetic datasets MJ and ST, and no lexicon is employed for evaluation. Specifically, LevOCR outperforms SATRN [22] and MASTER [29] that are transformer-based encoder-decoder models, showing the effectiveness of BERT-based framework for text recognition. In addition, SRN [47] and ABINet [8] achieve impressive performance by explicitly modelling linguistic information in their methods. The proposed LevOCR gains 2.4% improvement over SRN on average accuracy. Meanwhile, LevOCR surpasses the performance of ABINet on IIIT, IC15 and CUTE datasets and thus achieves the state-of-the-art performance on average accuracy. These results demonstrate the effectiveness of LevOCR.

4.8 Interpretability of LevOCR

Four intuitive examples to demonstrate the good interpretability of LevOCR are shown in Fig. 3. As in Fig. 3(a), the second character "n" is mis-classified as "m" in the image with GT string "snout". LevOCR is able to identify that 'm' is wrong and thus should be **deleted** (the probability of deletion is 0.87). Beyond that, one can easily examine the reason why LevOCR makes this decision through attention visualization and quantitative comparison. In this case, LevOCR relies more on visual information than on textual information (0.737 *vs.* 0.263) and the pixels near 'n' in the image contribute the most for this decision. Similarly, in the case of Fig. 3(b), where the GT string is "studios" and 'u' is

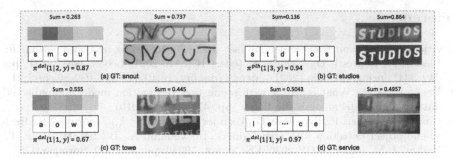

Fig. 3. Illustration of the interpretability of LevOCR. The details (attention maps and intermediate results) of the prediction of LevOCR are depicted. The sum attention weights of different modalities in the top layer are visualized. Best viewed in colors. (Color figure online)

intentionally removed, LevOCR manages to perceive that the third character is missing and thus should be *brought back* (the probability of inserting one character between 't' and 'd' is 0.94).

Additionally, when the initial prediction is incorrect and the image is severely corrupted or blurry, LevOCR will pay more attention to textual information in decision making, as shown in Fig. 3(c) and (d). Through the visualization and numbers produced by LevOCR, we can intuitively comprehend the character-level supporting evidences used by LevOCR in giving this prediction. Notably, good interpretability is an unique characteristic that distinguish the proposed LevOCR from other scene text recognition algorithms. Based on it, we can understand the underlying reason for a specific decision of LevOCR and diagnose its defects. We could even gain insights for designing better systems in the future.

4.9 Limitation

The *deletion* and *insertion* operations in LevOCR are relatively time-consuming, where one refinement iteration costs about 36 ms. Considering the time of visual feature extraction (11 ms) and alternative process, the elapsed time is about 47/83/119 ms for 1/2/3 iteration. The model size (109×10^6 parameters) is relatively large. Therefore, a more efficient architecture will be our future work.

5   Conclusion

In this paper, we have presented an effective and explainable algorithm LevOCR for scene text recognition. Based on Vision-Language Transformer (VLT), LevOCR is able to sufficiently exploit the information from both the vision modality and the language modality to make decisions in an iterative fashion. LevOCR can give fine-granularity (character-level) predictions and exhibits a special property of good interpretability. Extensive experiments verified the effectiveness and advantage of the proposed LevOCR algorithm.

References

1. Atienza, R.: Vision transformer for fast and efficient scene text recognition. In: Lladós, J., Lopresti, D., Uchida, S. (eds.) ICDAR 2021. LNCS, vol. 12821, pp. 319–334. Springer, Cham (2021). https://doi.org/10.1007/978-3-030-86549-8_21
2. Baek, J., et al.: What is wrong with scene text recognition model comparisons? dataset and model analysis. In: ICCV, pp. 4714–4722 (2019)
3. Carion, N., Massa, F., Synnaeve, G., Usunier, N., Kirillov, A., Zagoruyko, S.: End-to-end object detection with transformers. In: Vedaldi, A., Bischof, H., Brox, T., Frahm, J.-M. (eds.) ECCV 2020. LNCS, vol. 12346, pp. 213–229. Springer, Cham (2020). https://doi.org/10.1007/978-3-030-58452-8_13
4. Chen, X., Jin, L., Zhu, Y., Luo, C., Wang, T.: Text recognition in the wild: a survey. ACM Comput. Surv. (CSUR) **54**(2), 1–35 (2021)
5. Chen, Y.-C., et al.: UNITER: UNiversal Image-TExt representation learning. In: Vedaldi, A., Bischof, H., Brox, T., Frahm, J.-M. (eds.) ECCV 2020. LNCS, vol. 12375, pp. 104–120. Springer, Cham (2020). https://doi.org/10.1007/978-3-030-58577-8_7
6. Cheng, Z., Bai, F., Xu, Y., Zheng, G., Pu, S., Zhou, S.: Focusing attention: towards accurate text recognition in natural images. In: CVPR, pp. 5086–5094 (2017)
7. Dosovitskiy, A., et al.: An image is worth 16x16 words: transformers for image recognition at scale. In: ICLR (2021)
8. Fang, S., Xie, H., Wang, Y., Mao, Z., Zhang, Y.: Read like humans: autonomous, bidirectional and iterative language modeling for scene text recognition. In: CVPR, pp. 7098–7107 (2021)
9. Goodfellow, I.J., et al.: Generative adversarial nets. In: NeurIPS, pp. 2672–2680 (2014)
10. Gu, J., Wang, C., Zhao, J.: Levenshtein transformer. In: NeurIPS, pp. 11179–11189 (2019)
11. Gupta, A., Vedaldi, A., Zisserman, A.: Synthetic data for text localisation in natural images. In: CVPR, pp. 2315–2324 (2016)
12. He, K., Zhang, X., Ren, S., Sun, J.: Deep residual learning for image recognition. In: CVPR, pp. 770–778 (2016)
13. He, P., Huang, W., Qiao, Y., Loy, C.C., Tang, X.: Reading scene text in deep convolutional sequences. In: AAAI, pp. 3501–3508 (2016)
14. He, Y., et al.: Visual semantics allow for textual reasoning better in scene text recognition. In: AAAI, pp. 888–896 (2022)
15. Hu, W., Cai, X., Hou, J., Yi, S., Lin, Z.: GTC: guided training of CTC towards efficient and accurate scene text recognition. In: AAAI, pp. 11005–11012 (2020)
16. Jaderberg, M., Simonyan, K., Vedaldi, A., Zisserman, A.: Synthetic data and artificial neural networks for natural scene text recognition. In: NIPS Deep Learning Workshop (2014)
17. Jaderberg, M., Simonyan, K., Vedaldi, A., Zisserman, A.: Reading text in the wild with convolutional neural networks. Int. J. Comput. Vis. **116**(1), 1–20 (2016)
18. Karatzas, D., et al.: ICDAR 2015 competition on robust reading. In: ICDAR, pp. 1156–1160 (2015)
19. Karatzas, D., et al.: ICDAR 2013 robust reading competition. In: ICDAR, pp. 1484–1493 (2013)
20. Kim, W., Son, B., Kim, I.: Vilt: vision-and-language transformer without convolution or region supervision. In: ICML, vol. 139, pp. 5583–5594 (2021)

21. Lee, C., Osindero, S.: Recursive recurrent nets with attention modeling for OCR in the wild. In: CVPR, pp. 2231–2239 (2016)
22. Lee, J., Park, S., Baek, J., Oh, S.J., Kim, S., Lee, H.: On recognizing texts of arbitrary shapes with 2d self-attention. In: CVPR Workshops, pp. 2326–2335 (2020)
23. Li, M., et al.: Trocr: transformer-based optical character recognition with pre-trained models. CoRR abs/2109.10282 (2021)
24. Liao, M., Lyu, P., He, M., Yao, C., Wu, W., Bai, X.: Mask textspotter: An end-to-end trainable neural network for spotting text with arbitrary shapes. IEEE Trans. Pattern Anal. Mach. Intell. 43(2), 532–548 (2021)
25. Liao, M., et al.: Scene text recognition from two-dimensional perspective. In: AAAI, pp. 8714–8721 (2019)
26. Liu, H., et al.: Perceiving stroke-semantic context: hierarchical contrastive learning for robust scene text recognition. In: AAAI, pp. 1702–1710 (2022)
27. Liu, Z., et al.: Swin transformer: hierarchical vision transformer using shifted windows. CoRR abs/2103.14030 (2021)
28. Long, S., He, X., Yao, C.: Scene text detection and recognition: the deep learning era. IJCV 129(1), 161–184 (2021)
29. Lu, N., et al.: MASTER: multi-aspect non-local network for scene text recognition. PR 117, 107980 (2021)
30. Mishra, A., Alahari, K., Jawahar, C.V.: Scene text recognition using higher order language priors. In: BMVC, pp. 1–11 (2012)
31. Phan, T.Q., Shivakumara, P., Tian, S., Tan, C.L.: Recognizing text with perspective distortion in natural scenes. In: ICCV, pp. 569–576 (2013)
32. Qiao, Z., et al.: Pimnet: a parallel, iterative and mimicking network for scene text recognition. In: ACM MM, pp. 2046–2055 (2021)
33. Qiao, Z., Zhou, Y., Yang, D., Zhou, Y., Wang, W.: SEED: semantics enhanced encoder-decoder framework for scene text recognition. In: CVPR, pp. 13525–13534 (2020)
34. Risnumawan, A., Shivakumara, P., Chan, C.S., Tan, C.L.: A robust arbitrary text detection system for natural scene images. Expert Syst. Appl. 41(18), 8027–8048 (2014)
35. Sheng, F., Chen, Z., Xu, B.: NRTR: a no-recurrence sequence-to-sequence model for scene text recognition. In: ICDAR, pp. 781–786 (2019)
36. Shi, B., Bai, X., Yao, C.: An end-to-end trainable neural network for image-based sequence recognition and its application to scene text recognition. IEEE TPAMI 39(11), 2298–2304 (2017)
37. Shi, B., Yang, M., Wang, X., Lyu, P., Yao, C., Bai, X.: ASTER: an attentional scene text recognizer with flexible rectification. IEEE TPAMI 41(9), 2035–2048 (2019)
38. Su, W., et al.: VL-BERT: pre-training of generic visual-linguistic representations. In: ICLR (2020)
39. Vaswani, A., et al.: Attention is all you need. In: NeurIPS, pp. 5998–6008 (2017)
40. Wan, Z., He, M., Chen, H., Bai, X., Yao, C.: Textscanner: reading characters in order for robust scene text recognition. In: AAAI, pp. 12120–12127 (2020)
41. Wan, Z., Xie, F., Liu, Y., Bai, X., Yao, C.: 2d-ctc for scene text recognition. arXiv preprint arXiv:1907.09705 (2019)
42. Wan, Z., Zhang, J., Zhang, L., Luo, J., Yao, C.: On vocabulary reliance in scene text recognition. In: CVPR, pp. 11422–11431 (2020)
43. Wang, K., Babenko, B., Belongie, S.J.: End-to-end scene text recognition. In: ICCV, pp. 1457–1464 (2011)

44. Wang, T., et al.: Decoupled attention network for text recognition. In: AAAI, pp. 12216–12224 (2020)
45. Wang, Y., Xie, H., Fang, S., Wang, J., Zhu, S., Zhang, Y.: From two to one: a new scene text recognizer with visual language modeling network. In: ICCV, pp. 1–10 (2021)
46. Yang, M., et al.: Symmetry-constrained rectification network for scene text recognition. In: ICCV, pp. 9146–9155 (2019)
47. Yu, D., et al.: Towards accurate scene text recognition with semantic reasoning networks. In: CVPR, pp. 12110–12119 (2020)
48. Yue, X., Kuang, Z., Lin, C., Sun, H., Zhang, W.: RobustScanner: dynamically enhancing positional clues for robust text recognition. In: Vedaldi, A., Bischof, H., Brox, T., Frahm, J.-M. (eds.) ECCV 2020. LNCS, vol. 12364, pp. 135–151. Springer, Cham (2020). https://doi.org/10.1007/978-3-030-58529-7_9
49. Zeiler, M.D.: ADADELTA: an adaptive learning rate method. CoRR abs/1212.5701 (2012)
50. Zhan, F., Lu, S.: ESIR: end-to-end scene text recognition via iterative image rectification. In: CVPR, pp. 2059–2068 (2019)
51. Zhang, X., Zhu, B., Yao, X., Sun, Q., Li, R., Yu, B.: Context-based contrastive learning for scene text recognition. In: AAAI, pp. 888–896 (2022)
52. Zhu, Y., Yao, C., Bai, X.: Scene text detection and recognition: recent advances and future trends. Front. Comput. Sci. **10**(1), 19–36 (2016)

Multi-granularity Prediction for Scene Text Recognition

Peng Wang, Cheng Da, and Cong Yao[✉]

Alibaba DAMO Academy, Beijing, China
wdp0072012@gmail.com, dc.dacheng08@gmail.com, yaocong2010@gmail.com

Abstract. Scene text recognition (STR) has been an active research topic in computer vision for years. To tackle this challenging problem, numerous innovative methods have been successively proposed and incorporating linguistic knowledge into STR models has recently become a prominent trend. In this work, we first draw inspiration from the recent progress in Vision Transformer (ViT) to construct a conceptually simple yet powerful vision STR model, which is built upon ViT and outperforms previous state-of-the-art models for scene text recognition, including both pure vision models and language-augmented methods. To integrate linguistic knowledge, we further propose a Multi-Granularity Prediction strategy to inject information from the language modality into the model in an *implicit* way, *i.e.*, subword representations (BPE and WordPiece) widely-used in NLP are introduced into the output space, in addition to the conventional character level representation, while no independent language model (LM) is adopted. The resultant algorithm (termed MGP-STR) is able to push the performance envelop of STR to an even higher level. Specifically, it achieves an average recognition accuracy of 93.35% on standard benchmarks.

Keywords: Scene text recognition · ViT · Multi-granularity prediction

1 Introduction

Reading text from natural scenes is one of the most indispensable abilities when building an automated machine with high-level intelligence. This explains the reason why researchers from the computer vision community sedulously have explored and investigated this complex and challenging task for decades. Scene text recognition (STR) involves decoding textual content from natural images (usually cropped sub images), which is a key component in text reading pipelines.

Previously, a number of methods [5,30,39,41] have been proposed to address the problem of scene text recognition. Recently, there emerges a new trend that linguistic knowledge is introduced into the text recognition process. SRN [53] devised a global semantic reasoning module (GSRM) to model global semantic context. ABINet [9] proposed bidirectional cloze network (BCN) as the language model to learn bidirectional feature representation. Both SRN and ABINet adopt an independent and separate language model to capture rich language prior.

P. Wang and C. Da—Equal contribution.

© The Author(s), under exclusive license to Springer Nature Switzerland AG 2022
S. Avidan et al. (Eds.): ECCV 2022, LNCS 13688, pp. 339–355, 2022.
https://doi.org/10.1007/978-3-031-19815-1_20

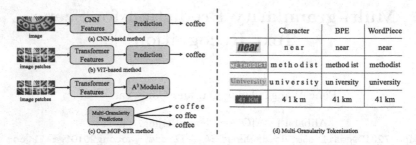

Fig. 1. Pipelines of classic CNN-based, ViT-based and the proposed MGP-STR scene text recognition methods are illustrated in (a), (b) and (c), respectively. (d) Examples of Character, BPE and WordPiece subword tokenization. (Best viewed in color.) (Color figure online)

In this paper, we propose to integrate linguistic knowledge in an *implicit* way for scene text recognition. Specifically, we first construct a pure vision STR model based on ViT [8] and a tailored Adaptive Addressing and Aggregation (A^3) module inspired by TokenLearner [36]. This model serves as a strong baseline, which already achieves better performance than previous methods for scene text recognition, according to the experimental comparisons. To further make use of linguistic knowledge to enhance the vision STR model, we explore a Multi-Granularity Prediction (MGP) strategy to inject information from the language modality. The output space of the model is expanded that subword representations (BPE and WordPiece) are introduced, *i.e.*, the augmented model would produce two extra subword-level predictions, besides the original character-level prediction. Notably, there is no independent and separate language model. In the training phase, the resultant model (named MGP-STR) is optimized with a standard multi-task learning paradigm (three losses for three types of predictions) and the linguistic knowledge is naturally integrated into the ViT-based STR model. In the inference phase, the three types of predictions are fused to give the final prediction result. Experiments on standard benchmarks verify that the proposed MGP-STR algorithm can obtain state-of-the-art performance. Another advantage of MGP-STR is that it does not involve iterative refinement, which could be time-consuming in the inference phase. The pipeline of the proposed MGP-STR algorithm as well as that of previous CNN-based and ViT-based methods are shown in Fig. 1. In a nutshell, the major difference between MGP-STR and other methods is that it generates three types of predictions, representing textual information at different granularities: from individual characters to short character combinations, and even whole words.

The contributions of this work are summarized as follows: (1) We construct a pure vision STR model, which combines ViT with a specially designed A^3 module. It already outperforms existing methods. (2) We explore an implicit way for incorporating linguistic knowledge by introducing subword representations to facilitate multi-granularity prediction, and prove that an independent language model (as used in SRN and ABINet) is not indispensable for STR models. (3) The proposed MGP-STR algorithm achieves state-of-the-art performance.

2   Related Work

Scene Text Recognition (STR) is a long-term subject of attention and research [4, 28,58]. With the popularity of deep learning methods [13,21,42], its effectiveness in the field of STR has been extensively verified. Depending on whether linguistic information is applied, we roughly divide STR methods into two categories, *i.e.*, language-free and language-augmented methods.

2.1   Language-Free STR Methods

The mainstream way for image feature extraction in STR methods is CNN [13, 42]. For example, previous STR methods [21,39,40] utilize VGG. Current STR methods [2,3,26,48] employ ResNet [13] for better performance. Based on the powerful CNN features, various methods [25,33,57] are proposed to tackle the STR problem. CTC-based methods [14,15,26,39,46] use the Connectionist Temporal Classication (CTC) [10] to accomplish sequence recognition. Segmentation-based methods [23,24,45,47] cast STR as a semantic segmentation problems.

Inspired by the great success of Transformer [44] in natural language processing (NLP) tasks, the application of Transformer in STR has also attracted more attention. Vision Transformer (ViT) [8] that directly processes image patches without convolutions opens the beginning of using Transformer blocks instead of CNNs to solve computer vision problems [27,52], leading to prominent results. ViTSTR [1] attempts to simply leverage the feature representations of the last layer of ViT for parallel character decoding. In general, language-free methods often fail to recognize low-quality images due to the lack of language information.

2.2   Language-Augmented STR Methods

Obviously, language information is favourable to the recognition of low-quality images. RNN-based methods [21,39,48] can effectively capture the dependency between sequential characters, which can be regarded as an implicit language model. However, they cannot execute decoding in parallel during training and inference. Recently, Transformer blocks are introduced into CNN-based framework to facilitate language content learning. SRN [53] proposes a Global Semantic Reasoning Module (GSRM) to capture the global semantic context through multiple parallel transmissions. ABINet [9] presents a Bidirectional Cloze Network (BCN) to explicitly model the language information, which is further used for iterative correction. VisionLAN [51] proposes a visual reasoning module that simultaneously captures visual and language information by masking input images at the feature level. The mentioned above approaches utilize a specific module to integrate language information. Meanwhile, most works [9,16] capture semantic information based on character-level or word-level. In this paper, we manage to utilize multi-granularity (character, subword and even word) semantic information based on BPE and WordPiece tokenizations.

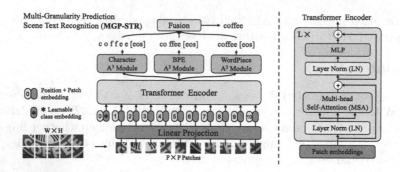

Fig. 2. The architecture of the proposed MGP-STR algorithm.

3   Methodology

The overview of the proposed MGP-STR method is depicted in Fig. 2, which is mainly built upon the original Vision Transformer (ViT) model [8]. We propose a tailored Adaptive Addressing and Aggregation (A^3) module to select a meaningful combination of tokens from ViT and integrate them into one output token corresponding to a specific character, denoted as Character A^3 module. Moreover, subword classification heads based on BPE A^3 module and WordPiece A^3 module are devised for subword predictions, so that the language information can be implicitly modelled. Finally, these multi-granularity predictions are merged via a simple and effective fusion strategy.

3.1   Vision Transformer Backbone

The fundamental architecture of MGP-STR is Vision Transformer [8,43], where the original image patches are directly utilized for image feature extraction by linear projection. As shown in Fig. 2, an input RGB image $\mathbf{x} \in \mathbb{R}^{H \times W \times C}$ is split into non-overlapping patches. Concretely, the image is reshaped into a sequence of flattened 2D patches $\mathbf{x}_p \in \mathbb{R}^{N \times (P^2 C)}$, where $(P \times P)$ is the resolution of each image patch and $(P^2 C)$ is the number of feature channels of $\mathbf{x}_p$. In this way, a 2D image is represented as a sequence with $N = HW/P^2$ tokens, which serve as the effective input sequence of Transformer blocks. Then, these tokens of $\mathbf{x}_p$ are linear transcribed into D dimension patch embeddings. Similar to the original ViT [8] backbone, a learnable [*class*] token embedding with D dimension is introduced into patch embeddings. And position embeddings are also added to each patch embedding to retain the positional information, where the standard learnable $1D$ position embedding is employed. Thus, the generation of patch embedding vector is formulated as follows:

$$\mathbf{z}_0 = [\mathbf{x}_{class}; \mathbf{x}_p^1 \mathbf{E}; \mathbf{x}_p^2 \mathbf{E}; \dots; \mathbf{x}_p^N \mathbf{E}] + \mathbf{E}_{pos}, \tag{1}$$

where $\mathbf{x}_{class} \in \mathbb{R}^{1 \times D}$ is the [*class*] embedding, $\mathbf{E} \in \mathbb{R}^{(P^2 C) \times D}$ is a linear projection matrix and $\mathbf{E}_{pos} \in \mathbb{R}^{(N+1) \times D}$ is the position embedding.

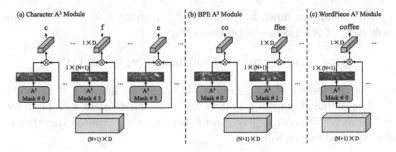

Fig. 3. The detailed architectures of the three A^3 modules.

The resultant feature sequence $\mathbf{z}_0 \in \mathbb{R}^{(N+1)\times D}$ serves as the input of Transformer encoder blocks, which are mainly composed of Multi-head Self-Attention (MSA), Layer Normalization (LN), Multilayer Perceptron (MLP) and residual connection as in Fig. 2. The Transformer encoder block is formulated as:

$$\mathbf{z}'_l = \text{MSA}(LN(\mathbf{z}_{l-1})) + \mathbf{z}_{l-1}$$
$$\mathbf{z}_l = \text{MLP}(LN(\mathbf{z}'_l)) + \mathbf{z}'_l. \qquad (2)$$

Here, L is the depth of Transformer block and $l = 1 \ldots L$. The MLP consists of two linear layers with GELU activation. Finally, the output embedding $\mathbf{z}_L \in \mathbb{R}^{(N+1)\times D}$ of Transformer is utilized for subsequent text recognition.

3.2 Adaptive Addressing and Aggregation (A^3) Modules

Traditional Vision Transformers [8,43] usually prepend a learnable $\mathbf{x}_{class}$ token to the sequence of patch embeddings, which directly collects and aggregates the meaningful information and serves as the image representation for the classification of the whole image. While the task of scene text recognition aims to produce a sequence of character predictions, where each character is only related to a small patch of the image. Thus, the global image representation $\mathbf{z}_L^0 \in \mathbb{R}^D$ is inadequate for text recognizing task. ViTSTR [1] directly employs the first T tokens of $\mathbf{z}_L$ for text recognition, where T is the maximum text length. Unfortunately, the rest tokens of $\mathbf{z}_L$ are not fully utilized.

In order to take full advantage of the rich information of the sequence $\mathbf{z}_L$ for text sequence prediction, we propose a tailored Adaptive Addressing and Aggregation (A^3) module to select a meaningful combination of tokens $\mathbf{z}_L$ and integrate them into one token corresponding to a specific character. Specifically, we manage to learn T tokens $\mathbf{Y} = [\mathbf{y}_i]_{i=1}^T$ from the sequence $\mathbf{z}_L$ for the subsequent text recognizing task. An aggregation function is, thus, formulated as $\mathbf{y}_i = A_i(\mathbf{z}_L)$, which converts the input $\mathbf{z}_L$ to a token vector $\mathbf{y}_i : \mathbb{R}^{(N+1)\times D} \mapsto \mathbb{R}^{1\times D}$. And such T functions are constructed for the sequential output of text recognition. Typically, the aggregation function $A_i(\mathbf{z}_L)$ is implemented via a spatial attention mechanism [36] to adaptively select the tokens from $\mathbf{z}_L$ corresponding to i_{th} character. Here, we employ function $\alpha_i(\mathbf{z}_L)$ and softmax function to generate precise spatial attention mask $\mathbf{m}_i \in \mathbb{R}^{(N+1) \times 1}$ from $\mathbf{z}_L \in \mathbb{R}^{(N+1) \times D}$. Thus, each output token $\mathbf{y}_i$ of A^3 module is produced by

$$\mathbf{y}_i = A_i(\mathbf{z}_L) = \mathbf{m}_i^T \tilde{\mathbf{z}}_L = \text{softmax}(\alpha_i(\mathbf{z}_L))^T (\mathbf{z}_L \mathbf{U})^T. \tag{3}$$

Here, $\alpha_i(\cdot)$ is implemented by group convolution with one 1×1 kernel. And $\mathbf{U} \in \mathbb{R}^{D \times D}$ is a linear mapping matrix for learning feature $\tilde{\mathbf{z}}_L$. Therefore, the resulting tokens of different aggregation functions are gathered together to form the final output tensor as follows:

$$\mathbf{Y} = [\mathbf{y}_1 \mathbf{y}_2; \ldots; \mathbf{y}_T] = [A_1(\mathbf{z}_L); A_2(\mathbf{z}_L); \ldots; A_T(\mathbf{z}_L)]. \tag{4}$$

Owing to the effective and efficient A^3 module, the ultimate representation of the text sequence is denoted as $\mathbf{Y} \in \mathbb{R}^{T \times D}$ in Eq. (4). Then, a character classification head is built by $\mathbf{G} = \mathbf{Y} \mathbf{W}^T \in \mathbb{R}^{T \times K}$ for text sequence recognition, where $\mathbf{W} \in \mathbb{R}^{K \times D}$ is a linear mapping matrix, K is the number of categories and $\mathbf{G}$ is the classification logist. We regard this module as Character A^3 for character-level prediction, of which the detailed structure is illustrated in Fig. 3(a).

3.3   Multi-granularity Predictions

Character tokenization that simply splits text into characters is commonly-used in scene text recognition methods. However, this naive and standard way ignores the language information of text. In order to effectively resort to linguistic information for scene text recognition, we incorporate subword [20] tokenization mechanism in NLP [7] into text recognition method. Subword tokenization algorithms aim to decompose rare words into meaningful subwords and remain frequently used words, so that the grammatical information of word has already been captured in the subwords. Meanwhile, since A^3 module is independent of Transformer encoder backbone, we can directly add extra parallel subword A^3 modules for subword predictions. In such a way, the language information can be implicitly injected into model learning for better performance. Notably, previous methods, *i.e.*, SRN [53] and ABINet [9], design an explicit transformer module for language modelling, while we cast linguistic information encoding problem as a character and subword prediction task without an explicit language model.

Specifically, we employ two subword tokenization algorithms Byte-Pair Encoding (BPE) [38] and WordPiece [37][1] to produce various combinations as shown in Fig. 1(b)(c). Thus, BPE A^3 module and WordPiece A^3 module are proposed for subword attention. And two subword-level classification heads are used for subword predictions. Since subwords could be whole words (such as "coffee" in WordPiece), subword-level and even word-level predictions can be generated by the BPE and WordPiece classification heads. Along with the original character-level prediction, we denote these various outputs as multi-granularity predictions

---

[1] Considering the potential out-of-vocabulary (OOV) issue in the inference phase, we did not directly predict whole words.

for text recognition. In this way, character-level prediction guarantees the fundamental recognition accuracy, and subword-level or word-level predictions can serve as complementary results for noised images via linguistic information.

Technically, the architecture of BPE or WordPiece A^3 module is the same as Character one. They are independent of each other with different parameters. And the numbers of categories are different for different classification heads, which depend on the vocabulary size of each tokenization method. The cross entropy loss is employed for classification. Additionally, the mask m_i precisely indicates the attention location of the i_{th} character in Character A^3 module, while it roughly shows the i_{th} subword region of the image in subword A^3 modules, due to the higher complexity and uncertainty of learning subword splitting.

3.4 Fusion Strategy for Multi-granularity Results

Multi-granularity predictions (Character, BPE and WordPiece) are generated by different A^3 modules and classification heads. Thus, a fusion strategy is required to merge these results. At the beginning, we attempt to fuse multi-granularity information by aggregating text features $\mathbf{Y}$ of the output of different A^3 modules at feature level. However, since these features are from different granularities, the i_{th} token $\mathbf{y}_i^{char}$ of character level is not aligned with the i_{th} token $\mathbf{y}_i^{bpe}$ (or $\mathbf{y}_i^{wp}$) of BPE level (or WordPiece level), so that these features cannot be added for fusion. Meanwhile, even if we concatenate features by $[\mathbf{Y}_i^{char}, \mathbf{Y}_i^{bpe}, \mathbf{Y}_i^{wp}]$, only one character-level head can be used for final prediction. The subword information will be greatly impaired in this way, resulting in less improvement.

Therefore, decision-level fusion strategy is employed in our method. However, perfectly fusing these predictions is a challenging problem [11]. We, thus, propose a compromised but efficient fusion strategy based on the prediction confidences. Specifically, the recognition confidence of each character or subword can be obtained by the corresponding classification head. Then, we present two fusion functions $f(\cdot)$ to produce the final recognition score based on atomic confidences:

$$f_{Mean}([c_1, c_2, \ldots, c_{eos}]) = \frac{1}{n} \sum_{i=1}^{eos} c_i, \tag{5}$$

$$f_{Cumprod}([c_1, c_2, \ldots, c_{eos}]) = \prod_{i=1}^{eos} c_i. \tag{6}$$

We only consider the confidence of valid character or subword and ending symbol eos, and ignore padding symbol pad. "Mean" recognition score is generated by the mean value function as in Eq. (5). And "Cumprod" represents the score produced by cumulative product function. Then, three recognition scores of three classification heads for one image can be obtained by $f(\cdot)$. We simply pick the one with the highest recognition score as the final predicted result.

4 Experiment

4.1 Datasets

For fair comparison, we use MJSynth [16,17] and SynthText [12] as training data. MJSynth contains $9M$ realistic text images and SynthText includes $7M$ synthetic text images. The test dataset consists of "regular" and "irregular" datasets. The "regular" dataset is mainly composed of horizontally aligned text images. IIIT 5K-Words (IIIT) [31] consists of 3,000 images collected on the website. Street View Text (SVT) [49] contains 647 test images. ICDAR 2013 (IC13) [19] contains 1,095 images cropped from mall pictures, but we eventually evaluate on 857 images, discarding images that contain non-alphanumeric characters or less than three characters. The text instances in the "irregular" dataset are mostly curved or distorted. ICDAR 2015 (IC15) [18] includes 2,077 images collected from Google Eyes, but we use 1,811 images without some extremely distorted images. Street View Text-Perspective (SVTP) [32] contains 639 images collected from Google Street View. CUTE80 (CUTE) [35] consists of 288 curved images.

4.2 Implementation Details

Model Configuration. MGP-STR is built upon DeiT-Base model [43], which is composed of 12 stacked transformer blocks. For each layer, the number of head is 12 and the embedding dimension D is 768. More importantly, square 224×224 images [1,8,43] are not adopted in our method. The height H and width W of the input image are set to 32 and 128. The patch size P is set to 4 and thus $N = 8 \times 32 = 256$ plus one [$class$] tokens $\mathbf{z}_L \in \mathbb{R}^{257 \times 768}$ can be produced. The maximum length T of the output sequence $\mathbf{Y}$ of A^3 module is set to 27. The vocabulary size K of Character classification head is set to 38, including $0-9$, $a-z$, pad for padding symbol and eos for ending symbol. The vocabulary sizes of BPE and WordPiece heads are set to $50,257$ and $30,522$.

Model Training. The pretrained weights of DeiT-base [43] are loaded the initial weights, except the patch embedding model, due to inconsistent patch sizes. Common data augmentation methods [6] for text image are applied, such as perspective distortion, affine distortion, blur, noise and rotation. We use 2 NVIDIA Tesla V100 GPUs to train our model with a batch size of 100. Adadelta [55] optimizer is employed with an initial learning rate of 1. The learning rate decay strategy is Cosine Annealing LR [29] and the training lasts 10 epochs.

4.3 Discussions on Vision Transformer and A^3 Modules

We analyse the influence of the patch size of Vision Transformer and the effectiveness of A^3 module in the proposed MGP-STR method (shown in Table 1). MGP-STR$_{P=16}$ represents the model that simply uses the first T tokens of $\mathbf{z}_L$ for text recognition as in ViTSTR [1], where the input image is reshaped to

Table 1. The ablation study of the proposed vision model and the accuracy comparisons with some SOTA methods based on only vision information.

Methods	Vision	Image size (Patch)	IC13	SVT	IIIT	IC15	SVTP	CUTE	AVG
MASTER [30]	CNN	–	95.3	90.60	95.0	79.4	84.5	87.5	89.5
SRN$_V$ [53]		–	93.2	88.1	92.3	77.5	79.4	84.7	86.9
ABINet$_V$ [9]		–	94.9	90.4	94.6	81.7	84.2	86.5	89.8
MGP-STR$_{P=16}$	ViT	$224 \times 224(16 \times 16)$	95.68	91.96	95.13	83.88	85.74	90.28	91.07
MGP-STR$_{P=4}$		$32 \times 128(4 \times 4)$	96.62	92.27	95.40	84.76	86.98	88.54	91.58
MGP-STR$_{Vision}$		$32 \times 128(4 \times 4)$	96.50	93.20	96.37	86.25	89.46	90.63	92.73

Table 2. The accuracies of MGP-STR$_{Fuse}$ with different fusion strategies.

Method	Mode	IC13	SVT	IIIT	IC15	SVTP	CUTE	AVG
MGP-STR$_{Fuse}$	Char	96.49	93.66	96.1	86.14	88.83	89.58	92.53
	Mean	97.31	94.28	96.60	86.97	90.23	90.97	93.28
	Cumprod	97.32	94.74	96.40	87.24	91.01	90.28	93.35

224×224 and the patch size is set to 16×16. In order to retain the significant information of the original text image, 32×128 images with 4×4 patches are employed in MGP-STR$_{P=4}$. MGP-STR$_{P=4}$ outperforms MGP-STR$_{P=16}$, which indicates that the standard image size of ViT [8,43] is incompatible with text recognition. Thus, 32×128 images with 4×4 patches are used in MGP-STR.

When the Character A^3 module is introduced into MGP-STR, denoted as MGP-STR$_{Vision}$, the recognition performance will be further improved. MGP-STR$_{P=16}$ and MGP-STR$_{P=4}$ cannot fully learn and utilize the all tokens, while the Character A^3 module can adaptively aggregate features of the last layer, resulting in more sufficient learning and higher accuracy. Meanwhile, compared with SOTA text recognition methods with CNN feature extractors, the proposed MGP-STR$_{Vision}$ method achieves substantially performance improvement.

4.4 Discussions on Multi-Granularity Predictions

Effect of Fusion Strategy. Since the subwords generated by subword tokenization methods contain grammatical information, we directly employ subwords as the targets of our method to capture the language information implicitly. As described in Sect. 3.2, two different subword tokenizations (BPE and Word-Piece) are employed for complementary multi-granularity predictions. Besides the character prediction, we propose two fusion strategies to further merge these three results, denoted as "Mean" and "Cumprod" as mentioned in Sect. 3.4. We denote this method that merges three results as MGP-STR$_{Fuse}$, and the accuracy results of MGP-STR$_{Fuse}$ with different fusion strategies are listed in Table 2. Additionally, the first line "Char" in Table 2 records the result of character classification head in MGP-STR$_{Fuse}$. It is clear to see that both "Mean" and "Cumprod" fusion strategies can significantly improve the recognition accuracy over single character-level result. Due the better performance of "Cumprod" strategy, we employ it as the fusion strategy in the following experiments.

Table 3. The accuracy results of the four variants of MGP-STR model. "Char", "BPE" and "WP" at "Output" represent predictions of Character, BPE and WordPiece classification head in each model, respectively. "Fuse" represents the fused results.

Methods	Char	BPE	WP	Output	IC13	SVT	IIIT	IC15	SVTP	CUTE	AVG
MGP-STR$_{Vision}$	✓	×	×	Char	96.50	93.20	96.37	86.25	89.46	90.63	92.73
MGP-STR$_{C+B}$	✓	✓	×	Char	97.43	93.82	96.53	85.92	89.15	90.28	92.84
				BPE	97.78	94.13	90.00	81.12	88.37	82.64	88.63
				Fuse	97.67	94.47	96.73	86.97	88.99	89.93	93.24
MGP-STR$_{C+W}$	✓	×	✓	Char	96.97	93.97	96.30	86.20	90.39	89.93	92.87
				WP	95.92	93.35	87.70	78.74	89.30	80.21	86.78
				Fuse	97.32	93.82	96.60	86.91	90.54	90.97	93.25
MGP-STR$_{Fuse}$	✓	✓	✓	Char	96.49	93.66	96.10	86.14	88.83	89.58	92.53
				BPE	95.56	93.66	88.73	79.84	89.76	83.33	87.63
				WP	95.79	94.59	86.37	77.36	89.61	79.86	85.99
				Fuse	97.32	94.74	96.40	87.24	91.01	90.28	93.35

Effect of Subword Representations. We evaluate four variants of the MGP-STR model, and the performances of these four methods are elaborately reported in Table 3, including the fused results and the results of each single classification. Specifically, MGP-STR$_{Vision}$ with only Character A^3 module has already obtained promising results. MGP-STR$_{C+B}$ and MGP-STR$_{C+W}$ incorporate Character A^3 module with BPE A^3 module and WordPiece A^3 module, respectively. No matter which subword tokenization is used alone, the accuracy of "Fuse" can exceed that of "Char" in both MGP-STR$_{C+B}$ and MGP-STR$_{C+W}$ methods, respectively. Notably, the performance of the classification of "BPE" or "WP" could be better than that of "Char" on SVP and SVTP datasets in the same model. These results show that subword predictions can boost text recognition performance by implicitly introducing language information. Thus, MGP-STR$_{Fuse}$ with three A^3 modules can produce complementary multi-granularity predictions (character, subword and even word). By fusing these multi-granularity results, MGP-STR$_{Fuse}$ obtains the best performance.

Comparison with BCN. Bidirectional cloze network (BCN) is designed in ABINet [9] for explicit language modelling, and it leads to favorable improvement over pure vision model. We equip MGP-STR$_{Vision}$ with BCN as a competitor of MGP-STR$_{Fuse}$ to verify the advantage of multi-granularity predictions. Concretely, we first reduce the dimension 768 of representation feature $\mathbf{Y}$ to 512 for feature fusion of the output of BCN. Following the training setting in [9], the model results are reported in Table 4. The accuracy of "V+L" is further improved over the pure vision prediction "V" in MGP-STR$_{Vision}$+BCN, and better than the original ABINet [9]. However, the performance of MGP-STR$_{Vision}$+BCN is a little worse than that of MGP-STR$_{Fuse}$. In addition, we provide the upper bound on the performance of MGP-STR$_{Fuse}$, denoted as MGP-STR$_{Fuse}^{*}$ in Table 4. If one of the three predictions ("Char", "BPE" and "WP") is right, the final prediction is considered correct. The highest score of MGP-STR$_{Fuse}^{*}$ demonstrates

Table 4. The accuracy results of MGP-STR$_{Vision}$ equipped with BCN and multi-granularity prediction. "V" represents the results of the pure vision output. "V+L" represents the results based on the both vision and language parts.

Methods	Mode	IC13	SVT	IIIT	IC15	SVTP	CUTE	AVG
MGP-STR$_{Vision}$+BCN	V	96.97	93.82	95.90	85.53	89.15	89.58	92.40
	V+L	97.32	95.36	95.97	86.69	91.78	89.93	93.14
MGP-STR$_{Fuse}$	V+L	97.32	94.74	96.40	87.24	91.01	90.28	93.35
MGP-STR$_{Fuse}^{*}$	V+L	97.66	96.29	96.97	89.06	92.09	92.01	94.38

Table 5. The accuracy results of MGP-STR$_{Fuse}$ with different ViT backbones.

Backbone	Output	IC13	SVT	IIIT	IC15	SVTP	CUTE	AVG
DeiT-Tiny	Char	93.47	90.57	93.93	82.94	81.71	84.38	89.36
	BPE	87.40	84.39	83.17	73.72	77.83	71.53	80.48
	WP	53.79	45.44	60.07	52.57	42.79	42.71	53.92
	Fuse	94.05	91.19	94.30	83.38	83.57	84.38	89.91
DeiT-Small	Char	95.92	91.04	94.97	84.59	85.89	86.81	91.01
	BPE	96.27	93.35	89.37	79.74	86.67	82.29	87.61
	WP	75.50	70.48	74.70	66.81	68.06	62.15	71.36
	Fuse	96.38	93.51	95.30	86.09	87.29	87.85	91.96
DeiT-Base	Char	96.49	93.66	96.10	86.14	88.83	89.58	92.53
	BPE	95.56	93.66	88.73	79.84	89.76	83.33	87.63
	WP	95.79	94.59	86.37	77.36	89.61	79.86	85.99
	Fuse	97.32	94.74	96.40	87.24	91.01	90.28	93.35

the good potential of multi-granularity predictions. Moreover, MGP-STR$_{Fuse}$ only requires two new subword prediction heads, rather than the design of a specific and explicit language model in [9,53].

4.5 Results with Different ViT Backbones

All of the proposed MGP-STR models mentioned earlier are based on DeiT-Base [43]. We also introduce two smaller models, namely DeiT-Small and DeiT-Tiny as presented in [43] to further evaluate the effectiveness of MGP-STR$_{Fuse}$ method. Specifically, the embedding dimensions of DeiT-Small and DeiT-Tiny are reduced to 384 and 192, respectively. Table 5 records the results of each prediction head of the MGP-STR$_{Fuse}$ method with different ViT backbones. Clearly, fusing multi-granularity predictions can still improve the performance of pure character-level prediction in every backbone. And bigger models achieve better performance in the same head. More importantly, the results of "Char" in DeiT-Small and even DeiT-Tiny have already surpassed the SOTA pure CNN-based vision models, referring to Table 1. Therefore, MGP-STR$_{Vision}$ with small or tiny ViT backbone is also a competitive vision model and multi-granularity prediction can also work well in different ViT backbones.

Table 6. The comparisons with SOTA methods on several public benchmarks.

Methods	Regular text			Irregular text			AVG
	IC13	SVT	IIIT	IC15	SVTP	CUTE	
TBRA [2]	93.6	87.5	87.9	77.6	79.2	74.0	84.6
ViTSTR [1]	93.2	87.7	88.4	78.5	81.8	81.3	85.6
ESIR [56]	91.3	90.2	93.3	76.9	79.6	83.3	87.1
DAN [50]	93.9	89.2	94.3	74.5	80.0	84.4	87.2
SE-ASTER [34]	92.8	89.6	93.8	80.0	81.4	83.6	88.3
RobustScanner [54]	94.8	88.1	95.3	77.1	79.5	90.3	88.4
TextScanner [45]	92.9	90.1	93.9	79.4	84.3	83.3	88.5
SATRN [22]	94.1	91.3	92.8	79.0	86.5	87.8	88.6
MASTER [30]	95.3	90.6	95.0	79.4	84.5	87.5	89.5
SRN [53]	95.5	91.5	94.8	82.7	85.1	87.8	90.4
VisionLAN [51]	95.7	91.7	95.8	83.7	86.0	88.5	91.2
ABINet [9]	**97.4**	93.5	96.2	86.0	89.3	89.2	92.6
MGP-STR$_{Vision}$	96.50	93.20	96.37	86.25	89.46	**90.63**	92.73
MGP-STR$_{Fuse}$	97.32	**94.74**	**96.40**	**87.24**	**91.01**	90.28	**93.35**

4.6   Comparisons with State-of-the-Arts

We compare the proposed MGP-STR$_{Vision}$ and MGP-STR$_{Fuse}$ methods with previous state-of-the-art scene text recognition methods, and the results on 6 standard benchmarks are summarized in Table 6. All of compared methods and ours are trained on synthetic datasets MJ and ST for fair evaluation. And the results are obtained without any lexicon based post-processing. Generally, language-aware methods (*i.e.*, SRN [53], VisionLAN [51], ABINet [9] and MGP-STR$_{Fuse}$) perform better than other language-free methods, showing the significance of linguistic information. Notably, MGP-STR$_{Vision}$ without any language information has already outperformed the state-of-the-art method ABINet with explicit language model. Owing to the multi-granularity prediction, MGP-STR$_{Fuse}$ obtains more impressive results further, which outperforms ABINet with 0.7% improvement on average accuracy.

4.7   Details of Multi-Granularity Predictions

We show the detailed prediction process of the proposed MGP-STR$_{Fuse}$ method on 6 test images from standard datasets. In the first three images, the results of character-level prediction are incorrect, due to irregular font, motion blur and curved shape, respectively. The scores of character prediction are very low, since the images are difficult to recognize and one character is wrong in each image. However, "BPE" and "WP" heads can recognize "table" image with high scores. And "BPE" can make correct predictions with two subwords on "dvisory" and "watercourse" images, while "WP" is wrong in "watercourse" image. After fusion, the mistakes can be corrected. From the rest three images,

Table 7. The details of multi-granularity prediction of MGP-STR$_{Fuse}$, including the scores of each prediction head, the intermediate multi-granularity (Gra.) results and the final prediction (Pred.). Best viewed in color.

Images	GT	Output	Char	BPE	WP	Fuse
		Score	0.1643	0.9813	0.9521	0.9813
	table	Gra.	tabbe	table	table	-
		Pred.	tabbe	table	table	table
		Score	0.0316	0.8218	0.2574	0.8218
	dvisory	Gra.	divsoory	d visory	dvisory	-
		Pred.	divsoory	dvisory	dvisory	dvisory
		Score	0.1565	0.8295	0.632	0.8295
	watercourse	Gra.	watercourss	water course	waterco	-
		Pred.	watercourss	watercourse	waterco	watercourse
		Score	0.9999	0.9207	0.0354	0.9999
	1869	Gra.	1869	18 69	18	-
		Pred.	1869	1869	18	1869
		Score	0.9998	0.5983	0.7638	0.9998
	thday	Gra.	thday	th day	today	-
		Pred.	thday	thday	today	thday
		Score	0.9675	0.6959	0.1131	0.9675
	guide	Gra.	guice	gu ice	guide	-
		Pred.	guice	guice	guide	guice

interesting phenomena can be observed. The predictions of "Char" and "BPE" conform to the images. The predictions of "WP", however, attempt to produce strings with more linguistic content, like "today" and "guide". Generally, "Char" aims to produce characters one by one, while "BPE" usually generates n-gram segments related to image and "WP" tends to directly predict words that are linguistically meaningful. These prove the predictions of different granularities convey text information in different aspects and are indeed complementary.

4.8   Visualization of Spatial Attention Maps of A³ Modules

Exemplar attention maps m_i of Character, BPE and WordPiece A^3 modules are shown in Fig. 4. Character A^3 module shows extremely precise addressing ability on a variety of text images. Specifically, for the "7" image with one character, the attention mask seems like the "7" shape. For the "day" and "bar" images with three characters, the attention masks of middle character "a" are completely different, verifying the adaptiveness of A^3 module. As depicted in Fig. 1(d) and in Table 7, BPE tends to generate short segments, thus the attention masks of BPE are spilt into 2 or 3 areas as shown in "leaves" and "academy" images. This is probably because that performing subword splitting and character addressing simultaneously is difficult. Moreover, WordPiece often produces a whole word, and the attention maps should be the whole feature map. Since the attention maps produced by the softmax function are usually sparse, the attention maps of

WordPiece are not as appealing as those of Character A^3 module. These results are consistent to those of Table 3, where the accuracies of "BPE" and "WP" are relatively lower than "Char", due to the difficulty of precise subword prediction.

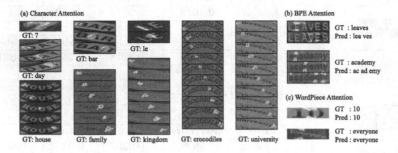

Fig. 4. The illustration of spatial attention masks on Character A^3 module, BPE A^3 module and WordPiece A^3 module, respectively.

4.9   Comparisons of Inference Time and Model Size

Table 8. Comparisons on inference time and model size.

Methods	Time (ms/image)	Parameters (1×10^6)
ABINet-S-iter1/iter2/iter3	13.7/18.6/24.3	32.8
ABINet-L-iter1/iter2/iter3	16.1/21.4/26.8	36.7
MGP-STR$_{Vision}$-tiny/small/base	10.6/10.8/10.9	5.4/21.4/85.5
MGP-STR$_{Fuse}$-tiny/small/base	12.0/12.2/12.3	21.0/52.6/148.0

The model sizes and latencies of the proposed MGP-STR with different settings as well as those of ABINet are depicted in Table 8[2]. Since MGP-STR is equipped with a regular Vision Transformer (ViT) and involves no iterative refinement, the inference speed of MGP-STR is very fast: 12.3 ms with ViT-Base backbone. Compared with ABINet, MGP-STR runs much faster (12.3 ms vs. 26.8 ms), while obtaining higher performance. The model size of MGP-STR is relatively large. However, a large portion of the model parameter is from the BPE and Word-Piece branches. For the scenarios that are sensitive to model size or with limited memory space, MGP-STR$_{Vision}$ is an excellent choice.

5   Conclusion

We presented a ViT-based pure vision model for STR, which shows its superiority in recognition accuracy. To further promote recognition accuracy of this

---

[2] All the evaluations are conducted on a NVIDIA V100 GPU.

baseline model, we proposed a Multi-Granularity Prediction strategy to take advantage of linguistic knowledge. The resultant model achieves state-of-the-art performance on widely-used datasets. In the future, we will extend the idea of multi-granularity prediction to broader domains.

References

1. Atienza, R.: Vision transformer for fast and efficient scene text recognition. In: Lladós, J., Lopresti, D., Uchida, S. (eds.) ICDAR 2021. LNCS, vol. 12821, pp. 319–334. Springer, Cham (2021). https://doi.org/10.1007/978-3-030-86549-8_21
2. Baek, J., et al.: What is wrong with scene text recognition model comparisons? dataset and model analysis. In: ICCV, pp. 4714–4722 (2019)
3. Borisyuk, F., Gordo, A., Sivakumar, V.: Rosetta: large scale system for text detection and recognition in images. In: Guo, Y., Farooq, F. (eds.) SIGKDD, pp. 71–79 (2018)
4. Chen, X., Jin, L., Zhu, Y., Luo, C., Wang, T.: Text recognition in the wild: a survey. ACM Comput. Surv. (CSUR) **54**(2), 1–35 (2021)
5. Cheng, Z., Bai, F., Xu, Y., Zheng, G., Pu, S., Zhou, S.: Focusing attention: towards accurate text recognition in natural images. In: CVPR, pp. 5086–5094 (2017)
6. Cubuk, E.D., Zoph, B., Shlens, J., Le, Q.V.: Randaugment: practical automated data augmentation with a reduced search space. In: CVPR Workshops, pp. 3008–3017 (2020)
7. Devlin, J., Chang, M., Lee, K., Toutanova, K.: BERT: pre-training of deep bidirectional transformers for language understanding. In: NAACL-HLT, pp. 4171–4186 (2019)
8. Dosovitskiy, A., et al.: An image is worth 16x16 words: transformers for image recognition at scale. In: ICLR (2021)
9. Fang, S., Xie, H., Wang, Y., Mao, Z., Zhang, Y.: Read like humans: Autonomous, bidirectional and iterative language modeling for scene text recognition. In: CVPR, pp. 7098–7107 (2021)
10. Graves, A., Fernández, S., Gomez, F.J., Schmidhuber, J.: Connectionist temporal classification: labelling unsegmented sequence data with recurrent neural networks. In: ICML. vol. 148, pp. 369–376 (2006)
11. Gu, J., Meng, G., Da, C., Xiang, S., Pan, C.: No-reference image quality assessment with reinforcement recursive list-wise ranking. In: AAAI, pp. 8336–8343 (2019)
12. Gupta, A., Vedaldi, A., Zisserman, A.: Synthetic data for text localisation in natural images. In: CVPR, pp. 2315–2324 (2016)
13. He, K., Zhang, X., Ren, S., Sun, J.: Deep residual learning for image recognition. In: CVPR, pp. 770–778 (2016)
14. He, P., Huang, W., Qiao, Y., Loy, C.C., Tang, X.: Reading scene text in deep convolutional sequences. In: AAAI, pp. 3501–3508 (2016)
15. Hu, W., Cai, X., Hou, J., Yi, S., Lin, Z.: GTC: guided training of CTC towards efficient and accurate scene text recognition. In: AAAI, pp. 11005–11012 (2020)
16. Jaderberg, M., Simonyan, K., Vedaldi, A., Zisserman, A.: Synthetic data and artificial neural networks for natural scene text recognition. In: NIPS Deep Learning Workshop (2014)
17. Jaderberg, M., Simonyan, K., Vedaldi, A., Zisserman, A.: Reading text in the wild with convolutional neural networks. Int. J. Comput. Vis. **116**(1), 1–20 (2016)

18. Karatzas, D., et al.: ICDAR 2015 competition on robust reading. In: ICDAR, pp. 1156–1160 (2015)
19. Karatzas, D., et al.: ICDAR 2013 robust reading competition. In: ICDAR, pp. 1484–1493 (2013)
20. Labeau, M., Allauzen, A.: Character and subword-based word representation for neural language modeling prediction. In: SWCN@EMNLP, pp. 1–13 (2017)
21. Lee, C., Osindero, S.: Recursive recurrent nets with attention modeling for OCR in the wild. In: CVPR, pp. 2231–2239 (2016)
22. Lee, J., Park, S., Baek, J., Oh, S.J., Kim, S., Lee, H.: On recognizing texts of arbitrary shapes with 2d self-attention. In: CVPR Workshops, pp. 2326–2335 (2020)
23. Liao, M., Lyu, P., He, M., Yao, C., Wu, W., Bai, X.: Mask textspotter: an end-to-end trainable neural network for spotting text with arbitrary shapes. IEEE Trans. Pattern Anal. Mach. Intell. **43**(2), 532–548 (2021)
24. Liao, M., Zhang, J., Wan, Z., Xie, F., Liang, J., Lyu, P., Yao, C., Bai, X.: Scene text recognition from two-dimensional perspective. In: AAAI. pp. 8714–8721 (2019)
25. Liu, H., et al.: Perceiving stroke-semantic context: Hierarchical contrastive learning for robust scene text recognition. In: AAAI, pp. 1702–1710 (2022)
26. Liu, W., Chen, C., Wong, K.K., Su, Z., Han, J.: Star-net: a spatial attention residue network for scene text recognition. In: BMVC (2016)
27. Liu, Z., et al.: Swin transformer: hierarchical vision transformer using shifted windows. CoRR abs/2103.14030 (2021)
28. Long, S., He, X., Yao, C.: Scene text detection and recognition: the deep learning era. IJCV **129**(1), 161–184 (2021)
29. Loshchilov, I., Hutter, F.: SGDR: stochastic gradient descent with warm restarts. In: ICLR (2017)
30. Lu, N., Yu, W., Qi, X., Chen, Y., Gong, P., Xiao, R., Bai, X.: MASTER: multi-aspect non-local network for scene text recognition. Pattern Recogn. **117**, 107980 (2021)
31. Mishra, A., Alahari, K., Jawahar, C.V.: Scene text recognition using higher order language priors. In: BMVC. pp. 1–11 (2012)
32. Phan, T.Q., Shivakumara, P., Tian, S., Tan, C.L.: Recognizing text with perspective distortion in natural scenes. In: ICCV, pp. 569–576 (2013)
33. Qiao, Z., et al.: Pimnet: a parallel, iterative and mimicking network for scene text recognition. In: ACM MM, pp. 2046–2055 (2021)
34. Qiao, Z., Zhou, Y., Yang, D., Zhou, Y., Wang, W.: SEED: semantics enhanced encoder-decoder framework for scene text recognition. In: CVPR, pp. 13525–13534 (2020)
35. Risnumawan, A., Shivakumara, P., Chan, C.S., Tan, C.L.: A robust arbitrary text detection system for natural scene images. Expert Syst. Appl. **41**(18), 8027–8048 (2014)
36. Ryoo, M.S., Piergiovanni, A.J., Arnab, A., Dehghani, M., Angelova, A.: Token-learner: what can 8 learned tokens do for images and videos? CoRR abs/2106.11297 (2021)
37. Schuster, M., Nakajima, K.: Japanese and Korean voice search. In: ICASSP, pp. 5149–5152 (2012)
38. Sennrich, R., Haddow, B., Birch, A.: Neural machine translation of rare words with subword units. In: ACL. The Association for Computer Linguistics (2016)
39. Shi, B., Bai, X., Yao, C.: An end-to-end trainable neural network for image-based sequence recognition and its application to scene text recognition. IEEE TPAMI **39**(11), 2298–2304 (2017)

40. Shi, B., Wang, X., Lyu, P., Yao, C., Bai, X.: Robust scene text recognition with automatic rectification. In: CVPR, pp. 4168–4176 (2016)
41. Shi, B., Yang, M., Wang, X., Lyu, P., Yao, C., Bai, X.: ASTER: an attentional scene text recognizer with flexible rectification. IEEE TPAMI **41**(9), 2035–2048 (2019)
42. Simonyan, K., Zisserman, A.: Very deep convolutional networks for large-scale image recognition. In: ICLR (2015)
43. Touvron, H., Cord, M., Douze, M., Massa, F., Sablayrolles, A., Jégou, H.: Training data-efficient image transformers & distillation through attention. In: ICML, vol. 139, pp. 10347–10357 (2021)
44. Vaswani, A., et al.: Attention is all you need. In: NeurIPS, pp. 5998–6008 (2017)
45. Wan, Z., He, M., Chen, H., Bai, X., Yao, C.: Textscanner: reading characters in order for robust scene text recognition. In: AAAI, pp. 12120–12127 (2020)
46. Wan, Z., Xie, F., Liu, Y., Bai, X., Yao, C.: 2d-ctc for scene text recognition. arXiv preprint arXiv:1907.09705 (2019)
47. Wan, Z., Zhang, J., Zhang, L., Luo, J., Yao, C.: On vocabulary reliance in scene text recognition. In: CVPR, pp. 11422–11431 (2020)
48. Wang, J., Hu, X.: Gated recurrent convolution neural network for OCR. In: NeurIPS, pp. 335–344 (2017)
49. Wang, K., Babenko, B., Belongie, S.J.: End-to-end scene text recognition. In: ICCV, pp. 1457–1464 (2011)
50. Wang, T., et al.: Decoupled attention network for text recognition. In: AAAI, pp. 12216–12224 (2020)
51. Wang, Y., Xie, H., Fang, S., Wang, J., Zhu, S., Zhang, Y.: From two to one: a new scene text recognizer with visual language modeling network. In: ICCV, pp. 1–10 (2021)
52. Xie, E., Wang, W., Yu, Z., Anandkumar, A., Alvarez, J.M., Luo, P.: Segformer: Simple and efficient design for semantic segmentation with transformers. CoRR abs/2105.15203 (2021)
53. Yu, D., et al.: Towards accurate scene text recognition with semantic reasoning networks. In: CVPR, pp. 12110–12119 (2020)
54. Yue, X., Kuang, Z., Lin, C., Sun, H., Zhang, W.: RobustScanner: dynamically enhancing positional clues for robust text recognition. In: Vedaldi, A., Bischof, H., Brox, T., Frahm, J.-M. (eds.) ECCV 2020. LNCS, vol. 12364, pp. 135–151. Springer, Cham (2020). https://doi.org/10.1007/978-3-030-58529-7_9
55. Zeiler, M.D.: ADADELTA: an adaptive learning rate method. CoRR abs/1212.5701 (2012)
56. Zhan, F., Lu, S.: ESIR: end-to-end scene text recognition via iterative image rectification. In: CVPR, pp. 2059–2068 (2019)
57. Zhang, X., Zhu, B., Yao, X., Sun, Q., Li, R., Yu, B.: Context-based contrastive learning for scene text recognition. In: AAAI, pp. 888–896 (2022)
58. Zhu, Y., Yao, C., Bai, X.: Scene text detection and recognition: recent advances and future trends. Front. Comp. Sci. **10**(1), 19–36 (2016)

Dynamic Low-Resolution Distillation for Cost-Efficient End-to-End Text Spotting

Ying Chen[2], Liang Qiao[1,2], Zhanzhan Cheng[2], Shiliang Pu[2(✉)], Yi Niu[2], and Xi Li[1(✉)]

[1] Zhejiang University, Hangzhou, China
{qiaoliang,xilizju}@zju.edu.cn
[2] Hikvision Research Institute, Hanzhou, China
{chenying30,chengzhanzhan,pushiliang.hri,niuyi}@hikvision.com

Abstract. End-to-end text spotting has attached great attention recently due to its benefits on global optimization and high maintainability for real applications. However, the input scale has always been a tough trade-off since recognizing a small text instance usually requires enlarging the whole image, which brings high computational costs. In this paper, to address this problem, we propose a novel cost-efficient Dynamic Low-resolution Distillation (DLD) text spotting framework, which aims to infer images in different small but recognizable resolutions and achieve a better balance between accuracy and efficiency. Concretely, we adopt a resolution selector to dynamically decide the input resolutions for different images, which is constraint by both inference accuracy and computational cost. Another sequential knowledge distillation strategy is conducted on the text recognition branch, making the low-res input obtains comparable performance to a high-res image. The proposed method can be optimized end-to-end and adopted in any current text spotting framework to improve the practicability. Extensive experiments on several text spotting benchmarks show that the proposed method vastly improves the usability of low-res models. The code is available at https://github.com/hikopensource/DAVAR-Lab-OCR/.

Keywords: End-to-end text spotting · Dynamic resolution · Sequential knowledge distillation

1 Introduction

Research on scene text spotting has achieved great process and been successfully applied in many fields such as finance, education, transportation, *etc.*. The

---

Y. Chen and L. Qiao—Contributed equally.

Supplementary Information The online version contains supplementary material available at https://doi.org/10.1007/978-3-031-19815-1_21.

© The Author(s), under exclusive license to Springer Nature Switzerland AG 2022
S. Avidan et al. (Eds.): ECCV 2022, LNCS 13688, pp. 356–373, 2022.
https://doi.org/10.1007/978-3-031-19815-1_21

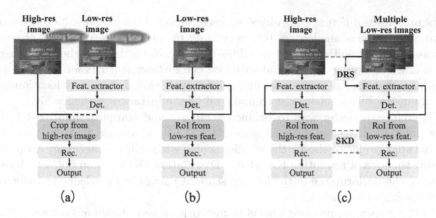

Fig. 1. (a) is the offline two-staged text spotter, which can use different resolutions for two tasks while cannot be globally optimized. (b) is the ordinary end-to-end text spotter, where the recognizer can only receive the low-res RoI features map when using the low-res input. (c) is our proposed DLD framework, where the low-res network can dynamically select small but feasible resolutions and reconstruct the high-res features.

traditional process of text spotting is usually divided into two sub-tasks: text detection [1,28,50,60] and recognition [7,9,43,46]. To reduce the error accumulation between two tasks and the maintenance cost, many works have been proposed in an end-to-end manner [3,17,25,26,38,39,44]. To further improve the real-time performance of the model, some works exquisitely design different geometric representations or lighter network architectures [30–32,49,51]. However, most works only report the results based on a fixed and carefully selected input resolution, but whose performances are usually seriously affected by the resolution changing in different situations.

In the traditional pipeline of two-staged text spotting, as shown in Fig. 1(a), to save the inference cost, we can firstly detect text from a down-sampled image and then crop text regions from the original high-res image for recognition. It will not damage the overall performance to some extent since the two tasks can be optimized separately. However, once enjoying the benefits such as global optimization and lower maintenance cost brought by end-to-end text spotters, we have to face the resolution choice problem: images can only be resized into a predefined scale. If we want to achieve a higher efficiency using low-res inputs, as illustrated in Fig. 1(b), many small texts will lose their discriminative features from the beginning of the network and are hard to be recognized. This makes end-to-end text spotter low practicability in many realistic situations.

This problem is mainly attributed to the different characteristics and resolution sensitivities of two sub-tasks of end-to-end text spotters [6]. When people read the text in a low-res image, they may easily identify whether an object belongs to a text. However, the blurred texture may influence the recognition since it is a more fine-grained sequential classification task. In fact, different texts may have different difficulties for recognition. People can sometimes correctly infer some of the low-res text according to the other recognizable characters and their semantic context meanings [5,9,57]. Nevertheless, when the image keeps down-sampling, it will gradually lose the distinct features for recognition. It means that for an image containing text with varied sizes and locations, a minimum resolution must exist to make all of the instances recognizable.

Therefore, a better way to balance accuracy and computational cost is to infer different images in different scales [45,55,61]. Moreover, in order to make the network prefer to choose the smaller scales with minimal accuracy drop, we borrow the idea of resolution Knowledge Distillation (KD) [24,36,56], which can enhance the performance of the low-res student using the knowledge transferred from the high-res teacher.

In this paper, we propose a novel framework named *Dynamic Low-resolution Distillation* (DLD) text spotting, which aims to dynamically choose feasible input resolutions for the end-to-end text spotter under a resolution KD schema, as shown in Fig. 1(c). Specifically, In DLD, the student network adopts a lightweight *Dynamic Resolution Selector* (DRS) to find a suitable down-sampled resolution to preserve the teacher's performance. Given a group of candidate down-sampled scales, DRS is optimized to find the best resolution with a minimal performance drop under both accuracy and computational cost supervision. On the other hand, to enhance the recognizability of low-res text, we emphasize the sequence information that the model extracts and integrate it with the *Sequential Knowledge Distillation* (SKD) strategy in the recognition part. The loss of SKD is composed of feature-based L2 loss and the sequence-level beam search output loss, which effectively increases the performance of those *low-res but recognizable* text instances. DLD is a self-consistent framework, where the proposed two tasks can work together organically and achieve effective mutual promotion. The SKD prompts the DRS to choose a relatively lower resolution, and the DRS provides varied ratios of resolution pairs to enhance the SKD to be more robust and focus on the scale-unrelated features.

The major contributions of this paper are as follows: (1) We first study the input resolution problem on end-to-end text spotting tasks and propose a Dynamic Low-resolution Distillation text spotting framework that can effectively enhance the performance and reduce the computational cost. (2) We propose a sequential KD strategy with a dynamic resolution selector that allows the model to choose a small but recognizable input scale. (3) Extensive experiments and ablation studies demonstrate the effectiveness of our method.

2   Related Works

2.1   End-to-End Text Spotting

Whether to employ Region of Interests (RoI) operations, current end-to-end text spotters can be divided into two types: two-staged and one-staged models.

Two-staged end-to-end text spotters usually involve RoI-like operations to crop detected regions from feature maps for the following recognition task.

Methods [25–27,34,39,59] usually follow the Faster-RCNN [41]/Mask-RCNN framework [14] to detect text regions and then crop the RoI regions into small features for recognition using RoI-pooling/RoI-Align operations. To recognize text in arbitrary shapes and improve detect efficiency, some works adopt the segmentation-based methods in the detection stage and then carefully design novel RoI operations to rectify the text into regular shapes, such as RoIRotate [30], RoI-Slide [10], TPS [38,47], BezierAlign [31,32], rectified RoI-Pooling [2], *etc.*.

In one-staged models, text instances are directly decoded from the global feature map without any RoI operation. [53] directly detects characters in different categories using multi-class segmentation. [49] decodes the gathered pixel-level feature vector into sequence with the proposed PG-CTC decoder. In the work of [37], the authors use mask attention to map different instances into different feature map channels and then predict individual text in each channel.

Both two types of methods suffer from the problem of input scales. Compared with two-staged methods that can reshape the RoI features into a uniform size, one-staged methods somehow face more challenges about text scales and usually require a large number of training samples.

2.2 Knowledge Distillation

Knowledge Distillation (KD) [18] was first proposed to transfer the capacity of a large teacher network to a small student. This learning paradigm continues to evolve in the following years and has been applied in many areas, such as image recognition [54], object detection [36], semantic segmentation [16], text recognition [4]. In addition to transferring knowledge between different networks, resolution KD [24,52,56] has also been widely used to train a low-res student with the help of a high-res teacher, which can be well adapted to improve some low-res applications like face recognition [11,12]. [36] firstly studies the low-res KD in object detection tasks and proposes an aligned multi-scale training method to align features in different levels.

However, these methods only conduct resolution KD in a fixed input resolution scale, which somehow limits the generalization ability of the model when objects are displayed in varied scales.

2.3 Dynamic Resolution

Since images have different difficulties to recognize, many works are proposed to assign images with dynamic input resolutions [45,48,55,61]. [45] proposes a reinforcement learning approach to dynamically identify when and where to use high-res data conditioned on the corresponding low-res data. [55] uses different sub-networks to cope with samples with different difficulties. [48] learns how to use different scaling strategies for different objects. [61] designs a resolution predictor to choose feasible input resolutions, which can reduce the computational cost while maintain performance.

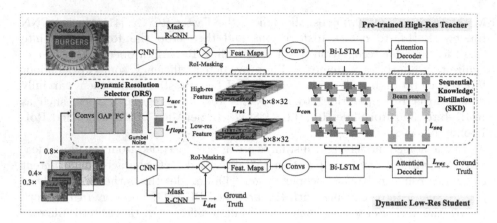

Fig. 2. Illustration of the proposed DLD framework. It contains a fixed pre-trained high-res teacher and a dynamic low-res student that aims to obtain comparable performance. The DRS dynamically selects a small resolution for the student with minimal performance reduction. The SKD process helps the student capture the inter-sequence information and be able to recognize text in low-resolution.

3   Methodology

3.1   Overview

As shown in Fig. 2, we propose a Dynamic Low-resolution Distillation (DLD) framework. It follows the setting of resolution distillation [24,52,56], where the teacher and student use the same network architecture but were input with images in different resolutions. The high-res teacher network is well pre-trained and then fixed in the following training. The student aims to achieve comparable performance in some lower resolutions. It mainly attributes to two parts: (1) a Dynamic Resolution Selector (DRS) to choose the appropriate resolution for different input images, and (2) a Sequential Knowledge Distillation (SKD) strategy to capture the semantic sequence information and improve the recognizability of the low-res instances. The whole framework is end-to-end trainable.

3.2   Baseline Text Spotting Model

We adopt a Mask-RCNN-based [14] two-staged end-to-end text spotting framework [26,27,34,39] as the base model. The detection branch follows the standard Mask-RCNN implementation, which can predict the mask region with its bounding box for any text shape. For the input image $I \in R^{H \times W \times 3}$, the multi-scale features are extracted through the backbone of ResNet-50 [15] and a feature pyramid network (FPN) [29]. For the text recognition task, the recognition features are firstly cropped from the global feature map via the RoI-Masking operation [39] and then uniformly resized into a fixed size $H_r \times W_r$. H_r and W_r are set to 8 and 32 pixels separately in all experiments. These feature maps go through six convolution layers and are then extracted the sequence information by the bidirectional long short-term memory (Bi-LSTM) [19] module. The final character sequences are decoded by an attention-based decoder [7].

We firstly train a strong high-resolution teacher and then fix it in following distillation training. The teacher network are trained under the supervision from both text detection and recognition annotations as follows,

$$L_{teacher} = L_{det} + L_{rec}, \tag{1}$$

where the detection part contains the losses from bounding boxes regression, classification, and instance segmentation.

3.3 Dynamic Resolution Selector

Inspired by [61], we propose a *Dynamic Resolution Selector* (DRS) to help model inference images in more feasible scales. Here, we predefine a group of candidate down-sampled scales for student network, *e.g.*, images can be selected in the range $[0.8\times, 0.3\times]$ of teacher's resolution. The target of DRS is to find a suitable scale in the group with minimal performance reduction compared to the teacher. The selection criteria are that decreasing the resolution should be rewarded while performance decline would be penalized. Specifically, The DRS is a lightweight residual network composed of 10 Convolution layers (Convs), a Global Average Pooling (GAP) layer, and a Fully Connected (FC) layer. Given a high-res image I and k candidate down-sampled scale factors $\{s_1, s_2, ..., s_k\}$, the DRS first predicts the probability vector $p = [p_1, p_2, ..., p_k]$ by the network and then transforms p into binary decisions $h = [h_1, h_2, ..., h_k] \in \{0, 1\}^k$ indicating which scale factor to select. To optimize DRS, the network first does forward calculations based on the given pre-trained teacher with the high-res input I and all of the corresponding low-res images $\{I_{s_1}, I_{s_2}, ..., I_{s_k}\}$. We use y and $\{y_{s_1}, y_{s_2}, ..., y_{s_k}\}$ to denote the predicted probability distribution of teacher and students, respectively. The loss generated in terms of accuracy can be formed as:

$$L_{acc} = KL(\sum_{i=1}^{k} h_i y_{s_i}, y), \tag{2}$$

where $KL(\cdot)$ is the KL divergence for the recognition results. The recognition feature maps are cropped according to the detection ground truth (GT) during training to ensure the number of recognition results is consistent. The optimization target is to make one of the h_i be 1, and the others are 0. The selected scale with the teacher's nearest recognition results and the highest detection accuracy will obtain the minimum loss.

To prevent the DRS module from converging to the maximum scale and encourage it to choose a smaller image as much as possible, we directly penalize it with its forward computation cost as follows:

$$L_{flops} = \sum_{i=1}^{k} h_i T_i, \tag{3}$$

where T_i is the forward FLOPS under input I_{s_i}. Since images containing different instances have different FLOPS, we use the pre-computed average value.

The overall supervision of DRS is as follows:

$$L_{DRS} = L_{acc} + \gamma L_{flops}, \tag{4}$$

where γ is the parameter to balance the weight between accuracy and computational cost.

Gumbel Softmax Trick. Notice that the process of converting p into one-hot h is non-differentiable. Here, we adopt the Gumbel-Softmax sampling trick [20]. Specifically, we first add Gumbel noise g_j to the discrete random variable p_j, and then draw discrete samples from the above distribution as:

$$h_i = \begin{cases} 1, & i = \arg\max_j(log(p_j) + g_j) \\ 0, & \text{otherwise} \end{cases}, \tag{5}$$

where $g_j = -log(-log(u_j))$ is calculated based on the i.i.d samples u_j, where $u_j \sim Uniform(0,1)$. In the above procedure, the arg max operation can be approximated by softmax operation as follows:

$$h_i = \frac{exp((log(p_i) + g_i)/\tau)}{\sum_{j=1}^{k} exp((log(p_j) + g_j)/\tau)}, \tag{6}$$

where τ is the temperature parameter. During training, using a lower τ can make the expectation of sampling closer to the result of arg max, but the gradient variance will be large. Adopting a higher τ can make the gradient variance smaller, but the expectation of sampling will be close to the average distribution. Here, we initialize with a larger τ at the beginning and gradually decrease it as $\tau = \sigma^{epoch}\tau_{init}$, where τ_{init} is the initial temperature and σ is a decay factor.

3.4   Sequential Knowledge Distillation

Text recognition is a sequential classification problem where the sequence information is vital for capturing the semantic meaning [9,43,57]. For example, although some characters are easily confused in low-res, such as 'i' and 'l' in Fig. 3, people can still recognize them in a word. This inspires us to dig out further the model's deeper potential, making DRS choose the smaller scale as much as possible. Therefore, we propose a *Sequential Knowledge Distillation* (SKD) strategy to help the low-res network extract semantic information under the supervision of its teacher. Here, we only explore the optimization problem of the text recognition task since it is more likely to be the bottleneck of the overall performance of the current end-to-end text spotting framework, which will also be demonstrated in the following experiments.

Specifically, given a high-res input I and the selected low-res image I_s, we use $\mathcal{F}^{roi}, \mathcal{F}_s^{roi} \in \mathbb{R}^{H \times W \times C}$ to separately represent the cropped recognition features of

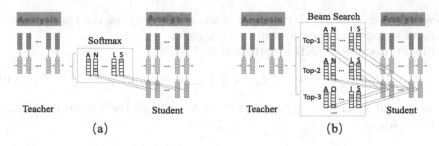

Fig. 3. The comparison of (a) logit-based Knowledge Distillation and (b) sequence-level Knowledge Distillation in sequence decoding.

teacher and student, where H, W, and C denote the feature map's height, width, and channel, respectively. These features are cropped using RoI-Masking with the detection GT and resized into a uniform shape. After a stack of convolutions and a Bi-LSTM module, the contextual information can be further extracted, which are represented as $\mathcal{F}^{con}, \mathcal{F}_s^{con} \in \mathbb{R}^{N \times C}$, where N is the length of the hidden state. In these two stages of the network, we adopt the feature-based KD strategy to set up L2 loss as:

$$L_{roi} = \frac{1}{HWC} \sum_{i=1}^{H} \sum_{j=1}^{W} \sum_{c=1}^{C} ||\mathcal{F}^{roi}[i,j,c] - \mathcal{F}_s^{roi}[i,j,c]||_2, \tag{7}$$

$$L_{con} = \frac{1}{NC} \sum_{i=1}^{N} \sum_{c=1}^{C} ||\mathcal{F}^{con}[i,c] - \mathcal{F}_s^{con}[i,c]||_2. \tag{8}$$

In the final decoding stage, different from the distillation process that aggregates logit-based loss [4] over the sequence, we borrow the idea of the sequence-level knowledge distillation [23] to better capture sequence information, as shown in Fig. 3. The student is trained based on the output from the top-k beam search [40] results of the teacher network. It helps the student retain the context information in a sequence as much as possible. To ensure the optimization speed, we only choose the results with the top-3 scores. Specifically, given the input $\mathcal{F}^{con}$ and the attention-based decoder, we use $p(q|\mathcal{F}^{con})$ to represent the predicted sequence distribution over all possible sequences $q \in \mathcal{Q}$. Then, the sequence-level knowledge distillation can be formulated and then approximated as follows:

$$
\begin{aligned}
L_{seq} &= -\sum_{q \in \mathcal{Q}} p(q|\mathcal{F}^{con}) \log p(q|\mathcal{F}_s^{con}) \\
&= -\sum_{q \in \mathcal{Q}} \mathbb{I}\{q = \hat{y}_1, \hat{y}_2, \hat{y}_3, ...\} \log p(q|\mathcal{F}_s^{con}) \\
&\approx -\log \sum_{k=1}^{K} p(q = \hat{y}_k|\mathcal{F}_s^{con})
\end{aligned}
\tag{9}
$$

where $\hat{y}_k$ is the result with the top-k beam search score of the teacher model. Here, we simply set K = 1 to save training time.

Finally, the overall SKD is optimized as:

$$L_{SKD} = L_{roi} + \eta_1 L_{con} + \eta_2 L_{seq}, \tag{10}$$

where η_1 and η_2 are the hyper-parameters to balance the magnitude of L_{roi}, L_{con} and L_{seq}.

3.5   Optimization

The proposed DLD framework is optimized to recognize images in both high accuracy and efficiency with end-to-end training. The overall loss of the student network is generated from three parts: the original text detection and recognition loss, the loss from DRS to balance accuracy and computational cost, and the loss from SKD to improve the representational capacity of the low-res model.

$$L = L_{det} + \lambda_1 L_{rec} + \lambda_2 L_{DRS} + \lambda_3 L_{SKD}, \tag{11}$$

where λ_1, λ_2 and λ_3 are weight balancing parameters.

In every epoch of the training stage, the student network will do forward calculations for k times for all candidate resolutions. The backward loss of L_{DRS} will only be propagated in the lightweight DRS module. The loss of L_{det}, L_{rec}, and L_{SKD} will only be conducted on the branch with the maximum h_i and will be not propagated to the DRS.

4   Experiments

4.1   Implementation Details

Datasets. We list the datasets used in this paper as follows. We evaluate our method on three popular text spotting benchmarks: (1) *ICDAR2013* [22] (*IC13*) that only contains horizontal text, (2) *ICDAR2015* [21] (*IC15*) that includes oriented text, and (3) *Total-Text* [8] (*TT*) that involves many curved text. For the teacher network, we firstly pre-train it on *SynthText-800K* [13] and then fine-tune with a mixture dataset which includes 7k images filtered from *ICDAR-MLT2017* [35] and all training images in *IC13*, *IC15*, and *TT*. In the following KD training stage, the teacher will be fixed, and the student network can be initialized using the teacher's weights.

Experiment Settings. The base model's architecture is described in Sect. 3.2. Teacher and student models share the same training settings. All models are trained by the AdamW [33] optimizer with batch-size = 3. The KD training lasts for 50 epochs and uses an initial learning rate of 1×10^{-3}. The learning rate is divided by 10 at the 30-th epoch and the 40-th epoch. The parameter τ_{init} is set as 5 and decay factor $\sigma = 0.965$. The Bi-LSTM module has 256 hidden units. For weight balancing parameters, we set $\gamma = 0.1$ and others as $\eta_1 = \eta_2 = \lambda_1 = \lambda_2 = \lambda_3 = 1$.

According to the scales of text instances in different datasets, we choose the basic inference resolutions for the teacher, *i.e.*, 'S-768' for IC13, 'S-1280' for IC15, and 'S-896' for Total-Text, where the prefix of '*S-*' represents the input images are resized by a fixed shorter side.

To obtain a strong baseline of the teacher network, we conduct widely-used data augmentation strategies as follows: (1) instance aware random cropping, (2) randomly scaling the shorter side of the input images to lengths in the range scales $[0.3\times, 1.0\times]$ of the basic resolutions, (3) random rotation with angle randomly chosen from $[-15°, +15°]$, (4) applying random brightness, jitters, and contrast to input images. In both training and testing stages, the student's DRS resolution ratios range is set as $\{0.8, 0.7, 0.6, 0.5, 0.4, 0.3\}$. All experiments are implemented in Pytorch with 8×32 GB-Tesla-V100 GPUs under CUDA-10.0 and CUDNN-7.6.3.

4.2 Results on Text Spotting Benchmarks

The effectiveness of the proposed DLD are compared with other three settings: (1) *Vanilla Multi-scale:* a single model that is trained in multiple scales and tested in a fixed scale. (2) *DRS-only:* with the proposed DRS, the student network removes the supervision from the distillation. (3) *SKD-only:* with the proposed SKD, the student keeps using the 1/2 scale compared with the teacher.

Table 1 shows the experimental results on three benchmarks. The result of *Vanilla Multi-scale* with high-res input can be treated as the original upper bound of the model. If the inputs are in low-resolutions, although the FLOPS can be optimized by approximately 75%, the accuracies will be dramatically decreased, *e.g.*, the *End-to-End* results of *General/None* are decreased by 8.5% (82.9% *vs.* 74.4%) in *IC13*, 6.6% (69.5% *vs.* 62.9%) in *IC15* and 6.9% (62.3% *vs.* 55.4%) in *Total-Text*, respectively. Using the SKD to transfer knowledge from the high-res teacher into the low-res student, in the result of *SKD-only*, we can see that the performances on low-res can be effectively increased by 4.4%/4.2%/4.2% in three datasets compared with *Vanilla Multiscale*, respectively.

Equipped with the DRS module, in *DRS-only*, we are able to tune the tendencies of the model to balance the accuracy and computational cost by different γ. When the model additionally integrates with SKD, under the entire *DLD* framework, where the student network can select more low-res scales without performance drop, the overall performances are further optimized. Specifically, when we set $\gamma = 0.1$, the model can achieve the comparable or even better accuracy (82.7% *vs.* 82.9%, 70.9% *vs.* 69.5%, 63.9% *vs.* 62.3%) than that of high-res input, and with about 50% FLOPS costs. Suppose we want the model more tend to be cost-efficient and set $\gamma = 0.3$. The models' FLOPS can be reduced to a similar level as that all using 1/2-resolution inputs, and the accuracies can be further improved by 2.8%/2.2%/2.3% compared with *SKD-only*, respectively. More statistical and visualized analysis are in the supplementary materials.

We conduct the following ablation experiments in Sects. 4.3, 4.4 and 4.5 on *Total-Text* [8] and use 'None' to denote lexicon-free End-to-End result and 'Full' to represent the result based on the lexicon combined all images.

Table 1. Results on three text spotting benchmarks. 'S', 'W' and 'G' separately mean recognition with strong, weak and generic lexicon [21]. 'Full' indicates lexicons of all images are combined, and 'None' means lexicon-free [8]. 'H' and 'L' in column 'Type' indicates whether the inference is carried out with high- or low-resolution input. FLOPS is the average *floating point operations*.

Dataset	Training method	Type	Input size	End-to-end (%)					Word spotting (%)					FLOPS
				S	W	G	None	Full	S	W	G	None	Full	
IC13	Vanilla Multi-Scale	H	S-768	86.9	86.6	82.9	–	–	91.4	91.0	86.3	–	–	142.9 G
		L	S-384	80.9	78.9	74.4	–	–	85.2	82.7	77.3	–	–	35.8 G
	SKD-only	L	S-384	84.1	82.8	78.8	–	–	88.0	86.5	81.7	–	–	35.8 G
	DRS-only ($\gamma = 0.1$)	L	Dynamic	85.7	84.8	80.7	–	–	90.1	88.9	84.0	–	–	80.7 G
	DRS-only ($\gamma = 0.3$)	L	Dynamic	83.7	82.0	77.6	–	–	87.8	85.8	80.5	–	–	48.8 G
	DLD ($\gamma = 0.1$)	L	Dynamic	86.5	85.7	82.7	–	–	90.9	89.9	86.1	–	–	71.5 G
	DLD ($\gamma = 0.3$)	L	Dynamic	85.6	84.4	81.6	–	–	90.0	88.6	84.9	–	–	41.6 G
IC15	Vanilla Multi-Scale	H	S-1280	78.0	74.4	69.5	–	–	81.4	77.2	71.7	–	–	517.2 G
		L	S-640	72.2	67.8	62.9	–	–	75.7	70.8	65.3	–	–	129.3 G
	SKD-only	L	S-640	75.4	71.7	67.1	–	–	78.9	74.6	69.6	–	–	129.3 G
	DRS-only ($\gamma = 0.1$)	L	Dynamic	76.2	72.1	66.8	–	–	79.8	75.2	69.3	–	–	298.8 G
	DRS-only ($\gamma = 0.3$)	L	Dynamic	73.6	68.9	63.7	–	–	76.4	71.5	66.3	–	–	163.6 G
	DLD ($\gamma = 0.1$)	L	Dynamic	79.0	75.7	70.9	–	–	82.4	78.6	73.3	–	–	261.8 G
	DLD ($\gamma = 0.3$)	L	Dynamic	78.1	73.5	69.3	–	–	81.1	76.4	71.2	–	–	148.3 G
TT	Vanilla Multi-Scale	H	S-896	–	–	–	62.3	71.4	–	–	–	65.2	75.9	206.7 G
		L	S-448	–	–	–	55.4	66.5	–	–	–	58.1	71.1	52.0 G
	SKD-only	L	S-448	–	–	–	59.6	68.9	–	–	–	62.6	73.5	52.0 G
	DRS-only ($\gamma = 0.1$)	L	Dynamic	–	–	–	60.9	70.4	–	–	–	63.5	75.0	119.2 G
	DRS-only ($\gamma = 0.3$)	L	Dynamic	–	–	–	58.8	68.9	–	–	–	61.6	73.6	75.0 G
	DLD ($\gamma = 0.1$)	L	Dynamic	–	–	–	63.9	73.7	–	–	–	66.4	77.8	103.0 G
	DLD ($\gamma = 0.3$)	L	Dynamic	–	–	–	61.9	71.9	–	–	–	64.0	75.9	62.1 G

4.3 Ablation Studies on Sequential Knowledge Distillation

Different Distillation Losses. SKD contains losses from three parts: the RoI feature's loss L_{roi}, the contexture feature's loss L_{con}, and the beam search output's loss L_{seq}. Here, we conduct different experiments based on the model of *SKD-only* to evaluate the importance degrees of these losses, and the result is shown in Table 2. It is easy to know that without any KD loss, the model will fall into the *Vanilla Multi-Scale* setting. From the result, we can see that L_{seq} has the greatest impact on distillation, which surpasses the result without distillation by 3.0% on 'None' and 1.4% on 'Full'. By combining all three losses, the model achieves 4.2%/2.4% improvements.

Different Knowledge Distillation Settings. We also conduct experiments on different KD strategies. Based on the setting of Resolution KD framework without DRS (teacher with S-896, and student with S-448), we compared our model with other two works: (1) Bhunia *et al.* [4]: contains four types of KD losses (Logits' Distillation, Character Localised Hint, Attention Distillation, Affinity Distillation) that are designed for text recognition, and (2) Qi *et al.* [36]: a KD strategy designed for the detection stage. Table 3 shows the experimental results. For the recognition KD, the results demonstrate that the performance of our proposed SKD surpasses [4] by 0.4%/0.6%. This is mainly because of the effectiveness of the sequence-level distillation strategy in some low-res texts. We simply replace the sequence-level distillation in SKD with the logits-based distillation adopted in [4], and we can see the performance will drop by 0.9% on 'None' and 1.4% on 'Full', respectively. For the detection KD, the results show that the enhancement of integration with detection distillation is limited. This is because, in the current model, the detection performance in low-resolution has only a small gap between that of high-resolution.

Different RoI Scales. Recognition feature scale is a factor that affects performance under the current Mask-RCNN-based framework. Here, we conduct experiments to evaluate its influence, whose results are illustrated in Table 4. The results show that larger RoI scales would help models obtain higher performance but inevitably bring extra computational cost. On the other hand, if teacher and student use different RoI scales, the model cannot directly perform distillation. So, we add a deconvolutional (deconv) module [58] to align the smaller student's features with the larger teacher's features. This also simulates a feature-level super-resolution process. From the results, we can see that compared with directly using a larger student RoI scale, conducting super-resolution will even degrade the performance and increase the FLOPS.

Table 2. Ablation on different distillation losses for SKD.

Training method	L_{roi}	L_{con}	L_{seq}	End-to-End (%)	
				None	Full
SKD-only (S-448)				55.4	66.5
	✓			56.9	66.9
		✓		57.5	67.2
			✓	58.4	67.9
	✓	✓	✓	59.6	68.9

Table 3. Ablation on different knowledge distillation settings.

Distillation method	End-to-end (%)	
	None	Full
SKD	59.6	68.9
Bhunia *et al.* [4]	59.2	68.3
SKD replaced Logits [4]	58.7	67.5
Qi *et al.* [36]	55.8	67.0
SKD+Qi *et al.* [36]	59.8	69.2

4.4 Ablation on Dynamic Resolution Selector

Different Candidate Scales. The set of candidate student scales is usually defined by experience. In Table 5, we compared the results under different candidate sets. The sets containing a single value are the same as the *SKD-only*

Table 4. Ablation on different RoI scales. '†' means model has extra deconv modules.

Training method	Type	Teacher RoI scale	Student RoI scale	End-to-End (%)		FLOPS
				None	Full	
Vanilla multi-scale	H	(8×32)	–	62.3	71.4	206.7G
	H	(16×64)	–	63.1	72.1	227.3G
DLD	L	(8×32)	(8×32)	63.9	73.7	103.0G
	L	(16×64)	(16×64)	64.8	74.1	112.3G
	L	(16×64)	(8×32)†	64.5	73.3	119.2G

model. We can see that the group of smaller candidates {0.5, 0.4, 0.3} obtains lower inference costs and accuracy than that of the larger group {0.8, 0.7, 0.6}. With more candidates values, the model can be optimized to find a better balance between accuracy and computational cost. Nevertheless, the training cost will be somehow increased.

Table 5. Ablation on different candidate scales. The training time reports the average time used to train the model for an epoch.

Training method	Resolution scales	End-to-end (%)		FLOPS	Training time (min/epoch)
		None	Full		
DLD	{0.5}	59.6	68.9	52.0G	7.8
	{0.8, 0.7, 0.6}	63.6	73.4	128.8G	9.0
	{0.5, 0.4, 0.3}	58.9	68.0	45.9G	8.4
	{0.8, 0.7, 0.6, 0.5, 0.4, 0.3}	63.9	73.7	103.0G	10.2

Table 6. Ablation on parameter γ.

Training method	γ	End-to-end (%)		FLOPS
		None	Full	
DLD	0.1	63.9	73.7	103.0G
	0.2	63.2	72.4	82.8G
	0.3	61.9	71.9	62.1G
	0.4	59.2	69.5	50.6G
	0.5	56.0	66.4	38.4G

Table 7. Ablation on parameter τ_{init}.

Training method	τ_{init}	End-to-end (%)		FLOPS
		None	Full	
DLD	1	63.6	71.9	115.8G
	3	63.5	73.2	110.2G
	5	63.9	73.7	103.0G
	7	63.8	72.6	96.7G
	9	63.2	72.5	98.5G

Balance Between Accuracy and Computational Cost. γ is a vital parameter to control the DRS's tendencies about accuracy and efficiency. Table 6 shows how the changes of γ influence the model. As the increasing of γ, the model tends to choose more minor input scales and achieves more efficient computational cost. However, the accuracy will be somehow reduced. This parameter can be controlled flexibly and provide a straightforward guide on the resolution choice under different requirements.

Different Temperature Parameter. Table 7 shows how τ_{init} influence the student's performance. This parameter affects the results of the convergence of the DRS module to some extent. It can be easily tuned once γ be fixed.

4.5 Studies on Different End-to-End Text Spotters

To demonstrate the effectiveness of our method, besides the basic Mask-RCNN-based text spotter, we also conducted experiments on the other two different frameworks based on the open-sourced code: (1) Text Perceptron [38], a two-staged text spotter whose text detection branch is segmentation-based, and (2) MANGO [37], a one-staged text spotter. Since MANGO has no explicit detection branch and directly recognizes text globally, we only report *End-to-End* result based on Intersection over Union(IoU) = 0.1 constraint as reported in [37]. Other results are reported based on IoU = 0.5. We calculate the *Text Recognition (Rec)* accuracy using the GT of detection in inference.

The experimental results are displayed in Table 8. In the *Vanilla Multi-Scale* setting, as the input scales decreases, it is not hard to understand that almost all of the accuracies will be declined. Nevertheless, in the Mask-RCNN-based framework, the performance drops in *Rec* and *End-to-End* are faster than that of *Det*. It means the text detection task can still work well in some relatively low resolutions, while the text recognition task becomes the overall bottleneck of End-to-End performance. This also proves the motivation we mentioned initially. In contrast, for the other two text spotters, the *Det* performance degrades faster when compressing the input size, which also jointly influences the End-to-End performance. This is because, in Mask-RCNN-based text spotters, there are a lot of preset anchors to capture different scales of text, but the segmentation task is relatively more sensitive to scales [42].

Table 8. The ablations experiments on scale changes in *Vanilla Multi-Scale* and the compared result when adopting DLD on different text spotting frameworks. '*Det*' is the Hmean metric of text detection task. '*Rec*' is the Accuracy metric of text recognition task. '*E2E*' stands for 'End-to-End'. 'Full' indicates lexicons of all images are combined and 'None' means lexicon-free. FPS is the average *frames per second*.

Training method	Input size	Mask-RCNN-based					Text perceptron [38]					MANGO [37]		
		Det (%)	Rec (%)	E2E (%)		FPS	Det (%)	Rec (%)	E2E (%)		FPS	E2E (%)		FPS
				None	Full				None	Full		None	Full	
Vanilla multi-scale	S-896	85.3	73.6	62.3	71.4	7.9	85.3	73.1	66.0	74.6	9.5	66.2	77.7	3.7
	S-768	85.7	72.8	61.2	71.1	8.6	85.1	72.6	64.7	74.2	11.4	67.1	78.1	4.7
	S-640	86.1	71.7	60.5	70.2	9.0	85.2	72.2	64.3	73.1	13.3	66.5	76.5	6.1
	S-512	84.9	66.9	58.7	69.3	9.4	82.5	68.9	61.3	70.5	14.8	61.9	73.3	7.7
	S-384	82.3	58.6	52.0	63.5	9.8	77.4	60.7	54.1	64.3	16.5	50.9	64.4	11.5
	S-256	76.5	42.5	38.3	48.5	12.0	62.2	45.2	40.5	50.2	17.8	29.2	46.3	13.9
DLD ($\gamma = 0.1$)	Dynamic	85.8	74.8	63.9	73.7	9.1	85.6	75.3	67.1	76.4	13.2	67.8	78.3	6.5
DLD ($\gamma = 0.3$)	Dynamic	85.1	73.1	61.9	71.9	9.7	81.7	73.5	63.6	72.8	15.8	62.5	73.8	10.4

When we adopt the proposed DLD on these text spotters, we can see that all the models with $\gamma = 0.1$ can obtain even higher accuracies and faster speed than that of high-res result in *Vanilla Multi-Scale*. Although the inference speed can be further accelerated with $\gamma = 0.3$, the *End-to-End* performance drops on Text Perceptron and MANGO are much larger than that on Mask-RCNN-based. Since DLD does not involve distillation loss in the text detection task, it is predictable that the *End-to-End* performance can be further improved with the help of the text detection knowledge transfer. Recall the results reported in Table 1, and we can find that the FLOPS is negatively correlated to the FPS but is not in equal proportion, because many operations are optimized to calculate in parallel and different platforms might behave differently. Nevertheless, reducing the computational cost is also vital for the low-end devices.

5   Conclusion

This paper proposes a novel *Dynamic Low-resolution Distillation* (DLD) framework for cost-efficient end-to-end text spotting, aiming to recognize images in different *low but recognizable* resolutions. The model integrates a dynamic low-resolution selector that can choose different down-sampled scales. A sequential knowledge distillation strategy is then adopted to make the model be able to recognize images with lower resolutions and hence achieve a better resolution-performance balance. Experiments show that our method can effectively enhance the practicability of end-to-end text spotters in many complicated situations.

References

1. Baek, Y., Lee, B., Han, D., Yun, S., Lee, H.: Character region awareness for text detection. In: CVPR, pp. 9365–9374 (2019)
2. Baek, Y., et al.: Character region attention for text spotting. In: Vedaldi, A., Bischof, H., Brox, T., Frahm, J.-M. (eds.) ECCV 2020. LNCS, vol. 12374, pp. 504–521. Springer, Cham (2020). https://doi.org/10.1007/978-3-030-58526-6_30
3. Bartz, C., Yang, H., Meinel, C.: See: towards semi-supervised end-to-end scene text recognition. In: AAAI, pp. 6674–6681 (2018)
4. Bhunia, A.K., Sain, A., Chowdhury, P.N., Song, Y.Z.: Text is text, no matter what: Unifying text recognition using knowledge distillation. In: ICCV. pp. 983–992 (2021)
5. Bhunia, A.K., Sain, A., Kumar, A., Ghose, S., Chowdhury, P.N., Song, Y.Z.: Joint visual semantic reasoning: multi-stage decoder for text recognition. In: ICCV, pp. 14940–14949 (2021)
6. Chen, X., Jin, L., Zhu, Y., Luo, C., Wang, T.: Text recognition in the wild: a survey. ACM Comput. Surv. **54**(2), 42:1–42:35 (2021)
7. Cheng, Z., Bai, F., Xu, Y., Zheng, G., Pu, S., Zhou, S.: Focusing attention: towards accurate text recognition in natural images. In: ICCV, pp. 5076–5084 (2017)
8. Ch'ng, C.K., Chan, C.S.: Total-text: a comprehensive dataset for scene text detection and recognition. In: ICDAR, vol. 1, pp. 935–942 (2017)
9. Fang, S., Xie, H., Wang, Y., Mao, Z., Zhang, Y.: Read like humans: autonomous, bidirectional and iterative language modeling for scene text recognition. In: CVPR, pp. 7098–7107 (2021)

10. Feng, W., He, W., Yin, F., Zhang, X., Liu, C.: Textdragon: an end-to-end framework for arbitrary shaped text spotting. In: ICCV, pp. 9075–9084 (2019)
11. Ge, S., Zhao, S., Li, C., Li, J.: Low-resolution face recognition in the wild via selective knowledge distillation. IEEE TIP **28**(4), 2051–2062 (2019)
12. Ge, S., Zhao, S., Li, C., Zhang, Y., Li, J.: Efficient low-resolution face recognition via bridge distillation. IEEE TIP **29**, 6898–6908 (2020)
13. Gupta, A., Vedaldi, A., Zisserman, A.: Synthetic data for text localisation in natural images. In: CVPR, pp. 2315–2324 (2016)
14. He, K., Gkioxari, G., Dollar, P., Girshick, R.: Mask R-CNN. In: ICCV, pp. 2980–2988 (2017)
15. He, K., Zhang, X., Ren, S., Sun, J.: Deep residual learning for image recognition. In: CVPR, pp. 770–778 (2016)
16. He, T., Shen, C., Tian, Z., Gong, D., Sun, C., Yan, Y.: Knowledge adaptation for efficient semantic segmentation. In: CVPR, pp. 578–587 (2019)
17. He, T., Tian, Z., Huang, W., Shen, C., Qiao, Y., Sun, C.: An end-to-end TextSpotter with explicit alignment and attention. In: CVPR, pp. 5020–5029 (2018)
18. Hinton, G.E., Vinyals, O., Dean, J.: Distilling the knowledge in a neural network. CoRR abs/1503.02531 (2015)
19. Hochreiter, S., Schmidhuber, J.: Long short-term memory. Neural Comput. **9**(8), 1735–1780 (1997)
20. Jang, E., Gu, S., Poole, B.: Categorical reparameterization with gumbel-softmax. In: ICLR (2017)
21. Karatzas, D., Gomez-Bigorda, L., Nicolaou, A., Ghosh, S., Bagdanov, A., Iwamura, M., Matas, J., Neumann, L., Chandrasekhar, V.R., Lu, S., et al.: ICDAR 2015 Competition on Robust Reading. In: ICDAR. pp. 1156–1160 (2015)
22. Karatzas, D., et al.: ICDAR 2013 robust reading competition. In: ICDAR, pp. 1484–1493 (2013)
23. Kim, Y., Rush, A.M.: Sequence-level knowledge distillation. In: Su, J., Carreras, X., Duh, K. (eds.) EMNLP, pp. 1317–1327 (2016)
24. Li, D., Yao, A., Chen, Q.: Learning to learn parameterized classification networks for scalable input images. In: Vedaldi, A., Bischof, H., Brox, T., Frahm, J.-M. (eds.) ECCV 2020. LNCS, vol. 12374, pp. 19–35. Springer, Cham (2020). https://doi.org/10.1007/978-3-030-58526-6_2
25. Li, H., Wang, P., Shen, C.: Towards end-to-end text spotting with convolutional recurrent neural networks. In: ICCV, pp. 5248–5256 (2017)
26. Liao, M., Lyu, P., He, M., Yao, C., Wu, W., Bai, X.: Mask textspotter: an end-to-end trainable neural network for spotting text with arbitrary shapes. IEEE TPAMI **1**(1) (2019)
27. Liao, M., Pang, G., Huang, J., Hassner, T., Bai, X.: Mask TextSpotter v3: segmentation proposal network for robust scene text spotting. In: Vedaldi, A., Bischof, H., Brox, T., Frahm, J.-M. (eds.) ECCV 2020. LNCS, vol. 12356, pp. 706–722. Springer, Cham (2020). https://doi.org/10.1007/978-3-030-58621-8_41
28. Liao, M., Wan, Z., Yao, C., Chen, K., Bai, X.: Real-time scene text detection with differentiable binarization. In: AAAI, pp. 11474–11481 (2020)
29. Lin, T.Y., Dollár, P., Girshick, R., He, K., Hariharan, B., Belongie, S.: Feature Pyramid Networks for Object Detection. In: CVPR, pp. 2117–2125 (2017)
30. Liu, X., Liang, D., Yan, S., Chen, D., Qiao, Y., Yan, J.: FOTS: fast oriented text spotting with a unified network. In: CVPR, pp. 5676–5685 (2018)
31. Liu, Y., Chen, H., Shen, C., He, T., Jin, L., Wang, L.: ABCNet: real-time scene text spotting with adaptive bezier-curve network. In: CVPR, pp. 9809–9818 (2020)

32. Liu, Y., et al.: Abcnet v2: adaptive bezier-curve network for real-time end-to-end text spotting. IEEE TPAMI (2021)
33. Loshchilov, I., Hutter, F.: Decoupled weight decay regularization. In: ICLR (2019)
34. Lyu, P., Liao, M., Yao, C., Wu, W., Bai, X.: Mask TextSpotter: an end-to-end trainable neural network for spotting text with arbitrary shapes. In: Ferrari, V., Hebert, M., Sminchisescu, C., Weiss, Y. (eds.) Computer Vision – ECCV 2018. LNCS, vol. 11218, pp. 71–88. Springer, Cham (2018). https://doi.org/10.1007/978-3-030-01264-9_5
35. Nayef, N., et al.: ICDAR2017 robust reading challenge on multi-lingual scene text detection and script identification - RRC-MLT. In: ICDAR, pp. 1454–1459 (2017)
36. Qi, L., et al.: Multi-scale aligned distillation for low-resolution detection. In: CVPR, pp. 14443–14453 (2021)
37. Qiao, L., et al.: MANGO: a mask attention guided one-stage scene text spotter. In: AAAI, pp. 2467–2476 (2021)
38. Qiao, L., et al.: Text perceptron: towards end-to-end arbitrary-shaped text spotting. In: AAAI, pp. 11899–11907 (2020)
39. Qin, S., Bissacco, A., Raptis, M., Fujii, Y., Xiao, Y.: Towards unconstrained end-to-end text spotting. In: ICCV, pp. 4704–4714 (2019)
40. Rabiner, L., R.: A tutorial on hidden Markov models and selected applications in speech recognition. Proc. IEEE **77**(2), 257–286 (1989)
41. Ren, S., He, K., Girshick, R., Sun, J.: Faster R-CNN: towards real-time object detection with region proposal networks. In: NeurIPS, pp. 91–99 (2015)
42. Richardson, E., et al.: It's all about the scale - efficient text detection using adaptive scaling. In: WACV, pp. 1833–1842 (2020)
43. Shi, B., Bai, X., Yao, C.: An end-to-end trainable neural network for image-based sequence recognition and its application to scene text recognition. IEEE TPAMI **39**(11), 2298–2304 (2017)
44. Sun, Y., Zhang, C., Huang, Z., Liu, J., Han, J., Ding, E.: Textnet: irregular text reading from images with an end-to-end trainable network. In: Jawahar, C.V., Li, H., Mori, G., Schindler, K. (eds.) ACCV, pp. 83–99 (2018)
45. Uzkent, B., Ermon, S.: Learning when and where to zoom with deep reinforcement learning. In: CVPR, pp. 12342–12351 (2020)
46. Wan, Z., He, M., Chen, H., Bai, X., Yao, C.: Textscanner: reading characters in order for robust scene text recognition. In: AAAI, pp. 12120–12127 (2020)
47. Wang, H., et al.: All you need is boundary: toward arbitrary-shaped text spotting. In: AAAI, pp. 12160–12167 (2020)
48. Wang, H., Kembhavi, A., Farhadi, A., Yuille, A.L., Rastegari, M.: ELASTIC: improving cnns with dynamic scaling policies. In: CVPR, pp. 2258–2267 (2019)
49. Wang, P., et al.: Pgnet: real-time arbitrarily-shaped text spotting with point gathering network. In: AAAI, pp. 2782–2790 (2021)
50. Wang, W., Xie, E., Li, X., Hou, W., Lu, T., Yu, G., Shao, S.: Shape robust text detection with progressive scale expansion network. In: CVPR, pp. 9336–9345 (June 2019)
51. Wang, W., et al.: Pan++: towards efficient and accurate end-to-end spotting of arbitrarily-shaped text. IEEE TPAMI (2021)
52. Wang, Y., Sun, F., Li, D., Yao, A.: Resolution switchable networks for runtime efficient image recognition. In: Vedaldi, A., Bischof, H., Brox, T., Frahm, J.-M. (eds.) ECCV 2020. LNCS, vol. 12360, pp. 533–549. Springer, Cham (2020). https://doi.org/10.1007/978-3-030-58555-6_32
53. Xing, L., Tian, Z., Huang, W., Scott, M.R.: Convolutional character networks. In: ICCV, pp. 9126–9136 (2019)

54. Xu, K., Rui, L., Li, Y., Gu, L.: Feature normalized knowledge distillation for image classification. In: Vedaldi, A., Bischof, H., Brox, T., Frahm, J.-M. (eds.) ECCV 2020. LNCS, vol. 12370, pp. 664–680. Springer, Cham (2020). https://doi.org/10.1007/978-3-030-58595-2_40

55. Yang, L., Han, Y., Chen, X., Song, S., Dai, J., Huang, G.: Resolution adaptive networks for efficient inference. In: CVPR, pp. 2366–2375 (2020)

56. Yang, T., Zhu, S., Chen, C., Yan, S., Zhang, M., Willis, A.: MutualNet: adaptive ConvNet via mutual learning from network width and resolution. In: Vedaldi, A., Bischof, H., Brox, T., Frahm, J.-M. (eds.) ECCV 2020. LNCS, vol. 12346, pp. 299–315. Springer, Cham (2020). https://doi.org/10.1007/978-3-030-58452-8_18

57. Yu, D., et al.: Towards accurate scene text recognition with semantic reasoning networks. In: CVPR, pp. 12110–12119 (2020)

58. Zeiler, M.D., Krishnan, D., Taylor, G.W., Fergus, R.: Deconvolutional networks. In: CVPR, pp. 2528–2535 (2010)

59. Zhang, P., et al.: TRIE: end-to-end text reading and information extraction for document understanding. In: ACM MM, pp. 1413–1422 (2020)

60. Zhou, X., et al.: EAST: an efficient and accurate scene text detector. In: CVPR, pp. 2642–2651 (2017)

61. Zhu, M., et al.: Dynamic resolution network. In: NeurIPS (2021)

Contextual Text Block Detection Towards Scene Text Understanding

Chuhui Xue[1,2], Jiaxing Huang[1], Wenqing Zhang[2], Shijian Lu[1(✉)],
Changhu Wang[2], and Song Bai[2]

[1] Nanyang Technological University, Singapore, Singapore
xuec0003@e.ntu.edu.sg, {jiaxing.huang,shijian.lu}@ntu.edu.sg
[2] ByteDance Inc., Singapore, Singapore
wenqingzhang@bytedance.com

Abstract. Most existing scene text detectors focus on detecting characters or words that only capture partial text messages due to missing contextual information. For a better understanding of text in scenes, it is more desired to detect contextual text blocks (CTBs) which consist of one or multiple integral text units (e.g., characters, words, or phrases) in natural reading order and transmit certain complete text messages. This paper presents contextual text detection, a new setup that detects CTBs for better understanding of texts in scenes. We formulate the new setup by a dual detection task which first detects integral text units and then groups them into a CTB. To this end, we design a novel scene text clustering technique that treats integral text units as tokens and groups them (belonging to the same CTB) into an ordered token sequence. In addition, we create two datasets SCUT-CTW-Context and ReCTS-Context to facilitate future research, where each CTB is well annotated by an ordered sequence of integral text units. Further, we introduce three metrics that measure contextual text detection in local accuracy, continuity, and global accuracy. Extensive experiments show that our method accurately detects CTBs which effectively facilitates downstream tasks such as text classification and translation. The project is available at https://sg-vilab.github.io/publication/xue2022contextual/.

Keyword: Scene text detection

1 Introduction

Scene texts often convey precise and rich semantic information that is very useful to visual recognition and scene understanding tasks. To facilitate reading and understanding by humans, they are usually designed and placed in the form of contextual text blocks which consist of one or multiple integral text units (e.g., a character, word, or phrase) that are arranged in natural reading order. Contextual text blocks deliver complete and meaningful text

Supplementary Information The online version contains supplementary material available at https://doi.org/10.1007/978-3-031-19815-1_22.

© The Author(s), under exclusive license to Springer Nature Switzerland AG 2022
S. Avidan et al. (Eds.): ECCV 2022, LNCS 13688, pp. 374–391, 2022.
https://doi.org/10.1007/978-3-031-19815-1_22

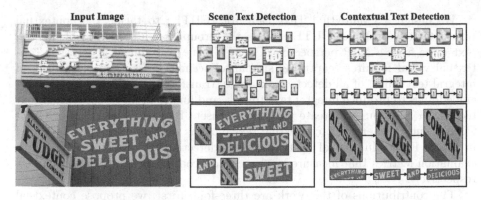

Fig. 1. Illustration of traditional scene text detection and the proposed contextual text detection: Traditional scene text detection detects integral text units (e.g., characters or words as shown in the second column) which usually deliver incomplete text messages and have large gaps towards scene text understanding. In contrast, the proposed contextual text detection detects contextual text blocks each of which consists of multiple integral text units in natural reading order. It facilitates the ensuing tasks in natural language processing and scene understanding greatly.

messages and detecting them is critical to the ensuing tasks such as natural language processing and scene image understanding.

Most existing scene text detectors [16,18,23,53] focus on detecting integral text units only as illustrated in the second column of Fig. 1. Their detection thus cannot convey complete text messages, largely because of two factors. First, they capture little contextual information, i.e., they have no idea which text units are from the same sentence and deliver a complete message. Second, they capture little text order information, i.e., they have no idea which is the previous or the next text unit in the natural reading order. Without contextual and text order information, the outputs of existing scene text detectors have a large gap towards natural understanding of scene texts and relevant scene images.

We propose a new text detection setup, namely contextual text detection, where the objective is to detect `contextual text blocks` (consisting of one or multiple ordered `integral text units`) instead of individual integral text units. This new setup has two challenges. First, it needs to detect and group the integral text units into a contextual text block that transmits a complete text message. Several studies [36,37] adopt a bottom-up approach by first detecting characters (or words) and then grouping them into a word (or a text line). However, their detected texts usually deliver partial text messages only, e.g., one text line in a contextual text block consisting of multiple text lines in Fig. 1. Second, it needs to order the detected integral text units belonging to the same contextual text block according to the natural reading order. Though some work [15] studies text sequencing in document images, it assumes a single block of text in document images and cannot handle scene images which often have multiple contextual text blocks with very different layouts and semantics.

We design a Contextual Text Detector (CUTE) to tackle the contextual text detection problem. CUTE models the grouping and ordering of integral text units from a NLP perspective. Given a scene text image, it extracts contextual visual features (capturing spatial adjacency and spatial orderliness of integral text units) of all detected text units, transform the features into feature embeddings to produce integral text tokens, and finally predicts contextual text blocks. In addition, we create two new datasets ReCTS-Context and SCUT-CTW-Context where each contextual text block is well annotated as illustrated in Fig. 1. For evaluation of contextual text detection, we also introduce three evaluation metrics that measure local accuracy, continuity, and global accuracy, respectively.

The contributions of this work are three-fold. First, we propose contextual text detection, a new text detection setup that aims to detect contextual text blocks that transmit complete text messages. To the best of our knowledge, this is the first work that studies the contextual text detection problem. Second, we design CUTE, a contextual text detector that detects integral text units and groups them into contextual text blocks in natural reading order. Third, we create two well-annotated datasets on contextual text detection and introduce three metrics to evaluate contextual text detection from multiple perspectives.

2 Related Works

2.1 Scene Text Detection

Recent scene text detectors can be broadly classified into two categories. The first category takes a bottom-up approach which first detects low-level text elements and then groups them into words or text lines. For example, CRAFT [2] and SegLink [31,35] detect characters or small segments of text instance and link them together to form text bounding boxes. The second category treats words as one specific type of objects and detects them directly by adapting various generic object detection techniques. For example, EAST [55], TextBoxes++ [17], RRD [19] and PSENet [41] detect text bounding boxes directly with generic object detection or segmentation techniques. Recent studies further improve by introducing border or counter awareness [8,42,47,56], local refinement [11,51], deformation convolution [39,43], Bezier curve [22], etc. Besides, document layout analysis [7,12,24,26,54] have been studied for years that usually take reading order of texts in document as consideration.

The existing scene text detectors have achieves very impressive performance. However, they are designed to detect individual text units like characters or words while the contextual information is missed. Differently, we propose a new setup that aims to detect contextual text blocks that deliver complete text messages.

2.2 Sequence Modeling

Sequence modeling has been widely studied in the field of NLP. Seq2Seq [34] presents an encoder-decoder structure for sequential natural language processing by using Recurrent Neural Network (RNN) [29]. Attention mechanisms [3, 25] is also introduced to relate different positions of a single sequence in order to compute a representation of the sequence. More recently, the advanced Transformer [38] is proposed which relies entirely on self-attention to compute representations of the input and output without using sequence-aligned RNNs or convolution.

Sequence modeling has also been adopted in computer vision tasks. RNNs [32, 33] and Transformers [44, 45, 49] have been widely used in recent scene text recognition studies since most scene texts are sequentially placed in scenes. Some work also studies visual permutation for Jigsaw puzzle [27, 30]. With the recent advances in Transformers, some work models different computer vision tasks sequentially in image recognition [9], object detection [5], etc. More recently, [15, 40] learn text sequences in document analysis by using Graph Convolution Network (GCN) [14].

We propose a contextual text detector which detects integral texts and groups them into contextual text blocks by attention mechanism. Different from existing work, the proposed CUTE can detect multiple contextual text blocks that convey different text messages in one image.

3   Problem Definition

In this section, we formalize the definition of terminologies in the contextual text detection problem.

Integral Text Unit: We define the basic detection units as integral text units which are usually integral components of a contextual text block. These units could be characters, words to text lines, depending on different real-world scenarios and applications. In contextual text detection problem, each integral text unit in image $I \in \mathbb{R}^{3 \times H \times W}$ is localized by using a bounding box t by:

$$t = (p_0, p_1, ..., p_{k-1}),$$
$$p_i = (x_i, y_i), x_i \in [0, W - 1], y_i \in [0, H - 1], \tag{1}$$

where k is the number of vertices in bounding boxes and it varies depending on different shapes of bounding boxes.

Contextual Text Block: A contextual text block is defined by a set of integral text units arranged in natural reading order. It delivers a complete text message which can be one or multiple sentences lying in one or multiple lines. Each contextual text block c is defined by:

$$c = (t_0, t_1, ..., t_{m-1}), \tag{2}$$

where m is the number of integral text units in C.

Contextual Text Detection: Given an input image $I \in \mathbb{R}^{3 \times H \times W}$, contextual text detection aims for a model f that can predict a set of contextual text blocks by :

$$C = f(I), \quad C = \{c_0, c_1, ..., c_{n-1}\}, \tag{3}$$

where n is the number of contextual text blocks in I.

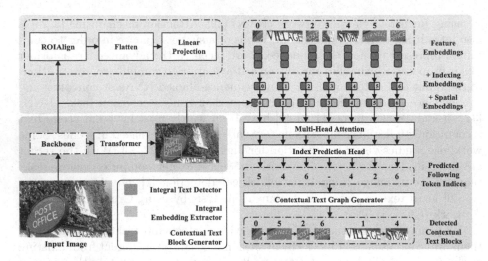

Fig. 2. The framework of the proposed contextual text detector (CUTE): Given a scene text image as input, CUTE first detects integral text units with an *Integral Text Detector*. For each detected integral text unit, it then learns textual *Feature Embeddings*, *Indexing Embeddings* and *Spatial Embeddings* that capture visual text features, text order features, and text spatial adjacency features, respectively. Finally, it models the relationship of integral text units by learning from the three types of embeddings with a *Contextual Text Block Generator* and produces contextual text blocks that convey complete text messages.

4   Method

We propose a network CUTE for contextual text detection which consists an *Integral Text Detector*, an *Integral Embedding Extractor* and a *Contextual Text Block Generator* as illustrated in Fig. 2. The *Integral Text Detector* first localizes a set of integral text units from input images. The *Integral Embedding Extractor* hence learns visual and contextual feature embeddings for each detected integral text unit. Finally, the *Contextual Text Block Generator* groups and arranges the detected integral texts in reading order to produce contextual text blocks.

4.1   Integral Text Detector

We adopt Transformer-based generic object detector [5] as the integral text detector in our CUTE which is built upon CNN and Transformer architecture. Given an input image $I \in \mathbb{R}^{3 \times H \times W}$, the DETR first extracts image features $x \in \mathbb{R}^{3 \times H_0 \times W_0}$ by using a CNN backbone (e.g., ResNet [10]). A Transformer hence predicts bounding boxes t (in Eq. 1) of integral text units from the extracted features x.

One of the major advances of the Transformer-based detector is that the Transformer models all interactions between elements of image features for object detection. Specifically, the feature map x is first flattened to a sequence of elements (i.e., pixels) accompanied with 2D positional embeddings. The Transformer hence focuses on image regions for each object by learning the relationships between each pair of elements in feature map x. As such, we adopt Transformer-based detector as the integral text detector in our CUTE for better modelling of element interactions in the visual features from network backbone. More details are available in the Supplementary Material.

4.2 Integral Embedding Extractor

Both visual and contextual features of integral text units are indispensable to accurate detection of contextual text blocks. We therefore design an Integral Embedding Extractor to extract three types of embeddings for each integral text unit including: (1) feature embeddings that are learnt from visual features of integral text units; (2) indexing embeddings that are encoded for integral ordering; (3) spatial embeddings that are predicted from spatial features of integral text units.

Feature Embeddings: We first extract visual features of integral text units and predict a set of feature embeddings. Given the image features x that are extracted from backbone network, the feature embeddings of the integral text units $v_{fe} \in \mathbb{R}^{r \times d}$ are defined by:

$$v_{fe} = (v_{fe}^0, v_{fe}^1, ..., v_{fe}^{r-1}),$$
$$v_{fe}^i = x_c^i W + b, \quad x_c^i = \text{flatten}(\text{ROIAlign}(x, t_i)). \tag{4}$$

Specifically, we first crop the visual features x_c for each of detected integral text units from the image features x by using the detected integral text boxes t from integral text detector. These features x_c are hence flattened and linearly projected to dimension d to produce feature embeddings v_{fe}, where r is the number of detected integral text units in image. More details about dimension d are available in Appendix.

Indexing Embeddings: We also introduce indexing embeddings for integral text ordering. Given a set of detected integral text units, we assign each integral text unit with an index number i, where $i \in [0, r-1]$ refers to the i-th integral text unit. Next, we adopt sinusoidal positional encoding [38] on these indices to produce indexing embeddings $v_{ie} \in \mathbb{R}^{r \times d}$ by:

$$v_{ie} = (v_{ie}^0, v_{ie}^1, ..., v_{ie}^{r-1}),$$
$$v_{ie}^i = \begin{cases} sin(i/10000^{2d_k/d}), & \text{if } d_k = 2n, \\ cos(i/10000^{2d_k/d}), & \text{if } d_k = 2n+1. \end{cases} \tag{5}$$

Spatial Embeddings: The spatial information of each detected integral text unit (i.e., size and position of integral texts in images) are lost because integral text features are extracted by cropping and resizing. For accurate contextual text block detection, we introduce spatial embeddings that encodes the spatial information to each integral text unit. Specifically, we use a vector v_s^i to represent the spatial information of i-th integral text unit which is defined by:

$$v_s^i = (w, h, x_1, y_1, x_2, y_2, w \times h), \tag{6}$$

where w, h, (x_1, y_1) and (x_2, y_2) refer to the width, height, top-left vertex coordinate, and bottom-right vertex coordinate of integral text bounding box t^i. The spatial embeddings $v_{se} \in \mathbb{R}^{r \times d}$ are hence obtained by two linear transformations:

$$\begin{aligned} v_{se} &= (v_{se}^0, v_{se}^1, ..., v_{se}^{r-1}), \\ v_{se}^i &= \max(0, \max(0, v_s^i W_1 + b_1) W_2 + b_2). \end{aligned} \tag{7}$$

The text tokens are hence obtained by:

$$v_{token} = \mathrm{Concat}(v_{fe}, v_{ie}, v_{se}). \tag{8}$$

4.3 Contextual Text Block Generator

Taking the integral tokens v_{token} as input, the Contextual Text Block Generator groups and arranges these integral tokens in reading order. As illustrated in Fig. 2, it learns the relationship between each pairs of integral tokens v_{token} by a multi-head attention layer and produces contextual text blocks by an index prediction head and a contextual text graph generator.

Multi-head Attention: We use multi-head self-attention mechanism to model the relationships between each pair of integral text units. Six stacked attention modules are adopted and each of them contains a multi-head self-attention layer following by a linear transformation layer. Layer normalization [1] is applied to the input of each layer. The text tokens v_{token} serve as values, keys, and queries of the attention function.

Index Prediction Head: We model the contextual information learning as an index classification problem by an index prediction head. We adopt a linear projection layer is predict a set of indices $\mathbf{INX} = (\mathrm{INX}^0, \mathrm{INX}^1, ..., \mathrm{INX}^{r-1})$, where v_{token}^j follows v_{token}^i in reading order if $\mathrm{INX}^i = j$. Cross-entropy loss is adopted for network optimization. Note we assign a random but unique index to each detected integral text unit as the detected integral text units are usually in random order.

For the i-th indexed query token v_{token}^i, three cases are considered including: (1) if v_{token}^i is not the last integral text in a contextual block, the index prediction head outputs index class j if v_{token}^j follows v_{token}^i; (2) if v_{token}^i is the last integral unit in a contextual block, the class i will be predicted; (3) if v_{token}^i is not a text (i.e., false alarms from Integral Text Detector), it will be classified to 'not a text' class. In this way, a $(N+1)$-way classification problem is defined for index prediction where 'N' refers the number of index categories and '$+1$' is the 'not a text' category. 'N' is a fixed number that is significantly larger than the possible number of integral text units in an image.

Contextual Text Graph Generator: A directed contextual text graph $G = (V, E)$ is constructed by a Contextual Text Graph Generator which considers the detected integral text units as vertices V. The E refers to the edges of the graph G that is obtained from the Index Prediction Head (IPH) by

Table 1. The **statistics** of the ReCTS-Context and SCUT-CTW-Context datasets: 'integral': Integral Text Units; 'block': Contextual Text Blocks; '#': Number.

Dataset	Integral Text	# integral	# block	# image	# integral per block	# integral per image	# block per image
ReCTS-Context	Character	440,027	107,754	20,000	4.08	22.00	5.39
SCUT-CTW-Context	Word	25,208	4,512	1,438	5.56	17.65	3.17

$E = \{(V_i, V_j)|\mathrm{IPH}(\boldsymbol{v}_{token}^i) = j, i \in |V|, j \in |V|\}$. A set of weakly connected components $G' = \{G'_0, G'_1, ... G'_n\}$ are produced from graph G where n refers to the number of contextual text blocks in the image. Each $G'_i = (V'_i, E'_i)$ represents a contextual text block in image where V'_i refers its integral text units and E'_i produces their reading order.

5   Datasets and Evaluation Metrics

5.1   Datasets

We create two contextual-text-block datasets ReCTS-Context and SCUT-CTW-Context as shown in Table 1. Figure 3 shows two samples where integral text units belonging to the same contextual text block are grouped in proper order. **ReCTS-Context (ReCTS):** We annotate contextual text blocks for images in dataset ICDAR2019-ReCTS [52], which are split into a training set and a test set with 15,000 and 5,000 images, respectively. It contains largely Chinese texts with characters as integral text units. **SCUT-CTW-Context (SCUT-CTW):** We annotate contextual text blocks for dataset SCUT-CTW-1500 dataset [50] which consists of 940 training images and 498 test images. Most integral text units in this dataset are words which have rich contextual information as captured in various scenes. More details about the two created datasets are available in Appendix.

5.2   Evaluation Metrics

We propose three evaluation metrics for the evaluation of contextual text detection: **Local Accuracy (LA):** We introduce LA to evaluate the accuracy of order prediction for neighbouring integral text units. Considering two correctly detected integral text units a and b (with b following a as ground-truth), a true positive is counted if the detection box of b is predicted as directly following that of a. We compute LA by $LA = TP/N$ where TP denotes the number of true positives and N is the total number of connected pairs in ground-truth.

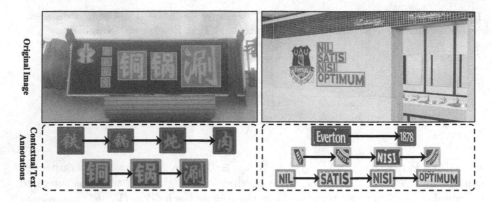

Fig. 3. Illustration of contextual text block annotation: We annotate each contextual text block by an ordered sequence of integral text units (characters or words) which together convey a complete textual message. The two sample images are picked from datasets ReCTS and SCUT-CTW, respectively.

Local Continuity (LC): We introduce LC to evaluate the continuity of integral text units by computing a modified n-gram precision score as inspired by BLEU [28]. Specifically, we compare n-grams of the predicted consecutive integral text units with the n-grams of the ground-truth integral texts and count the number of matches, where n varies from 1 to 5. For $n = 1$, we only consider the scenario that the contextual text block contains one integral text.

Global Accuracy (GA): Besides LA and LC which focus on local characteristics of integral text units ordering, we also evaluate the detection accuracy of contextual text blocks. TP is counted if all integral texts in a contextual text block are detected and the reading orders are accurately predicted. The global accuracy is hence computed by $GA = TP/N$ where N is the total number of contextual text blocks in ground-truth.

Besides, a detected integral text unit is determined to be matched with ground-truth text if the intersection-over-union (IoU) of these two bounding boxes are larger than a threshold. We adopt three IoU threshold standards that are widely-used in generic object detection task [20] including $IoU = 0.5, IoU = 0.75$ and $IoU = 0.5 : 0.05 : 0.95$ for thorough evaluation.

6   Experiments

6.1   Comparing with State-of-the-Art

We evaluate the proposed CUTE on ReCTS-Context and SCUT-CTW-Context datasets qualitatively and quantitatively as shown in Fig. 4 and Tables 2, 3 and 4.

Since there is little prior research on contextual text block detection, we develop a few baselines for comparisons. The first baseline is CLUSTERING that groups integral text units by mean shift clustering [6]. The second and the

Table 2. Quantitative comparison of CUTE with state-of-the-art methods on **ReCTS-Context**. LA: Local Accuracy; LC: Local Continuity; GA: Global Accuracy.

Model	IoU = 0.5			IoU = 0.75			IoU = 0.5:0.05:0.95		
	LA	LC	GA	LA	LC	GA	LA	LC	GA
CLUSTERING [6]	32.22	19.06	10.59	26.06	17.01	9.66	25.60	16.13	9.02
CRAFT-R50 [2]	63.66	53.26	45.96	51.22	48.39	36.76	50.06	45.46	35.60
LINK-R50 [46]	68.15	57.50	48.39	53.83	50.19	38.36	52.95	47.69	37.33
CUTE-R50	**70.43**	**64.74**	**51.55**	**54.39**	**56.63**	**39.52**	**53.92**	**53.56**	**38.92**
CRAFT-R101 [2]	65.21	54.59	47.02	52.01	48.65	37.21	51.56	46.10	36.33
LINK-R101 [46]	70.78	59.10	49.92	54.53	51.02	38.98	53.42	48.26	37.94
CUTE-R101	**72.36**	**67.33**	**53.76**	**55.14**	**57.03**	**40.21**	**54.56**	**53.94**	**39.42**

Table 3. Quantitative comparison of CUTE with state-of-the-art methods on **SCUT-CTW-Context**. LA: Local Accuracy; LC: Local Continuity; GA: Global Accuracy.

Model	IoU = 0.5			IoU = 0.75			IoU = 0.5:0.05:0.95		
	LA	LC	GA	LA	LC	GA	LA	LC	GA
CLUSTERING [6]	18.36	7.93	6.78	14.11	5.88	4.72	13.54	5.71	4.88
LINK-R50 [46]	25.47	3.33	18.88	20.25	3.15	14.70	19.31	2.93	14.26
CUTE-R50	**54.01**	**39.19**	**30.65**	**41.62**	**31.19**	**23.71**	**39.44**	**29.03**	**22.10**
LINK-R101 [46]	25.71	3.41	19.18	20.02	2.89	14.68	19.56	2.72	14.39
CUTE-R101	**55.71**	**39.38**	**32.62**	**40.61**	**29.04**	**22.77**	**39.95**	**28.30**	**22.69**

third baselines are CRAFT [2] and LINK [46], two bottom-up scene text detection methods that group characters/words to text lines. Since both CRAFT and LINK do not have the concept of contextual text blocks, we sort integral text units within each contextual text block according to the common reading order of left-to-right and top-to-down. In addition, we evaluate with two backbones ResNet-50 and ResNet-101 (denoted by 'R50' and 'R101') to study the robustness of the proposed CUTE.

We compare CUTE with the three baselines over ReCTS where integral text units are at character level. As Table 2 shows, the clustering-based method cannot solve the contextual text detection problem effectively because the integral text units are usually with different sizes, positions, and orientations. The bottom-up scene text detectors work better by focusing on visual features only. The proposed CUTE performs the best consistently as it models the relation between each pair of integral text units by considering both visual representative features and contextual information.

Fig. 4. Illustration of the proposed CUTE: Sample images are collected from SCUT-CTW-Context and ReCTS-Context datasets, where the color boxes highlight the detected integral text units and the green arrows show the predicted text orders. The integral text units of each contextual text block are highlighted in the same color. (Color figure online)

Table 4. Quantitative comparison of CUTE with state-of-the-art methods on **integral text grouping and ordering task**: The ground-truth integral text bounding boxes are adopted for evaluations on integral text grouping and ordering task only. LA: Local Accuracy; LC: Local Continuity; GA: Global Accuracy.

Model	SCUT-CTW			ReCTS		
	LA	LC	GA	LA	LC	GA
CLUSTERING [6]	27.94	12.74	10.76	69.70	49.15	32.20
LINK-R50 [46]	30.17	4.48	22.84	83.77	68.44	61.10
CUTE-R50	**71.48**	**58.53**	**49.67**	**92.08**	**82.79**	**76.02**
LINK-R101 [46]	45.54	6.28	31.69	86.66	75.03	69.55
CUTE-R101	**71.54**	**58.68**	**52.57**	**93.12**	**83.70**	**77.81**

We further conduct experiments over SCUT-CTW where integral text units are at word level. We compare CUTE with CLUSTERING and LINK only because CRAFT cannot group texts lying on different lines. As Table 3 shows, CLUSTERING achieves very low performance due to the complex contextual relations among integral text units. LINK obtains very low scores on LC, showing that only short contextual text blocks with small number of integral text units are detected. CUTE instead outperforms all three baselines by large margins consistently across LA, LC and GA. Note the detection performances over SCUT-CTW are relatively low because it contains many texts with more complex layouts as compared with ReCTS.

Additionally, to validate CUTE's effectiveness on the grouping and ordering of integral text units alone, we assume that all integral text units are accurately detected by feeding the bounding boxes of ground-truth integral text units to the *Integral Embedding Extractor* and *Contextual Text Block Generator*. As Table 4 shows, the proposed CUTE groups and orders integral text units effectively.

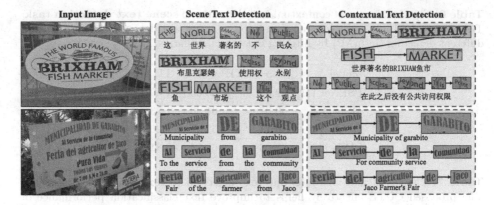

Fig. 5. Contextual text detection facilitates scene text translation significantly: The output of CUTE conveys complete text messages which can be better translated to other languages as 'natural language' with rich contextual information as shown in column 3. As a comparison, scene text detectors produce individual text units which can not be translated well as shown in column 2.

Table 5. Ablation studies of CUTE over SCUT-CTW. LA: Local Accuracy; LC: Local Continuity; GA: Global Accuracy.

Model	v_{fe}	v_{se}	v_{ie}	LA	LC	GA
1	✓			6.86	3.34	1.94
2	✓	✓		8.99	4.56	2.18
3	✓		✓	28.65	25.71	21.89
4	✓	✓	✓	**71.48**	**58.53**	**49.67**

6.2 Ablation Study

The proposed CUTE detects contextual text blocks by using both visual features (feature embeddings) and contextual features that capture spatial and ordering information, respectively. We conduct ablation studies over SCUT-CTW-Context to identify the contribution of each embedding. We trained four models with different combinations of the three embeddings. As Table 5 shows, CUTE does not work well with either feature embeddings alone or feature embeddings plus spatial embeddings. However, combining feature embeddings with indexing embeddings improves detection greatly as indexing embeddings introduce crucial text order information. The combination of all three embeddings performs the best by large margins, demonstrating the complementary nature of the three embeddings.

Table 6. The significance of contextual text detection to **scene text detection task**: The proposed CUTE effectively helps to improve scene text detection performance of different detectors (in mAP) by filtering out the false alarms.

Model	w/o CUTE	with CUTE
PSENet [41]	52.30	53.69 (+1.39)
MSR [48]	60.07	61.80 (+1.73)
DETR [5]	56.11	57.37 (+1.26)
LINK [46]	62.03	62.84 (+0.81)

Table 7. The significance of contextual text detection to **text classification task**: The proposed CUTE effectively helps to improve text classification performance of different text classifiers by learning from recognized texts in contextual text blocks.

Model	w/o CUTE	with CUTE
TextCNN [13]	90.56	92.40 (+1.84)
TextRNN [21]	79.55	87.20 (+7.65)
Fast Text [4]	90.96	91.82 (+0.86)
Transformer [38]	89.69	92.54 (+2.85)

6.3   Discussion

Contextual text detection facilitates downstream tasks: The proposed detection setup for contextual text blocks can facilitate both scene text detection and many downstream tasks. We first study how the proposed contextual text detection can improve the scene text detection task over SCUT-CTW. Specifically, traditional scene text detectors tend to produce false detection at image background that has similar visual representations as scene texts. CUTE can suppress such false detection effectively (i.e., classify the false detection into 'not a text' category) by learning the text ordering through not only visual features but also contextual information of texts (details in Sect. 4.3). As Table 6 shows, CUTE improves the scene text detection performance consistently across a number of scene text detectors that adopt different backbones and detection strategies.

We also study how the proposed contextual text detection can facilitate various downstream tasks. We focus on the scene text translation task that is very useful to scene understanding for visitors with different home languages. Specifically, we feed each detected text (i.e. a character, word, or contextual text block) to a neural machine translator (Google Translator) for translation across different languages. As Fig. 5 shows, CUTE groups and orders scene texts into contextual text blocks (delivering complete textual messages) which facilitates scene text translation greatly as compared with traditional scene text detectors without the concept of contextual text blocks.

Fig. 6. Typical Failure Cases of the Proposed CUTE: Correct, incorrect and missing orders or integral text units are highlighted by arrows in yellow, red and blue, respectively. The proposed CUTE may fail if the images contain complex text layouts. (Color figure online)

We additionally study how contextual text detection facilitates text classification task in NLP. Specifically, we classify and annotate the transcription of texts in ReCTS-Context into three categories (i.e., 'Address', 'Phone Number' or 'Restaurant Name') according to the text semantics. We train models by different text classification techniques and test on the detected texts from integral texts (denoted by 'w/o CUTE') and contextual text blocks (denoted by 'with CUTE'), respectively. As shown in Table 7, the use of CUTE helps to improve the text classification consistently across different text classifiers.

Typical Failure Cases: The proposed CUTE may fail if the images contain complex text layouts. As shown in Fig. 6, the proposed CUTE may fail if the texts from different contextual text blocks are in similar font styles and extremely close to (or far from) each other.

7 Conclusion and Future Work

We study contextual text detection, a new text detection setup that first detects integral text units and then groups them into contextual text blocks. We design CUTE, a novel method that detects contextual text blocks effectively by combining both visual and contextual features. In addition, we create two contextual text detection datasets within which each contextual text block is well annotated by an ordered text sequence. Extensive experiments show that CUTE achieves superior contextual text detection, and it also improves scene text detection and many downstream tasks significantly.

In the future, we will continue to study contextual text detection when scene texts have complex layouts. Specifically, we will expand and balance our datasets by including more complex scenes and text layouts. We will also study how to leverage text semantics (from scene text recognition) for better contextual text detection.

References

1. Ba, J.L., Kiros, J.R., Hinton, G.E.: Layer normalization. arXiv preprint arXiv:1607.06450 (2016)
2. Baek, Y., Lee, B., Han, D., Yun, S., Lee, H.: Character region awareness for text detection. In: Proceedings of the IEEE/CVF Conference on Computer Vision and Pattern Recognition, pp. 9365–9374 (2019)
3. Bahdanau, D., Cho, K., Bengio, Y.: Neural machine translation by jointly learning to align and translate. arXiv preprint arXiv:1409.0473 (2014)
4. Bojanowski, P., Grave, E., Joulin, A., Mikolov, T.: Enriching word vectors with subword information. Trans. Assoc. Comput. Linguist. **5**, 135–146 (2017)
5. Carion, N., Massa, F., Synnaeve, G., Usunier, N., Kirillov, A., Zagoruyko, S.: End-to-end object detection with transformers. In: Vedaldi, A., Bischof, H., Brox, T., Frahm, J.-M. (eds.) ECCV 2020. LNCS, vol. 12346, pp. 213–229. Springer, Cham (2020). https://doi.org/10.1007/978-3-030-58452-8_13
6. Cheng, Y.: Mean shift, mode seeking, and clustering. IEEE Trans. Pattern Anal. Mach. Intell. **17**(8), 790–799 (1995)
7. Clausner, C., Antonacopoulos, A., Pletschacher, S.: Icdar 2017 competition on recognition of documents with complex layouts-rdcl2017. In: 2017 14th IAPR International Conference on Document Analysis and Recognition (ICDAR), vol. 1, pp. 1404–1410. IEEE (2017)
8. Dai, P., Zhang, S., Zhang, H., Cao, X.: Progressive contour regression for arbitrary-shape scene text detection. In: Proceedings of the IEEE/CVF Conference on Computer Vision and Pattern Recognition, pp. 7393–7402 (2021)
9. Dosovitskiy, A., Beyer, L., Kolesnikov, A., Weissenborn, D., Zhai, X., Unterthiner, T., Dehghani, M., Minderer, M., Heigold, G., Gelly, S., et al.: An image is worth 16×16 words: Transformers for image recognition at scale. arXiv preprint arXiv:2010.11929 (2020)
10. He, K., Zhang, X., Ren, S., Sun, J.: Deep residual learning for image recognition. In: Proceedings of the IEEE Conference on Computer Vision and Pattern Recognition, pp. 770–778 (2016)
11. He, M., et al.: Most: a multi-oriented scene text detector with localization refinement. In: Proceedings of the IEEE/CVF Conference on Computer Vision and Pattern Recognition, pp. 8813–8822 (2021)
12. Jaume, G., Ekenel, H.K., Thiran, J.P.: Funsd: a dataset for form understanding in noisy scanned documents. In: 2019 International Conference on Document Analysis and Recognition Workshops (ICDARW), vol. 2, pp. 1–6. IEEE (2019)
13. Kim, Y.: Convolutional neural networks for sentence classification. In: Proceedings of the 2014 Conference on Empirical Methods in Natural Language Processing (EMNLP), pp. 1746–1751. Association for Computational Linguistics (2014). https://doi.org/10.3115/v1/D14-1181. https://www.aclweb.org/anthology/D14-1181
14. Kipf, T.N., Welling, M.: Semi-supervised classification with graph convolutional networks. In: International Conference on Learning Representations (ICLR) (2017)
15. Li, L., Gao, F., Bu, J., Wang, Y., Yu, Z., Zheng, Q.: An end-to-end OCR text re-organization sequence learning for rich-text detail image comprehension. In: Vedaldi, A., Bischof, H., Brox, T., Frahm, J.-M. (eds.) ECCV 2020. LNCS, vol. 12370, pp. 85–100. Springer, Cham (2020). https://doi.org/10.1007/978-3-030-58595-2_6

16. Liao, M., Pang, G., Huang, J., Hassner, T., Bai, X.: Mask TextSpotter v3: segmentation proposal network for robust scene text spotting. In: Vedaldi, A., Bischof, H., Brox, T., Frahm, J.-M. (eds.) Mask textspotter v3: Segmentation proposal network for robust scene text spotting. LNCS, vol. 12356, pp. 706–722. Springer, Cham (2020). https://doi.org/10.1007/978-3-030-58621-8_41

17. Liao, M., Shi, B., Bai, X.: Textboxes++: a single-shot oriented scene text detector. IEEE Trans. Image Process. 27(8), 3676–3690 (2018)

18. Liao, M., Wan, Z., Yao, C., Chen, K., Bai, X.: Real-time scene text detection with differentiable binarization. In: Proceedings of the AAAI (2020)

19. Liao, M., Zhu, Z., Shi, B., Xia, G.s., Bai, X.: Rotation-sensitive regression for oriented scene text detection. In: Proceedings of the IEEE Conference on Computer Vision and Pattern Recognition, pp. 5909–5918 (2018)

20. Liu, L., Ouyang, W., Wang, X., Fieguth, P., Chen, J., Liu, X., Pietikäinen, M.: Deep learning for generic object detection: A survey. Int. J. Comput. Vision 128(2), 261–318 (2020)

21. Liu, P., Qiu, X., Huang, X.: Recurrent neural network for text classification with multi-task learning. arXiv preprint arXiv:1605.05101 (2016)

22. Liu, Y., Chen, H., Shen, C., He, T., Jin, L., Wang, L.: Abcnet: real-time scene text spotting with adaptive bezier-curve network. In: Proceedings of the IEEE/CVF Conference on Computer Vision and Pattern Recognition, pp. 9809–9818 (2020)

23. Long, S., He, X., Yao, C.: Scene text detection and recognition: the deep learning era. Int. J. Comput. Vision 129(1), 161–184 (2021)

24. Long, S., Qin, S., Panteleev, D., Bissacco, A., Fujii, Y., Raptis, M.: Towards end-to-end unified scene text detection and layout analysis. In: Proceedings of the IEEE/CVF Conference on Computer Vision and Pattern Recognition, pp. 1049–1059 (2022)

25. Luong, M.T., Pham, H., Manning, C.D.: Effective approaches to attention-based neural machine translation. arXiv preprint arXiv:1508.04025 (2015)

26. Michael, J., Weidemann, M., Laasch, B., Labahn, R.: ICPR 2020 competition on text block segmentation on a NewsEye dataset. In: Del Bimbo, A., Cucchiara, R., Sclaroff, S., Farinella, G.M., Mei, T., Bertini, M., Escalante, H.J., Vezzani, R. (eds.) ICPR 2021. LNCS, vol. 12668, pp. 405–418. Springer, Cham (2021). https://doi.org/10.1007/978-3-030-68793-9_30

27. Noroozi, M., Favaro, P.: Unsupervised learning of visual representations by solving jigsaw puzzles. In: Leibe, B., Matas, J., Sebe, N., Welling, M. (eds.) ECCV 2016. LNCS, vol. 9910, pp. 69–84. Springer, Cham (2016). https://doi.org/10.1007/978-3-319-46466-4_5

28. Papineni, K., Roukos, S., Ward, T., Zhu, W.J.: Bleu: a method for automatic evaluation of machine translation. In: Proceedings of the 40th Annual Meeting of the Association for Computational Linguistics, pp. 311–318 (2002)

29. Rumelhart, D.E., Hinton, G.E., Williams, R.J.: Learning internal representations by error propagation. California Univ San Diego La Jolla Inst for Cognitive Science, Tech. rep. (1985)

30. Santa Cruz, R., Fernando, B., Cherian, A., Gould, S.: Deeppermnet: visual permutation learning. In: Proceedings of the IEEE Conference on Computer Vision and Pattern Recognition, pp. 3949–3957 (2017)

31. Shi, B., Bai, X., Belongie, S.: Detecting oriented text in natural images by linking segments. In: The IEEE Conference on Computer Vision and Pattern Recognition (CVPR), July 2017

32. Shi, B., Bai, X., Yao, C.: An end-to-end trainable neural network for image-based sequence recognition and its application to scene text recognition. IEEE Trans. Pattern Anal. Mach. Intell. **39**(11), 2298–2304 (2016)

33. Su, B., Lu, S.: Accurate scene text recognition based on recurrent neural network. In: Cremers, D., Reid, I., Saito, H., Yang, M.-H. (eds.) ACCV 2014. LNCS, vol. 9003, pp. 35–48. Springer, Cham (2015). https://doi.org/10.1007/978-3-319-16865-4_3

34. Sutskever, I., Vinyals, O., Le, Q.V.: Sequence to sequence learning with neural networks. In: Advances in Neural Information Processing Systems, pp. 3104–3112 (2014)

35. Tang, J., Yang, Z., Wang, Y., Zheng, Q., Xu, Y., Bai, X.: Seglink++: detecting dense and arbitrary-shaped scene text by instance-aware component grouping. Pattern Recogn. **96**, 106954 (2019)

36. Tian, S., Pan, Y., Huang, C., Lu, S., Yu, K., Lim Tan, C.: Text flow: a unified text detection system in natural scene images. In: Proceedings of the IEEE International Conference on Computer Vision, pp. 4651–4659 (2015)

37. Tian, Z., Huang, W., He, T., He, P., Qiao, Yu.: Detecting text in natural image with connectionist text proposal network. In: Leibe, B., Matas, J., Sebe, N., Welling, M. (eds.) ECCV 2016. LNCS, vol. 9912, pp. 56–72. Springer, Cham (2016). https://doi.org/10.1007/978-3-319-46484-8_4

38. Vaswani, A., et al.: Attention is all you need. In: Advances in Neural Information Processing Systems, pp. 5998–6008 (2017)

39. Wang, F., Zhao, L., Li, X., Wang, X., Tao, D.: Geometry-aware scene text detection with instance transformation network. In: Proceedings of the IEEE Conference on Computer Vision and Pattern Recognition, pp. 1381–1389 (2018)

40. Wang, R., Fujii, Y., Popat, A.C.: General-purpose ocr paragraph identification by graph convolutional neural networks. arXiv preprint arXiv:2101.12741 (2021)

41. Wang, W., Xie, E., Li, X., Hou, W., Lu, T., Yu, G., Shao, S.: Shape robust text detection with progressive scale expansion network. In: Proceedings of the IEEE/CVF Conference on Computer Vision and Pattern Recognition, pp. 9336–9345 (2019)

42. Wang, Y., Xie, H., Zha, Z.J., Xing, M., Fu, Z., Zhang, Y.: Contournet: taking a further step toward accurate arbitrary-shaped scene text detection. In: Proceedings of the IEEE/CVF Conference on Computer Vision and Pattern Recognition, pp. 11753–11762 (2020)

43. Xiao, S., Peng, L., Yan, R., An, K., Yao, G., Min, J.: Sequential deformation for accurate scene text detection. In: Vedaldi, A., Bischof, H., Brox, T., Frahm, J.-M. (eds.) Sequential deformation for accurate scene text detection. LNCS, vol. 12374, pp. 108–124. Springer, Cham (2020). https://doi.org/10.1007/978-3-030-58526-6_7

44. Xu, Y., Li, M., Cui, L., Huang, S., Wei, F., Zhou, M.: Layoutlm: pre-training of text and layout for document image understanding. In: Proceedings of the 26th ACM SIGKDD International Conference on Knowledge Discovery & Data Mining, pp. 1192–1200 (2020)

45. Xue, C., Lu, S., Bai, S., Zhang, W., Wang, C.: I2c2w: image-to-character-to-word transformers for accurate scene text recognition. arXiv preprint arXiv:2105.08383 (2021)

46. Xue, C., Lu, S., Hoi, S.: Detection and rectification of arbitrary shaped scene texts by using text keypoints and links. arXiv preprint arXiv:2103.00785 (2021)

47. Xue, C., Lu, S., Zhan, F.: Accurate scene text detection through border semantics awareness and bootstrapping. In: Ferrari, V., Hebert, M., Sminchisescu, C., Weiss, Y. (eds.) ECCV 2018. LNCS, vol. 11220, pp. 370–387. Springer, Cham (2018). https://doi.org/10.1007/978-3-030-01270-0_22

48. Xue, C., Lu, S., Zhang, W.: Msr: multi-scale shape regression for scene text detection. arXiv preprint arXiv:1901.02596 (2019)

49. Yu, D., Li, X., Zhang, C., Liu, T., Han, J., Liu, J., Ding, E.: Towards accurate scene text recognition with semantic reasoning networks. In: IEEE/CVF Conference on Computer Vision and Pattern Recognition (CVPR), June 2020

50. Yuliang, L., Lianwen, J., Shuaitao, Z., Sheng, Z.: Detecting curve text in the wild: new dataset and new solution. arXiv preprint arXiv:1712.02170 (2017)

51. Zhang, C., Liang, B., Huang, Z., En, M., Han, J., Ding, E., Ding, X.: Look more than once: An accurate detector for text of arbitrary shapes. In: Proceedings of the IEEE/CVF Conference on Computer Vision and Pattern Recognition, pp. 10552–10561 (2019)

52. Zhang, R., et al.: Icdar 2019 robust reading challenge on reading Chinese text on signboard. In: 2019 International Conference on Document Analysis and Recognition (ICDAR), pp. 1577–1581. IEEE (2019)

53. Zhang, W., Qiu, Y., Liao, M., Zhang, R., Wei, X., Bai, X.: Scene text detection with scribble line. In: Lladós, J., Lopresti, D., Uchida, S. (eds.) ICDAR 2021. LNCS, vol. 12824, pp. 79–94. Springer, Cham (2021). https://doi.org/10.1007/978-3-030-86337-1_6

54. Zhong, X., Tang, J., Yepes, A.J.: Publaynet: largest dataset ever for document layout analysis. In: 2019 International Conference on Document Analysis and Recognition (ICDAR), pp. 1015–1022. IEEE (2019)

55. Zhou, X., et al.: East: an efficient and accurate scene text detector. In: The IEEE Conference on Computer Vision and Pattern Recognition (CVPR), July 2017

56. Zhu, Y., Chen, J., Liang, L., Kuang, Z., Jin, L., Zhang, W.: Fourier contour embedding for arbitrary-shaped text detection. In: Proceedings of the IEEE/CVF Conference on Computer Vision and Pattern Recognition, pp. 3123–3131 (2021)

CoMER: Modeling Coverage for Transformer-Based Handwritten Mathematical Expression Recognition

Wenqi Zhao[ID] and Liangcai Gao[✉]

Wangxuan Institute of Computer Technology, Peking University, Beijing, China
wenqizhao@stu.pku.edu.cn, gaoliangcai@pku.edu.cn

Abstract. The Transformer-based encoder-decoder architecture has recently made significant advances in recognizing handwritten mathematical expressions. However, the transformer model still suffers from the lack of coverage problem, making its expression recognition rate (ExpRate) inferior to its RNN counterpart. Coverage information, which records the alignment information of the past steps, has proven effective in the RNN models. In this paper, we propose CoMER, a model that adopts the coverage information in the transformer decoder. Specifically, we propose a novel Attention Refinement Module (ARM) to refine the attention weights with past alignment information without hurting its parallelism. Furthermore, we take coverage information to the extreme by proposing self-coverage and cross-coverage, which utilize the past alignment information from the current and previous layers. Experiments show that CoMER improves the ExpRate by 0.61%/2.09%/1.59% compared to the current state-of-the-art model, and reaches 59.33%/59.81%/62.97% on the CROHME 2014/2016/2019 test sets. (Source code is available at https://github.com/Green-Wood/CoMER)

Keywords: Handwritten mathematical expression recognition · Transformer · Coverage · Alignment · Encoder-decoder model

1 Introduction

Handwritten mathematical expression recognition (HMER) aims to generate the corresponding LaTeX sequence from a handwritten mathematical expression image. The recognition of handwritten mathematical expressions has led to many downstream applications, such as online education, automatic scoring, and formula image searching. During the COVID-19 pandemic, an increasing number of education institutions chose to use online platforms for teaching and examing. The recognition rate of handwritten mathematical expressions is crucial to improving both learning efficiency and teaching quality in online education scenarios.

© The Author(s), under exclusive license to Springer Nature Switzerland AG 2022
S. Avidan et al. (Eds.): ECCV 2022, LNCS 13688, pp. 392–408, 2022.
https://doi.org/10.1007/978-3-031-19815-1_23

Handwritten mathematical expression recognition is an image-to-text task with more challenges than traditional text recognition. Besides various writing styles, we also need to model the relationships between symbols and contexts [2]. In LATEX, for example, the model needs to generate "^", "_", "{", and "}" to describe the position and hierarchical relationship between symbols in a two-dimensional image. Researchers use the encoder-decoder architecture widely in the HMER task [9,15,26,29,32–35] because of its feature extraction in the encoder part and language modeling in the decoder part.

Transformer [28], a neural network architecture based solely on the attention mechanism, has gradually replaced RNN as the preferred model in natural language processing (NLP) [8]. Through the self-attention mechanism in the transformer, tokens in the same sequence establish direct one-to-one connections. Such an architecture allows the transformer to better model long-term dependency [3] between tokens. Currently, Transformer is attracting more and more attention in the computer vision [10] and multimodal [7,17,23] community.

Although transformer has become the standard de-facto in NLP, its performance in the HMER task was unsatisfactory compared with its RNN counterparts [9,35]. We observe that the existing model using the transformer decoder still suffers from the lack of coverage problem [27,34]. This problem manifests itself in two ways: over-parsing means that some parts of the image are unnecessarily pasred multiple times, while under-parsing means that some areas remain unparsed. RNN decoder uses coverage attention [9,15,26,29,32–34] to alleviate this problem. However, the current transformer decoder uses vanilla dot-product attention without the coverage mechanism, which is the key factor limiting its performance.

The computation of each step in the transformer is independent of each other, unlike RNN, where the computation of the current step depends on the previous step's state. While this nature improves the parallelism in the transformer, it makes it difficult to use the coverage mechanism from previous works directly in the transformer decoder. To address the above issues, we propose a novel model for exploiting **Co**verage information in the transfor**MER** decoder, named CoMER. Inspired by the coverage mechanism in RNN, we want the transformer to allocate more attention to regions that have not yet been parsed. Specifically, we propose a novel and general Attention Refinement Module (ARM) that dynamically refines the attention weights with past alignment information without hurting its parallelism. To fully use the past alignment information generated from different layers, we propose self-coverage and cross-coverage to utilize the past alignment information from the current and previous layer, respectively. We further show that CoMER performs better than vanilla transformer decoder and RNN decoder in the HMER task. The main contributions of our work are summarized as follows:

- We propose a novel and general Attention Refinement Module (ARM) to refine the attention weight in the transformer decoder, which effectively alleviates the lack of coverage problem without hurting its parallelism.

– We propose self-coverage, cross-coverage, and fusion-coverage to fully use the past alignment information generated from different layers in the stack transformer decoder.
– Experiments show that CoMER outperforms existing state-of-the-art methods and achieves expression recognition rates (ExpRate)s of 59.33%/ 59.81%/ 62.97% on the CROHME 2014 [21]/2016 [22]/2019 [20] datasets.

2 Related Work

2.1 HMER Methods

The traditional approach usually divides the HMER task into two subtasks: symbol recognition and structure analysis [5]. Researchers represented the structural information of formulas through different predefined grammars, such as graph grammar [14], context-free grammar [1], and relational grammar [19]. These methods require researchers to develop hand-designed grammar rules, and their generalizability largely depends on the perfection of these grammar rules.

In recent years, encoder-decoder architectures have shown promising performance in various image-to-text tasks, such as scene text recognition [6] and image captioning [30]. In [34], a model called WAP was proposed to use encoder-decoder neural network for the first time to solve the HMER task and outperformed traditional grammar-based methods in the CROHME 2014 competition [21]. The WAP model uses a convolution neural network (CNN) encoder, a gated recurrent unit (GRU) decoder, and coverage attention to form the encoder-decoder architecture.

In terms of model architecture improvement, Zhang *et al.* [32] proposed DenseWAP, which uses a multi-scale DenseNet [12] encoder to improve the ability to handle multi-scale symbols. Ding *et al.* [9] then borrows the architecture design of the transformer to improve the RNN-based model performance by multi-head attention and stacked decoder.

In terms of data augmentation, Li *et al.* [15] proposed scale augmentation that scales the image randomly while maintaining the aspect ratio, which improves the generalization ability over multi-scale images. PAL-v2 [29] then uses printed mathematical expressions as additional data to help train the model.

In terms of training strategies, Truong *et al.* [26] proposed WS-WAP by introducing weakly supervised information about the presence or absence of symbols to the encoder. Besides, BTTR [35] was proposed to first use the transformer decoder for solving HMER task, and perform bidirectional language modeling with a single decoder.

2.2 Coverage Mechanism

The coverage mechanism was first proposed [27] to solve the over-translation and under-translation problems in the machine translation task.

All of the previous works in HMER [9,15,26,27,29,32–34] used the coverage attention in RNN, where a coverage vector is introduced to indicate whether an image feature vector has been parsed or not, leading the model to put more attention on the unparsed regions. It is a step-wise refinement, where the decoder needs to collect past alignment information for each step. For the RNN model, the decoder can naturally accumulate the attention weights in each step, but it is difficult for the transformer decoder which performs parallel decoding.

There is a work [25] that tried to introduce the coverage machenism in transformer decoder. They directly used the coverage mechanism in RNN to the transformer, which greatly hurts its parallelism and training efficiency. Our CoMER model, on the other hand, utilizes the coverage information as an attention refinement term in the transformer decoder without hurting its parallel decoding nature.

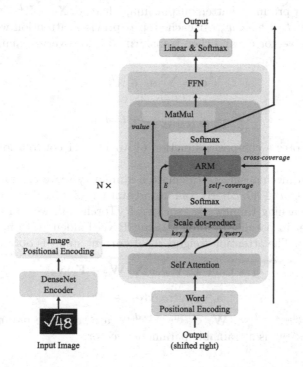

Fig. 1. The overview architecture of our proposed CoMER model. The attention weights generated by *key* and *query* are fed into a novel Attention Refinement Module (ARM). ARM utilizes the past alignment information generated from different layers through self-coverage and cross-coverage.

3   Methodology

In this section, we will first review the coverage attention in RNN and multi-head attention, then describe the architecture design of CoMER in detail. As illustrated in Fig. 1, the model consists of four main modules: 1) CNN Encoder, which extracts features from 2D formula images. 2) Positional Encoding that addresses position information for the transformer decoder. 3) Attention Refinement Module (ARM) is used to refine the attention weights with the past alignment information. 4) Self-coverage and cross-coverage utilize the past alignment information from the current and previous layers.

3.1 Background

Coverage Attention in RNN. Coverage attention has been widely used in RNN-based HMER models [9,15,26,27,29,32–34]. The coverage vector provides information to the attention model about whether a region has been parsed or not. Let encoder produces flatten output image feature $\mathbf{X}_f \in \mathbb{R}^{L \times d_{\text{model}}}$ with the sequence length $L = h_o \times w_o$. At each step t, previous attention weights $\mathbf{a}_k$ are accumulated as vector $\mathbf{c}_t$, and then transformed into coverage matrix $\mathbf{F}_t$.

$$\mathbf{c}_t = \sum_{k=1}^{t-1} \mathbf{a}_k \in \mathbb{R}^L \tag{1}$$

$$\mathbf{F}_t = \text{cov}(\mathbf{c}_t) \in \mathbb{R}^{L \times d_{\text{attn}}} \tag{2}$$

here $\text{cov}(\cdot)$ denotes a composite function of an 11×11 convolution layer and a linear layer.

In attention mechanism, we calculate a similarity score $e_{t,i}$ for every image feature at index $i \in [0, L)$. By taking advantage of broadcast operations in modern deep learning frameworks, such as PyTorch [24], we can compute similarity vector $\mathbf{e}_t$ in parallel by broadcasting RNN hidden state $\mathbf{h}_t \in \mathbb{R}^{d_{\text{model}}}$ to $\mathbf{H}_t \in \mathbb{R}^{L \times d_{\text{model}}}$. The attention weights $\mathbf{a}_t$ of current step t is obtained as follow:

$$\mathbf{e}_t = \tanh\left(\mathbf{H}_t \mathbf{W}_h + \mathbf{X}_f \mathbf{W}_x + \mathbf{F}_t\right) \mathbf{v}_a \tag{3}$$

$$\mathbf{a}_t = \text{softmax}(\mathbf{e}_t) \in \mathbb{R}^L \tag{4}$$

where $\mathbf{W}_h \in \mathbb{R}^{d_{\text{model}} \times d_{\text{attn}}}$, $\mathbf{W}_x \in \mathbb{R}^{d_{\text{model}} \times d_{\text{attn}}}$ are trainable parameters matrices, and $\mathbf{v}_a \in \mathbb{R}^{d_{\text{attn}}}$ is a trainable parameter vector.

Multi-head Attention. Multi-head attention is the most critical component of the transformer models [28]. With the model dimension size d_{model}, query sequence length T, and key sequence length L, we split the multi-head attention calculation for head $\mathbf{Head}_i$ into four parts: 1) project the query $\mathbf{Q}$, key $\mathbf{K}$, and value $\mathbf{V}$ into a subspace; 2) calculate the scaled dot-product $\mathbf{E}_i \in \mathbb{R}^{T \times L}$; 3) compute the attention weights $\mathbf{A}_i \in \mathbb{R}^{T \times L}$ by the softmax function; 4) obtain head $\mathbf{Head}_i$ by multiplying the attention weights $\mathbf{A}_i$ and value $\mathbf{V}_i$.

$$\mathbf{Q}_i, \mathbf{K}_i, \mathbf{V}_i = \mathbf{Q}\mathbf{W}_i^Q, \mathbf{K}\mathbf{W}_i^K, \mathbf{V}\mathbf{W}_i^V \tag{5}$$

$$\mathbf{E}_i = \frac{\mathbf{Q}_i \mathbf{K}_i^\mathsf{T}}{\sqrt{d_k}} \in \mathbb{R}^{T \times L} \tag{6}$$

$$\mathbf{A}_i = \text{softmax}(\mathbf{E}_i) \in \mathbb{R}^{T \times L} \tag{7}$$

$$\mathbf{Head}_i = \mathbf{A}_i \mathbf{V}_i \in \mathbb{R}^{T \times d_v} \tag{8}$$

where $\mathbf{W}_i^Q \in \mathbb{R}^{d_{\text{model}} \times d_k}, \mathbf{W}_i^K \in \mathbb{R}^{d_{\text{model}} \times d_k}, \mathbf{W}_i^V \in \mathbb{R}^{d_{\text{model}} \times d_v}$ denote the trainable projection parameter matrices. Then all h heads are concatenated and projected with a trainable projection matrix $\mathbf{W}^O \in \mathbb{R}^{h d_v \times d_{\text{model}}}$ to obtain the final output:

$$\text{MultiHead}(\mathbf{Q}, \mathbf{K}, \mathbf{V}) = [\mathbf{Head}_1; \ldots; \mathbf{Head}_h] \mathbf{W}^O \tag{9}$$

We follow this setting in CoMER and use the Attention Refinement Module (ARM) in Sect. 3.4 to refine the scale dot-product matrix $\mathbf{E}_i$ in Eq. (6).

3.2 CNN Encoder

In the encoder part, we use DenseNet [12] to extract features in the 2D formula image, following the same setting with BTTR [35]. The core idea of DenseNet is to enhance the information flow between layers through concatenation operation in the feature dimension. Specifically, in the DenseNet block b, the output feature of lth layer can be computed by the output features $\mathbf{X}_0, \mathbf{X}_1, \ldots, \mathbf{X}_{l-1} \in \mathbb{R}^{h_b \times w_b \times d_b}$ from the previous 0th to $(l-1)^{th}$ layers:

$$\mathbf{X}_\ell = H_\ell([\mathbf{X}_0; \mathbf{X}_1; \ldots; \mathbf{X}_{\ell-1}]) \in \mathbb{R}^{h_b \times w_b \times d_b} \tag{10}$$

where $[\mathbf{X}_0; \mathbf{X}_1; \ldots; \mathbf{X}_{\ell-1}] \in \mathbb{R}^{h_b \times w_b \times (l d_b)}$ denotes the concatenation operation in the feature dimension, d_b denotes the feature dimension size of DenseNet block, and $H_\ell(\cdot)$ function is implemented by: a batch normalization [13] layer, a ReLU [11] activation function, and a 3×3 convolution layer.

In order to align DenseNet output feature with the model dimension size d_{model}, we add a 1×1 convolution layer at the end of the encoder to obtain the output image feature $\mathbf{X}_o \in \mathbb{R}^{h_o \times w_o \times d_{\text{model}}}$.

3.3 Positional Encoding

Unlike the RNN decoders, which inherently consider the order of word tokens, the additional position information is necessary for the transformer decoder due to its permutation-invariant property. In CoMER, we are consistent with BTTR [35], employing both image positional encoding and word positional encoding.

For word positional encoding, we use the 1D positional encoding introduced in the vanilla transformer [28]. Given encoding dimension size d, position p, and the index i of feature dimension, the word positional encoding vector $\mathbf{p}_{p,d}^{\mathbf{W}} \in \mathbb{R}^d$ can be represented as:

$$\mathbf{p}_{p,d}^{\mathbf{W}}[2i] = \sin(p/10000^{2i/d})$$
$$\mathbf{p}_{p,d}^{\mathbf{W}}[2i+1] = \cos(p/10000^{2i/d}) \tag{11}$$

For image positional encoding, a 2D normalized positional encoding is used, which is the same as [4,35]. Since it is not the absolute position but the relative position that matters, the position coordinates should be normalized first. Given a 2D coordinates tuple (x, y) and the encoding dimension size d, the image positional encoding $\mathbf{p}_{x,y,d}^{\mathbf{I}} \in \mathbb{R}^d$ is computed by the concatenation of 1D positional encoding (11) of two dimensions.

$$\bar{x} = \frac{x}{h_o}, \quad \bar{y} = \frac{y}{w_o} \tag{12}$$

$$\mathbf{p}_{x,y,d}^{\mathbf{I}} = [\mathbf{p}_{\bar{x},d/2}^{\mathbf{W}}; \mathbf{p}_{\bar{y},d/2}^{\mathbf{W}}] \tag{13}$$

where h_o and w_o denote the shape of output image feature $\mathbf{X}_o \in \mathbb{R}^{h_o \times w_o \times d_{\text{model}}}$.

3.4 Attention Refinement Module

Although coverage attention has been widely used in the RNN decoder, it is difficult to use it directly in the transformer decoder due to transformer's parallel decoding. The inability to model the coverage information directly in the transformer leads to its unsatisfactory performance in the HMER task. We will first introduce the difficulty of using coverage information in the transformer in this subsection, then propose a novel Attention Refinement Module (ARM) to solve it.

A naive solution is to use the multi-head attention weight $\mathbf{A}$ in Eq. (7), accumulate it as $\mathbf{C}$, and then transform into a coverage matrix $\mathbf{F}$ using cov($\cdot$) function in Eq. (2). However, this naive solution is unacceptable considering space complexity. Assume that multi-head attention weight $\mathbf{A} \in \mathbb{R}^{T \times L \times h}$, then cov($\cdot$) function will be applied at every time step and every image feature location, which will produce coverage matrix $\mathbf{F} \in \mathbb{R}^{T \times L \times h \times d_{\text{attn}}}$ with space complexity $O(TLhd)$.

We can see that the bottleneck comes from the tanh($\cdot$) function in Eq. (3) where the coverage matrix needs to be summed with other feature vectors first, then multiplied by vector $\mathbf{v}_a \in \mathbb{R}^{d_{\text{attn}}}$. If we can multiply the coverage matrix with $\mathbf{v}_a$ first and then add the result of LuongAttention [18], the space complexity will be greatly reduced to $O(TLh)$. So we modify Eq. (3) as follows:

$$\begin{aligned}
\mathbf{e}_t' &= \tanh\left(\mathbf{H}_t \mathbf{W}_h + \mathbf{X}_f \mathbf{W}_x\right) \mathbf{v}_a + \mathbf{F}_t \mathbf{v}_a \\
&= \underbrace{\tanh\left(\mathbf{H}_t \mathbf{W}_h + \mathbf{X}_f \mathbf{W}_x\right) \mathbf{v}_a}_{\text{attention}} + \underbrace{\mathbf{r}_t}_{\text{refinement}}
\end{aligned} \tag{14}$$

where similarity vector $\mathbf{e}_t'$ can be divided into an attention term and a refinement $\mathbf{r}_t \in \mathbb{R}^L$ term. Notice that given accumulated vector $\mathbf{c}_t$ in Eq. (1), refinement term $\mathbf{r}_t$ could be directly produced by a coverage modeling function, avoiding intermediate representation with dimension d_{attn}. We name the process in Eq. (14) as the **Attention Refinement Framework**.

To use this framework in the transformer, we propose an **Attention Refinement Module (ARM)** shown in Fig. 2. The scale dot-product matrix $\mathbf{E} \in$

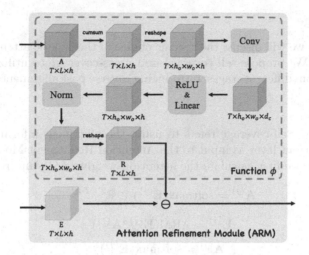

Fig. 2. The overview of Attention Refinement Module (ARM). Given the generic attention weights $\mathbf{A}$, we first calculate the refinement term $\mathbf{R}$ using function $\phi(\cdot)$. Then, we refine the attention term $\mathbf{E}$ by subtracting the refinement term $\mathbf{R}$.

$\mathbb{R}^{T \times L \times h}$ in Eq. (6) can be used as the attention term, and the refinement term matrix $\mathbf{R}$ needs to be calculated from the attention weights $\mathbf{A}$. Note that we use a generic attention weights $\mathbf{A}$ here to provide past alignment information, and the specific choice of it will be discussed in Sect. 3.5.

We define a function $\phi : \mathbb{R}^{T \times L \times h} \mapsto \mathbb{R}^{T \times L \times h}$ that takes the attention weights $\mathbf{A} \in \mathbb{R}^{T \times L \times h}$ as input and outputs the refinement matrix $\mathbf{R} \in \mathbb{R}^{T \times L \times h}$. With kernel size k_c, intermediate dimension $d_c \ll h \times d_{attn}$, and the output image feature shape $L = h_o \times w_o$, function $\phi(\cdot)$ is defined as:

$$\mathbf{R} = \phi(\mathbf{A}) = \mathrm{norm}\left(\max\left(0, \mathbf{K} * \widetilde{\mathbf{C}} + \mathbf{b}_c\right)\mathbf{W}_c\right) \tag{15}$$

$$\widetilde{\mathbf{C}} = \mathrm{reshape}(\mathbf{C}) \in \mathbb{R}^{T \times h_o \times w_o \times h} \tag{16}$$

$$\mathbf{c}_t = \sum_{k=1}^{t-1} \mathbf{a}_k \in \mathbb{R}^{L \times h} \tag{17}$$

where $\mathbf{a}_t$ is the attention weights at step $t \in [0, T)$, $\mathbf{K} \in \mathbb{R}^{k_c \times k_c \times h \times d_c}$ denotes a convolution kernel, $*$ denotes convolution operation over the reshaped accumulated matrix $\widetilde{\mathbf{C}} \in \mathbb{R}^{T \times h_o \times w_o \times h}$, $\mathbf{b}_c \in \mathbb{R}^{d_c}$ is a bias term, and $\mathbf{W}_c \in \mathbb{R}^{d_c \times h}$ is a linear projection matrix. Note that Eq. (17) can be efficiently computed by cumsum$(\cdot)$ function in modern deep learning frameworks [24].

We consider that function ϕ can extract local coverage features to detect the edge of parsed regions and identify the incoming unparsed regions. Finally, we refine the attention term $\mathbf{E}$ by subtracting the refinement term $\mathbf{R}$.

$$\begin{aligned} \mathrm{ARM}(\mathbf{E}, \mathbf{A}) &= \mathbf{E} - \mathbf{R} \\ &= \mathbf{E} - \phi(\mathbf{A}) \end{aligned} \tag{18}$$

3.5   Coverage

In this section, we will discuss the specific choice of the generic attention weights $\mathbf{A}$ in Eq. (15) We propose self-coverage and cross-coverage to utilize alignment information from different stages, introducing diverse past alignment information to the model.

Self-coverage. Self-coverage refers to using the alignment information generated by the current layer as input to the Attention Refinement Module. For the current layer j, we first calculate the attention weights $\mathbf{A}^{(j)}$, and refine itself.

$$\mathbf{A}^{(j)} = \mathrm{softmax}(\mathbf{E}^{(j)}) \in \mathbb{R}^{T \times L \times h} \tag{19}$$

$$\hat{\mathbf{E}}^{(j)} = \mathrm{ARM}(\mathbf{E}^{(j)}, \mathbf{A}^{(j)}) \tag{20}$$

$$\hat{\mathbf{A}}^{(j)} = \mathrm{softmax}(\hat{\mathbf{E}}^{(j)}) \tag{21}$$

where $\hat{\mathbf{E}}^{(j)}$ denotes the refined scale dot-product, and $\hat{\mathbf{A}}^{(j)}$ denotes the refined attention weights at layer j.

Cross-coverage. We propose a novel cross-coverage by exploiting the nature of the stacked decoder in the transformer. Cross-coverage uses the alignment information from the previous layer as input to the ARM of the current layer. For the current layer j, we use the refined attention weights $\hat{\mathbf{A}}^{(j-1)}$ from the previous $(j-1)$ layer and refine the attention term of the current layer.

$$\hat{\mathbf{E}}^{(j)} = \mathrm{ARM}(\mathbf{E}^{(j)}, \hat{\mathbf{A}}^{(j-1)}) \tag{22}$$

$$\hat{\mathbf{A}}^{(j)} = \mathrm{softmax}(\hat{\mathbf{E}}^{(j)}) \tag{23}$$

Notice that $\hat{\mathbf{A}}^{(j-1)} = \mathbf{A}^{(j-1)}$ holds if the previous layer do not use the ARM.

Fusion-Coverage. Combining the self-coverage and cross-coverage, we propose a novel fusion-coverage method to fully use the past alignment information generated from different layers.

$$\hat{\mathbf{E}}^{(j)} = \mathrm{ARM}(\mathbf{E}^{(j)}, [\mathbf{A}^{(j)}; \hat{\mathbf{A}}^{(j-1)}]) \tag{24}$$

$$\hat{\mathbf{A}}^{(j)} = \mathrm{softmax}(\hat{\mathbf{E}}^{(j)}) \tag{25}$$

where $[\mathbf{A}^{(j)}; \hat{\mathbf{A}}^{(j-1)}] \in \mathbb{R}^{T \times L \times 2h}$ denotes the concatenation of attention weights from the current layer and refined attention weights from the previous layer.

4 Experiments

4.1 Implementation Details

In the encoder part, we employ the same DenseNet to extract features from the formula image. Three densenet blocks are used in the encoder, each containing $D = 16$ bottleneck layers. A transition layer is inserted between every two densenet blocks to reduce the spatial and channel size of the feature map by $\theta = 0.5$. The growth rate is set to $k = 24$, and the dropout rate is set to 0.2.

In the decoder part, for hyperparameters in the transformer decoder, we set the model dimension to $d_{\text{model}} = 256$, the number of heads to $h = 8$, and the feedforward layer dimension size to $d_{ff} = 1024$. We use three stacked decoder layers and a 0.3 dropout rate. For the Attention Refinement Module that we proposed, we set the kernel size to $k_c = 5$, the intermediate dimension to $d_c = 32$. The normalization method we adopt in ARM is batch-normalization [13]. We use ARM starting with the second layer and share the same ARM between layers.

We use the same bidirectional training strategy as BTTR [35] to train CoMER with PyTorch [24] framework. We use SGD with a weight decay of 10^{-4} and momentum of 0.9. The learning rate is 0.08. We augment input images using scale augmentation [15] with uniformly sampled scaling factor $s \in [0.7, 1.4]$. All experiments are conducted on four NVIDIA 2080Ti GPUs with 4×11 GB memory.

In the inference phase, instead of the beam search, we perform the approximate joint search [16] that has been used in BTTR [35].

4.2 Datasets and Metrics

We use the Competition on Recognition of Online Handwritten Mathematical Expressions (CROHME) datasets [20–22] to conduct our experiments, which is currently the largest open dataset for HMER task. The training set contains a total of 8836 training samples, while the CROHME 2014/2016/2019 test set contains 986/1147/1199 test samples. The CROHME 2014 test set [21] is used as the validation set to select the best-performing model during the training process.

We use the evaluation tool officially provided by the CROHME 2019 [20] organizers to convert the predicted LaTeX sequences into symLG format. Then, metrics are reported by utilizing the LgEval library [31]. We choose "ExpRate", "≤ 1 error", "≤ 2 error", and "≤ 3 error" metrics to measure the performance of our proposed model. These metrics represent the expression recognition rate when we tolerate 0 to 3 symbol or structural errors.

4.3 Ablation Study

To verify the effectiveness of our proposed method, we performed ablation experiments on the CROHME 2014 test set [21]. In Table 1, the "Scale-aug" column indicates whether to adopt scale augmentation [15] for data augmentation. The

"Self-cov" column indicates whether self-coverage is used. The "Cross-cov" column suggests the use of cross-coverage.

First, since the original BTTR [35] did not use any data augmentation methods, we re-implement the BTTR model and achieve an ExpRate of 53.45%, which is similar to the original result in [35]. To compare BTTR as a baseline with our proposed CoMER, we also use scale augmentation to train BTTR and obtained an ExpRate of 55.17% for "BTTR (baseline)".

The performance of CoMER using ARM and coverage mechanism has been significantly improved compared to BTTR. Comparing the last four rows in Table 1, we can observe that:

1. When CoMER uses self-coverage to refine the attention weights, the performance is improved by 2.34% compared to "BTTR (baseline)". Experiment results validate the feasibility and effectiveness of using past alignment information in the transformer decoder.
2. Compared to self-coverage, using cross-coverage in CoMER can bring more performance gains owing to the more accurate alignment information from the previous layer.
3. "CoMER (Fusion)" obtains the best results by combining self-coverage and cross-coverage, outperforming the baseline model by 4.16%. This experiment results suggest that diverse alignment information generated from different layers helps ARM refine the current attention weights more accurately.

Table 1. Ablation study on the CROHME 2014 test set (in %). † denotes original reported results of BTTR [35]

Model	Scale-aug [15]	Self-cov	Cross-cov	ExpRate
BTTR† [35]	✗	✗	✗	53.96
BTTR	✗	✗	✗	53.45
BTTR (baseline)	✓	✗	✗	55.17 (+0.00)
CoMER (Self)	✓	✓	✗	57.51 (+2.34)
CoMER (Cross)	✓	✗	✓	58.11 (+2.94)
CoMER (Fusion)	✓	✓	✓	**59.33** (+4.16)

4.4 Comparison with State-of-the-Art Approaches

We compare the proposed CoMER with the previous state-of-the-art methods, as shown in Table 2. For the RNN-based models, we choose DenseWAP [32], DenseWAP-TD [33], WS-WAP [26], Li *et al.* [15], and Ding *et al.* [9] for comparison. For transformer-based models, we compare with BTTR [35] that uses a vanilla transformer decoder. Note that the approaches proposed by Li *et al.* [15] and Ding *et al.* [9] also use the scale augmentation [15].

Compared with the RNN-based models that use coverage attention, CoMER outperforms the previous state-of-the-art model proposed by Ding *et al.* [9] on each CROHME test set. In the ExpRate metric, CoMER improves by an average of 1.43% compared to the previous best-performing RNN-based model.

Compared with the transformer-based model, our proposed CoMER equipped with ARM and fusion-coverage significantly improves the performance. Specifically, CoMER outperforms "BTTR (baseline)" in all metrics and averages 3.6% ahead of "BTTR (baseline)" in ExpRate.

Table 2. Performance comparison with previous state-of-the-art approaches on the CROHME 2014/2016/2019 test sets (in %).

Dataset	Model	ExpRate	≤ 1 error	≤ 2 error	≤ 3 error
CROHME 14	DenseWAP [32]	43.0	57.8	61.9	–
	DenseWAP-TD [33]	49.1	64.2	67.8	–
	WS-WAP [26]	53.65	–	–	–
	Li *et al.* [15]	56.59	69.07	75.25	**78.60**
	Ding *et al.* [9]	58.72	–	–	–
	BTTR [35]	53.96	66.02	70.28	–
	BTTR (baseline)	55.17	67.85	72.11	74.14
	CoMER	**59.33**	**71.70**	**75.66**	77.89
CROHME 16	DenseWAP [32]	40.1	54.3	57.8	–
	DenseWAP-TD [33]	48.5	62.3	65.3	–
	WS-WAP [26]	51.96	64.34	70.10	72.97
	Li *et al.* [15]	54.58	69.31	73.76	76.02
	Ding *et al.* [9]	57.72	70.01	76.37	78.90
	BTTR [35]	52.31	63.90	68.61	–
	BTTR (baseline)	56.58	68.88	74.19	76.90
	CoMER	**59.81**	**74.37**	**80.30**	**82.56**
CROHME 19	DenseWAP [32]	41.7	55.5	59.3	–
	DenseWAP-TD [33]	51.4	66.1	69.1	–
	Ding *et al.* [9]	61.38	75.15	80.23	82.65
	BTTR [35]	52.96	65.97	69.14	–
	BTTR (baseline)	59.55	72.23	76.06	78.40
	CoMER	**62.97**	**77.40**	**81.40**	**83.07**

4.5   Performance at Different Lengths

Intuitively, we assume that the recognition accuracy of long sequences is lower than that of short ones because of the lack of coverage problem [27,34]. Thus, we consider the recognition accuracy of long sequences reflects the ability of a model to align the sequence and image. To verify that CoMER has better alignment and thus alleviates the lack of coverage problem, we calculate the recognition accuracy at different lengths on the CROHME 2014 test set, shown in Fig. 3.

By comparing "BTTR (baseline)" with the CoMER family of models, we found that CoMER equipped with ARM has better performance when dealing with various lengths of sequences, especially with longer ones. The performance of "CoMER (Fusion)" can reach even **5×** than "BTTR (baseline)" when recognizing sequences longer than 50. This experiment results show that the ARM and coverage mechanisms can improve the alignment quality and mitigates the lack of coverage problem.

Comparing the performance between self-coverage and cross-coverage, we find that cross-coverage performs better when parsing short sequences. In contrast, self-coverage is better at recognizing long sequences. We suppose this is because cross-coverage accumulates misalignments generated by the previous layer, causing it to incorrectly refine the attention weights in the current layer. In comparison, self-coverage performs alignment and refinement in each layer independently. "CoMER (Fusion)" uses both self-coverage and cross-coverage to exploit diverse alignment information and far outperforms other models in recognizing sequences longer than 20.

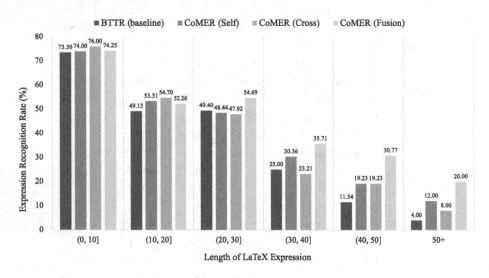

Fig. 3. Recognition accuracy (in %) for LATEX expressions of different lengths on the CROHME 2014 test set.

4.6   Refinement Term Visulization

As shown in Fig. 4, we visualize the refinement term **R** in the recognition process. We find that parsed regions are darker, which indicates ARM will suppress the attention weights in these parsed regions and encourage the model to focus on incoming unparsed regions. The visualization experiment shows that our proposed ARM can effectively alleviate the lack of coverage problem.

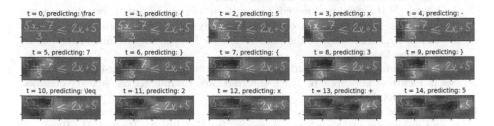

Fig. 4. The refinement term **R** visualization in recognizing formula image. The darker the color, the larger the value.

5 Conclusion and Future Work

In this paper, inspired by the coverage attention in RNN, we propose CoMER to introduce the coverage mechanism into the transformer decoder. We have the following four main contributions: **(1)** Our proposed CoMER alleviates the lack of coverage problem and significantly improves the recognition accuracy of long LATEX expressions. **(2)** We propose a novel Attention Refinement Module (ARM) that makes it possible to perform attention refinement in the transformer without harming its parallel computing nature. **(3)** We propose self-coverage, cross-coverage, and fusion-coverage to refine the attention weights using the past alignment information from the current and previous layers. **(4)** Experiments demonstrate the effectiveness of our proposed CoMER model. Specifically, we achieve new state-of-the-art performance on the CROHME 2014/2016/2019 test sets using a single CoMER model, reaching 59.33%/59.81%/62.97% in ExpRate.

We believe that our proposed attention refinement framework not only works for handwritten mathematical expression recognition. Our ARM can help refine the attention weights and improve the alignment quality for all tasks that require dynamic alignment. To this end, we intend to extend ARM in the transformer as a general framework for solving various vision and language tasks in the future work (e.g., machine translation, text summarization, image captioning).

Acknowledgements. This work is supported by the projects of National Key R&D Program of China (2019YFB1406303) and National Nature Science Foundation of China (No. 61876003), which is also a research achievement of Key Laboratory of Science, Technology and Standard in Press Industry (Key Laboratory of Intelligent Press Media Technology).

References

1. Alvaro, F., Sánchez, J.A., Benedí, J.M.: Recognition of on-line handwritten mathematical expressions using 2d stochastic context-free grammars and hidden markov models. Pattern Recogn. Lett. **35**, 58–67 (2014)
2. Anderson, R.H.: Syntax-directed recognition of hand-printed two-dimensional mathematics. In: Symposium on Interactive Systems for Experimental Applied Mathematics: Proceedings of the Association for Computing Machinery Inc., Symposium, pp. 436–459 (1967)
3. Bengio, Y., Frasconi, P., Simard, P.: The problem of learning long-term dependencies in recurrent networks. In: IEEE International Conference on Neural Networks, pp. 1183–1188. IEEE (1993)
4. Carion, N., Massa, F., Synnaeve, G., Usunier, N., Kirillov, A., Zagoruyko, S.: End-to-end object detection with transformers. In: Vedaldi, A., Bischof, H., Brox, T., Frahm, J.-M. (eds.) ECCV 2020. LNCS, vol. 12346, pp. 213–229. Springer, Cham (2020). https://doi.org/10.1007/978-3-030-58452-8_13
5. Chan, K.F., Yeung, D.Y.: Mathematical expression recognition: a survey. Int. J. Doc. Anal. Recogn. **3**(1), 3–15 (2000)
6. Cheng, Z., Bai, F., Xu, Y., Zheng, G., Pu, S., Zhou, S.: Focusing attention: towards accurate text recognition in natural images. In: Proceedings of the IEEE International Conference on Computer Vision, pp. 5076–5084 (2017)
7. Cornia, M., Stefanini, M., Baraldi, L., Cucchiara, R.: Meshed-memory transformer for image captioning. In: Proceedings of the IEEE/CVF Conference on Computer Vision and Pattern Recognition, pp. 10578–10587 (2020)
8. Devlin, J., Chang, M.W., Lee, K., Toutanova, K.: Bert: pre-training of deep bidirectional transformers for language understanding. In: North American Chapter of the Association for Computational Linguistics (2018)
9. Ding, H., Chen, K., Huo, Q.: An encoder-decoder approach to handwritten mathematical expression recognition with multi-head attention and stacked decoder. In: Lladós, J., Lopresti, D., Uchida, S. (eds.) ICDAR 2021. LNCS, vol. 12822, pp. 602–616. Springer, Cham (2021). https://doi.org/10.1007/978-3-030-86331-9_39
10. Dosovitskiy, A., et al.: An image is worth 16x16 words: Transformers for image recognition at scale. In: 9th International Conference on Learning Representations, ICLR 2021, Virtual Event, Austria, 3–7 May 2021. OpenReview.net (2021). https://openreview.net/forum?id=YicbFdNTTy
11. Glorot, X., Bordes, A., Bengio, Y.: Deep sparse rectifier neural networks. In: International Conference on Artificial Intelligence and Statistics (2011)
12. Huang, G., Liu, Z., van der Maaten, L., Weinberger, K.Q.: Densely connected convolutional networks. In: Computer Vision and Pattern Recognition (2017)
13. Ioffe, S., Szegedy, C.: Batch normalization: accelerating deep network training by reducing internal covariate shift. arXiv: Learning (2015)
14. Lavirotte, S., Pottier, L.: Mathematical formula recognition using graph grammar. In: Document Recognition V, vol. 3305, pp. 44–52. International Society for Optics and Photonics (1998)
15. Li, Z., Jin, L., Lai, S., Zhu, Y.: Improving attention-based handwritten mathematical expression recognition with scale augmentation and drop attention. In: 2020 17th International Conference on Frontiers in Handwriting Recognition (ICFHR), pp. 175–180. IEEE (2020)
16. Liu, L., Utiyama, M., Finch, A., Sumita, E.: Agreement on target-bidirectional neural machine translation. In: North American Chapter of the Association for Computational Linguistics (2016)

17. Luo, Y., et al.: Dual-level collaborative transformer for image captioning. In: Thirty-Fifth AAAI Conference on Artificial Intelligence, AAAI 2021, Thirty-Third Conference on Innovative Applications of Artificial Intelligence, IAAI 2021, The Eleventh Symposium on Educational Advances in Artificial Intelligence, EAAI 2021, Virtual Event, 2–9 February 2021, pp. 2286–2293. AAAI Press (2021). https://ojs.aaai.org/index.php/AAAI/article/view/16328
18. Luong, M.T., Pham, H., Manning, C.D.: Effective approaches to attention-based neural machine translation. In: Empirical Methods in Natural Language Processing (2015)
19. MacLean, S., Labahn, G.: A new approach for recognizing handwritten mathematics using relational grammars and fuzzy sets. Int. J. Doc. Anal. Recogn. (IJDAR) **16**(2), 139–163 (2013)
20. Mahdavi, M., Zanibbi, R., Mouchere, H., Viard-Gaudin, C., Garain, U.: Icdar 2019 crohme+ tfd: competition on recognition of handwritten mathematical expressions and typeset formula detection. In: 2019 International Conference on Document Analysis and Recognition (ICDAR), pp. 1533–1538. IEEE (2019)
21. Mouchere, H., Viard-Gaudin, C., Zanibbi, R., Garain, U.: Icfhr 2014 competition on recognition of on-line handwritten mathematical expressions (crohme 2014). In: 2014 14th International Conference on Frontiers in Handwriting Recognition, pp. 791–796. IEEE (2014)
22. Mouchère, H., Viard-Gaudin, C., Zanibbi, R., Garain, U.: Icfhr 2016 crohme: competition on recognition of online handwritten mathematical expressions. In: 2016 15th International Conference on Frontiers in Handwriting Recognition (ICFHR), pp. 607–612. IEEE (2016)
23. Pan, Y., Yao, T., Li, Y., Mei, T.: X-linear attention networks for image captioning. In: 2020 IEEE/CVF Conference on Computer Vision and Pattern Recognition, CVPR 2020, Seattle, WA, USA, 13–19 June 2020, pp. 10968–10977. Computer Vision Foundation/IEEE (2020). https://doi.org/10.1109/CVPR42600.2020.01098. https://openaccess.thecvf.com/content_CVPR_2020/html/Pan_X-Linear_Attention_Networks_for_Image_Captioning_CVPR_2020_paper.html
24. Paszke, A., et al.: Pytorch: an imperative style, high-performance deep learning library. In: Neural Information Processing Systems (2019)
25. Rosendahl, J., Herold, C., Petrick, F., Ney, H.: Recurrent attention for the transformer. In: Proceedings of the Second Workshop on Insights from Negative Results in NLP, pp. 62–66 (2021)
26. Truong, T.N., Nguyen, C.T., Phan, K.M., Nakagawa, M.: Improvement of end-to-end offline handwritten mathematical expression recognition by weakly supervised learning. In: 2020 17th International Conference on Frontiers in Handwriting Recognition (ICFHR), pp. 181–186. IEEE (2020)
27. Tu, Z., Lu, Z., Liu, Y., Liu, X., Li, H.: Modeling coverage for neural machine translation. In: Meeting of the Association for Computational Linguistics (2016)
28. Vaswani, A., et al.: Attention is all you need. In: Neural Information Processing Systems (2017)
29. Wu, J.W., Yin, F., Zhang, Y.M., Zhang, X.Y., Liu, C.L.: Handwritten mathematical expression recognition via paired adversarial learning. Int. J. Comput. Vis., 1–16 (2020)
30. Xu, K., et al.: Show, attend and tell: Neural image caption generation with visual attention. In: International Conference on Machine Learning, pp. 2048–2057 (2015)
31. Zanibbi, R., Mouchère, H., Viard-Gaudin, C.: Evaluating structural pattern recognition for handwritten math via primitive label graphs. In: Document Recognition and Retrieval (2013)

32. Zhang, J., Du, J., Dai, L.: Multi-scale attention with dense encoder for handwritten mathematical expression recognition. In: 2018 24th International Conference on Pattern Recognition (ICPR), pp. 2245–2250. IEEE (2018)
33. Zhang, J., Du, J., Yang, Y., Song, Y.Z., Wei, S., Dai, L.: A tree-structured decoder for image-to-markup generation. In: ICML. p. In Press (2020)
34. Zhang, J., Du, J., Zhang, S., Liu, D., Hu, Y., Hu, J., Wei, S., Dai, L.: Watch, attend and parse: An end-to-end neural network based approach to handwritten mathematical expression recognition. Pattern Recogn. **71**, 196–206 (2017)
35. Zhao, W., Gao, L., Yan, Z., Peng, S., Du, L., Zhang, Z.: Handwritten mathematical expression recognition with bidirectionally trained transformer. In: Lladós, J., Lopresti, D., Uchida, S. (eds.) ICDAR 2021. LNCS, vol. 12822, pp. 570–584. Springer, Cham (2021). https://doi.org/10.1007/978-3-030-86331-9_37

Don't Forget Me: Accurate Background Recovery for Text Removal via Modeling Local-Global Context

Chongyu Liu[1], Lianwen Jin[1,4,5(✉)], Yuliang Liu[2], Canjie Luo[1],
Bangdong Chen[1], Fengjun Guo[3], and Kai Ding[3]

[1] South China University of Technology, Guangzhou, Guangdong, China
{liuchongyu1996,canjie.luo}@gmail.com, eelwjin@scut.edu.cn
[2] Huazhong University of Science and Technology, Wuhan, Hubei, China
ylliu@hust.edu.cn
[3] IntSig Information Co. Ltd., Shanghai, China
{fengjun_guo,danny_ding}@intsig.net
[4] Pazhou Laboratory (Huangpu), Guangzhou, Guangdong, China
[5] Peng Cheng Laboratory, Shenzhen, Guangdong, China

Abstract. Text removal has attracted increasingly attention due to its various applications on privacy protection, document restoration, and text editing. It has shown significant progress with deep neural network. However, most of the existing methods often generate inconsistent results for complex background. To address this issue, we propose a Contextual-guided Text Removal Network, termed as CTRNet. CTRNet explores both low-level structure and high-level discriminative context feature as prior knowledge to guide the process of text erasure and background restoration. We further propose a Local-global Content Modeling (LGCM) block with CNNs and Transformer-Encoder to capture local features and establish the long-term relationship among pixels globally. Finally, we incorporate LGCM with context guidance for feature modeling and decoding. Experiments on benchmark datasets, SCUT-EnsText and SCUT-Syn show that CTRNet significantly outperforms the existing state-of-the-art methods. Furthermore, a qualitative experiment on examination papers also demonstrates the generalizability of our method. The code of CTRNet is available at https://github.com/lcy0604/CTRNet.

Keywords: GAN · Text removal · Context guidance · Transformer

1 Introduction

In recent years, text removal has attracted increasing research interests in the computer vision community. It aims to remove the text and fill the regions with

Supplementary Information The online version contains supplementary material available at https://doi.org/10.1007/978-3-031-19815-1_24.

© The Author(s), under exclusive license to Springer Nature Switzerland AG 2022
S. Avidan et al. (Eds.): ECCV 2022, LNCS 13688, pp. 409–426, 2022.
https://doi.org/10.1007/978-3-031-19815-1_24

plausible content. Text removal can help avoid privacy leaks by hiding some private messages such as ID numbers and license plate numbers. Besides, it can be widely used for document restoration in the field of intelligent education. It is also a crucial prerequisite step for text editing [20,37,49,52,53] and has wide applications in areas such as augmented reality translation.

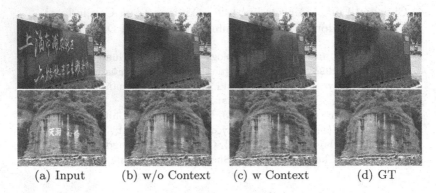

(a) Input   (b) w/o Context   (c) w Context   (d) GT

Fig. 1. Examples of scene text removal, which also show the comparison of the results with and without context guidance and feature modeling. Zoom-in for best view.

Recent text removal methods [23,38,40,48,56] have achieved significant improvements with the development of GAN [10,27,28]. Though the state-of-the-art methods [23,38,39,48] have reported promising performance, the restoration for complex backgrounds still remains a main challenge. To solve this problem, some researchers propose to directly predict the text stroke [3,38] and focus text region inpainting only on these stroke regions. However, text stroke prediction is an another challenging problem to be addressed, especially on image-level (with more than one text) [44,51]. Inspired by previous image inpainting methods [25,32,35], we consider that directly transforming the raw image to a final text-erased image in a unified framework is one of the major causes of inconsistent results for text removal. This is due to the imbalance between text erasure and the subsequent background restoration. The corruption of text region while erasing may mislead the reconstruction of the high-frequency textures. The results with blur and artifacts are shown in Fig. 1(b). To address this issue, we propose to mine more efficient context guidance from the existing data in a step-by-step manner to reduce the artifacts of text-erased regions and produce plausible content.

Specifically, we propose a novel text removal model, termed as CTRNet. CTRNet decouples the text removal task into four main components: Text Perception Head, Low-level/High-level Contextual Guidance blocks (LCG, HCG), and a Local-global Content Modeling (LGCM) block, as shown in Fig. 2. Text Perception Head is firstly introduced to detect the text regions and generate text masks. Subsequently, the LCG predicts the structure of text-erased images to provide low-level contextual priors, which is represented by the edge-preserved smoothing method RTV [50]. Besides, we incorporate an HCG block to learn the high-level discriminative context in latent feature space as another guidance. Structure is served as a local guide for the image encoder, while high-level context provides global knowledge. As the filling of text regions not only focuses on the information of their own and surroundings, but also uses the global affinity as reference, CTRNet introduces LGCM by the cooperation of CNNs and Transformer-Encoder [41] to extract local features and establish the long-term global relationship among the pixels, meanwhile incorporates context guidance for both feature modeling and decoding phase. Through such designs, CTRNet can capture sufficient contextual information to remove the text more thoroughly and restore backgrounds with more visually pleasing textures, as shown in Fig. 1(c).

Extensive experiments on the benchmark datasets, SCUT-EnsText [23] and SCUT-Syn [56] are conducted to verify the effectiveness of CTRNet. Additionally, qualitative experiment is conducted on an in-house examination paper dataset to verify the generalizability of our model.

Text removal takes complete text image as input and aims to preserve the original background of text regions, whereas image inpainting will directly mask the regions for restoration based only on the surrounding texture. Simply applying image inpainting methods to text removal will cause inaccurate background generation. We conduct experiments to compare our method with the state-of-the-art image inpainting models in Sect. 4.5/4.6, which practically illustrates the difference between these two tasks.

We summarize the contributions of this work as follows:

- We propose to learn both Low-level and High-level Contextual Guidance (LCG, HCG), which we find are important and useful as prior knowledge for text erasure and subsequent background texture synthesis.
- We propose Local-global Content Modeling blocks (LGCM) to extract local features and capture long-range dependency among the pixels globally.
- The context guidance is incorporated into LGCM for the feature modeling and decoding phase, which further promotes the performance of CTRNet.
- Extensive experiments on the benchmark datasets demonstrate the effectiveness of CTRNet not only in removing the text but recovering the background textures as well, significantly outperforming existing SOTA methods.

2   Related Work

Deep learning-based text removal can be categorized into one-stage methods and two-stage methods. One-stage methods are implemented in an end-to-end manner, requiring models to automatically detect the text regions and remove them in a unified framework. Nakamura et al. [29] proposed a patch-based auto-encoder [2] with skip connections, termed as SceneTextEraser. It was also the first DNN-based text removal method. Text removal can be also regarded as image-to-image translation. Following the idea of Pix2pix [14], EnsNet [56] adopted four refined losses and employed a local-aware discriminator to maintain the consistency of text-erased regions. Liu et al. [23] proposed EraseNet by introducing a coarse-to-refinement architecture and an additional segmentation head to help locate the text. MTRNet++ [39] shared the same spirit with EraseNet, but separately encoded the image content and text mask in two branches. Cho et al. [6] proposed to jointly predict the text stroke and inpaint the background, allowing the model to focus only on the restoration of text stroke regions. Wang et al. [48] presented PERT, which contained a novel progressive structure with shared parameters to remove text more thoroughly, and a region-based modification strategy to effectively guide the erasure process only on text regions.

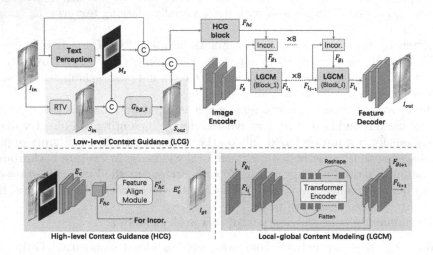

Fig. 2. The overview of the proposed CTRNet.

Two-stage methods follow the procedure of detecting the text, removing it, and then filling the background with plausible content. We further divide them into word-level and image-level. Word-level methods first crop the text regions according to the detected results, then operate the text removal process with single text [34,38]. Qin et al. [34] utilized cGAN [10,27] with one encoder and two decoders for both text stroke prediction and background inpaint. Tang et al. [38] proposed to predict the text strokes on word images, then both strokes and images were fed into an image inpainting network with Partial Convolution [24] to generate the text-erased results. For image-level methods, after obtaining the text mask through detection, they directly predict the results on the entire images. MTRNet [40], based on Pix2pix, implemented a text mask as an extra input. The method proposed by Keserwani et al. [18] was similar to MTRNet, but employed an additional local discriminator for better prediction. Zdenek et al. [55] considered the lack of pixel-wise training data and proposed a weak supervision method by introducing a pretrained PSENet [46] to detect the text, and then inpainted the text regions through another pretrained image inpainting method [58]. Conrad et al. [7] borrowed the concept developed by Zdenek et al. [55], but they proposed to further predict the text stroke before the application of a pretrained EdgeConnect [32] for background inpainting. Bian et al. [3] proposed a cascaded generative model, which decoupled text removal into text stroke detection and stroke removal.

3   Proposed Method

Figure 2 shows the pipeline of the proposed CTRNet. First, we introduce text perception head to detect the text regions and generate the text masks. To better restore the backgrounds of text regions, we propose to learn more contextual priors from the existing data, including low-level background structure with LCG and high-level context features with HCG. Structure information is served as a local guide and directly fed into the image encoder, while the high-level context feature is embedded into the high-dimensional feature space as a global guide with the Incor operation. Finally, we propose LGCM blocks to capture both local features and long-term correlation among all the pixels, so that CTRNet can make full use of different levels of information for feature decoding.

3.1   Text Perception Head

For scene text removal on image-level, purely feeding a text image into a model without any positional indication results in failed, mistaken, and incomplete erasures of text regions [23,48,56]. Therefore, we introduce a text perception head to help localize the text regions. With the detected results, we generate the corresponding masks and send them together with original images into the subsequent network. We propose to replace the original 0-1 mask (hard mask) with soft mask to help eliminate the defects and discontinuities between text regions and non-text regions. The procedure for soft mask generation is as follows: (1) The vanilla bounding boxes B are shrunk using the Vatti clipping algorithm [42] with the ratio of 0.9 to obtain B_s, meanwhile dilated with the same offset to B_d; (2) The soft border of text regions is defined as the minimum distance between the pixel in B_s and B_d. Figure 3(c) displays the example of soft-mask. Only the pixels in B_s are set to 1, while the range of pixels between B_s and B_d is $(0,1)$. The effectiveness of the soft mask is verified in Sect. 4.3.

3.2   Contextual Guidance Learning

Low-Level Contextual Guidance (LCG) Block: Scene text removal aims to not only erase the text, but also restore the backgrounds of text regions and synthesize their corresponding textures. Previous methods [23,39,48,56] follow an end-to-end training and inference procedure by directly predicting the results with scene text images as input. However, they suffer from some texture artifacts when dealing with complicated backgrounds, as shown in Fig. 4 and 5. We propose to first predict the low-frequency structure of the image, and take it as low-level guidance for the subsequent network. Inspired by Ren et al. [35]

and Liu et al. [25], the structure image is constructed by the edge-preserved smooth method RTV [50], which removes high-frequency textures with only sharp edges and smooth structure remain. RTV consists of a pixel-wise windowed total variation measure and a windowed inherent variation to remove image texture. Figure 3(d) and (e) display an example of the structure image S_{in} and its ground-truth S_{gt} generated from I_{in} and I_{gt}, respectively. Learning a mapping between two low-frequency structures, S_{in} and S_{gt}, is much easier than removing text directly. The structural clues for text regions can effectively simplify texture generation and enhance the performance by indicating the structure semantic of text regions, as shown in Fig. 4(e) (f) in the ablation study.

As shown in Fig. 2, LCG block consists of RTV method and a background structure generator G_{bg_s}. G_{bg_s} is an encoder-decoder architecture that takes both the structure S_{in} of scene text images and the soft mask M_s as input, and predicts the background structure S_{out} with text-erased. We take S_{out} as local guidance, and directly feed it into the image encoder with I_{in} to encode image features $F_s \in \mathbb{R}^{\frac{H}{4} \times \frac{W}{4} \times C}$.

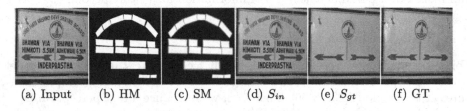

(a) Input   (b) HM   (c) SM   (d) S_{in} (e) S_{gt} (f) GT

Fig. 3. The basic elements of CTRNet. HM and SM denote hard mask and soft mask, respectively. S_{in} and S_{gt} represent the structure of the input and ground-truth. Zoom in for best view.

High-Level Contextual Guidance (HCG) Block: In addition to the low-level structure priors, we propose to explore potential high-level contextual guidance in latent feature spaces. Previous study [23,25,35] with Perceptual/Style Loss [9,15] demonstrates the effectiveness of high-level contextual supervision for image generation and translation. Therefore, we make our CTRNet to utilize such discriminative context as additional guidance information for both text removal and background restoration, instead of taking it merely as supervision for optimization. Inspired by Zhang et al. [57], we incorporate an HCG block into our CTRNet to learn high-level context features.

The architecture of HCG block is illustrated in the left-bottom of Fig. 2. The block consists of two feature encoders ($E_c(\cdot)$ and $E_c^{'}(\cdot)$), and a Feature Align Module (FAM), as done in [57]. $E_c(\cdot)$ encodes the concatenation of the original image I_{in} and its soft-mask M_s to obtain the features $F_{hc} \in \mathbb{R}^{\frac{H}{4} \times \frac{W}{4} \times C}$, whereas $E_c^{'}(\cdot)$ extracts the context features $F_{hc}^{'} \in \mathbb{R}^{\frac{H}{4} \times \frac{W}{4} \times C}$ from the paired labels I_{gt}. Here, $E_c^{'}(\cdot)$ is a classification model, termed as TResNet [36]. We directly use its pretrained model on the OpenImages datasets [21] to extract

F'_{hc} with frozen weights during the training procedure. After feature dimension mapping with 1×1 convolution layers in FAM, feature align loss L_{align} is applied to approximate the distribution of F_{hc} to F'_{hc}. The process can be formulated as

$$F'_{hc} = E'_c(I_{gt}); F_{hc} = E_c(I_{in}, M_s)$$
$$L_{align} = \left\| F_{hc} - F'_{hc} \right\|_1 * (1 + \alpha M_s) \tag{1}$$

α is set to 2.0. In this way, F_{hc} based on I_{in} can be transferred to contain context information of background I_{gt}, which can provide a high-level global guidance for feature modeling and decoding.

3.3 Local-Global Content Modeling (LGCM)

While erasing text regions and filling them with reasonable textures as background, beyond considering text regions as a reference, it is necessary for a text removal method to use the pixel information from the surrounding and global backgrounds. Therefore, we propose a feature content modeling block for both local (text regions) and global (surrounding and the entire background) levels. As shown in Fig. 2, the image content features $F_s \in \mathbb{R}^{\frac{H}{4} \times \frac{W}{4} \times C}$, incorporated with the high-level discriminative feature guidance, F_{hc} are sent to LGCM to model the local-global contextual features and enhance their representations. And the right-bottom of Fig. 2 displays the architecture of a single LGCM block.

CNNs operate locally at a fixed size (e.g. 3×3) to effectively extract features of specific regions and establish the relationship between the pixels in each local window. Therefore, four stacked vanilla 4×4 convolutions layers are utilized for local content modeling. In addition, features can be downsampled by CNNs to reduce the computation required for the subsequent global modeling operation. For global content modeling, we apply Transformer-Encoder as our basic module. Transformer-Encoder [41], which can effectively capture global interactions between pixels among the whole features and model their long-range dependency. Then two deconvolution layers are applied to upsample the modeled features and bring the inductive bias of CNN [22]. LGCM follows an iterative process with k stages ($k = 8$ empirically [57]). At the final convolution of each stage, F_{hc} are incorporated into the LGCM with ResSPADE [33,57]. The details for LGCM and ResSPADE are presented in supplement materials. The output of the $i - th$ LGCM is denoted as F_{l_i} ($F_{l_0} = F_s$).

Finally, Feature Decoder reconstructs the final text-erased output by decoding both features F_{l_8} from the final LGCM ($8th$) block and shadow content features F_s, which can be formulated as

$$I_{out} = H_{fd}(F_{l_8} + F_s) \tag{2}$$

3.4 Training Objective

We adopt the following losses to train our text removal network, including structure loss, multi-scale text-aware reconstruction loss, perceptual loss, style loss, and adversarial loss.

Structure Loss. The structure loss is used to measure the L_1 distance between the background structure output S_{out} and the ground truth S_{gt}, which is defined by:

$$L_{str} = \|S_{gt} - S_{out}\|_1 * (1 + \gamma M_s) \tag{3}$$

$(1 + \gamma M_s)$ denotes higher weight for text region. γ is set to 3.0.

Multi-scale Text-Aware Reconstruction Loss. The $L_1 - norm$ difference is proposed to measure the output and the ground truth. We first predict multi-layer outputs with text removed in different sizes, then assign higher weight to text regions when computing the loss:

$$L_{msr} = \sum_n \|(I_{out_n} - I_{gt_n})\|_1 * (1 + \theta_n M_s) \tag{4}$$

n denotes n-th output in the scales of $\frac{1}{16}, \frac{1}{4}$ and 1 of the input. $\theta_1, \theta_2, \theta_3$ is set to $2, 3, 4$, respectively.

Perceptual Loss. Except for low-level image-to-image supervision with reconstruction loss, we also adopt perceptual loss [15] to capture high-level semantics and try to simulate human perception of image quality. Both the straight output I_{out} and the original image with text-removed I_{com} are included as loss terms. Besides, the structure output S_{out} is also taken into consideration.

$$I_{com} = I_{in} * (1 - M_s) + I_{out} * M_s \tag{5}$$

$$L_{per} = \sum_i \sum_j \|\phi_j(I_i) - \phi_j(I_{gt})\|_1 + \sum_j \|\phi_j(S_{out}) - \phi_j(S_{gt})\|_1 \tag{6}$$

where I_i represent I_{out} and I_{com}. $\phi_j(.)$ denotes the activation maps of the j-th $(j = 1, 2, 3)$ pooling layer of VGG-16 pretrained on ImageNet [8].

Style Loss. We also utilize style loss to release the artifacts of the generated results. Style loss [9] construct a Gram matrix $Gr(.)$ from each selected activation map in perceptual loss. Style loss can be defined as

$$L_{style} = \sum_i \sum_j \frac{\|Gr_j(I_i) - Gr_j(I_{gt})\|_1}{H_j W_j C_j} + \sum_j \frac{\|Gr_j(S_{out}) - Gr_j(S_{gt})\|_1}{H_j W_j C_j} \tag{7}$$

Adversarial Loss. The adversarial loss encourages our model to generate more plausible details for the final results with text removed. Here we defined our adversarial loss as:

$$L_{adv} = E_{x \sim P_{\text{data}}(x)} [\log D(x)] + E_{x \sim P_{z(z)}} [\log (1 - D(G(z)))] \tag{8}$$

z is the input I_{in} and x represents the corresponding ground-truth I_{gt}.

Total Loss. The overall loss function for our text removal network is defined as:

$$L_{total} = \lambda_{al} L_{align} + \lambda_{str} L_{structure} + \lambda_m L_{msr}$$
$$+ \lambda_p L_{per} + \lambda_s L_{style} + \lambda_a L_{adv} \tag{9}$$

$\lambda_{al}, \lambda_{str}, \lambda_m, \lambda_p, \lambda_s, \lambda_a$ are the trade-off parameters. In our implementation, we empirically set $\lambda_{al} = 1.0, \lambda_{str} = 2.0, \lambda_m = 10.0, \lambda_p = 0.01, \lambda_s = 120, \lambda_a = 1.0$.

4   Experiments

4.1   Datasets and Evaluation Metrics

Datasets. To evaluate the effectiveness of our proposed CTRNet, we conduct experiments on the two widely used benchmarks, SCUT-Syn [56] and SCUT-EnsText [23].

(1) SCUT-Syn: SCUT-Syn contains a training set of 8,000 images and a testing set of 800 images. It is a synthetic dataset with [12]. The background images are mainly collected from ICDAR-2013 [17] and MLT-2017 [30], and the text instances are manually erased.

(2) SCUT-EnsText: SCUT-EnsText is a comprehensive real-world dataset with 2,749 images for training and 813 images for testing. These images are collected from public scene text benchmark, including ICDAR-2013 [17], ICDAR-2015 [16], MS COCO-Text [43], SVT [45], MLT-2017 [30], MLT-2019 [31], and ArTs [4], which consists of SCUT-CTW1500 [54] and Total-Text [5]. All the images are carefully annotated with Photoshop.

Table 1. Ablation study on SCUT-EnsText. MSSIM and MSE are represented by % in the table.

	Components				Evaluation on I_{out}				Evaluation on I_{com}			
	HCG	LGCM	SM	LCG	PSNR	MSSIM	MSE	FID	PSNR	MSSIM	MSE	FID
Baseline	-	-	-	-	32.39	95.45	0.13	20.75	33.21	95.52	0.11	22.15
Ours+	✓				32.90	96.62	0.11	17.40	34.88	97.09	0.10	19.42
Ours+	✓	✓			35.10	97.36	0.09	14.36	35.30	97.20	0.09	17.91
Ours+	✓	✓	✓		35.16	**97.38**	0.09	14.33	35.83	**97.42**	0.09	15.02
Ours+	✓	✓	✓	✓	**35.20**	97.36	**0.09**	**13.99**	**35.85**	97.40	**0.09**	**14.57**

Evaluation Metrics: To comprehensively evaluate the performance of our CTRNet, we utilize both Image-Eval and Detection-Eval as used in EraseNet [23]. (1) Image-Eval includes the following metrics for image quality evaluation. (1) Peak signal to noise ratio (PSNR); (2) Multi-scale Structural Similarity (MSSIM); (3) Mean Square Error (MSE); (4) Fréchet Inception Distance (FID) [13]. A higher PSNR, MSSIM and lower MSE, FID denotes better results. (2) Detection-Eval evaluates the Recall (R), Precision (P), F-measure (F), TIoU-Recall (TR), TIoU-Precision (TP), and TIoU-F-measure (TF) for the results under the protocols of ICDAR 2015 [16] and T-IoU [26]. CRAFT [1] is served as the text detector for evaluation. The lower R, P and F indicate that more text can be removed.

4.2   Implement Details

We utilize Pixel Aggregation Network (PAN) [47] as text perception head for CTRNet. The input size is set to 512×512. Adam solver [19] is used to optimized our method, and the β is set to (0.0, 0.9) as default. The batch size is set to 2. All experiments are conducted on a workstation with two NVIDIA 2080TI GPUs. More training details and the architectures of each component are provided in the supplementary materials.

4.3   Ablation Study

In this section, we conduct experiments on SCUT-EnsText to verify the contributions of different components in CTRNet. Our baseline model is implemented by a Pix2pix-based model, which takes both the images and the corresponding masks as input. As the text perception head is frozen when training the other components, the detected text regions remain the same in each experiment during inference; thus, we only employ Image-Eval to evaluate the performance. Apart from the direct output I_{out}, we also paste the erased text regions back to the input images based on the detected results to obtain I_{com}. The quantitative results for both outputs are presented in Table 1. The qualitative results are displayed in Fig. 4. Besides, we evaluate each loss item and their corresponding hyper-parameters, and the results are presented in our supplement materials.

HCG: HCG block aims to learn high-level discriminative context feature representation, which can effectively guide the process of feature modeling and decoding. As shown in Table 1, the incorporation of HCG into the modeling and decoding phase with ResSPADE blocks yields significant improvement on all metrics, with the increases of 0.51, 1.17, 0.02, 3.35 for I_{out} and 1.67, 1.57, 0.01, 2.73 for I_{com} in PSNR, MSSIM, MSE, and FID, respectively. The qualitative

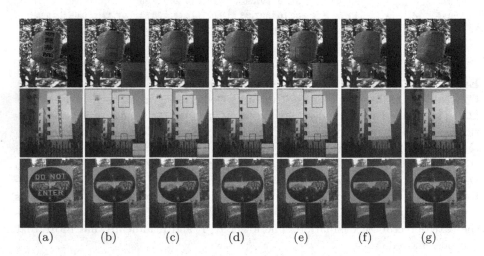

(a)   (b)   (c)   (d)   (e)   (f)   (g)

Fig. 4. Qualitative results for ablation studies on HCG, LGCM, LCG. (a) The input images; (b) Baseline results; (c) Baseline + HCG; (d) Baseline + HCG + LGCM; (e) Baseline + HCG + LGCM + LCG; (f) The structure output from LCG for the model (e); (g) The ground-truth. Zoom in for best view.

results shown in Fig. 4 also illustrate the effect of this component. Comparing with the results of the baseline model in Fig. 4(b), the results in Fig. 4(c) indicate that the HCG block can help generate a more plausible background and release more artifacts in the output.

LGCM: As shown in Table 1, the incorporation of our LGCM significantly facilitates performance improvement of 2.20, 0.74, 0.02, 3.04 for I_{out} in PSNR, MSSIM, MSE, and FID, respectively, while 0.42, 0.11, 0.01, 1.51 for I_{com}. Such a remarkable promotion benefits a lot from both the local and global modeling for the features and the learned context prior, which can capture not only the long-range dependency among pixels around the feature maps but their relationship at a fixed window as well. Therefore, LGCM enables our CTRNet to take advantage of both local and global information. The qualitative results are presented in Fig. 4(d). In comparison, the outputs of our model without LGCM exhibit some obvious defects on the text regions (the up/bottom row of Fig. 4(c)), while those with LGCM are more favorable, though there still exist mistaken erasure (e.g. the bottom of Fig. 4(d), but the restored background is smoother than (c)). Besides, with the long-rang dependency, the text can be removed more thoroughly with incorrect detection results, which is presented in the middle row of Fig. 4(c) and (d). Furthermore, we discuss the number of LGCM blocks in the supplementary materials.

(a) Input   (b) GT   (c) EN[23]   (d) Stroke[38]   (e) Ours

Fig. 5. Qualitative results on SCUT-EnsText for comparing our model with previous scene text removal methods. EN denotes EraseNet [23] and Stroke denotes the method proposed by Tang et al. [38]. Zoom in for best view.

LCG: According to the results shown in Table 1, under the same experimental setting, CTRNet with LCG yields slightly improvement in PSNR and FID by approximately 0.03 and 0.40 on average, respectively for both I_{out} and I_{com}, while the other metrics remain comparable. One of the basic challenges of scene text removal is the background restoration, the generated structure can indicate the region clues of text-erased so that provide the guidance for texture synthesis of the background. Figure 4(e) and (f) show the outputs of CTRNet with LCG and the generated background structure. With the background structure, our

Table 2. Comparison with state-of-the-art methods on SCUT-EnsText. The methods with "*" denote that the text mask are generated with the GT instead of the detected results. MSSIM and MSE are represented by % in the table. Bold indicates SOTA, while Underline indicates second best.

Methods	Image-Eval				Detection-eval					
	PSNR	MSSIM	MSE	FID	R	P	H	T-R	T-P	T-H
Original	-	-	-	-	69.5	79.4	74.1	50.9	61.4	55.7
Pix2pix [14]	26.70	88.56	0.37	46.88	35.4	69.7	47.0	24.3	52.0	33.1
STE [29]	25.46	90.14	0.47	43.39	5.9	40.9	10.2	3.6	28.9	6.4
EnsNet [56]	29.54	92.74	0.24	32.71	32.8	68.7	44.4	50.7	22.1	30.8
EraseNet [23]	32.30	95.42	0.15	19.27	4.6	53.2	8.5	2.9	37.6	5.4
PERT [48]	33.25	96.95	0.14	-	2.9	52.7	5.4	1.8	38.7	3.5
Ours (I_{out})	35.20	97.36	0.09	13.99	1.4	38.4	2.7	0.9	28.3	1.7
Tang et al. [38]	35.34	96.24	0.09	-	3.6	-	-	-	-	-
Ours (I_{com})	35.85	97.40	0.09	14.57	1.7	40.1	3.3	1.1	29.4	2.1
Tang et al.* [38]	37.08	96.54	0.05	-	-	-	-	-	-	-
Ours* (I_{com})	37.20	97.66	0.07	11.72	-	-	-	-	-	-

text removal network can restore a more natural background texture, as indicated by the red boxes in the figures. Besides, as shown in the bottom row of Fig. 4(e), there exist wrong detected results, but LCG can still help retain the corresponding region and predict more reasonable contents than others.

Soft Mask: The application of soft-mask mainly aims to eliminate the discontinuity and inconsistency at the junction of text/non-text regions on the output. Soft mask only achieves only a slight improvement on I_{out}, but a significant promotion on I_{com} by 0.53 in PSNR and 0.22 in MSSIM, respectively. Qualitative results of I_{com} for the comparison on hard-mask (0-1) and soft-mask are shown in the supplement file. With soft-mask, the output can preserve smoother edges between text and non-text regions. Besides, as the soft-mask is expanded, the texts are removed more completely and thoroughly.

4.4   Comparison with the State-of-the-Arts

In this section, we conduct experiments to evaluate the performance of CTRNet and the relevant SOTA methods on scene text removal on both SCUT-EnsText and SCUT-Syn. The quantitative results on SCUT-EnsText are given in Table 2, and the quantitative results on SCUT-Syn are given in Table 3. The results for these two datasets demonstrate that our proposed model outperforms existing state-of-the-art methods on both Image-Eval and Detection-Eval, indicating that our model can effectively remove the text on th images and meanwhile restore more reasonable background textures. Only the results of Tang et al. [38] preserve

(a) Input   (b) GT   (c) EN[23]   (d) Stroke[38]   (e) Ours

Fig. 6. Qualitative results on SCUT-Syn for comparing our model with previous scene text removal methods. EN denotes EraseNet [23] and Stroke denotes the method proposed by Tang et al. [38]. Zoom in for best view.

Table 3. Comparison with state-of-the-art methods on SCUT-Syn. MSSIM and MSE are represented by (%) in the table. Bold indicates SOTA, while Underline indicates second best.

Methods	Image-Eval			
	PSNR	MSSIM	MSE	FID
Pix2pix [14]	26.76	91.08	0.27	47.84
STE [29]	25.40	90.12	0.65	46.39
EnsNet [56]	37.36	96.44	0.21	-
EnsNet (reimplemented) [56]	36.23	96.76	0.04	19.96
EraseNet [23]	38.32	97.67	0.02	9.53
MTRNet++ [39]	34.55	98.45	0.04	-
Zdenek et al. [55]	37.46	93.64	-	-
Conrad et al. [7]	32.97	94.90	-	-
PERT [48]	39.40	97.87	0.02	-
Tang et al. [38]	38.60	97.55	0.02	-
Ours	**41.28**	**98.50**	**0.02**	**3.84**

non-text regions of the input (i.e. I_{com}) while the others are direct model output I_{out}, we evaluate all their performance for fair comparisons.

The qualitative comparison with other methods on SCUT-EnsText is shown in Fig. 5, and for SCUT-Syn in Fig. 6. In Fig. 5, the results generated by EraseNet [23] and Tang et al. [38] still contain artifacts and discontinuities on the output when dealing with complex text images. By utilizing local-global content modeling and different level contextual guidance, our model can predict more realistic textures for text regions and obtain significantly fewer noticeable inconsistencies. Besides, in Fig. 6, our model can also generate results of higher quality with more visually pleasing and plausible contents for synthetic data. More cases for comparison are given in the supplement materials.

Table 4. Comparison with state-of-the-art image inpainting methods on SCUT-EnsText. MSSIM and MSE are represented by (%) in the table.

Methods	Image-Eval			
	PSNR	MSSIM	MSE	FID
CTSDG [11]	33.10	95.55	0.14	20.01
SPL [57]	35.41	97.39	0.07	17.85
Ours	**37.20**	**97.66**	**0.07**	**11.72**

(a) Input   (b) GT   (c) CTDSG[11]   (d) SPL[57]   (e) Ours

Fig. 7. Qualitative results on SCUT-EnsText for comparing our model with state-of-the-art image inpainting methods. Zoom in for best view.

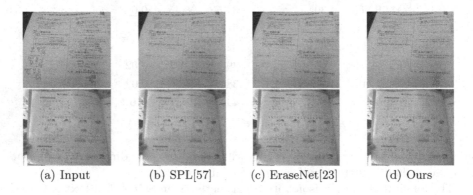

(a) Input   (b) SPL[57]   (c) EraseNet[23]   (d) Ours

Fig. 8. Qualitative results on examination papers. Zoom in for best view.

4.5   Comparison with State-of-the-Art Image Inpainting Methods

We conduct experiments to compare CTRNet with existing SOTA image inpainting methods, CTSDG [11] and SPL [57] on SCUT-EnsText. The quantitative and qualitative results are given in Table 4 and Fig. 7, respectively. Our model outperforms these two methods in all metrics with a remarkable margin, meanwhile can restore the text region background with more reasonable and realistic textures. The reason is that while we simply apply image inpainting methods on scene text removal, the text regions will be directly abandoned by masking according to the bounding boxes (blue boxes in Fig. 7(a)), causing that the model can not effectively deduce the background information.

4.6 Application on Handwritten Text Removal

In this section, we apply CTRNet to help restore document images to verify its generalizability. We collect 1,000 in-house examination paper images and manually annotate them by erasing the handwriting with PhotoShop. Then we train CTRNet and EraseNet [23] on the data and evaluate them with other paper images. Besides, we also train SPL [57] for comparison to further illustrate the difference between text removal and image inpainting. The visualization results are shown in Fig. 8. Our method can retain more printed words than SPL and EraseNet, which is more suitable for document restoration task. More results are given in the supplement materials.

5 Conclusion

In this paper, we propose a new text removal model called CTRNet. CTRNet introduces both low-level and high-level contextual guidance, which can effectively promote the performance on texture restoration for complex backgrounds. We further use smooth structure images and discriminative context features to represent the low-level and high-level context, respectively. Besides, the learned contextual guidance is incorporated into the image features and modeled in a local-global manner to effectively capture both sufficient context information and long-term correlation among all of the pixels. The experiments conducted on three benchmark datasets have demonstrated the effectiveness of the proposed CTRNet, outperforming previous state-of-the-art methods significantly.

Acknowledgement. This research is supported in part by NSFC (Grant No.: 61936003), GD-NSF (no. 2017A030312006, No. 2021A1515011870), and the Science and Technology Foundation of Guangzhou Huangpu Development District (Grant 2020GH17).

References

1. Baek, Y., Lee, B., Han, D., Yun, S., Lee, H.: Character region awareness for text detection. In: Proceedings of CVPR, pp. 9365–9374 (2019)
2. Bengio, Y., Courville, A., Vincent, P.: Representation learning: a review and new perspectives. IEEE Trans. Pattern Anal. Mach. Intell. **35**(8), 1798–1828 (2013)

3. Bian, X., Wang, C., Quan, W., Ye, J., Zhang, X., Yan, D.-M.: Scene text removal via cascaded text stroke detection and erasing. Comput. Vis. Media **8**(2), 273–287 (2021). https://doi.org/10.1007/s41095-021-0242-8

4. Chng, C.K., et al.: ICDAR2019 robust reading challenge on arbitrary-shaped text - RRC-ArT. In: Proceedings of ICDAR, pp. 1571–1576 (2019)

5. Ch'ng, C.K., Chan, C.S.: Total-Text: a comprehensive dataset for scene text detection and recognition. In: Proceedings of ICDAR, vol. 1, pp. 935–942 (2017)

6. Cho, J., Yun, S., Han, D., Heo, B., Choi, J.Y.: Detecting and removing text in the wild. IEEE Access **9**, 123313–123323 (2021)

7. Conrad, B., Chen, P.I.: Two-stage seamless text erasing on real-world scene images. In: Proceedings of ICIP, pp. 1309–1313. IEEE (2021)

8. Deng, J., Dong, W., Socher, R., Li, L.J., Li, K., Fei-Fei, L.: ImageNet: a large-scale hierarchical image database. In: Proceedings of CVPR, pp. 248–255 (2009)

9. Gatys, L.A., Ecker, A.S., Bethge, M.: Image style transfer using convolutional neural networks. In: Proceedings of CVPR, pp. 2414–2423 (2016)

10. Goodfellow, I., et al.: Generative adversarial nets. In: Proceedings of NIPS, pp. 2672–2680 (2014)

11. Guo, X., Yang, H., Huang, D.: Image inpainting via conditional texture and structure dual generation. In: Proceedings of ICCV, pp. 14134–14143 (2021)

12. Gupta, A., Vedaldi, A., Zisserman, A.: Synthetic data for text localisation in natural images. In: Proceedings of CVPR, pp. 2315–2324 (2016)

13. Heusel, M., Ramsauer, H., Unterthiner, T., Nessler, B., Hochreiter, S.: GANs trained by a two time-scale update rule converge to a local nash equilibrium. In: Proceedings of NIPS, pp. 6626–6637 (2017)

14. Isola, P., Zhu, J.Y., Zhou, T., Efros, A.A.: Image-to-image translation with conditional adversarial networks. In: Proceedings of CVPR, pp. 1125–1134 (2017)

15. Johnson, J., Alahi, A., Fei-Fei, L.: Perceptual losses for real-time style transfer and super-resolution. In: Leibe, B., Matas, J., Sebe, N., Welling, M. (eds.) ECCV 2016. LNCS, vol. 9906, pp. 694–711. Springer, Cham (2016). https://doi.org/10.1007/978-3-319-46475-6_43

16. Karatzas, D., et al.: ICDAR 2015 competition on robust reading. In: Proceedings of ICDAR, pp. 1156–1160 (2015)

17. Karatzas, D., et al.: ICDAR 2013 robust reading competition. In: Proceedings of ICDAR, pp. 1484–1493 (2013)

18. Keserwani, P., Roy, P.P.: Text region conditional generative adversarial network for text concealment in the wild. IEEE Trans. Circuits Syst. Video Technol. **32**(5), 3152–3163 (2021)

19. Kingma, D.P., Ba, J.: Adam: a method for stochastic optimization. In: Proceedings of ICLR (2014)

20. Krishnan, P., Kovvuri, R., Pang, G., Vassilev, B., Hassner, T.: TextStyleBrush: transfer of text aesthetics from a single example. arXiv preprint arXiv:2106.08385 (2021)

21. Kuznetsova, A., et al.: The open images dataset v4. Int. J. Comput. Vision **128**(7), 1956–1981 (2020)

22. Liang, J., Cao, J., Sun, G., Zhang, K., Van Gool, L., Timofte, R.: SwinIR: image restoration using swin transformer. In: Proceedings of ICCV, pp. 1833–1844 (2021)

23. Liu, C., Liu, Y., Jin, L., Zhang, S., Luo, C., Wang, Y.: EraseNet: end-to-end text removal in the wild. IEEE Trans. Image Process. **29**, 8760–8775 (2020)

24. Liu, G., Reda, F.A., Shih, K.J., Wang, T.C., Tao, A., Catanzaro, B.: Image inpainting for irregular holes using partial convolutions. In: Proceedings of ECCV, pp. 85–100 (2018)

25. Liu, H., Jiang, B., Song, Y., Huang, W., Yang, C.: Rethinking image inpainting via a mutual encoder-decoder with feature equalizations. In: Vedaldi, A., Bischof, H., Brox, T., Frahm, J.-M. (eds.) ECCV 2020. LNCS, vol. 12347, pp. 725–741. Springer, Cham (2020). https://doi.org/10.1007/978-3-030-58536-5_43

26. Liu, Y., Jin, L., Xie, Z., Luo, C., Zhang, S., Xie, L.: Tightness-aware evaluation protocol for scene text detection. In: Proceedings of CVPR, pp. 9612–9620 (2019)

27. Mirza, M., Osindero, S.: Conditional generative adversarial nets. arXiv preprint arXiv:1411.1784 (2014)

28. Miyato, T., Kataoka, T., Koyama, M., Yoshida, Y.: Spectral normalization for generative adversarial networks. In: Proceedings of ICLR (2018)

29. Nakamura, T., Zhu, A., Yanai, K., Uchida, S.: Scene text eraser. In: Proceedings of ICDAR, vol. 01, pp. 832–837 (2017)

30. Nayef, N., et al.: ICDAR2017 robust reading challenge on multi-lingual scene text detection and script identification - RRC-MLT. In: Proceedings of IDAR, vol. 01, pp. 1454–1459 (2017)

31. Nayef, N., et al.: ICDAR2019 robust reading challenge on multi-lingual scene text detection and recognition-RRC-MLT-2019. In: Proceedings of ICDAR, pp. 1582–1587 (2019)

32. Nazeri, K., Ng, E., Joseph, T., Qureshi, F., Ebrahimi, M.: EdgeConnect: structure guided image inpainting using edge prediction. In: Proceedings of ICCV Workshops (2019)

33. Park, T., Liu, M.Y., Wang, T.C., Zhu, J.Y.: Semantic image synthesis with spatially-adaptive normalization. In: Proceedings of CVPR, pp. 2337–2346 (2019)

34. Qin, S., Wei, J., Manduchi, R.: Automatic semantic content removal by learning to neglect. In: Proceedings of BMVC, pp. 1–12 (2018)

35. Ren, Y., Yu, X., Zhang, R., Li, T.H., Liu, S., Li, G.: StructureFlow: image inpainting via structure-aware appearance flow. In: Proceedings of ICCV, pp. 181–190 (2019)

36. Ridnik, T., et al.: Asymmetric loss for multi-label classification. In: Proceedings of ICCV, pp. 82–91 (2021)

37. Shimoda, W., Haraguchi, D., Uchida, S., Yamaguchi, K.: De-rendering stylized texts. In: Proceedings of ICCV, pp. 1076–1085 (2021)

38. Tang, Z., Miyazaki, T., Sugaya, Y., Omachi, S.: Stroke-based scene text erasing using synthetic data for training. IEEE Trans. Image Process. **30**, 9306–9320 (2021)

39. Tursun, O., Denman, S., Zeng, R., Sivapalan, S., Sridharan, S., Fookes, C.: MTR-Net++: one-stage mask-based scene text eraser. Comput. Vis. Image Underst. **201**, 103066 (2020)

40. Tursun, O., Zeng, R., Denman, S., Sivapalan, S., Sridharan, S., Fookes, C.: MTR-Net: a generic scene text eraser. In: Proceedings of ICDAR, pp. 39–44. IEEE (2019)

41. Vaswani, A., et al.: Attention is all you need. In: Proceedings of NIPS, pp. 6000–6010 (2017)

42. Vatti, B.R.: A generic solution to polygon clipping. Commun. ACM **35**(7), 56–63 (1992)

43. Veit, A., Matera, T., et al.: COCO-Text: Dataset and benchmark for text detection and recognition in natural images. arXiv preprint arXiv:1601.07140 (2016)

44. Wang, C., et al.: Semi-supervised pixel-level scene text segmentation by mutually guided network. IEEE Trans. Image Process. **30**, 8212–8221 (2021)

45. Wang, K., Belongie, S.: Word spotting in the wild. In: Daniilidis, K., Maragos, P., Paragios, N. (eds.) ECCV 2010. LNCS, vol. 6311, pp. 591–604. Springer, Heidelberg (2010). https://doi.org/10.1007/978-3-642-15549-9_43

46. Wang, W., et al.: Shape robust text detection with progressive scale expansion network. In: Proceedings of CVPR, pp. 9336–9345 (2019)
47. Wang, W., et al.: Efficient and accurate arbitrary-shaped text detection with pixel aggregation network. In: Proceedings of ICCV, pp. 8440–8449 (2019)
48. Wang, Y., Xie, H., Fang, S., Qu, Y., Zhang, Y.: A simple and strong baseline: Progressively region-based scene text removal networks. arXiv e-prints pp. arXiv-2106 (2021)
49. Wu, L., et al.: Editing text in the wild. In: Proceedings of ACM MM, pp. 1500–1508 (2019)
50. Xu, L., Yan, Q., Xia, Y., Jia, J.: Structure extraction from texture via relative total variation. ACM Trans. Graph. **31**(6), 1–10 (2012)
51. Xu, X., Zhang, Z., Wang, Z., Price, B., Wang, Z., Shi, H.: Rethinking text segmentation: a novel dataset and a text-specific refinement approach. In: Proceedings of CVPR, pp. 12045–12055 (2021)
52. Yang, Q., Huang, J., Lin, W.: Swaptext: image based texts transfer in scenes. In: Proceedings of CVPR, pp. 14700–14709 (2020)
53. Yu, B., Xu, Y., Huang, Y., Yang, S., Liu, J.: Mask-guided GAN for robust text editing in the scene. Neurocomputing **441**, 192–201 (2021)
54. Yuliang, L., Lianwen, J., Shuaitao, Z., Sheng, Z.: Curved scene text detection via transverse and longitudinal sequence connection. Pattern Recogn. **90**, 337–345 (2019)
55. Zdenek, J., Nakayama, H.: Erasing scene text with weak supervision. In: Proceedings of WACV (2020)
56. Zhang, S., Liu, Y., Jin, L., Huang, Y., Lai, S.: EnsNet: ensconce text in the wild. In: Proceedings of AAAI, vol. 33, pp. 801–808 (2019)
57. Zhang, W., et al.: Context-aware image inpainting with learned semantic priors. In: Proceedings of IJCAI, pp. 1323–1329 (2021)
58. Zheng, C., Cham, T.J., Cai, J.: Pluralistic image completion. In: Proceedings of CVPR, pp. 1438–1447 (2019)

TextAdaIN: Paying Attention to Shortcut Learning in Text Recognizers

Oren Nuriel[(✉)], Sharon Fogel, and Ron Litman

AWS AI Labs, Tel Aviv, Israel
{onuriel,shafog,litmanr}@amazon.com

Abstract. Leveraging the characteristics of convolutional layers, neural networks are extremely effective for pattern recognition tasks. However in some cases, their decisions are based on unintended information leading to high performance on standard benchmarks but also to a lack of generalization to challenging testing conditions and unintuitive failures. Recent work has termed this "shortcut learning" and addressed its presence in multiple domains. In text recognition, we reveal another such shortcut, whereby recognizers overly depend on local image statistics. Motivated by this, we suggest an approach to regulate the reliance on local statistics that improves text recognition performance.

Our method, termed TextAdaIN, creates local distortions in the feature map which prevent the network from overfitting to local statistics. It does so by viewing each feature map as a sequence of elements and deliberately mismatching fine-grained feature statistics between elements in a mini-batch. Despite TextAdaIN's simplicity, extensive experiments show its effectiveness compared to other, more complicated methods. TextAdaIN achieves state-of-the-art results on standard handwritten text recognition benchmarks. It generalizes to multiple architectures and to the domain of scene text recognition. Furthermore, we demonstrate that integrating TextAdaIN improves robustness towards more challenging testing conditions.

Keywords: Text recognition · Handwriting recognition · Scene text recognition · Shortcut learning · Regularization

1 Introduction

Reading someone else's handwriting is often a challenging task; some of the characters are unclear, the text is cursive, there is background clutter and the image quality can be low. When deciphering each character, we often rely on the surrounding area to compensate for the occasional obscurity of the text. The automation of reading text images has been a thriving field of research in

Supplementary Information The online version contains supplementary material available at https://doi.org/10.1007/978-3-031-19815-1_25.

© The Author(s), under exclusive license to Springer Nature Switzerland AG 2022
S. Avidan et al. (Eds.): ECCV 2022, LNCS 13688, pp. 427–445, 2022.
https://doi.org/10.1007/978-3-031-19815-1_25

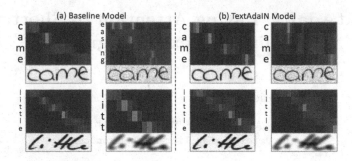

Fig. 1. Decoder attention maps. Each example shows the input image (bottom), attention map (top) and model prediction (left). Each line in the attention map is a time step representing the attention per character prediction. (a) The baseline model, which uses local statistics as a shortcut, misinterprets the corrupted images. (b) Our proposed method which overcomes this shortcut, enhances performance on both standard and challenging testing conditions

computer vision for decades. Recent deep learning methods have significantly improved recognition results [1,2,6,35,38,62].

However, previous works suggest that despite their super-human capabilities, deep learning methods are limited by their tendency to err even when introducing small (in some cases even invisible) modifications to the input. Numerous works have touched on this subject from various angles [10,23,41,46,53,54] and propose tailored solutions. Geirhos *et al.* [22] view each of these as a symptom of the same underlying problem, and terms this phenomenon *shortcut learning - decision rules that perform well on independent and identically distributed (i.i.d.) test data but fail on tests that are out-of-distribution (o.o.d)*. Shortcut learning occurs when there is an easy way to learn attributes which are highly correlated with the label (*i.e.*, "it stands on a grass lawn ⟹ it is a cow"). Thus, shortcuts are inherent in the data [23,27]. Yet, as they can depend on other various factors such as the architecture [15], and the optimization procedure [16,59] as well, revealing an instance of shortcut learning is non-trivial task. The fact that a model learned a shortcut can be discovered at test time when it encounters examples that the shortcut heuristic fails on (*i.e.*, a cow on the beach).

In this work, we reveal a shortcut pertaining to text recognizers, specifically, we reveal the unhealthy reliance of text recognizers on local statistics. Based on the observation that text recognizers operate on a local level, we hypothesize that they are susceptible to overly rely on local information which may even be indistinguishable to the naked eye (*i.e.*, a certain level of curvature is unique and highly correlated with the character "f"). As such in this case it is difficult to identify the exact shortcut heuristic, thus we provide intuition through quantitative and qualitative analyses. Figure 1(a) illustrates the decoder's attention maps for a state-of-the-art [35] recognizer before and after applying local corruptions to the image. In the first row, additive Gaussian noise is applied, which distorts local information while maintaining semantic information. As a conse-

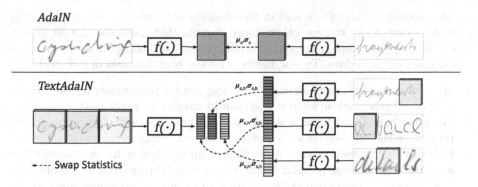

Fig. 2. TextAdaIN. TextAdaIN views each of the feature maps as a sequence of individual elements and swaps feature statistics between elements instead of entire images as in AdaIN. This feature-level distortion alleviates the model's tendency to rely on shortcuts in the form of local statistics

quence, the model diverges completely. In the second row, motion blur is applied, artificially imitating object motion. In this case, in order to successfully decode the corrupted image, global context is necessary (imagine reading the blurred image character by character without access to the surrounding characters). As one can tell from the attention maps, the model fails to do so and is unable to correctly decode the image. An in-depth analysis reveals that this phenomenon is apparent in standard text recognizers across both scene text and handwritten domains, as further elaborated in Sect. 3.

To prevent the model from using the aforementioned shortcut, we propose a simple, yet powerful, technique for moderating the reliance on local statistics. The key idea of our approach is to probabilistically swap fine-grained feature statistics in a manner that is adjusted to the task at hand. To that end, we propose TextAdaIN, a local variation of AdaIN [28], depicted in Fig. 2. In contrast to AdaIN which operates on the entire image, TextAdaIN splits the feature map into a sequence of elements and operates on each element independently. Furthermore, the normalization is performed over multiple dimensions. Both modifications increase the granularity level in which the statistics are modified and enable the usage of multiple donor images. Effectively, the representation space undergoes distortions derived from an induced distribution, namely other text images, at a sub-word level. Thus, forcing the encoder to account for information in surrounding areas as the local information cannot always be depended on. This is observed in Fig. 1(b), where in contrast to the baseline model, TextAdaIN successfully utilizes global context and properly decodes the images despite the corruptions.

We validate our method by comparing its performance with state-of-the-art approaches on several handwritten text benchmarks. TextAdaIN achieves state-of-the-art results, reducing the word error rate by **11.8%** and **16.4%** on IAM and RIMES, respectively. Furthermore, our method shows a consistent improvement across multiple architectures and in the domain of scene text recognition. Not only does our model surpass other, more complicated methods [2,9,20,38,62], but it is simple to implement and can effortlessly be integrated into any mini-batch training procedure. To summarize, the key contributions of our work are:

1. We reveal an instance of shortcut learning in text recognizers in the form of a heavy dependence on local statistics and suggest to regulate it.
2. We introduce TextAdaIN, a simple yet effective normalization approach to remediate the reliance on local statistics in text recognizers.
3. Extensive experimental validation shows our method achieves state-of-the-art results on several popular handwritten text benchmarks. In addition, it is applicable to the domain of scene text and can be used independent of the chosen architecture.
4. We demonstrate that our method leads to improved performance on challenging testing conditions.

2   Related Work

Shortcut Learning. An extensive amount of research has been conducted at understanding the behaviour of neural networks. One behavioural aspect under investigation is their unintended solutions, whereby a decision is made based on misleading information, thus limiting the performance under general conditions. A typical example of this is an intriguing discovery made by Szegedy *et al.* [53]. They showed the susceptibility of neural networks to adversarial examples, which are samples that undergo minimal, or even unnoticeable, modifications capable of altering model predictions. More recent works show other ill-desired sensitivities, [23] for texture, [3] for color constancy, [41,45] for global statistics and [8] for image background. These phenomena were classified by Geirhos *et al.* [22] as instances of the same underlying problem that they termed *shortcut learning*. So far, for shortcut learning in the domain of text recognition, we are only aware of [56], which exposed the decoder's high reliance on vocabulary.

Normalization and Style Transfer. Normalizing feature tensors is an effective and powerful technique that has been explored and developed over the years for a variety of tasks. Ioffe & Szegedy [29] were the first to introduce Batch Normalization, which inspired a series of normalization-based methods such as Layer Normalization [5], Instance Normalization [55], and Group Normalization [60].

The style of an image was characterized by [21] to be the statistics of activation maps in intermediate layers of convolutional neural networks. Instance Normalization (IN) [55] is a normalization layer which normalizes these statistics, removing the style representation from the activation map. Subsequently, Adaptive Instance Normalization (AdaIN) was proposed by [28] for real-time arbitrary style transfer. AdaIN changes the style of an image by incorporating statistics from an additional image.

Leveraging the benefits of this operation, Geirhos *et al.* [23] created Stylized-ImageNet, a stylized version of ImageNet. They demonstrated that classifiers trained on this dataset rely more on shape than on texture. More recently, Zhou *et al.* [63] proposed to probabilistically mix instance-level feature statistics during training across different domains, thus increasing the generalizability of the model. Furthermore, Nuriel *et al.* [41] demonstrated that a similar approach can reduce classifiers' reliance on global statistics, therefore increasing classification performance.

In this work we reveal a shortcut learning phenomenon in text recognizers. To remediate this problem, we also leverage AdaIN. However, instead of operating on a word (instance) level, we swap fine-grained statistics on a sub-word level. We do so by treating every few consecutive frames in the sequential feature map as individual elements.

Text Recognition. Text recognition has attracted considerable attention over the past few years. In particular, deep learning approaches have achieved remarkable results [1, 6, 18, 19, 35, 47, 51]. Still, current state-of-the-art methods struggle to train robust models when the amount of data is insufficient to capture the magnitude of styles. Various methods have been suggested to cope with this problem. Bhunia *et al.* [9] proposed an adversarial feature deformation module that learns ways to elastically warp extracted features, boosting the network's capability to learn highly informative features. Luo *et al.* [38] introduced an agent network that learns from the output of the recognizer. The agent controls a set of fiducial points on the image and uses a spatial transformer to generate "harder" training samples.

Unlike previous methods, our method does not require additional data, new models or complex training paradigms. Instead, we suggest a normalization-based method adjusted to text images and to sequence-to-sequence approaches. TextAdaIN is extremely easy to implement and can fit into any encoder as part of a mini-batch training process.

Throughout this work, unless mentioned otherwise, we integrate our proposed method with a state-of-the-art recognizer named SCATTER [35]. The SCATTER architecture consists of four main components: spatial transformation, feature extraction, visual feature refinement and a selective-contextual refinement block. For further details about the baseline architecture, we refer the reader to Appendix A.

3   Method

3.1   Shortcut Learning in Text Recognizers

As elaborated on in [22], shortcuts are dependent on various factors, including the architecture of the model and the data. We therefore draw our motivation for suspecting local statistics as a potential instance of shortcut learning in text recognizers based on two key observations pertaining to both the architecture and the nature of the data. First, the characters appear across a series of frames along the width axis of the image. Therefore, text recogni-

Table 1. Text recognizers' performance in challenging testing conditions. Mean accuracies of different state-of-the-art text recognizers while applying a series of subtle local image corruptions. The corruptions consist of local masking and pixel-wise distortions: Cutout, Dropout, Additive Guassian Noise, Elastic Transform and Motion Blur. Models are especially susceptible to learning shortcuts when the training data is limited, as in handwriting

Method	Scene text		Handwritten
	Regular text	Irregular text	IAM
Baek et al. (CTC) [6]	88.7	72.9	80.6
+Local Corruption	69.8 (-18.9)	44.1 (-28.8)	40.4 (-40.2)
Baek et al. (Attn) [6]	92.0	77.4	82.7
+Local Corruption	74.5 (-17.5)	50.5 (-26.9)	46.2 (-36.5)
SCATTER [35]	93.5	82.1	85.7
+Local Corruption	76.8 (-16.7)	55.3 (-26.8)	54.8 (-30.9)

tion approaches define the recognition task as a sequence character classification problem. This leads us to the second observation, the model's predictions are mostly based on local information which lies in consecutive frames [42,48]. Local information is referred to, in our work, as local feature statistics.

As illustrated in Fig. 1, when applying slight local modifications to the image distorting local information in a way which does not affect human reading capabilities (see Appendix B), the baseline model is unable to predict the words correctly. Table 1 quantitatively exemplifies this phenomenon, whereby the models fail to generalize to images under challenging testing conditions in the form of local corruptions. The table shows the performance of three different text recognition architectures - Baek et al. [6] with CTC and attention heads and SCATTER [35]. All models have been tested on the original scene-text and IAM datasets and on corrupted versions of these datasets. The corruptions used are the local-masking and pixel-wise distortions described in Table 6. All of the models suffer from a large decline in performance when adding the corruptions, and especially on handwriting where the training data is scarce.

An additional experiment validating text recognizers' sensitivity to local distortions is shown in Sect. 5.5, where we empirically demonstrate that text recognizers heavily rely on local information. Specifically, we show that profusely distorting global statistics has little to no effect on performance (unlike in classification models [41]). However, intensely distorting local statistics substantially degrades performance, which leads to the understanding that text recognizers do indeed rely on such information. The local statistics are an important cue, although they are not a determining factor. Thus, to regulate this ill-desired model bias, we propose TextAdaIN, a sequence-aware local variation of AdaIN.

3.2   AdaIN

To define AdaIN, we first begin with formally describing Instance Normalization (IN) [55]. Given an instance $x \in \mathbb{R}^{C \times H \times W}$, where C, H and W are the channels, height, and width respectively, IN is defined to be:

$$\text{IN}(x) = \gamma \left(\frac{x - \mu(x)}{\sigma(x)} \right) + \beta. \tag{1}$$

where $\gamma, \beta \in \mathbb{R}^C$ are learned parameters and $\mu(x)$, $\sigma(x) \in \mathbb{R}^C$ are calculated by taking the mean and standard deviation over H, W of x.

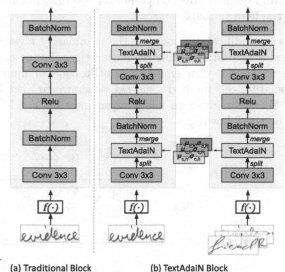

(a) Traditional Block   (b) TextAdaIN Block

Fig. 3. TextAdaIN block. (a) A standard residual block and (b) a TextAdaIN block. TextAdaIN is probabilistically employed after every Conv layer during training. *split* and *merge* refer to the mapping operations of reshaping each feature map and $\mu_{c,h}, \sigma_{c,h}$ refer to the feature statistics, as described in Sect. 3.3

Adaptive Instance Normalization (AdaIN), proposed in [28], is built upon IN. Given two image representations, $x_a, x_b \in \mathbb{R}^{C \times H \times W}$, AdaIN shifts the statistics of the representation of x_a to the representation of x_b. This is done in two steps. First, Instance Normalization is applied on x_a to remove x_a's style information. Then, the normalized activation map is scaled and shifted to match x_b's statistics. This operation is perceived to transfer x_b's style onto x_a.

$$\text{AdaIN}_c(x_a, x_b) = \sigma(x_b) \left(\frac{x_a - \mu(x_a)}{\sigma(x_a)} \right) + \mu(x_b). \tag{2}$$

AdaIN_c denotes the standard AdaIN operation in which σ, μ are calculated over the spatial dimensions, resulting in shifting corresponding channel statistics.

3.3   TextAdaIN

We wish to design a method that produces model decision rules which are not overly reliant on local information. To this end, we propose a method which distorts local feature statistics during training. Leveraging the recent development proposed by [41,63], we suggest two modifications to the vanilla AdaIN operation that correspond to the aforementioned observations:

1. Viewing the feature map as a sequence of individual elements and swapping the feature statistics between elements instead of entire images.
2. Modifying AdaIN to operate on two dimensions - the height and channels of the feature map.

These modifications increase the granularity level in which statistics are calculated and modified, thus regulating the reliance on local statistics. In addition, the sequential view enables the utilization of multiple donor images. Both are crucial for our method's success, as shown in Sect. 5.

Formally, given an image representation $x \in \mathbb{R}^{C \times H \times W}$, we define $\mu_{c,h}$, $\sigma_{c,h}$ to be the following:

$$\mu_{c,h}(x) = \frac{1}{W} \sum_{w=1}^{W} x_{c,h,w} \,, \tag{3}$$

$$\sigma_{c,h}(x) = \sqrt{\frac{1}{W} \sum_{w=1}^{W} (x_{c,h,w} - \mu_{c,h}(x))^2 + \epsilon} \,. \tag{4}$$

Therefore, a local variation of AdaIN_c can be defined as:

$$\text{AdaIN}_{c,h}(x_a, x_b) = \sigma_{c,h}(x_b) \left(\frac{x_a - \mu_{c,h}(x_a)}{\sigma_{c,h}(x_a)} \right) + \mu_{c,h}(x_b) \,. \tag{5}$$

This variant of AdaIN swaps statistics for every corresponding channel and height, thus impacting the feature map's statistics at a higher level of granularity. We note that backpropagating gradients only occur through $\mu_{c,h}(x_a), \sigma_{c,h}(x_a)$. The reason behind this is to avoid gradient flow from input image labels to the donor images. Given the definitions above, we formulate the TextAdaIN operation used during training. Let $X = \{x_i\}_{i=1}^{B}$ denote a mini-batch of B feature maps. We divide each sample x_i into K windows along its width. The result is a batch of elements pertaining to $B \cdot K$ windows. This operation can be defined as a mapping:

$$X \in \mathbb{R}^{B \times C \times H \times W} \rightarrow \widehat{X} \in \mathbb{R}^{B \cdot K \times C \times H \times \frac{W}{K}}. \tag{6}$$

Then, we employ a similar procedure to the one used in [41]. We randomly draw a permutation of the modified batch $\widehat{X}$ and apply $\text{AdaIN}_{c,h}$ between the modified batch and the permuted one. Namely, let

$$\pi(\widehat{X}) = [\hat{x}_{\pi(1)}, \hat{x}_{\pi(2)}...\hat{x}_{\pi(B \cdot K)}] \tag{7}$$

denote applying a permutation $\pi : [B \cdot K] \rightarrow [B \cdot K]$ on $\widehat{X}$. Then the output of TextAdaIN on the ith window of $\widehat{X}$ is defined by:

$$\text{TextAdaIN}(\hat{x}_i) = \text{AdaIN}_{c,h}(\hat{x}_i, \hat{x}_{\pi(i)}). \tag{8}$$

Table 2. Comparison to previous methods. Word and character error rates (WER and CER) are measured on IAM, RIMES and CVL handwriting datasets. '*' indicates using the unlabeled test for training. Our method achieves state-of-the-art across all datasets

Method	IAM			RIMES			CVL		
	WER	CER	Average	WER	CER	Average	WER	CER	Average
Bluche et al. [11]	24.7	7.3	16.00	-	-	-	-	-	-
Bluche et al. [12]	24.6	7.9	16.25	-	-	-	-	-	-
Sueiras et al. [52]	23.8	8.8	16.30	-	-	-	-	-	-
Alonso et al. [4]	-	-	-	11.9	4.0	7.95	-	-	-
ScrabbleGAN [20]	23.6	-	-	11.3	-	-	22.9	-	-
SSDAN* [62]	22.2	8.5	15.35	-	-	-	-	-	-
Bhunia et al. [9]	17.2	8.4	12.80	10.5	6.4	8.45	-	-	-
Kang et al.* [31]	17.3	6.8	12.05	-	-	-	-	-	-
SeqCLR [2]	20.1	9.5	14.80	7.6	2.6	5.10	22.2	-	-
Luo et al. [38]	14.1	**5.4**	9.75	8.7	2.4	5.50	-	-	-
SCATTER [35]	14.4	6.4	10.40	6.7	2.3	4.50	22.3	18.9	20.6
+MixStyle [63]	14.3	6.3	10.30	6.8	2.4	4.60	22.3	18.5	20.40
+pAdaIN [41]	14.6	6.4	10.50	6.4	2.2	4.30	22.3	18.2	20.25
+TextAdaIN	**12.7**	5.8	**9.25**	**5.6**	**1.9**	**3.70**	**21.8**	**18.0**	**19.90**

Subsequently, the batch of windows is rearranged back to its original form using the inverse mapping operation.

TextAdaIN is applied batch-wise with probability p after every convolutional layer in the encoder, as illustrated in Fig. 3(b). The permutation π is sampled uniformly, and p is a hyperparameter fixed ahead of training. TextAdaIN is only applied during training and not during inference.

4   Experiments

In this section, we begin by comparing our method's performance against state-of-the-art methods on several public handwriting datasets. Then, we demonstrate that TextAdaIN can be integrated into additional recognition architectures and applied to natural scene text images.

Datasets. We conduct experiments on several public handwriting and scene text datasets. For handwriting, we consider the English datasets IAM [39] and CVL [34], and the French dataset RIMES [25]. For scene text, we train on the synthetic datasets SynthText [26] and MJSynth [30] and test on four real-world regular text datasets: IIT5K [40], SVT [58], IC03 [37], IC13 [33] and three real-world irregular text datasets: ICDAR2015 [32], SVTP [43] and CUTE 80 [44]. We present samples from each dataset and include more details in Appendix C.

Metrics. To evaluate recognition performance, word-level accuracy is measured. For handwritten text recognition state-of-the-art comparison, Word Error Rate (WER) and Character Error Rate (CER) are adopted, similar to the convention used in [2,52,62].

Implementation Details. Unless mentioned otherwise, in all of our experiments, TextAdaIN is fused into the backbone of SCATTER [35]. The experimental settings, including the optimizer, learning rate, image size, and training datasets, are identical to SCATTER [35]. Full implementation details are described in Appendix D.

4.1   Comparison to State-of-the-Art

In Table 2, we measure the accuracy of our proposed method on public handwritten text benchmarks. Our method achieves state-of-the-art results across all datasets. Compared to current state-of-the-art methods, incorporating TextAdaIN achieves a performance increase of **+1.4** pp (85.9% vs. 87.3%) on IAM, **+2.0** pp (92.4% vs. 94.4%) on RIMES and **+0.4** pp (77.8% vs. 78.2%) on CVL. We wish to emphasize that previous methods, such as [2,9,31,38], introduced complex modifications to the training phase, including adversarial learning and contrastive pre-training. In contrast, TextAdaIN can be easily implemented in a few lines of code and seamlessly fit into any mini-batch training procedure. In addition, the effect of applying MixStyle [63] and pAdaIN [41] is displayed in Table 2. Both have little to no effect on the results, indicating that handwritten text recognizers are already invariant to changes in global statistics. We refer the reader to Appendix E to see failure cases of the model.

Table 3. Generalization to new domains and architectures. Similar to [35], we show weighted (by size) average results on the regular and irregular scene text datasets. All experiments are reproduced. Integrating TextAdaIN results in consistent improvements

Method	Scene text		Handwritten	
	Regular text	Irregular text	IAM	RIMES
	5,529	3,010	17,990	7,734
Baek et al. (CTC) [6]	88.7	72.9	80.6	87.8
+TextAdaIN	89.5 (+0.8)	73.8 (+0.9)	81.5 (+0.9)	90.7 (+2.9)
Baek et al. (Attn) [6]	92.0	77.4	82.7	90.2
+TextAdaIN	92.2 (+0.2)	77.7 (+0.3)	84.1 (+1.4)	93.0 (+2.8)
SCATTER [35]	93.6	83.0	85.7	93.3
+TextAdaIN	94.2 (+0.6)	83.4 (+0.4)	87.3 (+1.6)	94.4 (+1.1)
AbiNet [18]	93.9	82.0	85.4	92.0
+TextAdaIN	94.2 (+0.3)	82.8 (+0.8)	86.3 (+0.9)	93.0 (+1.0)

4.2   Generalization of Proposed Method

In this subsection, we explore our method's transferability to both the domain of scene text and to different recognition architectures. In addition to the SCATTER and AbiNet [18] architectures, we utilize the Baek *et al.* [6] framework, which can describe the building blocks of many text recognizers, including [13,14,20,35,36,47–50,57,61,62]. We choose to present TextAdaIN's performance when integrated into Baek *et al.* [6] framework while employing either a CTC [24] or an attention decoder [14,49]. As in [35], weighted (by size) average word accuracy is adopted where regular and irregular text datasets are distinguished.

In Table 3, we present the reproduced performance of the above methods. TextAdaIN shows consistent improvement on both scene and handwritten text benchmarks independent of the chosen architecture. The results are competitive with recent state-of-the-art methods.

5   Ablation Study

In this section, we conduct a series of experiments to further understand the performance improvements and analyze the impact of our key contributions. For this purpose, we adopt the IAM dataset, and the baseline model is the SCATTER architecture [35]. Similar to our previous experiments, implementation details are described in Appendix D.

We begin by exploring the different variants of AdaIN, demonstrating that our method significantly outperforms other variants. Then, we show the compatibility of our method

Table 4. AdaIN dimensions. Accuracy on the IAM dataset when applying the AdaIN operation over different dimensions. Our method, TextAdaIN, shows significant improvement upon the baseline of **+1.6** pp

Method	AdaIN Dim	Windows	IAM Accuracy
Baseline	-	-	85.7
AdaIN	C	-	85.4
AdaIN variations	W	-	85.7
	H	-	85.6
	H,W	-	85.7
	C,W	-	85.8
	C,H	-	85.9
	C	5	85.9
	W	5	85.5
	H	5	85.9
	H,W	5	85.8
	C,W	5	85.9
TextAdaIN	C,H	5	**87.3**

with other augmentation pipelines demonstrating its unique benefit as a complimentary method. To analyze the performance as a function of the granularity level, we then measure the accuracy while varying the number of windows. Subsequently, we demonstrate the reliance of text recognizers on local feature statistics by increasing the hyperparameter p. Lastly, we perform an analysis of our method's robustness towards challenging testing conditions, demonstrating its effectiveness on relieving the model of this shortcut.

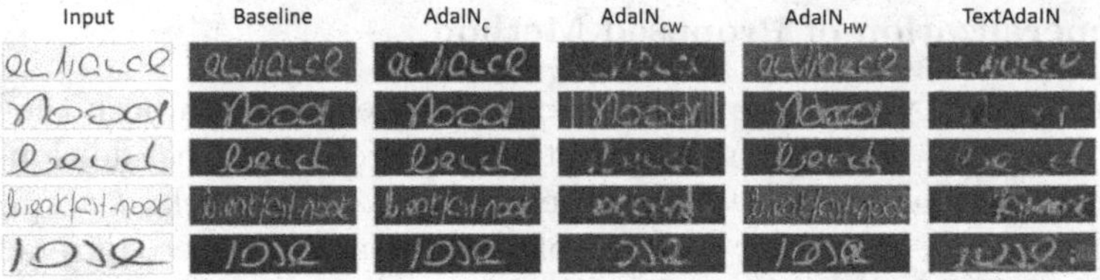

Fig. 4. Information encompassed in each dimension. Intensity maps of the features after the first convolution layer of the encoder are visualized. Each dimension of the feature space represents different information, hence, operating on different dimensions can influence the model accordingly. TextAdaIN has two noticeable effects: (1) injecting background distortions drawn from an induced distribution and (2) introducing masking on a local scale. Both regulate the reliance on local feature statistics, as further investigated in Sect. 5.4

5.1   AdaIN Variations

Each dimension of the feature space represents different information about the input. Hence, modifying AdaIN to operate across different dimensions can influence the model accordingly. Our method is employed over both the channel and height dimensions between different elements of samples in a batch. Each element consists of a pre-defined number of consecutive frames in the sequential feature map. As seen in Table 4, TextAdaIN significantly improves recognition performance as opposed to all other AdaIN variations.

To better understand the information encompassed in each of the dimensions, we visualize the feature maps of a trained baseline model in Fig. 4. For this purpose, we apply PCA on the spatial dimensions of the first convolutional layer's output, thus obtaining an $H \times W \times 1$ intensity map. An image depicting the spatial intensities is displayed after normalization.

As depicted in Fig. 4, applying $AdaIN_c$, the vanilla variation, has almost no effect on the learned features. This is in alignment with the quantitative results indicating that text recognizers are relatively invariant to changes in global statistics. As for $AdaIN_{c,w}$, modifying individual vertical frames introduces subtle changes to the feature map. The network can easily compensate for these distortions, leading to minimal impact on the training process. Interestingly, applying $AdaIN_{h,w}$ injects text from the donor image into the feature map. This phenomenon originates from shifting each corresponding spatial location in the representation space. Clearly, without the modification of the labels, this effect will not improve the performance.

TextAdaIN has two major effects, as visualized in Fig. 4. The first is injecting local perturbations drawn from an induced distribution into the feature space. The distribution is induced from the manner in which TextAdaIN operates, providing a correct balance between the coarse to fine distortion level. Namely, TextAdaIN's impact is more local than $AdaIN_c$, yet more global in the sequence dimension than $AdaIN_{c,w}$. Therefore, the impact aligns with both the nature of the data and sequence-to-sequence approaches.

Table 5. TextAdaIN's contribution is complimentary to data augmentations effect. Word accuracy for augmentation pipelines with (✗) and without (✓) TextAdaIN

Architecture	Augmentation pipeline	IAM		RIMES	
		✗	✓	✗	✓
SCATTER [35]	✗	84.6	**86.5**	91.6	**94.2**
	SCATTER [35]	85.7	**87.3**	93.3	**94.4**
	VisionLAN [19], ABINet [18]	86.3	**87.3**	93.4	**94.7**
	RandAug [17]	86.4	**87.0**	93.5	**94.4**
	Luo *et al.* [38]	85.7	**87.2**	93.5	**94.7**

Occasionally, statistics of smooth areas (without text) are injected into regions of the feature space which represent text. This generates the second effect of local masking, in which part of the textual features undergo masking. We hypothesize that this forces the model to rely on semi-semantic information, which compensates for the missing visual cues. This was partially observed by Aberdam *et al.* [2] while applying horizontal cropping and in the context of speech recognition by Baevski *et al.* [7]. As this analysis was performed on the feature space, we also show the influence of TextAdaIN on the input space in Sect. 5.4. Moreover, to see the importance of the induced distribution causing these effects, see Appendix F.

5.2   Compatibility with Augmentation Strategies

Similarly to TextAdaIN, data augmentation strategies can be used to relieve a model's propensity to shortcuts and increase their robustness. Hence, they have a similar effect, yet they operate at different levels. One at the input space and the other at the feature space. To validate the compatibility of our method with augmentation strategies, we apply a variety of augmentation strategies on top of the same architecture [35] with and without TextAdaIN. We choose augmentation strategies ranging from other text recognition frameworks [18,19], pseudo character-level augmentations [38] and state-of-the-art augmentation pipelines [17]. Table 5 displays the word accuracy for each augmentation pipeline with and without TextAdaIN. Applying TextAdaIN in conjunction with other augmentation strategies consistently improves performance and thus the contribution of TextAdaIN is complimentary to the chosen augmentation strategy. Furthermore, applying TextAdaIN without any augmentation outperforms all other independent augmentation pipelines, indicating the effectiveness and impact of our method over the most common regularization technique.

5.3   Number of Windows

TextAdaIN splits the feature map into windows along the width axis. Each window is perceived as an individual element in the AdaIN operation. As the

Table 6. Reducing the gap in challenging testing conditions. To demonstrate that TextAdaIN indeed regulates the usage of shortcuts, we evaluate it on corrupted versions of IAM. The corruptions are divided into three different categories based on their impact type. The normalized gap provides evidence for improved robustness, especially on local corruptions

Corruption type	None	Local masking		Pixel-wise distortions			Geometric	
		Dropout	Cutout	Additive Gaussian noise	Elastic Transform	Motion Blur	Shear & Rotate	Perspective
Baseline	85.7	51.4	53.7	62.0	66.7	70.5	76.8	74.0
TextAdaIN	87.3	57.7	59.6	72.0	72.4	73.6	78.9	75.2
Gap	+1.6	+6.3	+5.9	+10	+5.7	+3.1	+2.1	+1.2
Normalized Gap	1.00	3.94	3.69	6.25	3.56	1.94	1.31	0.75

features vary in size at different layers, we define K to represent the number of elements created per sample. Thus, K determines the window size at each layer. Modifying K has several different effects. For example, it controls the granularity level in which the statistics are calculated and modified and the number of donors. Therefore, an optimal value of K can be found to balance the different effects. In Appendix G, we plot the performance as a function of K. The best result is achieved when using $K = 5$. We note that the average length of English words is 4.7 characters. Thus, when $K = 5$, the statistics are normalized per character on average.

5.4   Challenging Testing Conditions

Notice that our approach leads to a similar boost on each of the datasets across all tested architectures and augmentation settings (for example $\approx +1\%$ on IAM). This suggests that this gap indeed stems from the shortcuts in the data and is not model dependent. Thus, we expect our method to perform similarly even on future and better-performing architectures. Moreover, we remind that one can detect shortcut learning at test time, given an image that violates the shortcut hypothesis (*i.e.*, an "f" with a different level of curvature than in the train). Thus, there are potentially even more undiscovered shortcuts than our improvements on standard test benchmarks reveal. To better demonstrate the existence of unrevealed shortcut learning, we perturb the test data in a way that changes its local style without modifying the semantic content. If the models are independent of the local style, one would expect that they will be robust to such modifications. Nevertheless, the significant performance drop (Table 1) reveals that these models are highly prone to shortcut learning, much more than discovered on the unperturbed test sets. To demonstrate that TextAdaIN indeed improves robustness towards challenging testing conditions, in Table 6, we evaluate its performance on several types of corruptions, comparing it to the baseline model.

The corruptions are divided into three categories: (1) local masking, (2) pixelwise methods and (3) geometric transformations. For each corruption, we display the gap between the performance of the baseline versus the TextAdaIN model. To accentuate the improvement provided by our method, we also display the normalized gap - the ratio between the gap on the corrupted data and the gap on the original data. This normalization removes the performance advantage of TextAdaIN on the original data. The results indicate that TextAdaIN improves the model's robustness towards *o.o.d* testing scenario. For example, the gap on additive noise is 10%. We note that the normalized gap, which represents TextAdaIN's robustness gains, is substantially higher in local-based corruptions rather than geometric corruptions which are applied globally. This provides further evidence that TextAdaIN regulates the reliance on local statistics in text recognizers. Despite the benefits of our method, Table 6 indicates that there are potentially even more undiscovered shortcuts as a significant gap exists when comparing to the original unperturbed test set.

5.5   Reliance on Local Statistics

In this subsection, we wish to further assert text recognizers' reliance on local statistics. Nuriel et al. [41] observed that applying AdaIN at high values of p resulted in a significant degradation of classification performance. We can thus infer that image classifiers depend on global statistics. For text recognizers, as shown in Table 7, this is not the case. Increasing the value of p, when applying AdaIN, only slightly affects the results. This indicates that global statistics are less significant in text recognition. In contrast, applying TextAdaIN with a high value of p decreases performance substantially. This implies that profusely applying TextAdaIN distorts important information that the model relies on. Therefore, text recognizers are prone to develop an unintended shortcut solution in the form of local statistics. If applied correctly, with the right p, TextAdaIN can alleviate this shortcut.

Table 7. Probability of applying TextAdaIN. Applying AdaIN at high values of p has little to no effect on the performance. In contrast, profusely applying TextAdaIN distorts important information that the model relies on.

Method	p	IAM Acc.
Baseline	–	85.7
AdaIN	0.01	85.4
	0.1	85.9
	0.25	85.8
TextAdaIN	0.001	86.1
	0.01	**87.3**
	0.05	86.8
	0.1	78.0
	0.25	74.7

6   Conclusion

Text recognizers leverage convolutional layers to extract rich visual features, and hence are extremely powerful. However, in this work, we expose their propensity towards learning an unintended "shortcut" strategy, whereby they overly rely on local statistics. Consequently, exhibiting a sensitivity towards subtle modifications that preserve image content. To relieve text recognizers' shortcut learning, we introduce TextAdaIN, a normalization-based method which distorts the feature space in a local manner and effectively regulates the reliance on local statistics. Our method achieves state-of-the-art results on handwritten text recognition benchmarks and improves robustness towards challenging testing conditions. TextAdaIN is also applicable to various recognition architectures and to the domain of scene text images. Furthermore, it can be implemented simply in a few lines of code and effortlessly integrated into a mini-batch training procedure.

By taking into account the nature of the data and the architectural characteristics, this shortcut was exposed. Yet, as we have seen, the prevalence of shortcuts is still at large. As future work, we wish to explore other shortcuts pertaining to text recognizers.

References

1. Aberdam, A., Ganz, R., Mazor, S., Litman, R.: Multimodal semi-supervised learning for text recognition. arXiv preprint arXiv:2205.03873 (2022)
2. Aberdam, A., et al.: Sequence-to-sequence contrastive learning for text recognition. arXiv preprint arXiv:2012.10873 (2020)
3. Afifi, M., Brown, M.S.: What else can fool deep learning? Addressing color constancy errors on deep neural network performance. In: Proceedings of the IEEE/CVF International Conference on Computer Vision, pp. 243–252 (2019)
4. Alonso, E., Moysset, B., Messina, R.: Adversarial generation of handwritten text images conditioned on sequences. In: 2019 International Conference on Document Analysis and Recognition (ICDAR), pp. 481–486. IEEE (2019)
5. Ba, J.L., Kiros, J.R., Hinton, G.E.: Layer normalization. arXiv preprint arXiv:1607.06450 (2016)
6. Baek, J., et al.: What is wrong with scene text recognition model comparisons? Dataset and model analysis. In: Proceedings of the IEEE International Conference on Computer Vision, pp. 4715–4723 (2019)
7. Baevski, A., Zhou, H., Mohamed, A., Auli, M.: wav2vec 2.0: A framework for self-supervised learning of speech representations. arXiv preprint arXiv:2006.11477 (2020)
8. Beery, S., Van Horn, G., Perona, P.: Recognition in terra incognita. In: Ferrari, V., Hebert, M., Sminchisescu, C., Weiss, Y. (eds.) ECCV 2018. LNCS, vol. 11220, pp. 472–489. Springer, Cham (2018). https://doi.org/10.1007/978-3-030-01270-0_28
9. Bhunia, A.K., Das, A., Bhunia, A.K., Kishore, P.S.R., Roy, P.P.: Handwriting recognition in low-resource scripts using adversarial learning. In: Proceedings of the IEEE/CVF Conference on Computer Vision and Pattern Recognition, pp. 4767–4776 (2019)
10. Bickel, S., Brückner, M., Scheffer, T.: Discriminative learning under covariate shift. J. Mach. Learn. Res. 10(9) (2009)
11. Bluche, T.: Deep neural networks for large vocabulary handwritten text recognition. Ph.D. thesis, Paris 11 (2015)
12. Bluche, T.: Joint line segmentation and transcription for end-to-end handwritten paragraph recognition. In: Advances in Neural Information Processing Systems, pp. 838–846 (2016)

13. Cheng, Z., Bai, F., Xu, Y., Zheng, G., Pu, S., Zhou, S.: Focusing attention: towards accurate text recognition in natural images. In: Proceedings of the IEEE International Conference on Computer Vision, pp. 5076–5084 (2017)
14. Cheng, Z., Bai, F., Xu, Y., Zheng, G., Pu, S., Zhou, S.: Focusing attention: towards accurate text recognition in natural images. In: Proceedings of the IEEE International Conference on Computer Vision, pp. 5076–5084 (2017)
15. d'Ascoli, S., Sagun, L., Bruna, J., Biroli, G.: Finding the needle in the haystack with convolutions: on the benefits of architectural bias. arXiv preprint arXiv:1906.06766 (2019)
16. De Palma, G., Kiani, B.T., Lloyd, S.: Deep neural networks are biased towards simple functions. arXiv preprint arXiv:1812.10156 (2018)
17. Cubuk, E.D., et al.: Randaugment: practical automated data augmentation with a reduced search space. In: CVPR (2020)
18. Fang, S., et al.: Read like humans: autonomous, bidirectional and iterative language modeling for scene text recognition (2021)
19. Wang, Y., et al.: From two to one: a new scene text recognizer with visual language modeling network. In: CVPR (2021)
20. Fogel, S., Averbuch-Elor, H., Cohen, S., Mazor, S., Litman, R.: ScrabbleGAN: semi-supervised varying length handwritten text generation. In: Proceedings of the IEEE/CVF Conference on Computer Vision and Pattern Recognition, pp. 4324–4333 (2020)
21. Gatys, L.A., Ecker, A.S., Bethge, M.: Image style transfer using convolutional neural networks. In: Proceedings of the IEEE Conference on Computer Vision and Pattern Recognition, pp. 2414–2423 (2016)
22. Geirhos, R., et al.: Shortcut learning in deep neural networks. Nat. Mach. Intell. 2(11), 665–673 (2020)
23. Geirhos, R., Rubisch, P., Michaelis, C., Bethge, M., Wichmann, F.A., Brendel, W.: Imagenet-trained CNNs are biased towards texture; increasing shape bias improves accuracy and robustness. In: International Conference on Learning Representations (2019). https://openreview.net/forum?id=Bygh9j09KX
24. Graves, A., Fernández, S., Gomez, F., Schmidhuber, J.: Connectionist temporal classification: labelling unsegmented sequence data with recurrent neural networks. In: Proceedings of the 23rd International Conference on Machine Learning, pp. 369–376 (2006)
25. Grosicki, E., El Abed, H.: ICDAR 2009 handwriting recognition competition. In: 2009 10th International Conference on Document Analysis and Recognition, pp. 1398–1402. IEEE (2009)
26. Gupta, A., Vedaldi, A., Zisserman, A.: Synthetic data for text localisation in natural images. In: Proceedings of the IEEE Conference on Computer Vision and Pattern Recognition, pp. 2315–2324 (2016)
27. Hermann, K.L., Chen, T., Kornblith, S.: The origins and prevalence of texture bias in convolutional neural networks. arXiv preprint arXiv:1911.09071 (2019)
28. Huang, X., Belongie, S.: Arbitrary style transfer in real-time with adaptive instance normalization. In: Proceedings of the IEEE International Conference on Computer Vision, pp. 1501–1510 (2017)
29. Ioffe, S., Szegedy, C.: Batch normalization: accelerating deep network training by reducing internal covariate shift. arXiv preprint arXiv:1502.03167 (2015)
30. Jaderberg, M., Simonyan, K., Vedaldi, A., Zisserman, A.: Synthetic data and artificial neural networks for natural scene text recognition. arXiv preprint arXiv:1406.2227 (2014)

31. Kang, L., Rusiñol, M., Fornés, A., Riba, P., Villegas, M.: Unsupervised adaptation for synthetic-to-real handwritten word recognition. In: 2020 IEEE Winter Conference on Applications of Computer Vision (WACV), pp. 3491–3500. IEEE (2020)

32. Karatzas, D., et al.: ICDAR 2015 competition on robust reading. In: 2015 13th International Conference on Document Analysis and Recognition (ICDAR), pp. 1156–1160. IEEE (2015)

33. Karatzas, D., et al.: ICDAR 2013 robust reading competition. In: 2013 12th International Conference on Document Analysis and Recognition, pp. 1484–1493. IEEE (2013)

34. Kleber, F., Fiel, S., Diem, M., Sablatnig, R.: CVL-database: an off-line database for writer retrieval, writer identification and word spotting. In: 2013 12th International Conference on Document Analysis and Recognition, pp. 560–564. IEEE (2013)

35. Litman, R., Anschel, O., Tsiper, S., Litman, R., Mazor, S., Manmatha, R.: Scatter: Selective context attentional scene text recognizer. In: Proceedings of the IEEE/CVF Conference on Computer Vision and Pattern Recognition (CVPR), June 2020

36. Liu, W., Chen, C., Wong, K.Y.K., Su, Z., Han, J.: Star-net: a spatial attention residue network for scene text recognition. In: BMVC, vol. 2, p. 7 (2016)

37. Lucas, S.M., Panaretos, A., Sosa, L., Tang, A., Wong, S., Young, R.: ICDAR 2003 robust reading competitions. In: Seventh International Conference on Document Analysis and Recognition, Proceedings, pp. 682–687. Citeseer (2003)

38. Luo, C., Zhu, Y., Jin, L., Wang, Y.: Learn to augment: joint data augmentation and network optimization for text recognition. In: Proceedings of the IEEE/CVF Conference on Computer Vision and Pattern Recognition, pp. 13746–13755 (2020)

39. Marti, U.V., Bunke, H.: The IAM-database: an English sentence database for offline handwriting recognition. Int. J. Doc. Anal. Recogn. 5(1), 39–46 (2002)

40. Mishra, A., Alahari, K., Jawahar, C.: Scene text recognition using higher order language priors (2012)

41. Nuriel, O., Benaim, S., Wolf, L.: Permuted Adain: reducing the bias towards global statistics in image classification. In: Proceedings of the IEEE/CVF Conference on Computer Vision and Pattern Recognition, pp. 9482–9491 (2021)

42. Qiao, Z., Zhou, Y., Yang, D., Zhou, Y., Wang, W.: Seed: semantics enhanced encoder-decoder framework for scene text recognition. In: Proceedings of the IEEE/CVF Conference on Computer Vision and Pattern Recognition, pp. 13528–13537 (2020)

43. Quy Phan, T., Shivakumara, P., Tian, S., Lim Tan, C.: Recognizing text with perspective distortion in natural scenes. In: Proceedings of the IEEE International Conference on Computer Vision, pp. 569–576 (2013)

44. Risnumawan, A., Shivakumara, P., Chan, C.S., Tan, C.L.: A robust arbitrary text detection system for natural scene images. Expert Syst. Appl. 41(18), 8027–8048 (2014)

45. Sakai, T., Nagao, M., Kanade, T.: Picture structure and its processing - the case of human-face photographs. In: Proceedings of Joint Conference of Electrical Engineers of Japan, October 1971

46. Schölkopf, B., Janzing, D., Peters, J., Sgouritsa, E., Zhang, K., Mooij, J.: On causal and anticausal learning. arXiv preprint arXiv:1206.6471 (2012)

47. Shi, B., Bai, X., Yao, C.: An end-to-end trainable neural network for image-based sequence recognition and its application to scene text recognition. IEEE Trans. Pattern Anal. Mach. Intell. 39(11), 2298–2304 (2016)

48. Shi, B., Bai, X., Yao, C.: An end-to-end trainable neural network for image-based sequence recognition and its application to scene text recognition. IEEE Trans. Pattern Anal. Mach. Intell. **39**(11), 2298–2304 (2016)

49. Shi, B., Wang, X., Lyu, P., Yao, C., Bai, X.: Robust scene text recognition with automatic rectification. In: Proceedings of the IEEE Conference on Computer Vision and Pattern Recognition, pp. 4168–4176 (2016)

50. Simonyan, K., Zisserman, A.: Very deep convolutional networks for large-scale image recognition. arXiv preprint arXiv:1409.1556 (2014)

51. Slossberg, R., et al.: On calibration of scene-text recognition models. arXiv preprint arXiv:2012.12643 (2020)

52. Sueiras, J., Ruiz, V., Sanchez, A., Velez, J.F.: Offline continuous handwriting recognition using sequence to sequence neural networks. Neurocomputing **289**, 119–128 (2018)

53. Szegedy, C., et al.: Intriguing properties of neural networks. arXiv preprint arXiv:1312.6199 (2013)

54. Torralba, A., Efros, A.A.: Unbiased look at dataset bias. In: CVPR 2011, pp. 1521–1528. IEEE (2011)

55. Ulyanov, D., Vedaldi, A., Lempitsky, V.: Instance normalization: the missing ingredient for fast stylization. arXiv preprint arXiv:1607.08022 (2016)

56. Wan, Z., Zhang, J., Zhang, L., Luo, J., Yao, C.: On vocabulary reliance in scene text recognition. In: Proceedings of the IEEE/CVF Conference on Computer Vision and Pattern Recognition, pp. 11425–11434 (2020)

57. Wang, J., Hu, X.: Gated recurrent convolution neural network for OCR. In: Advances in Neural Information Processing Systems, pp. 335–344 (2017)

58. Wang, K., Babenko, B., Belongie, S.: End-to-end scene text recognition. In: 2011 International Conference on Computer Vision, pp. 1457–1464. IEEE (2011)

59. Wu, L., Zhu, Z., et al.: Towards understanding generalization of deep learning: perspective of loss landscapes. arXiv preprint arXiv:1706.10239 (2017)

60. Wu, Y., He, K.: Group normalization. In: Ferrari, V., Hebert, M., Sminchisescu, C., Weiss, Y. (eds.) ECCV 2018. LNCS, vol. 11217, pp. 3–19. Springer, Cham (2018). https://doi.org/10.1007/978-3-030-01261-8_1

61. Yousef, M., Bishop, T.E.: OrigamiNet: weakly-supervised, segmentation-free, one-step, full page text recognition by learning to unfold. In: Proceedings of the IEEE/CVF Conference on Computer Vision and Pattern Recognition, pp. 14710–14719 (2020)

62. Zhang, Y., Nie, S., Liu, W., Xu, X., Zhang, D., Shen, H.T.: Sequence-to-sequence domain adaptation network for robust text image recognition. In: Proceedings of the IEEE Conference on Computer Vision and Pattern Recognition, pp. 2740–2749 (2019)

63. Zhou, K., Yang, Y., Qiao, Y., Xiang, T.: Domain generalization with mixstyle. In: ICLR (2021)

Multi-modal Text Recognition Networks: Interactive Enhancements Between Visual and Semantic Features

Byeonghu Na[1], Yoonsik Kim[2], and Sungrae Park[3](✉)

[1] Department of Industrial and Systems Engineering, KAIST, Daejeon, South Korea
wp03052@kaist.ac.kr
[2] Clova AI Research, NAVER Corp., Seongnam-si, South Korea
yoonsik.kim90@navercorp.com
[3] Upstage AI Research, Upstage, Yongin-si, South Korea
sungrae.park@upstage.ai

Abstract. Linguistic knowledge has brought great benefits to scene text recognition by providing semantics to refine character sequences. However, since linguistic knowledge has been applied individually on the output sequence, previous methods have not fully utilized the semantics to understand visual clues for text recognition. This paper introduces a novel method, called **M**ulti-mod**A**l **T**ext **R**ecognition **N**etwork (**MATRN**), that enables interactions between visual and semantic features for better recognition performances. Specifically, MATRN identifies visual and semantic feature pairs and encodes spatial information into semantic features. Based on the spatial encoding, visual and semantic features are enhanced by referring to related features in the other modality. Furthermore, MATRN stimulates combining semantic features into visual features by hiding visual clues related to the character in the training phase. Our experiments demonstrate that MATRN achieves state-of-the-art performances on seven benchmarks with large margins, while naive combinations of two modalities show less-effective improvements. Further ablative studies prove the effectiveness of our proposed components. Our implementation is available at https://github.com/wp03052/MATRN.

1 Introduction

Scene text recognition (STR), a major component of optical character recognition (OCR) technology, identifies a character sequence in a given text image patch (e.g. words in a traffic sign). Applications of deep neural networks have brought great improvements in the performance of STR models [2,26,27,29,33,34]. They typically consist of a visual feature extractor, abstracting the image patch, and a character sequence generator, responsible for character decoding. Despite wide explorations to find better visual feature extractors and character sequence generators, existing methods still suffer from challenging environments: occlusion, blurs, distortions, and other artifacts [2,3].

© The Author(s), under exclusive license to Springer Nature Switzerland AG 2022
S. Avidan et al. (Eds.): ECCV 2022, LNCS 13688, pp. 446–463, 2022.
https://doi.org/10.1007/978-3-031-19815-1_26

To address these remaining challenges, STR methods have tried to utilize linguistic knowledge on the output character sequence. The mainstream of the approaches had been to model recursive operations learning linguistic knowledge for next character prediction. RNN [2,27] and Transformer [16,25,32] have been applied to learn the auto-regressive language model (LM). However, the auto-regressive process requires expensive repeated computations and also learns limited linguistic knowledge from the uni-directional transmission.

To compensate for the issues, Yu *et al.* [33] propose SRN that refines an output sequence without auto-regressive operations. After identifying a seed character sequence, SRN re-estimates the character for each position at once by utilizing a Transformer encoder with a subsequent mask. Based on SRN, Fang *et al.* [7] improve the iterative refinement stages by explicitly dividing a vision model (VM) and an LM by blocking gradient flows and employing a bi-directional LM pre-trained on unlabeled text datasets. These methods incorporating semantic knowledge of LMs provide breakthroughs in recognizing challenging examples with ambiguous visual clues. However, the character refinements without visual features might lead to wrong answers by missing existent visual clues.

For better combinations of semantics and visual clues, Bhunia *et al.* [3] propose a multi-stage decoder referring to visual features multiple times to enhance semantic features. At each stage, a character sequence, designed as differentiable with Gumbel-softmax, is re-fined by re-assessing visual clues. Concurrently, Wang *et al.* [30] propose VisionLAN utilizing a language-aware visual mask that occludes selected character regions for enhancing the visual clues at the training phase. They prove that combining visual clues and semantic knowledge leads to better STR performances. Inspired by them, we raise a novel question: what is the best way to model the interactions between visual and semantic features identified by VM and LM, respectively?

To answer the question, this paper introduces a simple-but-effective extension of a STR model, named **M**ulti-mod**A**l **T**ext **R**ecognition **N**etwork (**MATRN**), that enhances visual and semantic features by referring to features in both modalities. MATRN consists of three proposed modules applied upon visual and semantic features: (1) multi-modal feature enhancement, incorporating bi-modalities to enhance each feature, (2) spatial encoding for semantics, linking two different modalities, (3) visual clue masking strategy, stimulating the cross-references between visual and semantic features. Figure 1 shows four types of visual and semantic feature fusions. MATRN is positioned in the bi-directional feature fusion (Fig. 1d) by applying multi-modal feature enhancement. To the best of our knowledge, this natural but simple extension has never been explored.

The resulting model, MATRN, is architecturally simple but effective. In addition, the visual and semantic feature fusions are not expensive because the whole process is conducted in parallel. When we evaluate simple combinations of visual and semantic features without our proposed components, the performance improvements are observed as less-effective. However, interestingly, the proposed components contribute to STR performances effectively and lead MATRNs to achieve superior performances with notable gains from the current state-of-the-

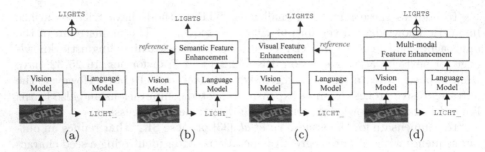

Fig. 1. Four types of visual and semantic feature fusions for STR: (a) simple combination of outputs from VM and LM, (b) visual-to-semantic feature fusion, (c) semantic-to-visual feature fusion, and (d) bi-directional feature fusion. SRN [33] is placed in (a) by applying LM to refine the output of VM. ABINet [7], PIMNet [22], and JVSR [3] can be aligned in (b) because their decoders refer to visual features iteratively during refining the final output sequence. VisionLAN [30] combines semantic information into visual features in a similar way to (c). Our method, MATRN, is positioned in (d) by enhancing both features through the bi-directional reference.

art. Consequently, our paper proves that semantics is helpful to capture better visual clues as well as that combining visual and semantic features reaches better STR performances.

Our contributions are threefold.

- We explore the combinations of visual and semantic features, identified by VM and LM, and prove their benefits. To the best of our knowledge, multi-modal feature enhancements with bi-directional fusions are novel components, that are natural extensions but have never been explored.
- We propose a STR method, named MATRN, that contains three major components, spatial encoding for semantics, multi-modal feature enhancements, and visual clue masking strategy, for better combinations of two modalities. Thanks to the effective contributions of the proposed components, MATRN achieves state-of-the-art performances on seven STR benchmarks.
- We provide empirical analyses that illustrate how our components improve STR performances as well as how MATRN contributes to the existing challenges.

2   Related Work

To utilize the benefits of a bi-directional Transformer, the non-autoregressive decoder has been introduced in the STR community. The general decoding process of them [1,7,22,30,33] lies in the effective construction of a sequence processed parallelly in the decoder. Specifically, positional embeddings describing the order of the output sequence are used to align visual (or semantic) features. Although the output sequence is generated in parallel, the bi-directional Transformer has shown comparable performances with the auto-regressive approaches.

ViTSTR [1] mainly focused on their VM without explicitly learning the LM. Inspired by the success of ViT [6], ViTSTR [1] has adopted ViT training scheme to STR. Specifically, its composition is very simple composed of the Transformer encoder and is trained with un-overlapped patches.

In order to incorporate linguistic knowledge, PIMNet [22], SRN [33] and ABINet [7] have been proposed. To learn linguistic knowledge from the auto-regressive model, PIMNet [22] proposed step-wise predictions and similarity distance between non-autoregressive and auto-regressive models. SRN and ABINet introduced a language modality that refines the output sequence of VM. Then, the final predictions are achieved by fusing the output sequences of LMs and VMs. In SRN [33], the LM is trained along with VM where the LM learns semantic information from other words. Based on SRN, ABINet [7] improves the iterative refinement stages by explicitly dividing the VM and LM. With a pretraining LM on unlabeled text datasets, it provides breakthroughs in recognizing challenging examples with ambiguous visual clues.

To interactively combine LM and VM, multi-modal recognizers are also introduced [3,30]. JVSR [3] proposes a multi-stage decoder referring to visual features multiple times to enhance semantic features. Specifically, it is based on an RNN-attention decoder with multi-stages where each stage generates an output sequence and visual features are employed for updating each hidden state. Since the decoder takes a hidden state as an input, the visual feature can iteratively enhance the semantic features. Concurrently, VisionLAN [30] proposes a language-aware visual mask that refers to semantic features for enhancing the visual features. Given a masking position of the word, the masking module occludes corresponding visual feature maps of the character region at the training phase. The previous multi-modal recognizers focus on one modality for final prediction and they utilize the other modality to improve their chosen one. In contrast, we explore the multiple combinations of multi-modal processes and propose MATRN which conducts both bi-directional enhancements.

3   MATRN

Here, we describe our recognition model, *MATRN*, which incorporates both visual and semantic features. We will provide an overview of our method, and then describe each component in detail.

3.1   Overview of MATRNs

Figure 2 shows the overview of our model. It includes a visual feature extractor and a seed text generator to embed an image and provide an initial sequence of characters, as traditional STR models do. LM is applied to the seed text to extract semantic features.

Our contributions are focused on incorporating the visual and semantic features for better STR performances. Our method first encodes spatial positions into semantic features by utilizing an attention map identified during the

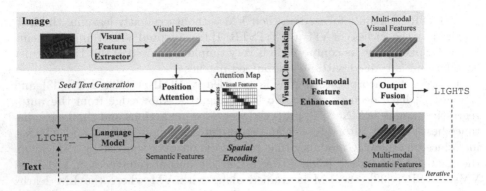

Fig. 2. An overview of MATRN. A visual feature extractor and an LM extract visual and semantic features, respectively. By utilizing the attention map, representing relations between visual features and character positions, MATRNs encode spatial information into the semantic features and hide visual features related to a randomly selected character. Through the multi-modal feature enhancement module, visual and semantic features interact with each other and the enhanced features in the two modalities are fused to finalize the output sequence.

seed text generation. The multi-modal feature enhancement module enriches individual visual and semantic features by incorporating multi-modalities. The enhanced features are named as *multi-modal visual features*, enhanced visual features with semantic knowledge, and *multi-modal semantic features*, enhanced semantic features with visual clues. Finally, both features are combined to provide the output sequence.

In the training phase of MATRN, the visual clue masking module hides visual features, related to a single character to stimulate the combination of semantics. Furthermore, the output sequence can be iteratively applied into the seed text for the LM, as follows [7].

3.2 Visual and Semantic Feature Extraction

To identify visual and semantic features, we construct three components: visual feature extractor, seed text generator, and language model. The following describes each module.

For the visual feature extractor, ResNet and Transformer units [7,33] are applied. The ResNet, $F^{\text{V.R}}$, with 45 layers embeds an input image, $\mathbf{X} \in \mathbb{R}^{H \times W \times 3}$, into convolution visual features, $\mathbf{V}^{\text{conv}} \in \mathbb{R}^{\frac{H}{4} \times \frac{W}{4} \times D}$. H, W are height and width of the image and D is the feature dimension. Before applying the Transformer, sinusoidal spatial position embeddings, $\mathbf{P}^{\text{V}} \in \mathbb{R}^{\frac{H}{4} \times \frac{W}{4} \times D}$, are added. Then, the Transformer, $F^{\text{V.T}}$, with three layers is applied:

$$\mathbf{V} = F^{\text{V.T}}(F^{\text{V.R}}(\mathbf{X}) + \mathbf{P}^{\text{V}}), \tag{1}$$

where $\mathbf{V} \in \mathbb{R}^{\frac{H}{4} \times \frac{W}{4} \times D}$ indicates visual features that are the outputs of the visual feature extractor.

For the seed text generation, an attention mechanism is utilized to transcribe visual features into character sequences. Specifically, an attention map, $\mathbf{A}^{\text{V-S}} \in \mathbb{R}^{T \times \frac{HW}{16}}$, is calculated by setting queries as text positional embeddings, $\mathbf{P}^{\text{S}} \in \mathbb{R}^{T \times D}$, and keys as $\mathcal{G}(\mathbf{V}) \in \mathbb{R}^{\frac{HW}{16} \times D}$ in the attention mechanism, where T is the maximum length of sequence and $\mathcal{G}(\cdot)$ is a mini U-Net. Through the attention map, visual features are abstracted upon sequential features, $\mathbf{E}^{\text{V}} = \mathbf{A}^{\text{V-S}}\widetilde{\mathbf{V}}$, where $\widetilde{\mathbf{V}} \in \mathbb{R}^{\frac{HW}{16} \times D}$ indicates the flattened visual features. By applying a linear layer and softmax function, a seed character sequence, $\mathbf{Y}_{(0)} \in \mathbb{R}^{T \times C}$, is generated, where C indicates the number of character classes. The whole process can be formalized as follows;

$$\mathbf{A}^{\text{V-S}} = \text{softmax}\left(\mathbf{P}^{\text{S}}\mathcal{G}(\mathbf{V})^{\top}/\sqrt{D}\right), \tag{2}$$

$$\mathbf{Y}_{(0)} = \text{softmax}\left(\mathbf{A}^{\text{V-S}}\widetilde{\mathbf{V}}\mathbf{W}\right), \tag{3}$$

where $\mathbf{W} \in \mathbb{R}^{D \times C}$ indicates a linear transition matrix.

The LM, introduced by [7], consists of four Transformer decoder blocks. It uses $\mathbf{P}^{\text{S}}$ as inputs and $\mathbf{Y}_{(0)}$ as the key/value of the attention layer. By processing the multiple decoder blocks, the LM identifies semantic features, $\mathbf{S} \in \mathbb{R}^{T \times D}$;

$$\mathbf{S} = F^{\text{LM}}(\mathbf{Y}_{(0)}), \tag{4}$$

where F^{LM} indicates the LM. We initialize the LM with the weights, pre-trained on WikiText-103, provided by [7].

3.3 Spatial Encoding to Semantic Features

One important point of combining the visual and semantic features is how to align each piece of information of different modalities. To guide the relationship between visual and semantic features, MATRN encodes spatial positions of visual features into semantic features. We call this process *spatial encoding to semantics (SES)*.

The key idea of SES is utilizing the attention map $\mathbf{A}^{\text{V-S}}$, used for the seed text generation, and the spatial position embedding $\mathbf{P}^{\text{V}}$, introduced in the visual feature extractor. Since $\mathbf{A}^{\text{V-S}}$ provides which visual features are used to estimate a character at each position, the spatial positions for semantic features, $\mathbf{P}^{\text{Align}} \in \mathbb{R}^{T \times D}$, are calculated as follows;

$$\mathbf{P}^{\text{Align}} = \mathbf{A}^{\text{V-S}}\widetilde{\mathbf{P}}^{\text{V}}, \tag{5}$$

where $\widetilde{\mathbf{P}}^{\text{V}} \in \mathbb{R}^{\frac{HW}{16} \times D}$ is the flattened sinusoidal spatial position embedding, $\mathbf{P}^{\text{V}}$. Then, we encode the spatial information into semantic features:

$$\mathbf{S}^{\text{Align}} = \mathbf{S} + \mathbf{P}^{\text{Align}}. \tag{6}$$

From this encoding process, the spatially aligned semantic features, $\mathbf{S}^{\text{Align}}$, contain spatial clues of visual features are highly related. It should be noted that SES does not need any additional parameters as well as it is simple and effective for the cross-references between visual and semantic features.

3.4   Multi-modal Features Enhancement

Now, we hold visual features, $\tilde{\mathbf{V}}$, that learn visual clues for character estimations, and semantic features, $\mathbf{S}^{\text{Align}}$, that contain linguistic knowledge for a character sequence. Previous methods [7,33] simply use a gated mechanism to seed character feature $\mathbf{E}^{\text{V}}$ and semantic feature $\mathbf{S}$. However, this simple fusion mechanism might not completely utilize these two features. Therefore, we propose a way in which the visual and semantic features refer to each other effectively and consequently enhance the features.

Multi-modal transformer [28], which consists of transformer layers processing multiple types of features at once, has been introduced in several domains such as visual question answering [10], vision-language navigation [4], autonomous driving [21], video retrieval [8], and many others. Inspired by them, we employ the multi-modal transformer for visual and semantic features enhancement for STR. The multi-modal transformers have multiple Transformer encoder blocks that consist of an attention layer and a feed-forward layer. At the attention layer, both visual and semantic features are processed through self-attentions. Since the queries determine their major modality, visual features are enhanced as multi-modal visual features, $\mathbf{V}^{\text{M}} \in \mathbb{R}^{\frac{HW}{16} \times D}$, and semantic features are updated into multi-modal semantic features, $\mathbf{S}^{\text{M}} \in \mathbb{R}^{T \times D}$.

3.5   Final Output Fusion

Both multi-modal features are utilized to finalize the output character sequence. While multi-modal semantic features are already aligned as a sequence, multi-modal visual features are required to be re-organized to estimate characters. To align the visual features into a sequence, we apply a character generator, which has the same architecture of the seed text generator, to aggregate $\mathbf{V}^{\text{M}}$ into sequential features, $\mathbf{E}^{\mathbf{V}^{\text{M}}}$ (See Sect. 3.2). Afterward, two sequential features, $\mathbf{E}^{\mathbf{V}^{\text{M}}}$ and $\mathbf{S}^{\text{M}}$, are combined through a gate mechanism to identify features, $\mathbf{F} \in \mathbb{R}^{T \times D}$, used for final character estimations:

$$\mathbf{G} = \sigma\left(\left[\mathbf{E}^{\mathbf{V}^{\text{M}}}; \mathbf{S}^{\text{M}}\right] \mathbf{W}^{\text{gated}}\right), \tag{7}$$

$$\mathbf{F} = \mathbf{G} \odot \mathbf{E}^{\mathbf{V}^{\text{M}}} + (1 - \mathbf{G}) \odot \mathbf{S}^{\text{M}}, \tag{8}$$

where $\mathbf{W}^{\text{gated}} \in \mathbb{R}^{2D \times D}$ is a weight, $[;]$ indicates concatenation, and $\odot$ is element-wise product. Finally, a linear layer and softmax function are applied on $\mathbf{F}$ to estimate a character sequence, $\mathbf{Y}_{(1)} \in \mathbb{R}^{T \times C}$.

3.6   Visual Clue Masking Strategy

To facilitate a better blend of the visual and semantic features, we propose a visual clue masking strategy, which is motivated by VisionLAN [30]. This strategy selects a single character randomly and hides corresponding visual features based on the attention map, $\mathbf{A}^{\text{V-S}}$, identified in the seed text generation. By

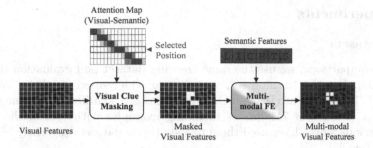

Fig. 3. Conceptual descriptions of visual clue masking strategy. Based on the attention map, representing relations between visual features and characters, influential features for a randomly selected character position are masked. In the multi-modal FE stage, semantic features are stimulated to be merged more strongly to compensate for the missing visual clues.

explicitly deleting influential features for the character estimation, the multi-modal FE module becomes stimulated to encode semantic knowledge into the visual features in order to compensate for the missing visual clues. Figure 3 provides the conceptual description of the visual clue masking strategy.

The masking process chooses a position randomly in a character sequence and finds the top-K visual features relevant to the chosen position. For example, if the fourth position is selected, the process identifies the front K visual features in the descending order of the attention scores at the fourth position. The identified visual features are replaced into $\mathbf{v}_{[MASK]} \in \mathbb{R}^D$. The visual clue masking is only applied in the training phase. To reduce the discrepancy between training and evaluating phases, we keep the identified features unchanged with probability 0.1, as like [5].

3.7 Training Objective

MATRN is trained as end-to-end learning with multi-task cross-entropy objectives from multi-level visual and semantic features. We denote $\mathcal{L}_*$ is a cross-entropy loss for estimated character sequences from a feature $*$. For the estimations, a linear layer and a softmax function are utilized. In addition, MATRN applies iterative semantic feature correction to resolve the noisy input for the LM, as follows [7,15]. At the iteration, the input of LM is replaced into the output of the output fusion layer (See Fig. 2). The loss of MATRN is formed as follows;

$$\mathcal{L} = \mathcal{L}_{\mathbf{E}^V} + \frac{1}{M} \sum_{i=1}^{M} \left(\mathcal{L}_{\mathbf{S}_{(i)}} + \mathcal{L}_{\mathbf{S}_{(i)}^M} + \mathcal{L}_{\mathbf{E}_{(i)}^{V^M}} + \mathcal{L}_{\mathbf{F}_{(i)}} \right), \quad (9)$$

where M is the number of iterations. Here, $\mathbf{S}_{(i)}$, $\mathbf{S}_{(i)}^M$, $\mathbf{E}_{(i)}^{V^M}$, and $\mathbf{F}_{(i)}$ indicate the semantic, multi-modal semantic, multi-modal visual, and final fused features at the i-th iteration, respectively.

4 Experiments

4.1 Datasets

For fair comparisons, we use the same training dataset and evaluation protocol with [7,33]. For the training set, we use two widely-used synthetic datasets, MJSynth [11] and SynthText [9]. MJSynth has 9M synthetic text images and SynthText consists of 7M images including examples with special characters. Most previous works have used these two synthetic datasets together: MJSynth + SynthText [2].

For evaluation, eight widely used real-world STR benchmark datasets are used as test datasets. The datasets are categorized into two groups: "regular" and "irregular" datasets, according to the geometric layout of texts. "regular" datasets mainly contain horizontally aligned text images. IIIT5K (IIIT) [19] consists of 3,000 images collected from the web. Street View Text (SVT) [12] has 647 images collected from Google Street View. ICDAR2013 (IC13) [13] represents images cropped from mall pictures and has two variants; 857 images (IC13$_S$) and 1015 images (IC13$_L$). We utilize all two variants for providing fair comparisons. We skipped the evaluation on ICDAR2003 [17] because it contains duplicated images with IC13 [2].

"irregular" datasets consist of more examples of text in arbitrary shapes. ICDAR2015 (IC15) consists of images taken from scenes and also has two versions; 1,811 images (IC15$_S$) and 2,077 images (IC15$_L$). Street View Text Perspective (SVTP) [20] contains 645 images of which texts are captured in perspective views. CUTE80 (CUTE) [24] consists of 288 images of which texts are heavily curved.

In our analyses, we measure the word prediction accuracy on each dataset. For "Total.", we evaluate the accuracy of unified evaluation datasets except for IC13$_L$ and IC15$_L$. It should be noted that we follow the philosophy of Baek *et al.* [2] which compares STR models upon the common evaluation datasets.

4.2 Implementation Details

The height and width of the input image are 32 and 128 by re-sizing text images and we apply image augmentation methods [7,18,33] such as rotation, color jittering, and noise injection. The number of character classes is 37; 10 for digits, 26 for alphabets, and a single padding token.

We borrow the network structures of the visual feature extractor, seed text generator, and language model from ABINet [7]. We set the feature dimension, D, as 512 and the maximum length of the sequence, T, as 25. For the multi-modal transformer, we use 2 Transformer blocks with 8 heads and a hidden size of 512. The iteration number M is set to 3 unless otherwise specified. We fixed the number of visual features mask, K, as 10.

We adopt the code from ABINet[1], and keep the experiment configuration. We use a pre-trained visual feature extractor and a pre-trained language model,

---

[1] https://github.com/FangShancheng/ABINet

which are provided by [7]. We use 4 NVIDIA GeForce RTX 3090 GPUs to train our models with batch size of 384. We used Adam [14] optimizer of initial learning rate 10^{-4}, and the learning rate is decayed to 10^{-5} after six epochs.

Table 1. Recognition accuracies (%) on eight benchmark datasets, including the variant versions. The underlined values represent the best performances among the previous STR methods and the bold values indicate the best performances among all models including ours. For our implementation, we conduct repeated experiments with three different random seeds and report the averaged accuracy with standard deviation.

Model	Year	Regular test dataset				Irregular test dataset			
		IIIT	SVT	IC13$_S$	IC13$_L$	IC15$_S$	IC15$_L$	SVTP	CUTE
CombBest [2]	2019	87.9	87.5	93.6	92.3	77.6	71.8	79.2	74.0
ESIR [35]	2019	93.3	90.2	-	91.3	-	76.9	79.6	83.3
SE-ASTER [23]	2020	93.8	89.6	-	92.8	80.0		81.4	83.6
DAN [29]	2020	94.3	89.2	-	93.9	-	74.5	80.0	84.4
RobustScanner [34]	2020	95.3	88.1	-	94.8	-	77.1	79.5	90.3
AutoSTR [37]	2020	94.7	90.9	-	94.2	81.8	-	81.7	-
Yang et al. [32]	2020	94.7	88.9	-	93.2	79.5	77.1	80.9	85.4
SATRN [16]	2020	92.8	91.3	-	94.1	-	79.0	86.5	87.8
SRN [33]	2020	94.8	91.5	95.5	-	82.7	-	85.1	87.8
GA-SPIN [36]	2021	95.2	90.9	-	94.8	82.8	79.5	83.2	87.5
PREN2D [31]	2021	95.6	<u>94.0</u>	96.4	-	83.0	-	87.6	<u>91.7</u>
JVSR [3]	2021	95.2	92.2	-	<u>95.5</u>	-	**84.0**	85.7	89.7
VisionLAN [30]	2021	95.8	91.7	95.7	-	83.7	-	86.0	88.5
ABINet [7]	2021	<u>96.2</u>	93.5	<u>97.4</u>	-	<u>86.0</u>	-	<u>89.3</u>	89.2
ABINet (reproduced)		96.2	93.7	97.2	95.4	85.9	82.1	89.3	89.0
		±0.2	±0.4	±0.2	±0.2	±0.2	±0.1	±0.4	±0.3
MATRN (ours)		**96.6**	**95.0**	**97.9**	**95.8**	**86.6**	82.8	**90.6**	**93.5**
		±0.1	±0.2	±0.1	±0.1	±0.1	±0.0	±0.2	±0.6

4.3   Comparison to State-of-the-Arts

Table 1 shows the existing STR methods and their performances on the eight STR benchmark datasets, including the variant versions of IC13 and IC15. In this comparison, we only consider the existing methods that are trained on MJSynth and SynthText.

When comparing the existing STR methods, PREN2D, JVSR, and ABINet showed state-of-the-art performances (See underlined values in the table). When compared to them, MATRN achieves the state-of-the-art performances on all evaluation datasets except IC15$_L$. Specifically, our model achieved superior performance improvements on SVTP and CUTE, 1.3% point (pp) and 1.8pp respectively, because these datasets contain low-quality images, curved images, or proper nouns. Therefore, we found that our multi-modal fusion modules resolve the difficulties of scene text images, which cannot solve alone. JVSR [3] still holds the best position on IC15$_L$, but MATRN shows huge performance gains on the other datasets: 1.4pp on IIIT, 2.8pp on SVT, 0.3pp on IC13$_L$, 4.9pp on SVTP, and 3.8pp on CUTE.

For apples-to-apples comparisons, we reproduced ABINet, which is one of the state-of-the-art methods and also our baseline before adding multi-modal fusion modules. In the sanity check, we observed that all reproduced performances are aligned upon confidence intervals from the reported scores. When comparing MATRN from the reproduced ABINet, the performance improvements are statistically significant over all datasets and the gaps are 0.4pp, 1.3pp, 0.7pp, 0.7pp, 1.3pp, and 4.5pp on IIIT, SVT, IC13$_S$, IC15$_S$, SVTP, and CUTE, respectively.

Many previous works, such as SE-ASTER, SRN, ABINet, JVSR, and Vision-LAN, also analyzed how semantic information can be utilized for text recognition. When compared to them, MATRN shows the best performances on all but one datasets. This result implies that our incorporation method for visual and semantic features is effective compared to the existing methods that utilized semantic information.

Table 2. Comparison of ABINet and MATRN under the comparable resources. *Param.* indicates the number of model parameters (M) and *Time* represents the inference time (ms/image) with batch size of 1 under AMD 32 cores, RTX 3090 GPU, and SSD 2TB. The underline indicates the similar or more resource when comparing from those of MATRN and the bold represents the best performer.

Model	Param.	Time	IIIT	SVT	IC13$_S$	IC15$_S$	SVTP	CUTE	Total
ABINet	36.7M	21.6 ms	96.2	93.7	97.2	85.9	89.3	89.0	92.6
ABINet w/ VM-*Big*	46.2M	22.6 ms	96.4	93.8	97.9	86.3	89.5	88.5	92.9
ABINet w/ LM-*Big*	46.2M	26.6 ms	96.0	94.3	97.5	86.3	89.9	88.9	92.8
ABINet w/ VM-*Bigger*	90.3M	29.7 ms	96.3	94.9	**98.0**	86.5	89.9	89.9	93.1
ABINet w/ LM-*Bigger*	52.5M	30.0 ms	96.1	94.3	97.7	86.0	90.1	89.2	92.8
MATRN (ours)	44.2M	29.6 ms	**96.6**	**95.0**	97.9	**86.6**	**90.6**	**93.5**	**93.5**
			±0.1	±0.2	±0.1	±0.1	±0.2	±0.6	±0.1

4.4   Performance Comparison Under the Comparable Resources

Since MATRN employs additional layers and modules upon ABINet, the performance gains might be considered as the effect of the additional memories and computational costs. To prove the pure benefits of the proposed methods, we evaluate large ABINets that utilize additional memories and computational costs as much as that MATRN requires. Specifically, the scale-up is conducted in two parts; adding transformer layers into VM (or LM) until the models have a similar number of parameters (*Big* models) and a similar inference speed (*Bigger* models). Table 2 shows the evaluation results. The *Big* models have similar parameters with MATRN but their speeds are faster since there is no cross-references between visual and semantic features. By scaling up the models, the *Bigger* models have similar inference speeds with MATRN but hold more parameters. When comparing the performances, the *Big* models provide relatively small performance improvements: 0.3pp of VM-*Big* and 0.2pp of LM-*Big* in Total. The *Bigger* models show better performance improvements than the *Big* models; 0.5pp of VM-*Bigger* and 0.2pp of LM-*Bigger* in Total. However, the performance gains from the scaling-up are restricted when comparing the performance improvements of MATRN; 0.9pp in Total. In addition, the performances of MATRN are statistically significant when comparing all large ABINets. The experiments prove that the benefits of MATRN have not solely lie in the increasing computation resources.

Table 3. Performance improvements through gradual applications of our proposed modules. At the last line, all modules are applied and the model becomes MATRN.

	Multi-modal FE	SES encoding	Visual clue masking	IIIT	SVT	IC13$_S$	IC15$_S$	SVTP	CUTE	Total
ABINet→				96.2	93.7	97.2	85.9	89.3	89.0	92.6
	✓			96.5	94.3	98.0	85.9	90.1	91.0	93.0
	✓	✓		96.4	94.7	**98.1**	**86.9**	90.4	89.9	93.3
MATRN→	✓	✓	✓	**96.6**	**95.0**	97.9	86.6	**90.6**	**93.5**	**93.5**

4.5 Ablation Studies on Proposed Modules

Here, we analyze how the proposed modules contribute to the final performances. Table 3 shows the ablation studies that start from ABINet and add the proposed modules one by one. As can be seen, the total performances increase when adding proposed modules gradually. The application of the multi-modal transformer provides 0.4pp performance improvements based on ABINet. By applying SES on the multi-modal transformer, the total performance increases by 0.3pp. When adding the visual clue masking, the total performance finally becomes 93.5% with the 0.2pp improvement. Consequently, the simple application of a multi-modal transformer brings 0.4pp and our novel modules provide 0.5pp of performance improvements. We should note that applying a multi-modal transformer requires additional computations and parameters but the other proposed modules use quite small computations without any additional parameters. The ablation study indicates that our proposed modules for better multi-modal fusion lead to better STR performances effectively.

Table 4. Comparisons between uni-modal and multi-model FEs.

Visual FE	Semantic FE	IIIT	SVT	IC13$_S$	IC15$_S$	SVTP	CUTE	Total
		96.5	93.2	97.0	85.9	89.0	89.2	92.7
	✓	**96.5**	93.8	97.2	85.8	89.0	90.3	92.8
✓		96.1	93.5	97.5	86.1	89.8	**91.3**	92.8
✓	✓	96.4	**94.7**	**98.1**	**86.9**	**90.4**	89.9	**93.3**

4.6 Discussion

Uni-modal vs. Multi-modal Feature Enhancement. The existing methods [3,30] focus on uni-modal FE by utilizing the other modality. To analyze the benefit of multi-modal FE, we compare the uni-modal FE that updates only a single modality utilizing the multi-modal transformer. In this experiment, we use SES for better fusion through the multi-modal transformer but do not apply the visual clue masking strategy for a fair comparison. Table 4 provides the comparison results. In the table, the first model is identical to ABINet with SES and the uni-modal FE models (the second and third models) update the target features through the multi-modal transformer. As can be seen, the uni-modal FEs provide marginal performance improvements; 0.1pp in Total. When enhancing both modalities (the last model), the STR model enjoys two benefits of the semantic and visual FE and shows large performance improvements in Total. Given these points, we found that combining visual and semantic features improves the recognition performance, but one-way information flows are not enough to fuse two modalities. Besides, the multi-modal FE enables the two features to communicate in both directions and provides better performance.

Table 5. STR Performances with each level of features from VM, LM, and their fusions. Each value indicates total STR accuracy (%). **V** and **S** represent the output features from VM and LM, respectively. $\mathbf{V}^M$ and $\mathbf{S}^M$ indicate the enhanced features through the cross-reference. **F** represents the combined features for the final output.

Model	V	S	$\mathbf{V}^M$	$\mathbf{S}^M$	F
ABINet	90.9	49.5	-	-	92.6
MATRN	91.2	52.6	93.4	93.4	93.5

STR Performance at Each Level of Features. MATRN utilizes multi-task cross-entropy objectives, described in Sect. 3.7. Here, we evaluate the STR performances from the multiple features; **V**, **S**, $\mathbf{V}^M$, $\mathbf{S}^M$, and **F**. Table 5 shows the results of ABINet and MATRN. Interestingly, the results of **S** show insufficient performances in both models by refining character sequences without consideration of visual clues. However, the semantic features are combined and lead to better performances; **F** (ABINet), $\mathbf{V}^{\mathrm{M}}$, and $\mathbf{S}^{\mathrm{M}}$ (MATRN). In addition, the multi-modal features in MATRN show better performances than the final performances of ABINet and their combination shows the best.

Target
Source
P I Z Z A
Target
Source
B A L L Y S
Target
Source
O R L A N D O

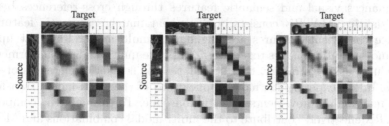

Fig. 4. Examples of self-attention maps in multi-modal FE. Attention maps on the top-right and the bottom-left indicate the cross attentions between two modalities.

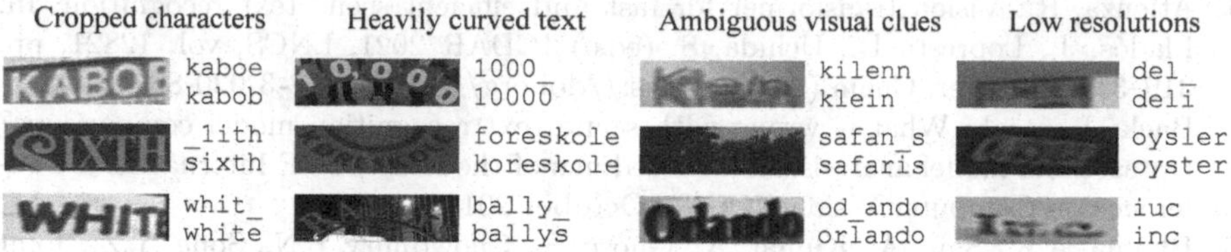

Cropped characters
kaboe
kabob
_lith
sixth
whit_
white
Heavily curved text
1000_
10000
foreskole
koreskole
bally_
ballys
Ambiguous visual clues
kilenn
klein
safan_s
safaris
od_ando
orlando
Low resolutions
del_
deli
oysler
oyster
iuc
inc

Fig. 5. Examples that ABINet fails (*first line*) but MATRN succeeds (*second line*).

Analysis on Cross-references. Figure 4 shows attention map examples identified by the multi-modal FE of MATRN. At each attention map, the top-left and the bottom-right show the uni-modal attentions referring to their uni-modal features and the others provide the cross attentions between two different modalities. As can be seen in the examples, visual and semantic features refer to their own modality as well as interact with each other.

Analysis on Previous Failure Cases. Figure 5 shows the test examples that ABINet fails but MATRN successes. As can be seen, MATRN provides robust results on "cropped characters", "heavily curved text", "ambiguous visual clues" and "low resolutions". The results show that MATRN tackles the existing challenges.

5   Conclusion

This paper explores the combinations of visual and semantic features identified by VM and LM for better STR performances. Specifically, we propose MATRN that enhances visual and semantic features through cross-references between two modalities. MATRN consists of SES, that matches semantic features on 2D space that visual features are aligned in, multi-modal FE, that updates visual and semantic features together through the multi-modal transformer, and visual clue masking strategy, that stimulates the semantic references of visual features. In our experiments, naive applications of the multi-modal transformer lead to marginal improvements from the baseline. To this end, the components of MATRN effectively contribute to the multi-modal combinations and MATRN finally achieves state-of-the-art performances on seven STR benchmarks with large margins.

References

1. Atienza, R.: Vision transformer for fast and efficient scene text recognition. In: Lladós, J., Lopresti, D., Uchida, S. (eds.) ICDAR 2021. LNCS, vol. 12821, pp. 319–334. Springer, Cham (2021). https://doi.org/10.1007/978-3-030-86549-8_21
2. Baek, J., et al.: What is wrong with scene text recognition model comparisons? Dataset and model analysis. In: Proceedings of the IEEE/CVF International Conference on Computer Vision (ICCV), October 2019
3. Bhunia, A.K., Sain, A., Kumar, A., Ghose, S., Chowdhury, P.N., Song, Y.Z.: Joint visual semantic reasoning: multi-stage decoder for text recognition. In: Proceedings of the IEEE/CVF International Conference on Computer Vision (ICCV), pp. 14940–14949, October 2021
4. Chen, S., Guhur, P.L., Schmid, C., Laptev, I.: History aware multimodal transformer for vision-and-language navigation. In: NeurIPS (2021)
5. Devlin, J., Chang, M.W., Lee, K., Toutanova, K.: BERT: pre-training of deep bidirectional transformers for language understanding. In: Proceedings of the 2019 Conference of the North American Chapter of the Association for Computational Linguistics: Human Language Technologies, Volume 1 (Long and Short Papers), Minneapolis, Minnesota, pp. 4171–4186. Association for Computational Linguistics, June 2019. https://doi.org/10.18653/v1/N19-1423. https://www.aclweb.org/anthology/N19-1423
6. Dosovitskiy, A., et al.: An image is worth 16x16 words: transformers for image recognition at scale. In: International Conference on Learning Representations (2021). https://openreview.net/forum?id=YicbFdNTTy
7. Fang, S., Xie, H., Wang, Y., Mao, Z., Zhang, Y.: Read like humans: autonomous, bidirectional and iterative language modeling for scene text recognition. In: Proceedings of the IEEE/CVF Conference on Computer Vision and Pattern Recognition (CVPR), pp. 7098–7107, June 2021
8. Gabeur, V., Sun, C., Alahari, K., Schmid, C.: Multi-modal transformer for video retrieval. In: Vedaldi, A., Bischof, H., Brox, T., Frahm, J.-M. (eds.) ECCV 2020. LNCS, vol. 12349, pp. 214–229. Springer, Cham (2020). https://doi.org/10.1007/978-3-030-58548-8_13

9. Gupta, A., Vedaldi, A., Zisserman, A.: Synthetic data for text localisation in natural images. In: IEEE Conference on Computer Vision and Pattern Recognition (2016)

10. Hu, R., Singh, A., Darrell, T., Rohrbach, M.: Iterative answer prediction with pointer-augmented multimodal transformers for TextVQA. In: Proceedings of the IEEE/CVF Conference on Computer Vision and Pattern Recognition, pp. 9992–10002 (2020)

11. Jaderberg, M., Simonyan, K., Vedaldi, A., Zisserman, A.: Synthetic data and artificial neural networks for natural scene text recognition. In: Workshop on Deep Learning, NIPS (2014)

12. Wang, K., Babenko, B., Belongie, S.: End-to-end scene text recognition. In: 2011 International Conference on Computer Vision, pp. 1457–1464 (2011). https://doi.org/10.1109/ICCV.2011.6126402

13. Karatzas, D., et al.: ICDAR 2013 robust reading competition. In: 2013 12th International Conference on Document Analysis and Recognition, pp. 1484–1493 (2013). https://doi.org/10.1109/ICDAR.2013.221

14. Kingma, D.P., Ba, J.: Adam: a method for stochastic optimization. In: Bengio, Y., LeCun, Y. (eds.) 3rd International Conference on Learning Representations, ICLR 2015, San Diego, CA, USA, 7–9 May 2015, Conference Track Proceedings (2015). http://arxiv.org/abs/1412.6980

15. Lee, J., Mansimov, E., Cho, K.: Deterministic non-autoregressive neural sequence modeling by iterative refinement. In: Proceedings of the 2018 Conference on Empirical Methods in Natural Language Processing, Brussels, Belgium, pp. 1173–1182. Association for Computational Linguistics, October-November 2018. https://doi.org/10.18653/v1/D18-1149. https://www.aclweb.org/anthology/D18-1149

16. Lee, J., Park, S., Baek, J., Oh, S.J., Kim, S., Lee, H.: On recognizing texts of arbitrary shapes with 2D self-attention. In: Proceedings of the IEEE/CVF Conference on Computer Vision and Pattern Recognition (CVPR) Workshops, June 2020

17. Lucas, S.M., Panaretos, A., Sosa, L., Tang, A., Wong, S., Young, R.: ICDAR 2003 robust reading competitions. In: Proceedings of Seventh International Conference on Document Analysis and Recognition, pp. 682–687 (2003). https://doi.org/10.1109/ICDAR.2003.1227749

18. Lyu, P., Liao, M., Yao, C., Wu, W., Bai, X.: Mask textspotter: an end-to-end trainable neural network for spotting text with arbitrary shapes. In: Proceedings of the European Conference on Computer Vision (ECCV), pp. 67–83 (2018)

19. Mishra, A., Alahari, K., Jawahar, C.: Scene text recognition using higher order language priors. In: Proceedings of the British Machine Vision Conference, pp. 127.1–127.11. BMVA Press (2012). https://doi.org/10.5244/C.26.127

20. Phan, T.Q., Shivakumara, P., Tian, S., Tan, C.L.: Recognizing text with perspective distortion in natural scenes. In: 2013 IEEE International Conference on Computer Vision, pp. 569–576 (2013). https://doi.org/10.1109/ICCV.2013.76

21. Prakash, A., Chitta, K., Geiger, A.: Multi-modal fusion transformer for end-to-end autonomous driving. In: Proceedings of the IEEE/CVF Conference on Computer Vision and Pattern Recognition, pp. 7077–7087 (2021)

22. Qiao, Z., et al.: PIMNet: a parallel, iterative and mimicking network for scene text recognition. In: Proceedings of the 29th ACM International Conference on Multimedia, pp. 2046–2055 (2021)

23. Qiao, Z., Zhou, Y., Yang, D., Zhou, Y., Wang, W.: Seed: semantics enhanced encoder-decoder framework for scene text recognition. In: Proceedings of the IEEE/CVF Conference on Computer Vision and Pattern Recognition (CVPR), June 2020

24. Risnumawan, A., Shivakumara, P., Chan, C.S., Tan, C.L.: A robust arbitrary text detection system for natural scene images. Expert Syst. Appl. **41**(18), 8027–8048 (2014). https://doi.org/10.1016/j.eswa.2014.07.008. https://www.sciencedirect.com/science/article/pii/S0957417414004060

25. Sheng, F., Chen, Z., Xu, B.: NRTR: a no-recurrence sequence-to-sequence model for scene text recognition. In: 2019 International Conference on Document Analysis and Recognition, ICDAR 2019, Sydney, Australia, 20–25 September 2019, pp. 781–786. IEEE (2019). https://doi.org/10.1109/ICDAR.2019.00130

26. Shi, B., Bai, X., Yao, C.: An end-to-end trainable neural network for image-based sequence recognition and its application to scene text recognition. IEEE Trans. Pattern Anal. Mach. Intell. **39**(11), 2298–2304 (2017). https://doi.org/10.1109/TPAMI.2016.2646371

27. Shi, B., Yang, M., Wang, X., Lyu, P., Yao, C., Bai, X.: Aster: an attentional scene text recognizer with flexible rectification. IEEE Trans. Pattern Anal. Mach. Intell. **41**(9), 2035–2048 (2019). https://doi.org/10.1109/TPAMI.2018.2848939

28. Tsai, Y.H.H., Bai, S., Liang, P.P., Kolter, J.Z., Morency, L.P., Salakhutdinov, R.: Multimodal transformer for unaligned multimodal language sequences. In: Proceedings of the 57th Annual Meeting of the Association for Computational Linguistics (Volume 1: Long Papers), Florence, Italy. Association for Computational Linguistics (2019)

29. Wang, T., et al.: Decoupled attention network for text recognition. In: Proceedings of the AAAI Conference on Artificial Intelligence, vol. 34, no. 07, pp. 12216–12224, April 2020. https://doi.org/10.1609/aaai.v34i07.6903. https://ojs.aaai.org/index.php/AAAI/article/view/6903

30. Wang, Y., Xie, H., Fang, S., Wang, J., Zhu, S., Zhang, Y.: From two to one: a new scene text recognizer with visual language modeling network. In: Proceedings of the IEEE/CVF International Conference on Computer Vision, pp. 14194–14203 (2021)

31. Yan, R., Peng, L., Xiao, S., Yao, G.: Primitive representation learning for scene text recognition. In: Proceedings of the IEEE/CVF Conference on Computer Vision and Pattern Recognition (CVPR), pp. 284–293, June 2021

32. Yang, L., Wang, P., Li, H., Li, Z., Zhang, Y.: A holistic representation guided attention network for scene text recognition. Neurocomputing **414**, 67–75 (2020). https://doi.org/10.1016/j.neucom.2020.07.010. https://www.sciencedirect.com/science/article/pii/S0925231220311176

33. Yu, D., et al.: Towards accurate scene text recognition with semantic reasoning networks. In: Proceedings of the IEEE/CVF Conference on Computer Vision and Pattern Recognition (CVPR), June 2020

34. Yue, X., Kuang, Z., Lin, C., Sun, H., Zhang, W.: RobustScanner: dynamically enhancing positional clues for robust text recognition. In: Vedaldi, A., Bischof, H., Brox, T., Frahm, J.-M. (eds.) ECCV 2020. LNCS, vol. 12364, pp. 135–151. Springer, Cham (2020). https://doi.org/10.1007/978-3-030-58529-7_9

35. Zhan, F., Lu, S.: ESIR: end-to-end scene text recognition via iterative image rectification. In: Proceedings of the IEEE/CVF Conference on Computer Vision and Pattern Recognition (CVPR), June 2019

36. Zhang, C., et al.: Spin: structure-preserving inner offset network for scene text recognition. In: Proceedings of the AAAI Conference on Artificial Intelligence, vol. 35, no. 4, pp. 3305–3314, May 2021. https://ojs.aaai.org/index.php/AAAI/article/view/16442

37. Zhang, H., Yao, Q., Yang, M., Xu, Y., Bai, X.: AutoSTR: efficient backbone search for scene text recognition. In: Vedaldi, A., Bischof, H., Brox, T., Frahm, J.-M. (eds.) ECCV 2020. LNCS, vol. 12369, pp. 751–767. Springer, Cham (2020). https://doi.org/10.1007/978-3-030-58586-0_44

SGBANet: Semantic GAN and Balanced Attention Network for Arbitrarily Oriented Scene Text Recognition

Dajian Zhong[1], Shujing Lyu[1(✉)], Palaiahnakote Shivakumara[2], Bing Yin[3], Jiajia Wu[3], Umapada Pal[4], and Yue Lu[1]

[1] Shanghai Key Laboratory of Multidimensional Information Processing, East China Normal University, Shanghai, China
djzhong@stu.ecnu.edu.cn, {sjlv,ylu}@cs.ecnu.edu.cn
[2] Faculty of Computer Science and Information Technology, University of Malaya, Kuala Lumpur, Malaysia
shiva@um.edu.my
[3] iFLYTEK Research, iFLYTEK, Hefei, China
{bingyin,jjwu}@iflytek.com
[4] CVPR Unit, Indian Statistical Institute, Kolkata, India
umapada@isical.ac.in

Abstract. Scene text recognition is a challenging task due to the complex backgrounds and diverse variations of text instances. In this paper, we propose a novel Semantic GAN and Balanced Attention Network (SGBANet) to recognize the texts in scene images. The proposed method first generates the simple semantic feature using Semantic GAN and then recognizes the scene text with the Balanced Attention Module. The Semantic GAN aims to align the semantic feature distribution between the support domain and target domain. Different from the conventional image-to-image translation methods that perform at the image level, the Semantic GAN performs the generation and discrimination on the semantic level with the Semantic Generator Module (SGM) and Semantic Discriminator Module (SDM). For target images (scene text images), the Semantic Generator Module generates simple semantic features that share the same feature distribution with support images (clear text images). The Semantic Discriminator Module is used to distinguish the semantic features between the support domain and target domain. In addition, a Balanced Attention Module is designed to alleviate the problem of attention drift. The Balanced Attention Module first learns a balancing parameter based on the visual glimpse vector and semantic glimpse vector, and then performs the balancing operation for obtaining a balanced glimpse vector. Experiments on six benchmarks, including regular datasets, i.e., IIIT5K, SVT, ICDAR2013, and irregular datasets, i.e., ICDAR2015, SVTP, CUTE80, validate the effectiveness of our proposed method.

Keywords: Semantic GAN · Semantic generator · Semantic discriminator · Balanced attention · Scene text recognition

© The Author(s), under exclusive license to Springer Nature Switzerland AG 2022
S. Avidan et al. (Eds.): ECCV 2022, LNCS 13688, pp. 464–480, 2022.
https://doi.org/10.1007/978-3-031-19815-1_27

1   Introduction

Scene text recognition has attracted growing research attention as a great need in real-life applications such as visual question answering [6], license plate recognition [54], driver-less vehicles [24]. Although previous works [1,3,5,21,26,56] have achieved great success, scene text recognition is still a challenging task because scene text images can be affected by multiple factors, such as complex background, arbitrarily shaped text, non-uniform spacing, etc.

With the development of Convolutional Neural Network (CNN) [18,20] and attention-based recognizer [9,25], text instances with simple background can be well recognized. Although, several models are proposed for addressing challenges of scene text recognition especially for regular text images, achieving good performance for arbitrarily oriented and irregularly shaped scene images is still considered as an open challenge. The key reason is that every character in the above two cases has a different orientation and shape in contrast to regular text. It can be observed from Fig. 1 that the existing methods [4,11] do not recognize the characters correctly for arbitrarily shaped text and text with complex backgrounds. Therefore, designing a robust method for recognizing arbitrarily shaped text is still a challenging task that remains to be solved.

Since it is easy to recognize clear images while those complex images are hard to recognize, there comes a question is it possible to transform complex images into simple ones? We can get inspiration from the existing works. Wang et al. [46] proposed a scene text dataset that contains paired real low-resolution and high-resolution images in the wild. Then the TSRNet is developed to reconstruct the high-resolution images for scene text images and recognize them. In this situation, the complex images (low-resolution images) can be transformed into clear images (high-resolution images). However, paired scene text images are needed in this method and it is hard to obtain these images and annotations. Besides, since the method can only deal with low-resolution images, scene text images with complex backgrounds are hard to recognize. Luo et al. [31] introduced the generative adversarial network [13,53] to remove the backgrounds while retaining the text content and then recognize the new reconstructed images. It satisfies the need for more scenarios, but it combines two networks into one. One network is for generating new images and another one is to recognize them. The method is time-consuming. The above mentioned methods used GAN for scene text recognition, but none of them used GAN as semantic generator and discriminator for scene text recognition. It motivated us to propose a novel model that explores GAN for extracting semantic features.

In this work, we introduce the Semantic GAN which consists of a Semantic Generator Module and a Semantic Discriminator Module. The Semantic Generator Module directly generates the semantic features upon the convolutional features for complex scene text images. Then the Semantic Discriminator Module distinguishes the semantic features between clear images and complex scene text images. In this way, the semantic feature distribution can be aligned and the generated features share more characteristics with those clear images and

Input				
GT	START	EBIZU	FRIKKIE	SAFARIS
Baek et al. [4]	STARI	BBIZU	FAR?KING	SABAttS
Fang et al. [11]	START	BBZZU	FRIKKLE	SAFA?NS

Fig. 1. Challenges of scene text recognition. GT represents the GroundTruth. Miss-recognized characters are marked in red and '?' represents the missed character. (Color figure online)

thus can be easier to recognize. In this framework, paired images and an extra image-to-image translation network are not needed.

Besides, the attention drift problem is first raised in [8]. They proposed the FANet method to draw back the drifted attention with a focusing attention mechanism. It first computes the attention center of each predicted label and then generates the probability distributions on the attention regions. Though the FANet method works well, the complex operations cost huge computations. In our work, we propose a Balanced Attention Module, which directly utilizes the convolutional features to correct the attention weights on the semantic features. The Balanced Attention Module significantly alleviates the problem of attention drift.

The Semantic GAN is capable of aligning the distribution between the support domain and target domain and the Balanced Attention is designed to address the problem of attention drift, thus alleviating the challenges. Our main contributions can be summarized as follows:

1. We propose a novel text recognition network, called SGBANet, which consists of Semantic GAN and Balanced Attention Module. The proposed method integrates GAN into the recognition network without introducing an extra image-to-image translation network, thus reducing the time complexity.
2. We introduce the Semantic GAN, which consists of a Semantic Generator Module and a Semantic Discriminator Module. To the best of our knowledge, it is the first time to use the Semantic Generator and Discriminator to generate semantic features for overcoming the challenge of scene text recognition.
3. We design a Balanced Attention Module, which automatically learns a balancing parameter based on the convolutional and semantic features. It corrects the attention weights on the semantic features and draws back the drifted attention to some extent.

2   Related Work

2.1   Scene Text Recognition

Scene text recognition aims to decode a character sequence from the scene images. The methods can be categorized into language-free methods and language-based methods. The language-free methods usually utilize convolutional features without consideration of the character dependency, such as segmentation-based methods and CTC-based methods. Segmentation-based methods [33,42,50] first segment the character regions and then recognize each character region to form the final character sequence. CTC-based methods [12,16,17] first extract visual features through CNN and then train with RNN and CTC loss to find the most possible combination. However, these methods lack linguistic information and thus easily miss one or two characters.

The language-based methods mainly employ the attention mechanism [38]. The encoder-decoder architecture makes use of linguistic information and character dependency. To boost the performance, some methods focus on learning a new feature representation. For example, [1] proposed a contrastive learning algorithm that first divides each feature map into a sequence of individual elements and performs the contrastive loss [15]. Then the learned representation features are fed to the recognizer. Yan et al. [51] proposed a primitive representation learning method that aims to exploit intrinsic representations of scene text images. Others may focus on integrating the rectification module [30,41,52,55] to reconstruct normal images for those irregular images. Then the reconstructed images are fed to the encoder-decoder module for further recognition. However, scene text usually has a variety of shapes and sizes. It is difficult for the rectification module to transform all the irregular text instances into regular ones. Since current attention-based methods suffer from the attention drift problem [8,27], directly decoding upon the convolutional features or linguistic features will degrade the recognition performance. Inspired by [44] which generates the character center masks to help focus attention on the right position. In this work, we introduce the Balanced Attention Module, which learns a balancing parameter based on the convolutional and semantic features and draws back the drifted attention. Through the method, the attention drift problem can be alleviated to some extent.

2.2   Generative Adversarial Network

With the development of GANs [34,36,58,59], image-to-image translation has achieved great success. Several methods integrate GANs to generate clear text images for scene text images [10]. This inspires the researchers to combine the GAN and recognition network. Thus, recent recognition methods focus on integrating the adversarial learning concept into the recognition network. For example, [57] introduced a gated attention similarity (GAS) unit to adaptively focus on aligning the distribution of the source and target sequence data. Luo et al. [31] introduced the generative adversarial network to generate a simple image without the complex background for each scene text image. However, it costs much computation if we first generate the required text image and then feed them to a recognition network. Since the two networks both contain huge convolution operations that can result in huge computation, our goal is to design a novel Semantic GAN to align the semantic feature distribution where the Semantic Generator Module directly generates the high-level semantic features and the

Semantic Discriminator Module distinguishes between the support domain and target domain.

3   Methodology

In this section, details of SGBANet are presented. We first describe the overall architecture of the proposed method. Then we dissect the Generator module and the Discriminator module. Finally, the Balanced Attention module is introduced.

3.1   Overall Architecture

As can be seen in Fig. 2, the overall architecture of the proposed method consists of the CNN Encoder, the Semantic GAN and the Balanced Attention Module. The CNN Encoder is used to extract the basic convolutional features. The Semantic GAN consists of the Semantic Generator Module(SGM) and the Semantic Discriminator Module (SDM). The Semantic Generator Module is applied to directly generate the high-level semantic features that can be easier to recognize and the Semantic Discriminator Module aims to distinguish between the support semantic features and target semantic features. After the adversarial learning, the semantic feature distribution between the source and target images can be aligned. The Balanced Attention Module is designed to draw back the drifted attention by learning a balancing parameter based on the convolutional and semantic features. Then the balancing operation can be performed to get the balanced glimpse vector.

There are two inputs for the whole architecture. One is the support image θ, which represents the simple image containing pure text instance. Another is the target image ϕ, which contains text instances with complex backgrounds. Firstly, the two images are fed into the CNN Encoder and visual feature map θ_v and ϕ_v are obtained. Secondly, they are fed to a Bi-LSTM layer and the Semantic Generator Module, respectively, and θ_s and ϕ_s are obtained. Then they are fed to the Semantic Discriminator Module. The Semantic Generator Module and the Semantic Discriminator Module contribute to generating simple semantic features. For the Semantic Generator Module, it generates the semantic feature that the discriminator can't distinguish from the support domain and target domain. At the same time, the Semantic Discriminator Module aims to distinguish them correctly. After the training of Semantic GAN, the Semantic Generator Module successfully generates the simple semantic feature for scene text images, which shares the same feature distribution with those of clear images. And ϕ_v and ϕ_s together with θ_v and θ_s are fed to the Balanced Attention Module for the final recognition.

3.2   CNN Encoder

Similar to [7], we take ResNet-based structure as the backbone network to extract basic visual features. We remove the CBAM module [47] and assemble an extra

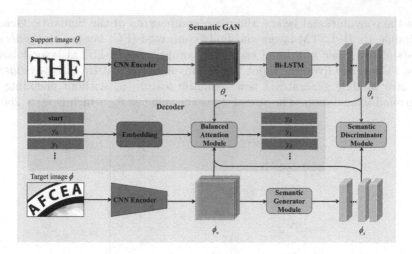

Fig. 2. Architecture of the proposed SGBANet. The support image θ and target image ϕ are fed to the CNN Encoders, which share the same parameters. The visual convolutional features θ_v and ϕ_v are fed to a Bi-LSTM and the Generator Module, respectively. Moreover, the semantic features θ_s and ϕ_s are fed to the Semantic Discriminator and Balanced Attention for discrimination and recognition. The Embedding module is to make a one-hot embedding on the input labels.

down-sampling layer. As a result, the size of θ_v and ϕ_v is restored to $\frac{H}{8} \times \frac{W}{8} \times C$, where H, W and C represent the height, width and channel of the input images, respectively. Since the size of text instances varies and there is no extra image-to-image network, FPN [28] is assembled to make the CNN Encoder capable of extracting different levels of features. The input support image and target image can be fed to a shared CNN Encoder for saving memory and computation cost.

3.3   Semantic GAN

The Semantic GAN consists of a Semantic Generator Module and a Semantic Discriminator Module. The Semantic Generator Module directly generates the semantic features for complex scene text images. A Bi-LSTM module is used to extract the semantic features of clear images. Then the Semantic Discriminator Module distinguishes the semantic features between support and target domain. In this way, the semantic feature distribution between the source and target images can be aligned and thus can be easier to recognize.

Semantic Generator Module. For the support image θ, the visual convolutional feature θ_v is directly fed to a Bi-LSTM layer and the semantic feature θ_s is obtained. As for the target image ϕ, the visual convolutional feature ϕ_v is fed to the Semantic Generator Module for generating the semantic feature ϕ_s so that the new generated feature shares the same feature distribution with those of support images. Different from the structure of the conventional generator that

stacks the convolutional layers, the main components of the Semantic Generator Module are Bi-LSTM layers and Fully connected (FC) layers. The generator
consists of two basic units and each unit comprises a Bi-LSTM layer followed
by two FC layers. Given the input visual convolutional feature ϕ_v, the Semantic
Generator Module generates a new semantic feature ϕ_s without encoding the
background information. The size of ϕ_s is the same as θ_s, which is $\frac{W}{8} \times 256$.

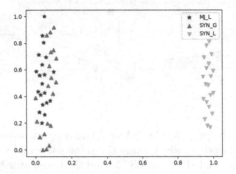

Fig. 3. T-SNE plot of learned feature representations. 'MJ_L' denotes learned features
from Bi-LSTM with sampled MJSynth images. 'SYN_G' and 'SYN_L' denote generated
semantic features and learned features from the Semantic Generator Module and Bi-
LSTM using sampled SynthText images, respectively.

Semantic Discriminator Module. The Semantic Discriminator Module is
used to discriminate the semantic features θ_s and ϕ_s and the architecture contains no convolutional layers. The Discriminator consists of two basic units and
an FC layer. Each unit comprises a Bi-LSTM layer and an FC layer. The first two
units are used to reduce the size of input features and the last FC layer is to do
the final discrimination. Given the semantic features θ_s and ϕ_s, the discriminator
distinguishes them between the support image and target image. The output size
of the discriminator is 1. To illustrate the effectiveness of the proposed Semantic
GAN, we randomly sample 20 MJSynth images and 20 SynthText images, which
represent the clear text images and complex scene text images respectively, and
visualize the learned features. As can be seen from Fig. 3, the Semantic Generator Module successfully generates the semantic features for the SynthText
images that share the same domain with those of MJSynth images.

3.4   Balanced Attention Module

Since convolutional features contain positions of characters, we can utilize the
convolutional features to correct the attention weights on the semantic features.
The Balanced Attention Module is designed to draw back the drifted attention
and recognize the character sequence. It works iteratively for T steps, producing

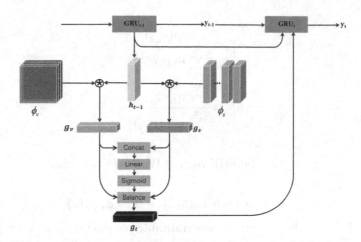

Fig. 4. Architecture of Balanced Attention Module. The 'Balance' operation means making a balance between the two glimpse vectors and it is defined by Eq. (3) and Eq. (4).

a target sequence of length T, denoted by $(y_1, y_2, ..., y_T)$. As can be seen in Fig. 4, at time step t, the output y_t for target images is defined by:

$$y_t = Softmax(W_{out}h_t + b_{out}) \tag{1}$$

where W_{out} and b_{out} are trainable parameters and h_t is the hidden state at the time step t. h_t is updated as follows:

$$h_t = GRU(y_{t-1}, h_{t-1}, g_t) \tag{2}$$

where y_{t-1} is the output at time step $t-1$ and g_t represents the glimpse vector defined by:

$$g_t = \lambda g_v + (1 - \lambda)g_s \, , \, \lambda \in R^n \tag{3}$$

where λ is learnable parameters. g_v and g_s are internal glimpse vectors. They are computed as follows:

$$\lambda = Sigmoid(W_\lambda cat(g_v, g_s) + b_\lambda) \tag{4}$$

$$g_v = \sum_{i=1}^{n} \alpha_{t,i}^v \times \phi_{v,i} \tag{5}$$

$$g_s = \sum_{i=1}^{n} \alpha_{t,i}^s \times \phi_{s,i} \tag{6}$$

where α_t^v and α_t^s are attention weights, which are defined by:

$$\alpha_{t,i}^v = \frac{\exp(e_{t,i}^v)}{\sum\limits_{j=1}^{n} \exp(e_{t,j}^v)} \tag{7}$$

$$\alpha_{t,i}^s = \frac{\exp(e_{t,i}^s)}{\sum\limits_{j=1}^{n} \exp(e_{t,j}^s)} \tag{8}$$

$$e_{t,i}^v = W_c \times \tanh(W_h h_{t-1} + W_v * AP(\phi_v) + b_v) \tag{9}$$

$$e_{t,i}^s = W_c \times \tanh(W_h h_{t-1} + W_s * \phi_s + b_s) \tag{10}$$

where W_c, W_h, W_v, W_s, b_v and b_s are trainable parameters and AP represents average pooling on the height of ϕ_v. Thus the size of $AP(\phi_v)$ is restored into $\frac{W}{8} \times C$ (C is set to 256), which is the same as that of ϕ_s. For the recognition of support images, the ϕ_v and ϕ_s can be replaced by θ_v and θ_s, and the above operations can be performed in the same way. As can be seen in Fig. 5, the balanced glimpse vector learns an accurate attention weight and guide the recognition of characters.

Fig. 5. An example of the balanced glimpse vector. The first image is the input and the others are attention maps under different time steps.

In the inference stage, since the input image can be a clear image or a complex scene text image, we feed the convolutional feature ϕ_v to the Bi-LSTM and Semantic Generator Module both. Then the two learned features are fed to the Balanced Attention Module for recognition and two character sequences are produced. Finally, we choose the character sequence with a higher confidence score as the final result and the other one will be discarded.

3.5 Training

The objective function L of our proposed SGBANet consists of two parts: the recognition loss L_R and the GAN loss L_G, as defined by:

$$L = L_R + \beta L_G \tag{11}$$

where β is the coefficient used to balance the importance of the recognition network and GAN network. We set β to 0 during the pre-training stage and 1 during the fine-tuning stage. The GAN loss is defined by:

$$L_G = L_g + \lambda L_d \tag{12}$$

$$L_d = E[\max(0, 1 - D(\theta_s))] + E[\max(0, 1 + D(G(\phi_v)))] \tag{13}$$

$$L_g = -E[D(G(\phi_v))] \tag{14}$$

where $G(\cdot)$ and $D(\cdot)$ denote the Semantic Generator Module and the Semantic Discriminator Module. θ_s and ϕ_v are semantic feature and visual convolutional feature of support image and target image, respectively.

As it is hard to train the recognition network combined with GAN, joint training of the recognition network and GAN will easily cause the instability of recognition loss. To make the whole network stable and robust enough, we have tried several loss functions for the GAN network, such as the original GAN loss [13], Wasserstein GAN Loss [2], and Hinge loss [48]. Additionally, we have tried several architectures of the Semantic Generator Module and the Semantic Discriminator Module, such as integrating convolution layers, LSTM layers and FC layers. As a result, we find that the Hinge loss, together with the architecture reported in Sect. 3.3 and Sect. 3.3, gets a robust training.

4   Experiments

4.1   Datasets

We train the proposed method SGBANet with the public available synthetic datasets, *i.e.* SynthText [14] and MJSynth [19] without fine-tuning on individual scene text datasets and lexicons. We evaluate the performance on the six widely used benchmarks, including three regular text datasets (IIIT5K, ICDAR2013, SVT), and three irregular text datasets (ICDAR2015, SVTP, CUTE80). Details of the datasets are as follows.

IIIT5K [35] contains 3000 test images cropped from natural scene images. Most of the text instances are regular with the horizontal layout.

ICDAR2013 (IC13) [23] has 1015 test images. The dataset only contains horizontal text instances.

Street View Text (SVT) [43] consists of 647 word patches cropped from Google Street View for testing. This dataset contains blur, noise and low-resolution text images.

ICDAR2015 (IC15) [22] contains 2077 test images collected by Google Glasses. Most of the text instances are irregular (oriented, perspective or curved). We discard the vertical text images, which results in 2002 test images.

Street View Text Perspective (SVTP) [37] contains 645 cropped images from side view angle snapshots in Google Street View. Most of the images are perspective distorted.

CUTE80 [39] contains 288 images cropped from high-resolution scene text images. Most of the images contain curved text.

4.2   Implementation Details

The proposed method is implemented by using PyTorch. All the experiments are conducted on an NVIDIA Tesla V100 GPU with 32 GB memory. In our experiments, all the input images are rescaled to the size of 64×256 with the aspect ratio preserved. The character set contains 64 classes, including 10 digits, 52 case-sensitive letters, the SOS token and the EOS token. The maximum sequence length is set to 32. AdaDelta is chosen as the optimizer and the batch size is set to 185.

The training process of the SGBANet is divided into two stages: the pre-training stage and the fine-tuning stage. In the pre-training stage, as we described in Eq. (11), we set the β to 0. Thus, we train the network on the SynthText and MJSynth from scratch for 2 epochs. Since images in MJSynth contain only pure text instances and images in SynthText contain complex backgrounds, images in the MJSynth and SynthText can be considered as support images and target images, respectively. In the fine-tuning stage, β is set to 1, and we jointly train the whole network for another 5 epochs.

4.3   Comparison with State-of-the-Art Approaches

We evaluate our method on the aforementioned six benchmark datasets and compare it with those state-of-the-art methods. For a fair comparison, all the methods are trained on the SynthText and MJSynth without fine-tuning on individual scene text datasets and no lexicons are used during the inference stage. Table 1 presents the details of the comparison results. It has been shown that our proposed SGBANet achieves the best on four datasets including IIIT5K, ICDAR2013, ICDAR2015 and SVTP, and achieves competitive performance on two datasets including SVT and CUTE80. Note that, for training the Semantic GAN, we have to divide the MJSynth and SynthText into support images and target images, respectively. Only the SynthText dataset is trained on the Semantic Generator Module. As a result, the proposed method doesn't achieve the best on the SVT and CUTE80. If we compare our method with SSDAN [57], which exploits the domain adaptation network, we can find that there is a large performance gap between the two methods on the regular text images. Qualitative results for text recognition of the existing methods and our proposed method are presented in Fig. 6. The existing methods [3,4] do not recognize the characters correctly, while the proposed method reports correct recognition results. In addition, We have calculated the average FPS of the proposed and existing methods [3,4] for all the 8 datasets and the results are 6.76, 6.68 and 7.58 for the methods [3,4] and SGBANet, respectively. This shows that our method is faster than the existing methods. The key reason is that the existing methods perform rectification before prediction while the proposed method does not.

Table 1. Comparison with state-of-the-art methods.

Methods	Regular text			Irregular text		
	IIIT5K	SVT	IC13	IC15	SVTP	CUTE80
Liao et al. [27]	92.0	82.1	91.4	–	–	–
Baek et al. [3]	87.9	87.5	92.3	71.8	79.2	74.0
Luo et al. [30]	91.2	88.3	92.4	68.8	76.1	77.4
Li et al. [25]	91.5	84.5	91.0	69.2	76.4	83.3
Shi et al. [40]	81.2	82.7	89.6	–	–	–
Zhang et al. [57]	83.8	84.5	91.8	–	–	–
Xie et al. [49]	–	–	–	68.9	70.1	82.6
Yue et al. [54]	95.3	88.1	94.8	77.1	79.5	**90.3**
Wang et al. [44]	90.5	82.2	–	–	–	83.3
Long et al. [29]	93.7	88.9	92.4	76.6	78.8	86.8
Wang et al. [45]	94.3	**89.2**	93.9	74.5	80.0	84.4
Luo et al. [32]	–	–	–	76.1	79.2	84.4
Aberdam et al. [1]	82.9	87.9	–	–	–	–
Baek et al. [4]	92.1	88.9	93.1	74.7	79.5	78.2
SGBANet	**95.4**	89.1	**95.1**	**78.4**	**83.1**	88.2

Input				
GT	BALLACK	LEST	CHELSEA	COMPANY
Baek et al. [3]	BALLACK	LEST	CHELSE?	COMPERS
Baek et al. [4]	BALLACH	? EST	CHELSEA	COMPANY
SGBANet	BALLACK	LEST	CHELSEA	COMPANY

Fig. 6. Qualitative results for text recognition of the existing methods and our proposed method.

4.4 Ablation Study

The proposed method mainly consists of three modules: the Semantic Generator Module, the Semantic Discriminator Module and the Balanced Attention Module. To demonstrate the effectiveness of the proposed method, we will first evaluate the performance of individual components and then make a further discussion on the Balance Attention Module.

The Effectiveness of the Individual Components. Since the Semantic GAN and Balanced Attention Module are two core components of the proposed method, we combine the baseline method with the individual components and conduct experiments on the six benchmarks. The proposed method without considering Semantic GAN and Balanced Attention Module is considered as the baseline method. The baseline method combined with Semantic GAN is considered as 'Baseline+SGAN'. In the same way, the baseline method combined with the two components is considered as 'Baseline+SGAN+BA'. It is observed from Table 2, 'Baseline+SGAN+BA' outperforms the 'Baseline' method on all the six benchmarks. It indicates that the Semantic GAN successfully generates simple semantic features that are easier to recognize. In the same way, 'Baseline+SGAN+BA' outperforms 'Baseline+SGAN', which attests to the effectiveness of the proposed Balance Attention Module.

Table 2. Effectiveness of the key components of the proposed method. 'SGAN' and 'BA' represent the Semantic GAN and Balance Attention.

Datasets	IIIT5K	SVT	IC13	IC15	SVTP	CUTE80
Baseline	90.1	84.5	91.8	70.5	76.8	80.0
Baseline+SGAN	92.1	86.6	91.1	72.5	77.1	80.5
Baseline+SGAN+BA	**95.4**	**89.1**	**95.1**	**78.4**	**83.1**	**88.2**

Discussions About the Balance Attention Module. The Balance Attention is the core component of our proposed method. The key step of the Balance Attention is the balancing operation, which learns a dynamic balancing parameter and makes a balance between the two glimpse vectors. The details of our balancing operation are defined in Eq. (3) and Eq. (4). We discuss the effectiveness of the proposed balancing operation and other balancing operations. In the experiment, we evaluate four balancing operations, including 'Single', 'Add', 'CL', and our 'Balance' operation. The 'Single' operation only uses the glimpse vector g_v. The 'Add' operation directly makes an add operation on g_v and g_s. The 'CL' operation generates a new glimpse vector by first concatenating the two glimpse vectors and then feeding it to an FC layer. 'Balance' is our proposed balancing operation. As can be seen in Table 3, the 'Single' operation gets the worst performance on the six benchmarks. Text instances with complex backgrounds and arbitrary shapes are challenging for the 'Single' operation. 'Add' and 'CL' operations improve the performance and achieve the best on SVT and CUTE80, respectively. Our 'Balance' operation further improves the performance and achieves the best performance on four datasets including IIIT5k, IC13, IC15, and SVTP, and there is only a gap of 0.3 on the other two datasets. Thus, our balancing operation gets the overall best performance.

Table 3. Evaluation of the balancing operations.

Datasets	IIIT5K	SVT	IC13	IC15	SVTP	CUTE80
Single	92.1	86.6	91.9	72.5	77.1	80.5
Add	94.2	**89.4**	94.0	77.3	81.7	87.1
CL	95.1	88.3	94.1	77.2	83.0	**88.5**
Balance	**95.4**	89.1	**95.1**	**78.4**	**83.1**	88.2

5   Conclusions

In this paper, we propose a novel Semantic GAN and Balanced Attention Network (SGBANet) for arbitrarily oriented scene Text recognition. The Semantic GAN is designed to align the semantic feature distribution between the support and target domain. The Semantic Generator Module focuses on generating simple semantic features for the scene text images. The Semantic Discriminator Module aims to distinguish the semantic features between the support domain and target domain. Experiments show that the Semantic GAN successfully generates simple semantic features for complex scene text images. The generated simple semantic features share the same feature distribution with those of clear images. Furthermore, to alleviate the problem of attention drift, the Balanced Attention Module is designed. It utilizes the convolutional features to correct the attention weights on the semantic features. A new balancing operation is performed on the two glimpse vectors and a balanced glimpse vector is learned. Ablation study on the baseline method combined with the proposed modules demonstrates the advantages of the designed modules. Extensive experiments on six benchmarks demonstrate the effectiveness of our proposed method.

Acknowledgements. This work is supported by the National Key Research and Development Program of China under Grant No. 2020AAA0107903, the National Natural Science Foundation of China under Grant No. 62176091, and the Shanghai Natural Science Foundation of China under Grant No. 19ZR1415900.

References

1. Aberdam, A., et al.: Sequence-to-sequence contrastive learning for text recognition. In: Proceedings of CVPR, pp. 15302–15312 (2021)
2. Arjovsky, M., Chintala, S., Bottou, L.: Wasserstein generative adversarial networks. In: Proceedings of ICML, pp. 214–223 (2017)
3. Baek, J., et al.: What is wrong with scene text recognition model comparisons? Dataset and model analysis. In: Proceedings of ICCV, pp. 4715–4723 (2019)
4. Baek, J., Matsui, Y., Aizawa, K.: What if we only use real datasets for scene text recognition? Toward scene text recognition with fewer labels. In: Proceedings of CVPR, pp. 3113–3122 (2021)
5. Bhunia, A.K., Ghose, S., Kumar, A., Chowdhury, P.N., Sain, A., Song, Y.Z.: MetaHTR: towards writer-adaptive handwritten text recognition. In: Proceedings of CVPR, pp. 15830–15839 (2021)

6. Biten, A.F., et al.: Scene text visual question answering. In: Proceedings of ICCV, pp. 4291–4301 (2019)
7. Cai, H., Sun, J., Xiong, Y.: CSTR: a classification perspective on scene text recognition. arXiv e-prints pp. arXiv-2102 (2021)
8. Cheng, Z., Bai, F., Xu, Y., Zheng, G., Pu, S., Zhou, S.: Focusing attention: towards accurate text recognition in natural images. In: Proceedings of ICCV, pp. 5076–5084 (2017)
9. Cheng, Z., Xu, Y., Bai, F., Niu, Y., Pu, S., Zhou, S.: Aon: towards arbitrarily-oriented text recognition. In: Proceedings of CVPR, pp. 5571–5579 (2018)
10. Fang, S., Xie, H., Chen, J., Tan, J., Zhang, Y.: Learning to draw text in natural images with conditional adversarial networks. In: Proceedings of IJCAI, pp. 715–722 (2019)
11. Fang, S., Xie, H., Wang, Y., Mao, Z., Zhang, Y.: Read like humans: autonomous, bidirectional and iterative language modeling for scene text recognition. In: Proceedings of CVPR, pp. 7098–7107 (2021)
12. Gao, Y., Chen, Y., Wang, J., Tang, M., Lu, H.: Reading scene text with fully convolutional sequence modeling. Neurocomputing **339**, 161–170 (2019)
13. Goodfellow, I., et al.: Generative adversarial nets. In: Advances in Neural Information Processing Systems, vol. 27 (2014)
14. Gupta, A., Vedaldi, A., Zisserman, A.: Synthetic data for text localisation in natural images. In: Proceedings of CVPR, pp. 2315–2324 (2016)
15. He, K., Fan, H., Wu, Y., Xie, S., Girshick, R.: Momentum contrast for unsupervised visual representation learning. In: Proceedings of CVPR, pp. 9729–9738 (2020)
16. He, P., Huang, W., Qiao, Y., Loy, C.C., Tang, X.: Reading scene text in deep convolutional sequences. In: Proceedings of AAAI, pp. 3501–3508 (2016)
17. Hu, W., Cai, X., Hou, J., Yi, S., Lin, Z.: GTC: guided training of CTC towards efficient and accurate scene text recognition. In: Proceedings of AAAI, pp. 11005–11012 (2020)
18. Jaderberg, M., Simonyan, K., Vedaldi, A., Zisserman, A.: Deep structured output learning for unconstrained text recognition. arXiv preprint arXiv:1412.5903 (2014)
19. Jaderberg, M., Simonyan, K., Vedaldi, A., Zisserman, A.: Synthetic data and artificial neural networks for natural scene text recognition. arXiv preprint arXiv:1406.2227 (2014)
20. Jaderberg, M., Simonyan, K., Vedaldi, A., Zisserman, A.: Reading text in the wild with convolutional neural networks. Int. J. Comput. Vision **116**(1), 1–20 (2016)
21. Kang, L., Rusinol, M., Fornés, A., Riba, P., Villegas, M.: Unsupervised writer adaptation for synthetic-to-real handwritten word recognition. In: Proceedings of WACV, pp. 3502–3511 (2020)
22. Karatzas, D., et al.: ICDAR 2015 competition on robust reading. In: Proceedings of ICDAR, pp. 1156–1160 (2015)
23. Karatzas, D., et al.: ICDAR 2013 robust reading competition. In: Proceedings of ICDAR, pp. 1484–1493 (2013)
24. Le, Q.N.N., Bhattacharyya, A., Chembakasseril, M.T., Hartanto, R.: Real-time sign detection and recognition for self-driving mini rovers based on template matching and hierarchical decision structure. In: Proceedings of ICAART, pp. 208–215 (2020)
25. Li, H., Wang, P., Shen, C., Zhang, G.: Show, attend and read: a simple and strong baseline for irregular text recognition. In: Proceedings of AAAI, pp. 8610–8617 (2019)

26. Liao, M., Pang, G., Huang, J., Hassner, T., Bai, X.: Mask TextSpotter v3: segmentation proposal network for robust scene text spotting. In: Vedaldi, A., Bischof, H., Brox, T., Frahm, J.-M. (eds.) ECCV 2020. LNCS, vol. 12356, pp. 706–722. Springer, Cham (2020). https://doi.org/10.1007/978-3-030-58621-8_41
27. Liao, M., et al.: Scene text recognition from two-dimensional perspective. In: Proceedings of AAAI (2019)
28. Lin, T.Y., Dollár, P., Girshick, R., He, K., Hariharan, B., Belongie, S.: Feature pyramid networks for object detection. In: Proceedings of CVPR, pp. 2117–2125 (2017)
29. Long, S., Guan, Y., Bian, K., Yao, C.: A new perspective for flexible feature gathering in scene text recognition via character anchor pooling. In: Proceedings of ICASSP, pp. 2458–2462 (2020)
30. Luo, C., Jin, L., Sun, Z.: MORAN: a multi-object rectified attention network for scene text recognition. Pattern Recogn. **90**, 109–118 (2019)
31. Luo, C., Lin, Q., Liu, Y., Jin, L., Shen, C.: Separating content from style using adversarial learning for recognizing text in the wild. Int. J. Comput. Vision **129**(4), 960–976 (2021)
32. Luo, C., Zhu, Y., Jin, L., Wang, Y.: Learn to augment: joint data augmentation and network optimization for text recognition. In: Proceedings of CVPR, pp. 13746–13755 (2020)
33. Lyu, P., Liao, M., Yao, C., Wu, W., Bai, X.: Mask textspotter: an end-to-end trainable neural network for spotting text with arbitrary shapes. In: Proceedings of ECCV, pp. 67–83 (2018)
34. Mao, X., Li, Q., Xie, H., Lau, R.Y., Wang, Z., Paul Smolley, S.: Least squares generative adversarial networks. In: Proceedings of ICCV, pp. 2794–2802 (2017)
35. Mishra, A., Alahari, K., Jawahar, C.: Top-down and bottom-up cues for scene text recognition. In: Proceedings of CVPR, pp. 2687–2694 (2012)
36. Odena, A., Olah, C., Shlens, J.: Conditional image synthesis with auxiliary classifier GANs. In: Proceedings of ICML, pp. 2642–2651. PMLR (2017)
37. Phan, T.Q., Shivakumara, P., Tian, S., Tan, C.L.: Recognizing text with perspective distortion in natural scenes. In: Proceedings of ICCV, pp. 569–576 (2013)
38. Qiao, Z., Zhou, Y., Yang, D., Zhou, Y., Wang, W.: Seed: semantics enhanced encoder-decoder framework for scene text recognition. In: Proceedings of CVPR, pp. 13528–13537 (2020)
39. Risnumawan, A., Shivakumara, P., Chan, C.S., Tan, C.L.: A robust arbitrary text detection system for natural scene images. Expert Syst. Appl. **41**(18), 8027–8048 (2014)
40. Shi, B., Bai, X., Yao, C.: An end-to-end trainable neural network for image-based sequence recognition and its application to scene text recognition. IEEE Trans. Pattern Anal. Mach. Intell. **39**, 2298–2304 (2016)
41. Shi, B., Yang, M., Wang, X., Lyu, P., Yao, C., Bai, X.: Aster: an attentional scene text recognizer with flexible rectification. IEEE Trans. Pattern Anal. Mach. Intell. **41**(9), 2035–2048 (2018)
42. Wan, Z., He, M., Chen, H., Bai, X., Yao, C.: Textscanner: reading characters in order for robust scene text recognition. In: Proceedings of AAAI (2020)
43. Wang, K., Babenko, B., Belongie, S.: End-to-end scene text recognition. In: Proceedings of ICCV, pp. 1457–1464 (2011)
44. Wang, Q., et al.: FACLSTM: ConvLSTM with focused attention for scene text recognition. Sci. China Inf. Sci. **63**(2), 1–14 (2020)
45. Wang, T., et al.: Decoupled attention network for text recognition. In: Proceedings of AAAI, pp. 12216–12224 (2020)

46. Wang, W., et al.: Scene text image super-resolution in the wild. In: Vedaldi, A., Bischof, H., Brox, T., Frahm, J.-M. (eds.) ECCV 2020. LNCS, vol. 12355, pp. 650–666. Springer, Cham (2020). https://doi.org/10.1007/978-3-030-58607-2_38

47. Woo, S., Park, J., Lee, J.Y., Kweon, I.S.: CBAM: convolutional block attention module. In: Proceedings of ECCV, pp. 3–19 (2018)

48. Xie, Y., Chen, X., Sun, L., Lu, Y.: DG-Font: deformable generative networks for unsupervised font generation. In: Proceedings of CVPR, pp. 5130–5140 (2021)

49. Xie, Z., Huang, Y., Zhu, Y., Jin, L., Liu, Y., Xie, L.: Aggregation cross-entropy for sequence recognition. In: Proceedings of CVPR, pp. 6538–6547 (2019)

50. Xing, L., Tian, Z., Huang, W., Scott, M.R.: Convolutional character networks. In: Proceedings of ICCV, pp. 9126–9136 (2019)

51. Yan, R., Peng, L., Xiao, S., Yao, G.: Primitive representation learning for scene text recognition. In: Proceedings of CVPR, pp. 284–293 (2021)

52. Yang, M., et al.: Symmetry-constrained rectification network for scene text recognition. In: Proceedings of ICCV, pp. 9147–9156 (2019)

53. Yang, S., Wang, Z., Wang, Z., Xu, N., Liu, J., Guo, Z.: Controllable artistic text style transfer via shape-matching GAN. In: Proceedings of ICCV, pp. 4442–4451 (2019)

54. Yue, X., Kuang, Z., Lin, C., Sun, H., Zhang, W.: RobustScanner: dynamically enhancing positional clues for robust text recognition. In: Vedaldi, A., Bischof, H., Brox, T., Frahm, J.-M. (eds.) ECCV 2020. LNCS, vol. 12364, pp. 135–151. Springer, Cham (2020). https://doi.org/10.1007/978-3-030-58529-7_9

55. Zhan, F., Lu, S.: ESIR: end-to-end scene text recognition via iterative image rectification. In: Proceedings of CVPR, pp. 2059–2068 (2019)

56. Zhang, C., Gupta, A., Zisserman, A.: Adaptive text recognition through visual matching. In: Vedaldi, A., Bischof, H., Brox, T., Frahm, J.-M. (eds.) ECCV 2020. LNCS, vol. 12361, pp. 51–67. Springer, Cham (2020). https://doi.org/10.1007/978-3-030-58517-4_4

57. Zhang, Y., Nie, S., Liu, W., Xu, X., Zhang, D., Shen, H.T.: Sequence-to-sequence domain adaptation network for robust text image recognition. In: Proceedings of CVPR, pp. 2740–2749 (2019)

58. Zhou, W., Ge, T., Xu, K., Wei, F., Zhou, M.: Self-adversarial learning with comparative discrimination for text generation. arXiv preprint arXiv:2001.11691 (2020)

59. Zhu, J.Y., Park, T., Isola, P., Efros, A.A.: Unpaired image-to-image translation using cycle-consistent adversarial networks. In: Proceedings of ICCV, pp. 2223–2232 (2017)

Pure Transformer with Integrated Experts for Scene Text Recognition

Yew Lee Tan[1]([✉]) [iD], Adams Wai-Kin Kong[1] [iD], and Jung-Jae Kim[2] [iD]

[1] Nanyang Technological University, Singapore, Singapore
yewlee001@e.ntu.edu.sg
[2] Institute for Infocomm Research, A*STAR, Singapore, Singapore

Abstract. Scene text recognition (STR) involves the task of reading text in cropped images of natural scenes. Conventional models in STR employ convolutional neural network (CNN) followed by recurrent neural network in an encoder-decoder framework. In recent times, the transformer architecture is being widely adopted in STR as it shows strong capability in capturing long-term dependency which appears to be prominent in scene text images. Many researchers utilized transformer as part of a hybrid CNN-transformer encoder, often followed by a transformer decoder. However, such methods only make use of the long-term dependency mid-way through the encoding process. Although the vision transformer (ViT) is able to capture such dependency at an early stage, its utilization remains largely unexploited in STR. This work proposes the use of a transformer-only model as a simple baseline which outperforms hybrid CNN-transformer models. Furthermore, two key areas for improvement were identified. Firstly, the first decoded character has the lowest prediction accuracy. Secondly, images of different original aspect ratios react differently to the patch resolutions while ViT only employ one fixed patch resolution. To explore these areas, Pure Transformer with Integrated Experts (PTIE) is proposed. PTIE is a transformer model that can process multiple patch resolutions and decode in both the original and reverse character orders. It is examined on 7 commonly used benchmarks and compared with over 20 state-of-the-art methods. The experimental results show that the proposed method outperforms them and obtains state-of-the-art results in most benchmarks.

Keywords: Transformer · Scene text recognition · Integrated experts

1 Introduction

Scene text recognition (STR) is useful in a wide array of applications such as document retrieval [36], robot navigation [33], and product recognition [22]. Furthermore, STR is able to improve the lives of visually impaired by providing them access to visual information through texts encountered in natural scenes [7,12].

Supplementary Information The online version contains supplementary material available at https://doi.org/10.1007/978-3-031-19815-1_28.

© The Author(s), under exclusive license to Springer Nature Switzerland AG 2022
S. Avidan et al. (Eds.): ECCV 2022, LNCS 13688, pp. 481–497, 2022.
https://doi.org/10.1007/978-3-031-19815-1_28

Traditionally, convolutional neural network (CNN) was used as a backbone in the encoder-decoder framework of STR to extract and encode features from the images [5]. Recurrent neural network (RNN) was then used to capture sequence dependency and decode the features into a sequence of characters. In recent times, transformer [37] has been employed in STR models because of its strong capability in capturing long-term dependency. Some researchers have designed transformer-inspired modules [41,50], while others have utilized it as a hybrid CNN-transformer encoder [8] and/or a transformer decoder in STR [20,23].

Scene text usually has the same font, color, and style, thus exhibiting a coherent pattern. These properties suggest that STR has strong long-term dependency. Henceforth, recent works based on hybrid CNN-transformer [8] outperform models with traditional architectures like CNN and RNN. A natural following question to ask is – will STR performance be improved by exploiting this dependency earlier, that is, by replacing the hybrid CNN-transformer encoder with a transformer-only encoder? The vision transformer (ViT) [6], is competitive against the most performant CNNs in various computer vision tasks. However, it remains largely unexploited in STR [1].

We discovered that employing ViT as an encoder followed by a transformer decoder gives competitive result in STR. However, there are two areas to improve on. First, ViT uses a linear layer to project image patches into encodings. The analysis in Sect. 3 shows that different patch resolutions can have detrimental impact on scene text images of certain word lengths and resizing scales. This finding may apply to other architectures that utilize patches.

Second, transformer decoder employs an autoregressive decoding process and therefore, lesser information is available to leading decoded characters as compared with trailing ones. Our analysis indicates that the first character, which is decoded without any information from previous character, has the highest error rate. This may also be prevalent in other autoregressive methods.

To address the aforementioned areas, we propose a transformer-only model that can process different patch resolutions and decode in both the original and reverse character orders (e.g. 'boy' and 'yob'). Inspired by the mixture of experts, we call this technique integrated experts. The model can effectively represent scene text images of multiple resizing scales. It also complements autoregressive decoding with minimal additional latency as opposed to ensemble.

In summary, the contribution of this work is as follows: (1) a strong transformer-only baseline model, (2) identification of areas for improvement in transformer for STR, (3) the integrated experts method which serves to address the areas for improvement, and (4) state-of-the-art results for 6 out of the 7 benchmarks.

The rest of the paper is organized as follows. Firstly, Sect. 2 explores related works. Secondly, Sect. 3 analyses the areas for improvement in using transformer in STR. Thirdly, Sect. 4 discusses the proposed methodology. Following which, Sect. 5 reports the experimental results on 7 scene text benchmarks. Lastly, Sect. 6 concludes this study.

2   Related Work

The encoder-decoder framework is a popular approach in the field of STR [30]. Traditionally, CNN was used to encode scene text images and RNN was used to model sequence dependency and translate the encoded features into a sequence of characters. Shi et al. [34] proposed a CNN encoder followed by deep bi-directional long-short term memory [13] for decoding. In a similar work [35], a rectification network was introduced into the encoder in order to rectify the image before features are extracted by a CNN.

As transformer became a de facto standard for sequence modeling tasks, works that incorporate transformer as the decoder are becoming more common in STR. Lu et al. [23] proposed a multi-aspect global context attention module, a variant of global context block [4], as part of the encoder network. A transformer decoder is then used to decode the image features into sequences of characters. A similar model was also proposed by Wu et al. [42], utilizing a transformer decoder which is preceded by a global context ResNet (GCNet). Zhang et al. [50] employed a combination of CNN and RNN as the encoder and a transformer inspired cross-network attention as a part of the decoder in their cascade attention network. Similarly, Yu et al. [45] introduced a global semantic reasoning module made up of transformer units, as a module in the decoder.

Apart from being used as/in the decoder, transformer has also been employed in the encoder in the form of a hybrid CNN-transformer [3]. Fu et al. [9] proposed the use of hybrid CNN-transformer to extract visual features from scene text images. It is then followed by a contextual attention module, which is made up of a variant of transformer, as part of the decoding process. Lee et al. [20] likewise utilized a hybrid CNN-transformer encoder and a transformer decoder as their recognition model. In addition, the authors proposed an adaptive 2D positional encoding as well as a locality-aware feed-forward module in the transformer encoder. With a focus on the positional encoding of transformer, Raisi et al. [31] applied a 2D learnable sinusoidal positional encoding which enables the CNN-transformer encoder to focus more on spatial dependencies.

Non-autoregressive forms of transformer decoder were also proposed in various works, coupled with an iterative decoding. Qiao et al. [29] proposed a parallel and iterative decoding strategy on a transformer-based decoder preceded by a feature pyramid network as an encoder. In a similar fashion, Fang et al. [8] utilized a hybrid CNN-transformer based vision model followed by a transformer decoder with iterative correction.

As ViT is becoming a more common approach at vision tasks, Ateinza [1] proposed ViT as both the encoder and non-autoregressive decoder to streamline the encoder-decoder framework of STR. The ViT is made up of the transformer encoder, where the word embedding layer is replaced with a linear layer. By utilizing this one stage process, the author is able to achieve a balance on the accuracy, speed, and efficiency for STR. However, its recognition accuracy does not achieve state-of-the-art performance.

3   Areas for Improvement in Transformer

3.1   Encoder: Impact of Patch Resolution

STR takes cropped images of text from natural scenes as inputs. Therefore, they come in different sizes and aspect ratios. As the images are needed to be of a fixed height and width before being passed as inputs into an STR model, one common approach is to ignore the original aspect ratios and resize them with varying scales. Preserving the original resolutions with padding results in worse performance in the work by Shi et al. [35] which is in line with our experimental result (in supplementary material). For ViT, resized images are split into patches, which will be flatten and passed through a linear layer followed by the transformer encoder.

Using a baseline architecture of ViT encoder with transformer decoder as described in Sect. 4, several models were trained with different patch resolutions. The distributions of correct predictions were analysed using the relative frequency distribution change [15] as defined in Eq. (1):

$$F_{l,s} = \frac{\frac{F_{l,s}^2 - F_{l,s}^1}{F_{l,s}^1}}{\frac{\sum_{l,s}(F_{l,s}^2 - F_{l,s}^1)}{\sum_{l,s} F_{l,s}^1}} \tag{1}$$

where the subscript l and s represent the word length and scaling factor. The scaling factor defined as $\frac{final\ width}{final\ height} \frac{initial\ height}{inital\ width}$, is the scaling of the initial aspect ratio to the final resized aspect ratio. $F_{l,s}^1$ and $F_{l,s}^2$ represent the frequency of the correct predictions at word length l with scale factor s of two models. The training dataset specified in Sect. 5.1 is used to compute $F_{l,s}$ because a large dataset is needed to reliably estimate $F_{l,s}$ at each l and s; the number of samples in the benchmark datasets is insufficient.

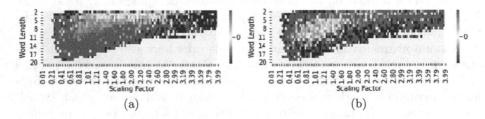

(a)   (b)

Fig. 1. Relative frequency distribution change in correct predictions (a) from a model trained using patch resolution 4×8 to a model trained using 8×4. (b) two models trained using input patch resolution of 8×4. All models were separately initialized and trained using the same hyperparameters (Color figure online)

Figure 1 visualizes the relative frequency distribution change, where the word length is ranged from 2 to 20 with scaling factor ranging from 0 to 4. Bins with frequency count lesser than 100 are removed. Noting that the remaining count account for 95% of total count, these arrangements will reduce the noise caused by bins with low frequency and provide better visuals. In Fig. 1a, $F_{l,s}^1$ and $F_{l,s}^2$

are calculated from the models trained with patch resolution of 4×8 and 8×4 respectively. In Fig. 1b, $F_{l,s}^1$ and $F_{l,s}^2$ are computed with two randomly initialized models trained with the same patch resolution of 8×4. As the denominator in Eq. (1) for Fig. 1a and Fig. 1b is positive, $F_{l,s} > 0$ signifies that $F_{l,s}^2$ produces more correct predictions at l and s than $F_{l,s}^1$ and vice-versa.

As plotted in Fig. 1a, the two models show clear contrast in terms of performance with respect to word length and scaling factor. In specifics, images with word length 3–5 and scaling factor of 1.2–2.4 are least affected by the patch resolution used (white region in Fig. 1. Images with (1) word length of 2–3, scaling factor < 1; and (2) word length 2–11, scaling factor > 2.6, favours patch resolution of 4×8 (blue regions). The red region represents images that performs better with 8×4. These findings suggest that models trained with different resolutions are experts for certain word lengths and scales. Furthermore, Fig. 1b shows no distinct contrast in the frequency between the two separately initialized models (trained with same patch resolution) as opposed to Fig. 1a. This provides a stronger evidence for the impact of different patch resolutions in STR.

3.2 Decoder: Errors in First Character Prediction

Two baseline models as described in Sect. 4.1 were randomly initialized and trained separately where one of them uses the original ground-truth texts while the other uses reversed ground-truths. Our experimental results for wrong predictions on train dataset are plotted in Fig. 2. It is to be noted that the incorrect predictions used to plot Fig. 2 are words with length 5 where there is only one incorrectly predicted character for Fig. 2a and Fig. 2b, and two incorrectly predicted characters for Fig. 2c and Fig. 2d.

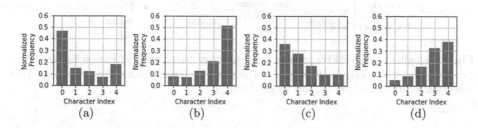

(a)   (b)   (c)   (d)

Fig. 2. Normalized frequency distributions of wrong predictions for word length 5 at the character indices, conditioned on ground truth characters. (a) Predictions with one wrong character. (b) Predictions with one wrong character trained on reversed ground-truths. (c) Predictions with two wrong characters. (d) Predictions with two wrong characters trained on reversed ground-truths

In Fig. 2a and Fig. 2c, the first decoded character is at index 0. Whereas in Fig. 2c and Fig. 2d, the order of character indices was flipped to reflect the reversed ground-truth texts. In the latter case, index 4 would be the first decoded character. As the transformer decoder is autoregressive, the predictions are conditioned on ground truth characters in order to evaluate the accuracy on individual character given the correct prior character(s).

The experimental results show that both models have the highest error rate when decoding the first character, and such observations can be seen in other word lengths as well as other numbers of incorrect characters. Also, characters that are decoded subsequently tend to have lower error rates, given the correct previous characters inputs. More analysis is in the supplementary material.

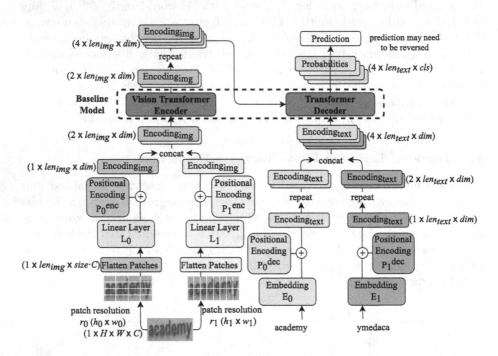

Fig. 3. Architecture of PTIE. It is to be noted that there is no attention between the concatenated Encoding$_{img}$. This is also the case for concatenated Encoding$_{text}$. The attention is utilized as per vanilla transformer

4   Methodology

4.1   Model Architecture and Approach

Architecture of the proposed baseline model is illustrated in Fig. 3. It consists of a ViT encoder and a transformer decoder. Inspired by the mixture of experts, we present a transformer with integrated experts, named PTIE, to improve on the areas discussed in Sect. 3. Each expert, denoted as $Exp_{i,j}$, requires image patches of resolution r_i and ground-truth texts of type j to be trained where $i, j \in \{0, 1\}$.

For this work, patch resolution r_0 has the dimension of $h_0 \times w_0 = 4 \times 8$, and r_1 has that of $h_1 \times w_1 = 8 \times 4$. Both patch resolutions have the same patch size $size = h_0 w_0 = h_1 w_1$. $j = 0$ represents the use of original ground-truth texts (e.g. 'academy'), and $j = 1$ for reversed ground-truths (e.g. 'ymedaca').

For expert $Exp_{i,j}$, the resized image of dimension $H \times W \times C$ (height $\times$ width $\times$ channels) will first be split up into patches of resolution r_i and then flatten. The sequence of flatten patches with length of len_{img} is passed through linear layer L_i. The output, Encoding$_{img}$, will then be summed with positional encoding P_i^{enc} before going through the encoder with encoding dimension of dim. Similarly, the ground-truths of type j will go through an embedding layer E_j and outputs Encoding$_{text}$ with sequence length, len_{text}. It is then summed with P_j^{dec} before being passed into the decoder which produces the probabilities over the total number of classes, cls. Cross-entropy loss will then be applied to the probabilities with their respective type j ground-truths.

In our design, all experts are integrated into 1 model. The parameters in the encoder and decoder are shared. The differentiating factors among them are the initial linear/embedding layers as well as the positional encodings. More precisely, each expert shares about 96% of the parameters with the others and each sample from the dataset will have 4 sets of input (1 for each expert), namely: (1) image split into patches of 4×8 with the original ground-truth text, (2) 4×8 patches with reversed ground-truth text, (3) 8×4 patches with original ground-truth, and (4) 8×4 patches with reversed ground-truth. It is to be noted that our baseline model mentioned in this work employs only 1 set of input (e.g. $i = 0, j = 0$: 4×8 patches with original ground-truth).

The manipulation of the dimensions with repeat and concatenation depicted in Fig. 3 ensures that PTIE decodes each sample image only once despite having 4 sets of initial input. This will allow the inference latency to be close to that of the baseline model. As an ensemble-inspired method, the model will generate 4 predictions for a given sample. The output with the highest word probability (calculated by the multiplications of characters probability) will then be selected as the final prediction. However, different from a standard ensemble, our proposed model requires only a quarter of the parameters and inference time while remaining competitive against an ensemble of models in terms of accuracy.

4.2 Positional Encoding

According to the study by Ke et al. [19], the positional encoding used in the vanilla transformer [37] causes noisy correlation with the embeddings of input tokens (e.g. characters) and may be detrimental to the model. Therefore, on top of the aforementioned proposed model, their strategy of untying the positional encoding from the input token embedding was also adopted.

Instead of summing the positional encoding, a positional attention is instead calculated and then added during the multi-head attention process. The positional attention for the encoder, α_i^{enc}, is calculated as in Eq. (2):

$$\alpha_i^{enc} = \frac{1}{\sqrt{2d}}(P_i^{enc}W_Q)(P_i^{enc}W_K)^T \tag{2}$$

where P_i^{enc} is the positional encoding of the patches with resolution r_i; d is the dimension of positional encodings; W_Q and W_K are linear layers with the same number of input and output dimensions. All layers in the encoder share the α_i^{enc}.

The decoder has masked self-attention and cross-attention layers. Their positional attentions, α_j^{dec} and $\alpha_{i,j}^{dec\_c}$, are calculated as in Eq. (3) and Eq. (4) respectively:

$$\alpha_j^{dec} = \frac{1}{\sqrt{2d}}(P_j^{dec}U_Q)(P_j^{dec}U_K)^T \tag{3}$$

$$\alpha_{i,j}^{dec\_c} = \frac{1}{\sqrt{2d}}(P_j^{dec}V_Q)(P_i^{enc}V_K)^T \tag{4}$$

where i and j denote the types of patch resolution and ground-truth and U_Q, U_K, V_Q, V_K are linear layers like W_Q and W_K. Similarly, all the layers in the decoder share the same positional attentions.

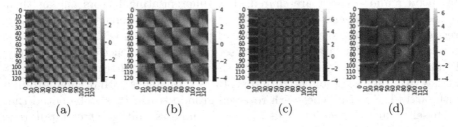

(a)   (b)   (c)   (d)

Fig. 4. Learned unnormalized positional attention maps in the encoder of PTIE for (a) head 1, resolution $= 4 \times 8$; (b) head 1, resolution $= 8 \times 4$; (c) head 2, resolution $= 4 \times 8$; (d) head 2, resolution $= 8 \times 4$. The axes represent the indices of the flatten patches

The image patches of both resolutions were flatten in row-major order. With a large amount of parameters sharing, the spatial layouts of flatten patches with different patch resolutions for PTIE are handled by the positional encodings as shown in Fig. 4. Thus, the unnormalized positional attention maps for patch resolution 4×8 and 8×4 are different.

4.3   Implementation Details

The network was implemented using PyTorch and trained with ADAM optimizer with a base learning rate of 0.02, betas of $(0.9, 0.98)$, and eps of $1e^{-9}$, warmup duration of 6000 steps with a decaying rate of $\min(steps^{-0.5}, steps \times warmup^{-1.5})$. The models were trained on 5 NVIDIA RTX3090, with a batch size of 640. All experiments were trained for 10 epochs. Images are grayscaled and resized to a height and width of 32 by 128 without retaining the original aspect ratios. Standard augmentation techniques following Fang et al.'s work [8] were applied. The models in all experiments contain 6 encoder layers and 6 decoder layers with dropout of 0.1. The encoding dimension is 512 with 16 heads for the multi-head attention. The feed forward layer has an intermediate dimension of 2048. The model recognizes 100 classes for training, including 10 digits, 52 case sensitive alphabets, 35 punctuation characters, a start token, an end token, and a pad token. For testing, only 36 case-insensitive alphanumeric characters were taken into consideration as per related works [8,35,43]. Greedy decoding was used with a maximum sequence length of 30. No rotation strategy [21] was used.

5   Experimental Results and Analysis

5.1   Datasets

Synthetic Datasets. Two synthetic datasets were used: *MJSynth* (MJ) [16], with 9 million samples, and *SynthText* (ST) [11], containing 8 million images. Some works utilized *SynthAdd* (SA) [21] due to the lack of punctuation in *MJSynth* and *SynthText*. SA was not used in our training.

Real Datasets. For evaluation, 6 datasets of real scene text images which contain 7 benchmarks were used. *IIIT 5K-Words* (IIIT5K) [26] contains 3000 test images. *ICDAR 2013* (IC13) [18] contains 1015 testing images as per related work [39]. Two verions of *ICDAR 2015* (IC15) [17], containing 2077 test images and 1811 images, were used for evaluation. *Street View Text* (SVT) [39] consists of 647 testing images. *Street View Text-Perspective* (SVT-P) [28] contains 645 testing images. *CUTE80* (CT) [32] contains 288 test images. *COCO-Text* [10] which contains 42, 618 training images were used for fine-tuning so as to compare with works which uses real datasets in training or fine-tuning.

5.2   Comparison with State-of-the-Art Methods

The results of PTIE are compared with recent works from top conferences and journals as shown in Table 1. PTIE achieves state-of-the-art results for most of the benchmarks, even though it has a simple architecture. In particular, PTIE–Untied attained the best results in 6 out of 7 benchmarks, outperforming the next best method by 0.9% for SVT, 2.9% for IC15 (2077), 1.8% for IC15 (1811), and 0.8% for SVTP. The model loses out to the best accuracy [8] on IC13 by 0.2% and achieved the third highest accuracy. Similarly, PTIE–Vanilla attained the highest accuracy in 5 benchmarks as compared with recent works. Figure 5 shows examples of success and failure cases.

Comparing with works that utilize real datasets, we fine-tune our PTIE models with real dataset (COCO-Text [10]) with results shown in Table. 2. Through fine-tuning, our proposed model attained some improvement in performance. The model is able to outperform the state-of-the-art methods for 4 of the benchmarks and achieved the second highest for 2 bechmarks. Between the PTIE models trained with ST+MJ, PTIE–Untied has a weighted average (over the benchmarks) of 0.1% higher than PTIE–Vanilla. For ST+MJ+R, PTIE–Untied has a weighted average of 0.4% higher than PTIE–Vanilla.

Table 1. Comparison of accuracies on benchmark datasets with works trained using synthetic datasets. PTIE–Untied uses the learnable positional encoding discussed in Sect. 4.2 while PTIE–Vanilla uses it as per vanilla transformer method. The best and second best results as compared with PTIE–Untied are in bold and underline respectively. Values in the parenthesis are the difference in accuracy between the proposed model with the best or next best result. Note that the comparison of results are only between a PTIE-based model and other related works

Method	Year	Train datasets	Regular text			Irregular text			
			IIIT	IC13	SVT	IC15		SVT-P	CT
			3000	1015	647	2077	1811	645	288
Luo et al. [24]	PR '19	ST+MJ	91.2	92.4	88.3	68.8	-	76.1	77.4
Yang et al. [44]	ICCV '19	ST+MJ	94.4	93.9	88.9	78.7	-	80.8	87.5
Zhan and Lu [47]	CVPR '19	ST+MJ	93.3	91.3	90.2	76.9	-	79.6	83.3
Wang et al. [40]	AAAI '20	ST+MJ	94.3	93.9	89.2	74.5	-	80.0	84.4
Wan et al. [38]	AAAI '20	ST+MJ	93.9	92.9	90.1	-	79.4	84.3	83.3
Zhang et al. [49]	ECCV '20	ST+MJ	94.7	94.2	90.9	-	81.8	81.7	-
Yue et al. [46]	ECCV '20	ST+MJ	95.3	94.8	88.1	77.1	-	79.5	90.3
Lee et al. [20]	CVPRW '20	ST+MJ	92.8	94.1	91.3	79.0	-	86.5	87.8
Yu et al. [45]	CVPR '20	ST+MJ	94.8	-	91.5	-	82.7	85.1	87.8
Qiao et al. [30]	CVPR '20	ST+MJ	93.8	92.8	89.6	80.0	-	81.4	83.6
Lu et al. [23]	PR '21	ST+MJ+SA	95.0	95.3	90.6	79.4	-	84.5	87.5
Raisi et al. [31]	CRV '21	ST+MJ	94.8	94.1	90.4	80.5	-	86.8	88.2
Qiao et al. [29]	ACMMM '21	ST+MJ	95.2	93.4	91.2	81.0	83.5	84.3	90.9
Atienza [1]	ICDAR '21	ST+MJ	88.4	92.4	87.7	72.6	78.5	81.8	81.3
Zhang et al. [48]	AAAI '21	ST+MJ	95.2	94.8	90.9	79.5	82.8	83.2	87.5
Wang et al. [41]	ICCV '21	ST+MJ	95.8	95.7	91.7	-	83.7	86.0	88.5
Wu et al. [42]	ICMR '21	ST+MJ	95.1	94.4	90.7	-	84.0	85.0	86.1
Fu et al. [9]	ICMR '21	ST+MJ	<u>96.2</u>	<u>97.3</u>	93.5	-	84.9	88.2	91.2
Zhang et al. [50]	ICMR '21	ST+MJ	90.3	96.8	89.5	76.0	-	78.5	78.9
Luo et al. [25]	IJCV '21	ST+MJ	95.6	96.0	92.9	<u>81.4</u>	83.9	85.1	<u>91.3</u>
Yan et al. [43]	CVPR '21	ST+MJ	95.6	-	<u>94.0</u>	-	83.0	87.6	**91.7**
Baek et al. [2]	CVPR '21	ST+MJ	92.1	93.1	88.9	74.7	-	79.5	78.2
Fang et al. [8]	CVPR '21	ST+MJ	<u>96.2</u>	97.4	93.5	-	<u>86.0</u>	<u>89.3</u>	89.2
PTIE–Vanilla		ST+MJ	96.7	97.1	95.5	83.4	87.4	89.8	91.3
			(+0.5)	(-0.3)	(+1.5)	(+2.0)	(+1.4)	(+0.5)	(-0.4)
PTIE–Untied		ST+MJ	**96.3**	97.2	**94.9**	**84.3**	**87.8**	**90.1**	**91.7**
			(+0.1)	(-0.2)	(+0.9)	(+2.9)	(+1.8)	(+0.8)	(0.0)

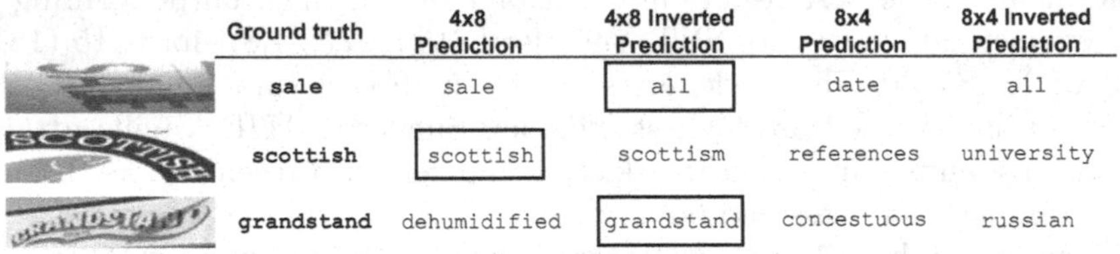

Ground truth	4x8 Prediction	4x8 Inverted Prediction	8x4 Prediction	8x4 Inverted Prediction
sale	sale	all (boxed)	date	all
scottish	scottish (boxed)	scottism	references	university
grandstand	dehumidified	grandstand (boxed)	concestuous	russian

Fig. 5. Sample images of success and failure cases. The boxed text represents final output from PTIE. More examples are in the supplementary material

5.3   Ablation Studies

Transformer-Only Encoder. In order to demonstrate the effectiveness of utilizing transformer-only encoder, 2 models were trained. We used a ViT encoder

Table 2. Comparison of accuracies on the benchmark datasets. The letter 'R' denotes the use of real dataset either in training or fine-tuning. The best and second best results in comparison with PTIE–Untied are in bold and underline respectively. Values in the parenthesis are the difference in accuracy between the proposed model with the best or next best result. Note that the comparison of results are only between a PTIE-based model and other related works

Method	Year	Train datasets	Regular text			Irregular text			
			IIIT	IC13	SVT	IC15		SVT-P	CT
			3000	1015	647	2077	1811	645	288
Li et al. [21]	AAAI '19	ST+MJ+SA+R	95.0	94.0	91.2	78.8	-	86.4	89.6
Yue et al. [46]	ECCV '20	ST+MJ+R	95.4	94.1	89.3	79.2	-	82.9	<u>92.4</u>
Wan et al. [38]	AAAI '20	ST+MJ+R	95.7	94.9	92.7	-	83.5	84.8	91.6
Hu et al. [14]	AAAI '20	ST+MJ+SA+R	95.8	94.4	92.9	79.5	-	85.7	92.2
Qiao et al. [29]	ACMMM '21	ST+MJ+R	**96.7**	95.4	<u>94.7</u>	**85.9**	<u>88.7</u>	<u>88.2</u>	**92.7**
Baek et al. [2]	CVPR '21	R	93.5	92.6	87.5	76.0	-	82.7	88.1
Luo et al. [25]	IJCV '21	ST+MJ+R	96.5	<u>95.6</u>	94.4	84.7	87.2	86.2	<u>92.4</u>
PTIE–Vanilla		ST+MJ+R	96.5	96.1	96.3	84.5	89.0	91.3	88.5
			(-0.2)	(+0.5)	(+1.6)	(-1.4)	(+0.3)	(+3.1)	(-4.2)
PTIE–Untied		ST+MJ+R	<u>96.6</u>	**96.6**	**95.8**	<u>85.1</u>	**89.2**	**92.1**	91.0
			(-0.1)	(+1.0)	(+1.1)	(-0.8)	(+0.5)	(+3.9)	(-1.7)

with transformer decoder as the baseline model and added a 45-layer ResNet [35] on top for the second model. Both models have the same hyperparameters. Comparison with works of similar architecture and method are given in Table 3.

Table 3. Comparison of accuracies with related works that are heavily based on transformer. The related works contain slight variations in the transformer architecture as discussed in Sect. 2. The reported accuracy is the weighted average over the 6 benchmarks. The total count of 7672 includes IC15 (2077) while 7406 uses IC15 (1811). Note that Lee et al. [20] uses two convolutional layers

Method	Encoder	Decoder	Parameters	Accuracy	
				7672	7406
Raisi et al. [31]	ResNet based + Trans	Trans	-	89.5	-
Lu et al. [23]	GCNet based	Trans	-	89.3	-
Wu et al. [42]	GCNet based + Trans	Trans	-	-	90.7
Lee et al. [20]	CNN based + Trans	Trans	55.0M	88.4	-
	ResNet based + Trans	Trans	67.8M	85.7	87.1
	Vision Trans	Trans	45.8M	**90.9**	**92.8**

The transformer-only model outperforms the other works that employ a hybrid CNN-transformer encoder. This shows that competitive results can be achieved with just a pure transformer model. Furthermore, our experimental results show that adding a ResNet on top of the transformer encoder has a lower performance as compared with just using a vision transformer. Overall, the results suggest that exploiting the long-term dependency at an earlier stage in an encoder-decoder framework appears to be beneficial for STR.

Comparison with Standard Ensemble. To evaluate the effectiveness of integrated experts, 4 separate models were each trained with one of the following inputs: (1) 8×4 patches with original ground-truth, (2) 8×4 patches with reversed ground-truth, (3) 4×8 patches with original ground-truth, and (4) 4×8 patches with reversed ground-truth. The ensemble of these 4 models is named Ensemble–Diverse and the PTIE trained with the 4 inputs is named PTIE–Diverse. The weighted average accuracies of the models over 6 benchmarks are tabulated in Table 4. It is to be noted that untied positional encoding was used in all experiments of this section.

Table 4. Weighted average accuracies of mutilple methods on 6 benchmark datasets (with 2077 samples from IC15). The naming convention for the methods starts with the patch resolution (e.g. 8×4) followed by the type of ground-truth used. "orig. GT" stands for the original ground-truth text, and "rev. GT" stands for the reversed ground-truth

Method	Parameters	Acc
		7672
8×4, orig. GT	45.8M	90.9
8×4, invt. GT	45.8M	90.0
4×8, orig. GT	45.8M	90.5
4×8, invt. GT	45.8M	90.1
Ensemble–Diverse	183.2M	**92.4**
8×4, orig. GT (1)	45.8M	90.9
8×4, orig. GT (2)	45.8M	90.7
8×4, orig. GT (3)	45.8M	90.5
8×4, orig. GT (4)	45.8M	90.7
Ensemble–Identical	183.2M	92.1
PTIE–Diverse	45.9M	**92.4**
PTIE–Identical	45.9M	91.0

Undoubtedly, the ensemble of the models brought about a significant performance boost. However, the improvement in accuracy comes at the price of requiring a greater amount of model parameters. Ensemble–Diverse needing 183.2M parameters, achieved an accuracy of 92.4%. In contrast, PTIE–Diverse is able to achieve the same result of 92.4% with only a quarter of the parameters.

The effectiveness of different patch resolutions and ground-truth types are also analyzed with 4 randomly initialized models trained with patch resolution of 8×4 and original ground-truth. Their accuracies are shown in Table 4 together with their ensemble (Ensemble–Identical) and PTIE–Identical. Although there is only one type of ground-truth and patch resolution, PTIE–Identical is still trained with separate positional encoding, linear layers, and embedding layers as per Sect. 4.1. From the experimental results, accuracy of Ensemble–Identical is lower than that of Ensemble–Diverse by 0.3% which highlights the effectiveness of using different resolutions and ground-truth types. Furthermore, PTIE–Identical suffers a 1.4% drop in accuracy indicating that different resolutions and ground-truth types are crucial for PTIE on leveraging the experts through different positional encoding, linear layers, and embedding layers.

Comparison of Latency. Table 5 shows a comparison of latency with other recent works that are open source. To tabulate the latency, inference on the test benchmarks was done with an RTX3090 and batch size of 1. Using 4 sets of well-designed inputs mentioned in Sect. 4.1, both PTIE–Diverse and Ensemble–Diverse achieved the highest average accuracy. Furthermore, the latency of 52 ms by PTIE–Diverse is comparable to the baseline (8×4, orig. GT) and is a quarter of Ensemble–Diverse. This is because PTIE–Diverse decodes only once per sample despite having 4 sets of input, while Ensemble–Diverse needs to decode 4 times. MLT-19 [27] containing 10,000 real images for end-to-end scene recognition averages 11.2 texts instances per image. Using a batch size of 11, the latency of PTIE is about 11ms per cropped scene text image (averaging to 0.12s per full image). Therefore, it may not be a problem for real-time applications. Furthermore, in situations such as applications in forensic science (e.g. parsing images from suspect's hard disk) or assistance to visually impaired, accuracy would be valued over latency.

Table 5. Inference time and weighted average accuracy of recent works. The total count of 7672 uses IC15 (2077) on top of the 5 other datasets mentioned in Sect. 5.1. 7406 uses IC15 (1811) and 7248 uses IC15 (1811) and a filtered version of IC13. The variation in total count is due to other works using varied set of benchmarks

Method	Year	Avg. accuracy			Parameters (mil.)	Time (ms)
		7672	7406	7248		
Wang et al. [40]	AAAI '20	86.9	-	-	18.4	22
Lu et al. [23]	PR '21	89.3	-	-	54.6	53
Fang et al. [8]	CVPR '21	-	92.8	-	36.7	27
Yan et al. [43]	CVPR '21	-	-	91.5	29.1	29
8×4, orig. GT		90.9	92.8	92.2	45.8	50
Ensemble–Diverse		**92.4**	93.7	**93.8**	183.2	202
PTIE–Diverse		**92.4**	**94.1**	93.5	45.9	52

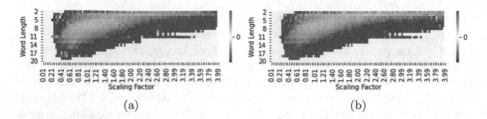

Fig. 6. Relative frequency distribution change in correct predictions of (a) PTIE from model trained with resolution 4 × 8 and original ground-truth. (b) PTIE from model trained with resolution 8 × 4 and original ground-truth

5.4   Addressing Areas for Improvement

As per Sect. 3.1, the relative frequency distribution changes of PTIE–Diverse from the models trained with (1) 4 × 8 patches and (2) 8 × 4 patches, are plotted in Fig. 6a and Fig. 6b respectively. Relative improvement in the predictions is seen in most of the lengths and scales for both patch resolutions. This shows that PTIE is effective in utilizing the advantages of both resolutions.

Furthermore, the frequency distributions in Fig. 7 demonstrate that PTIE–Diverse, trained with original and reversed ground-truth, is able to lower the prediction error of first character as discussed in Sect. 3.2. Overall, PTIE is able to improve the accuracy in STR by mitigating the problem of the weak first character prediction. Non-autoregressive decoding is explored in the supplementary material.

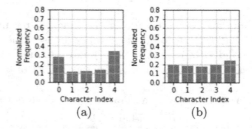

Fig. 7. Normalized frequency distributions of wrong predictions by PTIE for word length 5 conditioned on ground truth characters. (a) Predictions with one wrong character. (b) Predictions with two wrong characters

6   Conclusion

In this work, a simple and strong transformer-only baseline was introduced. By exploiting the long-term dependency of STR at an earlier stage in the model, the baseline is able to outperform related works which uses hybrid transformer. We then analyzed and discussed two areas for improvement for transformer in

STR. The integrated experts method was proposed to address them and state-of-the-art results were attained for most benchmarks. As the final predictions of PTIE were selected based on word probability, we will explore more selection methods and streamline the processes in PTIE for future work.

Acknowledgments. This work is partially supported by NTU Internal Funding - Accelerating Creativity and Excellence (NTU-ACE2020-03).

References

1. Atienza, R.: Vision transformer for fast and efficient scene text recognition. In: Lladós, J., Lopresti, D., Uchida, S. (eds.) ICDAR 2021. LNCS, vol. 12821, pp. 319–334. Springer, Cham (2021). https://doi.org/10.1007/978-3-030-86549-8_21
2. Baek, J., Matsui, Y., Aizawa, K.: What if we only use real datasets for scene text recognition? Toward scene text recognition with fewer labels. In: CVPR, pp. 3113–3122 (2021)
3. Bartz, C., Bethge, J., Yang, H., Meinel, C.: Kiss: keeping it simple for scene text recognition. arXiv preprint arXiv:1911.08400 (2019)
4. Cao, Y., Xu, J., Lin, S., Wei, F., Hu, H.: GCNet: non-local networks meet squeeze-excitation networks and beyond. In: ICCVW (2019)
5. Chen, X., Jin, L., Zhu, Y., Luo, C., Wang, T.: Text recognition in the wild: a survey. ACM Comput. Surv. **54**(2), 1–35 (2021)
6. Dosovitskiy, A., et al.: An image is worth 16x16 words: transformers for image recognition at scale. In: ICLR (2021)
7. Ezaki, N., Kiyota, K., Minh, B.T., Bulacu, M., Schomaker, L.: Improved text-detection methods for a camera-based text reading system for blind persons. In: ICDAR, pp. 257–261 (2005)
8. Fang, S., Xie, H., Wang, Y., Mao, Z., Zhang, Y.: Read like humans: autonomous, bidirectional and iterative language modeling for scene text recognition. In: CVPR, pp. 7098–7107 (2021)
9. Fu, Z., Xie, H., Jin, G., Guo, J.: Look back again: dual parallel attention network for accurate and robust scene text recognition. In: ICMR, pp. 638–644 (2021)
10. Gomez, R., et al.: ICDAR 2017 robust reading challenge on coco-text. In: ICDAR, vol. 1, pp. 1435–1443 (2017)
11. Gupta, A., Vedaldi, A., Zisserman, A.: Synthetic data for text localisation in natural images. In: CVPR, pp. 2315–2324 (2016). https://doi.org/10.1109/CVPR.2016.254
12. Gurari, D., et al.: Vizwiz grand challenge: answering visual questions from blind people. In: CVPR, pp. 3608–3617 (2018)
13. Hochreiter, S., Schmidhuber, J.: Long short-term memory. Neural Comput. **9**(8), 1735–1780 (1997)
14. Hu, W., Cai, X., Hou, J., Yi, S., Lin, Z.: GTC: guided training of CTC towards efficient and accurate scene text recognition. In: AAAI, vol. 34, pp. 11005–11012 (2020)
15. Huang, D., Lang, Y., Liu, T.: Evolving population distribution in China's border regions: spatial differences, driving forces and policy implications. PLoS ONE **15**(10), e0240592 (2020)
16. Jaderberg, M., Simonyan, K., Vedaldi, A., Zisserman, A.: Synthetic data and artificial neural networks for natural scene text recognition. arXiv preprint arXiv:1406.2227 (2014)

17. Karatzas, D., et al.: ICDAR 2015 competition on robust reading. In: ICDAR, pp. 1156–1160 (2015)
18. Karatzas, D., et al.: ICDAR 2013 robust reading competition. In: ICDAR, pp. 1484–1493 (2013)
19. Ke, G., He, D., Liu, T.Y.: Rethinking positional encoding in language pre-training. In: ICLR (2020)
20. Lee, J., Park, S., Baek, J., Oh, S.J., Kim, S., Lee, H.: On recognizing texts of arbitrary shapes with 2D self-attention. In: CVPRW, pp. 546–547 (2020)
21. Li, H., Wang, P., Shen, C., Zhang, G.: Show, attend and read: a simple and strong baseline for irregular text recognition. In: AAAI, vol. 33, pp. 8610–8617, July 2019
22. Long, S., He, X., Yao, C.: Scene text detection and recognition: The deep learning era. IJCV **129**(1), 161–184 (2021)
23. Lu, N., et al.: Master: multi-aspect non-local network for scene text recognition. PR **117**, 107980 (2021)
24. Luo, C., Jin, L., Sun, Z.: Moran: a multi-object rectified attention network for scene text recognition. PR **90**, 109–118 (2019)
25. Luo, C., Lin, Q., Liu, Y., Jin, L., Shen, C.: Separating content from style using adversarial learning for recognizing text in the wild. IJCV **129**(4), 960–976 (2021)
26. Mishra, A., Alahari, K., Jawahar, C.: Scene text recognition using higher order language priors. In: BMVC (2012)
27. Nayef, N., et al.: ICDAR 2019 robust reading challenge on multi-lingual scene text detection and recognition-RRC-MLT-2019. In: ICDAR, pp. 1582–1587. IEEE (2019)
28. Phan, T.Q., Shivakumara, P., Tian, S., Tan, C.L.: Recognizing text with perspective distortion in natural scenes. In: ICCV, pp. 569–576 (2013). https://doi.org/10.1109/ICCV.2013.76
29. Qiao, Z., et al.: Pimnet: a parallel, iterative and mimicking network for scene text recognition. In: ACMMM, pp. 2046–2055 (2021)
30. Qiao, Z., Zhou, Y., Yang, D., Zhou, Y., Wang, W.: Seed: semantics enhanced encoder-decoder framework for scene text recognition. In: CVPR, June 2020
31. Raisi, Z., Naiel, M.A., Younes, G., Wardell, S., Zelek, J.: 2LSPE: 2D learnable sinusoidal positional encoding using transformer for scene text recognition. In: CRV, pp. 119–126 (2021)
32. Risnumawan, A., Shivakumara, P., Chan, C.S., Tan, C.L.: A robust arbitrary text detection system for natural scene images. Expert Syst. Appl. **41**(18), 8027–8048 (2014). https://doi.org/10.1016/j.eswa.2014.07.008. https://www.sciencedirect.com/science/article/pii/S0957417414004060
33. Schulz, R., et al.: Robot navigation using human cues: a robot navigation system for symbolic goal-directed exploration. In: ICRA, pp. 1100–1105 (2015)
34. Shi, B., Bai, X., Yao, C.: An end-to-end trainable neural network for image-based sequence recognition and its application to scene text recognition. PAMI **39**(11), 2298–2304 (2016)
35. Shi, B., Yang, M., Wang, X., Lyu, P., Yao, C., Bai, X.: Aster: an attentional scene text recognizer with flexible rectification. PAMI **41**(9), 2035–2048 (2018)
36. Tsai, S.S., Chen, H., Chen, D., Schroth, G., Grzeszczuk, R., Girod, B.: Mobile visual search on printed documents using text and low bit-rate features. In: ICIP, pp. 2601–2604 (2011)
37. Vaswani, A., et al.: Attention is all you need. In: NIPS, vol. 30 (2017)
38. Wan, Z., He, M., Chen, H., Bai, X., Yao, C.: Textscanner: reading characters in order for robust scene text recognition. In: AAAI, vol. 34, pp. 12120–12127, April 2020

39. Wang, K., Babenko, B., Belongie, S.: End-to-end scene text recognition. In: ICCV, pp. 1457–1464 (2011)

40. Wang, T., et al.: Decoupled attention network for text recognition. In: AAAI, vol. 34, pp. 12216–12224, April 2020. https://doi.org/10.1609/aaai.v34i07.6903

41. Wang, Y., Xie, H., Fang, S., Wang, J., Zhu, S., Zhang, Y.: From two to one: a new scene text recognizer with visual language modeling network. In: ICCV, pp. 14194–14203 (2021)

42. Wu, L., Liu, X., Hao, Y., Ma, Y., Hong, R.: Naster: non-local attentional scene text recognizer. In: ICMR, pp. 331–338 (2021)

43. Yan, R., Peng, L., Xiao, S., Yao, G.: Primitive representation learning for scene text recognition. In: CVPR, pp. 284–293 (2021)

44. Yang, M., et al.: Symmetry-constrained rectification network for scene text recognition. In: ICCV, October 2019

45. Yu, D., et al.: Towards accurate scene text recognition with semantic reasoning networks. In: CVPR, pp. 12113–12122 (2020)

46. Yue, X., Kuang, Z., Lin, C., Sun, H., Zhang, W.: RobustScanner: dynamically enhancing positional clues for robust text recognition. In: Vedaldi, A., Bischof, H., Brox, T., Frahm, J.-M. (eds.) ECCV 2020. LNCS, vol. 12364, pp. 135–151. Springer, Cham (2020). https://doi.org/10.1007/978-3-030-58529-7_9

47. Zhan, F., Lu, S.: ESIR: end-to-end scene text recognition via iterative image rectification. In: CVPR, June 2019

48. Zhang, C., et al.: Spin: structure-preserving inner offset network for scene text recognition. In: AAAI, vol. 35, pp. 3305–3314 (2021)

49. Zhang, H., Yao, Q., Yang, M., Xu, Y., Bai, X.: AutoSTR: efficient backbone search for scene text recognition. In: Vedaldi, A., Bischof, H., Brox, T., Frahm, J.-M. (eds.) ECCV 2020. LNCS, vol. 12369, pp. 751–767. Springer, Cham (2020). https://doi.org/10.1007/978-3-030-58586-0_44

50. Zhang, M., Ma, M., Wang, P.: Scene text recognition with cascade attention network. In: ICMR, pp. 385–393 (2021)

OCR-Free Document Understanding Transformer

Geewook Kim[1(✉)], Teakgyu Hong[4], Moonbin Yim[2], JeongYeon Nam[1],
Jinyoung Park[5], Jinyeong Yim[6], Wonseok Hwang[7], Sangdoo Yun[3],
Dongyoon Han[3], and Seunghyun Park[1]

[1] NAVER CLOVA, Seongnam-si, South Korea
gwkim.rsrch@gmail.com
[2] NAVER Search, Seongnam-si, South Korea
[3] NAVER AI Lab, Seongnam-si, South Korea
[4] Upstage, Yongin-si, South Korea
[5] Tmax, Seongnam-si, South Korea
[6] Google, Seoul, South Korea
[7] LBox, Seoul, South Korea

Abstract. Understanding document images (*e.g.*, invoices) is a core but
challenging task since it requires complex functions such as *reading text*
and a *holistic understanding of the document*. Current Visual Document
Understanding (VDU) methods outsource the task of reading text to off-
the-shelf Optical Character Recognition (OCR) engines and focus on the
understanding task with the OCR outputs. Although such OCR-based
approaches have shown promising performance, they suffer from 1) high
computational costs for using OCR; 2) inflexibility of OCR models on
languages or types of documents; 3) OCR error propagation to the subsequent process. To address these issues, in this paper, we introduce a
novel OCR-free VDU model named **Donut**, which stands for **Do**cument
understanding **t**ransformer. As the first step in OCR-free VDU research,
we propose a simple architecture (*i.e.*, Transformer) with a pre-training
objective (*i.e.*, cross-entropy loss). Donut is conceptually simple yet effective. Through extensive experiments and analyses, we show a simple
OCR-free VDU model, Donut, achieves state-of-the-art performances on
various VDU tasks in terms of both speed and accuracy. In addition, we
offer a synthetic data generator that helps the model pre-training to be
flexible in various languages and domains. The code, trained model, and
synthetic data are available at https://github.com/clovaai/donut.

Keywords: Visual document understanding · Document information
extraction · Optical character recognition · End-to-end transformer

T. Hong, M. Yim, J. Park, J. Yim and W. Hwang—This work was done while the
authors were at NAVER CLOVA.

Supplementary Information The online version contains supplementary material
available at https://doi.org/10.1007/978-3-031-19815-1_29.

ⓒ The Author(s), under exclusive license to Springer Nature Switzerland AG 2022
S. Avidan et al. (Eds.): ECCV 2022, LNCS 13688, pp. 498–517, 2022.
https://doi.org/10.1007/978-3-031-19815-1_29

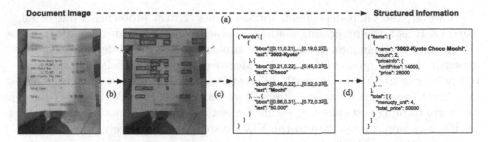

Fig. 1. The schema of the conventional document information extraction (IE) pipeline. (a) The goal is to extract the structured information from a given semi-structured document image. In the pipeline, (b) text detection is conducted to obtain text locations and (c) each box is passed to the recognizer to comprehend characters. (d) Finally, the recognized texts and its locations are passed to the following module to be processed for the desired structured form of the information

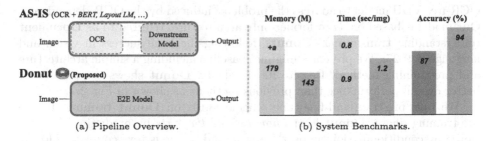

Fig. 2. The pipeline overview and benchmarks. The proposed end-to-end model, **Donut**, outperforms the recent OCR-dependent VDU models in memory, time cost and accuracy. Performances on visual document IE [43] are shown in (b). More results on various VDU tasks are available at Sect. 3 showing the same trend

1   Introduction

Document images, such as commercial invoices, receipts, and business cards, are easy to find in modern working environments. To extract useful information from such document images, Visual Document Understanding (VDU) has not been only an essential task for industry, but also a challenging topic for researchers, with applications including document classification [1,25], information extraction [21,40], and visual question answering [42,55].

Current VDU methods [17,21,23,60,61] solve the task in a two-stage manner: 1) reading the texts in the document image; 2) holistic understanding of the document. They usually rely on deep-learning-based Optical Character Recognition (OCR) [3,4] for the text reading task and focus on modeling the understanding part. For example, as shown in Fig. 1, a conventional pipeline for extracting structured information from documents (a.k.a. document parsing) consists of three separate modules for text detection, text recognition, and parsing [21,23].

However, the OCR-dependent approach has critical problems. First of all, using OCR as a pre-processing method is expensive. We can utilize pre-trained off-the-shelf OCR engines; however, the computational cost for inference would be expensive for high-quality OCR results. Moreover, the off-the-shelf OCR methods rarely have flexibility dealing with different languages or domain changes, which may lead to poor generalization ability. If we train an OCR model, it also requires extensive training costs and large-scale datasets [3,4,37,44]. Another problem is, OCR errors would propagate to the VDU system and negatively influence subsequent processes [22,52]. This problem becomes more severe in languages with complex character sets, such as Korean or Chinese, where the quality of OCR is relatively low [48]. To deal with this, post-OCR correction module [10,48,49] is usually adopted. However, it is not a practical solution for real application environments since it increases the entire system size and maintenance cost.

We go beyond the traditional framework by modeling a direct mapping from a raw input image to the desired output without OCR. We introduce a new OCR-free VDU model to address the problems induced by the OCR-dependency. Our model is based on Transformer-only architecture, referred to as **Do**cument **u**nderstanding **t**ransformer (**Donut**), following the huge success in vision and language [8,9,27]. We present a minimal baseline including a simple architecture and pre-training method. Despite its simplicity, **Donut** shows comparable or better overall performance than previous methods as shown in Fig. 2.

We take pre-train-and-fine-tune scheme [8,61] on **Donut** training. In the pre-training phase, **Donut** learns *how to read the texts* by predicting the next words by conditioning jointly on the image and previous text contexts. **Donut** is pre-trained with document images and their text annotations. Since our pre-training objective is simple (*i.e.*, reading the texts), we can realize domain and language flexibility straightforwardly pre-training with synthetic data. During fine-tuning stage, **Donut** learns *how to understand the whole document* according to the downstream task. We demonstrate **Donut** has a strong understanding ability through extensive evaluation on various VDU tasks and datasets. The experiments show a simple OCR-free VDU model can achieve state-of-the-art performance in terms of both speed and accuracy.

The contributions are summarized as follows:

1. We propose a novel OCR-free approach for VDU. To the best of our knowledge, this is the first method based on an OCR-free Transformer trained in end-to-end manner.
2. We introduce a simple pre-training scheme that enables the utilization of synthetic data. By using our generator SynthDoG, we show **Donut** can easily be extended to a multi-lingual setting, which is not applicable for the conventional approaches that need to retrain an off-the-shelf OCR engine.
3. We conduct extensive experiments and analyses on both public benchmarks and private industrial datasets, showing that the proposed method achieves not only state-of-the-art performances on benchmarks but also has many practical advantages (e.g., *cost-effective*) in real-world applications.
4. The codebase, pre-trained model, and synthetic data are available at GitHub.[1]

---

[1] https://github.com/clovaai/donut.

2   Method

2.1   Preliminary: Background

There have been various visual document understanding (VDU) methods to understand and extract essential information from the semi-structured documents such as receipts [17,19,23], invoices [47], and form documents [6,14,41].

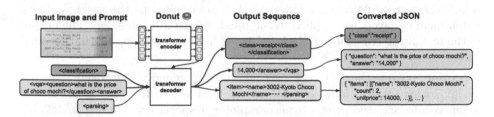

Fig. 3. The pipeline of Donut. The encoder maps a given document image into embeddings. With the encoded embeddings, the decoder generates a sequence of tokens that can be converted into a target type of information in a structured form

Earlier VDU attempts have been done with OCR-independent visual backbones [1,12,15,25,29], but the performances are limited. Later, with the remarkable advances of OCR [3,4] and BERT [8], various OCR-dependent VDU models have been proposed by combining them [21–23]. More recently, in order to get a more general VDU, most state-of-the-arts [17,60] use both powerful OCR engines and large-scale real document image data (e.g., IIT-CDIP [30]) for a model pre-training. Although they showed remarkable advances in recent years, extra effort is required to ensure the performance of an entire VDU model by using the off-the-shelf OCR engine.

2.2   Document Understanding Transformer

Donut is an end-to-end (i.e., self-contained) VDU model for general understanding of document images. The architecture of Donut is quite simple, which consists of a Transformer [9,56]-based visual encoder and textual decoder modules. Note that Donut does not rely on any modules related to OCR functionality but uses a visual encoder for extracting features from a given document image. The following textual decoder maps the derived features into a sequence of subword tokens to construct a desired structured format (e.g., JSON). Each model component is Transformer-based, and thus the model is trained easily in an end-to-end manner. The overall process of Donut is illustrated in Fig. 3.

Encoder. The visual encoder converts the input document image $\mathbf{x} \in \mathbb{R}^{H \times W \times C}$ into a set of embeddings $\{\mathbf{z}_i | \mathbf{z}_i \in \mathbb{R}^d, 1 \leq i \leq n\}$, where n is feature map size or the number of image patches and d is the dimension of the latent vectors of the encoder. Note that CNN-based models [16] or Transformer-based models [9,38] can be used as the encoder network. In this study, we use Swin Transformer [38] because it shows the best performance in our preliminary study in document parsing. Swin Transformer first splits the input image $\mathbf{x}$ into non-overlapping patches. Swin Transformer blocks, consist of a shifted window-based multi-head self-attention module and a two-layer MLP, are applied to the patches. Then, patch merging layers are applied to the patch tokens at each stage. The output of the final Swin Transformer block $\{\mathbf{z}\}$ is fed into the following textual decoder.

Decoder. Given the $\{\mathbf{z}\}$, the textual decoder generates a token sequence $(\mathbf{y}_i)_{i=1}^m$, where $\mathbf{y}_i \in \mathbb{R}^v$ is an one-hot vector for the i-th token, v is the size of token vocabulary, and m is a hyperparameter, respectively. We use BART [31] as the decoder architecture. Specifically, we initialize the decoder model weights with those from the publicly available[2] pre-trained multi-lingual BART model [36].

Model Input. Following the original Transformer [56], we use a teacher-forcing scheme [59], which is a model training strategy that uses the ground truth as input instead of model output from a previous time step. In the test phase, inspired by GPT-3 [5], the model generates a token sequence given a prompt. We add new special tokens for the prompt for each downstream task in our experiments. The prompts that we use for our applications are shown with the desired output sequences in Fig. 3. Illustrative explanations for the teacher-forcing strategy and the decoder output format are available in Appendix A.4.

Output Conversion. The output token sequence is converted to a desired structured format. We adopt a JSON format due to its high representation capacity. As shown in Fig. 3, a token sequence is one-to-one invertible to a JSON data. We simply add two special tokens [START_*] and [END_*], where * indicates each field to extract. If the output token sequence is wrongly structured, we simply treat the field is lost. For example, if there is only [START_name] exists but no [END_name], we assume the model fails to extract "name" field. This algorithm can easily be implemented with simple regular expressions [11].

2.3   Pre-training

Task. The model is trained to read all texts in the image in reading order (from top-left to bottom-right, basically). The objective is to minimize cross-entropy loss of next token prediction by jointly conditioning on the image and previous contexts. This task can be interpreted as a pseudo-OCR task. The model is trained as a visual language model over the visual corpora, i.e., document images.

---

[2] https://huggingface.co/hyunwoongko/asian-bart-ecjk.

Fig. 4. Generated English, Chinese, Japanese, and Korean samples with SynthDoG. Heuristic random patterns are applied to mimic the real documents

Visual Corpora. We use IIT-CDIP [30], which is a set of 11M scanned english document images. A commercial CLOVA OCR API is applied to get the pseudo text labels. As aforementioned, however, this kind of dataset is not always available, especially for languages other than English. To alleviate the dependencies, we build a scalable *Synthetic Document Generator*, referred to as **SynthDoG**. Using the SynthDog and Chinese, Japanese, Korean and English Wikipedia, we generated 0.5M samples per language.

Synthetic Document Generator. The pipeline of image rendering basically follows Yim et al. [63]. As shown in Fig. 4, the generated sample consists of several components; background, document, text, and layout. Background image is sampled from ImageNet [7], and a texture of document is sampled from the collected paper photos. Words and phrases are sampled from Wikipedia. Layout is generated by a simple rule-based algorithm that randomly stacks grids. In addition, several image rendering techniques [13,39,63] are applied to mimic real documents. The generated examples are shown in Fig. 4. More details of SynthDoG are available in the code[1] and Appendix A.2.

2.4   Fine-Tuning

After the model learns *how to read*, in the application stage (i.e., fine-tuning), we teach the model *how to understand* the document image. As shown in Fig. 3, we interpret all downstream tasks as a JSON prediction problem.

The decoder is trained to generate a token sequence that can be converted into a JSON that represents the desired output information. For example, in the document classification task, the decoder is trained to generate a token sequence [START_class] [memo] [END_class] which is 1-to-1 invertible to a JSON { "class": "memo"}. We introduce some special tokens (e.g., [memo] is used for representing the class "memo"), if such replacement is available in the target task.

3   Experiments and Analyses

In this section, we present **Donut** fine-tuning results on three VDU applications on six different datasets including both public benchmarks and private industrial service datasets. The samples are shown in Fig. 5.

3.1   Downstream Tasks and Datasets

Document Classification. To see whether the model can distinguish across different types of documents, we test a classification task. Unlike other models that predict the class label via a softmax on the encoded embedding, Donut generate a JSON that contains class information to maintain the uniformity of the task-solving method. We report overall classification accuracy on a test set.

RVL-CDIP. The RVL-CDIP dataset [15] consists of 400K images in 16 classes, with 25K images per class. The classes include letter, memo, email, and so on. There are 320K training, 40K validation, and 40K test images.

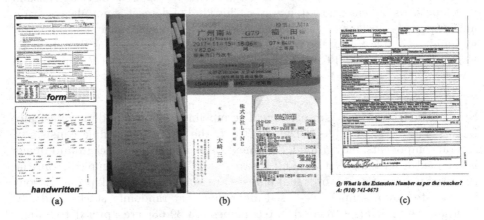

Fig. 5. Samples of the downstream datasets. (a) Document Classification. (b) Document Information Extraction. (c) Document Visual Question Answering

Document Information Extraction. To see the model fully understands the complex layouts and contexts in documents, we test document information extraction (IE) tasks on various real document images including both public benchmarks and real industrial datasets. In this task, the model aims to map each document to a structured form of information that is consistent with the target ontology or database schema. See Fig. 1 for an illustrative example. The model should not only read the characters well, but also understand the layouts and semantics to infer the groups and nested hierarchies among the texts.

We evaluate the models with two metrics; field-level F1 score [17,21,61] and Tree Edit Distance (TED) based accuracy [22,64,66]. The F1 checks whether the extracted field information is in the ground truth. Even a single character is missed, the score assume the field extraction is failed. Although F1 is simple and easy to understand, there are some limitations. First, it does not take into account partial overlaps. Second, it can not measure the predicted structure (e.g., groups and nested hierarchy). To assess overall accuracy, we also use another metric based on TED [64], that can be used for any documents represented as trees. It is calculated as, $\max(0, 1 - \mathrm{TED}(\mathrm{pr}, \mathrm{gt})/\mathrm{TED}(\phi, \mathrm{gt}))$, where gt, pr, and ϕ

stands for ground truth, predicted, and empty trees respectively. Similar metrics are used in recent works on document IE [22,66]

We use two public benchmark datasets as well as two private industrial datasets which are from our active real-world service products. Each dataset is explained in the followings.

CORD. The Consolidated Receipt Dataset (CORD)[3] [43] is a public benchmark that consists of 0.8K train, 0.1K valid, 0.1K test receipt images. The letters of receipts is in Latin alphabet. The number of unique fields is 30 containing menu name, count, total price, and so on. There are complex structures (i.e., nested groups and hierarchies such as `items>item>{name, count, price}`) in the information. See Fig. 1 for more details.

Ticket. This is a public benchmark dataset [12] that consists of 1.5K train and 0.4K test Chinese train ticket images. We split 10% of the train set as a validation set. There are 8 fields which are ticket number, starting station, train number, and so on. The structure of information is simple and all keys are guaranteed to appear only once and the location of each field is fixed.

Business Card (In-Service Data). This dataset is from our active products that are currently deployed. The dataset consists of 20K train, 0.3K valid, 0.3K test Japanese business cards. The number of fields is 11, including name, company, address, and so on. The structure of information is similar to the *Ticket* dataset.

Receipt (In-Service Data). This dataset is also from one of our real products. The dataset consists of 40K train, 1K valid, 1K test Korean receipt images. The number of unique field is 81, which includes store information, payment information, price information, and so on. Each sample has complex structures compared to the aforementioned datasets. Due to industrial policies, not all samples can publicly be available. Some real-like high-quality samples are shown in Fig. 5 and in the supplementary material.

Document Visual Question Answering. To validate the further capacity of the model, we conduct a document visual question answering task (DocVQA). In this task, a document image and question pair is given and the model predicts the answer for the question by capturing both visual and textual information within the image. We make the decoder generate the answer by setting the question as a starting prompt to keep the uniformity of the method (See Fig. 3).

DocVQA. The dataset is from Document Visual Question Answering competition[4] and consists of 50K questions defined on more than 12K documents [42]. There are 40K train, 5K valid, and 5K test questions. The evaluation metric is ANLS (Average Normalized Levenshtein Similarity) which is an edit-distance-based metric. The score on the test set is measured via the evaluation site.

---

[3] https://huggingface.co/datasets/naver-clova-ix/cord-v1.
[4] https://rrc.cvc.uab.es/?ch=17.

Table 1. Classification results on the RVL-CDIP dataset. Donut achieves state-of-the-are performance with reasonable speed and model size efficiency. **Donut** is a general purpose backbone but does not rely on OCR while other recent backbones (e.g., LayoutLM) do. [†]# parameters for OCR should be considered for non-E2E models

	OCR	#Params	Time (ms)	Accuracy (%)
BERT	✓	$110M + \alpha^\dagger$	1392	89.81
RoBERTa	✓	$125M + \alpha^\dagger$	1392	90.06
LayoutLM	✓	$113M + \alpha^\dagger$	1396	91.78
LayoutLM (w/ image)	✓	$160M + \alpha^\dagger$	1426	94.42
LayoutLMv2	✓	$200M + \alpha^\dagger$	1489	95.25
Donut (Proposed)		143M	**752**	**95.30**

3.2 Setups

We use Swin-B [38] as a visual encoder of **Donut** with slight modification. We set the layer numbers and window size as $\{2, 2, 14, 2\}$ and 10. In further consideration of the speed-accuracy trade-off, we use the first four layers of BART as a decoder. As explained in Sect. 2.3, we train the multi-lingual **Donut** using the 2M synthetic and 11M IIT-CDIP scanned document images. We pre-train the model for 200K steps with 64 A100 GPUs and a mini-batch size of 196. We use Adam [28] optimizer, the learning rate is scheduled and the initial rate is selected from 1e-5 to 1e-4. The input resolution is set to 2560×1920 and a max length in the decoder is set to 1536. All fine-tuning results are achieved by starting from the pre-trained multi-lingual model. Some hyperparameters are adjusted at fine-tuning and in ablation studies. We use 960×1280 for Train Tickets and Business Card parsing tasks. We fine-tune the model while monitoring the edit distance over token sequences. The speed of Donut is measured on a P40 GPU, which is much slower than A100. For the OCR based baselines, states-of-the-art OCR engines are used, including MS OCR API used in [60] and CLOVA OCR API[5] used in [22,23]. An analysis on OCR engines is available in Sect. 3.4. More details of OCR and training setups are available in Appendix A.1 and A.5.

3.3 Experimental Results

Document Classification. The results are shown in Table 1. Without relying on any other resource (e.g., off-the-shelf OCR engine), Donut shows a state-of-the-art performance among the general-purpose VDU models such as LayoutLM [61] and LayoutLMv2 [60]. In particular, Donut surpasses the LayoutLMv2 accuracy reported in [60], while using fewer parameters with the 2x faster speed. Note that the OCR-based models must consider additional model

---

[5] https://clova.ai/ocr.

parameters and speed for the entire OCR framework, which is not small in general. For example, a recent advanced OCR-based model [3, 4] requires more than 80M parameters. Also, training and maintaining the OCR-based systems are costly [22], leading to needs for the Donut-like end-to-end approach.

Table 2. Performances on various document IE tasks. The field-level F1 scores and tree-edit-distance-based accuracies are reported. **Donut** shows the best accuracies for all domains with significantly faster inference speed. †Parameters for vocabulary are omitted for fair comparisons among multi-lingual models. ‡# parameters for OCR should be considered. *Official multi-lingual extension models are used

	OCR	#Params	CORD [43]			Ticket [12]			Business card			Receipt		
			Time (s)	F1	Acc.	Time (s)	F1	Acc.	Time (s)	F1	Acc.	Time (s)	F1	Acc.
BERT* [21]	✓	$86_M^\ddagger + \alpha^\ddagger$	1.6	82.2	78.2	1.7	86.7	91.7	1.5	55.6	86.9	2.5	80.2	77.3
BROS [17]	✓	$86_M^\ddagger + \alpha^\ddagger$	1.7	83.7	80.3									
LayoutLMv2* [60,62]	✓	$179_M^\ddagger + \alpha^\ddagger$	1.7	88.9	87.0	1.8	96.3	90.1	1.6	68.8	92.0	2.6	86.0	89.0
Donut		$143_M^\dagger$	**1.2**	**91.6**	**93.5**	**0.6**	**97.0**	**98.8**	**1.4**	**74.2**	**95.1**	**1.9**	**88.2**	**94.4**
SPADE* [23]	✓	$93_M^\dagger + \alpha^\ddagger$	4.0	83.1	84.5	4.5	13.9	59.8	4.3	48.1	83.5	7.3	74.8	79.8
WYVERN* [20]	✓	$106_M^\ddagger + \alpha^\ddagger$	1.2	62.8	70.5	1.5	63.5	76.2	1.7	46.5	88.8	3.4	85.0	92.0

Document Information Extraction. Table 2 shows the results on the four different document IE tasks. The first group uses a conventional BIO-tagging-based IE approach [21]. We follows the conventions in IE [17, 61]. OCR extracts texts and bounding boxes from the image, and then the serialization module sorts all texts with geometry information within the bounding box. The BIO-tagging-based named entity recognition task performs token-level tag classification upon the ordered texts to generate a structured form. We test three general-purpose VDU backbones, BERT [8], BROS [17], and LayoutLMv2 [60, 62].

We also test two recently proposed IE models, SPADE [23] and WYVERN [22]. SPADE is a graph-based IE method that predicts relations between bounding boxes. WYVERN is an Transformer encoder-decoder model that directly generates entities with structure given OCR outputs. WYVERN is different from Donut in that it takes the OCR output as its inputs.

For all domains, including public and private in-service datasets, Donut shows the best scores among the comparing models. By measuring both F1 and TED-based accuracy, we observe not only Donut can extract key information but also predict complex structures among the field information. We observe that a large input resolution gives robust accuracies but makes the model slower. For example, the performance on the CORD with 1280×960 was 0.7 sec./image and 93.6 accuracy. But, the large resolution showed better performances on the low-resource situation. The detailed analyses are in Sect. 3.4. Unlike other baselines, Donut shows stable performance regardless of the size of datasets and complexity of the tasks (See Fig. 5). This is a significant impact as the target tasks are already actively used in industries.

Table 3. Average Normalized Levenshtein Similarity (ANLS) scores on DocVQA. Donut shows a promising result without OCR. *__Donut__ shows a high ANLS score on the handwritten documents which are known to be challenging due to the difficulty of handwriting OCR (See Fig. 6). †Token embeddings for English is counted for a fair comparison. ‡# parameters for OCR should be considered

	Fine-tuning set	OCR	#Params†	Time (ms)	ANLS test set	ANLS* handwritten
BERT [60]	train set	✓	110M + $\alpha^{\ddagger}$	1517	63.5	n/a
LayoutLM [61]	train set	✓	113M + $\alpha^{\ddagger}$	1519	69.8	n/a
LayoutLMv2 [60]	train set	✓	200M + $\alpha^{\ddagger}$	1610	78.1	n/a
Donut	train set		176M	**782**	67.5	**72.1**
LayoutLMv2-Large-QG [60]	train + dev + QG	✓	390M + $\alpha^{\ddagger}$	1698	**86.7**	67.3

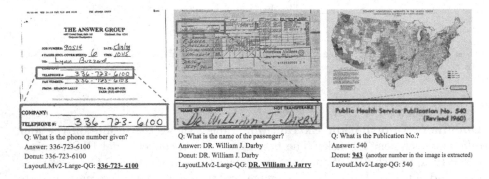

Q: What is the phone number given?
Answer: 336-723-6100
Donut: 336-723-6100
LayoutLMv2-Large-QG: **336-723- 4100**

Q: What is the name of the passenger?
Answer: DR. William J. Darby
Donut: DR. William J. Darby
LayoutLMv2-Large-QG: **DR. William J. Jarrv**

Q: What is the Publication No.?
Answer: 540
Donut: **943** (another number in the image is extracted)
LayoutLMv2-Large-QG: 540

Fig. 6. Examples of Donut and LayoutLMv2 outputs on DocVQA. The OCR-errors make a performance upper-bound of the OCR-dependent baselines, e.g., LayoutLMv2 (left and middle examples). Due to the input resolution constraint of the end-to-end pipeline, Donut miss some tiny texts in large-scale images (right example) but this could be mitigated by scaling the input image size (See Sect. 3.4)

Document Visual Question Answering. Table 3 shows the results on the DocVQA dataset. The first group is the general-purposed VDU backbones whose scores are from the LayoutLMv2 paper [60]. We measure the running time with MS OCR API used in [60]. The model in the third group is a DocVQA-specific-purposed fine-tuning model of LayoutLMv2, whose inference results are available in the official leader-board.[6]

As can be seen, **Donut** achieves competitive scores with the baselines that are dependent on external OCR engines. Especially, Donut shows that it is robust to the handwritten documents, which is known to be challenging to process. In the conventional approach, adding a post-processing module that corrects OCR errors is an option to strengthen the pipeline [10,48,49] or adopting an encoder-decoder architecture on the OCR outputs can mitigate the problems of OCR errors [22]. However, this kind of approaches tend to increase the entire system size and maintenance cost. Donut shows a completely different direction. Some

---

[6] https://rrc.cvc.uab.es/?ch=17&com=evaluation&task=1.

inference results are shown in Fig. 6. The samples show the current strengths of Donut as well as the left challenges in the Donut-like end-to-end approach. Further analysis and ablation is available in Sect. 3.4.

3.4 Further Studies

In this section, we study several elements of understanding Donut. We show some striking characteristics of Donut through the experiments and visualization.

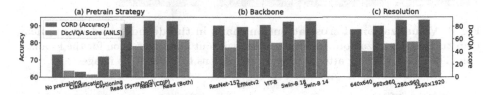

Fig. 7. Analysis on (a) pre-training strategies, (b) image backbones, and (c) input resolutions. Performances on CORD [43] and DocVQA [42] are shown

On Pre-training Strategy. We test several pre-training tasks for VDUs. Figure 7(a) shows that the Donut pre-training task (i.e., text reading) is the most simple yet effective approach. Other tasks that impose a general knowledge of images and texts on models, e.g., image captioning, show little gains in the fine-tuning tasks. For the text reading tasks, we verify three options, SynthDoG only, IIT-CDIP only, and both. Note that synthetic images were enough for the document IE task in our analysis. However, in the DocVQA task, it was important to see the real images. This is probably because the image distributions of IIT-CDIP and DocVQA are similar [42].

On Encoder Backbone. Here, we study popular image classification backbones that show superior performance in traditional vision tasks to measure their performance in VDU tasks. The Fig. 7(b) shows the comparison results. We use all the backbones pre-trained on ImageNet [7]. EfficientNetV2 [53] and Swin Transformer [38] outperform others on both datasets. We argue that this is due to the high expressiveness of the backbones, which were shown by the striking scores on several downstream tasks as well. We choose Swin Transformer due to the high scalability of the Transformer-based architecture and higher performance over the EfficientNetV2's.

On Input Resolution. The Fig. 7(c) shows the performance of Donut grows rapidly as we set a larger input size. This gets clearer in the DocVQA where the images are larger with many tiny texts. But, increasing the size for a precise result incurs bigger computational costs. Using an efficient attention mechanism [58] may avoid the matter in architectural design, but we use the original Transformer [56] as we aim to present a simpler architecture in this work.

On Text Localization. To see how the model behaves, we visualize the corss attention maps of the decoder given an unseen document image. As can be seen in Fig. 8, the model shows meaningful results that can be used as an auxiliary indicator. The model attends to a desired location in the given image.

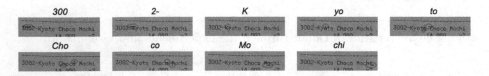

Fig. 8. Visualization of cross-attention maps in the decoder and its application to text localization. Donut is trained without any supervision for the localization. The Donut decoder attends proper text regions to process the image

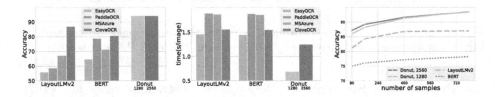

Fig. 9. Comparison of BERT, LayoutLMv2 and Donut on CORD. The performances (i.e., speed and accuracy) of the OCR-based models extremely varies depending on what OCR engine is used (left and center). Donut shows robust performances even in a low resourced situation showing the higher score only with 80 samples (right)

On OCR System. We test four widely-used public OCR engines (See Fig. 9). The results show that the performances (i.e., speed and accuracy) of the conventional OCR-based methods heavily rely on the off-the-shelf OCR engine. More details of the OCR engines are available in Appendix A.1.

On Low Resourced Situation. We evaluate the models by limiting the size of training set of CORD [43]. The performance curves are shown in the right Fig. 9. Donut shows a robust performances. We also observe that a larger input resolution, 2560 × 1920, shows more robust scores on the extremely low-resourced situation, e.g., 80 samples. As can be seen, Donut outperformed the LayoutLMv2 accuracy only with 10% of the data, which is only 80 samples.

4   Related Work

4.1   Optical Character Recognition

Recent trends of OCR study are to utilize deep learning models in its two sub-steps: 1) text areas are predicted by a detector; 2) a text recognizer then recognizes all characters in the cropped image instances. Both are trained with a large-scale datasets including the synthetic images [13,24] and real images [26,45].

Early detection methods used CNNs to predict local segments and apply heuristics to merge them [18,65]. Later, region proposal and bounding box regression based methods were proposed [34]. Recently, focusing on the homogeneity and locality of texts, component-level approaches were proposed [4,54].

Many modern text recognizer share a similar approach [35,50,51,57] that can be interpreted into a combination of several common deep modules [3]. Given the cropped text instance image, most recent text recognition models apply CNNs to encode the image into a feature space. A decoder is then applied to extract characters from the features.

4.2 Visual Document Understanding

Classification of the document type is a core step towards automated document processing. Early methods treated the problem as a general image classification, so various CNNs were tested [1,15,25]. Recently, with BERT [8], the methods based on a combination of CV and NLP were widely proposed [32,61]. As a common approach, most methods rely on an OCR engine to extract texts; then the OCR-ed texts are serialized into a token sequence; finally they are fed into a language model (e.g., BERT) with some visual features if available. Although the idea is simple, the methods showed remarkable performance improvements and became a main trend in recent years [2,33,60].

Document IE covers a wide range of real applications [21,40], for example, given a bunch of raw receipt images, a document parser can automate a major part of receipt digitization, which has been required numerous human-labors in the traditional pipeline. Most recent models [22,23] take the output of OCR as their input. The OCR results are then converted to the final parse through several processes, which are often complex. Despite the needs in the industry, only a few works have been attempted on end-to-end parsing. Recently, some works are proposed to simplify the complex parsing processes [22,23]. But they still rely on a separate OCR to extract text information.

Visual QA on documents seeks to answer questions asked on document images. This task requires reasoning over visual elements of the image and general knowledge to infer the correct answer [42]. Currently, most state-of-the-arts follow a simple pipeline consisting of applying OCR followed by BERT-like transformers [60,61]. However, the methods work in an extractive manner by their nature. Hence, there are some concerns for the question whose answer does not appear in the given image [55]. To tackle the concerns, generation-based methods have also been proposed [46].

5   Conclusions

In this work, we propose a novel end-to-end framework for visual document understanding. The proposed method, **Donut**, directly maps an input document image into a desired structured output. Unlike conventional methods, **Donut** does not depend on OCR and can easily be trained in an end-to-end fashion. We also propose a synthetic document image generator, SynthDoG, to alleviate the dependency on large-scale real document images and we show that **Donut** can be easily extended to a multi-lingual setting. We gradually trained the model from *how to read* to *how to understand* through the proposed training pipeline. Our extensive experiments and analysis on both external public benchmarks and private internal service datasets show higher performance and better *cost-effectiveness* of the proposed method. This is a significant impact as the target tasks are already practically used in industries. Enhancing the pretraining objective could be a future work direction. We believe our work can easily be extended to other domains/tasks regarding document understanding.

References

1. Afzal, M.Z., et al.: Deepdocclassifier: document classification with deep convolutional neural network. In: 2015 13th International Conference on Document Analysis and Recognition (ICDAR), pp. 1111–1115 (2015). https://doi.org/10.1109/ICDAR.2015.7333933
2. Appalaraju, S., Jasani, B., Kota, B.U., Xie, Y., Manmatha, R.: Docformer: end-to-end transformer for document understanding. In: Proceedings of the IEEE/CVF International Conference on Computer Vision (ICCV), pp. 993–1003, October 2021
3. Baek, J., et al.: What is wrong with scene text recognition model comparisons? Dataset and model analysis. In: Proceedings of the IEEE/CVF International Conference on Computer Vision (ICCV), October 2019
4. Baek, Y., Lee, B., Han, D., Yun, S., Lee, H.: Character region awareness for text detection. In: 2019 IEEE/CVF Conference on Computer Vision and Pattern Recognition (CVPR), pp. 9357–9366 (2019). https://doi.org/10.1109/CVPR.2019.00959
5. Brown, T., et al.: Language models are few-shot learners. In: Larochelle, H., Ranzato, M., Hadsell, R., Balcan, M.F., Lin, H. (eds.) Advances in Neural Information Processing Systems, vol. 33, pp. 1877–1901. Curran Associates, Inc. (2020). https://proceedings.neurips.cc/paper/2020/file/1457c0d6bfcb4967418bfb8ac142f64a-Paper.pdf
6. Davis, B., Morse, B., Cohen, S., Price, B., Tensmeyer, C.: Deep visual template-free form parsing. In: 2019 International Conference on Document Analysis and Recognition (ICDAR), pp. 134–141 (2019). https://doi.org/10.1109/ICDAR.2019.00030
7. Deng, J., Dong, W., Socher, R., Li, L.J., Li, K., Fei-Fei, L.: Imagenet: a large-scale hierarchical image database. In: 2009 IEEE Conference on Computer Vision and Pattern Recognition, pp. 248–255. IEEE (2009)
8. Devlin, J., Chang, M.W., Lee, K., Toutanova, K.: BERT: pre-training of deep bidirectional transformers for language understanding. In: Proceedings of the 2019 Conference of the North American Chapter of the Association for Computational Linguistics: Human Language Technologies, Volume 1 (Long and Short Papers), Minneapolis, Minnesota, pp. 4171–4186. Association for Computational Linguistics, June 2019. https://doi.org/10.18653/v1/N19-1423. https://aclanthology.org/N19-1423
9. Dosovitskiy, A., et al.: An image is worth 16x16 words: transformers for image recognition at scale. In: 9th International Conference on Learning Representations, ICLR 2021, Virtual Event, Austria, 3–7 May 2021. OpenReview.net (2021). https://openreview.net/forum?id=YicbFdNTTy

10. Duong, Q., Hämäläinen, M., Hengchen, S.: An unsupervised method for OCR post-correction and spelling normalisation for Finnish. In: Proceedings of the 23rd Nordic Conference on Computational Linguistics (NoDaLiDa), Sweden, Reykjavik, Iceland, 31 May–2 June 2021, pp. 240–248. Linköping University Electronic Press (2021). https://aclanthology.org/2021.nodalida-main.24

11. Friedl, J.E.F.: Mastering Regular Expressions, 3 edn. O'Reilly, Beijing (2006). https://www.safaribooksonline.com/library/view/mastering-regular-expressions/0596528124/

12. Guo, H., Qin, X., Liu, J., Han, J., Liu, J., Ding, E.: Eaten: entity-aware attention for single shot visual text extraction. In: 2019 International Conference on Document Analysis and Recognition (ICDAR), pp. 254–259 (2019). https://doi.org/10.1109/ICDAR.2019.00049

13. Gupta, A., Vedaldi, A., Zisserman, A.: Synthetic data for text localisation in natural images. In: Proceedings of the IEEE Conference on Computer Vision and Pattern Recognition (CVPR), June 2016

14. Hammami, M., Héroux, P., Adam, S., d'Andecy, V.P.: One-shot field spotting on colored forms using subgraph isomorphism. In: 2015 13th International Conference on Document Analysis and Recognition (ICDAR), pp. 586–590 (2015). https://doi.org/10.1109/ICDAR.2015.7333829

15. Harley, A.W., Ufkes, A., Derpanis, K.G.: Evaluation of deep convolutional nets for document image classification and retrieval. In: 2015 13th International Conference on Document Analysis and Recognition (ICDAR), pp. 991–995 (2015). https://doi.org/10.1109/ICDAR.2015.7333910

16. He, K., Zhang, X., Ren, S., Sun, J.: Deep residual learning for image recognition. In: 2016 IEEE Conference on Computer Vision and Pattern Recognition (CVPR), pp. 770–778 (2016). https://doi.org/10.1109/CVPR.2016.90

17. Hong, T., Kim, D., Ji, M., Hwang, W., Nam, D., Park, S.: Bros: a pre-trained language model focusing on text and layout for better key information extraction from documents. In: Proceedings of the AAAI Conference on Artificial Intelligence, vol. 36, no. 10, pp. 10767–10775, June 2022. https://doi.org/10.1609/aaai.v36i10.21322. https://ojs.aaai.org/index.php/AAAI/article/view/21322

18. Huang, W., Qiao, Yu., Tang, X.: Robust scene text detection with convolution neural network induced MSER trees. In: Fleet, D., Pajdla, T., Schiele, B., Tuytelaars, T. (eds.) ECCV 2014. LNCS, vol. 8692, pp. 497–511. Springer, Cham (2014). https://doi.org/10.1007/978-3-319-10593-2_33

19. Huang, Z., et al.: ICDAR 2019 competition on scanned receipt OCR and information extraction. In: 2019 International Conference on Document Analysis and Recognition (ICDAR), pp. 1516–1520 (2019). https://doi.org/10.1109/ICDAR.2019.00244

20. Hwang, A., Frey, W.R., McKeown, K.: Towards augmenting lexical resources for slang and African American English. In: Proceedings of the 7th Workshop on NLP for Similar Languages, Varieties and Dialects, Barcelona, Spain, pp. 160–172. International Committee on Computational Linguistics (ICCL), December 2020. https://aclanthology.org/2020.vardial-1.15

21. Hwang, W., et al.: Post-OCR parsing: building simple and robust parser via bio tagging. In: Workshop on Document Intelligence at NeurIPS 2019 (2019)

22. Hwang, W., Lee, H., Yim, J., Kim, G., Seo, M.: Cost-effective end-to-end information extraction for semi-structured document images. In: Proceedings of the 2021 Conference on Empirical Methods in Natural Language Processing, pp. 3375–3383. Association for Computational Linguistics, Online and Punta Cana, Dominican Republic, November 2021. https://doi.org/10.18653/v1/2021.emnlp-main.271. https://aclanthology.org/2021.emnlp-main.271

23. Hwang, W., Yim, J., Park, S., Yang, S., Seo, M.: Spatial dependency parsing for semi-structured document information extraction. In: Findings of the Association for Computational Linguistics: ACL-IJCNLP 2021, pp. 330–343. Association for Computational Linguistics, August 2021. https://doi.org/10.18653/v1/2021.findings-acl.28. https://aclanthology.org/2021.findings-acl.28

24. Jaderberg, M., Simonyan, K., Vedaldi, A., Zisserman, A.: Synthetic data and artificial neural networks for natural scene text recognition. In: Workshop on Deep Learning, NIPS (2014)

25. Kang, L., Kumar, J., Ye, P., Li, Y., Doermann, D.S.: Convolutional neural networks for document image classification. In: 2014 22nd International Conference on Pattern Recognition, pp. 3168–3172 (2014)

26. Karatzas, D., et al.: ICDAR 2015 competition on robust reading. In: 2015 13th International Conference on Document Analysis and Recognition (ICDAR), pp. 1156–1160 (2015). https://doi.org/10.1109/ICDAR.2015.7333942

27. Kim, W., Son, B., Kim, I.: ViLT: vision-and-language transformer without convolution or region supervision. In: Meila, M., Zhang, T. (eds.) Proceedings of the 38th International Conference on Machine Learning. Proceedings of Machine Learning Research, 18–24 July 2021, vol. 139, pp. 5583–5594. PMLR (2021). http://proceedings.mlr.press/v139/kim21k.html

28. Kingma, D.P., Ba, J.: Adam: A method for stochastic optimization. In: Bengio, Y., LeCun, Y. (eds.) 3rd International Conference on Learning Representations, ICLR 2015, San Diego, CA, USA, May 7–9, 2015, Conference Track Proceedings (2015), http://arxiv.org/abs/1412.6980

29. Klaiman, S., Lehne, M.: DocReader: bounding-box free training of a document information extraction model. In: Lladós, J., Lopresti, D., Uchida, S. (eds.) ICDAR 2021. LNCS, vol. 12821, pp. 451–465. Springer, Cham (2021). https://doi.org/10.1007/978-3-030-86549-8_29

30. Lewis, D., Agam, G., Argamon, S., Frieder, O., Grossman, D., Heard, J.: Building a test collection for complex document information processing. In: Proceedings of the 29th Annual International ACM SIGIR Conference on Research and Development in Information Retrieval, SIGIR 2006, pp. 665–666. Association for Computing Machinery, New York (2006). https://doi.org/10.1145/1148170.1148307

31. Lewis, M., et al.: BART: denoising sequence-to-sequence pre-training for natural language generation, translation, and comprehension. In: Proceedings of the 58th Annual Meeting of the Association for Computational Linguistics, pp. 7871–7880. Association for Computational Linguistics, July 2020. https://doi.org/10.18653/v1/2020.acl-main.703. https://aclanthology.org/2020.acl-main.703

32. Li, C., et al.: StructuralLM: structural pre-training for form understanding. In: Proceedings of the 59th Annual Meeting of the Association for Computational Linguistics and the 11th International Joint Conference on Natural Language Processing (Volume 1: Long Papers), pp. 6309–6318. Association for Computational Linguistics, August 2021. https://doi.org/10.18653/v1/2021.acl-long.493. https://aclanthology.org/2021.acl-long.493

33. Li, P., et al.: SelfDoc: self-supervised document representation learning. In: 2021 IEEE/CVF Conference on Computer Vision and Pattern Recognition (CVPR), pp. 5648–5656 (2021). https://doi.org/10.1109/CVPR46437.2021.00560

34. Liao, M., Shi, B., Bai, X., Wang, X., Liu, W.: Textboxes: a fast text detector with a single deep neural network. In: Proceedings of the AAAI Conference on Artificial Intelligence, vol. 31, no. 1, February 2017. https://doi.org/10.1609/aaai. v31i1.11196. https://ojs.aaai.org/index.php/AAAI/article/view/11196

35. Liu, W., Chen, C., Wong, K.Y.K., Su, Z., Han, J.: Star-net: a spatial attention residue network for scene text recognition. In: Richard C. Wilson, E.R.H., Smith, W.A.P. (eds.) Proceedings of the British Machine Vision Conference (BMVC), pp. 43.1–43.13. BMVA Press, September 2016. https://doi.org/10.5244/C.30.43

36. Liu, Y., et al.: Multilingual denoising pre-training for neural machine translation. Trans. Assoc. Comput. Linguist. **8**, 726–742 (2020). https://aclanthology.org/2020. tacl-1.47

37. Liu, Y., Chen, H., Shen, C., He, T., Jin, L., Wang, L.: ABCNet: real-time scene text spotting with adaptive Bezier-curve network. In: Proceedings of the IEEE/CVF Conference on Computer Vision and Pattern Recognition (CVPR), June 2020

38. Liu, Z., et al.: Swin transformer: hierarchical vision transformer using shifted windows. In: Proceedings of the IEEE/CVF International Conference on Computer Vision (ICCV), pp. 10012–10022, October 2021

39. Long, S., Yao, C.: Unrealtext: synthesizing realistic scene text images from the unreal world. arXiv preprint arXiv:2003.10608 (2020)

40. Majumder, B.P., Potti, N., Tata, S., Wendt, J.B., Zhao, Q., Najork, M.: Representation learning for information extraction from form-like documents. In: Proceedings of the 58th Annual Meeting of the Association for Computational Linguistics, pp. 6495–6504. Association for Computational Linguistics, July 2020. https://doi.org/10.18653/v1/2020.acl-main.580. https://www.aclweb. org/anthology/2020.acl-main.580

41. Majumder, B.P., Potti, N., Tata, S., Wendt, J.B., Zhao, Q., Najork, M.: Representation learning for information extraction from form-like documents. In: Proceedings of the 58th Annual Meeting of the Association for Computational Linguistics, pp. 6495–6504. Association for Computational Linguistics, July 2020. https://doi. org/10.18653/v1/2020.acl-main.580. https://aclanthology.org/2020.acl-main.580

42. Mathew, M., Karatzas, D., Jawahar, C.: DocVQA: a dataset for VQA on document images. In: Proceedings of the IEEE/CVF Winter Conference on Applications of Computer Vision, pp. 2200–2209 (2021)

43. Park, S., et al.: Cord: a consolidated receipt dataset for post-OCR parsing. In: Workshop on Document Intelligence at NeurIPS 2019 (2019)

44. Peng, D., et al.: SPTS: Single-Point Text Spotting. CoRR abs/2112.07917 (2021). https://arxiv.org/abs/2112.07917

45. Phan, T.Q., Shivakumara, P., Tian, S., Tan, C.L.: Recognizing text with perspective distortion in natural scenes. In: Proceedings of the IEEE International Conference on Computer Vision (ICCV), December 2013

46. Powalski, R., Borchmann, Ł, Jurkiewicz, D., Dwojak, T., Pietruszka, M., Pałka, G.: Going full-TILT boogie on document understanding with text-image-layout transformer. In: Lladós, J., Lopresti, D., Uchida, S. (eds.) ICDAR 2021. LNCS, vol. 12822, pp. 732–747. Springer, Cham (2021). https://doi.org/10.1007/978-3-030-86331-9_47

47. Riba, P., Dutta, A., Goldmann, L., Fornés, A., Ramos, O., Lladó, J.: Table detection in invoice documents by graph neural networks. In: 2019 International Conference on Document Analysis and Recognition (ICDAR), pp. 122–127 (2019). https://doi.org/10.1109/ICDAR.2019.00028

48. Rijhwani, S., Anastasopoulos, A., Neubig, G.: OCR post correction for endangered language texts. In: Proceedings of the 2020 Conference on Empirical Methods in Natural Language Processing (EMNLP), pp. 5931–5942. Association for Computational Linguistics, November 2020. https://doi.org/10.18653/v1/2020.emnlp-main.478. https://aclanthology.org/2020.emnlp-main.478

49. Schaefer, R., Neudecker, C.: A two-step approach for automatic OCR postcorrection. In: Proceedings of the The 4th Joint SIGHUM Workshop on Computational Linguistics for Cultural Heritage, Social Sciences, Humanities and Literature, pp. 52–57. International Committee on Computational Linguistics, December 2020. https://aclanthology.org/2020.latechclfl-1.6

50. Shi, B., Bai, X., Yao, C.: An end-to-end trainable neural network for image-based sequence recognition and its application to scene text recognition. IEEE Trans. Pattern Anal. Mach. Intell. **39**, 2298–2304 (2017)

51. Shi, B., Wang, X., Lyu, P., Yao, C., Bai, X.: Robust scene text recognition with automatic rectification. In: 2016 IEEE Conference on Computer Vision and Pattern Recognition (CVPR), pp. 4168–4176 (2016). https://doi.org/10.1109/CVPR.2016.452

52. Taghva, K., Beckley, R., Coombs, J.: The effects of OCR error on the extraction of private information. In: Bunke, H., Spitz, A.L. (eds.) DAS 2006. LNCS, vol. 3872, pp. 348–357. Springer, Heidelberg (2006). https://doi.org/10.1007/11669487_31

53. Tan, M., Le, Q.: Efficientnetv2: smaller models and faster training. In: Meila, M., Zhang, T. (eds.) Proceedings of the 38th International Conference on Machine Learning. Proceedings of Machine Learning Research, 18–24 July 2021, vol. 139, pp. 10096–10106. PMLR (2021). https://proceedings.mlr.press/v139/tan21a.html

54. Tian, Z., Huang, W., He, T., He, P., Qiao, Y.: Detecting text in natural image with connectionist text proposal network. In: Leibe, B., Matas, J., Sebe, N., Welling, M. (eds.) ECCV 2016. LNCS, vol. 9912, pp. 56–72. Springer, Cham (2016). https://doi.org/10.1007/978-3-319-46484-8_4

55. Tito, R., Mathew, M., Jawahar, C.V., Valveny, E., Karatzas, D.: ICDAR 2021 competition on document visual question answering. In: Lladós, J., Lopresti, D., Uchida, S. (eds.) ICDAR 2021. LNCS, vol. 12824, pp. 635–649. Springer, Cham (2021). https://doi.org/10.1007/978-3-030-86337-1_42

56. Vaswani, A., et al.: Attention is all you need. In: Guyon, I., et al. (eds.) Advances in Neural Information Processing Systems, vol. 30. Curran Associates, Inc. (2017). https://proceedings.neurips.cc/paper/2017/file/3f5ee243547dee91fbd053c1c4a845aa-Paper.pdf

57. Wang, J., Hu, X.: Gated recurrent convolution neural network for OCR. In: Guyon, I., et al. (eds.) Advances in Neural Information Processing Systems, vol. 30. Curran Associates, Inc. (2017). https://proceedings.neurips.cc/paper/2017/file/c24cd76e1ce41366a4bbe8a49b02a028-Paper.pdf

58. Wang, S., Li, B., Khabsa, M., Fang, H., Ma, H.: Linformer: self-attention with linear complexity. arXiv preprint arXiv:2006.04768 (2020)

59. Williams, R.J., Zipser, D.: A learning algorithm for continually running fully recurrent neural networks. Neural Comput. **1**(2), 270–280 (1989)

60. Xu, Y., et al.: LayoutLMv2: multi-modal pre-training for visually-rich document understanding. In: Proceedings of the 59th Annual Meeting of the Association for Computational Linguistics and the 11th International Joint Conference on Natural Language Processing (Volume 1: Long Papers), pp. 2579–2591. Association for Computational Linguistics, August 2021. https://doi.org/10.18653/v1/2021.acl-long.201. https://aclanthology.org/2021.acl-long.201

61. Xu, Y., Li, M., Cui, L., Huang, S., Wei, F., Zhou, M.: Layoutlm: pre-training of text and layout for document image understanding. In: Proceedings of the 26th ACM SIGKDD International Conference on Knowledge Discovery & Data Mining, KDD 2020, pp. 1192–1200. Association for Computing Machinery, New York (2020). https://doi.org/10.1145/3394486.3403172

62. Xu, Y., et al.: Layoutxlm: multimodal pre-training for multilingual visually-rich document understanding. arXiv preprint arXiv:2104.08836 (2021)

63. Yim, M., Kim, Y., Cho, H.-C., Park, S.: SynthTIGER: synthetic text image GEneratoR towards better text recognition models. In: Lladós, J., Lopresti, D., Uchida, S. (eds.) ICDAR 2021. LNCS, vol. 12824, pp. 109–124. Springer, Cham (2021). https://doi.org/10.1007/978-3-030-86337-1_8

64. Zhang, K., Shasha, D.: Simple fast algorithms for the editing distance between trees and related problems. SIAM J. Comput. **18**, 1245–1262 (1989). https://doi.org/10.1137/0218082

65. Zhang, Z., Zhang, C., Shen, W., Yao, C., Liu, W., Bai, X.: Multi-oriented text detection with fully convolutional networks. In: 2016 IEEE Conference on Computer Vision and Pattern Recognition (CVPR), pp. 4159–4167 (2016). https://doi.org/10.1109/CVPR.2016.451

66. Zhong, X., ShafieiBavani, E., Jimeno Yepes, A.: Image-based table recognition: data, model, and evaluation. In: Vedaldi, A., Bischof, H., Brox, T., Frahm, J.-M. (eds.) ECCV 2020. LNCS, vol. 12366, pp. 564–580. Springer, Cham (2020). https://doi.org/10.1007/978-3-030-58589-1_34

CAR: Class-Aware Regularizations for Semantic Segmentation

Ye Huang[1], Di Kang[2], Liang Chen[3], Xuefei Zhe[2], Wenjing Jia[1],
Linchao Bao[2], and Xiangjian He[4(✉)]

[1] University of Technology Sydney, Ultimo, Australia
[2] Tencent AI Lab, Shenzhen, China
[3] Fujian Normal University, Fuzhou, China
[4] University of Nottingham Ningbo China, Ningbo, China
xiangjian.he@gmail.com

Abstract. Recent segmentation methods, such as OCR and CPNet, utilizing "class level" information in addition to pixel features, have achieved notable success for boosting the accuracy of existing network modules. However, the extracted class-level information was simply concatenated to pixel features, without explicitly being exploited for better pixel representation learning. Moreover, these approaches learn soft class centers based on coarse mask prediction, which is prone to error accumulation. In this paper, aiming to use class level information more effectively, we propose a universal Class-Aware Regularization (CAR) approach to optimize the intra-class variance and inter-class distance during feature learning, motivated by the fact that humans can recognize an object by itself no matter which other objects it appears with. Three novel loss functions are proposed. The first loss function encourages more compact class representations within each class, the second directly maximizes the distance between different class centers, and the third further pushes the distance between inter-class centers and pixels. Furthermore, the class center in our approach is directly generated from ground truth instead of from the error-prone coarse prediction. Our method can be easily applied to most existing segmentation models during training, including OCR and CPNet, and can largely improve their accuracy at no additional inference overhead. Extensive experiments and ablation studies conducted on multiple benchmark datasets demonstrate that the proposed CAR can boost the accuracy of all baseline models by up to 2.23% mIOU with superior generalization ability. The complete code is available at https://github.com/edwardyehuang/CAR.

Keywords: Class-aware regularizations · Semantic segmentation

Supplementary Information The online version contains supplementary material available at https://doi.org/10.1007/978-3-031-19815-1_30.

© The Author(s), under exclusive license to Springer Nature Switzerland AG 2022
S. Avidan et al. (Eds.): ECCV 2022, LNCS 13688, pp. 518–534, 2022.
https://doi.org/10.1007/978-3-031-19815-1_30

1   Introduction

Semantic segmentation, which assigns a class label for each pixel in an image, is a fundamental task in computer vision. It has been widely used in many real-world scenarios that require the results of scene parsing for further processing, *e.g.*, image editing, autopilot, etc. It also benefits many other computer vision tasks such as object detection and depth estimation.

After the early work FCN [15] which used fully convolutional networks to make the dense per-pixel segmentation task more efficient, many works [2,34] have been proposed which have greatly advanced the segmentation accuracy on various benchmark datasets. Among these methods, many of them have focused on better fusing spatial domain context information to obtain more powerful feature representations (termed *pixel features* in this work) for the final per-pixel classification. For example, VGG [20] utilized large square context information by successfully training a very deep network, and DeepLab [2] and PSPNet [34] utilized multi-scale features with the ASPP and PPM modules.

Recently, methods based on dot-product self-attention (SA) have become very popular since they can easily capture the long-range relationship between pixels [6,7,11,19,21,25,30,33,35]. SA aggregates information dynamically (by different attention maps for different inputs) and selectively (using weighted averaging spatial features according to their similarity scores). Using multi-scale and self-attention techniques during spatial information aggregation has worked very well (*e.g.*, 80% mIOU on Cityscapes [16] (single-scale w/o flipping)).

As complements to the above methods, many recent works have proposed various modules to utilize class-level contextual information. The class-level information is often represented by the class center/context prior which are the mean features of each class in the images. OCR [29] and ACFNet [31] extract "soft" class centers according to the predicted coarse segmentation mask by using the weighted sum. CPNet [28] proposed a context prior map/affinity map, which indicates if two spatial locations belong to the same class, and used this predicted context prior map for feature aggregation. However, they [28,29,31] simply concatenated these class-level features with the original pixel features for the final classification.

In this paper, we also focus on utilizing class level information. Instead of focusing on how to better extract class-level features like the existing methods [28,29,31], we use the simple, but accurate, average feature according to the GT mask, and focus on maximizing the inter-class distance during feature learning. This is because it mirrors how humans can robustly recognize an object by itself no matter what other objects it appears with.

Learning more separable features makes the features of a class less dependent upon other classes, resulting in improved generalization ability, especially when the training set contains only limited and biased class combinations (*e.g.*, cows and grass, boats and beach). Figure 1 illustrates an example of such a problem, where the classification of dog and sheep depends on the classification of grass class, and has been mis-classified as cow. In comparison, networks trained with our proposed CAR successfully generalize to these unseen class combinations.

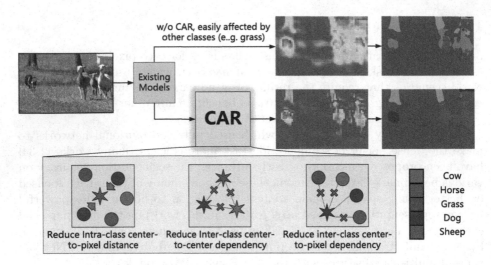

Fig. 1. The concept of the proposed CAR. Our CAR optimizes existing models with three regularization targets: 1) reducing pixels' intra-class distance, 2) reducing inter-class center-to-center dependency, and 3) reducing pixels' inter-class dependency. As highlighted in this example (indicated with a red dot in the image), with our CAR, the grass class does not affect the classification of dog/sheep as much as before, and hence successfully avoids previous (w/o CAR) mis-classification.

To better achieve this goal, we propose CAR, a class-aware regularizations module, that optimizes the class center (intra-class) and inter-class dependencies during feature learning. Three loss functions are devised: the first encourages more compact class representations within each class, and the other two directly maximize the distance between different classes. Specifically, an intra-class center-to-pixel loss (termed as "intra-c2p", Eq. (3)) is first devised to produce more compact representation within a class by minimizing the distance between all pixels and their class center. In our work, a class center is calculated as the averaged feature of all pixels belonging to the same class according to the GT mask. More compact intra-class representations leave a relatively large margin between classes, thus contributing to more separable representations. Then, an inter-class center-to-center loss ("inter-c2c", Eq. (6)) is devised to maximize the distance between any two different class centers. This inter-class center-to-center loss alone does not necessarily produce separable representations for every individual pixels. Therefore, a third inter-class center-to-pixel loss ("inter-c2p", Eq. (13)) is proposed to enlarge the distance between every class center and all pixels that do not belong to the class.

In summary, our contributions in this work are:

1. We propose a universal class-aware regularization module that can be integrated into various segmentation models to largely improve the accuracy.

2. We devise three novel regularization terms to achieve more separable and less class-dependent feature representations by minimizing the intra-class variance and maximizing the inter-class distance.
3. We calculate the class centers directly from ground truth during training, thus avoiding the error accumulation issue of the existing methods and introducing no computational overhead during inference.
4. We provide image-level feature-similarity heatmaps to visualize the learned inter-class features with our CAR are indeed less related to each other.

2   Related Work

Self-Attention. Dot-product self-attention proposed in [22,25] has been widely used in semantic segmentation [7,30,33,35]. Specifically, self-attention determines the similarity between a pixel with every other pixel in the feature map by calculating their dot product, followed by softmax normalization. With this attention map, the feature representation of a given pixel is enhanced by aggregating features from the whole feature map weighted by the aforementioned attention value, thus easily taking long-range relationship into consideration and yielding boosted performance. In self-attention, in order to achieve correct pixel classification, the representation of pixels belonging to the same class should be similar to gain greater weights in the final representation augmentation.

Class Center. In 2019 [29,31], the concept of *class center* was introduced to describe the overall representation of each class from the categorical context perspective. In these approaches, the center representation of each class was determined by calculating the dot product of the feature map and the coarse prediction (*i.e.*, weighted average) from an auxiliary task branch, supervised by the ground truth [34]. After that, those intra-class centers are assigned to the corresponding pixels on feature map. Furthermore, in 2020 [28], a learnable kernel and one-hot ground truth were used to separate the intra-class center from inter-class center, and then concatenated with the original feature representation.

All of these works [28,29,31] have focused on extracting the intra (inter) class centers, but they then simply concatenated the resultant class centers with the original pixel representations to perform the final logits. We argue that the categorical context information can be utilized in a more effective way so as to reduce the inter-class dependency.

To this end, we propose a CAR approach, where the extracted class center is used to directly regularize the feature extraction process so as to boost the differentiability of the learned feature representations (see Fig. 1) and reduce their dependency on other classes. Figure 2 contrasts the two different designs. More details of the proposed CAR are provided in Sect. 3.

Inter-Class Reasoning. Recently, [5,13] studied the class dependency as a dataset prior and demonstrated that inter-class reasoning could improve the classification performance. For example, a car usually does not appear in the sky, and therefore the classification of sky can help reduce the chance of misclassifying an object in the sky as a car. However, due to the limited training

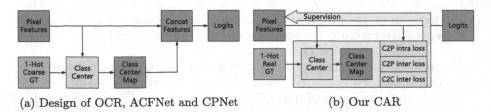

(a) Design of OCR, ACFNet and CPNet   (b) Our CAR

Fig. 2. The difference between the proposed CAR and previous methods that use class-level information. Previous models focus on extracting class center while using simple concatenation of the original pixel feature and the class/context feature for later classification. In contrast, our CAR uses direct supervision related to class center as regularization during training, resulting in small intra-class variance and low inter-class dependency. See Fig. 1 and Sect. 3 for details.

data, such class-dependency prior may also contain bias, especially when the desired class relation rarely appears in the training set.

Figure 1 shows such an example. In the training set, cow and grass are dependent on each other. However, as shown in this example, when there is a dog or sheep standing on the grass, the class dependency learned from the limited training data may result in errors and predict the target into a class that appears more often in the training data, *i.e.*, cow in this case. In our CAR, we design inter-class and intra-class loss functions to reduce such inter-class dependency and achieve more robust segmentation results.

3   Methodology

3.1   Extracting Class Centers from Ground Truth

Denote a feature map and its corresponding resized one-hot encoded ground-truth mask as $\mathbf{X} \in \mathbb{R}^{H \times W \times C1}$ and $\mathbf{Y} \in \mathbb{R}^{H \times W \times N_{\text{class}}}$, respectively. We first get the spatially flattened class mask $\mathbf{Y}_{\text{flat}} \in \mathbb{R}^{HW \times N_{\text{class}}}$ and flattened feature map $\mathbf{X}_{\text{flat}} \in \mathbb{R}^{HW \times C}$. Then, the class center[2], which is the average features of all pixel features of a class, can be calculated by:

$$\boldsymbol{\mu}_{image} = \frac{\mathbf{Y}_{\text{flat}}^{T} \cdot \mathbf{X}_{\text{flat}}}{\mathbf{N}_{\text{non-zero}}} \in \mathbb{R}^{N_{\text{class}} \times C}, \tag{1}$$

where $\mathbf{N}_{\text{non-zero}}$ denotes the number of non-zero values in the corresponding map of the ground-truth mask $\mathbf{Y}$. In our experiments, to alleviate the negative impact of noisy images, we calculate the class centers using all the training images in a batch, and denote them as $\boldsymbol{\mu}_{\text{batch}}$[3].

---

[1] H, W and C denote images' height and width, and number of channels, respectively.
[2] It is termed as *class center* in [31] and *object region representations* in [29].
[3] We use $\boldsymbol{\mu}$ and omit the subscript *batch* for clarity.

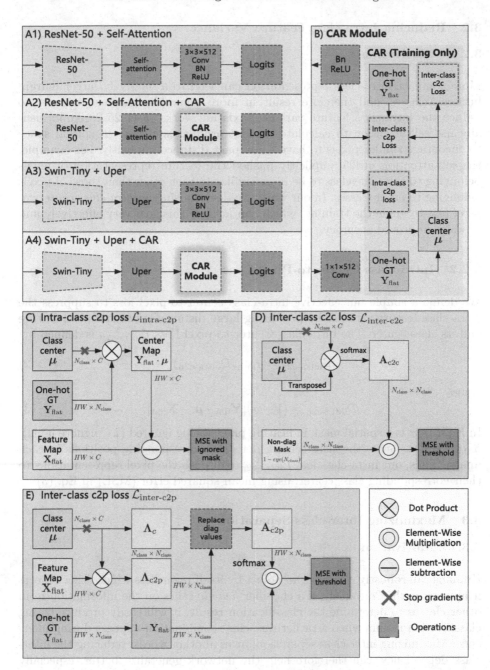

Fig. 3. The proposed CAR approach. CAR can be inserted into various segmentation models, right before the logit prediction module (A1-A4). CAR contains three regularization terms, including (C) intra-class center-to-center loss $\mathcal{L}_{\text{intra-c2p}}$ (Sect. 3.2.2), (D) inter-class center-to-center loss $\mathcal{L}_{\text{inter-c2c}}$ (Sect. 3.3.2), and (E) inter-class center-to-pixel loss $\mathcal{L}_{\text{inter-c2p}}$ (Sect. 3.3.3).

3.2   Reducing Intra-class Feature Variance

3.2.1   Motivation

More compact intra-class representation can lead to a relatively larger margin between classes, and therefore result in more separable features. In order to reduce the intra-class feature variance, existing works [7,11,25,28,30,35] usually use self-attention to calculate the dot-product similarity in spatial space to encourage similar pixels to have a compact distance implicitly. For example, the self-attention in [25] implicitly pushed the feature representation of pixels belonging to the same class to be more similar to each other than those of pixels belonging to other classes. In our work, we devise a simple *intra-class center-to-pixel loss* to guide the training, which can achieve this goal very effectively and produce improved accuracy.

3.2.2   Intra-class Center-to-Pixel Loss

We define a simple but effective intra-class center-to-pixel loss to suppress the intra-class feature variance by penalizing large distance between a pixel feature and its class center. The Intra-class Center-to-pixel Loss $\mathcal{L}_{\text{intra-c2p}}$ is defined by:

$$\mathcal{L}_{\text{intra-c2p}} = f_{\text{mse}}(\mathcal{D}_{\text{intra-c2p}}), \tag{2}$$

where

$$\mathcal{D}_{\text{intra-c2p}} = (1 - \sigma)|\mathbf{Y}_{\text{flat}} \cdot \boldsymbol{\mu} - \mathbf{X}_{\text{flat}}|. \tag{3}$$

In Eq. (3), σ is a spatial mask indicating pixels being ignored (*i.e.*, ignore label), $\mathbf{Y}_{\text{flat}} \cdot \boldsymbol{\mu}$ distributes the class centers $\boldsymbol{\mu}$ to the corresponding positions in each image. Thus, our intra-class loss $\mathcal{L}_{\text{intra-c2p}}$ will push the pixel representations to their corresponding class center, using mean squared error (MSE) in Eq. (3).

3.3   Maximizing Inter-class Separation

3.3.1   Motivation

Humans can robustly recognize an object by itself regardless which other objects it appears with. Conversely, if a classifier *heavily* relies on the information from other classes to determine the classification result, it will easily produce wrong classification results when a rather rare class combination appears during inference. Maximizing inter-class separation, or in another words, reducing the inter-class dependency, can therefore help the network generalize better, especially when the training set is small or is biased. As shown in Fig. 1, the dog and sheep are mis-classified as the cow because cow and grass appear together more often in the training set. To improve the robustness of the model, we propose to reduce this inter-class dependency. To this end, the following two loss functions are defined.

3.3.2   Inter-class Center-to-Center Loss

The first loss function is to maximize the distance between any two different class centers. Inspired by the center loss used in face recognition [26], we propose to reduce the similarity between class centers μ, which are the averaged features of each class calculated according to the GT mask. The *inter-class relation* is defined by the dot-product similarity [22] between any two classes as:

$$\mathbf{A}_{c2c} = \text{softmax}(\frac{\mu^T \cdot \mu}{\sqrt{C}}), \quad \mathbf{A}_{c2c} \in \mathbb{R}^{N_{class} \times N_{class}}. \tag{4}$$

Moreover, since we only need to constrain the inter-class distance, only the non-diagonal elements are retained for the later loss calculation as:

$$\mathbf{D}_{\text{inter-c2c}} = \Big(1 - eye(N_{class})\Big)\mathbf{A}_{c2c}. \tag{5}$$

We only penalize larger similarity values between any two different classes than a pre-defined threshold $\frac{\epsilon_0}{N_{class}-1}$, *i.e.*,

$$\mathcal{D}_{\text{inter-c2c}} = f_{\text{sum}}\Big(\max(\mathbf{D}_{\text{inter-c2c}} - \frac{\epsilon_0}{N_{class}-1}, 0)\Big). \tag{6}$$

Thus, the Inter-class Center-to-center Loss $\mathcal{L}_{\text{inter-c2c}}$ is defined by:

$$\mathcal{L}_{\text{inter-c2c}} = f_{\text{mse}}(\mathcal{D}_{\text{inter-c2c}}). \tag{7}$$

Here, a small margin is used in consideration of the feature space size and the mislabeled ground truth.

3.3.3   Inter-class Center-to-Pixel Loss

Maximizing only the distances between class centers does not necessarily result in separable representation for every individual pixels. We further maximize the distance between a class center and any pixel that does not belong to this class. More concretely, we first compute the center-to-pixel dot product as:

$$\mathbf{\Lambda}_{c2p} = \mu^T \cdot \mathbf{X}_{\text{flat}}, \quad \mathbf{\Lambda}_{c2p} \in \mathbb{R}^{HW \times N_{class}}. \tag{8}$$

Ideally, with the previous loss $\mathcal{L}_{\text{inter-c2c}}$, the features of all pixels belonging to the same class should be equal to that of the class center. Therefore, we replace the intra-class dot product with its ideal value, namely using the class center μ for calculating the intra-class dot product as:

$$\mathbf{\Lambda}_c = diag(\mu^T \cdot \mu), \tag{9}$$

and the replacement effect is achieved by using masks as:

$$\mathbf{\Lambda}' = \mathbf{\Lambda}_{c2p}(1 - \mathbf{Y}_{\text{flat}}) + \mathbf{\Lambda}_c. \tag{10}$$

This updated dot product $\mathbf{\Lambda}'$ is then used to calculate similarity across class axis with a softmax as:

$$\mathbf{A}_{\text{c2p}} = \text{softmax}(\mathbf{\Lambda}'), \quad \mathbf{A}_{\text{c2p}} \in \mathbb{R}^{HW \times N_{\text{class}}}. \quad (11)$$

Similar to the calculation of $\mathcal{L}_{\text{inter-c2c}}$ in the previous subsection, we have

$$\mathbf{D}_{\text{inter-c2p}} = (1 - \mathbf{Y}_{\text{flat}})\mathbf{A}_{\text{c2p}}, \quad (12)$$

$$\mathcal{D}_{\text{inter-c2p}} = f_{\text{sum}}\left(\max(\mathbf{D}_{\text{inter-c2p}} - \frac{\epsilon_1}{N_{\text{class}} - 1}, 0)\right). \quad (13)$$

Thus, the Inter-class Center-to-pixel Loss $\mathcal{L}_{\text{inter-c2p}}$ is defined by:

$$\mathcal{L}_{\text{inter-c2p}} = f_{\text{mse}}(\mathcal{D}_{\text{inter-c2p}}). \quad (14)$$

3.4   Differences with OCR, ACFNet, CPNet, and CIPC

Methods that are closely related to ours are OCR [29], ACFNet [31] and CPNet [28], which all focus on better utilizing class-level features and differ on how to extract the class centers and context features. However, they all use a **simple concatenation** to fuse the original pixel feature and the complementary context feature. For example, OCR and ACFNet first produce a coarse segmentation, which is supervised by the GT mask with a categorical cross-entropy loss, and then use this predicted coarse mask to generate the (soft) class centers by weighted summing all the pixel features. OCR then aggregates these class centers according to their similarity to the original pixel feature termed as "pixel-region relation", resulting in a "contextual feature". Slightly differently from OCR, ACFNet directly uses the probability (from the predicted coarse mask) to aggregate class center, obtaining a similar context feature termed as "attentional class feature". CPNet defines an affinity map, which is a binary map indicating if two spatial locations belong to the same class. Then, they use a sub-network to predict their ideal affinity map and use the soft version affinity map termed as "Context Prior Map" for feature aggregation, obtaining a class feature (center) and a context feature. Note that CPNet concatenates class feature, which is the updated pixel feature, and the context feature.

We also propose to utilize class-level contextual features. Instead of extracting and fusing pixel features with sub-networks, we propose three loss functions to directly regularize training and encourage the learned features to maintain certain desired properties. The approach is simple but more effective thanks to the direct supervision (validated in Table 2). Moreover, our class center estimate is more accurate because we use the GT mask. This strategy largely reduces the complexity of the network and introduces no computational overhead during inference. Furthermore, it is compatible with all existing methods, including OCR, ACFNet and CPNet, demonstrating great generalization capability.

We also notice that Cross-Image Pixel Contrast (CIPC) [24] shares a similar high-level goal as our CAR, *i.e.*, learning more similar representations for pixels belonging to the same class than to a different class. However, the approaches of achieving this goal are very different. CIPC is motivated by contrastive learning while our CAR is motivated by the compositionality of the scene, for better generalization in the cases of rare class combinations. Therefore, CIPC adopts the *one-vs-rest* style InfoNCE loss, including the typical pixel-to-pixel loss and a special pixel-to-center loss. In contrast, **(1)** we propose an additional *center-to-center* loss to regularize the inter-class dependency explicitly and effectively (see Table 1); **(2)** we use *one-vs-one* style inter-class losses while CIPC uses *one-vs-rest* style NCE loss. Compared to our *one-vs-one* loss, using *one-vs-rest* loss for training does not necessarily result in small inter-class similarity between the current class and every individual "other" classes and may increase the inter-class similarity among those "other" classes. **(3)** we leave margins to prevent CAR regularizations, which is not the primary task of pixel classification, from dominating the learning process.

Table 1. Ablation studies of adding CAR to different methods on Pascal Context dataset. All results are obtained with single scale test without flip. "A" means replacing the 3×3 conv with 1×1 conv (detailed in Sect. 4.2.1). CAR improves the performance of different types of backbones (CNN & Transformer) and head blocks (SA & Uper), showing the generalizability of the proposed CAR.

	Methods	$\mathcal{L}_{\text{intra-c2p}}$	$\mathcal{L}_{\text{inter-c2c}}$	$\mathcal{L}_{\text{inter-c2p}}$	A	mIOU (%)
R1	ResNet-50 + Self-Attention [25]	–	–			48.32
R2					✓	48.56
R3	+ CAR	✓				49.17
R4		✓	✓			49.79
R5		✓	✓	✓		50.01
R6		✓			✓	49.62
R7		✓	✓		✓	50.00
R8		✓	✓	✓	✓	**50.50**
S1	Swin-Tiny + UperNet [27]	–	–			49.62
S2					✓	49.82
S3	+ CAR	✓				49.01
S4		✓	✓			50.63
S5		✓	✓	✓		50.26
S6		✓			✓	49.62
S7		✓	✓		✓	50.58
S8		✓	✓	✓	✓	**50.78**

4   Experiments

4.1   Implementation

Training Settings. For both CAR and baselines, we apply the settings common to most works [10,11,32,33,35], including SyncBatchNorm, batch size = 16, weight decay (0.001), 0.01 initial LR, and poly learning decay with SGD during training. In addition, for the CNN backbones (*e.g.*, ResNet), we set *output stride* = 8 (see [3]). Training iteration is set to 30k iterations unless otherwise specified. For the thresholds in Eq. 6 and Eq. 13, we set $\epsilon_0 = 0.5$ and $\epsilon_1 = 0.25$.

Determinism and Reproducibility. Our implementations are based on the latest NVIDIA deterministic framework (2022), which means exactly the same results can be always reproduced with the same hardware and same training settings (including random seed). To demonstrate the effectiveness of our CAR with equal comparisons, we reproduced all the baselines that we compare, all conducted with exactly the same settings unless otherwise specified.

4.2 Experiments on Pascal Context

The Pascal Context [18] dataset is split into 4,998/5,105 for training/test set. We use its 59 semantic classes following the common practice [29,33]. Unless otherwise specified, both baselines and CAR are trained on the training set with 30k iterations. The ablation studies are presented in Sect. 4.2.1.

4.2.1 Ablation Studies on Pascal Context

CAR on ResNet-50 + Self-Attention. We firstly test the CAR with "ResNet-50 + Self-Attention" (w/o image-level block in [33]) to verify the effectiveness of the proposed loss functions, *i.e.*, $\mathcal{L}_{\text{intra-c2p}}$, $\mathcal{L}_{\text{inter-c2c}}$, and $\mathcal{L}_{\text{inter-c2p}}$.

As shown in Table 1, using $\mathcal{L}_{\text{intra-c2p}}$ directly improves 1.30 mIOU (48.32 vs 49.62); Introducing $\mathcal{L}_{\text{inter-c2c}}$ and $\mathcal{L}_{\text{inter-c2p}}$ further improves 0.38 mIOU and 0.50 mIOU; Finally, with all three loss functions, the proposed CAR improves 2.18 mIOU from the regular ResNet-50 + Self-attention (48.32 vs 50.50).

CAR on Swin-Tiny + Uper. "Swin-Tiny + Uper" is a totally different architecture from "ResNet-50 + Self-Attention [25]". Swin [14] is a recent Transformer-based backbone network. Uper [27] is based on the pyramid pooling modules (PPM) [34] and FPN [12], focusing on extracting multi-scale context information. Similarly, as shown in Table 1, after adding CAR, the performance of Swin-Tiny + Uper also increases by 1.16, which shows our CAR can generalize to different architectures well.

The Devil Is In the Architecture's Detail. We find it important to replace the leading 3×3 conv (in the original method) with 1×1 conv (Fig. 3B). For example, $\mathcal{L}_{\text{intra-c2p}}$ and $\mathcal{L}_{\text{inter-c2p}}$ did not improve the performance in Swin-Tiny + Uper (Row S3 vs S1, and S5 vs S4 in Table 1). A possible reason is that the network is trained to maximize the separation between different classes. However, if the two pixels lie on different sides of the segmentation boundary, a 3×3 conv will merge the pixel representations from different classes, making the proposed losses harder to optimize.

To keep simplicity and maximize generalization, we use the same network configurations in our **all** experiments. However, performance may be further improved with some minor dedicated modifications for each baseline when deploying our CAR. For example, decreasing the filter number to 256 for the last conv layer of ResNet-50 + Self-Attention + CAR results in a further improvement to 51.00 mIOU (from 50.50). Replacing the conv layer after PPM (inside Uper block, A3 in Fig. 3) from 3×3 to 1×1 in Swin-Tiny + UperNet boosts Swin (tiny & large) + UperNet + CAR by an extra 0.5–1.0 mIOU. We intentionally did *not* exhaustively search these variants and *not* report these results in any table since they did not generalize.

CAR on Different Baselines. After we have verified the effectiveness of each part of the proposed CAR, we then tested CAR on multiple well-known baselines. All of the baselines were reproduced under similar conditions (see Sect. 4.1). Experimental results shown in Table 2 demonstrate the generalizability of our CAR on different backbones and methods.

Table 2. Ablation studies of adding CAR to different baselines on Pascal Context [18] and COCOStuff-10K [1]. We deterministically reproduced all the baselines with the same settings. All results are single-scale without flipping. CAR works very well in most existing methods. § means reducing the class-level threshold to 0.25 from 0.5. We found it is sensitive for some model variants to handle a large number of class. Affinity loss [28] and Auxiliary loss [34] are applied on CPNet and OCR, respectively, since they highly rely on those losses.

Methods	Backbone	Reference	mIOU(%)	
			Pascal Context	COCO-Stuff10K
FCN [15]	ResNet-50 [8]	CVPR2015	47.72	34.10
FCN + CAR	ResNet-50 [8]		48.40(+0.68)	34.91(+0.81)§
FCN [15]	ResNet-101 [8]	CVPR2015	50.93	35.93
FCN + CAR	ResNet-101 [8]		51.39(+0.49)	36.88(+0.95)§
DeepLabV3 [4]	ResNet-50 [8]	ECCV2018	48.59	34.96
DeepLabV3 + CAR	ResNet-50 [8]		49.53(+0.94)	35.13(+0.17)
DeepLabV3 [4]	ResNet-101 [8]	ECCV2018	51.69	36.92
DeepLabV3 + CAR	ResNet-101 [8]		52.58(+0.89)	37.39(+0.47)
Self-Attention [25]	ResNet-50 [8]	CVPR2018	48.32	34.35
Self-Attention + CAR	ResNet-50 [8]		50.50(+2.18)	36.58(+2.23)§
Self-Attention [25]	ResNet-101 [8]	CVPR2018	51.59	36.53
Self-Attention + CAR	ResNet-101 [8]		52.49(+0.9)	38.15(+1.62)
CCNet [10]	ResNet-50 [8]	ICCV2019	49.15	35.10
CCNet + CAR	ResNet-50 [8]		49.56(+0.41)	36.39(+1.29)
CCNet [10]	ResNet-101 [8]	ICCV2019	51.41	36.88
CCNet + CAR	ResNet-101 [8]		51.97(+0.56)	37.56(+0.68)
DANet [7]	ResNet-101 [8]	CVPR2019	51.45	35.80
DANet + CAR	ResNet-101 [8]		52.57(+1.12)	37.47(+1.67)
CPNet [28]	ResNet-101 [8]	CVPR2020	51.29	36.92
CPNet + CAR	ResNet-101 [8]		51.98(+0.69)	37.12(+0.20)§
OCR [29]	HRNet-W48 [23]	ECCV2020	54.37	38.22
OCR + CAR	HRNet-W48 [23]		54.99(+0.62)	39.53(+1.31)
UperNet [27]	Swin-Tiny [14]	ICCV2021	49.62	36.07
UperNet + CAR	Swin-Tiny [14]		50.78(+1.16)	36.63(+0.56)§
UperNet [27]	Swin-Large [14]	ICCV2021	57.48	44.25
UperNet + CAR	Swin-Large [14]		58.97(+1.49)	44.88(+0.63)
CAA [9]	EfficientNet-B5 [17]	AAAI2022	57.79	43.40
CAA + CAR	EfficientNet-B5 [17]		58.96(+1.17)	43.93(+0.53)

Visualization of Class Dependency Maps. In Fig. 4, we present the class dependency maps calculated on the complete Pascal Context *test* set, where every pixel stores the dot-product similarities between every two class centers. The maps indicate the inter-class dependency obtained with the standard ResNet-50 + Self-Attention and Swin-Tiny + UperNet, and the effect of applying our CAR. A hotter color means that the class has higher dependency on the corresponding class, and vice versa. According to Fig. 4 a1–a2, we can easily observe that the inter-class dependency has been significantly reduced with CAR on ResNet50 + Self-Attention. Figure 4 b1-b2 show a similar trend when tested with different backbones and head blocks. This partially explains the reason why baselines with CAR generalize better on rarely seen class combinations (Figs. 1 and 5). Interestingly, we find that the class-dependency issue is more serious in Swin-Tiny + Uper, but our CAR can still reduce its dependency level significantly.

Visualization of Pixel-relation Maps. In Fig. 5, we visualize the pixel-to-pixel relation energy map, based on the dot-product similarity between a red-dot marked pixel and other pixels, as well as the predicted results for different methods, for comparison. Examples are from Pascal Context test set. As we can see, with CAR supervision, the existing models focus better on objects themselves rather than other objects. Therefore, this reduces the possibility of the classification errors because of the class-dependency bias.

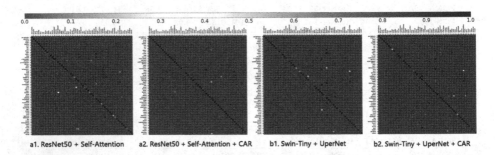

Fig. 4. Class dependency maps generated on Pascal Context test set. One may zoom in to see class names. A hotter color means that the class has higher dependency to the corresponding class, and vice versa. It is obvious that our CAR reduces the inter-class dependency, thus providing better generalizability (see Figs. 1 and 5).

4.3   Experiments on COCOStuff-10K

COCOStuff-10K dataset [1] is widely used for evaluating the robustness of semantic segmentation models [11,29]. The COCOStuff-10k dataset is a very challenging dataset containing 171 labeled classes and 9000/1000 images for training/test. As shown in Table 2, all of the tested baselines gain performance

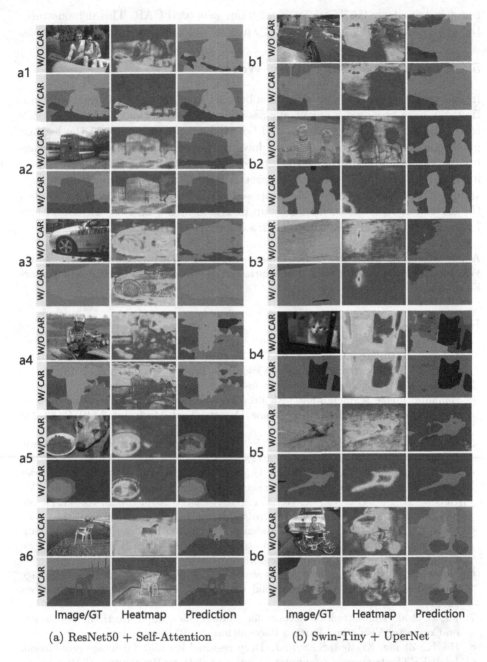

(a) ResNet50 + Self-Attention   (b) Swin-Tiny + UperNet

Fig. 5. Visualization of the feature similarity between a given pixel (marked with a red dot in the image) and all pixels, as well as the segmentation results on Pascal Context test set. A hotter color denotes larger similarity value. Apparently, our CAR reduces the inter-class dependency and exhibits better generalization ability, where energies are better restrained in the intra-class pixels. (Color figure online)

boost ranging from 0.17% to 2.23% with our proposed CAR. This demonstrates the generalization ability of our CAR when handling a large number of classes.

5   Conclusions and Future Work

In this paper, we have aimed to make a better use of class level context information. We have proposed a universal class-aware regularizations (CAR) approach to regularize the training process and boost the differentiability of the learned pixel representations. To this end, we have proposed to minimize the intra-class feature variance and maximize the inter-class separation simultaneously. Experiments conducted on benchmark datasets with extensive ablation studies have validated the effectiveness of the proposed CAR approach, which has boosted the existing models' performance by up to 2.18% mIOU on Pascal Context and 2.23% on COCOStuff-10k with no extra inference overhead.

Acknowledgement. This research depends on the NVIDIA determinism framework. We appreciate the support from @duncanriach and @reedwm at NVIDIA and Tensor-Flow team.

References

1. Caesar, H., Uijlings, J., Ferrari, V.: COCO-stuff: thing and stuff classes in context. In: IEEE Conference on Computer Vision and Pattern Recognition (2018)
2. Chen, L.C., Papandreou, G., Kokkinos, I., Murphy, K., Yuille, A.L.: Deeplab: semantic image segmentation with deep convolutional nets, atrous convolution, and fully connected CRFs. IEEE Trans. Pattern Anal. Mach. Intell. **40**(4), 83–848 (2017)
3. Chen, L.C., Papandreou, G., Schroff, F., Adam, H.: Rethinking atrous convolution for semantic image segmentation (2017)
4. Chen, L.-C., Zhu, Y., Papandreou, G., Schroff, F., Adam, H.: Encoder-decoder with atrous separable convolution for semantic image segmentation. In: Ferrari, V., Hebert, M., Sminchisescu, C., Weiss, Y. (eds.) ECCV 2018. LNCS, vol. 11211, pp. 833–851. Springer, Cham (2018). https://doi.org/10.1007/978-3-030-01234-2_49
5. Choi, S., Kim, J.T., Choo, J.: Cars can't fly up in the sky: improving urban-scene segmentation via height-driven attention networks. In: IEEE Conference on Computer Vision and Pattern Recognition (2020)
6. Dosovitskiy, A., et al.: An image is worth 16x16 words: transformers for image recognition at scale. In: International Conference on Learning Representations (2021)
7. Fu, J., et al.: Dual attention network for scene segmentation. In: IEEE Conference on Computer Vision and Pattern Recognition (2019)
8. He, K., Zhang, X., Ren, S., Sun, J.: Deep residual learning for image recognition. In: IEEE Conference on Computer Vision and Pattern Recognition (2016)
9. Huang, Y., Kang, D., Jia, W., He, X., liu, L.: Channelized axial attention - considering channel relation within spatial attention for semantic segmentation. In: AAAI (2022)
10. Huang, Z., et al.: CCNet: criss-cross attention for semantic segmentation. IEEE Trans. Pattern Anal. Mach. Intell. (2020)

11. Li, X., Zhong, Z., Wu, J., Yang, Y., Lin, Z., Liu, H.: Expectation-maximization attention networks for semantic segmentation. In: International Conference on Computer Vision (2019)
12. Lin, T.Y., Dollá, P., Girshick, R., He, K., Hariharan, B., Belongie, S.: Feature pyramid networks for object detection. In: IEEE Conference on Computer Vision and Pattern Recognition (2017)
13. Liu, M., Schonfeld, D., Tang, W.: Exploit visual dependency relations for semantic segmentation. In: IEEE Conference on Computer Vision and Pattern Recognition (2021)
14. Liu, Z., et al.: Swin transformer: Hierarchical vision transformer using shifted windows. In: ICCV (2021)
15. Long, J., Shelhamer, E., Darrell, T.: Fully convolutional networks for semantic segmentation. In: IEEE Conference on Computer Vision and Pattern Recognition (2015)
16. Marius, C., et al.: The cityscapes dataset for semantic urban scene understanding. In: IEEE Conference on Computer Vision and Pattern Recognition (2016)
17. Mingxing, T., Quoc, L.: Efficientnet: rethinking model scaling for convolutional neural networks. In: International Conference on Machine Learning (2019)
18. Mottaghi, R., et al.: The role of context for object detection and semantic segmentation in the wild. In: IEEE Conference on Computer Vision and Pattern Recognition (2014)
19. Ranftl, R., Bochkovskiy, A., Koltun, V.: Vision transformers for dense prediction. In: ICCV (2021)
20. Simonyan, K., Zisserman, A.: Very deep convolutional networks for large-scale image recognition. In: International Conference on Learning Representations (2015)
21. Sixiao, Z., et al.: Rethinking semantic segmentation from a sequence-to-sequence perspective with transformers. In: IEEE Conference on Computer Vision and Pattern Recognition (2021)
22. Vaswani, A., et al.: Attention is all you need. In: Conference on Neural Information Processing Systems (2017)
23. Wang, J., et al.: Deep high-resolution representation learning for visual recognition. IEEE Trans. Pattern Anal. Mach. Intell. **43**, 3349–3364 (2020)
24. Wang, W., Zhou, T., Yu, F., Dai, J., Konukoglu, E., Van Gool, L.: Exploring cross-image pixel contrast for semantic segmentation. In: ICCV, pp. 7303–7313 (2021)
25. Wang, X., Girshick, R., Gupta, A., He, K.: Non-local neural networks. In: IEEE Conference on Computer Vision and Pattern Recognition (2018)
26. Chen, L.-C., Zhu, Y., Papandreou, G., Schroff, F., Adam, H.: Encoder-decoder with atrous separable convolution for semantic image segmentation. In: Ferrari, V., Hebert, M., Sminchisescu, C., Weiss, Y. (eds.) ECCV 2018. LNCS, vol. 11211, pp. 833–851. Springer, Cham (2018). https://doi.org/10.1007/978-3-030-01234-2_49
27. Xiao, T., Liu, Y., Zhou, B., Jiang, Y., Sun, J.: Unified perceptual parsing for scene understanding. In: Ferrari, V., Hebert, M., Sminchisescu, C., Weiss, Y. (eds.) ECCV 2018. LNCS, vol. 11209, pp. 432–448. Springer, Cham (2018). https://doi.org/10.1007/978-3-030-01228-1_26
28. Yu, C., Wang, J., Gao, C., Yu, G., Shen, C., Sang, N.: Context prior for scene segmentation. In: IEEE Conference on Computer Vision and Pattern Recognition (2020)
29. Yuan, Y., Chen, X., Wang, J.: Object-contextual representations for semantic segmentation. In: Vedaldi, A., Bischof, H., Brox, T., Frahm, J.-M. (eds.) ECCV 2020.

LNCS, vol. 12351, pp. 173–190. Springer, Cham (2020). https://doi.org/10.1007/978-3-030-58539-6_11

30. Yuan, Y., Huang, L., Guo, J., Zhang, C., Chen, X., Wang, J.: OCNet: object context for semantic segmentation. Int. J. Comput. Vis. **129**(8), 2375–2398 (2021). https://doi.org/10.1007/s11263-021-01465-9

31. Zhang, F., et al.: ACFNet: attentional class feature network for semantic segmentation. In: International Conference on Computer Vision (2019)

32. Zhang, H., et al.: Context encoding for semantic segmentation. In: IEEE Conference on Computer Vision and Pattern Recognition (2018)

33. Zhang, H., Zhan, H., Wang, C., Xie, J.: Semantic correlation promoted shape-variant context for segmentation. In: IEEE Conference on Computer Vision and Pattern Recognition (2019)

34. Zhao, H., Shi, J., Qi, X., Wang, X., Jia, J.: Pyramid scene parsing network. In: IEEE Conference on Computer Vision and Pattern Recognition (2017)

35. Zhu, Z., Xu, M., Bai, S., Huang, T., Bai, X.: Asymmetric non-local neural networks for semantic segmentation. In: International Conference on Computer Vision (2019)

Style-Hallucinated Dual Consistency Learning for Domain Generalized Semantic Segmentation

Yuyang Zhao[1(✉)], Zhun Zhong[2], Na Zhao[1], Nicu Sebe[2], and Gim Hee Lee[1]

[1] National University of Singapore, Singapore, Singapore
yuyang.zhao@u.nus.edu
[2] University of Trento, Trento, Italy
https://github.com/HeliosZhao/SHADE

Abstract. In this paper, we study the task of synthetic-to-real domain generalized semantic segmentation, which aims to learn a model that is robust to unseen real-world scenes using only synthetic data. The large domain shift between synthetic and real-world data, including the limited source environmental variations and the large distribution gap between synthetic and real-world data, significantly hinders the model performance on unseen real-world scenes. In this work, we propose the **Style-HA**llucinated **D**ual consist**E**ncy learning (**SHADE**) framework to handle such domain shift. Specifically, SHADE is constructed based on two consistency constraints, Style Consistency (SC) and Retrospection Consistency (RC). SC enriches the source situations and encourages the model to learn consistent representation across style-diversified samples. RC leverages real-world knowledge to prevent the model from overfitting to synthetic data and thus largely keeps the representation consistent between the synthetic and real-world models. Furthermore, we present a novel style hallucination module (SHM) to generate style-diversified samples that are essential to consistency learning. SHM selects basis styles from the source distribution, enabling the model to dynamically generate diverse and realistic samples during training. Experiments show that our SHADE yields significant improvement and outperforms state-of-the-art methods by 5.05% and 8.35% on the average mIoU of three real-world datasets on single- and multi-source settings, respectively.

1 Introduction

Semantic segmentation, *i.e.*, predicting a semantic category for each pixel, plays a crucial role in autonomous driving. With modern deep neural networks [19,20] and abundant annotated data [5,6], fully-supervised methods [2,21,39] have achieved remarkable success on many public datasets. Nonetheless, annotating

---

Supplementary Information The online version contains supplementary material available at https://doi.org/10.1007/978-3-031-19815-1_31.

© The Author(s), under exclusive license to Springer Nature Switzerland AG 2022
S. Avidan et al. (Eds.): ECCV 2022, LNCS 13688, pp. 535–552, 2022.
https://doi.org/10.1007/978-3-031-19815-1_31

each pixel for a high-resolution image is expensive and time-consuming. For example, it takes more than 1.5 h to annotate a 1024×2048 driving scene [5], and the time is even doubled for scenes under adverse weather [32] and poor lighting conditions [31]. To alleviate the heavy annotation cost, unsupervised domain adaptive semantic segmentation (UDA-Seg) [35,46,47] has been introduced to learn models that can perform well on a target set, given the labeled (source) data and unlabeled (target) data. Considering that synthetic data can be automatically generated and annotated by a pre-designed engine [29,30], existing works of UDA-Seg commonly use synthetic data as the source domain and real-world data as the target domain.

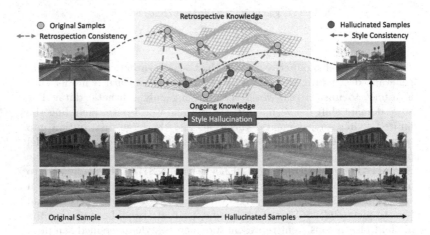

Fig. 1. Illustration of dual consistency constraints and examples of style hallucination. We generate hallucinated samples (brown circle) from the style hallucination module and then utilize the paired samples and real-world (retrospective) knowledge to learn style consistency (blue dash line) and retrospection consistency (gray dash line). (Color figure online)

Despite the success of UDA-Seg, the limitations are still severe. First, the adapted model achieves remarkable performance on the target data, but still degrades when facing unseen out-of-distribution samples. Second, it is almost impractical to collect diverse enough real-world data that can cover all the conditions. For example, a model trained with Singapore scenes cannot well address the snowy road in Switzerland. To mitigate such limitations, a more practical but challenging setting, domain generalized semantic segmentation (DG-Seg) [4,41,43], is introduced in the community. DG-Seg only leverages annotated source data to train a robust model that can cope with different unseen conditions. Similar to UDA-Seg, synthetic data are commonly used as the source data to release expensive annotation cost in DG-Seg. In this paper, we aim to solve the synthetic-to-real DG task in semantic segmentation.

The main challenge for synthetic-to-real DG-Seg is to cope with the significant domain shift between source and unseen target domains, which can be roughly divided into two aspects. First, the environmental variations in source data are very limited compared to those of unseen target data. Second, there exists large distribution gap between synthetic and real-world data, *e.g.*, image styles and characteristics of objects. To learn the domain-invariant model that can address the domain shift, previous works design tailor-made modules [4, 26] to remove domain-specific information, or leverage extra real-world data to transfer synthetic data [14, 41] to real-world styles for narrowing the distribution gap. However, the removal of domain-specific information [4, 26] is not complete and explicit due to the lack of real-world information; the real-world style transfer [14, 41] heavily relies on extra data, which are not always available in practice, and ignores the invariant representation within the source domain. Taking the above into account, in this paper, we aim to explicitly learn domain-invariant representation with the stylized samples in the source domain and bridge the gap between synthetic and real-world data without using extra real-world data.

To this end, we introduce a novel dual consistency learning framework that can jointly achieve the above two goals. As shown in Fig. 1, we introduce two consistency constraints, *style consistency* (SC) and *retrospection consistency* (RC), which explicitly encourage the model to learn style invariant representation and to be less overfitting to the synthetic data respectively. Specifically, we first diversify the samples in SC by style variation, and then enforce the consistency between them. To obtain the diverse samples, we adopt the style features, *i.e.*, channel-wise mean and standard deviation, to generate new data. Compared with directly transferring the whole image (*e.g.*, CycleGAN [48]), changing style features can maintain the pixel alignment to the utmost extent. This forces the model to learn pixel-level consistency between paired samples. In addition, our RC lies in the guidance of real-world information. We leverage ImageNet [6] pre-trained model which is available in all the DG-Seg models. The pre-trained model contains general knowledge of classifying some "things" class, *e.g.*, bicycle, bus and car. Furthermore, the features of these classes in the pre-trained model reflect the representation in the context of real-world. Consequently, such features can serve as the guidance for the ongoing model to retrospect what the real-world looks like and to lead the model less overfitting to the synthetic data.

Style diversifying is crucial for the success of dual consistency learning. Previous works [33, 44] commonly mix or swap styles within the source domain, which will generate more samples of the dominant styles (*e.g.*, daytime in GTAV [29]). Nevertheless, it is not the best way since the target styles may be quite different from the dominant styles. To fully take the advantage of all the source styles, we propose style hallucination module (SHM), which leverages C basis styles to represent the style space of C dimension and thus to generate new styles. Ideally, the basis styles should be linearly independent so the linear combination of basis styles can represent all the source styles. However, many unrealistic styles that impair the model training are generated when we directly take C orthogonal unit vectors as the basis. To reconcile diversity and realism, we use farthest point sampling (FPS) [28] to select C styles from all the source styles as basis styles. Such basis styles contain many rare styles since rare styles are commonly far away from the dominant ones. With these basis styles that represent the style space in a better way, we utilize linear combination to generate new styles. To summarize, we propose the **Style-HA**llucinated **D**ual consist**E**ncy learning (**SHADE**) framework for domain generalization in the context of semantic segmentation, and our contributions are as follows:

- We propose the dual consistency constraints for domain generalized semantic segmentation, which learn the style invariant representation among diversified styles and narrow the domain gap between synthetic and real domains by retrospecting the real-world knowledge.
- We propose the style hallucination module to generate new and diverse styles with the representative basis styles, enhancing the dual consistency learning.
- Experiments on single-source and multi-source DG benchmark demonstrate the effectiveness of.the proposed method and we achieve new state-of-the-art performance.

2   Related Work

Domain Generalization. To tackle the performance degradation in the out-of-distribution conditions, domain generalization [4,14,23,41,44] is introduced to learn a robust model with one or multiple source domains, aiming to perform well on unseen domains. Considering the expensive annotation cost in semantic segmentation, synthetic data are commonly adopted as the source domain in recent DG-Seg works. The large domain shift and the restricting conditions in the training data greatly limit the performance on the unseen real-world test data. To address these problems, one main stream of previous works [14,41] focuses on diversifying training data with real-world templates and learning the invariant representation from all the domains. Another main stream aims at directly learning the explicit domain-invariant features within the source domain [4,26,33]. IBN-Net [26] and ISW [4] leverage tailor-made instance normalization block and whitening transformation to reduce the impact of domain-specific information. Different from previous methods, we generate new styles only with the synthetic source domain and learn the invariant representation across styles.

Consistency learning (CL). CL is adopted by many computer vision tasks and settings. One main stream is leveraging CL to exploit the unlabeled samples in semi-supervised learning [8,34] and unsupervised domain adaptation [25,45, 49] since the consistency between two view samples can be used for pseudo-labeling. CL is also applied to address the corruptions and perturbations [12,36] by maximizing the similarity between different augmentations. In addition, CL is also used in self-supervised learning [3,10] as the contrastive loss to utilize totally unlabeled data. We introduce CL into domain generalization, leading the model robust to various styles. We also leverage consistency with real-world knowledge to narrow the domain gap between synthetic and real-world data.

Style Variation. Style features are widely explored in style transfer [7,16], which aims at changing the image style but maintaining the content. Inspired by this, recent domain generalization methods leverage the style features to generate diverse data of different styles to improve the generalization ability. Swapping [33, 42] and mixing [44] existing styles within the source domains is an effective way and generating new styles [38] by specially designed modules can also make sense. We also only leverage the styles within the source domain but take the relatively rare styles in the source domains into account, thus generating more diverse samples to improve generalization ability.

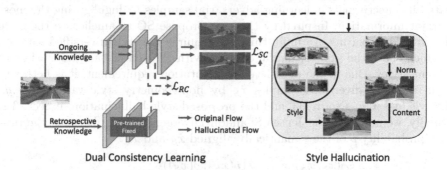

Dual Consistency Learning   **Style Hallucination**

Fig. 2. Overview of the proposed style-hallucinated dual consistency learning (SHADE) framework. Training images are fed into the segmentation model (ongoing knowledge) and the ImageNet pre-trained model (retrospective knowledge). The style hallucination module is inserted into a certain layer of the segmentation model to generate stylized samples. Finally, the model is optimized by the dual consistency losses: style consistency $\mathcal{L}_{SC}$ and retrospection consistency $\mathcal{L}_{RC}$. Note that the cross entropy loss is also used and we omit it here for brevity.

3   Methodology

Preliminary. In synthetic-to-real domain generalized semantic segmentation, one or multiple labeled source domains $\mathcal{S} = \{x^i_S, y^i_S\}^{N_S}_{i=i}$, where N_S is the number of source domains, are used to train a segmentation model, which is deployed to unseen real-world target domains $\mathcal{T}$ directly. In general, the source and target domains share the same label space $Y_S, Y_T \in (1, N_C)$ but belong to different distributions. The goal of this task is to improve the generalization ability of model in unseen domains using only the source data.

Overview. To solve the above challenging problem, we propose the **St**y**le-HA**llucinated **D**ual consist**E**ncy learning (**SHADE**) framework, which is quipped with dual consistency constraints and a Style Hallucination Module (SHM). The dual consistency constraints effectively learn the domain-invariant representation and reduce the gap between the real and synthetic data. SHM enriches the training samples by dynamically generating diverse styles, which catalyzes the advantage of dual consistency learning. The overall framework is shown in Fig. 2.

3.1 Dual Consistency Constraints

In SHADE, we introduce two consistency learning constraints: (1) Style Consistency (SC) that aims at learning the consistent predictions across stylized samples. (2) Retrospection Consistency (RC) that focuses on narrowing the distribution shift between synthetic and real-world data in the feature-level.

Style Consistency (SC). Different from traditional cross entropy constraint focusing on the high-level semantic information, logit pairing [12,17] has demonstrated its effectiveness in learning adversarial samples by highlighting the most invariant information. Inspired by this, we propose SC to ameliorate the style shift with logit pairing. To fulfill this, SC requires the style-diversified samples $\tilde{x}_S$ which share the same semantic content with the source samples x_S but of different styles. Due to the pixel-level segmentation requirement, it is better to obtain the style-diversified samples $\tilde{x}_S$ by non-geometry style variation, *e.g.*, MixStyle [44], CrossNorm [33] and the proposed style hallucination in Sect. 3.2. Formally, we minimize the Jensen-Shannon Divergence (JSD) between the posterior probability p of the semantically aligned $\tilde{x}_S$ and x_S:

$$
\begin{aligned}
\mathcal{L}_{SC}(x_S, \tilde{x}_S) &= JSD\left(p(x_S); p(\tilde{x}_S)\right) \\
&= \frac{1}{2}\left(D[p(x_S)\|Q] + D[p(\tilde{x}_S)\|Q]\right),
\end{aligned}
\tag{1}
$$

where $Q = (p(x_S) + p(\tilde{x}_S))/2$ is the average information of the original and style-diversified samples. D denotes the KL Divergence between the posterior probability $p \in \{p(x_S), p(\tilde{x}_S)\}$ and Q. JSD highlights the invariant pixel-level semantic information across two styles, impelling the model to be stable and insensitive to varied styles.

Retrospection Consistency (RC). Backbones of semantic segmentation models commonly start from ImageNet [6] pre-trained weights since the pre-trained backbones have learned general representation of many "things" categories in the real-world, including some classes in the self-driving scenes, *e.g.*, bicycle, bus, and car. However, the model learns more task-specific information and fit to the synthetic data when training with synthetic semantic segmentation data. As the model is required to deploy on unseen real-world scenarios, it is important to obtain some knowledge for the real-world objects. Previous works [14,41] leverage the abundant and even carefully selected images from real-world data, which may not be readily fulfilled in applications. Since ImageNet pre-trained weights are available to every segmentation model as the initialization, we propose RC to leverage such knowledge to lead the model less overfitting to the synthetic data and to retrospect the real-world knowledge lying in initialization. As the ImageNet pre-trained model is trained by image classification, only "things" classes are learned instead of "stuff" classes like road and wall. Consequently, RC is implemented as the feature-level distance minimization on those pixels of "things" classes. In addition, the style-diversified samples $\tilde{x}_S$ in style consistency is also used in RC, which can lead the generated samples close to the real-world style. We define RC as:

$$\mathcal{L}_{RC}(x_S, \tilde{x}_S) = \frac{1}{\sum_m M_{things}^{(m)}} \sum_m M_{things}^{(m)} \cdot \left(\left(f(x_S; \theta_S)^{(m)} - f(x_S; \theta_{IN})^{(m)} \right)^2 \right.$$
$$\left. + \left(f(\tilde{x}_S; \theta_S)^{(m)} - f(x_S; \theta_{IN})^{(m)} \right)^2 \right),$$

$$(2)$$

where M_{things} denotes the mask of "things" classes. $f(x_S; \theta_S)$ and $f(\tilde{x}_S; \theta_S)$ denote the bottleneck feature of original sample x_S and style-diversified sample $\tilde{x}_S$ respectively, which are obtained from the ongoing segmentation model θ_S. $f(x_S; \theta_{IN})$ denotes the bottleneck feature of original sample x_S in the retrospective ImageNet pre-trained model θ_{IN}.

Discussion. Our retrospection consistency is inspired by the Feature Distance (FD) in DAFormer [13] but with different motivation and implementation. *First*, DAFormer focuses on unsupervised domain adaptation in semantic segmentation with unlabeled real-world data available, so it only focuses on fitting to the specific target domain (CityScapes [5]) rather than addressing unseen domain shift. *Second*, FD in DAFormer is used to better classify those similar classes (*e.g.*, bus and train) with the classification knowledge from ImageNet. Since we have no idea about the target distribution in DG-Seg, RC in our framework serves as an important guidance for the real-world knowledge, especially for more complex real-world scenes (*e.g.*, BDD100K [40] and Mapillary [24]). In addition, RC can also enhance the learning of real-world styles by taking the style-diversified samples into account.

3.2 Style Hallucination

Background. Style transfer [1,16] and domain generalization [33,44] methods show that the channel-wise mean and standard deviation can represent the non-content style of the image, which plays an important role in the domain shift. The style features can be readily used by AdaIN [16] which can transfer the image to an arbitrary style while remaining the content:

$$\text{AdaIN}(x, y) = \sigma(y) \left(\frac{x - \mu(x)}{\sigma(x)} \right) + \mu(y), \tag{3}$$

where x and y denotes the feature maps providing the content and style respectively. $\mu(*)$ and $\sigma(*)$ denotes the channel-wise mean and standard deviation. In domain generalization, as only one or multiple source domains are accessible, previous works modify AdaIN by replacing style features with other source styles. Those styles can be directly obtained from other samples [33] or can be generated by mixing other styles with its own styles [44].

Style Hallucination Module (SHM). Unlike image classification benchmarks where images are commonly of the same style in one dataset, even one semantic segmentation dataset contains various styles, *e.g.*, daytime, nighttime and twilight. This is why existing style variation methods [33,44] can work in single-source domain generalized segmentation. However, the ways of these methods in generating extra styles are sub-optimal, since they just randomly swap or mix source styles without considering the frequency and diversity of the source styles. As a result, more samples of the dominant style (*e.g.*, daytime) will be generated, yet the generated distribution may be quite different from the real-world one. Since we have no idea about the real-world target set, it is better to diversify the source samples as much as possible. We next introduce the Style Hallucination Module (SHM) for generating diverse source samples.

Definition 1: *A basis B of a vector space V over a field F is a linearly independent subset of V that spans V. When the field is the reals* $\mathbb{R}$*, the resulting basis vectors are n-tuples of reals that span n-dimensional Euclidean space* $\mathbb{R}^n$ *[9].*

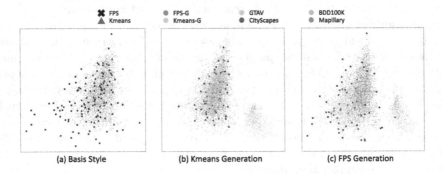

(a) Basis Style   (b) Kmeans Generation   (c) FPS Generation

Fig. 3. Visualization of distributions of different domains. (a) Comparison of two kinds of basis styles; (b) generated style with Kmeans basis style; (c) generated style with FPS basis style. (Zoom in for details.)

According to Definition 1, style space can be viewed as a subspace of C-dimensional vector space, and thus all possible styles can be represented by the basis vectors. However, if we directly take C linearly independent vectors as the basis, *e.g.*, orthogonal unit vectors, many unrealistic styles are generated since the realistic styles are only in a small subspace, and such generated styles can impair the model training. To reconcile the diversity and realism, we use farthest point sampling (FPS) [28] to select C styles from all the source styles as basis styles. FPS is widely used for point cloud downsampling, which can iteratively choose C points from all the points, such that the chosen points are the most distant points with respect to the remaining points. Despite not strictly linearly independent, basis styles obtained by FPS can represent the style space to the utmost extent, and also contain many rare styles since rare styles are commonly far away from dominant ones. In addition, we recalculate the dynamic basis styles every k epochs instead of fixing basis style, as the style space is changing along with the model training. To generate new styles, we sample the combination weight $W = [w_1, \cdots, w_C]$ from Dirichlet distribution $B([\alpha_1, \cdots, \alpha_C])$ with the concentration parameters $[\alpha_1, \cdots, \alpha_C]$ all set to $1/C$. The basis styles are then linearly combined by W:

$$\mu_{HS} = W \cdot \mu_{base}, \qquad \sigma_{HS} = W \cdot \sigma_{base}, \qquad (4)$$

where $\mu_{base} \in \mathbb{R}^{C \times C}$ and $\sigma_{base} \in \mathbb{R}^{C \times C}$ are the C basis styles. With the generated styles, style hallucinated samples $\tilde{x}_S$ can be obtained by:

$$\tilde{x}_S = \sigma_{HS} \left(\frac{x_S - \mu(x_S)}{\sigma(x_S)} \right) + \mu_{HS}. \qquad (5)$$

Discussion. Selecting representative basis styles is crucial for SHM. FPS is adopted in our method as it can cover the rare styles to the utmost extent. Another way is taking the Kmeans [22] clustering centers as the basis. As shown in Fig. 3(a), FPS samples (black cross) spread out more than Kmeans centers (teal triangle), and can cover almost all possible source styles (lightskyblue point). When using the basis styles for style generation, styles obtained from Kmeans centers (Fig. 3(b)) are still within the source distributions and even ignore some possible rare styles. In contrast, FPS basis styles can generate more diverse styles (Fig. 3(c)), and even generate some styles close to the real-world ones (yellow, pink and orange point). Table 4 further demonstrates the effectiveness of FPS basis styles and shows that the Kmeans basis styles are even worse than directly swapping and mixing source styles.

3.3 Training Objective

The overall training objective is the combination of pixel-level cross entropy loss and the proposed two consistency constraints:

$$
\begin{aligned}
\mathcal{L} = \frac{1}{2} \left(\mathcal{L}_{CE}(x_S, y_S) + \mathcal{L}_{CE}(\tilde{x}_S, y_S) \right) \\
+ \lambda_{SC} \mathcal{L}_{SC}(x_S, \tilde{x}_S) + \lambda_{RC} \mathcal{L}_{RC}(x_S, \tilde{x}_S),
\end{aligned}
\qquad (6)
$$

where λ_{SC} and λ_{RC} are the weights for style consistency and retrospection consistency, respectively.

4   Experiments

4.1   Experimental Setup

Datasets. Two synthetic datasets (GTAV [29] and SYNTHIA [30]) are taken as the source domains. GTAV [29] contains 24,966 images with the size of 1914×1052, splitting into 12,403 training, 6,382 validation, and 6,181 testing images. SYNTHIA [30] contains 9,400 images of 960×720, where 6,580 images are used for training and 2,820 images for validation. We evaluate the model on the validation sets of the three real-world datasets. CityScapes [5] contains

Table 1. Comparison with state-of-the-art methods on single-source DG with ResNet-50 and ResNet-101 as backbone, respectively. "Extra Data" denotes using extra real-world data during training. § denotes selecting best checkpoint for each target dataset.

Net	Methods (GTAV)	Extra Data	CityScapes	BDD100K	Mapillary	Mean
ResNet-50	Baseline	✗	28.95	25.14	28.18	27.42
	SW [27]	✗	29.91	27.48	29.71	29.03
	IterNorm [15]	✗	31.81	32.70	33.88	32.79
	IBN-Net [26]	✗	33.85	32.30	37.75	34.63
	DRPC [41]§	✓	37.42	32.14	34.12	34.56
	ISW [4]	✗	36.58	35.20	40.33	37.37
	Ours	✗	**44.65**	**39.28**	**43.34**	**42.42**
ResNet-101	Baseline	✗	32.97	30.77	30.68	31.47
	IBN-Net [26]	✗	37.37	34.21	36.81	36.13
	ISW [4]	✗	37.20	33.36	35.57	35.38
	DRPC [41]§	✓	42.53	38.72	38.05	39.77
	FSDR [14]§	✓	44.80	41.20	43.40	43.13
	Ours	✗	**46.66**	**43.66**	**45.50**	**45.27**

500 validation images of 2048×1024. BDD-100K [40] and Mapillary [24] contain 1,000 1280×720 images and 2,000 1920×1080 images for validation, respectively.

Implementation Details. Following [4], we use DeepLabV3+ [2] as the segmentation model. The segmentation model is equipped with two backbones, ResNet-50 and ResNet-101 [11]. The SHM is inserted after the first Conv-BN-ReLU layer (layer0). We re-select the basis styles with the interval $k = 3$. We set $\lambda_{SC} = 10$ and $\lambda_{RC} = 1$. Models are optimized by the SGD optimizer with the learning rate 0.01, momentum 0.9 and weight decay 5×10^{-4}. The polynomial decay [18] with the power of 0.9 is used as the learning rate scheduler. All models are trained with the batch size of 8 for 40K iterations. During training, four widely used data augmentation techniques are adopted, including color jittering, Gaussian blur, random flipping, and random cropping of 768×768.

Protocols. We conduct experiments on both single-source DG and multi-source DG. For *single-source DG*, to conduct a fair comparison with [4] and [14], we train the model with GTAV training data (12,403 images) when using ResNet-50 backbone (same with [4]), and with the whole GTAV datasets (24,966 images) when using ResNet-101 backbone (same with [14]). For *multi-source DG*, we follow [4] to train the model with the training set of GTAV (12,403 images) and SYNTHIA (6,580 images) using ResNet-50 backbone. **Note that** several state-of-the-art works, *e.g.,* [14] and [41], select the *best checkpoint* for each target dataset respectively, which is impractical since we cannot estimate the model performance on unseen domains in real-world applications. Instead, we directly use the *last checkpoint* to evaluate the three target datasets, which is more in line with the practical purpose of domain generalization.

Baseline. The baseline in each protocol is the model trained with the corresponding source training data by cross entropy loss function.

Evaluation Metric. We use the 19 shared semantic categories for training and evaluation. The mean intersection-over-union (mIoU) of the 19 categories on the three real-world datasets is adopted as the evaluation metric.

4.2 Comparison with State-of-the-Art Methods

Single-source DG. In Table 1, we compare SHADE with state-of-the-art methods under single source setting, including SW [27], IterNorm [15], IBN-Net [26], ISW [4], DRPC [41] and FSDR [14]. *First*, we compare models that are trained with GTAV training set, using ResNet-50 backbone. SHADE achieves an average mIoU of 42.42% on the three real-world target datasets, yielding an improvement of 15.00% mIoU over the baseline and outperforming the previous best method (ISW) by 5.05%. *Second,* we further compare methods under the training protocol of DRPC [41] and FSDR [14], using ResNet-101 backbone and taking the whole set of GTAV (24,966 images) as the training data. Note that DRPC [41] and FSDR [14] utilize extra real-world data from ImageNet [6] or even driving scenes. Moreover, they select the best checkpoint for each target dataset, which is impractical in the real-world applications. Even so, we achieve the best results on all three datasets, **46.66% on CityScapes, 43.66% on BDD100K, 45.50% on Mapillary**, outperforming FSDR [14] by 2.14% in the average mIoU. These results show that we produce new state of the art in domain generalized semantic segmentation.

Table 2. Comparison with state-of-the-art methods on multi-source DG. All models use ResNet-50 backbone and are trained with training sets of GTAV and SYNTHIA.

Methods (G+S)	CityScapes	BDD100K	Mapillary	Mean
Baseline	35.46	25.09	31.94	30.83
IBN-Net [26]	35.55	32.18	38.09	35.27
ISW [4]	37.69	34.09	38.49	36.76
Ours	**47.43**	**40.30**	**47.60**	**45.11**

Table 3. Ablation studies on loss functions. All models use ResNet-50 backbone and are trained with GTAV training set. SHM: our style hallucination module; EMA: using exponential moving average model instead of ImageNet pre-trained model.

SHM	$\mathcal{L}_{SC}$	$\mathcal{L}_{RC}$	EMA	CityScapes	BDD100K	Mapillary	Mean
✗	✗	✗	✗	28.95	25.14	28.18	27.42
✓	✗	✗	✗	38.68	32.40	35.96	35.68
✓	✓	✗	✗	42.66	35.92	40.42	39.67
✓	✗	✓	✗	41.43	37.65	41.77	40.29
✓	✓	✗	✓	42.38	38.04	42.34	40.92
✓	✓	✓	✗	**44.65**	**39.28**	**43.34**	**42.42**

Multi-source DG. To further verify the effectiveness of SHADE, we compare SHADE with IBN-Net [26] and ISW [4] under the multi-source setting. We use ResNet-50 as the backbone and take the training set of GTAV and SYNTHIA as the source domains. As shown in Table 2, SHADE gains an improvement of 14.28% in average mIoU over the baseline, and outperforms ISW and IBN-Net by 8.35% and 9.84% respectively. The significant improvement over ISW and IBN-Net is mainly benefited from the various samples. With richer source samples, our SHM can generate more informative and diverse styles, which can effectively facilitate the dual consistency learning.

4.3   Ablation Studies

To investigate the effectiveness of each component in SHADE, we conduct ablation studies in Table 3.

Table 4. Comparison of different style variation methods. All models use ResNet-50 backbone and are trained with GTAV training set.

Methods (GTAV)	CityScapes	BDD100K	Mapillary	Mean
Baseline	28.95	25.14	28.18	27.42
Random Style	37.99	37.63	38.06	37.89
MixStyle [44]	43.14	37.94	42.22	41.10
CrossNorm [33]	43.13	37.20	41.83	40.72
Kmeans Basis	40.50	37.62	39.46	39.19
Ours	**44.65**	**39.28**	**43.34**	**42.42**

Effectiveness of Style Hallucination Module (SHM). SHM is the basis of SHADE. When using SHM only, we directly apply cross entropy loss on the style hallucinated samples. As shown in the second row of Table 3, our SHM can largely improves the model performance even without using the proposed dual consistency learning. This demonstrates the importance of training the model with diverse samples and the effectiveness of our SHM.

Effectiveness of Style Consistency (SC). SC is the consistency constraint that leads the model to learn style invariant representation. In Table 3, compared with only applying SHM, SC yields an improvement of 3.99% in average mIoU, demonstrating the superiority of the proposed logit pairing over cross entropy loss in learning style invariant model.

Effectiveness of Retrospection Consistency (RC). *First*, RC serves as an important guidance for narrowing the domain gap between synthetic and real data. Applying RC on top of SHM can yield an improvement of 4.61%, while removing RC will degrade the performance of SHADE by 2.75% in mIoU. *Second*, we conduct experiments to verify that the effectiveness of RC lies in the real-world knowledge instead of feature-level distance minimization of the paired samples. As directly minimizing the feature-level absolute distance of paired samples will lead to sub-optimal results (lead all the features close to zero), we replace the ImageNet pre-trained model in RC by exponential moving average (EMA) model. Comparing the fifth row and the sixth row in Table 3, EMA model only gains 1.25% improvement while RC improves the SC model by 2.75%. The results verify the significance of the retrospective knowledge in RC.

4.4   Further Evaluation

In this section, we compare other style variation methods with SHM and evaluate two important factors influencing SHM, *i.e.*, basis style selection interval k and the insert location of SHM.

Comparison of Different Style Variation Methods. We compare SHM with random style, MixStyle [44], CrossNorm [33] and style hallucination with Kmeans basis in Table 4. Random style utilizes the randomly sampled new styles from the standard normal distribution to form new samples. MixStyle [44] generates new styles by mixing the original style with the random shuffled style within a mini-batch, and CrossNorm [33] swaps the original style with another style within the shuffled mini-batch. SHM and Kmeans basis both use the linear combination of basis style to generate new styles, but the basis styles of SHM are selected by FPS [28] while those of Kmeans basis are obtained by Kmeans clustering centers. We can make four observations from Table 4. **First**, we cannot make full use of dual consistency to achieve significant performance with the unrealistic random styles since standard normal distribution cannot represent the source nor the target domains. **Second**, despite the use of realistic source styles, random utilization of MixStyle and CrossNorm leads to the generation of more samples from the dominant styles that may be different from the real-world target styles. When using MixStyle and CrossNorm, the model achieves an average mIoU of 41.10% and 40.72%, respectively. **Third**, as shown in Fig. 3(b), Kmeans basis suffers from the similar but more severe dominant

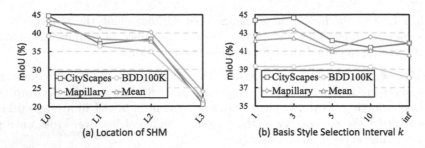

Fig. 4. Parameter analysis on the location of SHM and the basis style selection interval.

style issue in style generation. As a result, rare styles are discarded and thus the model achieves poorer performance than the above two. **Fourth**, SHM selects basis styles with FPS, and thus the selection can cover the source distribution to a large extent, especially those rare styles. With such basis styles, SHM generates styles from all the source distributions, and some generated styles are even close to the target domains (Fig. 3(c)). Consequently, combining SHM with dual consistency learning, SHADE can reap the benefit of the source data and outperforms other methods on all three target datasets.

Location of SHM. We investigate the impact of inserting SHM in different locations in Fig. 4(a). "L0" denotes inserting SHM after the first Conv-BN-ReLU layer (layer0) and "L1" to "L3" denote inserting SHM after the corresponding (1–3) ResNet layer. As shown in Fig. 4(a), "L0" achieves the best result while the performance of "L1" and "L2" drops a little. However, the model suffers from drastic performance degradation when inserting SHM after layer3. The reasons are two-fold. First, the channel-wise mean and standard deviation represent more style information in the shallow layers of deep neural networks while they contain more semantic information in deep layers [7,16]. Second, the residual connections in ResNet will lead the ResNet activations of deep layers to have large peaks and small entropy, which makes the style features biased to a few dominant patterns instead of the global style [37].

Basis Style Selection Interval. The distribution of source styles is varied along with the model training. To better represent the style space, we re-select the basis styles with the interval of k epochs. The abscissa of Fig. 4(b) denotes the selection interval k and "inf" denotes only selecting the basis style once in the beginning of training. As shown in Fig. 4(b), the model achieves consistent and good performance with frequent re-selection ($k <= 3$) while the performance degrades with the increase of selection interval, and the average mIoU is lower than 41% when only selecting once. Taking both the performance and computational cost into consideration, we set $k = 3$ in SHADE.

4.5   Real-to-Others Domain Generalization

To further demonstrate the effectiveness of SHADE, we leverage CityScapes [5] as the source domain and generalize to real (BDD100K [40] and Mapillary [24]) and synthetic (GTAV [29] and SYNTHIA [30]) domains. As shown in Table 5, SHADE consistently outperforms ISW [4] and IBN-Net [26] on both real and synthetic datasets. These results verify the versatility of our method.

Table 5. Comparison with state-of-the-art methods trained on CityScapes.

Methods	GTAV	SYNTHIA	BDD100K	Mapillary
IBN-Net [26]	45.06	26.14	48.56	57.04
ISW [4]	45.00	26.20	50.73	58.64
Ours	**48.61**	**27.62**	**50.95**	**60.67**

5   Conclusion

In this paper, we propose a novel framework (SHADE) for synthetic-to-real domain generalized semantic segmentation. SHADE leverages two consistency constraints to learn the domain-invariant representation by seeking consistent representation across styles and the guidance of retrospective knowledge. In addition, the style hallucination module (SHM) is equipped into our framework, which can effectively catalyze the dual consistency learning by generating diverse and realistic source samples. Experiments on three real-world dataset show that SHADE achieves state-of-the-art performance under both single- and multi-source domain generalization settings with different backbones.

Acknowledgment. This research/project is supported by the National Research Foundation Singapore and DSO National Laboratories under the AI Singapore Programme (AISG Award No: AISG2-RP-2020-016), the Tier 2 grant MOE-T2EP20120-0011 from the Singapore Ministry of Education, and the EU H2020 project AI4Media (No. 951911).

References

1. Chen, H., et al.: Diverse image style transfer via invertible cross-space mapping. In: ICCV (2021)
2. Chen, L.-C., Zhu, Y., Papandreou, G., Schroff, F., Adam, H.: Encoder-decoder with atrous separable convolution for semantic image segmentation. In: Ferrari, V., Hebert, M., Sminchisescu, C., Weiss, Y. (eds.) ECCV 2018. LNCS, vol. 11211, pp. 833–851. Springer, Cham (2018). https://doi.org/10.1007/978-3-030-01234-2_49
3. Chen, T., Kornblith, S., Norouzi, M., Hinton, G.: A simple framework for contrastive learning of visual representations. In: ICML (2020)

4. Choi, S., Jung, S., Yun, H., Kim, J.T., Kim, S., Choo, J.: Robustnet: Improving domain generalization in urban-scene segmentation via instance selective whitening. In: CVPR (2021)
5. Cordts, M., et al.: The cityscapes dataset for semantic urban scene understanding. In: CVPR (2016)
6. Deng, J., Dong, W., Socher, R., Li, L.J., Li, K., Fei-Fei, L.: Imagenet: a large-scale hierarchical image database. In: CVPR (2009)
7. Dumoulin, V., Shlens, J., Kudlur, M.: A learned representation for artistic style. In: ICLR (2017)
8. French, G., Laine, S., Aila, T., Mackiewicz, M., Finlayson, G.: Semi-supervised semantic segmentation needs strong, varied perturbations. In: BMVC (2020)
9. Halmos, P.R.: Finite-Dimensional Vector Spaces. Springer, New York (1987)
10. He, K., Fan, H., Wu, Y., Xie, S., Girshick, R.: Momentum contrast for unsupervised visual representation learning. In: CVPR (2020)
11. He, K., Zhang, X., Ren, S., Sun, J.: Deep residual learning for image recognition. In: CVPR (2016)
12. Hendrycks, D., Mu, N., Cubuk, E.D., Zoph, B., Gilmer, J., Lakshminarayanan, B.: AugMix: a simple data processing method to improve robustness and uncertainty. In: ICLR (2020)
13. Hoyer, L., Dai, D., Van Gool, L.: Daformer: improving network architectures and training strategies for domain-adaptive semantic segmentation. In: CVPR (2022)
14. Huang, J., Guan, D., Xiao, A., Lu, S.: FSDR: frequency space domain randomization for domain generalization. In: CVPR (2021)
15. Huang, L., Zhou, Y., Zhu, F., Liu, L., Shao, L.: Iterative normalization: Beyond standardization towards efficient whitening. In: CVPR (2019)
16. Huang, X., Belongie, S.: Arbitrary style transfer in real-time with adaptive instance normalization. In: ICCV (2017)
17. Kannan, H., Kurakin, A., Goodfellow, I.: Adversarial logit pairing. In: ICML (2018)
18. Liu, W., Rabinovich, A., Berg, A.C.: Parsenet: Looking wider to see better. In: CoRR (2015)
19. Liu, Z., et al.. Swin transformer: hierarchical vision transformer using shifted windows. In: ICCV (2021)
20. Liu, Z., Mao, H., Wu, C.Y., Feichtenhofer, C., Darrell, T., Xie, S.: A convnet for the 2020s. arXiv preprint arXiv:2201.03545 (2022)
21. Long, J., Shelhamer, E., Darrell, T.: Fully convolutional networks for semantic segmentation. In: CVPR (2015)
22. MacQueen, J.: Some methods for classification and analysis of multivariate observations. In: Proceedings of the Fifth Berkeley Symposium on Mathematical Statistics and Probability (1967)
23. Meng, R., et al.: Attention diversification for domain generalization. arXiv preprint arXiv:2210.04206 (2022)
24. Neuhold, G., Ollmann, T., Rota Bulo, S., Kontschieder, P.: The mapillary vistas dataset for semantic understanding of street scenes. In: ICCV (2017)
25. Pan, F., Shin, I., Rameau, F., Lee, S., Kweon, I.S.: Unsupervised intra-domain adaptation for semantic segmentation through self-supervision. In: CVPR (2020)
26. Pan, X., Luo, P., Shi, J., Tang, X.: Two at once: enhancing learning and generalization capacities via IBN-net. In: Ferrari, V., Hebert, M., Sminchisescu, C., Weiss, Y. (eds.) ECCV 2018. LNCS, vol. 11208, pp. 484–500. Springer, Cham (2018). https://doi.org/10.1007/978-3-030-01225-0_29
27. Pan, X., Zhan, X., Shi, J., Tang, X., Luo, P.: Switchable whitening for deep representation learning. In: ICCV (2019)

28. Qi, C.R., Yi, L., Su, H., Guibas, L.J.: Pointnet++: deep hierarchical feature learning on point sets in a metric space. In: NeurIPS (2017)
29. Richter, S.R., Vineet, V., Roth, S., Koltun, V.: Playing for data: ground truth from computer games. In: Leibe, B., Matas, J., Sebe, N., Welling, M. (eds.) ECCV 2016. LNCS, vol. 9906, pp. 102–118. Springer, Cham (2016). https://doi.org/10. 1007/978-3-319-46475-6_7
30. Ros, G., Sellart, L., Materzynska, J., Vazquez, D., Lopez, A.M.: The synthia dataset: a large collection of synthetic images for semantic segmentation of urban scenes. In: CVPR (2016)
31. Sakaridis, C., Dai, D., Gool, L.V.: Guided curriculum model adaptation and uncertainty-aware evaluation for semantic nighttime image segmentation. In: ICCV (2019)
32. Sakaridis, C., Dai, D., Van Gool, L.: ACDC: the adverse conditions dataset with correspondences for semantic driving scene understanding. In: ICCV (2021)
33. Tang, Z., Gao, Y., Zhu, Y., Zhang, Z., Li, M., Metaxas, D.: Selfnorm and crossnorm for out-of-distribution robustness. In: ICCV (2021)
34. Tarvainen, A., Valpola, H.: Mean teachers are better role models: weight-averaged consistency targets improve semi-supervised deep learning results. In: NeurIPS (2017)
35. Tsai, Y.H., Hung, W.C., Schulter, S., Sohn, K., Yang, M.H., Chandraker, M.: Learning to adapt structured output space for semantic segmentation. In: CVPR (2018)
36. Wang, H., Xiao, C., Kossaifi, J., Yu, Z., Anandkumar, A., Wang, Z.: Augmax: adversarial composition of random augmentations for robust training. In: NeurIPS (2021)
37. Wang, P., Li, Y., Vasconcelos, N.: Rethinking and improving the robustness of image style transfer. In: CVPR (2021)
38. Wang, Z., Luo, Y., Qiu, R., Huang, Z., Baktashmotlagh, M.: Learning to diversify for single domain generalization. In: ICCV (2021)
39. Xie, E., Wang, W., Yu, Z., Anandkumar, A., Alvarez, J.M., Luo, P.: Segformer: simple and efficient design for semantic segmentation with transformers. In: NeurIPS (2021)
40. Yu, F., et al.: Bdd100k: a diverse driving dataset for heterogeneous multitask learning. In: CVPR (2020)
41. Yue, X., Zhang, Y., Zhao, S., Sangiovanni-Vincentelli, A., Keutzer, K., Gong, B.: Domain randomization and pyramid consistency: simulation-to-real generalization without accessing target domain data. In: ICCV (2019)
42. Zhao, Y., Zhong, Z., Luo, Z., Lee, G.H., Sebe, N.: Source-free open compound domain adaptation in semantic segmentation. In: IEEE TCSVT (2022)
43. Zhong, Z., Zhao, Y., Lee, G.H., Sebe, N.: Adversarial style augmentation for domain generalized urban-scene segmentation. arXiv preprint arXiv:2207.04892 (2022)
44. Zhou, K., Yang, Y., Qiao, Y., Xiang, T.: Domain generalization with mixstyle. In: ICLR (2021)
45. Zhou, Q., et al.: Uncertainty-aware consistency regularization for cross-domain semantic segmentation. In: Computer Vision and Image Understanding (2022)
46. Zhou, Q., et al.: Context-aware mixup for domain adaptive semantic segmentation. arXiv preprint arXiv:2108.03557 (2021)
47. Zhou, Q., Zhuang, C., Yi, R., Lu, X., Ma, L.: Domain adaptive semantic segmentation with regional contrastive consistency regularization. In: ICME (2022)

48. Zhu, J.Y., Park, T., Isola, P., Efros, A.A.: Unpaired image-to-image translation using cycle-consistent adversarial networks. In: ICCV (2017)
49. Zou, Y., Yu, Z., Vijaya Kumar, B.V.K., Wang, J.: Unsupervised domain adaptation for semantic segmentation via class-balanced self-training. In: Ferrari, V., Hebert, M., Sminchisescu, C., Weiss, Y. (eds.) ECCV 2018. LNCS, vol. 11207, pp. 297–313. Springer, Cham (2018). https://doi.org/10.1007/978-3-030-01219-9_18

SeqFormer: Sequential Transformer for Video Instance Segmentation

Junfeng Wu[1], Yi Jiang[2], Song Bai[2], Wenqing Zhang[1], and Xiang Bai[1(✉)]

[1] Huazhong University of Science and Technology, Wuhan, China
xbai@hust.edu.cn
[2] ByteDance Inc., Singapore, Singapore

Abstract. In this work, we present SeqFormer for video instance segmentation. SeqFormer follows the principle of vision transformer that models instance relationships among video frames. Nevertheless, we observe that a stand-alone instance query suffices for capturing a time sequence of instances in a video, but attention mechanisms shall be done with each frame independently. To achieve this, SeqFormer locates an instance in each frame and aggregates temporal information to learn a powerful representation of a video-level instance, which is used to predict the mask sequences on each frame dynamically. Instance tracking is achieved naturally without tracking branches or post-processing. On YouTube-VIS, SeqFormer achieves 47.4 AP with a ResNet-50 backbone and 49.0 AP with a ResNet-101 backbone without bells and whistles. Such achievement significantly exceeds the previous state-of-the-art performance by 4.6 and 4.4, respectively. In addition, integrated with the recently-proposed Swin transformer, SeqFormer achieves a much higher AP of 59.3. We hope SeqFormer could be a strong baseline that fosters future research in video instance segmentation, and in the meantime, advances this field with a more robust, accurate, neat model. The code is available at https://github.com/wjf5203/SeqFormer.

Keywords: Video instance segmentation · Video transformer

1 Introduction

Video Instance Segmentation (VIS) [30,45] is an emerging vision task that aims to simultaneously perform detection, classification, segmentation, and tracking of object instances in videos. Compared to image instance segmentation [11], video instance segmentation is much more challenging since it requires accurate tracking of objects across an entire video.

Previous VIS algorithms can be roughly divided into two categories. The first mainstream follows the tracking-by-detection paradigm, extending image

J. Wu and W. Zhang—Work done during an internship at ByteDance.

Supplementary Information The online version contains supplementary material available at https://doi.org/10.1007/978-3-031-19815-1_32.

© The Author(s), under exclusive license to Springer Nature Switzerland AG 2022
S. Avidan et al. (Eds.): ECCV 2022, LNCS 13688, pp. 553–569, 2022.
https://doi.org/10.1007/978-3-031-19815-1_32

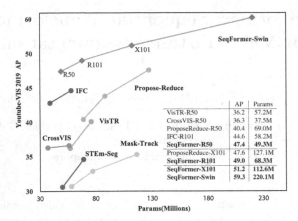

Fig. 1. Performance *vs*. Model Size. All results are reported with single model and single-scale inference. SeqFormer significantly outperforms the previous method with similar parameters.

instance segmentation models with a tracking branch [4,10,21,28,45,46]. These methods first predict candidate detection and segmentation frame-by-frame, and then associate them by classification [45,46] or re-identification [4,21] to track the instance through a video. Nevertheless, the tracking process is sensitive to occlusions and motion blur that are common in videos. Another mainstream is to predict clip-level instance masks by taking a video clip [2,3] or the entire video [14,39] as input. It divides a video into multiple overlapping clips and generates mask sequences with clip-by-clip matching on overlapping frames. More recently, VisTR [39] first adapts transformer [37] to VIS and uses instance queries to obtain instance sequence from video clips. After that, IFC [14] improves the performance and efficiency of VisTR by building communications between frames in a transformer encoder.

In this paper, we present Sequential Transformer (SeqFormer), which follows the principle of vision transformer [5,39] and models instance relationships among video frames. As in [14], we observe that a stand-alone instance query suffices although an object may be of different positions, sizes, shapes, and various appearances. Nevertheless, it is witnessed that the attention process shall be done with each frame independently, so that the model will attend to locations following with the movement of instance through the video. This observation aligns with the conclusion drawn in action recognition [29,47], where the 1D time domain and 2D space domain have different characteristics and should be handled in a different fashion.

Considering the movement of an instance in a video, a model is supposed to attend to different spatial locations following the motion of the instance. We decompose the shared instance query into frame-level box queries for the attention mechanism to guarantee that the attention focuses on the same instance on each frame. The box queries are kept on each frame and used to predict the bounding box sequences. Then the features within the bounding boxes are aggregated to refine the box queries on the current frame. By repeating this refinement through decoder layers, SeqFormer locates the instance in each frame in a coarse-to-fine manner, in a similar way to Deformable DETR [49].

However, to mitigate redundant information from non-instance frames, those box queries are aggregated in a weighted manner, where the weights are end to end learned upon the box embeddings. The generated representation, which retains richer object cues, is used to predict the category and generate dynamic convolution weights of mask head. Since the box sequences are predicted and refined in the decoder, SeqFormer naturally and succinctly establishes the association of instances across frames.

In summary, SeqFormer enjoys the following advantages:

- SeqFormer is a neat and efficient end-to-end framework. Given an arbitrary long video as input, SeqFormer predicts the classification results, box sequences, and mask sequences in one step without the need for additional tracking branches or hand-craft post-processing.
- As shown in Fig. 1, SeqFormer sets the new state-of-the-art performance on YouTube-VIS 2019 benchmark [45]. SeqFormer achieves 47.4 AP with a ResNet-50 backbone and 49.0 AP with a ResNet-101 backbone without bells and whistles. Such achievement significantly exceeds the previous state-of-the-art performance by 4.6 and 4.4, respectively. With a ResNext-101 backbone, SeqFormer achieves 51.2 AP, which is the first time that an algorithm achieves an AP above 50. In addition, integrated with the recently-proposed Swin transformer, SeqFormer achieves a much higher AP of 59.3.
- With the query decomposition mechanism, SeqFormer attends to locations following with the movement of instance through the video and learns a powerful representation for instance sequences.
- The code and the pre-trained models are publicly available. We hope the SeqFormer, with the idea of making attention follow with the movement of object, could be a strong baseline that fosters future research in video instance segmentation, and in the meantime, advances this field with a more robust, accurate, neat model.

2 Related Work

Image Instance Segmentation. Instance Segmentation is the most fundamental and challenging task in computer vision, which aims to detect every instance and segment every pixel respectively in static images. Instance segmentation was dominated by Mask R-CNN architecture [11,13,22] for a long time, Mask R-CNN [11] directly introduces fully convolutional mask head to Faster R-CNN [31] in a multi-task learning manner. Recently, one stage models [6,35,38,41] emerged as excellent frameworks for instance segmentation. Solo [38] and CondInst [35] propose one stage instance segmentation pipeline and achieve comparable performance. CondInst [35] proposes to dynamically generate the mask head parameters for each instance, which is used to predict the mask of the corresponding instance. QueryInst [8] proposes a query based instance segmentation framework based on Sparse R-CNN [34], which also take advantage of the Dynamic mask head. Dynamic mask head can be efficiently adopted into video segmentation tasks because instances with the same identity on different frames can share the same mask head parameters.

Video Instance Segmentation. Video instance segmentation is extended from the traditional image instance segmentation, and aims to simultaneously segment and track all object instances in the video sequence. The baseline method MaskTrack R-CNN [45] is built upon Mask R-CNN [11] and introduces a tracking head to associate each instance in the video. SipMask [4] proposes a spatial preservation module to generate spatial coefficients for mask predictions based on the one-stage FCOS [36]. STMask [17] proposes a spatial feature calibration to extract features for frame-level instance segmentation on each frame, and further introduces a temporal fusion module to aggregate temporal information from adjacent frames. STEm-Seg [2] models a video clip as a single 3D spatial-temporal volume and enables inference procedure based on clustering. CrossVIS [46] proposes a learning scheme that uses the instance feature in the current frame to pixel-wisely localize the same instance in other frames. MaskProp [3] and Propose-Reduce [18] take advantage of mask propagation, which can achieve high performance, but it is very computationally intensive.

Transformers. Transformer [37] was first proposed for the sequence-to-sequence machine translation task and became the basic component in most Natural Language Processing tasks. Recently, Transformer has been successfully applied in many visual tasks such as Object detection [5,34,49], segmentation [39,40,42,48], tracking [26,33,44], video recognition [1,16,23,29]. VIT [7] firstly applies transformer in image recognition and model an image as sequence of patches, which achieves comparable performance with traditional CNN architecture. DETR [5] proposes a new detection paradigm upon transformers, which simplifies the traditional detection framework and abandons the hand-crafted post-processing module. Deformable DETR [49] achieves better performance by using local attention and multi-scale feature maps. VisTR [39] is the first method that adapts Transformer to the VIS task. However, VisTR has a fixed number of input queries hardcoded by video length and maximum number of instances. Each query corresponds to an object on every single frame. In our method, instances with the same identity share a same query, which aggregates information across the video and learn a global feature representation for efficient segmentation. IFC [14] improves the performance and efficiency of VisTR by building communications between frames in the transformer encoder instead of flatting the space-time features into one dimension, but it still flatten the space-time features for the transformer decoder. Our model is designed to carry out the instance feature capturing independently on different frames, which makes the model attend to locations following with the movement of instance through the video.

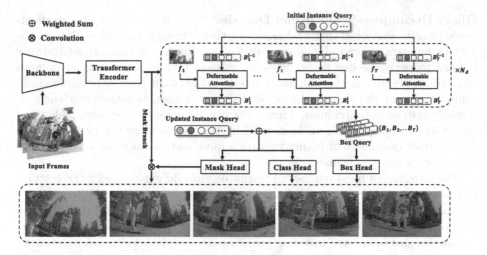

Fig. 2. The overall architecture of SeqFormer. Given the feature maps of input frames, the initial instance query is decomposed into frame-level box queries at the first decoder layer. The box queries are kept on each frame and serve as anchors without interacting with each other. The features extracted by box queries from each frame are aggregated to the instance query after each decoder layer, which is used for predicting dynamic mask head parameters. Then the mask head convolves the encoded feature maps to generate the mask sequences.

3   Method

3.1   Architecture

The network architecture is visualized in Fig. 2. SeqFormer has a CNN backbone and a transformer encoder for extracting feature maps from each frame independently. Next, a transformer decoder is adapted to locate the instance sequences and generate a video-level instance representation. Finally, three output heads are used for instance classification, instance sequences segmentation, and bounding box prediction, respectively.

Backbone. Given an input video $x_v \in \mathbb{R}^{T \times 3 \times H \times W}$ with 3 color channels and T frames of resolution $H \times W$, the CNN backbone (*e.g.*, ResNet [12]) extracts feature maps for each frame independently.

Transformer Encoder. First, a 1×1 convolution is used to reduce the channel dimension of the all the feature maps to $C = 256$, creating new feature maps $\{\mathbf{f}'_t\}_{t=1}^T, \mathbf{f}'_t \in \mathbb{R}^{C \times H' \times W'}, t \in [1, T]$. After adding fixed positional encodings [5], the transformer encoder performs deformable attention [49] on the feature maps, resulting in the output feature maps $\{\mathbf{f}_t\}_{t=1}^T$, with the same resolutions as the input. To perform attention mechanisms on each frame independently, we keep the spatial and temporal dimensions of feature maps rather than flattening them into one dimension.

Query Decompose Transformer Decoder. Given a video, humans can effort-lessly identify every instance and associate them through the video, despite the various appearance and changing positions on different frames. If an instance is hard to recognize due to occlusion or motion blur in some frames, humans can still re-identify it through the context information from other frames. In other words, for the same instance on different frames, humans treat them as a whole instead of individuals. This is the crucial difference between video and image instance segmentation. Motivated by this, we propose Query Decompose Transformer Decoder, which aims to learn a more and robust video-level instance representation across frames.

We introduce a fixed number of learnable embeddings to query the features of the same instance from each frame, termed Instance Queries. Different from the instance queries corresponding to frame-level instances in VisTR [39], which has a fixed number of input queries hardcoded by video length and maximum number of instances, our instance queries correspond to video-level instances. Since the changing appearance and position of the instance, the model should attend to different exact spatial locations of each frame. To achieve this goal, we propose to decompose the instance query into T frame-specific box queries, each of which serves as an anchor for retrieving and locating features on the corresponding frame.

At the first decoder layer, an instance query $\mathbf{I}_q \in \mathbb{R}^C$ is used to query the instance features on features maps of each frame independently:

$$\mathbf{B}_t^1 = \text{DeformAttn}(\mathbf{I}_q, \mathbf{f}_t), \tag{1}$$

where $\mathbf{B}_t^1 \in \mathbb{R}^C$ is the box query on frame t from the 1-st decoder layer, and DeformAttn indicates deformable attention module in [49] . Given a query element and the frame feature map $\mathbf{f}_t$, deformable attention only attends to a small set of key sampling points. At the l-th $(l > 1)$ layer, the box query $\mathbf{B}_t^{l-1}$ from last layer is used as input:

$$\mathbf{B}_t^l = \text{DeformAttn}(\mathbf{B}_t^{l-1}, \mathbf{f}_t), \tag{2}$$

and the instance query aggregates the temporal features by a weighted sum of all the box queries at the end of every decoder layers, where the weights are end to end learned upon the box embedding:

$$\mathbf{I}_q^l = \frac{\sum_{t=1}^T \mathbf{B}_t^l \times \text{FC}(\mathbf{B}_t^l)}{\sum_{t=1}^T \text{FC}(\mathbf{B}_t^l)} + \mathbf{I}_q^{l-1}. \tag{3}$$

After N_d decoder layers, we get an instance query and T box queries for each instance. The instance query is a shared video-level instance representation, and the box query contains the position information for predicting the bound box on each frame. We define the instance query $I_q^{N_d}$ and box queries $\{B_t^{N_d}\}_{t=1}^T$ from the last layer of decoder as output instance embedding and box embeddings $\{\mathbf{BE}_t\}_{t=1}^T, \mathbf{BE}_t \in \mathbb{R}^{N \times d}$.

Output Heads. As shown in Fig. 2, we add mask head, box head, class head on the top of the decoder outputs. A linear projection acts as the class head to produce the classification results. Given the instance embedding from the transformer decoder with index $\sigma(i)$, class head output a class probability of class $\mathbf{c}_i$ (which may be $\varnothing$) as $\hat{p}_{\sigma(i)}(\mathbf{c}_i)$.

The box head is a 3-layer feed forward network (FFN) with ReLU activation function and a linear projection layer. For $\mathbf{BE}_t$ of each frame, the FFN predicts the normalized center coordinates, height and width of the box w.r.t. the frame. Thus, for the instance with index $\sigma(i)$, we denote the predicted box sequence as $\hat{\mathbf{b}}_{\sigma(i)} = \{\hat{\mathbf{b}}_{(\sigma(i),1)}, \hat{\mathbf{b}}_{(\sigma(i),2)}, ..., \hat{\mathbf{b}}_{(\sigma(i),T)}\}$.

As for mask head, we leverage dynamic convolution [35] as our mask head. The output instance embedding of decoder contains the information of instance on all frames, thus it can be regarded as a more robust instance representation. We can use instance embedding to efficiently generate the entire mask sequences. First, a 3-layer FFN encodes the instance embedding into parameters ω_i of mask head with index $\sigma(i)$, which has three 1×1 convolution layers. The instances with the same identity on different frames share the same mask head parameters, which makes the segmentation very efficient. Each convolution layer has 8 channels and uses ReLU as the activation function except for the last one, following [35]. As shown in Fig. 2, there is a mask branch that provides the feature maps for mask head to predict instance masks. We employ an FPN-like architecture as the mask branch to make use of multi-scale feature maps from transformer encoder and generate feature maps sequences $\{\hat{\mathbf{F}}_{\text{mask}}^{1}, \hat{\mathbf{F}}_{\text{mask}}^{2}, ..., \hat{\mathbf{F}}_{\text{mask}}^{T}\}$ that are $\frac{1}{8}$ of the input resolution and have 8 channels for each frame independently. Then the feature map $\hat{\mathbf{F}}_{\text{mask}}^{t}$ is concatenated with a map of the relative coordinates from center of $\hat{\mathbf{b}}_{(\sigma(i),t)}$ in corresponding frames to provide a location cue for predicting the instance mask. Thus we get the $\{\mathbf{F}_{\text{mask}}^{t}\}_{t=1}^{T}, \mathbf{F}_{\text{mask}}^{t} \in \mathbb{R}^{10 \times \frac{H}{8} \times \frac{W}{8}}$. The mask head performs convolution on these high-resolution sequence feature maps $\mathbf{F}_{\text{mask}}^{t}$ to predict the mask sequences:

$$\{\mathbf{m}_i^t\}_{t=1}^{T} = \{\text{MaskHead}(\mathbf{F}_{\text{mask}}^{t}, \omega_i)\}_{t=1}^{T}, \tag{4}$$

where MaskHead performs three-layer 1×1 convolution on given feature maps with the kernels reshaped from ω. By sharing the same mask head parameters for instances with the same identity on different frames, our method can efficiently perform instance segmentation on each frame. Similar to DETR [5], we add output heads and Hungarian loss after each decoder layer as an auxiliary loss to supervise the training stage.

3.2 Instance Sequences Matching and Loss

Our method predicts a fixed-size set of N predictions in a single pass through the decoder, and N is set to be significantly larger than the number of instances in a video. To train our network, we first need to find a bipartite graph matching between the prediction and the ground truth. Let $\mathbf{y}$ denotes the ground truth set of video-level instance, and $\hat{\mathbf{y}}_i = \{\hat{\mathbf{y}}_i\}_{i=1}^{N}$ denotes the predicted instance set. Each element i of the ground truth set can be seen as $\mathbf{y}_i = \{\mathbf{c}_i, (\mathbf{b}_{i,1}, \mathbf{b}_{i,2}, ..., \mathbf{b}_{i,T})\}$, where $\mathbf{c}_i$ is the target class label including $\varnothing$, and $\mathbf{b}_{i,t} \in [0,1]^4$ is a vector that defines ground truth bounding box center coordinates and its relative height and width in the frame t. For the predictions of instance with index $\sigma(i)$, we take the output of class head $\hat{p}_{\sigma(i)}(\mathbf{c}_i)$ and predicted bounding box $\hat{\mathbf{b}}_{\sigma(i)}$. Then we define the pair-wise matching cost between ground truth y_i and a prediction with index $\sigma(i)$.

$$\mathcal{L}_{\text{match}}(\mathbf{y}_i, \hat{\mathbf{y}}_{\sigma(i)}) = -\hat{p}_{\sigma(i)}(\mathbf{c}_i) + \mathcal{L}_{\text{box}}(\mathbf{b}_i, \hat{\mathbf{b}}_{\sigma(i)}), \tag{5}$$

where $\mathbf{c}_i \neq \varnothing$. Note that Eq. 5 does not consider the similarity between mask prediction and mask ground truth, as such mask-level comparison is computationally expensive. To find the best assignment of a ground truth to a prediction, we search for a permutation of N elements $\sigma \in S_n$ with the lowest cost:

$$\hat{\sigma} = \arg\min_{\sigma \in S_n} \sum_i^N \mathcal{L}_{\text{match}}(\mathbf{y}_i, \hat{\mathbf{y}}_{\sigma(i)}). \tag{6}$$

Following prior work [5,39], the optimal assignment is computed with the Hungarian algorithm [15]. Given the optimal assignment $\hat{\sigma}$, we use Hungarian loss for all matched pairs to train our network:

$$\mathcal{L}_{\text{Hung}}(\mathbf{y}, \hat{\mathbf{y}}) = \sum_{i=1}^N \Big[-\log \hat{p}_{\hat{\sigma}(i)}(\mathbf{c}_i) + \mathbb{1}_{\{\mathbf{c}_i \neq \varnothing\}} \mathcal{L}_{\text{box}}(\mathbf{b}_i, \hat{\mathbf{b}}_{\hat{\sigma}}(i))$$
$$+ \mathbb{1}_{\{\mathbf{c}_i \neq \varnothing\}} \mathcal{L}_{\text{mask}}(\mathbf{m}_i, \hat{\mathbf{m}}_{\hat{\sigma}}(i)) \Big] . \tag{7}$$

For $\mathcal{L}_{\text{box}}$, we use a linear combination of the $\mathcal{L}_1$ loss and the generalized IoU loss [32]. The mask sequences $\{m_i^t\}_{t=1}^T$ from mask head with $\frac{1}{8}$ of the video resolution which may loss some details, thus we upsample the predicted mask to $\frac{1}{4}$ of the video resolution, and downsample the ground truth mask to the same resolution for mask loss, following [35]. The mask loss $\mathcal{L}_{\text{mask}}$ is defined as a combination of the Dice [27] and Focal loss [19]. We calculate box loss and mask loss on each frame and take the average for Hungarian loss.

4   Experiment

4.1   Datasets and Metrics

We evaluate our method on YouTube-VIS 2019 [45] and YouTube-VIS 2021 [43] datasets. YouTube-VIS 2019 is the first and largest dataset for video instance segmentation, which contains 2238 training, 302 validation, and 343 test high-resolution YouTube video clips. It has a 40-category label set and 131k high-quality instance masks. In each video, objects with bounding boxes and masks are labeled every five frames. YouTube-VIS 2021 is an improved and extended version of YouTube-VIS 2019 dataset, it contains 3,859 high-resolution videos and 232k instance annotations. The newly added videos in the dataset include more instances and frames.

Video instance segmentation is evaluated by the metrics of average precision (AP) and average recall (AR). Different from image instance segmentation, each instance in a video contains a sequence of masks. To evaluate the spatio-temporal consistency of the predicted mask sequences, the IoU computation is carried out in the spatial-temporal domain. This requires a model not only to obtain accurate segmentation and classification results at frame-level but also to track instance masks between frames accurately.

4.2 Implementation Details

Model Settings. ResNet-50 [12] is used as our backbone network unless otherwise specified. Similar to [49], we use the features from the last three stages as {C3, C4, C5} in ResNet, which correspond to the feature maps with strides {8, 16, 32}. And adding the lowest resolution feature map C6 obtained via a 3 × 3 stride 2 convolution on the C5. We set sampled key numbers $K = 4$ and eight attention heads for deformable attention modules. We use six encoder and six decoder layers of hidden dimension 256 for the transformer, and the number of instance queries is set to 300.

Training. We used AdamW [25] optimizer with base learning rate of 2×10^{-4}, $\beta 1 = 0.9$, $\beta 2 = 0.999$, and weight decay of 10^{-4}. Learning rates of the backbone and linear projections used for deformable attention modules are multiplied by a factor of 0.1. We first pre-train the model on COCO [20] by setting the number of input frames $T = 1$. Given the pretrained weights, we train our models on the YouTube-VIS dataset with input frames $T = 5$ sampled from the same video.

The training data of the YouTube-VIS dataset is not sufficient, which makes a model prone to overfitting. To address this problem, we adopt 80K training images in the COCO for compensation, following [2,18]. We only use the images with 20 overlapping categories in COCO and augment them with ±10° rotation to generate a five-frame pseudo video. We train our model on the mixed dataset including COCO and the video dataset for 12 epochs, and the learning rate is decayed at the 6-th and 10-th epoch by a factor of 0.1. The input frame sizes are downsampled so that the longest side is at most 768 pixels. The model is implemented with PyTorch-1.7 and is trained on 8 V100 GPUs of 32G RAM, with 2 video clips per GPU.

Inference. SeqFormer is able to model a video of arbitrary length without grouping frames into subsequences. We take the whole video as input during inference, which is downscaled to 360p, following MaskTrack R-CNN [45]. SeqFormer learns a video-level instance representation used for dynamic segmentation on each frame and classification, and the box sequences are generated by the decoder. Thus, no post-processing is needed for associating instances.

4.3 Main Results

The comparison of SeqFormer with previous state-of-the-art methods on YouTube-VIS 2019 are listed in Table 1. MaskProp [3] and ProposeReduce [18]

Table 1. Quantitative results of video instance segmentation on YouTube-VIS 2019 validation set. The result with superscript "†" is obtained without coco joint training. The best results with the same backbone are in **bold**.

Backbone	Method	Params	FPS	AP	AP_{50}	AP_{75}	AR_1	AR_{10}
ResNet-50	MaskTrack R-CNN [45]	58.1M	20.0	30.3	51.1	32.6	31.0	35.5
	STEm-Seg [2]	50.5M	7.0	30.6	50.7	33.5	37.6	37.1
	SipMask [4]	33.2M	30.0	33.7	54.1	35.8	35.4	40.1
	CompFeat [9]	-	-	35.3	56.0	38.6	33.1	40.3
	SG-Net [21]	-	-	34.8	56.1	36.8	35.8	40.8
	VisTR [39]	57.2M	69.9	36.2	59.8	36.9	37.2	42.4
	MaskProp [3]	-	-	40.0	-	42.9	-	-
	CrossVIS [46]	37.5M	39.8	36.3	56.8	38.9	35.6	40.7
	Propose-Reduce [18]	69.0M	-	40.4	63.0	43.8	41.1	49.7
	IFC [14]	39.3M	107.1	42.8	65.8	46.8	43.8	51.2
	SeqFormer†	49.3M	72.3	45.1	66.9	50.5	**45.6**	54.6
	SeqFormer	49.3M	72.3	**47.4**	**69.8**	**51.8**	45.5	**54.8**
ResNet-101	MaskTrack R-CNN [45]	77.2M	-	31.8	53.0	33.6	33.2	37.6
	STEm-Seg [2]	69.6M	-	34.6	55.8	37.9	34.4	41.6
	SG-Net [21]	-	-	36.3	57.1	39.6	35.9	43.0
	VisTR [39]	76.3M	57.7	40.1	64.0	45.0	38.3	44.9
	MaskProp [3]	-	-	42.5	-	45.6	-	-
	CrossVIS [46]	56.6	35.6	36.6	57.3	39.7	36.0	42.0
	Propose-Reduce [18]	88.1M	-	43.8	65.5	47.4	43.0	53.2
	IFC [14]	58.3M	89.4	44.6	69.2	49.5	44.0	52.1
	SeqFormer	68.4M	64.6	**49.0**	**71.1**	**55.7**	**46.8**	**56.9**
ResNeXt-101	MaskProp [3]	-	-	44.3	-	48.3	-	-
	Propose-Reduce [18]	127.1M	-	47.6	71.6	51.8	46.3	56.0
	SeqFormer	112.7M	30.7	**51.2**	**75.3**	**58.0**	**46.5**	**57.3**
Swin-L	**SeqFormer**	220.0M	27.7	**59.3**	**82.1**	**66.4**	**51.7**	**64.4**

are the state-of-the-art methods, which take a strong backbone to extract spatial features and use mask propagation to improve the segmentation and tracking, but suffer from low inference speed. We list the methods with different backbones for fair comparison. It can be observed that SeqFormer significantly surpasses all the previous best reported results by at least 4 AP with the same backbone. Training our model with coco pseudo videos improves the AP from 45.1 to 47.4. SeqFormer with a ResNet-50 backbone can even achieve competitive performance against state-of-the-art methods with a ResNeXt-101 backbone. By adopting Swin transformer [24] as our backbone without further modifications, SeqFormer can first achieve 59.3 AP on this benchmark, outperforming the best previous results by a large margin of 11.7 AP. To understand the runtime efficiency, we measure FPS of SeqFormer excluding the data loading process of multiple images on NVIDIA Tesla V100. With an input size of 360p and a ResNet-50 backbone on YouTube-VIS, the inference FPS is 72.3. While surpassing the stateof-the-art AP by a large margin, SeqFormer is the second fast

Table 2. Quantitative results of video instance segmentation on YouTube-VIS 2021 validation set. The best results with the same backbone are in **bold**.

Backbone	Method	AP	AP$_{50}$	AP$_{75}$	AR$_1$	AR$_{10}$
ResNet-50	MaskTrack R-CNN [45]	28.6	48.9	29.6	26.5	33.8
	SipMask [4]	31.7	52.5	34.0	30.8	37.8
	CrossVIS [46]	34.2	54.4	37.9	30.4	38.2
	IFC [14]	36.6	57.9	39.3	-	-
	SeqFormer	**40.5**	**62.4**	**43.7**	**36.1**	**48.1**
Swin-L	**SeqFormer**	**51.8**	**74.6**	**58.2**	**42.8**	**58.1**

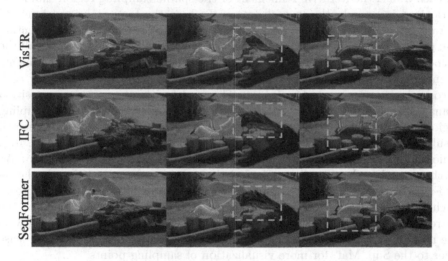

Fig. 3. Qualitative comparisons with other methods.

one following IFC. An example of qualitative comparison with previous methods is given in Fig. 3, the mask predictions of SeqFormer are more stable over time. Please refer to the Sup. Mat. for more qualitative results. We also evaluate our approach on the recently introduced YouTube-VIS 2021 dataset, which is a more challenging dataset with more videos and a higher number of instances and frames. As shown in Table 2, SeqFormer achieves 40.5 AP with a ResNet-50 backbone, surpassing previous methods by 3.9 AP. We believe that our effective method will serve as a strong baseline on these benchmarks and facilitate future research in video instance segmentation.

4.4   Ablation Study

This section conducts extensive ablation experiments to study the effects of different settings in our proposed method. All the ablation experiments are conducted with the ResNet-50 backbone and training on YouTube-VIS 2019 dataset rather than the mixed dataset.

Table 3. Instance query decomposition. Decomposing instance query into frame-level box queries is critical for SeqFormer.

Decompose	AP	AP_{50}	AP_{75}	AR_1	AR_{10}
w/o	34.1	53.7	34.9	34.8	40.9
w	45.1	66.9	50.5	45.6	54.6

Instance Query Decomposition. Instance query decomposition plays an important role in our method. Since an instance may have different positions on each frame, the iterative refinement of the spatial sampling region should be performed independently on each frame. To keep the temporal consistency of instances, we use the temporal-shared instance query for deformable attention and get box queries for each frame. The box queries will be kept through all the decoder layers and serve as frame anchors for the same instance. Experiments of models without box queries and using the shared instance query for each decoder layer are presented in Table 3. The model without query decomposition manages to achieve only 34.1 AP. It is because the query controls the sampling region of deformable attention. Using the same instance query for each frame will result in the same spatial sampling region on each frame, as shown in Fig. 4(a), which is inaccurate and insufficient for video-level instance representation. We further visualize the sampling points of the second and the last decoder layers in Fig. 4(b) and (c). The box queries decoupled from instance query serve as anchors for locating features and iteratively refining the sampling region on the current frame. It can be seen that SeqFormer attends to locations following with the movement of instance through the video in a coarse-to-fine manner. Please refer to the Sup. Mat. for more visualization of sampling points.

Spatial Temporal Dimensions. Previous transformer-based methods [14,39] flatten the spatial and temporal dimensions of video features into one dimension for the transformer decoder. We argue that the temporal dimension should not be flattened with spatial dimensions, since it was recognized that the 2D space domain and 1D time domain have different characteristics and should be intuitively handled in a different way [47]. Thus, we retain the complete 3D spatio-temporal dimensions and perform explicit region sampling and information aggregation on all frames. In this experiment, we study the effect of this architecture by replacing deformable transformer with vanilla transformer and flattening the spatial and temporal dimensions, termed as 'flatten' in Table 4. For fair comparison, we use single-scale deformable attention as the baseline, termed as 'single-scale', which use the same scale feature map with 'flatten', the default setting termed as 'multi-scale'. By keeping spatial-temporal dimensions of video features, the AP increased from 35.1 to 42.5. The use of multi-scale feature maps can only improve 2.6 AP, which proves that the success of our method mainly comes from the preservation of the temporal dimension and the explicit spatial sampling.

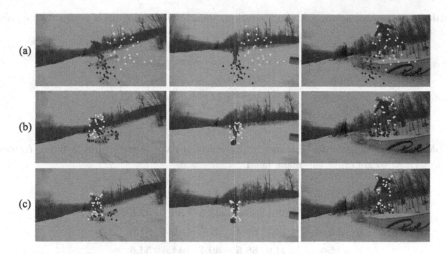

Fig. 4. The sampling points from the first decoder layer is shown in (a), which is coarse and inaccurate. The refined accurate sampling points from the second and last decoder layer are shown in (b) and (c).

Table 4. Spatial and temporal dimensions. Keeping spatial-temporal feature dimensions and performing instance feature capture independently on different frames brings about 7.4 AP gains. Multi-scale feature maps can further bring 2.6 AP.

Feature	AP	AP_{50}	AP_{75}	AR_1	AR_{10}
Flatten	35.1	56.8	35.6	38.1	41.8
Single-scale	42.5	64.6	46.5	41.5	50.9
Multi-scale	45.1	66.9	50.5	45.6	54.6

Aggregation of Temporal Information. The frame-level box queries and the predicted boxes can align the instance features from all frames, there are several ways to aggregate the aligned features into the instance query. We conduct an experiment to evaluate the different aggregation ways for these features, as shown in Table 5. In the 'sum' setting, the features from different frames are directly added together as the instance feature of this decoder layer. In the 'average' setting, the feature on each frame is averaged as the instance feature. In the 'weighted-sum' setting, we apply a softmax layer and a fully-connected layer on box embeddings to get the weights of each frame, and the features are aggregated in a weighted sum in Eq. 3. The result is 30.6 AP and 43.2 AP for 'sum' and 'average' settings respectively. Direct summation will cause the value to be unstable with different frame numbers. Since some instances only appear in a few frames, directly averaging features from all frames may cause the information to be diluted. Please refer to the Sup. Mat. for more details and visualization of different frame weights.

Table 5. Temporal information aggregation. Weighted sum brings a performance gain of 1.9 in AP.

Aggregation	AP	AP_{50}	AP_{75}	AR_1	AR_{10}
Sum	30.6	44.5	34.3	37.2	45.0
Average	43.2	65.2	48.5	43.4	52.8
Weighted-sum	45.1	66.9	50.5	45.6	54.6

Table 6. Fewer frames for instance representation. We evenly sample fewer frames from a video to generate the mask head.

Frames	AP	AP_{50}	AP_{75}	AR_1	AR_{10}
1	38.1	58.3	41.3	38.7	47.5
3	43.4	65.4	47.6	42.4	51.3
5	44.6	66.5	49.7	44.8	54.6
10	44.7	66.9	49.5	44.3	53.5
all	45.1	66.9	50.5	45.6	54.6

Robust Instance Representation. Our decoder explicitly aligns and aggregates the information from each frame to learn a video-level instance representation. In this experiment, we try to generate instance representation with fewer frames. We use the instance representation to generate a mask head and apply the mask head on each frame to get the mask sequences, as shown in Table 6. Surprisingly, with only one frame as input, the generated mask head can produce a competitive result of 38.1 AP. With five frames as input, the performance is only 0.5 AP worse than taking all frames as input. This result shows that the mask head learned by our method can generalize well to unseen frames.

5   Conclusion

In this paper, we have proposed an effective transformer architecture for video instance segmentation, named SeqFormer, which performs attention mechanisms on each frame independently and learns a shared powerful instance query for each video-level instance. With the proposed instance query decomposition, our network can align the instance features and naturally tackle the instance tracking without additional tracking branches or post-processing. We demonstrated that our method surpasses all state-of-the-art methods by a large margin. We believe that our neat and efficient approach will serve as a strong baseline for future research in video instance segmentation.

Acknowledgment. We thank Xiaoding Yuan for the support and discussions about implementation details. We thank the anonymous reviewers for their efforts and valuable feedback to improve our work.

References

1. Arnab, A., Dehghani, M., Heigold, G., Sun, C., Lučić, M., Schmid, C.: ViViT: a video vision transformer. In: Proceedings of the IEEE/CVF International Conference on Computer Vision, pp. 6836–6846 (2021)
2. Athar, A., Mahadevan, S., Ošep, A., Leal-Taixé, L., Leibe, B.: STEm-Seg: spatio-temporal embeddings for instance segmentation in videos. In: Vedaldi, A., Bischof, H., Brox, T., Frahm, J.-M. (eds.) ECCV 2020. LNCS, vol. 12356, pp. 158–177. Springer, Cham (2020). https://doi.org/10.1007/978-3-030-58621-8_10
3. Bertasius, G., Torresani, L.: Classifying, segmenting, and tracking object instances in video with mask propagation. In: CVPR (2020)
4. Cao, J., Anwer, R.M., Cholakkal, H., Khan, F.S., Pang, Y., Shao, L.: SipMask: spatial information preservation for fast image and video instance segmentation. In: Vedaldi, A., Bischof, H., Brox, T., Frahm, J.-M. (eds.) ECCV 2020. LNCS, vol. 12359, pp. 1–18. Springer, Cham (2020). https://doi.org/10.1007/978-3-030-58568-6_1
5. Carion, N., Massa, F., Synnaeve, G., Usunier, N., Kirillov, A., Zagoruyko, S.: End-to-end object detection with transformers. In: Vedaldi, A., Bischof, H., Brox, T., Frahm, J.-M. (eds.) ECCV 2020. LNCS, vol. 12346, pp. 213–229. Springer, Cham (2020). https://doi.org/10.1007/978-3-030-58452-8_13
6. Chen, X., Girshick, R., He, K., Dollár, P.: Tensormask: a foundation for dense object segmentation. In: ICCV (2019)
7. Dosovitskiy, A., et al.: An image is worth 16x16 words: transformers for image recognition at scale. arXiv preprint arXiv:2010.11929 (2020)
8. Fang, Y., et al.: Instances as queries. In: ICCV (2021)
9. Fu, Y., Yang, L., Liu, D., Huang, T.S., Shi, H.: Compfeat: comprehensive feature aggregation for video instance segmentation. arXiv preprint arXiv:2012.03400 (2020)
10. Goel, V., Li, J., Garg, S., Maheshwari, H., Shi, H.: MSN: efficient online mask selection network for video instance segmentation. arXiv preprint arXiv:2106.10452 (2021)
11. He, K., Gkioxari, G., Dollar, P., Girshick, R.: Mask R-CNN. In: ICCV (2017)
12. He, K., Zhang, X., Ren, S., Sun, J.: Deep residual learning for image recognition. In: CVPR (2016)
13. Huang, Z., Huang, L., Gong, Y., Huang, C., Wang, X.: Mask scoring R-CNN. In: Proceedings of the IEEE/CVF Conference on Computer Vision and Pattern Recognition, pp. 6409–6418 (2019)
14. Hwang, S., Heo, M., Oh, S.W., Kim, S.J.: Video instance segmentation using inter-frame communication transformers. In: NeurIPS (2021)
15. Kuhn, H.W.: The Hungarian method for the assignment problem. Nav. Res. Logist. Q. 2(1–2), 83–97 (1955)
16. Li, K., et al.: Uniformer: unified transformer for efficient spatiotemporal representation learning. arXiv preprint arXiv:2201.04676 (2022)
17. Li, M., Li, S., Li, L., Zhang, L.: Spatial feature calibration and temporal fusion for effective one-stage video instance segmentation. In: CVPR (2021)
18. Lin, H., Wu, R., Liu, S., Lu, J., Jia, J.: Video instance segmentation with a propose-reduce paradigm. arXiv preprint arXiv:2103.13746 (2021)
19. Lin, T.Y., Goyal, P., Girshick, R., He, K., Dollár, P.: Focal loss for dense object detection. In: ICCV (2017)

20. Lin, T.-Y., et al.: Microsoft COCO: common objects in context. In: Fleet, D., Pajdla, T., Schiele, B., Tuytelaars, T. (eds.) ECCV 2014. LNCS, vol. 8693, pp. 740–755. Springer, Cham (2014). https://doi.org/10.1007/978-3-319-10602-1_48

21. Liu, D., Cui, Y., Tan, W., Chen, Y.: SG-Net: spatial granularity network for one-stage video instance segmentation. In: CVPR (2021)

22. Liu, S., Qi, L., Qin, H., Shi, J., Jia, J.: Path aggregation network for instance segmentation. In: Proceedings of the IEEE Conference on Computer Vision and Pattern Recognition, pp. 8759–8768 (2018)

23. Liu, X., et al.: End-to-end temporal action detection with transformer. IEEE Trans. Image Process. (TIP) **31**, 5427–5441 (2022)

24. Liu, Z., et al.: Swin transformer: hierarchical vision transformer using shifted windows. arXiv preprint arXiv:2103.14030 (2021)

25. Loshchilov, I., Hutter, F.: Decoupled weight decay regularization. In: ICLR (2019)

26. Meinhardt, T., Kirillov, A., Leal-Taixe, L., Feichtenhofer, C.: TrackFormer: multi-object tracking with transformers. arXiv preprint arXiv:2101.02702 (2021)

27. Milletari, F., Navab, N., Ahmadi, S.A.: V-net: fully convolutional neural networks for volumetric medical image segmentation. In: 2016 Fourth International Conference on 3D Vision (3DV) (2016)

28. Nguyen, T.C., Tang, T.N., Phan, N.L., Nguyen, C.H., Yamazaki, M., Yamanaka, M.: 1st place solution for youtubevos challenge 2021: video instance segmentation. arXiv preprint arXiv:2106.06649 (2021)

29. Patrick, M., et al.: Keeping your eye on the ball: trajectory attention in video transformers. arXiv preprint arXiv:2106.05392 (2021)

30. Qi, J., et al.: Occluded video instance segmentation: a benchmark. Int. J. Comput. Vis. 1–18 (2022)

31. Ren, S., He, K., Girshick, R., Sun, J.: Faster R-CNN: towards real-time object detection with region proposal networks. In: NeurIPS (2015)

32. Rezatofighi, H., Tsoi, N., Gwak, J., Sadeghian, A., Reid, I., Savarese, S.: Generalized intersection over union: a metric and a loss for bounding box regression. In: CVPR (2019)

33. Sun, P., et al.: Transtrack: multiple object tracking with transformer. arXiv preprint arXiv:2012.15460 (2020)

34. Sun, P., et al.: Sparse R-CNN: end-to-end object detection with learnable proposals. In: CVPR (2021)

35. Tian, Z., Shen, C., Chen, H.: Conditional convolutions for instance segmentation. In: Vedaldi, A., Bischof, H., Brox, T., Frahm, J.-M. (eds.) ECCV 2020. LNCS, vol. 12346, pp. 282–298. Springer, Cham (2020). https://doi.org/10.1007/978-3-030-58452-8_17

36. Tian, Z., Shen, C., Chen, H., He, T.: FCOS: fully convolutional one-stage object detection. In: ICCV (2019)

37. Vaswani, A., et al.: Attention is all you need. In: NeurIPS (2017)

38. Wang, X., Kong, T., Shen, C., Jiang, Y., Li, L.: SOLO: segmenting objects by locations. In: Vedaldi, A., Bischof, H., Brox, T., Frahm, J.-M. (eds.) ECCV 2020. LNCS, vol. 12363, pp. 649–665. Springer, Cham (2020). https://doi.org/10.1007/978-3-030-58523-5_38

39. Wang, Y., et al.: End-to-end video instance segmentation with transformers. In: CVPR (2021)

40. Wu, J., Jiang, Y., Sun, P., Yuan, Z., Luo, P.: Language as queries for referring video object segmentation. In: CVPR, pp. 4974–4984 (2022)

41. Xie, E., et al.: Polarmask: single shot instance segmentation with polar representation. In: CVPR, pp. 12193–12202 (2020)

42. Xie, E., Wang, W., Yu, Z., Anandkumar, A., Alvarez, J.M., Luo, P.: Segformer: simple and efficient design for semantic segmentation with transformers. Adv. Neural. Inf. Process. Syst. **34**, 12077–12090 (2021)

43. Xu, N., et al.: Youtubevis dataset 2021 version. https://youtube-vos.org/dataset/vis/

44. Yan, B., Peng, H., Fu, J., Wang, D., Lu, H.: Learning spatio-temporal transformer for visual tracking. In: ICCV (2021)

45. Yang, L., Fan, Y., Xu, N.: Video instance segmentation. In: ICCV (2019)

46. Yang, S., et al.: Crossover learning for fast online video instance segmentation. arXiv preprint arXiv:2104.05970 (2021)

47. Zhao, Y., Xiong, Y., Lin, D.: Trajectory convolution for action recognition. In: NeurIPS (2018)

48. Zheng, S., et al.: Rethinking semantic segmentation from a sequence-to-sequence perspective with transformers. In: Proceedings of the IEEE/CVF Conference on Computer Vision and Pattern Recognition, pp. 6881–6890 (2021)

49. Zhu, X., Su, W., Lu, L., Li, B., Wang, X., Dai, J.: Deformable DETR: deformable transformers for end-to-end object detection. arXiv preprint arXiv:2010.04159 (2020)

Saliency Hierarchy Modeling
via Generative Kernels for Salient Object Detection

Wenhu Zhang[1], Liangli Zheng[2], Huanyu Wang[3], Xintian Wu[3], and Xi Li[3,4,5](✉)

[1] Polytechnic Institute, Zhejiang University, Hangzhou, China
wenhuzhang@zju.edu.cn
[2] School of Software Technology, Zhejiang University, Hangzhou, China
lianglizheng@zju.edu.cn
[3] College of Computer Science and Technology, Zhejiang University,Hangzhou, China
{huanyuhello,xilizju}@zju.edu.cn
[4] Shanghai Institute for Advanced Study, Zhejiang University, Hangzhou, China
[5] Shanghai AI Laboratory, Hangzhou, China

Abstract. Salient Object Detection (SOD) is a challenging problem that aims to precisely recognize and segment the salient objects. In ground-truth maps, all pixels belonging to the salient objects are positively annotated with the same value. However, the saliency level should be a relative quantity, which varies among different regions in a given sample and different samples. The conflict between various saliency levels and single saliency value in ground-truth, results in learning difficulty. To alleviate the problem, we propose a Saliency Hierarchy Network (SHNet), modeling saliency patterns via generative kernels from two perspectives: region-level and sample-level. Specifically, we construct a Saliency Hierarchy Module to explicitly model saliency levels of different regions in a given sample with the guide of prior knowledge. Moreover, considering the sample-level divergence, we introduce a Hyper Kernel Generator to capture the global contexts and adaptively generate convolution kernels for various inputs. As a result, extensive experiments on five standard benchmarks demonstrate our SHNet outperforms other state-of-the-art methods in both terms of performance and efficiency.

Keywords: Salient object detection · Saliency hierarchy modeling · Region-level · Sample-level · Generative kernel

1 Introduction

Salient Object Detection (SOD) aims to accurately detect and segment the most eye-catching area in a given image, mimicking the human visual perception.

Supplementary Information The online version contains supplementary material available at https://doi.org/10.1007/978-3-031-19815-1_33.

© The Author(s), under exclusive license to Springer Nature Switzerland AG 2022
S. Avidan et al. (Eds.): ECCV 2022, LNCS 13688, pp. 570–587, 2022.
https://doi.org/10.1007/978-3-031-19815-1_33

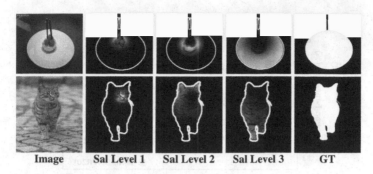

Fig. 1. The illustration of saliency hierarchy. Although all pixels in the salient objects are positively annotated with the same value in ground-truth maps (GT), the saliency levels (Sal Level) of different regions are inherently hierarchical.

In recent years, deep learning based SOD methods have achieved huge success by introducing dense feature interactions [6,27,45], various attention modules [11,36,54], and multi-task learning pipelines [43,51,53]. In essence, tahese approaches leverage the strong abilities of the deep neural networks to learn a mapping function from raw images to ground-truth saliency maps, in which the whole salient object is positively annotated with the same saliency level.

However, it shows evident saliency divergence among different regions (in a given sample) and samples, due to various colors, sizes, layouts, etc.. For example, in the first row of Fig. 1, the fruits, cake and plate obviously possess diverse saliency levels. Similarly, in the second row, different regions inside the cat also show different saliency levels. It is difficult to learn a mapping function from pixels with divergent saliency levels to the same value in a ground-truth map. To solve this problem, we propose a novel framework modeling the hierarchical saliency levels with generative kernels for different regions and samples.

In order to model the region-level hierarchical saliency, a straightforward solution is to learn annotated hierarchical labels. As a matter of fact, there is no acknowledged standard for saliency level division in the literature. Therefore, we explore several saliency level decomposition strategies and generate sub-saliency masks of different saliency levels. Based on these sub-saliency masks, we design a Saliency Hierarchy Module (SHM). Firstly, the SHM extracts local features within regions of different saliency levels. An SHM contains multiple branches and regions of features belonging to the same saliency level are processed in an independent branch. Then, it aggregates all the region level features together forming an integrated feature map. Through cascading several SHMs together, we achieve a hierarchy saliency modeling scheme at every stage of our framework. In this way, we not only depict the saliency levels explicitly, but also model hierarchical saliency levels with different patterns.

Moreover, considering the sample-level saliency divergence, we propose to adaptively generate convolution kernels for different samples. We design a Hyper Kernel Generator (HKG) to capture a global view of the input image. Specifi-

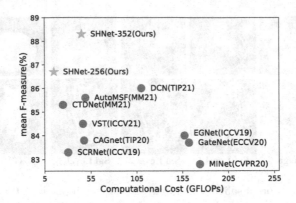

Fig. 2. Mean F-measure against GFLOPs on DUTS-TE [40]. Our SHNet (Red Stars) outperforms other SOTA approaches on both performance and efficiency. (Color figure online)

cally, we introduce a Transformer decoder [38] to generate a set of hyper-kernels by constructing dense attention between several learnable queries and flattened image patches. Through sufficient interactions, the hyper-knowledge of different saliency patterns are embedded in the hyper-kernels. Each hyper-kernel corresponds to a specific saliency level in SHMs. With these hyper-kernels, HKG further produces different convolution kernels for all branches in SHMs. Different from previous works [4,7], who utilize transformer to predict task-specific elements, our HKG aims to generate convolutional kernels for the decoder, improving the capacity and flexibility of our framework. As a result, we generate convolutional kernels to model saliency divergence among different samples with the proposed HKG, and model region-level saliency with SHMs. Our framework achieves the state-of-the-art performance, as shown in Fig. 2.

The main contributions are summarized as follows:

- We propose a novel framework to model salient objects hierarchically from the perspective of regions and samples.
- We design Saliency Hierarchy Modules (SHM), which model the region-level saliency hierarchy within a given sample.
- We introduce a Hyper Kernel Generator (HKG) to generate adaptive kernels to model the saliency divergence among samples.
- Extensive experiments on five widely used benchmarks demonstrate our method achieves SOTA results *w.r.t.*, performance and efficiency.

2   Related Work

2.1   Salient Object Detection

Early SOD methods [1,2,15,18,19,26,41] mainly focus on the hand-crafted features to detect and segment the salient objects, such as color contrast [2], frequency prior [1], etc. Recently, deep learning based SOD approaches [5,16,32,48] have achieved a qualitative leap in performance due to the powerful feature extraction capability in visual representation. The existing SOD approaches can be roughly divided into architecture based methods [12,25,27,30,36,39,42,56] and regularization based methods [21,24,37,43,47,48].

Architecture Based Methods. The architecture based methods mainly concentrate on designing novel models for the complex feature interaction. For example, Pang et al. [30] used mutual learning and the self-interaction module to reduce the noise during feature fusion. Wei et al.(F3Net) [42] used the cascaded feedback decoder to release the feature redundancy between various levels. Ma et al. [27] proposed a pyramidal feature shrinking network to aggregate adjacent feature nodes in pairs and discard interference information. Other methods [12,25,36,39,56] also verify the effectiveness of dense interaction for SOD.

Regularization Based Methods. As for the regularization based approaches, they improve the performance by building auxiliary supervision. For example, Wei et al. [43] (LDF) used the body map and detail map as auxiliary supervision to avoid the interference between the center area and boundary. Liu et al. [24] introduced edge detection and skeleton extraction, trying to solve them with SOD jointly. Tang et al. [37] designed an uncertainty-based saliency map to disentangle high-resolution SOD into two tasks and achieve good results. With similar purpose, various auxiliary loss functions [21,47,48] are proposed for regularizing the training of deep SOD models.

Different from these methods, which directly map the whole images to corresponding binary saliency maps, we focus on hierarchically modeling saliency patterns and alleviating the learning difficulty caused by the saliency divergence.

2.2 Hypernetworks and Transformers

Hypernetworks. Hypernetwork [13,17] can directly generate instance-wise parameters for the network with another independent weight generation model at test time. It is a powerful modeling tool providing the network adaptivity in a parameter-efficient manner. Similar design is used for many tasks, such as image-to-image translation [17], semantic segmentation [29], 3D reconstruction [23], and so on. Inspired by hypernetworks, we utilize a shared HKG module for generating sample-adaptive kernels for all the HSMs, improving the model capacity with a computational-efficient manner.

Transformers. Vaswani et al. [38] proposed the first transformer encoder-decoder architecture for NLP tasks. Recently, various computer vision tasks introduce transformer models and achieve exciting results, including image classification [9], semantic segmentation [57], object detection [4] and saliency object detection [25]. Different from CNN-based models, transformer relies on the attention mechanism to model the long-term dependencies from a sequence perspective. VST [25] first introduces the transformer architecture to SOD task for capturing the global contexts and contrast, which achieves huge success. In this paper, our HKG can be treated as a meta block or hypernetwork, which aims to generate unique convolution kernels for per image and per saliency level, modeling the sample-level saliency divergence adaptively.

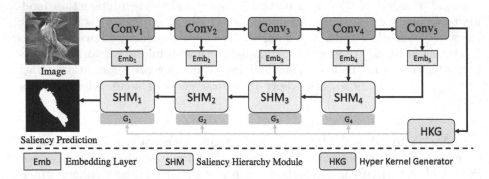

Fig. 3. An overview of our proposed Saliency Hierarchy Network. The whole network consists of a CNN backbone with embedding layers, a Hyper Kernel Generator and five stacked Saliency Hierarchy Modules.

3   Method

In this section, we illustrate our Saliency Hierarchy Network (SHNet) in detail. The proposed SHNet mainly consists of two modules, Saliency Hierarchy Module (SHM) and Hyper Kernel Generator (HKG), as shown in Fig. 3. Within an SHM, we produce several sub-saliency masks through a saliency level classifier and utilize these masks to decompose the input features into several parts for hierarchical saliency modeling in respective branches. Note that the sub-saliency masks are regularized by prior knowledge to depict the hierarchy decomposition process explicitly. Within an HKG, we utilize a transformer decoder to generate sample-adaptive hyper-kernels, which are further parsed into convolution kernel groups corresponding to all the cascaded SHMs. We utilize the traditional CNN backbone (e.g., ResNet [14], VGG [35]) as the encoder, containing K-layer convolution blocks. Formally, we denote the number of saliency levels as N and the outputs of each encoder layers as $\{F_1, F_2, ..., F_K\}$.

3.1   Saliency Hierarchy Module

In this section, we describe the detail of Saliency Hierarchy Module in detail. The SHM focuses on region-level hierarchical saliency modeling within a given sample. As shown in Fig. 4, an SHM includes two processes: Saliency Feature Decomposition and Hierarchical Saliency Modeling.

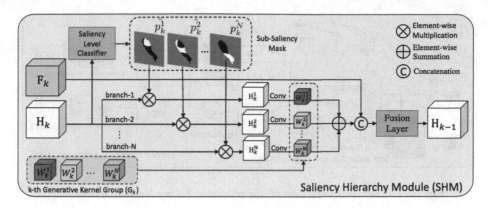

Fig. 4. The detailed depiction of our proposed Saliency Hierarchy Module.

Saliency Feature Decomposition. In order to decompose the input features according to their different saliency levels, we propose to depict the saliency hierarchy with generated sub-saliency masks. Specifically, we introduce an N-class classifier to predict the pixel-wise saliency levels:

$$\hat{P}_k = \text{softmax}(\text{Conv}_{3\times3}(H_k)), \tag{1}$$

where H_k is the input features of k-th SHM, $\hat{P}_k$ is the stacked sub-saliency masks, softmax($\cdot$) is the softmax normalization along the channel dimension, and $\text{Conv}_{3\times3}(\cdot)$ is a learnable convolution layer. Then, we unfold the obtained $\hat{P}_k$ and get N predicted sub-saliency masks $\{\hat{p}_k^1, ..., \hat{p}_k^N\}$, corresponding to N different levels in the salient objects.

Moreover, to assign different saliency patterns to various regions, we decompose the input features into sub-features corresponding to respective saliency levels under the guidance of the obtained sub-saliency masks:

$$H_k^n = (\hat{p}_k^n \otimes H_k), \quad n = 1, 2, ..., N, \tag{2}$$

where $\otimes$ denotes the element-wise multiplication and H_k^n is the obtained sub-feature for the n-th saliency level.

It has to be mentioned that several prior knowledge is introduced for providing pseudo-labels $\{p_k^1, ..., p_k^N\}$ to regularize the predicted sub-saliency masks. During the regularization, we explicitly guide the learning process of the sub-saliency masks and inject the prior knowledge into our framework to mimic the saliency hierarchy.

Hierarchical Saliency Modeling. In order to detect salient objects in different levels, we input the decomposed features $\{H_k^1, ..., H_k^N\}$ in multiple branches. Specifically, we use the different convolution kernels to extract features from different levels, achieving more dedicated saliency modeling schemes as:

$$H_k^{n\prime} = H_k^n * W_k^n, \quad n = 1, 2, ..., N, \tag{3}$$

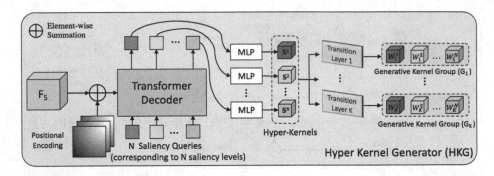

Fig. 5. The detailed depiction of our proposed Hyper Kernel Generator.

where W_k^n is the n-th kernel of the input Generative Kernel Groups, $*$ is the convolution operation, and $H_k^{n'}$ indicates the features from different regions. Finally, we aggregate all regional features $\{H_k^{1'}, ..., H_k^{N'}\}$ with the input feature F_k from the k-th CNN block. The whole process can be formulated as:

$$H_{k-1} = \text{Conv}_{3\times3}(\text{Concat}(\sum_{n=1}^{N} H_k^{n'}, F_k)), \tag{4}$$

where $\text{Concat}(\cdot)$ is the concatenation operator and H_{k-1} is the output of SHM_k.

Overall, SHM not only explicitly depicts the hierarchical saliency levels inside an image based on sub-saliency masks, but also models the saliency patterns of different saliency levels to capture more details within respective branches.

3.2 Hyper Kernel Generator

In this section, we illustrate the proposed Hyper Kernel Generator (HKG), which further promotes our hierarchy saliency modeling scheme adaptive to different samples, as shown in Fig. 5. Inspired by hypernetworks, we utilize a unified HKG to generate the cascaded Generative Kernel Groups for all the HSM modules. First, the shared hyper-kernels are produced by a transformer block. Each hyper-kernel corresponds to a saliency level. Next, these shared hyper-kernels are parsed into different kernel groups prepared for the cascaded SHMs.

Hyper-Kernels. In order to get the hyper-kernels, we introduce transformer architecture to establish dense attention between several learnable queries and flattened image patches. The transformer block is composed of L stacked transformer decoding layers. Each layer of the transformer constructs interactions between the learnable saliency queries Q_0 and the flattened image patches. In this way, the l-th transformer decoding layer is formulated as:

$$Q_l = \text{MLP}(\text{MCA}(\text{MSA}(Q_{l-1}), T)), \tag{5}$$

where MSA($\cdot$) is the multi-head self-attention, MCA($\cdot$) is the multi-head cross-attention, and MLP($\cdot$) is the multi-layer perceptron blocks. T stands for the flattened input F_K with standard positional encoding. Denote Q_L as the output of the last transformer layer. We use a shared MLP to project the output feature Q_L into hyper-kernels:

$$\mathbb{S}^n = \text{MLP}(Q_L^n), \quad n = 1, 2, ..., N, \tag{6}$$

where Q_L^n is the n-th token in Q_L and $\mathbb{S}^n$ is the hyper-kernel for the n-th saliency level. By utilizing transformer, we achieve a group of sample-adaptive hyper-kernels $\{\mathbb{S}^1, \mathbb{S}^2, ..., \mathbb{S}^N\}$ for a given sample.

Transition Layers. After that, we assign K transition layers parsing the generated hyper-kernels, i.e., $\mathbb{S}^n$, into K different kernel groups:

$$W_k^n = \phi_k(\mathbb{S}^n), \quad k = 1, 2, ..., K, n = 1, 2, ..., N, \tag{7}$$

where $\phi_k(\cdot)$ is the k-th transition layer. Each transition layer is prepared for a specific decoder block (i.e., SHM). Finally, the k-th Generative Kernel Group $G_k = \{W_k^1, W_k^2, ..., W_k^N\}$ is fed into SHM$_k$ to conduct the sample-adaptive convolution operations. It is worth noting that the hyper-kernels are shared across the all SHMs.

Overall, our HKG module learns the hyper-knowledge of diverse saliency patterns to generate the cascaded sample-adaptive kernel groups for decoder blocks, enhancing the flexibility and capacity of the framework dramatically.

3.3 Optimization

Sub-saliency Masks Regularization. As a matter of fact, it is a daunting task to generate sub-saliency masks in a completely unconstrained situation. To alleviate the learning difficulty, we introduce a prior guidance G_{sal} to divide the salient objects of a ground-truth label into several parts $\{p^1, p^2, ..., p^N\}$. p^n denotes the sub-saliency label of the n-th saliency level, and all pixels belong to the n-th saliency level are annotated as positive, otherwise negative. For example, we use Grad-CAM [34] to obtain the gradient response map of the input sample and divide the ground-truth label according to the level of the gradient response. More prior algorithms and corresponding experiments are discussed in Sect. 4.4.

Objective Function. Based on the obtained sub-saliency labels $\{p^1, p^2, ..., p^N\}$, we propose to regularize the predicted sub-saliency masks $\{\hat{p^1}, \hat{p^2}, ..., \hat{p^N}\}$. Note that we only regularize the pixels that belong to the salient objects y_{pos}, i.e., white and black regions in the sub-saliency mask $\hat{p^n}$ in Fig. 4. Those pixels in gray are ignored. Thus, the saliency hierarchy loss for n-th saliency level in the k-th SHM is denoted as:

$$\mathcal{L}_{hierarchy}^{n,k} = \sum_{(i,j) \in y_{pos}} (\hat{p_k^n}(i,j) - p^n(i,j))^2, \tag{8}$$

where $\hat{p}_k^n(i,j)$ and $p^n(i,j)$ are pixels at location (i,j) from the predicted sub-saliency mask and sub-saliency label, respectively.

Finally, the overall objective function is the combination between $\mathcal{L}_{hierarchy}^{n,k}$ and a pixel position aware loss L_{ppa} [42], denoted as:

$$\mathcal{L}_{total} = \mathcal{L}_{ppa}(\hat{y}, y) + \rho \sum_{k=1}^{K} \sum_{n=1}^{N} \mathcal{L}_{hierarchy}^{n,k}, \tag{9}$$

where ρ is a hyper-parameter, $\hat{y}$ and y are the predicted and ground-truth saliency maps, respectively.

4   Experiments

4.1   Datasets and Evaluation Metrics

Datasets. We perform experiments on five widely used benchmark datasets, including DUTS [40], ECSSD [49], HKU-IS [20], DUT-O [50] and PASCAL-S [22]. DUTS contains 10,553 training images (DUTS-TR) and 5,019 test images (DUTS-TE). ECSSD contains 1000 images with structurally complex natural contents. HKU-IS is composed of 4,447 complex scenes that contain multiple salient objects. DUT-O contains 5,168 images with complex backgrounds. PASCAL-S consists of 850 challenging images.

Evaluation Metrics. To comprehensively and fairly evaluate various methods, we employ three widely used metrics, including mean F-measure ($\mathcal{F}_\beta$) [1], mean absolute error ($\mathcal{M}$) [3] and E-measure ($\mathcal{E}_\xi$) [10]. Specifically, the mean F-measure can evaluate the overall performance based on the region similarity. The Mean Absolute Error represents the average absolute difference between the saliency map and ground truth. The E-measure can jointly utilize image-level statistics and local pixel-level statistics for evaluating the binary saliency map. Besides, we also report the floating point of operations (FLOPs) to evaluate their complexity.

4.2   Implementation Details

Our method is implemented with PyTorch toolbox [31], and can be conducted on a single NVIDIA GTX 1080Ti GPU. The proposed model is trained on DUTS-TR and tested on the above mentioned five datasets. As for training, we adopt ResNet-50 [14] and VGG-16 [35] as our backbone networks, which are pretrained on the ImageNet [8] dataset. To reduce overfitting, we utilize image augmentation techniques (i.e., random flipping, rotating, cropping and color enhancing). The maximum learning rates are set to $2e-5$ for the convolution backbone network and $2e-4$ for other parts, with warm-up and linear decay strategies. Training batch size and epochs are set to 16 and 100, respectively. Totally, the whole network is trained in an end-to-end manner using Adam optimizer. For more fair comparison, we conduct experiments on two kinds of resolutions (i.e., 256×256 and 352×352) with different channel settings. As for testing, each image is simply resized to the corresponding resolution and then fed into our network to get the saliency prediction without any post-processing.

Table 1. Performance comparison of SOTA methods over 5 datasets. MAE ($\mathcal{M}$ ↓, smaller is better), mean F-measure (F_β ↑, larger is better) and mean E-measure (E_ξ ↑, larger is better) are used to measure the model performance. '†' means inputs of 256 resolution. '*' means inputs of 352 resolution. The best two results are marked in red and blue. Our method outperforms other approaches on both performance and efficiency.

Method	GFLOPs	DUTS-TE			ECSSD			HKU-IS			DUT-O			PASCAL-S		
		$\mathcal{M}$	F_β	E_ξ	$\mathcal{M}$	F_β	E_ξ	$\mathcal{M}$	F_β	E_ξ	$\mathcal{M}$	F_β	E_ξ	$\mathcal{M}$	F_β	E_ξ
VGG-Based methods																
CPD* [45]	118.86	.043	.813	.902	.040	.915	.938	.033	.896	.940	.057	.745	.845	.074	.825	.882
AFN [11]	–	.046	.812	.893	.042	.905	.935	.036	.888	.934	.057	.742	.846	.071	.824	.883
MLMS* [44]	256.81	.045	.802	.893	.038	.914	.943	.034	.893	.942	.056	.742	.853	.069	.838	.890
EGN† [53]	–	.043	.826	.898	.044	.910	.936	.034	.894	.938	.056	.752	.853	.076	.818	.877
CAGN* [28]	154.25	.044	.823	.904	.042	.915	.939	.033	.906	.947	.057	.744	.860	.077	.831	.881
GateN [55]	216.47	.045	.817	.893	.041	.905	.932	.035	.891	.934	.061	.733	.840	.070	.826	.886
MIN [30]	292.52	.039	.823	.912	.036	.922	.943	.030	.906	.955	.057	.741	.864	.065	.843	.898
ITSD [58]	114.93	.042	.833	.905	.040	.910	.937	.035	.894	.938	.063	.752	.853	.074	.831	.891
DCN* [47]	411.25	.041	–	.918	.032	–	.945	.034	–	.949	.055	–	.871	.069	–	.892
AMSF† [52]	87.71	.039	.842	.920	.036	.924	.951	.029	.908	.955	.056	.763	.866	.068	.840	.899
SHNet†	44.97	.035	.851	.926	.033	.926	.950	.028	.913	.955	.054	.765	.868	.060	.842	.906
SHNet*	95.02	.034	.861	.928	.031	.930	.952	.026	.917	.957	.056	.769	.868	.058	.849	.910
ResNet/Transformer-Based methods																
CPD* [45]	35.48	.043	.805	.898	.037	.917	.942	.034	.891	.938	.056	.747	.847	.072	.824	.882
EGN† [53]	157.21	.039	.839	.907	.041	.918	.943	.031	.902	.944	.052	.760	.857	.074	.823	.881
SCRN* [46]	30.13	.040	.833	.900	.038	.916	.939	.034	.894	.935	.056	.749	.848	.064	.833	.892
CAGN* [28]	47.47	.040	.838	.914	.037	.921	.944	.030	.910	.950	.054	.753	.862	.067	.847	.896
GateN [55]	162.13	.040	.837	.906	.040	.913	.936	.033	.897	.937	.055	.757	.855	.069	.826	.886
F3N* [42]	32.86	.035	.852	.920	.033	.928	.948	.028	.910	.952	.053	.766	.864	.061	.830	.898
MIN [30]	174.06	.037	.828	.917	.033	.924	.953	.028	.908	.956	.055	.756	.873	.064	.842	.899
LDF* [43]	31.02	.034	.855	.910	.034	.930	.925	.027	.914	.954	.051	.773	.873	.060	.848	.865
VST† [25]	46.32	.037	.845	.919	.034	.920	.951	.030	.907	.952	.058	.774	.871	.067	.835	.902
CTDN* [56]	24.66	.034	.853	.929	.032	.927	.950	.027	.919	.955	.052	.779	.875	.061	.841	.901
DCN* [47]	110.22	.035	.860	.927	.032	.931	.955	.027	.915	.958	.051	.779	.878	.062	.839	.901
AMSF† [52]	48.96	.034	.856	.931	.033	.929	.954	.027	.914	.959	.050	.778	.876	.061	.850	.902
SHNet†	15.26	.032	.867	.936	.030	.933	.958	.026	.918	.958	.049	.784	.883	.057	.849	.912
SHNet*	44.87	.030	.883	.938	.028	.939	.957	.025	.926	.959	.048	.790	.880	.056	.855	.910

4.3 Comparison with State-of-the-Art

Quantitative Comparison. As shown in Table 1, we present the quantitative comparison in terms of four evaluation metrics on five datasets. On one hand, our SHNet surpasses these SOTA methods by a large margin across all the datasets in most metrics. Specifically, the VGG-based SHNet outperforms other methods across all datasets, except that it ranks second on E_ξ of DUT-O dataset. The ResNet-based SHNet obtains the best results on all five datasets. Especially, the F_β of ResNet-based SHNet-352 is significantly better than other best result on DUTS-TE (88.3% against 86.0%) and DUT-O (79.0% against 77.9%). Meanwhile, it also possesses an evident advantage on $\mathcal{M}$ with 11.7% and 12.5% improvements on DUTS-TE and ECSSD.

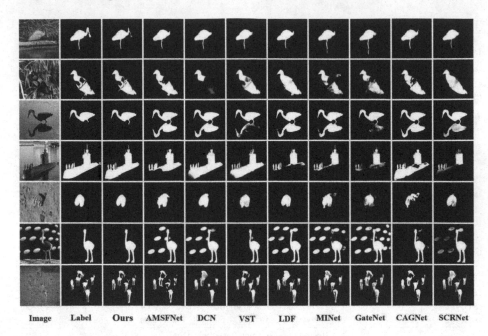

| Image | Label | Ours | AMSFNet | DCN | VST | LDF | MINet | GateNet | CAGNet | SCRNet |

Fig. 6. Qualitative comparison between the state-of-the-art SOD methods and our SHNet. Obviously, saliency maps produced by our model are more clear and more accurate than that of other methods in various challenging scenarios.

Table 2. Ablation study of different prior guidance G_{sal}. 'w/o' means no extra supervision. 'Baseline' means framework without saliency hierarchy modeling.

#	G_{sal}	DUTS-TE		ECSSD		DUT-O	
		$\mathcal{F}_\beta \uparrow$	$\mathcal{M} \downarrow$	$\mathcal{F}_\beta \uparrow$	$\mathcal{M} \downarrow$	$\mathcal{F}_\beta \uparrow$	$\mathcal{M} \downarrow$
1	w/o	.830	.038	.909	.039	.745	.056
2	Erode	.849	.036	.922	.034	.761	.054
3	DT	.850	.035	.920	.034	.764	.054
4	Grad-Cam	**.854**	**.034**	**.927**	**.031**	**.772**	**.050**
*	Baseline	.820	.041	.901	.041	.734	.060

On the other hand, our method (SHNet-256) achieves the state-of-the-art performance using the lowest cost (i.e., VGG-based: 44.97 GFLOPs, ResNet-based: 15.26 GFLOPs) among all the compared methods. Moreover, both the VGG-based and ResNet-based SHNet-352 achieve higher performance without consuming much computation cost. The reason might be a larger input is helpful to more accurate modeling of region-level saliency divergence.

Qualitative Comparisons. To further illustrate the effectiveness of our method, we visualize a qualitative comparison between our method and other

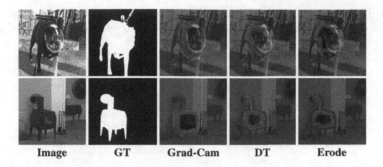

Fig. 7. The visualization results of prior guidance G_{sal}. Red, yellow and green represent the saliency level division results, when the number of saliency levels (N) equals 3. **Best viewed in color.** (Color figure online)

state-of-the-art approaches. As shown in Fig. 6, our method not only highlights the salient object regions clearly, but also well suppresses the background noises. The proposed SHNet is able to accurately segment salient objects under various challenging scenarios, including images with fine structures (1st and 7th rows), partial occlusion (2nd row), reflection interference (3rd row), low contrast foreground and background (4th and 5th rows), and cluttered distractions (6th and 7th rows). It is worth noting that SHNet achieves better results than other methods under an extremely challenging scenario (7th row), where multiple salient objects are similar with the background in terms of color and texture.

4.4   Ablation Analysis

In this section, we perform a series of ablation studies and further estimate each component in the proposed framework. First, we explore different prior guidance estimation methods. Second, we study the region-level saliency modeling scheme and visualize the activation maps in different branches. Next, we show the effectiveness of Hyper Kernel Generator. Finally, we show the ablation studies on the proposed components in our method. Experiments are conducted with inputs at a resolution of 256 × 256, based on ResNet-50 backbone.

Prior Guidance Estimation. In this part, we explore several prior guidance G_{sal} to assist the learning process. As shown in Fig. 7, we show three kinds of saliency division results under different G_{sal} to illustrate the proposed method: including DT, Erode, Grad-Cam. Specifically, 'DT' [33] refers to calculating the nearest distance of each pixel to the boundary and decomposing the ground-truth map with given thresholds. 'Erode' means we iteratively erode the ground-truth label to get the annular saliency level division. 'Grad-Cam' [34] is a data-driven method that decompose the ground-truth salient objects according to the gradient response maps of each regions, which are provided by a standard classification model (i.e. ResNet-50 pre-trained on ImageNet).

Table 3. Performance (mean F-measure) and computational cost comparison of different approaches. These approaches use different strategies to generate kernel groups.

#	Settings	GFLOPs	Params	DUTS-TE	ECSSD
1	Static	13.2	25.1	.854	.927
2	Hyper Conv	15.3	31.4	.859	.927
3	Build-in Trans	15.7	61.0	.866	**.933**
4	**Hyper Trans**	15.1	32.4	**.867**	**.933**

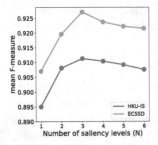

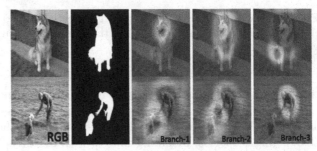

Fig. 8. Ablation on the number of saliency levels (from 1 to 6).

Fig. 9. The visualization of feature activation maps (Grad-Cam) from different branches in SHM₄. **Best viewed in color.** (Color figure online)

As shown in Table 2, the method without extra guidance achieves 83% on $\mathcal{F}_\beta$ of DUTS-TE. Through explicit guidance on the sub-saliency masks with 'Erode' and 'DT', the performance gains 1.9%, and 2.0%, respectively. Furthermore, when applying the 'Grad-Cam' to generate sub-saliency labels, the performance further increases to 85.4%. These results indicate that our framework supports various knowledge to mimic the hierarchy patterns for region-level modeling and the data-driven method (e.g., 'Grad-Cam') is more friendly to our framework.

Region-Level Saliency Modeling. The number of saliency levels (N) is an important hyper-parameter. As shown in Fig. 8, we compare the mean F-measure on two datasets, and the qualitative results indicate that applying multi-branch learning patterns on the decomposed sub-saliency regions can significantly boost the performance. However, over decomposition may do harm to the global context, resulting in a slight performance drop. We achieve the best performance in our framework when N equals 3. Moreover, as shown in Fig. 9, we provide the visualization of feature activation maps (Grad-Cam) from different branches in SHM₄ (i.e., $\{H_4^{1'}, H_4^{2'}, H_4^{3'}\}$ in Eq. 3). Different regions are activated in corresponding branches, which evidently justifies that our model achieves the region-level saliency hierarchy modeling by a divide-and-conquer strategy.

Table 4. Ablation study of each module in our SHNet. 'Baseline' denotes the vanilla U-Net with ResNet-50 backbone. 'SHM (Static)' denotes the SHM with static kernels in the branches.

Settings	DUTS-TE		ECSSD		HKU-IS		PASCAL-S		DUT-O	
	$\mathcal{F}_\beta \uparrow$	$\mathcal{M} \downarrow$	$\mathcal{F}_\beta \uparrow$	$\mathcal{M} \downarrow$	$\mathcal{F}_\beta \uparrow$	$\mathcal{M} \downarrow$	$\mathcal{F}_\beta \uparrow$	$\mathcal{M} \downarrow$	$\mathcal{F}_\beta \uparrow$	$\mathcal{M} \downarrow$
Baseline (B)	.820	.041	.901	.041	.886	.036	.827	.067	.734	.060
B + SHM(Static)	.854	.034	.927	.031	.912	.028	.848	.059	.772	.050
B + SHM+HSG	**.867**	**.032**	**.933**	**.030**	**.918**	**.026**	**.849**	**.057**	**.784**	**.049**

Sample-Level Saliency Modeling. In order to verify the effectiveness of our proposed HKG, we conduct a series of experiments with different kernel generation strategies, as shown in Table 3. Our strategy is denoted as 'Hyper Trans', which uses shared hyper-kernels for all SHMs. 'Hyper Conv' means utilizing the convolutional architecture to generate the shared hyper-kernels. 'Build-in Trans' stands for using multiple transformer architecture for generating different hyper-kernels for respective SHMs instead of the shared one. The results demonstrate that the proposed HKG is an effective way to produce the two-dimensional (layer, branch) kernel matrix for our decoder. Meanwhile, the shared hyper-kernels could reduce computational costs without any performance drop, which further verifies our module could excavate the hyper-knowledge for the diverse saliency patterns.

Effectiveness of the Proposals. As shown in Table 4, we use the vanilla U-Net with ResNet-50 backbone as our baseline model. 'SHM (Static)' indicates the Saliency Hierarchy Modules with static kernels in the multiple branches. The mean F-measure of 'SHM (Static)' is better than that of the baseline on DUTS-TE (85.4% against 82.0%) and DUT-O (77.2% against 73.4%). Moreover, with the HKG module, the performance is further improved to 78.4% in mean F-measure on DUT-O, and surpasses the state-of-the-art results with a low computational cost.

5   Conclusion

In this paper, we propose a framework named SHNet for SOD, which aims to model saliency hierarchically with generative kernels. We design a Saliency Hierarchy Module to model the hierarchical saliency levels in a given sample with the guide of prior knowledge. Furthermore, we design a Hyper Kernel Generator to automatically adjust our network parameters to the saliency divergence among different samples by generating cascaded kernel groups, which achieves a sample adaptive inference pattern. Extensive experiments demonstrate the effectiveness of our method on both performance and efficiency.

Acknowledgment. This work is supported in part by National Key Research and Development Program of China under Grant 2020AAA0107400, Zhejiang Provincial Natural Science Foundation of China under Grant LR19F020004, National Natural Science Foundation of China under Grant U20A20222.

References

1. Achanta, R., Hemami, S., Estrada, F., Susstrunk, S.: Frequency-tuned salient region detection. In: IEEE Conference on Computer Vision and Pattern Recognition, pp. 1597–1604. IEEE (2009)
2. Achanta, R., Hemami, S.S., Estrada, F.J., Süsstrunk, S.: Frequency-tuned salient region detection. In: IEEE Conference on Computer Vision and Pattern Recognition (2009)
3. Borji, A., Cheng, M.M., Jiang, H., Li, J.: Salient object detection: a benchmark. IEEE Trans. Image Process. **24**(12), 5706–5722 (2015)
4. Carion, N., Massa, F., Synnaeve, G., Usunier, N., Kirillov, A., Zagoruyko, S.: End-to-end object detection with transformers. In: Vedaldi, A., Bischof, H., Brox, T., Frahm, J.-M. (eds.) ECCV 2020. LNCS, vol. 12346, pp. 213–229. Springer, Cham (2020). https://doi.org/10.1007/978-3-030-58452-8_13
5. Chen, S., Tan, X., Wang, B., Hu, X.: Reverse attention for salient object detection. In: Ferrari, V., Hebert, M., Sminchisescu, C., Weiss, Y. (eds.) ECCV 2018. LNCS, vol. 11213, pp. 236–252. Springer, Cham (2018). https://doi.org/10.1007/978-3-030-01240-3_15
6. Chen, Z., Xu, Q., Cong, R., Huang, Q.: Global context-aware progressive aggregation network for salient object detection. In: AAAI, vol. 34, pp. 10599–10606 (2020)
7. Cheng, B., Schwing, A., Kirillov, A.: Per-pixel classification is not all you need for semantic segmentation. In: Advances in Neural Information Processing Systems, vol. 34 (2021)
8. Deng, J., Dong, W., Socher, R., Li, L.J., Li, K., Fei-Fei, L.: Imagenet: a large-scale hierarchical image database. In: IEEE Conference on Computer Vision and Pattern Recognition, pp. 248–255. IEEE (2009)
9. Dosovitskiy, A., et al.: An image is worth 16x16 words: transformers for image recognition at scale. In: International Conference on Learning Representations (2021)
10. Fan, D.P., Gong, C., Cao, Y., Ren, B., Cheng, M.M., Borji, A.: Enhanced-alignment measure for binary foreground map evaluation. In: IJCAI (2018)
11. Feng, M., Lu, H., Ding, E.: Attentive feedback network for boundary-aware salient object detection. In: IEEE Conference on Computer Vision and Pattern Recognition, pp. 1623–1632 (2019)
12. Gu, Y.C., Gao, S.H., Cao, X.S., Du, P., Lu, S.P., Cheng, M.M.: INAS: integral NAS for device-aware salient object detection. In: International Conference on Computer Vision, pp. 4934–4944 (2021)
13. Ha, D., Dai, A., Le, Q.V.: Hypernetworks. In: International Conference on Learning Representations (2016)
14. He, K., Zhang, X., Ren, S., Sun, J.: Deep residual learning for image recognition. In: IEEE Conference on Computer Vision and Pattern Recognition, pp. 770–778 (2016)
15. Itti, L., Koch, C., Niebur, E.: A model of saliency-based visual attention for rapid scene analysis. IEEE Trans. Pattern Anal. Mach. Intell. **20**(11), 1254–1259 (1998)

16. Ji, W., Li, X., Wei, L., Wu, F., Zhuang, Y.: Context-aware graph label propagation network for saliency detection. IEEE Trans. Image Process. **29**, 8177–8186 (2020)
17. Jia, X., De Brabandere, B., Tuytelaars, T., Gool, L.V.: Dynamic filter networks. Adv. Neural Inform. Process. Syst. **29**, 667–675 (2016)
18. Jiang, H., Wang, J., Yuan, Z., Wu, Y., Zheng, N., Li, S.: Salient object detection: a discriminative regional feature integration approach. In: International Journal Computer Vision, pp. 2083–2090 (2013)
19. Jiang, Z., Davis, L.S.: Submodular salient region detection. In: IEEE Conference on Computer Vision and Pattern Recognition, pp. 2043–2050 (2013). https://doi.org/10.1109/CVPR.2013.266
20. Li, G., Yu, Y.: Visual saliency based on multiscale deep features. In: CVPR, pp. 5455–5463. IEEE Computer Society (2015)
21. Li, J., Su, J., Xia, C., Ma, M., Tian, Y.: Salient object detection with purificatory mechanism and structural similarity loss. IEEE Trans. Image Process. **30**, 6855–6868 (2021)
22. Li, Y., Hou, X., Koch, C., Rehg, J.M., Yuille, A.L.: The secrets of salient object segmentation. In: CVPR, pp. 280–287. IEEE Computer Society (2014)
23. Littwin, G., Wolf, L.: Deep meta functionals for shape representation. In: International Conference on Computer Vision, pp. 1824–1833 (2019)
24. Liu, J.J., Hou, Q., Cheng, M.M.: Dynamic feature integration for simultaneous detection of salient object, edge, and skeleton. IEEE Trans. Image Process. **29**, 8652–8667 (2020)
25. Liu, N., Zhang, N., Wan, K., Shao, L., Han, J.: Visual saliency transformer. In: International Conference on Computer Vision, pp. 4722–4732 (2021)
26. Liu, T., et al.: Learning to detect a salient object. IEEE Trans. Pattern Anal. Mach. Intell. **33**(2), 353–367 (2010)
27. Ma, M., Xia, C., Li, J.: Pyramidal feature shrinking for salient object detection. In: AAAI, vol. 35, pp. 2311–2318 (2021)
28. Mohammadi, S., Noori, M., Bahri, A., Majelan, S.G., Havaei, M.: Cagnet: content-aware guidance for salient object detection. Pattern Recogn. **103**, 107303 (2020)
29. Nirkin, Y., Wolf, L., Hassner, T.: Hyperseg: patch-wise hypernetwork for real-time semantic segmentation. In: IEEE Conference on Computer Vision and Pattern Recognition, pp. 4061–4070 (2021)
30. Pang, Y., Zhao, X., Zhang, L., Lu, H.: Multi-scale interactive network for salient object detection. In: IEEE Conference on Computer Vision and Pattern Recognition, pp. 9413–9422 (2020)
31. Paszke, A., et al.: Pytorch: an imperative style, high-performance deep learning library. In: Advances in Neural Information Processing Systems (2019)
32. Qin, X., Zhang, Z., Huang, C., Gao, C., Dehghan, M., Jagersand, M.: Basnet: boundary-aware salient object detection. In: IEEE Conference on Computer Vision and Pattern Recognition, pp. 7479–7489 (2019)
33. Rosenfeld, A., Pfaltz, J.L.: Distance functions on digital pictures. Pattern Recogn. **1**(1), 33–61 (1968)
34. Selvaraju, R.R., Cogswell, M., Das, A., Vedantam, R., Parikh, D., Batra, D.: Grad-cam: Visual explanations from deep networks via gradient-based localization. In: International Conference on Computer Vision, pp. 618–626 (2017)
35. Simonyan, K., Zisserman, A.: Very deep convolutional networks for large-scale image recognition. International Conference on Learning Representations (2014)
36. Sun, P., Zhang, W., Wang, H., Li, S., Li, X.: Deep RGB-D saliency detection with depth-sensitive attention and automatic multi-modal fusion. In: IEEE Conference on Computer Vision and Pattern Recognition, pp. 1407–1417 (2021)

37. Tang, L., Li, B., Zhong, Y., Ding, S., Song, M.: Disentangled high quality salient object detection. In: International Conference on Computer Vision, pp. 3580–3590 (2021)
38. Vaswani, A., et al.: Attention is all you need. In: Advances in Neural Information Processing Systems, pp. 5998–6008 (2017)
39. Wang, B., Chen, Q., Zhou, M., Zhang, Z., Jin, X., Gai, K.: Progressive feature polishing network for salient object detection. In: AAAI, vol. 34, pp. 12128–12135 (2020)
40. Wang, L., et al.: Learning to detect salient objects with image-level supervision. In: CVPR, pp. 3796–3805. IEEE Computer Society (2017)
41. Wang, T., Zhang, L., Lu, H., Sun, C., Qi, J.: Kernelized subspace ranking for saliency detection. In: Leibe, B., Matas, J., Sebe, N., Welling, M. (eds.) ECCV 2016. LNCS, vol. 9912, pp. 450–466. Springer, Cham (2016). https://doi.org/10.1007/978-3-319-46484-8_27
42. Wei, J., Wang, S., Huang, Q.: F^3net: Fusion, feedback and focus for salient object detection. In: AAAI, pp. 12321–12328 (2020)
43. Wei, J., Wang, S., Wu, Z., Su, C., Huang, Q., Tian, Q.: Label decoupling framework for salient object detection. In: Proceedings of the IEEE/CVF Conference on Computer Vision and Pattern Recognition, pp. 13025–13034 (2020)
44. Wu, R., Feng, M., Guan, W., Wang, D., Lu, H., Ding, E.: A mutual learning method for salient object detection with intertwined multi-supervision. In: 2019 IEEE/CVF Conference on Computer Vision and Pattern Recognition (CVPR) (2020)
45. Wu, Z., Su, L., Huang, Q.: Cascaded partial decoder for fast and accurate salient object detection. In: IEEE Conference on Computer Vision and Pattern Recognition, pp. 3907–3916 (2019)
46. Wu, Z., Su, L., Huang, Q.: Stacked cross refinement network for edge-aware salient object detection. In: International Conference on Computer Vision, pp. 7264–7273 (2019)
47. Wu, Z., Su, L., Huang, Q.: Decomposition and completion network for salient object detection. IEEE Trans. Image Process. **30**, 6226–6239 (2021)
48. Xu, B., Liang, H., Liang, R., Chen, P.: Locate globally, segment locally: a progressive architecture with knowledge review network for salient object detection. In: AAAI, vol. 35, pp. 3004–3012 (2021)
49. Yan, Q., Xu, L., Shi, J., Jia, J.: Hierarchical saliency detection. In: CVPR, pp. 1155–1162. IEEE Computer Society (2013)
50. Yang, C., Zhang, L., Lu, H., Ruan, X., Yang, M.: Saliency detection via graph-based manifold ranking. In: CVPR, pp. 3166–3173. IEEE Computer Society (2013)
51. Zhang, L., Zhang, J., Lin, Z., Lu, H., He, Y.: CAPSAL: Leveraging captioning to boost semantics for salient object detection. In: IEEE Conference on Computer Vision and Pattern Recognition, pp. 6024–6033 (2019)
52. Zhang, M., Liu, T., Piao, Y., Yao, S., Lu, H.: Auto-msfnet: Search multi-scale fusion network for salient object detection. In: ACM International Conference on Multimedia (2021)
53. Zhao, J.X., Liu, J.J., Fan, D.P., Cao, Y., Yang, J., Cheng, M.M.: EGNet: edge guidance network for salient object detection. In: International Conference on Computer Vision, pp. 8779–8788 (2019)
54. Zhao, T., Wu, X.: Pyramid feature attention network for saliency detection. In: IEEE Conference on Computer Vision and Pattern Recognition, pp. 3085–3094 (2019)

55. Zhao, X., Pang, Y., Zhang, L., Lu, H., Zhang, L.: Suppress and balance: a simple gated network for salient object detection. In: Vedaldi, A., Bischof, H., Brox, T., Frahm, J.-M. (eds.) ECCV 2020. LNCS, vol. 12347, pp. 35–51. Springer, Cham (2020). https://doi.org/10.1007/978-3-030-58536-5_3
56. Zhao, Z., Xia, C., Xie, C., Li, J.: Complementary trilateral decoder for fast and accurate salient object detection. In: ACM International Conference on Multimedia, pp. 4967–4975 (2021)
57. Zheng, S., et al.: Rethinking semantic segmentation from a sequence-to-sequence perspective with transformers. In: IEEE Conference on Computer Vision and Pattern Recognition, pp. 6881–6890 (2021)
58. Zhou, H., Xie, X., Lai, J.H., Chen, Z., Yang, L.: Interactive two-stream decoder for accurate and fast saliency detection. In: IEEE Conference on Computer Vision and Pattern Recognition, pp. 9141–9150 (2020)

In Defense of Online Models for Video Instance Segmentation

Junfeng Wu[1], Qihao Liu[2], Yi Jiang[3], Song Bai[3(✉)], Alan Yuille[2],
and Xiang Bai[1]

[1] Huazhong University of Science and Technology, Wuhan, China
[2] Johns Hopkins University, Baltimore, USA
[3] ByteDance Inc., Singapore, Singapore
songbai.site@gmail.com

Abstract. In recent years, video instance segmentation (VIS) has been largely advanced by offline models, while online models gradually attracted less attention possibly due to their inferior performance. However, online methods have their inherent advantage in handling long video sequences and ongoing videos while offline models fail due to the limit of computational resources. Therefore, it would be highly desirable if online models can achieve comparable or even better performance than offline models. By dissecting current online models and offline models, we demonstrate that the main cause of the performance gap is the error-prone association between frames caused by the similar appearance among different instances in the feature space. Observing this, we propose an online framework based on contrastive learning that is able to learn more discriminative instance embeddings for association and fully exploit history information for stability. Despite its simplicity, our method outperforms all online and offline methods on three benchmarks. Specifically, we achieve 49.5 AP on YouTube-VIS 2019, a significant improvement of 13.2 AP and 2.1 AP over the prior online and offline art, respectively. Moreover, we achieve 30.2 AP on OVIS, a more challenging dataset with significant crowding and occlusions, surpassing the prior art by 14.8 AP. The proposed method won **first place** in the video instance segmentation track of the 4th Large-scale Video Object Segmentation Challenge (CVPR2022). We hope the simplicity and effectiveness of our method, as well as our insight on current methods, could shed light on the exploration of VIS models. The code is available at https://github.com/wjf5203/VNext.

Keywords: Video instance segmentation · Online model · Contrastive learning

---

J. Wu and Q. Liu—First two authors contributed equally.Work done during an internship at ByteDance.

Supplementary Information The online version contains supplementary material available at https://doi.org/10.1007/978-3-031-19815-1_34.

ⓒ The Author(s), under exclusive license to Springer Nature Switzerland AG 2022
S. Avidan et al. (Eds.): ECCV 2022, LNCS 13688, pp. 588–605, 2022.
https://doi.org/10.1007/978-3-031-19815-1_34

1   Introduction

Video instance segmentation aims at detecting, segmenting, and tracking object instances simultaneously in a given video. It attracted considerable attention after first defined [45] in 2019 due to the huge challenge and the wide applications in video understanding, video editing, autonomous driving, augmented reality, etc. Current VIS methods can be categorized as online or offline methods. Online methods [4,8,18,20,45,46] take as input a video frame by frame, detecting and segmenting objects per frame while tracking instances and optimizing results across frames. Offline methods [1,3,16,21,37,40], in contrast, take the whole video as input and generate the instance sequence of the entire video with a single step.

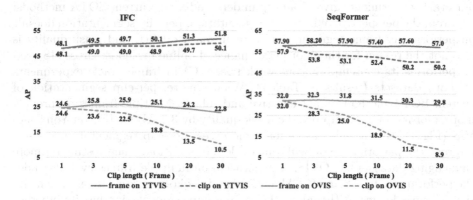

Fig. 1. Oracle experiments on SOTA offline methods: We analyze current VIS methods and visualize some results here. More results can be found in Sect. 4.2. 'YTVIS' is short for YouTube-VIS 2019. 'Frame' and 'clip' stand for frame oracle and clip oracle experiments, respectively. For frame oracles, we provide the ground-truth instance ID both within each clip and between adjacent clips. Thus the performance only depends on the quality of the estimated segmentation masks. For clip oracles, we only provide the ground-truth instance ID between adjacent clips, and the method is required to do association within the clips by itself. Therefore the gaps between frame oracles and clip oracles show the effect of the black-box association done within current offline models. When clip length is 1, the method is doing per-frame segmentation.

Despite high performance, the requirement of full videos limits the application scenarios of offline models, especially for scenarios involving long video sequences (videos exceed 50 frames on GPU of 32G RAM [40]) and ongoing videos (*e.g.*, videos in autonomous driving and augmented reality). However, online models are usually inferior to the contemporaneous offline models by over 10 AP, which is a huge drawback. Previously, little work tries to explain the performance gap between these two paradigms, or gives insight into the high performance of the offline paradigm. A common attempt of the latter is made from the inherent advantages of offline models being able to skip the error-accumulating tracking steps [21] and utilize the richer information provided by multiple frames to improve segmentation [1,16,38,40]. However, does that really explain the high performance of current offline methods? What's the main problem causing the poor performance of online models? Can online models achieve performance comparable to, or even better than, SOTA offline ones?

To deeply understand the performance of both online and offline models, we analyze in detail three SOTA methods (offline: IFC [16] and SeqFormer [40], online: CrossVIS [46]) on two datasets (YouTube-VIS [45] and OVIS [30]) that have different difficulty levels. 'Simple video' refers to the video in YouTube-VIS. These videos are much shorter and only contain very slight occlusions, simple motions, and smooth changes in illumination and object shapes. 'Complex video' refers to the video in OVIS. Please see Sect. 4.1 for details. The results (Fig. 1) of our oracle experiments give us a deep understanding of current SOTA methods:

From the perspective of instance segmentation, per-clip segmentation doesn't outperform per-frame segmentation a lot in mask quality, and mask quality is also not the reason for the poor performance of online methods: CrossVIS even outperforms its contemporaneous work (*i.e.* IFC) in frame oracle experiments on both datasets (results in Table 1). What's more, per-clip segmentation of current SOTA methods is not effective and robust. Multiple frames do provide more information and improve the mask quality by 3.7 AP for IFC on YouTube-VIS (Fig. 1). But it only works for some cases: per-clip segmentation doesn't improve the performance of SeqFormer a lot. In addition, when testing on more challenging datasets like OVIS, segmentation on multiple frames even degrades the performance by 1.8 and 2.2 AP on IFC and SeqFormer respectively when clip size becomes longer. Although in theory, per-clip segmentation has its inherent advantage to using multiple frames, it still requires further exploration, especially in how to utilize information in multiple frames and how to handle complex motion patterns, occlusion, and object deformation. Currently, we don't see an obvious gap between the mask qualities of per-clip and per-frame segmentation.

From the perspective of association, a huge advantage of the offline methods is their ability to avoid the use of hand-designed association modules. It works well on simple cases of the YouTube-VIS dataset. We demonstrate that it is the main reason causing the performance gap between the current online and offline paradigms. However, this black-box association process done within offline models also gets worse rapidly when the video becomes complex (degrades the performance of IFC by 12.3 AP and SeqFormer by 20.9 AP on OVIS). In addition, when handling longer videos, *e.g.* videos in the real world or from OVIS dataset, offline methods require splitting the input video into clips to avoid exceeding computational limits, and thus hand-designed clip matching is still inevitable, which will further decrease the overall performance. To sum up, matching/association is the main reasoning for the performance gap, and it is still inevitable and of great importance for offline models.

To improve the matching performance and thus bridge the performance gap, we propose a framework **In Defense of OnLine** models for video instance segmentation, termed IDOL. The key idea is to ensure, in the embedding space, the similarity of the same instance across frames and the difference of different instances in all frames, even for instances that belong to the same category and have similar appearances. It provides more discriminative instance features with better temporal consistency, which guarantees more accurate association results. However, previous method [29] selects positive and negative samples by a hand-craft setting, introducing false positives in occlusions and crowded scenes, thus impairing contrastive learning. To address it, we formulate the problem of sample selection as an Optimal Transport problem in Optimization Theory, which reduces false positives and further improves the quality of the embedding. During inference, by using one-to-many temporally weighted softmax, we utilize the learned prior of the embedding to re-identify missing instances caused by occlusions and to enforce the consistency and integrality of associations.

Our thorough analysis gives us a deep understanding of current online and offline VIS methods. Based on our observation, we bridge the performance gap from the perspective of feature embeddings and propose IDOL. We conduct extensive experiments on YouTube-VIS 2019, YouTube-VIS 2021, and OVIS datasets. Despite its simplicity, our method sets a new state-of-the-art achieving 62.2 AP, 56.1 AP, and 42.6 AP on the validation set of these three benchmarks, respectively. More importantly, compared with previous online methods, we achieve a consistent improvement ranging from 13.2 AP to 14.7 AP on these datasets. We even surpass the previous SOTA offline method by up to 2.1 AP. We believe the simplicity and effectiveness of our method shall benefit further research. In addition, our thorough analysis provides insights for current methods and suggests useful directions for future work in both online and offline VIS.

2 Related Work

Online Video Instance Segmentation. Most online VIS methods are built upon image-level instance segmentation with an additional tracking head to associate instances across the video. The baseline method MaskTrack R-CNN [45] is built upon Mask R-CNN and proposes to leverage multi cues such as appearance similarity, semantic consistency, spatial correlation, and detection confidence to determine the instance labels. Most online methods [4,8,17,20,46] follow this pipeline. CrossVIS [46] proposes a new learning scheme that uses the instance feature in the current frame to segment the same instance in another frame. Multi-Object Tracking and Segmentation (MOTS) [7,36] aims to simultaneously segment and track all object instances of a given video sequence in real-time, which is similar to online VIS. MOTS methods are usually built upon multiple object trackers [2,18,29,32,44,47–49]. Track R-CNN [36] firstly extends the popular task of multi-object tracking to MOTS based on Mask R-CNN [13]. Point-Track [43] proposes a new online tracking-by-points paradigm with learning discriminative instance embeddings. Trackformer [25] adopts the transformer architecture for MOTS and introduces track query embeddings that follow objects through a video sequence. Online models have a wider range of application scenarios, however, they are usually inferior to offline art by over 10 AP. We find that the current SOTA online models fail to achieve accurate associations, causing the performance gap. We aim to tackle this problem in this work.

Offline Video Instance Segmentation. Offline methods for VIS take the whole video as input and predict the instance sequence of the entire video (or video clip) with a single step. MaskProp [3] and Propose-Reduce [21] perform mask propagation in a video clip to improve mask and association. However, the propagation process is time-consuming, which limits its application. Recently, VisTR [37] adopts the transformer [35] to VIS and models the instance queries for the whole video. However, it learns an embedding for each instance of each frame, which makes it hard to apply to longer videos and more complex scenes. IFC [16] proposes inter-frame communication transformers and significantly reduces computation and memory usage. SeqFormer [40] dynamically allocates spatial attention on each frame and learns a video-level instance embedding, which greatly improves the performance. We deeply analyze the current SOTA offline models, IFC and SeqFormer, find that their improvement mainly comes from the blackbox association between frames, but this advantage is gradually lost in complex scenarios. In contrast, our online method can be applied to both ongoing and long videos and complex scenarios, with more stable association quality and higher performance.

Contrastive Learning has made significant progress in representation learning [6,11,12,15,28,29,33,41]. MOCO [12] and SimCLR [6] use contrastive learning for image-level self-supervised training and learn strong feature representations for downstream tasks. Some methods [11,19,26] extend the contrastive learning into multiple positive samples format to obtain better feature representations. We absorb ideas from contrastive learning and propose to learn contrastive embeddings between frames for each instance.

3   Method

Given a video clip that consists of multiple image frames, online VIS models [45,46] utilize additional association head upon on instance segmentation models [13,34]. We have already discussed that achieving more stable and discriminative instance embeddings between frames is the key to improve the performance of online models. To achieve this, we propose a contrastive learning framework to extract more discriminative features for instance association (Fig. 2). We first introduce the instance segmentation pipeline in Sect. 3.1. Then the details of our contrastive learning framework and the cross-frame instance association strategy are introduced in Sect. 3.2 and Sect. 3.3 respectively. More implementation details can be found in the supplementary.

3.1   Instance Segmentation

For fair comparisons with the state-of-the-art offline method [40], we take DeformableDETR [50] with dynamic mask head [34] as our instance segmentation pipeline in this paper. Our method can be coupled with other instance segmentation methods with minor modifications.

Given an input frame $x \in R^{3 \times H \times W}$ of a video, a CNN backbone extracts multi-scale feature maps. The Deformable DETR module takes the feature maps with additional fixed positional encodings [5] and N learnable object queries as input. The object queries are first transformed into output embeddings $E \in R^{N \times C}$ by the transformer decoder. After that, they are decoded into box coordinates and class labels by 3-layer feed-forward network (FFN) separately. For per-frame mask generation, we employ an FPN-like [22] mask branch to make the use of multi-scale feature maps from transformer encoder and generate feature map F_{mask} that are 1/8 resolution of the input frame. Another FFN encode outputs embeddings into parameters ω of mask head, which performs three-layer 1×1 convolution on the given feature map F_{mask}:

$$\mathbf{m}_i = \text{MaskHead}(\mathbf{F}_{\text{mask}}, \omega_i). \tag{1}$$

Then we calculate pair-wise matching cost which takes into account both the class prediction and the similarity of predicted and ground truth boxes. For each ground truth, we assign multi predictions to it by selecting the top k predictions with the least cost by an optimal transport method [9,10]. Finally, the whole model is optimized with a multi-task loss function

$$\mathcal{L} = \mathcal{L}_{cls} + \lambda_1 \mathcal{L}_{box} + \lambda_1 \mathcal{L}_{mask} + \lambda_2 \mathcal{L}_{embed}, \tag{2}$$

where loss weights λ_1 and λ_2 are set to 2.0 and 1.0 by default. For $\mathcal{L}_{box}$, we use a combination of $\mathcal{L}_1$ loss and the generalized IoU loss [31]. The $\mathcal{L}_{mask}$ is defined as a combination of the Dice loss [27] and Focal loss [23]. $\mathcal{L}_{embed}$ is the contrastive loss described in the next section.

3.2 Contrastive Learning Between Frames

More discriminative feature embeddings can help distinguish instances on different frames, thereby improving the quality of cross-frame association. To this end, we introduce contrastive learning between frames to make the embedding of the same object instance closer in the embedding space, and the embedding of different object instances farther away. Object queries are used to query the features of instances from each frame in our instance segmentation pipeline. Therefore, the output embeddings can be regarded as features of different instances. We employ an extra light-weighted FFN as a contrastive head to decode the contrastive embeddings from the instance features.

Given a key frame for instance segmentation training, we select a reference frame from the temporal neighborhood. The instances appearing on the key frame may have different positions and appearances on the reference frame, but their contrastive embeddings should be as close as possible in embedding space. For each instance in the key frame, we send the output embedding with the lowest cost to the contrastive head and get the contrastive embedding $\mathbf{v}$. Different from

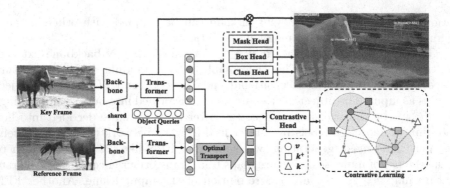

Fig. 2. The training pipeline of IDOL. Given a key frame and a reference frame, the shared-weight backbone and transformer predict the instance embeddings on them respectively. The embeddings on the key frame are used to predict masks, boxes, and categories, while the embeddings on the reference frame are selected as positive and negative embeddings dynamically by our optimal transport progress. Embeddings of the same color belong to the same video instance. Best viewed in color. (Color figure online)

previous method [29], which selects positive and negative samples by a hand-craft setting, if the same instance appears on the reference frame, we take top $m1$ predictions with the least cost as positive and top $m2$ predictions with the highest cost as negatives. $m1$ and $m2$ are calculated dynamically by the optimal transport method [9,10]. Please refer to the supplementary for more details. The contrastive loss function for a positive pair of examples is defined as follows:

$$
\begin{aligned}
\mathcal{L}_{embed} &= -\log \frac{\exp(\mathbf{v} \cdot \mathbf{k}^+)}{\exp(\mathbf{v} \cdot \mathbf{k}^+) + \sum_{\mathbf{k}^-} \exp(\mathbf{v} \cdot \mathbf{k}^-)} \\
&= \log[1 + \sum_{\mathbf{k}^-} \exp(\mathbf{v} \cdot \mathbf{k}^- - \mathbf{v} \cdot \mathbf{k}^+)],
\end{aligned}
\tag{3}
$$

where $\mathbf{k}^+$ and $\mathbf{k}^-$ are positive and negative feature embeddings from the reference frame, respectively. We extend Eq. 3 to multiple positive scenarios:

$$
\mathcal{L}_{embed} = \log[1 + \sum_{\mathbf{k}^+} \sum_{\mathbf{k}^-} \exp(\mathbf{v} \cdot \mathbf{k}^- - \mathbf{v} \cdot \mathbf{k}^+)].
\tag{4}
$$

3.3 Instance Association

Previous online methods [45,46] take semantic consistency, spatial correlation, and detection confidence as cures. They are then leveraged to determine the instance labels. Other clip-based nearly online methods [1,3,16] match instances using the predicted masks of overlapping frames by masking soft IoU metric between clips. However, the online models perform instance segmentation on each frame independently, and therefore, the prediction quality on each frame is unstable. What makes it worse is the complex motion patterns, severe occlusions, false positives, duplicate predictions, error accumulation in long videos, and the frequently disappear and reappear objects, which makes instance association very challenging. Therefore, a strong instance association method should be robust to these cases. To this end, we propose a temporally weighted softmax score for instance matching and a memory bank-based association strategy to address these problems and improve the association quality of the online model.

Temporally Weighted Softmax. Considering scenarios with fast motion, occlusion, and crowded objects, box-based matching introduces wrong association due to ambiguous location priors. However, the contrastive embedding learned by our method is able to maintain discriminative in embedding space when the position and shape change. Therefore, the contrastive embeddings are used to calculate the embedding similarity between the instances on the current and the previous frames. Assume there are N predicted instances with N contrastive embeddings $\mathbf{d}_i \in \mathbb{R}^C$, and M instances in the memory bank, each of which has multiple temporal contrastive embeddings $\{\mathbf{e}_j^t\}^{T_{t=1}}, e_j^t \in \mathbb{R}^C$ from previous T frames. These embeddings are combined by a temporally weighted sum:

$$\hat{\mathbf{e}}_j = \frac{\sum_{t=1}^T \mathbf{e}_j^t \times (\tau + T/t)}{\sum_{t=1}^T \tau + T/t}. \tag{5}$$

Then we compute bi-directional similarity f between predicted instance i and memory instance j by:

$$\mathbf{f}(i,j) = [\frac{\exp(\hat{\mathbf{e}}_j \cdot \mathbf{d}_i) + \sigma_j}{\sum_{k=1}^M \exp(\hat{\mathbf{e}}_k \cdot \mathbf{d}_i) + \sigma_k} + \frac{\exp(\hat{\mathbf{e}}_j \cdot \mathbf{d}_i)}{\sum_{k=1}^N \exp(\hat{\mathbf{e}}_j \cdot \mathbf{d}_k)}]/2, \tag{6}$$

where σ_j is the existing time of instance j in the memory, it serves as the confidence scores of each instance in the memory. By introducing the temporal contrastive embeddings and the confidence scores determined by the duration of existence, the learned prior information is able to reidentify missing instances caused by occlusions, enforcing the consistency and integrality of associations.

Association Strategy. To take full advantage of the learned contrastive embedding, we propose a new association strategy during inference. Given a test video, we initialize an empty memory bank for it and perform instance segmentation on each frame sequentially in an online scheme. For the prediction of each frame, we first perform inter-class duplicate removal by NMS with a threshold of 0.5. Then we compute matching scores $\mathbf{f}(i,j)$ between predictions and memory bank by Eq. 6, and search for the best assignment for instance i by:

$$\hat{j} = \arg\max \mathbf{f}(i,j), \forall j \in \{1, 2, ..., M\}. \tag{7}$$

If $\mathbf{f}(i, \hat{j}) > 0.5$, we assign the instance i on current frame to the memory instance $\hat{j}$. For the prediction without an assignment but has a high class score, we start a new instance ID in the memory bank.

4   Experiments

4.1   Dataset and Metrics

We report our results on YouTube-VIS 2019 [45], YouTube-VIS 2021 [42], and OVIS [30] datasets. YouTube-VIS 2019 is the first and largest dataset for video instance segmentation. It contains 2,238 training, 302 validation, and 343 test high-resolution YouTube video clips, with an average video duration of 4.61s. YouTube-VIS 2021 is an extended version of YouTube-VIS 2019. Both datasets have 40 object categories, but the category label set is slightly different. OVIS dataset is a relatively new and challenging dataset. It consists of 607 training videos, 140 validation videos, and 154 test videos. Compared with YouTube-VIS, its videos are much longer and last 12.77s on average, and more importantly, it contains much more videos that record objects with severe occlusion, complex motion patterns, and rapid deformation. All these features make OVIS an ideal dataset to evaluate and analyze different methods. We report standard metrics such as AP, AP_{50}, AP_{75}, AR_1, and AR_{10}. IoU threshold is used during evaluation.

Table 1. Oracle experiments on association quality. Frame oracle means gt instance ID is provided (same to Fig. 1). We set the clip length of IFC to 10. AP is reported.

Dataset	Method	Publish	Predicted	Frame oracle
YouTube-VIS	CrossVIS	ICCV 2021	43.4	52.8
	IFC	NeurIPS 2021	46.8	50.1
OVIS	CrossVIS	ICCV 2021	10.1	29.9
	IFC	NeurIPS 2021	8.7	25.1

Table 2. Oracle experiments on clip length for offline models. AP is reported.

Dataset	Method	Oracle type	Clip length (frame)					
			1	3	5	10	20	30
YouTube-VIS	IFC	frame	48.1	49.5	49.7	50.1	51.3	51.8
		clip	48.1	49.1	49.0	48.9	49.7	50.1
	SeqFormer	frame	57.9	58.2	57.9	57.4	57.6	57.0
		clip	57.9	53.8	53.14	52.4	50.2	50.2
OVIS	IFC	frame	24.6	25.8	25.9	25.1	24.2	22.8
		clip	24.6	23.6	22.5	18.8	13.5	10.5
	SeqFormer	frame	32.0	32.3	31.8	31.5	30.3	29.8
		clip	32.0	28.3	25.0	18.9	11.5	8.9

4.2 Analysis of Current SOTA VIS Models

Since no annotation for the validation set is available, we split the original training set into custom training split and validation split. All models are trained on the training split and evaluated on the validation split. YouTube-VIS 2019 and OVIS are used. We analyze the results as follows:

Performance Gaps Between Online and Offline Models: First, we compare the mask quality of two recent online and offline methods in Table 1. They are both published in 2021 thus can be considered as work in the same period. When ground-truth instance ID is provided (the column of 'frame oracle'), CrossVIS outperforms IFC on both YouTube-VIS and OVIS. However, when the instance ID is not provided (the column of 'predicted'), the methods are required to match the results, and the performance of CrossVIS drops dramatically by 9.4 AP while the performance of IFC drops by 3.3 AP on YouTube-VIS, leading to the poor performance of CrossVIS. Offline methods enable the model to match predicted masks by itself and avoid using hand-designed association modules. It works well on simple datasets and benefits current offline models, but it still fails on challenging datasets like OVIS.

Analysis of Current Offline Models: In Table 2, we give detailed analyses for SOTA offline models, hoping to provide insights for future research. Compared with online methods, offline models in theory have two inherent advantages:

First, as we mentioned above, it avoids hand-designed association. However, this step is very sensitive to the occlusion and the complexity of videos, especially when the clip becomes longer. For example, when clip length is equal to 5, the black-box association degrades the performance of IFC and SeqFormer on OVIS by 3.4 AP (25.9 AP *vs.* 22.5 AP) and 6.8 AP (31.8 AP *vs.* 25.0 AP), respectively. When clip length is set to 30, the performance drops by 12.3 AP (22.8 AP *vs.* 10.5 AP) and 20.9 AP (29.8 AP *vs.* 8.9 AP), respectively. What's more, even a clip length of 30 still doesn't meet the requirement of real-world application. Clip matching is still inevitable, and it further decreases the overall performance.

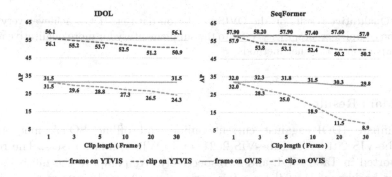

Fig. 3. Oracle experiments on IDOL and SeqFormer.

Another inherent advantage of offline models is the ability to use multiple frames for instance segmentation, which provides more information to handle occlusion and optimize the results. However, current models still fail to fully utilize this feature. Currently, it only works for simple videos: compared with per-frame segmentation (clip length = 1), it improves the mask quality by at most 3.7 AP for IFC (when clip length = 30) and 0.3 AP for SeqFormer (when clip length = 3). When testing on OVIS, multiple frames segmentation only improves the mask quality by at most 1.3 AP for IFC (clip length = 5) and 0.3 AP for SeqFormer (clip length = 3), and even degrades the performance by 1.8 AP for IFC and 2.2 AP for SeqFormer when clip size becomes longer (clip length = 30). What's more, the improvement is even less obvious in practice when no ground-truth instance ID is provided, even for simple videos, due to the association problem. It only improves the performance of IFC on YouTube-VIS by 2.0 AP, but degrades the performance in all the other experiments.

To prove the effectiveness of our method, we further analyze IDOL with oracle experiments in Fig. 3. Since IDOL is an online model, the results of frame oracles with different clip lengths are the same as per-frame segmentation oracle results. For clip oracles, IDOL is required to do association within the clips by itself. Compared with SeqFormer, the gaps between frame oracles and clip oracles of IDOL are much smaller on OVIS, proving that IDOL performs a more robust association between frames than the offline model on challenging datasets.

Fig. 4. Qualitative results on the OVIS validation dataset. IDOL achieves very good results on complex scenes. Please refer to the supplementary for more qualitative results and comparison with other methods.

4.3   Main Results

We compare IDOL against current online and offline SOTA methods on YouTube-VIS 2019, YouTube-VIS 2021, and OVIS validation sets. The results are reported in Tables 3, 4, and 5, respectively. We compare the methods with different backbones [14,24] for a fair comparison. Notably, our method significantly surpasses all previous online methods by at least 10.1 AP. In addition, we also outperform all previous offline methods under all evaluation metrics when training on the same data. More importantly, our method achieves an overall first place [39] in the YouTube-VIS Challenge 2022, which proves our SOTA performance. In addition, our method only decreases the inference speed of the adopted instance segmentation pipeline by 1.1 FPS on an RTX-2080Ti, which proves our efficiency. In general, our method is simple and very effective compared with all baseline methods. Qualitative results on sample videos of the challenging OVIS dataset are shown in Fig. 4. More qualitative results can be found in the supplementary. We analyze the performance in detail as follows:

YouTube-VIS 2019: It is the most commonly used dataset. We reported the results in Table 3. When using the same backbones, IDOL significantly outperforms previous online methods by 10.1 AP (on ResNet-50) and 10.6 AP (on ResNet-101). Compared with offline methods, we achieve better performance when no extra data is used for training, surpassing previous methods by 1.3 AP and 2.2 AP with ResNet-50 and Swin-L as the backbone, respectively. For the result with superscript "†", we randomly crop images from COCO twice to form pseudo key-reference frame pairs to pre-train the contrastive embedding part of our model before training on real video datasets. It improves the performance by 3.1 AP on ResNet-50 and 0.7 AP on Swin-L backbone, outperforming previous SOTA models comprehensively.

YouTube-VIS 2021: It is an extended version of YouTube-VIS 2019. It contains more videos with a larger number of instances and frames. As shown in Table 4, we achieve 43.9 AP with a ResNet-50 backbone, surpassing the previous best online method and offline method by 9.7 AP and 3.4 AP, respectively.

OVIS: As mentioned before, OVIS contains long video sequences with heavy occlusion and complex motion, thus it is extremely difficult for all algorithms and exceeds the capability of offline methods due to the limit of computational resources. STEm-Seg [1] is the only offline method that can be directly evaluated on OVIS since its design enables it to run in a nearly online manner. To compare with the SOTA offline methods (*e.g.* IFC [16] and SeqFormer [40]), we split the video into short clips and apply the clipping matching method provided in IFC on these two methods (SeqFormer doesn't provide its matching method). The results are provided in Table 5. Note that the previous best method only gains 15.4 AP on the validation set. IDOL with the same ResNet-50 backbone achieves 2× performance and gains 30.2 AP, surpassing the previous method by 14.8 AP. What's more, when using a stronger backbone (*i.e.*, Swin-L) to extract better features, IDOL achieves the state-of-the-art performance of 42.6 AP, which is a huge improvement over previous best results.

4.4 Ablation Study

In this section, we conduct extensive ablation experiments to study the importance of the core factors of our method on YouTube-VIS 2019. In the "Contrastive" setting, we use box IoU between predictions and ground truth for positive and negative embeddings selection following [29]. We further evaluate our

Table 3. Comparison on YouTube-VIS 2019 val set. The best results with the same backbone are in **bold** and second underline. 'V' means only YouTube-VIS training set is used. 'V+I' means synthetic videos from COCO with overlapping categories are also used for joint training. Note that offline models take advantage of larger batch sizes thus having much bigger FPS, while online models handle video frame by frame. The result with superscript "†" is obtained by pre-training on COCO pseudo key-reference frame pairs, and resolution of 480p is used during inference.

Backbone	Method	Type	FPS	Data	AP	AP_{50}	AP_{75}	AR_1	AR_{10}
ResNet-50	MaskTrack R-CNN [45]	online	20.0	V	30.3	51.1	32.6	31.0	35.5
	SipMask [4]	online	30.0	V	33.7	54.1	35.8	35.4	40.1
	CompFeat [8]	online	–	V	35.3	56.0	38.6	33.1	40.3
	CrossVIS [46]	online	39.8	V	36.3	56.8	38.9	35.6	40.7
	PCAN [18]	online	–	V	36.1	54.9	39.4	36.3	41.6
	STEm-Seg [1]	offline	7.0	V+I	30.6	50.7	33.5	37.6	37.1
	VisTR [37]	offline	69.9	V	36.2	59.8	36.9	37.2	42.4
	MaskProp [3]	offline	–	V	40.0	–	42.9	–	–
	Propose-Reduce [21]	offline	–	V+I	40.4	63.0	43.8	41.1	49.7
	IFC [16]	offline	107.1	V	42.8	65.8	46.8	43.8	51.2
	SeqFormer [40]	offline	72.3	V	45.1	66.9	50.5	<u>45.6</u>	54.6
	SeqFormer [40]	offline	72.3	V+I	<u>47.4</u>	69.8	51.8	45.5	54.8
	IDOL(ours)	online	30.6	V	46.4	<u>70.7</u>	<u>51.9</u>	44.8	<u>54.9</u>
	IDOL(ours)†	online	30.6	V	**49.5**	**74.0**	**52.9**	**47.7**	**58.7**
ResNet-101	MaskTrack R-CNN [45]	online	–	V	31.8	53.0	33.6	33.2	37.6
	CrossVIS [46]	online	35.6	V	36.6	57.3	39.7	36.0	42.0
	PCAN [18]	online	–	V	37.6	57.2	41.3	37.2	43.9
	STEm-Seg [1]	offline	-	V+I	34.6	55.8	37.9	34.4	41.6
	VisTR [37]	offline	57.7	V	40.1	64.0	45.0	38.3	44.9
	MaskProp [3]	offline	–	V	42.5	–	45.6	–	–
	Propose-Reduce [21]	offline	-	V+I	43.8	65.5	47.4	43.0	53.2
	IFC [16]	offline	89.4	V	44.6	69.2	49.5	44.0	52.1
	SeqFormer [40]	offline	64.6	V+I	<u>49.0</u>	71.1	<u>55.7</u>	<u>46.8</u>	<u>56.9</u>
	IDOL(ours)	online	26.0	V	48.2	**73.6**	52.5	45.6	55.5
	IDOL(ours)†	online	26.0	V	**50.1**	<u>73.1</u>	**56.1**	**47.0**	**57.9**
Swin-L	SeqFormer [40]	offline	27.7	V+I	59.3	82.1	66.4	51.7	64.4
	IDOL(ours)	online	17.6	V	<u>61.5</u>	<u>84.2</u>	**69.3**	<u>53.3</u>	<u>65.6</u>
	IDOL(ours)†	online	17.6	V	**62.2**	**86.5**	<u>69.2</u>	**54.6**	**68.1**

optimal transport method to dynamically select positive and negative embeddings, termed as "OT". For ablation study on inference strategy, "multi-cues" setting combines semantic consistency, spatial correlation, detection confidence and appearance similarity together to perform association following [45, 46]. Our association strategy is termed "embedding".

Table 4. Comparison on YouTube-VIS 2021 val set. Best in **bold**, second <u>underline</u>.

Backbone	Method	Type	AP	AP_{50}	AP_{75}	AR_1	AR_{10}
ResNet-50	MaskTrack R-CNN [45]	online	28.6	48.9	29.6	26.5	33.8
	SipMask [4]	online	31.7	52.5	34.0	30.8	37.8
	STMask [20]	online	31.1	50.4	33.5	26.9	35.6
	CrossVIS [46]	online	34.2	54.4	37.9	30.4	38.2
	IFC [16]	offline	36.6	57.9	39.3	-	-
	SeqFormer [40]	offline	<u>40.5</u>	<u>62.4</u>	<u>43.7</u>	<u>36.1</u>	<u>48.1</u>
	IDOL(ours)	online	**43.9**	**68.0**	**49.6**	**38.0**	**50.9**
Swin-L	SeqFormer [40]	offline	51.8	74.6	58.2	42.8	58.1
	IDOL(ours)	online	**56.1**	**80.8**	**63.5**	**45.0**	**60.1**

Table 5. Comparison on OVIS 2021 val set. Best in **bold** and second <u>underline</u>. The results with superscript "†" are not reported in [16,40]. Videos in OVIS are much longer than those in YTVIS, offline models are unable to take the entire video as input due to the limit of computational resources. We split the video into clips of length 10 and perform clip matching provided by [16] on overlapping frames to get the final results.

Backbone	Method	Type	AP	AP_{50}	AP_{75}	AR_1	AR_{10}
ResNet-50	MaskTrack R-CNN [45]	online	10.8	25.3	8.5	7.9	14.9
	SipMask [4]	online	10.2	24.7	7.8	7.9	15.8
	CMaskTrack R-CNN [30]	online	<u>15.4</u>	<u>33.9</u>	13.1	9.3	20.0
	CrossVIS [46]	online	14.9	32.7	12.1	10.3	19.8
	STEm-Seg [1]	offline	13.8	32.1	11.9	9.1	20.0
	IFC† [16]	offline	13.1	27.8	11.6	9.4	23.9
	SeqFormer† [40]	offline	15.1	31.9	<u>13.8</u>	<u>10.4</u>	<u>27.1</u>
	IDOL(ours)	online	**30.2**	**51.3**	**30.0**	**15.0**	**37.5**
Swin-L	**IDOL(ours)**	online	**42.6**	**65.7**	**45.2**	**17.9**	**49.6**

Contrastive Training. To evaluate the importance of our contrastive embeddings, we apply the same association method on the embeddings predicted by ID Head and contrastive head. As shown in Table 6, contrastive training only improves 1.5 AP with the multi-cues association but improves 8.9 AP when it comes to the embedding-based association. Furthermore, optimal transport matching (OT) improves the results by 2.3 AP, which indicates that the choice of positive and negative embeddings plays an important role in learning discriminative embeddings. OT provides a better selection of positive and negative embeddings during training, and thus improves the quality of the embedding. We show the visualization of positive and negative embeddings selected by these two strategies in supplementary.

Table 6. Ablation study on contrastive learning and inference strategies on YTVIS.

Training			Inference		AP	AP$_{75}$	AR$_1$
ID Head	Contrastive	OT	Matching	Temporal			
✓	–	–	multi-cues	–	30.3	30.5	31.5
✓	–	–	embeddings	–	33.6	36.8	38.7
✓	–	–	embeddings	✓	34.8	37.6	39.4
–	✓	–	multi-cues	–	31.8	35.3	31.9
–	✓	–	embeddings	–	42.5	45.7	42.2
–	✓	✓	embeddings	–	44.8	49.9	43.4
–	✓	✓	embeddings	✓	46.4	51.9	44.8

Association Strategy and Temporally Weighted Softmax. As shown in Table 6, compared with "multi-cues", our embedding association strategy takes advantage of the discriminative embedding learned by contrastive learning, and improves the AP from 31.8 to 42.5 on YouTube-VIS. In addition, when temporally weighted softmax is added, it can be further improved by 1.6 AP. Utilizing information and priors from multiple previous frames improve robustness of association. Considering the problem of false positives and disappearing-and-reappearing that the online model needs to deal with, we believe this strategy helps maintain temporal consistency. We provide more visualization results, detailed analysis, and additional ablation experiments on OVIS in.

5   Conclusions

Online video instance segmentation methods have their inherent advantage in handling long/ongoing videos, but they are inferior to the offline models in performance. In this work, we aim to bridge the performance gap. We first deeply analyze the current online and offline models and find that the gap mainly comes from the error-prone association between frames. Based on this observation, we propose IDOL, which enables models to learn more discriminative and robust instance features for VIS tasks. It significantly outperforms all online and offline methods and achieves new SOTA on three benchmarks. We believe our insights on VIS methods will inspire future work in both online and offline methods.

Acknowledgment. This work was supported by NSF 1763705. We thank the reviewers for their efforts and valuable feedback to improve our work.

References

1. Athar, A., Mahadevan, S., Ošep, A., Leal-Taixé, L., Leibe, B.: STEm-seg: spatiotemporal embeddings for instance segmentation in videos. In: Vedaldi, A., Bischof, H., Brox, T., Frahm, J.-M. (eds.) ECCV 2020. LNCS, vol. 12356, pp. 158–177. Springer, Cham (2020). https://doi.org/10.1007/978-3-030-58621-8_10

2. Bergmann, P., Meinhardt, T., Leal-Taixe, L.: Tracking without bells and whistles. In: ICCV (2019)
3. Bertasius, G., Torresani, L.: Classifying, segmenting, and tracking object instances in video with mask propagation. In: CVPR (2020)
4. Cao, J., Anwer, R.M., Cholakkal, H., Khan, F.S., Pang, Y., Shao, L.: SipMask: spatial information preservation for fast image and video instance segmentation. In: Vedaldi, A., Bischof, H., Brox, T., Frahm, J.-M. (eds.) ECCV 2020. LNCS, vol. 12359, pp. 1–18. Springer, Cham (2020). https://doi.org/10.1007/978-3-030-58568-6_1
5. Carion, N., Massa, F., Synnaeve, G., Usunier, N., Kirillov, A., Zagoruyko, S.: End-to-end object detection with transformers. In: Vedaldi, A., Bischof, H., Brox, T., Frahm, J.-M. (eds.) ECCV 2020. LNCS, vol. 12346, pp. 213–229. Springer, Cham (2020). https://doi.org/10.1007/978-3-030-58452-8_13
6. Chen, T., Kornblith, S., Norouzi, M., Hinton, G.: A simple framework for contrastive learning of visual representations. In: ICML (2020)
7. Dendorfer, P., et al.: Motchallenge: a benchmark for single-camera multiple target tracking. Int. J. Comput. Vision $129(4)$, 845–881 (2021)
8. Fu, Y., Yang, L., Liu, D., Huang, T.S., Shi, H.: Compfeat: comprehensive feature aggregation for video instance segmentation. arXiv preprint arXiv:2012.03400 (2020)
9. Ge, Z., Liu, S., Li, Z., Yoshie, O., Sun, J.: Ota: optimal transport assignment for object detection. In: CVPR (2021)
10. Ge, Z., Liu, S., Wang, F., Li, Z., Sun, J.: Yolox: Exceeding yolo series in 2021. arXiv preprint arXiv:2107.08430 (2021)
11. Han, T., Xie, W., Zisserman, A.: Self-supervised co-training for video representation learning. In: NeurIPS (2020)
12. He, K., Fan, H., Wu, Y., Xie, S., Girshick, R.: Momentum contrast for unsupervised visual representation learning. In: CVPR (2020)
13. He, K., Gkioxari, G., Dollar, P., Girshick, R.: Mask R-CNN. In: ICCV (2017)
14. He, K., Zhang, X., Ren, S., Sun, J.: Deep residual learning for image recognition. In: CVPR (2016)
15. Henaff, O.: Data-efficient image recognition with contrastive predictive coding. In: ICML (2020)
16. Hwang, S., Heo, M., Oh, S.W., Kim, S.J.: Video instance segmentation using inter-frame communication transformers. In: NeurIPS (2021)
17. Jiang, Z., et al.: STC: spatio-temporal contrastive learning for video instance segmentation. arXiv preprint arXiv:2202.03747 (2022)
18. Ke, L., Li, X., Danelljan, M., Tai, Y.W., Tang, C.K., Yu, F.: Prototypical cross-attention networks for multiple object tracking and segmentation. In: NeurIPS (2021)
19. Khosla, P., et al.: Supervised contrastive learning. In: NeurIPS (2020)
20. Li, M., Li, S., Li, L., Zhang, L.: Spatial feature calibration and temporal fusion for effective one-stage video instance segmentation. In: CVPR (2021)
21. Lin, H., Wu, R., Liu, S., Lu, J., Jia, J.: Video instance segmentation with a propose-reduce paradigm. In: ICCV (2021)
22. Lin, T.Y., Dollar, P., Girshick, R., He, K., Hariharan, B., Belongie, S.: Feature pyramid networks for object detection. In: CVPR (2017)
23. Lin, T.Y., Goyal, P., Girshick, R., He, K., Dollár, P.: Focal loss for dense object detection. In: ICCV (2017)
24. Liu, Z., et al.: Swin transformer: hierarchical vision transformer using shifted windows. arXiv preprint arXiv:2103.14030 (2021)

25. Meinhardt, T., Kirillov, A., Leal-Taixe, L., Feichtenhofer, C.: TrackFormer: multi-object tracking with transformers. arXiv preprint arXiv:2101.02702 (2021)
26. Miech, A., Alayrac, J.B., Smaira, L., Laptev, I., Sivic, J., Zisserman, A.: End-to-end learning of visual representations from uncurated instructional videos. In: CVPR (2020)
27. Milletari, F., Navab, N., Ahmadi, S.A.: V-net: fully convolutional neural networks for volumetric medical image segmentation. In: 2016 fourth international conference on 3D vision (3DV) (2016)
28. Van den Oord, A., Li, Y., Vinyals, O.: Representation learning with contrastive predictive coding. arXiv e-prints pp. arXiv-1807 (2018)
29. Pang, J., et al.: Quasi-dense similarity learning for multiple object tracking. In: CVPR (2021)
30. Qi, J., et al.: Occluded video instance segmentation: a benchmark. Int. J. Comput. Vision 130, 1–18 (2022)
31. Rezatofighi, H., Tsoi, N., Gwak, J., Sadeghian, A., Reid, I., Savarese, S.: Generalized intersection over union: a metric and a loss for bounding box regression. In: CVPR (2019)
32. Sun, P., et al.: TransTrack: multiple-object tracking with transformer. arXiv preprint arXiv:2012.15460 (2020)
33. Sun, Y., et al.: Circle loss: a unified perspective of pair similarity optimization. In: CVPR (2020)
34. Tian, Z., Shen, C., Chen, H.: Conditional convolutions for instance segmentation. In: Vedaldi, A., Bischof, H., Brox, T., Frahm, J.-M. (eds.) ECCV 2020. LNCS, vol. 12346, pp. 282–298. Springer, Cham (2020). https://doi.org/10.1007/978-3-030-58452-8_17
35. Vaswani, A., et al.: Attention is all you need. In: NeurIPS (2017)
36. Voigtlaender, P., et al.: Mots: multi-object tracking and segmentation. In: Proceedings of the IEEE/CVF Conference on Computer Vision and Pattern Recognition, pp. 7942–7951 (2019)
37. Wang, Y., et al.: End-to-end video instance segmentation with transformers. In: CVPR (2021)
38. Wu, J., et al.: Efficient video instance segmentation via tracklet query and proposal. In: CVPR (2022)
39. Wu, J., Bai, X., Jiang, Y., Liu, Q., Yuan, Z., Bai, S.: 1st place solution for YouTubeVOS challenge 2022: video instance segmentation. In: CVPR Workshops (2022)
40. Wu, J., Jiang, Y., Bai, S., Zhang, W., Bai, X.: Seqformer: Sequential transformer for video instance segmentation. In: Avidan, S., et al. (eds.) Computer Vision ECCV 2022. LNCS, pp. xx–yy. Springer, Cham (2022)
41. Wu, Z., Xiong, Y., Yu, S.X., Lin, D.: Unsupervised feature learning via non-parametric instance discrimination. In: CVPR (2018)
42. Xu, N., et al.: Youtubevis dataset 2021 version. https://youtube-vos.org/dataset/vis/
43. Xu, Z., Yang, W., Zhang, W., Tan, X., Huang, H., Huang, L.: Segment as points for efficient and effective online multi-object tracking and segmentation. In: TPAMI (2021)
44. Yan, B., et al.: Towards grand unification of object tracking. arXiv preprint arXiv:2207.07078 (2022)
45. Yang, L., Fan, Y., Xu, N.: Video instance segmentation. In: ICCV (2019)
46. Yang, S., et al.: Crossover learning for fast online video instance segmentation. In: ICCV (2021)

47. Zhang, Y., et al.: Bytetrack: multi-object tracking by associating every detection box. arXiv preprint arXiv:2110.06864 (2021)
48. Zhang, Y., Wang, C., Wang, X., Zeng, W., Liu, W.: FairMOT: on the fairness of detection and re-identification in multiple object tracking. IJCV (2021)
49. Zhou, X., Koltun, V., Krähenbühl, P.: Tracking objects as points. In: Vedaldi, A., Bischof, H., Brox, T., Frahm, J.-M. (eds.) ECCV 2020. LNCS, vol. 12349, pp. 474–490. Springer, Tracking objects as points (2020). https://doi.org/10.1007/978-3-030-58548-8_28
50. Zhu, X., Su, W., Lu, L., Li, B., Wang, X., Dai, J.: Deformable detr: deformable transformers for end-to-end object detection. In: ICLR (2021)

Active Pointly-Supervised Instance Segmentation

Chufeng Tang[1], Lingxi Xie[2], Gang Zhang[1], Xiaopeng Zhang[2],
Qi Tian[2(✉)], and Xiaolin Hu[1,3,4(✉)]

[1] Department of Computer Science and Technology, Institute for AI, BNRist,
State Key Laboratory of Intelligent Technology and Systems,
Tsinghua University, Beijing, China
{tcf18,zhang-g19}@mails.tsinghua.edu.cn, xlhu@mail.tsinghua.edu.cn
[2] Huawei Inc., Shenzhen, China
198808xc@gmail.com, zxphistory@gmail.com, tian.qi1@huawei.com
[3] Chinese Institute for Brain Research (CIBR), Beijing, China
[4] IDG/McGovern Institute for Brain Research, Tsinghua University, Beijing, China

Abstract. The requirement of expensive annotations is a major burden
for training a well-performed instance segmentation model. In this paper,
we present an economic active learning setting, named active pointly-
supervised instance segmentation (APIS), which starts with box-level
annotations and iteratively samples a point within the box and asks if it
falls on the object. The key of APIS is to find the most desirable points to
maximize the segmentation accuracy with limited annotation budgets.
We formulate this setting and propose several uncertainty-based sampling strategies. The model developed with these strategies yields consistent performance gain on the challenging MS-COCO dataset, compared
against other learning strategies. The results suggest that APIS, integrating the advantages of active learning and point-based supervision, is
an effective learning paradigm for label-efficient instance segmentation.

Keywords: Instance segmentation · Active learning · Point-based
supervision · Label-efficient learning

1 Introduction

Instance segmentation aims to predict a pixel-wise mask with a category label for
each instance in the given image. Despite the rapid development of the instance
segmentation methods, the requirement of a massive amount of labeled data is
still a heavy burden of training a well-performed instance segmentation model.
For example, the annotation of a polygon-based mask for an object in MS-COCO
requires 79.2 s [33] on average and even higher for the more precise mask annotations in LVIS [17], which is considerably more time-consuming than annotating
a bounding box (*e.g.*, 7 s via clicking extreme points [38]).

Supplementary Information The online version contains supplementary material
available at https://doi.org/10.1007/978-3-031-19815-1_35.

© The Author(s), under exclusive license to Springer Nature Switzerland AG 2022
S. Avidan et al. (Eds.): ECCV 2022, LNCS 13688, pp. 606–623, 2022.
https://doi.org/10.1007/978-3-031-19815-1_35

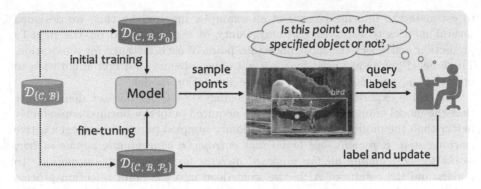

Fig. 1. Overview of the training pipeline for the proposed APIS setting where the annotator is asked for labeling whether the point falls on the specified object (*i.e.*, the bird) or not. The expected label in this case is 'yes'. $\mathcal{D}$ is the training data and $\mathcal{C}, \mathcal{B}, \mathcal{P}$ are the category, bounding box, and point annotations, respectively (see Sect. 3.1 for details).

In general, weak supervision and active learning are usually two effective ways to reduce the annotation cost. For the task of instance segmentation, a number of existing works attempted to predict instance masks with weak supervisions, such as category tags [3,40,61], bounding boxes [21,26,28,51], and points [9,29]. However, active learning for instance segmentation has been less investigated. Wang *et al.*. [52] first explored the possibility on medical image analysis, but, to the best of our knowledge, no existing work has studied this setting on more complex and larger-scale datasets (*e.g.*, MS-COCO [33]).

In this paper, we present a new setting named **active pointly-supervised instance segmentation (APIS)** to study active learning algorithms for instance segmentation with point supervisions. Under the proposed setting where each image in the data pool has been annotated with category labels and bounding boxes, the goal of the algorithms is selecting the most informative *points* for labeling to maximize the model's performance. Figure 1 illustrates the training pipeline of APIS. Compared to the typical active learning settings that the most informative *images* or *instances* are selected and annotated with boxes and masks, APIS can be studied in a more fine-grained manner because it allocates annotation budgets to *pixels*, and the annotation of points is considerably faster and cheaper. As stated in a previous work [9], labeling whether a point falls on the specified object or not takes only 0.9 s on average. Note that active learning is a training strategy that point labels are only queried during the training phase of APIS, while no annotations are provided for testing.

APIS raises an important problem that has not been studied before, *i.e.*, *how to estimate the informativeness of a point*, where the informativeness can be roughly defined as the potential gain of segmentation accuracy (*e.g.*, in terms of mAP) if this point is annotated. However, estimating the precise accuracy gain for each point is obviously infeasible. In the literature, uncertainty is widely used to estimate the informativeness of an example. Inspired by this, we designed several metrics to estimate the uncertainty of a point based on the model's prediction and select the most uncertain point of each instance for annotation. The labeled points are used together with the category and box annotation to update (*e.g.*, fine-tuning) the instance segmentation model.

Extensive experiments on the challenging MS-COCO dataset demonstrate that the model trained with the actively acquired points performed consistently better than the model trained with randomly sampled points during each active learning step. *Especially, we found that entropy, a conceptually simple metric, works the best among all the proposed metrics for uncertainty estimation.* To understand the results of APIS, we went deep into the point selection process and studied the training dynamics, point distribution and point difficulties. The analyses reveal that the proposed sampling metric provides a good estimation of the point informativeness and therefore leads to higher performance. In addition to the random sampling baseline, we further compared APIS against a setting of active instance segmentation with full supervisions, where the most informative images or instances are selected for mask annotation. Conditioned on the same annotation budget and training time, the model developed under the APIS setting outperformed all other competitors. *The results suggest that active learning cooperates effectively with point supervisions, which can further boost the instance segmentation performance under a limited annotation budget.* We hope the promising results, as well as the comprehensive analysis presented in this work, will draw the attention of the community to APIS and other label-efficient visual recognition techniques.

The contribution of this work is summarized as follows:

- We present a new active instance segmentation setting APIS where the goal is to sample the most informative points to maximize the model's performance. To our knowledge, this work is the first to explore active learning for instance segmentation with point supervisions.
- We estimate the informativeness with the uncertainty of point predictions, and the model trained with the actively acquired points consistently outperformed the random sampling counterparts on MS-COCO.
- We provide comprehensive comparisons and analyses to understand the results of APIS and concluded that APIS successfully combines the advantages of active learning and point-based supervision to reduce the annotation burden of instance segmentation.

2   Related Work

Instance Segmentation. Currently, the fully supervised methods still dominate the popular instance segmentation benchmarks [11,17,33]. Mask R-CNN [20] and its follow-up methods [7,22,34] predict masks based on the region-level features. One-stage methods like CondInst [50] and SOLO [54] directly segment instances at image-level by learning instance-aware kernels. Recently, some query-based methods [8,14,15] further boost the segmentation performance. For the weakly supervised paradigm, category tags [3,40,61] are the simplest supervision but the results are usually uncompetitive. With bounding box annotations, the recently proposed BoxInst [51] and DiscoBox [28] significantly outperformed previous methods [21,26] on MS-COCO. In addition, PointSup [9] further reduced the gap to the fully-supervised methods by training with boxes and several randomly sampled points for each instance, which is similar the random sampling baseline in APIS where the points are accessed for training step by step. However, there are still great differences that APIS focus on active learning for instance segmentation while PointSup [9] is for weakly-supervised learning.

Active Learning. Over the past decades, a great number of active learning algorithms have been proposed but mostly designed for image classification, which can be roughly divided into two categories: uncertainty-based [5,16,24,30,53] and diversity-based [1,18,44,47] algorithms. In recent years, some researchers shifted their attention to the downstream visual recognition tasks such as object detection [2,10,19,25,35,43,58] and semantic segmentation [46,55,57]. However, for the task of instance segmentation, the potential of active learning has been less explored. Only one published work [52] preliminarily studied this problem on the medical image datasets where a triplet uncertainty metric was calculated with the predicted mask IoU scores of Mask Scoring R-CNN [22], which makes the metric relying on a specialized architecture. By contrast, we first studied this problem on the most commonly used MS-COCO dataset and the proposed metrics are model-agnostic. Furthermore, different from all existing settings where images or instances [12] are selected for labeling, the proposed APIS setting performs in a fine-grained and weakly supervised manner, *i.e.*, selecting and labeling points. A few works [13,39] studied weak supervisions for active object detection while they focused on how to decide the annotation scheme (strongly or weakly) for an image, which are complementary to APIS.

Point-Based or Click-Based Segmentation. Point-based supervision has been studied in various image segmentation tasks, including semantic segmentation [4,41], instance segmentation [9,29], and panoptic segmentation [31]. In addition, point clicks are widely used in interactive annotation [6,23,32,36,56] methods, which usually requires mask annotations for training the model. During testing (*i.e.*, annotating an unseen image), the user is asked to provide some corrective point clicks iteratively. APIS is intrinsically different to these methods that the model only interacts with users during training and no additional labels are required during testing.

3   Method

3.1   Problem Formulation

In this section, we formally define the proposed active pointly-supervised instance segmentation (APIS) setting. Suppose we collect a large training dataset of N images denoted as $\mathcal{D} = \{\mathcal{I}_i\}_{i=1}^N$ with annotations $\{\mathcal{C}, \mathcal{B}\}$, where $\mathcal{C} = \{\mathcal{C}_i\}_{i=1}^N$ is the category annotation, $\mathcal{B} = \{\mathcal{B}_i\}_{i=1}^N$ is the box annotation, and $Q_i = |\mathcal{B}_i| = |\mathcal{C}_i|$ is the number of instances in the ith image. We studied a typical setting of APIS that each instance is sampled with the same number of points and all the points should be located in the corresponding ground-truth bounding box. Additionally, we also studied a scenario where *not* all instances were labeled with the same number of points, see *Supp. Material* for details.

Before the active learning cycle starts, we randomly sample and annotate one point for each instance. The initial set of points is denoted as:

$$\mathcal{P}_0 = \{(x_{ij}^0, y_{ij}^0, u_{ij}^0) \mid 1 \le i \le N, 1 \le j \le Q_i\}, \tag{1}$$

where (x_{ij}^0, y_{ij}^0) is the coordinates of a point that is located in the jth bounding box of the ith image, and $u_{ij}^0 \in \{0, 1\}$ is the point label which indicates whether the point falls on the foreground object or not. The size of $\mathcal{P}_0$ is $Q = \sum_{i=1}^N Q_i$ that equals to the total number of instances in $\mathcal{D}$. The instance segmentation model $\mathcal{M}_0$ is initialized by training with the above annotations $\{\mathcal{C}, \mathcal{B}, \mathcal{P}_0\}$.

At the sth ($s \ge 1$) active learning step, the informativeness of points is estimated based on the predictions of the previous model $\mathcal{M}_{s-1}$. We designed several uncertainty-based metrics to estimate the point informativeness, which will be explained in Sect. 3.2. The most informative point of each instance is selected and the annotators are asked to label it. The newly labeled points are merged with $\mathcal{P}_{s-1}$ and formed the new point set $\mathcal{P}_s$:

$$\mathcal{P}_s = \mathcal{P}_{s-1} \cup \{(x_{ij}^s, y_{ij}^s, u_{ij}^s) \mid 1 \le i \le N, 1 \le j \le Q_i\}, \tag{2}$$

where the number of points in $\mathcal{P}_s$ is $(s+1) \times Q$. Subsequently, the model $\mathcal{M}_s$ is fine-tuned from $\mathcal{M}_{s-1}$ with all available annotations $\{\mathcal{C}, \mathcal{B}, \mathcal{P}_s\}$. The above process is repeated multiple steps until the annotation budget has been exhausted or a satisfactory performance has been achieved.

3.2   Point Selection for APIS

In this section, we tackle the core problem raised by APIS that how to define a point's informativeness. Note that informativeness is not totally determined by correctness, *e.g.*, if the model predicts a point as positive with a high confidence while the ground-truth is negative, annotating it may not be an ideal solution (see Sect. 4.3). That said, even provided the mask labels, it is still difficult to determine which point has a potentially large contribution. We refer to some existing active learning methods [5,16,24,30,53] to study uncertainty, and use the uncertainty of points to rank their informativeness.

In modern instance segmentation models, a ground-truth instance is usually assigned as the learning target for multiple predictions during training, known as label assignment [60], which makes NMS (Non-Maximum Supression) being a necessary process during inference. Suppose there are K mask predictions $\{\mathbf{m}^k\}_{k=1}^K$ matching to a given instance in $\mathcal{D}$, where $\mathbf{m}^k \in [0,1]^{H \times W}$ is an image-level probability matrix and $H \times W$ is the shape of the image. Note that for

CondInst [50] the prediction is already image-level while for Mask R-CNN [20] the region-level prediction should be transformed to image-level. Denote the element of $\mathbf{m}^k$ with coordinates (x, y) as p_{xy}^k that indicates the probability of a point located at (x, y) falling on the object. We designed several metrics to estimate the uncertainty for a point based on its predictive probability of p_{xy}^k.

(1) Entropy of the Averaged Predictions. The Shannon Entropy [45] metric is commonly used in existing active learning algorithms [2, 16, 19, 53]. In our case, since mask prediction is a binary classification problem for points, the entropy metric can be defined as:

$$\mathcal{H}(p) = -p \log p - (1 - p) \log(1 - p), \tag{3}$$

where p is the probability of any point. We simply average multiple predictions on the same point to calculate the entropy value, and the point with the highest entropy value is selected for the corresponding instance:

$$(\hat{x}, \hat{y}) = \arg\max_{(x,y)\in\Omega} \mathcal{H}(\bar{p}_{xy}), \quad \bar{p}_{xy} = \frac{1}{K} \sum_{k=1}^{K} p_{xy}^k, \tag{4}$$

where $(\hat{x}, \hat{y})$ is the coordinates of the actively selected point for the given instance and Ω is the spatial constraint for the point candidates. In our setting, the selected points are expected to fall inside the ground-truth bounding boxes. The intuition behind the above sampling strategy is straightforward yet reasonable, *i.e., the more the probability close to 0.5, the higher the entropy, and the more likely the point should be selected.* Designing the constraint Ω carefully or averaging multiple predictions with some adaptive weights can make the above strategy more sophisticated, however it is not the focus of this work.

(2) Disagreement Among Multiple Predictions. The intuition behind the disagreement metric is that *if multiple predictions for the same point varied significantly, the model should be highly uncertain about that point and we should select that point for labeling.* This idea can be traced back to the classical *query by committee* paradigm [37]. A number of works implicitly or explicitly followed this idea to select samples actively. For example, in the task of active object detection, the offsets between the boxes generated from different SSD layers [43], or the IoU scores between the proposals and final detected boxes [25] were used to measure the disagreement. In our case, we adopt the *variance* across different predictions for a point to measure the disagreement and the point with the largest *variance* is selected for the corresponding instance:

$$(\hat{x}, \hat{y}) = \arg\max_{(x,y)\in\Omega} \mathbb{V}(\mathbf{p}_{xy}), \tag{5}$$

where $\mathbf{p}_{xy} \in \mathbb{R}^K$ is the probability vector at the location (x, y) and $\mathbb{V}(\cdot)$ calculates the variance of it.

In addition to sampling metrics mentioned above, how to form the prediction set $\{\mathbf{m}^k\}_{k=1}^K$ for a given instance is an important problem. In this work, by considering the properties of the APIS setting, we propose and compare several solutions. (a) *Multiple Anchors*: Since a ground-truth instance is usually assigned to multiple anchors (where anchors are the positive locations for CondInst [50], or the positive proposals for Mask R-CNN [20], *etc.*) during training, we naturally have multiple predictions for one instance. (b) *Multiple Models*: Another solution is training the same models multiple times with different initializations to get multiple predictions, which is usually called Deep Ensembles [5,27] in the literature. (c) *Multiple Scales*: Training multiple models is computationally inefficient. An alternative is to forward the same model multiple times under different conditions. In our case, the model is usually trained with multi-scale inputs, thus we can forward the model with an individual scale each time to get multiple predictions. The concept of multi-scale here can be freely replaced by other types of data augmentations (*e.g.*, flipping, rotation).

We calculate the entropy and disagreement metrics on the above prediction sets individually and obtain several different point sampling strategies. Note that the case of multiple anchors also appear in each model or each forward pass, and we simply concatenate them as a single prediction set. For the instance that was not predicted ($K = 0$), we randomly sample a point for it. For the instance that has only one prediction ($K = 1$), we only use entropy as the metric.

3.3   Baseline for APIS

Note that there is no existing work can be directly compared to APIS since the problem of active instance segmentation has been less investigated. In addition to the *random sampling* baseline, inspired by the existing works for active image classification or object detection where the full labels are usually queried, we create a baseline setting for comparison, named *active fully-supervised instance segmentation (AFIS)*, where the mask annotations are queried during each active learning step. Note that the category and box annotations $\{\mathcal{C}, \mathcal{B}\}$ are also provided in advance. We designed several sampling strategies under the AFIS setting, which will serve as the baselines for APIS. A straightforward strategy is selecting the most informative *images* and labeling masks for all instances in the image. An alternative is selecting and annotating the most informative *instances*, which is a fine-grained solution that not all instances in the image are labeled. We call them *image-level* selection and *instance-level* selection for AFIS. See *Supp. Material* for more description of AFIS.

Under the AFIS setting, we propose two metrics to define the informativeness of an image or an instance. (a) *Mean Entropy*: Inspired by the aforementioned uncertainty-based metrics of APIS, we defined the instance uncertainty as the mean entropy of all points inside the ground-truth bounding box, and the uncertainty of an image is defined as the mean uncertainty of all instances in that image. The most uncertain images and instances are selected for the image-level and instance-level cases, respectively. (b) *Detection Quality*: The quality of mask prediction is usually dependent on the detection quality. For an instance that was not accurately detected, the potential of the mask label, if provided, may not be fully utilized. Therefore, we propose to select the instances with the

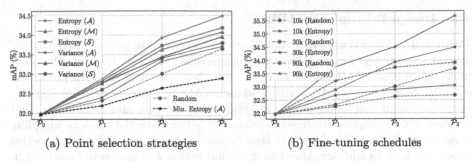

(a) Point selection strategies   (b) Fine-tuning schedules

Fig. 2. (a) Comparison of different point selection strategies. $\mathcal{A}$, $\mathcal{M}$ and $\mathcal{S}$ indicate the prediction sets constructed from multiple anchors, multiple models, and multiple scales, respectively. (b) Comparison of different fine-tuning schedules.

higher detection quality for labeling masks. Since the ground-truth boxes are provided, we can easily use the detection loss (*e.g.*, GIoU Loss [42]) as the metric for instance selection. For the image-level selection, we calculate the average detection loss of all instances for an image, and the images with the lowest loss are selected.

4 Experiments

4.1 Experimental Settings

We report results on the MS-COCO [33] dataset. All the active selection strategies were applied on the `train2017` split, including 118k images with 860k instances, where the annotation for points was simulated by adopting the labels of the ground-truth instance masks on the corresponding location. All models were evaluated on the `val2017` split.

Implementation Details. We mainly took CondInst [50] with ResNet-50 as the instance segmentation model and adopted the `AdelaiDet` [49] codebase. To train the model with point supervision, we followed the same training protocol as PointSup [9] where the point prediction was sampled from the prediction map using bilinear interpolation and the per-pixel cross-entropy loss was calculated on the labeled points only. The initial model $\mathcal{M}_0$ was trained for 90k iterations with the initial learning rate being 0.01 and decayed at iteration 60k and 80k, respectively. Other training settings were the same as CondInst. After that, the active learning process was repeated multiple times. At the sth active learning step, $(s + 1)$ points were labeled in total for each instance where s points were actively acquired, denoted as $\mathcal{P}_s$ in the following experiments. By default, at each step, the model was fine-tuned for 30k iterations with the initial learning rate being 0.01 and decayed every 10k iterations. All models were trained with the SGD optimizer and multi-scale data augmentation with mini-batch of 16 images on 8 NVIDIA Tesla V100 GPUs. The results were measured by the mask mAP(%) metric of instance segmentation.

4.2   Design Principles of APIS

Point Selection Strategy. As introduced in Sect. 3.2, we propose two metrics, named *Entropy* and *Variance* (*i.e.*, the disagreement) here, to estimate the point uncertainty based on the prediction set, and there are three types of prediction sets: *Multiple-Anchors* ($\mathcal{A}$), *Multiple-Models* ($\mathcal{M}$), and *Multiple-Scales* ($\mathcal{S}$). We composed them into six different point selection strategies, and we observed that all these six strategies performed consistently better than the random sampling baseline, as shown in Fig. 2(a). The results demonstrate the effectiveness of active point selection. In addition, the strategies that taking *Entropy* as the metric usually performed better than the *Variance* counterparts. When using *Entropy* as the metric, constructing the prediction set from multiple anchors ($\mathcal{A}$) performed better than from multiple models ($\mathcal{M}$) or scales ($\mathcal{S}$), and the latter two solutions are obviously inefficient in computation. The best-performing strategy is calculating the entropy value for each point based on the predictions from multiple anchors, which surpassed random sampling by 0.56%, 0.92% and 0.80% mAP at the first three steps. Surprisingly, the result at the second step ($\mathcal{P}_2$) even outperformed the random sampling counterparts with larger annotation costs and longer training time ($\mathcal{P}_3$). Unless otherwise specified, we use *Entropy* to denote this best-performing strategy in the rest of this paper.

For the *Entropy* strategy mentioned above, we always chose the most uncertain point of each instance for labeling, and we were also curious about the inverse situation that the most certain points (*i.e.*, point with the lowest entropy value) were selected instead. As shown in Fig. 2(a) (black dashed line), the points with the lowest entropy even performed worse than the randomly sampled points, which verified that the proposed entropy metric is a simple yet effective way to estimate the point informativeness.

Fine-Tuning Schedule. We compared different fine-tuning schedules at each active learning step. For the 10k schedule (~1.3 epoch), the learning rate was fixed at 0.0001. For the 90k schedule (12 epochs), the initial learning rate was 0.01 and reduced by a factor of 10 at iteration 60k and 80k, respectively. As shown in Fig. 2(b), we observed that the longer the training time, the larger the gaps between active point selection and random sampling. When adopting the 90k schedule, the gap reached to +1.77% at the third step ($\mathcal{P}_3$). The results suggest that the actively acquired point is indeed more informative, and the longer training time can further release its potential. In this paper, unless otherwise specified, the 30k schedule was used in experiments for convenience.

Instance Segmentation Model. In our experiments, we mainly used the CondInst with ResNet-50 backbone as the instance segmentation model. Actually, the proposed APIS setting can be studied with a diverse set of models, and we also studied two alternatives. (a) *Larger backbone*: Using the higher-capacity ResNet-101 as the backbone, the similar observation can be made that active selection works consistently better than random sampling, as shown in Fig. 3(a). (b) *Boxly-supervised model*: Recall that $\mathcal{P}_0$ in above experiments is a set of randomly sampled points which is used to initialize the model to obtain the initial

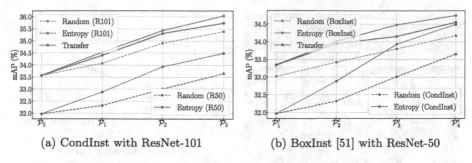

(a) CondInst with ResNet-101   (b) BoxInst [51] with ResNet-50

Fig. 3. The results of taking CondInst with ResNet-101 and BoxInst [51] as the instance segmentation model, respectively. *Transfer* indicates that the points are acquired from CondInst with ResNet-50 and transferred to this model. (Color figure online)

mask predictions. A number of works [21,26,28,51] attempted to predict masks by training with box annotations only. By adopting these models as the initial model in APIS, we can eliminate the need of $\mathcal{P}_0$. In Fig. 3(b), we adopted BoxInst [51], a dominant method in the boxly-supervised instance segmentation area, as the initial model, and each instance was labeled with s points in $\mathcal{P}'_s$ (in comparison, $s + 1$ in $\mathcal{P}_s$). As shown, the proposed strategy also worked in this case. With the power of BoxInst, similar or even better results were achieved with fewer points, *e.g.*, the result of $\mathcal{P}'_1$ surpassed $\mathcal{P}_1$ (in Fig. 2(a)) by 0.47% mAP, although $\mathcal{P}_1$ has more points.

Transferability. We studied the transferability of the actively acquired points. As shown in Fig. 3 (blue lines), we transferred the points acquired from one model (CondInst with ResNet-50) to other models, CondInst with ResNet-101 and BoxInst, respectively. Specifically, the point set $\mathcal{P}_s$ of the former model served as the supervision for the latter two models in the sth step. As shown, the results of the transferred points are slightly lower than the results of selecting points for those models from scratch, but still higher than random sampling.

4.3   Analysis for APIS

Visualization Analysis. To better understand how the point is selected and how it works, we visualized the mask predictions, uncertainty maps, and the selected points for some instances, as shown in Fig. 4a. We observed that the highlighted regions in uncertainty maps often corresponded to the two types of mistakes in the mask predictions. One is the typical over-segmented or under-segmented regions (*e.g.*, holes on the object, or patches on the background). Another one is the error around the boundaries of the predicted masks (*i.e.*, imprecise boundaries). Therefore, the points selected from these misclassified regions can provide a valuable feedback about how the model performs and it is possible to correct the mistakes by fine-tuning with the selected points in the subsequent active learning steps (*e.g.*, the last column). Interestingly, some prediction errors were still corrected even without sampling the points from

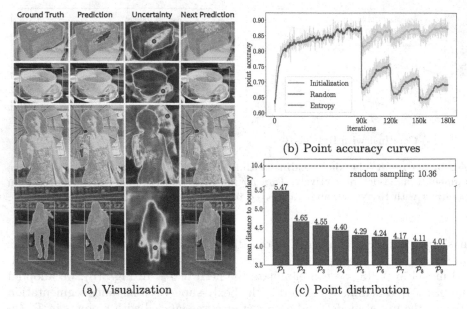

(a) Visualization   (c) Point distribution

Fig. 4. (a) Visualization of (from left to right): ground-truth masks, mask predictions, uncertainty maps, and mask predictions after fine-tuning with the selected points (red spots) for some instances. (b) Accuracy curves of the actively acquired points and random points during training. (c) The mean distances to the object boundaries of the actively acquired points for each step. The mean distance for random points is provided for reference (dash line). (Color figure online)

those regions (*e.g.*, dashed boxes in the 3rd row). The reason might be that the patterns of these error regions also appeared in other instances that have the desired annotations. On the other side, there were also some failure cases where the prediction around the selected point even got worse after fine-tuning (*e.g.*, the 4th row). More visualized results are included in *Supp. Material*.

Point Accuracy Curves. In addition to the case studies above, the accuracy (*i.e.*, accuracy of binary classification for points during training) curves of the actively acquired points and randomly sampled points are plotted in Fig. 4b. As shown, the accuracy of the actively acquired points dropped dramatically at the beginning of each step (iteration 90k, 120k and 150k, respectively), which shows that the selected points were often misclassified at the previous step and it is possible to correct the errors by fine-tuning the model with their labels (*e.g.*, the first three rows of Fig. 4a). In contrast, the accuracy of random points dropped slightly at each time and always stayed at a high level, which indicates that most of these points were already handled by the model and of course less informative. In addition, the accuracy improvements usually decreased with more steps. It suggests that, with more steps, the mask prediction gets gradually better and the selected point usually gets harder.

Table 1. Sampling points with different difficulties. $\star$ indicates that mask labels were used for selection.

Strategy	$\mathcal{P}_0$	$\mathcal{P}_1$	$\mathcal{P}_2$	$\mathcal{P}_3$
Random	31.97	32.32	33.01	33.69
Entropy	31.97	**32.88**	**33.93**	**34.49**
*Max Error	31.97	7.95	12.45	14.24
*Least Error	31.97	32.16	32.50	32.95

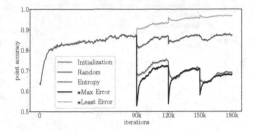

Fig. 5. The point accuracy (measured on train2017) curves of sampling points with different difficulties. At the first step ($\mathcal{P}_1$), the misclassification ratio was 82% and 7% for *Max Error* and *Least Error*, respectively.

Point Distribution. We calculated the distance between the actively acquired points and the ground-truth instance boundaries, and show the mean distances at each step in Fig. 4c. As shown, the selected points were usually closer to boundaries than the random points and the mean distance became smaller with more steps. This is as expected—as the model gets gradually better (*e.g.*, over/under-segmented regions has been corrected), the predicted boundaries get closer to the actual object boundaries, thus the remaining high-entropy points are mostly located around object boundaries (see the 2nd column of Fig. 4a). However, the points around object boundaries are inherently hard to classify even with full supervisions, as studied in previous works [48,59], and their labels might be noisy due to the coarse polygon-based mask annotations in MS-COCO. In summary, with more steps, the algorithm tends to select points around object boundaries, yet these annotations, though being difficult, often bring marginal performance gain, which confirmed the observations in above analysis.

Point Difficulty. From the accuracy decrements (after adding new points) in Fig. 4b we can calculated that about 51% of the actively acquired points ($\mathcal{P}_1$) were misclassified by the previous model ($\mathcal{M}_0$), while the ratio is 23% for random sampling, which suggests that the actively acquired points are more difficult for the model to learn. To study the influence of point difficulty, two experiments were conducted where we selected the points with maximum error or with minimum error at each step. The results were compared in terms of both mask mAP (Table 1) and point accuracy (Fig. 5). For *Least Error*, although the point accuracy (orange line) always stayed at a high level, the results of mAP still lagged behind random sampling, which suggests that these well-classified points were too easy for the model and of course less informative. For *Max Error*, the results of mAP were extremely poor while the point accuracy (black line) still increased during each training step. The reason might be that these points were mostly the hard cases and training with them directly made the model overfitted. Two conclusions can be drawn from the above results: (a) Point difficulty can heavily impact the performance of active learning, where neither the easiest nor the

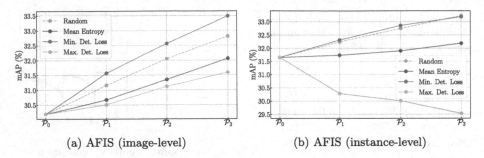

(a) AFIS (image-level)   (b) AFIS (instance-level)

Fig. 6. Comparison of different image-level and instance-level selection strategies designed for AFIS. See Sect. 3.3 and *Supp. Material* for details.

most difficult points should be selected. The proposed *Entropy* metric achieves a reasonable balance in this factor. (b) APIS is a challenging but non-trivial problem. It is still difficult to determine which point has a potentially large contribution even provided the mask labels. The results and analyses suggest that uncertainty is a better solution towards the right direction than correctness.

4.4   Comparison to Other Learning Strategies

Comparison of APIS and AFIS. As introduced in Sect. 3.3, a baseline setting AFIS was established for comparison. For fair comparison, the annotation budget and training time should be the same with APIS during each step. As stated in previous works [9,33], it takes 0.9 s on average to label a point and 79.2 s to create a polygon-based instance mask in MS-COCO. In above experiments, one point was labeled for each instance at each step, thus 860000 points in total. If the same budget is allocated to instances, we can annotate masks for $860000/(79.2/0.9) \approx 9773$ instances. Unlike previous works that the annotation cost for different images are treated identical, in our case the cost is proportional to the number of instances in the image, which varies across images. Therefore, given a fixed annotation budget, the number of annotated images is dependent on the sampling strategy.

We compared different sampling strategies for the case of *image-level* selection and *instance-level* selection, respectively. $\mathcal{P}_s$ here indicates that the cost for labeling images or instances is exactly the same as $\mathcal{P}_s$ in APIS. Similarly, some images or instances were randomly selected (with the same budget as $\mathcal{P}_0$) for model initialization. As shown in Fig. 6, the results of the *Mean Entropy* strategy were unsatisfactory in both cases, even lagging behind random sampling. On the other hand, the strategy that selecting instances with the lowest detection loss (*Min. Det. Loss*) usually produced on par or even better results than other competitors. Since AFIS is not the focus of this paper, we provided more results and analyses of AFIS in *Supp. Material*.

The best-performing strategies found above were adopted for comparison in Fig. 7. Three conclusions can be drawn from the results: (1) Point-based supervision is an effective way for training instance segmentation models. Even with

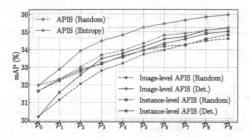

Fig. 7. Comparison of APIS and AFIS with the same annotation budget and training time. Det. indicates the *Min. Det. Loss* strategy.

Table 2. Comparison of APIS and weakly-supervised instance segmentation methods (with ResNet-50 backbone). †: our impl. (no point aug.).

Method	Anno.	Iter.	mAP
CondInst [50]	Fully sup.	270k	37.5
DiscoBox [28]	$\{\mathcal{C}, \mathcal{B}\}$	270k	31.4
BoxInst [51]	$\{\mathcal{C}, \mathcal{B}\}$	270k	31.8
PointSup† [9]	$\{\mathcal{C}, \mathcal{B}, \mathcal{P}_{10}\}$	270k	35.4
APIS (ours)	$\{\mathcal{C}, \mathcal{B}, \mathcal{P}_7\}$	270k	35.4
APIS (ours)	$\{\mathcal{C}, \mathcal{B}, \mathcal{P}_{10}\}$	360k	36.0

random points, the model can still outperformed those trained with mask supervisions under the same annotation costs and training time. (2) Active learning is a label-efficient training strategy for instance segmentation, especially when the annotation budget is limited. As shown, the active selection strategy usually performed better than random sampling in all settings. (3) The proposed APIS setting, combining active learning and point-based supervision, is a more powerful yet economic choice to train instance segmentation models under limited annotation budgets. The model developed under this setting consistently outperformed all other competitors at each active learning step. For example, at the 5th step ($\mathcal{P}_5$), our model achieved on par or even better results than other models with more points and longer training time (*e.g.*, $\mathcal{P}_9$).

Comparison to Weakly-Supervised Methods. In Table 2, we compared APIS with some existing weakly-supervised instance segmentation methods. Compared to boxly-supervised methods [28,51], labeling points additionally usually leads to considerable improvements. Compared to PointSup [9] (based on CondInst with ResNet50) trained with 10 randomly sampled points, APIS achieved the same results with 3 fewer points per instance. We argue that random sampling not considered the informativeness of different points, thus leading to sub-optimal results. In spite of this, we have to realize that APIS and PointSup varied significantly in motivation, which optimized for active learning and weakly-supervised learning, respectively.

5   Conclusion

In this paper, we propose APIS, a new active learning setting for instance segmentation where the most informative points are selected for annotation. We formulate this setting and propose several sampling strategies. Extensive experiments and detailed analysis on MS-COCO demonstrate that APIS is a powerful but economic learning strategy for training instance segmentation models with limited annotation budgets. We hope this work could inspire future researches on related topics, *e.g.*, point-based supervision and label-efficient learning.

Acknowledgment. This work was supported in part by the National Natural Science Foundation of China (Nos. U19B2034, 62061136001 and 61836014).

References

1. Agarwal, S., Arora, H., Anand, S., Arora, C.: Contextual diversity for active learning. In: Vedaldi, A., Bischof, H., Brox, T., Frahm, J.-M. (eds.) ECCV 2020. LNCS, vol. 12361, pp. 137–153. Springer, Cham (2020). https://doi.org/10.1007/978-3-030-58517-4_9
2. Aghdam, H.H., Gonzalez-Garcia, A., Weijer, J.V.D., López, A.M.: Active learning for deep detection neural networks. In: International Conference on Computer Vision, pp. 3672–3680 (2019)
3. Arun, A., Jawahar, C.V., Kumar, M.P.: Weakly supervised instance segmentation by learning annotation consistent instances. In: Vedaldi, A., Bischof, H., Brox, T., Frahm, J.-M. (eds.) ECCV 2020. LNCS, vol. 12373, pp. 254–270. Springer, Cham (2020). https://doi.org/10.1007/978-3-030-58604-1_16
4. Bearman, A., Russakovsky, O., Ferrari, V., Fei-Fei, L.: What's the point: semantic segmentation with point supervision. In: Leibe, B., Matas, J., Sebe, N., Welling, M. (eds.) ECCV 2016. LNCS, vol. 9911, pp. 549–565. Springer, Cham (2016). https://doi.org/10.1007/978-3-319-46478-7_34
5. Beluch, W.H., Genewein, T., Nürnberger, A., Köhler, J.M.: The power of ensembles for active learning in image classification. In: IEEE Conference on Computer Vision and Pattern Recognition, pp. 9368–9377 (2018)
6. Benenson, R., Popov, S., Ferrari, V.: Large-scale interactive object segmentation with human annotators. In: IEEE Conference on Computer Vision and Pattern Recognition, pp. 11700–11709 (2019)
7. Chen, K., et al.: Hybrid task cascade for instance segmentation. In: Conference on Computer Vision and Pattern Recognition, pp. 4974–4983 (2019)
8. Cheng, B., Misra, I., Schwing, A.G., Kirillov, A., Girdhar, R.: Masked-attention mask transformer for universal image segmentation. In: IEEE Conference on Computer Vision and Pattern Recognition, pp. 1290–1299 (2022)
9. Cheng, B., Parkhi, O., Kirillov, A.: Pointly-supervised instance segmentation. In: IEEE Conference on Computer Vision and Pattern Recognition, pp. 2617–2626 (2022)
10. Choi, J., Elezi, I., Lee, H.J., Farabet, C., Alvarez, J.M.: Active learning for deep object detection via probabilistic modeling. In: International Conference on Computer Vision (2021)
11. Cordts, M., et al.: The cityscapes dataset for semantic urban scene understanding. In: IEEE Conference on Computer Vision and Pattern Recognition, pp. 3213–3223 (2016)
12. Desai, S.V., Balasubramanian, V.N.: Towards fine-grained sampling for active learning in object detection. In: Conference on Computer Vision and Pattern Recognition and Workshops, pp. 924–925 (2020)
13. Desai, S.V., Chandra, A.L., Guo, W., Ninomiya, S., Balasubramanian, V.N.: An adaptive supervision framework for active learning in object detection. In: British Machine Vision Conference (2019)
14. Dong, B., Zeng, F., Wang, T., Zhang, X., Wei, Y.: SOLQ: segmenting objects by learning queries. In: Advances in Neural Information Processing Systems (2021)
15. Fang, Y., et al.: Instances as queries. In: International Conference on Computer Vision, pp. 6910–6919 (2021)

16. Gal, Y., Islam, R., Ghahramani, Z.: Deep Bayesian active learning with image data. In: International Conference on Machine Learning, pp. 1183–1192 (2017)
17. Gupta, A., Dollar, P., Girshick, R.: Lvis: a dataset for large vocabulary instance segmentation. In: IEEE Conference on Computer Vision and Pattern Recognition, pp. 5356–5364 (2019)
18. Hasan, M., Roy-Chowdhury, A.K.: Context aware active learning of activity recognition models. In: International Conference on Computer Vision, pp. 4543–4551 (2015)
19. Haussmann, E., et al.: Scalable active learning for object detection. In: 2020 IEEE Intelligent Vehicles Symposium (IV), pp. 1430–1435 (2020)
20. He, K., Gkioxari, G., Dollár, P., Girshick, R.: Mask R-CNN. In: International Conference on Computer Vision, pp. 2961–2969 (2017)
21. Hsu, C.C., Hsu, K.J., Tsai, C.C., Lin, Y.Y., Chuang, Y.Y.: Weakly supervised instance segmentation using the bounding box tightness prior. In: Advances in Neural Information Processing Systems, pp. 6586–6597 (2019)
22. Huang, Z., Huang, L., Gong, Y., Huang, C., Wang, X.: Mask scoring R-CNN. In: IEEE Conference on Computer Vision and Pattern Recognition, pp. 6409–6418 (2019)
23. Jang, W.D., Kim, C.S.: Interactive image segmentation via backpropagating refinement scheme. In: IEEE Conference on Computer Vision and Pattern Recognition, pp. 5292–5301 (2019)
24. Joshi, A.J., Porikli, F., Papanikolopoulos, N.: Multi-class active learning for image classification. In: IEEE Conference on Computer Vision and Pattern Recognition, pp. 2372–2379 (2009)
25. Kao, C.C., Lee, T.Y., Sen, P., Liu, M.Y.: Localization-aware active learning for object detection. In: Asian Conference on Computer Vision, pp. 506–522 (2018)
26. Khoreva, A., Benenson, R., Hosang, J., Hein, M., Schiele, B.: Simple does it: weakly supervised instance and semantic segmentation. In: IEEE Conference on Computer Vision and Pattern Recognition, pp. 876–885 (2017)
27. Lakshminarayanan, B., Pritzel, A., Blundell, C.: Simple and scalable predictive uncertainty estimation using deep ensembles. In: Advances in Neural Information Processing Systems (2017)
28. Lan, S., et al.: Discobox: weakly supervised instance segmentation and semantic correspondence from box supervision. In: International Conference on Computer Vision (2021)
29. Laradji, I.H., Rostamzadeh, N., Pinheiro, P.O., Vazquez, D., Schmidt, M.: Proposal-based instance segmentation with point supervision. In: IEEE International Conference on Image Processing, pp. 2126–2130 (2020)
30. Lewis, D.D., Catlett, J.: Heterogeneous uncertainty sampling for supervised learning. In: International Conference on Machine Learning (1994)
31. Li, Y., et al.: Fully convolutional networks for panoptic segmentation with point-based supervision. arXiv preprint arXiv:2108.07682 (2021)
32. Li, Z., Chen, Q., Koltun, V.: Interactive image segmentation with latent diversity. In: IEEE Conference on Computer Vision and Pattern Recognition, pp. 577–585 (2018)
33. Lin, T.-Y., et al.: Microsoft COCO: common objects in context. In: Fleet, D., Pajdla, T., Schiele, B., Tuytelaars, T. (eds.) ECCV 2014. LNCS, vol. 8693, pp. 740–755. Springer, Cham (2014). https://doi.org/10.1007/978-3-319-10602-1_48
34. Liu, S., Qi, L., Qin, H., Shi, J., Jia, J.: Path aggregation network for instance segmentation. In: IEEE Conference on Computer Vision and Pattern Recognition, pp. 8759–8768 (2018)

35. Liu, Z., Ding, H., Zhong, H., Li, W., Dai, J., He, C.: Influence selection for active learning. In: International Conference on Computer Vision, pp. 9274–9283 (2021)
36. Maninis, K.K., Caelles, S., Pont-Tuset, J., Van Gool, L.: Deep extreme cut: From extreme points to object segmentation. In: IEEE Conference on Computer Vision and Pattern Recognition, pp. 616–625 (2018)
37. Melville, P., Mooney, R.J.: Diverse ensembles for active learning. In: International Conference on Machine Learning (2004)
38. Papadopoulos, D.P., Uijlings, J.R., Keller, F., Ferrari, V.: Extreme clicking for efficient object annotation. In: International Conference on Computer Vision, pp. 4930–4939 (2017)
39. Pardo, A., Xu, M., Thabet, A., Arbelaez, P., Ghanem, B.: Baod: budget-aware object detection. In: IEEE Conference on Computer Vision and Pattern Recognition Workshops, pp. 1247–1256 (2021)
40. Pont-Tuset, J., Arbelaez, P., Barron, J.T., Marques, F., Malik, J.: Multiscale combinatorial grouping for image segmentation and object proposal generation. IEEE Trans. Pattern Anal. Mach. Intell. **39**(1), 128–140 (2016)
41. Qian, R., Wei, Y., Shi, H., Li, J., Liu, J., Huang, T.: Weakly supervised scene parsing with point-based distance metric learning. In: AAAI, pp. 8843–8850 (2019)
42. Rezatofighi, H., Tsoi, N., Gwak, J., Sadeghian, A., Reid, I., Savarese, S.: Generalized intersection over union: a metric and a loss for bounding box regression. In: IEEE Conference on Computer Vision and Pattern Recognition, pp. 658–666 (2019)
43. Roy, S., Unmesh, A., Namboodiri, V.P.: Deep active learning for object detection. In: British Machine Vision Conference (2018)
44. Sener, O., Savarese, S.: Active learning for convolutional neural networks: a core-set approach. arXiv preprint arXiv:1708.00489 (2017)
45. Shannon, C.E.: A mathematical theory of communication. ACM SIGMOBILE Mob. Comput. Commun. Rev. **5**(1), 3–55 (2001)
46. Shin, G., Xie, W., Albanie, S.: All you need are a few pixels: Semantic segmentation with pixelpick. In: IEEE Conference on Computer Vision and Pattern Recognition Workshops, pp. 1687–1697 (2021)
47. Sinha, S., Ebrahimi, S., Darrell, T.: Variational adversarial active learning. In: International Conference on Computer Vision, pp. 5972–5981 (2019)
48. Tang, C., Chen, H., Li, X., Li, J., Zhang, Z., Hu, X.: Look closer to segment better: Boundary patch refinement for instance segmentation. In: IEEE Conference on Computer Vision and Pattern Recognition, pp. 13926–13935 (2021)
49. Tian, Z., Chen, H., Wang, X., Liu, Y., Shen, C.: AdelaiDet: a toolbox for instance-level recognition tasks. https://git.io/adelaidet (2019)
50. Tian, Z., Shen, C., Chen, H.: Conditional convolutions for instance segmentation. In: Vedaldi, A., Bischof, H., Brox, T., Frahm, J.-M. (eds.) ECCV 2020. LNCS, vol. 12346, pp. 282–298. Springer, Cham (2020). https://doi.org/10.1007/978-3-030-58452-8_17
51. Tian, Z., Shen, C., Wang, X., Chen, H.: Boxinst: high-performance instance segmentation with box annotations. In: IEEE Conference on Computer Vision and Pattern Recognition, pp. 5443–5452 (2021)
52. Wang, J., et al.: Semi-supervised active learning for instance segmentation via scoring predictions. In: British Machine Vision Conference (2020)
53. Wang, K., Zhang, D., Li, Y., Zhang, R., Lin, L.: Cost-effective active learning for deep image classification. IEEE Trans. Circuits Syst. Video Technol. **27**(12), 2591–2600 (2016)

54. Wang, X., Zhang, R., Shen, C., Kong, T., Li, L.: Solo: a simple framework for instance segmentation. IEEE Trans. Pattern Anal. Mach Intell. **4**, 8587–8601 (2021)
55. Wu, T.H., et al.: Redal: region-based and diversity-aware active learning for point cloud semantic segmentation. In: International Conference on Computer Vision, pp. 15510–15519 (2021)
56. Xu, N., Price, B., Cohen, S., Yang, J., Huang, T.S.: Deep interactive object selection. In: IEEE Conference on Computer Vision and Pattern Recognition, pp. 373–381 (2016)
57. Yang, L., Zhang, Y., Chen, J., Zhang, S., Chen, D.Z.: Suggestive annotation: a deep active learning framework for biomedical image segmentation. In: International Conference on Medical Image Computing and Computer-Assisted Intervention, pp. 399–407 (2017)
58. Yuan, T., et al.: Multiple instance active learning for object detection. In: IEEE Conference on Computer Vision and Pattern Recognition, pp. 5330–5339 (2021)
59. Zhang, G., et al.: Refinemask: towards high-quality instance segmentation with fine-grained features. In: IEEE Conference on Computer Vision and Pattern Recognition, pp. 6861–6869 (2021)
60. Zhu, B., et al.: Autoassign: differentiable label assignment for dense object detection. arXiv preprint arXiv:2007.03496 (2020)
61. Zhu, Y., Zhou, Y., Xu, H., Ye, Q., Doermann, D., Jiao, J.: Learning instance activation maps for weakly supervised instance segmentation. In: IEEE Conference on Computer Vision and Pattern Recognition, pp. 3116–3125 (2019)

A Transformer-Based Decoder for Semantic Segmentation with Multi-level Context Mining

Bowen Shi[1], Dongsheng Jiang[2], Xiaopeng Zhang[2], Han Li[1], Wenrui Dai[1],
Junni Zou[1], Hongkai Xiong[1], and Qi Tian[2(✉)]

[1] Shanghai Jiao Tong University, Shanghai, China
{sjtu_shibowen,qingshi9974,daiwenrui,zoujunni,xionghongkai}@sjtu.edu.cn
[2] Huawei Cloud EI, Shenzhen, China
tian.qi1@huawei.com

Abstract. Transformers have recently shown superior performance than CNN on semantic segmentation. However, previous works mostly focus on the deliberate design of the encoder, while seldom considering the decoder part. In this paper, we find that a light weighted decoder counts for segmentation, and propose a pure transformer-based segmentation decoder, named SegDeformer, to seamlessly incorporate into current varied transformer-based encoders. The highlight is that SegDeformer is able to conveniently utilize the tokenized input and the attention mechanism of the transformer for effective context mining. This is achieved by two key component designs, *i.e.*, the internal and external context mining modules. The former is equipped with internal attention within an image to better capture global-local context, while the latter introduces external tokens from other images to enhance current representation. To enable SegDeformer in a scalable way, we further provide performance/efficiency optimization modules for flexible deployment. Experiments on widely used benchmarks ADE20K, COCO-Stuff and Cityscapes and different transformer encoders (*e.g.*, ViT, MiT and Swin) demonstrate that SegDeformer can bring consistent performance gains. Code is available at https://github.com/lygsbw/segdeformer.

1 Introduction

Semantic segmentation is a fundamental computer vision task and has attracted broad interest for its wide applications. Current solutions for semantic segmentation usually follow an encoder-decoder architecture proposed in FCN [22], which enables efficient transferring from the classification pretrained backbone for segmentation via per-pixel classification. Recently, great performance benefits have

---

B. Shi and D. Jiang—Equal contribution.

Supplementary Information The online version contains supplementary material available at https://doi.org/10.1007/978-3-031-19815-1_36.

© The Author(s), under exclusive license to Springer Nature Switzerland AG 2022
S. Avidan et al. (Eds.): ECCV 2022, LNCS 13688, pp. 624–639, 2022.
https://doi.org/10.1007/978-3-031-19815-1_36

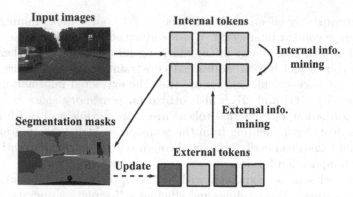

Fig. 1. The internal tokens from the current image and the introduced leanable external tokens can easily interacted with each other for multi-level context mining in a transformer-based framework.

been achieved in image classification by replacing Convolutional Neural Networks (CNN) with transformer-based networks [11,12,21], and many works [24,30,37] have pushed the segmentation performance by adapting these structures.

However, previous transformer-based methods mostly focus on designing the encoder, while ignoring the decoder part. These frameworks are usually equipped with a cumbersome transformer encoder for better performance, which inevitably suffers high computational costs. Considering this issue, there have been several context modeling designs at the decoder for CNN-based models. Among them, ASPP [4] and PPM [35] enlarge the spatial scale of contexts to utilize multi-scale contexts. OCNet [32] and CCNet [15] augment the representation of a position by aggregating the representations of its contextual positions. The highlight is that, the decoder part has stronger feature integration capability compared to the encoder. Since there exist co-occurrent visual patterns among pixels, designing context modeling schemes in the decoder is a more direct and effective practice. Considering that the context introduced by these works all comes from pixels within a single image, some recent works [17,27] introduce cross-image context mining and validate that it helps improve feature representation.

Different from previous complex context mining schemes, this paper pursues a simple but effective design for the decoder based on a light weighted transformer module. *The motivation is that we find transformer enjoys several advantages which are suitable for context mining.* First, the attention mechanism is very conducive to contextual information interaction since it has a global receptive field. Second, the flexible tokenized input of the transformer makes it convenient to model cross-image information. As shown in Fig. 1, by leveraging transformer, we can conveniently integrate context from different levels.

Based on these observations, this paper proposes a pure transformer-based decoder, named SegDeformer, for semantic segmentation. SegDeformer considers using two different kinds of context modules to help model pixel-level representation. One is an internal context mining module to capture global-local context within an image, which contains only one internal attention layer but the straight design is surprisingly effective. Another is an external context mining module for cross-image context interaction. We introduce additional learnable tokens in this module which take charge of summarizing information from other images. We also decouple and impose additional constraints on these tokens to make each token category-specific and ensure that the extracted information is helpful. Compared to [17] and [27] which utilize huge memory space to store the external information, our external tokens are more flexible and can bring more hierarchical features. Benefiting from the transformer structure, internal tokens and external tokens can easily interact through several external attention layers with little computation burden.

SegDeformer can be combined with other optimization modules, such as multi-stage feature fusion modules and efficient self-attention operation, for further performance/efficiency trade off. SegDeformer is also applicable to different kinds of transformer encoders, *e.g.*, ViT [11], MiT [30] and Swin [21], and bring consistent performance gains. To demonstrate the power of SegDeformer, we conduct massive experiments on three widely used segmentation benchmarks, ADE20K, COCO-Stuff and Cityscapes, and experimental results demonstrate its superior performance.

In a nutshell, this paper makes the following contributions:

– We propose a novel transformer-based decoder for semantic context mining, which is applicable to different encoders with varied structures.
– We design simple but effective internal and external context mining modules in the decoder for different levels of feature augmentation.
– We propose optimization techniques for further expansion and analysis the effect of SegDeformer on segmentation benchmarks.

2   Related Work

Transformer-Based Semantic Segmentation. Great performance breakthroughs have been achieved in semantic segmentation since the introduction of transformers [11,21,26] into computer vision tasks. Among the transformer-based methods, some works [10,21] directly transfer the transformer encoder designed for classification into semantic segmentation by fine-tuning together with the segmentation decoders [18,29]. Recent works [6,16,24,30] consider to design the overall segmentation framework for better adaptation. Among them, SegFormer [30] adopts a hierarchical encoder design for fine-to-coarse feature extraction as well as a light-weighted decoder design for efficient prediction. Segmenter [24] adds additional class-related tokens that aggregate embeddings of image patches for predicting class labels. MaskFormer [6] utilizes mask classification that predicts the class labels for binary masks related to regions or segments rather than focusing on each pixel. SeMask [16] introduces semantic attention layers into the encoder to improve the ability to encapsulate semantic information in features. Different from these methods, we pay more attention to the decoder and utilize the transformer for context interactions while ensuring our design can adapt to different encoders.

Context Scheme. It is efficient and effective to aggregate contextual information for boosting semantic segmentation. ASPP [2–4] and PPM [35] exploit multi-scale contexts by introducing pyramid pooling representations and parallel dilated convolutions, respectively. Recently, contextual information is further aggregated to augment the pixel representation using the spatial positions [36], channels [13] and objects [32] attention mechanisms, and these strategies are then enhanced by using the non-local operation [28] and criss-cross attention [15] to exploit the long-term dependency and criss-cross path. Furthermore, pixels are grouped in [19,31,33] to consider the relations within different object regions and augment the features with the group representation. Considering that these methods leverage the contexts from the same (current) image, MCIBI [17] improves the pixel representations with cross-image information stored in the memory bank. In this work, we consider both intra- and extra-image context mining by exploiting the input and interaction schemes of the transformer.

Discussion. Our design is inspired by MCIBI [17], which also introduces cross-image information for context mining. The main difference is that we bring the benefits of the transformer into the decoder design, while MCIBI is still limited to the CNN framework. Besides, we introduce learnable external tokens, which are proved useful in the following section to model more hierarchical cross-image information and achieve better performance than the use of memory bank in MCIBI. Segmenter [24] also introduces external class-map tokens, whereas they only use the similarity between these tokens and the internal tokens of the image for class prediction. However, we experimentally demonstrate that their structures are difficult to transfer. Our SegDeformer also goes one step further in the usage of external tokens, *i.e.*, we use external tokens serve only as key for feature augmentation and enable more specialized designs for external tokens. More details will be introduced in the following.

3   Methods

3.1   Overall Architecture

An overview of our architecture is shown in Fig. 2. Given an $H \times W \times 3$ input image, we first divide it into patches and pass these patches to the vision transformer encoder to obtain multi-stage feature map $F_i \in \mathbb{R}^{C_i \times H_i \times W_i}$, where $i \in \{1, 2, 3, 4\}$. Vision transformer encoder can benefit from our architecture regardless of their kinds, so it can be both flat structures like ViT, where the feature maps pass through each stage are all at $\frac{1}{16}$ of the original image resolution, and deep-narrow structures like MiT and Swin, where the feature maps are at $\{\frac{1}{4}, \frac{1}{8}, \frac{1}{16}, \frac{1}{32}\}$ of the original image resolution. Similarly, the channel dimension of the feature maps increases with the deepening of the deep-narrow structures but keeps the same in the flat structures.

After obtaining these multi-stage features, we then pass them to our proposed SegDeformer to augment the representations and predict the final segmentation

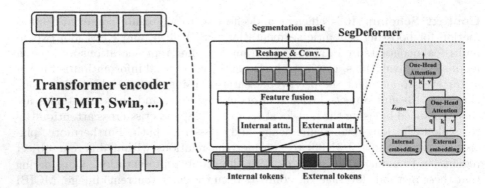

Fig. 2. The overall architecture. SegDeformer contains two key components: internal attention and external attention, for internal and external context mining. It is a general decoder that is applicable to different kinds of transformer encoders.

mask M of size $H \times W \times N_{cls}$, where N_{cls} is the number of categories. The proposed SegDeformer consists of the following main steps. First, following Seg-Former [30], basic MLP layers and optional up-sampling operations are used to unify the channel dimension and feature scale of multi-stage features:

$$\hat{F}_i = \text{Linear}\,(C_i, C)\,(F_i)\,, \forall i,$$
$$\hat{F}_i = \text{Upsample}\,(H_1 \times W_1)\left(\hat{F}_i\right), \forall i, \tag{1}$$
$$F = \text{Linear}(4C, C)\left(\text{Concat}\left(\hat{F}_i\right)\right), \forall i,$$

where $\text{Linear}(C_{in}, C_{out})(\cdot)$ denotes a linear layer and C_{in} and C_{out} are input and output vector dimensions respectively and F denotes the fused feature. Then, we flatten F back to the internal token sequence X_{inter} with size $N \times C$, where $N = H_1 \times W_1$ denotes the length of X_{inter}, and conduct internal and external context mining as follows:

$$Y_{inter} = \mathcal{M}_{inter}(X_{inter}),$$
$$Y_{exter} = \mathcal{M}_{exter}(X_{inter}, X_{exter}), \tag{2}$$

where $\mathcal{M}_{inter}$ and $\mathcal{M}_{exter}$ denotes the internal context mining module and external context mining module, respectively, and Y_{inter} and Y_{exter} are their outputs. $X_{exter} \in \mathbb{R}^{N_{cls} \times C}$ is a learnable external token sequence which will be introduced in the following. Next, the augmented feature $F_{aug} \in \mathbb{R}^{H_1 \times W_1 \times C}$ is obtained by a feature fusion operation $\mathcal{F}$ and a reshape operation:

$$F_{aug} = \text{Reshape}(\mathcal{F}(X_{inter}, Y_{inter}, Y_{exter})), \tag{3}$$

where $\mathcal{F}$ is simply set to an element-wise adding operation in our architecture. Finally, the predicted segmentation mask M is obtained by:

$$M = \text{Upsample}(H \times W)(\mathcal{H}(F_{aug})), \tag{4}$$

where $\mathcal{H}$ denotes the classification head.

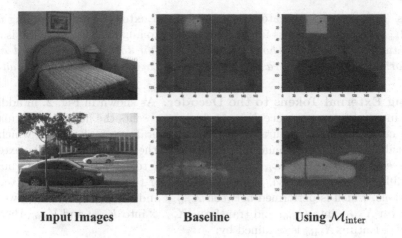

Input Images   **Baseline**   **Using $\mathcal{M}_{\text{inter}}$**

Fig. 3. Feature consistency visualization. The feature consistency of a given pixel (red dots in images) is calculated by the similarity between its feature and the features of other pixels. (Color figure online)

3.2   Internal Context Mining

Although the highest layers of transformer architecture are proved to have global respective field [30], we observe that the following multi-stage feature unification operation (Eq. 1) still brings feature confusion and leads to noncontinuous and incorrect mask prediction. We think this is because attention at different stages usually focuses on different contents, some aggregated information may not be suitable for segmentation and requires re-integration. Besides, for transformer encoders with deep-narrow designs, features are organized in a fine-to-coarse way, and regions represented by tokens at different stages have scale differences.

The internal context mining module $\mathcal{M}_{inter}$ with global aggregation capabilities is therefore designed to *reintegrate information from other related pixels. Such that confused pixels can aggregate relevant high-quality information from other pixels*, and improve the representation. We do not adopt complicated designs for $\mathcal{M}_{inter}$ because we empirically find only a one-head self-attention operation is enough to solve the feature confusion problem, as shown in Fig. 3. For computing self-attention in $\mathcal{M}_{inter}$, X_{inter} is first transformed into $Q_{inter}, K_{inter}, V_{inter}$ with the same dimensions $N \times C$ by projecting. Then Y_{inter} is computed by:

$$Y_{inter} = \text{SoftMax}\left(\frac{Q_{inter}K_{inter}^T}{\sqrt{C}}\right) V_{inter}. \tag{5}$$

3.3   External Context Mining

Besides the internal information, the contextual information from other images can also enrich features and benefit globally consistent representation across images. This section elaborates the details of our external context mining module $\mathcal{M}_{exter}$, which uses cross-image information to augment features and is complimentary to $\mathcal{M}_{inter}$. *We hope to convey that the tokenized input used in the transformer is flexible and easily expandable to carry cross-image information.*

Adding External Tokens to the Decoder. As shown in Fig. 2, in addition to the internal token sequence X_{inter}, which represents the intrinsic information of the current image, we further introduce several external tokens, which are responsible for bring cross-image information to the current image. The external token sequence contains N_{cls} tokens, and each token aggregates information with different meanings. $\mathcal{M}_{exter}$ is composed of two one-head cross-attention operations, which is performed between X_{inter} and X_{exter}. Specifically, we first transform X_{inter} into Q_{mid} and transform X_{exter} into K_{mid} and V_{mid}, then the mid-level feature X_{mid} is obtained by:

$$Attn_{mid} = \frac{Q_{mid}K_{mid}^T}{\sqrt{C}},$$
$$X_{mid} = \text{SoftMax}(Attn_{mid})V_{mid}. \tag{6}$$

Then we project X_{inter} again to Q_{exter} and project X_{mid} to K_{exter} and V_{exter}, and the augmented feature Y_{exter} is finally obtained by:

$$Y_{exter} = \text{SoftMax}\left(\frac{Q_{exter}K_{exter}^T}{\sqrt{C}}\right)V_{exter}. \tag{7}$$

Adding Constraint to External Tokens. As part of the network parameters, X_{exter} can continuously update itself along with the learning process. However, we find that adding additional constraints to X_{exter} to make each token category-specific can bring better performance. The category specialization can be achieved by applying additional cross-entropy loss on the mid output M^{mid} arising from $Attn_{mid} \in \mathbb{R}^{N \times N_{cls}}$:

$$M^{mid} = \text{Upsample}(H \times W)(\text{Reshape}(Attn_{mid})),$$
$$\mathcal{L}_{attn} = \frac{1}{H \times W}\sum_{i,j}\mathcal{L}_{ce}\left(M^{mid}_{[i,j,*]}, \S\left(\mathcal{GT}_{[ij]}\right)\right), \tag{8}$$

Here, $\S$ denotes for converting the ground truth class label stored in $\mathcal{GT}$ into a one-hot format, $\sum_{i,j}$ denotes that the summation is carried out over all the pixels of the $\mathcal{GT}$, and $\mathcal{L}_{ce}$ is the cross-entropy loss. Similarly, we can also get the final segmentation loss $\mathcal{L}_{seg}$ using the mask prediction M:

$$\mathcal{L}_{seg} = \frac{1}{H \times W}\sum_{i,j}\mathcal{L}_{ce}\left(M_{[i,j,*]}, \S\left(\mathcal{GT}_{[ij]}\right)\right),$$
$$\mathcal{L}_{total} = \mathcal{L}_{seg} + \alpha\mathcal{L}_{attn}, \tag{9}$$

where α is the hyper-parameters to balance the losses. We empirically set $\alpha = 0.4$ by default.

Decoupling External Tokens. In the above basic framework, X_{exter} is responsible for both information interaction and category prediction, which increases the difficulty of its ability to compress information. We find that decoupling X_{exter} into two parts that take the two responsibilities separately can further enhance expressiveness. So in practice, we first enlarge the dimension of X_{exter} to $\hat{X}_{exter}$ with size $N \times 2C$. Then, for one external token $\hat{x}_{exter} \in \hat{X}_{exter}$ with size $2C$, we decouple it into two parts:

$$\hat{x}_{exter} = [\hat{x}_{info}, \hat{x}_{class}], \qquad (10)$$

where $\hat{x}_{info} \in \mathbb{R}^C$ takes charge of exchanging information and $\hat{x}_{class} \in \mathbb{R}^C$ is used for mid-level prediction. The decoupling of responsibilities can be easily achieved by substituting K_{mid} and V_{mid} in Eq. 6 with the projection of $\hat{X}_{class}$ and $\hat{X}_{info}$, respectively.

3.4 Optimization Modules

SegDeformer can be seamlessly integrated with other modules for further adaptation and expansion. We list part of the optimization techniques we used in this section, *i.e.*, multi-stage feature fusion and efficient self-attention.

Multi-stage Feature Fusion. SegDeformer mainly utilizes the attention mechanism to augment features while only using basic MLP (Eq. 1) for multi-stage feature fusion. Some other multi-level feature aggregation techniques, *e.g.*, Semantic-FPN [18], UperNet [29], and FAPN [14], can be used in conjunction with our method and bring further performance gains. Following Swin [21], We additionally introduce UperNet in some cases to pursue better feature representation.

Efficient Self-Attention. Despite SegDeformer can make good use of the characteristics of the transformer, the computational cost of the attention operations, mainly coming from Eq. 5 and 7, makes it unable to adapt to some real-time structures. In this case, we can introduce efficient self-attention to reduce the calculation amount. Denote the reduction ratio as R, we can use a $R \times R$ convolution with stride R to reduce the scale of K and V in Eq. 5 and 7. As a result, the complexity of the self-attention is reduced from $O\left(N^2\right)$ to $O\left(\frac{N^2}{R}\right)$.

4 Experiments

4.1 Experimental Settings

Datasets. We conduct experiments on three wildly used datasets, namely:

- **ADE20K** [9] is a scene parsing dataset. It contains around 25K images spanning 150 semantic categories, of which 20K for training, 2K for validation, and another 3K for testing.

Table 1. Benchmark results on ADE20K (val). † means using UperNet. ‡ means using ImageNet-22K for pretraining. SeMask-L in the encoder is short for SeMask Swin-L.

Method	Encoder	Crop size	Params↓	mIoU↑	MS mIoU↑
FCN [22]	ResNet101	512 × 512	68.59	39.91	41.40
EncNet [34]	ResNet101	512 × 512	55.05	42.61	44.01
PSPNet [35]	ResNet101	512 × 512	68.07	44.39	45.35
CCNet [15]	ResNet101	512 × 512	68.92	43.71	45.04
DeeplabV3+ [5]	ResNet101	512 × 512	62.68	45.47	46.35
Deit-B† [25]	Deit-B	512 × 512	120.57	45.36	47.16
DPT [23]	ViT-B	512 × 512	109.71	46.97	48.34
SETR-PUP [37]	ViT-L	512 × 512	317.29	48.24	49.99
Twins† [7]	SVT-L	512 × 512	132.78	49.65	50.63
SegFormer-B1 [30]	MiT-B1	512 × 512	13.72	40.97	42.54
SegFormer-B5 [30]	MiT-B5	512 × 512	82.01	49.13	50.22
Swin-L†‡ [21]	Swin-L	512 × 512	233.96	51.61	52.98
Swin-L‡ [21]	Swin-L	640 × 640	203.65	50.85	52.95
SeMask-L‡ [16]	SeMask-L	640 × 640	211.79	51.89	53.52
Swin-L†‡ [21]	Swin-L	640 × 640	233.96	52.09	53.47
Deit-B† + SegDeformer	Deit-B	512 × 512	122.96	46.07	47.94
SegFormer-B1 + SegDeformer	MiT-B1	512 × 512	14.35	44.05	45.98
SegFormer-B5 + SegDeformer	MiT-B5	512 × 512	82.65	50.32	51.29
Swin-L†‡ + SegDeformer	Swin-L	512 × 512	236.35	52.77	53.90
Swin-L†‡ + SegDeformer	Swin-L	640 × 640	236.35	**53.12**	**54.13**

– **COCO-Stuff** [1] is a large scale dataset, which includes 118K training images and 5K validation images from COCO 2017 [20], which contains annotations for 80 object classes and 91 stuff classes.
– **Cityscapes** [8] is an urban scene dataset which contains 5,000 finely annotated images, with 2,975 for training, 500 for validation and 1,524 for testing, respectively. It contains 19 categories, such as person, sky and car *etc.*

Implementation Details. We train our model with 8 Tesla V100 using the *mmsegmentation*[1] codebase. Unless specified, the encoder is pretrained on Imagenet-1K dataset and the decoder is randomly initialized. Most training and evaluation settings follow [30]. Specifically, during training, we randomly crop the training images to 512 × 512 for ADE20K and COCO-Stuff and to 1024 × 1024 for Cityscapes. Other data augmentation strategies follow [30]. We train the models for 160K iterations and use a batch size of 16 for ADE20K and COCO-Stuff and 8 for Cityscapes. We use AdamW optimizer and the learning rate is set to an initial value of $6e - 5$ with "poly" LR schedule. During the evaluation, we keep the aspect ratio and rescale the short side of the image to training cropped size. For

---

[1] https://github.com/open-mmlab/mmsegmentation.

Table 2. Benchmark results on COCO-Stuff. † means using UperNet. ‡ means using ImageNet-22K for pretraining.

Method	Encoder	mIoU↑
Deit-B† [25]	Deit-B	45.68
SegFormer-B5 [30]	MiT-B5	46.71
Swin-L†‡ [21]	Swin-L	49.05
Deit-B† + SegDeformer	Deit-B	46.02
SegFormer-B5 + SegDeformer	MiT-B5	47.51
Swin-L†‡ + SegDeformer	Swin-L	**49.51**

Table 3. Benchmark results on Cityscapes (val). † means using UperNet. ‡ means using ImageNet-22K for pretraining. ⋆ means using efficient self-attention.

Method	Encoder	mIoU↑
Deit-B† [25]	Deit-B	79.09
SegFormer-B5 [30]	MiT-B5	82.07
Swin-L†‡ [21]	Swin-L	82.80
Deit-B† + SegDeformer	Deit-B	80.10
SegFormer-B5⋆ + SegDeformer	MiT-B5	82.46
Swin-L†‡⋆ + SegDeformer	Swin-L	**83.52**

COCO-Stuff and Cityscapes, we additionally conduct inference using the sliding window test. Following the standard, we use mean Intersection-over-Union (mIoU) averaged over all classes for evaluation. *It should be noted that for fair comparisons, the results reported following are all based on mmsegmentation.*

4.2 Main Results

This section compares our results with other methoss on ADE20K, COCO-Stuff and Cityscapes, as well as the qualitative results on Cityscapes.

Results on ADE20K. Table 1 summarizes our results for ADE20K. The top part of the table reports some CNN-based methods and the middle includes some transformer-based methods, which achieve higher performance and are served as our primary research objective. At the bottom, we report the results of our SegDeformer with different encoders. As shown, Segdocoder achieves 43.88%, 46.07%, 50.32% and 52.77% mIoU based on MiT-B1, Deit-B, MiT-B5 and Swin-L, respectively, which is 2.91%, 0.71%, 1.19% and 1.16% better than corresponding baselines with only a small increase in the number of parameters. We also conducted multi-scale inference following standard practice [21], and the performance gains are consistent, which are 3.44% for MiT-B1, 0.78% for Deit-B, 1.07% for MiT-B5 and 0.92% for Swin-L. Besides, SegDeformer can improve the

Fig. 4. Visual comparisons between Deit-B and Deit-B + SegDeformer on Cityscapes.

result when using larger input for Swin-L, from 52.09% to 53.12%. A recent work, SeMask [16], achieves close performance growth when using Swin-L with FPN as the baseline. Its design requires adding attention modules to every encoder layer, while our decoder design only introduces a small number of external tokens with three attention operations, which is simpler and more effective.

Results on COCO-Stuff. We then evaluate SegDeformer on the COCO-Stuff dataset. Since *mmsegmentation* does not provide results on COCO-Stuff, we reproduce the Deit-B, Mit-B5 and Swin-L baseline for fair comparisons. The results shown in Table 2 are still positive. We achieve 0.34% gains for Deit-B, 0.80% gains for MiT-B5 and 0.46% gains for Swin-L.

Results on Cityscapes. We also report benchmark results on Cityscapes. To meet the larger input size, we replace self-attention with efficient self-attention when using MiT-B5 and Swin-L. As shown in Table 3, we achieve 1.01% gains for Deit-B, 0.39% gains for MiT-B5 and 0.72% gains for Swin-L. Figure 4 shows the qualitative results, where SegDeformer provides smoother predictions and better details than the baseline.

4.3   Ablation Study

This section ablates different variants of our SegDeformer framework on ADE20K, including the components of $\mathcal{M}_{inter}$ and $\mathcal{M}_{exter}$, and the use of $\mathcal{M}_{inter}$ and $\mathcal{M}_{exter}$. Some other discussions and comparisons are also included.

Designs of X_{inter}. This section studies the structure design of $\mathcal{M}_{inter}$. As shown in Table 4, Equipping $\mathcal{M}_{inter}$ with only a one-head self-attention can already boost the performance by a large margin, from 40.97% to 42.65%. The experimental results are robust and no additional performance gains are brought when using more complex designs, so we choose to keep the simplest design.

Table 4. Studies on the structure of internal context mining modules based on SegFormer-B1, including the number of heads, depths, and the use of MLP after the internal attention.

Heads	Depths	MLP	mIoU
0	0		40.97
1	1		42.65 (1.68 ↑)
1	2		42.53 (1.56 ↑)
2	1		42.62 (1.65 ↑)
1	1	✓	**42.81** (1.84 ↑)

Table 5. Studies on the design of external context mining modules based on SegFormer-B1, including the type of X_{exter}, the use of $\mathcal{L}_{attn}$ and Y_{exter}, and the decoupling ($De.$) operation.

Type of X_{exter}		$\mathcal{L}_{attn}$	Y_{exter}	$De.$	mIoU↑
Mom.	Learn.				
					40.97
✓			✓		41.44 (0.47 ↑)
✓		✓	✓		41.74 (0.77 ↑)
	✓		✓		41.57 (0.60 ↑)
	✓	✓			41.86 (0.89 ↑)
	✓	✓	✓		42.37 (1.40 ↑)
	✓	✓	✓	✓	**42.84** (1.87↑)

Type of X_{exter}. We first replace the learnable external tokens with momentum update tokens to analyze the influence of the type of X_{exter}. The momentum update schedule is the same as [17]. The results are shown in Table 5. Compared to baseline, it achieves minor improvement (0.47%) and adds mid-level supervision merely bringing 0.30% additional gains, which is still 0.63% lower than our learnable external tokens under the same setting. We believe this is because the momentum updated features are relatively similar to the internal features, so their augmentation effect is limited, while our method can bring more hierarchical features. More analysis is included in the appendix.

Influence of $\mathcal{L}_{attn}$, Y_{exter} and the Decoupling Operation. Then we study $\mathcal{L}_{attn}$, Y_{exter} and the decoupling operation. As shown in Table 5, although learning X_{exter} freely can also bring performance improvements, it is not as effective as adding additional regularization to each token (41.57% vs 42.37%). Removing Y_{exter} and directly using X_{mid} for feature fusion means merely using one attention layer in $\mathcal{M}_{exter}$, which causes 0.51% performance loss compared to our final module. Decoupling X_{exter} can bring further performance gain, from 42.37% to 42.84%, which indicates that fully mining external information has more potential benefits.

Table 6. Effectiveness of internal and external context mining based on SegFormer-B1.

Mining type		mIoU↑
Internal	External	
		40.97
✓		42.65 (1.68 ↑)
	✓	42.84 (1.87 ↑)
✓	✓	**44.05** (3.08 ↑)

Table 7. Studies on the applicability of SegDeformer and optimization modules. †
means using UperNet. ⋆ means using efficient self-attention.

Method	Params↓	fps↑	mIoU↑
Deit-S†	52.09	30.30	42.87
Deit-S + SegDeformer	27.21	**33.65**	43.93
Deit-S† + SegDeformer	54.48	28.52	**44.10**
Swin-S†	81.26	**15.89**	47.72
Swin-S + SegDeformer	54.02	4.83	48.16
Swin-S† + SegDeformer	83.65	4.34	**48.94**
Swin-S†⋆ + SegDeformer	92.43	11.44	48.42
SegFormer-B2	24.91	**33.47**	45.58
SegFormer-B2 + SegDeformer	25.40	7.80	**47.49**
SegFormer-B2⋆ + SegDeformer	27.59	24.63	47.09

Effectiveness of $\mathcal{M}_{inter}$ and $\mathcal{M}_{exter}$. Table 6 inspects the influence of internal
and external mining. It reveals that both kinds of mining bring performance
gains (1.68% for $\mathcal{M}_{inter}$ and 1.87% for $\mathcal{M}_{exter}$), and combining them brings
larger improvement (3.08%). The results reflect the effectiveness of mining in
both global-local and cross-image contexts, and their effects are complementary.

Adaptability of SegDeformer. In Table 7, we investigate the adaptability of
our SegDeformer. As shown, our method can bring performance improvement to
all the encoders. For Deit-B and Swin-L, replacing the original UperNet decoder
with SegDeformer can respectively bring 1.06% and 0.44% gains, and integrating SegDeformer with UperNet decoder can lead to another 0.27% and 0.78%
improvement. For SegFormer-B2, our SegDeformer can also boost the performance from 45.58% to 47.49%, which demonstrates its adaptability.

Complexity Analysis. Table 7 also reports the parameters and latency for a
comprehensive comparison. For flat structures like DeiT-S, SegDeformer enjoys
fewer parameters and less latency (27.21 M and 33.65 fps) compared to the Uper-
Net decoder (52.09 M and 30.30 fps). For deep-narrow structures like MiT-B2 and

Table 8. Ablation studies on SegFormer-B2 with different depths and widths at base decoders, denoted as (*depth,width*). ⋆ means using efficient self-attention.

Method	Params↓	mIoU↑
SegFormer-B2 (2,256)	**24.91**	45.58
SegFormer-B2 (8,256)	25.46	45.68
SegFormer-B2 + SegDeformer (-,256)	25.40	**47.49**

Method	fps↑	mIoU↑
SegFormer-B2 (2,256)	**33.47**	45.58
SegFormer-B2 (8,512)	24.33	46.08
SegFormer-B2⋆ + SegDeformer (-,256)	24.63	**47.09**

Swin-S, although the amount of parameters is still small (54.02 M and 25.40 M), the latency of SegDeformer becomes hard to tolerate (4.83 fps and 7.80 fps). This is because the final output size of the deep-narrow network is larger, which increases the computational burden of self-attention, and we can resort to efficient self-attention for better performance and efficiency trade off. The latency can be great optimized when using efficient self-attention, *i.e.*, 4.83 fps → 11.44 fps for MiT-B2 and 7.80 fps → 24.63 fps for Swin-S, with a tiny performance penalty.

Comparison with Decoders with Varying Depths and Widhts. We deliberately design decoders with varying depths and widths for fair comparisons with our SegDeformer under roughly the same parameters and fps. As shown in Table 8, merely adding depths or widths brings marginal gains, and SegDeformer enjoys better performance, which validates that the advantage comes from the architecture rather than the capacity. Note that for fps, we provide an efficient self-attention optimization to fit some deep-narrow encoders, and SegDeformer with efficient self-attention achieves better performance under close fps. We also provide comparisons with some other representative decoders in the appendix.

5   Conclusion

This paper proposed a pure transformer-based decoder termed SegDeformer for semantic segmentation, which can effectively model the intra- and inter-image context for better feature representation. The main contributions are two folds. First, we propose an internal context mining module equipped with an internal attention layer to capture global-local context within an image. Second, we model cross-image context via introducing learnable external tokens and designing an external context mining module for cross-image feature interaction. We also provide several optimization modules for scalable deployment. SegDeformer can be integrated with different encoders and experiments demonstrate its effectiveness.

Acknowledgment. This work was supported in part by the National Natural Science Foundation of China under Grant 61932022, Grant 61931023, Grant 61971285, Grant 62120106007, and in part by the Program of Shanghai Science and Technology Innovation Project under Grant 20511100100.

References

1. Caesar, H., Uijlings, J., Ferrari, V.: Coco-stuff: thing and stuff classes in context. In: CVPR (2018)
2. Chen, L., Papandreou, G., Kokkinos, I., et al: Semantic image segmentation with deep convolutional nets and fully connected crfs. In: ICLR (2015)
3. Chen, L., Papandreou, G., Kokkinos, I., et al.: Deeplab: semantic image segmentation with deep convolutional nets, atrous convolution, and fully connected crfs. TPAMI **40**, 834–848 (2017)
4. Chen, L., Papandreou, G., Schroff, F., et al: Rethinking atrous convolution for semantic image segmentation. arXiv (2017)
5. Chen, L., Zhu, Y., Papandreou, G., et al: Encoder-decoder with atrous separable convolution for semantic image segmentation. In: ECCV (2018)
6. Cheng, B., Schwing, A., Kirillov, A.: Per-pixel classification is not all you need for semantic segmentation. In: NeurIPS (2021)
7. Chu, X., Tian, Z., Wang, Y., et. al: Twins: revisiting the design of spatial attention in vision transformers. In: NeurIPS (2021)
8. Cordts, M., Omran, M., Ramos, S., et al: The cityscapes dataset for semantic urban scene understanding. In: CVPR (2016)
9. Cordts, M., Omran, M., Ramos, S., et al: Semantic understanding of scenes through the ade20k dataset. In: CVPR (2017)
10. Dong, X., Bao, J., Chen, D., et al.: Cswin transformer: a general vision transformer backbone with cross-shaped windows. arXiv (2021)
11. Dosovitskiy, A., Beyer, L., Kolesnikov, A., et al: An image is worth 16×16 words: transformers for image recognition at scale. In: ICLR (2021)
12. Fang, J., Xie, L., Wang, X., et al: Msg-transformer: exchanging local spatial information by manipulating messenger tokens. arXiv (2021)
13. Fu, J., Liu, J., Tian, H., et al: Dual attention network for scene segmentation. In: CVPR (2019)
14. Huang, S., Lu, Z., Cheng, R., et al: FaPN: feature-aligned pyramid network for dense image prediction. In: ICCV (2021)
15. Huang, Z., Wang, X., Wei, Y., et al: Ccnet: criss-cross attention for semantic segmentation. In: TPAMI (2020)
16. Jain, J., Singh, A., Orlov, N., et al.: Semask: semantically masking transformer backbones for effective semantic segmentation. arXiv (2021)
17. Jin, Z., Gong, T., Yu, D., et al.: Mining contextual information beyond image for semantic segmentation. In: ICCV (2021)
18. Kirillov, A., Girshick, R., He, K., et al: Panoptic feature pyramid networks. In: CVPR (2019)
19. Li, X., Zhong, Z., Wu, J., et al: Expectation-maximization attention networks for semantic segmentation. In: ICCV (2019)
20. Lin, T.-Y., et al.: Microsoft COCO: common objects in context. In: Fleet, D., Pajdla, T., Schiele, B., Tuytelaars, T. (eds.) ECCV 2014. LNCS, vol. 8693, pp. 740–755. Springer, Cham (2014). https://doi.org/10.1007/978-3-319-10602-1_48

21. Liu, Z., Lin, Y., Cao, Y., et al.: Swin transformer: hierarchical vision transformer using shifted windows. In: ICCV (2021)
22. Long, J., Shelhamer, E., Darrell, T.: Fully convolutional networks for semantic segmentation. In: CVPR (2015)
23. Ranftl, R., Bochkovskiy, A., Koltun, V.: Vision transformers for dense prediction. arXiv (2021)
24. Strudel, R., Garcia, R., Laptev, I., et al: Segmenter: transformer for semantic segmentation. In: ICCV (2021)
25. Touvron, H., Cord, M., Douze, M., et al: Training data-efficient image transformers & distillation through attention. arXiv (2020)
26. Vaswani, A., Shazeer, N., Parmar, N., et al.: Attention is all you need. In: NeurIPS (2017)
27. Wang, W., Zhou, T., Yu, F., et al: Exploring cross-image pixel contrast for semantic segmentation. In: ICCV (2021)
28. Wang, X., Girshick, R., Gupta, A., et al: Non-local neural networks. In: CVPR (2018)
29. Xiao, T., Liu, Y., Zhou, B., et al: Unified perceptual parsing for scene understanding. In: ECCV (2018)
30. Xie, E., Wang, W., Yu, Z., et al.: Segformer: simple and efficient design for semantic segmentation with transformers. In: NeurIPS (2021)
31. Yuan, Y., Chen, X., Wang, J.: Object-contextual representations for semantic segmentation. arXiv (2019)
32. Yuan, Y., Wang, J.: Ocnet: object context network for scene parsing. arXiv (2018)
33. Zhang, F., C, Y., Li, Z., et al: Acfnet: attentional class feature network for semantic segmentation. In: ICCV (2019)
34. Zhang, H., Dana, K., Shi, J., et al.: Context encoding for semantic segmentation. arXiv (2018)
35. Zhao, H., Shi, J., Qi, X., et al: Pyramid scene parsing network. In: CVPR (2017)
36. Zhao, H., Zhang, Y., Liu, S., et. al: PSANet: point-wise spatial attention network for scene parsing. In: ECCV (2018)
37. Zheng, S., Lu, J., Zhao, H., et al: Rethinking semantic segmentation from a sequence-to-sequence perspective with transformers. In: CVPR (2021)

XMem: Long-Term Video Object Segmentation with an Atkinson-Shiffrin Memory Model

Ho Kei Cheng$^{(\boxtimes)}$ and Alexander G. Schwing

University of Illinois Urbana-Champaign, Champaign, USA
{hokeikc2,aschwing}@illinois.edu

Frame 0 (input)   Frame 295   Frame 460   Frame 1285   Frame 2327

Abstract. We present XMem, a video object segmentation architecture for long videos with unified feature memory stores inspired by the Atkinson-Shiffrin memory model. Prior work on video object segmentation typically only uses one type of feature memory. For videos longer than a minute, a single feature memory model tightly links memory consumption and accuracy. In contrast, following the Atkinson-Shiffrin model, we develop an architecture that incorporates multiple independent yet deeply-connected feature memory stores: a rapidly updated *sensory memory*, a high-resolution *working memory*, and a compact thus sustained *long-term memory*. Crucially, we develop a memory potentiation algorithm that routinely consolidates actively used working memory elements into the long-term memory, which avoids memory explosion and minimizes performance decay for long-term prediction. Combined with a new memory reading mechanism, XMem greatly exceeds state-of-the-art performance on long-video datasets while being on par with state-of-the-art methods (that do not work on long videos) on short-video datasets.

1   Introduction

Video object segmentation (VOS) highlights specified target objects in a given video. Here, we focus on the semi-supervised setting where a first-frame annotation is provided by the user, and the method segments objects in all other frames

Supplementary Information The online version contains supplementary material available at https://doi.org/10.1007/978-3-031-19815-1_37.

© The Author(s), under exclusive license to Springer Nature Switzerland AG 2022
S. Avidan et al. (Eds.): ECCV 2022, LNCS 13688, pp. 640–658, 2022.
https://doi.org/10.1007/978-3-031-19815-1_37

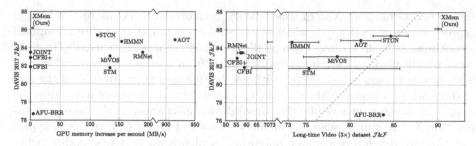

Fig. 1. Do state-of-the-art VOS algorithms scale well? **Left**: Memory scaling with respect to short-term segmentation quality. **Right**: Segmentation quality scaling from standard short videos (y-axis) to long videos (x-axis) – the dashed line indicates a 1:1 performance ratio. Error bars show standard deviations in memory sampling if applicable. See Sect. 4.1 for details.

as accurately as possible while preferably running in real-time, online, and while having a small memory footprint even when processing long videos[1].

As information has to be propagated from the given annotation to other video frames, most VOS methods employ a *feature memory* to store relevant deep-net representations of an object. Online learning methods [3,42,49] use the weights of a network as their feature memory. This requires training at test-time, which slows down prediction. Recurrent methods propagate information often from the most recent frames, either via a mask [39] or via a hidden representation [20,47]. These methods are prone to drifting and struggle with occlusions. Recent state-of-the-art VOS methods use attention [9,18,36,54,60] to link representations of past frames stored in the feature memory with features extracted from the newly observed query frame which needs to be segmented. Despite the high performance of these methods, they require a large amount of GPU memory to store past frame representations. In practice, they usually struggle to handle videos longer than a minute on consumer-grade hardware.

Methods that are specifically designed for VOS in long videos exist [27,29]. However, they often sacrifice segmentation quality. Specifically, these methods reduce the size of the representation during feature memory insertion by merging new features with those already stored in the feature memory. As high-resolution features are compressed right away, they produce less accurate segmentations. Figure 1 shows the relation between GPU memory consumption and segmentation quality in short/long video datasets (details are given in Sect. 4.1).

We think this undesirable connection of performance and GPU memory consumption is a direct consequence of using a single feature memory type. To address this limitation we propose a unified memory architecture, dubbed XMem. Inspired by the Atkinson-Shiffrin memory model [1] which hypothesizes that the human memory consists of three components, XMem maintains three independent yet deeply-connected feature memory stores: a rapidly updated *sensory memory*, a high-resolution *working memory*, and a compact thus sustained

---

[1] Code is available at https://hkchengrex.github.io/XMem.

long-term memory. In XMem, the sensory memory corresponds to the hidden representation of a GRU [11] which is updated every frame. It provides temporal smoothness but fails for long-term prediction due to representation drift. To complement, the working memory is agglomerated from a subset of historical frames and considers them equally [9,36] without drifting over time. To control the size of the working memory, XMem routinely consolidates its representations into the long-term memory, inspired by the consolidation mechanism in the human memory [46]. XMem stores long-term memory as a set of highly compact prototypes. For this, we develop a memory potentiation algorithm that aggregates richer information into these prototypes to prevent aliasing due to sub-sampling. To read from the working and long-term memory, we devise a space-time memory reading operation. The three feature memory stores combined permit handling long videos with high accuracy while keeping GPU memory usage low.

We find XMem to greatly exceed prior state-of-the-art results on the Longtime Video dataset [29]. Importantly, XMem is also on par with current state-of-the-art (that cannot handle long videos) on short-video datasets [41,57]. In summary:

- We devise XMem. Inspired by the Atkinson-Shiffrin memory model [1], we introduce memory stores with different temporal scales and equip them with a memory reading operation for high-quality video object segmentation on both long and short videos.
- We develop a memory consolidation algorithm that selects representative prototypes from the working memory, and a memory potentiation algorithm that enriches these prototypes into a compact yet powerful representation for longterm memory storage.

2   Related Works

General VOS Methods. Most VOS methods employ a *feature memory* to store information given in the first frame and to segment any new frames. Online learning approaches either train or fine-tune their networks at test-time and are therefore typically slow in inference [3,32,49]. Recent improvements are more efficient [2,34,37,42], but they still require online adaptation which is sensitive to the input and has diminishing gains when more training data is available. In contrast, tracking-based approaches [5,10,19,20,22,35,39,47,52,56,63] perform frame-to-frame propagation and are thus efficient at test-time. They however lack long-term context and often lose track after object occlusions. While some methods [6,23,26,48,53,59] also include the first reference frame for global matching, the context is still limited and it becomes harder to match as the video progresses. To address the context limitation, recent state-of-the-art methods use more past frames as feature memory [13,16,21,28,36,58,64]. Particularly, Space-Time Memory (STM) [36] is popular and has been extended by many follow-up works [8,9,18,31,33,43,44,50,54]. Among these extensions, we use STCN [9] as our working memory backbone as it is simple and effective. However, most variants cannot handle long videos due to the ever-expanding feature memory

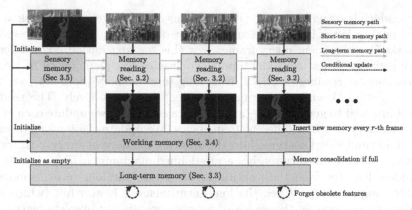

Fig. 2. Overview of XMem. The memory reading operation extracts relevant features from all three memory stores and uses those features to produce a mask. To incorporate new memory, the sensory memory is updated every frame while the working memory is only updated every r-th frame. The working memory is consolidated into the long-term memory in a compact form when it is full, and the long-term memory will forget obsolete features over time.

bank of STM. AOT [60] is a recent work that extends the attention mechanism to transformers but does not solve the GPU memory explosion problem. Some methods [14,33] employ a local feature memory window that fails to consider long-term context outside of this window. In contrast, *XMem* uses multiple memory stores to capture different temporal contexts while keeping the GPU memory usage strictly bounded due to our long-term memory and consolidation.

Methods that Specialize in Handling Long Videos. Liang *et al.* [29] propose AFB-URR which selectively uses exponential moving averages to merge a given memory element with existing ones if they are close, or to add it as a new element otherwise. A least-frequently-used-based mechanism is employed to remove unused features when the feature memory reaches a predefined limit. Li *et al.* [27] propose the global context module. It averages all past memory into a single representation, thus having zero GPU memory increase over time. However, both of these methods *eagerly* compress new high-resolution feature memory into a compact representation, thus sacrificing segmentation accuracy. Our multi-store feature memory avoids eager compression and achieves much higher accuracy in both short-term and long-term predictions.

3   XMem

3.1   Overview

Figure 2 provides an overview of XMem. For readability, we consider a single target object. However, note that XMem is implemented to deal with multiple objects, which is straightforward. Given the image and target object mask at the first frame (top-left of Fig. 2), XMem tracks the object and generates corresponding masks for subsequent query frames. For this, we first initialize the different feature memory stores using the inputs. For each subsequent query frame, we perform memory reading (Sect. 3.2) from long-term memory (Sect. 3.3), working memory (Sect. 3.4), and sensory memory (Sect. 3.5) respectively. The readout features are used to generate a segmentation mask. Then, we update each of the feature memory stores at different frequencies. We update the sensory memory every frame and insert features into the working memory at every r-th frame. When the working memory reaches a pre-defined maximum of $T_{\max}$ frames, we consolidate features from the working memory into the long-term memory in a highly compact form. When the long-term memory is also full (which only happens after processing thousands of frames), we discard obsolete features to bound the maximum GPU memory usage. These feature memory stores work in conjunction to provide high-quality features with low GPU memory usage even for very long videos.

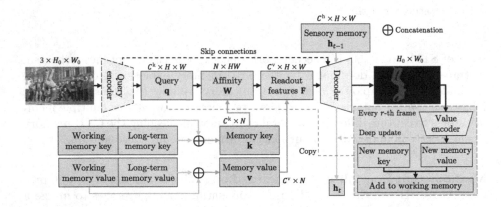

Fig. 3. Process of memory reading and mask decoding of a single query frame. We extract query $\mathbf{q}$ from the image and perform attention-based memory reading from the working/long-term memory to obtain features F. Together with the sensory memory, it is fed into the decoder to generate a mask. For every r-th frame, we store new features into the working memory and perform a deep update to the sensory memory.

XMem consists of three end-to-end trainable convolutional networks as shown in Fig. 3: a *query encoder* that extracts query-specific image features, a *decoder* that takes the output of the memory reading step to generate an object mask, and a *value encoder* that combines the image with the object mask to extract new memory features. See Sect. 3.6 for details of these networks. In the following, we will first describe the memory reading operation before discussing each feature memory store in detail.

3.2   Memory Reading

Figure 3 illustrates the process of memory reading and mask generation for a single frame. The mask is computed via the decoder which uses as input the short-term sensory memory $\mathbf{h}_{t-1} \in \mathbb{R}^{C^h \times H \times W}$ and a feature $\mathbf{F} \in \mathbb{R}^{C^v \times H \times W}$ representing information stored in both the long-term and the working memory.

The feature $\mathbf{F}$ representing information stored in both the long-term and the working memory is computed via the readout operation

$$\mathbf{F} = \mathbf{v}\mathbf{W}(\mathbf{k}, \mathbf{q}). \tag{1}$$

Here, $\mathbf{k} \in \mathbb{R}^{C^k \times N}$ and $\mathbf{v} \in \mathbb{R}^{C^v \times N}$ are C^k- and C^v-dimensional keys and values for a total of N memory elements which are stored in both the long-term and working memory. Moreover, $\mathbf{W}(\mathbf{k}, \mathbf{q})$ is an affinity matrix of size $N \times HW$, representing a readout operation that is controlled by the key $\mathbf{k}$ and a query $\mathbf{q} \in \mathbb{R}^{C^k \times HW}$ obtained from the query frame through the query encoder. The readout operation maps every query element to a distribution over all N memory elements and correspondingly aggregates their values $\mathbf{v}$.

The affinity matrix $\mathbf{W}(\mathbf{k}, \mathbf{q})$ is obtained by applying a softmax on the memory dimension (rows) of a similarity matrix $\mathbf{S}(\mathbf{k}, \mathbf{q})$ which contains the pairwise similarity between every key element and every query element. For computing the similarity matrix we note that the L2 similarity proposed in STCN [9] is more stable than the dot product [36], but it is less expressive, e.g., it cannot encode the confidence level of a memory element. To overcome this, we propose a new similarity function (*anisotropic L2*) by introducing two new scaling terms that break the symmetry between key and query. Figure 4 visualizes their effects.

Concretely, the key is associated with a shrinkage term $\mathbf{s} \in [1, \infty)^N$ and the query is associated with a selection term $\mathbf{e} \in [0, 1]^{C^k \times HW}$. Then, the similarity between the i-th key element and the j-th query element is computed via

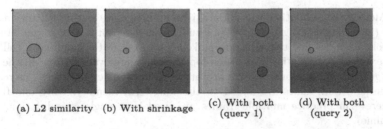

(a) L2 similarity   (b) With shrinkage   (c) With both (query 1)   (d) With both (query 2)

Fig. 4. Visualization of similarity functions in 2D with the background color showing the influence of each memory element (RGB). L2 similarity (a) [9] considers all memory elements uniformly. The shrinkage term (b) allows encoding element-level confidence (visualized by the size of dots) that accounts for the area of influence and sharpness of the mixing weights. The selection term allows query-specific interpretation of the memory – (c) and (d) show its effect with two different queries that focus on the vertical and horizontal dimension respectively. (b) can be seen as a case where the selection term is isotropic. When combined, we can model more complex similarity relations. (Color figure online)

$$\mathbf{S}(\mathbf{k}, \mathbf{q})_{ij} = -\mathbf{s}_i \sum_c^{C^k} \mathbf{e}_{cj} \left(\mathbf{k}_{ci} - \mathbf{q}_{cj}\right)^2, \tag{2}$$

which equates to the original L2 similarity [9] if $\mathbf{s}_i = \mathbf{e}_{cj} = 1$ for all i, j, and c. The shrinkage term $\mathbf{s}$ directly scales the similarity and explicitly encodes confidence – a high shrinkage represents low confidence and leads to a more local influence. Note that even low-confidence keys can have a high contribution if the query happens to coincide with it – thus avoiding the memory domination problem of the dot product, as discussed in [9]. Differently, the selection term $\mathbf{e}$ controls the relative importance of each channel in the key space such that attention is given to the more discriminative channels.

The selection term $\mathbf{e}$ is generated together with the query $\mathbf{q}$ by the query encoder. The shrinkage term $\mathbf{s}$ is collected together with the key $\mathbf{k}$ and the value $\mathbf{v}$ from the working and the long-term memory.[2] The collection is simply implemented as a concatenation in the last dimension: $\mathbf{k} = \mathbf{k}^{\mathrm{w}} \oplus \mathbf{k}^{\mathrm{lt}}$ and $\mathbf{v} = \mathbf{v}^{\mathrm{w}} \oplus \mathbf{v}^{\mathrm{lt}}$, where superscripts 'w' and 'lt' denote working and long-term memory respectively. The working memory consists of key $\mathbf{k}^{\mathrm{w}} \in \mathbb{R}^{C^k \times THW}$ and value $\mathbf{v}^{\mathrm{w}} \in \mathbb{R}^{C^v \times THW}$, where T is the number of working memory frames. The long-term memory similarly consists of keys $\mathbf{k}^{\mathrm{lt}} \in \mathbb{R}^{C^k \times L}$ and values $\mathbf{v}^{\mathrm{lt}} \in \mathbb{R}^{C^v \times L}$, where L is the number of long-term memory prototypes. Thus, the total number of elements in the working/long-term memory is $N = THW + L$.

Next, we discuss the feature memory stores in detail.

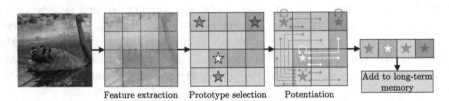

Feature extraction   Prototype selection   Potentiation   Add to long-term memory

Fig. 5. Memory consolidation procedure. Given an image, we extract features as memory keys (image stride exaggerated). We visualize these features with colors. For memory consolidation, we first select prototype keys (stars) from the candidates (all grids). Then, we invoke potentiation which non-locally aggregates values from all the candidates to generate more representative prototype values (golden outline). The resultant prototype keys and values are added to the long-term memory. Only one frame is shown here – in practice multiple frames are used in a single consolidation. (Color figure online)

3.3   Long-Term Memory

Motivation. A long-term memory is crucial for handling long videos. With the goal of storing a set of compact (consume little GPU memory) yet representative (lead to high segmentation quality) memory features, we design a *memory*

---

[2] For brevity, we omit the handling of these two scaling terms in memory updates for the rest of the paper. They are updated in the same way as the value.

consolidation procedure that selects *prototypes* from the working memory and enriches them with a *memory potentiation* algorithm, as illustrated in Fig. 5.

We perform memory consolidation when the working memory reaches a pre-defined size $T_{\max}$. The first frame (with user-provided ground-truth) and the most recent $T_{\min} - 1$ memory frames will be kept in the working memory as a high-resolution buffer while the remainder ($T_{\max} - T_{\min}$ frames) are *candidates* for being converted into long-term memory representations. We refer to the keys and values of these candidates as $\mathbf{k}^c \subset \mathbf{k}^w$ and $\mathbf{v}^c \subset \mathbf{v}^w$ respectively. In the following, we describe the prototype selection process that picks a compact set of prototype keys $\mathbf{k}^p \subset \mathbf{k}^c$, and the memory potentiation algorithm that generates enriched prototype values $\mathbf{v}^p$ associated with these prototype keys. Finally, these prototype keys and values are appended to the long-term memory $\mathbf{k}^{lt}$ and $\mathbf{v}^{lt}$.

Prototype Selection. In this step, we sample a small representative subset $\mathbf{k}^p \subset \mathbf{k}^c$ from the candidates as *prototypes*. It is essential to pick only a small number of prototypes, as their amount is directly proportional to the size of the resultant long-term memory. Inspired by human memory which moves frequently accessed or studied patterns to a long-term store, we pick candidates with high *usage*. Concretely, we pick the top-P frequently used candidates as prototypes. "Usage" of a memory element is defined by its cumulative total affinity (proba-bility mass) in the affinity matrix $\mathbf{W}$ (Eq. (1)), and normalized by the duration that each candidate is in the working memory. Note that the duration for each candidate is at least $r \cdot (T_{\min} - 1)$, leading to stable usage statistics. We obtain the keys of these prototypes as $\mathbf{k}^p \in \mathbb{R}^{C^k \times P}$.

Memory Potentiation. Note that, so far, our sampling of prototype keys $\mathbf{k}^p$ from the candidate keys $\mathbf{k}^c$ is both *sparse* and *discrete*. If we were to sample the prototypes values $\mathbf{v}^p$ in the same manner, the resultant prototypes would inevitably under-represent other candidates and would be prone to *aliasing*. The common technique to prevent aliasing is to apply an anti-aliasing (e.g., Gaussian) filter [15]. Similarly motivated, we perform filtering and aggregate more information into every sampled prototype. While standard filtering can be easily performed on the image plane (2D) or the spatial-temporal volume (3D), it leads to blurry features – especially near object boundaries. To alleviate, we instead construct the neighbourhood for the filtering in the high dimensional (C^k) key space, such that the highly expressive adjacency information given by the keys $\mathbf{k}^p$ and $\mathbf{k}^c$ is utilized. As these keys have to be computed and stored for memory reading anyway, it is also economical in terms of run-time and memory consumption.

Concretely, for each prototype, we aggregate values from all the value candi-dates $\mathbf{v}^c$ via a weighted average. The weights are computed using a softmax over the key-similarity. For this, we conveniently re-use Eq. (2). By substituting the memory key $\mathbf{k}$ with the candidate key $\mathbf{k}^c$, and the query $\mathbf{q}$ with the prototype keys $\mathbf{k}^p$, we obtain the similarity matrix $\mathbf{S}(\mathbf{k}^c, \mathbf{k}^p)$. As before, we use a softmax to obtain the affinity matrix $\mathbf{W}(\mathbf{k}^c, \mathbf{k}^p)$ (where every prototype corresponds to a distribution over candidates). Then, we compute the prototype values $\mathbf{v}^p$ via

$$\mathbf{v}^p = \mathbf{v}^c \mathbf{W}(\mathbf{k}^c, \mathbf{k}^p). \tag{3}$$

Finally, $\mathbf{k}^p$ and $\mathbf{v}^p$ are appended to the long-term memory $\mathbf{k}^{lt}$ and $\mathbf{v}^{lt}$ respectively – concluding the memory consolidation process. Note, similar prototypical approximations have been used in transformers [38,55]. Differently, our approach uses a novel prototype selection scheme suitable for video object segmentation.

Removing Obsolete Features. Although the long-term memory is extremely compact with a high ($> 6000\%$) compression ratio, memory can still overflow since we are continuously appending new features. Empirically, with a 6GB memory budget (e.g., a consumer-grade mid-end GPU), we can process up to 34,000 frames before running into any memory issues. To handle even longer videos, we introduce a least-frequently-used (LFU) eviction algorithm similar to [29]. Unlike [29], our "usage" (as defined in Sect. 3.3, Prototype Selection) is defined by the cumulative affinity after top-k filtering [8] which circumvents the introduction of an extra threshold hyperparameter. Long-term memory elements with the least usage will be evicted when a pre-defined memory limit is reached.

The long-term memory is key to enabling efficient and accurate segmentation of long videos. Next, we discuss the working memory, which is crucial for accurate short-term prediction. It acts as the basis for the long-term memory.

3.4   Working Memory

The working memory stores high-resolution features in a temporary buffer. It facilitates accurate matching in the temporal context of a few seconds. It also acts as a gateway into the long-term memory, as the importance of each memory element is estimated by their usage frequency in the working memory.

In our multi-store feature memory design, we find that a classical instantiation of the working memory is sufficient for good results. We largely employ a baseline STCN-style [9] feature memory bank as our working memory, which we will briefly describe for completeness. We refer readers to [9] for details. However, note that our memory reading step (Sect. 3.2) differs significantly. The working memory consists of keys $\mathbf{k}^w \in \mathbb{R}^{C^k \times THW}$ and values $\mathbf{v}^w \in \mathbb{R}^{C^v \times THW}$, where T is the number of working memory frames. The key is encoded from the image and resides in the same embedding space as the query $\mathbf{q}$ while the value is encoded from both the image and the mask. Bottom-right of Fig. 3 illustrates the working memory update process. At every r-th frame, we 1) copy the query as a new key; and 2) generate a new value by feeding the image and the predicted mask into the value encoder. The new key and value are appended to the working memory and are later used in memory reading for subsequent frames. To avoid memory explosion, we limit the number of frames in the working memory T: $T_{\min} \leq T < T_{\max}$ by consolidating extra frames into the long-term memory store as discussed in Sect. 3.3.

3.5   Sensory Memory

The sensory memory focuses on the short-term and retains low-level information such as object location which nicely complements the lack of temporal locality in the working/long-term memory. Similar to the working memory, we find a classical baseline to work well.

Concretely, the sensory memory stores a hidden representation $h_t \in \mathbb{R}^{C^h \times H \times W}$, initialized as the zero vector, and propagated by a Gated Recurrent Unit (GRU) [11] as illustrated in Fig. 6. This sensory memory is updated every frame using multi-scale features of the decoder. At every r-th frame, whenever a new working memory frame is generated, we perform a *deep update*. Features from the value encoder are used to refresh the sensory memory with

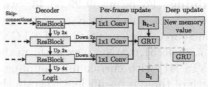

Fig. 6. Sensory memory update overview. Multi-scale features from the decoder are downsampled and concatenated as inputs to a GRU. In the deep update, a separate GRU is additionally used to refresh the sensory memory

another GRU. This allows the sensory memory to 1) discard redundant information that has already been saved to the working memory, and 2) receive updates from a deep network (i.e., the value encoder) with minimal overhead as we are reusing existing features.

3.6   Implementation Details

Here, we describe some key implementation details. To fully reproduce both training and inference, please see our open-source implementation (footnote 1).

Networks. Following common practice [9,29,36,43], we adopt ResNets [17] as the feature extractor, removing the classification head and the last convolutional stage. This results in features with stride 16. The query encoder is based on a ResNet-50 and the value encoder is based on a ResNet-18, following [9]. To generate the query q, the shrinkage term s, and the selection term e, we apply separate 3×3 convolutional projections to the query encoder feature output. Note that both the query and the shrinkage term are used for the current query frame, while the selection term is copied to the memory (along the copy path in Fig. 3) for later use if and only if we are inserting new working memory. We set $C^k = 64$, $C^v = 512$ following [9], and $C^h = 64$. To control the range of the shrinkage factor to be in $[1, \infty)$, we apply $(\cdot)^2 + 1$, and to control the range of the selection factor to be in $[0, 1]$, we apply a sigmoid.

The decoder concatenates hidden representation h_{t-1} and readout feature F. It then iteratively upsamples by $2\times$ at a time until stride 4 while fusing skip-connections from the query encoder at every level, following STM [36]. The stride 4 feature map is projected to a single channel logit via a 3×3 convolution, and is bilinearly upsampled to the input resolution. In the multi-object scenario, we use soft-aggregation [36] to fuse the final logits from different objects. Note that the bulk of the computation (i.e., query encoder, affinity $\mathbf{W}$) can be shared between different objects as they are only conditioned on the image [9].

Training. Following [9,29,36,43], we first pretrain our network on synthetic sequences of length three generated by deforming static images. We adopt the open-source implementation of STCN [9] without modification, which trains on [7,25,45,51,62]. Next, we perform the main training on YouTubeVOS [57] and DAVIS [41] with curriculum sampling [36]. We note that the default sequence length of three is insufficient to train the sensory memory as it would be heavily dependent on the initial state. Thus, we instead sample sequences of length eight. To reduce training time and for regularization, a maximum of three (instead of all) past frames are randomly selected to be the working memory for any query in training time. The entire training process takes around 35 h on two RTX A6000 GPUs. Deep updates are performed with a probability of 0.2, which is $1/r$ as we use $r = 5$ by default following [9]. Optionally, we also pretrain on BL30K [4,8,12] which gives a further boost in accuracy. We label any method that uses BL30K with an asterisk (*).

We use bootstrapped cross entropy loss and dice loss with equal weighting following [60]. For optimization, we use AdamW [24,30] with a learning rate of 1e-5 and a weight decay of 0.05, for 150K iterations with batch size 16 in static image pretraining, and for 110K iterations with batch size 8 in main training. We drop the learning rate by a factor of 10 after the first 80K iterations. For a fair comparison, we also retrain the STCN [9] baseline with the above setting. There is no significant difference in performance for STCN (see appendix).

4 Experiments

Unless otherwise specified, we use $T_{\min} = 5$, $T_{\max} = 10$, and $P = 128$, resulting in a compression ratio of 6328% from working memory to long-term memory. We set the maximum number of long-term memory elements to be 10,000 which means XMem never consumes more than 1.4GB of GPU memory, possibly enabling applications even on mobile devices. We use top-k filtering [8] with $k = 30$. 480p videos are used by default. To evaluate we use standard metrics (higher is better) [40]: Jaccard index $\mathcal{J}$, contour accuracy $\mathcal{F}$, and their average $\mathcal{J}\&\mathcal{F}$. For YouTubeVOS [57], $\mathcal{J}$ and $\mathcal{F}$ are computed for "seen" and "unseen" classes separately, denoted by subscripts S and U respectively. $\mathcal{G}$ is averaged $\mathcal{J}\&\mathcal{F}$ for both seen and unseen classes. For AOT [60], we compare with their R50 variant which has the same ResNet backbone as ours.

4.1 Long-Time Video Dataset

To evaluate long-term performance, we test models on the Long-time Video dataset [29] which contains three videos with more than 7,000 frames in total.

We also synthetically extend it to even longer variants by playing the video back and forth. $n\times$ denotes a variant that has n times the number of frames. For comparison, we select state-of-the-art methods with available implementation as we need to re-run their models. Most SOTA methods cannot handle long videos natively. We first measure their GPU memory increase per frame by averaging the memory consumption difference between the 100-th and 200-th frame in 480p.[3] Figure 1 (left) shows our findings, assuming 24FPS. For methods with prohibitive memory usage on long videos, we limit their feature memory insertion frequency accordingly, using 50 memory frames in STM as a baseline following [29]. Our method uses less memory than this baseline. We note that a low memory insertion frequency leads to high variances in performance, thus we run these experiments with 5 evenly-spaced offsets to the memory insertion routine and show "mean ± standard deviation" if applicable. In this dataset, we use $r = 10$. We do not find BL30K [8] pretraining to help here.

Table 1 tabulates the quantitative results, and Fig. 1 (right) plots the short-term performance against the long-term performance. Methods that use a temporally local feature window (CFBI(+) [59,61], JOINT [33]) have a constant memory cost but fail when they lose track of the context. Methods with a fast-growing memory bank (e.g., STM [36], AOT [60], STCN [9]) are forced to use a low feature memory insertion frequency and do not scale well to long videos. Figure 7 shows the scaling behavior of STCN vs. XMem in more detail.

AFB-URR [29] is designed to handle long videos and scales well with no degradation – but due to eager feature compression it has relatively low performance in the short term compared to other methods. In contrast, XMem not only holds up well in scaling to longer videos but also performs well in the short-term as shown in the next section. We provide qualitative comparisons in the appendix.

Table 1. Quantitative comparisons on the Long-time Video dataset [29]

| Method | Long-time Video (1×) | | | | | | Long-time Video (3×) | | | | | | $\Delta_{1\times\rightarrow3\times}$ |
	$\mathcal{J}\&\mathcal{F}$		$\mathcal{J}$		$\mathcal{F}$		$\mathcal{J}\&\mathcal{F}$		$\mathcal{J}$		$\mathcal{F}$		$\mathcal{J}\&\mathcal{F}$
CFBI+ [61]	50.9		47.9		53.8		55.3		54.0		56.5		4.4
RMNet [54]	59.8	±3.9	59.7	±8.3	60.0	±7.5	57.0	±1.6	56.6	±1.5	57.3	±1.8	−2.8
JOINT [33]	67.1	±3.5	64.5	±4.2	69.6	±3.9	57.7	±0.2	55.7	±0.3	59.7	±0.2	−9.4
CFBI [59]	53.5		50.9		56.1		58.9		57.7		60.1		5.4
HMMN [44]	81.5	±1.8	79.9	±1.2	83.0	±1.5	73.4	±3.3	72.6	±3.1	74.3	±3.5	−8.1
STM [36]	80.6	±1.3	79.9	±0.9	81.3	±1.0	75.3	±13.0	74.3	±13.0	76.3	±13.1	−5.3
MiVOS* [8]	81.1	±3.2	80.2	±2.0	82.0	±3.1	78.5	±4.5	78.0	±3.7	79.0	±5.4	−2.6
AOT [60]	84.3	±0.7	83.2	±3.2	85.4	±3.3	81.2	±2.5	79.6	±3.0	82.8	±2.1	−3.1
AFB-URR [29]	83.7		82.9		84.5		83.8		82.9		84.6		0.1
STCN [9]	87.3	±0.7	85.4	±1.1	89.2	±1.1	84.6	±1.9	83.3	±1.7	85.9	±2.2	−2.7
XMem (Ours)	**89.8**	±0.2	**88.0**	±0.2	**91.6**	±0.2	**90.0**	±0.4	**88.2**	±0.3	**91.8**	±0.4	0.2

---

[3] We make sure to exclude any caching or input buffering overhead.

4.2   Short Video Datasets

Table 2 and Table 3 tabulate our result on YouTubeVOS [57] 2018 validation, DAVIS [40] 2016/2017 validation, and DAVIS 2017 [41] test-dev. Results on YouTubeVOS [57] 2019 validation can be found in the appendix. The test set for YouTubeVOS is closed at the time of writing. We use $r = 5$ for these datasets. Following standard practice [9,36,59], we report single/multi-object FPS on DAVIS 2016/2017 validation. We additionally report FPS on YouTubeVOS 2018 validation which has longer videos on average. We measure FPS on a V100 GPU. For a fair comparison, we re-time prior works that report FPS on a slower GPU if possible and label this with a †. We note that some methods (not ours) are faster on a 2080Ti than on a V100. In these cases, we always give competing methods the benefit. Our speed-up solely comes from the use of long-term memory – a compact feature memory representation is faster to read from.

Table 2. Quantitative comparisons on three commonly used short-term datasets. * denotes BL30K [8] pretraining. Bold and underline denote the best and the second-best respectively in each column. † denotes FPS re-timed on our hardware. On YouTubeVOS, we re-run AOT with all input frames (improving its performance) for a fair comparison

Method	YT-VOS 2018 val [57]						DAVIS 2017 val [41]				DAVIS 2016 val [40]			
	$\mathcal{G}$	$\mathcal{J}_s$	$\mathcal{F}_s$	$\mathcal{J}_u$	$\mathcal{F}_u$	FPS	$\mathcal{J}\&\mathcal{F}$	$\mathcal{J}$	$\mathcal{F}$	FPS	$\mathcal{J}\&\mathcal{F}$	$\mathcal{J}$	$\mathcal{F}$	FPS
STM [36]	79.4	79.7	84.2	72.8	80.9	–	81.8	79.2	84.3	11.1†	89.3	88.7	89.9	14.0†
AFB-URR [29]	79.6	78.8	83.1	74.1	82.6	–	76.9	74.4	79.3	6.8†	–	–	–	–
CFBI [59]	81.4	81.1	85.8	75.3	83.4	3.4	81.9	79.1	84.6	5.9	89.4	88.3	90.5	6.2
RMNet [54]	81.5	82.1	85.7	75.7	82.4	–	83.5	81.0	86.0	4.4†	88.8	88.9	88.7	11.9
HMMN [44]	82.6	82.1	87.0	76.8	84.6	–	84.7	81.9	87.5	9.3†	90.8	89.6	92.0	13.0†
MiVOS* [8]	82.6	81.1	85.6	77.7	86.2	–	84.5	81.7	87.4	11.2	91.0	89.6	92.4	16.9
STCN [9]	83.0	81.9	86.5	77.9	85.7	13.2†	85.4	82.2	88.6	20.2†	91.6	**90.8**	92.5	26.9†
JOINT [33]	83.1	81.5	85.9	78.7	86.5	–	83.5	80.8	86.2	6.8†	–	–	–	–
STCN* [9]	84.3	83.2	87.9	79.0	87.3	13.2†	85.3	82.0	88.6	20.2†	<u>91.7</u>	90.4	<u>93.0</u>	26.9†
AOT [60]	85.5	84.5	<u>89.5</u>	79.6	88.2	6.4	84.9	82.3	87.5	18.0	91.1	90.1	92.1	18.0
XMem (Ours)	<u>85.7</u>	<u>84.6</u>	89.3	<u>80.2</u>	<u>88.7</u>	**22.6**	<u>86.2</u>	<u>82.9</u>	<u>89.5</u>	**22.6**	91.5	90.4	92.7	**29.6**
XMem* (Ours)	**86.1**	**85.1**	**89.8**	**80.3**	**89.2**	**22.6**	**87.7**	**84.0**	**91.4**	**22.6**	**92.0**	<u>90.7</u>	**93.2**	**29.6**

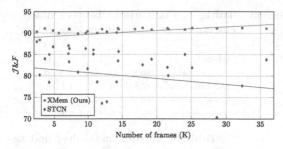

Fig. 7. Least-square fits of performance over video length for XMem and STCN [9] on variants of the Long-time Video dataset [29] from 1× to 10×. In longer videos, STCN decays due to missing context while ours stabilizes as we gain sufficient context

Table 3. Results on DAVIS 2017 test-dev. ‡: uses 600p videos

Method	DAVIS 2017 td		
	$\mathcal{J}\&\mathcal{F}$	$\mathcal{J}$	$\mathcal{F}$
STM‡ [36]	72.2	69.3	75.2
RMNet [54]	75.0	71.9	78.1
STCN [9]	76.1	73.1	80.0
CFBI+‡ [61]	78.0	74.4	81.6
HMMN [44]	78.6	74.7	82.5
MiVOS* [8]	78.6	74.9	82.2
AOT [60]	79.6	75.9	83.3
STCN* [9]	79.9	76.3	83.5
XMem (Ours)	81.0	77.4	84.5
XMem* (Ours)	81.2	77.6	84.7
XMem*‡ (Ours)	**82.5**	**79.1**	**85.8**

Table 4. Ablation on our memory stores. Standard deviations for $L_{1\times}$ are omitted

Setting	Y_{18}	D_{17}	$L_{1\times}$	FPS_{D17}	FPS_{Y18}
All memory stores	85.7	86.2	**89.8**	22.6	22.6
No sensory memory	84.4	85.1	87.9	23.1	23.1
No working memory	72.7	77.6	38.7	**31.8**	**28.1**
No long-term memory	**85.9**	**86.3**	n/a	17.6	10.0

Table 5. Ablation on the two scaling terms in memory reading

Setting	Y_{18}	D_{17}
With both terms	**85.7**	**86.2**
With shrinkage s only	85.1	85.6
With selection e only	84.8	84.8
With neither	85.0	85.1

4.3 Ablations

We perform ablation studies on validation sets of YouTubeVOS 2018 [57] (Y_{18}), DAVIS 2017 [41] (D_{17}), and Long-time Video ($n\times$) [29] ($L_{n\times}$). We report the most representative metric ($\mathcal{G}$ for YouTubeVOS, $\mathcal{J}\&\mathcal{F}$ for DAVIS/Long-time Video). FPS is measured on DAVIS 2017 validation unless otherwise specified. We highlight our final configuration with cyan .

Memory Stores. Table 4 tabulates the performance of XMem without any one of the memory stores. If the working memory is removed, long-term memory cannot function and it becomes "sensory memory only" with a constant memory cost. If the long-term memory is removed, all the memory frames are stored in the working memory. Although it has a slightly better performance due to its higher resolution feature, it cannot handle long videos and is slower.

Memory Reading. Table 5 shows the importance of the two scaling terms in the anisotropic L2 similarity. Interestingly, the selection term **e** alone does not help. We hypothesize that the selection term allows attention on a different subset of memory elements for every query, thus increasing the relative importance of each memory element. The shrinkage term **s** allows element-level modulation of confidence, thus avoiding too much emphasis on less confident elements. There is a synergy between the two terms, and our final model benefits from both.

Table 6. Comparisons between different memory consolidation methods

Setting		$L_{3\times}$	Compress ratio
Random	$P = 64$	89.5 ± 0.8	**12625%**
K-means centroid	$P = 64$	89.5 ± 0.5	**12625%**
Usage-based	$P = 64$	**89.6**± 0.4	**12625%**
Random	$P = 128$	89.7 ± 0.7	6328%
K-means centroid	$P = 128$	82.4 ± 10.3	6328%
Usage-based	$P = 128$	**90.0 $\pm$ 0.4**	6328%
Random	$P = 256$	89.8 ± 0.7	3164%
K-means centroid	$P = 256$	74.5 ± 17.0	3164%
Usage-based	$P = 256$	**90.1 $\pm$ 0.4**	3164%
No potentiation		87.9 ± 0.2	
With potentiation		**90.0 $\pm$ 0.4**	

Table 7. Comparisons between different strategies for handling long videos

Setting	$L_{1\times}$	$L_{3\times}$	$\Delta_{1\times \to 3\times}$
Consolidation	**89.8 $\pm$ 0.2**	**90.0 $\pm$ 0.4**	0.2
Eager compression	87.8 ± 0.3	87.3 ± 1.3	-0.5
Sparse insertion	89.8 ± 0.4	87.3 ± 1.0	-2.5
Local window	86.2 ± 1.5	85.5 ± 0.9	-0.7

Table 8. Ablation on the deep update frequency of sensory memory

Setting	Y_{18}	D_{17}	FPS
Every r-th frame	**85.7**	**86.2**	**22.6**
Every single frame	85.5	86.1	18.5
No deep update	85.3	85.4	**22.6**

Long-term Memory Strategies. Table 6 compares different prototype selection strategies and shows the importance of potentiation. We run all algorithms 5 times with evenly-spaced memory insertion offsets and show standard deviations. We choose the usage-based selection scheme with $P = 128$ for a balance between performance and memory compression. Table 7 compares additional strategies used by prior works, employed on our model. Eager compression is inspired by AFB-URR [29]. We set $T_{\min} = 1$ and $T_{\max} = 2$. Note, since we cannot compute usage statistics in this setting, we use random prototype selection with the same compression ratio. Sparse insertion follows our treatment to methods with a growing memory bank [9,36]. We set the maximum number of memory frames to be 50 following [29]. Local window follows [14,33,59], where we simply discard the oldest memory frame when the memory bank reaches its capacity. We always keep the first reference frame and set the memory bank capacity to be 50. Our memory consolidation algorithm is the most effective among these.

Deep Update. Table 8 shows different configurations of the deep update. Employing deep update every r-th frame results in a performance boost, with no noticeable speed drop (recall that we have to use the value encoder every r-th frame for our working memory anyway). However, using deep updates more often requires extra invocations of the value encoder and leads to a slowdown.

Pretraining. There are prior works that do not use static image pretraining [2, 14,33,61]. We provide our results without pretraining in the appendix.

4.4 Limitations

Our method sometimes fails when the target object moves too quickly or has severe motion blur as even the fastest updating sensory memory cannot catch up. See the appendix for examples. We think a sensory memory with a large receptive field that is more powerful than our baseline instantiation could help.

5   Conclusion

We present XMem – to our best knowledge the first multi-store feature memory model used for video object segmentation. XMem achieves excellent performance with minimal GPU memory usage for both long and short videos. We believe XMem is a good step toward accessible VOS on mobile devices, and we hope to draw attention to the more widely-applicable long-term VOS task.

Acknowledgment. Work supported in part by NSF under Grants 1718221, 2008387, 2045586, 2106825, MRI 1725729, and NIFA award 2020-67021-32799.

References

1. Atkinson, R.C., Shiffrin, R.M.: Human memory: a proposed system and its control processes. In: Psychology of learning and motivation, vol. 2, pp. 89–195. Elsevier (1968)
2. Bhat, G., et al.: Learning what to learn for video object segmentation. In: Vedaldi, A., Bischof, H., Brox, T., Frahm, J.-M. (eds.) ECCV 2020. LNCS, vol. 12347, pp. 777–794. Springer, Cham (2020). https://doi.org/10.1007/978-3-030-58536-5_46
3. Caelles, S., Maninis, K.K., Pont-Tuset, J., Leal-Taixé, L., Cremers, D., Van Gool, L.: One-shot video object segmentation. In: CVPR (2017)
4. Chang, A.X., et al.: ShapeNet: an information-rich 3D model repository. arXiv:1512.03012 (2015)
5. Chen, X., Li, Z., Yuan, Y., Yu, G., Shen, J., Qi, D.: State-aware tracker for real-time video object segmentation. In: CVPR (2020)
6. Chen, Y., Pont-Tuset, J., Montes, A., Van Gool, L.: Blazingly fast video object segmentation with pixel-wise metric learning. In: CVPR (2018)
7. Cheng, H.K., Chung, J., Tai, Y.W., Tang, C.K.: Cascadepsp: toward class-agnostic and very high-resolution segmentation via global and local refinement. In: CVPR (2020)
8. Cheng, H.K., Tai, Y.W., Tang, C.K.: Modular interactive video object segmentation: interaction-to-mask, propagation and difference-aware fusion. In: CVPR (2021)
9. Cheng, H.K., Tai, Y.W., Tang, C.K.: Rethinking space-time networks with improved memory coverage for efficient video object segmentation. In: NeurIPS (2021)
10. Cheng, J., Tsai, Y.H., Hung, W.C., Wang, S., Yang, M.H.: Fast and accurate online video object segmentation via tracking parts. In: CVPR (2018)
11. Cho, K., Van Merriënboer, B., Bahdanau, D., Bengio, Y.: On the properties of neural machine translation: encoder-decoder approaches. arXiv (2014)
12. Denninger, M., et al.: Blenderproc. arXiv:1911.01911 (2019)
13. Duarte, K., Rawat, Y.S., Shah, M.: Capsulevos: semi-supervised video object segmentation using capsule routing. In: ICCV (2019)
14. Duke, B., Ahmed, A., Wolf, C., Aarabi, P., Taylor, G.W.: Sstvos: sparse spatiotemporal transformers for video object segmentation. In: CVPR (2021)
15. Forsyth, D., Ponce, J.: Computer Vision: A Modern Approach. Prentice hall, Upper Saddle River (2011)
16. Ge, W., Lu, X., Shen, J.: Video object segmentation using global and instance embedding learning. In: CVPR (2021)

17. He, K., Zhang, X., Ren, S., Sun, J.: Deep residual learning for image recognition. In: CVPR (2016)
18. Hu, L., Zhang, P., Zhang, B., Pan, P., Xu, Y., Jin, R.: Learning position and target consistency for memory-based video object segmentation. In: CVPR (2021)
19. Hu, P., Wang, G., Kong, X., Kuen, J., Tan, Y.P.: Motion-guided cascaded refinement network for video object segmentation. In: CVPR (2018)
20. Hu, Y.T., Huang, J.B., Schwing, A.: Maskrnn: instance level video object segmentation. In: NIPS (2017)
21. Huang, X., Xu, J., Tai, Y.W., Tang, C.K.: Fast video object segmentation with temporal aggregation network and dynamic template matching. In: CVPR (2020)
22. Jang, W.D., Kim, C.S.: Online video object segmentation via convolutional trident network. In: CVPR (2017)
23. Johnander, J., Danelljan, M., Brissman, E., Khan, F.S., Felsberg, M.: A generative appearance model for end-to-end video object segmentation. In: CVPR (2019)
24. Kingma, D.P., Ba, J.: Adam: a method for stochastic optimization. In: ICLR (2015)
25. Li, X., Wei, T., Chen, Y.P., Tai, Y.W., Tang, C.K.: Fss-1000: a 1000-class dataset for few-shot segmentation. In: CVPR (2020)
26. Li, X., Loy, C.C.: Video object segmentation with joint re-identification and attention-aware mask propagation. In: Ferrari, V., Hebert, M., Sminchisescu, C., Weiss, Y. (eds.) ECCV 2018. LNCS, vol. 11207, pp. 93–110. Springer, Cham (2018). https://doi.org/10.1007/978-3-030-01219-9_6
27. Li, Yu., Shen, Z., Shan, Y.: Fast video object segmentation using the global context module. In: Vedaldi, A., Bischof, H., Brox, T., Frahm, J.-M. (eds.) ECCV 2020. LNCS, vol. 12355, pp. 735–750. Springer, Cham (2020). https://doi.org/10.1007/978-3-030-58607-2_43
28. Liang, S., Shen, X., Huang, J., Hua, X.S.: Video object segmentation with dynamic memory networks and adaptive object alignment. In: ICCV (2021)
29. Liang, Y., Li, X., Jafari, N., Chen, J.: Video object segmentation with adaptive feature bank and uncertain-region refinement. In: NeurIPS (2020)
30. Loshchilov, I., Hutter, F.: Decoupled weight decay regularization. In: ICLR (2019)
31. Lu, X., Wang, W., Danelljan, M., Zhou, T., Shen, J., Van Gool, L.: Video object segmentation with episodic graph memory networks. In: Vedaldi, A., Bischof, H., Brox, T., Frahm, J.-M. (eds.) ECCV 2020. LNCS, vol. 12348, pp. 661–679. Springer, Cham (2020). https://doi.org/10.1007/978-3-030-58580-8_39
32. Maninis, K.K., et al.: Video object segmentation without temporal information. PAMI 41, 1515–1530 (2018)
33. Mao, Y., Wang, N., Zhou, W., Li, H.: Joint inductive and transductive learning for video object segmentation. In: ICCV (2021)
34. Meinhardt, T., Leal-Taixé, L.: Make one-shot video object segmentation efficient again. In: NeurIPS (2020)
35. Oh, S.W., Lee, J.Y., Sunkavalli, K., Kim, S.J.: Fast video object segmentation by reference-guided mask propagation. In: CVPR (2018)
36. Oh, S.W., Lee, J.Y., Xu, N., Kim, S.J.: Video object segmentation using space-time memory networks. In: ICCV (2019)
37. Park, H., Yoo, J., Jeong, S., Venkatesh, G., Kwak, N.: Learning dynamic network using a reuse gate function in semi-supervised video object segmentation. In: CVPR (2021)
38. Patrick, M., et al.: Keeping your eye on the ball: trajectory attention in video transformers. In: NeurIPS (2021)
39. Perazzi, F., Khoreva, A., Benenson, R., Schiele, B., Sorkine-Hornung, A.: Learning video object segmentation from static images. In: CVPR (2017)

40. Perazzi, F., Pont-Tuset, J., McWilliams, B., Van Gool, L., Gross, M., Sorkine-Hornung, A.: A benchmark dataset and evaluation methodology for video object segmentation. In: CVPR (2016)
41. Pont-Tuset, J., Perazzi, F., Caelles, S., Arbeláez, P., Sorkine-Hornung, A., Van Gool, L.: The 2017 davis challenge on video object segmentation. arXiv:1704.00675 (2017)
42. Robinson, A., Lawin, F.J., Danelljan, M., Khan, F.S., Felsberg, M.: Learning fast and robust target models for video object segmentation. In: CVPR (2020)
43. Seong, H., Hyun, J., Kim, E.: Kernelized memory network for video object segmentation. In: Vedaldi, A., Bischof, H., Brox, T., Frahm, J.-M. (eds.) ECCV 2020. LNCS, vol. 12367, pp. 629–645. Springer, Cham (2020). https://doi.org/10.1007/978-3-030-58542-6_38
44. Seong, H., Oh, S.W., Lee, J.Y., Lee, S., Lee, S., Kim, E.: Hierarchical memory matching network for video object segmentation. In: ICCV (2021)
45. Shi, J., Yan, Q., Xu, L., Jia, J.: Hierarchical image saliency detection on extended cssd. TPAMI **38**, 717–729 (2015)
46. Squire, L.R., Genzel, L., Wixted, J.T., Morris, R.G.: Memory consolidation. In: Cold Spring Harbor perspectives in biology. Cold Spring Harbor Lab (2015)
47. Ventura, C., Bellver, M., Girbau, A., Salvador, A., Marques, F., Giro-i Nieto, X.: Rvos: end-to-end recurrent network for video object segmentation. In: CVPR (2019)
48. Voigtlaender, P., Chai, Y., Schroff, F., Adam, H., Leibe, B., Chen, L.C.: Feelvos: fast end-to-end embedding learning for video object segmentation. In: CVPR (2019)
49. Voigtlaender, P., Leibe, B.: Online adaptation of convolutional neural networks for video object segmentation. In: BMVC (2017)
50. Wang, H., Jiang, X., Ren, H., Hu, Y., Bai, S.: Swiftnet: real-time video object segmentation. In: CVPR (2021)
51. Wang, L., et al.: Learning to detect salient objects with image-level supervision. In: CVPR (2017)
52. Wang, Q., Zhang, L., Bertinetto, L., Hu, W., Torr, P.H.: Fast online object tracking and segmentation: a unifying approach. In: CVPR (2019)
53. Wang, Z., Xu, J., Liu, L., Zhu, F., Shao, L.: Ranet: ranking attention network for fast video object segmentation. In: ICCV (2019)
54. Xie, H., Yao, H., Zhou, S., Zhang, S., Sun, W.: Efficient regional memory network for video object segmentation. In: CVPR (2021)
55. Xiong, Y., et al.: Nyströmformer: A nyström-based algorithm for approximating self-attention. In: AAAI (2021)
56. Xu, K., Wen, L., Li, G., Bo, L., Huang, Q.: Spatiotemporal CNN for video object segmentation. In: CVPR (2019)
57. Xu, N., et al.: Youtube-vos: a large-scale video object segmentation benchmark. In: ECCV (2018)
58. Xu, X., Wang, J., Li, X., Lu, Y.: Reliable propagation-correction modulation for video object segmentation. In: AAAI (2022)
59. Yang, Z., Wei, Y., Yang, Y.: Collaborative video object segmentation by foreground-background integration. In: Vedaldi, A., Bischof, H., Brox, T., Frahm, J.-M. (eds.) ECCV 2020. LNCS, vol. 12350, pp. 332–348. Springer, Cham (2020). https://doi.org/10.1007/978-3-030-58558-7_20
60. Yang, Z., Wei, Y., Yang, Y.: Associating objects with transformers for video object segmentation. In: NeurIPS (2021)

61. Yang, Z., Wei, Y., Yang, Y.: Collaborative video object segmentation by multi-scale foreground-background integration. PAMI (2021)
62. Zeng, Y., Zhang, P., Zhang, J., Lin, Z., Lu, H.: Towards high-resolution salient object detection. In: ICCV (2019)
63. Zhang, L., Lin, Z., Zhang, J., Lu, H., He, Y.: Fast video object segmentation via dynamic targeting network. In: ICCV (2019)
64. Zhang, Y., Wu, Z., Peng, H., Lin, S.: A transductive approach for video object segmentation. In: CVPR (2020)

Self-Distillation for Robust LiDAR Semantic Segmentation in Autonomous Driving

Jiale Li[1][iD], Hang Dai[2]([✉])[iD], and Yong Ding[1]([✉])[iD]

[1] Zhejiang University, Hangzhou, China
dingy@vlsi.zju.edu.cn
[2] MBZUAI, Abu Dhabi, United Arab Emirates
hang.dai@mbzuai.ac.ae

Abstract. We propose a new and effective self-distillation framework with our new Test-Time Augmentation (TTA) and Transformer based Voxel Feature Encoder (TransVFE) for robust LiDAR semantic segmentation in autonomous driving, where the robustness is mission-critical but usually neglected. The proposed framework enables the knowledge to be distilled from a teacher model instance to a student model instance, while the two model instances are with the same network architecture for jointly learning and evolving. This requires a strong teacher model to evolve in training. Our TTA strategy effectively reduces the uncertainty in the inference stage of the teacher model. Thus, we propose to equip the teacher model with TTA for providing privileged guidance while the student continuously updates the teacher with better network parameters learned by itself. To further enhance the teacher model, we propose a TransVFE to improve the point cloud encoding by modeling and preserving the local relationship among the points inside each voxel via multi-head attention. The proposed modules are generally designed to be instantiated with different backbones. Evaluations on SemanticKITTI and nuScenes datasets show that our method achieves state-of-the-art performance. Our code is publicly available at https://github.com/jialeli1/lidarseg3d.

Keywords: Semantic segmentation · LiDAR · Self-distillation

1 Introduction

LiDAR point cloud semantic segmentation network as a visual recognition module in autonomous driving system, which is vital for driving scenario understanding [4,6]. The previous works [17,18,38] show that slight disturbances to the input data may impair the prediction results of neural networks, such as noise, missing part, and so on [38]. As shown in Fig. 1, the LiDAR semantic

---

Supplementary Information The online version contains supplementary material available at https://doi.org/10.1007/978-3-031-19815-1_38.

© The Author(s), under exclusive license to Springer Nature Switzerland AG 2022
S. Avidan et al. (Eds.): ECCV 2022, LNCS 13688, pp. 659–676, 2022.
https://doi.org/10.1007/978-3-031-19815-1_38

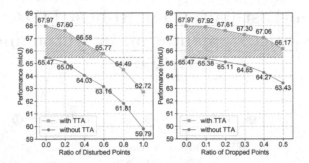

Fig. 1. Robustness test by disturbing point cloud samples in SemanticKITTI [4] dataset using the following settings: 1) add point-wise random noise uniformly distributed in $[-0.05, +0.05]$ m, 2) randomly drop points. We plot the performance mIoU (%) of the models with and without TTA against disturbing.

segmentation network gets undesirable performance degradation when imposing the point-wise random noise and the random dropping on the input point cloud. The unexpected conditions, such as weather changes and unstable data transmission, may cause the disturbances. Thus, boosting robustness is mission-critical but neglected in LiDAR segmentation for autonomous driving.

Training a robust model can be achieved by means of data augmentation [11,15] as well as knowledge distillation [19,41,45]. The standard types of data augmentation transformations for LiDAR point cloud include random flip, random rotation, random scaling, and random translation [8,39,56,59], which have been widely applied. Recently, the knowledge distillation [19] is broadly developed for model compression purposes in 2D semantic segmentation [2,30,45], showing a promising way to robustly train a compact student model with the guidance from a cumbersome teacher model. But there are three main limitations: (i) A cumbersome teacher model with higher performance is required to be designed and trained. (ii) The differences of the feature distributions between the heterogeneous teacher model and student model are detrimental for distillation [45]. Although many efforts are made to adapt the feature map for alleviating the distribution gap in 2D semantic segmentation [2,30,45], the gap still exists in such two heavy and lightweight models. (iii) The student model yields a better performance with distillation than individually training, but not a new state-of-the-art performance due to the limited distillation efficiency.

Inspired by 2D semi-supervised learning works [40,41] that can train a model with the unlabeled image mainly by the consistency regularization between outputs of two instances of the same model, we propose to perform self-distillation to learn from the segmentation model itself without the cumbersome teacher model. We follow these 2D works [29,40,41] to instantiate a teacher model to provide predictions as the soft labels for training a student model, and update the teacher model with the temporal assembly of student model. In such a self-distillation, the above limitations (i) and (ii) can be effectively avoided. Unlike the purpose of training on extra unlabeled data [29,40], we aim to further address the limitation

(iii) above by self-distillation to achieve robust LiDAR semantic segmentation with stronger performance. As privileged guidance from the teacher is critical for transferring useful knowledge to a student, the quality guarantee should be considered for further enhancing the teacher. Thus, two additional components on robustness boost in the inference stage and the point cloud encoding aspect, which are further proposed as follows and tailored on LiDAR semantic segmentation field.

As shown in Fig. 1, the robustness in the inference stage is susceptible to external disturbances, thus the robustness boost is necessary to be addressed when the soft labels are inferred from the teacher. Test-Time Augmentation (TTA) is a effective and general idea for boosting the models in image-based 2D computer vision [7, 20, 60] by averaging the predictions of input variants to reduce the uncertainty. It is feasible to equip the teacher model with TTA when inferring predictions as distillation guidance. But TTA is barely used for distillation in 2D semantic segmentation and not well-investigated on LiDAR 3D semantic segmentation yet. Only the flip and multi-scale tests are independently used in 2D semantic segmentation [20, 48, 60], since the other transformations like rotation and translation will make the pixel-wise results overflow the image boundaries and spatially un-aligned. Differently, as long as the order of points is unchanged in a point cloud, the point-wise results of different input variants are naturally aligned for merging so that more types of transformations should account for LiDAR semantic segmentation. Thus, we firstly introduce the TTA into this field by reusing a proposed compound transformation instead of any individual transformations multiple times. The compound transformation can provide more diversity and flexibility than individual transformations in point cloud variants generation. In Fig. 1, for the input samples with the ratio of disturbance within the shaded area, the LiDAR segmentation model with TTA can still achieve better performance than the model without TTA on clean input samples. The proposed TTA is potential to improve the soft labels from the teacher model for better self-distillation.

To enhance the point cloud encoding in a large-scale autonomous driving scene, we mainly focus on the voxel methods since they [39, 56, 59] are significantly more effective and efficient than point methods [21, 42, 50] due to the better structured representation and the deeper convolutional network architecture. The major concern for voxel-based methods is the quantization error introduced in the voxelization process, where a cluster of local points inside a voxel are encoded as the average of their input features (e.g. 3D coordinates and reflection intensity) [12, 37, 39, 51, 57]. The average operation encoded voxel features can also be treated as introducing some noise to the initial point features. Encoding a cluster of points as the average reduces the consumption resource of feature extraction, it is also equivalent to losing object details as well as dropping points. The larger voxel size worsens these cases and weakens the robustness of point cloud encoding. To address this, we propose a novel Voxel Feature Encoder (VFE) with Transformer [43] on the local points inside a voxel, termed as TransVFE. Transformer can naturally accommodate the unordered sequence data like point clouds and model the relationship among local points via multi-head attention [14]. Thus, the proposed TransVFE can serve as a performance enhancement module in our teacher and student models, which models and preserves the local geometric relationship during the conversion from points to voxels at the point cloud encoding level.

Notably, teacher and student models in our method are designed with the same network architectures for jointly learning and evolving without requiring the additional cumbersome teacher model. The model equipped with the proposed TTA as the teacher can provide privileged guidance while the student continuously updates the teacher with better network parameters learned by itself. The proposed TransVFE also are integrated into the models to enhance the voxel feature learning. In such a manner, even the teacher and student are homogeneous, the robust model training can proceed with the self-distillation.

Our main **contributions** are 4-fold: (**i**) We propose a novel method for robust LiDAR semantic segmentation in autonomous driving, achieving new state-of-the-art performance on SemanticKITTI and nuScenes datasets; (**ii**) we propose to perform self-distillation for LiDAR semantic segmentation, which enables the homogeneous models of teacher and student to jointly learn and evolve; (**iii**) We propose a simple yet efficient LiDAR semantic segmentation TTA strategy with a compound transformation, which can improve the teacher model for better self-distillation as well as be utilized independently in the inference stage with mIoU improvements; (**iv**) We propose a novel TransVFE that can enhance the robust point cloud voxel feature learning in our teacher and student models by modeling and preserving the local relationship among the points in each voxel.

2 Related Work

2.1 LiDAR Semantic Segmentation

Semantic segmentation on large-scale point clouds [4,6] measured by the LiDAR sensors are of more challenges than the synthetic and indoor point clouds [3,52]. The LiDAR semantic segmentation methods mostly follow the network architecture of U-Net [36] with skip-connections incorporated symmetrical encoder and decoder, but are differently designed with point cloud representations of point, 2D image and 3D voxel.

The **point** representation usually takes large computation costs on gathering the disordered neighbors for feature extraction. To trade off the computation burden and segmentation performance, PointASNL [50] and RandLA-Net [21] propose the learnable adaptive and the efficient random down-sampling algorithms to improve the classic farthest point sampling [34], respectively. The expressive local feature extractors developed in KPConv [42], BAAFNet [35] and others perform well on small point clouds but not that well on LiDAR point clouds. Besides, the **2D images** methods of PolarNet-series [56,58] and others [4,32,46,47,49] project the 3D point cloud as 2D images in Bird's-Eye-View (BEV) and range view, achieving the most efficient LiDAR semantic segmentation with the mature 2D Convolutional Neural Networks (CNNs) on GPUs. But the 3D-to-2D projection inevitably suffers from the loss of the 3D structure

Table 1. Comparing with other distillation related semantic segmentation methods.

Task	2D semantic segmantation	3D semantic segmantation	
Method	He et al. [16], SKD [30], IFVD [45], CSC [33], An et al. [2]	PSD [55]	Ours
Purpose	Model compression	Weakly supervised learning	Achieving higher performance
Cumbersome teacher	√	✗	✗
Parameters of teacher model	Pretrained & Fixed	Independently trained	Updated from student itself
Equip teacher with TTA	✗	✗	√

information of objects, resulting in unsatisfactory segmentation performance. The recent **3D voxel** methods Cylinder3D [59] and SPVNAS [39] yield top performances by designing deeper 3D sparse CNNs to explicitly explore the 3D structure information in the cylindrical [59] or cartesian [39] coordinate system. The 3D sparse convolutions are performed only on the non-empty voxels with acceptable memory consumption and significant computational acceleration [9,13,39]. As a fundamental module in 3D voxel methods, the VFE implemented by the average operation [12,39,51] or a PointNet [24,34] ignore the relationship of local points in voxel at the point cloud encoding level.

2.2 Semantic Segmentation with Knowledge Distillation

Knowledge distillation [19] is recently researched for compressing a cumbersome teacher as a compact student model in 2D semantic segmentation. An additional auto-encoder is employed to translate the high-level features for distillation in a latent domain by He et al. [16]. SKD [30] proposes to structurally transfer the pairwise relation on features, pixel-wise outputs, and holistic representations to the student. Unlike the dense distillation, IFVD [45] computes the intra-class feature variation to guide the student to mimic the class-wise prototype. The long-range dependence, spatial and channel correlations also are extracted as the knowledge for distillation by An et al. [2] and CSC [33], respectively. The above methods make efforts to adapt the feature map for alleviating the differences of feature distributions between the heterogeneous teacher model and student model, but the distribution gap still exists in such two heavy and lightweight models. Instead, we aim at achieving higher LiDAR semantic segmentation performance by performing self-distillation without any cumbersome teacher.

In LiDAR semantic segmentation, only the recently published weakly-supervised PSD [55] shares the closest distillation manner in terms of using two model instances of the same network architecture. However, the differences between PSD and ours still appear in Table 1 as follows. (**i**) Different model training strategies. Given a point cloud with only a tiny fraction of point-wise labels provided, PSD has two branches of disturbed and undisturbed input point clouds, where the undisturbed branch is termed as the teacher for providing robust feature representation as the knowledge to guide the disturbed branch termed as the student. The teacher and student are independently trained and only the consistency regularization effectiveness can aid the training. Instead, our teacher and student models are designed to be jointly evolved, where the more privileged guidance from the teacher can be transferred to the student while the student continuously updates the teacher with better network parameters learned by itself. (ii) Our teacher model is equipped with the proposed TTA strategy for the quality grantee of the distillation guidance, while no such quality grantee is considered in PSD. (iii) Different purposes. PSD mainly focuses on indoor point clouds and relies on consistency regularization to achieve weakly-supervised segmentation for reducing the labeling burden on an input point cloud, while our self-distillation aims to achieve more robust LiDAR semantic segmentation with stronger performance in large-scale driving scenarios.

2.3 Test-Time Augmentation

Since few efforts have been made on the TTA for LiDAR semantic segmentation, we mainly review the TTA applied in image-based 2D vision works [7,20,22,31,60]. The pixel-wise segmentation and object-wise axis-aligned boxes of the flipped and scaled input images can be averaged easily by the corresponding inverse transformation in 2D segmentation [20,48,60] and detection [7,54]. But the translation and rotation can cause some content pixels to overflow the image boundaries and coordinate quantization errors, resulting in unacceptable misalignment among transformed images. Image recognition tasks with image-wise classifications can additionally employ the rotation and translation transformations to perform TTA. For the point cloud with unstructured and unordered points, the point-wise semantic predictions can be easily averaged across the input variants from different types of transformations, as long as the order of points is unchanged. Some greedy [31] and learnable [22] policies search the combination of different TTA input variants in image recognition with carefully tuned search parameters and loss functions. However, as a pioneer of introducing the TTA into the LiDAR segmentation field, we employ a compound transformation based on the four types of transformations in TTA. It is simple yet effective, demonstrating the beauty of science.

3   Method

This section describes the proposed LiDAR semantic segmentation method. Since the teacher and student models in our method are related to the TransVFE and TTA, we begin with the overview of our network architecture in Sect. 3.1 followed by the description of a novel TTA strategy for LiDAR segmentation in Sect. 3.2. The proposed self-distillation framework and the loss function are presented in Sect. 3.3 and Sect. 3.4.

3.1   Network

TransVFE. Let $\left\{ \left(x_i, f_i^{\text{in}} \right) : i = 1, \cdots, N_{\text{P}} \right\}$ denote a input point cloud X within the range of $[x_{\text{Min}}, x_{\text{Max}}]$, where $x \in \mathbb{R}^{3 \times 1}$ represents the 3D point coordinates, and $f^{\text{in}} \in \mathbb{R}^{C_{\text{in}} \times 1}$ represents the C_{in}-dimensional point-wise input features such as coordinates x and reflection intensity r. We rearrange X as the structural non-empty voxels by voxelization. The point coordinates x are discretized into integer values $\bar{v} = \lfloor \frac{x - x_{\text{Min}}}{d} \rfloor$ by a step d. The points with the same $\bar{v}$ are gathered into a voxel and denoted as $\mathcal{N} = \left\{ \left(\bar{v}_i, f_i^{\text{in}} \right) : i = 1, \cdots, T \right\}$. The unique values of $\bar{v}$ are set as the voxel indices v. The VFE is defined on the $\mathcal{N}$ to encode the all the local point features $F^{\text{in}} \in \mathbb{R}^{C_{\text{in}} \times T}$ in $\mathcal{N}$ as the voxel-wise feature.

Given a voxel with T local points inside it, we use a VFE with Transfomer [43], termed as TransVFE, to model the relationship of local points in voxel via Multi-Head Self-Attention $MHSA(\cdot)$ and Feed-Forward Network $FFN(\cdot)$:

$$F' = Norm(W^{\text{in}} F^{\text{in}}), \tag{1}$$

$$F^{\text{att}} = F' + MHSA(F'), \tag{2}$$

$$F^{\text{trans}} = F^{\text{att}} + FFN(F^{\text{att}}), \tag{3}$$

where the input features F^{in} are initially projected to C_{trans} dimension by a linear layer with learnable parameters W^{in}. $Norm$ indicates LayerNorm operation. The $MHSA(\cdot)$ can be decomposed into N_{H} heads with features H as

$$MHSA(F') = [H_j : j = 1, \cdots N_{\text{H}}], \tag{4}$$

$$H_j^T = Softmax(\frac{Q_j^T K_j}{\sqrt{C^{\text{trans}} / N_{\text{H}}}}) V_j^T, \tag{5}$$

$$Q_j, K_j, V_j = W_j^{\text{q}} F', W_j^{\text{k}} F', W_j^{\text{v}} F'. \tag{6}$$

The $W_j^{\text{q}}, W_j^{\text{k}}, W_j^{\text{v}}$ are the learnable parameters in linear layers for feature projection, and each local point in F' interacts with others as defined in Eq. 5. After stacking three blocks of Transformer, we follow [14] to employ a max-pooling operation along the point-axis to get the expressive voxel-wise feature $f^{\text{trans}} \in \mathbb{R}^{C_{\text{trans}} \times 1}$ from $F^{\text{trans}} \in \mathbb{R}^{C_{\text{trans}} \times T}$, and apply another linear layer to compress $f^{\text{trans}} \in \mathbb{R}^{C_{\text{trans}} \times 1}$ to $f^{\text{vfe}} \in \mathbb{R}^{C_0 \times 1}$ with less channels for saving computation in the subsequent network. Thus, our TransVFE explicitly encodes local points into the voxel features as $\mathcal{V} = \left\{ \left(v_i, f_i^{\text{vfe}} \right) : i = 1, \cdots, N_{\text{V}} \right\}$, where each item (v, f^{vfe}) indicates the non-empty voxel located at v with the corresponding voxel-wise feature f^{vfe}.

3D Sparse U-Net. Without loss of generalization, we leverage the universal U-Net from [37] as our backbone, which is implemented with the computationally efficient 3D sparse convolutions [13,51] following [37,59]. We rearrange the voxels in $\mathcal{V}$ as a sparse tensor for feature learning with the 3D sparse convolutional blocks. The details are in the supplementary material.

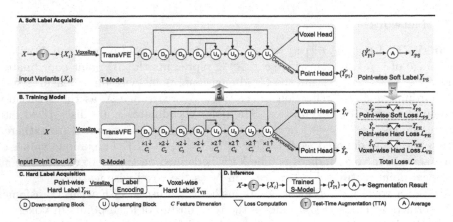

Fig. 2. Overview of self-distillation for robust LiDAR semantic segmentation.

Voxel Head and Point Head. Voxelization makes feature extraction efficient [25,27], but LiDAR segmentation requires point-wise outputs. The existing methods [56,59] reverse the pair-wise mapping from the voxel-wise outputs back to the points, and associate all the points in the same voxel with the same category. This inevitably has the risk of classifying points of different categories into the same category, especially for object boundaries. Thus, we devoxelize the voxel-wise features into point-wise features to predict point-wise output $\hat{Y}_P$ following [39]. For each point, we interpolate the point feature from its K nearest neighboring voxels [26]. We set the K to 3 for computation efficiency.

We construct segmentation heads composed of fully connected layers on voxel-wise and point-wise features, respectively. The voxel-wise prediction $\hat{Y}_V$ is for auxiliary supervision only, while we apply an *argmax* function to the point-wise prediction $\hat{Y}_P$ for obtaining the predicted classes as the segmentation results. To avoid ambiguity in voxel-wise supervision, we ignore the voxels containing points of multiple classes in the auxiliary voxel-wise loss.

3.2 Test-Time Augmentation for LiDAR Semantic Segmentation

We choose four standard types of data augmentation transformations with the common hyper-parameters widely used in the training phase of a LiDAR segmentation network [8,39,56,59]: global scaling (τ_{scale}) with a random scaling factor in $[0.95, 1.05]$, random flipping (τ_{flip}) along the X, Y axis, global rotation (τ_{rot}) around the Z axis with a random angle in $\left[-\frac{\pi}{4}, +\frac{\pi}{4}\right]$, global translation ($\tau_{\text{tran}}$) with a random vector ($\Delta x, \Delta y, \Delta z$) sampled from a Gaussian distribution with mean zero and the standard deviation 0.5. The random value controls the magnitude of applying each transformation.

We can apply the above transformations in test-time and assemble the predictions from the input and its augmented samples to boost the robustness of LiDAR segmentation model. Given a model with weights θ', the assembled prediction $\hat{Y}'$ from the naive version of point cloud TTA can be formulated as

$\hat{Y}' = \frac{1}{M}\sum_{i=1}^{M}\theta'(X_i)$, where $\mathcal{X} = \{X_i\}$ is the set of input variants and M denotes the number of samples in $\mathcal{X}$. The naive strategy is to generate the $\mathcal{X}$ as a set of $\{X, X_{\text{scale}}, X_{\text{flip}}, X_{\text{rot}}, X_{\text{tran}}\}$, which consist of the identical input X and the augmented input samples generated by the four types of transformations. Although we can apply each type of transformation multiple times with different magnitudes to generate more input variants, the flexibility of data augmentation is still within the individual transformation.

Instead, we develop a more effective strategy for increasing the diversity and flexibility of the augmented samples. We define a compound transformation $\tau_{\text{comp}}(X)$ as $\tau_{\text{tran}}(\tau_{\text{rot}}(\tau_{\text{flip}}(\tau_{\text{scale}}(X))))$, which combines individual transformations. The magnitude of τ_{comp} can be independently controlled by each individual transformation. The X is augmented into a set of $\mathcal{X}^* = \{X, X_{\text{comp},j}\}$ with different magnitudes, where "j" indexes the augmented samples in the set. The diversity and the flexibility in the input point cloud variants help reduce the uncertainty with the assembled prediction from multiple input point cloud variants in the inference stage.

3.3 Self-distillation

For training a robust model with stronger performance without a cumbersome teacher model (T-Model) providing the distillation guidance, we propose to perform self-distillation on two model instances of the same network architecture.

Teacher Model Configuration. The quality of the guidance from the T-Model is critical to training a good student model (S-Model) [16,29,41,57]. Hence, we decide the configuration of the T-Model in two terms of the performance boost and the network parameters updating. Since TTA always improves the performance of a model robustly, it is feasible to equip the T-Model with TTA when inferring predictions as distillation guidance. But it is barely used for distillation in 2D semantic segmentation, and we show that our TTA strategy can be involved in the T-Model configuration for better self-distillation. With the aid of TTA, the parameters of the T-Model can naively be copied from the current S-Model or loaded from the pretrained parameters. Besides these, updating T-Model with the successive network parameters of S-Model is widely used to provide the predictions as the reliable soft labels on unlabeled images in the semi-supervised 2D vision works [29,40,41]. Inspired by this, we can also update the T-Model with weights θ' as the Exponential Moving Average (EMA) of the S-Model with weights θ in successive training step t [41], which can be formulated as $\theta'_t = \alpha\theta'_{t-1} + (1-\alpha)\theta_t$, where $\alpha = \min(1 - \frac{1}{t}, 0.999)$. The smoothing coefficient α makes the T-Model a temporal assembly of S-Models from different training steps, so that the T-Model is more likely to have better soft labels to regularize the learning process [41].

As the combination of different manners in updating T-Model and TTA, we investigate five strategies for self-distillation. Specifically, we describe all the five optional configurations for T-Model as follows. (**i**) We copy the T-Model from the current S-Model at each training step t, but its prediction is improved by our TTA[1]. (ii) The T-Model is a pre-trained model, then frozen when training the S-Model following [19,44]. (iii) We pre-train and freeze the T-Model, and boost it with TTA in distillation[1]. (iv) The T-Model is the EMA of the S-Model following [41,57]. (v) The T-Model is the EMA of the S-Model with our TTA[1].

We finally employ configuration (v) to excavate instructive knowledge in our self-distillation with the most significant improvements achieved.

Training with Soft Labels. Since there are different numbers of non-empty voxels but the same number of points between the augmented point clouds in TTA, we only consider the point-wise outputs for self-distillation. As shown at the 2nd row of Fig. 2, we use the generated soft label Y_{PS} to compute an additional soft loss term $\mathcal{L}_{PS}$ between the soft label Y_{PS} and the S-Model prediction $\hat{Y}_{P}$ as a useful knowledge transfer for helping the S-Model learn better. It is a self-distillation procedure between the T-Model from the EMA of the S-Model with the proposed TTA and the S-Model in our case where the T-Model and the S-Model are with the same network architecture, excavating instructive knowledge from the S-Model itself. After self-distillation, only the S-Model is used for inference, which avoids the computation consumption from the T-Model. In the inference stage, we can also apply TTA to the S-Model to get the final output for further performance improvement. More discussions on the differences of other knowledge distillation related semantic segmentation methods and ours can be retrieved in Sect. 2.2 and Table 1.

3.4 Loss Function

We can train our model individually with voxel-wise hard label Y_{VH} and point-wise hard label Y_{PH} only, or jointly with the additional point-wise soft label Y_{PS} for achieving self-distillation. When training without self-distillation, the total loss $\mathcal{L}$ is the sum of the hard label loss $\mathcal{L}_{VH}$ on voxel-wise prediction and the hard label loss $\mathcal{L}_{PH}$ on point-wise prediction as $\mathcal{L} = \mathcal{L}_{VH} + \mathcal{L}_{PH}$. Let $\alpha \in \{V, P\}$ denote the voxel-wise and point-wise, respectively. The hard label loss term $\mathcal{L}_{\alpha H}$ in $\mathcal{L}$ is a combination of the commonly used cross-entropy loss $\mathcal{L}_{ce}$ and lovasz-softmax loss $\mathcal{L}_{lovasz}$ [5] as $\mathcal{L}_{\alpha H} = \mathcal{L}_{ce}(\hat{Y}_{\alpha}, Y_{\alpha H}) + \mathcal{L}_{lovasz}(\hat{Y}_{\alpha}, Y_{\alpha H})$.

When training the full framework of self-distillation, we formulate the overall loss $\mathcal{L}$ as $\mathcal{L}_{VH} + \mathcal{L}_{PH} + \mathcal{L}_{PS}$. Inspired by knowledge distillation [19,44] in image recognition, the soft loss $\mathcal{L}_{PS}$ is implemented with the cross-entropy loss between the point-wise prediction $\hat{Y}_{P}$ and the point-wise soft label Y_{PS} as $\gamma \mathcal{L}_{ce}(\hat{Y}_{P}, Y_{PS})$. When the mIoU of the soft label Y_{PS} is larger, the dynamic coefficient γ of $\exp(mIoU(Y_{PS}, Y_{PH}))$ assigns a larger weight value to the soft loss $\mathcal{L}_{PS}$.

4 Experiments

4.1 Dataset and Metric

SemanticKITTI Dataset. SemanticKITTI [4] dataset for LiDAR semantic segmentation is collected in Germany with the Velodyne-HDL64E LiDAR.

---

[1] The new soft label acquisition strategies proposed in this paper.

Table 2. Performance comparison on IoU (%) between our method and state-of-the-art LiDAR Segmentation methods on SemanticKITTI testing set [4]. The methods are divided into the branches of point, 2D image, and 3D voxel, according to their main point cloud representations (PC Rep.). Bold and underlined indicate the best and the second best results, respectively.

PC Rep.	Methods	mIoU	Car	Bicycle	Motorcycle	Truck	Other-vehicle	Person	Bicyclist	Motorcyclist	Road	Parking	Sidewalk	Other-ground	Building	Fence	Vegetation	Trunk	Terrain	Pole	Traffic-sign
Point	PointASNL [50]	46.8	87.4	0.0	25.1	39.0	29.2	34.2	57.6	0.0	87.4	24.3	74.3	1.8	83.1	43.9	84.1	52.2	70.6	57.8	36.9
	RandLA-Net [21]	53.9	94.2	26.0	25.8	40.1	38.9	49.2	48.2	7.2	90.7	60.3	73.7	20.4	86.9	56.3	81.4	61.3	66.8	49.2	47.7
	KPConv [42]	58.8	96.0	32.0	42.5	33.4	44.3	61.5	61.6	11.8	88.8	61.3	72.7	31.6	90.5	64.2	84.8	69.2	69.1	56.4	47.4
	BAAF-Net [35]	59.9	95.4	31.8	35.5	48.7	46.7	49.5	55.7	53.0	90.9	62.2	74.4	29.6	89.8	60.8	82.7	63.4	67.9	53.7	52.0
2D Image	RangeNet++ [32]	52.2	91.4	25.7	34.4	25.7	23.0	38.3	38.8	4.8	91.8	65.0	75.2	27.8	87.4	58.6	80.5	55.1	64.6	47.9	55.9
	PolarNet [56]	54.3	93.8	40.3	30.1	22.9	28.5	43.2	40.2	5.6	90.8	61.7	74.4	21.7	90.0	61.3	84.0	65.5	67.8	51.8	57.5
	SqueezeSegv3 [49]	55.9	92.5	38.7	36.5	29.6	33.0	45.6	46.2	20.1	91.7	63.4	74.8	26.4	80.0	59.4	82.0	58.7	65.4	49.6	58.9
	SalsaNext [10]	59.5	91.9	48.3	38.6	38.9	31.9	60.2	59.0	19.4	91.7	63.7	75.8	29.1	90.2	64.2	81.8	63.6	66.5	54.3	62.1
	KPRNet [23]	63.1	95.5	54.1	47.9	23.0	42.6	65.9	65.0	16.5	93.2	73.9	80.6	30.2	91.7	68.4	85.7	69.8	71.2	58.7	64.1
3D Voxel	Darknet53 [4]	49.9	86.4	24.5	32.7	25.5	22.6	36.2	33.6	4.7	91.8	64.8	74.6	27.9	84.1	55.0	78.3	50.1	64.0	38.9	52.2
	MinkNet42 [9]	54.3	94.3	23.1	26.2	26.1	36.7	43.1	36.4	7.9	91.1	63.8	69.7	29.3	92.7	57.1	83.7	68.4	64.7	57.3	60.1
	3D-MiniNet [1]	55.8	90.5	42.3	42.1	28.5	29.4	47.8	44.1	14.5	91.6	64.2	74.5	25.4	89.4	60.8	82.8	60.8	66.7	48.0	56.6
	FusionNet [53]	61.3	95.3	47.5	37.7	41.8	34.5	59.5	56.8	11.9	91.8	68.8	77.1	30.8	92.5	69.4	84.5	69.8	68.5	60.4	66.5
	SPVNAS-Lite [39]	63.7	-	-	-	-	-	-	-	-	-	-	-	-	-	-	-	-	-	-	-
	SPVNAS [39]	66.4	-	-	-	-	-	-	-	-	-	-	-	-	-	-	-	-	-	-	-
	Cylinder3D [59]	67.8	97.1	67.6	64.0	59.0	58.6	73.9	67.9	36.0	91.4	65.1	75.5	32.3	91.0	66.5	85.4	71.8	68.5	62.6	65.6
	(AF)²-S3Net [8]	69.7	94.5	65.4	86.8	39.2	41.1	80.7	80.4	74.3	91.3	68.8	72.5	53.5	87.9	63.2	70.2	68.5	53.7	61.5	71.0
	Ours (w.o. TTA)	68.0	97.0	54.4	48.1	55.9	61.6	65.5	69.4	51.1	91.3	67.0	77.0	35.6	92.2	67.8	84.9	72.2	69.3	63.4	68.0
	Ours (w. TTA)	70.4	97.4	58.7	54.2	54.9	65.2	70.2	74.4	52.2	90.9	69.4	76.7	41.9	93.2	71.1	86.1	74.3	71.1	65.4	70.6

Table 3. Performance comparison on IoU (%) between our method and other LiDAR Segmentation methods on nuScenes [6] validation set. Bold and underlined indicate the best and the second best results, respectively.

Methods	mIoU	Barrier	Bicycle	Bus	Car	Construction	Motorcycle	Pedestrian	Traffic-cone	Trailer	Truck	Driveable	Other	Sidewalk	Terrain	Manmade	Vegetation
(AF)²-S3Net [8]	62.2	60.3	12.6	82.3	80.0	20.1	62.0	59.0	49.0	42.2	67.4	94.2	68.0	64.1	68.6	82.9	82.4
RangeNet++ [32]	65.5	66.0	21.3	77.2	80.9	30.2	66.8	69.6	52.1	54.2	72.3	94.1	66.6	63.5	70.1	83.1	79.8
PolarNet [56]	71.0	74.7	28.2	85.3	90.9	35.1	77.5	71.3	58.8	57.4	76.1	96.5	71.1	74.7	74.0	87.3	85.7
SalsaNext [10]	72.2	74.8	34.1	85.9	88.4	42.2	72.4	72.2	63.1	61.3	76.5	96.0	70.8	71.2	71.5	86.7	84.4
AMVNet [28]	76.1	79.8	32.4	82.2	86.4	62.5	81.9	75.3	72.3	83.5	65.1	97.4	67.0	78.8	74.6	90.8	87.9
Cylinder3D [59]	76.1	76.4	40.3	91.2	93.8	51.3	78.0	78.9	64.9	62.1	84.4	96.8	71.6	76.4	75.4	90.5	87.4
Ours (w.o. TTA)	77.7	77.5	49.4	93.9	92.5	54.9	86.7	80.1	67.8	65.7	86.0	96.4	74.0	74.9	74.5	86.0	82.8
Ours (w. TTA)	78.7	78.2	52.8	94.5	93.1	54.5	88.1	82.2	69.4	67.3	86.6	96.4	74.5	75.2	75.3	87.1	84.1

It contains 22 sequences: sequences 00 to 10 (excluding 08) containing 19,130 point clouds as the training set, sequence 08 containing 4,071 point clouds as the validation set, and the remaining sequences 11 to 21 with 20,351 point clouds as the testing set. For the setting of single scan input, the official evaluation protocol merges classes with different motion states and ignores classes with only a few points, so 19 valid classes are preserved from 28 annotated classes.

nuScenes Dataset. nuScenes [6] dataset for LiDAR semantic segmentation is collected in different areas of Boston and Singapore with the Velodyne-HDL32E LiDAR. It officially splits 28,130 point clouds for training, 6,019 point clouds for validation. After merging similar classes and ignoring rare classes, 16 valid classes remain for semantic segmentation evaluation.

Evaluation Metric. We adopt the mean Intersection-over-Union (mIoU) over all classes as the evaluation metric defined in [4,6], which can be formulated as $\text{mIoU} = \frac{1}{C} \sum_{c=1}^{C} \frac{\text{TP}_c}{\text{TP}_c + \text{FP}_c + \text{FN}_c}$, where TP_c, FP_c, FN_c correspond to the number of true positive, false positive, and false negative predictions for the c-th class in C classes.

4.2   Implementation Details

We configure TransVFE with the number of multi-head N_H of 4, the hidden feature dimension C_{trans} of 64, the compressed feature dimension C_0 of 16, which

Table 4. Latency analysis on SemanticKITTI testing set.

Methods	RandLA-Net [21]	SqueezeSegV3 [49]	SPVNAS-Lite [39]	Ours
Latency (s)	0.416	0.113	0.150	0.148
mIoU (%)	53.9	55.9	63.7	68.0

are mentioned in Eq. 5. In the 3D sparse U-Net, the feature dimensions C_1 - C_8 are set as 32, 64, 128, 128, 128, 128, 64, 32, respectively. We only use the point-wise outputs as the inferred segmentation results, while the voxel-wise outputs are used in the training phase only. More details on point cloud voxelization and model training are provided in the supplementary material.

4.3   Evaluation

Results on SemanticKITTI. Table 2 presents the performance of our method without (w.o.) and with (w.) TTA after self-distillation against other methods on the testing set of SemanticKITTI dataset. Our full pipeline achieves the best result on mIoU. The efficient 3D convolution facilitates the exploration of 3D object structures, so 3D voxel methods achieve better performance than point and 2D image methods. Our method achieves the largest number of Top-1 and Top-2 results (8/20 & 13/20) among the overall 19 object classes and mIoU, which shows the reliable and robust LiDAR segmentation performance of various object categories. Qualitative visualizations are in supplementary material.

Results on nuScenes. We also evaluate our method on the nuScenes dataset. In Table 3, our method outperforms the Cylinder3D [59] and AMVNet [28] in mIoU of 2.6%. In terms of all metrics, our full method still achieves the 7/17 Top-1 results and the largest number of Top-2 results (12/17). Considering the different collection environments and collection LiDAR sensors between the SemanticKITTI and nuScenes, our method generalizes well in different datasets.

Table 5. Effects of VFE. All models are trained without self-distillation and inferred without TTA. "Improv." is the improvement compared to average-based model.

VFE module	SemanticKITTI		nuScenes	
	mIoU	Improv	mIoU	Improv
Average	64.90	–	75.94	–
PointNet	65.08	+0.18	75.96	+0.02
TransVFE (Ours)	65.47	+0.57	76.42	+0.48

Latency. Table 4 shows the latency analysis under the same experimental settings with the same machine. Our method achieves much higher mIoU with close latency against SqueezeSegV3 [49] and SPVNAS-Lite [39].

4.4   Ablation Study

We conduct extensive ablation experiments on SemanticKITTI and nuScenes datasets following the official evaluation protocol on the validation sets. Since the T-Model in our method is related to the TransVFE and TTA, Table 5 and 6 first demonstrate the effects of the TransVFE and TTA without the self-distillation followed by the further analyses on our full framework in Table 7 and Fig. 3.

Table 6. Effects of the different augmentation strategies for TTA. M and j are the number and index of input variants in $\mathcal{X}$, respectively. "Row" and "Improv." denote the row index and the mIoU improvements compared with the baseline in the first row.

Row	$\mathcal{X}$	M	SemanticKITTI		nuScenes	
			mIoU	Improv	mIoU	Improv
1	$\{X\}$	1	65.47	–	76.42	–
2	$\{X, X_{\text{scale},j} : j = 1, \cdots, 4\}$	5	66.32	+0.85	77.13	+0.71
3	$\{X, X_{\text{flip},j} : j = 1, \cdots, 4\}$	5	66.49	+1.02	76.87	+0.45
4	$\{X, X_{\text{rot},j} : j = 1, \cdots, 4\}$	5	66.53	+1.06	77.04	+0.62
5	$\{X, X_{\text{tran},j} : j = 1, \cdots, 4\}$	5	66.57	+1.10	77.06	+0.64
6	$\{X, X_{\text{scale}}, X_{\text{flip}}, X_{\text{rot}}, X_{\text{tran}}\}$	5	66.64	+1.17	77.27	+0.85
7	$\{X, X_{\text{comp},j} : j = 1, \cdots, 4\}$	5	67.75	+2.28	77.54	+1.12
8	$\{X, X_{\text{comp},j} : j = 1, \cdots, 5\}$	6	67.97	+2.50	77.70	+1.28
9	$\{X, X_{\text{comp},j} : j = 1, \cdots, 6\}$	7	67.82	+2.35	77.67	+1.25
10	$\{X, X_{\text{comp},j} : j = 1, \cdots, 7\}$	8	68.04	+2.57	77.72	+1.30

Table 7. Effects of self-distillation. "Exp.", "EMA", and "Improv." indicate experiment tags, Exponential Moving Average, and Improvements compared to the baseline in Exp. A. The setting of the baseline (Exp. A) is mentioned in **TransVFE**. Note that TTA is only used in self-distillation for this experiment setting.

Exp.	S-model initialization	T-model configuration	T-model parameter	SemanticKITTI		nuScenes	
			TTA	mIoU	Improv.	mIoU	Improv.
A	Scratch	–	–	65.47	–	76.42	–
B		Copy	√	65.61	+0.14	76.62	+0.20
C		Pre-trained & fixed	×	65.89	+0.42	76.83	+0.41
D		Pre-trained & fixed	√	66.09	+0.62	76.98	+0.56
E		EMA	×	66.18	+0.71	76.93	+0.51
F		EMA	√	66.64	+1.17	77.31	+0.89
G	Pre-trained	Pre-trained & fixed	√	66.81	+1.34	77.50	+1.08
H		EMA	√	**67.11**	**+1.64**	**77.74**	**+1.32**

TransVFE. Table 5 shows that our TransVFE of modeling the local relationship can improve the performance compared with the VFE modules implemented by average operation in [39,51] and PointNet in [56,59] in terms of point cloud encoding. Thus, we use this model shown in the last row of Table 5 as the **baseline model** for the ablation studies of TTA and self-distillation.

TTA Strategy. In Table 6, the improvements in rows 2–5 first demonstrate that all the four types of transformations can be taken into account for TTA. Rows 6 and 2–5 then show that combining the four individual TTA transformations is slightly better than reusing any individual transformations multiple times, when an input variant set $\mathcal{X}$ with a fixed capacity ($M = 5$) is given. Reusing compound transform in row 7 achieves much more significant improvements than combining the four individual TTA transformations in row 6 on both datasets, indicating that our compound transform is simple yet effective enough. The last three rows validate that the performance can be further improved with the increased capacity of $\mathcal{X}$ but gradually saturated after $M = 6$. Thus, we set M to 6 in this work.

Self-distillation. The Exp. B-F in Table 7 inspect the effectiveness of the five optional T-Model configurations as described in Sect. 3.3. The mIoU of Exp. B, D, and F is consistently higher than the mIoU of Exp. A, C, and E, showing that applying the TTA to acquire soft labels with higher quality is effective for better self-distillation. Among different manners of updating the T-Model network parameters, the EMA shows the most significant improvements. Especially, the Exp. F that applies both the EMA and TTA achieves the best mIoU

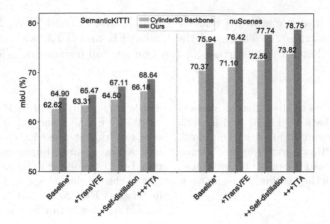

Fig. 3. Continuous improvements of our method and **Cylinder3D backbone** [59] in our framework. Baseline* is the model with average-based VFE.

on both datasets. The dual assemblies of the S-Model network parameters and the T-Model predictions guarantee the quality of the soft labels thus enhancing the self-distillation. Finally, the last two rows suggest that we can initialize the parameters of both the S-Model and T-Model from the pre-trained baseline model with higher overall performances. The Exp. H that applies both the EMA and our TTA with pre-trained model initialization yields the best mIoU on two datasets. We thus use this self-distillation strategy in the proposed framework.

Backbone. The proposed method is agnostic to the backbone architectures under voxel representation of LiDAR point cloud. Since the codes of Cylinder3D [59] and SPVNAS [39] are not completely released yet, we choose our backbone as a general U-Net from the LiDAR perception work [37]. The experiments in Fig. 3 validate that our framework can also achieve significant improvements when using Cylinder3D backbone. Therefore, all the proposed components can be instantiated with other backbones for LiDAR semantic segmentation.

5   Conclusions

In this paper, we propose a novel self-distillation framework and firstly use it for robust LiDAR semantic segmentation in autonomous driving. The proposed framework enables the self-distillation from a teacher model instance to a student model instance with the same network architecture for jointly learning and evolving in training. Our method achieves state-of-the-art performance on SemanticKITTI and nuScenes datasets, demonstrating the effectiveness of the overall self-distillation framework. Extensive experiments validate that all the proposed components are effective with significant improvements and general to be instantiated with different backbones for LiDAR semantic segmentation.

Acknowledgement. This work was supported by the National Key Research and Development Program of China (2018YFE0183900) and YUNJI Technology Co. Ltd.

References

1. Alonso, I., Riazuelo, L., Montesano, L., Murillo, A.C.: 3D-MiniNet: learning a 2D representation from point clouds for fast and efficient 3D LiDAR semantic segmentation. IEEE Rob. Autom. Lett. **5**(4), 5432–5439 (2020)
2. An, S., Liao, Q., Lu, Z., Xue, J.H.: Efficient semantic segmentation via self-attention and self-distillation. IEEE Trans. Intell. Transp. Syst. **23**, 1–11 (2022)
3. Armeni, I., et al.: 3D semantic parsing of large-scale indoor spaces. In: CVPR, pp. 1534–1543 (2016)
4. Behley, J., et al.: SemanticKITTI: a dataset for semantic scene understanding of LiDAR sequences. In: ICCV, pp. 9296–9306 (2019)
5. Berman, M., Triki, A.R., Blaschko, M.B.: The lovász-softmax loss: a tractable surrogate for the optimization of the intersection-over-union measure in neural networks. In: CVPR, pp. 4413–4421 (2018)
6. Caesar, H., et al.: nuScenes: a multimodal dataset for autonomous driving. In: CVPR, pp. 11618–11628 (2020)
7. Chen, Y., Zhang, Z., Cao, Y., Wang, L., Lin, S., Hu, H.: RepPoints v2: verification meets regression for object detection. In: NeurIPS (2020)
8. Cheng, R., Razani, R., Taghavi, E., Li, E., Liu, B.: (AF)2–S3Net: attentive feature fusion with adaptive feature selection for sparse semantic segmentation network. In: CVPR, pp. 12547–12556 (2021)
9. Choy, C.B., Gwak, J., Savarese, S.: 4D spatio-temporal ConvNets: minkowski convolutional neural networks. In: CVPR, pp. 3075–3084 (2019)
10. Cortinhal, T., Tzelepis, G., Aksoy, E.E.: SalsaNext: fast, uncertainty-aware semantic segmentation of LiDAR point clouds for autonomous driving. arXiv preprint arXiv:2003.03653 (2020)
11. Cubuk, E.D., Zoph, B., Mané, D., Vasudevan, V., Le, Q.V.: AutoAugment: learning augmentation strategies from data. In: CVPR, pp. 113–123 (2019)
12. Deng, J., Shi, S., Li, P., Zhou, W., Zhang, Y., Li, H.: Voxel R-CNN: towards high performance voxel-based 3D object detection. In: AAAI, pp. 1201–1209 (2021)
13. Graham, B., Engelcke, M., van der Maaten, L.: 3D semantic segmentation with submanifold sparse convolutional networks. In: CVPR, pp. 9224–9232 (2018)
14. Guo, M., Cai, J., Liu, Z., Mu, T., Martin, R.R., Hu, S.: PCT: point cloud transformer. Comput. Visual Media **7**(2), 187–199 (2021)
15. Hataya, R., Zdenek, J., Yoshizoe, K., Nakayama, H.: Faster AutoAugment: learning augmentation strategies using backpropagation. In: Vedaldi, A., Bischof, H., Brox, T., Frahm, J.-M. (eds.) ECCV 2020. LNCS, vol. 12370, pp. 1–16. Springer, Cham (2020). https://doi.org/10.1007/978-3-030-58595-2_1
16. He, T., Shen, C., Tian, Z., Gong, D., Sun, C., Yan, Y.: Knowledge adaptation for efficient semantic segmentation. In: CVPR, pp. 578–587 (2019)
17. Hendrycks, D., Dietterich, T.G.: Benchmarking neural network robustness to common corruptions and perturbations. In: ICLR (2019)
18. Hendrycks, D., Mu, N., Cubuk, E.D., Zoph, B., Gilmer, J., Lakshminarayanan, B.: AugMix: a simple data processing method to improve robustness and uncertainty. In: ICLR (2020)
19. Hinton, G.E., Vinyals, O., Dean, J.: Distilling the knowledge in a neural network. CoRR abs/1503.02531 (2015). http://arxiv.org/abs/1503.02531
20. Hu, H., Cui, J., Wang, L.: Region-aware contrastive learning for semantic segmentation. In: ICCV, pp. 16271–16281 (2021)

21. Hu, Q., et al.: RandLA-Net: efficient semantic segmentation of large-scale point clouds. In: CVPR, pp. 11105–11114 (2020)
22. Kim, I., Kim, Y., Kim, S.: Learning loss for test-time augmentation. In: NeurIPS (2020)
23. Kochanov, D., Nejadasl, F.K., Booij, O.: KPRNet: improving projection-based LiDAR semantic segmentation. In: ECCV (2020)
24. Lang, A.H., Vora, S., Caesar, H., Zhou, L., Yang, J., Beijbom, O.: PointPillars: fast encoders for object detection from point clouds. In: CVPR, pp. 12689–12697 (2019)
25. Li, J., Dai, H., Shao, L., Ding, Y.: Anchor-free 3D single stage detector with mask-guided attention for point cloud. In: ACM MM, pp. 553–562 (2021)
26. Li, J., Dai, H., Shao, L., Ding, Y.: From voxel to point: IoU-guided 3D object detection for point cloud with voxel-to-point decoder. In: ACM MM (2021)
27. Li, J., et al.: P2V-RCNN: point to voxel feature learning for 3D object detection from point clouds. IEEE Access **9**, 98249–98260 (2021)
28. Liong, V.E., Nguyen, T.N.T., Widjaja, S., Sharma, D., Chong, Z.J.: AMVNet: assertion-based multi-view fusion network for LiDAR semantic segmentation. CoRR abs/2012.04934 (2020). http://arxiv.org/abs/2012.04934
29. Liu, Y., et al.: Unbiased teacher for semi-supervised object detection. In: ICLR (2021)
30. Liu, Y., Chen, K., Liu, C., Qin, Z., Luo, Z., Wang, J.: Structured knowledge distillation for semantic segmentation. In: CVPR, pp. 2604–2613 (2019)
31. Lyzhov, A., Molchanova, Y., Ashukha, A., Molchanov, D., Vetrov, D.P.: Greedy policy search: a simple baseline for learnable test-time augmentation. In: Adams, R.P., Gogate, V. (eds.) UAI, vol. 124, pp. 1308–1317 (2020)
32. Milioto, A., Vizzo, I., Behley, J., Stachniss, C.: RangeNet++: fast and accurate LiDAR semantic segmentation. In: IROS, pp. 4213–4220 (2019)
33. Park, S., Heo, Y.S.: Knowledge distillation for semantic segmentation using channel and spatial correlations and adaptive cross entropy. Sensors **20**(16), 4616 (2020)
34. Qi, C.R., Su, H., Mo, K., Guibas, L.J.: PointNet: deep learning on point sets for 3D classification and segmentation. In: CVPR, pp. 77–85 (2017)
35. Qiu, S., Anwar, S., Barnes, N.: Semantic segmentation for real point cloud scenes via bilateral augmentation and adaptive fusion. In: CVPR, pp. 1757–1767 (2021)
36. Ronneberger, O., Fischer, P., Brox, T.: U-Net: convolutional networks for biomedical image segmentation. In: Navab, N., Hornegger, J., Wells, W.M., Frangi, A.F. (eds.) MICCAI 2015. LNCS, vol. 9351, pp. 234–241. Springer, Cham (2015). https://doi.org/10.1007/978-3-319-24574-4_28
37. Shi, S., Wang, Z., Shi, J., Wang, X., Li, H.: From points to parts: 3D object detection from point cloud with part-aware and part-aggregation network. IEEE TPAMI **43**(8), 2647–2664 (2021)
38. Taghanaki, S.A., Luo, J., Zhang, R., Wang, Y., Jayaraman, P.K., Jatavallabhula, K.M.: Robustpointset: a dataset for benchmarking robustness of point cloud classifiers. In: ICLR (2021)
39. Tang, H., Liu, Z., Zhao, S., Lin, Y., Lin, J., Wang, H., Han, S.: Searching efficient 3D architectures with sparse point-voxel convolution. In: Vedaldi, A., Bischof, H., Brox, T., Frahm, J.-M. (eds.) ECCV 2020. LNCS, vol. 12373, pp. 685–702. Springer, Cham (2020). https://doi.org/10.1007/978-3-030-58604-1_41
40. Tang, Y., Chen, W., Luo, Y., Zhang, Y.: Humble teachers teach better students for semi-supervised object detection. In: CVPR, pp. 3132–3141 (2021)

41. Tarvainen, A., Valpola, H.: Mean teachers are better role models: Weight-averaged consistency targets improve semi-supervised deep learning results. In: NeurIPS, pp. 1195–1204 (2017)
42. Thomas, H., Qi, C.R., Deschaud, J., Marcotegui, B., Goulette, F., Guibas, L.J.: KPConv: flexible and deformable convolution for point clouds. In: ICCV, pp. 6410–6419 (2019)
43. Vaswani, A., et al.: Attention is all you need. In: NeurIPS, pp. 5998–6008 (2017)
44. Wang, H., Zhao, H., Li, X., Tan, X.: Progressive blockwise knowledge distillation for neural network acceleration. In: IJCAI, pp. 2769–2775 (2018)
45. Wang, Y., Zhou, W., Jiang, T., Bai, X., Xu, Y.: Intra-class feature variation distillation for semantic segmentation. In: Vedaldi, A., Bischof, H., Brox, T., Frahm, J.-M. (eds.) ECCV 2020. LNCS, vol. 12352, pp. 346–362. Springer, Cham (2020). https://doi.org/10.1007/978-3-030-58571-6_21
46. Wu, B., Wan, A., Yue, X., Keutzer, K.: SqueezeSeg: convolutional neural nets with recurrent CRF for real-time road-object segmentation from 3D LiDAR point cloud. In: ICRA, pp. 1887–1893 (2018)
47. Wu, B., Zhou, X., Zhao, S., Yue, X., Keutzer, K.: SqueezeSegV2: improved model structure and unsupervised domain adaptation for road-object segmentation from a LiDAR point cloud. In: ICRA, pp. 4376–4382 (2019)
48. Xie, E., Wang, W., Yu, Z., Anandkumar, A., Alvarez, J.M., Luo, P.: SegFormer: simple and efficient design for semantic segmentation with transformers. CoRR abs/2105.15203 (2021)
49. Xu, C., et al.: SqueezeSegV3: spatially-adaptive convolution for efficient point-cloud segmentation. In: Vedaldi, A., Bischof, H., Brox, T., Frahm, J.-M. (eds.) ECCV 2020. LNCS, vol. 12373, pp. 1–19. Springer, Cham (2020). https://doi.org/10.1007/978-3-030-58604-1_1
50. Yan, X., Zheng, C., Li, Z., Wang, S., Cui, S.: PointASNL: robust point clouds processing using nonlocal neural networks with adaptive sampling. In: CVPR, pp. 5588–5597 (2020)
51. Yan, Y., Mao, Y., Li, B.: SECOND: sparsely embedded convolutional detection. Sensors 18(10), 3337 (2018)
52. Yi, L., et al scalable active framework for region annotation in 3D shape collections. ACM TOG 35(6), 210:1–210:12 (2016)
53. Zhang, F., Fang, J., Wah, B., Torr, P.: Deep FusionNet for point cloud semantic segmentation. In: Vedaldi, A., Bischof, H., Brox, T., Frahm, J.-M. (eds.) ECCV 2020. LNCS, vol. 12369, pp. 644–663. Springer, Cham (2020). https://doi.org/10.1007/978-3-030-58586-0_38
54. Zhang, S., Chi, C., Yao, Y., Lei, Z., Li, S.Z.: Bridging the gap between anchor-based and anchor-free detection via adaptive training sample selection. In: CVPR, pp. 9756–9765 (2020)
55. Zhang, Y., Qu, Y., Xie, Y., Li, Z., Zheng, S., Li, C.: Perturbed self-distillation: weakly supervised large-scale point cloud semantic segmentation. In: ICCV, pp. 15520–15528 (2021)
56. Zhang, Y., et al.: PolarNet: an improved grid representation for online LiDAR point clouds semantic segmentation. In: CVPR, pp. 9598–9607 (2020)
57. Zheng, W., Tang, W., Jiang, L., Fu, C.: SE-SSD: self-ensembling single-stage object detector from point cloud. In: CVPR, pp. 14494–14503 (2021)
58. Zhou, Z., Zhang, Y., Foroosh, H.: Panoptic-PolarNet: proposal-free LiDAR point cloud panoptic segmentation. In: CVPR, pp. 13194–13203 (2021)

59. Zhu, X., et al.: Cylindrical and asymmetrical 3D convolution networks for LiDAR segmentation. In: CVPR, pp. 9939–9948 (2021)
60. Zhu, Z., Xu, M., Bai, S., Huang, T., Bai, X.: Asymmetric non-local neural networks for semantic segmentation. In: ICCV, pp. 593–602. IEEE (2019)

2DPASS: 2D Priors Assisted Semantic Segmentation on LiDAR Point Clouds

Xu Yan[1], Jiantao Gao[2], Chaoda Zheng[1], Chao Zheng[3], Ruimao Zhang[1], Shuguang Cui[1], and Zhen Li[1(✉)]

[1] The Future Network of Intelligence Institute,
Shenzhen Research Institute of Big Data,
The Chinese University of Hong Kong (Shenzhen), Shenzhen, China
`xuyan1@link.cuhk.edu.cn`, `lizhen@cuhk.edu.cn`
[2] Shanghai University, Shanghai, China
[3] Tencent Map, T Lab, Beijing, China

Abstract. As camera and LiDAR sensors capture complementary information in autonomous driving, great efforts have been made to conduct semantic segmentation through multi-modality data fusion. However, fusion-based approaches require paired data, *i.e.*, LiDAR point clouds and camera images with strict point-to-pixel mappings, as the inputs in both training and inference stages. It seriously hinders their application in practical scenarios. Thus, in this work, we propose the 2D Priors Assisted Semantic Segmentation (**2DPASS**) method, a general training scheme, to boost the representation learning on point clouds. The proposed 2DPASS method fully takes advantage of 2D images with rich appearance during training, and then conduct semantic segmentation without strict paired data constraints. In practice, by leveraging an auxiliary modal fusion and multi-scale fusion-to-single knowledge distillation (MSFSKD), 2DPASS acquires richer semantic and structural information from the multi-modal data, which are then distilled to the pure 3D network. As a result, our baseline model shows significant improvement with only point cloud inputs once equipped with the 2DPASS. Specifically, it achieves the state-of-the-arts on two large-scale recognized benchmarks (*i.e.*, SemanticKITTI and NuScenes), *i.e.*, ranking the top-1 in both single and multiple scan(s) competitions of SemanticKITTI.

Keywords: Semantic segmentation · Multi-modal · Knowledge distillation · LiDAR point clouds

1 Introduction

Semantic segmentation plays a crucial role in large-scale outdoor scene understanding, which has broad applications in autonomous driving and robotics [1–3].

X. Yan, J. Gao and C. Zheng—Equal first authorship.

Supplementary Information The online version contains supplementary material available at https://doi.org/10.1007/978-3-031-19815-1_39.

© The Author(s), under exclusive license to Springer Nature Switzerland AG 2022
S. Avidan et al. (Eds.): ECCV 2022, LNCS 13688, pp. 677–695, 2022.
https://doi.org/10.1007/978-3-031-19815-1_39

Front-Camera Image and Perspective Projection   360° LiDAR Point Cloud   Point Cloud in Camera Perspective

Fig. 1. Limitation of fusion-based methods. When the self-driving car only has front-cameras with limited perspective such as SemanticKITTI [16] dataset while the 360-degree LiDAR has a much larger sensing range, fusion-based methods that require strict alignment between camera and LiDAR can only identify a small proportion of the point cloud (see the red region). (Color figure online)

In the past few years, the research community has devoted significant effort to understanding natural scenes using either camera images [4–7] or LiDAR point clouds [2,8–12] as the input. However, these single-modal methods inevitably face challenges in complex environments due to the inherent limitations of the input sensors. Concretely, cameras provide dense color information and fine-grained texture, but they are ambiguous in depth sensing and unreliable in low light conditions. In contrast, LiDARs robustly offer accurate and wide-ranging depth information regardless of lighting variances but only capture sparse and textureless data. Since cameras and LiDARs complement each other, it is better to perceive the surrounding with both sensors.

Recently, many commercial cars have been equipped with both cameras and LiDARs. This excites the research community to improve the semantic segmentation by fusing the information from two complementary sensors [13–15]. These approaches first establish the mapping between 3D points and 2D pixels by projecting the point clouds onto the image planes using the sensor calibrations. Based on the point-to-pixel mapping, the models fuse the corresponding image features into the point features, which are further processed to obtain the final semantic scores. Despite the improvements, fusion-based methods have the following unavoidable limitations: **1)** Due to the difference of FOVs (field of views) between cameras and LiDARs, the point-to-pixel mapping cannot be established for points that are out of the image planes. Typically, the FOVs of LiDAR and cameras only overlap in a small portion (see Fig. 1), which significantly limits the application of fusion-based methods. **2)** Fusion-based methods consume more computational resources since they process both images and point clouds (through multitask or cascade manners) at runtime, which introduces a great burden on real-time applications.

To address the above two issues, we focus on improving semantic segmentation by leveraging both images and point clouds through an effective design in this work. Considering the sensors are moving in the scenes, the non-overlap part of the 360-degree LiDAR point clouds corresponding to image in the same time-stamp (see the gray region of the right part in Fig. 1) can be covered by images from other time-stamp. Besides, the dense and structural information of images provides useful regularization for both seen and unseen point cloud regions.

Based on these observations, we propose a "model-independent" training scheme, namely 2D Priors Assisted Semantic Segmentation (**2DPASS**), to enhance the representation learning of any 3D semantic segmentation networks with minor structure modification. In practice, on the one hand, for above-mentioned non-overlap regions, 2DPASS takes pure point clouds as the inputs to train the segmentation model. On the other hand, for subregions with well-aligned point-to-pixel mappings, 2DPASS adopts an auxiliary multi-modal fusion to aggregate image and point features in each scale, and then aligns the 3D predictions with the fusion predictions. Unlike previous cross-modal alignment [17] apt to contaminate the modal-specific information, we design a multi-scale fusion-to-single knowledge distillation (MSFSKD) strategy to transfer extra knowledge to the 3D model as well as retaining its modal-specific ability. Compared with fusion-based methods, our solution has the following preferable properties: **1) Generality**: It can be easily integrated with any 3D segmentation model with minor structural modification; **2) Flexibility**: The fusion module is only used during the training to enhance the 3D network. After training, the enhanced 3D model can be deployed without image inputs. **3) Effectively**: Even with only a small section of overlapped multi-modality data, our method can significantly boost the performance. As a result, we evaluate 2DPASS with a simple yet strong baseline implemented with sparse convolutions [3]. The experiments show 2DPASS brings noticeable improvements even over this strong baseline. Equipped with 2DPASS using multi-modal data, our model achieves the **top-1** results on the single and multiple-scan leaderboards of SemanticKITTI [16]. The state-of-the-art results on the NuScenes [18] dataset further confirm the generality of our method.

In general, the main contributions are summarized as follows.

- We propose 2D Priors Assisted Semantic Segmentation (2DPASS) that assists 3D LiDAR semantic segmentation with 2D priors from cameras. To the best of our knowledge, 2DPASS is the first method that distills multi-modal knowledge to single point cloud modality for semantic segmentation.
- Equipped with the proposed multi-scale fusion-to-single knowledge distillation (MSFSKS) strategy, 2DPASS achieves the significant performance gains on SemanticKITTI and NuScenes benchmarks, ranking the **1st** on single and multiple tracks of SemanticKITTI.

2   Related Work

2.1   Single-Sensor Methods

Camera-Based Methods. Camera-based semantic segmentation aims to predict the pixel-wise labels for input 2D images. FCN [19] is the pioneer in semantic segmentation, which proposes an end-to-end fully convolutional architecture based on image classification networks. Recent works have achieved significant improvements via exploring multi-scale features learning [4,20,21], dilated convolution [5,22], and attention mechanisms [7,23]. However, camera-only methods are ambiguous in depth sensing and not robust in low light conditions.

LiDAR-Based Methods. The LiDAR data is generally represented as point clouds. There are several mainstreams to process point clouds with different representations. **1) Point-based** methods approximate a permutation-invariant set function using a per-point Multi-Layer Perceptron (MLP). PointNet [24] is the pioneer in this field. Later on, many studies design point-wise MLP [25,26], adaptive weight [27,28] and pseudo grid [29,30] based methods to extract local features of point clouds or exploit nonlocal operators [31–33] to learn long distance dependency. However, point-based methods are not efficient in the LiDAR scenario since their sampling and grouping algorithms are generally time-consuming. **2) Projection-based** methods are very efficient approaches for LiDAR point clouds. They project point clouds onto 2D pixels so that traditional CNN can play a normal role. Previous works project all points scanned by the rotating LiDAR onto 2D images by plane projection [34–36], spherical projection [37,38] or both [39]. However, the projection inevitably causes information loss. And the projection-based methods currently meet the bottleneck of the segmentation accuracy. **3)** Most recent works adopt **voxel-based** frameworks since they balance the efficiency and effectiveness, where sparse convolution (SparseConv) [3] are most commonly utilized. Compared to traditional voxel-based methods (*i.e.*, 3DCNN) directly transforming all points into the 3D voxel grids, SparseConv only stores non-empty voxels in a Hash table and conducts convolution operations only on these non-empty voxels in a more efficient way. Recently, many studies have used SparseConv to design more powerful network architectures. Cylinder3D [40] changes original grid voxels to cylinder ones and designs an asymmetrical network to boost the performance. AF^2-S3Net [41] applies multiple branches with different kernel sizes, aggregating multi-scale features via an attention mechanism. **4)** Very recently, there is a trend of exploiting **multi-representation fusion** methods. These methods combine multiple representations above (*i.e.*, points, projection images, and voxels) and design feature fusion among different branches. Tang *et.al.* [10] combines point-wise MLPs in each sparse convolution block to learn a point-voxel representation and uses NAS to search for a more efficient architecture. RPVNet [42] proposes range-point-voxel fusion network to utilizes information from three representations. Nevertheless, these methods only take sparse and textureless LiDAR point clouds as inputs, thus appearance and texture in the camera images have not been fully utilized.

2.2 Multi-sensor Methods

Multi-sensor methods attempt to fuse information from two complementary sensors and leverage the benefits of both camera and LiDAR [14,15,43,44]. RGBAL [14] converts RGB images to a polar-grid mapping representation and designs early and mid-level fusion strategies. PointPainting [15] exploits the segmentation logits of images and projects them to the LiDAR space by bird's-eye projection [23] or spherical projection [45] for LiDAR network performance improvement. Recently, PMF [13] exploits a collaborative fusion of two modalities in camera coordinates. However, these methods require multi-sensor inputs in both training and inference phases. Moreover, the paired multi-modality data is usually computation-intensive and unavailable in practical application.

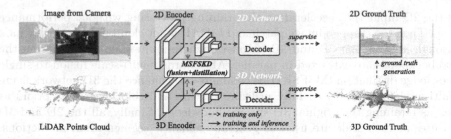

Fig. 2. 2D Priors Assisted Semantic Segmentation (2DPASS). It first crops a small patch from the original camera image as the 2D input. Then the cropped image patch and LiDAR point cloud independently pass through the 2D and 3D encoders to generate multi-scale features in parallel. Afterwards, for each scale, complementary 2D knowledge is effectively transferred to the 3D network via the multi-scale fusion-to-single knowledge distillation (MSFSKD). The feature maps (in the form of either pixel grid or point set) are used to generate the final semantic scores using modal-specific decoders, which are supervised by pure 3D labels.

2.3 Cross-modal Knowledge Transfer

Knowledge distillation was initially proposed for compressing the large teacher network to a small student one [46]. Over the past few years, several subsequent studies enhanced knowledge transferring through matching feature representations in different manners [47–50]. For instance, aligning attention maps [49] and Jacobean matrixes [50] were independently applied. With the development of multi-modal computer vision, recent research apply knowledge distillation to transfer priors across different modalities, *e.g.*, exploiting extra 2D images in the training phase and improving the performance in the inference [51–55]. Specifically, [56] introduces the 2D-assisted pre-training, [57] inflates the kernels of 2D convolution to the 3D ones, and [58] applies well-designed teacher-student framework. Inspired but different from the above, we transfer 2D knowledge through a multi-scale fusion-to-single manner, which additionally takes care of the modal-specific knowledge.

3 Method

3.1 Framework Overview

This paper focuses on improving the LiDAR point cloud semantic segmentation, which aims to assign the semantic label to each point. To handle difficulties in large-scale outdoor LiDAR point clouds, *i.e.*, sparsity, varying density, and lack of texture, we introduce the strong regularization and priors from 2D camera images through a **fusion-to-single** knowledge transferring.

The workflow of our 2D Priors Assisted Semantic Segmentation (2DPASS) is shown in Fig. 2. Since the camera images are pretty large (*e.g.*, 1242 × 512), sending the original ones to our multi-modal pipeline is intractable. Therefore, we randomly sample a small patch (480 × 320) from the original camera image as the 2D input [17], accelerating the training processing without performance drop. Then the cropped image patch and LiDAR point cloud independently pass through independent 2D and 3D encoders, where multi-scale features from the two backbones are extracted in parallel. Afterwards, multi-scale fusion-to-single knowledge distillation (MSFSKD) is conducted to enhance the 3D network using multi-modal features, *i.e.*, fully utilizing texture and color-aware 2D priors as well as retaining the original 3D-specific knowledge. Finally, all the 2D and 3D features at each scale are used to generate semantic segmentation predictions, which are supervised by pure 3D labels. During inference, the 2D-related branch can be discarded, which effectively prevents extra computational burden in real application compared with fusion-based approaches.

3.2   Modal-Specific Architectures

Multi-scale Feature Encoders. As shown in Fig. 2, we use two different networks to independently encode multi-scale features from 2D image and 3D point cloud. We apply ResNet34 [59] encoder with 2D convolution as the 2D network. For the 3D network, we adopt sparse convolution [3] to construct the 3D network. One merit of sparse convolution lies in the sparsity, with which the convolution operation only considers the non-empty voxels. Specifically, we design a hierarchical encoder as SPVCNN [10], and we adopt the ResNet bottleneck [59] design in each scale while replacing the ReLU activation with Leaky ReLU activation [60]. In both network, we extract L feature maps from different scales, obtaining the 2D and 3D features, *i.e.*, $\{F_l^{2D}\}_{l=1}^L$ and $\{F_l^{3D}\}_{l=1}^L$.

Prediction Decoders. After processing the features from images and point clouds at each scale, two modal-specific prediction decoders are independently applied to restore the down-sampled feature maps to their original sizes.

For the 2D network, we adopt FCN [19] decoder to up-sample the features from each encoder layer. Specifically, the feature map D_l^{2D} from the l-th decoder layer can be gained by up-sampling the feature map from the $(L - l + 1)$-th encoder layer, where all the up-sampled feature maps will be merged through element-wise addition. Finally, the semantic segmentation of the 2D network is obtained by passing the fused feature map through a linear classifier.

For the 3D network, we do not adopt the U-Net decoder used in previous methods [10,40,41]. In contrast, we up-sample the features from different scales to the original size and concatenate them together before feeding them into the classifier. We find out that such a structure can better learn hierarchical information while gaining the prediction in a more efficient way.

3.3   Point-to-Pixel Correspondence

Since the 2D features and 3D features are generally represented as pixels and points, respectively, it is difficult to directly transfer information between two modalities. In this section, we aim to generate paired features of two modalities for further knowledge distillation, using the point-to-pixel correspondence. The details of paired feature generation in two modalities are demonstrated in Fig. 3.

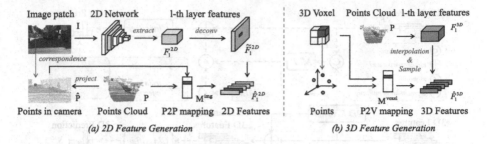

Image patch   2D Network   l-th layer features   3D Voxel   Points Cloud l-th layer features

(a) 2D Feature Generation   (b) 3D Feature Generation

Fig. 3. 2D and 3D feature generation. Part (a) demonstrates the 2D feature generation, where the point cloud will first be projected onto the image patch and generate the point-to-pixel (P2P) mapping. After that, it transfers the 2D feature map to the point-wise 2D features according to P2P mapping. Part (b) shows the 3D feature generation. The point-to-voxel (P2V) mapping is easy to obtain, and the voxel features will be interpolated onto the point cloud.

2D Features. The process of 2D feature generation is illustrated in Fig. 3(a). By cropping a small patch $I \in \mathbb{R}^{H \times W \times 3}$ from the original image and passing it through a 2D network, multi-scale features can be extracted in the hidden layers with different resolution. Taking the feature map $F_l^{2D} \in \mathbb{R}^{H_l \times W_l \times D_l}$ from l-th layer as an example, we first conduct a decovolution operation to upscale its resolution to the original one $\tilde{F}_l^{2D}$. Similar to the recent multi-sensor method [13], we adopt perspective projection and calculate a point-to-pixel mapping between point clouds and images. Specifically, given a LiDAR point cloud $P = \{p_i\}_{i=1}^{N} \in \mathbb{R}^{N \times 3}$, the projection of each 3D point $p_i = (x_i, y_i, z_i) \in \mathbb{R}^3$ to a point $\hat{p}_i = (u_i, v_i) \in \mathbb{R}^2$ in the image plane is given as:

$$[u_i, v_i, 1]^T = \frac{1}{z_i} \times K \times T \times [x_i, y_i, z_i, 1]^T, \tag{1}$$

where $K \in \mathbb{R}^{3 \times 4}$ and $T \in \mathbb{R}^{4 \times 4}$ are the camera intrinsic and extrinsic matrices respectively. K and T are directly provided in KITTI [61]. Since the lidar and cameras operate at different frequencies in NuScenes [18], we need to transform the LiDAR frame at timestamp t_l to camera frame at timestamp t_c via the global coordinate system. The extrinsic matrix T in NuScenes dataset [18] is given as:

$$T = T_{\text{camera} \leftarrow \text{ego}_{t_c}} \times T_{\text{ego}_{t_c} \leftarrow \text{global}} \times T_{\text{global} \leftarrow \text{ego}_{t_l}} \times T_{\text{ego}_{t_l} \leftarrow \text{lidar}} \tag{2}$$

After the projection, the point-to-pixel mapping is represented as

$$M^{img} = \{(\lfloor v_i \rfloor, \lfloor u_i \rfloor)\}_{i=1}^{N} \in \mathbb{R}^{N \times 2}, \tag{3}$$

where $\lfloor \cdot \rfloor$ is the floor operation. According to the point-to-pixel mapping, we extract a point-wise 2D feature $\hat{F}^{2D} \in \mathbb{R}^{N^{img} \times D_l}$ from the original feature map F^{2D} if any pixel on the feature map is included in M^{img}. Here $N^{img} < N$ represents the number of points that are included in M^{img}.

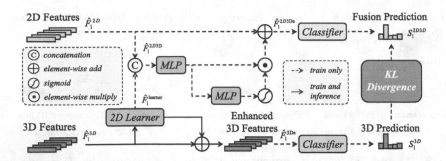

Fig. 4. Internal structure of **Multi-Scale Fusion-to-Single Knowledge Distilla-tion (MSFSKD)**, which consists of the modality fusion and Modality-Preserving KD. For each scale, modality fusion is first ultilized to achieve an enhanced multi-modality feature $\hat{F}_l^{2D3De}$. Afterwards, the enhanced feature $\hat{F}_l^{2D3De}$ promotes the 3D represen-tation $\hat{F}_l^{3De}$ through the uni-directional Modality-Preserving KD.

3D Features. The process of 3D features is relatively straightforward (as shown in Fig. 3(b)). Specifically, for the point cloud $P = \{(x_i, y_i, z_i)\}_{i=1}^N$, we obtain a point-to-voxel mapping in the l-th layer through

$$M_l^{voxel} = \{(\lfloor x_i/r_l \rfloor, \lfloor y_i/r_l \rfloor, \lfloor z_i/r_l \rfloor)\}_{i=1}^N \in \mathbb{R}^{N \times 3}, \tag{4}$$

where r_l is the voxelization resolution in the l-th layer. After that, given the 3D feature $F_l^{3D} \in \mathbb{R}^{N'_l \times D_l}$ from a sparse convolution layer, we gain a point-wise 3D feature $\tilde{F}_l^{3D} \in \mathbb{R}^{N \times D_l}$ through nearest interpolation on the original feature map F_l^{3D} according to M_l^{voxel}. Finally, we filter the points by discarding points outside the image FOV:

$$\hat{F}_l^{3D} = \{f_i | f_i \in \tilde{F}_l^{3D}, M_{i,1}^{img} \leq H, M_{i,2}^{img} \leq W\}_{i=1}^N \in \mathbb{R}^{N^{img} \times D_l}, \tag{5}$$

2D Ground Truths. Considering only 2D images is provided, the 2D ground-truths are obtained by projecting the 3D point labels to the corresponding image plane using above point-to-pixel mapping. Afterwards, the projected 2D ground truths can work as the supervision for the 2D branch.

Features Correspondence. Since both 2D and 3D feature use the same point-to-pixel mapping, 2D features $\hat{F}_l^{2D}$ and 3D features $\hat{F}_l^{3D}$ in arbitrary l-th layer have the same number of point N^{img} and point-to-pixel correspondence.

3.4   Multi-scale Fusion-to-Single Knowledge Distillation (MSFSKD)

As the key of 2DPASS, MSFSKD aims at improving the 3D representation in each scale using auxiliary 2D priors through a fusion-then-distillation manner. The knowledge distillation (KD) design of MSFSKD is partially inspired by [17]. However, [17] conducts KD in a naive cross-modal manner, *i.e.*, simply aligning the outputs from two sets of single modal features (*i.e.* either 2D or

3D), which inevitably pushes the features from two modals to their overlapped space. Therefore, such a manner actually discards the modal-specific information, which is crucial in multi-sensor segmentation. Although this issue can be relieved by introducing extra segmentation heads [17], it is inherent for the cross-modal distillation, resulting in biased predictions. To this end, we propose multi-scale fusion-to-single knowledge distillation (MSFSKD) module as shown in Fig. 4, which first fuses features of both images and point clouds and then conducts unidirectional alignment between the fused and the point cloud features. In our fusion-then-distillation manner, the fusion well retains the complete information from multi-modal data. Besides, the unidirectional alignment ensures boosted point cloud features from fusion without losing modal-specific information.

Modality Fusion. For each scale, considering the 2D and 3D feature gaps owing to different backbones, it is ineffective to directly fuse the raw 3D features $\hat{F}_l^{3D}$ into their 2D counterparts $\hat{F}_l^{2D}$. Thus, we firstly transform $\hat{F}_l^{3D}$ to $\hat{F}_l^{learner}$ through a "2D learner" MLP, which struggles to narrow the feature gap. Afterwards, the $\hat{F}_l^{learner}$ not only flows into the subsequent concatenation with 2D features $\hat{F}_l^{2D}$ to gain the fused features $\hat{F}_l^{2D3D}$ through another MLP, but also goes back into the original 3D features via a skip connection to yield enhanced 3D features $\hat{F}_l^{3D_e}$. Besides, similar to attention mechanism, the final enhanced fused features $\hat{F}_l^{2D3D_e}$ is obtained by:

$$\hat{F}_l^{2D3D_e} = \hat{F}_l^{2D} + \sigma(\text{MLP}(\hat{F}_l^{2D3D})) \odot \hat{F}_l^{2D3D}, \tag{6}$$

where σ denotes Sigmoid activation function.

Modality-Preserving KD. Although the $\hat{F}_l^{learner}$ is generated from pure 3D features, it is influenced by the segmentation loss of the 2D decoder as well, which takes enhanced fused feature $\hat{F}_l^{2D3D_e}$ as inputs. Acting like a residual between fused and point features, the 2D learner feature $\hat{F}_l^{learner}$ well prevents the distillation from contaminating the modal-specific information in $\hat{F}_l^{3D}$, achieving a Modality-Preserving KD. Finally, two independent classifiers (fully-connected layers) are respectively applied on top of $\hat{F}_l^{2D3D_e}$ and $\hat{F}_l^{3D_e}$ to obtain the semantic scores S_l^{2D3D} and S_l^{3D}. We choose KL divergence as the distillation loss L_{xM} as follows:

$$L_{xM} = D_{KL}(S_l^{2D3D} \| S_l^{3D}), \tag{7}$$

In our implementation, we detach S_l^{2D3D} from the computational graph when computing L_{xM}, enforcing the uni-directional distillation by only pushing S_l^{3D} closer to S_l^{2D3D}.

By taking such a knowledge distillation scheme, there are several advantages in our framework: **1)** The 2D learner and the fusion-to-single distillation provides rich texture information and structural regularization to enhance the 3D feature learning without losing any modal-specific information in 3D. **2)** The fusion branch is only adopted in the training phase. Therefore, the enhanced model can almost run without extra computational cost during the inference.

Table 1. Semantic segmentation results on the *SemanticKITTI* test benchmark. Only approaches published before 03/08/2022 are compared.

Method	mIoU	Road	Sidewalk	Parking	Other-ground	Building	Car	Truck	Bicycle	Motorcycle	Other-vehicle	Vegetation	Trunk	Terrain	Person	Bicyclist	Motorcyclist	Fence	Pole	Traffic sign	Speed (ms)
SqueezeSegV2 [38]	39.7	88.6	67.6	45.8	17.7	73.7	81.8	13.4	18.5	17.9	14.0	71.8	35.8	60.2	20.1	25.1	3.9	41.1	20.2	26.3	-
DarkNet53Seg [16]	49.9	91.8	74.6	64.8	27.9	84.1	86.4	25.5	24.5	32.7	22.6	78.3	50.1	64.0	36.2	33.6	4.7	55.0	38.9	52.2	-
RangeNet53++ [45]	52.2	91.8	75.2	65.0	27.8	87.4	91.4	25.7	25.7	34.4	23.0	80.5	55.1	64.6	38.3	38.8	4.8	58.6	47.9	55.9	83.3
3D-MiniNet [62]	55.8	91.6	74.5	64.2	25.4	89.4	90.5	28.5	42.3	42.1	29.4	82.8	60.8	66.7	47.8	44.1	14.5	60.8	48.0	56.6	-
SqueezeSegV3 [8]	55.9	91.7	74.8	63.4	26.4	89.0	92.5	29.6	38.7	36.5	33.0	82.0	58.7	65.4	45.6	46.2	20.1	59.4	49.6	58.9	238
PointNet++ [25]	20.1	72.0	41.8	18.7	5.6	62.3	53.7	0.9	1.9	0.2	0.2	46.5	13.8	30.0	0.9	1.0	0.0	16.9	6.0	8.9	5900
TangentConv [36]	40.9	83.9	63.9	33.4	15.4	83.4	90.8	15.2	2.7	16.5	12.1	79.5	49.3	58.1	23.0	28.4	8.1	49.0	35.8	28.5	3000
PointASNL [31]	46.8	87.4	74.3	24.3	1.8	83.1	87.9	39.0	0.0	25.1	29.2	84.1	52.2	70.6	34.2	57.6	0.0	43.9	57.8	36.9	-
RandLA-Net [1]	55.9	90.5	74.0	61.8	24.5	89.7	94.2	43.9	29.8	32.2	39.1	83.8	63.6	68.5	48.4	47.4	9.4	60.4	51.0	50.7	880
KPConv [29]	58.8	90.3	72.7	61.3	31.5	90.5	95.0	33.4	30.2	42.5	44.3	84.8	69.2	69.1	61.5	61.6	11.8	64.2	56.4	47.4	-
PolarNet [63]	54.3	90.8	74.4	61.7	21.7	90.0	93.8	22.9	40.3	30.1	28.5	84.0	65.5	67.8	43.2	40.2	5.6	61.3	51.8	57.5	62
JS3C-Net [2]	66.0	88.9	72.1	61.9	31.9	92.5	95.8	54.3	59.3	52.9	45.0	84.5	69.8	67.9	69.5	65.4	39.9	70.8	60.7	68.7	471
SPVNAS [10]	67.0	90.2	75.4	67.6	21.8	91.6	97.2	56.6	50.6	50.4	58.0	86.1	73.4	71.0	67.4	67.1	50.3	66.9	64.3	67.3	259
Cylinder3D [40]	68.9	92.7	77.0	65.0	32.3	90.7	97.1	50.8	67.6	63.8	58.5	85.6	72.5	69.8	73.7	69.2	48.0	66.5	62.4	66.2	131
RPVNet [42]	70.3	93.4	80.7	70.3	33.3	93.5	97.6	44.2	68.4	68.7	61.1	86.5	75.1	71.7	75.9	74.4	43.4	72.1	64.8	61.4	168
(AF)²-S3Net [41]	70.8	92.0	76.2	66.8	45.8	92.5	94.3	40.2	63.0	81.4	40.0	78.6	68.0	63.1	76.4	81.7	77.7	69.6	64.0	73.3	-
Baseline	67.4	89.8	73.8	62.1	33.5	91.9	96.3	54.9	51.1	55.8	51.6	86.5	72.3	71.3	76.8	79.8	30.3	68.7	63.7	70.2	62
2DPASS(Ours)	72.9	89.7	74.7	67.4	40.0	93.5	97.0	61.1	63.6	63.4	61.5	86.2	73.9	71.0	77.9	81.3	74.1	72.9	65.0	70.4	62

4   Experiments

4.1   Experiment Setups

Datasets. We extensively evaluate 2DPASS on two large-scale outdoor benchmarks: SemanticKITTI [16] and Nuscenes [18]. **SemanticKITTI** provides dense semantic annotations for each individual scan of sequences 00–10 in KITTI dataset [61]. According to the official setting, sequence 08 is the validation split, while the remaining are the train split. SemanticKITTI uses sequences 11–21 in KITTI as the test set, whose labels are held on for blind online testing[1]. **NuScenes** contains 1000 scenes which show a great diversity in inner cities traffic and weather conditions. It officially divides the data into 700/150/150 scenes for train/val/test. Similar to SemanticKITTI, the test set of NuScenes is used for online benchmarking[2]. For 2D sensors, KITTI has only two front-view cameras, while NuScenes has six cameras covering the full 360° fields of view.

Evaluation Metrics. We evaluate methods mainly using mean intersection over union (mIoU), which is defined as the average IoU over all classes. Additionally, we report the overall accuracy (Acc)/ frequency-weighted IOU (FwIOU) provided by the online leaderboard of two benchmarks. FwIoU is similar to mIoU except that each IoU is weighted by the point-level frequency of its class.

Network Setup. We apply ResNet34 [59] encoder with 2D convolution as the 2D network, where features after each down-sampling layers are extracted to generate 2D features. The 3D encoder is a modified SPVCNN [10] (voxel size 0.1) with fewer parameters, whose hidden dimensions are 64 for SemanticKITTI and 128 for NuScenes to speed up the network. The number of layers L for MSFSKD is set to 4 and 6 for SemanticKITTI and NuScenes, respectively. In each scale of knowledge distillation, 2D and 3D features are reduced to 64 dimensions through deconvolution or MLPs. Similarly, the hidden size of MLPs and 2D learner in MSFSKD are identically 64.

---

[1] https://competitions.codalab.org/competitions/20331.
[2] https://eval.ai/web/challenges/challenge-page/720/leaderboard/1967.

Table 2. Comparison to the state-of-the-art methods on the test set of SemanticKITTI multiple scans challenge. *-s* indicates static and *-m* stands for moving.

Method	mIoU	Acc	Car-s	Car-m	Truck-s	Truck-m	Other-s	Other-m	Person-s	Person-m	Bicyclist-s	Bicyclist-m	Motorcyclist-s	Motorcyclist-m
LatticeNet [64]	45.2	89.3	91.1	54.8	29.7	3.5	23.1	0.6	6.8	49.9	0.0	44.6	0.0	64.3
TemporalLidarSeg [65]	47.0	89.6	92.1	68.2	39.2	2.1	35.0	12.4	14.4	40.4	0.0	42.8	0.0	12.9
KPConv [29]	51.2	89.3	93.7	69.4	42.5	5.8	38.6	4.7	21.6	67.5	0.0	67.4	0.0	47.2
Cylinder3D [40]	52.5	91.0	94.6	74.9	41.3	0.0	38.8	0.1	12.5	65.7	1.7	68.3	0.2	11.9
(AF)²-S3Net [41]	56.9	88.1	91.8	65.3	15.7	5.6	27.5	3.9	16.4	67.6	15.1	66.4	67.1	59.6
2DPASS(Ours)	62.4	91.4	96.2	82.1	48.2	16.1	52.7	3.8	35.4	80.3	7.9	71.2	62.0	73.1

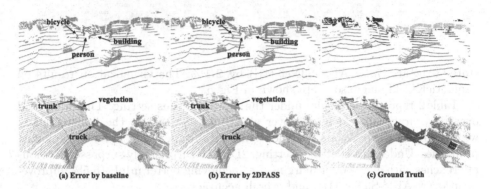

(a) Error by baseline   (b) Error by 2DPASS   (c) Ground Truth

Fig. 5. Qualitative results of 2DPASS on the validation set of SemanticKITTI. Our baseline has a higher error recognizing small objects and region boundaries, while 2DPASS recognizes small objects better thanks to the prior of 2D modality.

Training and Inference Details. We employ the cross-entropy and Lovasz losses as [40] for semantic segmentation. For the knowledge distillation, we set the proportion of segmentation loss and KL divergence as 1 : 0.05. Test-time augmentation [40] is applied during the inference. Training details will be introduced in supplementary material.

4.2 Benchmark Results

SemanticKITTI. SemanticKITTI evaluates segmentation performance using two settings: single scan and multiple scans. For methods using a single scan as input, moving and non-moving are mapped to a single class. While methods using multiple scans as inputs should distinguish between moving and non-moving objects, which is more challenging. All the reported results are from the official blind test competition website of SemanticKITTI.

Table 1 shows our performance under the single scan setting. Our baseline without 2DPASS already performs on par with a strong model Cylinder3D [40] while runs at a faster speed. Even so, the application of 2DPASS still brings a significant improvement over the baseline. Thanks to the auxiliary knowledge distillation, 2DPASS does not put any extra burden on the original model and thus does not sacrifice the running speed of the baseline. Overall, 2DPASS achieves the best result in terms of mIoU and running speed, outperforming the

Table 3. Semantic segmentation results on the *Nuscenes* test benchmark. Only approaches published before 03/08/2022 are compared. *L* and *C* stand for LiDAR and camera, respectively. (*) The speed reported in PMF [13] is accelerated by TensorRT, and we test their model without such technique in the same environment.

Method	Input	mIoU	FW mIoU	Barrier	Bicycle	Bus	Car	Construction	Motorcycle	Pedestrian	Traffic cone	Trailer	Truck	Driveable	Other flat	Sidewalk	Terrain	Manmade	Vegetation	speed (ms)
PolarNet [63]	L	69.4	87.4	72.2	16.8	77.0	86.5	51.1	69.7	64.8	54.1	69.7	63.5	96.6	67.1	77.7	72.1	87.1	84.5	–
JS3C-Net [2]	L	73.6	88.1	80.1	26.2	87.8	84.5	55.2	72.6	71.3	66.3	76.8	71.2	96.8	64.5	76.9	74.1	87.5	86.1	–
Cylinder3D [40]	L	77.2	89.9	82.8	29.8	84.3	89.4	63.0	79.3	77.2	73.4	84.6	89.1	**97.7**	70.2	80.3	75.5	90.4	87.6	63
AMVNet [39]	L	77.3	90.1	80.6	32.0	81.7	88.9	67.1	84.3	76.1	73.5	**84.9**	67.3	97.5	67.4	79.4	75.5	91.5	88.7	85
SPVCNN [10]	L	77.4	89.7	80.0	30.0	91.9	90.8	64.7	79.0	75.6	70.9	81.0	74.6	97.4	69.2	80.0	76.1	89.3	87.1	63
(AF)²-S3Net [41]	L	78.3	88.5	78.9	52.2	89.9	84.2	**77.4**	74.3	77.3	72.0	83.9	73.8	97.1	66.5	77.5	74.0	87.7	86.8	270
PMF [13]	L+C	77.0	89.0	82.0	40.0	81.0	88.0	64.0	79.0	80.0	**76.0**	81.0	67.0	97.0	68.0	78.0	74.0	90.0	88.0	125*
2D3DNet [66]	L+C	80.0	90.1	**83.0**	59.4	88.0	85.1	63.7	84.4	**82.0**	**76.0**	84.8	71.9	96.9	67.4	79.8	**76.0**	**92.1**	**89.2**	–
Baseline	L	77.6	88.5	80.8	37.9	92.7	90.5	65.4	77.6	71.5	70.9	83.1	75.3	97.0	69.3	78.1	75.6	89.1	86.8	44
2DPASS(Ours)	L	**80.8**	90.1	81.7	55.3	**92.0**	**91.8**	73.3	**86.5**	78.5	72.5	84.7	**75.5**	97.6	69.1	79.9	75.5	90.2	88.0	44

state-of-the-art (*i.e.*, (AF)²-S3Net [41]) by **2.1%**. The visualization results on SemanticKITTI single scan are shown in Fig. 5.

Table 2 reports the results under the multiple scans setting. The mIoU and overall accuracy are calculated over all 25 classes. Due to the limited space, we only report the per-class IOUs for dynamic objects with non-moving/moving properties. Under this challenge setting, 2DPASS surprisingly surpasses previous approaches with even larger margins, *i.e.*, achieving better mIoU (5.5% improvement over (AF)²-S3Net [41]) and overall accuracy.

NuScenes. The results on NuScenes are reported in Table 3, where 2DPASS achieves the 1st place as well. Note that we only include published works in Table 3 and the results are directly taken from the official leaderboard of NuScenes, where our model also ranks the 3rd place with slight disadvantage when considering unpublished works. Besides surpassing all single-modal methods, 2DPASS surprisingly outperforms those fusion-based approaches (the last two rows in Table 3). Note that NuScenes provides images covering the whole FOV of the LiDAR, and fusion-based approaches achieve such results by using both point clouds and image features during the inference. In contrast, our method only takes point clouds as input.

Table 4. Comparison with different knowledge distillation.

Method	SemanticKITTI
Hinton *et.al.* [46]	66.34
Huang *et.al.* [67]	66.46
Yang *et.al.* [68]	66.75
xMUDA [17]	67.88
2DPASS	**69.32**

Table 5. Ablation study on the SemanticKITTI validation set.

baseline	MSFSKD			SemanticKITTI
	KL Div	Modality fusion	2D learner	
✓				65.58
✓	✓			66.34
✓	✓	✓		69.13
✓	✓	✓	✓	**69.32**

4.3   Comprehensive Analysis

Comparing with Other Knowledge Distillation. To further verify the effectiveness of our fusion-to-single knowledge distillation paradigm upon common teach-student architecture and other cross-modal manners, we compare 2DPASS with typical approaches of knowledge transfer in Table 4, where we utilize these methods in each scale for fair comparison. Among all the methods, Hinton *et. al.* [46], Huang *et. al.* [67] and Yang *et. al.* [68] are pure knowledge distillation designs, where the former is the pioneer for the research field and the latter is newly proposed. As shown in the Table 4, pure knowledge distillation manners cannot be directly adopted on the LiDAR semantic segmentation, and their improvement upon the baseline model is limited. Recently, [17] adopts cross-modal feature alignment technique in the task of domain adaptation on semantic segmentation. However, their improvement is still marginal. To the end, in the Table 4, 2DPASS significantly performs better, which illustrates the effectiveness of our multi-scale fusion-to-single knowledge distillation (MSFSKD).

Design Analysis of MSFSKD. Table 5 demonstrates the ablation study on SemanticKITTI validation set. As shown in the table, our baseline only achieves a lower result of 65.58 mIoU. Note that simply using feature alignment between two modalities cannot effectively improve the result, where the metric of mIoU will be only increased to 66.34. After using 2D-3D fusion in each knowledge distillation scale, there is a significant improvement to 69.13. This improvement mainly comes from the knowledge provided by the stronger fusion prediction. Finally, we find out that 2D learner design can slightly improve the performance by about 0.2%. Note that the results on SemanticKITTI validation set is lower than that on benchmark since small object category (*i.e.*, motocyclist) only occupies a small proportion.

Distance-Based Evaluation. We investigate how segmentation is affected by distance of the points to the ego-vehicle, and compare 2DPASS, current state-of-the-art and the baseline on the SemanticKITTI validation set. Figure 6(a) illustrates the mIoU of 2DPASS as opposed to the baseline and $(AF)^2$-S3Net. The results of all the methods get worse by increasing the distance since points are relatively sparse in the long distance. 2DPASS improves the performance greatly within 10 m, *i.e.*, from 61.2 to 89.1, which is the best distance for the camera to capture objects' color and texture. There is also a significant improvement upon $(AF)^2$-S3Net within this distance, *i.e.*, 84.4 v.s. 89.1.

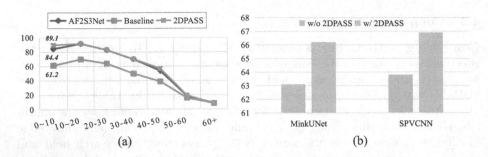

(a)   (b)

Fig. 6. Extensive experiment results. The part (a) shows the results on SemanticKITTI validation set with different distance-range. Part (b) demonstrates the results before and after exploiting 2DPASS on MinkowskiNet [10] and SPVCNN [10].

Generality. We show our 2DPASS can be a "model-independent" training scheme that boosts the performance of other networks. We additionally trained two open-sourced baselines, *i.e.*, MinkowskiNet and SPVCNN implemented in [10] with 2DPASS. During the experiment, we keep all the setups the same except for the 2D-related components. As shown in Fig. 6(b), 2DPASS improves the former one from 63.1 to 66.2 and the latter from 63.8 to 66.9. These results sufficiently demonstrate the effectiveness and generality of 2DPASS.

5   Conclusion

This work proposes the 2D Priors Assisted Semantic Segmentation (**2DPASS**), a general training scheme, to boost the performance of LiDAR point cloud semantic segmentation via 2D prior-related knowledge distillation. By leveraging an auxiliary modal fusion and knowledge distillation in a multi-scale manner, 2DPASS acquires richer semantic and structural information from the multi-modal data, effectively enhancing the performance of a pure 3D network. Eventually, it achieves the state-of-the-arts on two large-scale benchmarks (*i.e.*, SemanticKITTI and NuScenes). We believe that our work can be applied to a wider range of other scenarios in the future, such as 3D detection and tracking.

Acknowledgement. This work was supported in part by NSFC-Youth 61902335, by the Basic Research Project No. HZQB-KCZYZ-2021067 of Hetao Shenzhen HK S&T Cooperation Zone, by the National Key R&D Program of China with grant No. 2018YFB1800800, by Shenzhen Outstanding Talents Training Fund, by Guangdong Research Project No. 2017ZT07X152 and No. 2019CX01X104, by the Guangdong Provincial Key Laboratory of Future Networks of Intelligence (Grant No. 2022B1212010001), by zelixir biotechnology company Fund, by Tencent Open Fund, and by ITSO at CUHKSZ.

References

1. Hu, Q., et al.: Randla-net: efficient semantic segmentation of large-scale point clouds. In: Proceedings of the IEEE Conference on Computer Vision and Pattern Recognition (2020)
2. Yan, X., et al.: Sparse single sweep lidar point cloud segmentation via learning contextual shape priors from scene completion. In: Proceedings of the AAAI Conference on Artificial Intelligence, vol. 35, pp. 3101–3109 (2021)
3. Graham, B., Engelcke, M., van der Maaten, L.: 3D semantic segmentation with submanifold sparse convolutional networks. In: Proceedings of the IEEE Conference on Computer Vision and Pattern Recognition, pp. 9224–9232 (2018)
4. Chen, L.C., Papandreou, G., Kokkinos, I., Murphy, K., Yuille, A.L.: Deeplab: semantic image segmentation with deep convolutional nets, atrous convolution, and fully connected crfs. IEEE Trans. Pattern Anal. Mach. Intell. **40**(4), 834–848 (2017)
5. Chen, L.C., Papandreou, G., Schroff, F., Adam, H.: Rethinking atrous convolution for semantic image segmentation. arXiv preprint arXiv:1706.05587 (2017)
6. Song, S., Yu, F., Zeng, A., Chang, A.X., Savva, M., Funkhouser, T.: Semantic scene completion from a single depth image. In: Proceedings of the IEEE Conference on Computer Vision and Pattern Recognition, pp. 1746–1754 (2017)
7. Huang, Z., Wang, X., Huang, L., Huang, C., Wei, Y., Liu, W.: Ccnet: criss-cross attention for semantic segmentation. In: Proceedings of the IEEE/CVF International Conference on Computer Vision, pp. 603–612 (2019)
8. Xu, C.: SqueezeSegV3: spatially-adaptive convolution for efficient point-cloud segmentation. In: Vedaldi, A., Bischof, H., Brox, T., Frahm, J.-M. (eds.) ECCV 2020. LNCS, vol. 12373, pp. 1–19. Springer, Cham (2020). https://doi.org/10.1007/978-3-030-58604-1_1
9. Zhu, X., et al.: Cylindrical and asymmetrical 3D convolution networks for lidar segmentation. In: Proceedings of the IEEE/CVF Conference on Computer Vision and Pattern Recognition, pp. 9939–9948 (2021)
10. Tang, H.: Searching efficient 3D architectures with sparse point-voxel convolution. In: Vedaldi, A., Bischof, H., Brox, T., Frahm, J.-M. (eds.) ECCV 2020. LNCS, vol. 12373, pp. 685–702. Springer, Cham (2020). https://doi.org/10.1007/978-3-030-58604-1_41
11. Zheng, C., et al.: Beyond 3D siamese tracking: a motion-centric paradigm for 3D single object tracking in point clouds. arXiv preprint arXiv:2203.01730 (2022)
12. Zheng, C., et al.: Box-aware feature enhancement for single object tracking on point clouds. In: Proceedings of the IEEE/CVF International Conference on Computer Vision, pp. 13199–13208 (2021)
13. Zhuang, Z., Li, R., Jia, K., Wang, Q., Li, Y., Tan, M.: Perception-aware multi-sensor fusion for 3D lidar semantic segmentation. In: Proceedings of the IEEE/CVF International Conference on Computer Vision, pp. 16280–16290 (2021)
14. El Madawi, K., Rashed, H., El Sallab, A., Nasr, O., Kamel, H., Yogamani, S.: Rgb and lidar fusion based 3D semantic segmentation for autonomous driving. In: IEEE Intelligent Transportation Systems Conference (ITSC), vol. 2019, pp. 7–12. IEEE (2019)
15. Vora, S., Lang, A.H., Helou, B., Beijbom, O.: Pointpainting: sequential fusion for 3D object detection. In: Proceedings of the IEEE/CVF Conference on Computer Vision and Pattern Recognition, pp. 4604–4612 (2020)

16. Behley, J., et al.: Semantickitti: a dataset for semantic scene understanding of lidar sequences. In: Proceedings of the IEEE International Conference on Computer Vision, pp. 9297–9307 (2019)
17. Jaritz, M., Vu, T.H., Charette, R.d., Wirbel, E., Pérez, P.: xmuda: cross-modal unsupervised domain adaptation for 3D semantic segmentation. In: Proceedings of the IEEE/CVF Conference on Computer Vision and Pattern Recognition, pp. 12605–12614 (2020)
18. Caesar, H., et al.: nuscenes: a multimodal dataset for autonomous driving. In: CVPR (2020)
19. Long, J., Shelhamer, E., Darrell, T.: Fully convolutional networks for semantic segmentation. In: Proceedings of the IEEE Conference on Computer Vision and Pattern Recognition, pp. 3431–3440 (2015)
20. Lin, G., Shen, C., Van Den Hengel, A., Reid, I.: Efficient piecewise training of deep structured models for semantic segmentation. In: Proceedings of the IEEE Conference on Computer Vision and Pattern Recognition, pp. 3194–3203 (2016)
21. Zhao, H., Shi, J., Qi, X., Wang, X., Jia, J.: Pyramid scene parsing network. In: Proceedings of the IEEE Conference on Computer Vision and Pattern Recognition, pp. 2881–2890 (2017)
22. Wang, P., et al.: Understanding convolution for semantic segmentation. In: IEEE Winter Conference on Applications of Computer Vision (WACV), vol. 2018, pp. 1451–1460. IEEE (2018)
23. Yuan, Y., Huang, L., Guo, J., Zhang, C., Chen, X., Wang, J.: Ocnet: object context network for scene parsing. arXiv preprint arXiv:1809.00916 (2018)
24. Qi, C.R., Su, H., Mo, K., Guibas, L.J.: Pointnet: deep learning on point sets for 3D classification and segmentation. In: Proceedings of the IEEE Conference on Computer Vision and Pattern Recognition, pp. 652–660 (2017)
25. Qi, C.R., Yi, L., Su, H., Guibas, L.J.: Pointnet++: deep hierarchical feature learning on point sets in a metric space. In: Advances in Neural Information Processing Systems, pp. 5099–5108 (2017)
26. Wang, Y., Sun, Y., Liu, Z., Sarma, S.E., Bronstein, M.M., Solomon, J.M.: Dynamic graph cnn for learning on point clouds. ACM Trans. Graph. (TOG) **38**(5), 1–12 (2019)
27. Wu, W., Qi, Z., Fuxin, L.: Pointconv: deep convolutional networks on 3D point clouds. In: Proceedings of the IEEE Conference on Computer Vision and Pattern Recognition, pp. 9621–9630 (2019)
28. Liu, Y., Fan, B., Xiang, S., Pan, C.: Relation-shape convolutional neural network for point cloud analysis. In: Proceedings of the IEEE/CVF Conference on Computer Vision and Pattern Recognition, pp. 8895–8904 (2019)
29. Thomas, H., Qi, C.R., Deschaud, J.E., Marcotegui, B., Goulette, F., Guibas, L.J.: Kpconv: flexible and deformable convolution for point clouds. In: The IEEE International Conference on Computer Vision (ICCV) (2019)
30. Hua, B.S., Tran, M.K., Yeung, S.K.: Pointwise convolutional neural networks. In: Proceedings of the IEEE Conference on Computer Vision and Pattern Recognition, pp. 984–993 (2018)
31. Yan, X., Zheng, C., Li, Z., Wang, S., Cui, S.: Pointasnl: robust point clouds processing using nonlocal neural networks with adaptive sampling. In: Proceedings of the IEEE/CVF Conference on Computer Vision and Pattern Recognition, pp. 5589–5598 (2020)
32. Zhao, H., Jiang, L., Jia, J., Torr, P.H., Koltun, V.: Point transformer. In: Proceedings of the IEEE/CVF International Conference on Computer Vision, pp. 16259–16268 (2021)

33. Engel, N., Belagiannis, V., Dietmayer, K.: Point transformer. IEEE Access **9**, 134826–134840 (2021)

34. Lawin, F.J., Danelljan, M., Tosteberg, P., Bhat, G., Khan, F.S., Felsberg, M.: Deep projective 3D semantic segmentation. In: Felsberg, M., Heyden, A., Krüger, N. (eds.) CAIP 2017. LNCS, vol. 10424, pp. 95–107. Springer, Cham (2017). https://doi.org/10.1007/978-3-319-64689-3_8

35. Boulch, A., Le Saux, B., Audebert, N.: Unstructured point cloud semantic labeling using deep segmentation networks. 3DOR **2**, 1–8 (2017)

36. Tatarchenko, M., Park, J., Koltun, V., Zhou, Q.Y.: Tangent convolutions for dense prediction in 3D. In: Proceedings of the IEEE Conference on Computer Vision and Pattern Recognition, pp. 3887–3896 (2018)

37. Wu, B., Wan, A., Yue, X., Keutzer, K.: Squeezeseg: convolutional neural nets with recurrent crf for real-time road-object segmentation from 3D lidar point cloud. In: 2018 IEEE International Conference on Robotics and Automation (ICRA), pp. 1887–1893. IEEE (2018)

38. Wu, B., Zhou, X., Zhao, S., Yue, X., Keutzer, K.: Squeezesegv 2: improved model structure and unsupervised domain adaptation for road-object segmentation from a lidar point cloud. In: 2019 International Conference on Robotics and Automation (ICRA), pp. 4376–4382. IEEE (2019)

39. Liong, V.E., Nguyen, T.N.T., Widjaja, S., Sharma, D., Chong, Z.J.: Amvnet: assertion-based multi-view fusion network for lidar semantic segmentation. arXiv preprint arXiv:2012.04934 (2020)

40. Zhou, H., et al.: Cylinder3d: an effective 3D framework for driving-scene lidar semantic segmentation. arXiv preprint arXiv:2008.01550 (2020)

41. Cheng, R., Razani, R., Taghavi, E., Li, E., Liu, B.: Af2-s3net: attentive feature fusion with adaptive feature selection for sparse semantic segmentation network. In: Proceedings of the IEEE/CVF conference on computer vision and pattern recognition, pp. 12547–12556 (2021)

42. Xu, J., Zhang, R., Dou, J., Zhu, Y., Sun, J., Pu, S.: Rpvnet: a deep and efficient range-point-voxel fusion network for lidar point cloud segmentation. In: Proceedings of the IEEE/CVF International Conference on Computer Vision, pp. 16024–16033 (2021)

43. Krispel, G., Opitz, M., Waltner, G., Possegger, H., Bischof, H.: Fuseseg: lidar point cloud segmentation fusing multi-modal data. In: Proceedings of the IEEE/CVF Winter Conference on Applications of Computer Vision, pp. 1874–1883 (2020)

44. Meyer, G.P., Charland, J., Hegde, D., Laddha, A., Vallespi-Gonzalez, C.: Sensor fusion for joint 3D object detection and semantic segmentation. In: Proceedings of the IEEE/CVF Conference on Computer Vision and Pattern Recognition Workshops (2019)

45. Milioto, A., Vizzo, I., Behley, J., Stachniss, C.: Rangenet++: fast and accurate lidar semantic segmentation. In: Proceedings of the IEEE/RSJ International Conference on Intelligent Robots and Systems (IROS) (2019)

46. Hinton, G., Vinyals, O., Dean, J.: Distilling the knowledge in a neural network. In: NeurIPS Workshops (2014)

47. Ba, L.J., Caruana, R.: Do deep nets really need to be deep? In: NeurIPS, pp. 2654–2662 (2014)

48. Chen, G., Choi, W., Yu, X., Han, T., Chandraker, M.: Learning efficient object detection models with knowledge distillation. In: Proceedings of the 31st International Conference on Neural Information Processing Systems, pp. 742–751 (2017)

49. Zagoruyko, S., Komodakis, N.: Paying more attention to attention: improving the performance of convolutional neural networks via attention transfer. In: ICLR (2017)

50. Srinivas, S., Fleuret, F.: Knowledge transfer with jacobian matching. In: International Conference on Machine Learning, pp. 4723–4731. PMLR (2018)

51. Gupta, S., Hoffman, J., Malik, J.: Cross modal distillation for supervision transfer. In: Proceedings of the IEEE Conference on Computer Vision and Pattern Recognition, pp. 2827–2836 (2016)

52. Wang, L., et al.: An efficient approach to informative feature extraction from multimodal data. In: Proceedings of the AAAI Conference on Artificial Intelligence, vol. 33, pp. 5281–5288 (2019)

53. Yuan, S., Stenger, B., Kim, T.K.: Rgb-based 3D hand pose estimation via privileged learning with depth images. arXiv preprint arXiv:1811.07376 (2018)

54. Liu, Z., Qi, X., Fu, C.W.: 3D-to-2D distillation for indoor scene parsing. In: CVPR (2021)

55. Zhao, L., Peng, X., Chen, Y., Kapadia, M., Metaxas, D.N.: Knowledge as priors: Cross-modal knowledge generalization for datasets without superior knowledge. In: Proceedings of the IEEE/CVF Conference on Computer Vision and Pattern Recognition, pp. 6528–6537 (2020)

56. Liu, Y.C., et al.: Learning from 2D: pixel-to-point knowledge transfer for 3D pretraining. arXiv preprint arXiv:2104.04687 (2021)

57. Xu, C., et al.: Image2point: 3D point-cloud understanding with pretrained 2D convnets. arXiv preprint arXiv:2106.04180 (2021)

58. Yuan, Z., Yan, X., Liao, Y., Guo, Y., Li, G., Cui, S., Li, Z.: X-trans2cap: crossmodal knowledge transfer using transformer for 3D dense captioning. In: Proceedings of the IEEE/CVF Conference on Computer Vision and Pattern Recognition, pp. 8563–8573 (2022)

59. He, K., Zhang, X., Ren, S., Sun, J.: Deep residual learning for image recognition. In: Proceedings of the IEEE Conference on Computer Vision and Pattern Recognition, pp. 770–778 (2016)

60. Maas, A.L., Hannun, A.Y., Ng, A.Y., et al.: Rectifier nonlinearities improve neural network acoustic models. In: Proceedings of ICML, vol. 30, p. 3. Citeseer (2013)

61. Geiger, A., Lenz, P., Urtasun, R.: Are we ready for autonomous driving? the KITTI vision benchmark suite. In: Proceedings of the IEEE Conference on Computer Vision and Pattern Recognition (CVPR), pp. 3354–3361 (2012)

62. Alonso, I., Riazuelo, L., Montesano, L., Murillo, A.C.: 3D-mininet: learning a 2D representation from point clouds for fast and efficient 3D lidar semantic segmentation. arXiv preprint arXiv:2002.10893 (2020)

63. Zhang, Y., et al.: Polarnet: an improved grid representation for online lidar point clouds semantic segmentation. In: Proceedings of the IEEE/CVF Conference on Computer Vision and Pattern Recognition, pp. 9601–9610 (2020)

64. Rosu, R.A., Schütt, P., Quenzel, J., Behnke, S.: Latticenet: fast point cloud segmentation using permutohedral lattices. arXiv preprint arXiv:1912.05905 (2019)

65. Duerr, F., Pfaller, M., Weigel, H., Beyerer, J.: Lidar-based recurrent 3D semantic segmentation with temporal memory alignment. In: 2020 International Conference on 3D Vision (3DV), pp. 781–790. IEEE (2020)

66. Genova, K., et al.: Learning 3D semantic segmentation with only 2D image supervision. In: 2021 International Conference on 3D Vision (3DV), pp. 361–372. IEEE (2021)

67. Huang, Z., et al.: Revisiting knowledge distillation: an inheritance and exploration framework. In: Proceedings of the IEEE/CVF Conference on Computer Vision and Pattern Recognition, pp. 3579–3588 (2021)
68. Yang, J., Martinez, B., Bulat, A., Tzimiropoulos, G.T.: Knowledge distillation via softmax regression representation learning. In: ICLR2021 (2021)

Extract Free Dense Labels from CLIP

Chong Zhou[1], Chen Change Loy[1(✉)], and Bo Dai[2]

[1] S-Lab, Nanyang Technological University, Singapore, Singapore
{chong033,ccloy}@ntu.edu.sg
[2] Shanghai AI Laboratory, Shanghai, China
daibo@pjlab.org.cn

Abstract. Contrastive Language-Image Pre-training (CLIP) has made a remarkable breakthrough in open-vocabulary zero-shot image recognition. Many recent studies leverage the pre-trained CLIP models for image-level classification and manipulation. In this paper, we wish examine the intrinsic potential of CLIP for pixel-level dense prediction, specifically in semantic segmentation. To this end, with minimal modification, we show that MaskCLIP yields compelling segmentation results on open concepts across various datasets *in the absence of annotations and fine-tuning*. By adding pseudo labeling and self-training, MaskCLIP+ surpasses SOTA transductive zero-shot semantic segmentation methods by large margins, *e.g.*, mIoUs of unseen classes on PASCAL VOC/PASCAL Context/COCO Stuff are improved from 35.6/20.7/30.3 to 86.1/66.7/54.7. We also test the robustness of MaskCLIP under input corruption and evaluate its capability in discriminating fine-grained objects and novel concepts. Our finding suggests that MaskCLIP can serve as a new reliable source of supervision for dense prediction tasks to achieve annotation-free segmentation. Source code is available here.

1 Introduction

Large-scale visual-language pre-training models such as CLIP [44] capture expressive visual and language features. Various downstream vision tasks, *e.g.*, text-driven image manipulation [41], image captioning [24], view synthesis [29], and object detection [18], have attempted to exploit such features for improved generality and robustness. For instance, conducting zero-shot image classification based on raw CLIP features leads to a competitive approach that matches the performance of fully-supervised counterparts [44].

In this paper, we take a step further to explore the applicability of CLIP features for pixel-level dense prediction tasks such as semantic segmentation. This investigation is meaningful in that previous studies mainly leverage CLIP

B. Dai—Completed this work when he was with S-Lab, NTU.

Supplementary Information The online version contains supplementary material available at https://doi.org/10.1007/978-3-031-19815-1_40.

© The Author(s), under exclusive license to Springer Nature Switzerland AG 2022
S. Avidan et al. (Eds.): ECCV 2022, LNCS 13688, pp. 696–712, 2022.
https://doi.org/10.1007/978-3-031-19815-1_40

Fig. 1. Here we show the original image in (a), the segmentation result of MaskCLIP+ in (b), and the confidence maps of MaskCLIP and MaskCLIP+ for *Batman* in (c) and (d) respectively. Through the adaptation of CLIP, MaskCLIP can be directly used for segmentation of fine-grained and novel concepts (e.g., *Batman* and *Joker*) without any training operations and annotations. Combined with pseudo labeling and self-training, MaskCLIP+ further improves the segmentation result.

features as a global image representation. In contrast, our exploration wishes to ascertain the extent of CLIP features in encapsulating object-level and local semantics for dense prediction. Different from the conventional pre-training task of image classification on iconic images, CLIP learns from images of complex scenes and their descriptions in natural language, which (1) encourages it to embed local image semantics in its features, (2) enables it to learn concepts in open vocabulary, and (3) captures rich contextual information, such as the co-occurrence/relation of certain objects and priors of the spatial locations. We believe all these merits contribute significantly to its potential for dense prediction tasks.

In this paper, we summarize both our success and failure experience on leveraging CLIP features for dense prediction. We find it essential to not break the visual-language association in the original CLIP feature space. In our earlier exploration, we experienced failures with the attempt to fine-tune the image encoder of CLIP for the segmentation task, *e.g.*, initializing DeepLab [5] with the weights of CLIP's image encoder and fine-tune the backbone on segmentation. In addition, we found it is of utmost importance to avoid any unnecessary attempts to manipulate the text embeddings of CLIP. Such an approach would fail in segmenting unseen classes.

In our successful model, named **MaskCLIP**, we show that one can simply extract dense patch-level features from the CLIP's image encoder, *i.e.*, the *value* features of the last attention layer, without breaking the visual-language association. Classification weights for dense prediction, which are essentially 1×1 convolutions, can be directly obtained from the text embeddings of CLIP's text encoder without any deliberate mapping. In our empirical study, MaskCLIP yields reasonable predictions in both quantitative performance measured by mIoU metric and qualitative results. Besides, MaskCLIP can be based on all variants of CLIP, including ResNets and ViTs. And we provide side-by-side comparisons between the two popular backbone networks. We also propose two mask refinement techniques for MaskCLIP to further improve its performance, namely *key smoothing* and *prompt denoising*, both require no training. Specifically, key smoothing computes the similarity between the *key* features (of the last attention layer) of different patches, which are used to smooth the predictions. Prompt denoising removes prompts with classes that unlikely exist in the image, thus with fewer distractors, predictions become more accurate.

However, it is hard to further improve the segmentation capacity of MaskCLIP as its architecture is restricted to be the image encoder of CLIP. To relax MaskCLIP from the architectural constraint and to incorporate more advanced architectures such as PSPNet [54] and DeepLab [5], we notice that instead of deploying MaskCLIP at the inference time, we can deploy it at the training time, where it serves as a generalizable and robust annotator that provides high-quality pseudo labels. Together with a standard self-training strategy, the resulting model, termed **MaskCLIP+**, achieves a strikingly remarkable performance.

Apart from annotation-free and open-vocabulary segmentation, MaskCLIP+ can also be applied to the transductive zero-shot semantic segmentation task, where MaskCLIP only generates pseudo labels for the unseen classes. On the three standard segmentation benchmarks, namely PASCAL VOC [14], PASCAL Context [37], and COCO Stuff [2], MaskCLIP+ improves the state-of-the-art results in terms of mIoU of unseen classes, by 50.5%, 46%, and 24.4%, respectively ($35.6 \rightarrow 86.1$, $20.7 \rightarrow 66.7$, and $30.3 \rightarrow 54.7$). Thanks to the the generality and robustness of CLIP features, MaskCLIP+ can be readily applied to various extended settings of semantic segmentation, including the segmentation of fine-grained classes (*e.g.*, attribute-conditioned classes like *white car* and *red bus*) or novel concepts (such as *Batman* and *Joker* as shown in Fig. 1), as well as the segmentation of moderately corrupted inputs. We show more interesting results in the experiment section.

Semantic segmentation is notorious for its high dependency on labeled training data. Many methods have been explored to get around such stringent requirement, *e.g.*, through using weak labels like image tags, bounding boxes, and scribbles. Our study, for the first time, shows that features learned via large-scale visual-language pre-training can be readily used to facilitate open vocabulary dense prediction. The proposed model, MaskCLIP, shows promising potential in providing rich and meaningful dense pseudo labels for training existing methods.

2 Related Work

Transferable Representation Learning. Pre-training is widely used for dense prediction tasks. Yosinski *et al.* [51] show that ImageNet [10] pre-training greatly speeds up the convergence of the downstream object detection task. Later, extensive research is conducted on making the pre-training a human-labor-free process. In particular, self-supervised representation learning constructs pretext tasks [12,13,38] or relies on contrastive learning [6,9,21], clustering [3], and bootstrapping [17] to obtain supervision signals. Another line of work seeks to learn visual representation from natural language. Some studies [11,15,16,43,47,52] propose to learn from image-caption pairs. Recently, CLIP [44] and ALIGN [30] perform contrastive learning on very large-scale web-curated image-text pairs and show promising pre-trained representations with impressive zero-shot transferability. The success of CLIP inspires a new way of studies that transfer the pre-trained CLIP model to various downstream tasks such as text-driven image manipulation [41], image captioning [24], view synthesis [29], and object detection [18]. Different from these methods that typically apply CLIP right off the shelf for image encoding, we explore ways to adapt CLIP for pixel-level dense prediction. A concurrent work, DenseCLIP [45], aims to better fine-tune the CLIP pre-trained weights on target semantic segmentation datasets without keeping the zero-shot transferability, which are different from our setting. To examine the intrinsic potential of CLIP for dense prediction tasks, we refrain from any fine-tuning and major architectural modification.

Zero-Shot Visual Recognition. Zero-shot learning aims at classifying instances of those categories that are not seen during training. Common clues to infer unseen categories include shared attributes and visual-semantic mapping. As the latter does not require extra annotations, the paradigm is well-suited for zero-shot dense prediction tasks. Zhao *et al.* [53] project image pixel features and word concepts into a joint space. Kato *et al.* [31] fuse semantic features into visual features as guidance. ZS3Net [1] proposes to generate fake pixel-level features from semantic features for the unseen. SPNet [49] learns a projection from visual space to semantic space. Other studies like [25], [33], and [19], improve the generative ZS3Net in terms of uncertainty, structural consistency, and context, respectively, while STRICT [40] boosts the SPNet through self-training. Depending on whether the unlabeled pixels are observed during training, the setting can be split into inductive (not observed) and transductive. We show that the proposed MaskCLIP not only achieves new SOTA on the zero-shot segmentation setting but can also deal with more difficult settings where all the categories are unseen during training.

Self-Training. Self-training leverages the model trained on labeled data to generate pseudo labels for the unlabeled, which then are used to iteratively improve the previous model. Self-training has firstly become popular in the semi-supervised classification task [28,32,34,42] and is also recently applied in the semi-supervised/zero-shot semantic segmentation settings [4,7,26,27,35,36,39, 55]. Our MaskCLIP+ adopts the same philosophy where the pseudo labels are obtained from both frozen MaskCLIP and MaskCLIP+ itself.

3   Methodology

Our study serves as an early attempt that explores the applicability of CLIP features for pixel-level dense prediction tasks. We start with a brief introduction of CLIP and a naïves solution as the preliminary, followed by presenting the proposed MaskCLIP in detail.

3.1   Preliminary on CLIP

CLIP [44] is a visual-language pre-training method that learns both visual and language representations from large-scale raw web-curated image-text pairs. It consists of an image encoder $\mathcal{V}(\cdot)$ and a text encoder $\mathcal{T}(\cdot)$, both jointly trained to respectively map the input image and text into a unified representation space. CLIP adopts contrastive learning as its training objective, where ground-truth image-text pairs are regarded as positive samples, and mismatched image-text pairs are constructed as negative ones. In practice, the text encoder is implemented as a Transformer [48]. As for the image encoder, CLIP provides two alternative implementations, namely a Transformer and a ResNet [22] with global attention pooling layer. Our method can be based on both encoder architectures.

We believe CLIP has inherently embedded local image semantics in its features as it learns to associate image content with natural language descriptions, the latter of which contain complex and dense semantic guidance across multiple granularities. For example, to correctly identify the image corresponds to the description *the man at bat readies to swing at the patch while the umpire looks on* [8], CLIP must divide image semantics into local segments and properly align image semantics with singular mentioned concepts like *man, bat, swing, patch, man at bat, man at patch,* and *man readies to swing,* instead of handling the image as a whole. Such uniqueness is absent from training with solely image labels.

3.2   Conventional Fine-Tuning Hinders Zero-Shot Ability

The current de facto pipeline of training a segmentation network is (1) initializing the backbone network with the ImageNet [10] pre-trained weights, (2) adding segmentation-specific network modules with randomly initialized weights, and (3) jointly fine-tuning the backbone and newly added modules.

It is natural to follow these standard steps to adapt CLIP for segmentation. Here, we start our exploration by applying this pipeline on DeepLab [5] with two CLIP-specific modifications. Specifically, we first replace the ImageNet pre-trained weights with weights of the image encoder of CLIP. Second, we adopt a mapper $\mathcal{M}$ that maps text embeddings of CLIP to the weights of DeepLab classifier (the last 1×1 convolutional layer). The modified model can be formulated as follows:

$$\text{DeepLab}(x) = \mathcal{C}_\phi(\mathcal{H}(\mathcal{V}_{*l}(x))), \tag{1}$$

$$\phi = \mathcal{M}(t), \tag{2}$$

where $\mathcal{V}_{*l}(\cdot)$ denotes the DeepLab backbone, which is a ResNet dilated by a factor of l. $H(\cdot)$ denotes the randomly initialized ASPP module [5], and $\mathcal{C}_\phi(\cdot)$ is the DeepLab classifier, whose weights, denoted as ϕ, are determined by the text embedding of CLIP via the mapper $\mathcal{M}$. Ideally, by updating the classifier weights with the corresponding text embedding, the adapted DeepLab is able to segment different classes without re-training.

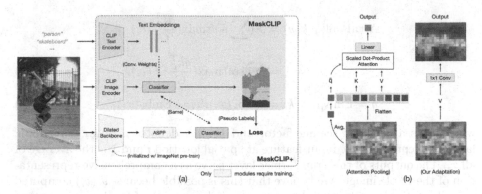

Fig. 2. Overview of MaskCLIP/MaskCLIP+. Compared to the conventional fine-tuning method, the key to the success of MaskCLIP is keeping the pre-trained weights frozen and making minimal adaptation to preserve the visual-language association. Besides, to compensate for the weakness of using the CLIP image encoder for segmentation, which is designed for classification, MaskCLIP+ uses the outputs of MaskCLIP as pseudo labels and trains a more advanced segmentation network such as DeepLabv2 [5]

To evaluate the segmentation performance of this modified DeepLab on both seen and unseen classes, we train it on a subset of classes in the dataset, considering the remaining classes as unseen ones. We have tried a series of mapper architectures. Although they perform well on seen classes, in all these cases the modified DeepLab fails to segment unseen classes with satisfying performance. We hypothesize that this is mainly because the original visual-language association of CLIP features has been broken: (1) the backbone is slightly different from the image encoder in terms of network architecture; (2) weights initialized from the image encoder have been updated during fine-tuning; (3) an extra mapper, which is trained only on data of seen classes, is introduced therefore leading to insufficient generality.

3.3 MaskCLIP

Failing the fine-tuning attempt, we turn to a solution that avoids introducing additional parameters and modifying the feature space of CLIP. To this end, we carefully revisit the image encoder of CLIP, especially its unique global attention pooling layer. As shown in Fig. 2(b), different from conventional global averaged pooling, the image encoder of CLIP adopts a Transformer-style multi-head attention layer where globally average-pooled feature works as the query, and feature at each spatial location generates a key-value pair. Consequently, the output of this layer is a spatial weighted-sum of the incoming feature map followed by a linear layer $\mathcal{F}(\cdot)$:

$$\text{AttnPool}(\bar{q}, k, v) = \mathcal{F}(\sum_i \text{softmax}(\frac{\bar{q}k_i^{\mathsf{T}}}{C})v_i)$$

$$= \sum_i \text{softmax}(\frac{\bar{q}k_i^{\mathsf{T}}}{C})\mathcal{F}(v_i), \tag{3}$$

$$\bar{q} = \text{Emb}_{\text{q}}(\bar{x}), \ k_i = \text{Emb}_{\text{k}}(x_i), \ v_i = \text{Emb}_{\text{v}}(x_i), \tag{4}$$

where C is a constant scaling factor and $\text{Emb}(\cdot)$ denotes a linear embedding layer[1]. x_i represents the input feature at spatial location i and $\bar{x}$ is the average of all x_i. The outputs of the Transformer layer serve as a comprehensive representation of the whole image. We believe that this is possible because $\mathcal{F}(v_i)$ computed at each spatial location already captures a rich response of local semantics that correspond well with tokens in the text embeddings of CLIP.

Based on such a hypothesis, as shown in Fig. 2(b), we directly modify the image encoder of CLIP in our new attempt: (1) removing the query and key embedding layers; (2) reformulating the value-embedding layer and the last linear layer into two respective 1×1 convolutional layers. Moreover, we keep the text encoder unchanged and it takes prompts with target classes as the input. The resulting text embedding of each class is used as the classifier. We name the resulting model as MaskCLIP since it yields pixel-level mask predictions instead of a global image-level prediction. We then evaluate MaskCLIP on various standard segmentation benchmarks as well as web-crawled images. As shown in Fig. 1, MaskCLIP can output reasonable results without any fine-tuning nor annotations. More qualitative results and quantitative results with respect to the mIoU metric are included in the experiment section.

One might argue that, since the global attention pooling is a self-attention layer, even without modification, it can also generate dense features. However, since query $\bar{q}$ is the only query trained during the CLIP pre-training, this naïve solution fails. We treat this solution as the baseline and compare its results with ours in the experiments. Moreover, the Transformer layer in ViT is very similar to the global attention pooling. In fact, the only two differences are: (1) the global query is generated by a special [CLS] token instead of the average among all spatial locations; (2) Transformer layer has a residual connection. Therefore, by replacing $\bar{q}$ with $q_{[cls]}$ and adding input x to the output, MaskCLIP can work with the ViT backbone.

Despite the simplicity of MaskCLIP in comparison to existing segmentation approaches, the proposed method enjoys multiple unique merits inherited from CLIP. First, MaskCLIP can be used as a free segmentation annotator to provide rich and novel supervision signals for segmentation methods working with limited labels. Second, since the visual-language association of CLIP is retained in MaskCLIP, it naturally possesses the ability to segment open vocabulary classes, as well as fine-grained classes described by free-form phrases, such as

---

[1] Here we have simplified the formula by ignoring the channel-wise splitting and concatenation.

white car and *red bus*. Third, since the CLIP is trained on raw web-curated images, CLIP demonstrates great robustness to natural distribution shift [44] and input corruptions [46]. We verify that MaskCLIP preserves such robustness to some extent.

Key Smoothing and Prompt Denoising. To further improve the performance of MaskCLIP, we propose two refinement strategies, namely *key smoothing* and *prompt denoising*. Recall that, in Eq. 3, besides $\bar{q}$, key features k_i also get trained during CLIP pre-training. However, in the original MaskCLIP, k_i is simply discard. Hence, here we seek to utilize this information to refine the final output. Key features can be viewed as the descriptor of the corresponding patch, therefore patches with similar key features should yield similar predictions. With this hypothesis, we propose to smooth the predictions with:

$$\text{pred}_i = \sum_j \cos(\frac{k_i}{\|k_i\|_2}, \frac{k_j}{\|k_j\|_2})\text{pred}_i, \tag{5}$$

where k_i and pred_i are key features and class confidence predictions at spatial location i, while $\|\cdot\|_2$ and $\cos(\cdot)$ denote L2 normalization and cosine similarity. We name this strategy as key smoothing.

In addition, we also observe that when dealing with many target classes, since only a small proportion of the classes appear in a single image, the rest classes are in fact distractors and undermine the performance. Therefore, we propose prompt denoising, which removes the prompt with target class if its class confidence at all spatial locations is all less than a threshold $t = 0.5$.

3.4   MaskCLIP+

While MaskCLIP does not require any training, its network architecture is rigid because it adopts the image encoder of CLIP. To relax it from this constraint and benefit from more advanced architectures tailored for segmentation, such as DeepLab [5] and PSPNet [54], we propose MaskCLIP+. Instead of directly applying MaskCLIP for test-time prediction, MaskCLIP+ regard its predictions as training-time pseudo ground-truth labels. Together with an adopted self-training strategy, MaskCLIP+ is thus free from the restriction on its backbone architecture. As shown in Fig. 2(a), we take DeepLabv2 [5] as the backbone of MaskCLIP+ to ensure a fair comparison with previous segmentation methods.

MaskCLIP-Guided Learning. In MaskCLIP+, we leverage the predictions of MaskCLIP to guide the training of another target network comprising an architecture tailored to segmentation task. In parallel to the target network, we feed the same pre-processed image input to the MaskCLIP and use the predictions of MaskCLIP as pseudo ground-truth labels to train the target network.

In addition, we replace the classifier of the target network with that of MaskCLIP, to preserve the network's ability for open vocabulary prediction.

MaskCLIP-guided learning is also applicable in the transductive zero-shot segmentation setting. Specifically, while pixels of both seen and unseen classes are observed, only annotations of seen classes are available. In this case, we only use MaskCLIP to generate pseudo labels for the unlabeled pixels. Compared to SOTA methods, MaskCLIP+ obtains remarkably better results across three standard benchmarks, namely PASCAL VOC 2012 [14], PASCAL Context [37], and COCO Stuff [2], where the results of MaskCLIP+ are even on par with that of fully-supervised baselines.

We note that some related attempts [18,50], targeting object detection, perform knowledge distillation between the image-level visual features of CLIP and the features of a target model. Different from such feature-level guidance, we adopt pseudo labels in our case. This is because our target network, with a segmentation-tailored architecture, is structurally distinct from the image encoder of CLIP. Therefore, distillation by feature matching may be a suboptimal strategy. In fact, as reported by [18], under zero-shot setting, such feature-level guidance indeed results in conflicts between the performance of seen and unseen classes. On the contrary, by adopting pseudo labels in MaskCLIP+, we do not observe any performance drop on seen classes.

Self-Training. It is expected that after certain training iterations, the target network guided by MaskCLIP will outperform MaskCLIP, rendering the latter suboptimal for further guidance as it gradually becomes an inferior model over time. Empirically, we also find that MaskCLIP-guided learning reaches an upper bound at around 1/10 of the standard training schedule. To further improve the performance, we swap out MaskCLIP and let the target model generate pseudo labels for itself. This is commonly referred to as self-training.

4   Experiments

Datasets. We conduct experiments on three standard segmentation benchmarks, namely PASCAL VOC 2012 [14], PASCAL Context [37], and COCO Stuff [2]. PASCAL VOC 2012 contains 1,426 training images with 20 object classes plus a background class. Following common practice, we augment it with the Semantic Boundaries Dataset [20]. PASCAL Context labels PASCAL VOC 2010 (4,998/5,105 train/validation images) with segmentation annotations of 520 object/stuff classes, from which the most common 59 classes are treated as foreground while the rest are regarded as background. COCO Stuff extends the COCO dataset, which contains segmentation annotations of 80 object classes on 164K images, with additional 91 stuff classes.

Text Embedding. We follow the same process to construct text embeddings as Gu *et al.* [18]. Specifically, we feed prompt engineered texts into the text encoder

Table 1. Annotation-free segmentation (mIoU). (a) We evaluate the performance of MaskCLIP(+) on two standard datasets. For Pascal Context, we ignore the evaluation on the background class. The target model of MaskCLIP+ is Deeplabv2-ResNet101. KS and PD denote key smoothing and prompt denoising respectively. And they are not used in MaskCLIP+. **(b)** We test the robustness of MaskCLIP on Pascal Context under various types of corruption

(a)

Method	CLIP	PASCAL Context	COCO Stuff
Baseline	r50	8.3	4.6
	vit16	9.0	4.3
MaskCLIP	r50	18.5	10.2
	+KS	21.0	12.4
	+PD	19.0	10.8
	+KS+PD	21.8	12.8
	vit16	21.7	12.5
	+KS	23.9	13.8
	+PD	23.1	13.2
	+KS+PD	25.5	14.6
MaskCLIP+	r50	23.9	13.6
	vit16	31.1	18.0

(b)

Corruption	Level 1		Level 5	
	r50	vit16	r50	vit16
None	18.5	21.7	18.5	21.7
Gaussian noise	13.7	19.6	2.1	6.8
Shot noise	14.0	19.6	2.4	7.5
Impulse noise	9.9	17.3	2.1	7.2
Speckle noise	15.1	20.0	5.6	11.4
Gaussian blur	17.4	21.6	4.3	14.1
Defocus blur	15.7	20.8	6.6	15.5
Spatter	17.1	20.5	7.8	12.2
JPEG	15.7	20.8	7.6	14.5

of CLIP with 85 prompt templates, such as *there is a {class name} in the scene*, and average the resulting 85 text embeddings of the same class.

Implementation Details. We implement our method on the *MMSegmentation*[2] codebase and inherit its training configurations. Input resolutions are set as 512×512. When using ViT, the pre-trained positional embeddings adopt bicubic interpolation. MaskCLIP requires no training and we train MaskCLIP+ on 4 T V100 GPUs with a batch size of 16. For annotation-free segmentation, we perform MaskCLIP-guided learning for 4k/8k iterations on PASCAL Context/COCO Stuff with DeepLabv2-ResNet101 as the backbone segmentor. Self-training is not used in this setting. For zero-shot segmentation, we choose the lightest training schedule provided by *MMSegmentation*, which is 20k/40k/80k for PASCAL VOC/PASCAL Context/COCO Stuff. The first 1/10 training iterations adopt MaskCLIP-guided learning and the rest adopts self-training. For fair comparisons, we choose DeepLabv2 as the target model for PASCAL VOC and COCO Stuff and DeepLabv3+ for PASCAL Context. All use the ResNet-101 backbone initialized with the ImageNet pre-trained weights. Finally, we use the publicly available CLIP-ResNet-50 and CLIP-ViT-B/16 models[3].

---

[2] https://github.com/open-mmlab/mmsegmentation.
[3] https://github.com/openai/CLIP.

4.1   Annotation-Free Segmentation

In this challenging setting, no annotation is provided during training. We first evaluate the mIoU performance on two standard datasets, PASCAL Context and COCO-Stuff. Then we collect images from Flickr to show interesting qualitative results on novel concepts, such as *Batman* and *Joker*. Finally, we test the robustness of MaskCLIP under various image corruptions.

Performance on Standard Datasets. In Table 1a, we show mean Intersection over Union (mIoU) results on PASCAL Context and COCO-Stuff. The baseline in the table refers to directly using dense features from the CLIP's image encoder without any modification. As shown in the table, MaskCLIP outperforms the baseline by huge margins, indicating it is essential to avoid computing attention of the last attention layer and instead value features should be directly used. The results also show that key smoothing and prompt denoising are effective and are orthogonal to each other. Therefore, we empirically conclude that for each spatial location, the query features should be discarded and key/value features can be re-organized into final predictions. Furthermore, with the predictions of MaskCLIP as pseudo labels, MaskCLIP+ significantly improves the performance, *e.g.*, on PASCAL Context, without any human annotation, MaskCLIP+(ViT-B/16) obtains 31.1 mIoU. One may notice that ViT almost consistently surpasses ResNet. Apart from ViT-B/16 has more FLOPs than ResNet-50, another possible reason is that ViT only downsamples the input by 16 times whereas ResNet downsamples 32 times, which particularly matters

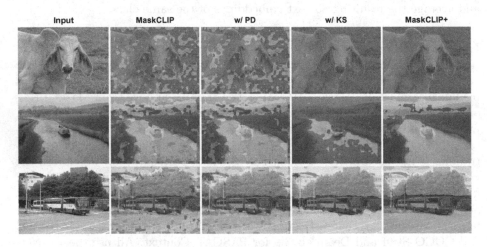

Fig. 3. Qualitative results on PASCAL Context. Here all results are obtained **without** any annotation. PD and KS refer to prompt denoising and key smoothing respectively. With PD, we can see some distraction classes are removed. KS is more aggressive. Its outputs are much less noisy but are dominated by a small number of classes. Finally, MaskCLIP+ yields the best results

for dense prediction tasks. Besides quantitative results, in Fig. 3, we also visualize the outputs of each MaskCLIP variant.

Open-Vocabulary Segmentation on Web-Crawled Images. MaskCLIP inherits the open-vocabulary ability from CLIP and does not require annotations. Therefore, we can deploy it on several interesting setups where the target classes are (1) more fine-grained, such as *red car, yellow car*; (2) of certain imagery properties, *e.g.*, blurry; (3) novel concepts like *Batman, Joker*. To this end, we collect images from Flickr then directly evaluate these images on MaskCLIP and train MaskCLIP+ with only MaskCLIP-guided learning. Note that, for the background, we enumerate a set of classes that might appear in the background and regard them as a whole as the background class. Results in Fig. 4 are impressive given the open-vocabulary targets and being annotation-free. Besides, results from MaskCLIP+ are less noisy and more accurate than MaskCLIP, which is complementary to the quantitative results.

Fig. 4. Qualitative results on Web images. Here we show the segmentation results of MaskCLIP and MaskCLIP+ on various **unseen classes**, including fine-grained classes such as cars in different colors/imagery properties, celebrities, and animation characters. All results are obtained **without** any annotation

Robustness Under Corruption. CLIP is trained on web-curated images, whose quality and distribution are more diverse than well-pre-processed datasets. Radford *et al.* [44] and Ravula *et al.* [46] demonstrate the robustness of CLIP on natural distribution shift and artificial corruption respectively. While these explorations are done for image classification, we benchmark its robustness for dense prediction tasks. Specifically, we impose various corruptions used in ImageNet-C [23] with different severity levels on images in PASCAL Context and evaluate on MaskCLIP. In Table 1b, MaskCLIP models based on CLIP-ViT-B/16 are much more robust than CLIP-ResNet-50. In particular, CLIP-ViT-B/16 rarely suffers from degradation across a wide range of corruptions

Table 2. Zero-shot segmentation performances. ST stands for self-training. mIoU(U) denotes mIoU of the unseen classes. SPNet-C is the SPNet with calibration. On PASCAL Context, all methods use DeepLabv3+-ResNet101 as the backbone segmentation model and the rest two datasets use DeepLabv2-ResNet101. For MaskCLIP+, CLIP-ResNet-50 is used to generate pseudo labels

Method	PASCAL-VOC			COCO-stuff			PASCAL-context		
	mIoU(U)	mIoU	hIoU	mIoU(U)	mIoU	hIoU	mIoU(U)	mIoU	hIoU
Inductive									
SPNet	0.0	56.9	0.0	0.7	31.6	1.4	·	·	·
SPNet-C	15.6	63.2	26.1	8.7	32.8	14.0	·	·	·
ZS3Net	17.7	61.6	28.7	9.5	33.3	15.0	12.7	19.4	15.8
CaGNet	26.6	65.5	39.7	12.2	33.5	18.2	18.5	23.2	21.2
Transductive									
SPNet+ST	25.8	64.8	38.8	26.9	34.0	30.3	·	·	·
ZS3Net+ST	21.2	63.0	33.3	10.6	33.7	16.2	20.7	26.0	23.4
CaGNet+ST	30.3	65.8	43.7	13.4	33.7	19.5	·	·	·
STRICT	35.6	70.9	49.8	30.3	34.9	32.6	·	·	·
MaskCLIP+	**86.1**	**88.1**	**87.4**	**54.7**	**39.6**	**45.0**	**66.7**	**48.1**	**53.3**
	+50.5	+17.2	+37.6	+24.4	+4.7	+12.4	+46.0	+22.1	+29.9
Fully Sup	·	88.2	·	·	39.9	·	·	48.2	·

with level 1 severity and is cable of generating reasonable labels even under the most severe corruptions (level 5^4).

4.2   Zero-Shot Segmentation

Apart from annotation-free segmentation, MaskCLIP+ can also be applied to the zero-shot segmentation task with minor effort. Specifically, in the zero-shot setting, pixels of certain classes do not have annotations, to which MaskCLIP can assign reliable pseudo labels.

Zero-Shot Setups. Traditionally, zero-shot segmentation methods train on a subset of classes, named seen classes, with ground-truth annotations, and during inference, both seen and unseen classes are evaluated. Depending on whether the unlabeled pixels are observed during training, the setting can be split into inductive (not observed) and transductive (observed). Our method conforms to the transductive setting.

The selection of seen classes varies among previous works and we follow the most common setups, where for PASCAL VOC, the background class is ignored and *potted plant, sheep, sofa, train, tv monitor* are chosen as the 5 unseen classes;

---

[4] The severity level is controlled by certain coefficients, such as kernel size, specified in ImageNet-C [23].

for PASCAL Context, the background is not ignored and *cow, motorbike, sofa, cat, boat, fence, bird, tv monitor, keyboard, aeroplane* are unseen; and for COCO Stuff, *frisbee, skateboard, cardboard, carrot, scissors, suitcase, giraffe, cow, road, wall concrete, tree, grass, river, clouds, playing field* are unseen. We report the mean Intersection over Union (mIoU) of seen, unseen, and all classes as well as the harmonic mean (hIoU) of seen and unseen mIoUs as evaluation metrics.

We compare MaskCLIP+ with SOTA methods including SPNet [49], ZS3Net [1], CaGNet [19], and STRICT [40]. ZS3Net and CaGNet are generative approaches, while SPNet is non-generative and more simple but requires post-possessing step of calibration (SPNet-C). STRICT improves SPNet by a self-training strategy and is free of calibration. Compare with these methods, our MaskCLIP+ does not rely on any particular network architecture nor post-possessing. Note that similar to CLIP, all methods, except for ZS3Net, do not exclude unseen classes during pre-training. Besides, MaskCLIP+ also follows the rule that pixel-level annotations of unseen classes are prohibited. Thus, the comparison is fair.

Despite being simple, MaskCLIP+ achieves a strikingly good result. As shown in Table 2, it surpasses all methods on all datasets with large margins. On PASCAL VOC, PASCAL Context, and COCO Stuff, in terms of unseen mIoUs, MaskCLIP+ improves the previous SOTA by 50.5, 24.4, and 46.0 respectively (on a scale of 100). Note that the overall mIoU of MaskCLIP+ is on par with that of fully supervised baselines. Please refer to Table 2 for more specific numbers.

Table 3. Ablations of MaskCLIP+. Experiments are performed on the PASCAL VOC dataset under the zero-shot setting

Method	mIoU(S)	mIoU(U)	mIoU	hIoU
Adapted DeepLabv2	83.4	3.7	63.5	7.0
+MaskCLIP-Guided	**89.5**	72.8	85.3	80.3
+Self-Training	88.8	**86.1**	**88.1**	**87.4**

Ablation Studies of MaskCLIP+. We perform ablation studies on the PASCAL VOC zero-shot segmentation setting. As shown in Table 3, we first examine the two proposed strategies in MaskCLIP+. Compared to the adapted DeepLabv2, whose classifier is replaced with the MaskCLIP classifier, MaskCLIP-guided learning improves the unseen mIoU from 3.7 to 72.8 and the result is further improved by self-training to 86.1. However, there is a slight degradation on seen classes when using self-training (from 89.5 to 88.8) partially due to model drifting. Overall, MaskCLIP+ performs better than MaskCLIP on unseen classes and surpasses the baseline DeepLabv2 on seen classes in the same time.

5   Conclusion

This paper presents our exploration of applying CLIP in semantic segmentation, as an early attempt that studies the applicability of pre-trained visual-language models in pixel-level dense prediction tasks. While the conventional fine-tuning paradigm fails to benefit from CLIP, we find the image encoder of CLIP already possesses the ability to directly work as a segmentation model. The resulting model, termed MaskCLIP, can be readily deployed on various semantic segmentation settings without re-training. On top of the success of MaskCLIP, we further propose MaskCLIP+ that leverages MaskCLIP to provide training-time pseudo labels for unlabeled pixels, which thus can be applied to more segmentation-tailored architectures beyond just the image encoder of CLIP. On standard transductive zero-shot segmentation benchmarks, MaskCLIP+ significantly improves previous SOTA results. More importantly, MaskCLIP+ can be readily employed for segmenting more challenging unseen classes, such as celebrities and animation characters.

Acknowledgement. This study is supported under the RIE2020 Industry Alignment Fund - Industry Collaboration Projects (IAF-ICP) Funding Initiative, as well as cash and in-kind contribution from the industry partner(s). This study is also supported by Singapore MOE AcRF Tier 2 (MOE-T2EP20120-0001) and Shanghai AI Laboratory.

References

1. Bucher, M., Vu, T.H., Cord, M., Pérez, P.: Zero-shot semantic segmentation. In: NeurIPS (2019)
2. Caesar, H., Uijlings, J., Ferrari, V.: Coco-stuff: thing and stuff classes in context. In: CVPR (2018)
3. Caron, M., Misra, I., Mairal, J., Goyal, P., Bojanowski, P., Joulin, A.: Unsupervised learning of visual features by contrasting cluster assignments. In: NeurIPS (2020)
4. Chen, L.-C., et al.: Naive-Student: leveraging semi-supervised learning in video sequences for urban scene segmentation. In: Vedaldi, A., Bischof, H., Brox, T., Frahm, J.-M. (eds.) ECCV 2020. LNCS, vol. 12354, pp. 695–714. Springer, Cham (2020). https://doi.org/10.1007/978-3-030-58545-7_40
5. Chen, L.-C., Zhu, Y., Papandreou, G., Schroff, F., Adam, H.: Encoder-decoder with atrous separable convolution for semantic image segmentation. In: Ferrari, V., Hebert, M., Sminchisescu, C., Weiss, Y. (eds.) ECCV 2018. LNCS, vol. 11211, pp. 833–851. Springer, Cham (2018). https://doi.org/10.1007/978-3-030-01234-2_49
6. Chen, T., Kornblith, S., Norouzi, M., Hinton, G.: A simple framework for contrastive learning of visual representations. In: ICML (2020)
7. Chen, X., Yuan, Y., Zeng, G., Wang, J.: Semi-supervised semantic segmentation with cross pseudo supervision. In: CVPR (2021)
8. Chen, X., et al.: Microsoft coco captions: data collection and evaluation server. arXiv preprint (2015)
9. Chen, X., He, K.: Exploring simple siamese representation learning. In: CVPR (2021)
10. Deng, J., Dong, W., Socher, R., Li, L.J., Li, K., Fei-Fei, L.: Imagenet: a large-scale hierarchical image database. In: CVPR (2009)

11. Desai, K., Johnson, J.: Virtex: learning visual representations from textual annotations. In: CVPR (2021)

12. Doersch, C., Gupta, A., Efros, A.A.: Unsupervised visual representation learning by context prediction. In: ICCV (2015)

13. Dosovitskiy, A., Springenberg, J.T., Riedmiller, M., Brox, T.: Discriminative unsupervised feature learning with convolutional neural networks. In: NeurIPS (2014)

14. Everingham, M., Eslami, S.A., Van Gool, L., Williams, C.K., Winn, J., Zisserman, A.: The pascal visual object classes challenge: a retrospective. IJCV **111**, 98–136 (2015)

15. Gomez, L., Patel, Y., Rusiñol, M., Karatzas, D., Jawahar, C.: Self-supervised learning of visual features through embedding images into text topic spaces. In: CVPR (2017)

16. Gordo, A., Larlus, D.: Beyond instance-level image retrieval: leveraging captions to learn a global visual representation for semantic retrieval. In: CVPR (2017)

17. Grill, J.B., et al.: Bootstrap your own latent: a new approach to self-supervised learning. In: NeurIPS (2020)

18. Gu, X., Lin, T.Y., Kuo, W., Cui, Y.: Open-vocabulary object detection via vision and language knowledge distillation. arXiv preprint (2021)

19. Gu, Z., Zhou, S., Niu, L., Zhao, Z., Zhang, L.: Context-aware feature generation for zero-shot semantic segmentation. In: ACM MM (2020)

20. Hariharan, B., Arbeláez, P., Bourdev, L., Maji, S., Malik, J.: Semantic contours from inverse detectors. In: ICCV (2011)

21. He, K., Fan, H., Wu, Y., Xie, S., Girshick, R.: Momentum contrast for unsupervised visual representation learning. In: CVPR (2020)

22. He, K., Zhang, X., Ren, S., Sun, J.: Deep residual learning for image recognition. In: CVPR (2016)

23. Hendrycks, D., Dietterich, T.: Benchmarking neural network robustness to common corruptions and perturbations. In: ICLR (2019)

24. Hessel, J., Holtzman, A., Forbes, M., Bras, R.L., Choi, Y.: Clipscore: a reference-free evaluation metric for image captioning. In: EMNLP (2021)

25. Hu, P., Sclaroff, S., Saenko, K.: Uncertainty-aware learning for zero-shot semantic segmentation. In: NeurIPS (2020)

26. Hung, W.C., Tsai, Y.H., Liou, Y.T., Lin, Y.Y., Yang, M.H.: Adversarial learning for semi-supervised semantic segmentation. In: BMVC (2018)

27. Ibrahim, M.S., Vahdat, A., Ranjbar, M., Macready, W.G.: Semi-supervised semantic image segmentation with self-correcting networks. In: CVPR (2020)

28. Iscen, A., Tolias, G., Avrithis, Y., Chum, O.: Label propagation for deep semi-supervised learning. In: CVPR (2019)

29. Jain, A., Tancik, M., Abbeel, P.: Putting nerf on a diet: semantically consistent few-shot view synthesis. In: ICCV (2021)

30. Jia, C., et al.: Scaling up visual and vision-language representation learning with noisy text supervision. In: ICML (2021)

31. Kato, N., Yamasaki, T., Aizawa, K.: Zero-shot semantic segmentation via variational mapping. In: ICCVW (2019)

32. Lee, D.H.: Pseudo-label: the simple and efficient semi-supervised learning method for deep neural networks. In: ICMLW (2013)

33. Li, P., Wei, Y., Yang, Y.: Consistent structural relation learning for zero-shot segmentation. In: NeurIPS (2020)

34. Li, X., et al.: Learning to self-train for semi-supervised few-shot classification. In: NeurIPS (2019)

35. Mendel, R., de Souza, L.A., Rauber, D., Papa, J.P., Palm, C.: Semi-supervised segmentation based on error-correcting supervision. In: Vedaldi, A., Bischof, H., Brox, T., Frahm, J.-M. (eds.) ECCV 2020. LNCS, vol. 12374, pp. 141–157. Springer, Cham (2020). https://doi.org/10.1007/978-3-030-58526-6_9

36. Mittal, S., Tatarchenko, M., Brox, T.: Semi-supervised semantic segmentation with high-and low-level consistency. IEEE TPAMI **43**, 1369–1379 (2019)

37. Mottaghi, R., et al.: The role of context for object detection and semantic segmentation in the wild. In: CVPR (2014)

38. Noroozi, M., Favaro, P.: Unsupervised learning of visual representations by solving jigsaw puzzles. In: Leibe, B., Matas, J., Sebe, N., Welling, M. (eds.) ECCV 2016. LNCS, vol. 9910, pp. 69–84. Springer, Cham (2016). https://doi.org/10.1007/978-3-319-46466-4_5

39. Ouali, Y., Hudelot, C., Tami, M.: Semi-supervised semantic segmentation with cross-consistency training. In: CVPR (2020)

40. Pastore, G., Cermelli, F., Xian, Y., Mancini, M., Akata, Z., Caputo, B.: A closer look at self-training for zero-label semantic segmentation. In: CVPRW (2021)

41. Patashnik, O., Wu, Z., Shechtman, E., Cohen-Or, D., Lischinski, D.: Styleclip: text-driven manipulation of stylegan imagery. In: ICCV (2021)

42. Pham, H., Dai, Z., Xie, Q., Le, Q.V.: Meta pseudo labels. In: CVPR (2021)

43. Quattoni, A., Collins, M., Darrell, T.: Learning visual representations using images with captions. In: CVPR (2007)

44. Radford, A., et al.: Learning transferable visual models from natural language supervision. In: ICML (2021)

45. Rao, Y., et al.: Denseclip: language-guided dense prediction with context-aware prompting. arXiv preprint (2021)

46. Ravula, S., Smyrnis, G., Jordan, M., Dimakis, A.G.: Inverse problems leveraging pre-trained contrastive representations. In: NeurIPS (2021)

47. Sariyildiz, M.B., Perez, J., Larlus, D.: Learning visual representations with caption annotations. In: Vedaldi, A., Bischof, H., Brox, T., Frahm, J.-M. (eds.) ECCV 2020. LNCS, vol. 12353, pp. 153–170. Springer, Cham (2020). https://doi.org/10.1007/978-3-030-58598-3_10

48. Vaswani, A., et al.: Attention is all you need. In: NeurIPS (2017)

49. Xian, Y., Choudhury, S., He, Y., Schiele, B., Akata, Z.: Semantic projection network for zero-and few-label semantic segmentation. In: CVPR (2019)

50. Xie, J., Zheng, S.: Zsd-yolo: zero-shot yolo detection using vision-language knowledge distillation. arXiv preprint (2021)

51. Yosinski, J., Clune, J., Bengio, Y., Lipson, H.: How transferable are features in deep neural networks? In: NeurIPS (2014)

52. Yuan, X., et al.: Multimodal contrastive training for visual representation learning. In: CVPR (2021)

53. Zhao, H., Puig, X., Zhou, B., Fidler, S., Torralba, A.: Open vocabulary scene parsing. In: ICCV (2017)

54. Zhao, H., Shi, J., Qi, X., Wang, X., Jia, J.: Pyramid scene parsing network. In: CVPR (2017)

55. Zou, Y., et al.: Pseudoseg: designing pseudo labels for semantic segmentation. In: ICLR (2021)

3D Compositional Zero-Shot Learning with DeCompositional Consensus

Muhammad Ferjad Naeem[1]([✉])[ID], Evin Pınar Örnek[2][ID], Yongqin Xian[1][ID],
Luc Van Gool[1][ID], and Federico Tombari[2,3][ID]

[1] ETH Zürich, Zürich, Switzerland
ferjad.naeem@vision.ee.ethz.ch
[2] TUM, Munich, Germany
[3] Google Zurich, Zürich, Switzerland

Abstract. Parts represent a basic unit of geometric and semantic similarity across different objects. We argue that part knowledge should be composable beyond the observed object classes. Towards this, we present 3D Compositional Zero-shot Learning as a problem of part generalization from seen to unseen object classes for semantic segmentation. We provide a structured study through benchmarking the task with the proposed Compositional-PartNet dataset. This dataset is created by processing the original PartNet to maximize part overlap across different objects. The existing point cloud part segmentation methods fail to generalize to unseen object classes in this setting. As a solution, we propose DeCompositional Consensus, which combines a part segmentation network with a part scoring network. The key intuition to our approach is that a segmentation mask over some parts should have a consensus with its part scores when each part is taken apart. The two networks reason over different part combinations defined in a per-object part prior to generate the most suitable segmentation mask. We demonstrate that our method allows compositional zero-shot segmentation and generalized zero-shot classification, and establishes the state of the art on both tasks.

Keywords: 3D compositional zero-shot learning · Compositionality

1 Introduction

A centaur is a mythological creature with the upper body of a human and the bottom body of a horse. This creature was never observed in our world, yet even a child can label its body parts from the human head to the horse legs. We humans can dissect the knowledge of basic concepts as primitives, like parts from human head to horse legs, to generalize to unseen objects. Cognitive studies have shown

---

M. F. Naeem and E. P. Örnek—Author contributed equally.

Supplementary Information The online version contains supplementary material available at https://doi.org/10.1007/978-3-031-19815-1_41.

© The Author(s), under exclusive license to Springer Nature Switzerland AG 2022
S. Avidan et al. (Eds.): ECCV 2022, LNCS 13688, pp. 713–730, 2022.
https://doi.org/10.1007/978-3-031-19815-1_41

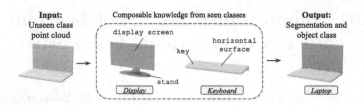

Fig. 1. We aim to compose parts (*e.g.,* display screen, key, horizontal surface) from seen (*e.g., Display, Keyboard*) to unseen object classes (*e.g., Laptop*) for semantic segmentation and classification in 3D point clouds.

that humans learn part-whole relations in hippocampal memory to achieve object understanding through compositionality [18,47]. Compositionality has evolved as a survival need since every combination of every primitive cannot be observed.

Parts represent a basic primitive of geometric and semantic similarity across objects. Recently, PartNet dataset has been introduced to study fine-grained semantic segmentation of parts [35]. This has inspired several architectural works towards improving supervised fine-grained segmentation in 3D models [5,54, 57]. A parallel line of work uses the concept of parts to improve tasks like 3D reconstruction with hierarchical decomposition [39], unsupervised segmentation by finding repeated structural patterns [29], and instance segmentation in unseen objects [9]. However, these works do not predict semantic part classes.

With the availability of RGB-D sensors and the ease of acquiring 3D data in domains from augmented reality to robotic perception, the need for object understanding beyond seen object classes has emerged [2,38,51]. A model is unlikely to be trained for all possible existing objects [10,12], however, man-made environments consist of objects that share similarities through their parts. In this scenario, reasoning over learned parts can present an avenue for generalization to unseen objects classes. Zero-shot learning with 3D data has received far less attention compared to 2D domain. In this work, we introduce a new task, namely 3D Compositional Zero-Shot Learning (3D-CZSL), aiming at jointly segmenting and classifying 3D point clouds of both seen and unseen object classes (see Fig. 1). 3D-CZSL is a challenging task as it requires generalizing parts from seen object classes to unseen classes that can be composed entirely of these parts.

Our contributions are as follows: (1) We formalize zero-shot compositionality for 3D object understanding with semantic parts and introduce the 3D-CZSL task. To the best of our knowledge, we present the first work for joint classification and semantic part labeling for compositional zero-shot learning in 3D. (2) We establish a novel benchmark through Compositional PartNet (C-PartNet), which enables research in 3D-CZSL through 16 seen and 8 unseen object classes. (3) We show that existing point cloud models fail to generalize beyond the seen object classes, whereas the performance of existing 2D zero-shot methods is severely limited in the 3D domain. (4) We propose a novel method, DeCompositional Consensus, which maximizes agreement between a segmentation hypothesis and its decomposed parts. Our method sets the state of the art for 3D-CZSL.

2   Related Work

Our work lies at the intersection of compositionality, zero-shot learning, and 3D point cloud part segmentation and discovery.

Compositionality is the notion of describing a whole through its parts, studied thoroughly in many disciplines such as mathematics, physics, and linguistics. Hoffman [19] and Biederman [4] suggested that human object recognition is based on compositionality. They heavily influenced both traditional and modern computer vision research, such as describing objects by their primitives in Deformable Part Models [15], images as a hierarchy of features in Convolutional Neural Networks [26,61], understanding a scene through its components as in Scene Graphs [22], events as a set of actions as in Space-Time Region Graphs [53]. Parts have been used as semantic and geometric object primitives, which were seen to be captured within CNN kernels implicitly [16,17].

Zero-Shot Learning (ZSL) addresses the task of recognizing object classes whose instances have not been seen during training [25,49,56]. This is attained through auxiliary information in the form of attributes (ALE [1]), word embeddings (SPNet [55]), or text descriptions [46]. *Compositional zero-shot learning (CZSL)* focuses on detecting unseen compositions of already observed primitives. The current literature on the topic focuses on state-object compositionality. Towards this, one line of research aims to learn a transformation between objects and states [28,34,37]. Another line proposes a joint compatibility function with respect to the image, state, and object [31,42,58]. Graph methods are also recently used in this direction including learning a causal graph of state object transformations [3] and using the dependency structure of state object compositions to learn graph embeddings [30,36]. There have been some preliminary works exploring *zero-shot learning in 3D* as an extension of 2D methods including projecting on word embeddings [12], using transductive approaches [10], along with some unlabelled data [11], and using generative models to learn the label distribution of unseen classes [32].

3D Part Segmentation and Discovery aims at parsing 3D objects into semantically and geometrically significant parts. The PartNet dataset [35] enabled studying fine-grained 3D semantic segmentation, hierarchical segmentation, and instance segmentation. The existing point cloud processing methods accomplish the task through conditioning the model over the known object class. PointNet models [43,44] provide multi-layer-perceptron (MLP) based solutions, DGCNN [54] uses graph convolutions for point clouds, ConvPoint [5] preprocesses points to define neighborhoods for convolutions, GDANet [57] uses attention in addition to MLP and currently holds state of the art for part semantic segmentation. Capsule Networks [48,62] propose architectural changes that implicitly model parts for tasks like object classification and segmentation.

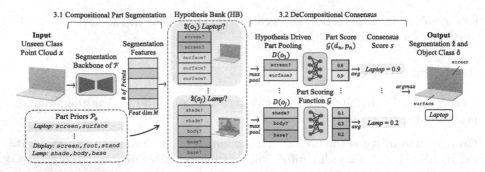

Fig. 2. DeCompositional Consensus(DCC) combines our compositional part segmentation function $\mathcal{F}$ with our part scoring function $\mathcal{G}$. We use the Part Prior $\mathcal{P}_o$ of which parts can exist in each object class to populate the Hypothesis Bank with multiple segmentation masks. These hypotheses are used in a Hypothesis Driven Part Pooling to get a part descriptor of each part as an input to the part scoring function $\mathcal{G}$ to calculate the DCC Score. This score measures the agreement of the segmentation mask with its part scores when each part is taken apart like lego blocks. Hypothesis with the maximum DCC score is selected for compositional zero-shot segmentation and zero-shot classification.

An alternate line of work uses the idea of parts in objects for downstream tasks like instance segmentation and point cloud reconstruction. This includes discovering geometrically similar part prototypes, similar to superpixels [29], predicting category-agnostic segmentation through a clustering approach [52], finding repetitive structural patterns in instances of an object [9], modeling 3D objects as compositions of cuboids [50], superquadrics [21,39,40], convex functions [13], and binary space partitioning planes [8] through deep learning.

Our work lies at the intersection of these three areas. Similar to CZSL works [3,28,34,36,37], we study the compositionality of learned primitives, however, we are interested in parts of objects rather than state-object relations. Similar to ZSL works [1,25,46,49,55,56], we learn classification scores of unseen object classes, however, our method only uses parts as side information and does not rely on any pretrained models like word embeddings. Similar to part discovery in objects [9,23,29,39,62], we rely on parts as a basic unit of understanding an object. However, instead of geometric primitives, we use human-defined semantic parts, which tightly couple geometry, semantics, and affordances [14]. Our method further has parallels to ensemble learning, where a combination of learners solves the same downstream task [7], however, we use an agreement between different tasks to improve generalization.

3 Proposed Approach

In the following, we formalize the problem and explain the proposed solution.

Problem Formulation. Let T define the training set with instances (x, o, z), where x is an input object point cloud described as a set of points in $\mathbb{R}^3$, o is the object class label from the set of seen object classes $\mathcal{O}_s$ and z is the part segmentation mask labelled with parts p from the set of all possible parts $\mathcal{P}$. We task a model to generalize to a set of unseen object classes $\mathcal{O}_u$, i.e., $\mathcal{O}_s \cap \mathcal{O}_u = \emptyset$. We assume that $\mathcal{O}_u$ is labelled with the same part set P for part segmentation that was completely observed in seen object classes $\mathcal{O}_s$. This makes the part segmentation task as a compositional zero-shot problem and the object classification task as a generalized zero-shot problem, i.e., we predict over the full object set $\mathcal{O} = \mathcal{O}_s \cup \mathcal{O}_u$ at inference for object classification. We further assume that the model has access to a **part prior** for all object classes. For an object class o, this prior is defined as the set of parts $\mathcal{P}_o = \{p_1, ..., p_l\}$ that it can be labelled with for part segmentation.

Method Overview. Part segmentation is a challenging task, as it requires one model to adapt to parts of varying scale, orientation, and geometry for all objects. Existing point cloud part segmentation methods simplify this by learning an object class conditioned model, either by training separate models specialized for each object class [35], or by feeding the object class label as an input to the model (one-hot class vector [43,54,57,62]). However, this requires an object class input at test time which is not available for unseen object classes. In this work, we refer to this case as **object prior**, i.e., the model has access to the ground truth object class. The first step of our approach removes the object prior assumption and proposes Compositional Part Segmentation. In the second step, we propose our model DeCompositional Consensus which predicts the object class using the part segmentation from the previous step. It learns an agreement over a segmentation hypothesis and its part-based object classification score based on the idea of an object being taken apart like Lego blocks. The full model is depicted in Fig. 2.

3.1 Compositional Part Segmentation

We reformulate part segmentation to allow compositional reasoning by encoding the part prior into the optimization criterion and the model inference. Formally, given an input point cloud x, we define $\mathcal{F}(x, p)$ as the part segmentation function, with learnable parameters W, which returns a part score for each part p in the full part set $\mathcal{P}$. At training time, we compute the segmentation loss L_{Seg} from [43,44] as a cross entropy over parts in the part prior $\mathcal{P}_o$ of the ground truth object class o rather than the full part set $\mathcal{P}$. At inference, the predicted part segmentation mask $\hat{z}(o)$ of an object class o is computed over the scores of parts in its part prior:

$$\hat{z}(o) = \arg\max_{p \in \mathcal{P}_o}(\mathcal{F}(x,p)) \tag{1}$$

With the proposed changes, a part segmentation model such as PointNet [43] can now compositionally generate a part segmentation mask for any object class we have a part prior for. Furthermore, the proposed improvements also prevent unintended biases against similar parts in different object classes as shown experimentally later in Table 3b. Notably, when an object prior is available as ground truth class, it defines the upper bound of the part segmentation performance for a model (see Table 1a "Object Prior"). In the absence of an object prior (GT object class), we can predict $|\mathcal{O}|$ segmentation masks (hypotheses) for each object class we have a part prior for, generating the **Hypothesis Bank (HB)**. Next, we introduce our novel method which allows for selecting the most suitable segmentation hypothesis for an input point cloud.

3.2 DeCompositional Consensus

We propose a novel method, **DeCompositional Consensus (DCC)**, which learns an agreement (Consensus) over a segmentation hypothesis and its part-based object classification score when the object is taken apart (DeComposed) into parts like lego blocks as segmented in the hypothesis. DCC is based on the idea that we can learn what a valid part descriptor is from seen object classes to generalize to unseen object classes.

Hypothesis Driven Part Pooling. We extract a part descriptor for each part in a segmentation hypothesis from the point-wise features of the segmentation backbone as shown in Fig. 2. Part segmentation models like PointNet [43] generate this feature representation in the penultimate layer of the model, *i.e.*, before the final per-part segmentation scoring layer. We use the segmentation hypothesis as the pooling mask to pool over the point dimensions of the feature map for each part. This results in a permutation invariant part feature vector for each part, *i.e.*, part descriptor representing the features responsible for that part segmentation in this hypothesis. We choose maxpool as the pooling operation due to its wide adoption in point cloud literature [43,44]. For the segmentation hypothesis $\hat{z}(o)$ of an object class o, this operation returns a set $\mathcal{D}(o)$ with part descriptors d for each part p found in this hypothesis. Note that $|\mathcal{D}(o)|$ is not always equal to $|\mathcal{P}_o|$ as a segmentation hypothesis might not contain all parts defined in the $\mathcal{P}_o$, *e.g.*, an instance of a chair might or might not contain sidearms.

Learning DeCompositional Consensus. Our DCC model learns a part scoring function $\mathcal{G}$ with weights Θ. For a part descriptor d, the function returns a score $\mathcal{G}(d,p)$ which measures the likelihood of this part descriptor to belong to the part p. We define DeCompositional Consensus score as the agreement between the segmentation hypothesis and the part scores. For an object hypothesis $\hat{z}(o)$, the DCC score is defined as:

$$s(x, o) = \frac{1}{|\mathcal{D}(o)|} \sum_{n=1}^{|\mathcal{D}(o)|} \mathcal{G}(d_n, p_n) \qquad (2)$$

Our novel DCC score measures the individual consensus of each part descriptor with the full segmentation mask to define an object classification score. We optimize DCC score for classification with a cross entropy loss over $\mathcal{O}_s$ as:

$$L_{DeComp} = -log(\frac{\exp s(x, o)}{\sum_{o' \in \mathcal{O}_s} \exp s(x, o')}) \qquad (3)$$

Since L_{DeComp} is computed over the Hypothesis Bank generated by $\mathcal{F}$, an additional part classification loss L_{Part} is computed using the ground truth segmentation mask z of each input to prevent bias against parts that are hard to segment. L_{Part} uses the ground truth segmentation mask to extract part descriptor set $\mathcal{D}_{gt}$ and optimizes them for part classification over $\mathcal{P}$.

$$L_{Part} = \sum_{n=1}^{|\mathcal{D}_{gt}|} -log(\frac{\exp \mathcal{G}(d_n, p_n)}{\sum_{p' \in \mathcal{P}} \exp \mathcal{G}(d_n, p')}) \qquad (4)$$

Inference. For generalized zero-shot inference, the HB is populated over all object classes $\mathcal{O} = \mathcal{O}_s + \mathcal{O}_u$. The object class prediction $\hat{o}$ for an input point cloud x is retrieved by selecting the object class with the highest DeCompositional Consensus score:

$$\hat{o} = \arg \max_{o' \in \mathcal{O}}(s(x, o')) \qquad (5)$$

The corresponding hypothesis of the predicted class $\hat{o}$ becomes the final part segmentation output, *i.e.*, $\hat{z}(\hat{o})$. Our technical novelty lies in defining part descriptors as features responsible for part segmentation in a hypothesis; and using their likelihood to define an object class level consensus score to achieve zero-shot compositionality. In contrast to several zero-shot baselines [36,55], our method does not require any supervised calibration step over the unseen classes.

4   Compositional PartNet Benchmark

Zero-shot compositionality in machine learning algorithms has mainly been studied for state-object relations in image datasets like MIT-States [20], UT-Zappos [60], AO-CLEVr [3], and more recent C-GQA [36]. These datasets have several limitations such as including label noise [3,20], lacking visual cues [36,60], being too simple [3], or missing multilabel information [36].

We believe that 3D part object relations provide an ideal avenue to study zero-shot compositionality, as they tend to be more well-defined albeit challenging. There have been several attempts in a part-based benchmark [6,59] for 3D

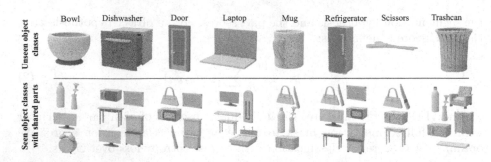

Fig. 3. Compositional PartNet refines the labels of PartNet dataset to maximize shared parts across different object classes, and enables studying 3D-CZSL task. The available 24 object classes are divided into 16 seen classes for training and 8 unseen classes for inference in zero-shot. We depict the shared labels between seen and unseen object classes in same colors.

object understanding. Recently, ShapeNet has been extended with fine-grained part labels to form the new dataset PartNet [35]. PartNet provides 24 distinct object classes, annotated with fine-grained, instance-level, and hierarchical 3D part information, consisting of around 26K 3D models with over 500K part instances and 128 part classes. However, these part class labels are not unified across different object categories, preventing a study into zero-shot compositionality. We refine PartNet into **Compositional PartNet (C-PartNet)** with a new labeling scheme that relates the compositional knowledge between objects by merging and renaming the repeated labels as shown in Fig. 3.

Unifying Part Labels. While PartNet provides three levels of hierarchical part labels, not all objects are labeled at the deepest level. We take the **deepest level** available for each object. We find similar parts within and across different objects by training a supervised segmentation model and compute pairwise similarities between parts across PartNet. Parts that share a high similarity and have the same semantic meaning (*e.g.,* `bed horizontal surface` in object Bed and `horizontal surface` in Storage Furniture) are merged into a single general part label (`horizontal surface`). Furthermore, parts with a similar function but different name (*e.g.,* `screen side` of Laptop and `display screen` of Display) are merged together. The relabelled C-PartNet consists of 96 parts compared to 128 distinct part labels in the original PartNet. Details in the supplementary.

Selecting Test Time Unseen Object Classes. Objects that share a similar function tend to have similar parts [4]. We divide PartNet objects into several functional categories. Details of this categorization and the dataset statistics can be found in the supplementary. We identify three easy to compose unseen object classes (*i.e.,* Mug, Bowl and TrashCan), that share large similarities with seen object classes (Bottle and Vase). Furthermore, we choose three object classes of medium difficulty that require generalizing parts beyond the context they were observed in (*i.e.*, Dishwasher, Refrigerator, and Laptop). Finally, Scissors and Door present two hard-to-compose object classes that require generalizing beyond scale, context, and number instances of parts compared to seen object classes. The validation set contains all seen and 2 unseen object classes (Bowl and Dishwasher). The test set consists of 16 seen O_s and 8 unseen classes O_u.

5   Experiments

Since our proposed benchmark lies at the intersection of point cloud processing, attribute learning, zero-shot learning, and its specialized sub-domain compositional zero-shot learning, we adapt baselines representing these lines of works.

Baselines. *Object Prior* uses a point cloud part segmentation model trained with our framework and evaluates the segmentation performance on the ground truth object. This is the oracle upper bound for the zero-shot models. *Direct Seg* trains a point cloud part segmentation model $\mathcal{F}$ without a part prior to predict over all parts $\mathcal{P}$ in the dataset. *PartPred* is inspired from a classic zero-shot baseline DAP [24] and trains a part prediction network from the global feature of each point cloud. The predicted parts are used as P_o for Eq. 1 to condition the compositional part segmentation network [24]. For zero-shot classification baselines, we use the predicted class to select the corresponding segmentation mask from the Hypothesis Bank. Among these, *SPNet* [55] learns classification by projecting the global feature of an input on a pretrained distribution where both seen and unseen objects lie *e.g.*, word embeddings. *CGE* [36] proposes to model compositional relations using a graph consisting of parts connected to objects they occur in. We reformulate CGE to a multitask setup and use part nodes for segmentation and object nodes for classification. *PartPred DCC* uses the part prediction network's scores for parts found in each segmentation hypothesis to calculate the consensus score from Eq. 2. Finally, *3D Capsule Networks* [62] aim to discover part prototypes through unsupervised reconstruction. Segmentation is subsequently learned by a linear mapper from capsules to part labels. We give additional details about these baselines in the supplementary and also compare with the current SOTA for part class agnostic segmentation method, Learning to Group [29], on unseen object classes.

Metrics. The proposed benchmark consists of two jointly learned tasks. For the **compositional zero-shot segmentation**, we report the mean object classwise Intersection-over-Union (mIoU) for part labels over seen and unseen object classes. We also report the harmonic mean over seen and unseen object classes to study the best generalized zero-shot performance. In addition, we report a perobject mIoU to study model performance on each unseen object across the three difficulty levels. For **generalized zero-shot classification**, we report for the per-object class top-1 classification accuracy over unseen classes, mean accuracy over seen classes, unseen classes and their harmonic mean. For models that apply joint classification and segmentation, we choose the checkpoint with the best segmentation performance to encourage compositional part understanding. Part based classification baselines can give the same scores across two objects if an instance does not have all parts, *e.g.,* an empty Vase has the same parts in Vase Hypothesis and Bowl. This is counted as an accurate classification, since the ground truth object still receives the highest score and achieves compositional segmentation.

Training Details. For its simplicity and competitive performance in our ablations (see Table 3), we choose PointNet [43] as the backbone model for $\mathcal{F}$ in our baseline comparisons in Table 1a, 1b. We also report further results on DGCNN [54], ConvPoint [5] and GDANet [57] in Table 3 . All backbones are pretrained with the author's implementations extended by our framework. The pretrained models are then used as initialization for the zero-shot models and are finetuned. For our model DCC, we use a 2-layer MLP with 512 hidden dimensions, ReLU, and dropout followed by a linear layer as function $\mathcal{G}$. We use a step size learning rate scheduler between $1e^{-3}$ and $1e^{-5}$ with Adam optimizer. We use cross entropy as segmentation loss L_{Seg} for part segmentation similar to [43,44,54,57].

Table 1. Baseline comparison. We compare our proposed method, DeCompositional Consensus (DCC), against baseline and report results for the two tasks. * marks baselines that require supervised calibration. For (a), we report mIoU % over part labels per object class over seen objects, unseen objects, and their harmonic mean. We also report the mIoU over each unseen object class. For (b), we report the top-1 classification accuracy. DCC achieves SOTA on both tasks.

(a) Compositional zero-shot segmentation											
Method	Unseen object classes										
	HM	S	U	Bowl	Dish	Door	Lap	Mug	Refr	Scis	Trash
Object Prior [43]	47.9	52.8	43.8	77.0	40.2	25.1	72.4	47.1	31.9	22.5	34.2
Direct Seg [43]	28.5	**48.7**	20.1	62.9	4.0	1.6	19.9	35.7	0.9	0.0	33.9
SPNet* [55]	8.5	28.5	5.0	12.6	2.5	0.5	0.0	2.6	2.6	0.0	15.8
CGE* [36]	30.8	37.0	26.4	67.0	19.5	0.3	35.1	39.6	11.2	0.0	33.6
3D-PointCapsNet [62]	4.4	9.4	2.9	4.3	0.0	0.2	1.2	11.2	0.1	0.1	6.5
PartPred [24]	26.3	33.6	21.6	66.2	2.3	7.2	19.4	43.1	0.5	0.0	32.5
PartPred DCC [24]	20.9	41.3	14.0	35.5	2.1	**7.2**	17.2	29.2	0.7	0.0	20.0
DCC (ours)	**35.2**	38.0	**32.7**	66.1	30.9	5.3	**56.3**	40.4	**28.4**	0.0	**34.2**
(b) Generalized zero-shot classification											
Method	Unseen object classes										
	HM	S	U	Bowl	Dish	Door	Lap	Mug	Refr	Scis	Trash
SPNet* [55]	3.8	46.7	2.0	12.0	0.0	3.1	0.0	0.0	0.0	0.0	0.0
CGE* [36]	33.1	54.3	23.8	31.9	0.0	0.0	52.0	1.0	33.7	0.0	**71.9**
PartPred DCC [24]	19.9	**74.0**	11.5	4.3	3.3	**25.8**	0.0	13.5	0.0	0.0	45.2
DCC(ours)	**55.9**	73.2	**45.2**	79.8	57.1	5.3	**55.4**	71.9	55.6	0.0	36.8

L_{Seg}, L_{DeComp} and L_{Part} are equally weighted and the network is trained until convergence on the validation set. We use Word2Vec [33] for models that rely on word embeddings [36,55]. For CGE, we choose the graph configuration that achieved the best result on the validation set at 2 layers of GCN with a hidden dimension of 1024. Our framework is implemented in PyTorch [41] and all experiments are conducted using Nvidia A100 GPUs. The dataset and experimental framework will be released upon acceptance.

5.1   Comparing with State of the Art

We compare our method with baselines on compositional zero-shot segmentation in Table 1a and generalized zero-shot classification in Table 1b. Our method outperforms all baselines on almost all metrics and establishes state of the art on both tasks.

Compositional Zero-Shot Segmentation Performance. Our method demonstrates remarkable performance gains on all unseen classes and achieves the best harmonic mean on compositional zero-shot segmentation in Table 1a. We achieve a 50% improvement over the direct segmentation demonstrating that the introduction of object class conditioned inference with DCC can improve compositional zero-shot segmentation in point cloud models. This improvement is observed most in unseen object classes that have large variations in parts from the seen object classes like Dishwasher (7.5×), Laptop (2.5×) and Refrigerator (28×) as shown in Fig. 4. Unseen object classes that share large geometric and semantic similarities with respect to parts to seen object classes also have significant improvements. This includes improvements in Bowl (4%), Mug (14%), and TrashCan (1.4%) that have very similar parts with seen Bottle and Vase.

Comparing with zero-shot learning baselines, we observe that our method achieves the best performance in 6 out of 8 classes and establishes a state of the art in overall harmonic mean and unseen mIoU while achieving competitive seen IoU. PartPred [24] learns to dynamically predict parts and generalizes to unseen objects that share part and geometric similarities with seen objects in the Container category but fails in other objects. As SPNet [55] does not use any part information, it fails to generalize to unseen objects by projecting on word embeddings alone. Compared to SPNet, CGE [36] performs much better as it uses the part prior and refines the word embeddings by using the dependency structure defined in the graph. Although being competitive on Bowl, Dishwasher, Mug and TrashCan, it performs much poorer on other unseen objects. 3D-PointCapsNet [62], while conceptually engineered for part-whole relations, fails to generalize to unseen objects, likewise having very low performance on seen objects. We relate this performance to the capsules' inability to generalize without object prior as further shown in the supplementary material. Finally, PartPred DCC, achieves impressive performance on seen objects but fails on the unseen objects showing the importance of learning consensus over the features responsible for a hypothesis. We observe that while some methods have almost zero classification

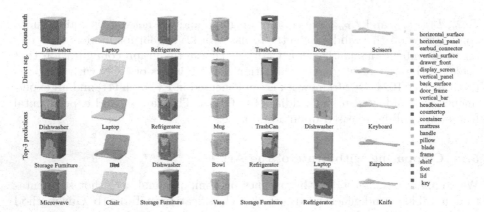

Fig. 4. Qualitative results. Direct segmentation tends to segment an input point cloud to parts from seen objects with large geometric similarities. While this works for the objects from Container category, it fails in more complex objects that share similarity with Furniture while being composed of parts from other categories. In contrast, DeCompositional Consensus builds an implicit understanding of what parts can occur together in different categories, and achieves meaningful segmentations for all object classes but Door and Scissors.

accuracy, they can still achieve some segmentation performance due to confusion with objects that share some parts with the ground truth object. All methods fail to generalize to challenging object classes Door and Scissors. We discuss that in qualitative analysis in Sect. 5.3.

Zero-Shot Classification Performance. Our method also achieves significant gains on generalized zero-shot classification as seen in Table 1b. DCC attains the best harmonic mean and unseen classification accuracy while maintaining a competitive seen performance. In fact, the best seen performance is achieved by PartPred DCC which extends our DCC score to a simple attribute (part) prediction model. This shows the power of enforcing consensus in different decisions of a model. Specifically, DCC is able to classify 6 out of the 8 unseen object classes with an outstanding accuracy. SPNet is only able to classify Bowl with a low accuracy of 12%. CGE is again a competitive baseline here. However, it is only able to receive reasonable classification scores on 4 of the 8 unseen object classes while maintaining a competitive seen class performance.

5.2   Ablations

We ablate our design choices and compare performance against different point cloud backbones.

Optimization Criteria. We ablate over the two optimization criteria for DCC in Table 2. As seen from row a) that only training for L_{DeComp} is unable to

Table 2. Ablating over L_{DeComp} **and** L_{Part}, we see that both the criterion complement each other to achieve the best performance.

	Hyperparameters			Classification			Segmentation		
	L_{DeComp}	L_{Part}	Segonly	HM	S	U	HM	S	U
a)	✓		✓	29.0	38.1	23.4	23.3	24.2	22.5
b)		✓		14.9	34.8	9.4	24.8	22.1	28.3
c)	✓	✓		52.6	54.4	50.9	39.1	35.9	42.9
d)	✓	✓	✓	**72.8**	**76.6**	**69.3**	**45.1**	**40.9**	**50.2**

Table 3. Backbone ablation. (a) We see DCC results in a large improvement compared to direct segmentation across all ablated point cloud models (b) We further see that our Part Prior optimization criterion greatly benefits all backbones under oracle evaluation especially on unseen objects.

CZSL segmentation						Oracle performance						
Backbone	Direct seg.			DCC			Backbone	L_{Seg} Over $\mathcal{P}$			L_{Seg} Over $\mathcal{P}_o$		
	HM	S	U	HM	S	U		HM	S	U	HM	S	U
PointNet [43]	28.5	48.7	20.1	35.2	38.0	**32.7**	PointNet [43]	43.2	51.7	37.1	47.9	52.8	43.8
DGCNN [54]	**29.5**	**50.0**	**20.9**	36.2	45.1	30.2	DGCNN [54]	**44.6**	52.4	**38.8**	50.0	**55.0**	46.3
ConvPoint [5]	2.9	5.2	2.0	29.5	35.0	25.5	ConvPoint [5]	29.1	28.7	29.5	43.5	42.4	43.0
GDANet [57]	28.7	47.7	20.5	33.5	**46.2**	26.4	GDANet [57]	43.4	**53.1**	36.8	48.0	53.7	43.4

attain high performance as it can introduce bias against hard to predict parts to increase classification performance. Similarly, only training for L_{Part} in row b) achieves low performance as the model is not optimized for the downstream classification task of predicting the consensus score. Row c) and d) combine both of these losses and see a big performance gain. In row c) we replace the predicted segmentation mask corresponding to the ground truth object class in HB with the ground truth segmentation mask. Comparing row c) and d) in Table 2, we see that when we learn DCC score exclusively on the model's predicted segmentation instead of using ground truth segmentation mask, we see a large improvement in seen and unseen performance. We conjecture that the part scoring function $\mathcal{G}$ learns the segmentation network's limitations in this setting, *i.e.*, if a part is not predicted well by $\mathcal{F}$, $\mathcal{G}$ can look for cues from other parts.

Comparing Point Cloud Backbones. We compare point cloud backbones under Direct Segmentation and DCC in Table 3a. We see that all models are unable to achieve competitive performance over unseen object classes with direct segmentation. In fact, ConvPoint [5] completely fails under this setting. The introduction of DCC to every backbone leads to a major increase in performance on the unseen object while being competitive over seen classes. This shows that our model can be readily extended to various families of point cloud backbones. In Table 3b, we compare the oracle segmentation performance over the ground truth object class when trained with and without our part prior optimization criterion (L_{Seg} over $\mathcal{P}_o$ or over $\mathcal{P}$) . In absence of our criterion, we observe a large difference between the performance on seen and unseen object classes. We conjecture that the model overfits to seen object classes, limiting compositionality to unseen object classes. With our criterion, *e.g.,* PointNet segmentation network improves up to 19% on unseen and 1% on seen classes.

5.3   Qualitative and Model Limitation

In Fig. 4, we show some qualitative results for direct segmentation versus top-3 results of our model across unseen objects. We further validate our results from Table 1a, and see that for the easy object Mug, the direct segmentation can give a meaningful result. However, it fails for other relatively harder objects, which can be attributed to the lack of affordance, *i.e.,* how an agent interacts with an object. Our method, despite not having access to affordances, builds an implicit understanding of what parts occur in each object category and is thus able to learn a reasonable consensus score. This brings about an increased generalization and meaningful results for all objects. We see a correct prediction for even Dishwasher and Refrigerator, which are closer geometrically to Furniture than Microwave, their closest functional seen object. However, although less, DCC also suffers from lack of affordances. For example, among the top-3 result for a Laptop in Fig. 4 is a Chair which shares geometrical similarity to an open Laptop. This indicates an upper bound to the performance that can be achieved from visual data alone [27,45]. An affordance prior can help address this limitation for part-object relations.

Another aspect that limits our model performance is the generalization limitations of point cloud backbones. In Fig. 5, we compare the object prior per part performance on the unseen objects between PointNet [43] and GDANet [57], which were released five years apart. A surprising insight we observe is that years of progress in point cloud processing, while making a significant advance on seen object classes, does not translate to improvement on unseen object classes. We see that there is no clear consensus on which model is better for unseen object class generalization. Even using the right part prior, some parts are unlikely to be segmented in unseen classes. An example of this is handle, which is unable to be reasonably segmented for Mug, Dishwasher, and Refrigerator. A more extreme case of this is observed in Door and Scissors, where the segmentation fails completely as shown in last two columns of Fig. 4. These objects have a large variation with respect to parts from the seen objects in scale, the number of instances (two blades in Scissors vs one in Knife), and orientation.

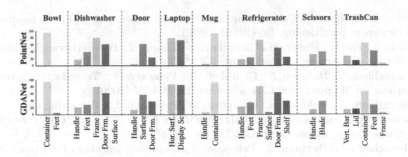

Fig. 5. Error plots. We find that PointNet [43] is comparable in mIoU to a much newer model, GDANet [57], across unseen objects.

6   Conclusion and Future Work

We introduce 3D-CZSL as a joint compositional zero-shot segmentation and generalized zero-shot classification task. We provide a structured study into zero-shot compositionality through a novel benchmark on the proposed C-PartNet dataset and show that previous models do not generalize beyond the training object classes. Towards this, our novel approach, DeCompositional Consensus, maximizes the agreement between a segmentation hypothesis and its parts when taken apart, and sets a new SOTA. We also show that while there has been a lot of progress in part segmentation in a supervised setting, simple models like PointNet are still competitive in unseen object classes, arguably because the current research has not focused on this task. There are several future directions that can stem from this work, including introducing affordance priors and extension of the capsules paradigm for part reasoning on unseen object classes. We also hope to inspire future research into compositional point cloud models.

References

1. Akata, Z., Perronnin, F., Harchaoui, Z., Schmid, C.: Label-embedding for attribute-based classification. In: CVPR (2013)
2. Armeni, I., et al.: 3D semantic parsing of large-scale indoor spaces. In: CVPR (2016)
3. Atzmon, Y., Kreuk, F., Shalit, U., Chechik, G.: A causal view of compositional zero-shot recognition. In: NeurIPS (2020)
4. Biederman, I.: Recognition-by-components: a theory of human image understanding. Psychol. Rev. **94**, 115–147 (1987)
5. Boulch, A.: Convpoint: continuous convolutions for point cloud processing. Comput. Graph. **88**, 24–34 (2020)
6. Chen, X., Golovinskiy, A., Funkhouser, T.: A benchmark for 3D mesh segmentation. In: SIGGRAPH (2009)
7. Chen, Z., Wang, S., Li, J., Huang, Z.: Rethinking generative zero-shot learning: an ensemble learning perspective for recognising visual patches. In: Proceedings of the 28th ACM International Conference on Multimedia (2020)

8. Chen, Z., Tagliasacchi, A., Zhang, H.: Bsp-net: generating compact meshes via binary space partitioning. In: CVPR (2020)
9. Chen, Z., Yin, K., Fisher, M., Chaudhuri, S., Zhang, H.: Bae-net: branched autoencoder for shape co-segmentation. In: ICCV (2019)
10. Cheraghian, A., Rahman, S., Campbell, D., Petersson, L.: Transductive zero-shot learning for 3D point cloud classification. In: WACV (2020)
11. Cheraghian, A., Rahman, S., Campbell, D., Petersson, L.: Mitigating the hubness problem for zero-shot learning of 3D objects. In: BMVC (2019). https://bmvc2019.org/wp-content/uploads/papers/0233-paper.pdf
12. Cheraghian, A., Rahman, S., Petersson, L.: Zero-shot learning of 3D point cloud objects. In: MVA (2019)
13. Deng, B., Genova, K., Yazdani, S., Bouaziz, S., Hinton, G., Tagliasacchi, A.: Cvxnet: learnable convex decomposition. In: CVPR (2020)
14. Deng, S., Xu, X., Wu, C., Chen, K., Jia, K.: 3D affordancenet: a benchmark for visual object affordance understanding. In: CVPR (2021)
15. Felzenszwalb, P., McAllester, D., Ramanan, D.: A discriminatively trained, multi-scale, deformable part model. In: CVPR (2008)
16. Gonzalez-Garcia, A., Modolo, D., Ferrari, V.: Do semantic parts emerge in convolutional neural networks? Int. J. Comput. Vis. **126**, 476–494 (2018)
17. Gonzalez-Garcia, A., Modolo, D., Ferrari, V.: Objects as context for detecting their semantic parts. In: CVPR (2018)
18. Hinton, G.: Some demonstrations of the effects of structural descriptions in mental imagery. Cogn. Sci. **3**(3), 231–250 (1979)
19. Hoffman, D.D., Richards, W.A.: Parts of recognition. Cognition **18**(1–3), 65–96 (1984)
20. Isola, P., Lim, J.J., Adelson, E.H.: Discovering states and transformations in image collections. In: CVPR (2015)
21. Jaklic, A., Leonardis, A., Solina, F., Solina, F.: Segmentation and Recovery of Superquadrics, vol. 20. Springer, Heidelberg (2000). https://doi.org/10.1007/978-94-015-9456-1
22. Johnson, J., et al.: Image retrieval using scene graphs. In: CVPR (2015)
23. Kawana, Y., Mukuta, Y., Harada, T.: Unsupervised pose-aware part decomposition for 3D articulated objects (2021)
24. Lampert, C.H., Nickisch, H., Harmeling, S.: Learning to detect unseen object classes by between-class attribute transfer. In: CVPR (2009)
25. Larochelle, H., Erhan, D., Bengio, Y.: Zero-data learning of new tasks. In: AAAI (2008)
26. LeCun, Y.: Backpropagation applied to handwritten zip code recognition. Neural Comput. **1**(4), 541–551 (1989)
27. Li, X., Liu, S., Kim, K., Wang, X., Yang, M.H., Kautz, J.: Putting humans in a scene: learning affordance in 3D indoor environments. In: CVPR (2019)
28. Li, Y.L., Xu, Y., Mao, X., Lu, C.: Symmetry and group in attribute-object compositions. In: CVPR (2020)
29. Luo, T., et al.: Learning to group: a bottom-up framework for 3D part discovery in unseen categories. ICLR (2020)
30. Mancini, M., Naeem, M.F., Xian, Y., Akata, Z.: Learning graph embeddings for open world compositional zero-shot learning. In: arXiv (2021)
31. Mancini, M., Naeem, M.F., Xian, Y., Akata, Z.: Open world compositional zero-shot learning. In: CVPR (2021)

32. Michele, B., Boulch, A., Puy, G., Bucher, M., Marlet, R.: Generative zero-shot learning for semantic segmentation of 3D point cloud. CoRR abs/2108.06230 (2021). https://arxiv.org/abs/2108.06230
33. Mikolov, T., Sutskever, I., Chen, K., Corrado, G.S., Dean, J.: Distributed representations of words and phrases and their compositionality. In: NeurIPS (2013)
34. Misra, I., Gupta, A., Hebert, M.: From red wine to red tomato: composition with context. In: CVPR (2017)
35. Mo, K., et al.: PartNet: a large-scale benchmark for fine-grained and hierarchical part-level 3D object understanding. In: CVPR (2019)
36. Naeem, M.F., Xian, Y., Tombari, F., Akata, Z.: Learning graph embeddings for compositional zero-shot learning. In: CVPR (2021)
37. Nagarajan, T., Grauman, K.: Attributes as operators: factorizing unseen attribute-object compositions. In: Ferrari, V., Hebert, M., Sminchisescu, C., Weiss, Y. (eds.) ECCV 2018. LNCS, vol. 11205, pp. 172–190. Springer, Cham (2018). https://doi.org/10.1007/978-3-030-01246-5_11
38. Newcombe, R.A., et al.: Kinectfusion: real-time dense surface mapping and tracking. In: ISMAR (2011)
39. Paschalidou, D., Gool, L.V., Geiger, A.: Learning unsupervised hierarchical part decomposition of 3D objects from a single RGB image. In: CVPR (2020)
40. Paschalidou, D., Ulusoy, A.O., Geiger, A.: Superquadrics revisited: learning 3D shape parsing beyond cuboids. In: CVPR (2019)
41. Paszke, A., et al.: Pytorch: an imperative style, high-performance deep learning library. In: NeurIPS (2019)
42. Purushwalkam, S., Nickel, M., Gupta, A., Ranzato, M.: Task-driven modular networks for zero-shot compositional learning. In: ICCV (2019)
43. Qi, C.R., Su, H., Mo, K., Guibas, L.J.: Pointnet: deep learning on point sets for 3D classification and segmentation. In: CVPR (2017)
44. Qi, C.R., Yi, L., Su, H., Guibas, L.J.: Pointnet++: deep hierarchical feature learning on point sets in a metric space. In: NeurIPS (2017)
45. Qi, W., Mullapudi, R.T., Gupta, S., Ramanan, D.: Learning to move with affordance maps. In: ICLR (2020)
46. Reed, S., Akata, Z., Lee, H., Schiele, B.: Learning deep representations of fine-grained visual descriptions. In: CVPR (2016)
47. Rolls, E.T., Treves, A.: Neural networks in the brain involved in memory and recall. In: Van Pelt, J., Corner, M., Uylings, H., Lopes Da Silva, F. (eds.) The Self-Organizing Brain: From Growth Cones to Functional Networks, Progress in Brain Research, vol. 102, pp. 335–341. Elsevier, Amsterdam (1994)
48. Sabour, S., Frosst, N., Hinton, G.E.: Dynamic routing between capsules. In: ICLR (2017)
49. Socher, R., Ganjoo, M., Manning, C.D., Ng, A.: Zero-shot learning through cross-modal transfer. In: NeurIPS (2013)
50. Tulsiani, S., Su, H., Guibas, L.J., Efros, A.A., Malik, J.: Learning shape abstractions by assembling volumetric primitives. In: CVPR (2017)
51. Wald, J., Avetisyan, A., Navab, N., Tombari, F., Niessner, M.: Rio: 3D object instance re-localization in changing indoor environments. In: ICCV (2019)
52. Wang, X., Sun, X., Cao, X., Xu, K., Zhou, B.: Learning fine-grained segmentation of 3D shapes without part labels. In: CVPR (2021)
53. Wang, X., Gupta, A.: Videos as space-time region graphs. In: Ferrari, V., Hebert, M., Sminchisescu, C., Weiss, Y. (eds.) ECCV 2018. LNCS, vol. 11209, pp. 413–431. Springer, Cham (2018). https://doi.org/10.1007/978-3-030-01228-1_25

54. Wang, Y., Sun, Y., Liu, Z., Sarma, S.E., Bronstein, M.M., Solomon, J.M.: Dynamic graph cnn for learning on point clouds. ACM Trans. Graph. (TOG) **38**, 1–12 (2019)
55. Xian, Y., Choudhury, S., He, Y., Schiele, B., Akata, Z.: Semantic projection network for zero-and few-label semantic segmentation. In: CVPR (2019)
56. Xian, Y., Lampert, C.H., Schiele, B., Akata, Z.: Zero-shot learning-a comprehensive evaluation of the good, the bad and the ugly. IEEE TPAMI **41**(9), 2251–2265 (2019). https://doi.org/10.1109/TPAMI.2018.2857768
57. Xu, M., Zhang, J., Zhou, Z., Xu, M., Qi, X., Qiao, Y.: Learning geometry-disentangled representation for complementary understanding of 3D object point cloud. In: AAAI (2021)
58. Yang, M., Deng, C., Yan, J., Liu, X., Tao, D.: Learning unseen concepts via hierarchical decomposition and composition. In: CVPR (2020)
59. Yi, L., et al.: A scalable active framework for region annotation in 3D shape collections. In: SIGGRAPH Asia (2016)
60. Yu, A., Grauman, K.: Fine-grained visual comparisons with local learning. In: CVPR (2014)
61. Zeiler, M.D., Fergus, R.: Visualizing and understanding convolutional networks. In: Fleet, D., Pajdla, T., Schiele, B., Tuytelaars, T. (eds.) ECCV 2014. LNCS, vol. 8689, pp. 818–833. Springer, Cham (2014). https://doi.org/10.1007/978-3-319-10590-1_53
62. Zhao, Y., Birdal, T., Deng, H., Tombari, F.: 3D point capsule networks. In: CVPR (2019)

Video Mask Transfiner for High-Quality Video Instance Segmentation

Lei Ke[1,2], Henghui Ding[1], Martin Danelljan[1], Yu-Wing Tai[3],
Chi-Keung Tang[2], and Fisher Yu[1(✉)]

[1] Computer Vision Lab, ETH Zürich, Zürich, Switzerland
i@yf.io
[2] The Hong Kong University of Science and Technology, Hong Kong, China
[3] Kuaishou Technology, Beijing, China
http://vis.xyz/pub/vmt

Abstract. While Video Instance Segmentation (VIS) has seen rapid progress, current approaches struggle to predict high-quality masks with accurate boundary details. Moreover, the predicted segmentations often fluctuate over time, suggesting that temporal consistency cues are neglected or not fully utilized. In this paper, we set out to tackle these issues, with the aim of achieving highly detailed and more temporally stable mask predictions for VIS. We first propose the Video Mask Transfiner (VMT) method, capable of leveraging fine-grained high-resolution features thanks to a highly efficient video transformer structure. Our VMT detects and groups sparse error-prone spatio-temporal regions of each tracklet in the video segment, which are then refined using both local and instance-level cues. Second, we identify that the coarse boundary annotations of the popular YouTube-VIS dataset constitute a major limiting factor. Based on our VMT architecture, we therefore design an automated annotation refinement approach by iterative training and self-correction. To benchmark high-quality mask predictions for VIS, we introduce the HQ-YTVIS dataset, consisting of a manually re-annotated test set and our automatically refined training data. We compare VMT with the most recent state-of-the-art methods on the HQ-YTVIS, as well as the Youtube-VIS, OVIS and BDD100K MOTS benchmarks. Experimental results clearly demonstrate the efficacy and effectiveness of our method on segmenting complex and dynamic objects, by capturing precise details.

Keywords: Video instance segmentation · Multiple object tracking and segmentation · Video mask transfiner · Iterative training · Self-correction

---

Supplementary Information The online version contains supplementary material available at https://doi.org/10.1007/978-3-031-19815-1_42.

© The Author(s), under exclusive license to Springer Nature Switzerland AG 2022
S. Avidan et al. (Eds.): ECCV 2022, LNCS 13688, pp. 731–747, 2022.
https://doi.org/10.1007/978-3-031-19815-1_42

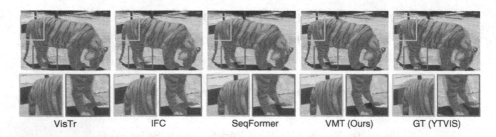

VisTr   IFC   SeqFormer   VMT (Ours)   GT (YTVIS)

Fig. 1. Video instance segmentation results by VisTr [35], IFC [14], SeqFormer [36], and VMT (Ours) along with the YTVIS Ground Truth. All methods adopt R101 as backbone. VMT achieves highly accurate boundary details, e.g. at the feet and tail regions of the tiger, even exceeding the quality of the GT annotations.

1 Introduction

Video Instance Segmentation (VIS) requires tracking and segmenting all objects from a given set of categories. Most recent state-of-the-art methods [11,14,35,36] are transformer-based, using learnable object queries to represent each tracklet in order to predict instance masks for each object. While achieving promising results, their predicted masks suffer from oversmoothed object boundaries and temporal incoherence, leading to inaccurate mask predictions, as shown in Fig. 1. This motivates us to tackle the problem of *high-quality* video instance segmentation, with the aim to achieve accurate boundary details and temporally stable mask predictions.

Although high-resolution instance segmentation [15,19] has been explored in the image domain, video opens the opportunity to leverage rich temporal information. Multiple temporal views can help to accurately identify object boundaries, and allow the use of correspondences across frames to achieve temporally consistent and robust segmentation. However, high-quality VIS poses major challenges, most importantly: 1) utilizing long-range spatio-temporal cues in the presence of dynamic and fast-moving objects; 2) the large computational and memory costs brought by high-resolution video features for capturing low-level details; 3) how to fuse fine-grained local features and with global instance-aware context for accurate boundary prediction; 4) the inaccurate boundary annotation of existing large-scale datasets [37]. In this work, we set out to address all these challenges, in order to achieve VIS with highly accurate mask boundaries.

We propose Video Mask Transfiner (VMT), an efficient video transformer that performs spatio-temporal segmentation refinement for high-quality VIS. To achieve efficiency, we take inspiration from Ke et al. [15] and identify a set of sparse error-prone regions. However, as illustrated in Fig. 2, we detect 3D spatio-temporal points, which are often located along object motion boundaries. These regions are represented as a sequence of quadtree points to encapsulate various spatial and temporal scales. To effectively utilize long-range temporal ques, we group all points and jointly process them using a spatio-temporal refinement transformer. Thus, the input sequence for the transformer contains both detailed spatial and temporal information. To effectively integrate instance-aware global context, besides using the aggregated points as both input queries and keys of the transformer, we design an additional instance guidance layer (IGL). It makes our transformer aware of both local boundary details and global semantic context.

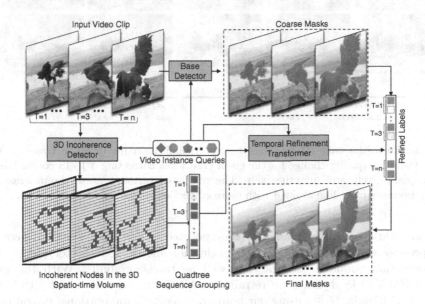

Fig. 2. We propose VMT for high-quality video instance segmentation. It adopts a temporal refinement transformer to jointly correct the 3D error-prone regions in the spatio-temporal volume. We employ VMT for automatically correcting the YTVIS with an iterative training paradigm by taking its annotation as coarse masks input.

While our VMT already achieves higher segmentation performance, we observed the boundary quality of the YTVIS [37] training annotations to be the next major bottleneck in the strive towards higher-quality mask predictions and evaluation on this popular, large-scale, and highly challenging dataset. Most importantly, we notice that many videos in YTVIS suffer object boundary inflation issues, as shown in Fig. 1 and Fig. 5. This introduces a learned bias in the trained model and prohibits very accurate evaluation. In fact, high-quality training data for VIS is difficult to obtain since dense pixel-wise annotations are costly for a large number videos. To address this difficulty, instead of manual relabeling the training data, we design an automatic refinement procedure by employing VMT with iterative training. To self-correct mask annotations of YTVIS, both VMT model and training data are alternately evolved, as in Fig. 3. To initialize the training of VMT annotation refinement, we use recently proposed OVIS [28] with better boundary annotations.

To enable benchmarking of high-quality VIS, we introduce the High-Quality YTVIS (HQ-YTVIS) dataset, consisting of our automatically refined train-

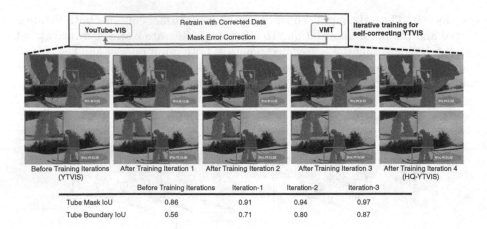

Fig. 3. Illustration and intermediate results visualization for iterative training. We show the mask quality change for the given case when correcting YTVIS coarse labels both qualitatively and quantitatively. The predicted instance masks boundaries by VMT becomes more fine-grained with more correction iterations on the YTVIS.

ing annotations and a manually re-annotated val & test split. Moreover, we propose the Tube-Boundary AP evaluation metric that better focuses on segmentation boundary accuracy as well as tracking ability. With the proposed HQ-YTVIS dataset, we retrain our VMT and several recent VIS baselines [11,14,16,35,37,38] using our boundary-accurate annotations, providing a comprehensive comparison with current state-of-the-art. We also compare our VMT with state-of-the-art methods on the OVIS [28] and BDD MOTS [39] benchmarks with better annotated boundaries. Quantitative and qualitative results on all three benchmarks demonstrate that VMT not only consistently outperforms existing VIS methods, but also predicts masks at much higher resolution size with small additional computation costs to current video transformer-based methods. We hope our VMT and HQ-YTVIS benchmark could facilitate the community in achieving ever more accurate video instance segmentation.

2   Related Work

Video Instance Segmentation (VIS). Extended from image instance segmentation, existing VIS methods can be divided into three categories: two-stage, one-stage, and transformer-based. Earlier methods [3,21,37] widely adopted the two-stage Mask R-CNN family [12,13,17] by introducing a tracking head for object association. Later works [5,20,23] adopted a one-stage instance segmentation framework by using anchor-free detectors [31] and linear combination of mask bases [4]. For longer temporal information modeling [22], CrossVIS [38] proposes instance-to-pixel relation learning and PCAN [16] introduces prototypical cross-attention operations for reading space-time memory. For the transformer-based approach, VisTr [35] first uses vision transformer [6] for VIS, which is then improved by IFC [14] using memory token communication. Seqformer [36] designs query decomposition mechanism. The aforementioned approaches put very limited emphasis on generating very accurate boundary details necessary of high-quality video object masks. In contrast, VMT is the first method targeting for very high-quality video instance segmentation.

Multiple Object Tracking and Segmentation (MOTS). MOTS methods [25,26,33] mainly follow the tracking-by-detection paradigm. To utilize temporal features, different from [2,16] in clustering/grouping spatio-temporal feature, VMT directly detects the sparse error-prone points in the 3D feature space w/o feature compression and yield highly accurate boundary details.

Refinement for Segmentation. Existing works [19,30] on instance segmentation refinement are single-image based and thus neglect temporal information. Most of them adopt convolutional networks [30] or MLPs [19]. The latest image-based method Mask Transfiner [15] detects incoherent regions and adopts quadtree transformer for correcting region errors. Some methods [9,10,29,34,40] focus on refining semantic segmentation details. However, they apply on images without temporal object associations.

We build VMT based on [15], due to its efficiency and accuracy for single image segmentation. The key design of our VMT lies in leveraging temporal information and multi-view object associations of the input video clip. We explore new ways of using video instance queries to detect 3D incoherent points and correct spatio-temporal segmentation errors. Besides, VMT is also a part of our iterative training and self-correction to construct the HQ-YTVIS benchmark.

Self Training. To reduce the expense of large-scale human-annotation on pixels, some semantic segmentation methods produce pseudo labels for unlabeled data using teacher model [7,42] or data augmentation [43]. Then, their models are jointly trained on both human-labeled and pseudo labels. In contrast, VMT aims at self-correcting the coarsely or wrongly annotated VIS data. Considering that high-quality VIS requires very accurate video mask annotations to reveal object boundary details, our proposed self-correction and iterative training become even more valuable by eliminating such exhaustive manual labeling.

3   High-Quality Video Instance Segmentation

We tackle the problem of high-quality Video Instance Segmentation (VIS), by proposing an efficient temporal refinement transformer, Video Mask Transfiner (VMT), in Sect. 3.1. We further introduce a new iterative training paradigm for automatically correcting inaccurate annotations of YTVIS in Sect. 3.2. To facilitate the research in high-quality VIS, we contribute a large-scale HQ-YTVIS benchmark, and propose the Tube-Boundary AP metric in Sect. 3.3. The proposed benchmark and metric contribute to existing and future VIS models, with high-quality annotations for both better training and more precise evaluation.

3.1 Video Mask Transfiner

Figure 4 depicts the overall architecture of Video Mask Transfiner (VMT). Our design is inspired by the image-based instance segmentation method Mask Transfiner [15]. This single-image method first detects incoherent regions, where segmentation errors most likely occur in the coarse mask prediction. A quadtree transformer is then used to refine the segmentation in these regions. However, in case of video, the usage of temporal information, including object associations between different frames, is not accounted for by Mask Transfiner. This limits its segmentation performance in the video domain, leading to temporally incoherent mask results. To effectively and efficiently leverage the high-resolution temporal features, we propose three new components for our VMT: 1) an instance query based 3D incoherent points detector; 2) quadtree sequence grouping for temporal information aggregation; and 3) instance query guided incoherent points segmentation. We will describe each of these key components in this section, after a brief summary of the employed base detector in the following.

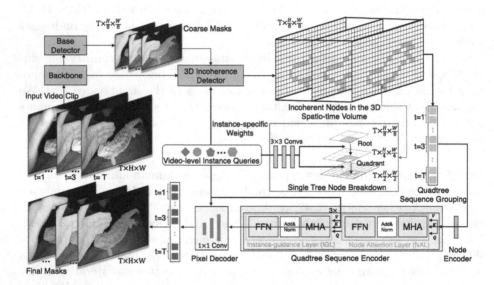

Fig. 4. Our VMT framework. A sequence of quadtrees are first constructed in the spatio-time volume by the 3D incoherence detector. Then, these incoherent nodes are concatenated across frames by Quadtree Sequence Grouping. The produced new spatio-temporal node sequences are corrected by temporal refinement transformer under the guidance of video instance queries with global instance context.

Backbone and Base Detector. Given a video clip that consists of multiple image frames as input, we first use CNN backbone and transformer encoder [41] to extract feature maps for each frame. Then, we adopt video-level instance queries to detect and segment objects for each frame following [36]. This base detector [36] generates initial coarse mask predictions of the video tracklets at low resolution $T \times \frac{H}{8} \times \frac{W}{8}$, where T, H and W are the length, height and width of the input video clip. Given this input data, our goal is to predict highly accurate video instance segmentation masks at $T \times H \times W$.

Query-based 3D Incoherent Points Detection. To detect the incoherent regions in the video clip, where segmentation errors are concentrated, a lightweight 3D incoherent region detector is designed. The detector, which encodes the video-level instance query embedding to generate a set of dynamic convolutional weights, consists of three 3×3 convolution layers with ReLU activations. The predicted instance-specific weights are then convolved with the spatio-temporal feature volume at resolution $T \times \frac{H}{8} \times \frac{W}{8}$, followed by a binary classifier to detect the 3D sparse incoherent tree roots.

We further break down these predicted incoherent points in the 3D volume into each frame. Each point serves as root node in a tree, by branching each node into its four quadrants on the corresponding lower-level frame feature map, which is 2× higher in resolution. The branching is recursive until reaching the largest feature resolution. We share this 3-layer dynamic instance weights to detect incoherent points for the same video instance across backbone feature sizes at $\{\frac{H}{8} \times \frac{W}{8}, \frac{H}{4} \times \frac{W}{4}, \frac{H}{2} \times \frac{W}{2}\}$, as visualized in Fig. 4. This allows VMT to save a huge computational and memory cost, because only a small part of the high-resolution video features are processed, occupying less than 10% of the all the points in the 3D temporal volume. Video-level instance query captures both positional and appearance information for a time sequence of the same instance in a video clip. The instance-specific information are already contained in the correlation weights. Thus, different from [15], instance query-based detection removes the necessity of constructing ROI pooling feature pyramid for each video object. Our 3D incoherent region detector directly operates on the spatio-temporal feature volume from the backbone.

Quadtree Sequence Grouping. After detecting 3D incoherent points, we build a sequence of quadtree points within the video clip, each of which resides in a single frame. To effectively utilize the temporal information across frames, VMT groups together all the tree nodes from all frames of the quadtree sequence, and concatenate them in the token dimension for the transformer. The resulting new sequence is the input for the temporal refinement transformer, which contains tree nodes across both spatial and temporal scales, thus encapsulating both detailed spatial and temporal information. We study the influence of different video clip lengths in Table 1, which reveals that the input sequence from longer video clips with more diverse and rich information boosts the accuracy of temporal segmentation refinement.

Instance Query Guided Temporal Refinement. For segmenting the newly formed incoherent sequence above, instead of solely leveraging the incoherent points as both input queries and keys [15], our Node Attention Layer (NAL) utilizes video-level instance queries as additional semantic guidance. In Fig. 4, to inject each point with instance-specific information, we introduce the Instance Guidance Layer (IGL) after each NAL in a level-wise manner. IGL uses incoherent points only as queries, and adopts the video-level instance embedding as the keys and values. This helps our temporal refinement transformer be aware of both local boundary details and global instance-level context, thus better separating incoherent points among different foreground instances. Besides, we add a low-level RGB feature embedding, produced by a network consisting of three 3×3 Conv. layers directly operating on the image. This further encapsulates fine-grained object edge details as input to the node encoder. Finally, the output is sent into the dynamic pixel decoder for final prediction.

3.2 Iterative Training Paradigm for Self-correcting YTVIS

We observed the boundary annotation quality of the YTVIS dataset to be an important bottleneck when aiming to learn highly accurate segmentation masks. We show the inaccurate and coarse boundary annotations of YTVIS in Fig. 5, Fig. 1 and the supplemental video. In particular, we randomly sample 200 videos from the original YTVIS annotations, and find around 28% of the cases suffer from the boundary inflation problem, where a halo about 5 pixels is around the real object contour. These coarse annotations may due to small number of selected polygon points during instance labeling, which introduces a severe bias in the training, leading to inaccurate boundary prediction. Based on VMT, we therefore design a method for automatic annotation refinement, and apply it to correct the inaccurate annotations of YTVIS. The core idea is to take the coarse mask annotations from HQ-YTVIS as input and alternate between refining the training data and training the model to achieve gradually improved annotations.

At the beginning, to equip VMT with initial boundary correction ability, we pretrain VMT on the better annotated OVIS dataset as the first iteration, which has similar data categories and sources as YTVIS. We train the temporal refinement transformer of VMT in a class-agnostic way, leveraging only the incoherent points and video-level instance queries as the input. To simulate various shapes and output of inaccurate segmentation, we degrade the video mask annotations of OVIS [28] by subsampling the boundary regions followed by random dilations and erosions. Examples of such degraded masks are in the supplemental file. VMT is trained to correct the errors in the ground-truth incoherent regions, and we further enlarge the regions by dilating 3 pixels to introduce both the diversity and the balance of foreground and background pixels ratio in this region.

After training on OVIS, we employ the trained VMT to correct the mask boundary annotations of YTVIS, where the mask annotations of YTVIS are regarded as the coarse mask inputs. We only correct the mask labels when the confidence of the most likely predicted class (foreground or background) is larger than 0.65. Then, we obtain a corrected version of YTVIS and use this new corrected YTVIS data to retrain the temporal refinement transformer of VMT as the 2nd iteration. We iterate this process until the model performance on the manually labeled validation set reaches saturation, requiring 4 iterations. We illustrate the iterative training process and show the intermediate visualizations in Fig. 3. After each iteration, the produced annotations masks of YTVIS become more fine-grained until final convergence. We compare the training results using different iterated versions of the YTVIS data, and evaluate their performance on the human-relabeled *val* set in Table 3.

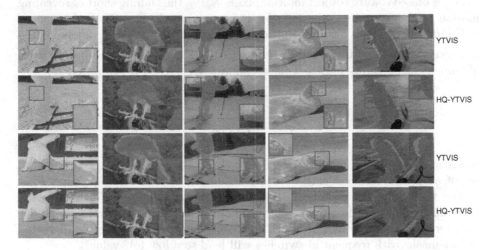

Fig. 5. Masks quality comparisons between YTVIS [37] and HQ-YTVIS annotations.

3.3 The HQ-YTVIS Benchmark

To facilitate the research in high-quality VIS, we further contribute a new benchmark HQ-YTVIS and design a new evaluation metric Tube-Boundary AP.

HQ-YTVIS. To construct the HQ-YTVIS, we first randomly re-split the original YTVIS training set (2238 videos) with coarse mask boundary annotations into train (1678 videos, 75%), val (280 videos, 12.5%) and test (280 videos, 12.5%) subsets following the splitting ratios in YTVIS. Then, the masks annotations on the train subset is self-corrected automatically by VMT using iterative training as described in Sect. 3.2. The smaller set of validation and test videos are carefully relabeled by human annotators to ensure high mask boundary quality. Figure 5 shows the mask annotation differences of the same image from the training set between HQ-YTVIS and YTVIS. HQ-YTVIS has much more accurate object boundary annotations. We retrained VMT and all baselines [11,14,16,35,37,38] on HQ-YTVIS from scratch, and compare the results with those obtained by training them on the original YTVIS annotations with the same set of images. We conduct quantitative results comparisons results in Table 4, which clearly shows the advantage brought by HQ-YTVIS. We also include the relevant qualitative comparisons in the Supp. file. We hope HQ-YTVIS can serve a new and more accurate benchmark to facilitate future development of VIS methods aiming at higher mask quality.

Tube-Boundary AP. We propose a new segmentation measure Tube-Boundary AP for high-quality video instance segmentation. The standard tube mask AP in [37] is biased towards object interior pixels [8,19], thus falling short of revealing motion boundary errors, especially for large moving objects. Given a sequence of GT masks $G^i_{b...e}$ for instance i, a sequence detected masks $P^j_{\hat{b}...\hat{e}}$ for predicted instance j, we extend frame index b and $\hat{b}$ to 1, e and $\hat{e}$ to T for temporal length alignment using empty masks. Tube-Boundary AP (AP^B) is computed as,

$$\mathrm{AP}^B(i,j) = \frac{\sum_{t=1}^{t=T} \left| (G^i_t \cap g^i_t) \cap (P^j_t \cap p^j_t) \right|}{\sum_{t=1}^{t=T} \left| (G^i_t \cap g^i_t) \cup (P^j_t \cap p^j_t) \right|} \tag{1}$$

where spatio-temporal boundary regions g and p are respectively the sequential set of all pixels within d pixels distance from the contours of $G^i_{b...e}$ and $P^i_{\hat{b}...\hat{e}}$ in the video clip. By definition, Tube-Boundary AP not only focuses on the boundary quality of the objects, but also considers spatio-temporal consistency between the predicted and ground truth object masks. For example, detected object masks with frequent id switches will lead to a low IoU value.

4   Experiments

4.1   Experimental Setup

HQ-YTVIS & YTVIS. We conduct experiments on YTVIS [37] and our HQ-YTVIS datasets. YTVIS contains 2,883 videos with 131k annotated object instances belonging to 40 categories. We identify its inaccurate mask boundaries issues in Fig. 5 and Sect. 3.2, which influences both model training and accuracy in testing evaluation. For HQ-YTVIS, we split the original YTVIS training set (2238 videos) into a new *train* (1678 videos, 75%), *val* (280 videos 12.5%) and *test* (280 videos 12.5%) sets following the ratios in YTVIS. The masks annotations on the *train* subset of HQ-YTVIS is self-corrected by VMT, while the smaller sets of *val* and *test* are carefully relabeled by human annotators to ensure high mask boundary quality. We employ both the standard tube mask **AP^M** in [37] and our Tube-Boundary **AP^B** as evaluation metrics.

OVIS. We also report results on OVIS [28], a recently proposed VIS benchmark on occlusion learning. OVIS has better-annotated boundaries for instance masks with 607, 140 and 154 videos for train, valid and test respectively.

BDD100K MOTS. We further train and evaluate Video Mask Transfiner on the large-scale BDD100K [39] MOTS, which is a self-driving benchmark with high-quality instance masks. It contains 154 videos (30,817 images) for training, 32 videos (6,475 images) for validation, and 37 videos (7,484 images) for testing.

4.2 Implementation Details

Video Mask Transfiner is implemented on the query-based detector [41], and employ [36] to provide coarse mask predictions for video instances. For the temporal refinement transformer, we adopt 3 multi-head attention layers, setting the hidden dimension to 64 and using 4 attention heads. The instance queries are shared between temporal refinement transformer with the base object detector. During training, we follow the setting in [36] and use video clips consisting of 5 frames and sample them from the whole video. We train VMT for 12 epochs and use AdamW [24] as optimizer, with initial learning rate set to 2e-4. Our VMT executes at 8.2 FPS on Swin-L backbone. The learning rate is decayed at the 5th and 11th epochs by factor of 0.1. More details are in the Supp. file.

Table 1. Quadtree sequence grouping (QSG) across frames in varying video clip lengths on HQ-YTVIS *val* set.

Length	QSG	AP^B	AP^B_{50}	AR^B_1	AP^M	AP^M_{50}	AR^M_1
1		26.1	59.8	23.8	44.5	64.2	40.1
5		30.2	63.3	29.6	47.5	69.8	43.5
5	✓	31.4	64.2	30.7	48.2	70.5	44.1
10		31.2	64.1	30.3	48.9	70.6	44.3
10	✓	32.5	65.3	31.2	49.6	71.2	44.9
All		32.3	66.0	30.6	49.7	71.8	45.5
All	✓	**33.7**	**67.2**	**31.8**	**50.5**	**72.4**	**46.2**

Table 2. Ablation on 3D incoherent region detector, and refinement region types comparison on HQ-YTVIS validation set. IQ: Instance Query.

Region type	Incoherence detector	AP^B	AP^B_{50}	AR^B_1	AP^M	AP^M_{50}	AR^M_1
Detected object boundary	FCN	31.8	65.4	30.5	48.7	71.0	45.0
	IQ (Frame-level)	31.3	64.8	29.9	48.1	69.9	44.3
	IQ (Video-level)	32.8	66.2	31.0	49.8	71.6	45.7
3D Incoherent region	FCN	32.2	65.1	30.7	49.1	70.9	45.3
	IQ (Frame-level)	31.8	65.2	30.5	48.9	70.6	45.1
	IQ (Video-level)	**33.7**	**67.2**	**31.8**	**50.5**	**72.4**	**46.2**

4.3 Ablation Experiments

We conduct detailed ablation studies for VMT using ResNet-101 as backbone on HQ-YTVIS and OVIS *val* sets. We analyze the impact of each proposed component. Besides, we study the effect of iterative training for self-correcting YTVIS, and compare the same models trained on our HQ-YTVIS vs. YTVIS.

Effect of the Quadtree Sequence Grouping. Table 1 analyzes the influence of video clip lengths to the Quadtree Sequence Grouping (QSG). It reveals that the longer video clips with richer temporal amount indeed brings more performance gain to our VMT. When we increase the tube length from 1 to all frames in the video, a remarkable gain in tube boundary AP^B from 26.1 to 33.7 is achieved. This demonstrate that our approach effectively leverages temporal information, since a tube length 1 performs independent prediction for each frame. Moreover, models **w/o** QSG are refining the inherent points in each frame separately as [15]. The multiple boundary view of the same object brings an gain in temporal refinement for over 1.0 AP^B.

Ablation on the 3D Incoherence Detector. We study the design choices of our 3D incoherence detector in Table 2. We compare fixed FCN and dynamic FCN (three 3×3 Convs) with weights produced by frame-level or video-level instance queries used in [36]. Video-level instance queries achieve the highest AP^B, improving 1.9 point compared to the frame-level queries, which shows the effect of temporally aggregated video-level instance information. We also compare 3D incoherent regions with detected object mask boundaries, where the 3D incoherent regions achieves 0.9 AP^B gain.

Table 3. Comparison on iterative training. Models after each correction is evaluated on HQ-YTVIS *val* by taking **GT** classes, ids and coarse masks as input.

Table 4. Training on YTVIS **vs.** HQ-YTVIS with the same images from scratch. We evaluate the trained models on HQ-YTVIS and OVIS *val* sets.

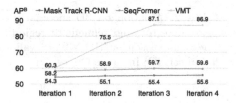

Method	YTVIS	HQ-YTVIS	HQ-YTVIS			OVIS	
			AP^B	AP^B_{50}	AP^M	AP^M	AP^M_{50}
MaskTrack [37]	✓		19.8	48.9	40.2	9.3	24.2
MaskTrack [37]		✓	**21.7**	**50.5**	**41.1**	**10.5**	**25.1**
SeqFormer [36]	✓		28.9	64.2	48.6	13.8	32.1
SeqFormer [36]		✓	**31.0**	**66.1**	**50.5**	**15.2**	**33.7**
VMT (Ours)	✓		30.5	64.7	48.9	15.9	33.8
VMT (Ours)		✓	**33.7**	**67.2**	**50.5**	**17.1**	**35.0**

Effect of Iterative Training. In Table 3, we compare MaskTrack [37], SeqFormer [36] and VMT for correcting coarse masks of YTVIS in the iterative training. We observe that the improvement scales after each iteration of MaskTrack and SeqFormer on HQ-YTVIS *val* is minor, where the boundary quality AP^B after the 3rd iteration are still coarse (around 60.0 using **GT** object classes, identities and corresponding coarse masks). In contrast, VMT achieves consistent and large mask quality improvements after three training iterations, which reveals the design advantages of our temporal refinement transformer.

Training on YTVIS vs. HQ-YTVIS. In Table 4, we evaluate the performance of three different approaches when training on either YTVIS or HQ-YTVIS. We train MaskTrack [37], SeqFormer [36] and our VMT from scratch with the same set of images. We use HQ-YTVIS and OVIS for evaluation due to the better annotated mask boundaries. For evaluation on OVIS, we train the mask heads of all these methods in a class-agnostic way, and fix the model weights of the mask head when finetuning them on OVIS for object detection and tracking parts. All three methods trained using HQ-YTVIS obtain consistent and large performance gain of over 2.0 AP^B on the manually labeled

HQ-YTVIS val set, and over 1.0 AP^M on the OVIS val set. This shows our self-corrected HQ-YTVIS dataset consistently improves existing VIS methods for segmentation quality, without overfitting to the specific dataset.

Temporal Attention Visualization. In Fig. 6, we visualize the temporal attention distribution for incoherent nodes in a video-clip of length 5. The attention weights are extracted from the last NAL of the refinement transformer. For the sampled point R1 at T=3, it attends more to the feet regions of the giraffe with semantic correspondence in both the current and neighboring frames. Also, the attention weights for the temporally farther frames are smaller.

4.4 Comparison with State-of-the-art Methods

We compare VMT with the state-of-the-art methods on the benchmarks HQ-YTVIS, YTVIS, OVIS and BDD100K MOTS. Note that we only conduct iterative training when producing the training annotations of HQ-YTVIS. When retraining VMT and all other baselines on the HQ-YTVIS benchmark, all methods are trained from scratch and only once on the same data for fair comparison.

HQ-YTVIS & YTVIS. Table 5 compares VMT with state-of-the-art instance segmentation methods on both HQ-YTVIS and YTVIS benchmarks. VMT achieves consistent performance advantages on different backbones, showing its effectiveness by surpassing SeqFormer [36] by around 2.8 AP^B_{75} on HQ-YTVIS using ResNet-50. As in Fig. 5 and Sect. 3.2, the mask boundary annotation in YTVIS is less accurate. Therefore, the advantages brought by our approach are not fully revealed on this dataset. Yet, VMT exceeds SeqFormer by about 0.5 AP^M on YTVIS with ResNet-50 with higher mask quality as in Fig. 7. Moreover, masks predicted by our approach are 16× larger than those of SeqFormer, while only increasing negligible amount of the model parameters.

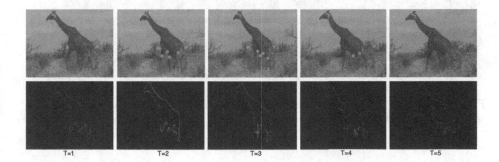

Fig. 6. Temporal attention visualizations on the sparse incoherent regions for a video clip of length 5. The sampled red node R1 attends more to the feet regions of the giraffe with semantic correspondence in both the current and neighboring frames. The top 10 attended incoherent node regions are marked in yellow. (Color figure online)

Table 5. Comparison with state-of-the-art methods on HQ-YTVIS test set and YTVIS [37] validation set. All methods, including VMT, are retrained on HQ-YTVIS and YTVIS training sets respectively from scratch for fair comparisons. Results are reported in terms of Tube-Mask AP^M [37] and our Tube-boundary AP^B. VMT predicts mask at output sizes $16\times$ larger than SeqFormer [36]. The advantage of VMT is not fully revealed on YTVIS due to its inaccurate and coarse boundary annotation.

Method	Backbone	Params	HQ-YTVIS						YTVIS		
			AP^B	AP^B_{75}	AR^B_1	AP^M	AP^M_{75}	AR^M_1	AP^M	AP^M_{75}	AR^M_1
MaskTrack [37]	R50	58.1M	19.8	10.6	21.1	38.8	48.6	40.3	30.3	32.6	31.0
CrossVIS [38]	R50	37.5M	23.6	16.2	24.9	43.0	52.3	44.0	36.3	38.9	35.6
VisTr [35]	R50	57.2M	24.0	16.3	25.1	43.3	52.9	44.5	36.2	36.9	37.2
PCAN [16]	R50	36.9M	23.9	16.1	25.2	42.2	51.8	43.9	36.1	39.4	36.3
IFC [14]	R50	39.3M	26.5	19.6	27.5	46.6	51.5	46.9	42.8	46.8	43.8
SeqFormer [36]	R50	49.3M	28.6	21.4	29.3	48.5	52.2	48.5	47.4	51.8	45.5
VMT (Ours)	R50	51.5M	**30.7**	**24.2**	**31.5**	**50.5**	**54.5**	**50.2**	**47.9**	**52.0**	**45.8**
MaskTrack [37]	R101	77.2M	21.7	13.1	22.8	41.1	49.1	41.7	31.8	33.6	33.2
CrossVIS [38]	R101	56.6M	24.5	19.7	26.5	44.1	52.6	44.5	36.6	39.7	36.0
VisTr [35]	R101	76.3M	25.1	20.5	27.7	45.3	53.2	45.1	40.1	45.0	38.3
PCAN [16]	R101	54.8M	24.8	20.1	27.0	44.0	52.1	44.3	37.6	41.3	37.2
IFC [14]	R101	58.3M	27.2	23.6	28.3	48.2	51.8	47.6	44.6	49.5	44.0
SeqFormer [36]	R101	68.4M	30.7	27.3	30.1	49.0	52.3	46.6	49.0	55.7	**46.8**
VMT (Ours)	R101	70.5M	**32.5**	**28.9**	**32.6**	**51.2**	**55.1**	**49.3**	**49.4**	**56.4**	46.7
SeqFormer [36]	Swin-L	220.0M	43.3	41.5	41.6	63.7	69.7	58.7	59.3	66.4	51.7
VMT (Ours)	Swin-L	222.3M	**44.8**	**43.4**	**43.0**	**64.8**	**70.1**	**59.3**	**59.7**	**66.7**	**52.0**

OVIS. The results of OVIS dataset are reported in Table 6, where VMT achieves the best mask AP 19.8 using Swin-L backbone, improving 1.9 point compared to the baseline SeqFormer [36].

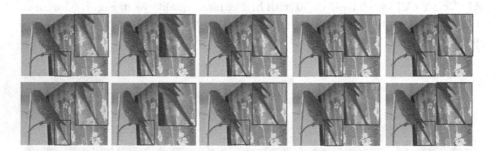

Fig. 7. Seqformer (1st row) vs. ours (2rd row) on YTVIS, in terms of mask quality & temporal consistency. Please refer to the Supp. file for more video results comparisons.

Table 6. Comparison with state-of-the-art on the OVIS validation set.

Method	Backbone	AP	AP_{50}	AP_{75}	AR_1	AR_{10}
MaskTrack [37]	R50	10.8	25.3	8.5	7.9	14.9
SipMask [5]	R50	10.2	24.7	7.8	7.9	15.8
CrossVIS [38]	R50	14.9	32.7	12.1	10.3	19.8
STMask [20]	R50	15.4	33.8	12.5	8.9	21.3
CMTrack RCNN [28]	R50	15.4	33.9	13.1	9.3	20.0
SeqFormer [36]	R50	15.6	34.3	12.1	9.6	21.8
VMT (Ours)	R50	**16.9**	**36.4**	**13.7**	**10.4**	**22.7**
SeqFormer [36]	R101	16.2	35.1	13.1	10.3	22.9
VMT (Ours)	R101	**17.8**	**35.7**	**15.4**	**10.5**	**23.8**
SeqFormer [36]	Swin-L	17.9	35.6	15.6	10.7	24.1
VMT (Ours)	Swin-L	**19.8**	**39.6**	**17.2**	**11.2**	**26.3**

Table 7. State-of-the-art comparison on the BDD100K segmentation tracking validation set using ResNet-50. I: ImageNet. C: COCO. S: Cityscapes. B: BDD100K.

Method	Pretrained	mMOTSA↑	mMOTSP↑	mIDF↑	ID sw.↓	mAP↑
SortIoU	I, C, S	10.3	59.9	21.8	15951	22.2
MaskTrack [32]	I, C, S	12.3	59.9	26.2	9116	22.0
STEm-Seg [2]	I, C, S	12.2	58.2	25.4	8732	21.8
QDTrack [27]	I, C, S	22.5	59.6	40.8	1340	22.4
QDTrack-fix [27]	I, B	23.5	66.3	44.5	973	25.5
PCAN [16]	I, B	27.4	66.7	45.1	876	26.6
VMT (Ours)	I, B	**28.7**	**67.3**	**45.7**	**825**	**28.3**

BDD100K MOTS. Table 7 shows results on BDD100K MOTS, where Mask Transfiner obtains the highest mMOTSA of 28.7 and outperforms the PCAN [16] by 1.3 points by sharing the same object detection tracking heads. The large gain reveals the high quality of temporal masks prediction by VMT.

5   Conclusion

We present Video Mask Transfiner, the first high-quality video instance segmentation method. Enabled by the efficient video transformer design, VMT utilizes the high-resolution spatio-temporal features for temporal mask refinement and achieves large boundary and mask AP gains on the HQ-YTVIS, OVIS, and BDD100K. To refine the coarse annotation of YTVIS, we design an iterative training paradigm and adopt VMT to correct the annotations errors of the training data instead of tedious manual relabeling. We build the new HQ-YTVIS benchmark with more accurate mask boundary annotations than YTVIS, and introduce Tube Boundary AP for accurate performance measure. We believe our method, the new benchmark HQ-YTVIS and evaluation metric will facilitate future video instance segmentation works on improving their mask quality and benefit real-world applications such as video editing [1,18].[1]

References

1. Alldieck, T., Magnor, M., Xu, W., Theobalt, C., Pons-Moll, G.: Video based reconstruction of 3D people models. In: CVPR (2018)
2. Athar, A., Mahadevan, S., Ošep, A., Leal-Taixé, L., Leibe, B.: STEm-Seg: spatio-temporal embeddings for instance segmentation in videos. In: Vedaldi, A., Bischof, H., Brox, T., Frahm, J.-M. (eds.) ECCV 2020. LNCS, vol. 12356, pp. 158–177. Springer, Cham (2020). https://doi.org/10.1007/978-3-030-58621-8_10
3. Bertasius, G., Torresani, L.: Classifying, segmenting, and tracking object instances in video with mask propagation. In: CVPR (2020)

[1] This work is supported in part by the Research Grant Council of the Hong Kong SAR under grant no. 16201420 and Kuaishou Technology.

4. Bolya, D., Zhou, C., Xiao, F., Lee, Y.J.: Yolact: real-time instance segmentation. In: ICCV (2019)
5. Cao, J., Anwer, R.M., Cholakkal, H., Khan, F.S., Pang, Y., Shao, L.: SipMask: spatial information preservation for fast image and video instance segmentation. In: Vedaldi, A., Bischof, H., Brox, T., Frahm, J.-M. (eds.) ECCV 2020. LNCS, vol. 12359, pp. 1–18. Springer, Cham (2020). https://doi.org/10.1007/978-3-030-58568-6_1
6. Carion, N., Massa, F., Synnaeve, G., Usunier, N., Kirillov, A., Zagoruyko, S.: End-to-End object detection with transformers. In: Vedaldi, A., Bischof, H., Brox, T., Frahm, J.-M. (eds.) ECCV 2020. LNCS, vol. 12346, pp. 213–229. Springer, Cham (2020). https://doi.org/10.1007/978-3-030-58452-8_13
7. Chen, L.-C., et al.: Naive-Student: leveraging semi-supervised learning in video sequences for urban scene segmentation. In: Vedaldi, A., Bischof, H., Brox, T., Frahm, J.-M. (eds.) ECCV 2020. LNCS, vol. 12354, pp. 695–714. Springer, Cham (2020). https://doi.org/10.1007/978-3-030-58545-7_40
8. Cheng, B., Girshick, R., Dollár, P., Berg, A.C., Kirillov, A.: Boundary iou: improving object-centric image segmentation evaluation. In: CVPR (2021)
9. Cheng, H.K., Chung, J., Tai, Y.W., Tang, C.K.: Cascadepsp: toward class-agnostic and very high-resolution segmentation via global and local refinement. In: CVPR (2020)
10. Ding, H., Jiang, X., Liu, A.Q., Thalmann, N.M., Wang, G.: Boundary-aware feature propagation for scene segmentation. In: ICCV (2019)
11. Fang, Y., et al.: Instances as queries. In: ICCV (2021)
12. He, K., Gkioxari, G., Dollár, P., Girshick, R.: Mask r-cnn. In: ICCV (2017)
13. Huang, Z., Huang, L., Gong, Y., Huang, C., Wang, X.: Mask scoring r-cnn. In: CVPR (2019)
14. Hwang, S., Heo, M., Oh, S.W., Kim, S.J.: Video instance segmentation using inter-frame communication transformers. In: NeurIPS (2021)
15. Ke, L., Danelljan, M., Li, X., Tai, Y.W., Tang, C.K., Yu, F.: Mask transfiner for high-quality instance segmentation. In: CVPR (2022)
16. Ke, L., Li, X., Danelljan, M., Tai, Y.W., Tang, C.K., Yu, F.: Prototypical cross-attention networks for multiple object tracking and segmentation. In: NeurIPS (2021)
17. Ke, L., Tai, Y.W., Tang, C.K.: Deep occlusion-aware instance segmentation with overlapping bilayers. In: CVPR (2021)
18. Ke, L., Tai, Y.W., Tang, C.K.: Occlusion-aware video object inpainting. In: ICCV (2021)
19. Kirillov, A., Wu, Y., He, K., Girshick, R.: Pointrend: image segmentation as rendering. In: CVPR (2020)
20. Li, M., Li, S., Li, L., Zhang, L.: Spatial feature calibration and temporal fusion for effective one-stage video instance segmentation. In: CVPR (2021)
21. Lin, C.C., Hung, Y., Feris, R., He, L.: Video instance segmentation tracking with a modified vae architecture. In: CVPR (2020)
22. Lin, H., Wu, R., Liu, S., Lu, J., Jia, J.: Video instance segmentation with a propose-reduce paradigm. In: ICCV (2021)
23. Liu, D., Cui, Y., Tan, W., Chen, Y.: Sg-net: spatial granularity network for one-stage video instance segmentation. In: CVPR (2021)
24. Loshchilov, I., Hutter, F.: Decoupled weight decay regularization. In: ICLR (2019)
25. Meinhardt, T., Kirillov, A., Leal-Taixe, L., Feichtenhofer, C.: Trackformer: multi-object tracking with transformers. arXiv preprint arXiv:2101.02702 (2021)

26. Milan, A., Leal-Taixé, L., Schindler, K., Reid, I.: Joint tracking and segmentation of multiple targets. In: CVPR (2015)
27. Pang, J., et al.: Quasi-dense similarity learning for multiple object tracking. In: CVPR (2021)
28. Qi, J., et al.: Occluded video instance segmentation. arXiv preprint arXiv:2102.01558 (2021)
29. Takikawa, T., Acuna, D., Jampani, V., Fidler, S.: Gated-scnn: gated shape cnns for semantic segmentation. In: ICCV (2019)
30. Tang, C., Chen, H., Li, X., Li, J., Zhang, Z., Hu, X.: Look closer to segment better: Boundary patch refinement for instance segmentation. In: CVPR (2021)
31. Tian, Z., Shen, C., Chen, H., He, T.: Fcos: fully convolutional one-stage object detection. In: ICCV (2019)
32. Voigtlaender, P., Chai, Y., Schroff, F., Adam, H., Leibe, B., Chen, L.C.: Feelvos: fast end-to-end embedding learning for video object segmentation. In: CVPR (2019)
33. Voigtlaender, P., et al.: Mots: multi-object tracking and segmentation. In: CVPR (2019)
34. Wang, J., et al.: Deep high-resolution representation learning for visual recognition. TPAMI **43**, 3349–3364 (2020)
35. Wang, Y., et al.: End-to-end video instance segmentation with transformers. In: CVPR (2021)
36. Wu, J., Jiang, Y., Zhang, W., Bai, X., Bai, S.: Seqformer: a frustratingly simple model for video instance segmentation. arXiv preprint arXiv:2112.08275 (2021)
37. Yang, L., Fan, Y., Xu, N.: Video instance segmentation. In: ICCV (2019)
38. Yang, S., et al.: Crossover learning for fast online video instance segmentation. In: ICCV (2021)
39. Yu, F., et al.: Bdd100k: a diverse driving dataset for heterogeneous multitask learning. In: CVPR (2020)
40. Yuan, Y., Xie, J., Chen, X., Wang, J.: SegFix: model-agnostic boundary refinement for segmentation. In: Vedaldi, A., Bischof, H., Brox, T., Frahm, J.-M. (eds.) ECCV 2020. LNCS, vol. 12357, pp. 489–506. Springer, Cham (2020). https://doi.org/10.1007/978-3-030-58610-2_29
41. Zhu, X., Su, W., Lu, L., Li, B., Wang, X., Dai, J.: Deformable detr: deformable transformers for end-to-end object detection. arXiv preprint arXiv:2010.04159 (2020)
42. Zhu, Y., et al.: Improving semantic segmentation via self-training. arXiv preprint arXiv:2004.14960 (2020)
43. Zou, Y., et al.: Pseudoseg: designing pseudo labels for semantic segmentation. In: International Conference on Learning Representations (ICLR) (2021)

Author Index

Printed in the United States
by Baker & Taylor Publisher Services

Printed in the United States
by Baker & Taylor Publisher Services